# BUSINESS AND ITS ENVIRONMENT

FIFTH EDITION

# BUSINESS AND ITS ENVIRONMENT

**David P. Baron**

*Stanford University*

PEARSON

Prentice
Hall

Upper Saddle River, New Jersey 07458

**Library of Congress Cataloging-in-Publication Data**

Baron, David P.
   Business and its environment / David P. Baron.—5th ed.
      p.  cm.
   Includes bibliographical references and index.
   ISBN 0-13-187355-5
   1. Social responsibility of business.  2. Industrial policy.  3. Commercial law.  4. Business
ethics.  I. Title.
   HD60.B37 2005
   658.4'08—dc22

                              2005014666

**VP/Editorial Director:** Jeff Shelstad
**Senior Acquisitions Editor:** Jennifer Simon
**Assistant Editor:** Richard Gomes
**Editorial Assistant:** Denise Vaughn
**Marketing Manager:** Anke Braun
**Marketing Assistant:** Patrick Danzuso
**Associate Director:** Judy Leale
**Production Editor:** Suzanne Grappi
**Permissions Supervisor:** Charles Morris
**Manufacturing Buyer:** Michelle Klein
**Production Manager, Manufacturing:** Arnold Vila
**Cover Design Manager:** Jayne Conte
**Composition/Full-Service Project Management:** Progressive Publishing Alternatives
**Printer/Binder:** Hamilton
**Typeface:** 10/12 Times Ten

Credits and acknowledgments borrowed from other sources and reproduced, with permission, in this textbook appear on appropriate page within text.

---

**Pearson Prentice Hall™** is a trademark of Pearson Education, Inc.
**Pearson®** is a registered trademark of Pearson plc
**Prentice Hall®** is registered trademark of Pearson Education, Inc.

Pearson Education LTD.
Pearson Education Singapore, Pte. Ltd
Pearson Education, Canada, Ltd
Pearson Education—Japan

Pearson Education Australia PTY, Limited
Pearson Education North Asia Ltd
Pearson Educación de Mexico, S.A. de C.V.
Pearson Education Malaysia, Pte. Ltd

10 9 8 7 6 5
ISBN 0-13-187355-5

To Mary

# Brief Contents

# Contents

# List of Cases

# Preface

The environment of business has interrelated market and nonmarket components. The market environment is characterized by the structure of the markets in which a firm operates and the rules that govern market competion. The nonmarket environment is characterized by the legal, political, and social arrangements in which the firm is embedded. The nonmarket environment determines the rules of the game for the market environment through government policies and public expectations. Just as firms compete in their market environment, they also compete in their nonmarket environment. Nonmarket competition is more complex, however, because that competition includes not only other firms but also activists, interest groups, the public, and government. *Business and Its Environment* is concerned with the inter-relationships among the market and nonmarket environments and the effective management of the issues therein. In contrast to a public policy perspective, the approach taken is managerial. That is, it takes the perspective of firms and managers, not of government or the public. It focuses on issues central to the performance of firms, as measured by both shareholder value and conduct in accord with ethics principles and social responsibilities.

The emphasis in the book is on strategy—nonmarket strategy and its integration with the market strategy of a firm. A nonmarket strategy is composed of objectives and a course of action for participating effectively and responsibly in the nonmarket competition on issues arising in the environment of business. The approach taken in the book emphasizes frameworks, principles, and analysis as the foundations for formulating effective and responsible strategies.

The fifth edition of *Business and Its Environment* represents continuity and change. It retains the structure, much of the subject matter, and the conceptual frameworks of the fourth edition. It also retains the strategy orientation and the guidance of the normative subjects of ethics and social responsibility. The fifth edition includes chapter cases for class discussion of managerial issues and applications of the conceptual frameworks and institutional material. At the end of each of the five parts of the book are integrative cases on an activist challenge to Citigroup, fuel economy standards, pharmaceutical regulation, globalization, and the pricing of AIDS drugs for poor countries. The fifth edition continues the focus on strategies for improving performance by addressing the challenges in the nonmarket environment and their effects on the market environment. The approach draws on the disciplines of economics, political science, law, and ethics to provide a foundation for strategy formulation and a deeper understanding of the environment of business and nonmarket issues. An integrated perspective strengthens the managerial orientation of the book and also enhances the usefulness of the conceptual materials for other parts of the business curriculum.

The principal changes in the fifth edition are a thorough updating of all the chapters, further development of strategy concepts such as nonmarket positioning, new frameworks such as that of private politics, new and updated applications, and new material on current challenges for firms. The new material includes entrepreneurial positioning, social entrepreneurship, the strategy of activists, social litigation as in the case of obesity, pharmaceutical responsbility, privacy, the fair trade movement, reputation management, and the regulation of broadband and media ownership.

The fifth edition contains 72 cases, including 21 new cases on Citigroup, Google, Exclusive Resorts, the Rainforest Action Network, McDonald's, Merck, Pfizer, Enron Power Marketing, GlaxoSmithKline, UPS, Wal-Mart, Home Depot, and Japan Post, as well as on industry-wide issues including CAFE standards, fair trade, FCC regulation, personal injury litigation, and pharmaceutical responsibility. The new cases are set in the 21st century and address issues in antitrust and regulation, pharmaceuticals, information technology, environmental protection, international business, the activist environment, and business ethics and responsibility. Twenty-one of the cases concern global and international nonmarket issues, and 21 deal with environmental and health issues. Each case poses a managerial problem that requires analysis and strategy formulation.

The book is organized in five parts. Part I introduces the nonmarket environment and nonmarket strategy with a focus on issues involving the public, activists, and the news media. Part II is concerned with issues addressed in the context of government institutions and with nonmarket strategies for dealing with those issues. The frameworks developed in this part provide a foundation for Parts III and IV. Part III focuses on the interactions between government and markets with an emphasis on antitrust, regulation, environmental protection, the law of intellectual property, contracts, and torts, and the economics and politics of information industries. Part IV is explicitly international and provides frameworks for understanding the political economy of countries and the relationships between business and government as a foundation for formulating effective strategies. Japan, the European Union, and China are considered, and international trade policy is used to bring the policy and strategy issues together. Part V is normative and focuses on ethics and corporate social responsibility. The complexities involved in operating in developing countries are considered both through conceptual frameworks and cases.

I would like to thank David Brady, Daniel Diermeier, Timothy Feddersen, Thomas Gilligan, Kirk Hanson, Daniel Kessler, Keith Krehbiel, and Romian Wacziarg for contributing cases to the fifth edition. The Graduate School of Business of Stanford University provided institutional support for the work underlying this book.

David P. Baron
Stanford, California

CHAPTER 1

# Market and Nonmarket Environments

## Introduction

Some companies are successful in both their market environment and the social, political, and legal nonmarket environment in which they operate. Intel, British Petroleum, and eBay have had continuing success in their markets, and they have also conducted themselves in a manner that has earned the confidence and respect of the public and government. Other companies have had great success in their markets but stumbled before the public and government. Nike became synonymous with athletic footwear and earned a reputation as an aggressive competitor, but public concerns about the working conditions in its suppliers' factories in Asia tarnished its image and affected its market performance. Wal-Mart, the world's largest company, was targeted by activists, unions, and politicians for its work practices in the United States, for allegedly depressing wages in the labor market, and for driving small merchants out of business and weakening the culture of small towns. Microsoft is one of the great successes in the history of business, but its market conduct has resulted in recurring antitrust judgments in the United States and the European Union. Citigroup, the world's largest financial institution, had a decade of strong growth but was hit with a series of costly scandals. As a result of its $31 billion acquisition of subprime lender Associates First Capital, Citigroup faced private lawsuits for abusive practices, state legislation restricting subprime lending, and fines of $285 million imposed by the Federal Reserve and the Federal Trade Commission. Citigroup also paid $2.8 billion to settle lawsuits for its role in structuring financial instruments for Enron and WorldCom and $735 million for biased securities research. In 2004 Citigroup increased its reserves to $6.7 billion for "Enron and pending litigation," and Japan ordered Citigroup to close its private banking business in the country. In addition to the fines and settlements and the damage to its reputation, Citigroup was targeted by the Rainforest Action Network, an environmental activist group, for its financing of environmentally destructive projects in developing countries.

The problems encountered by Nike, Wal-Mart, Microsoft, and Citigroup originated in their market environments, but the challenges to their operations came from the nonmarket environment. That is, the challenges resulted not from the actions of competitors but instead from the public, interest groups, the legal system, and government. These companies underappreciated the importance of the nonmarket environment and have paid a price for doing so.

Firms have more control over their fate in the markets in which they operate than they have in their nonmarket environment, but successful companies must understand that if they do not manage their nonmarket environment, it will manage them. Indeed, the long-run sustainability of competitive advantage requires managing effectively in the nonmarket environment. Companies like Intel, British Petroleum, and eBay have learned that they can participate both responsibly and effectively in influencing developments in their nonmarket environment. This book is about managing successfully in the nonmarket environment. The perspective taken is that of strategy—nonmarket strategy for a firm—and its implementation. That strategy is considered not in isolation but in conjunction with the firm's market or competitive strategy.

This chapter introduces the environment of business, identifies the role of management in the nonmarket environment, and presents a framework for analyzing that environment. The framework is illustrated using the automobile industry as an example. The sources of change in the nonmarket environment are then considered, and a framework for assessing the progress of nonmarket issues is presented.

## The Environment of Business

The environment of business consists of market and nonmarket components. The market environment includes those interactions between firms, suppliers, and customers that are governed by markets and contracts. These interactions typically involve voluntary economic transactions and the exchange of property. To succeed, firms must operate effectively in their market environment. They must be efficient in production and responsive to consumer demand. They must anticipate and adapt to change, innovate through research and development, and develop new products and services. Effective management in the market environment is a necessary condition for success, but it is not sufficient.

The performance of a firm, and of its management, also depends on its activities in its nonmarket environment. The nonmarket environment is composed of the social, political, and legal arrangements that structure interactions outside of, but in conjunction with, markets and contracts. The nonmarket environment encompasses those interactions between the firm and individuals, interest groups, government entities, and the public that are intermediated not by markets but by public and private institutions. Public institutions differ from markets because of characteristics such as majority rule, due process, broad enfranchisement, collective action, and publicness. Activities in the nonmarket environment may be voluntary, as when the firm cooperates with government officials or an environmental group, or involuntary, as in the case of government regulation or a boycott of a firm's product led by an activist group. Effective management in the nonmarket environment has become a necessary condition for success just as has effective management in the market environment.

The nonmarket environment has grown in importance and complexity over time and commands increased managerial attention. Nonmarket issues high on firms' agendas include environmental protection, health and safety, regulation and deregulation, intellectual property protection, human rights, international trade policy, regulation and antitrust, activist pressures, media coverage of business, corporate social responsibility, and ethics. Although the saliency of particular issues ebbs and flows, nonmarket issues arise sufficiently often to have important consequences for managerial and firm performance. Nonmarket issues, the forces that influence their development, and the strategies for addressing them are the focus of the field of business and its environment. The managerial objective is to improve the overall performance of firms by effectively addressing nonmarket issues and the forces associated with them.

Developments in the nonmarket environment affect performance on a number of dimensions. In the automobile industry, emissions and fuel economy standards affect research and development, design, production, pricing, and marketing. Safety regulation and liability standards have similar broad effects. Import competition and access to international markets affect competitive strategies involving product design, pricing, and capacity planning. Each of these examples has two components—an underlying issue and its impact on firm performance. The fuel economy issue, for example, is related to global climate change and security and has broad implications for performance. The focus for management in the nonmarket environment is on how an automobile company can participate effectively and responsibly in the public and private processes addressing these issues. Activity in the nonmarket environment is generally organized around specific issues and is motivated by the impacts of those issues. The legislative process, for example, focuses on bills to address a specific issue, such as fuel economy standards. Managerial attention thus focuses on specific issues affecting performance, the forces driving those issues, and the institutions governing the resolution of those issues.

## The Role of Management

Because of its importance for managerial and organizational performance, nonmarket strategy is the responsibility of managers. As illustrated in Figure 1-1, managers operate in both the market and the nonmarket environments. Managers are in the best position to assess the impact of their firm's market activities on its nonmarket environment and the impact of developments in the nonmarket environment on market opportunities and performance. Management thus is responsible for formulating and implementing nonmarket as well as market strategies.

Firms typically deal with nonmarket issues in proportion to their potential impacts on performance. Managers are in the best position to assess those impacts and, with the assistance of specialists, to formulate strategies to address the underlying issues. The implementation of nonmarket strategies also involves the active participation of managers. They may address the public on issues, communicate with the media, testify in regulatory and antitrust proceedings, lobby government, participate in coalitions and associations, serve on government advisory panels, meet with activists, negotiate with interest groups, build relationships with stakeholders, and participate in constituency programs.

Successful management requires frameworks for analyzing nonmarket issues, principles for reasoning about them, and strategies to address them. These frameworks, principles, and strategies enable managers to address issues in a systematic manner and

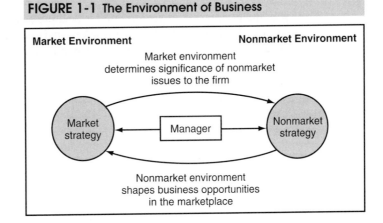

**FIGURE 1-1 The Environment of Business**

Market Environment                     Nonmarket Environment

Market environment
determines significance of nonmarket
issues to the firm

Market strategy ← Manager → Nonmarket strategy

Nonmarket environment
shapes business opportunities
in the marketplace

guide their firms successfully and responsibly in their nonmarket environments. In formulating nonmarket strategies, managers may draw on the expertise of lawyers, public affairs specialists, Washington representatives, and community relations specialists. Managers, however, ultimately must evaluate the quality of the advice they receive and combine it with their own knowledge of the market and nonmarket environments. Most firms have found that managers must be involved in all stages of their efforts to address nonmarket issues.

## Market and Nonmarket Environments

As illustrated in Figure 1-1, the market and nonmarket environments of business are interrelated. A firm's activities in its market environment can generate nonmarket issues and change in its nonmarket environment. That change may take the form of actions by government, such as legislation, regulation, antitrust lawsuits, and international trade policies. Similarly, the actions of interest groups and activists may force a firm to change its market practices. As an example of the market origins of nonmarket issues, in the 1990s lower real gasoline prices and changing consumer demand resulted in sport utility vehicles (SUVs) and light trucks capturing half the light-vehicle market. This reduced average fuel economy and, in conjunction with the global climate change and security issues, generated pressure to increase fuel economy standards. Moreover, the size and weight of SUVs raised concerns about the safety of the occupants of other vehicles in the event of a collision.

Nonmarket issues and actions also shape the market environment. Higher fuel economy standards would affect virtually all aspects of automobile design and manufacturing. Similarly, political action against Microsoft's alleged anticompetitive practices in the software industry put pressure on the Department of Justice and state attorneys general to file an antitrust lawsuit. The market environment is also shaped by the actions of interest and activist groups and the public sentiment for their causes. The Exxon Valdez oil spill increased environmental pressure on firms through liability for damages, more stringent regulations, and direct public pressure.

Both the market and nonmarket environments of business are competitive. In the market environment, performance is determined by competition among firms as directed by their market or competitive strategies. In the nonmarket environment, legislation, regulation, administrative decisions, and public pressure are the result of competition involving individuals, activist and interest groups, and firms. In the market environment, strategies are intermediated by markets, whereas in the nonmarket environment, strategies are intermediated by public and private institutions, including legislatures, courts, regulatory agencies, and public sentiment. Just as the market environment of business changes and competitive advantage evolves, the nonmarket environment changes and the issues on a firm's nonmarket agenda evolve.

The nonmarket environment should thus be understood as responsive to the strategies of firms and other interested parties. Those strategies can affect market opportunities. Robert Galvin (1992), who led Motorola for over three decades, described Motorola's approach to its nonmarket environment as "writing the rules of the game."[1]

> The first step in any defined strategy is writing the rules of the game honorably and fairly in a manner that gives everyone a chance with predictable rules. Our company has started industries. We have helped write standards. We have

---

[1]See Yoffie (1988a, 1988b) for analysis of aspects of this strategy.

helped write trade rules. We have helped influence policies. We have helped write national laws of countries where we have engaged, always in a respectful way. We have never taken for granted that the rules of the game would just evolve in a fashion that would make for the greatest opportunity.... With the right rules of the game, one's opportunity for success is enhanced.

Galvin's point is not that companies dictate the rules of the game but rather that those rules are shaped by the strategies of firms and other interested parties and by the governing institutions. Companies and their leaders can shape those rules by participating responsibly in the public and private processes that address market and nonmarket issues.

## Analysis of the Nonmarket Environment: The Four I's

The nonmarket environment of a firm or industry is characterized by four I's:

- issues
- interests
- institutions
- information

Issues are the basic unit of analysis and the focus of nonmarket action. Using the agricultural biotechnology industry as an example, the central nonmarket issues have been the formulation of regulatory policies for bioengineered plant and animal foods and the public reaction to those products. Interests include the individuals and groups with preferences about, or a stake in, the issue. The principal interests are the agricultural biotechnology companies, the interest groups and activists concerned about biotechnology issues, and the public. Institutions include government entities such as legislatures and regulatory agencies as well as nongovernmental institutions such as the news media and public sentiment. The Environmental Protection Agency, the Department of Agriculture, the Food and Drug Administration, and Congress are the principal public institutions in whose arenas the issues are addressed.

Information pertains to what the interested parties know or believe about the issues and the forces affecting their development. In the case of agricultural biotechnology, information pertains to the risks associated with individual products and with the technology. The public acceptance of bioengineered crops and animals is influenced by both scientific evidence and fear of the unknown, which are shaped by the information provided by firms, activists, government institutions, and media coverage of the issues. The task for management is to formulate and implement strategies that effectively address the nonmarket issues in competition with the strategies of other interests in the context of institutions in which information plays an important role.

Each firm and industry has a set of issues that it must address, and these issues constitute its nonmarket issue agenda. Associated with each issue are the institutional arenas in which the issue will be addressed, the interests likely to be involved, and the information available. Many issues on a firm's nonmarket agenda require issue-specific strategies, and the analysis of the associated interests, institutions, and information provides a foundation for strategy formulation, as considered in Chapter 2. The remainder of this chapter is concerned with the origin and development of nonmarket issues. The nonmarket environment of the automobile industry is considered next to illustrate the framework.

# The Nonmarket Environment of the Automobile Industry

This section identifies selected issues facing the automobile industry and then examines the associated interests, institutions, and information.

## Issues

**Fuel Economy Regulation** Heightened concerns about security and global warming coupled with declining fuel economy due to the greater market share of SUVs and light trucks led to the introduction of bills in Congress to increase the Corporate Average Fuel Economy (CAFE) standard by 40 percent. The auto industry argued that such an increase would hurt car buyers, increase prices, cost jobs, and increase traffic fatalities. The National Academy of Sciences had estimated that 1,300 to 2,600 additional fatalities a year resulted from the downsizing of cars in the 1970s and 1980s as a result of higher fuel economy standards.

**Fuel Economy Activism** Explaining that "we're going now to the customers," the Sierra Club began a 3-year private politics campaign to pressure through public sentiment the big-three auto manufacturers to increase their fuel economy. It conducted a radio and television advertising campaign challenging the automobile companies and calling on Ford CEO Bill Ford "to do his part" to improve fuel economy. The Bluewater Network, Global Exchange, and Rainforest Action Network also launched campaigns targeting Ford.

**Global Climate Change** The California legislature enacted a law written by the environmental activist group Bluewater Network requiring a 30 percent reduction in greenhouse gasses emissions by vehicles by the year 2014. Under federal environmental regulation, California had the authority to set more stringent pollution standards than required by federal regulation, and the law named carbon dioxide as a pollutant, since it contributes to global warming. The only means of reducing emissions by 30 percent was to increase the fuel economy of motor vehicles. The automobile industry filed a lawsuit challenging the law, claiming that it would regulate fuel economy, which only the federal government has the authority to do.

**Diesel Emissions** Current diesel automobiles could not be registered in California, New York, or three other states because of their emissions. The oil industry was required by the EPA to upgrade its refineries by 2007 to produce lower sulfur diesel fuel, which in addition to reducing particulates (soot) would allow reductions in nitrogen oxides. Engine manufacturers planned new engines by 2007 to reduce emissions further.

**Clean Gasoline** To alleviate the high price of gasoline, Senator Jeff Bingaman (D-NM) proposed temporarily suspending low-sulfur gasoline standards to allow gasoline that did not meet the standards to be imported. The proposal was opposed by the American Petroleum Institute and the Alliance of Automobile Manufacturers (AAM). The AAM argued for additional reductions in the sulfur content of gasoline to allow a new line of more efficient engines to be introduced.

**Power Window Safety** After seven children were killed by power windows in 3 months, safety advocates led by Kids and Cars advocated immediate action. The National Highway Traffic Safety Administration (NHTSA) prepared a proposed rule to reduce the hazard, and the Senate passed a measure requiring safer power windows and a government database to track fatalities. The Senate measure was in conference with the House of Representatives. Automakers began installing safer lift-closing switches and studying bounce-back windows.

**News Media**   Suzuki and Consumers Union settled a libel lawsuit over an article in *Consumer Reports* showing a Samurai tipping on two wheels and stating that it "easily rolls over in turns." In a joint statement, Consumers Union stated that its description "was limited to the severe turns" used in the test.[2] The settlement came after the Supreme Court refused to hear an appeal by Suzuki of a lower court decision.

**Gas Guzzler Tax**   A gas guzzler tax was imposed on all automobiles getting less than 22.5 miles per gallon, but the tax did not pertain to light trucks. The Sierra Club asked Congress to extend the tax to light vehicles.

**Safety in SUV Passenger Cars Collisions**   The administrator of NHTSA stated in public and in private meetings with automobile executives that they must change the design of SUVs to reduce the risk to occupants of passenger cars. Under threat of regulation, the automakers agreed to develop voluntary standards to reduce injuries in the event of a collision. The Insurance Institute for Highway Safety, an opponent of the auto industry, joined in the effort on the condition that real progress be made quickly. Clarence Ditlow, the director of the Center for Auto Safety, said, "This voluntary cooperation is not the solution. NHTSA needs to step forward with regulation."[3]

**Recalls**   NHTSA and Honda agreed that a recall was not needed after Honda agreed to make changes in oil filters that leaked and caused fires in 84 CR-Vs. NHTSA asked Chrysler to recall voluntarily 600,000 Dodge Durango and Dakota pickup trucks because of failures in a suspension joint. Chrysler replied that the failures that caused the frame to collapse did not constitute a safety defect.

**Liability**   Trial lawyers entered new territory in 2004 when they filed lawsuits in state courts based on the theory of "compatibility." The theory alleged that automakers were obligated to produce automobiles that were compatible with large SUVs and trucks so that the larger vehicles could not override the bumpers and the most crash-resistant parts of cars. The Association of Trial Lawyers of America supported networks of lawyers who pooled information on compatibility cases. The automakers were concerned about jury awards for pain and suffering and punitive damages. They supported liability reform to cap such awards.

**International Trade**   The Australia–United States free trade agreement of 2004 eliminated the 25 percent tariff on light truck imports from Australia. The tariff remained in effect for imports from other countries, except Canada and Mexico under the North American Free Trade Agreement (NAFTA).

**Discrimination**   The Consumer Federation of America (CFA) commissioned a study of dealer markups on loans arranged through Honda's automobile financing arm. The study concluded that African-American borrowers were charged a higher markup than white borrowers. An earlier study estimated that dealer markups cost consumers $1 billion a year. Trial lawyers filed several lawsuits alleging discrimination against their clients.

**Alternative Vehicles**   The Clinton administration and the big-three automakers had joined in the Partnership for a New Generation of Vehicles (PNGV) to develop an 80-mpg family car. The PNGV was abandoned because of consensus that the goal was infeasible. The Bush administration and the big-three U.S. automakers then established the FreedomCAR research program with emphasis on fuel cell technology.

---

[2]*The New York Times,* July 9, 2004.
[3]*The New York Times,* February 14, 2003.

**Zero-Emissions Vehicles (ZEVs)**  In 1990 the California Air Resources Board (CARB) mandated that by 2003, 10 percent of new vehicles sold in the state have zero emissions (ZEV). Automakers invested billions of dollars in electric vehicles, which proved to be a failure. In 2003 CARB mandated the sale of fuel cell, hybrid, and partial ZEV vehicles. A spokesperson for the Union of Concerned Scientists said, "The question remains, will automakers bring their lawyers or their engineers to the table in California?"[4]

**Labor Relations**  Workers at Nissan's Smyrna, Tennessee, plant had twice under federal labor law rejected United Auto Workers (UAW) attempts to represent them. Workers at other foreign-owned plants had also rejected the UAW. The next opportunity for the UAW was Nissan's newly opened plant in Canton, Alabama, which was expected to employ 5,300 workers. The UAW faced declining membership as the big-three automakers continued to lose market share and nonunion foreign-owned plants expanded.

**Global Climate Change in the European Union (EU)**  At the end of 2003 the European Automobile Manufacturers Association wrote to the Commission of the European Union (EU) stating that compliance with the voluntary agreement to reduce carbon dioxide emission of light vehicles by 25 percent by 2010 would add £2,700 to the price of a car, or £33.5 billion over the European Union. The Association stated, "Car buyers are not prepared to pay any extra for cleaner, more environmentally-friendly cars," and compliance would result in "a move of car production to non-EU countries, disappearance of large/premium cars, plant closures, sizeable job losses, decreased trade balance, reduced income tax, and lowered economic growth."[5] The Japan Automobile Manufacturers Association also wrote to the Commission urging that it take into account the economic situation of the industry.

## Interests

Interests include those who have an economic stake in an issue. U.S., Asian, and European automobile companies have interests that are opposed on some issues, such as the unionization of the plants of Japanese companies, but are aligned on others, such as liability reform and carbon dioxide emissions in the European Union. Other interests with direct stakes in these issues are car buyers, passengers, employees, insurance companies, and oil companies. The automobile and oil industries are on opposite sides of the issue of who should be responsible for further emissions reductions. Some interests are organized, as in the case of workers represented by the UAW, and others, such as car buyers and passengers in cars that collide with SUVs, are unorganized.

Interests include special interest, activist, and advocacy groups and other non-governmental organizations (NGOs). Special interest groups pursue issues because of the benefits that accrue to their members, as in the case of the Association of Trial Lawyers of America. Watchdog groups, such as the Center for Auto Safety, monitor the activities of firms and call those activities to the attention of the media, government, and public. Advocacy groups, such as the Consumer Federation of America, represent the interests of individuals, such as Honda borrowers. Activist groups, such as the Sierra Club, take direct action against firms to force them to change their policies. Public institutions are frequently the arbiters of such conflicts.

---

[4]*The New York Times,* April 25, 2003.
[5]*Sunday Herald,* March 21, 2004.

The interests may be grouped as follows:[6]

***Organized Interests***
Automakers
United Auto Workers
Insurance industry
Trial lawyers
Oil industry

***Unorganized Interests***
Car buyers
Borrowers
Passengers

***NGOs***
Environmental groups such as Sierra Club, Bluewater Network, Rainforest Action Network
Center for Auto Safety
Consumer Federation of America
Union of Concerned Scientists

## Institutions

The market and nonmarket environments in Figure 1-1 include activities that take place both within and outside government institutions. The principal government institutions are legislatures, the executive branch, the judiciary, administrative agencies, regulatory agencies, and international organizations such as the World Trade Organization (WTO). These institutions both make decisions and serve as arenas in which interests compete over issues. The nonmarket environment includes the set of laws established by these institutions, such as the gas guzzler tax and labor laws, as well as regulations, such as safety and fuel economy standards, established by administrative and regulatory agencies. The nonmarket environment also includes the common, or judge-made, law of torts, which governs the liability system.

Institutions can also be established by private means. Such institutions include markets, the insurance system, and voluntary agreements such as those pertaining to SUV collision safety and carbon dioxide reduction in the European Union. The nonmarket environment also includes nongovernmental institutions such as the news media and public sentiment. As considered in Chapter 3, the news media plays an important role in informing those in the nonmarket environment about issues, but it also serves as an institution. That is, firms and other interests attempt to communicate to the public through the news media. The Sierra Club and other activist groups engage in private politics, as considered in Chapter 4, and attempt to influence companies such as Ford through public sentiment.

Institutions are not unitary bodies. Congress is composed of two chambers and 535 members who represent constituencies with varied interests. Institutions also have internal structures that affect how nonmarket issues are addressed. Congress acts by majority rule, has a committee system, and follows a complex set of procedures for enacting legislation. Understanding the workings of these institutions, their procedures, and the forces that operate within them is essential for effective management in the nonmarket environment. Managers must also be familiar with the mandates, agendas, and procedures of regulatory agencies, such as NHTSA, EPA, and CARB.

---

[6]Not all relevant interests are listed.

Government officeholders may be active on nonmarket issues, and their actions to some extent reflect their personal interests. Their actions, however, are usually constrained by the mandates, procedures, and policies of the institutions in which they hold office and by the preferences of their political principals. The head of the EPA, for example, is accountable to the president, Congress, and the public. Legislators not only must follow legislative procedures and respect committee jurisdictions, but they also must be attentive to the preferences of their electoral constituents. Regulators must respect the mandates in their enabling legislation and follow a complex set of administrative procedures, both of which provide bases for judicial review. In addition, regulators must be attentive to their political principals in Congress and the Office of the President. For these reasons, institutional officeholders, such as the administrator of NHTSA and Senator Bingaman, are considered as part of the institution rather than as an interest.[7]

The institutions in whose arenas the nonmarket issues for the automobile industry are addressed can be categorized as follows:

### Legislative
Congress
California legislature

### Administrative and Regulatory Agencies
Bush administration
Environmental Protection Agency
National Highway Traffic Safety Administration
California Air Resources Board
Commission of the European Union

### Private Regulation
Voluntary SUV collision standards
Voluntary carbon dioxide reduction in the EU

### Judicial
Federal courts
State courts

### International
Australia–United States free trade agreement
North American Free Trade Association

### Nongovernmental
Public sentiment
News media

## Information

Information refers to what interests and institutional officeholders know about the issues, the consequences of alternative courses of action, and the preferences of those concerned with an issue. Issues are often contested because interests have conflicting preferences regarding their resolution, as in the case of the proponents and opponents of higher fuel economy standards. Issues can also be contested because interests have different information. Auto companies have superior information about the preferences of car buyers for higher fuel economy, and environmentalists may

---

[7]The exception is when the jobs of officeholders, the budget, or the status of the office is at stake.

have superior information about the extent of public concern about climate change. Organizations such as the National Academy of Sciences and universities play an important role in providing scientific assessments of issues such as fuel economy and auto safety.

Information is also frequently at the heart of strategies for addressing nonmarket issues. Lobbying, for example, involves providing information to officeholders about the likely consequences of policy alternatives for their constituents and the public more broadly. Information provision is also important in regulatory rule making because of the complexity of most regulatory issues and because agencies are required to develop a record supporting their actions. Information can also be an instrument of nonmarket competition. On the issue of California's law to reduce $CO_2$ emissions, the Union of Concerned Scientists estimated that compliance would increase the cost of a Ford Explorer by $1,960, whereas the Alliance of Automobile Manufacturers estimated that the cost increase would be $4,361.

Information can also be important to the progress of issues. The information provided by automakers and the National Academy of Sciences about the effect of downsizing on safety shifted the focus of fuel economy improvements away from designing smaller cars. Information can also lead to resolution of an issue. Mounting evidence and growing public concern about climate change led automakers in the European Union to adopt a voluntary carbon dioxide reduction goal, and the environmental groups' campaigns targeting Ford sought to mobilize the public to support greater fuel economy.

The chapter cases, *The Nonmarket Environment of the Pharmaceutical Industry* and *The Nonmarket Environment of McDonald's,* provide opportunities to characterize the issues, interests, institutions, and information in their nonmarket environments and to consider the progress of the issues. The chapter case, *An Emerging Issue: MTBE,* addresses the origin and development of a nonmarket issue.

## Change in the Nonmarket Environment

The nonmarket environment changes as issues are resolved, current issues progress, and new issues arise. This section focuses on the origins of issues and the forces that give rise to them. The following sections address the anticipation of nonmarket issues and their progression and resolution.

Nonmarket issues originate from both external forces and a firm's own actions. Most changes in the tax law originate in response to ideas that capture a degree of political support. However, the issue of eliminating the investment tax credit, which had been a component of U.S. tax policy for over 20 years, arose in part because of political action by service industries that viewed the credit as a subsidy to capital-intensive industries. As indicated in a subsequent section, the issue of automobile safety regulation arose from an automobile accident and articles by two young policy activists. The issue of a possible health risk from the electromagnetic field generated by high-voltage electricity transmission lines arose from a small-scale inferential study linking power lines to leukemia in children. As the varied origins of these issues indicate, managers must be sensitive to the sources of nonmarket issues—even those such as possible health risks from the electromagnetic field generated by transmission lines—that initially seem remote or even far-fetched.

Nonmarket issues have five basic sources:

- scientific discovery and technological advancement
- new understandings

- institutional change
- interest group activity
- moral concerns

Scientific discovery and technological advancement can produce fundamental changes in both the market and nonmarket environments. In the market environment, they create opportunities for new products and processes, new applications of existing knowledge, and future discoveries. They also give rise to nonmarket issues. Measurements suggesting that the earth was warming spawned issues ranging from higher fuel economy standards to the deforestation of tropical rain forests. The discovery of an ozone hole above the Antarctic confirmed theories of ozone depletion and propelled a number of nonmarket issues ranging from the elimination of CFCs to measures to reduce the incidence of skin cancer. When the theory of ozone depletion was initially advanced, DuPont came under pressure to stop producing CFCs. DuPont argued that there was yet no evidence that CFCs actually caused ozone depletion and pledged in a public advertisement that it would cease production if scientific evidence showed a relationship. When a National Academy of Sciences study concluded that there was a causal link, DuPont announced the next day that it would cease production.

Nonmarket issues can also arise from new technology and scientific uncertainty. The spectacular success of the cellular telephone industry was interrupted one day when a man called the *Larry King Live* television talk show and claimed that his wife had died from brain cancer caused by extensive use of a cellular telephone. Earlier in the day, a CEO of a major corporation announced that he had brain cancer, and the previous day, a CEO of another major corporation had died of brain cancer. The call and speculation that the CEOs might have been heavy users of cellular telephones caused a panic. The stock prices of McCaw Communications, the nation's largest cellular telephone company, and Motorola, the largest manufacturer of cellular telephones, dropped by over 5 percent. Fears were calmed by statements of government officials that there was no scientific evidence linking cellular telephones to cancer. The industry pledged to conduct additional research into whether radio-frequency radiation emitted by the telephones was harmful. The Cellular Telecommunications Industry Association earmarked $25 million for research and established a Scientific Advisory Group on Cellular Telephone Research to oversee the research program. The promise of research to fill the gap in scientific information reassured cellular telephone users, and the growth in usage resumed.

Nonmarket issues also arise from changes in understandings. The environmental movement brought to the attention of the public the damage to the natural environment and the associated health risks. Renewed confidence in markets and the failure of socialist economic systems spurred a wave of privatization in both developed and developing countries. Increasing evidence of the economic benefits of international trade led not only to further reductions in trade barriers through the World Trade Organization but also to market integration in North America through NAFTA and in the European Union through the Single European Act. Antitrust policy and enforcement changed substantially during the 1980s as a consequence of new understandings about the effects of the competitive practices of firms. Changes in the membership of the Supreme Court during the 1980s and the understandings the new members brought with them resulted in changes in affirmative action policies.

Issues also become salient because groups organize to advance their own interests. Interest groups formed around the issue of extending the period of daylight saving time and worked for nearly a decade to obtain an extension by Congress. The growth and developing effectiveness of AARP led it to push for congressional enactment of a catastrophic illness insurance plan, only to have a grassroots revolt among its members lead to repeal of the act before it had taken effect. Consumer groups have similarly organized to take political action to stem the increases in pharmaceutical prices. Interest groups can also stop change, as in the case of the auto industry and higher fuel economy standards.

Nonmarket issues also arise because of institutional actions. A Supreme Court decision in 1988 supported a new theory of "fraud on the market," under which a firm could be held liable if its stock price fell significantly when the firm's projections of future earnings had been favorable. This provided incentives for trial lawyers to file class action lawsuits against high-technology companies when their naturally volatile stock price fell by 10 percent or more. No evidence of fraud was required to file a lawsuit, and filing allowed the lawyers to conduct discovery and depose company executives. To avoid the costs and disruptions of discovery and depositions, and the subsequent costs of a trial, many companies were willing to settle the lawsuits even if they expected to win. Settlements totaled nearly $7 billion. Viewing the practice as extortionary and the lawsuits as frivolous, companies backed federal legislation granting a safe harbor for forward-looking projections, and Congress enacted the statute over President Clinton's veto. In response, the trial lawyers brought their cases under state laws and backed a ballot initiative in California to increase their likelihood of extracting settlements. The high-tech companies and other targets of the lawsuits then successfully backed new federal legislation to require such cases to be filed in federal courts.

Change in the nonmarket environment also comes from market forces. In the mid-1990s, new markets associated with the Internet, wireless systems, and integrated services resulted in a restructuring of the telecommunications industry, including mergers, acquisitions, and strategic alliances. Congress then struggled with legislation to lift the archaic restrictions on competition left over from the era of telecommunications regulation. The Federal Communications Commission also struggled to formulate rules for transitioning from regulation to competition that would stand up to security by the courts.

Nonmarket issues also arise because of heightened moral concerns. The increased saliency of personal privacy resulted in a ban on the use of polygraph tests by employers, who responded with a variety of pencil and paper tests, including some designed to test for honesty and loyalty. These tests ultimately became a nonmarket issue. Privacy concerns associated with the Internet resulted in both self-regulation by Internet service providers and Web sites and calls for new legislation. In the European Union, privacy concerns led to strong legislation on the handling and use of personal information on the Internet. Moral concerns were also raised about subprime lending to borrowers who did not qualify for bank loans, leading to charges of predatory lending. Moral concerns about the spread of AIDS in developing countries and the suffering of its victims put pressure on pharmaceutical firms to provide greater access to their drugs.

## Anticipating Change in the Nonmarket Environment

The effectiveness with which a firm and its managers address nonmarket issues depends on their approach to the nonmarket environment. One approach is to respond to nonmarket issues only when they are strong enough to force the firm to act. A second approach emphasizes limiting the extent of the damage once the firm has been challenged by an issue. A third approach is anticipatory and is intended to prepare the firm to take advantage of opportunities as they arise and address issues before they become problems. A fourth approach is proactive with the firm and its managers not only anticipating nonmarket issues but also acting to affect which issues arise and how they will be framed. This approach recognizes that nonmarket issues and their development are affected by the way business is conducted. The fourth approach is the most effective, but it requires considerable sensitivity to the sources of nonmarket issues and how they progress.

Proactive managers attempt to identify potential issues and act to reduce their adverse, or enhance their beneficial, impacts. A fundamental step in anticipating nonmarket issues is to view the potential issue or business practice from the perspective of others who might be concerned about it. The Graduation Cards example illustrates this point.

---

EXAMPLE

## Graduation Cards

Graduation represents an important market for the greeting card industry. In its preparation for the college graduation season, Hallmark Cards was considering the array of cards it would market. Cards could reflect a variety of themes, but two traditionally popular ones were transition and celebration. One transition was coming of legal drinking age, and Hallmark was considering cards featuring alcoholic beverages. Alcoholic beverages were also associated with celebration, so the cards would draw on two themes. One card being considered had a photo of a Budweiser can with a small cherubic character saying, "You're graduating?" Another card portrayed a beer and eggs breakfast on graduation day, and a third suggested a robe large enough to cover two champagne bottles.

Graduation cards are bought by friends and relatives of the graduate, and it is from their perspective that the cards must be considered—for both their market and nonmarket potentials. The proposed cards were intended for the college graduation market, and virtually all those recipients would be of legal drinking age. College students, however, were not the only ones graduating. Twice as many students graduate from high school each year, and virtually none of them is of legal drinking age. Some parents and relatives

may well view the cards as promoting alcoholic beverages and contributing to underage drinking and driving, a major cause of accidents and deaths. Parents and others concerned about underage drinking provide the potential for a nonmarket reaction to the cards.

The next step is to assess whether people concerned about the cards are likely to act in the nonmarket environment. Some parents and relatives will be concerned about the cards, but they are dispersed and most have limited means of generating a nonmarket issue. Some, however, participate in organizations such as the PTA and Mothers Against Drunk Driving (MADD) that are experienced in dealing with nonmarket issues and know how to attract the news media to bring an issue to the attention of the public and hence to put it on a firm's agenda. This does not mean that a nonmarket reaction is certain, but it certainly is possible.

Hallmark chose to market the cards, and the reaction was swift. MADD activists began to pressure store owners to stop selling the cards, and the media picked up the story. Faced with public criticism, Hallmark withdrew the cards from the market and subsequently decided not to produce any graduation cards with a reference to alcoholic beverages.

# The Nonmarket Issue Life Cycle

The progression of nonmarket issues can often be understood in terms of a life cycle. The nonmarket issue life cycle relates the stage of development of an issue to its impact on a firm and its management.[8] This is not a theory, since it does not provide an explanation for how or why an issue develops or a basis for predicting its likely development. In particular, it does not identify the causal factors that govern an issue's progress. The life cycle concept is useful, however, because it identifies a pattern and serves as a reminder that issues with simple origins can garner support, propelling them through a series of stages and resulting in significant impacts. Issues do not, however, have a life of their own. Instead, their progression is governed by the attention they receive from the public, firms, interest groups, and government.

Nonmarket issues can progress through five stages: (1) issue identification, (2) interest group formation, (3) legislation, (4) administration, and (5) enforcement. As an issue progresses through its life cycle, its impact on the firm and its management tends to increase. As the impact increases, management's range of discretion in addressing the issue correspondingly decreases. The impact may take the form of government actions such as regulation or changes in public sentiment that limit the options available to management.

To illustrate the nonmarket life cycle, consider the issue of automobile safety regulation. The progression of the issue is illustrated along the horizontal axis in Figure 1-2, and the vertical axis represents the impact on automobile manufacturers. In the 1950s, automobile safety was viewed primarily as a function of road conditions and the driver's skill. In 1957, as Congressman Kenneth Roberts of Alabama and his wife were returning from their honeymoon, their car was rear-ended. Both were injured, but their

**FIGURE 1-2 Nonmarket Issue Life Cycle**

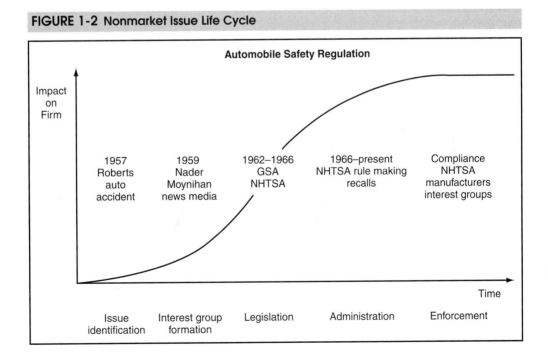

---

[8]The life cycle concept was originated by Ian Wilson while at General Electric.

well-packaged glass and china wedding presents in the backseat were undamaged. Roberts recognized that an ignored dimension of the auto safety issue was the vehicle itself and how safely it contained its passengers.

Roberts held congressional hearings on the issue, but no action resulted. In 1959 two articles on the issue were published. A young attorney named Ralph Nader published an article on automobile safety that focused on automobile design. A young official in the Department of Labor, Daniel Patrick Moynihan, published an article arguing for a broader perspective on the automobile safety issue. Interest group activity began to develop, and the media was attracted to the issue, particularly when it was revealed that General Motors had hired a private detective to investigate Nader. In 1962 the issue entered the legislative stage when the General Services Administration (GSA) issued a standard for brake fluid. Legislation was introduced in Congress and, after considerable deliberation and intense politics, the Motor Vehicle Safety Act of 1966 was enacted. The act established NHTSA, which was given administrative rule-making authority to establish mandatory automobile safety standards.

The enforcement phase for auto safety regulation has been multifaceted. Auto manufacturers test their models extensively, not only for compliance with regulations but often to exceed government standards. NHTSA enforces the regulations and can order the recall of vehicles. Advocacy groups such as the Center for Auto Safety monitor both the industry and the enforcement activities of NHTSA. Safety regulations are also enforced through the courts as a result of lawsuits filed by individuals and trial lawyers.

Nonmarket issues that complete their life cycles do not always result in more restrictions on business, as evidenced by the issue of airline deregulation. Economists analyzing the performance of airlines regulated by the Civil Aeronautics Board (CAB) concluded that regulation was inducing inefficiencies and increasing costs. The issue attracted attention because of the large differences between the fares of the CAB-regulated airlines and airlines such as Southwest that operated only intrastate routes and hence were not subject to CAB regulation. Regulatory oversight hearings brought additional attention to the issue and planted the seeds of legislative action. These developments coincided with increased public criticism of economic regulation and decreased confidence in government. As congressional and executive branch attention increased, the issue entered the legislative stage. At the same time, economist Alfred Kahn was appointed to head the CAB. He moved quickly to take administrative action to deregulate the industry, which spurred the legislative process. The result was legislation that eliminated the economic regulation of the domestic airline industry. After transferring some of its nonregulatory functions to other government agencies, the CAB ceased to exist. Similar concerns about the economic consequences of surface transportation regulation resulted in the elimination of the Interstate Commerce Commission, the first federal regulatory agency.

Not all nonmarket issues, of course, garner enough support to pass through all five stages, and many do not survive the legislative stage. The fact that an issue does not pass through all the stages does not mean that it has no impact. The attention an issue receives can produce change even in the absence of institutional action. The consumer movement has not progressed as far as its supporters had hoped, and Congress has not passed major consumer legislation since 1976. Despite the consumer movement's failure to become broader and more powerful, it has resulted in a variety of significant changes. Furthermore, interest groups have been formed to advocate consumer interests.

# Summary

Firms operate in both market and nonmarket environments. The field of business and its environment is concerned with issues in the nonmarket environment that have potentially important effects on organizational and managerial performance. Managers are in the best position to understand how the firm's market activities give rise to nonmarket issues and to assess the significance of nonmarket issues for overall performance. Managers thus have the responsibility for addressing nonmarket issues and formulating nonmarket as well as market strategies.

The nonmarket environment of a firm is characterized by four I's: issues, interests, institutions, and information. As indicated by the example of the automobile industry, nonmarket issues have important implications for firms and their market and nonmarket performance. Nonmarket issues may be identified externally or by management and may arise from scientific discovery, new understandings, interest group activity, institutional change, and moral concerns. Because these factors change over time, the nonmarket environment and a firm's nonmarket issue agenda evolve.

Management must not only deal effectively with nonmarket issues but must also anticipate issues and take proactive steps to address them. Many nonmarket issues pass through stages—issue identification, interest group formation, legislation, administration, and enforcement—that constitute a life cycle. This pattern serves as a reminder that issues evolve, even seemingly minor issues can have substantial effects, and the impact increases as issues move through the stages of their life cycle. Not all nonmarket issues pass through all five stages, however, and some, such as deregulation, result in fewer rather than more restrictions. The progress of an issue is shaped by the actions of interests and the characteristics of the institutions in whose arenas the issue is addressed.

# Organization of the Book

The book is organized in five parts, and cases for discussion are provided in each chapter. An integrative case is provided at the conclusion of each part. Part I introduces the nonmarket environment, the nonmarket issues firms face, and the factors, including activist pressures and the news media and public sentiment, that affect the development of those issues. The focus is on the formulation of strategies for addressing nonmarket issues and the integration of those strategies with market strategies. Part II considers issues addressed in the context of government institutions with an emphasis on legislatures. The substantive focus is on conceptual frameworks for analyzing political issues affecting companies and formulating effective strategies for addressing them. The frameworks developed in this part provide a foundation for Parts III and IV. Part III focuses on the interactions between government and markets with an emphasis on antitrust, regulation, environmental protection, court-adjudicated law, and information industries. Part IV is explicitly international and provides frameworks for understanding the political economy of countries and the relationships between business and government. Japan, the European Union, and China are considered, and international trade policy is used to bring the policy and strategy issues together. Part V is normative and focuses on the social responsibilities of firms and the guidance that ethics provides. Ethics systems and reasoning are the centerpieces of Part V, and the applications focus on corporate responsibility and operating across borders.

# The Nonmarket Environment of the Pharmaceutical Industry

U.S. spending on pharmaceuticals increased by 19 percent to $131.9 billion in 2000, the fifth consecutive year of increases above 13 percent. Expenditures were expected to top $150 billion in 2001. The expenditures reflected the importance of drugs as health care therapies and the continuing discoveries of new treatments as a result of the industry's research and development efforts. A study by a research center supported by the pharmaceutical industry reported that the cost of developing a new drug had increased from $231 million in 1987 to $802 million in 2000 (in inflation-adjusted dollars). The expenditures also reflected high prices, heavy marketing expenditures, and high profits. These factors attracted the attention of government officials, activists, and advocacy groups.

Public Citizen, a consumer activist organization, published a report arguing that the pharmaceutical industry exaggerated the cost of developing new drugs.[9] The Pharmaceutical Research and Manufacturers Association (PhRMA) hired Ernst & Young to evaluate the Public Citizen report.[10] Ernst & Young criticized the report and concluded that the pharmaceutical industry paid a higher percentage of its revenues as taxes than all other industries in the United States. Critics responded that the tax payments were large because the industry's profit margins were so high.

In a study based on the annual reports of nine pharmaceutical companies, Families USA reported that eight of the companies spent more than twice as much on marketing as on research and development. Six of the companies had net incomes that exceeded their research and development expenditures. Families USA also reported that prices for the 50 most prescribed drugs for seniors had increased at twice the rate of inflation.

PhRMA replied, "The Families USA 'study' condemns the pharmaceutical industry for being a success at developing medicines upon which millions of patients depend. When the pharmaceutical industry does well, patients do even better. Because the pharmaceutical industry is profitable, Americans have the best chance in the world of getting the cure for Alzheimer's, cancer, diabetes or AIDS."[11]

One reason pharmaceutical profits were high was that the brand-name companies faced buyers that controlled only small shares of the market. One fear of the brand-name companies was that buyers would join together and use their bargaining power to drive prices down. Maine had passed a law empowering the state to negotiate and purchase prescription drugs for its citizens. PhRMA filed a lawsuit against the state, and a federal court issued a preliminary injunction preventing the state from implementing the law. The Court of Appeals, however, reversed the lower court decision.

The state of Florida passed new legislation to use its purchasing power on drugs included under Medicaid, the federal program administered by the states that funded medical care for the poor. Florida included in its formulary—the list of drugs for which reimbursement would be provided—only those drugs for which the manufacturers agreed to pay rebates to the state beyond the rebates required by Medicaid. Rather than give in to the pressure, Pfizer reached an agreement with the state under which its prescription drugs were included in the formulary without any price discount. Instead, Pfizer agreed to pay for nurses to monitor tens of thousands of patients to make sure they took their medications

---

[9]Public Citizen, "Rx R&D Myths: The Case Against the Drug Industry's R&D 'Scare Card,'" Washington, DC, July 2001.
[10]Ernst & Young, LLP, "Pharmaceutical Industry R&D Costs: Key Findings about the Public Citizen Report," August 8, 2001.

[11]www.pharma.org.

and had checkups on a regular basis. PhRMA had a different response to Florida's program. It filed a lawsuit arguing that federal law required that all prescription drugs be available to Medicaid recipients unless a drug had been shown to have no therapeutic benefits.

Florida also adopted a counter-detailing program in which pharmacists employed by the state visited doctors to encourage them to prescribe generic drugs rather than the more expensive brand-name drugs.[12] The pharmacists provided a "report card" to each doctor indicating the doctor's Medicaid prescriptions record.

On a regular basis the news media carried articles on developments in the pharmaceutical industry. Since the fortunes of companies depended on the results of clinical trials and the FDA's drug approval decisions, the business press covered the FDA closely. The business press also covered patent extension decisions and the progress of patent infringement cases. Congress and the Bush administration had pharmaceutical issues high on their agenda, resulting in media coverage of legislative and regulatory reform issues. The nonbusiness media also covered the industry, focusing more on the impact of drugs—and their prices—on consumers.

The media was also concerned about the sponsorship of research and clinical testing. Pharmaceutical companies financed research in universities and hospitals and retained the intellectual property rights to the resulting discoveries. The scientific and medical press had become concerned about the implications of this trend for the integrity of their publications. The British journal *Nature* required authors to disclose any financial interests related to the studies they published in the journal.

Journals were also concerned about the symmetry of what was published. Pharmaceutical companies were hesitant to disclose negative research results that might undermine products.[13] The *New England Journal of Medicine,* the *Journal of the American Medical Association,* and other journals adopted a policy to force pharmaceutical companies that sponsor clinical research to allow researchers to publish unfavorable as well as favorable results.

Judges had also become concerned about links between expert witnesses and the pharmaceutical industry. Some judges required expert witnesses to disclose their financial connections to the industry.

In an unprecedented action, Blue Cross of California, a unit of WellPoint Health Networks, filed a Citizen Petition with the FDA to switch from prescription-only to over-the-counter (OTC) status three second-generation antihistamines— Allegra, produced by Aventis; Claritin, produced by Schering-Plough; and Zyrtec, marketed in the United States by Pfizer.[14] This would benefit consumers because the second-generation antihistamines were nonsedating, whereas the 100 first-generation antihistamines sold on the OTC market were sedating. A switch would put the second-generation antihistamines under considerable price pressure.

In January 2001, Schering-Plough's third-generation antihistamine Clarinex was approved for sale in the European Union, and in the same month the FDA issued an "approvable" letter for the drug indicating that there were no outstanding clinical or scientific issues. The FDA, however, withheld approval because of quality control problems in Schering-Plough's New Jersey and Puerto Rico manufacturing facilities. Public Citizen had put pressure on the FDA by writing to the Secretary of Health and Human Services, citing consultants' reports on the production facilities and FDA warning letters to Schering-Plough.

Public Citizen also asked the secretary of Health and Human Services to undertake criminal prosecution of Schering-Plough. A study by Public Citizen concluded that the probable cause of 17 deaths was asthma inhalers sold without the active medication albuterol. In 1999 and 2000 Schering-Plough had recalled 59 million inhalers because advocacy groups had raised concerns about them. A Schering-Plough spokesperson said that 5,000 people a year died from asthma and that there was "no evidence that a patient was ever harmed by an inhaler subject to any recalls." He added that "every inhaler returned to the company by a patient claiming injury and alleging the canister lacked active ingredient has been tested and found to contain active ingredient."[15]

The pricing and marketing of prescription drugs was of concern to state and federal law enforcement

---

[12]Marketing of drugs directly to doctors is referred to as detailing.
[13]See the Chapter 21 case, *Reporting of Clinical Trial Results.*

[14]See the Part III integrative case *Pharmaceutical Switching.*
[15]*The Wall Street Journal,* August 10, 2001.

agencies. Twenty pharmaceutical companies were under investigation for price reporting practices associated with the sale of drugs to Medicaid and Medicare. One focus of the investigations was the reporting of high wholesale prices while providing deep discounts to doctors. This increased the doctor's margin, providing incentives to prescribe the drugs.

In 1997 the FDA had revised its regulations, allowing direct-to-consumer (DTC) advertising of prescription drugs in the broadcast media. Schering-Plough and other pharmaceutical companies began to advertise directly to consumers through television, radio, and print. The advertisements gave a toll-free number to call for information, referred to magazine advertisements where warnings were given, and instructed viewers to "ask your doctor." The marketing strategy was to induce consumers to ask their doctors for the drug by brand name. The strategy proved to be quite successful, pushing Claritin sales to $2.5 billion in the United States. In 2000 Merck spent $161 million on DTC advertising for Vioxx, which was more than Budweiser spent advertising its beers. PhRMA explained that DTC advertising helped educate consumers and involve them more in their own health care.

The National Institute for Health Care Management, a research institute funded by Blue Cross Blue Shield, reported that DTC advertising had increased from $700 million in 1996 to $2.5 billion in 2000 and that the increase was concentrated in 50 drugs. The Institute also reported that the increase in pharmaceutical spending was due to an increase in prescriptions written and not to price increases. PhRMA explained, "We have an epidemic of undertreatment of serious illnesses in the United States."[16]

The American Medical Association (AMA) took an interest in the DTC advertising issue. The AMA supported the objectives of educating patients and involving them in their own health care but was concerned that the doctor–patient relationship could be strained when patients asked for a drug by brand name. An AMA ethics committee stated, "Physicians should resist commercially induced pressure to prescribe drugs that

may not be indicated. Physicians should deny requests for inappropriate prescriptions and educate patients as to why certain advertised drugs may not be suitable treatment options. . . ."[17] In 2001 the AMA wrote to the Senate Commerce Committee stating, "Our physician members have expressed concern about the impact that direct-to-consumer advertising has on the physician/patient relationship and on health care costs." The AMA asked the committee to direct the FDA to study the impact of DTC advertising. The FDA began a review.

DTC advertising also attracted the attention of activist and advocacy groups. The Prescription Access Litigation Project filed a lawsuit against Schering-Plough claiming that its advertising of Claritin was deceptive and boosted demand and the price of the drug. Some policy specialists observed that if DTC advertising were restricted, consumers would simply turn to the Internet for information on prescription drugs.

The Commission of the European Union (EU) proposed a fast-track approval process for new drugs. The objective was to reduce the approval time from 18 months to 9 to 12 months, which would be faster than the approval time of 14 months in the United States. The Commission also proposed a relaxation of restrictions on DTC advertisements, but not broadcast advertising, for treatments of certain diseases, including diabetes, AIDS, and asthma.

In 2001 Bayer withdrew its newly introduced and fast-selling cholesterol-lowering drug Baycol because over 50 deaths were associated with its use. The drug had been approved in the United Kingdom, and other EU member states had adopted the U.K. decision. Responsibility for monitoring the safety of the drug, however, was unclear. The European Agency for the Evaluation of Medical Products said it had little role in safety because it had not participated in the licensing. The recall brought home to the European governments the confusion in drug safety regulation and the poor communication among the member states. The Medicines Control Agency of Germany faulted Bayer for not having disclosed problems earlier.

---

[16]*The New York Times,* November 11, 2001.

[17]American Medical Association, "E-5.015 Direct-to-Consumer Advertisements of Prescription Drugs," www.ama-assn.org.

Post-marketing monitoring of drugs was also an issue in the United States. One concern was the rapid adoption of drugs as a result of aggressive marketing by the brand-name pharmaceutical companies. This meant that if there were side effects not identified in the clinical testing, problems would spread quickly.[18] *Business Week* called for an independent body such as the National Transportation Safety Board to investigate problems with drugs.

Many developing countries faced an AIDS crisis, and the cost of the cocktail of drugs used to treat AIDS was beyond the means of those countries. South Africa used its Medicines Act to threaten the pharmaceutical industry with compulsory licensing and parallel imports of AIDS drugs. Thirty-nine international pharmaceutical companies filed a lawsuit against the South African government but later dropped the lawsuit and agreed to substantial price reductions.[19]

PhRMA opposed the practice of deep discounts for drugs for developing countries because it contributed to "parallel trade." Parallel trade was the importation of drugs that had been exported with deep discounts to developing countries. The industry argued that parallel trade resulted in the importation of adulterated and counterfeit drugs or drugs that had been improperly stored and handled and thus imposed a safety risk to the (re)importing country. A bill introduced in Congress, however, would authorize pharmacies and wholesalers to purchase prescription drugs that had been exported from the United States.

Brazil faced high costs of purchasing AIDS drugs and negotiated price reductions with several drug companies, but Roche refused to offer a substantial reduction. Brazil then announced that it would issue a license to a Brazilian company to produce a generic version of Roche's drug.[20] Roche conceded and reduced the price to Brazil by an additional 40 percent.

The protection of intellectual property rights was an important issue for the brand-name pharmaceutical companies. The industry supported the World Trade Organization (WTO) and its enforcement of the TRIPS (Trade-Related Aspects of Intellectual Property Rights) Agreement. The industry participated in the U.S. government's Special 301 process to identify countries and their practices that violated TRIPS. The industry in particular pointed to Argentina, India, Israel, and Taiwan and argued that they should be priority countries for the U.S. government's enforcement activities. The United States filed a trade complaint with the WTO against Brazil for its law allowing compulsory licensing for drugs not manufactured in the country.

The pharmaceutical industry criticized India for restrictions on imports of pharmaceuticals and for encouraging a domestic industry that copied drugs under patent. A 1972 law allowed companies to copy a patented drug if they used a different manufacturing process. Pharmacists prescribed much of the drugs in India, and the drug companies competed for their attention. Brand-name companies began offering gifts to pharmacists if they prescribed the company's drugs, and Indian companies began to provide bonuses of free drugs. GlaxoSmithKline provided color television sets to pharmacists who met certain targets.

Patents provided the most important protection for intellectual property in the pharmaceutical industry. The patent on Schering-Plough's Claritin was scheduled to expire in December 2002, and the company sought without success before the FDA and in Congress to extend the market exclusivity. To delay the entry of competitors, Schering-Plough filed a patent infringement lawsuit against ten generic pharmaceutical companies, claiming that their versions of Claritin would, when ingested, necessarily produce a metabolite on which Schering-Plough held a patent. The courts had not upheld this "metabolite defense," but neither had they rejected it. At a minimum, the lawsuit could delay entry of the generics.

To resolve a lawsuit, Schering-Plough reached a settlement with Upsher-Smith Laboratories and American Home Products regarding their generic versions of K-Dur. Schering-Plough paid $60 million to Upsher-Smith, which then did not market its drug. Upsher-Smith had received a 180-day exclusivity period as a result of being the first company to develop a generic version, so other companies could not market their generic drugs. In April 2001 the

---

[18]See the Chapter 19 cases, *Merck and Vioxx* and *Pfizer and Celebrex.*

[19]See the Part V integrative case, *GlaxoSmithKline and AIDS Drug Policy.*

[20]The Brazilian constitution allowed the country to violate a patent in the case of abusive practices.

Federal Trade Commission voted unanimously to file civil charges challenging the agreement as a violation of the antitrust laws.

In addition to using patent infringement defenses, brand-name pharmaceutical companies used FDA rules to stave off generics. The patent on Bristol-Myers Squibb's blockbuster diabetes drug Glucophage expired in September 2000, and the company had initially been successful in staving off the generics by inducing patients to switch to two new versions of the drug that were not chemically equivalent to Glucophage. Based on new clinical tests, the FDA had approved Glucophage as safe for children, and Bristol-Myers received exclusive rights until 2004 for use by children. A 1994 FDA rule required that labels contain dosage and use information for children, but generics could not include such information on their labels because Bristol-Myers had exclusive rights to the data. The dilemma for the FDA was that its rule technically might block all generic versions of Glucophage. The dilemma had delayed the FDA approval of 14 generic versions for months, and Bristol-Myers was prepared to file a lawsuit if the FDA allowed provision of dosage and use information.

Medicare did not provide prescription drug benefits, and only about one-third of the elderly had pharmaceuticals insurance coverage. Congress wanted to provide prescription drug benefits under Medicare, but Democrats in Congress sought to provide roughly twice the coverage supported by the Bush administration. The pharmaceutical industry had opposed the legislation based on concerns that it would increase buyers' bargaining power relative to the pharmaceutical companies.

In response to congressional attempts to provide prescription drug coverage under Medicare, the Bush administration reached an agreement with pharmacy-benefits managers (PBMs) to negotiate drug discounts with pharmaceutical companies. The pharmaceutical companies opposed the plan because of the price pressures it would create. Two pharmacy associations, the National Association of Chain Drug Stores and the National Community Pharmacist Association (NCPA), filed a lawsuit to block the drug discount plan. The pharmacists opposed the plan because they feared being forced to shoulder the discounts.

The pharmacists were also concerned about direct competition from PBMs. In attempting to lower pharmaceutical expenditures, PBMs had begun to operate mail-order prescription refill services, making them direct competitors to the independent pharmacists. The NCPA, with 25,000 members nationwide, responded by launching a campaign to pressure state governments to increase their regulation of PBMs. The PBMs argued that the NCPA campaign was intended to increase its members' profits.

Public clamor and interest group activity against managed care organizations focused primarily on the denial of care sought by patients. Managed care organizations had been formed to hold down the cost of health care, and one means of doing so was to limit the opportunity of patients to receive whatever care they wanted. Patient advocacy groups and the Association of Trial Lawyers in particular sought to eliminate those limits by allowing patients to sue any provider that denied the care. Bills had passed the House and Senate, but the bills differed on where patients could file a lawsuit against a health care plan. The Democratic majority in the Senate passed a bill allowing lawsuits in state courts, believed to be more sympathetic to patients, and the Republican majority in the House restricted lawsuits to federal court and capped awards. The bills would require health plans to provide drugs not on their formulary at no additional cost if a doctor stated they were necessary. ■

## PREPARATION QUESTIONS

1. Characterize the issues, interests, institutions, and information in the environment of the pharmaceutical industry.
2. Which issues will be addressed in which institutional arenas, and which interests will be active on those issues?
3. Where are these issues in their life cycles?

# An Emerging Issue: MTBE

The Clean Air Act of 1990 addressed automobile emissions in a novel manner by focusing not only on the automobile and its emissions control system but also on the fuel used. To reduce carbon monoxide emissions that are a principal cause of smog, the act mandated that in ozone nonattainment areas, gasoline contain 15 percent oxygenates or be reformulated to achieve an equivalent reduction in emissions. This reformulated gasoline (RFG) had been required by the Environmental Protection Agency (EPA) in wintertime in several cities and throughout the year in a few areas. The principal substance chosen by refiners to meet the RFG mandate was methyl tertiary-butyl ether (MTBE). In 1995, 11 percent MTBE gasoline was used in nonattainment areas, and to meet standards set by the California Air Resources Board, virtually all gasoline sold in California since 1995 contained 11 percent MTBE. This oxygenate was a natural selection because oil companies had been blending 1 to 2 percent MTBE in gasoline since 1979 to increase octane. Using MTBE also solved a waste disposal problem, since it was produced from isobutylene, a by-product of refining.

The EPA estimated that RFG reduced hydrocarbon emissions by at least 15 percent. The California Air Resources Board credited the RFG program with major reductions in emissions equivalent to the elimination of 3.5 million cars. The board claimed to be "oxygenate neutral," however, expressing no preference for MTBE over other oxygenates.

RFG using MTBE had several drawbacks. MTBE cost approximately 20 cents a gallon more than gasoline. It also had less energy content than conventional gasoline, and hence mileage could be reduced by 2 to 3 percent. MTBE could also make ignition more difficult in cold weather and could affect fuel system seals and hoses, possibly causing fuel leaks. Chevron conducted a 115-vehicle, matched sets study of the effects of MTBE on elastometric fuel system parts and found a statistically significant higher number of fuel system leaks with gasoline blended with MTBE, particularly in older cars. Chevron posted a warning on its pumps in California.

MTBE also had an odor somewhat different from that of gasoline. Complaints about RFG with MTBE began in 1992 in Alaska, where motorists filling their gas tanks complained that the fumes made them ill. The RFG mandate had been enacted without substantial research on the oxygenates, and the auto and oil industries began a research program on the side effects of clean fuels only in 1990.

MTBE had high water solubility and chemical stability and did not biodegrade, making it a potential groundwater pollutant. In 1996 the city of Santa Monica, California, closed half its drinking water wells because of contamination with MTBE leaking from underground storage tanks at service stations. Both Chevron and Shell agreed to pay at least $5 million in the first year to clean up wells, but obtained the right to cease the cleanup if they found they were not responsible for the contamination. In 1998 Mobil agreed to pay $2.2 million to the city of Santa Monica and could be responsible for further cleanup costs.

The EPA had designated MTBE as a "possible," and gasoline as a "probable," carcinogen and argued that gasoline with MTBE was less hazardous than conventional gasoline. Some environmentalists and local residents, however, complained about the possible risks, particularly to drinking water.

Several other oxygenates were available, including the alkyl ethers (TAME [tertiary-amyl methyl ether], ETBE [ethyl tertiary-butyl ether], and DIPE [diisopropyl ether]) and alcohols (ethanol, methanol, and TBA [tertiary-butyl alcohol]). Little was known about the health effects of many of these oxygenates.

Ethanol was the second leading oxygenate used in RFG but had only 13 percent of the market. According to Chevron, ethanol was more expensive than the conventional refinery blendstocks despite a federal tax subsidy. Ethanol also had the disadvantage that it evaporated easily, thus adding to smog. RFG with ethanol was also difficult to ship by pipeline because the ethanol could separate out. The energy content of ethanol was approximately 66 percent of conventional gasoline, whereas the energy content of MTBE was 81 percent of conventional gasoline. The ethanol industry had worked intensely to preserve the ethanol tax credit through the year 2007. Lobbying for the ethanol industry was conducted by Fuels for the Future, the National Corn Growers Association, and Archer Daniels Midland.[21]

---

[21]Chemical Business Newsbase, March 13, 1998.

Several organizations had formed to oppose oxygenated fuels. The most active grassroots organization was Oxybusters, founded in 1993 in New Jersey by Barry Grossman. Oxybusters of California was formed by Jodi Walters of Lodi, who complained, "I've experienced short-term memory loss—light-headedness." Oxybusters groups were also established in Connecticut, Maine, Pennsylvania, and Texas. Oxybusters repeated arguments that MTBE reduced carbon monoxide emissions only in older cars and then only by 20 percent. Radio talk show hosts jumped on the campaign opposing RFG.

In 1997 the contamination of the wells in Santa Monica and the activities of Oxybusters resulted in a movement in California to overturn the RFG mandate. One activist group supporting the overturn was CALPIRG, the California Public Interest Research Group, with 60,000 members. CALPIRG stated, "Ethanol poses a substantially smaller risk of water pollution. It is readily absorbed into soil, unlike MTBE. It is biodegradable and non-carcinogenic." The Sierra Club and the Natural Resources Defense Council expressed reservations, however, arguing that the use of ethanol could be worse than what it replaced.[22] Environmentalists defending the use of MTBE focused on reducing leaks in gasoline storage tanks.

Tosco Corporation, the third largest refiner in California, wrote in October 1997 to the California Air Resources Board, calling for the reduction or elimination of MTBE. Citing a 1995 study by the auto and oil industries, Duane Bordvick of Tosco stated, "Theoretically, we can get oxygenates like MTBE down to zero in the new gasoline and still achieve the same goals. Water contamination is what is driving us. This problem is growing every day, and it is going to be very costly to solve. So we think it is better to deal with it now rather than look back and say we should have done something sooner."[23] The 1995 study concluded, "No significant differences were observed between California Reformulated Gasoline with and without oxygenate (MTBE)" in emissions and "The addition of an oxygenate (MTBE) had no significant effects on total exhaust toxics."

In October 1997 Governor Pete Wilson of California signed a bill directing the University of California to conduct a study of the health risks of MTBE. Earlier in the year, the EPA had written

to the American Petroleum Institute identifying research needed on MTBE. Under the Clean Air Act, the industry was responsible for research on the health effects of gasoline components. Bill Teaser, a senior scientist with Environmental Defense, said, "The fact there was a mandate to clean up the air did not justify ignoring potential water-quality problems. The bottom line is that companies need to do a more thorough assessment of all the characteristics of the compounds they put in gasoline."[24]

In December 1997 Senator Barbara Boxer (D-CA) wrote to EPA Administrator Carol Browner asking for safety standards for MTBE in drinking water and for a plan to phase out MTBE. The EPA issued an advisory identifying the levels at which the odor and taste of MTBE could be detected in drinking water. The advisory recommended that MTBE levels not exceed 20 to 40 parts per billion, which was 20,000 to 100,000 times lower than the level at which cancer was observed in animal toxicology studies.[25] The EPA reiterated its conclusion that the benefits of MTBE use "far exceed any known risks from the substance." In January 1998 Senator Diane Feinstein (D-CA) introduced legislation that would preclude the use of RFG in nonattainment areas in California.

In December 1998, Chevron Corporation followed Tosco by asking Congress to eliminate the RFG requirements if clean air goals could be met through other means. "Oxygenates in gasoline do little to reduce smog, but they have raised legitimate environmental concerns about MTBE in groundwater," said Dave O'Reilly, president of Chevron Products Co.[26]

The MTBE industry had grown to annual sales of $3 billion with 27 companies producing MTBE in the United States. MTBE was also imported from Canada and Argentina. The largest U.S. producer was ARCO Chemical Company, which had an MTBE capacity of 3,610 million pounds at its Channelview, Texas, plant and 1,140 million pounds at its Corpus Christi, Texas, plant. Ned Griffith of ARCO Chemical and vice chairman of the Oxygenated Fuels Association said, "We're disappointed and don't agree with [Tosco's] conclusions. While there has been some water contamination and it needs to be dealt with, there are no cases where people have

---

[22]Copley News Service, March 20, 1998.
[23]*San Francisco Chronicle,* October 30, 1997.

[24]*San Francisco Chronicle,* December 2, 1997.
[25]*API Soil & Groundwater Research Bulletin (Summary),* No. 3, March 1998.
[26]Chevron Press Release, December 1, 1997.

been directly exposed to MTBE through their water system."[27] Neither Tosco nor Chevron produced MTBE. ∎

## PREPARATION QUESTIONS

1. Identify the issues, interests, institutions, and information in the case.
2. Which companies have the strongest interests in the MTBE issue?
3. Are the interests of the oil companies homogeneous or heterogeneous?
4. Where is the MTBE issue in its life cycle and how it likely to progress?
5. As an oil company such as Chevron or Tosco, what strategy should be adopted to advance the campaign to eliminate the RFG mandate?

# The Nonmarket Environment of McDonald's

McDonald's, the world's largest restaurant chain with 30,000 restaurants in 118 countries serving 46 million customers daily, faced a host of nonmarket issues in the early 2000s.

## Obesity

The body mass index (BMI) of Americans increased throughout the 20th century, and the proportion of people considered obese increased from 15 to 31 percent from 1980 to 2000.[28] Sixty-four percent of American adults were overweight or obese. Interest in the obesity issue intensified after the release in February 2004 of a report by the Centers for Disease Control and Prevention estimating that 400,000 deaths anually were caused by obesity-released illnesses compared to 435,000 deaths caused by tobacco. The Surgeon General estimated that health care costs resulting from obesity were $117 billion annually.

Economists studied the increase in the BMI and concluded that it was due to several factors. Calorie intake had increased about 10 percent, and the strenuousness of work had decreased. Moreover, technological change had substantially reduced the relative cost of food, leading people to eat more.

In contrast to the economists, activists blamed fast food and the failure to provide nutritional information about menu items. Trial lawyers sought a new mass tort after their success in litigation against tobacco companies and saw obesity as an opportunity. Professor John Banzhaf, a law professor at George Washington University, who advised trial lawyers in obesity lawsuits against McDonald's, said, "A fast-food company like McDonald's may not be responsible for the entire obesity epidemic, but let's say they're 5 percent responsible. Five percent of $117 billion is still an enormous amount of money."[29] The first two obesity lawsuits had been dismissed.[30]

## The Cheeseburger Bill

The restaurant and food industries argued that obesity was a matter of individual responsibility and lobbied Congress for protection from obesity lawsuits. In 2004 the House quickly passed the Personal Responsibility in Food Consumption Act, dubbed the cheeseburger bill, on a 276–139 vote. The bill provided protection from obesity and weight-based lawsuits unless the weight gain was due to the violation of a state or federal law. Author of the bill Ric Keller (R-FL) said, "We need to get back to the old-fashioned principles of common sense and personal responsibility and get

---

[27]*San Francisco Chronicle,* October 30, 1997.
[28]Cutler, Glaeser, and Shapiro concluded that demographic changes did not explain the increase in obesity. David M. Cutler, Edward L. Glaeser, and Jesse M. Shapiro, "Why Have Americans Become More Obese?" Working paper, National Bureau of Economic Research, no date.

[29]*Time,* August 3, 2003.
[30]See the Chapter 12 case *Obesity and McLawsuits* for more information on the issue.

away from this new culture where everybody plays the victim and blames other people for their problems."[31] James Sensenbrenner (R-WI) was more direct, stating that "fat people should 'look in the mirror' and that parents need to monitor children's eating habits to make sure that 'little Johnny' doesn't become 'big Johnny.' "[32] House Speaker Dennis Hastert (R-IL) commented, "We as Americans need to realize that suing your way to better health is not the answer. Trial lawyers need to stop encouraging consumers to blame others for the consequences of their actions just so they can profit from frivolous lawsuits against restaurants."[33]

Referring to the cheeseburger bill, Representative James McGovern (D-MA) argued, "It protects an industry that doesn't need to be protected at this particular point and we're dealing with a problem that doesn't exist. The problem that does exist is that we have an obesity problem in this country."[34] Neil Barnard, president of the Physicians Committee for Responsible Medicine, commented, "[The bill] is an unsavory attempt to protect corporate profits at the expense of American health. The bill strips the public of its right to seek any redress against food manufacturers for their contribution to the obesity crisis, and the related epidemics of heart disease and diabetes."[35]

The restaurant industry backed the Commonsense Consumption Act, the state version of the cheeseburger bill, which would shield restaurants and food processors from obesity liability. As of mid-2004 the cheeseburger bill had been introduced in 23 state legislatures, and eight states had enacted it.

## Filmmaking Activism

The news media extensively covered the fast-food and obesity issue, and the issue became the subject of films. McDonald's was the target of a 98-minute film *Super Size Me* by filmmaker Morgan Spurlock. Spurlock ate only at McDonald's for 30 days, gained 25 pounds, and received warnings from doctors about his health. "Spurlock's approach was undeniably extreme. He supersized his meals whenever a counter worker made the offer, and ordered everything on the menu at least once. He also stopped exercising.

As a result he was often eating twice as many calories a day as he needed. And as any nutritionist will tell you, it only takes an extra 100 calories a day to gain 10 pounds a year."[36]

In response to Spurlock's film, the Competitive Enterprise Institute (CEI) supported preparation of a film by Soso Whaley in which for two 30-day periods she ate only at McDonald's. She lost 18 pounds by controlling her calorie intake. The CEI stated, "Whaley's documentary project, focusing on personal responsibility, obesity, and public health, is taking on the increasing victim mentality being fostered by public health activists and the dishonest bashing of the fast food industry."[37]

## Meal and Menu Nutrition Information

The public attention to the obesity issue led to the introduction of the Menu Education and Labeling Act (MEAL) in the House and the Senate. The so-called McMenu bills applied to chains with 20 or more locations operating under one trade name. The Senate bill required disclosure "in a statement adjacent to the name of the food on any menu . . . the number of calories, grams of saturated fat plus trans fat, and milligrams of sodium contained in a serving of the food. . . ."

The participants in the news conference accompanying the bill submission were Senator Tom Harkin (D-IA), Representative Rosa DeLauro (D-CN), and Margo Wootan, nutrition policy director of the Center for Science in the Public Interest (CSPI). Harkin said, "So many people are getting suckered into these supersized gimmicks because they are led to believe that bigger is better value. But if you continue to choose supersized, the odds are you will be supersized." Wootan said, "People have good nutrition information in the supermarkets, but people can only guess what they're eating at chain restaurants."[38] The National Restaurant Association, representing 870,000 restaurants with 11.7 million workers, opposed the "one-size-fits-all" and "pre-packaged" MEAL bill. The Association observed, "When Americans do dine out at one of

---

[31]The Daily Buzz, www.foodservice.com, March 11, 2004.
[32]The Daily Buzz, www.foodservice.com, March 11, 2004.
[33]Associated Press Online, March 10, 2004.
[34]Associated Press Online, March 10, 2004.
[35]The Daily Buzz, www.foodservice.com, March 9, 2004.

[36]*San Francisco Chronicle,* April 21, 2004. The film included John Banzhaf, who commented that the documentary would result in more lawsuits.
[37]Competitive Enterprise Institute, Washington, DC, April 15, 2004.
[38]Copely News Service, November 24, 2003.

the nation's 870,000 restaurants they find a wide variety of venues, menu items, and portion sizes—meeting customers' demands for choice, value and flexibility, as well as their tastes and dietary needs."[39]

## Healthy Lifestyles

As a result of the concern about obesity, McDonald's suspended its promotion of supersize meals and developed a "healthy lifestyles" program, initially offering additional items, including fruit and salads. In April 2004 the company launched a Lifestyles Platform to address obesity and physical well-being. The Platform included new food choices and ordering options such as the "Go Active" adult Happy Meal, education and easily accessible nutrition information, and physical activity, including the distribution of 15 million Stepometers and walking/fitness booklets. In 2004 it announced that by the end of the year it would introduce a new "core menu" and phase-out supersize options.

The CSPI continued to focus on McDonald's. In response to McDonald's announcement that it would add salads and healthy meals to its menu, Executive Director Michael F. Jacobson declared, "Consumers have good reason to be skeptical about the company's latest promises, since the company broke its promise to reformulate its trans-fat-laden cooking oil. By frying in partially hydrogenated vegetable oil, McDonald's recklessly promotes heart disease among its consumers."[40]

## Children's Advertising

Advertising to children had long been of concern to children's advocates and members of Congress, which had restricted advertising on children's television programs. McDonald's promoted its trademark golden arches on Barbie dolls and backpacks, and some schools had McDonald's days for lunch. McDonald's also used plastic toy promotions often timed with the release of a movie. "'It seems very clear it's a breach of duty,' says John Banzhaf. . . . 'Schools get paid a kickback for every sugary soft drink or burger sold.'"[41] Professor Walter Willett of Harvard University's School of Public Health, said,

"The vast majority of what they sell is junk. . . . We don't sell children guns, alcohol or drugs, but we do allow them to be exploited by food companies."[42]

## Obesity in the Workplace

McDonald's also faced obesity issues in the workplace. A 6 feet 1 inch, 420-pound man was offered a job as a cook but was told that he could not begin work until his specially ordered uniform with a 54-inch waistband arrived. After waiting 4 months for the uniform he filed a lawsuit against McDonald's alleging violation of the Americans with Disabilities Act (ADA).[43] The ADA did not prohibit discrimination based on appearance, but some plaintiffs argued that they were not hired or not treated fairly because employers wrongly concluded that they had a disability. A 5 feet 1 inch, 320-pound woman had filed a lawsuit on this theory. In 1997 the U.S. Court of Appeals ruled that "obesity, except in special cases where the obesity relates to a physiological disorder, is not a 'physical impairment.'"

## Acrylamide

Researchers in Sweden detected the chemical acrylamide in a variety of foods but particularly in carbohydrates cooked at high temperatures. The researchers specifically mentioned french fries from McDonald's and Burger King. Researchers in other countries, including those at the Food and Drug Administration (FDA), confirmed the findings. Activists, including the CSPI, argued that the concentrations of acrylamide exceeded the EPA and WHO standards for water. Author Steven Milloy countered that in the study on which the EPA based its drinking water standard, the lowest concentration at which rats had a significant increase in cancer was 500 micrograms per kilogram of body weight.[44] Milloy stated that for a 154-pound man this was equivalent to 35,000 micrograms, which would require eating 486 large servings of McDonald's french fries every day for life. He added, "Acrylamide hysteria is nothing more than a

---

[39]U.S. Newswire, November 5, 2003.
[40]Press Release, CSPI, April 15, 2004.
[41]*The New York Times*, August 3, 2004.

[42]*The New York Times*, August 3, 2004.
[43]During this period, McDonald's sold the restaurant to a franchisee who was unaware of the employment offer. (*The New York Times*, August 4, 2003.)
[44]Steven Milloy, *Junk Science Judo: Self-Defense Against Health Scares and Scams*, Washington, DC: Cato Institute, 2001.

convenient, if not cynical, tactic of CSPI to advance its anti-fun food agenda."[45]

The issue of consumer warnings regarding acrylamide resurfaced in California in April 2004. The Safe Drinking Water and Toxic Enforcement Act required a public notice for substances "known to the state to cause cancer, birth defects or other reproductive harm." In 1990 California had declared acrylamide, which was used in treating sewage water, to be such a substance. The concern was for workers who produced or worked with acrylamide. Private attorneys filed lawsuits to force the state to require fast-food companies to warn the public. The State began conducting studies to determine if there was any danger to people.

## Mad Cow Disease

In December 2003 the first case of mad cow disease documented in the United States was detected in Washington state in a downer (immobile) cow that had been purchased from Canada.[46] The FDA immediately began an informational campaign, as did the beef industry and the food and restaurant industries, to assure the public that there was no threat to humans. The National Cattlemen's Beef Association (NCBA) had been preparing for such an event by providing information to the public on beef safety.

McDonald's, which did not buy meat from downer cattle nor cattle parts that could carry the disease, stated that the recall of beef by the federal government had "absolutely no connection whatsoever to McDonald's or our suppliers." McDonald's had dealt with the issue of mad cow disease in a number of other countries and had used that experience to prepare for such an event in the United States. McDonald's posted on its Web site a letter to its customers and also distributed copies to customers in its restaurants. McDonald's reported that its sales were not affected.

The critics of the FDA and U.S. Department of Agriculture (USDA) continued to sound the alarm, and the media reported their claims, but no one seemed to pay attention. The CSPI criticized the actions of the USDA, stating that "consumer protec-

tion has certainly fallen short." Concerned about the ban on American beef imposed by a number of countries, the USDA set up an international panel to assess the situation. The panel recommended that the United States adopt stronger standards, consistent with international standards, and stated that more cases were likely in the future and that the present case should not be viewed as an "imported case." The NCBA criticized the recommendation as not taking into account the steps the United States and Canada had taken since 1989 to reduce the likelihood of BSE.

## Antibiotics and Growth Hormones

Human health concerns had been raised about the possible development of antibiotic resistance in humans as a result of the use of antibiotics in food animals. Recognizing the importance of antibiotics for both human and veterinary medicine, McDonald's developed a policy based on the principle that "All users of antibiotics, including those who supervise use in animals and those who supervise use in humans, must work to sustain the long-term efficacy of antibiotics for human and veterinary medicine."[47] McDonald's established Sustainable Use Guiding Principles to govern their use. In the absence of a specific disease or likely threat of a specific disease, "antibiotics belonging to classes of compounds approved for use in human medicine" were to be phased out.

McDonald's, Environmental Defense, and Elanco Animal Health joined together to create the Antibiotics Coalition. "By working together, McDonald's and Environmental Defense have leveraged the company's purchasing power to reverse the trend of antibiotics overuse in animal agriculture. McDonald's new policy demonstrates that reducing antibiotic use is both feasible and affordable."[48]

In 2000 McDonald's began phasing out growth-promoting antibiotics in Europe, and by the end of 2001, it had eliminated all such antibiotics in its suppliers' chicken feed. Antibiotics in the fluoroquinolone class were discontinued in the United States in 2001. In 2003 it announced that use of

---

[45]Steven Milloy, "French Fry Scare," www.cato.org. Americans ate 28 pounds of potato chips and french fries a year on average.
[46]Mad cow disease is bovine spongiform encephalopathy (BSE), and in humans it is known as variant Creutzfeldt-Jakob disease (vCJD).

[47]McDonald's Global Policy on Antibiotic Use in Food Animals. www.mcdonalds.com.
[48]PR Newswire, June 19, 2003.

growth-promoting hormones would be phased out by all its suppliers.

## Animal Welfare

McDonald's was targeted by People for the Ethical Treatment of Animals (PETA) and other animal welfare groups over the treatment of food animals. In response McDonald's adopted new standards for its beef suppliers, including minimum space standards for cattle in feedlots. McDonald's market power quickly led feedlot operators to meet the standards, bringing about change in the entire industry. Standards were also set for animal transport and care.

In 2000 PETA distributed "Unhappy Meals" boxes similar to the boxes used for Happy Meals. Each box contained a doll resembling Ronald McDonald with a bloody butcher's knife in his hand. McDonald's pledged to improve the welfare of chickens, and PETA suspended its campaign.[49]

Change had begun when the USDA hired Dr. Temple Gradin, a professor at Colorado State University who researched animal welfare, to evaluate the conditions in 24 meat-processing plants.[50] Her report startled the government and the industry. She documented substantial, and unnecessary, animal suffering. In 1997 McDonald's decided to visit Gradin and was impressed by her scientific, quantitative approach to evaluating the slaughter of animals. "We went to Colorado State and saw her, and it was magic. She pitched her program, and we thought it was perfect."[51] Gradin demonstrated how she "measured animal behavior and conditions, how she paid attention to animal vocalizations, how she studied their responses to electric prods, how she cataloged their adaptations to various conditions."[52]

The American Meat Association held workshops attended by farmers, slaughterhouse managers, and truck drivers on topics such as "Inside the Mind of a Steer," "Humane Turkey Production," and "Creating an Animal Welfare Mind-Set in Your Company." Truck drivers took workshops to become certified as humane handlers. Paul Whitfield, of Odom's Tennessee Pride sausage plant, commented about no longer using an electric prod, "We sure don't have to

be as aggressive as before. It's a lot less stressful, on us and on them." PETA applauded the improvements with Bruce Friedrich stating, "We've achieved societal sea change." But he quickly added, "The level of abuse is still such that it would horrify any compassionate person."[53]

In response to pressure from McDonald's and other large customers, the United Egg Producers (UEP), which represented virtually all egg producers in the United States, developed an "animal care certified" logo that retailers could carry on their egg cartons. To qualify, producers had to file monthly reports and have an on-site compliance audit annually. Adele Douglass, former director of the American Humane Association, commented, "What the UEP has done is incredible. They've moved a whole industry forward." Paul Shapiro, of Compassion Over Killing, however, said, "What the UEP is trying to do is increase space minimally to prevent an inevitable legislative ban on cages. We find animal abuse is the norm in the egg industry and not the exception. These hens never see daylight, never touch earth, and never even flap their wings."[54]

## Defamation

In 2001 Carmen Calderón complained to the public health agency in Chile that her son had come down with food poisoning after eating in a McDonald's restaurant. McDonald's filed a $1.25 million lawsuit against Calderón, seeking an apology for what it viewed as an unsubstantiated claim.

## The Environment

McDonald's established an environmental policy pertaining to natural resources, rainforests, sustainability, and waste management. It refused to purchase beef from "rainforest or recently deforested rainforest land." McDonald's also participated in the European Union's Greenlights Programme and the U.S. Green Lights program to reduce electricity use in its restaurants. In Denmark McDonald's opened the first HFC/CFC-free restaurant. Minister of the Environment Hans Chr. Schmidt, said, "Today McDonald's is showing how companies can make a difference by setting new standards for environmental performance, . . . It's a good day for the

[49]*Associate* Press Online, March 24, 2002.
[50]www.gradin.com.
[51]*The International Herald Tribune,* June 26, 2003.
[52]*The International Herald Tribune,* June 26, 2003.

[53]*Los Angeles Times,* April 29, 2003.
[54]The Business Press/California, March 31, 2003.

environment."[55] Greenpeace claimed credit for forcing McDonald's to open the restaurant.

## Suppliers

As a result of concerns in the 1990s about the treatment of workers in overseas suppliers' factories, McDonald's developed a Code of Conduct for Suppliers. The code covered employment practices pertaining to the use of prison and forced labor, child labor, working hours, compensation, nondiscrimination, and the workplace environment. McDonald's refused to do business with suppliers that did not abide by the Code and reserved the right to conduct unannounced inspections of suppliers' facilities.

## Franchisees

By 2000 McDonald's was the largest employer in Brazil and was named employer of the year by *Exame* magazine. The economic downturn and the rise of the U.S. dollar, however, squeezed McDonald's franchisees. In response McDonald's purchased hundreds of franchises, and by 2003 only 184 of 582 restaurants in Brazil were owned by franchisees. The remaining franchisees filed a lawsuit against McDonald's alleging that it squeezed them by overcharging for rent and opening too many restaurants.[56]

## Vegetarianism

A 2000 Roper poll commissioned by the Vegetarian Resource Group found that 6 percent of girls and 2 percent of boys between 6 and 17 years never eat meat. "Janet Carr, nutrition director at Remuda Ranch, a clinic for women with bulimia and anorexia in Wichenberg, Arizona, says about 25 percent of her teen clients classify themselves as vegetarians. 'Can someone be a healthy vegetarian? I would say yes, absolutely, but it's a difficult challenge, you have to put a lot of effort into it,' Carr, says."[57] The National Cattlemen's Beef Association began a marketing campaign aimed at 8 to 12-year-old girls emphasizing beef as a source of protein, iron, and B12, of which the USDA indicated young girls did not get nearly enough.

## Brand Name Attractions

In April 2003 two incendiary devices failed to ignite at a Chico, California, McDonald's where Animal Liberation Front (ALF) activists had written "Meat is Murder" on the restaurant. The next day, firebombs exploded at a McDonald's and an Arby's in Albuquerque, New Mexico. The Earth Liberation Front (ELF) produced a videotape, "Igniting the Revolution," that featured McDonald's as a target. "Wherever they are, McDonald's are a legitimate target for people who want to protect the earth. McDonald's is a symbol of international animal abuse and environmental destruction," said Rodney Coronado, who had spent four years in prison for a firebombing in 1992.[58] Directions on building firebombs were available on the ALF and ELF Web sites. ■

---

### PREPARATION QUESTIONS

1. Characterize the four I's.
2. What is the time frame of each issue?
3. Which issues should have the highest priority?

4. What overall strategy should McDonald's adopt for dealing with these nonmarket issues?

---

[55]McDonald's Corporate Press Release, January 16, 2003.
[56]*The Wall Street Journal*, October 21, 2003.

[57]*Morning Call*, May 23, 2003.
[58]Associated Press State & Local Wire, April 28, 2003.

# CHAPTER 2

# Integrated Strategy

## Introduction

A business strategy guides a firm in its market and nonmarket environments and has both market and nonmarket components. A market strategy is a concerted pattern of actions taken in the market environment to create value by improving the economic performance of a firm. A nonmarket strategy is a concerted pattern of actions taken in the nonmarket environment to create value by improving overall performance. A firm that decides to enter a country that has open markets relies primarily on a market strategy. A firm that decides to enter a country that has erected trade barriers needs a nonmarket strategy in addition to a market strategy. An effective business strategy integrates these two components and tailors them to the firm's market and nonmarket environments as well as to its competencies.[1]

Market and nonmarket strategies focus on the pursuit of opportunity and advantage in the face of market and nonmarket competition with the objective of achieving superior performance. In this book, performance is considered at two levels. Initially, it is measured by the value created for the firm's owners. Then, in Part V the objective is broadened using concepts of corporate social responsibility and ethics.

This chapter focuses on nonmarket analysis and strategy and their integration with their market counterparts. As illustrated in Figure 2-1, effective management in the nonmarket environment requires conceptual frameworks for (1) analyzing nonmarket issues and the broader environment, (2) formulating effective strategies for addressing those issues, and (3) positioning the firm in its nonmarket environment. The strategy concept is introduced first, and the integration of market and nonmarket analysis and strategy formulation are considered. Strategic positioning in the nonmarket environment is then considered and illustrated using the examples of eBay and BP (British Petroleum). Nonmarket analysis is then considered, and a framework for analysis is presented and illustrated using an example involving Citibank.

---

[1]This material is adapted from Baron (1995b). Copyright © 1995 by the Board of Regents of the University of California. Reprinted from the *California Management Review*, Vol. 37., No. 2. By permission of The Regents.

# Strategy in the Nonmarket Environment

## The Importance of Nonmarket Strategy

The importance of nonmarket strategies is related to the control of a firm's opportunities, as illustrated in Figure 2-2. Opportunities can be controlled by government at one extreme and markets at the other extreme. Nonmarket strategies are more important the more opportunities are controlled by government and are less important, but often still important, when opportunities are controlled by markets. In some industries, such as consumer electronics and computer software, government exercises relatively little control over firms and their activities. In contrast, government exercises considerable control over pharmaceuticals and local telecommunications service. The automobile industry is somewhere in between. One important role of nonmarket strategy is to unlock opportunities controlled by government, as illustrated by the strategies of firms to deregulate the telecommunications industry. Another important role of nonmarket strategy is to avoid control of opportunities by government, as in the case of self-regulation by business of Internet privacy protection.

Over time, industries can move along the control dimension. In many countries the government had controlled telecommunications services through ownership of a monopoly supplier. In the pursuit of improved performance, many of these countries privatized their telecommunications firms and replaced ownership with regulation and competition. In the United States the regulation of telecommunications is being replaced by market competition, with long-distance and information services being the most extensively controlled by markets and local service the least. The Internet has been at the right in Figure 2-2, but nonmarket issues such as privacy, taxation of electronic commerce, and protection of intellectual property have made nonmarket strategy more important, as considered in Chapter 13.

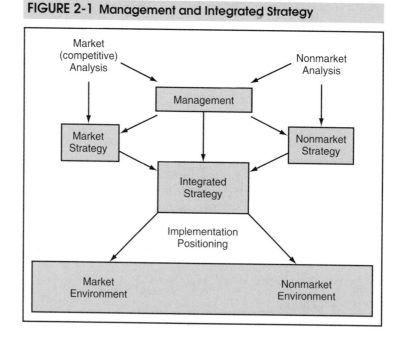

FIGURE 2-1 Management and Integrated Strategy

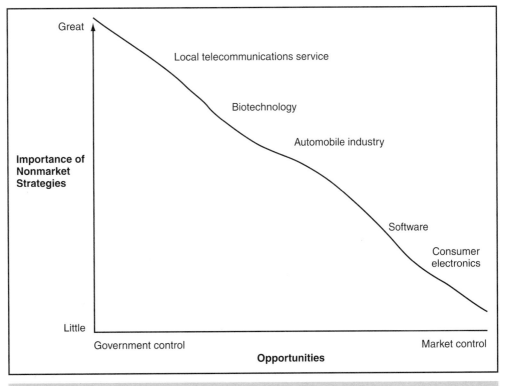

**FIGURE 2-2** Nonmarket Strategy and the Control of Opportunities

In addition to government and markets, two other factors affect opportunities. First, opportunities can be controlled by private politics, which includes actions such as protests, boycotts, and public criticism by activist, advocacy, and interest groups as well as the public climate in which a firm operates. The control of opportunities typically centers on the conjunction of an issue and the practices of a firm or industry. The more intense is private politics, the more important is nonmarket strategy, as illustrated in Figure 2-3. Issues such as the environment, human rights, privacy, health, and safety attract private politics, as considered in Chapter 4. In contrast, issues such as intellectual property protection, liability reform, and antitrust seldom attract private politics but are the subject of public politics. Issues such as genetically modified organisms in food attract intense private politics in Europe and less in the United States.

Second, opportunities can be affected by moral concerns, which may call for restraint in the pursuit of some opportunities. Part V of the book provides principles to guide firms and their managers in reasoning about moral concerns and broader social responsibilities and whether they require self-regulation on the part of a firm. For example, before the issue became salient, Levi Strauss & Co. used moral principles in formulating a policy governing working conditions at its overseas suppliers' factories, as considered in Chapter 21.

## Competition and Change in the Nonmarket Environment

Market strategies typically take the nonmarket environment as given and focus on the competitive positions of firms in the industry, the threats from substitutes and potential

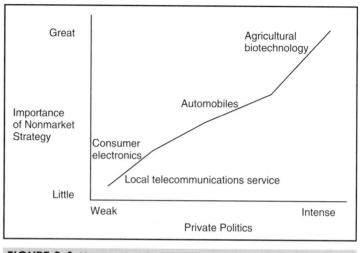

**FIGURE 2-3 Nonmarket Strategy and Private Politics**

entrants, and the bargaining power of suppliers and customers.[2] When a firm looks ahead, however, neither the market nor the nonmarket environments can be viewed as fixed. Moreover, change depends importantly on the strategies that firms and other interested parties employ to influence those environments.

When a firm chooses a market strategy, that strategy competes with the strategies of other participants in the market. Similarly, when a firm chooses a nonmarket strategy, that strategy competes with the strategies of others, including other firms, activists, interest groups, and government agencies. That competition shapes the nonmarket environment and often the market environment as well. The nonmarket environment thus should be thought of as competitive, as is the market environment. Nonmarket competition focuses on specific issues, such as a bill to increase fuel economy standards, as well as on broader issues, such as replacing fuel economy regulation with a carbon tax. A broader set of participants is typically present in the nonmarket than in the market environment, so a firm often has a more complex strategy problem in the nonmarket environment. Nonmarket strategy is essential, since in its absence competitors in the nonmarket environment will influence the outcome of issues and shape the environment to their advantage.

## Strategy and the Nonmarket Issue Life Cycle

The timing of a nonmarket strategy can be crucial to success. Using the life cycle concept from Chapter 1, Figure 2-4 identifies strategies as a function of the stage at which a firm begins to address a nonmarket issue. The firm has more flexibility and a wider range of alternatives the earlier it addresses an issue. If an issue is addressed at the issue identification stage, strategies can be directed at affecting the development of the issue. The firm may also be able to frame the issue prior to interest group formation. Levi Strauss was one of the first companies to address the issue of working conditions in its suppliers' factories, and the policies it developed kept it out of the line of attack of activists.

---

[2]See Porter (1980); Oster (1999); Besanko, Dranove, Schaefer, and Shanley (2004); and Saloner, Shepard, and Podolny (2001).

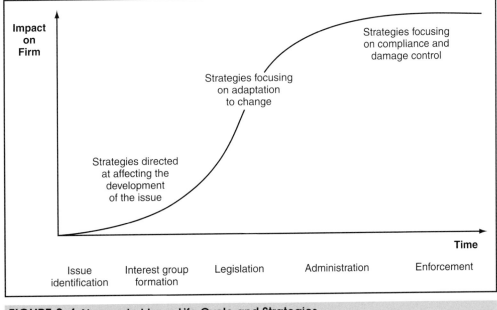

**FIGURE 2-4 Nonmarket Issue Life Cycle and Strategies**

If a firm addresses the issue once interest groups have formed and the issue is in the legislative stage, the firm has less flexibility and its range of alternatives is narrower. Nike was late in addressing the issue of working conditions at its suppliers' factories in Asia, and it became a target for activists, as considered in Chapter 4. Nike found itself in the position of reacting to the nonmarket strategies of others rather than shaping the development of the issue. Its opportunity to participate in the resolution of the nonmarket issue was largely limited to the enforcement stage. Nike's nonmarket strategy basically involved damage control.

## Strategies and Borders

Bartlett and Ghoshal (1989) characterize market strategies as multidomestic (multinational), international, and global. A global market strategy is one in which "products and strategies are developed to exploit an integrated unitary world market." Global market strategies often focus on achieving cost advantages through global-scale operations, as exemplified by Honda's early strategy of selling the same motorcycles in all the markets it entered. In the nonmarket environment, examples of global strategies are (1) working for free trade globally, (2) building constructive working relationships with host governments, (3) applying universal ethics principles, and (4) implementing the same environmental standards in all countries.

An international strategy centers on transferring the parent's expertise to foreign markets. Yahoo!, for example, took its online auction service to other countries. International strategies are specific applications of policy and expertise in other countries.

A global or international nonmarket strategy may not be successful, however, because strategies must take into account the specific nonmarket issues in a country, the institutions in whose context the issues are addressed, the organization of interests, and other country-specific factors. In France, Yahoo! was quickly met with a lawsuit because World War II Nazi items were auctioned on its U.S. Web site. French law prohibits buying or selling Nazi items, and France filed a lawsuit against Yahoo! Yahoo! refused to ban the items because it was legal to sell them in other countries, including the United States. In contrast, eBay designs its online auction venues in strict accord with the laws of each country in which it operates. Many nonmarket issues have a strong domestic component, so nonmarket strategies are more likely than market strategies to be multidomestic when issues, institutions, and interests differ across countries.

The success of a multidomestic strategy requires issue-specific action plans tailored to the institutions and the organization of interests in individual countries. Examples of nonmarket issues that require a multidomestic approach include legislation, antitrust policy, liability rules, safety regulation, pharmaceuticals approval, intellectual property rights, and environmental regulation. Although there are common principles, such as information provision as the key to effective lobbying, that underlie the strategies used to address such issues, differences in the institutions typically require country-specific strategies. In the United States lobbying focuses on Congress and its committees. In Japan lobbying focuses more on the bureaucracy and political parties and their leaders. In the European Union, lobbying focuses on the Commission and the Directorates-General as well as on national institutions as a means of influencing the Council of Ministers. In Germany, lobbying occurs through peak business and labor associations and their chambers, as well as directly between individual firms and the bureaucracy and political parties.

## Integrated Strategy

An effective market strategy is necessary for successful firm performance, but it is not always sufficient. An effective nonmarket strategy is rarely sufficient, but for most firms it is necessary for successful performance. Market strategies serve the objective of superior performance by developing and sustaining the competitive advantage required to pursue market opportunities. Nonmarket strategies serve the objective of superior performance by participating effectively and responsibly in the public processes that affect the control of opportunities. The performance of a firm also depends on how well its nonmarket analysis and strategy are integrated with its market analysis and strategy. Because performance is the responsibility of management, managers are responsible for both market and nonmarket strategies and for their integration, as illustrated in Figure 2-1.

The focus of nonmarket strategy is on issues that affect the opportunities of a firm, its positioning in its market and nonmarket environments, and its reputation and sustainability. A nonmarket strategy consists of objectives and a plan of action to address the issues on a firm's agenda, and that strategy must be tailored to the institutions in whose arenas the issues will be addressed. That strategy must also anticipate the strategies of other interests, including those aligned with and those opposed to the objectives of the firm.

Both market and nonmarket strategies have the objective of superior performance and focus on securing market opportunities and addressing threats to those opportunities. Synergies can be present between market and nonmarket strategies, and the overall business strategy is more effective the more that those synergies can be exploited. A synergy is present if a nonmarket action increases the return from a market action or, conversely, a market action increases the return from a nonmarket action.

As an example, the automobile industry faces market pressure from higher gasoline prices and nonmarket pressure for improved fuel economy to address the global climate change and security issues. Diesel engines provide 20 to 30 percent better fuel economy than gasoline engines, yet in California, New York, and three other states existing diesel engines cannot meet current emissions standards and will not be able to meet the 2007 federal standards for particulates emissions. Synergies are present because the more an automaker commits to diesel technology in its market strategy, the stronger is the incentive in its nonmarket strategy to lobby Congress for cleaner diesel fuel. Conversely, the more progress an automaker makes convincing Congress to mandate cleaner diesel fuel, the stronger is the incentive to deploy current-technology diesel engines in automobiles and to develop more efficient engines.

One approach to integrating market and nonmarket strategies is to incorporate both into the market strategy process. For example, regulation pertaining to who may provide services, as in telecommunications, could be incorporated into the analysis of the rivalry among existing firms and the assessment of potential new entrants and the threat of substitutes. The drawback to this approach is that the institutions in which regulatory policies are established are quite different from the institution of markets, so the nature of the analysis is different. Moreover, in markets only the parties that transact play a role, whereas in nonmarket institutions a wide range of interests is enfranchised to participate.

Market and nonmarket strategies could also be viewed as separate. Just as market analysis focuses on competitive forces, nonmarket analysis can focus on assessing threats (such as those arising from government, interest groups, and activist pressures) and on unlocking market opportunities. Viewing nonmarket issues as a separate force, however, risks missing the interrelationships between market and nonmarket issues and the synergies between strategies to address those issues.[3]

The most effective means of integrating market and nonmarket strategies is to incorporate both into the business strategy process. That is, both market and nonmarket strategies should be chosen together in addressing forces in the market and nonmarket environments.[4] The nonmarket strategy component then focuses on specific nonmarket issues that affect market threats and opportunities and on nonmarket actions as complements to market actions.

Because nonmarket strategies must be tailored to the specific issues, interests, institutions, and information in the nonmarket environment, there is no short list of generic nonmarket strategies. Moreover, the nonmarket agenda of a firm is in part set externally in the environment rather than by the firm, and strategies must attend to that agenda. The chapter cases, *Envirotest Systems Corporation (A)* and *Personal Watercraft, aka Jet Skis,* provide opportunities to assess market and nonmarket strategies and the effectiveness of their integration.

---

[3]Gale and Buchholz (1987) discuss the relationship between political strategies and Porter's (1980) five forces. Yoffie (1987) characterizes strategies by the approach taken to political issues.
[4]Baron (1997a, 1999, 2001) provides formal models of integrated strategies and a nontechnical presentation in (1996).

# Nonmarket Positioning

Firms strategically position themselves in the markets in which they operate, focusing on the benefits to customers and costs to the firm.[5] They also strategically position their products in attribute space, both in an absolute sense and relative to rival products. Positioning is a foundation for market or competitive strategy because it can be a source of competitive advantage.

Just as firms position themselves strategically in their market environments, they also position themselves strategically in their nonmarket environments. Positioning provides a foundation for nonmarket strategy and can enhance a market strategy and its integration with a nonmarket strategy. Positioning also affects the set of nonmarket issues and challenges a firm faces, including challenges from activist and interest groups, governments, and competitors.[6] Market positioning also affects the set of nonmarket issues a firm encounters. Nike, the Gap, and other footwear and apparel manufacturers positioned themselves as design and marketing companies and sourced their products from independent contractors, primarily in Asia. The working conditions in the contractors' factories, however, generated a host of nonmarket issues for the firms.

Nonmarket positioning should be a conscious choice rather than dictated by a firm's market positioning or by those in its environment. Nonmarket positioning thus is a fundamental part of the strategy process. Exclusive Resorts was conceived as a luxury vacation residence alternative to a second home without the hassles and expense associated with ownership. The principal form of vacation residence was a timeshare in which a consumer purchased a fraction of a year at a resort development. Timeshares had earned a bad reputation as a result of high-pressure marketing techniques, and most states closely regulated them. Exclusive Resorts faced the challenge of designing its business so that it served the market opportunity it had identified yet avoided the regulatory burden imposed on timeshares. The challenge was to position itself in its market environment to serve the demand for luxury vacation residences and to position itself in the nonmarket environment to avoid timeshare and other regulations. Exclusive Resorts was an instant success, and that success attracted new entrants with similar business models. The luxury vacation residence model then posed a market threat to the timeshare industry. Moreover, some of the new entrants were not as well capitalized as Exclusive Resorts, which raised the possibility that promises to consumers might not be kept. This could result in complaints that could attract the attention of regulators. The chapter case, *Exclusive Resorts: Entrepreneurial Positioning and Nonmarket Defense,* provides an opportunity to assess its positioning and formulate an integrated strategy for addressing the threats resulting from its market success.

Too often firms find themselves in a position they wish they had avoided. A firm may find itself confronted by protests over its environmental practices, disadvantaged by a regulatory action, or exposed to avoidable liabilities. Alternatively, a firm may benefit from having established a relationship of trust with a regulatory agency, joined with an environmental group to resolve a wildlife habitat problem, or provided expertise to a congressional committee addressing a complex issue in pharmaceutical patent protection. Not only is nonmarket positioning important for avoiding problems and attracting benefits, but it also provides a platform on which both market and nonmarket strategies can be constructed. Nonmarket positioning thus should be a strategic choice just as positioning a product in attribute space is a strategic choice. The eBay example illustrates this choice.

---

[5]See Besanko, Dranove, Schaefer, and Shanley (2004); Saloner, Shepard, and Podolny (2001); and Porter (1980, 1985).
[6]The contributors in Aggarwal (2001) consider positioning of firms in Asia, although most of the analysis focuses on market positioning.

## eBay's Positioning in Legal Space

eBay, the market leader in person-to-person online auctions, had 34 million members in its trading community in 2001 and hosted 5 million auctions on a given day. eBay had carefully positioned itself relative to state and federal laws, and that positioning shielded it from certain liabilities. In turn, the scope of its activities was influenced by that shield. eBay provided a venue for online auctions, and unlike an offline auction house, it did not review the listings of items posted by sellers, see the items auctioned, or verify their authenticity. It also did not participate in the transaction, other than to charge fees for each listing and item sold. eBay did not act as an agent of the seller or the buyer.

A critical issue for eBay was whether it could be held liable for the listings provided by sellers or for postings on its bulletin boards. The Communications Decency Act (CDA) of 1996 shielded an Internet service provider (ISP) from liability for what was said or written on an Internet site, whereas an Internet content provider could be liable for postings. eBay positioned itself as an ISP, thus receiving protection under the CDA. That positioning, however, meant that eBay had to be careful not to provide content, such as commenting on the authenticity of items listed for sales. Instead, eBay provided links to Internet sites where members could obtain opinions, authentication, and grading of items ranging from coins to Beanie Babies to comic books.

Offline auction houses were regulated by state laws, and eBay carefully avoided the jurisdiction of those and other state laws. eBay argued that it was similar to the newspaper classified ads rather than an offline auction house. Nevertheless, under a California law allowing actions against companies that violated laws, eBay was sued by individuals claiming that pirated software and fake sports memorabilia were sold on its site. In both cases the judges ruled that eBay was protected by the CDA from liability for what sellers offered on its site.[1]

eBay also positioned itself relative to violations of the law by the buyers and sellers on its site. A small number of sellers engaged in fraud, others sold items that violated copyrights, and others sold banned items. eBay monitored its site for possible fraud, as did members of its trading community. For example, eBay used shill-hunter software to identify shill bidding rings, and community members reported possible shill bidders.

Although eBay monitored for fraud, it did not monitor for copyright violations because doing so might make it liable for any infringing items it failed to find. A federal Court of Appeals decision in *Fonovisa, Inc. v. Cherry Auctions, Inc.* held that a swap meet owner was liable for copyright violations because pirated recordings were sold on its venue.[2] The Court ruled that the owner had the ability to monitor its site for illegal items and failed to do so. eBay could monitor its site for possible copyright violations, but with nearly one million new listings a day, complete monitoring was virtually impossible.

The Digital Millennium Copyright Act of 1998 clarified the monitoring issue by stating that Web sites could be liable if they monitored for intellectual property infringements and failed to find an infringing item. A site, however, had a safe harbor if it did not monitor, provided that it removed violating items when notified by a copyright holder. eBay had already implemented such a program, now referred to as VeRO (verified rights owners), and it continued its policy. Monitoring was thus performed by the copyright holders, who asked eBay to remove infringing items. eBay assisted the copyright holders by creating a system in which VeRO members could query on key words and automatically receive email notification of any listing with those key words.

This did not satisfy the Business Software Alliance (BSA), which developed a model code requiring Internet sites to pre-screen listings for

---

[1]The text of one opinion, which was not officially published, can be found at www.2001law.com/article_429.htm. The other case, *Gentry v. eBay, Inc.,* can be found at http://legal.web.aol.com/decisions/dldecen/gentry.html.

[2]For the text of the ruling, see http://www.law.cornell.edu/copyright/cases/76_F3d_259.htm.

*(Continued)*

*(Continued)*

copyright violations. Even though Amazon.com agreed to the code, eBay refused to do so. It subsequently began restricted monitoring by examining only what was within the "Four Corners" of a seller's listing and dropping from its site items so identified as infringing a copyright. eBay believed that the CDA provided protection from liability if it relied only on the listing provided by the seller.[3] The Four Corners policy also strengthened eBay's bargaining position relative to the BSA as the two parties attempted to find a mutually agreeable policy.

Intellectual property law provided little protection for eBay's database. In a 1991 decision, *Feist Publications, Inc. v. Rural Telephone Service Co.,* 499 U.S., 340, the U.S. Supreme Court held that "facts," even if collected through "sweat and effort," remained in the public domain. Earlier court decisions had held that databases were protected by copyright under the "sweat of the brow" doctrine. This doctrine prevailed despite 1976 amendments to the Copyright Act that required a degree of creativity or originality for compilations of data to receive copyright protection. In *Feist* the court affirmed the originality and creativity requirement and stated that "all facts—scientific, historical, biographical and news of the day . . . are part of the public domain available to every person." This ruling gave auction aggregators a legal basis for extracting "facts" from eBay and other online auction sites.[4]

Bidders' Edge, an auction aggregator, used a robot to copy all of eBay's auction listings and make them available to users of its Web site. Bidders' Edge argued that the listings were compilations of facts and hence under *Feist* were not protected by copyright. Legal space often provides a number of avenues for pursuing an issue. eBay might have been able to meet the creativity test, but in doing so it would risk being viewed as an Internet content provider and subject to other litigation. eBay was successful in protecting its database from robotic searches by relying on the law outside the realm of intellectual property.

By either good fortune or considerable foresight, eBay had also positioned itself well in another part of legal space. A competitor, BidBay, entered the online auction market with a logo and cover page that closely resembled eBay's. In addition to the similarity of its name, BidBay's cover page used the same color scheme, location of the company name and menu bar, search window, and category list as did eBay. In intellectual property law, the most defensible trademarks are those that are "arbitrary and fanciful." An eBay attorney explained, "eBay is a completely coined name. It means nothing."[5] eBay filed a trademark infringement lawsuit against BidBay, which agreed to change its name.

[3]In political space eBay attempted to obtain an amendment to the DMCA to provide a safe harbor for responsible monitoring for copyright violations.

[4]See the case *eBay and Database Protection* in Chapter 12.
[5]*San Jose Mercury News,* July 31, 2001.

## Nonmarket Positioning and Market Strategies

Nonmarket positioning is influenced by a firm's market strategy. Starbucks Coffee has cultivated a particular market segment and established a nonmarket image of social awareness, concern, and action. It stated that "contributing positively to our communities and environment" is "a guiding principle of the company's mission." This positioning was appealing to a clientele of socially aware, higher income consumers, and contributed to its cachet. Starbucks backed this image with action. For example, in conjunction with Conservation International it financed Mexican farmers to grow coffee beans in the forest shade so that land would not be cleared for agricultural purposes.

As they do in the market environment, some firms attempt to differentiate themselves in the nonmarket environment. Starbucks has done so by its commitment to social responsibility. BP has positioned itself as a green oil company.

A position such as that taken by BP may serve as a platform from which it can elicit support in other components of its environment. BP may have benefited from its green positioning when it sought U.S. government approval for its acquisitions of Amoco and Arco in 1998 and 1999, respectively. Its positioning, however, may have hindered it in entering Iran. Instead of directly entering into contracts with Iran for the development of its vast oil and gas reserves, BP sought a nod from the U.S. government that it would not impose sanctions on the company. The nod was not forthcoming, and its European rivals TotalFinaElf and Royal Dutch/Shell entered Iran first.

Nike experienced rapid growth in part as a result of aggressive marketing. Nike was in the face of the public. It was also driven by an aggressive and combative competitive attitude. That combination made Nike the largest U.S. footwear and apparel company. Nike's success and its in-your-face market position also made it a natural target for union activists who sought to improve the working conditions in overseas factories that supplied the footwear and apparel industries.

Frequently, firms seek cover rather than visibility in their nonmarket environment so that their positioning is obscured from the view of the public. Pharmaceutical companies often prefer the anonymity of working through the Pharmaceutical Research and Manufacturers Association (PhRMA) to taking action themselves. Moreover, in implementing nonmarket strategies pharmaceutical companies prefer to work behind the scenes, focusing on relationship building and lobbying. The firms opposing the Kyoto Protocol did not have sufficient anonymity in the Global Climate Coalition when individual firms were members. The Coalition then restructured itself so that its members were trade associations. The firms opposing the Kyoto Protocol then had two layers of cover.

Nonmarket positioning can provide opportunity in the nonmarket as well as market environment. The automobile industry has been under pressure from environmentalists, government, and the public to improve the fuel economy of the light-vehicle fleet. The instrument for fuel economy improvements has been fuel economy standards, but those standards have changed little over the past 20 years. The U.S. automobile industry opposed fuel economy standards as an inflexible command-and-control regulatory approach. The industry argued that technology should be the instrument of improved fuel economy. The most promising near-term technologies were the diesel engine and the hybrid engine, which combined a conventional internal combustion engine and an electric motor that operated primarily at low speed where the gasoline engine was least efficient. Honda and Toyota were positioned as the leaders in hybrid vehicles, and DaimlerChrysler was the leader in diesel vehicles.

Hybrid technology was expensive, however, and demand was likely to be limited unless gasoline prices were high or the vehicles were subsidized by the manufacturers or the government. Auto manufacturers naturally favored government subsidies and took the position that any subsidy should apply to any hybrid automobile, even if the electric motor was used to improve performance rather than fuel economy. Environmentalists argued that any subsidy should be restricted to improvements in fuel economy and that the amount of the subsidy should vary with the improvement achieved. Ford broke ranks with General Motors and DaimlerChrysler and supported the environmentalists' position of a graduated subsidy. General Motors criticized that approach because a graduated subsidy could be seen as providing support for the fuel economy standards system, which it argued should be scrapped. Ford's position won praise from environmentalists, but would its position bring it benefits in either its market or nonmarket environment?

One possible benefit is providing opportunities to work with NGOs to address nonmarket issues. A number of companies have turned to environmental groups both to find better solutions to problems and to solidify their nonmarket positioning. Conservation International (CI) works with "environment-friendly companies" to find innovative solutions to their environmental problems. In 2001 CI and Ford, which provided the $25 million funding, launched the Center for Environmental Leadership in Business to engage the private sector. The Center worked for positive environmental changes with programs in agriculture and fisheries, energy and mining, forestry, and travel and leisure. Despite funding the Center and suppporting other environmental projects, as indicated in Chapter 1, Ford was targeted by several environmental activist groups seeking improved fuel economy.

Nonmarket positioning can also affect the set of issues a firm faces. As the eBay example indicates, positioning can affect the legal liabilities to which a firm is exposed. Nonmarket positioning can also affect the likelihood of targeting by activists and interest groups. BP's green stance and its demonstrated commitment reduced the risk of criticism by environmental groups. ExxonMobil had quite a different stance, opposing the Kyoto Protocol, for example. BP's positioning helped shift the environmentalists' attention toward ExxonMobil. Environmental activists launched a boycott of Esso gas stations in Europe.

## Positioning Spaces

Nonmarket positioning takes place in three interrelated spaces: public sentiment, political (lawmaking and rule making), and legal (existing laws and regulation).

**Positioning in the Space of Public Sentiment**   Public sentiment is determined by the diverse interests, viewpoints, and preferences of the individuals in a society. These individuals may be organized or unorganized with respect to a particular nonmarket issue. Workers may be represented by a union. Those interested in the environment may be members of the Sierra Club or Greenpeace, and farmers may join organizations because they support or oppose free trade. Other individuals may be unorganized, but they may individually act, as when they participate in a boycott led by an activist group.

BP provides an example of positioning in the space of public sentiment. It withdrew from the Global Climate Coalition because of the Coalition's opposition to the Kyoto Protocol and then joined the Pew Trust's climate change program—the Business Environmental Leadership Council—that requires members to implement a voluntary carbon emissions reduction program. BP also joined the International Climate Change Partnership, the World Resources Institute, the Energy and Biodiversity Initiative, the Papua Conservation Fund, and the Climate, Community, and Biodiversity Alliance. In addition, the BP Conservation Program provided conservation grants in 58 countries. More importantly, BP made substantial investments in solar energy and implemented an aggressive, voluntary $CO_2$ reduction program in cooperation with the environmental group Environmental Defense. To establish credibility with the public, Environmental Defense published audited inventories of the company's emissions. BP also used product design in reducing pollution. Five years before federal regulations were to take effect, BP marketed a gasoline that contained 80 percent less sulfur than ordinary premium gasoline.[7]

To solidify its positioning before the public, BP changed its corporate symbol to a starburst and adopted the slogan "Beyond Petroleum." The slogan, however, created confusion. Some activists interpreted it as a commitment to withdraw from the petroleum industry. Company officials hurriedly explained that it instead meant that the company was looking beyond the petroleum industry. BP was forced to relaunch its public positioning by taking out two-page advertisements in *The New York Times, The Wall Street Journal, Business Week,* and *Fortune* extolling its environmental achievements and

---

[7]The gasoline earned BP sulfur emissions credits that it could use or sell. Emissions credits are considered in Chapter 11.

restating its slogan as "Responsibilities Beyond Petroleum." The ad featured the company's low-sulfur gasoline, $CO_2$ reduction program, solar energy business, and the hydrogen-powered buses it and DaimlerChrysler planned to introduce in Europe.

**Positioning in Political Space**   Lawmaking and rule making take place in political space, where the rules of the game are made. Positioning in political space affects the opportunity to participate effectively in lawmaking and rule-making processes.

Because of the importance of nonmarket issues to the profitability of the industry, the pharmaceutical industry has developed a position of strength in political space. The industry has positioned itself by building relationships with members of Congress and the executive branch. According to the Center for Responsive Politics, the pharmaceutical industry was 12th in political contributions in the 2000 election cycle, contributing $26.3 million. Sixty percent was in soft money contributions to political parties and other political organizations. Schering-Plough was sixth among the pharmaceutical companies, with $1.2 million in contributions. Pfizer was first, with $2.4 million.

More important than the political contributions were the lobbying and relationship-building activities of the industry. The Center for Responsive Politics reported that Schering-Plough spent $9.2 million on lobbying in 1999, of which $2.3 million went to 17 lobbying firms. Pfizer spent $3.8 million on lobbying. In addition, the companies have their own in-house lobbyists, and their managers also lobby. The industry association PhRMA also contributes lobbying as well as positioning the industry in the space of public sentiment.

The brand-name pharmaceutical companies used their positioning in political space to obtain the opportunity to market prescription drugs directly to consumers rather than solely to doctors. In 1997 the Food and Drug Administration approved revised marketing guidelines that allowed direct-to-consumer (DTC) advertising on broadcast media. The approval was based on the theory that the advertising would better educate consumers about their medical alternatives and engage them in their own health care. DTC advertising proved to be highly successful in increasing demand for prescription drugs—so successful that it resulted in a backlash. Doctors complained that they were pressured to prescribe particular brand-name drugs because patients had seen DTC ads. Insurers and health care activists raised concerns about DTC advertising raising prices, as well as demand, and contributing to double-digit increases in spending for drugs. The Prescription Access Litigation Project filed a lawsuit against Schering-Plough, claiming that the advertising of its blockbuster antihistamine Claritin was deceptive and boosted demand and the price of the drug.

In contrast to the pharmaceutical industry, some companies have decided to make no political contributions. For example, Home Depot makes no political contributions in the United States, and BP makes no political contributions in any country. In the 2004 election cycle an increased number of firms decided not to make soft money contributions.

The most important source of positioning in political space comes from constituents. Firms have stakeholders—employees, suppliers, retailers, shareholders, pensioners, and customers—who are constituents of government officeholders. This constituency base can be an important component of positioning if the constituents can represent their own interests on nonmarket issues, the firm can represent them, or officeholders can claim credit for serving them. Many firms track their supply contracts by congressional district so they can inform members of Congress about how much business they do in their districts. The pharmaceutical companies have sought to position themselves in political space by enlisting the support of patients who have benefited from drug therapies. PhRMA conducted a television advertising campaign that included personal testimony about the benefits of prescription drugs.

Some positioning in political space may become untenable. Automakers in the United States have successfully blocked increases in fuel economy standards for light vehicles despite growing evidence about global warming. Beginning in 2000 the average fuel economy of the new, light vehicle fleet began to decrease as the market share of SUVs and light trucks passed 50 percent. Coupled with growing concern about global climate change, Ford pledged to increase its light truck/SUV fuel economy by 25 percent over the next 5 years. General Motors and DaimlerChrysler quickly followed suit. The Bush administration followed with an 8.3 percent increase in the fuel economy standard for the light-truck fleet. The pressure for higher fuel economy standards continued unabated.

**Positioning in Legal Space**  Positioning in legal space affects not only the liabilities to which a company is exposed but also a company's market and nonmarket strategies. eBay's positioning as an ISP provides protection under the CDA, but it also means that the company is limited in its ability to provide content on its Web site. Even though it might be able to compete profitably online with high-end off-line auction houses by serving as an agent and authenticating auction items, it has been careful not to do so because that could make it an Internet content provider as well as expose it to off-line auction house regulations.

In legal space, patents provide the most important protection for intellectual property for many industries, and perhaps nowhere are patents more important than in the pharmaceutical industry. The pharmaceutical industry regularly seeks patent extensions and was successful in obtaining a 6-month patent extension for approved drugs that were subsequently tested for use on children. Schering-Plough, however, conducted without success a multimillion dollar campaign to extend the patent on Claritin.

Microsoft has taken an aggressive approach to its markets and had largely ignored its legal environment, as considered in the Chapter 9 case, *The Microsoft Antitrust Case*. In contrast to Microsoft's approach to its antitrust environment, Cisco Systems and Intel, which both have dominant market shares, have sought to avoid antitrust problems and fix potential problems before they develop. Their positioning begins with respect for government officials and with a commitment to invest in relationships with antitrust enforcers so that potential problems can be fixed before they lead to a lawsuit. Cisco also works to educate antitrust enforcers about high-technology industries and stands ready to provide technical expertise to regulators. Both Cisco and Intel make regular assessments of their antitrust status and look for early warning signs of potential problems.

Part of their legal positioning is training their personnel to avoid antitrust problems and actions that might lead to problems. Sales representatives at Cisco receive antitrust training and are told to avoid aggressive competitive language that might be construed as anticompetitive. At Intel employees are trained not to use aggressive language toward competitors or partners and to avoid certain terms that might be associated with antitrust violations. For example, the word *leveraging* (i.e., leveraging from a dominant position) is not used.

## The Perils of Positioning

Positioning is intended to improve overall performance by affecting the set of issues a firm faces and by providing a foundation for both market and nonmarket strategies. Positioning can, at times, however, be perilous. Demand for large SUVs increased to the point that in 2003 Ford was forced to announce that it would be unable to achieve the 25 percent improvement in the fuel economy of its SUVs it had pledged. As Bill Ford, an avowed environmentalist, assumed the position of CEO, activists saw the backtracking on its pledge as an opportunity to target him and the company with private politics campaigns to force an increase in fuel economy. Although Ford was the first company to offer a hybrid SUV, the Bluewater Network, Global Exchange, the Rainforest Action Network (RAN), and the Sierra Club targeted Ford with advertisements and demonstrations at Ford's 100th anniversary celebration. Global Exchange and RAN prepared for a 5-year campaign against Ford.

Along with its 3,500 outlets, Starbucks' positioning in the space of public sentiment has made it a convenient arena for a variety of activists seeking to appeal to its clientele as well as to the company itself. Activists were concerned with the working conditions in coffee-producing plantations and targeted Starbucks despite its considerable efforts to support coffee-producing families and to protect the environment. Anarchists and antiglobalization activists protesting the Seattle World Trade Organization meeting laid seige to a Starbucks store.

Starbucks' positioning also created expectations about its business practices, and activists demanded more of the company than it was willing to do. In conjunction with demonstations at the Republican national convention in 2004, several hundred demonstators protested Starbucks' business practices, including its opposition to unionization, and also used Starbucks stores as a site for antiglobalization protests.

In addition, its positioning attracted activists who sought to promote causes with no connection to Starbucks. Local activist groups in Seattle targeted Starbucks to attract attention and media coverage to their causes with the hope that the company would take up their cause. Opponents of the use of recombinant bovine growth hormone picketed Starbucks to pressure it to stop using milk produced from cows treated with the hormone. Starbucks agreed to stop using such milk, but the protests resumed the following year to try to force Starbucks to be more aggressive in promoting the cause.

In response to a boycott intended to force Starbucks to demand reform of the Seattle police department, a Starbucks spokesperson commented, "We are not an activist or a political organization. When people say that we should do more than take money from the community, we do give back. What we are willing to do is to help invigorate the community by providing jobs, supporting educational and philanthropic programs for youth, and it hurts us when a small group of people decide that we need to be doing something else, which happens to be on their agenda."[8]

When it positioned itself as a green oil company, BP created expectations among governments and the public about how it would deal with issues. But, just as Ford and Starbucks became symbols and targets, so had BP, as activists sought to use its positioning to push the company further in pursuit of their agenda. Environmental activists seeking to pressure oil companies to begin planning for phasing out oil and gas production placed a shareholder resolution on the agenda for the BP annual meeting.[9] A Greenpeace campaigner observed that BP "built their brand on how environmentally-friendly they are. This has given us the impetus to push them to fulfill the implicit promises they've made." Referring to the company's commitment to solar energy, the campaigner said, "They're one of the best-placed companies to make that change."[10]

Positioning can also be disrupted by nonmarket entrepreneurship. With its patent on Claritin scheduled to expire in December 2002, Schering-Plough developed a third-generation antihistamine, Clarinex, that it planned to introduce in early 2001. The firm's strategy was to use DTC marketing to switch prescription demand from Claritin and Clarinex and then shift Claritin to the OTC market just prior to patent extension.

---

[8]*The Los Angeles Times,* June 26, 2001.
[9]The resolution received only 7 percent of the vote but attracted considerable public attention, particularly in the United Kingdom.
[10]*The Wall Street Journal,* April 16, 2001.

This strategy, if successful, would position Clarinex to capture the prescription sales and take the generics to the OTC market along with Claritin, which would be the only brand-name, second-generation antihistamine on the OTC market.

This positioning was disrupted both by a blunder by Schering-Plough and nonmarket entrepreneurship by WellPoint Health Services. The blunder was in allowing production quality problems to develop in its plants, which led the FDA to withhold approval of Clarinex. The nonmarket entrepreneurship took the form of a citizen petition by WellPoint to the FDA to force an early switch of Claritin to the OTC market, threatening Schering-Plough's opportunity to shift demand to Clarinex. WellPoint's argument was that Claritin and the other second-generation, nonsedating antihistamines were safer than the antihistamines currently sold OTC. Moreover, Schering-Plough's advertisements for Claritin stated that it was safe, like "a sugar pill." An FDA advisory panel voted overwhelmingly that Claritin could be safely sold on the OTC market. The Part III integrative case, *Pharmaceutical Switching,* concerns the strategy responses by Schering-Plough and WellPoint.

## Nonmarket Assets, Competencies, and Reputation

Just as firms create value by deploying market assets, firms deploy nonmarket assets to add value. Nonmarket assets take several forms. One is expertise in dealing with government, the news media, interest and activist groups, and the public. Another is knowledge of the procedures and functioning of the institutions in whose arenas nonmarket issues are resolved. A reputation for responsible actions earned with government, stakeholders, and the public also constitutes a nonmarket asset.

These nonmarket assets, and the competencies that flow from them, can give a firm a nonmarket advantage.[11] Distinctive competencies and firm-specific nonmarket assets generate value as a function of how costly it is for market and nonmarket rivals to replicate them and for competitors, activists, and interest groups to dissipate them. As indicated in Chapter 1, Wal-Mart was criticized by activists, unions, and politicians for allegedly depressing wages and driving small merchants out of business. In a public referendum, voters in Ingelwood, California, defeated a proposal to change a zoning requirement to allow Wal-Mart to build a superstore. The criticism not only damaged its reputation but also threatened its expansion strategy, as considered in the Chapter 7 case, *Wal-Mart and Its Urban Growth Strategy.* Wal-Mart belatedly began to develop competencies and improve its reputation. It began an advertising campaign featuring employees telling how happy they were working for Wal-Mart. It also opened a Washington office to develop better relationships with the federal government, sponsored PBS and NPR programs, and started a fellowhip program for minority journalism students. In 2005 the company held its first news conference.

Some competencies can be developed internally, and some can be contracted for externally. Firms can hire outside legal counsel, public affairs experts, ethicists, and lobbyists. For example, Wal-Mart hired Washington lobbyists to represent its interests. The principal nonmarket competency that cannot be replicated, however, is the knowledge, expertise, and skill of managers in addressing nonmarket issues. Members of Congress are more interested in speaking with the company's CEO or local store managers than with its Washington lobbyist. The better the CEO and other managers understand the issues, interests, and institutions that comprise the nonmarket environment, the more effective they will be in developing and implementing nonmarket strategies.

---

[11]See Prahalad and Hamel (1990) for a discussion of core competencies.

The value of a nonmarket competency also depends on the effectiveness of a firm's allies in addressing nonmarket issues. On many issues, a firm's market rivals may be its nonmarket allies, as when an issue affects firms in an industry in a similar manner. Consequently, industry members frequently work through a trade association or an ad hoc coalition to implement nonmarket strategies. In markets, firms are prohibited by antitrust laws from colluding. In the nonmarket environment, the law generally allows firms to join forces to formulate and implement nonmarket strategies. Pharmaceutical companies thus work through PhRMA on issues such as patent policy that affect companies in a similar manner. In the case of a patent extension for an individual drug, a company typically acts on its own.

An important nonmarket asset is a reputation for responsible actions and principled behavior. In lobbying, for example, providing incorrect or strategically biased information can harm a reputation and impair future lobbying. Nevertheless, in some cases reputations can be changed, as BP has done and as Wal-Mart is attempting to do.

Reputations, however, are ultimately established, and destroyed, by actions. Many firms invest in their public reputations just as they invest in their market reputations for service or quality. A reputation can be durable if sustained by actions consistent with it, and BP's environmental programs support its reputation. Reputations, however, can be fragile and quickly lost. A tarnished reputation is difficult to rebuild, as ExxonMobil, Drexel Burnham Lambert, Nike, and others have learned.

# A Framework for the Analysis of Nonmarket Issues

Nonmarket issues are typically complex and require conceptual frameworks to guide analysis and strategy formulation. This section presents such a framework and illustrates its use with an example involving Citibank. The chapter case, *Envirotest Systems Corporation (A),* provides an opportunity to consider nonmarket issues using this framework.

In this framework the unit of analysis is the nonmarket issue. The initial step involves generating strategy alternatives. Managers must exercise creativity in generating alternatives beyond those that immediately suggest themselves. For example, as an alternative to higher fuel economy standards, General Motors advocated a tax on carbon fuels as a means of addressing the global climate change issue. Subsequently, the Clinton administration tried, but failed, to have a closely related Btu tax enacted.

Once alternatives have been identified, they are to be evaluated in three stages— *screening, analysis,* and *choice,* as illustrated in Figure 2-5. In the screening stage, alternatives that are contrary to the law, widely shared ethics principles, or a well-evaluated company policy are eliminated. In the case of the automobile industry, an alternative involving noncompliance with mandatory NHTSA safety standards would be screened out. Several automobile companies, however, routinely pay a fine, as provided for by law, for not meeting fuel economy standards.

The alternatives that remain after the screening stage are then analyzed to predict their likely consequences. The analysis stage is based on the positive methods of economics, political science, and other social sciences and focuses on predicting the actions of interests and the consequences of alternative strategies. For example, automobile manufacturers must predict how successful their opposition to higher fuel economy standards is likely to be. This prediction focuses on interests, institutions and their officeholders, and information and takes into account the likely actions of the other

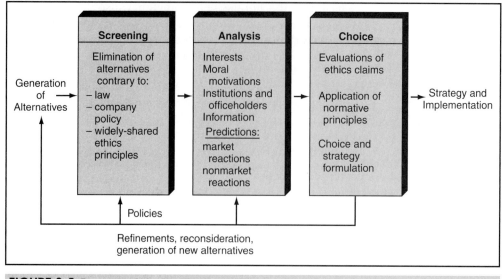

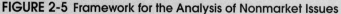

**FIGURE 2-5 Framework for the Analysis of Nonmarket Issues**

interested parties. The analysis stage also considers moral motivations of nonmarket behavior and thus how others evaluate the firm's actions.

The alternatives are evaluated and a choice made in the third stage. On issues that do not involve significant moral concerns, choice is based on the interests of the firm and its stakeholders. The objective is typically value creation, taking into account the impact of alternatives on stakeholders who are important to long-run performance. If the issue involves significant moral concerns, normative principles pertaining to well-being, rights, and justice are to be applied, as considered in Part V of this book.

In the nonmarket environment, moral claims about rights are frequently made. Some rights are "granted" in the sense that the government or moral consensus has both established them and clearly assigned the associated duty to respect them. When the duty has not been clearly assigned or the right itself has not been established by government or through moral consensus, the right is said to be "claimed." Granted rights are to be used to screen out alternatives in the first stage, whereas claimed rights are to be evaluated in the choice stage. For example, there is a general consensus that firms should not exploit children. There may be disagreement, however, about what constitutes exploitation, as in the case of advertising children's toys on Saturday morning television.[12] When moral consensus is absent, the claim is to be evaluated in the choice stage of the framework.

The process illustrated in Figure 2-5 yields specific strategies—concerted sets of actions to be taken by identified individuals or business units—and policies that guide managers in addressing market and nonmarket issues. Those policies can be stated as rules to be followed or as principles to be used in reasoning about what to do in a particular situation. For example, BP's policy for evaluating environmental protection alternatives is to take their costs into account only when the environmental impacts of alternatives are the same. Policies are to be used in the first stage to screen out alternatives that are inconsistent with the firm's business strategy.

---

[12]See Hamilton (1998) for a study of the political economy of TV violence and children.

The framework presented in Figure 2-5 is to be viewed as dynamic. The evaluations in the choice stage and the consequences of the choices made provide a basis for learning, refinement of policies and strategies, and methods.

# Example: Citibank and Credit Cards for Undergraduates

In 1987 Citibank decided to offer VISA and MasterCard credit cards to undergraduate college students. Its objective was to develop an early relationship with individuals likely to be frequent users of the cards once they joined the workforce. To assess the credit worthiness and future earnings potential of an applicant, Citibank used several indicators. For students who were not employed or worked only on a part-time basis, it used their undergraduate major as one measure of creditworthiness. According to Bill McGuire, a spokesman for Citibank, "using the major [is] a good indicator of future earning potential and of students' ability to pay debt."[13]

## Application of the Framework
### First Stage: Screening
The nonmarket issue is whether it is acceptable to use students' undergraduate majors as a basis for issuing credit cards. The first stage of the framework involves determining whether use of an applicant's undergraduate major is contrary to the law, widely shared ethics principles, or company policy. Use of undergraduate major as a predictor of creditworthiness is neither illegal discrimination nor a violation of the Equal Credit Opportunity Act. Similarly, individuals do not have a granted right to have a credit card, and moral consensus on using an applicant's undergraduate major is not evident. The use of undergraduate major thus passes the screening stage.

Several moral claims, however, remain to be considered in the subsequent stages of the analysis. As some people claim, should everyone have a right to credit with that right withdrawn only upon failure to make the required payments? If not, which measures are acceptable predictors of creditworthiness? Is it better to use undergraduate major as a predictor, with the result that at least some students receive credit cards, or is it better not to offer cards to undergraduates? Instead of resolving these difficult questions in the screening stage, the framework calls for their resolution in the choice stage following the second stage analysis.

### Second Stage: Analysis
The second stage of the framework focuses on predicting consequences of alternatives not only for Citibank but also for others, including any moral concerns that may motivate action affecting Citibank. The anticipated market consequences are lower credit losses and higher usage than if Citibank did not use undergraduate major. Although many lower income people are good credit risks because they match their purchases to their income, people with higher incomes are more likely to have higher credit card usage. Based on similar considerations, Citibank had instituted the Citidollars program, which operated like a frequent-flyer program, providing discounts on products based on credit card usage.

---

[13]*Peninsula Times Tribune,* March 20, 1988. The following is the application of the framework to the Citibank case and is not Citibank's analysis.

The possible nonmarket consequences of using undergraduate major are more difficult to quantify than the market consequences, but that does not mean that they are less important or that managers cannot reason about them. Failure to anticipate the consequences of nonmarket behavior is a frequent cause of failed managerial decisions. Citibank's use of undergraduate major is a case in point. An application of the framework might have led Citibank to use other predictors of creditworthiness, thereby avoiding what turned out to be an embarrassing episode.

The first question in the analysis is whether people are likely to become aware of Citibank's policy and, if so, whether they would be motivated to take action. The law requires that a person denied credit be notified of the reasons for the denial. Those denied will be disappointed, and some will be angry. That anger could be based on self-interest, but some students could be concerned about the principle underlying Citibank's policy. Some might believe on moral grounds that creditworthiness should be based on credit history and the ability to pay rather than on undergraduate major or likely future earnings. Others might believe that basing creditworthiness on undergraduate major could distort students' choices of majors and ultimately of professions. Some might be concerned that Citibank's practices could induce lying by students who might falsely report their majors to increase their chances of receiving a credit card.

The predictive focus is on whether nonmarket action might be expected, what form that action might take, and what impact it might have. Indeed, Citibank contributed directly to the nonmarket action and to the issue becoming public. At the University of California–Berkeley, a Citibank canvasser, who had set up a table at the student union to take applications, was asked by a reporter from the student newspaper if it were true that some students were being rejected as a result of their major. "The canvasser advised her to fill in the credit application by listing business administration or electrical engineering as her major, instead of English."[14]

The next step is to predict whether the issue will become public. Students have various means of making an issue public, ranging from bringing it before the student government to complaining to university administrators to organizing demonstrations. The most effective way to call attention to the issue, however, is to attract the news media. How likely the media is to cover this issue can be assessed using the theory presented in the next chapter. In brief, the media finds claims of discrimination and unfairness to be newsworthy. Furthermore, students know how to make the issue more newsworthy by organizing protests and taking symbolic actions. This does not imply that protests can be expected on all college campuses, but a manager should ask how many protests are necessary to attract the news media. The answer may be "one."

This analysis does not predict that the issue will inevitably become public, but it does indicate that it might. Citibank, however, need not abandon the use of undergraduate major simply because a market action might generate a nonmarket issue. Most of the public would never learn of the issue, and many of those who did might believe that Citibank's policy was appropriate. Those who view the use of undergraduate major as inappropriate, however, are the concern.

With regard to immediate effects, few students had a business relationship with Citibank that they could end in protest. Nor, due to the costs of switching banks, were they likely to be able to persuade any significant number of Citibank customers to withdraw their business. The immediate market consequences were thus likely to be

---

[14]*Peninsula Times Tribune,* March 20, 1988.

small. The effect on future business, however, might be more significant. Some students might choose not to deal with Citibank in the future. Furthermore, Citibank's recruiting on college campuses might be affected, either through boycotts or other direct action. At Berkeley, student protesters demanded that Citibank be barred from recruiting on campus as a result of the issue. In addition, Citibank's reputation could be affected by a controversy. Certainly, Citibank management could be embarrassed by protests or media coverage.

## The Outcome

The issue became public through student protests at Berkeley, and the national media was quickly attracted to the issue. As the pressure mounted, Citibank changed its market strategy and abandoned using a student's undergraduate major. Citibank subsequently developed a new application form for college students that asked only for the name of the college attended, the class, and the expected graduation date, in addition to information on bank accounts, income, and sources of funds.

Had Citibank conducted a positive analysis and been sensitive to the types of concerns—in particular the moral motivations of nonmarket action—that can result from a market strategy, it could have avoided a situation that at a minimum was an embarrassment. In this case, the use of the framework in Figure 2-5 obviates the need for an evaluation in the third stage, since even from a consideration of Citibank's self-interest alone, it was not worthwhile to use undergraduate major.[15] The Chapter 21 case, *Citigroup and Subprime Lending*, provides another example.

## Organization of the Nonmarket Strategy Function

During the 1970s several companies formed strategic planning departments to assist management in developing long-range market strategies. These staff departments were typically attached to, but separate from, top management, which proved to be the cause of many failures. Similarly, several companies formed issues management groups to identify and address nonmarket issues. That experiment also produced failures, particularly when the group focused on societal issues rather than on specific issues impacting the firm's performance.[16]

Wartick and Rude (1986) analyzed the problems experienced by issues management groups in eight firms.[17] They identified four conditions necessary for success:

- Top management must support and be involved in the effort.
- Field units and relevant staff departments must be involved.
- The issues management unit must fill a void in the managerial decision-making process.
- Results must come from the effort.

---

[15]One possible qualification to this conclusion is that the likelihood of the issue becoming public may have been sufficiently low that Citibank's best strategy was to use undergraduate major as a measure of credit-worthiness as long as the practice did not draw public attention, and if it did, to discontinue the practice. It is more likely, however, that Citibank did not anticipate a public reaction. Certainly, the canvasser at Berkeley had not been informed about the potential sensitivity of the issue.

[16]Littlejohn (1986) describes the issues management activities of Monsanto and Gulf Oil.

[17]Also see Sigman and McDonald (1987).

The perspective taken here is that there should be no void for an issues management unit to fill. That is, the responsibility for addressing nonmarket issues should reside with operating managers and not with a separate staff unit.

Management rather than staff now formulates a firm's market strategy, and the same is true for nonmarket strategies. Managers must be centrally involved because they are in the best position to assess the consequences of nonmarket factors for market strategies and overall performance. The nonmarket environment is often more complex than the market environment, however, because public institutions are complex and a larger set of interests are enfranchised to participate. Moreover, successfully addressing a nonmarket issue may require expertise in the law, government institutions, and public communication. In such cases, managers may need the advice of specialists. Managers must, however, be able to evaluate the advice they receive. To do so, they need to be as knowledgeable about the relevant nonmarket issues as they are about the markets in which the firm operates. Because managers operate continuously in their market environment and often only on an episodic basis in their nonmarket environment, frameworks such as that in Figure 2-5 can be particularly helpful in structuring analysis and strategy formulation.

## Summary

A business strategy must be congruent with the competencies of a firm and the characteristics of its environment—both the market and nonmarket environments. Just as the environment has two components, a business strategy has both market and nonmarket components, and these components should be integrated. The nonmarket component is of greater importance when the opportunities of a firm are controlled by government, challenged by private politics, or raise moral concerns. Nonmarket strategies can be directed at competitive forces or at unlocking opportunities blocked by the nonmarket environment. Because strategies depend on the issues, interests, institutions, and information that characterize the nonmarket environment, they are more likely to be multidomestic than global. Nonmarket strategies are based on assets such as the knowledge and experience of managers in addressing nonmarket issues and the reputation of the firm for responsible actions. Nonmarket assets can be developed, and over the long run their development is part of a business strategy.

Positioning in the nonmarket environment provides a foundation for strategy and hence is a strategic choice of the firm. Positioning can attract opportunities and affect the set of issues the firm faces. Positioning takes place in legal, political, and public sentiment spaces. eBay's positioning in legal space has shielded it from certain liabilities and responsibilities. The brand-name pharmaceutical companies have established a strong position in political space, and BP has established a green position in the space of public sentiment. The benefits from positioning may not spill over from one space to another or even from one issue to another, as BP has learned. Positioning thus is often issue-specific.

Most companies focus on those nonmarket issues with a potentially significant impact on performance. Addressing nonmarket issues in an effective manner requires a framework that organizes analysis, reasoning, and strategy formulation. The framework illustrated in Figure 2-5 is composed of three stages: screening, analysis, and choice. The screening stage rules out those alternatives that are contrary to the law, company policy, or ethical consensus. The analysis stage focuses on the prediction of nonmarket actions and their likely consequences. The choice stage involves evaluating those consequences and any ethics claims and making choices based on those evaluations. The results of the choice stage are strategies for addressing the issue and policies that can be used to guide managers in the screening stage for future issues.

# Exclusive Resorts: Entrepreneurial Positioning and Nonmarket Defense

Brad Handler had just retired from eBay, where he had been the first lawyer and 35th employee at the company. In May 2002 he and his family joined his brother Brent and his family for a much deserved vacation at a luxury resort in Hawaii. The accommodations were fine but lacked many of the comforts of a home, such as a kitchen, space for young children, a room for a nanny, and accommodations for grandparents. While sitting on the beach, he realized there was a demand for luxury vacation residences that avoided the hassles of owning a second home and being tied to a single location. Brad and Brent decided to establish a luxury vacation residence venture. Brad's retirement lasted only a few months.

When he returned to California, Brad began researching the formats for such a venture. The first challenge was to position the new venture in both the market and nonmarket environments.

In the market environment, Brad and Brent identified a set of criteria for positioning the venture:

1. Serve the luxury end of the market.
2. Provide accommodations equivalent to a second home.
3. Provide the services and convenience of a fine hotel or resort.
4. Offer a choice of locations and accommodations.
5. Provide customers with liquidity of any deposits and refundable fees.
6. Provide assurance of availability of accommodations.
7. Separate the vacation aspect from the investment aspect.
8. Own rather than lease the residences.
9. Structure the revenue to cover the costs of the venture in a manner that reduced the risks to the principals.
10. Enter rapidly with a scalable format.

In the nonmarket environment the positioning criteria were to (1) avoid the onerous state regulation that accompanied certain forms of real estate ventures, (2) avoid the risk that promises to customers would be viewed as a security and hence subject to Securities and Exchange Commission (SEC) regulation, and (3) mitigate any nonmarket opposition to the venture.

The existing formats for vacation residence ventures were timeshares, fractionals, private vacation clubs, and destination clubs.[18] Timeshares were the largest segment of the vacation residence market. Purchasers obtained either a deed or a right-to-use in a unit in a development, so the vacation and investment aspects were inexorably linked. Some timeshares had earned a bad reputation because of high-pressure sales tactics, although practices had improved.

Private vacation clubs provided a variety of accommodations, including residences, at popular tourist destinations. These clubs were often operated by hotel chains such as Hilton, Hyatt, and Marriott and had been growing in popularity. Marriott Vacation Club International sold deeded units on a fractional basis in resorts and allowed owners to trade their weeks or exchange them for points redeemable at Club resorts. Other vacation clubs did not provide ownership but rather a right to use a room in the hotels owned or leased by the club. Vacation clubs were timeshares, but their marketing was softer.

A destination club provided both residences and travel and tour services, such as those offered by Abercrombie & Kent Destination Clubs. In 2000 Private Retreats offered a club that leased or owned residences in the $800,000 range in a variety of locations, and members could reserve the residences on a space available basis.

---

[18]Definitions from California law are presented in the Appendix.

## Positioning in the Nonmarket Environment

Positioning in the nonmarket environment was influenced by local, state, and federal law. Zoning was generally city or county law, and real estate law was state law, which meant that a venture with multiple locations could be subject to a myriad of regulations. No federal legislation pertained to timeshares and fractionals, but they were subject to regulation in most states.

The basic principle of timeshare law was that a promise made must be kept. This had a number of implications for the industry. First, a developer could not finance the development with a mortgage because, if the developer defaulted, the timeshare owners would be stuck with the mortgage obligation. Second, developers were not allowed to remove or substitute inventory. That is, they could not easily swap out owners from one timeshare development to a newer development. Third, most developers left once all the timeshares had been sold, leaving the timeshare owners responsible for the management of the facility under a homeowners association.

Under the regulatory system in California and other states, in addition to a fee interest in real estate, timeshare owners received a "right to use" that could take one of three forms: (1) a recurring basis, such as the 20th and 21st weeks of every year; (2) a fixed date, such as May 15 to May 29; or (3) a periodic right to use—some portion of a year, such as one month a year. Brad reasoned that it should be possible to avoid regulation if members did not have any of the three forms of use. The appendix of this case provides excerpts from the California law.

The federal Securities Act of 1933 required that, absent any available exemption, all securities be registered with the Securities and Exchange Commission (SEC) before they were offered to the public. The definition of *security* was broad and included an *investment contract*, which the Supreme Court ruled was a security if "a person invests his money in a common enterprise and is led to expect profits solely from the efforts of the promoter or a third party."[19]

Federal securities law had several implications for timeshares and the vacation residency industry.

First, the buyers' investments in timeshares were not liquid. Second, timeshares substituted "exchanges" for liquidity, whereby one owner exchanged use of his or her time slot for use of another person's slot, possibly at a different location. Third, for the private vacation club and destination clubs, promotions that made promises based on the value of the real estate holdings could be viewed as securities and subjected to SEC and/or state registration requirements.

The Federal Trade Commission (FTC) provided scrutiny over the vacation residence industry because of the possibility of unfair or deceptive practices. In its "Timeshare Tips" the FTC stated, "Never consider the purchase of a timeshare as an investment. Timeshare resales usually are difficult."[20] The resale price of a timeshare was generally far less than the purchase price, since the purchase price covered the developer's sales and marketing expenses, which were roughly 50 percent of the sale price.

With respect to the third positioning criterion, whether rivals would take nonmarket action to restrict the new venture or attempt to put it under the same regulatory framework as timeshares would depend on how successful it was. If it were very successful, a challenge in the nonmarket environment was quite possible.

## Positioning in the Market Environment

In the market environment, the principals, Brad and Brent Handler and Tom Fillipini, chose a country club model in which members belonged to the club but did not own any of the facilities. The three would own the club through a limited-liability company, and Brad would serve as chairman and CEO. They named the venture Exclusive Resorts and designed it for those seeking accommodations in luxury residences in attractive vacation locations that provided skiing, golf, beaches, natural beauty, and the style of major cities. The residences would have concierge and maid service as well as provide conveniences such as initial grocery shopping, trip planning, and reservations for activities and events. To accommodate members' demands, Exclusive Resorts pledged to maintain a ratio of no more than 6 members per residence.

---

[19]*SEC v. Howey Co.* U.S. Supreme Court. 328 U.S. 293 (1946).

[20]FTC, "Timeshare Tips," March 1997; Time shares were traded on eBay.

As of this writing, the membership fee was $375,000, of which 80 percent was refundable.[21] Current annual dues ranged from $15,000 to $25,000 depending on whether the member selected 2 to 4 weeks of advanced reservations with total usage up to 60 days. Members would have access to the accommodations any time, and the club guaranteed accommodations at any of its locations with notice of at least 90 days. If all the residences in a location were occupied, Exclusive Resorts pledged to rent an equivalent residence for the member. Exclusive Resorts planned to purchase multiple residences in the same location, both to accommodate members' demand and so that a concierge could be assigned to the residences. The first residences were in Beaver Creek, Colorado; Kohala Coast, Hawaii; New York, New York; and Los Cabos, Mexico.

After the initial residence purchases, Exclusive Resorts used the refundable portion of the membership deposit to purchase additional residences and used the annual dues to cover the maintenance of the residences. Exclusive Resorts also used mortgage financing but never more than 50 percent of the aggregate residence value.

Exclusive Resorts opened for memberships in the spring of 2003 and was an instant success. By mid-2004 it had over 750 members, 130 residences in 25 locations, 200 residences under contract or in the late stages of furnishings, and a substantial waiting list.[22] The average value of the residences was $2.5 million. Exclusive Resorts anticipated selling its residences on average after 7 years to replenish its inventory.

During its growth one of the biggest challenges was finding residences fast enough to accommodate those seeking membership. Exclusive Resorts concluded that it was necessary to develop some of its own properties and launched its first captive development in Hawaii.

As it expanded, Exclusive Resorts formed alliances and purchased other luxury residence companies. Alliances were formed with Virtuoso, a $3 billion luxury travel network; The Timbers,

a developer and owner of resort club communities; and Marquis Jet Partnership, which made private jet service available for members. Exclusive Resorts also acquired two competitors, the Odyssey Club and Mirabella Estates.

To avoid being classified as a security, Brad and Brent structured the venture so that membership could not provide a profit. Paragraph 12 of the Club Membership Agreement stated that membership "is not an investment" and the member has no "interest in the Club's income" and "will not share in any appreciation in the value of Club assets."

The paragraph also made it clear that a member had no "recurrent use or occupancy of a specific Club Property or Properties, or on an annual or other periodic schedule, or any specific time period of use. Rather, such rights are based on all Club Members' rights to occupy available Club Properties on a first-come, first-served basis, subject to the Club's reservation policies, including Club Members' use of non-Club Properties pursuant to the Availability Policy."

In recognition of possible regulatory risk, Paragraph 13 of the Club Membership Agreement stated, "Although the Club makes regular, prudent efforts to qualify its tax, regulatory and other legal obligations, government authorities could impose fees, taxes, charges, fines, penalties, cost or other liabilities on the Club related to (a) any new regulation applicable to the Club or the Club's failure to comply with any existing regulation, or (b) the Club's failure to pay any taxes associated with the sale of Club Memberships, Annual Dues, occupancy of Club Properties by Club Members, or any other aspect of the Club's business (collectively, '**Imposed Fees**')." If any Imposed Fees were incurred, Exclusive Resorts had the sole discretion to bill members or increase the annual dues.

## Competition and Entry

In the marketplace Private Retreats and Abercrombie & Kent entered into a licensing arrangement and began selling memberships in Abercrombie & Kent Destination Clubs with two tiers. Private Retreats offered a luxury vacation residence club with residence values between $700,000 and $1.5 million. As a result of the success of Exclusive Resorts, Abercrombie & Kent offered another club, Distinctive Retreats, with average residence values of $2.5 million. These clubs were structured somewhat differently

---

[21]Refunds were governed by a three-in one-out rule under which a refund was provided once three new members had joined. Through mid-2004 fewer than 10 members had sought and received refunds. The membership could also terminate the club on a 75 percent vote, sell the properties, and distribute the proceeds, up to their 80 percent deposit, to the members.
[22]It received a membership inquiry from Steve Case, founder of AOL, who subsequently bought half the company.

from Exclusive Retreats. First, members could use the residences for any length of time. Second, a Residence Daily Fee ranging from $75 to $250 per person was charged. Third, the membership fees were 100 percent refundable. Fourth, membership dues were in the $8,000 to $16,000 range. Abercrombie & Kent also offered access to its safaris, yachts, and tours.

The success of Exclusive Resorts spurred entry into the luxury vacation residence club industry. In addition to Abercrombie & Kent Destination Clubs, entrants included the Portofino Club with an 80 percent refundable $210,000 initial membership fee and annual dues of $15,000; Private Escapes with a fully refundable membership fee of $75,000, annual dues of $6,000, and a daily fee of $75; BelleHavens with residences with an average value of $1 million for a membership deposit of $200,000, annual fees from $8,000 to $18,000, and a refund of 90 percent of the membership deposit at the time of sale. BelleHavens was unique in that the members actually owned the properties and hence could "sell" their memberships with sales governed by a two-in one-out rule.

Private Escapes introduced its Platinum Club with a pledge to share the appreciation of its real estate holdings: "Each year, the club will distribute 18% of the appreciation from its resort real estate holdings as dividends to you and the membership. No catch. When the properties appreciate, you get dividends. But if the market goes soft, you have no exposure. You may also choose to have your appreciation dividends issued as club credits, making them tax free and essentially doubling their value."[23]

## Nonmarket Threats

As Exclusive Resorts' market success continued, nonmarket threats began to grow. Entry into the luxury vacation residence club business was surprisingly easy, and by mid-2004 a dozen or so clubs were being offered. These clubs were typically not as well capitalized as was Exclusive Resorts, and one concern was that some of them might fail and tarnish the image of the industry. This could scare away some prospective members and raise concerns among current members. Moreover,

bankruptcies could lead to regulation. In addition, "equity" like club offerings could attract the SEC's attention. Bankruptcies or new regulatory activity had the potential to harm the timeshare industry as well.

Exclusive Resorts and the other luxury vacation residence clubs posed a threat to traditional timeshares and particularly to the luxury vacation clubs. Taking members away from the luxury vacation clubs could ripple through the timeshare industry. Similarly, failures by undercapitalized luxury residence or vacation clubs could raise concerns among consumers and weaken demand for fractionals and timeshares.

The American Resort Development Association (ARDA) represented the timeshare industry, including among its members timeshare developers and vacation club companies. ARDA members also included law firms, consulting firms, and others that provided services to the resort development industry. ARDA reported that in 2003 there were 5,425 timeshares worldwide with 1,590 in the United States. Sales of timeshares in the United States were $5.5 billion in 2002, and 3 million U.S. consumers owned timeshares with 92 percent using them on average nearly 2 weeks a year. The average size of a timeshare resort was 83 units.

Since timeshares were regulated by state laws, ARDA had developed considerable strength in states that regulated developments as well as those that regulated marketing to their residents. ARDA's objective was not to overturn state regulations but to obtain sensible re-regulation. ARDA had developed Model Timesharing Act Guiding Principles that it advocated as a basis for state regulation.

ARDA expressed concerns about whether luxury vacation residence clubs were operating outside the law, since consumers did not have the protections of state timeshare law. In particular, club plans were not vetted by state regulators. ARDA was also concerned that the contractual arrangements were not transparent to consumers and that the promises made might not be kept. ARDA not only was concerned with risks to consumers but also feared that possible fraud or failures among the clubs could tarnish the entire resort development industry. ARDA was particularly concerned because entry into the luxury vacation residence club business was relatively easy. For example, Private Escapes' Platinum Club offering was made with only one residence,

---

[23]www.private-escapes.com/platinum/dividends.html August 16, 2004.

one yacht under contract, reciprocal privileges at six original Private Escapes properties, and 22 properties "coming soon."

ARDA wanted everyone in the resort development industry to play by the same rules even though their respective business models were different. ARDA sought to have the luxury vacation residence clubs registered in the states in which they held properties and in which they sold memberships.

ARDA asked four of its member law firms to construct a "model club" based on three luxury vacation residence clubs, including Exclusive Resorts. The law firms then assessed whether the model club would be required to register in each of seven states. The law firms concluded, consistent with ARDA's position, that registration was required in each state, including California, except where the law specifically allowed the club, as in Colorado.[24] Registration would subject the model club to the same requirements as timeshares. The law firms also examined the securities issue as well as whether club members were protected in

the event of bankruptcy. ARDA sent the analysis to the Association of Real Estate Licenses Law Officials (ARELLO), the association of state real estate regulatory officials. Additionally, private lawyers from law firms within the industry contacted state regulators.

Several states wrote to Exclusive Resorts seeking additional information about its offering. The question was whether it might be required to register with the state under the laws and regulations that pertained to timeshares. If that were required, Exclusive Resorts would be subject to costly and burdensome regulations. In California the cost to register a timeshare development could run as high as $150,000. Moreover, a core component of the Exclusive Resorts model, that of inventory replacement via the sale of appreciated assets, would be prohibited. Several state attorneys general had contacted ARDA for its views on the luxury vacation residence club industry. ∎

SOURCE: This case was written by Professor David P. Baron based on interviews with Brad Handler and Howard C. Nusbaum of ARDA as well as information from public sources. Copyright © 2004 by the Board of Trustees of the Leland Stanford Junior University. All rights reserved. Reprinted with permission.

---

[24]Exclusive Resorts LLC was a Delaware company whose principal place of business was in Denver, Colorado.

# Appendix

## California Real Estate Law and Subdivided Lands Law

Section 10250.1 of Part 2. Regulation of Transactions, Chapter 1 Subdivided Lands, Article 1 General Provisions defined the subdivision projects that were required to register and hence were subject to regulation.

11003.5 **(a)** A "time-share project" is one in which a purchaser receives a right in perpetuity, for life, or for a term of years, to the recurrent, exclusive use or occupancy of a lot, parcel, unit, or segment of real property, annually or on some other periodic basis. . . .

**(b)** A "time-share estate" is a right of occupancy in a time-share project which is coupled with an estate in the real property.

**(c)** A "time-share use" is a license or contractual or membership right of occupancy in a time-share project which is not coupled with an estate in real property.

**(d)** An "exchange program" is any method, arrangement, or procedure for the voluntary exchange of the right to use and occupy accommodations and facilities among purchasers of time-share interests or other property interests.

**(f)** A "multisite time-share project" is any method, arrangement, or procedure, with respect to which a purchaser obtains, by any means, a recurring right to use and occupy accommodations or facilities in a time-share project consisting of more than one component site, only through use of a reservation system, on a nonpriority basis.

**(g)** A "reservation system" is the method, arrangement, or procedure by which a purchaser of a time-share interest, (1) in order to reserve the use and occupancy of any accommodation or facility. . . . In the event that an owner of a time-share interest is required to use an exchange program as the owner's principal means of obtaining the right to use and occupy the accommodations and facilities of any time-share project, that arrangement shall be a reservation system.

## PREPARATION QUESTIONS

1. How well is Exclusive Resorts positioned in its market environment?
2. How well is it positioned in its nonmarket environment?
3. How serious are the nonmarket threats?
4. What should Exclusive Resorts do about the nonmarket threats?
5. Looking to the future, formulate an integrated strategy for Exclusive Resorts.

# Envirotest Systems Corporation (A)

## The Opportunity

The Clean Air Act of 1990 called for an average 24 percent reduction in vehicle emissions by the end of the century and directed the Environmental Protection Agency (EPA) to issue revised regulations to expand and enhance state inspection and maintenance (I/M) programs. Not only would additional areas of the country be required to have an I/M program, but the programs currently in place in several states would have to be improved. Nearly all the existing programs were "decentralized" with testing and repairs conducted by service stations and repair shops. In many parts of the country these decentralized systems were believed to be ineffective in attaining clean air standards. Proponents of enhanced emissions testing argued that centralized testing using more sophisticated technology was required to achieve air quality standards. In a centralized system a motorist drove to a test-only facility where emissions were tested using a dynamometer, a treadmill-like machine that allowed emissions to be tested at various speeds rather than at idle, as in decentralized testing. Several centralized systems were in operation in 1990.

## Seizing the Opportunity

In 1988 Chester Davenport and Slivy Edwards established an investment fund to acquire companies that were expected to benefit from stricter government regulations. Davenport, a lawyer, had worked in several government positions, including serving as assistant secretary of transportation in the Carter administration. He also had practiced law and had successfully invested in several commercial real estate properties in Washington. His experience had brought him a wide set of contacts and considerable expertise in dealing with both government and the financial community. Edwards was an experienced corporate finance specialist who brought financial expertise to the venture.

Recognizing the opportunity created by the Clean Air Act, in 1990 Davenport and Edwards formed Envirotest Systems Corporation to acquire Hamilton Test Systems, Inc., from United Technologies Corporation for $51 million. Hamilton

had been founded in 1974 in Arizona to operate the nation's first centralized, contractor-operated emissions testing facility. Envirotest provided test-only facilities and did no repairs. In 1990 it had four emissions testing contracts in effect. Although it was clear that the demand for emissions testing would increase substantially, there was uncertainty about how large an expansion the EPA would mandate and whether it would recommend the type of testing program Envirotest provided. Davenport was confident about the EPA's recommendations. As he explained, "It was my business to know these things."[25]

The success of Envirotest depended on the forthcoming EPA regulations, and in 1992 Davenport's expectations were realized. The EPA regulations required 182 metropolitan areas in 35 states to have either a basic or an enhanced I/M program. Fifty-three metropolitan areas with 15 million vehicles had no I/M program, and 15 states had either no program or a decentralized program. Envirotest estimated that a total of 59 million vehicles would be required to have an enhanced I/M program.

In addition to the I/M mandate, the EPA concluded that no decentralized program could be as effective as a centralized program. One of the EPA's concerns with decentralized systems was the inherent conflict of interest in a system in which the tester also made the repairs.

This concern was emphasized by proponents of centralized testing such as the Natural Resources Defense Council. A spokesperson said, "Under the old program, mechanics had an incentive to fail cars that should pass and a mechanic had an incentive to pass a car once he worked on it." The EPA concluded that a centralized program was superior to a decentralized program and decided that the pollution credits given for implementation of a decentralized program would be 50 percent less than for centralized systems.

The EPA estimated that centralized testing would cost less than decentralized testing and take less of a motorist's time. A test for nitrogen oxide, which was not included in many existing programs, would be added, causing more vehicles to fail. Under the EPA's regulations motorists could be

---

[25]*The Wall Street Journal,* March 4, 1994.

required to pay up to $450 for repairs. Existing programs had caps of from $50 to $300.

The EPA required enhanced programs in 83 areas, and in those areas decentralized programs were not permitted unless the jurisdiction demonstrated that a decentralized program was as effective as a centralized program.[26] Under the Clean Air Act, implementation of the National Ambient Air Quality Standards was delegated to the states, and states could choose either a centralized or a decentralized program as well as the test procedures required. The EPA's regulations, however, placed the burden of proof on the states to demonstrate that a decentralized program could be as effective as a centralized program. The EPA, in effect, told the states that they would not be able to demonstrate equivalent effectiveness. If a state failed to adopt an acceptable program by November 1994, the EPA had the authority to ask the Department of Justice and the Department of Transportation to impose penalties on the states. Those penalties included withholding federal highway funds and reducing pollution offset credits that could be used for plant expansions in the state. For Pennsylvania, for example, nearly $1 billion of federal highway funds could be withheld.

Because of the EPA's rule making, in 1992 Envirotest acquired for $83.5 million virtually all of its largest competitor, Systems Control, Inc., renamed ETI, from a unit of Electronic Data Systems, a subsidiary of General Motors.[27] GM was forced to sell because of a conflict of interest between manufacturing and testing vehicles. The acquisition made Envirotest the nation's largest vehicle emissions testing company.

## Market Strategy

Envirotest's market strategy focused on vehicle testing programs and direct service extensions. Envirotest designed, owned, and operated the test-only facilities and provided complete systems including public education about vehicle emissions testing. To avoid conflicts of interests, it made no repairs. This was a marketing advantage because

---

[26]An association of state air-pollution-control officials met to review the EPA's regulations and generally concluded that states should switch to centralized testing.
[27]Envirotest sold the name Systems Control and its 50 percent interest in a joint venture in an I/M program in the state of Washington to the joint venture partner Sun Electric Corporation.

one of the EPA's reasons for favoring centralized programs over decentralized programs was the inherent conflict of interest that arose when the same party did both testing and repairs.

Envirotest had two types of customers: governments and motorists. Emissions testing contracts were let by states and municipalities through a competition typically involving the submission of bids in response to a request for proposals. Contracts with states extended for 7 years and provided for an exclusive emissions testing operator. Contracts could be terminated at will by a state, but damages could be imposed in that event.

Envirotest's other customer was the motorist, and Envirotest emphasized customer convenience and user-friendliness. Motorists were also constituents and voters, so states were particularly sensitive to the public reception of emissions testing. Contracts thus required centralized testing facilities to be located within specified distances of the bulk of the population—for example, within 5 miles of all the population in urban areas and within 10 miles of 80 percent of the population in rural areas. Contracts also provided for fines on the operator based on the length of time for completing the tests—for example, if 95 percent of the tests were not completed in 20 minutes or less.

Envirotest formed alliances as part of its bidding strategy. For its successful bid in Colorado, Envirotest formed an alliance with the leader in mechanics hot-line services, experts in advanced troubleshooting and vehicle diagnostics, the developer of an onboard diagnostics technology, and a vehicle diagnostic database/expert system company.

Envirotest planned to invest $150 million to purchase land and construct testing facilities in Pennsylvania. In April 1993 it made an initial public offering raising $55 million in equity and $125 million in long-term debt. Envirotest also arranged a $130 million credit facility and project financing of up to $400 million from its investment bank. As important as having the funds available to build and operate several testing systems simultaneously was having the organizational capacity to manage multiple contracts. One benefit of acquiring ETI was obtaining experienced personnel.

A component of Envirotest's market strategy was to have leading-edge technologies, and hence it invested in research and development through its R&D facilities in Tucson. In addition to its centralized testing technologies, in 1993 Envirotest acquired Remote Sensing Technologies (RST) from Sun Electric Corporation, which had commercialized a remote sensing device.[28]

Envirotest engaged in a limited set of product extensions. It provided pre-emissions safety inspections, a quality assurance service, and a referee service. The referee service in Anchorage, Alaska, resolved disputes between motorists and repair shops. The quality assurance program in California provided inspection of the state's 9,300 smog check stations. Its safety inspection services were operated both separately and within its emissions testing facilities.

## Competitive Advantage and Competencies

Envirotest had a competitive advantage because of its experience. Of the 16 centralized testing systems in the United States and British Columbia, Envirotest operated 10. Emissions testing had learning curve economies along two dimensions. The first was the usual development of technical sophistication and operational expertise. The other pertained to dealing with the public. An advantage of being the largest and most experienced company was that states could have a measure of confidence that Envirotest would effectively manage its interactions with the public.

Envirotest had many distinctive technical, operational, and organizational competencies. It had unparalleled proprietary technologies that it had extended through several strategic alliances. It had two emissions testing technologies, one from Hamilton and the other from ETI, and had acquired a remote testing technology. It had extensive operating experience and a reputation for effective service. It also had the largest number of experienced professionals.

## Nonmarket Strategy

One foundation of Envirotest's nonmarket strategy was its knowledge of governments in their three roles. Governments created demand (EPA), were customers (states and municipalities), and chose technology through the type of emissions testing system they selected (states and municipalities). Envirotest developed relationships with the EPA and was successful in being selected to develop the demonstration facility for the I/M 240 enhanced test required by the EPA for centralized testing facilities. This gave the company a marketing advantage that it could use as evidence that it was the most experienced contractor and had an unparalleled technology. Part of Envirotest's nonmarket strategy with respect to governments as customers was to encourage states to choose centralized testing rather than to attempt to demonstrate that an alternative system could perform as well.

A second foundation of its nonmarket strategy was sensitivity to the concerns of interest groups and the public. An important part of an emissions testing program was public education intended to build acceptance for the program. Envirotest participated in both the development and implementation of these programs. Envirotest also sought to manage effectively its interactions with "key participant groups," the most important of which were motorists and repair shops. Envirotest was willing to support exemptions for fleet operators, automobile dealers, and government agencies that wished to operate their own testing facilities.

The company also sought to develop effective relationships with interest groups at the state level. In Colorado, for example, it interacted with and attempted to be responsive to the concerns of the American Automobile Association, the American Lung Association, the Automobile Service Association, the Colorado Automobile Dealers Association, the Colorado Building and Construction Trades Council, and Coloradans for Clean Air.

As part of its constituency efforts, Envirotest lined up local suppliers and partners. For example, one of its partners was a Colorado firm that manufactured dynamometers. It also pointed to the number of people it would hire in a state and established a Minority/Women Business Enterprise program for minority and women contractors.

In bidding for state contracts, Envirotest used a three-stage contract award approach in which nonmarket strategies comprised the first of the three stages.[29] The first stage, called Pre-Bid Marketing, was founded on the premise that "participation in the

---

[28]Remote sensing technologies involved portable roadside infrared monitors that examined vehicle emissions and photographed the license plates of vehicles. Vehicles emitting more than allowable levels were sent notices to go to a testing facility or repair shop.

[29]The second stage involved the preparation of proposals/bids, and the final stage involved program implementation.

legislative and regulatory authorization process for emissions testing programs [is] an important initial step in marketing its services. With the help of legislative consultants, the Company's marketing staff educates states and municipalities on the environmental and operational benefits associated with contractor-operated centralized programs, and attempts to build support for adoption of such a program among environmental and health organizations." Once legislation had been enacted, "interested parties (including the Company and its competitors) are often asked to assist the appropriate governmental authority in drafting the technical aspects of a bid request. This effort often includes reviewing bid criteria and recommending specified test programs."[30]

## Competitive Advantage and Nonmarket Competencies

Envirotest's three principal nonmarket competencies were (1) its knowledge of and experience with government, (2) its sensitivity to the concerns of the public and interest groups, and (3) its reputation for dealing effectively with public concerns. Davenport not only had considerable experience and expertise, but he also had a set of relationships with influential members of the federal government and the public. As the company had grown and obtained additional emissions testing contracts, it had hired additional executives to manage its interactions with government.

Its sensitivity to public concerns led Envirotest to seek effective relationships with both organized interest groups, such as repair shops and automobile dealers, and unorganized interests such as motorists. Its educational and outreach programs constituted a competency that could be transferred to other states.

Its reputation for dealing effectively with interests and the public was an important competency, as government officials wanted to avoid a public outcry against emissions testing. A reputation for and experience with these matters provided a degree of assurance that served Envirotest well in contractor selection.

## Market Threats

Envirotest faced a number of threats in its market environment. The centralized testing industry included four rivals: Sun-Systems Control, Gordon-Darby, Allen-MATRA, and Environmental Systems Products. Envirotest operated more testing programs than all the others combined and was the most formidable firm in the industry, but nevertheless it faced competition.

The threat of new entry came both from new firms that might enter the centralized testing business and from states that could choose to provide their own centralized testing facilities. With the pressure on government to become slimmer and the movement toward privatization and outsourcing, however, few states were likely to provide centralized testing themselves.

The threats from substitutes came at two levels. First, states had the authority to achieve air quality standards through a variety of means. For example, they could institute programs to scrap old cars, which accounted for a substantial proportion of the emissions in many states.[31] States could also implement remote testing programs directed at detecting vehicles with excessive emissions. Second, states could choose an alternative emissions testing approach—decentralized or remote testing—provided they demonstrated to the EPA that it would be as effective as centralized testing. Although Envirotest did not have a clear technological advantage in remote testing, it had pursued opportunities for remote testing programs. Remote testing had the advantage of identifying the worst polluting vehicles, including those whose emissions control systems had been tampered with, and requiring them to undergo repair and further testing, while not requiring testing of clean vehicles. California, for example, spent $250 million annually testing clean vehicles and $117 million annually repairing dirty ones.[32] ■

---

[30]Envirotest Systems Corp. Form 10-K for the fiscal year ended September 30, 1993. Securities and Exchange Commission, Washington, DC, 1993, pp. 11–13.

[31]Pre-1982 vehicles accounted for 25 percent of the vehicles on the road.
[32]California Research Bureau, "Motor Vehicle Inspection and Maintenance in California," Sacramento, CA, August 24, 1993.

## PREPARATION QUESTIONS

1. What forces gave rise to the opportunity for Davenport and Edwards?
2. Assess the effectiveness of Envirotest's market strategy. Is the company likely to be able to take full advantage of the opportunities presented by the Clean Air Act?
3. How effectively integrated are its market and nonmarket strategies? Are its market and nonmarket competencies complementary?
4. How significant are the threats in its market environment? Is it capable of dealing with those threats?
5. Does it face threats from its nonmarket environment? If so, how should it deal with them?

# Personal Watercraft, aka Jet Skis

Personal watercraft, popularly known as water bikes or jet skis, are vessels powered by a jet pump with engines up to 135 horsepower and capable of reaching speeds of over 60 mph. Jet skis skyrocketed in popularity during the 1990s with sales reaching $1.2 billion in 1996, accounting for 37 percent of the boats sold in the United States. The average jet ski cost $6,328 in 1996, and over a million were in operation. The leading producer with nearly half the market was Bombardier, based in Montreal, producer of Sea Doo personal watercraft. Other producers included Polaris Industries, Kawasaki, and Yamaha. Despite, or perhaps because of, their popularity jet skis were under attack from several quarters.

Safety concerns resulted from the speed of jet skis and from some of their operating characteristics. One characteristic was that they were nearly impossible to control when an operator lost hold of the throttle. A study published in the *Journal of the American Medical Association* reported that injuries associated with personal watercraft increased dramatically with an estimated 12,000 people treated in hospital emergency rooms in 1995, including four fatalities. The study also indicated that the accident rate for personal watercraft was substantially higher than for regular motorboats. In California, jet skis accounted for 55 percent of boating injuries but only 18 percent of registered boats. The industry responded that surveys had shown that the average personal watercraft was used more per year than larger boats, making the accident rates "roughly comparable" to water skiing. Kawasaki stated, "More fatalities are routinely recorded for kayaking and canoeing." The National Transportation Safety Board had begun a study of jet ski safety, and a number of states and interest groups were pressuring the U.S. Coast Guard to examine jet ski accidents.

John Donaldson, executive director of the Personal Watercraft Industry Association, said, "This is just a recreational activity—it's fun. It's not a firearm. . . . It's not a proven health risk like cigarettes." Pat Hartman of Polaris Industries said that jet skis were "as safe as the driver. It's like a loaded gun. If it's in the wrong hands, it's not safe."

EPA regulations that took effect in 1998 set new hydrocarbon and nitrogen oxide emissions standards for boats, and those standards would become more stringent each year until 2006 when a 75 percent reduction in emissions would have been achieved. The standards were applied on a "corporate average" basis that required all of a company's certified engines, on average, to achieve the standards. This allowed greater flexibility to manufacturers. The Earth Island Institute, an environmental activist group, criticized the EPA regulations as too weak.

The California Air Resources Board had begun a study to determine if jet skis should be regulated for their emissions. Other state and local agencies in California began to examine jet ski operations as a source of MTBE, a gasoline additive that reduced automobile emissions but could contaminate water supplies.[33] The Northern California Marine Association expressed concern about the effect of a boating ban on recreation and the businesses that serviced boating. Administrative Director Mary Kirin Velez said, "Our whole emphasis is on getting the governor

---

[33] See the Chapter 1 case An Emerging Issue: MTBE.

to give a waiver to let the oil companies produce gasoline without using MTBE."[34]

Local environmental groups also took up the cause. The Bluewater Network organized a public demonstration in San Francisco comparing jet skis with two-stroke and four-stroke engines. The two-stroke engine left an oily residue in the water, whereas the four-stroke engine left no apparent residue. Russell Long, director of the Bluewater Network, called jet skis "America's No. 1 water polluter. . . . We don't want to take away anyone's Jet Ski. Our focus is the new ones that haven't been built yet."[35]

Two-stroke engines used gasoline mixed with oil, and critics argued that the fuel did not burn completely. In four-stroke engines the lubricating oil was kept separate from the combustion compartment.[36] Two-stroke engines, however, delivered more power and faster acceleration. Two-stroke engines had been banned in motorcycles because of their emissions. The Tahoe Regional Planning Agency voted to ban two-cycle engines from Lake Tahoe to reduce water pollution. The EPA issued regulations taking effect in 1999 that required fuel injection, which would substantially reduce pollution.

In addition to water pollution, homeowners and others complained of the noise made by personal watercraft. Mark Desmeules, director of Maine's Natural Resources Division, referred to jet skis as "the Ninja bikes of the water." He added, "That's why there is such a public outcry—the ability of just one of them to degrade the quality of the natural experience for so many people."[37] Vermont responded by banning jet skis from lakes with less than 300 acres. Legislation introduced in Minnesota would have banned personal watercraft on lakes with less than 200 acres, but opposition by the Jetsporters Association of Minnesota led to defeat of the bill. Jim Medema of the International Jet Sports Boating Association said, "The vote sent a clear message to those that would discriminate against PWC owners. We want to ensure that Minnesotans can continue to ride their PWC safely and responsibly without any unfair restrictions that do not apply to other boaters."

The National Park Service, an agency of the Department of the Interior, was considering regula-

tions that would allow individual park superintendents to designate personal watercraft usage areas. The regulations were supported by over 100 conservation organizations, including the American Canoe Association, the National Parks and Conservation Association, and the Earth Island Institute. The International Jet Sports Boating Association opposed the regulations. Both sides urged their members to write to the secretary of the interior. Mark Speaks of Yamaha Motors said, "I have not read a study that personal watercraft are particularly annoying to wildlife. I don't know why they would be more annoying to wildlife than any other boat."[38]

Local governments also were addressing personal watercraft issues. For example, the city council of Evanston, Illinois, recommended that PWC operators be charged permit fees twice as high as for other boats. The Illinois Department of Natural Resources notified Evanston that such fees were discriminatory and that it could lose state grants if they were imposed.

The industry implemented several nonmarket strategies to address the issues it faced. Industry members had formed the Personal Watercraft Industry Association (PWIA), which acted on behalf of industry members in public arenas. "Where conflict exists, the PWIA seeks to support resolution through the careful balancing of the interests of all parties, including PWC and other boat operators, swimmers, fishermen, paddlesports enthusiasts, environmentalists, and shoreline residents or recreationists."[39]

At the state level the PWIA developed model legislation intended to make waterways safer and to reduce conflicts. Twenty-six states enacted regulations based on the model legislation, which included a minimum age requirement of 16 years for operators, defined and restricted unsafe operation, prohibited nighttime operation, required that operators and passengers wear personal flotation devices, required operators of personal watercraft equipped with engine shutoff lanyards to use them, prohibited tow lines, and required safety instruction.[40] Mandatory instruction had been required in Connecticut since 1989 and was credited with keeping accidents down. The PWIA supported state legislation such as that in North Carolina that would prohibit nighttime use and increase the minimum age to 16 unless the

[34]*San Jose Mercury News,* February 14, 1998.
[35]*San Francisco Chronicle,* March 26, 1997.
[36]*The Wall Street Journal,* February 18, 1998.
[37]*San Francisco Chronicle,* December 30, 1997.
[38]*San Francisco Chronicle,* December 30, 1997.
[39]Yamaha Web site, www.yamaha-motor.com.
[40]Yamaha Web site. Many states, for example, had no age requirement to operate a personal watercraft.

person was between 12 and 16 and had an adult onboard or had taken a boat safety course.

Manufacturers' Web sites provided instructions on watercraft safety, rules of the road, and self-tests on operation safety. Jet skis came with a videotape, booklets, and warning labels on the watercraft. Web sites for jet skis also provided an environmental guide, including instructions to fuel and clean watercraft engines away from the water and shore. Operators were also instructed to avoid bird habitats and shallow waters where the watercraft could stir up sediment.

Legislative and regulatory activity took place at the federal, state, and local levels as well as in special jurisdictions such as the Tahoe Regional Planning Agency. The PWIA Web site provided tracking information on legislative and regulatory activity at each of these levels. Manufacturers also encouraged watercraft owners to take political action on issues pertaining to jet skis. Bombardier asked owners to contact their government entities to learn about possible legislative and regulatory action and also provided advice about how to participate effectively in public processes. It recommended that individuals ask their legislators about any restrictions being considered, identify key legislators including committee chairpersons, and ask about hearings schedules. Bombardier also provided guides for effective testimony; for example, "When testifying at the hearing, thank the legislators for the opportunity to make your views known, and state your position on the issue in a clear and concise manner. Be prepared to answer questions, and do not be confrontational or react defensively."

In response to the criticisms, manufacturers made changes in their watercraft in an attempt to reduce complaints and regulatory pressure. Bombardier announced that all its 1999 Sea-Doo models would include sound reduction technologies adapted from the automotive industry. The technologies included a new muffler, new composite parts that reduced noise levels, and a resonator that suppressed certain frequencies. Bombardier announced that the sound pressure level had been reduced by 50 percent on one of its models.

One strategy of the industry was to lend jet skis to government agencies, and in 1997 nearly 2,000 were on loan to game wardens, search and rescue teams, firefighters, and police and sheriff departments. Mary Ann Anderson, who had led the fight against jet skis in the San Juan Islands of Washington, said, "What they are doing is very ironic—producing a machine that needs to be highly regulated because of the way it is built and the power involved in it. Then they give this product to law enforcement, which are supposed to be policing them. It's ridiculous."[41]

The issues associated with jet skis were similar in some regards to those of snowmobiles in the 1970s. Bombardier and Polaris also manufactured snowmobiles and along with other manufacturers had taken measures, such as developing trails, to defuse criticism by landowners. Bombardier credited the strategy of loaning snowmobiles to law enforcement agencies and search and rescue teams as helping gain their acceptance. As public acceptance increased, the market for snowmobiles continued to grow. ∎

SOURCE: Copyright © 1999 by the Board of Trustees of the Leland Stanford Junior University. All rights reserved. Reprinted with permission.

---

[41]*San Francisco Chronicle,* December 30, 1997.

---

## PREPARATION QUESTIONS

1. Identify the issues, interests, institutions, and information associated with jet skis.
2. How have the jet ski manufacturers used market and nonmarket strategies to address the issues they face?
3. Should the jet ski manufacturers join the National Marine Manufacturers Association, which represents power boat manufacturers?
4. Should the jet ski industry seek to be included in the same regulatory category as power boats, or should it seek to have its own regulatory category, for example, with respect to no-wake zones?
5. What nonmarket strategy should a company such as Bombardier adopt? How should it be integrated with its market strategy?

# CHAPTER 3

# The News Media and Nonmarket Issues

## Introduction

The news media plays an important role in society by providing information to the public about matters affecting people's lives and the society in which they live. The news media also plays an important role in identifying nonmarket issues and stimulating action that affects their progress. The news media finds business of interest, and with stories instantly transmitted worldwide by the broadcast media and the Internet, a firm's actions are in the eye of the media and under the scrutiny of interest groups, activists, and government. Phil Knight, chairman and CEO of Nike, stated in Nike's 1996 annual report, "Yet no sooner had the great year ended than we were hit by a series of blasts from the media about our practices overseas." As this comment suggests, many companies dread media coverage of their nonmarket issues and have had to develop a capability for interacting effectively with the media.

The essential role the news media plays in a democracy is accompanied by a responsibility to provide information in an accurate and unbiased manner so that individuals can formulate their own conclusions about issues. News organizations, however, face incentives, including those provided by profits, and pressures from competition among news organizations. Similarly, journalists face incentives associated with career and professional advancement. These incentives and pressures complicate the fulfillment of that responsibility. The news media itself is a diverse collection of organizations, including television, radio, Internet services, newspapers, magazines, and journals, and each faces its own set of challenges.

This chapter considers the role of the news media in the development of nonmarket issues. To analyze that role, a theory of media coverage and treatment is presented. This theory provides a basis for anticipating the impact of the news media on the progress of issues through their life cycles. The news media as an institution is then considered, focusing on the business and professional incentives that motivate news organizations, their editors, and journalists. Lastly, approaches to dealing with the news media are presented, including recourse in the event of a dispute.

# The Role of the News Media in Nonmarket Issues

In Chapter 1 the news media was identified as one of the institutions in whose arena nonmarket issues are addressed. Indeed, Cater (1959) referred to the news media as the "fourth branch" of government, formalizing Thomas Carlyle's 1841 description of British statesman Edmund Burke's characterization of reporters as the "Fourth Estate."[1] Editors and journalists are the "officeholders" of the institution. In addition to serving as an arena in which nonmarket issues are addressed, the news media plays an important role in identifying nonmarket issues and placing issues on the agendas of firms. Media coverage can

- alert the public, activists, interest groups, and government officeholders to nonmarket issues
- raise concerns about the policies and practices of firms
- provide information about the likely effects of alternative courses of action
- reduce the costs of collective nonmarket action
- enhance a nonmarket strategy by conveying information generated by an interest group
- represent certain interests and principles consistent with the news media's perception of its role in society.

Interest groups and activist organizations, as well as government officeholders, are prepared to act on a variety of issues, and media coverage can inform them and spur action. Media coverage can also make a message common knowledge among the public and thereby reduce the cost of collective action. An interest group such as a union or trial lawyers may seize the opportunity created by media coverage of an event to further its interests. Media coverage can also provide a natural opportunity for a politician to advance an issue, represent constituents affected by it, or claim credit for addressing it.[2]

Nonmarket entrepreneurs outside of public office have developed strategies for attracting media coverage to call attention to issues, influence the public, and stimulate private and public politics. As considered in Chapter 11, environmental groups use the release of the EPA's annual Toxic Substances Inventory to hold press conferences to name the nation's largest polluters and call for more stringent environmental standards. Similarly, Greenpeace is effective in using media coverage to advance the issues on its agenda, as illustrated by the Chapter 4 case, *Shell, Greenpeace, and Brent Spar.*

A striking example of the role the news media can play in an activist group's strategy was provided by the Natural Resources Defense Council's (NRDC) campaign on Alar, a chemical used to make apples ripen more uniformly and stay crisp when stored. In a 1989 policy study, "Intolerable Risk: Pesticides in Our Children's Food," the NRDC argued that Alar increased the risk of cancer in children and called for a ban on its use. To advance its position through the media, the NRDC hired Fenton Communications. After the media campaign, David Fenton described their strategy.[3]

> Our goal was to create so many repetitions of NRDC's message that average American consumers (not just the policy elite in Washington) could not avoid hearing it—from many different media outlets within a short period of time. The idea was for the "story" to achieve a life of its own, and continue for weeks and months to affect policy and consumer habits. Of course this had to be achieved with extremely limited resources. . . .
>
> It was agreed that one week after the study's release, [Meryl] Streep and other prominent citizens would announce the formation of NRDC's new project,

---

[1] Quoted in Sparrow (1999, p. 5).
[2] See Cook (1989) and Graber (2000).
[3] *The Wall Street Journal,* October 3, 1989.

Mothers and Others for Pesticide Limits. This group would direct citizen action at changing the pesticide laws, and help consumers lobby for pesticide-free produce at their grocery stores.

The separation of these two events was important in ensuring that the media would have two stories, not one, about this project. Thereby, more repetition of NRDC's message was guaranteed.

As the report was being finalized, Fenton Communications began contacting various media. An agreement was made with *60 Minutes* to "break" the story of the report in late February. Interviews were also arranged several months in advance with major women's magazines like *Family Circle, Women's Day,* and *Redbook* (to appear in mid-March). Appearance dates were set with the *Donahue Show, ABC's Home Show,* double appearances on NBC's *Today Show* and other programs. . . .

In addition, we arranged for Meryl Streep and Janet Hathaway of NRDC to grant 16 interviews by satellite with local TV major market anchors. . . .

In the ensuing weeks, the controversy kept building. Articles appeared in food sections of newspapers around the country. Columnists and cartoonists took up the story. *McNeil/Lehrer, The New York Times* and *Washington Post* did follow-up stories, as did the three network evening programs and morning shows. Celebrities from the casts of *L.A. Law* and *thirtysomething* joined NRDC for a Los Angeles news conference.

This episode illustrates the responsiveness of the media to an issue such as pesticide use and its role in stimulating nonmarket action that can advance an issue through its life cycle. Media coverage made the NRDC's message common knowledge, leading to demands by the public to ban Alar. Not only did the NRDC orchestrate newsworthy events, but it also timed them to extend the media attention. This was despite very little scientific basis for NRDC's claims.[4]

This example is not intended to suggest that it is easy to use the media in a nonmarket strategy. The news media guards the independence of its editorial judgments and is careful to avoid being used as part of a nonmarket strategy. However, when an issue is of interest to viewers and readers, the news media has incentives to cover it. That coverage can serve the interests of activists, interest groups, public officeholders, or businesses. When those parties can make the issue more interesting to an audience, the impact of news coverage of the issue increases. The Alar episode serves as a reminder of the potential effect of media coverage on the progress of an issue. Addressing the issue then is considerably more difficult, as indicated in the chapter case, *The Alar Episode.*

## Messages and Their Interpretation

Because of the importance of the news media, firms and their managers must anticipate which issues will attract media coverage and how the media will treat them. Figure 3-1 illustrates the role of the media in informing the public and facilitating nonmarket action. Issues and events are observed by the media, which then decides whether to cover them and how to treat those it covers. Coverage and treatment provide messages to which readers and viewers are exposed and on which interest groups, politicians, firms, and others condition their perceptions and actions. Those actions can themselves be newsworthy, attracting further coverage and giving the issue a life of its own.

---

[4]See the chapter case *The Alar Episode.*

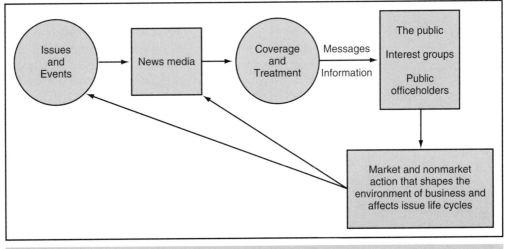

**FIGURE 3-1** The News Media and the Environment of Business

The messages provided by the news media are interpreted in a variety of ways depending on individuals' prior information, beliefs, and preferences. Even though the interpretation of messages can vary, their impact can be systematic and hence important. In a series of laboratory experiments, Iyengar and Kinder (1987) investigated the agenda-setting role of the news media and the ways in which news stories affected viewers' attitudes toward issues and political leaders. Their research indicated that viewers attached greater importance to an issue after seeing news coverage of it. They also found that news coverage primes viewers by affecting "what springs to mind and what is forgotten or ignored."[5] These agenda-setting and priming effects are important to both the development of nonmarket issues and management's efforts to address them.

## A Theory of News Media Coverage and Treatment

To assess the role of the news media in nonmarket issues, a theory is needed for the stages of the process shown in Figure 3-1 in which the media observes issues and events and chooses whether to cover them and how to treat those it covers. The unit of analysis is the issue, and the theory is intended to explain and predict coverage and treatment. Treatment may take several forms:

- a straightforward presentation of facts and description of events
- an interpretation of the facts and events
- an exploration of their potential significance and ramifications
- advocacy of a course of action.

Advocacy is, in principle but not always in practice, to be restricted to the editorial page.

A variety of explanatory variables could be used in a theory of media coverage and treatment, but in the interest of parsimony only two are considered—the intrinsic audience interest in the issue and its societal significance as perceived by the news media. As indicated in the previous section, audience interest and societal significance may themselves be influenced by media coverage and treatment.

---

[5]Iyengar and Kinder (1987, p. 114).

## Intrinsic Audience Interest

The audience interest perspective begins with the observation that coverage and treatment decisions are influenced by revenue and hence audience considerations. Subscription and advertising revenues are based on circulation and ratings, and the objective is to attract an audience by covering issues of interest to readers and viewers and treating those issues in a manner that will hold their attention. From this perspective, predicting which issues the media will cover requires determining which issues are of intrinsic interest to readers and viewers. Similarly, predicting the treatment an issue will receive requires determining what attracts and holds their attention. The principal predictions of the audience theory are that (1) coverage increases with audience interest and (2) treatment will be chosen to appeal to and retain an audience.

Assessing intrinsic audience interest in issues such as international trade policy, product safety, environmental protection, and employment practices of overseas suppliers generally lies in the realm of judgment rather than measurement. A product safety issue centering on a hazard to consumers attracts an instant audience, whereas many international trade issues have limited audience interest due to their complexity and their indirect effects on people. Environmental issues matter to many people, so environmental stories have a natural audience. Even an issue remote in its origins and distant in its effects can attract interest, as in the case of the destruction of Amazon Basin rain forests. The more proximate the consequences, however, the greater the audience interest.

## Societal Significance

The societal significance perspective views coverage and treatment as a reflection of the news media's perception of the significance of an issue to society. This perspective reflects the news media's role in serving democracy by providing the information that citizens need. Veteran journalist Edwin Newman (1984, p. 19) said, "We in the news business help to provide the people with the information they need to frame their attitudes and to make, or at any rate to authorize or ratify, the decisions on which the well-being of the nation rests." Louis H. Young (1978), former editor-in-chief of *Business Week,* stated, "Reporters see themselves as guardians of the public's right to know." Applied to business issues, he described an incident involving a company's board of directors meeting and explained, "The magazine's position was—and is—that what the directors ate or drank was their business; but when they considered replacing the chief executive of a company it was the business of stockholders, both present and future."

A duty to provide information to the public places the news media in a watchdog role, and that role frequently is an adversarial one. Louis Banks, former managing editor of *Fortune,* noted, "The editorial mind-set is influenced by the periodic—and important—feats of investigative reporting or crisis coverage that bring out the natural adversarial aspects of the business-media relationship and reassure the media about their watchdog, top-dog role."[6]

The societal significance perspective emphasizes issues important to the social fabric and to tensions in that fabric. Two similar events will receive quite different coverage if one has a racial dimension and the other does not. Similarly, issues that have a human cause are more likely to be covered. Two similar health risks associated with food products will receive different coverage if one involves a man-made risk and the other a natural risk. The societal significance perspective also emphasizes forerunners of changes in the social fabric, particularly when moral concerns are raised. An issue

---

[6]*Fortune,* October 14, 1985, p. 207.

such as the responsibility of U.S. companies for the working conditions in the factories of their overseas suppliers has societal significance, as Nike painfully learned.[7]

The societal significance perspective can be summarized as follows. The news media has a special role in a democracy and is assigned, or has assumed, the duty of serving the people's right to know about issues important to the fabric of society. This duty is recognized in the First Amendment, which protects the news media in its role of providing the information people need. The greater the media's perception of an issue's societal significance, the more likely it is to be covered. Also, the greater the perceived societal significance, the more likely the treatment will be characterized by advocacy consistent with the media's vision of an informed democracy. Issues high on the societal significance dimension include health, safety, environmental protection, human rights, security, and social justice.

## Combining the Perspectives

Combining these two perspectives provides a theory of news coverage and treatment as a function of intrinsic audience interest and the media's assessment of the societal significance of the issue. In this theory, treatment depends more on societal significance than on audience interest, whereas coverage depends more on audience interest.

Figure 3-2 illustrates the predictions of the theory, which are refined in the next section. The theory predicts that issues low on both the audience interest dimension

**FIGURE 3-2** Theory of Media Coverage and Treatment

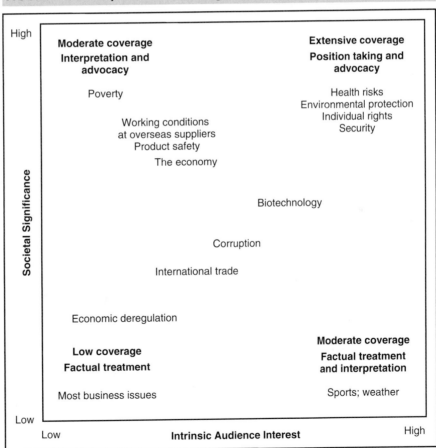

[7]See the Chapter 4 case, *Nike in Southeast Asia.*

and the societal significance dimension will receive little coverage. Most routine business news is in this category and at most is covered by the business press. Deregulation of the electric power or telecommunication industry has a major impact on economic efficiency, but economic deregulation has neither high audience interest nor high perceived societal significance. Furthermore, economic deregulation is complex and thus difficult for the media to explain or for readers or viewers to understand. The treatment of such issues tends to be factual, objective, and balanced.

Issues that are high on the audience interest dimension but low on the societal significance dimension include the daily weather, sports, and the entertainment industry. These issues receive moderate coverage and are generally treated in a factual and balanced manner.

Issues low on the audience interest dimension but high on the societal significance dimension include poverty and much of politics. Such issues are likely to receive only moderate coverage because of their limited audience interest. Their treatment, however, may involve a degree of position taking or advocacy. The working conditions in overseas factories are a distant issue for most readers and viewers, but because of its high societal significance as perceived by the media, the issue received considerable coverage. In its role as a protector of the public's right to know, the news media may advocate a course of action. Treatment of the issue, for example, frequently used the term *sweatshops.*

Issues high on both the intrinsic audience interest and societal significance dimensions receive extensive coverage, and their treatment may involve both factual reporting and position taking and advocacy. These issues include health, safety, the environment, and human rights. A health risk, particularly the protection of society from such a risk, is high on both the audience interest and the societal significance dimensions. Consequently, the Alar issue received considerable coverage, and its treatment reflected the media's perceived duty to warn the public. The media covered the events organized by the NRDC because those events made the story more appealing to audiences. The coverage conveyed the NRDC's message, and by implication the media's treatment advocated that precautions be taken, including governmental action.

Coverage and treatment can differ between the print and broadcast media, between *The New York Times* and the *New York Post,* and Fox News and CBS News. Moreover, over time issues may change their location in the audience interest–societal significance space. Over the past three decades issues involving health risks and environmental protection have moved to the upper right in Figure 3-2.

This theory of news media coverage and treatment is based on two sufficient conditions—societal significance and intrinsic audience interest. Other features of stories, such as visual effects, human interest, confrontation, and controversy, are also important. The theory is extended along these dimensions in the next section.

## Extending the Theory

### Newsworthiness

The concept of newsworthiness extends the intrinsic audience interest and perceived societal significance dimensions. An issue is more newsworthy if it has a degree of immediacy or urgency. The massive television coverage of a natural disaster results in part because it is a breaking story. The risk to life and property makes it urgent. The burning of Amazon Basin rain forests has less urgency, but its link to global climate change makes it more immediate than it would otherwise be. A groundwater contamination issue has a greater degree of urgency if there is a threat to health.

An issue is more newsworthy if it has a human interest dimension with which the audience can identify, as in stories about victims of injustice, accidents, or natural disasters. A story is also more interesting if it is told by someone involved in the issue rather than by a correspondent. In an era of remote channel changers, television producers are reluctant to air a "talking head" segment with a correspondent telling a long and complex story. When the story is told by participants, however, the result is often more than just an eyewitness account, since the participants have an opportunity to make judgments about the issue or advocate action.

An issue often is more newsworthy if it involves a celebrity. The NRDC was correct in thinking that Meryl Streep would attract coverage for the Alar issue. Similarly, the news media may choose to cover an issue because it is entertaining, or it may add an entertaining dimension to the story. Particularly for television, an issue is more newsworthy if it has visual appeal.

A story is more newsworthy if it involves confrontation or controversy. An environmental issue is more newsworthy if it contains allegations that apple growers are creating hazards for an unsuspecting public. A story is more newsworthy if it ties to an issue such as health with high intrinsic audience interest. In particular, linking it to the health of children not only provides a human interest dimension but also demonstrates that the news media is fulfilling its role by protecting the public's right to know. A common approach to developing confrontation and controversy in a story is to have each side tell its version of the issue. This provides balance, but it also highlights the controversy.

In contrast, stories about ideas are often difficult to write and present, particularly for a medium such as television. Stories about ideas provide limited opportunities to develop controversy, drama, and human interest or to include visual effects. The media thus may not give as much coverage to issues centering on ideas as they might merit in terms of their societal significance. To explain why the national news media was slow to cover the savings and loan crisis that cost the economy tens of billions of dollars, Ellen Hume wrote: "It was all too complicated and boring to interest many mainstream journalists. Regulatory changes—such as the accounting tricks and reduced capital requirements that helped paper over the first phase of the savings and loan crisis in the early 1980s—weren't big news. . . . When asked why TV hadn't covered the crisis much even after it made headlines in 1988, the president of NBC News, Michael Gartner, observed that the story didn't lend itself to images, and without such images, 'television can't do facts.'"[8] Hume added that as the issue developed, the victims (the depositors) did not complain, because their deposits were federally insured. Controversy and conflict were absent. Media interest subsequently developed as the magnitude of the crisis became evident and as information about malfeasance was revealed.

## The Cost of Coverage

News coverage is also a function of the costs of obtaining information and producing a story. Costs include those of assigning journalists to stories and beats, maintaining bureau offices, getting reporters to where the stories are breaking, and providing editorial and administrative support. Once journalists are assigned to a story and are on location, the marginal cost of coverage is reduced and the media is more likely to use stories from that source. As Edwin Newman (1984, p. 29) stated, "What is news on television often depends on where your reporters and cameramen are. If you keep people at the White House, you will be tempted to use stories from there, if only for economic

---

[8]Ellen Hume, "Why the Press Blew the S&L Scandal," *The New York Times*, May 24, 1990.

reasons. . . . If you send reporters and camera crews on a trip with the secretary of state, you tend to use what they send back. If you staff a story day after day, you will have it on the air day after day."

Both the costs of obtaining information and the budget pressures on most media organizations have forced them to rely increasingly on low-cost sources of information such as interest groups, government agencies, and businesses rather than developing the information firsthand. Firms and interest groups thus are frequently sources of the information the news media needs to present stories. These sources often strategically provide information, and journalists may end up relying on what their sources' claims about facts rather than gathering those facts directly.[9] Brooks Jackson, a Cable News Network correspondent and former *Wall Street Journal* reporter, observed, "We usually depend on governmental institutions or groups like Common Cause or Ralph Nader or General Motors or somebody to make sense out of all this data for us."[10]

## Balance and Fairness

Journalism standards and editorial controls require that a story be accurate and the treatment provide balance and fairness. Accuracy involves not only verifying facts but also ensuring that the story as presented portrays the situation correctly. Balance requires presenting both sides of an issue, which often involves providing an opportunity for the various sides to present their views on the issue. Fairness involves not only ensuring that the participants in an issue have an opportunity to present their views but that a person or subject is not presented or treated in an unjust manner. The latter is particularly relevant on those issues high on the societal significance dimension on which the media may take an advocacy position.

# The Nature of the News Media

## News Organizations as Businesses

In the United States, news organizations are owned by for-profit companies, so profit is a primary objective. ABC is owned by Walt Disney, CBS by Viacom, NBC by General Electric, and Fox by the News Corporation. As profit-oriented firms, news media companies are interested in attracting readers and viewers, since subscription and advertising revenue depend on audience size. Reuven Frank (1991, p. 222), former president of NBC News, said "The product of commercial television is not programs. If one thinks of making goods to sell, the viewers are not the customers, those who buy the product. Advertisers buy the product, pay money for it. Programs are not what they buy, what they pay for is audience, people to heed their messages. The bigger the audience, the more they pay. . . . "

News organizations are in a highly competitive industry. They compete not only against other companies in the same medium but also across media. The traditional competition has been intensified with the rise of Internet news organizations that exploit synergies with broadcast news organizations. Competitive pressures have increased the importance of attracting an audience.[11] Competitive pressures also mean that there are strong incentives to be first with a breaking story, and this can affect accuracy.

---

[9]Baron (2005a) provides a theory of strategic provision of information by sources.
[10]Quoted in Ellen Humes, "Why the Press Blew the S&L Scandal," *The New York Times*, May 24, 1990.
[11]The same type of competitive and performance pressures are present in government-owned media. Küng-Shankleman (2000) provides an analysis of the BBC and CNN as businesses in their market and nonmarket environments.

Young (1978, p. 2) offered a perspective on the implications:

> As more organs of the media are owned by large corporations, whose prime interest is financial, the journalistic principles of a publication can be compromised by—or dissipated in—the business needs. The demand [is] for more circulation, more advertising, and more profit. To achieve these, the media will cater to populist—meaning antibusiness—fears and prejudices, entertain instead of enlighten, pander instead of lead. They reduce big issues to oversimplified personality battles, because both people and disputes make good reading and viewing.

This statement is surely too strong, but it indicates the tension between the incentives to attract an audience and the standards of the journalism profession.

## The Profession

Media decisions are made by the people who choose careers in journalism. Journalists are younger, better educated, and more liberal than the American public. A survey by the American Society of Newspaper Editors (ASNE) found, "At the bigger papers, 61 percent of newsroom respondents described themselves as Democrats (or leaning toward Democrat) and only 10 percent as Republicans (or leaning toward Republican)."[12] In 1992, 89 percent of the Washington journalists surveyed voted for Bill Clinton and 7 percent for George Bush. Sixty-one percent of the journalists rated themselves as liberal or liberal to moderate and 9 percent as conservative or conservative to moderate.[13] Editors were more evenly balanced in their orientation and political preferences.

A widely shared perspective among journalists is that they are serving the public. Some journalists joined the profession in the wake of Robert Woodward and Carl Bernstein's triumph in the Watergate affair. Not only had journalists succeeded in uncovering illegal activity, but their work led to the resignation of a U.S. president. Journalists seek the "scoop that will echo around the world."

Writing before Watergate, Epstein (1973, p. 219), who studied the operations of network television news programs, addressed journalists' views of their role and power.

> Privately almost all network correspondents expressed a strong belief in their ability to effect change in public policy through their work, if not as individuals, then certainly as a group. Some considered their self-perceived political powers "frightening" and "awesome," while others merely depicted them as a necessary part of the political process.

Journalism is governed by standards enforced by the news media organizations and professional associations.[14] A journalist is trained to present the who, what, where, when, and why of a story. Journalistic judgments, however, can lead to quite different treatments of stories. As an example, the Institute of Medicine, a unit of the National Academies, released a report on the health effects of indoor mold and moisture. On May 26, 2004, the headline in *The Wall Street Journal* read, "Indoor Mold Linked to

---

[12]ASNE, Chapter "Characteristics of the Respondents." www.asne.org.
[13]Povich (1996, p. 137).
[14]The Poynter Institute provides information on journalistic ethics: www.poynter.org. Codes of ethics and responsibilities for journalists can be found at www.asne.org/ideas/codes.

Problems Such as Asthma and Coughing," the headline in the *San Jose Mercury News* read, "Report: Mold seen as irritant, but not as bad as feared," and *The New York Times* headline read, "Panel Finds Mold in Buildings Is No Threat to Most People."

Journalists seek professional attainment, recognition, and reward. A necessary condition for attainment is that a journalist's work be published or aired and have an impact. Journalists thus have strong incentives to present stories that will pass editorial scrutiny and be sufficiently newsworthy that editors will print or air them. Stories must also be read or viewed, so journalists seek to make their stories engaging. These factors can result in inaccuracies, bias, and in some cases fabrication. The chapter case, *General Motors Like a Rock (A)?,* considers such a situation.

## Does the News Media Treat Issues Selectively?

The media may not cover every issue under the same criteria. Most issues are treated under controls and editorial standards. On some issues, however, the media takes an advocacy approach, suspending the standards of fairness and balance. Epstein (1973, p. 233) wrote that

> controls tend to be disregarded when executives, producers and correspondents all share the same view and further perceive it to be a view accepted by virtually all thoughtful persons. News reports about such subjects as pollution, hunger, health care, racial discrimination, and poverty fall in this category. On such consensus issues, correspondents are expected by executives openly to advocate the eradication of the presumed evil and even put it in terms of a "crusade," as a CBS vice-president suggested with respect to the pollution issue. At times, however, what are assumed to be commonly held values turn out to be disputed ones in some parts of the country; and when executives are apprised of this (by affiliates and others), the usual "fairness" controls are applied to the subject.

There is certainly consensus on preferring less to more pollution, but often the real issue, as in the case of global climate change, is how much reduction in emissions is warranted by the cost and how the cost is to be distributed. On these dimensions, considerable disagreement exists. For example, the UAW and automobile manufacturers oppose raising fuel economy standards, whereas the Sierra Club supports higher standards.

When editorial controls are disregarded, unbalanced reporting can result. In the wake of the firing of Jayson Blair for the fabrication of stories, *The New York Times* created the position of public editor devoted "to receiving, investigating, and answering outsiders' concerns about our coverage." The public editor Daniel Okrent described his conclusions about the coverage of social issues: "And if you think *The Times* plays it down the middle on any of [the social issues], you've been reading the paper with your eyes closed. . . . [It is] quite another thing to tell only the side of the story your co-religionists wish to hear. I don't think it's intentional when *The Times* does this. But negligence doesn't have to be intentional. . . . *Times* editors have failed to provide the three-dimensional perspective balanced journalism requires."[15] Okrent referred to *The Times'* coverage as "cheerleading," and his assessment is consistent with Epstein's observation about "consensus issues." The publisher of *The Times* described its consensus viewpoint as "urban." Unbalanced reporting is a source of concern to firms and their managers.

---

[15]*The New York Times,* July 25, 2004.

## Bias, Accuracy, and Fairness

The public widely views the media as biased. A survey by the ASNE (1999) revealed that 78 percent of the public believed that there was bias in news reporting.[16] There was little consensus, however, on the nature and direction of the perceived bias. The ASNE wrote, "The public appears to diagnose the root causes of media bias in two forms. First, (and at best), bias is a lack of dispassion and impartiality that colors the decision of whether or not to publish a story, or the particular facts that are included in a news report and the tone of how those facts are expressed. Second (and at worst), they see bias as an intent to persuade."

Most nonmarket issues involving business are complex, and the ability to present that complexity and achieve accuracy, balance, and fairness differs considerably among media organizations. Some newspapers and magazines can present complex stories in a comprehensive manner and in enough detail to provide accuracy and balance. Television, however, may not be well suited to presenting complex stories, in part because of the brief time that can be allocated to a story. As Epstein (1980, p. 127) stated, "This enforced brevity leaves little room for presenting complex explanations or multifaceted arguments." As importantly, the need to retain viewer interest requires that a story be attractive and entertaining. The desire to develop human interest and controversy in a limited time slot can lead to sacrifices in balance and accuracy. Qualification and complexity, even when written into a story, may be edited out to provide time for other stories. Many complaints by business executives about television news coverage are due to the simplification needed to fit a story into a restricted time slot. Distortion in a story thus could result from simplification rather than bias.

Because journalists write for the audience and not for the protagonists in a story, the protagonists may view a story as not giving sufficient attention or credence to their side. The difference between the objective of providing information to the public and the subject's interest in a favorable portrayal can lead to a perception of bias.

The treatment of an issue, particularly when advocacy journalism is practiced and editorial controls are suspended, can put firms in a difficult position. News coverage of fires due to the use of space heaters may involve the victims telling of their plight and demanding that the manufacturer and the government take action. Given the framing of the issue, manufacturers may have considerable difficulty providing information about the safety features already incorporated, the possibility that the victims may have misused the heaters, and the measures taken to reduce the likelihood of misuse. The fact that no space heater can be perfectly safe reduces the credibility of such explanations.[17]

Media coverage can also be alarmist, which can put firms in a difficult position. The media coverage in the Alar episode was alarmist, as was coverage of the outbreak of SARS in 2003. Health scares are frequently fanned by the media because "fear sells," but the media can also exercise restraint. Michael Fumento, writing in the *Washington Post*, commented on the media's restraint in the coverage of the first, and only, case of mad cow disease in the United States:[18]

---

[16]Groseclose and Milyo (2004) found "a very significant liberal bias" in the news media. Eighteen of the 20 news outlets studied were found to be more liberal than the average U.S. voter and average member of Congress and "closer to the average Democrat in Congress than to the median member of the House of Representatives." Their methodology required no judgments about which media outlets were liberal or conservative or the degree of bias. They simply counted the number of citations a news publication made to each of 50 think tanks and computed a score by comparing those citations to citations of those think tanks in speeches by members of Congress. The positions of Congress members on a left–right scale were determined using a statistical procedure standard in political science based on rankings by interest groups. Baron (2005b) provides a supply side theory of bias based on the career interests of journalists.
[17]See the Chapter 12 case, *California Space Heaters (A)*.
[18]*Washington Post*, January 18, 2004.

Part of the explanation for the paucity of panic, though probably only a minor one, may be that there's no cause for it—and even the media know this. . . . Watching the British over the last decade may also have helped us keep our heads level. . . . The United Kingdom's top BSE official said in 1996 that as many as half a million Britons would die from the bad beef, while an estimate in the *British Food Journal* a year earlier pegged potential deaths at as many as 10 million. . . . A 2001 study in *Science* magazine estimated the number [of cases] will probably top out at 200.

Sales at McDonald's and other restaurants were largely unaffected by the case.

Cost pressures on news organizations, journalists' incentives to have stories aired or published, deadlines and space constraints, and competitive pressures can result in inaccuracies in stories. Cost pressures, for example, led some news organizations to shift some fact-checking responsibilities to their reporters. This resulted in a number of serious violations of professional standards. News organizations responded by strengthening their internal controls. CNN, for example, established an internal watchdog office, the Journalistic Standards and Practices office. Cost and competitive pressures, however, work against stronger internal controls.

## Business Interactions with the News Media

Business concerns with media coverage and treatment stem from several considerations. First, few companies like their activities to be publicly scrutinized. The media guards its independence and in particular does not serve as a public relations arm of firms. Second, the desire for balance and the incentive to develop controversy to make stories appealing often gives critics of the company an opportunity to deliver their message to the public. Third, some executives agree with Young that the media caters to antibusiness sentiments. Fourth, particularly in the case of television interviews, the control of the editing process gives the media the opportunity to select the parts of an interview that make the best story, and those may not be the parts business wants to have aired. Fifth, media treatment almost always results in oversimplification that can preclude the presentation of a full account of a company's side of the story. Because of these concerns many firms have developed competencies for interacting with the media.

In interacting with the media, managers should be both cautious and realistic in their expectations. In a 1995 case against ABC's *Primetime Live,* Court of Appeals judge Richard Posner wrote, "Investigative journalists well known for ruthlessness promise to wear kid gloves. They break their promise, as any person of normal sophistication would expect. If this is 'fraud,' it is a kind against which potential victims can easily arm themselves by maintaining a minimum skepticism about journalistic goals and method."[19]

## The Need for Information

Many business issues are newsworthy, and frequently only business has the information that can serve as the basis for a story. This provides firms with an opportunity to develop a relationship with news organizations in which they provide the information needed in exchange for stories that will be fair and balanced. As one prominent journalist commented, "We need access [to information] and sources can trade on access."

---

[19]*The New York Times,* July 13, 1998.

Many firms sustain those relationships through their forthrightness and the credibility of the information they provide. Many firms have professionalized their interactions with the media by employing communications specialists and by giving their managers media training. Business interactions with the media are also broadening as more managers assume a role in interacting with the media.

## Media Strategies

Media strategies guide interactions with the media and communication with stakeholders and the public. Evans (1987, pp. 84–87) identified six elements of an effective media strategy:

- The unusual is usual.
- Emphasize the consistency of business and the public interest.
- Remember your audience.
- Communicate through the press.
- The medium is the message.
- Establish credibility—not friendship.

A firm's interactions with the media should be tailored to the audience. In interacting with the media the firm is speaking not only with the journalist but, more importantly, with the audience. The information presented thus should be directed at the likely audience. In the case of an issue that will be covered only by the business press, the information should be tailored for a knowledgeable audience. If the audience is more general, the information should be accessible to the layperson.

For most nonmarket issues the interests of a firm are consistent with some aspect of the public interest or at least with the interests of stakeholders. Emphasizing the effects of the issue not on profits but on stakeholders can be effective, as can pointing out that the practice in question is consistent with the same component of the public interest. In interviews, managers thus should not only answer questions but also take the opportunity to make affirmative statements about the firm's position.

The development of relationships of confidence is easier with the business press than with the general media because of the business press's greater need for information and because it typically assigns journalists to regular beats. The journalist then has an incentive to develop both expertise and a relationship with the firm, and the resulting stories may be more accurate and balanced. If a journalist demonstrates an understanding of the industry and the issues, the firm may choose to release its information first to him or her as a reward.

Developing relationships with journalists from the more general news media, particularly television, is often more difficult because fewer journalists are assigned to business beats. For those journalists, the incentive to develop expertise on the issues can be weak. A journalist assigned to an issue high on the social significance dimension—products with a health risk to children, for instance—may not have expertise on the issue. In such cases it is particularly important for a manager to communicate effectively with the journalist and not leave a media vacuum for others to fill.

## Responses and Vacuums

On many issues—particularly those that may generate nonmarket action—business prefers to avoid media coverage. One tempting strategy is not to comment to the media in the hope that no story will appear. If it seems likely that the story will appear anyway, a "no comment" strategy can be risky. Especially on issues that are high on the societal significance dimension, the media may take an advocacy approach either directly or by airing the allegations of others. Leaving a vacuum that the firm's critics can fill with their side of the story can often be more damaging than having the firm tell its side of the story, even if that story is not compelling. Providing facts and demonstrating concern, even if the facts are not all favorable to the firm, can narrow the space in which critics can maneuver.

Just as allowing critics to fill a vacuum is generally not a good strategy, attacking critics is often not a good strategy, since it can create a second story that can prolong an issue. After a half-time employee of Électricité de France wrote a book criticizing French corporations for their rigid social norms and urging French workers to adopt "calculated loafing" and to "spread gangrene through the system from inside," her employer sent her a letter calling her before a disciplinary hearing for "spreading gangrene from within." The letter was given to the news media, and coverage of the episode caused sales of the book to skyrocket.[20]

Many firms have concluded that there are some media representatives or programs with which it is better to not talk. Many will not talk with investigative journalism programs such as *60 Minutes* because of concerns about how they and their firm will be portrayed. They prefer a statement such as "The company refused to comment" to risking an interview from which the editors will extract a 15-second clip to be interspersed among interviews with the critics of the firm.

## Media Interviews

Because of the importance of the media in the development of nonmarket issues, managers frequently grant interviews to the media and are called on to speak to the public. Media training is customary in many firms, and a communications consulting industry has developed to support that training. Many firms provide guidelines for their managers in dealing with journalists. The Hewlett-Packard Company's guidelines are presented in Figure 3-3.

Perhaps the best advice for media interviews was given by the publisher of a major newspaper. He said that when dealing with the press, there were three cardinal rules.

---

### FIGURE 3-3 Hewlett-Packard Company Guidelines

**HEWLETT-PACKARD COMPANY'S TWELVE GUIDES FOR CONDUCTING A MEDIA INTERVIEW**

- Assume everything you say is "on the record."
- Speak in plain English.
- State your main point or conclusion first.
- If you don't understand a question, say so.
- If presented with a "laundry list" of questions, identify the one question you are responding to before answering it.
- Don't hesitate to repeat an answer.
- Volunteer information to make your points and to give perspective.
- Use anecdotes and illustrations involving people.
- Have fun doing the interview, without being flippant, of course.
- Don't be afraid to admit mistakes.
- Don't expect the editor to clear the story with you before it is published.
- Never, never, never stretch the truth.

---

[20]*The New York Times,* August 14, 2004. Corine Maier, *Bonjour Paresse,* Éditions Michalon, Paris, 2004.

The first is "Tell the truth." The second is "Tell the truth." The third is "Always remember the first two." A pragmatic version of the publisher's cardinal rules was provided by a judge who said, "Always tell the truth—it's easier to remember." Answering truthfully is always a good policy, but simply responding to questions is not. Managers must be prepared to make affirmative points when responding to an interviewer's questions and seize opportunities to tell the company's side of the story.

When asked to appear for a television interview, some business executives ask to go on live so that their comments cannot be edited. Stations, however, typically will not agree to an unedited interview. The interviewee thus is often advised to answer questions in a manner that makes them difficult to edit. Sometimes a manager may ask the reporter to submit questions in advance, but that request is usually rejected. When agreeing to an interview, some firms find it prudent to audiotape or videotape the interview. Taping the interview provides a record of what transpired and can be useful if a dispute with the media arises. Taping may also caution journalists to be careful about what they write or broadcast. When agreeing to an interview, it is important to recognize that at times the media may already have the story in the can and may be seeking an interview to develop controversy. The chapter case, *Illinois Power Company (A),* presents such a situation.

## Anticipating Issues

Many firms attempt to educate the media about important issues in their nonmarket environment. Some go further and attempt to communicate directly with the interest groups that are likely to be concerned with issues. To the extent that a firm can anticipate an issue, it is better positioned to deal effectively with it as it progresses through its life cycle.

When a nonmarket issue can be anticipated, the theory of the news media can be used to assess whether the issue is likely to be covered and, if so, the type of treatment it is likely to receive. For those stories that will be covered only by the business press, a firm can hope, and in many cases expect, that the journalist has a degree of expertise in the subject matter of the story. If, in addition, the issue is low on the societal significance dimension, the firm may need do little more than provide the media with facts and present its side of the issue.

A broader set of news organizations is likely to be attracted to issues that are high on the societal significance dimension, making interactions with the media more complex. Such issues also may attract or be initiated by activist groups, as in the case of Alar. Those groups can be expected to advance their side of the issue in providing information to the media. The Alar episode was more orchestrated than most, but the point is clear. Interest and activist groups can orchestrate events to advance their causes both in a planned manner and in response to an issue brought to their—and the public's—attention by the media.

When media coverage of an issue can be anticipated, the firm has the opportunity to prepare. Preparation includes gathering the relevant information about the issue and its context and assigning a spokesperson to interact with the media. Preparation also includes considering the messages likely to be conveyed by the media and its sources. As discussed in the context of Figure 3-1, the messages are a function not only of the coverage and treatment given to the issue but also of the information the audience already has. Individuals, interest groups, and politicians may evaluate a story in different ways. Some may consider the story in terms of their own self-interest, whereas others may look at it in terms of broader principles. These varied evaluations can result in market and nonmarket actions that affect the progress of the issue and cause change in the firm's environment. Firms and their managers thus must be sensitive to how those in the audience will evaluate its messages.

# Unanticipated Events

Because events such as environmental accidents can occur, firms should have a routine to follow in the event of a breaking story. For serious matters firms should have a crisis management plan. If the issue is one that need not be made public—embezzlement, for example—the first decision is whether to release the information to the news media or attempt to keep it confidential. The latter can be successful in many cases, but leaks occur more often than most managers expect.

If the incident is public, the first step is to gather as much information as possible as quickly as possible. There is little that can damage a firm more than having others uncover information that management itself does not have. An important precaution is an accurate record-keeping system that, for example, keeps track of the toxic wastes generated by a plant and where they are disposed. Having the facts readily accessible not only allows the firm to be in the position of being the best source of information for the media but also provides a basis on which management can develop a strategy. In implementing a strategy, it is also often wise for the firm to speak with a single voice. The spokesperson must have all the information on the issue so as not to be blindsided and to better anticipate the story's likely development.

The Body Shop example illustrates an ineffective response to a critical article on the company. Its response resulted in continuing problems with the media and the public.

---

### EXAMPLE

## The Body Shop

By 1994 the Body Shop had achieved both financial and social success. Emphasizing cosmetics made from natural ingredients, the company had grown from a single shop to 1,100 stores in 40 countries. Part of its strategy was to do social good at the same time as making profits. It developed a widely publicized Trade Not Aid program in which it bought raw materials from indigenous peoples. It purchased blue corn from the Santa Ana Pueblo tribe in New Mexico and nuts from the Kayapo people in Brazil. It also used those programs in its promotional and public relations activities. The Body Shop had become one of the darlings of the social responsibility community, winning praise for its activities and making an international celebrity of its founder, Anita Roddick, who along with her husband, Gordon Roddick, ran the company.

The image they had crafted came under attack when an investigative journalist wrote an article criticizing the accomplishments of the company.[1]

The journal in which it was to appear intended to make a splash and promoted the article in advance of publication. The British and American press picked up the issue and others joined in the criticism of the Body Shop; for example, British labor unions renewed their criticism of the company for its opposition to unionization at its main plant in England. The article detailed alleged mistakes and shortcomings by the company, but the principal message was that the company was not living up to the image its promotional activities had created.

The Roddicks were incensed and leaped into action. They viewed the image they had created in their publicity as an aspiration toward which they worked, and they disputed both the facts and the message of the article. Before the article appeared, Anita Roddick wrote daily to the company's staff, franchisees, and other supporters, rejecting the allegations in the article and reassuring the stockholders of the company's record. The Body Shop had both its British solicitor and its U.S. law firm write

[1]Jon Entine, "Shattered Image," *Business Ethics,* September–October 1994, pp. 23–28.

*(Continued)*

*(Continued)*

the journal about the author and requested a copy of the article in advance. The letters led the journal to take out libel insurance.[2] After publication of the article, the Body Shop sent out lengthy press releases countering the alleged facts presented in the article and attacking the credibility of the author and the journal editor. The company admitted that its record was not perfect but argued that it was far better than others in the cosmetics industry and that the company should not be judged against a standard of perfection. The company's press releases were countered by letters and press releases from the author of the article and the journal editor defending the article and the information on which it was based.

The Body Shop also elicited testimonials from its business partners and others sympathetic with the causes it espoused. The Roddicks convinced Ben Cohen, founder of Ben & Jerry's ice cream company, to resign from the advisory board of the journal. Gordon Roddick also wrote to all the advisory board members and sent a 10-page letter to every one of the journal's subscribers, defending the company's record and challenging the motives of the journal's editor. Criticism continued, however, as Franklin Research and Development, an investment firm that provided investment advice about socially responsible firms, issued a report critical of the company's record. Franklin, which had previously given its highest social rating to the Body Shop, indicated that its investigation had corroborated some of the information in the article. Franklin also criticized the Body Shop for its attacks on its critics.[3] Franklin's basic criticisms were not only that the Body Shop had not lived up to the standards it had set for itself but also that it had benefited financially from the image it had promoted. Hence, not living up to that image was of greater concern.

To address the substance of the criticism, the Body Shop decided to undergo an independent social audit and publish the audit regardless of its conclusions. The results of that audit are considered in Chapter 21.

---

[2]The Body Shop had earned a reputation for aggressive actions with respect to the media. In 1992 it had won a libel case against a British television station for a critical documentary. For public figures, libel cases are easier to win in the United Kingdom than in the United States because the protection of *New York Times v. Sullivan* is not available to the media.

[3]Franklin Research and Development, "Investing for a Better World," September 15, 1994.

## Recourse in Disputes with the Media

### Private Recourse

The subjects of news coverage at times perceive stories to be incomplete, inaccurate, or unfair. Some take actions ranging from writing to the editor to correct inaccuracies to initiating legal action. Firms may also take economic measures against the media by, for example, withdrawing advertising in response to a story that management believes has misrepresented the facts. The Procter & Gamble example describes one such case. When neither economic measures nor legal action is warranted, companies can bring concerns about a story to the attention of the media. Some firms make a practice of notifying editors about their concerns, with the objectives of improving future stories and establishing a reputation for being ready to act.

---

EXAMPLE

## Procter & Gamble and Neighbor to Neighbor

Neighbor to Neighbor, an activist group located in San Francisco, opposed U.S. support for the government in El Salvador and called for the end of military aid to that country. The group claimed that coffee growers in El Salvador financed right-wing death squads with money obtained from exporting coffee to the United States. From the group's perspective, U.S. coffee companies that imported Salvadoran coffee beans were supporting the death squads.

Neighbor to Neighbor took its message to the American public by placing advertisements in *The New York Times, The New London Day* (Connecticut), and *The Progressive* magazine. The group also advocated a consumer boycott of U.S. coffee brands. The best-selling U.S. brand was Folgers, produced by the Procter & Gamble Company (P&G). To generate support for the boycott, the group produced a 30-second television commercial that it planned to air on several television stations. The commercial, narrated by Ed Asner, named only Folgers and showed an upside-down coffee cup dripping blood.[1] The inscription on the cup read "Seal of Salvadoran Coffee," and Asner said, "The murderous civil war in El Salvador has been supported by billions of American tax dollars and by the sale of Salvadoran coffee. . . . Boycott Folgers. What it brews is misery and death."[2]

Of the 30 television stations approached by Neighbor to Neighbor, all but two rejected the commercial. After reviewing it for taste and content, investigating its content, and obtaining legal advice on the possibility of libel suits, the CBS affiliate WHDH-TV in Boston broadcast the commercial twice in May 1990. Seymour L. Yamoff, president and general manager of WHDH-TV, stated, "The information on this particular commercial is correct. . . . We screen them for accuracy, libel, slander and 'Do they meet a standard of fairness?' " He also stated that the station had never broadcast such "issue advertisements" other than in election campaigns, and he could not recall any such advertisement being aired in Boston during the 20 years he had lived there.

P&G was shocked by the commercial. It purchased coffee from 30 countries, and less than 2 percent of its supply came from El Salvador. P&G was one of the largest television advertisers and provided advertising revenue of $1 million annually to WHDH-TV. That represented nearly 2 percent of the station's advertising revenue. The revenue from broadcasting the Neighbor to Neighbor commercial totaled less than $1,000.

P&G decided to withdraw its advertising from WHDH-TV and threatened to withdraw its advertising from any other station that broadcast the ad. WHDH-TV hired a *Washington Post* reporter, Scott Armstrong, to conduct an inquiry into the commercial. In the draft of his report, he concluded "that certain conclusions . . . were not substantiated."[3] As a result of the report, WHDH-TV adopted a new policy: "Any public-issue commercials submitted to the station in the future will be broadcast only after the truth of their claims has been determined."[4] "A Procter & Gamble spokesman said, 'We were satisfied that WHDH had on further review concluded that certain representations in the anti-Folgers ad were not substantiated and . . . it was an appropriate time to resume advertising on that station.' "[5] As a result of a peace accord between the government and rebels in El Salvador in March 1992, the boycott was called off.

---

[1]The print advertisements had mentioned other coffee brands in addition to Folgers.
[2]*Boston Globe,* December 12, 1990. A similar commercial calling for a boycott of Hills Brothers Coffee was aired on the West Coast where Hills Brothers had its largest market share.

[3]*Boston Globe,* December 12, 1990.
[4]*Boston Globe,* December 12, 1990.
[5]*Boston Globe,* December 12, 1990.

The news media is governed by professional standards, and journalists and editors develop and maintain reputations for professionalism. Organizations such as the Society of Professional Journalists, Sigma Delta Chi, and the ASNE work to foster high professional standards and ethics in journalism. Media organizations discipline their correspondents, editors, and managers who violate professional standards. Correspondents may be suspended, reassigned, or fired for violations. In the chapter case, *General Motors Like a Rock (A)?*, NBC took disciplinary actions when it was revealed that its *Dateline* producers and correspondents had used a model rocket engine to ignite a fire during a test collision of a GM truck. NBC reassigned the correspondent and fired the producer of the *Dateline* segment. The senior producer and the executive producer of *Dateline* resigned, and Michael Gartner, president of NBC News, also resigned. NBC also created the position of ombudsman to supplement its professional standards and review segments produced for its news programs as well as programs such as *Dateline*.

## Recourse to the Law: Defamation and Libel

Defamation is a branch of torts pertaining to false statements made to a third party that damage a person's reputation.[21] The category of "person" includes humans as well as legal entities such as corporations. Defamation takes the form of either libel or slander. Libel pertains to statements that are either written or broadcast, whereas slander pertains to statements that are spoken. A finding of slander requires a showing of actual damages, but a finding of libel generally does not require such a showing. Defamation cases are governed by state law and the common law. Defamation cases generally center on statements made in public, but in *Dun & Bradstreet v. Greenmoss Builders* 472 U.S. 749 (1985), Greenmoss Builders was awarded $350,000 when Dun & Bradstreet issued an erroneous credit report. Thus, defamation more generally applies to a statement made to a third party.

A defendant in a defamation suit has several possible defenses, which fall into the categories of "truth" and "privilege." A defendant always has the defense that what was said, written, or broadcast was the truth. In some states truth constitutes an absolute defense, whereas in others it may be subject to limitations such as those arising from laws on privacy. For example, in some states it is illegal to disclose that someone has been convicted of a crime or has a disease.

The courts exercise judgment in assessing a truth defense. In 1990, 20 Washington State apple growers filed suit against CBS and the NRDC seeking $250 million in damages, alleging that the *60 Minutes* segment on Alar had led to a panic among consumers that cost the state's growers $150 million in sales. A federal district judge dismissed the suit because the plaintiffs had not shown that the broadcast was false. The judge stated, "Even if CBS's statements are false, they were about an issue that mattered, cannot be proven as false and therefore must be protected."[22] CBS had argued that its story was based on an EPA report, and the judge stated, "A news reporting service is not a scientific testing lab, and these services should be able to rely on a scientific Government report when they are relaying the report's contents."[23]

A degree of privilege is provided to the media by the First Amendment, which extends protection but does not provide an absolute defense. In *New York*

---

[21]A tort is a civil wrong that damages a person or property.
[22]*Auvil v. CBS "60 Minutes,"* 836 F. Supp. 740 [E.D. Wash.].
[23]*The New York Times*, September 15, 1993.

*Times v. Sullivan,* 376 U.S. 254 (1964), the Supreme Court delineated a standard of proof required of plaintiffs in a defamation suit.[24] The ruling requires plaintiffs who are "public figures" to show that the statement in question was made with actual malice—that is, either with knowledge that it was false or with "reckless disregard" for whether it was true.[25] Being careless or sloppy with the facts is not sufficient for a finding of libel. In a complex case, the court attempts to balance the rights of the plaintiff with the rights of the media as provided by the First Amendment. Although plaintiffs win some libel suits against the media, the media is generally successful in defending itself given the protection provided by the Constitution and Supreme Court rulings.

The rationale for the standard enunciated in *Sullivan* is that although individuals retain rights to privacy, they lose a degree of privateness when they participate in "public" activities. The publicness of a plaintiff is not restricted to public officeholders but also pertains to private citizens who voluntarily appear in public. A corporate executive who makes public speeches or testifies in public hearings may be held to be a public figure in a defamation suit. Thus, a corporate plaintiff in a defamation suit may have to meet the standard of proof delineated in *Sullivan.*

To illustrate the application of this standard, in 1981 anchorman Walter Jacobson of CBS's Chicago television station WBBM stated in a commentary that Brown & Williamson Tobacco Corporation was trying to lure young people to its Viceroy cigarette by using a marketing strategy that related the cigarette to "pot, wine, beer, and sex." Jacobson based his commentary on a Federal Trade Commission (FTC) study that reported that a Brown & Williamson advertising agency had hired a consultant who had proposed such a strategy. The FTC study, however, did not indicate that Brown & Williamson had adopted the consultant's recommendations. Indeed, Jacobson's assistant had told him prior to the broadcast that the company had rejected the proposed strategy. In spite of having been so informed, Jacobson made his commentary. The jury concluded that Jacobson made a statement that he knew to be false and held for Brown & Williamson. The jury awarded $3 million in compensatory damages and $2 million in punitive damages against CBS and WBBM and $50,000 in punitive damages against Jacobson. A federal judge reduced the compensatory damages to $1, but the Court of Appeals reinstated $1 million in compensatory damages. The decision was appealed to the Supreme Court, which allowed the Court of Appeals decision to stand.[26]

A relatively untested aspect of the law pertains to information posted on the Internet. Such postings can be widely disseminated and could form the basis for a defamation lawsuit. Online service companies could also be the potential subject of a lawsuit if they played a role in maintaining a bulletin board or exercising editorial control over postings or access. The Communications Decency Act of 1996 provides a degree of protection to Internet service providers, and that law has

---

[24]This case arose when supporters of Martin Luther King placed an advertisement in *The New York Times* describing the activities of the Alabama police. The advertisement contained "several minor inaccuracies and exaggerations" (Schmidt, 1981), and an Alabama jury found that the supporters and the newspaper were guilty of defamation under state law. The Supreme Court viewed a standard requiring complete accuracy as conflicting with the First Amendment's protection of freedom of the press.

[25]If the plaintiff proves actual malice, the court presumes there is actual damage, relieving the plaintiff of the burden of proving damages.

[26]Juries often award large judgments against the news media in libel cases, and judges frequently view the awards as excessive and reduce them.

protected eBay against defamation and other lawsuits, as indicated in Chapter 2. No case has yet reached the Supreme Court to clarify the application of the law, but the Court of Appeals ruled that AOL was not liable for postings on its Web site.

## Political Recourse

The First Amendment provides protection to the news media, and *Sullivan* strengthens that protection in the case of public figures. Commercial speech, however, receives less protection. Although the apple industry failed to obtain relief in the courts, the Alar episode generated considerable sympathy for the industry. The American Feed Industry Association (AFIA), a trade association, seized the opportunity and hired a law firm specializing in food and drug issues to draft a model "food-disparagement bill" for introduction in state legislatures. The model bill would change state libel laws to provide a cause for action against a party that made "disparaging statements" or disseminated "false information" about the safety of a food product. Steve Kopperud, senior vice president of AFIA, said, "There has been long-standing frustration ... that an activist organization, for the price of a full-page ad in *USA Today,* can say whatever it wishes to scare the public."[27]

The model bill was based on court decisions on commercial speech in which a firm could be held liable if it intentionally made disparaging statements about a competitor's product for the purpose of harming its sales. Kopperud stated that the food disparagement laws were intended "to impose the same kind of burdens of proof you see in commercial speech cases ... you can't say, 'This sugar pill will cure cancer,' but an activist can say, 'This egg will kill you.'"[28] By mid-1997, 13 states had enacted versions of the model bill, which have become known as "veggie-libel" laws. Larry Gearhardt of the Ohio Farm Bureau said that Ohio's disparagement law "gives protection to people who could not protect themselves—individual farmers who could be hurt by a disparaging comment."[29]

Critics of these laws argued that they placed the burden of proof on defendants to demonstrate conclusive scientific evidence, which they argued was a standard that would stifle free speech. John Stauber, director of the Center on Media and Democracy, argued, "Under this definition, it would have been illegal in the 1960s to criticize pesticides such as DDT, which were believed 'safe' for the environment according to data that was then considered 'reasonable' and 'reliable.'"[30] Sarah Delea, a spokeswoman for the United Fresh Fruit and Vegetable Association, said, "We feel these laws serve as a reminder to groups and individuals that they need to stay within legal boundaries when disseminating information. Groups or individuals should not defame a product or the way it is grown/produced without factual, scientific basis in order to further their own agendas and cause unnecessary public fear."[31] Whether such laws will be found to restrict speech remains to be seen.[32]

---

[27]Marianne Lavelle, *The National Law Journal,* May 5, 1997.
[28]Marianne Lavelle, *The National Law Journal,* May 5, 1997.
[29]*The Columbus Dispatch,* June 29, 1997.
[30]Marianne Lavelle, *The National Law Journal,* May 5, 1997.
[31]Marianne Lavelle, *The National Law Journal,* May 5, 1997.
[32]The first case centering on statements against beef made on the *Oprah Winfrey Show* was dismissed because of a failure to prove damages.

## Summary

The news media is a source of information for those in the nonmarket environment. It alerts the public, activists, public officeholders, and interest groups to nonmarket issues and the activities of firms. Those interested in advancing an issue may attempt to use the media as a component of their nonmarket strategies. Although the media guards its independence, it may at times find components of those strategies to be newsworthy, as in the Alar episode.

Because the news media plays an important role in the development of nonmarket issues, managers must assess which issues the media is likely to cover and the treatment those issues are likely to receive. The theory of coverage and treatment predicts that the news media will cover issues with intrinsic audience interest or perceived societal significance. Stories are more likely to be newsworthy if they have broad audience interest, immediacy, human interest, controversy and conflict, and, for television, visual appeal. Societal significance pertains to the media's role as a protector of the public's right to know. In this role, the media may at times engage in advocacy by making judgments or supporting particular policies.

The media needs information for its stories, and on many issues business is the best and least-costly source of information. Firms thus have an opportunity to develop relationships with journalists who cover business issues on a regular basis. Managers may be called on to interact with the media, and to prepare for those interactions, they need to be fully informed about the issue in question as well as about the intended audience.

Business issues are often complex and may be difficult for television and the general media to cover. Although the media applies standards of accuracy, fairness, and balance to a story, it has incentives to make the story appealing to the audience and therefore may overemphasize conflict and controversy. It may also simplify a story to fit a time slot, a space limit, or a deadline. Many of the complaints about news coverage of business result from oversimplification.

The news media is both a business and a profession. Media companies are motivated by profit considerations, and journalists have career interests. Editorial controls govern conduct, and journalists are guided by professional standards. A tension, however, exists between those standards and corporate and individual incentives. That tension can at times compromise accuracy, fairness, and balance.

The subjects of media stories frequently believe that they were unfairly treated or that a story was inaccurate or unbalanced. One recourse is a defamation lawsuit, but such lawsuits are typically costly and difficult to win. The standard under which a case will be judged is important to its eventual outcome. For a public figure, the standard is articulated in *New York Times v. Sullivan*. This standard provides considerable protection for the media because a plaintiff must show actual malice and a "reckless disregard" for the truth.

Some critics have called for restraints on the news media. Despite its lapses and occasional abuses, the news media plays an essential role in a democracy, and the imperfections in the coverage and treatment of stories may be the cost borne for the benefits provided. As Thomas Jefferson wrote, "Were it left to me to decide whether we should have a government without newspapers or newspapers without a government, I should not hesitate to prefer the latter."[33]

---

[33]Letter to E. Carrington, 1787.

# The Alar Episode

Alar, which had been licensed for use on apples in 1968, is the brand name for daminozide, a chemical produced by the Uniroyal Chemical Company, a unit of Avery, Incorporated. Alar first became an issue in 1986 when Ralph Nader and several consumer and environmental groups urged the EPA to ban the chemical. In 1985, studies on animals had shown that daminozide and a by-product, UDMH, might cause cancer. An EPA science advisory panel, however, advised the agency to delay its decision in favor of additional study.

In response to the concerns raised by the activists, 15 food companies announced that they would no longer use apples treated with Alar. Over the next 3 years, Alar use decreased to approximately 5 percent of the apple crop from 40 percent in 1985. As of 1989, sales of Alar were approximately $5 million annually, with approximately half accounted for by exports. In 1989 the NRDC executed a carefully designed media strategy that alleged a health risk for children who ate apples treated with Alar. In its study of 23 chemicals and pesticides and the diets of preschool children, the NRDC concluded that 0.03 percent of children aged 1 to 5 years would eventually get cancer from pesticides in the food they eat. The NRDC estimated that the risk was 240 times the EPA's acceptable level. Alar was cited by the NRDC as one of the most hazardous of the 23 chemicals.

*The Economist* (March 18, 1989, p. 25) characterized the NRDC's study as follows: "Few paused to assess the science on which the NRDC's report was based. The group took some old toxicology studies that the EPA had rejected in 1985 as flawed, ignored some new ones commissioned by the EPA which showed daminozide as causing only benign tumors in mice (and not rats) only at absurdly high concentrations, did a small survey of how many apples children eat, inserted a factor for the greater vulnerability of children than adults,

ignored the fact that 95 percent of apples never have daminozide applied to them, and came out with a figure that one in 4,200 children is likely to get cancer solely because of eating contaminated apples, 100 times the risk the EPA calculates. The EPA says the data were discredited and the logic faulty."

After the *60 Minutes* broadcast highlighting the NRDC's allegations, the media leaped on the issue. Thousands of parents protested to their representatives in Washington, and politicians jumped on the bandwagon. Apple growers, supermarkets, producers of apple-based foods, and the producer of Alar came under attack. Even though the EPA estimated that in 1988 only 4 to 8 percent of apples were treated with Alar, parents, politicians, and activists called for apples to be removed from school cafeterias and demanded that they be banned altogether. Congressional hearings were held, and Meryl Streep testified before a Senate committee and also visited the White House to meet with an advisor to President Bush.

The FDA, EPA, and Department of Agriculture responded to the Alar scare by issuing a joint statement in March 1989 stating, "There is not an imminent hazard posed to children in the consumption of apples at this time, despite claims to the contrary." The agencies added, "The federal government encourages school systems and others responsible for the diets of children to continue to serve apples and other nutritious fruit to American children."[34] Tests by the Los Angeles Unified School District convinced the district to resume serving fresh apples, apple juice, and several other processed apple products.

Supermarkets were worried by the scare, and many immediately removed apples from their shelves, pledging to sell only Alar-free apples. In

---

[34]*Peninsula Times Tribune*, Palo Alto, CA, March 17, 1989.

checking supermarkets' compliance with their Alar-free policies, Consumers Union found traces of the chemical in 55 percent of 20 samples of fresh apples tested.[35] It also reported that it tested 50 samples of apple juice and found residues of Alar in three-quarters of the samples. The manufacturers of 26 of the brands claimed not to use Alar-treated apples.[36]

Apple growers claimed that Consumers Union's testing procedure was unapproved and inaccurate. Consumers Union had used a new testing procedure capable of detecting concentrations as low as 0.02 parts per million (ppm). The testing equipment used by most apple processors was capable of detecting Alar at a concentration of only 1 ppm. The Processed Apple Institute reported that it found Alar in only 8 of 4,623 samples.

In 1986 Safeway instituted a policy of accepting only Alar-free apples for its supermarkets. Instead of doing the testing itself, however, Safeway relied on its suppliers and buyers to ensure that the apples it sold were Alar-free. In 1988 consumer groups alleged that Safeway continued to sell apples treated with Alar. An independent laboratory, under contract from WMAQ-TV of Chicago, had found traces of the chemical in apples sold in Safeway supermarkets in Los Angeles and Sacramento. The highest concentration found was 2.52 ppm, compared to the EPA limit of 20 ppm.

The EPA commissioned additional studies of daminozide, and the "studies showed no strong evidence of carcinogenicity."[37] The concern about UDMH, however, remained. Preliminary results from a study conducted by Uniroyal showed that a high dose of UDMH caused a high incidence of cancer in mice. The EPA believed that a limit lower than 20 ppm was appropriate for UDMH and began the required rule-making process, which would take from 18 to 24 months, that could lead to a ban on Alar. Although the EPA disagreed with the estimation procedures used by the NRDC, it believed that the risks from Alar and UDMH might be great enough to justify banning Alar. ■

---

### PREPARATION QUESTIONS

1. How did the NRDC strategy and the media coverage affect the life cycle of the Alar issue? Which firms have this issue on their nonmarket issue agenda?
2. How should the apple industry respond to the campaign against Alar? Should it seek rebuttal time on *60 Minutes,* file a lawsuit against the program and CBS News, or take no action?
3. How should Safeway implement its Alar-free policy?
4. What, if anything, should Uniroyal do about the production of Alar while the EPA considers a ban on its use?

---

[35] *Consumer Reports,* May 1989, p. 291.
[36] Alar can be absorbed by the tree itself, so it could be possible to find traces of Alar in apples that had not been treated.

[37] *Consumer Reports,* May 1989, p. 289.

# General Motors Like a Rock (A)?

In 1992 the General Motors Corporation struggled through rocky management shake-ups and its third consecutive year of red ink. If any silver lining could be found in GM's financial cloud, it was its line of pickup trucks. Large pickups were one of GM's few profitable products from its ailing North American operations. Sales of Chevy and GMC full-size pickups exceeded half a million in 1991. Greater expectations for 1992 and 1993 coincided with a beefed-up marketing campaign centering on the theme "Like a Rock." However, as events unfolded, GM management found itself between a rock and a hard place.

In 1992 the Center for Auto Safety (CAS) petitioned NHTSA to recall some 5 million Chevrolet and GMC full-size pickup trucks. The CAS claimed that more than 300 people had died in side-impact accidents involving the trucks. Unlike most other pickups, GM class C/K pickups built during the years 1973 to 1987 were equipped with twin "side-saddle" gasoline tanks positioned outside the main frame rails. In 1987 GM made a design change in its trucks and brought the tanks inside the frame.

The CAS petition was not the first sign of a potential problem in GM's pickups. For years GM had managed to avoid the eye of the media by fighting on a case-by-case basis as many as 140 fuel tank–related lawsuits. Most were settled out of court with settlements occasionally exceeding $1 million. Throughout these legal proceedings, GM steadfastly defended the overall safety of its trucks. GM regularly pointed out that the NHTSA standard called for crashworthiness at 20 mph, and its pickups easily met that standard. In the 1970s GM regularly tested its trucks with side-impact crashes at 30 mph. In the mid-1980s it increased its internal standard to 50 mph. That fires sometimes broke out in the highest speed tests was not disputed but rather was viewed by GM as evidence that it was pushing its tests to the limit in an effort to make its trucks safer.

Data and interpretations concerning the relative safety of GM trucks were mixed. According to NHTSA, GM's side-saddle trucks were 2.4 times as likely as Ford's to be involved in deadly side-impact crashes. According to the Insurance Institute for Highway Safety—a research group supported by

insurance companies—the GM trucks might be slightly more prone to fire than similar models built by Ford and Chrysler, but they could be far safer in certain kinds of accidents. This conclusion, according to GM, suggested a need for a broader and more appropriate criterion of safety—that of overall crashworthiness. At least one large database on accidents indicated that in terms of the overall probability of a fatal accident, GM trucks were marginally safer than their competitors.

In November 1992, NBC's *Dateline* aired a 15-minute segment entitled, "Waiting to Explode?" Its focus was the GM series C/K pickup trucks. In preparation for the segment, the NBC news crew hired three "safety consultants" to assist in conducting two crash tests of GM pickups on a rural Indiana road on October 24. Each test simulated a side-impact crash by using a tow truck to push a Chevy Citation along the road into a pickup. The pickup was parked on the road perpendicular to the oncoming car, which slammed into the pickup's passenger side. A minute-long videotape of the tests was aired, and correspondent Michele Gillen stated that the tests were "unscientific." In the first of the tests, Gillen stated that the car was moving at about 40 mph. The truck was jolted significantly, but no fire ensued. In the second test, a fire broke out at a speed stated to be 30 mph. In the broadcast one safety consultant described the fire as "a holocaust."

After the nationally televised broadcast that reached approximately 11 million viewers, GM officials examined the NBC test segment in slow motion. Suspicions arose. GM wrote to NBC almost immediately, stating that the show was unfair and requesting NBC's test data. NBC refused to comply. In a follow-up contact, GM asked NBC to allow it to inspect the pickups. On January 4 the producer of *Dateline* told GM the vehicles were "junked and therefore are no longer available for inspection."

In the meantime, 32-year-old Pete Pesterre, editor of the magazine *Popular Hot Rodding,* had been pursuing some suspicions of his own. He was intimately familiar with GM trucks. He had owned four of them and once was involved in a side-impact crash from which he emerged unscathed. After Pesterre wrote an editorial criticizing the *Dateline* segment, a reader from Indiana called Pesterre and informed him that he knew a Brownsburg, Indiana, firefighter who was at the scene of the NBC crash tests. When the Brownsburg Fire Department is on assignment, as it was the day NBC staged the crashes, its firefighters customarily videotape the action for subsequent use in training. GM contacted the fire chief, who provided a copy of the tape. Similarly, GM learned that an off-duty sheriff's deputy was on site and had also videotaped the tests. GM also acquired his tape.

To analyze the tapes (including NBC's), GM called on its Hughes Aircraft subsidiary to deploy digital-enhancement techniques for sophisticated frame-by-frame analysis. These investigations revealed that NBC had been less than precise about both the sequence and speeds of the two tests. The first test conducted was the second test aired. The GM/Hughes analysis suggested the actual speed was 39 mph instead of the 30 mph stated in the *Dateline* segment.[38] This test yielded the so-called holocaust. In the other test NBC claimed a speed of 40 mph, but GM/Hughes concluded the speed was 47 mph. No fire occurred in this test.

Another revelation came from the audio portion of the firefighter's tape. After the first test—which, although slower, did produce a fire—the firemen were noticeably unimpressed with the outcome. It was clear that the fire was confined to the grass, short lived, and not life endangering. One firefighter laughed, and one said, "So much for that theory."

Meanwhile, GM was able to locate and acquire the two wrecked Citations and the two wrecked pickups. The recovered pickups were sent to GM's plant in Indianapolis where workers discovered a model rocket engine in the bed of one truck. Inspections of the bottom of the truck uncovered flare marks and remnants of duct tape in two places where GM's video analysis had curiously shown both smoke and fire in frames prior to impact in the crash. Additional inspection of tapes and photographs fueled suspicions that a detonator or starter device had been wired to the rocket engine.

GM officials wanted to examine the trucks' fuel tanks but they had been stripped from the trucks. GM immediately went to court seeking a restraining order to bar one of the NBC consultants from disposing of the fuel tanks. Days later, through his attorney,

GM learned that the consultant had given the tanks to a neighbor. Eventually GM obtained the tanks.

Having obtained the pickups and the tanks, GM identified and contacted the trucks' previous owners. From the owner of the truck that was struck and caught fire, GM learned that the gas cap was nonstandard. The owner had lost gas caps several times and in the last instance obtained one that did not fit correctly. GM also strongly suspected that the tank had been "topped off" with gasoline prior to the test. (Tanks are designed with 5 gallons of excess space to make topping off impossible with properly functioning fuel pumps.) GM sent the gas tank of the truck to an X-ray lab and a metallurgist to test whether, as NBC correspondent Gillen claimed, the tank was punctured and therefore was responsible for the fire. According to the experts, it was not punctured. GM had therefore amassed considerable data that supported a different theory about the crash results and the *Dateline* segment. The pieces of the puzzle were as follows:

- a possibly topped-off tank
- a faulty fuel cap in the truck involved in the fiery accident
- rocket engines that flared prior to impact
- footage indicating that the fire was confined primarily to grass and did not engulf the cab of the pickup
- fuel tanks that, contrary to NBC claims, had not been punctured

Additionally, GM conducted background checks on NBC's "safety experts" and learned the following:

- The consultant referred to by NBC as "vice president of the Institute for Safety Analysis" had no engineering background but was a former stock-car driver with a BA in Asian studies.
- The second consultant worked as a "safety consultant" for trial lawyers and had worked as a consultant for ABC News in seven segments on auto safety. He majored in industrial design but did not complete college.
- The third was from the Institute for Injury Reduction, a nonprofit organization that tests products for plaintiffs' attorneys. He had no college degree but studied Japanese and had a diploma in Korean from the U.S. Government's Defense Language School.

On Monday February 1, 1993, GM's executive vice president and general counsel, Harry Pearce,

---

[38]The 9 mph is important because energy is a function of the square of the velocity. To be precise, $e = .5MV^2$, where $e$ is kinetic energy, $M$ is mass, and $V$ is velocity.

presented these findings to GM's board of directors. When asked how the directors responded, Pearce said, "They were shocked."

In January, GM had sent yet another letter to Robert Read, the *Dateline* producer, this time detailing GM's specific findings. Read responded without informing either NBC President Robert Wright or NBC News President Michael Gartner. In a subsequent letter to Read dated February 2, GM carbon-copied Wright and Gartner, finally bringing the case to the attention of top NBC officials. NBC management responded by having its top public relations advisers and NBC General Counsel Richard Cotton draft a letter from Gartner to GM. The letter asserted three separate times that the NBC story was entirely accurate. "NBC does not believe that any statements made . . . were either false or misleading . . . the *Dateline* report was and remains completely factual and accurate."[39]

On February 4, 1993, an Atlanta jury awarded $101 million in punitive damages and $4.2 million in compensatory damages to the parents of a 17-year-old boy killed in a fiery death in a GM C/K pickup. The parents had argued that the placement of the fuel tank outside the frame of the pickup made it vulnerable to puncturing during a collision. GM's defense in the trial had been that the boy had died instantly during the collision which, the GM attorney argued, occurred at such a high speed that the death could not be blamed on the truck's design.

On Friday, February 5—the morning after the verdict in the liability case and a few days before a scheduled press conference by the CAS—GM management had a weekend to consider some delicate strategic options. One major option was to file a defamation suit against NBC. Defamation was the communication (e.g., by journalists) to a third party (e.g., viewers) of an untrue statement of fact that injures the plaintiff (GM). A second major option was to go public with the information it had developed on the *Dateline* segment. With the liability verdict and its aftermath fresh in the news, GM would be taking a significant risk in drawing still more attention to its pickups. Said one Wall Street analyst, "A successful rebuttal won't make anybody go out and buy trucks. The publicity [of an aggressive defense by GM and an attack on GM's critics] can't do anything but harm GM."[40] This perspective reflected the rule of thumb that "any news is bad news" when it involves a major company, a less-than-perfectly safe product, and a high level of public sensitivity toward product safety. ■

SOURCE: This is an abridged version of a case written by Professor Keith Krehbiel. Royal Bryson provided valuable comments. Copyright © 1994 by the Board of Trustees of the Leland Stanford Junior University. All rights reserved. Reprinted with permission.

---

## PREPARATION QUESTIONS

1. From GM's perspective, what are the nonmarket issues? What are their sources? Where are they in their life cycles?
2. Should GM fight the *Dateline* issue as a matter of principle? Why or why not?
3. What kind of media coverage should GM anticipate over the next week? Does GM have any control or influence over this situation?
4. Should GM file a defamation suit and/or go public with its findings about the *Dateline* segment?
5. In the position of Mr. Gartner at NBC, what would you have done upon receiving GM's letter and findings?

---

[39] *The Wall Street Journal*, February 11, 1993.

[40] *The Wall Street Journal*, February 8, 1993.

# Illinois Power Company (A)

At 8 A.M. on November 26, 1979, the executives of Illinois Power Company, a medium-size utility headquartered in Decatur, Illinois, met to decide how to respond to a *60 Minutes* program that had been broadcast the night before.[41]

The *60 Minutes* segment had used Illinois Power's Clinton Nuclear Power Plant as an example of severe cost overruns and excessive delays, which the CBS report said were typical of nuclear power plant construction. In late 1979 public interest in the cost and safety of nuclear power was at a peak; the Three Mile Island nuclear accident had occurred in March 1979.

*60 Minutes* was among the most popular programs on television and frequently led the list of the most watched television shows. The program, which featured pugnacious reporters Mike Wallace, Dan Rather, Morley Safer, and Harry Reasoner, prided itself on being the advocate of the "average American." Each 1-hour program consisted of three 15- to 18-minute segments or stories. Usually, two of the three weekly stories focused on individual or bureaucratic malfeasance or misfeasance. The program's producers particularly liked to stage interviews during which one of the star reporters and a camera crew would burst unannounced into the office of the person to be interviewed.

The *60 Minutes* segment on Illinois Power featured interviews with three former Illinois Power employees, who claimed the cost overruns and production delays were due to mismanagement. The company believed that the three employees were using the charges as revenge for alleged mistreatment by the company. One employee had been fired; another resigned over wage increases he found unsatisfactory. The former employee who had suggested that *60 Minutes* do the story on Clinton had been denied permission to appear as an expert witness in state regulatory hearings after it was discovered he had falsified his academic credentials and work experience. Nevertheless, CBS featured him as Illinois Power's "sharpest critic."

More troubling to Illinois Power was that Harry Reasoner, who reported the story on the air, appeared to be misstating several key facts that had been discussed with him and explained at length. The story left the strong impression that Illinois Power was mismanaging the construction of the Clinton Nuclear Power Plant and expected its customers to pay higher rates to compensate for this mismanagement. Reasoner stated that the nuclear facility would come on line much later and at a much higher cost than Illinois Power was now predicting.

Illinois Power executives felt betrayed. They had welcomed the *60 Minutes* producer, reporter, and camera crews. Illinois Power had taken one precaution, however; it had filmed everything the *60 Minutes* cameras had filmed on Illinois Power property. Company executives believed they could show with these films that Harry Reasoner had deliberately misrepresented the facts in at least three instances.

Company executives were particularly concerned about the impact such a negative report would have on the company's customers ("the residents of one-third of Illinois"), its shareholders, its employees, and its case for a 14 percent rate increase then before the Illinois utility regulatory commission. What could the company do now to counteract whatever damage had been done?

Among the alternatives suggested were to ignore the whole incident, sue CBS for damages (it would be necessary to show deliberate misrepresentation), request equal time under the Fairness Doctrine by petitioning the FCC, and seek a public judgment against CBS from the National News Council, a self-regulatory group of the media that published its decisions in the *Columbia Journalism Review*. Illinois Power's management wondered which would be the most effective in controlling the damage to the company, or whether the company ought to consider other alternatives. ■

SOURCE: This case was prepared by Kirk O. Hanson, Senior Lecturer in Business Administration, from publicly available sources as a basis for class discussion rather than to illustrate the effective or ineffective handling of an administrative situation. Copyright © 1981 by the Board of Trustees of the Leland Stanford Junior University. Reprinted by permission. All rights reserved.

---

[41]A transcript of the *60 Minutes* segment is found in CBS News, *60 Minutes Verbatim*, Arno Press, New York, 1980, pp. 149–153.

## PREPARATION QUESTIONS

1. Where is the *60 Minutes* story located in Figure 3-2? What makes it newsworthy?
2. If Illinois Power files a libel suit, under what standard is it likely to be tried? Is Illinois Power likely to win?

3. What should Illinois Power do about the impact of the story on its constituents and its nonmarket environment?

# CHAPTER 4

# Private Politics

## Introduction

Many nonmarket issues are addressed in public institutions, as considered in parts II and III of this book, which deal with lawmaking, regulation, and the legal system. The competition between firms and other interests over the resolution of these issues in the context of the institutions of government is called *public politics*. Other nonmarket issues are addressed largely outside, but often in the shadow of, public institutions. These issues are advanced by strategies of individuals, interest groups, activists, and NGOs that range from direct pressure on firms, as in the case of consumer boycotts, to attempts to influence public sentiment. The primary objective of these strategies is to cause a firm to change its policies or practices. The competition between firms and these other interests over the resolution of issues outside of government institutions is called *private politics*.

Private politics can be motivated by self-interest as well as broader concerns. In some cases it arises because an individual becomes concerned about an issue, as in the instance in Chapter 1 of the person who telephoned Larry King and said that his wife had died from brain cancer caused by radiation from heavy use of a cellular telephone. More often, private politics originates from interest groups, as when U.S. labor unions act to demand higher wages and improved working conditions in the overseas factories supplying the apparel and footwear industries. Private politics is also initiated by activist and advocacy groups that serve the interests of others in addition to the interests of their members. The causes these individuals, interest groups, and activists pursue are important components of the nonmarket environment, and the issues on their agendas are frequently thrust onto the agendas of firms. Understanding their concerns, organization, and strategies is essential to formulating strategies to address the issues they advance and the pressures they exert.

Private politics affects the issues, interests, institutions, and information that comprise the nonmarket environment. First, the groups initiating private politics can identify issues about which management either is unaware or has not understood as important to others, as in the case of the possible health risks from cellular telephone radiation. Similarly, the actions of Greenpeace calling attention to Shell UK's plan to sink the oil storage platform, Brent Spar, in the North Atlantic generated private politics in Europe even though the plan had been approved by the UK government. Individuals and interest and activist groups thus play an important role in setting the nonmarket agendas of firms and in advancing issues through their life cycles. Moreover, the issues they raise and the concerns they express may point in the direction of more effective and responsible management.

Second, these groups can affect the organization of interests by forming watchdog and advocacy groups and by mobilizing people to work for causes. These groups have been instrumental in advancing the causes of environmental protection, health and safety protection for consumers, and civil and human rights. The organizations they form are an increasingly important component of the nonmarket environment.

Third, the pressure these groups exert can affect the institutional configuration of the nonmarket environment. In public politics their actions have led to new laws, expanded regulatory authority, court orders, legislative oversight activities, and executive branch initiatives. These groups were the prime movers behind the creation of the Environmental Protection Agency (EPA) and the Consumer Products Safety Commission, and organized labor worked for the creation of the Occupational Safety and Health Administration. In private politics activists have spurred the formation of private governance institutions such as the Fair Labor Association and the Forest Stewardship Council that govern the private regulation of labor practices in overseas apparel and footwear factories and in timber harvesting and forest management, respectively. This private regulation has been growing as an alternative to government regulation.

Fourth, individuals, interest groups, and activists provide information that influences public and private politics. Rachel Carson's *Silent Spring* spurred the environmental movement by calling attention to the harmful effects of DDT. Activists at the Earth Island Institute spurred a public outcry and boycotts of tuna products when they produced a film showing dolphins drowning in nets used to catch tuna.[1] The news media plays a major role in disseminating this information, and an important component of private politics strategies is to attract media coverage, as illustrated by the campaign against the apple-ripening chemical Alar considered in Chapter 3.

Regardless of whether these groups are right in their causes, their actions can damage a firm, its reputation, and its constituents. Some products, rightly or wrongly, have been doomed by the actions of activists. Ralph Nader's attacks on the safety of the General Motors Corvair, for instance, contributed to the car's elimination. Activists have been vocal opponents of agricultural biotechnology, causing delays in new products and increased costs. The strength of activist groups varies across countries. The opposition to agricultural biotechnology has waned in the United States as more products have been brought to market without the harmful effects claimed by their critics. Opposition to agricultural biotechnology, however, remains strong in much of Europe. Because of private politics, a major Swiss pharmaceutical company located biotechnology units just over the French border and connected those units by pipeline to its plant just inside Switzerland. In effect, the plant lies on both sides of the border with the biotechnology components located in France.

This chapter first considers the nature of private politics using activist campaigns as an example. The strategies used by interest and activist groups are then considered more generally, followed by a discussion of the organization of these groups. Strategies of firms for dealing with private politics challenges are then considered.

---

[1]Putnam (1993) provides an analysis of the boycott of H. J. Heinz over the killing of dolphins in conjunction with tuna fishing.

# Campaigns

Activists organize corporate campaigns to advance the issues on their agendas, and a frequent component of a campaign is a boycott. Some boycotts are more symbolic than real, but many attract media and public attention. Boycotts against such companies as Starkist Tuna, General Electric, the Walt Disney Company, Shell, Citigroup, Boise Cascade, and Coca-Cola have attracted national and international attention. The Walt Disney Company was the subject of several boycotts. The National Hispanic Media Coalition organized a boycott because of Disney's record in hiring Hispanics. The Southern Baptist Convention organized a boycott to protest Disney's decision to extend employee benefits to gay and lesbian domestic partners. A leader of the boycott said, "Do they expect Mickey to leave Minnie and move in with Donald? That's goofy!" International labor groups called for boycotts of Disney toys because of the working conditions in the factories of its Asian suppliers. The Texas State Board of Education sold 1.2 million shares in Disney to protest violence and sexually explicit movies produced by its Miramax Films subsidiary. The Immune Deficiency Foundation called for a boycott of Disney because of its movie *Bubble Boy,* and civil rights groups called for a boycott because of a racially offensive promotion on a radio station owned by Disney.

In the early 1990s General Electric came under attack for its operation of nuclear weapons facilities. A boycott and other pressures were directed at the company by the United Methodist Church, Physicians for Social Responsibility, and INFACT, an activist group that had led the campaign against Nestlé for its marketing of infant formula in developing countries. INFACT produced a documentary film, *Deadly Deception: General Electric, Nuclear Weapons and the Environment,* that won an Academy Award for best documentary in 1992. The award provided the filmmaker an opportunity to criticize General Electric in her acceptance speech, which was broadcast worldwide.

Campaigns such as those against Disney and General Electric target the company directly, but activists are increasingly targeting the markets in which a company operates. Physicians for Social Responsibility claimed that its campaign against General Motors had caused physicians to switch purchases of $43 million of medical equipment, such as magnetic resonance imaging machines, from General Electric to other suppliers. General Electric denied that the campaign had any effect, and in 1993 it sold its aerospace division, which included its nuclear weapons business.

The Rainforest Action Network (RAN) now focuses primarily on market campaigns. To stop timber harvesting in old growth forests, RAN first targeted companies selling lumber and wood products, including Home Depot, Kinko's, and Lowe's, and then targeted home builders. Once it had affected the market for old growth products, it turned its attention to timber companies, beginning with Boise Cascade and moving to Weyerhaeuser.

Boycott targets may also be chosen because of opportunity. Greenpeace used the 2000 Olympics in Australia to launch a boycott against Coca-Cola, which was an official sponsor of the Olympics. The objective was to stop Coca-Cola from using hydrofluorocarbons (HFCs) as a refrigerant in its dispensing machines. Greenpeace Australia produced a downloadable poster under the caption "Enjoy Climate Change" depicting Coke's family of polar bears worriedly sitting on a melting ice cap. Greenpeace urged the public to download the posters and paste them on Coke machines.

Activist and interest groups often use both private and public politics strategies, as the Pizza Hut example illustrates.

Do campaigns and boycotts have an effect on either the performance of firms or on their policies? Nearly all companies state that a boycott had no significant effect on their performance, yet some customers do stop purchasing the products of a boycott target. A boycott of Mitsubishi Electric organized by RAN led Circuit City to stop carrying

---

**EXAMPLE**

## Pizza Hut and Health Insurance Reform

In the summer of 1994 Congress was occupied with Clinton administration proposals to change the health care system. Interest group activity was intense. In July the Health Care Reform Project, an interest group formed by a coalition of organizations led by labor unions, released a report attacking Pizza Hut and McDonald's for providing less health care coverage for their employees in the United States than they provided in other countries.[1] The group sought mandatory employer-provided health insurance and universal coverage. To publicize its campaign, the group held a press conference and placed full-page advertisements in *The New York Times* and the *Washington Post*. The headline read "No Matter How You Slice It . . . Pizza Hut Does Not Deliver the Same Health Benefits in America as It Does in Germany and Japan." The group also produced a commercial it planned to show on four New York and Washington television stations. Showing a young man delivering a pizza by bicycle, the commercial said that Pizza Hut provided health coverage for all its employees in Germany and Japan, "but for many workers in America, Pizza Hut pays no health insurance. Zero." Neither the advertisement nor the commercial mentioned McDonald's. The strategy of the interest groups was coordinated with one of its allies in Congress, Senator Edward Kennedy (D-MA), chairman of the Senate Labor Committee, who appeared at the press conference and asked, "What do they have against American workers?" He announced plans to hold committee hearings the next week on the issue and asked Pizza Hut and McDonald's to appear.

Under attack, Pizza Hut first addressed the immediate problem of the television commercial. Its Washington law firm wrote to the television stations pointing out its concerns with the commercial. The letter stated, "If you cause to be broadcast any statement to the effect that Pizza Hut does not offer health care coverage for its employees in the United States, the company will regard that false broadcast as having been made with knowledge of

falsity or in reckless disregard of falsity."[2] This thinly-veiled threat of a libel suit caused the television stations not to broadcast the advertisement.

Pizza Hut then sought to explain more fully the underlying issue and defend its policies. It indicated that health care coverage was not provided for part-time, hourly employees for the first 6 months of employment, although employees could purchase a basic plan for $11 a month. After 6 months the company paid for a modest supplement to that insurance. Pizza Hut had 120,000 employees who worked 20 hours a week or less, and most of them had health care coverage through their families. Moreover, few part-time workers remained on the job for 6 months. Pizza Hut also explained that health care coverage was mandatory in Germany and Japan and was one of the reasons a pizza that sold for $11 in the United States sold for $19 in Germany and $25 in Japan. Pizza Hut claimed that the cost of a pizza would increase by 10 percent if the plan supported by the interest groups and Senator Kennedy were adopted.

Pizza Hut also had allies in Congress, and its home state senators, Robert Dole (R-KS) and Nancy Kassenbaum (R-KS), defended the company. Speaking on the floor of the Senate, Senator Dole said, "I don't know what company or industry will next be attacked by the White House, the Democratic National Committee or their allies, but from the arguments they use, I know they like their pizzas with a lot of baloney."[3]

Pizza Hut CEO Allan S. Huston appeared before Senator Kennedy's committee and defended the company's record and practices. Choosing to let Pizza Hut take all the heat, McDonald's declined to appear. Committee staffers placed a Big Mac, fries, and a soft drink on the table in front of the empty chair provided for McDonald's CEO. Senator Kennedy attacked the companies for "an unacceptable double standard."

---

[1]Health Care Reform Project, "Do As We Say, Not As We Do," Washington, DC, July 1994.

[2]*The New York Times,* July 16, 1994. See the section "Recourse to the Law" in Chapter 3 for the explanation for this language as a basis for a libel lawsuit.
[3]*The New York Times,* July 24, 1994.

(*Continued*)

*(Continued)*

Shortly afterwards, the Clinton administration's health care reform efforts collapsed in disarray, and the Health Care Reform Project closed its doors. Although Pizza Hut had incurred only minor damage, the issue of health care coverage for part-time workers was unlikely to go away. The issue had attracted considerable media attention because of the societal significance of health issues and the attention being given to health care reform. Moreover, organized labor and other interest and activist groups, as well as some members of Congress, would continue to raise the issue—perhaps with different tactics.

Mitsubishi televisions. The loss of a large retailer must have hurt Mitsubishi sales. The question is thus better posed in terms of the magnitude of the effect on company performance.

Several studies have measured the stock price performance of companies that were the target of a boycott relative to the stock price performance of companies not subject to a boycott. The empirical evidence is largely inconclusive.[2] Despite the inconclusive evidence, most firms are concerned about the possibility of a boycott not only because of possible lost sales but also because the public attention, frequently under the scrutiny of the media, can harm their reputation and public image.

Many campaigns are organized not to lead a boycott but instead to threaten the reputation or public image of a firm. RAN does not attempt to organize boycotts because it believes that it is too difficult to demonstrate to a target the effect of a boycott. Instead, in its campaigns RAN focuses on the public face and brand equity of its targets. The objective is to call attention to the objectionable practices of the target, casting doubt on the public face the company has created through its public relations and advertising. RAN primarily targets companies with branded products and a consumer presence so that consumers can take individual actions against the target. In the Part I integrative case, *Anatomy of a Corporate Campaign: Rainforest Action Network and Citigroup (A),* RAN conducted an aggressive campaign against Citigroup, focusing on its public face, and some consumers cut up their Citibank credit cards and some students pledged not to do business with Citigroup.

Which companies are most susceptible to boycotts or reputation damage? Figure 4-1 identifies characteristics of companies, their products, and their operating environment that make them susceptible. A consumer products company is susceptible because consumers can take action by switching to competing products. This is easiest when switching costs are low, as in the case of gasoline, tuna, or televisions. A company with a brand name is also susceptible because customers can punish it by not buying a variety of products. General Electric experienced this even outside its consumer product lines.

A company whose activities produce harmful externalities such as pollution or a health hazard could be subject to protests from those affected or from advocacy groups

---

[2]A number of event studies of the stock market reaction to boycotts have been conducted. Davidson, Worrell, and El-Jelly (1995) found that the announcements of 40 boycotts between 1969 and 1991 resulted in a statistically significant decrease in the share price of the targets. Friedman (1985), Pruitt and Friedman (1986), and Pruitt, Wei, and White (1988) found evidence that boycotts significantly reduced the market values of target firms. Koku, Akhigbe, and Springer (1997), however, found that the market values of 54 target firms increased significantly. Teoh, Welch, and Wazzan (1999) found no significant effect of the boycott of South Africa on either U.S. firms or on shares traded on the Johannesburg Stock Exchange. Epstein and Schnietz (2002) studied the effect on the stock prices of firms identified as "abusive" by the antiglobalization demonstrations at the 1999 Seattle World Trade Organization meeting. Firms that were identified as abusive because of environmentally damaging activities had significantly lower stock returns, whereas firms with allegedly abusive labor practices experienced normal returns. Friedman (1999), Manheim (2001), and Vogel (1978) have studied individual boycotts in more detail.

- Products
  - consumer products
  - products with low switching costs
  - a brand name that can be damaged
- Operating environment
  - activities that produce harmful externalities
  - operating in an interest group–rich environment
  - multinational/global operations—issues can spill over to other units and countries
  - operating in developing countries
- Organization
  - a decentralized organization, so that external effects, including intracompany, are not naturally considered

**FIGURE 4-1 Susceptibility to Private Politics and Boycotts**

that support them. Operating in an interest group–rich environment, as in Europe or the United States, provides a ready set of groups that could initiate private politics. Also, multinational companies must be concerned about the effects of operations taken in one country on interest groups and activists in other countries. Operations in developing countries may encounter fewer organized interest and activist groups, but groups in developed countries closely monitor activities in developing countries. Shell learned this from its decision not to intervene when the Nigerian government executed nine activists, including a Nobel peace prize nominee, who were protesting environmental degradation from oil fields operated by Shell. The organization of a company can also increase susceptibility. In a highly decentralized company, a subsidiary in one country may not take into account or even be aware of the potential effects of its activities on private politics against subsidiaries in other countries.

The characteristics identified in Figure 4-1 can be used in the chapter cases, *Shell, Greenpeace, and Brent Spar* and *Nike in Southeast Asia,* to assess whether campaigns are likely to be successful.

# Private or Public Politics?

The choice between public and private politics is strategic, and activists are increasingly choosing private politics. What can private politics accomplish that public politics cannot? One answer is that private politics can succeed when public politics faces interest group opposition or institutional gridlock.

During the 1970s and 1980s activists primarily focused on public politics, seeking legislation and regulation to compel firms to change their practices. In the 1990s many activist groups recognized that it was difficult to obtain change through government and turned to private politics by directly pressuring firms to change their practices. Commenting on the boycott campaign against ExxonMobil for its stance on climate change, Paul Gilding, former head of Greenpeace, said, "The smart activists are now saying, 'OK, you want to play markets—let's play.' [Lobbying government] takes forever and can easily be counter-lobbied by corporations. No, no, no. They start with consumers at the pump, get them to pressure the gas stations, get the station owners to pressure the companies and the companies to pressure governments. After all, consumers do have choices where they buy their gas, and there are differences now. Shell and BPAmoco (which is also the world's biggest solar company) both withdrew from the oil industry lobby that has been dismissing climate change."[3]

---

[3] *The New York Times,* June 2, 2001.

Michael Brune, executive director of RAN, said, "Companies were more responsive to public opinion than certain legislatures were. We felt we could create more democracy in the marketplace than in the government." Democracy in the marketplace means that citizen consumers express in markets their views on the performance of firms. If they object to logging in old growth forests, they can impose their will on the logging companies by refusing to buy old growth products.

Another example is fuel economy standards. With the exception of a small increase in fuel economy standards to take effect in model year 2007, fuel economy standards are basically the same as in 1985. Moreover, the actual fuel economy of the new-vehicle fleet has decreased in recent years as the market share of light trucks and SUVs has increased. Environmental groups have worked in Congress to mandate higher standards, as indicated in the Part II integrative case *CAFE Standards 2002.* When opposition to increased standards mounted in Congress, the Sierra Club turned to private politics. It began a 3-year campaign to pressure the big-three auto manufacturers to increase the fuel economy of their light vehicles. As Carl Pope of the Sierra Club explained, "We're going now to the customers." A number of other activist groups also launched private politics campaigns against automakers and in particular SUVs. Those groups included the Detroit Project, Earth on Empty, Evangelical Environmental Network, and RAN, in addition to the Sierra Club.

In many cases activists integrate private and public politics campaigns. To address the issue of fuel economy, the Bluewater Network launched both public and private politics campaigns. In the latter Bluewater targeted Ford using advertisements, demonstrations, public criticism, and a consumer boycott. In commenting on Ford's planned introduction of its hybrid Escape SUV, executive director Russell Long said, "It's ridiculous for Bill Ford to portray his company as an environmental leader because of the hybrid Escape. Ford's new vehicles create more global warming pollution than any other major auto company."[4] Its public politics campaign focused on legislation in California that would require automakers to improve their fuel economy. Under federal law California is allowed to set more stringent pollution standards than federal standards. The Bluewater Network drafted legislation calling for sharp reductions in pollutants, and included carbon dioxide. The only way to appreciably reduce carbon dioxide emissions was to reduce the consumption of fossil fuels, and a major reduction could only be accomplished by reducing the fuel burned in automobiles and trucks. The legislation was enacted and signed into law by the governor.

The innovation in the California law was to classify carbon dioxide as a pollutant to give the state regulatory jurisdiction. Carbon dioxide, however, had never been considered a pollutant under federal law, and the EPA had explicitly refused to list it as a pollutant. The auto industry saw the California law as back-door regulation of fuel economy, which only the federal government has the authority to regulate.[5] Elisa Lynch of the Bluewater Network said, "We wrote a bill that will stand up well in court. This is not related to fuel economy."[6] The California law would have its day in court.

In 2003 the AIDS Healthcare Foundation (AHF) launched a public and private politics campaign against GlaxoSmithKline (GSK) to force the company to make its AIDS drugs accessible to developing countries. AHF asked investors, including

---

[4]*Los Angeles Times,* no date.
[5]In an earlier court case the Department of Justice had filed a brief stating, "The Energy Policy and Conservation Act provides that when a federal fuel economy standard is in effect, a state or a political subdivision of a state may not enact nor adopt or enforce a law or regulation related to fuel economy standards." Associated Press, October 10, 2002.
[6]*Automotive News,* July 8, 2002.

CalPERS, to pressure GSK to lower its drug prices for developing countries. It filed a lawsuit in the United States challenging GSK's patent on AZT, the first antiretroviral drug. It also filed a complaint in South Africa challenging GSK's pricing practices and a lawsuit in California alleging that GSK engaged in false advertising of its AIDS drugs. AHF lobbied the California state government to put pressure on GSK and its pricing policies. AHF organized protests and demonstrations against GSK in the United States and barred company personnel from its AIDS outpatient facilities in the United States.

# Activist Strategies

Activists choose nonmarket strategies just as firms do. They seek to pressure firms to change their practices, and although some have a large membership that could be mobilized for action against a target, most are small with limited resources and a small membership base. Activists thus face a collective action problem, and a campaign serves as a coordinating mechanism for those with concerns about the practices of firms. Citizen consumers must learn about the issue of concern to the activist and the firm's practices. The news media plays a central role by creating a degree of common knowledge about the issue, the practices, and the target. Activists often take out advertisements in newspapers and magazines as part of their attempt to inform the public, but they also rely on "earned" media—that is, media coverage of the activist campaign. The chapter case, *Strategic Activism: The Rainforest Action Network,* examines the strategy and organization of a small, successful activist group. The Part I integrative case, *Anatomy of a Corporate Campaign: Rainforest Action Network and Citigroup,* illustrates RAN's approach to influencing a target.

Common knowledge and the concerns of activists must be turned into action. This requires a strategy. The two basic strategies of activists are putting direct pressure on firms through private politics and working through public institutions using public politics. Direct pressure is applied by calling attention to the activities of a firm, as in the Pizza Hut example. This may involve attracting the media to the issue, communicating through community groups, or attempting to reach opinion leaders and public officeholders. The media may be attracted by events such as demonstrations, hanging banners on buildings, or press conferences at which studies are released or allegations made. Some activists have access to a network of organizations through which their concerns can be communicated. Others may enlist the aid of public officeholders, such as Senator Kennedy in the Pizza Hut example.

Pressure can be applied through centralized and decentralized activities. The campaign against Pizza Hut was centralized through labor unions. As an example of decentralized strategy, the Emergency Planning and Community Right-to-Know Act requires the federal government to publish annually the Toxics Release Inventory, which lists for every plant in the country the emissions of over 300 possibly hazardous chemicals. Using data from the Inventory, the Natural Resources Defense Council holds an annual press conference and releases a study of the nation's biggest polluters. The Inventory and the media coverage alert local community groups to the emissions in their areas. Local groups, using private politics, then pressure firms in their areas to reduce their emissions. Partly as a result of these activities, several major companies, including DuPont and Dow Chemical, have reduced emissions below the levels required by EPA regulations.[7]

---

[7]In addition to the Toxics Release Inventory, the government makes available on the Internet mortgage lending data by census tracts and the chemical composition of drinking water.

The Internet has helped activists coordinate and mount their campaigns on a broader and decentralized basis. Carol Browner, former head of the Environmental Protection Agency, said, "Environmental groups have become truly sophisticated in using the Web to move information to millions of people literally overnight, and to attack companies on a global scale."[8] The coordinated antiglobalization protests against international institutions that began in 1999 in Seattle against the World Trade Organization and continued against the International Monetary Fund, World Bank, and G-8 are ample evidence.

A first-mover advantage is often available to an activist. Moving first typically allows the activist both to attract the media with an event and frame the issue by raising concerns or making allegations about the target. Moving first can also provide an advantage if surprise leads the target to make a tactical mistake in responding to the activist's campaign. RAN begins its campaigns with a letter to the CEO of the target, often followed shortly thereafter by speaking at the target's annual meeting.

Activist groups also use their standing before courts, legislatures, and administrative organizations to petition, sue, and advocate action. Environmental legislation and certain health and safety legislation were written to give citizens the right to petition regulatory agencies for action and sue those agencies if they fail to act. In the Chapter 3 case, *General Motors Like a Rock? (A)*, the Center for Auto Safety petitioned NHTSA to recall General Motors pickup trucks with side-mounted gas tanks. As illustrated in the Pizza Hut example, many activist groups have as allies legislators and officials in executive branch agencies who can influence agendas. Access to public institutions is a lever activists often use to pressure firms to negotiate on an issue. The public politics strategies used by activists are similar to those used by firms, as considered in Part II of the book.

Litigation is an important strategy for many groups. A lawsuit may serve as a bargaining lever in an activist campaign or may be used to force action by the target or government. The Natural Resources Defense Council initially followed an aggressive litigation strategy to spur enforcement of environmental regulations. Community groups coordinated by ACORN routinely filed lawsuits to block acquisitions of federally chartered banks as a means of obtaining lending commitments in their communities.

Some activists and NGOs choose to work directly with firms and industries to implement new policies. Two prominent such groups are Conservation International and Environmental Defense. Other groups, such as RAN and the Bluewater Network, prefer negative campaigns. RAN believes that praising a company that had good environmental policies would have little effect in inducing other companies to adopt similar policies. Instead, negative campaigns can catch the attention of the public, the media, and the target.

These two approaches to achieving change can leave activist groups on opposite sides of an issue. Forest products are certified by independent third parties to have come from forests managed with certain minimum social, environmental, and conservation practices. Two competing certification systems have been established. The Forest Stewardship Council (FSC) was supported by RAN, Greenpeace, the Sierra Club, and other NGOs. The Sustainable Forestry Institute (SFI) was developed by the timber industry in cooperation with Conservation International and the Nature Conservancy. The groups backing the FSC criticized the SFI as letting the fox guard the henhouse.

## Advocacy Science

A frequently used strategy of activists is to conduct a policy study or scientific investigation to call attention to an issue. Even when it involves only secondary sources, this

---

[8]*The New York Times,* September 9, 2001.

practice of "advocacy science" can advance the activists' cause. As in the Alar case considered in Chapter 3, a study can attract the media, and hence the public, which gives a degree of credibility to the claims of the activists. It can also attract sympathetic legislators, who can provide support, introduce bills, and hold hearings at which activists can testify. Advocacy science is most effective if it can be coordinated with other actions to prolong attention to the issue and provide a series of newsworthy events.

Activists may also sieze the release of studies by others to advance their causes, as illustrated by the fish farm activism example.

---

**EXAMPLE**

## Fish Farm Activism

In 2004 a study published in the journal *Science* reported higher levels of polychlorinated biphenyls (PCBs) and dioxin in salmon raised in fish farms than in salmon caught in the wild.[1] The concentrations exceeded Environmental Protection Agency (EPA) standards. David Carpenter, of the University of Albany, one of the authors of the study, said, "We're not telling people not to eat fish, ... We're telling them to eat less farmed salmon."[2] Wild salmon cost $15 a pound compared to $5 a pound for farmed salmon.

The Environmental Working Group and Center for Environmental Health (CEH) filed a notice with the State of California of their intent to file a lawsuit against fish farms, producers, and retailers for failing to notify consumers of the PCBs and dioxin. Michael Green, executive director of CEH, said, "We believe it's the responsibility of these companies to ensure the fish they sell is not contaminated with toxic chemicals. Our goal is to challenge them to change their practices so their fish is safe to eat."[3]

The tolerance level for PCBs set by the Food and Drug Administration was 2000 parts per billion, which was 50 times greater than the level in fish farm salmon. Also, "'The study tested salmon raw, with the skin on. Removing the skin and grilling it removes a significant amount of PCBs, dioxins and other pollutants stored in fish fat,' the FDA said."[4] "We do think the levels [in farmed salmon] should be lowered," said Terry Troxell, an FDA division director and toxicologist. "However, we don't believe there is a public health concern with the levels seen here. ... Our message for consumers is not to alter their consumption of wild or farmed salmon."[5] The guidelines used in the research study were set by the EPA for recreationally caught fish and by the FDA standards for commercially caught fish. The EPA stood by its guidelines.

Salmon were an important source of omega-3 fatty acids, which reduce the risk of heart disease. Salmon were also low in mercury. Martha Daviglus of the Northwestern University Medical School observed, "The benefits (of salmon) in my opinion are way over the risks of having cancer."[6] A Purdue University food toxicologist, Charles Santere, criticized the study for ignoring the benefits of salmon: "I would calculate 6,000 people getting cancer over their lifetime, that's an approximation, versus potentially saving the lives of 100,000 individuals every year."[7] He added, "In my view, the study says we should be eating more farmed salmon."[8] Eric Rimm of the Harvard School of Public Health commented, "To alarm people away from fish because of some potential, at this point undocumented, risk of long-term cancer—that does worry me."[9]

---

[1] The study was financed by the Pew Charitable Trust.
[2] *Associated Press*, January 8, 2004.
[3] *The Vancouver Sun*, January 23, 2004.
[4] *Associated Press*, January 8, 2004.

[5] *The Oakland Tribune*, January 10, 2004.
[6] *Philadelphia Inquirer*, January 21, 2004.
[7] *Los Angeles Times*, January 9, 2004.
[8] *The Times (London)*, January 9, 2004.
[9] *Associated Press*, January 8, 2004.

## Target Selection

An important component of a private politics campaign is selection of a target. Targeting is largely driven by strategic calculations, and activists frequently do not target a company directly but instead target companies in its value chain, that is, its suppliers or customers. Target selection strategies vary widely. Activists sometimes target "worst offenders." For example, environmental activists concluded that ExxonMobil was the most obstinate opponent of measures to address global climate change. As a result, European activists led a boycott of Esso products. In contrast, hoping that they would be quickly responsive, activists sometimes target firms, such as BP and Starbucks as considered in Chapter 2, that have positioned themselves as socially responsible and environmentally friendly. Sometimes activists target the most well-known company or largest company in an industry. In the campaign against the prevailing labor practices in overseas apparel and footwear plants, activists targeted Nike. RAN chooses targets with a strong retail presence, brand identity, and a "public face." RAN chose Citigroup not only because of these characteristics but also because it was the industry leader and the worst offender. Because it was the industry leader, success with Citigroup could ripple throughout the industry.

In its global climate change campaign RAN chose as its target Ford rather than General Motors, even though GM had shown greater opposition to higher fuel economy standards. RAN's rationale was that (1) Ford had the lowest fleet fuel economy of the U.S. automakers. (2) Ford had a primary brand in the United States, whereas GM sold vehicles under a larger number of domestic brands (Chevrolet, Buick, Oldsmobile, Pontiac, Cadillac, GMC, Hummer, Saturn, and Saab). Thus, Ford's brand equity was a clearer target. (3) CEO and Chairman Bill Ford had been a supporter of the environmental movement and was thought to be sympathetic to environmental causes. A campaign would provide an opportunity to go further in embracing higher fuel economy. (4) Ford had broken its promise by announcing that it would be unable to meet its fuel economy goal for SUVs. (5) Ford had been targeted by other environmental activist groups, including the Bluewater Network and the Sierra Club, and RAN's campaign would add to the pressure.

Activists also target individuals in both their personal and professional roles. Attention typically focuses on those perceived as influential and possibly influenceable. RAN directed attention to Citigroup CEO Sandy Weill by putting his picture in advertisements and on posters, and school children sent him valentines asking him to stop Citigroup's financing of environmentally destructive projects. Pro-choice demonstrators participating in the National Organization of Women's nationwide boycott picketed Domino's Pizza outlets, claiming that the chain opposed abortion rights. Although Domino's Pizza had no policy on abortion, its owner, Thomas S. Monaghan, had made a personal contribution of $50,000 to the Committee to End Tax-Funded Abortions.

## A Generic Strategy of Activists

Although some campaign activities may be coercive, particularly when an individual is the target, the examples above indicate the range of strategies used by interest and activist groups. Potential targets must anticipate the actions of activist groups and be prepared to deal with the issues they place on the firm's agenda. Figure 4-2 characterizes a generic strategy used by many activist groups in advancing the issues on their agendas. This characterization draws on the role of the news media in informing the public about issues, as considered in Chapter 3. The activist group first identifies an issue such as health insurance or fuel economy and selects a target such as Pizza Hut or Ford. The activist group may have a first-mover advantage and frame the issue by identifying its societal significance and the company's role in the issue. The audience interest in an issue

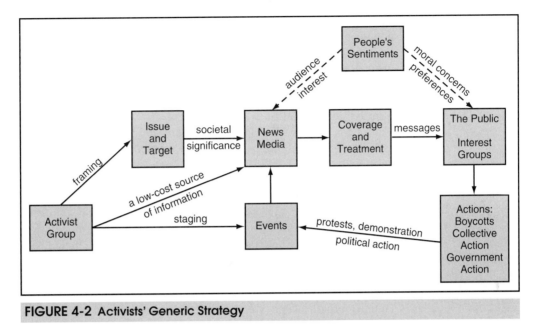

**FIGURE 4-2** Activists' Generic Strategy

is determined by people's sentiments, and those sentiments may be based on moral concerns, as in the case of workers without health care insurance. To attract the news media, the activists may orchestrate events. The activists also seek to become a low-cost source of information for the journalists. For example, Greenpeace has photographers and camera crews that broadcast its actions worldwide. When media coverage is difficult to attract, some activist groups take out advertisements in newspapers.

People's responses to this strategy depend on their sentiments and concerns about the issue. The hope of the activists is that individuals and interest groups will take action in the form of protests, boycotts, and collective action, which may attract further news media coverage. In addition, government officials may be attracted to the issue. Greenpeace's actions in the chapter case, *Shell, Greenpeace, and Brent Spar,* attracted the support of motorists, labor unions, and government officials. The basic strategy of the activists thus is to frame the issue to attract the interest of the public and the news media and induce people and government officeholders to take actions that give the issue a life of its own.

# Activist Organizations

## Activists and Their Organizations

Activism can be a means of furthering interests, as when a labor union leads a boycott of a company whose workers it seeks to organize, as in the Pizza Hut example. Or, a union may pressure companies regarding wages in their suppliers' factories in Asia with the objective of reducing the competitiveness of imports that threaten union jobs in the United States. For some, activism provides training for political office or for advancement in the network of interest groups participating in public policy processes. For others, an activist group provides a forum to express personal visions. Most activists, however, are motivated by concerns about specific issues. Some are concerned about an environmental or health issue or about the well-being of workers in Asian factories. Some are concerned about human and civil rights. Some advocate specific policies such as higher fuel economy, whereas others see activism as a means of advancing a broader social agenda to reform corporate conduct.

The nonmarket environment is populated by thousands of interest and activist groups, although some of them have only brief life spans. Because these groups shape the nonmarket environment of business and the agendas of firms, managers must be aware of their capabilities, networks, and agendas.[9] A number of activist groups were founded in association with Ralph Nader. These include the nucleus organizations: Center for Study of Responsive Law, U.S. Public Interest Research Group, Corporate Accountability Research Group, and Essential Information.[10] Less directly connected with Nader personally is Public Citizen, which sponsors the Health Research Group, Critical Mass Energy Project, Buyers Up!, Congress Watch, Global Trade Watch, and the Litigation Group. Other organizations include the Aviation Consumer Action Project, Center for Auto Safety, Center for Science in the Public Interest, Clean Water Action Project, Disability Rights Center, National Insurance Consumer Organization, Pension Rights Center, and Telecommunications Research and Action Center.[11]

Another set of activist organizations was spawned by David Brower, former executive director of the Sierra Club, who founded the Earth Island Institute (EII). Organizations founded through EII include the International Rivers Network and RAN. Activist organizations frequently form coalitions to advance particular issues. The antiglobalization activists have a broad network coordinated over the Internet and are capable of demonstrating wherever international economics organizations convene. The Ruckus Society provides training camps for participants in demonstrations and campaigns, and RAN contracts with Ruckus to supplement its own training camps. For demonstrations, protests, and other actions, RAN relies on four national networks of student organizations: Free The Planet, the Student Environmental Action Coalition, Students Transforming and Resisting Corporations, and the Sierra Student Coalition.

Activist organizations such as these are important components of the nonmarket environment. These groups are often staffed by dedicated people pursuing a cause they view as just or at least opportune. They are also an important source of information for citizens, politicians, and the media.

## Greenpeace

Greenpeace International has 2.8 million members from over 100 countries, offices in 40 countries, and a worldwide budget of €120 million. Greenpeace began in 1971 with a high-profile effort to stop nuclear testing in the Aleutian Islands, and its most widely known incident occurred in 1985 when French commandos sank the Greenpeace ship *Rainbow Warrior* in New Zealand, where it was attempting to block French nuclear testing. That incident caused membership in the United States to climb to 1.2 million in 1991. Because of Greenpeace's opposition to the Persian Gulf War and due to the successes of the environmental movement, such as the ban on hunting whales, U.S. membership declined to 400,000 in 1997. Nevertheless, Greenpeace remains one of the most formidable environmental activist groups, particularly in Europe.

Greenpeace has eight campaigns: climate change, toxic chemicals, nuclear power, oceans, genetic engineering, ancient forests, stop war, and trade and the environment. Internally, Greenpeace has two competing factions. The rubber suits argue for continued

---

[9]Rothenberg (1992) examines agenda setting in the citizens group Common Cause. Mundo (1992) provides an analysis of the history, evolution, organization, and activities of the Sierra Club.

[10]Griffin (1987) presents Nader's approach of forming public interest groups on college campuses.

[11]This list is based on Internet sites, the Encyclopedia of Associations, 24th edition, 1990; "Ralph Nader, Inc.," *Forbes,* September 17, 1990; and "The Resurrection of Ralph Nader," *Fortune,* May 22, 1989.

emphasis on high-profile, dramatic actions to call attention to issues. The technocrats argue for participation in policy processes and the search for alternative solutions to environmental problems. For example, Greenpeace supported development of a new, environmentally safe cooling system for refrigerators, which it argued should be adopted as an alternative to current HFC-based refrigerators. Its boycott of Coca-Cola in conjunction with the 2000 Olympics led to an announcement by the company, along with McDonald's and Unilever, that it would eliminate the use of HFCs in refrigeration by the 2004 Athens Olympics. The chapter case, *Shell, Greenpeace, and Brent Spar,* deals with another of Greenpeace's high-profile actions.

RAN is a tax-exempt organization, and contributions are tax deductible for the donor. The Sierra Club is also tax-exempt, but contributions are not tax deductible because the Club engages in political activities, such as lobbying and endorsing candidates. In 2001 the Sierra Club spent $370,000 on outside lobbyists, and in addition 9 other internal lobbyists and 11 staff lobbied. The Sierra Club Political Committee was a "hard money" PAC, and the Sierra Club Educational Fund raised soft money contributions.[12]

The organization of RAN, a much smaller environmental activist group than Greenpeace or the Sierra Club, is described in the chapter case, *Strategic Activism: The Rainforest Action Network.*

# Interacting with Activist Groups

## Assessment

When the nonmarket environment is populated by interest and activist groups, firms must develop approaches to dealing with these groups. Figure 4-3 highlights several basic steps successful firms have taken. A firm must assess its position and any possible private politics challenges to that position. This assessment begins by answering the question of what is demanded of the firm by the activists and, more importantly, by the public. A firm like McDonald's has a major public presence, making it the subject of a wide set of demands, identified in the Chapter 1 case, *The Nonmarket Environment of McDonald's.* The demands made on an investment banking firm or consulting firm are much more limited.

The next step is to assess vulnerability to a private politics campaign. This involves assessing not only the firm's vulnerability but also the vulnerability of those in its value chain. The determinants of vulnerability are identified in Figure 4-1 and are the same as used by activists in selecting their targets.

It is also important to assess the extent of public support for the activists' agendas. A number of firms have established forums with activist groups for exchanging information and viewpoints on issues. Firms generally prefer to interact with more moderate groups and avoid those that emphasize confrontation. Some interactions can lead to cooperative

---

**FIGURE 4-3 Addressing the Activist Environment**

- identify the relevant interest groups and activist organizations in your market and nonmarket environments
- understand their agenda, preferences, and capabilities
- understand the broader public support for their agenda
- consult with them on important issues; a number of companies have established regular forums for exchanging information and views
- cooperate when that is beneficial
- fight when you are right and can win—but be careful

---

[12]"Political Finance, The Newsletter," September 2002.

efforts to resolve problems, as in the McDonald's and Environmental Defense episode discussed later. On some issues, however, firms fight the activists when they are confident that they are both right and can win the fight. In some cases such as that of Nike and Disney, firms have underestimated the resolve of the activists.

If a firm is potentially vulnerable, the next step is to consider whether it is possible to forestall a possible campaign through self-regulation, by working with constructive NGOs, or by making public commitments to new policies. Interacting with an outside group can provide benefits, particularly when the group has expertise. When it considered establishing oil operations in Iran, Shell met with Amnesty International to discuss how it might handle human rights matters in the country. When partnering with an NGO, firms frequently prefer science-based NGOs with reputations for working with companies. Environmental Defense, Conservation International, and the World Wildlife Fund are frequent partners of companies. In some cases the formation of new organizations may be warranted. Staples joined with NatureServe, Conservation International, and the Nature Conservancy to form the Forest and Biodiversity Conservation Alliance. Major global banks worked with Conservation International to develop the Equator Principles for governing the financing of major development projects.

When a firm is challenged by an activist group or even a moderate NGO, the specific issues of concern must be evaluated and possible developments assessed. The frameworks developed in the previous chapters may be used to assess the challenge. Management should assess where the issue is in its life cycle and how rapidly it is progressing. Often the issues generated by activists and interest groups are early in their life cycles, and thus firms have an opportunity to affect their progress. The next step involves identifying other potentially interested parties and assessing how likely they are to become involved in the issue. As indicated in Figure 4-2, activists may attempt to bring the issue to the attention of the public and government officials through media strategies. The theory of the news media presented in Chapter 3 can be used to assess how the media may cover and treat the issue. Assessing the effectiveness of alternative strategies is often difficult when the issue is the subject of media and public attention, and that attention may advance an issue quickly through its life cycle. In the case of a boycott, the firm must assess whether people are likely to become aware of the issue and be sympathetic to the position of the activists. Sympathy, however, does not necessarily translate into action, so the likelihood that individuals will actually respond must be assessed.

Many firms choose to meet with activist groups to show their concern about the issue, explain the steps being taken to address it, or indicate the difficulties involved in addressing it. Meetings may help the firm understand the motivations of the activists and how likely they are to persist in their efforts. When targeted by RAN, Citigroup quickly initiated discussions. Developing understanding and trust was difficult, however, because Citigroup found that it was not on the same wave length as RAN. Citigroup eventually hired as a facilitator a former member of Greenpeace who subsequently had earned an MBA. In its meetings with RAN, Weyerhaeuser also used the services of a facilitator.

## Strategy and Negotiations

Determining the most effective strategy requires understanding the nature and strength of the activists, the concerns that motivate them, the likelihood of media coverage, how much damage they might cause, how central the issue is to their agenda, and whether they are led by professionals or amateurs. Professionals are more difficult to co-opt, but they may be more practical as well. With limited resources, activists and interest groups must determine which issues to address, and they may abandon an issue that appears to be unwinnable or requires too much of their available resources.

When confronted with private nonmarket action, a natural reaction is to be defensive. A better response is to evaluate the claims and demands made by the activists and determine whether they have merit. In some cases a firm may conclude that the activist's position is correct. RAN targeted Kinko's as part of its Old Growth Campaign, and within a few weeks received a letter from Kinko's stating that RAN's demands were consistent with Kinko's environmental policies. In disbelief, RAN called Kinko's to argue for its demands. Kinko's was surprised, since its letter stated that it agreed with RAN—Kinko's would stop sourcing supplies from old growth forests.

McDonald's faced a major solid-waste disposal problem, and when asked by Environmental Defense (ED) to discuss the problem, it decided to accept. The result was a voluntary working arrangement with ED to develop a plan of action that included waste reduction, recycling, and substitute packaging.[13] The arrangement provided McDonald's fresh ideas for addressing the waste disposal problem.

If the interactions with an activist group reach the point of bargaining over the resolution of the issues, a firm must assess the benefits and costs of alternative resolutions. It is also important to determine how an agreement will be monitored and how misunderstandings that might subsequently develop will be resolved. A firm also must assess whether its competitors will follow suit or whether the playing field will be uneven. Most firms prefer that the playing field be level, with their competitors taking the same steps on the issue.

An important component of a strategy for addressing a private politics campaign is to shore up the support of a firm's employees, some of whom may be sympathetic with the demands made by the activists. During the Old Growth Campaign, a Home Depot employee gave RAN the intercom code used in all its stores. RAN's staff and others went into stores, entered the intercom code, and recorded messages such as "Lumber from old growth forests is on sale on Aisle 3," or "Tropical lauan from the habitat of the orangutan and Sumatran tiger on sale on Aisle 4." The intercom system provided an opportunity to review a message before it was broadcast. Activists thus could be gone with their shopping carts before the message was broadcast or could be in the next aisle recording another message, making it difficult for Home Depot personnel to find them. This was repeated by dozens of activists in stores across the United States.

Weyerhaeuser was targeted by RAN after Boise Cascade had agreed to no longer harvest old growth timber. After an initial demonstration in Seattle and speaking at Weyerhaeuser's annual meeting, RAN paused its campaign as it prepared for a series of actions against the company later in the year. During the pause Weyerhaeuser published in its employee newsletter a lengthy interview with the executive responsible for sustainable forestry and for meeting with RAN. She explained the company's position and also warned of the actions that might be taken against the company. The objective was to protect employee morale by explaining the extensive steps the company already takes to protect forests and manage them in an environmentally sound manner.

Negotiations with activists can be voluntary, as in the case of McDonald's decision to join with ED to address solid-waste problems. In many cases, however, the objectives of the activists and the interests of the firm are in direct conflict. In such cases, negotiations between the activists and the firm may be required to resolve the issue. Often negotiations take place in the shadow of threats. Examples of negotiations are the OnBank example and the Part I integrative case, *Anatomy of a Campaign: Rainforest Action Network and Citigroup (A)*. RAN and Citigroup discussed the issue for 2 years with neither making any concessions.

---

[13]The McDonald's–ED partnership is considered in Chapter 11.

---

## EXAMPLE

### Negotiating with Activists: OnBank[1]

In response to charges that some financial institutions limited lending in inner-city neighborhoods, Congress enacted the Community Reinvestment Act (CRA). The CRA required federally chartered banks to lend in the communities in which their depositors lived. The Home Mortgage Disclosure Act (HMDA) required banks to report their mortgage lending by census tract. When two banks announced a merger, activist groups frequently seized the opportunity to challenge the merger. The groups asserted that the merging banks had not complied with the CRA, and they backed that assertion with data on mortgage lending by census tract filed in compliance with the HMDA.

In 1992 OnBank announced it would acquire another local bank, Merchants National Bank & Trust. When an inner-city resident's application to refinance his mortgage was rejected by OnBank, he turned to a community organization. The organization examined OnBank's lending record and found that it had seldom made loans in the community, had no branches in the inner city, and refused to participate in the city's Syracuse Housing Partnership. Merchants, however, had four branches in the inner city, participated in the Housing Partnership, and made significantly more loans in the inner city. Community organizations feared that the acquisition might result in Merchants operating as OnBank did. The community organizations began a letter-writing campaign to state and federal regulators calling attention to OnBank's lending record. OnBank countered with data showing that its record compared favorably with other banks in the state of New York.

OnBank received endorsements from local organizations such as the United Way and the Urban League.

The community organizations gave OnBank a list of 26 concerns and proposed that they and the bank meet. The two sides met to discuss the issues, but the bank was unwilling to conclude an agreement. Meanwhile, OnBank was negotiating with state regulators, and when the state approved the acquisition, the community groups protested and attracted considerable media coverage. The acquisition still required approval by the Federal Reserve Bank, and the protests led to a second meeting at which regulators were present as observers. Little progress was made until the bank agreed to participate in a number of smaller working groups to address specific issues. The smaller groups made rapid progress and, with a threat of direct action against the bank and federal approval still pending, the bank and the community organizations reached an agreement to increase lending in the inner city.[2] The threat of direct action against the bank, the required regulatory approval, and the reporting of lending data by census tract provided the opportunity to pressure OnBank and obtain lending commitments.

---

[1]This example is based on an article in *The Wall Street Journal,* September 22, 1992.
[2]This process is repeated throughout the nation. Community organizations have formed an organization, the Association of Community Organizations for Reform Now (ACORN), that helps local organizations intervene in the bank merger approval process.

---

In the OnBank case the activists had a one-shot opportunity—the required approval by the Federal Reserve Bank—to extract concessions from the bank. This made it relatively easy for the bank to "buy off" the activists, and since the bank had a strong incentive to resolve the issue and complete the merger, an agreement was reached quickly. RAN and Citigroup did not have a one-shot opportunity, and the discussions and negotiations were lengthy.

In cases where the stakes are high and monitoring of the firm's actions is difficult, the parties may require more than a simple agreement. To resolve issues of working conditions in factories in Southeast Asia, activists and footwear and apparel companies formed the Fair Labor Association (FLA) to govern working conditions in suppliers' factories. The FLA is considered in more detail in Chapter 22, but in brief it is a private governance institution established to maintain the agreement between the companies and the activists. The FLA has no enforcement powers, but it has informational powers stemming from its authority to inspect the working conditions in overseas factories and release its findings. The FLA is an institution of private regulation.

To monitor its agreement with Home Depot, RAN used local volunteers. With some training it is possible to distinguish lumber from old growth trees from lumber from younger trees. The volunteers then walked through Home Depot aisles visually checking the lumber and reporting to RAN on their findings. RAN's only enforcement mechanism, however, was the threat of relaunching its campaigns against the company.

## Challenging the Activists

The demands made in a campaign often are unreasonable or too costly to meet, and firms resist or fight back. Some firms decide that they will agree to disagree with the activist and bear whatever heat the activist can muster. A target of a campaign may also fight back. This may involve filing a lawsuit against the activist organization. BP, for example, filed a lawsuit against Greenpeace as a result of its boarding a drilling rig under tow to an exploration location. A lawsuit, however, carries the risk of creating a second media story.

When targeted by RAN, Boise Cascade wrote to all of RAN's donors and wrote to the Internal Revenue Service challenging the tax status of RAN. This strategy only developed sympathy for RAN, and Boise Cascade subsequently conceded to RAN's demands. Many firms, when opposing an activist campaign, choose not to attack the activist group but instead provide information about the issues in question in the hope of weakening public support for the campaign. A target may invest in reputation management by providing positive information about its record and making sure that employees are on board. Targets may also develop an alternative organization. The timber industry established the Sustainable Forest Initiative to implement forest management standards that were more practical and less costly than those of the activist-backed Forest Stewardship Council.

In some cases, a firm may change the boundaries of the organization. Boise Cascade eventually agreed to RAN's demands, but doing so was not costly to Boise because it was in the process of selling its entire timber operations to a private equity firm and becoming a consumer products company. A number of cosmetics and pharmaceutical companies stopped animal testing of their products because of protests and violence by PETA and other animal rights organizations. Some of those companies have farmed out their testing to independent companies, such as Huntingdon Life Sciences, which has become the subject of an intense and at times violent campaign by activists opposed to animal testing. SHAC (Stop Huntingdon Animal Cruelty) has targeted pharmaceutical companies that use Huntingdon. SHAC picketed the homes of Chiron executives, including sending a hearse to the house of a Chiron executive to pick up her very-alive body. SHAC also engaged in violence. Environmental extremists bombed Chiron's facilities. In 2004 the FBI arrested seven people for violence against Huntingdon and Chiron.

As indicated in the chapter case *Strategic Activism: The Rainforest Action Network*, the Center for the Defense of Free Enterprise (CDFE) and the Frontiers of Freedom Institute (FFI) portrayed RAN as an anticapitalist attack group that used intimidation, force, and unlawful actions and should therefore have its tax status revoked. The House Ways and Means Committee decided to hold a hearing on whether organizations that intentionally break laws should have their tax-free status withdrawn.

The opponents of activists have also sought to shed light on activists and their practices. Taking a page from the activists' book, opponents have begun to provide information on those who fund groups such as RAN.[14]

---

[14]See www.ngowatch.org, www.eco-terrorism.com, and www.activistcash.org.

Activists and NGOs have been criticized for being both "unelected" and unaccountable. They do not stand for election to allow the public to express its evaluation of their performance. They do not have to abide by governance requirements, such as Sarbanes-Oxley, considered in Chapter 18, that apply to firms. Some opponents of activists seek to apply Sarbanes-Oxley to NGOs and nonprofits. Independently of Sarbanes-Oxley many corporations issue public reports on their social activities, and those reports increasingly discuss shortcomings as well as accomplishments. For example, in 2004 the Gap released its first corporate social responsibility report, which revealed shortcomings in the practices of some of its overseas suppliers. NGOs typically do not report on their shortcomings.

Activists and NGOs could be accountable to the public, government, their members, and financial supporters. SustainAbility, Ltd., a London consulting firm, published a report (2002) "The 21st Century NGO: In the Market for Change," asking for greater public accountability. The American Enterprise Institute (AEI) started a Web site, http://ngowatch.org, to monitor NGO activity. Danielle Pletka, of the AEI, said, "It is in all of our interests to have NGOs, even NGOs we agree with, be accountable and transparent and have a role in international institutions that is clear to everybody. I don't think there's any disagreement from the left or the right."[15]

# Summary

Private politics takes place outside the arenas of government institutions and typically is intended to cause a firm to change its practices. Private politics is often led by activist organizations that attempt to advance issues on their agendas through direct pressure. Activists play an important role in the nonmarket environment because they can (1) alert management to issues of concern to others, (2) affect the organization of interests, (3) lead to changes in institutions in the nonmarket environment, and (4) provide information to the public and government officials.

Private politics strategies are frequently integrated with public politics strategies. A private politics strategy may be composed of target selection, actions to attract the media, and efforts to develop public support. These strategies may involve advocacy science, policy studies, and media strategies to bring issues to the attention of a broader public. Activist organizations frequently interact with each other, and some form networks. Activist organizations employ a variety of strategies to advance the issues on their agendas, and frequently those strategies are organized as a campaign. The objective is to shine the spotlight of public attention on the firm with the hope that attention will cause it to change its practices. This is often complemented by using public politics as a lever to encourage negotiations on the issue. An alternative private politics strategy is decentralized and centers on mobilizing individuals and local groups to take action, as in the case of a boycott. The framework presented in Figure 4-2 summarizes the strategy of many activist organizations.

In dealing with activist organizations, firms take a variety of approaches. Some ignore the issues and the activists in the hope that their interest will wane or that they will fail to generate broader support. Many negotiate directly with the activists, as in the OnBank case. Others collaborate with the activists to find a solution to the problems identified, as in the case of McDonald's and ED. When a firm believes that its practices are appropriate or that the activist group is weak, it may oppose the activists. Most firms, however, prefer to negotiate rather than become engaged in a protracted confrontation that could attract the attention of the media, the public, and government officials.

---

[15]*The New York Times,* January 3, 2004.

# Shell, Greenpeace, and Brent Spar

The North Sea was a mature petroleum province where several facilities had already been abandoned or were approaching the ends of their useful lives. There were about 400 offshore petroleum platforms in the North Sea, about half of which were in the United Kingdom sector. The removal of platforms was governed by a variety of international regulatory principles. According to the guidelines of the International Maritime Organization, any installation in shallow waters had to be completely removed and dismantled on land. A substantial portion (about 50 in UK waters) of the current installations, however, were in deeper water, and if approved, could be disposed of at sea. According to the British interpretation of international conventions and guidelines as well as UK legislation, operators had to submit their preferred disposal option, the Best Practical Environmental Option (BPEO), for government approval. Each such case for disposal then was individually considered on its merits. If the platforms were disposed of at sea, any remains had to be left at least 55 meters below the surface. Proposals had to be well documented and include a review of the options considered. The costs of abandonment were to be borne by the field licensee. Part of the cost (50 to 70 percent) was tax deductible.

## Royal Dutch/Shell

The Royal Dutch/Shell Group of Companies was a multinational holding of service and operating companies engaged in various branches of the oil, natural gas, chemicals, coal, and related businesses throughout the greater part of the world.[16] The parent companies, Royal Dutch Petroleum Company (domiciled in The Netherlands) and "Shell" Transport and Trading Company, plc (domiciled in the United Kingdom), did not themselves engage in operational activities. There were about 295,000 shareholders of Royal Dutch and

some 300,000 of Shell Transport. Royal Dutch and Shell Transport owned the shares in the Group Holding Companies, Shell Petroleum NV (The Netherlands), Shell Petroleum Company Limited (United Kingdom), and Shell Petroleum Inc. (USA). These Group Holding Companies held all Group interests in the operating companies, such as Shell UK and Shell Germany (Deutsche Shell AG). The management of each operating company, although bound by common standards, was fairly independent in its decision making and was responsible for the performance and long-term viability of its own operations. It could, however, draw on the experience and expertise of other operating companies.

By most international standards Royal Dutch/Shell was one of the most successful companies in the world. It was the largest corporation in Europe and the third largest in the world. In recent years Royal Dutch/Shell was Europe's most profitable company. Since 1992, however, it had been in the process of restructuring. One reason was that its return on capital lagged behind its main competitor, Exxon. According to C.A.J. Herkstroeter, president of the Group, the process of restructuring, although encouraging, was not yet satisfactory in terms of return on capital employed. Group companies had about 106,000 employees in 1994 (down from 117,000 in 1993). Its net income in 1994 was £4,070 million (up 36 percent from 1993), its return on capital was 10.4 percent (up from 7.9 percent from 1993), and its debt-to-capital ratio was 16.7 percent (down from 17.8 percent in 1993).

## The Issue—Disposal of Large Offshore Petroleum Facilities

The Brent Spar was a cylindrical buoy, 463 feet high and weighing about 14,500 tons. Between 1976 and 1991 it was used as an oil storage facility and tanker loading buoy for the Brent field (which along with Brent Spar was 50 percent owned by Esso AG, a unit

---

[16]Royal Dutch Petroleum Company, Annual Report, 1994.

of Exxon Corporation). In 1991 a review concluded that the necessary refurbishing of the facility was economically unjustifiable. Brent Spar was thus decommissioned in September 1991. Shell UK, one of the operating companies of the Royal Dutch/Shell Group, considered several disposal options. These options were evaluated according to engineering complexity, risk to health and safety of workforce, environmental impact, cost, and acceptability to the British authorities and other officially designated parties. The latter included government bodies such as the Scottish National Heritage and the Joint Nature Conservancy Committee, as well as "legitimate users of the sea" (as specified in the 1987 Petroleum Act), mainly fishermen's associations and British Telecom International.[17]

Two options survived the initial screening process: horizontal onshore dismantling and deepwater disposal. The former consisted of the rotation of the buoy to the horizontal, transport to shore, and onshore dismantling. The latter involved towing the structure to a deepwater disposal site in the Northeast Atlantic and sinking the platform. The study commissioned by Shell UK concluded that deepwater disposal dominated on the grounds of engineering complexity, risk to health and safety of the workforce, and cost (about £11 million versus £46 million). Both alternatives were acceptable to the other parties consulted.

With respect to possible environmental impacts, the study concluded that both options were equally balanced. Whereas the environmental impact was expected to be minimal for both options, horizontal dismantling (due to its considerably higher engineering complexity) would involve an increased potential for mishaps that, if one were to occur in shallow inshore water, could have a significant impact on other users of the sea. In addition, a research team at the University of Aberdeen recommended deep-sea disposal. Consequently, Shell UK proposed deepwater disposal as its BPEO to the British Department of Energy, the relevant regulatory agency. In mid-February 1995 the British Energy minister, Tim Eggart, announced that Shell's BPEO was accepted. The European governments were informed about the decision and were given 3 months to protest the decision. Although some of the European governments, including Germany, were generally critical of deep-sea

disposal, no government officially protested, and so Shell UK scheduled the towing of Brent Spar to the disposal site in the North Atlantic for mid-June.

## Greenpeace

Founded in 1971, Greenpeace had grown to be the world's largest environmental group. It had about 3.1 million contributors worldwide and a budget of about $140 million. Offices were located in 30 countries with a full-time staff of about 1,200. In addition, Greenpeace owned four ships, a helicopter, and modern communications equipment. It could also draw on a wide network of thousands of volunteers. In 1994 Greenpeace was forced to cut its budget by about 10 percent and dismiss more than 90 staff members because of a drop in contributions mainly due to Greenpeace USA's opposition to the Persian Gulf War. The Greenpeace offices were fairly independent but coordinated their decisions through Greenpeace International, located in Amsterdam. Greenpeace strongholds were in Germany, the Netherlands, and the United States.[18]

One of the largest and most active Greenpeace sections was in Germany. Greenpeace e.V. (Germany) had about 120 full-time staff members, a budget of roughly $50 million, and could rely on over 500,000 enlisted volunteers.[19] Its German headquarters and the North Sea logistic centers were located in Hamburg. Greenpeace enjoyed high acceptance and popularity among the German public and had frequently captured center stage through spectacular actions, which was reflected in donations that reached a record in 1994. Greenpeace Germany alone contributed over 40 percent of the total budget of Greenpeace International. Recently, Greenpeace Germany had also been active in developing alternative solutions to environmental problems.

One of Greenpeace's principal strategies was to attract the public's attention through high-profile, confrontational actions, which were covered by Greenpeace photographers and film crews. "We try to keep it simple," said Steve D'Esposito, an American who was executive director of Greenpeace International. "One, we raise environmental awareness. Two, we want to push the world toward solutions, using the most egregious examples. The

---

[17]Rudall Blanchard Associates Ltd. (for Shell UK Exploration and Production), Brent Spar Abandonment BPEO, December 1994.

[18]*Frankfurter Allgemeine Zeitung,* June 12, 1995.
[19]Interview with Harald Zindler, Greenpeace Germany, August 11, 1995.

whole point is to confront; we try to get in the way. Confrontation is critical to get coverage in the press or to reach the public some other way."[20]

## The Brent Spar Protests

After being informed about Shell UK's plans concerning Brent Spar in summer 1994, Greenpeace commissioned a policy study to consider the arguments for deep-sea disposal. The study concluded that total removal and not deep-sea disposal should be adopted as the BPEO, especially from the viewpoint of the environment.[21] By March, Greenpeace had devised a plan to board the Brent Spar. To win public support through television coverage, Greenpeace acquired satellite communications and video equipment.

On April 30, 1995, 14 Greenpeace activists from the United Kingdom, the Netherlands, and Germany landed on the Brent Spar by boat. They were joined by a group of nine journalists who with Greenpeace filmed the incident and broadcast it by satellite. After a 3-week occupation, the group was expelled by Shell. Although the UK media gave little coverage to the Greenpeace campaign, German television extensively broadcast footage of soaked activists. Harald Zindler, head of the section Campaigns of Greenpeace Germany, who organized the Brent Spar landing, recalled, "We were very happy when Shell decided to clear the platform. It portrayed Shell as an unresponsive and inconsiderate big business."[22] In response to the media coverage, expressions of outrage and protest in Germany and the Netherlands grew. Members of all German political parties and the German minister of the environment, Angelika Merkel, condemned Shell's decision to dump the rig in the deep sea. On May 22, the worker representatives on Shell Germany's supervisory board expressed "concern and outrage" at Shell's decision to "turn the sea into a trash pit."[23]

Under pressure, executives of Shell Germany met with Jochen Lorfelder of Greenpeace, who argued that 85 percent of German motorists would participate in a boycott. He told Shell that "in the four weeks it would take to tow the Brent Spar to its

dumping site, Greenpeace would make life a nightmare for Shell." The chairman of Shell Germany explained that Shell UK's studies indicated that deep-sea disposal was the best alternative for the environment. Lorfelder answered, "But Joe Six-Pack won't understand your technical details. All he knows is that if he dumps his can in a lake, he gets fined. So he can't understand how Shell can do this."[24]

On June 7 Greenpeace activists again landed on the Brent Spar but were soon expelled. The next day the Fourth International North Sea Conference began in Esbjerg, Denmark. One of the main topics was the disposal of petroleum facilities. Germany introduced a proposal that would rule out any disposal at sea. Norway, France, and the United Kingdom, however, blocked the proposal.[25] In the meantime, calls for an informal boycott of Shell by German motorists were mounting. Proponents included members of all German political parties, unions, motorists' associations, the Protestant Church, and the former chief justice of the German Constitutional Court, Ernst Benda.

In its media campaign, Greenpeace successfully appealed to the German enthusiasm for recycling. In their homes many Germans separated garbage into bags for metal, glass, paper, chemicals, plastic, and organic waste. Harald Zindler pointed out the appeal of Greenpeace's strategy to the general public: "The average citizen thinks: 'Here I am dutifully recycling my garbage, and there comes big business and simply dumps its trash into the ocean.'" Greenpeace always tried to keep its message simple and connect it to the public's everyday experiences and values.

Despite the mounting protests and another attempt by Greenpeace to board the rig, Shell began towing the Brent Spar to its dumping site on June 11 as scheduled. During the following week the boycott of German Shell gas stations was in full swing. Sales were off 20 to 30 percent[26] and in some areas up to 40 percent.[27] The mayor of Leipzig banned city vehicles from using Shell gasoline. Boycotts also spread to the Netherlands and Denmark. During the G7-summit at Halifax, Canada, German Chancellor Helmut Kohl criticized Shell and the British government for

[20]*The New York Times,* July 8, 1995.
[21]Simon Reddy (for Greenpeace International), No Grounds for Dumping, April 1995.
[22]Interview, August 11, 1995.
[23]*The Wall Street Journal,* July 7, 1995.

[24]*The Wall Street Journal,* July 7, 1995.
[25]Accepted proposals of this conference were non-binding.
[26]*The Wall Street Journal,* July 7, 1995.
[27]*Wirtschaftswoche,* June 22, 1995.

persisting with the proposed deep-sea dumping. Two days later a firebomb exploded at a Shell gas station in Hamburg.

Shell had used high-powered water cannons to keep a Greenpeace helicopter from approaching the Brent Spar, but on June 16, two Greenpeace activists again succeeded in landing on the rig by arriving before the water cannons had been turned on. They managed to stay on Brent Spar while the rig was being towed to its chosen disposal site. On June 19, the German economics minister, Guenther Rexrodt, announced that his ministry, too, would join the boycott. During this period the German public received inconsistent messages from Shell. Although Shell Germany suggested that the project could be halted, Shell UK refused to stop the towing. Meanwhile in the United Kingdom, Prime Minister John Major was repeatedly attacked in Parliament but refused to reconsider the government's decision to approve Shell's proposal.

## Shell's Climb Down

After a meeting of the Royal Dutch/Shell Group's managing directors in The Hague on June 20, Christopher Fay, chairman of Shell UK, announced that Shell would abandon its plans to sink the Brent Spar. Fay stressed that he still believed that deep-sea disposal offered the best environmental option but admitted that Shell UK had reached an "untenable position" because of its failure to convince other governments around the North Sea.[28] Shell UK would now attempt to dismantle the platform on land and sought approval from Norwegian authorities to anchor the Brent Spar temporarily in a fjord on the Norwegian coast.

The decision was received with joy by environmentalists and with an angry response by the British government. John Jennings, chairman of Shell Transport, apologized in a letter to the British Prime Minister. A variety of public relations experts criticized Shell's handling of the protests and its decision to abandon its original plans. Mike Beard, former president of the Institute of Public Relations, commented, "They failed to communicate the benefits of the course they believed to be right; they lost what they believed to be their case; and now

they're having to defend something they don't consider to be defensible."[29]

In response, Dick Parker, production director of Shell Expro, defended the company's decision not to involve environmental interest groups like Greenpeace: "Greenpeace does not have formal consultative status under the guidelines set out for an offshore installation proposal. Other bodies who represent a wide range of interests or who are accountable to their members are part of the process, and we consulted them."[30] Following the decision to halt the project, Shell started an advertising campaign admitting mistakes and promising change.

## Aftermath

In the June 29 issue of *Nature,* two British geologists at the University of London argued that the environmental effects of Shell UK's decision to dump the Brent Spar in the deep sea would "probably be minimal." Indeed, the metals of the Brent Spar might even be beneficial to the deep-sea environment. Disposing of the Brent Spar on land could pose greater risks to the environment.[31] Robert Sangeorge of the Switzerland-based Worldwide Fund for Nature said, "Deep-sea disposal seemed the least harmful option." He called the Brent Spar episode "a circus and sideshow that distracted from the big environmental issues affecting the world."[32] In response, however, a spokesperson for Shell UK reiterated that the company would stick to its decision to abandon deep-sea disposal.

The Brent Spar remained anchored in Erfjord, Norway. After an independent Norwegian inspection agency, Det Norske Veritas, had surveyed the contents of the Brent Spar, some doubts arose about Greenpeace's estimates of the oil sludge remaining on Brent Spar. Shell had previously estimated that the Spar contained about 100 tons of sludge. Greenpeace had estimated 5,000 tons. On September 5, Greenpeace UK's executive director, Lord Peter Melchett, admitted that the estimates were inaccurate and apologized to Christopher Fay. Shell UK welcomed the apology and announced its intention to

---

[28]*Financial Times,* June 21, 1995.

[29]*Financial Times,* June 23, 1995.
[30]Shell UK (Sarah James, ed.), Brent Spar, July 1995.
[31]E. G. Nisbet and C. M. R. Fowler. "Is Metal Disposal Toxic to Deep Oceans?" *Nature* 375:715, June 29, 1995.
[32]*The Wall Street Journal,* July 7, 1995.

include Greenpeace among those to be consulted in its review of options and the development of a new BPEO.[33] ∎

SOURCE: This case was prepared by Daniel Diermeier from public sources, including materials supplied by the Shell Petroleum Co. Ltd. (London, UK) and Greenpeace e.V. (Hamburg, Germany), as well as an interview with Harald Zindler, head of the section Campaigns (Bereichsleiter Aktionen) of Greenpeace Germany. Copyright © 1995 by Daniel Diermeier. All rights reserved. Reprinted with permission.

---

## PREPARATION QUESTIONS

1. From Shell UK's perspective, what was the issue in this case, and where was it in its issue life cycle?
2. In which institutional arenas was this issue addressed? Which interests were active on this issue?
3. Evaluate Shell UK's decision process in choosing a BPEO. Could it have effectively communicated its rationale for deep-sea disposal to the public? Was Shell UK right in abandoning its initial plan? How should Shell have managed the Brent Spar disposal? From the perspective of a major multinational corporation such as Royal Dutch/Shell, what strategy should be adopted to participate in, influence, and prepare for the development of this or similar issues? In what way, if any, might the organization structure of Shell have contributed to the Brent Spar debacle? Should the management of issues such as the disposal of the Brent Spar be centralized?
4. How did Greenpeace view this issue? What were its objectives and strategy? Why was it able to win the public opinion war? Could Greenpeace use the estimated costs of deep-sea and on-land disposal to its advantage? Why was Shell unable to explain its position and reasoning to the public?
5. Why did the German government not protest Shell's plan before the boycott? Why did the German government oppose deep-sea dumping? Why did the British government approve Shell's BPEO?
6. What should Shell UK do now about the Brent Spar?

---

[33] *Financial Times*, September 5–9, 1995.

# Nike in Southeast Asia

Phil Knight, chairman of the board and CEO, opened Nike's 1996 annual report with an account of the record revenues of $6.5 billion. One paragraph later, though, he added: "Yet no sooner had the great year ended than we were hit by a series of blasts from the media about our practices overseas." Nike had been widely criticized by labor and human rights groups over the working conditions and wages at its suppliers' factories in Asia. The media followed developments closely as revelations of sweatshops in the United States added to the public interest in Nike. *Doonesbury* likened Nike factories to Dickensian sweatshops.

Sourcing shoes from low-wage countries in Asia had been one of the foundations of the company's strategy. Nike had never owned a factory in Asia; instead the company contracted production from independent companies. Shoes and apparel thus were manufactured in independently owned and operated factories, and Nike took ownership of the product only when it left the factory. The factories were mostly owned by Korean and Taiwanese companies with whom Nike maintained long-term relationships.

In 1997 Nike bought the bulk of its shoes from China, Vietnam, and Indonesia. As the company's visibility increased, so did the scrutiny of its practices. Nike had to deal with allegations of subcontractors running sweatshops marked by poor working conditions, worker abuse, and below-subsistence wages. Shoes that sold for up to $140 were manufactured by workers earning about $2 a day in such countries as Vietnam and Indonesia.

Nike had contracts with a dozen factories in Indonesia in 1997, employing around 120,000 people. Both Nike's South Korean and Taiwanese manufacturing partners had come to Indonesia to take advantage of the low labor costs. In Nike audits, several incidents involving Korean and Taiwanese plant managers had been reported. The workers considered some managers too strict, or even abusive, shouting at or striking workers, or issuing punishments considered excessive for bad work or tardiness. In one case, a worker had to run laps around the factory because the shoes she assembled had defects.[34] Nike insisted that managers who were found to be abusive be transferred or removed. Employees and union activists from the Union of Needletrade, Industrial and Textile Employees (UNITE) in the United States confirmed that Nike's audits had been effective; at the Nikomas plant, for example, a security guard who hit a worker had been quickly fired by the owners.[35]

Underpayment of wages had led to several cases of unrest at Nike's Indonesian contract factories. In April 1997 workers at PT HASI staged a mass strike and protest. They demanded to be paid the new basic minimum monthly wage of 172,500 rupiah ($71.37), excluding allowances, that went into effect on April 1. A representative of the workers said that the company had included their "attendance" allowance in their basic wage, which meant that their minimum wage had actually stayed at last year's levels. The *Jakarta Post* quoted the personnel manager of the company as saying that because of its financial situation, it had been given permission by the manpower ministry to delay paying the 1997 minimum wage.

About 10,000 of the 13,000 workers at the factory marched 6 miles to the district parliament to demand the increase. Later in the week they burned cars and ransacked the factory's offices. The company then agreed to pay the minimum wage without including allowances for attendance, overtime, transport, holiday pay, and meals.[36] Nike claimed that its contract factories paid more than what most laborers would earn in other jobs. "We turn away more prospective employees than we could hire," Knight commented. "It sounds like a low wage and

it is. But it's a wage that's greater than they used to make."[37]

In Vietnam, Nike's footwear plants had been under attack by both workers and media since 1996 when a 29-year-old Korean forewoman at the Sam Yang factory lined up 15 female Vietnamese workers and beat them around the face with an unfinished shoe because she was angered by the quality of their work. Workers staged an immediate strike, and the forewoman was fired the same day. Later, she was found guilty in a Vietnam court of "humiliating" workers.[38] In another incident a Taiwanese manager from the Pao Chen factory forced 56 slow workers to run laps until a dozen fainted. The manager was sentenced to 6 months in prison for physically abusing workers.[39]

The monthly minimum wage at foreign-owned factories in Vietnam was $45 in 1997, compared with about $20 per month at state-owned factories. The Nike contract factories were believed to pay the minimum wage, but some had been accused of paying the workers less than this in the first 3 months of employment, which was illegal.

When it came to average per-capita income, cost of living, and the value of workers' benefits, statements from Nike and claims from human rights groups such as the Vietnam Labor Watch (VLW) differed. Although Nike said that the annual per-capita income in areas where Nike factories were located was $200, VLW claimed it was $925. A *San Jose Mercury News* investigation found the average to be $446 in the areas where 14 of the 15 factories were located. According to Nike, most workers saved enough of their salary to send money home to their families. VLW interviewed 35 workers, and none said they could save money. The *Mercury News* found that 12 of 24 workers could save money. Nike claimed that workers received free health care, whereas the VLW said workers' health insurance was deducted from their paychecks. The *Mercury News* found that employers, by law, deducted and contributed 1 percent of employees' salaries to government medical insurance.[40]

---

[34]"Sweatshops Haunt U.S. Consumers," *Business Week,* July 29, 1996.
[35]"Sweatshops Haunt U.S. Consumers," *Business Week,* July 29, 1996.
[36]"Workers Win Pay Raise at Nike Plant in Indonesia," *The Reuters Asia-Pacific Business Report,* April 23, 1997.

[37]"Protests as Nike CEO Addresses Stanford Students." *San Francisco Examiner,* April 30, 1997.
[38]"Culture Shock: Korean Employers Irk Vietnamese Workers," *Far Eastern Economic Review,* August 22, 1996.
[39]"Nike Aide in Vietnam Convicted," *The Wall Street Journal,* June 1997.
[40]"Nike's Fancy Footwork in Vietnam," *San Jose Mercury News,* June 25, 1997.

Nike had its first "Code of Conduct" for its contract factories in 1992, after the initial criticism of its labor practices in Asia. In a Memorandum of Understanding signed by all Nike contractors, the contractors were required to comply with all local government regulations, including those on occupational health and safety. Nike banned the use of forced labor, and required environmental responsibility, nondiscrimination, and equal opportunity practices. The rights of association and collective bargaining were to be guaranteed. Nike's production managers, who were stationed at the factories, monitored working conditions on a daily basis. Enforcement was not a problem according to Nike; many factories produced exclusively for Nike, which gave the company tremendous leverage. Beginning in 1994 Nike hired the Indonesian office of the international accounting firm Ernst & Young to monitor the plants for worker pay, safety conditions, and attitudes toward the job. The auditors were to pull workers off the assembly line at random and ask them questions that the workers would answer anonymously. In September 1997 Nike severed contracts with four factories in Indonesia that did not pay workers the minimum wage. This was the first time Nike had fired contractors for noncompliance with its code of conduct.

In 1996 Nike established a Labor Practices Department to monitor subcontracted manufacturing facilities and upgrade conditions for factory workers around the world. The creation of the department was "a further step in Nike's ongoing commitment to have products made only in the best facilities with the best working conditions in the sports and fitness industry." Specific emphasis would be on Indonesia, China, and Vietnam.[41]

Nike had long promised independent monitoring of its factories, and in February 1997 it hired Andrew Young, civil rights activist and former U.S. ambassador to the United Nations and mayor of Atlanta, to review its labor practices. The appointment received a mixed reception; Nike and Young emphasized his independence, but critics claimed he was hired to promote the company's image.

Young's report was released in June 1997 and called conditions in Nike's overseas factories comparable with those in U.S. factories. The report stated, "The factories that we visited which produce NIKE goods were clean, organized, adequately ventilated and well lit.... I found no evidence or pattern of widespread or systematic abuse or mistreatment of workers in the twelve factories." The Young report did not specifically address the wage issue, which Young considered too complex and beyond the capacity of his firm. Phil Knight said, "We will take action to improve in areas where he suggests we need to improve. For although his overall assessment is that we are doing a good job, good is not the standard Nike seeks in anything we do."[42] When the Young report was released, Nike took out full-page advertisements in major papers summarizing the key recommendations from the report.

The report was immediately criticized by human rights and labor groups. Thuyen Nguyen, director of VLW, noted that Young spent only 10 days visiting factories in China, Vietnam, and Indonesia; his tours were conducted by management, and he talked to workers through Nike interpreters. "Workers are not about to complain in front of the boss, especially in authoritarian countries where workers labeled troublemakers can be fired and jailed," wrote Nguyen.[43] Medea Benson, director of the human rights group Global Exchange, said, "I think it was an extremely shallow report. I was just amazed that he even admitted that he spent three hours in factories using Nike interpreters and then could come and say he did not find systematic abuse."[44]

In a letter to Phil Knight, a coalition of women's groups including the National Organization of Women, the Ms. Foundation for Women, the Black Women's Agenda, and the Coalition of Labor Union Women wrote, "While the women who wear Nike shoes in the United States are encouraged to perform their best, the Indonesian, Vietnamese, and Chinese women making the shoes often suffer from inadequate wages, corporal punishment, forced overtime, and/or sexual harassment."[45] Fifty-three members of Congress wrote to Phil Knight accusing Nike of "ruthlessly exploiting" workers. Knight invited the Congress members to visit the factories.

---

[41]"Nike Establishes Labor Practices Department," Canada NewsWire, October 3, 1996.

[42]*The New York Times*, June 25, 1997.
[43]"Report on Nike Work Force Glossed over Issues," Thuyen Nguyen. Letter, *The New York Times*, June 30, 1997.
[44]*The New York Times*, June 25, 1997.
[45]*The New York Times*, October 20, 1997.

The criticism and actions against Nike also occurred at the local level. Protesters distributed leaflets at a Nike-sponsored event at Stanford University where Phil Knight had received his MBA.

Five months after Andrew Young's report, the heat was turned up further when an audit by Ernst & Young, initially intended for Nike's internal use, was leaked to the media. The report revealed unsafe conditions at the Tae Kwang Vina Industrial Ltd. Factory in Vietnam, including chemical levels 6 to 177 times that allowed by Vietnamese regulations. The audit also stated that dust in the mixing room was 11 times the standard and that a high percent of the employees had respiratory problems. Major problems detailed in the report were the unprotected use of dangerous materials, poor air quality, and overtime-law violations. Over 75 percent of the workers in the factory were said to suffer from respiratory problems. Nike said that the shortcomings in the audit had been addressed.

The publicity surrounding labor practices was worrisome to Nike management. In some regions around the world, surveys showed that the bad publicity had affected consumers' perceptions of Nike. Consumers were used to considering Nike a leader in its field, but here the company was stumbling. Bob Wood, vice president of U.S. marketing, stated, "It's obviously not good. It's something that we're really concerned about, but we haven't noticed any literal decline in demand or sell-through of our products because of it."

Knight admitted that Nike had been ill prepared for the media offensive. "Our communications staff is woefully inadequate to deal with this problem right now," he explained. "Our Washington, DC, office essentially is one guy, and he's always dealt essentially with the [international] trade, with the quota issues." In 1997 Nike's public relations department had a staff of approximately 10 people. According to Knight, "They should probably have fifty people in there, but they have to be the right people, and organized right." Martha Benson, a Nike spokesperson in Asia, explained, "We are about sports, not Manufacturing 101."[46]

Phil Knight could not have been more sure that Nike was a force for positive change in Asia. "Whether you like Nike or don't like Nike, good corporations are the ones that lead these countries out of poverty," he said in an interview. "When we started in Japan, factory labor there was making $4 a day, which is basically what is being paid in Indonesia and being so strongly criticized today. Nobody today is saying, 'The poor old Japanese.' We watched it happen all over again in Taiwan and Korea, and now it's going on in Southeast Asia." ∎

## PREPARATION QUESTIONS

1. How serious are the criticisms of the practices in the factories of Nike's suppliers in Indonesia and Vietnam? Are Nike's sales likely to be hurt by the criticisms and the actions of activists?
2. How effectively has Nike addressed the sequence of episodes? Was hiring Andrew Young wise?
3. What, if anything, should Nike do about the wages paid in its suppliers' factories in Asia? Is Phil Knight right in saying that companies like Nike can "lead countries out of poverty"?
4. How should Nike deal with the inevitable continued scrutiny its practices will receive?

[46] *The Wall Street Journal,* September 26, 1997.

# Strategic Activism: The Rainforest Action Network

The Rainforest Action Network (RAN) worked "to protect the Earth's rainforests and support the rights of their inhabitants through education, grassroots organizing, and nonviolent direct action."[47] RAN accomplished its mission by organizing campaigns to redirect corporations away from the destruction and exploitation of nonsustainable forest resources. RAN worked with other non-governmental organizations (NGOs), student groups, and indigenous forest communities. Founded in 1985, RAN had 10,000 members and an annual budget of $2.0 million in 2003. RAN's three campaigns in 2004 were the Old Growth Campaign, the Global Finance Campaign, and Jumpstart Ford.

In its early years RAN's campaigns were often in direct support of indigenous communities or in direct opposition to specific projects. RAN would attempt to stop a company from carrying out a specific project but would not try to change the overall policies of the company or stop similar projects. For instance, RAN campaigned to drive Conoco out of the rainforests of Ecuador rather than drive Conoco out of endangered ecosystems worldwide. Although it was often successful in stopping destructive activities, such as a logging operation or road building, RAN was only stopping individual projects. RAN had some successful campaigns, such as convincing Burger King to stop selling rainforest beef, but Brune said, "RAN was losing the bigger battle and definitely losing the war."

In the mid-1990s RAN changed its strategy. Campaigns would be broader in scope—not focusing on a specific road or plant that RAN considered destructive but on the policies of a company, and eventually its industry. For greater impact RAN decided to target companies with established brands. RAN consolidated activities into two main campaigns—the Old Growth Campaign and Beyond Oil.

RAN took it as given that the public wanted to protect the environment. Board member Michael Klein said, "The amount of information on the environment is overwhelming. I still don't know if paper or plastic cups are better. Instead of trying to educate the public on this, like many other NGOs, we think it's easier to just tell people who the bad guy is."

In April 2003 RAN's board of directors appointed as executive director Michael Brune, the former campaigns director for the organization. Brune and the board of directors began a review of RAN's strategy and mission in light of the expanded scope of RAN's campaigns.

## RAN's Position among NGOs

NGOs were private, nonprofit organizations that typically focused on development, the environment, and human rights. Their activities included research, information distribution, training, community service, legal advocacy, public pressure, and civil disobedience. NGOs ranged in size from just a few people with a particular cause to national and international organizations with huge memberships.[48]

RAN characterized itself as a "responsible radical." Among the thousands of groups working for environmental and human rights, RAN was a radical organization, but one of the most stable and mainstream of such groups. Organizations more radical than RAN included antiglobalization and anticapitalism groups such as EarthFirst! and the Earth Liberation Front, which in 5 years carried out over 100 acts of violence, causing $37 million worth of damage, and was classified by the FBI as the leading domestic terror threat.[49] RAN, on the other hand, described itself as a peaceful organization and denounced violence. More mainstream NGOs than RAN included the World Wildlife Fund, the Sierra Club, and the Nature Conservancy.

RAN was significantly smaller than its more widely known peers. Although RAN and Greenpeace had similar styles, Greenpeace was a larger, international, and membership-based organization.

---

[47]www.ran.org, May 11, 2004.

[48]www2.ucsc.edu/atlas/glossary.html;bch-cbd.naturalsciences.be/belgium/glossary/glos_n.htm, May 17, 2004.

[49]http://abcnews.go.com/sections/us/DailyNews/elf010130.html.

| | Year | Revenues | Assets | Year | Members/Supporters |
|---|---|---|---|---|---|
| RAN | 2002 | $2.3 million | $1.6 million | 2004 | 10,000 |
| The Sierra Club | 2002 | $85 million | $45 million | 2004 | 700,000 |
| The Nature Conservancy | 2003 | $668 million | $3.7 billion | 2004 | 1 million |
| Greenpeace | 2002 | €165 million | €122 million | 2004 | 2.8 million |

## Public Politics or Private Politics?

Historically, most NGOs targeted governments to change public policy. RAN was one of the first organizations to target corporations solely with the objective of changing private policies that it viewed as destructive to the environment and, in particular, to rainforests. RAN differed from many other radical NGOs that used aggressive corporate campaigns in that it was willing to work with its target companies to find economically feasible ways for companies to meet its demands. Although RAN's demands might result in higher costs for a company, Klein said, "RAN is not out to hurt corporations. If the playing field is leveled across an industry, then corporations can still thrive and be successful."

RAN, however, was sometimes accused of being anticapitalist. George Landrith, executive director of the Frontiers of Freedom Institute,[50] called RAN "fundamentally radical, anticapitalist and lawless."[51]

RAN understood the importance of the marketplace and felt that change could better be achieved through corporations than through government—once industry leaders changed their practices, they would pressure government to change regulations to level the playing field. Brune said:

> The unique role of RAN is that while we engage in marches, banner hangs, and so on, we are not at the outside—we also sit with CEOs and negotiate agreements with the largest companies of the world. I'm as likely to give interviews to *The Wall Street Journal* as the *EarthFirst! Journal*.

### Campaigns and Commitment

RAN believed that praising a company that had good environmental policies would have little effect in inducing other companies to adopt similar policies. Instead, negative campaigns could catch the attention of the public, the media, and the target. RAN viewed companies with a public image and a strong brand as the most susceptible to its campaign tactics. RAN initiated a campaign with a letter to its target presenting a series of demands. Many of RAN's campaign tactics were designed to call public attention to companies whose actions and policies RAN deemed destructive. RAN hung banners ("banner hangs"), organized Days of Action, coordinated with other NGOs and student groups, paid for advertisements in publications such as *The New York Times*, and garnered media attention.[52] Some of its actions, such as trespassing and blocking access to roads or buildings, broke laws, resulting in arrests of protestors.

RAN differed from many NGOs in the duration of its campaigns. Many NGOs (including RAN before the mid-1990s) organized campaigns that lasted only a few months. RAN now sought to change practices in an entire sector, such as timber, and the changes it sought were often profound. Because of the scope of its objectives and the dramatic changes demanded, RAN committed 3 to 5 years to a campaign.

## RAN Campaigns

### Mitsubishi Campaign

In the 1990s RAN targeted Mitsubishi Corporation's role in rainforest harvesting in Asia. The Mitsubishi Corporation produced industrial products, and to pressure it, RAN targeted the U.S. operations of Mitsubishi Motors and Mitsubishi Electric, which

---

[50]According to the FFI' 10 tenets, "The environment is best protected and preserved where free markets thrive, capitalism is robust, and property rights are respected." www.ff.org/about/tentenets.html, May 13, 2004.

[51]Glen Martin, "Attack on tax status of environment group—Conservatives ask IRS for new ruling," www.sfgate.com, June 25, 2001.

[52]On a Day of Action anywhere from several dozen to over 100 demonstrations were conducted to raise awareness of an issue. Participants included RAN staff, volunteers, students, members of other NGOs, and concerned citizens. The activities on a Day of Action varied, depending on the campaign. Examples included passing out flyers in front of a store, delivering a letter to a store manager, and lockdowns, which could include shutting down a store, hanging banners, and commandeering a store's intercom system. RAN let local groups decide which activities to carry out.

were independent of Mitsubishi Corporation and not involved in the logging. The campaign lasted nearly 8 years and resulted in some new policies from both Mitsubishi Motors and Mitsubishi Electric and new forestry policies from Al-Pac, a Canadian subsidiary of Mitsubishi Corporation. RAN, however, failed to achieve the comprehensive policy from Mitsubishi Corporation it had sought.

### Beyond Oil Campaign

As part of its larger effort targeting the oil industry, in the 1990s RAN tried to protect the indigenous U'wa people from the harmful effects of planned oil exploration and development by Occidental Petroleum in Colombia rainforests. Because of the difficulty in gaining leverage over Occidental, the campaign failed to drive Occidental out of U'wa territory. In addition, RAN had no exit strategy, since stopping Occidental would not solve the problem—in fact, Occidental eventually abandoned its plans but sold the lease to a local company. That company drilled several exploratory wells but did not find oil.

Lessons from the Mitsubishi and Beyond Oil campaigns helped shape RAN's strategy for future campaigns. RAN learned that target selection was crucial—targets with a strong retail presence and brand identity and a "public face" would be much more susceptible to its campaigns.

### Old Growth Campaign

RAN was not against all logging, but wanted it to be sustainable. In 1992 RAN asked Home Depot to stop using old growth tropical timber. Little happened until 1997 when RAN initiated the Old Growth Campaign. After two years of the campaign, Home Depot agreed to stop selling wood from old growth forests. Within a year, 8 out of the top 10 retailers had followed suit. RAN then focused on the American home construction industry, and within 6 months, convinced three of the top five homebuilders not to build with old growth wood.

In 2000 RAN used its new market leverage to pressure the logging industry itself. Boise Cascade, a market leader in the timber industry, was RAN's next target. Boise countered by writing to RAN's supporters and filing a complaint with the IRS to revoke RAN's 501(c)(3) tax status. Recognizing that its attacks on RAN were ineffective, in 2002 Boise announced a new domestic policy to "no longer harvest timber from old-growth forests in the

United States" by 2004.[53] By mid-2004 the list of companies agreeing to stop using old growth pulp, paper, and lumber included Home Depot, Boise Cascade, Lowe's, Kinko's, 3M, IBM, Hallmark, and Hewlett-Packard, among hundreds of others.[54] RAN continued its campaign against other timber companies and forest product retailers, with Weyerhaeuser the next target.

## RAN's Strategy

### Campaign Strategies and Target Selection

As a relatively small NGO with limited resources, RAN needed leverage to have impact. RAN gained leverage by selecting as campaign targets large, brand-oriented, U.S.-based, multinational companies that were dominant in their industries. Describing why brand was important, Klein said, "Brand is about customers identifying with a corporation's set of values. As a result, global winners have, and need to defend, high standards." RAN did not use the term *boycott* because it was too difficult to demonstrate an effect on sales, just as it was difficult to demonstrate an endorsement effect. RAN instead referred to the impact on brand equity.

RAN's goal was to shift the practices of entire sectors, not just individual companies, so it relied on the ripple effect of targeting a market leader. RAN also tried to select targets that were the largest abusers in the industry, since they were "demonizable." After succeeding with its initial target, RAN would expand a campaign to include other companies in the industry with the objective of obtaining industry-wide change.

When formulating strategies for a campaign, RAN tried to understand the mind-set of its corporate target—its marketing and customers. Home Depot and Lowe's had very different market strategies for the home improvement market. Brune cited data showing that 70 percent of all home improvement decisions were made by women. Home Depot was oriented toward men. Its stores were busier and more muscular looking, with exposed ceilings, lots of steel, masculine orange colors, narrow aisles, and muted

---

[53]www.ran.org/about_ran/programs.html, May 10, 2004.
[54]In the spring of 1997 RAN targeted Kinko's. Within a few weeks RAN received a letter from Kinko's stating that RAN's demands were consistent with Kinko's environmental policies. In disbelief, RAN called Kinko's to argue for its demands. Kinko's was surprised that RAN was calling to argue, since its letter to RAN stated that it agreed with RAN—Kinko's would take this environmental issue seriously and would stop sourcing from old growth forests.

lighting. Home Depot took pride in skid marks on its floors. In contrast, Lowe's was tailored to women—its stores had wider aisles, better lighting, and softer colors, and its advertising was geared to women. RAN designed its campaign advertisements and materials for Lowe's principal clientele. Brune said:

> Women support environmental issues more strongly than men, so we knew that Lowe's would be sensitive to environmental pressure from RAN. So although we targeted Home Depot first because it was larger and growing faster, we knew that once Home Depot moved, Lowe's would not only match Home Depot's policies, but try to exceed them. We wanted them to compete against each other on their environmental values and compliance with policies. We expected leapfrogging, and that's exactly what happened.

Lowe's agreed to a new policy before RAN began its advertising.

Attracting media coverage was essential to pressuring companies and communicating with the public, RAN supporters, and donors. Much of RAN's media attention was "earned"—media coverage that RAN did not pay for, such as press coverage of Days of Action or articles written about campaigns. In addition, RAN paid for advertisements in newspapers and magazines.

RAN's style of campaigning was different from that of many NGOs. While publicly pressuring the target, RAN sought to negotiate agreements with the company to obtain policy changes that the target company could feasibly implement. After an agreement with a target company, RAN stopped its pressure tactics and publicly praised the target.

### Leveraging the Activist Network

RAN leveraged its resources by working with other NGOs and student groups. Enlisting students was particularly important to RAN's success—students at many universities were eager to participate in its campaigns. RAN campaigners traveled to campuses to spur interest and mobilize student groups. In addition RAN hired organizers from Green Corps, an organization that trained young environmental activists for future leadership.[55] Green Corps organizers were hired on a short-term basis to saturate campuses—educating students, organizing Days of Action, and

establishing groups (or relationships with existing student groups) with which RAN could coordinate after the organizers had gone.

Days of Action were also coordinated using "super organizers," which were affiliated with national student groups such as Free The Planet, the Student Environmental Action Coalition, Students Transforming and Resisting Corporations, and the Sierra Student Coalition. In the summer months, student groups held training programs. RAN provided training on conducting demonstrations, holding press conferences, and designing campaign materials, as well as informational updates on environmentally destructive activities. RAN worked with the student groups to organize Days of Action, which were then promoted by the groups throughout their own networks to boost participation.

### Work with Other NGOs

RAN typically engaged in grassroots activism to spur its corporate negotiations and often worked with other NGOs in a loosely coordinated but complementary manner. For instance, RAN would cite egregious wood sales from the Amazon or Congo Basin, while other organizations would push to create a demand for potential alternatives, such as certified, ecologically sustainable wood products.

RAN worked with a diverse coalition to support its long-term campaign goals. Many of its campaign allies had similar long-term objectives and worked in close collaboration with RAN on its campaigns. Other organizations, such as the World Wildlife Fund, World Resources Institute, and the Nature Conservancy, often took a less confrontational approach, making close partnership difficult. However, these groups and RAN shared a commitment to conservation and thus worked together on a more limited set of issues, such as promoting certified wood products or criticizing Bush administration policies.

NGOs addressing the same concerns sometimes found themselves on opposite sides. In the Old Growth Campaign environmentalists and logging companies battled over which of two groups should certify wood as coming from forests managed with certain minimum social, environmental, and conservation practices. Two certification systems were established. The Forest Stewardship Council (FSC) was supported by RAN, Greenpeace, the Sierra Club, and other NGOs. The Sustainable Forestry Institute (SFI) was supported by the logging industry. Advisors to the SFI included Conservation International and

---

[55]Green Corps had historically been politically aggressive but had not promoted civil disobedience.

the Nature Conservancy, much to the chagrin of other environmental organizations. Brune said the SFI was like "the fox guarding the henhouse."[56]

### Training

Training was important to prevent activists from getting hurt and ensure that campaign activities were carried out without negatively affecting the public perception of RAN. RAN offered training to staff and volunteers, and it contracted with the Ruckus Society to coordinate some of its activist training camps. Ruckus was an independent organization that trained individuals and local groups to protest. Training provided by Ruckus helped RAN with high-profile direct actions or acts of civil disobedience, such as banner hangs and blockades. Training included tactics for nonviolent acts of civil disobedience, earning media coverage, fundraising, grassroots organizing, facilitation, delivering meaningful sound bites, climbing buildings for banners hangs, calming angry protestors, dealing with nervous police, and conducting surveillance.[57]

Civil disobedience—such as scaling buildings, chaining oneself to the doors of a bank branch with U-locks or Kryptonite chains, and blocking entrances with concrete filled barrels—was usually conducted by RAN employees, the Ruckus Society, or most often by volunteer activists trained by RAN or Ruckus. Such activities were not always controlled by RAN—for instance, a student group in Illinois that decided to shut down local Home Depot stores on a Saturday may have told RAN about their plans or may have done it autonomously, possibly without proper training.

## Nonmarket Assets

### Competencies

Once RAN achieved success with a target, the target sometimes acted as an ally. During the Old Growth Campaign, after Lowe's had agreed to stop sourcing old growth products, Lowe's hosted meetings between RAN and Boise Cascade to help move those negotiations along. Kinko's stopped purchasing from Boise Cascade. This helped spread RAN's policies throughout the industry. Brune said, "RAN's power base is not the size of our member base, but our wins with Home Depot, Lowe's, Boise Cascade, and others. We have a non-traditional source of power because Home Depot and the others act as surrogates or partners."

RAN also occasionally received assistance from employees of the target who were sympathetic to its campaign goals. A Home Depot employee gave RAN the intercom code used in all its stores. Brune and others went into stores, entered the intercom code, and recorded messages such as "Lumber from old-growth forests is on sale on Aisle 3," or "Tropical lauan from the habitat of the orangutan and Sumatran tiger on sale on Aisle 4." The intercom system provided an opportunity to review a message before it was broadcast. Activists thus could be gone with their shopping carts before the message was broadcast or be in another aisle recording another message, making it difficult for Home Depot personnel to find them. This was repeated by dozens of activists in stores across the United States.

### Resources

RAN's budget had been relatively constant for years, in the $2 to $3 million range. Over half of RAN's income went for staff; over one quarter, for additional campaign expenses; and the remainder covered overhead and administrative expenses. Although needs varied, about $1 million per year was needed per campaign. RAN's budget increased to $2.4 million for 2004, and Brune expected it to reach $5 million over the next 5 years. To meet its budget growth, RAN had to boost its fundraising.

RAN raised funds from membership dues, wealthy donors, and grants from foundations, such as the Ford Foundation, Rockefeller Brothers Fund, Ruben & Elisabeth Rausing Trust, Educational Foundation of America, Tides Foundation, and Wallace Global Fund. RAN did not accept contributions from its targets or from corporations, with the exception of a few "friends of RAN," which included small businesses with environmentally friendly policies.

With its existing resources RAN was stretched to run three campaigns. James Gollin, chair of RAN's board, said "On a scale of 1 to 10, RAN is an 11 or 12 in goal achievement, but only a 3 for fundraising—RAN has a great product, but does not have a representative amount of the dollars raised for environmental work." Gollin was not sure this was a problem, however. More money would enable RAN to run more campaigns, pay for more ads, and

---

[56]Efforts to reduce support for SFI were organized under the www.dontbuysfi.com/ Web site.
[57]www.ruckus.org/training/, May 10, 2004; David Postman, "Protestors hit training camp to prepare for WTO meeting," *The Seattle Times*, September 20, 1999.

train more protestors, but Gollin thought RAN was successful in part because it was lean, mean, and focused on campaigns about which it felt strongly.

### Organization

In 2004 RAN had about two dozen employees, all in the United States. RAN's staff was organized into four departments: operations, development (fundraising), communications, and campaigns. Within the campaigns department RAN typically had a director for each campaign and used an organizing staff of about five to support the campaigns collectively. To supplement its limited resources, RAN relied on volunteers. RAN did not have a lawyer on its staff and relied on pro bono lawyers for legal work and for representing arrested staff members.

Although RAN was located in the United States, its reach was broader. RAN was allied with local groups in other countries that would report on activities such as harvesting rainforests. RAN put that information, along with pictures, on its Web site. Activist groups in other countries also joined in Days of Action.

RAN's board of directors oversaw the organization—choosing the executive director, directing and supporting the general mission, supporting fundraising efforts, helping with some negotiations, and offering campaign ideas. The board was generally hands-off, meeting once a quarter, and delegated day-to-day activities, including staffing, to the executive director. Some board members filled specific functional roles, such as finance, accounting, governance, and communications. Other board members were more general strategists and idea generators.

Board members were usually consulted at some stages of negotiations with campaign targets. Brune and the campaign director typically sent the first and last drafts of negotiation agreements to the board. In addition, Brune worked closely with three or four board members discussing the negotiations and strategies as campaigns progressed. Draft campaign demands, campaign strategies, and agreements were sent to the board for input, but not for approval.

### Victory, Monitoring, and Enforcement

At the beginning of a campaign RAN laid out demands and the goals it hoped to achieve. RAN typically declared victory and praised the target company not when all of the goals were achieved, but when significant and notable progress was made. RAN wanted to reward steps in the right direction, occasionally to the chagrin of more radical activists.

Since an agreement between RAN and a target was not legally enforceable, RAN relied on the threat of resuming its campaign if the company did not adhere to its new policies or make the needed improvements. RAN had not had to restart a campaign against any of its targets.

Monitoring of agreements was performed differently for each campaign. For the Old Growth Campaign, RAN trained local volunteers to spot old growth lumber in Home Depot stores. These volunteers periodically walked up and down store aisles to examine the lumber and reported back to RAN if they found old growth products.

### Selecting the Agenda

In spring 2003 RAN launched a campaign—the Clean Car Campaign, beginning with Jumpstart Ford—that was seemingly far from its mission to protect rainforests. RAN partnered with Global Exchange, a comparably sized activist group that had focused on human rights issues. They wrote to CEO Bill Ford stating that the United States had a fuel addiction and that the Ford Motor Company was harming the climate, forests, and national security. RAN asked Ford to attain an average fleet fuel economy of 50 mpg by 2010 and stop producing vehicles that emitted greenhouse gases at the tailpipe by 2020. RAN recognized that the federal government would not significantly increase fuel economy standards, so it turned to private politics.

RAN hired Jacob Harold as an independent contractor for 3 months to launch the Jumpstart Ford campaign, culminating with Ford's 100th anniversary shareholder meeting on June 16, 2003. Harold created marketing materials, worked to build a network and relationships with other NGOs targeting Ford, met with ex–Ford insiders to learn the dynamics of the organization, organized activities to coincide with Ford's shareholder meeting, and developed a 2- to 3-year campaign strategy. Some of the activities RAN organized included a banner hang (in which Ruckus assisted and a number of activists were arrested) at Ford's 100th anniversary celebration festivities in Dearborn. Across the street from Ford's celebrations they inflated a 100-foot dinosaur with the slogan, "I love guzzling gas." RAN also organized a small protest and handed out thousands of flyers that illustrated a 25 mpg Model T and a 12 mpg Ford

Expedition. Harold also met with Ford personnel and spoke at Ford's annual meeting, questioning Bill Ford and the board on fuel economy. After the meeting, Ford's chief of security thanked Harold for his professionalism. RAN expected the campaign to last as long as 5 years and planned to take the campaign to other companies once it achieved success with Ford.

When RAN decided to target an automaker for contributing to global climate change, it considered Ford, General Motors, and Chrysler. Ford was selected for a number of reasons. Naming Bill Ford personally was viewed as an advantage, since it gave him the opportunity to become a leader—Bill Ford thought of himself as both an industrialist and an environmentalist. Ford also had broken a promise to improve SUV fuel economy by 25 percent by mid-decade, and according to Brune, the company had the worst fuel economy of any of the world's major automakers. Ford was also the target of other NGOs, such as the Sierra Club, Bluewater Network, and Global Exchange, among others, and RAN believed that multiple voices, demands, and strategies would help. Ford also had a concentrated brand, unlike GM. Brand targeting was a key part of RAN's strategy, and communicating with the public on all of GM's brands—Chevrolet, Pontiac, Buick, Cadillac, GMC, Oldsmobile, Saturn, Hummer, and Saab—would have been difficult.

The NGOs targeting Ford had different strategies and goals, and although they shared thoughts on the campaigns, they stopped short of integrating their strategies. RAN, for example, talked frequently with the Sierra Club and the Bluewater Network about their campaign plans, but they did not join in campaign activities.

## Strategy Review

RAN was founded with the goal of protecting tropical rainforests. Over time, its campaigns expanded to include temperate rainforests (e.g., in British Columbia and the Pacific Northwest) and old growth forests, some of which were not rainforests (e.g., public lands in Idaho and Montana, or national forests in the Rocky Mountains). As RAN's campaign scope broadened beyond forests with the Jumpstart Ford campaign, the board and Brune decided to review its mission statement and strategy. Brune said:

> We were considering expanding the mission statement to state that RAN's primary strategy is to transform the global marketplace in order to preserve forests and their inhabitants; and

also to expand beyond forests to include all natural systems that sustain life, whether it be clean air, clean water, or climate. So although RAN would be rooted in forests, RAN would also look at other issues that might have a long-term impact on forests.

Brune wanted not only to update the mission statement to reflect RAN's current work, but to look ahead to the next 10 years and encompass future work that might be broader in scope—to enable RAN to work on climate and energy issues in a manner consistent with its core competencies and the threat of climate change to rainforests and other ecosystems.

## Challenges

### Finding Opportunities

RAN's biggest challenge would be picking future campaigns for which RAN could have significant impact. Klein said, "The easy targets are disappearing." As a result, RAN was broadening its mission to allow for evolution.

### Jumpstart Ford: A Campaign Too Far?

What RAN and Global Exchange asked of Ford was considerably more aggressive than what RAN had asked of companies in the Old Growth and other campaigns. While the demands were believed to be technologically feasible, they were economically very demanding—some might say impossible. Ford already faced financial problems and was struggling to sell more cars. RAN's campaign position was that Ford could not afford not to make changes—RAN tried to tie Ford's fiscal health to its environmental performance. Brune said, "In order not to lose market share to Japanese automakers, Ford will have to innovate and produce cars that are more compelling to the public. Hybrid engines should not just be a niche market, but should be incorporated into all engines." Ford planned to market an Escape SUV hybrid for model year 2005, but a hybrid generally cost $3,000 to $5,000 more than a vehicle with a standard engine.

### House Ways and Means Oversight Investigation

Nonprofit organizations were either 501(c)(3) or 501(c)(4) organizations.[58] The 501(c)(3) organizations were tax-exempt, and donations to them were

---

[58] RAN, Greenpeace, and the Nature Conservancy were 501(c)(3) organizations. The Sierra Club had given up its 501(c)(3) status, opting for a 501(c)(4) status instead, since it lobbied government and endorsed candidates for public offices.

tax deductible by the donors. These organizations included charities, schools, and hospitals, with missions to educate and provide services to the public. The 501(c)(4) category was used for organizations that lobbied. They were also tax-exempt, but donations to them were not tax deductible by donors.[59]

The Center for the Defense of Free Enterprise (CDFE) and the Frontiers of Freedom Institute (FFI) portrayed RAN as an anticapitalist attack group that used intimidation, force, and unlawful actions and should therefore have its 501(c)(3) tax status revoked.[60] Starting in 2001 (coinciding with RAN's actions against Boise Cascade as part of the Old Growth Campaign), the CDFE and FFI asked the IRS to review RAN's tax status.

As a result of the CDFE and FFI efforts, the House Ways and Means Subcommittee on Oversight subpoenaed RAN at the end of 2003, demanding all e-mails, newspaper articles, board minutes, Web site entries, and press releases. RAN complied but blacked out the names and addresses of individuals. Brune said, "Nonviolent direct action is in RAN's mission statement. We decided it wasn't effective to fight the subpoena and are anxious to make our case that civil disobedience should be embraced as a vital part of a democratic society."[61] Addressing this issue took time and money, neither of which RAN had in abundance. The subcommittee was considering whether organizations that performed acts of civil disobedience should be eligible for any tax benefit status—including both 501(c)(3) and 501(c)(4).

Revocation of 501(c)(3) and 501(c)(4) tax statuses would be devastating to NGOs involved in civil disobedience, including RAN.

### High Turnover

Brune said, "Turnover is high at RAN but has been better in the last year. Still, half of our staff will be gone by the time the Ford campaign is done." The high turnover was not unique to RAN. Staff members at cause-related NGOs tended to work hard and immerse themselves emotionally in their work, which often resulted in burnout and required breaks from work. Turnover was also a function of demographics—NGO staff members tended to be young, in their 20s or early 30s, and life changes such as marriage or graduate school often led to resignations or movements from one NGO to another. In addition, Brune said, "NGOs tend to pay barely enough money for staff to afford beer, pizza, and a couch in a friend's apartment." RAN tried to improve the lifestyle of its employees and reduce turnover by raising wages, improving health care, and instituting family leaves, among other practices. ∎

SOURCE: This is an abridged version of a case written by Research Associate Erin Yurday, Cornell MBA 1998, under the supervision of David P. Baron. This case would not have been possible without the help of Michael Brune, James Gollin, Michael Klein, and Jacob Harold. Copyright © 2004 by the Board of Trustees of the Leland Stanford Junior University. All rights reserved. Reprinted with permission.

---

### PREPARATION QUESTIONS

1. Should RAN expand its mission to include any additional issues such as agribusiness, water, climate, corporate responsibility and power, genetically modified organisms, overall levels of consumption, and soon.? If so, how should RAN attract new funding? Should it raise funds using the Internet as moveon.org has successfully done? Should RAN use offshoot organizations, such as local chapters, to grow membership and dues and boost fundraising? Might a larger membership be a more conservative membership?

2. What has made RAN and its strategy effective? What changes, if any, should it make in its strategy? If RAN expanded its mission or changed its strategy, what additional competencies should it build?

3. Given the long time horizon of its campaigns and its limited number of campaigns, target selection was crucial for RAN. Was Ford a good target?

4. As CEO of a potential target, should you take preemptive steps to avoid targeting by RAN or one of its peers? Which steps?

---

[59]"Logging Giant Boise Cascade and Anti-Environment Activists on the Attack Against Rainforest Action Network," RAN Press Release, June 21, 2001.
[60]Ibid.
[61]Ellen Komp, "Rainforest Action Network Targeted in Congressional Probe," www.civilliberties.org/RAN.html, May 10, 2004.

# Anatomy of a Corporate Campaign: Rainforest Action Network and Citigroup (A)

Citigroup, the world's largest project finance bank, provided financing for extractive projects such as mining, logging, and oil exploration. Some of these projects took place in developing countries and in rainforests and other endangered ecosystems. In 2000 the Rainforest Action Network (RAN) launched its Global Finance Campaign with Citigroup as the target. The goal was to convince Citigroup, and eventually all lenders, to stop financing destructive activities in endangered ecosystems.

Project finance referred to the financing of long-term industrial (e.g., pulp and paper mills), public service, and infrastructure (e.g., telecommunications) projects. The cash flows generated by a project were used to repay the debt financing.[1]

Creditors did not have recourse to the project companies (contractors) for failure to repay the debt—only to a project's specific assets, rights, and interests, which served as collateral for the funding. Most project finance deals were highly leveraged with project companies providing 20 to 40 percent of the required funds as equity. Typically, a lead bank arranged a project's financing and then opened the deal to participation by other banks and investors. The project finance market peaked in 2000, when $379 billion was funded globally.

## Extractive Projects and Rainforests

Environmental NGOs (non-governmental organizations) had historically targeted logging and mining companies directly. In the late 1990s, however, some environmental activist organizations, such as RAN, began to focus on the commercial banks financing extractive industries. The objective was to cut off funding for projects that led to the destruction of rainforests in developing countries. Through project finance, revolving credit facilities, or general corporate loans, many banks funded the extraction of timber, wood pulp, wood chip, and oil, in addition to open-pit mining for ores and land clearing for cattle farming, all of which contributed to the destruction of rainforests.

Tropical rainforests received between 4 and 8 meters of rain a year. Rainforests covered only 2 percent of the Earth's surface, yet they housed about half of the world's 5 to 10 million plant and animal species. According to the National Academy of Science, a 4-square-mile area of rainforest typically housed 1,500 species of flowering plants, 750 of trees, 125 of mammals, 400 of birds, 100 of reptiles, 60 of amphibians, and 150 of butterflies. Drugs for cancer treatment, heart problems, arthritis, and birth control came (in some cases exclusively) from rainforest plants. Rainforests also held years and years of carbon buildup in their vegetation. When this vegetation was burned or cut and left to decay, the carbon was released as $CO_2$. $CO_2$ released in this manner was the second largest factor contributing to the greenhouse effect.

The primary rainforests in India, Bangladesh, Sri Lanka, and Haiti had been destroyed. By 1985, 55 and 45 percent, respectively, of the Philippines' and Thailand's rainforests had been destroyed. According to the National Academy of Science, over 50 million acres of rainforest were destroyed a year.

[1]Michelle Chan-Fishel, "Project Finance Trends: Key players, regions, and sectors," Friends of the Earth-US, September 22, 2003.

**131**

# The Rainforest Action Network

RAN was founded in 1985 with the mission of protecting tropical rainforests and the human rights of people living in them. RAN used tools such as citizen protests, media, nonviolent civil disobedience, and publications to bring awareness to the issues and pressure governments, corporations, and lending institutions. RAN had about two dozen employees, all in the United States, organized in three departments: operations, development (fundraising), and campaigns. RAN had a full-time media specialist who interacted with the news media and participated in campaign planning. Within the campaigns department, RAN typically had a campaign manager for each campaign and used an organizing staff of about five to support whichever campaign was active at the time.

In the mid-1990s RAN changed its focus from public policy to the private sector with the objective of changing the practices of companies with environmentally destructive practices. RAN executive director Michael Brune said, "Companies were more responsive to public opinion than certain legislatures were. We felt we could create more democracy in the marketplace than in the government."

# RAN's Global Finance Campaign

## Selecting a Target

In late 1999 RAN was concluding a successful 2-year campaign (led by Brune) targeting Home Depot, which had agreed to end by 2003 the sale of wood from endangered forests. For the Global Finance Campaign, RAN planned to use a model similar to the one used for Home Depot—target a large, brand-oriented, U.S.-based multinational company that had a strong retail presence, was a leader in its industry, and had a key role in facilitating the destruction of old growth forests and supporting extractive industries. Because RAN was a small organization with the goal of shifting the practices of entire sectors, not just individual companies, it relied on the ripple effect of targeting a market leader.

One company stood out as the best target— Citigroup, the world's largest bank. Citigroup was the leading global, emerging market project finance bank, and developing country project finance bank. Citigroup also had a key role in a number of specific projects that alarmed RAN, such as the Camisea pipeline in Peru (Citigroup was the financial advisor

on the project but did not directly fund it) and the Chad-Cameroon pipeline under construction by ExxonMobil, Chevron, and a consortium of central African oil companies.[2] In researching Citigroup's involvement, RAN relied on data from Dealogic's ProjectWare, a database of project finance deals.

In 2000 Citigroup had net income of $13.5 billion on revenues of $111.8 billion and had customers in over 100 countries and territories. Citigroup's activities included global consumer banking, global corporate and investment banking, global investment management and private banking, and investment activities. Citigroup's global consumer group offered banking, lending, investment services, and credit cards to customers in over 50 countries and territories. The global consumer group reported core net income of $5.3 billion on $30.4 billion of revenues in 2000.[3]

Citigroup had a public image and a brand to protect (in particular, its large consumer banking operation and credit card business), which made it an attractive target. Ilyse Hogue, RAN's campaign manager for the Global Finance Campaign, said:

> Citigroup had poured $100 million into its brand image, most recently on its "Live Richly" marketing campaign, which was predicated on the notion that "there is more to life than money." We saw a company that was investing a lot in making the public believe that they operated in line with common social values. Part of Citi's vulnerability was the juxtaposition of what it articulated to the public with what we saw on the ground from Citi's finance activities.

RAN began the campaign expecting it to last up to 5 years but hoping to win in 3 years. RAN dedicated three staff members, including Hogue, full time to the Global Finance Campaign.

RAN had such limited resources and Citigroup was such a large target that many people thought RAN could not win the campaign. RAN believed, however, that Citigroup's vulnerability was its sensitivity to public opinion, so exploiting that vulnerability by publicizing Citigroup's environmental practices became the heart of RAN's strategy.

---

[2]For years RAN had developed relationships with allies (e.g., other NGOs, indigenous federations, and others) on the front lines of the affected areas. These allies kept RAN apprised of project developments and enabled it to track the projects and their financing.
[3]Citigroup Inc. 2000 Annual Report.

## RAN's Strategy during the First Two Years of the Campaign[4]

In developing its strategy, RAN drew heavily on past campaigns and consulted with allies that had interacted with Citigroup and were interested in helping. RAN dubbed Citibank the "World's Most Destructive Bank" and on April 13, 2000 wrote to Citigroup CEO Sandy Weill, asking the company to recognize its role in, and take action to address, the destruction of the world's old-growth forests and acceleration of climate change. As with most of RAN's campaigns, this introductory letter presented the issues and a set of demands. Five days later a group of RAN campaigners addressed the board of directors and Sandy Weill at Citigroup's annual meeting, voicing their concerns in front of a room of shareholders. On April 19, Citigroup agreed to meet with RAN to discuss its connection with the fossil fuel and forest industries. Citigroup, however, took no action to address the issues.

After Citigroup's annual meeting, RAN organized a 3-day strategic brainstorming session, attended by about 20 ally organizations, to generate ideas, increase awareness, and spur interest in the campaign. Some of RAN's strategies included shareholder resolutions, high-profile media attention, paid advertisements, Days of Action with student networks, disruptions of Citibank branches, and other nonviolent civil disobedience (e.g., banner hangs). Hogue believed the media was one of the best arrows in RAN's quiver when going after a target's brand image.

In September 2000 RAN launched the campaign on college campuses, encouraging a boycott of Citigroup credit cards and job recruitment. Many of RAN's actions were designed to call the public's attention to the campaign objectives and attract media coverage, which was essential to informing the public. In October, RAN organized a Day of Action that included demonstrations in which participants cut up their Citibank credit cards and closed their Citibank accounts. In December, carolers gathered at Citigroup's headquarters and sang "Oil Wells" to the tune of "Jingle Bells." The campaign also targeted Sandy Weill. For Valentine's Day 2001, Weill received hundreds of valentines, asking him to show the Earth some love and stop funding rainforest destruction. April 2001 saw the second Day of Action, with 80 actions in 12 countries on five continents. The actions included hanging banners, marches, and leaving symbolic piles of wood chips and oil at Citibank branches. Also in April, 500 schoolchildren sent drawings to Weill asking him to stop funding rainforest destruction. In October, an oil pipeline under construction in an Ecuadorian cloudforest reserve was obstructed by dozens of indigenous women and children. Students across the United States gathered at local Citibank branches, bringing pledges from 12,000 students who refused to do business with the "#1 funder of global warming." In February 2002 students at 60 U.S. colleges participated in a National Student Week of Action, which included demonstrations as well as telephone calls and letters delivered to Citigroup.[5]

Much of RAN's media attention was "earned"— media coverage that RAN did not pay for, such as press coverage of Days of Action or articles written about the Global Finance Campaign. In addition, RAN paid for a number of advertisements in various newspapers and magazines criticizing Citigroup and challenging it to take leadership in protecting the environment.

Enlisting students was important to the success of the campaign, and RAN found that students at many universities were eager to participate. To mobilize student groups, RAN campaigners traveled to campuses to spur interest in the campaign. In addition, RAN hired organizers from Green Corps, an organization that trained young environmental activists to become future leaders. Green Corps had historically been politically aggressive but had not promoted the use of civil disobedience. Green Corps organizers were hired on a short-term basis and saturated campuses—educating students, organizing Days of Action, and establishing groups (or relationships with existing student groups) with which RAN could coordinate.

Students at Columbia University, through SEEJ (Students for Environmental and Economic Justice), played a significant role in the campaign over time. Citigroup had a substantial presence at Columbia— it had an affinity agreement with Columbia, and Citigroup's logo appeared on student identification cards. Nearly 4,000 Columbia students opened accounts with Citibank each year.[6]

RAN's ability to gain the support of young people, such as college students, was critical in getting

---

[4]www.ran.org

[5]During campaign activities, no activists were injured or served jail time. However, there were many arrests—of RAN staff, students, concerned citizens, and volunteers. Arrests sometimes led to fines or community service, but most charges were dropped.
[6]"SEEJ Members Influence Citigroup Corporate Agenda," *Columbia Daily Spectator,* February 3, 2004.

Citigroup's attention. Many students refused Citibank credit cards as a result of the campaign and wrote letters to Citigroup to that effect. Hogue said, "Cards issued to college students are kind of a gateway drug, in Citigroup's mind. If Citigroup breeds brand loyalty by issuing credit cards to young people, then Citigroup has their business for college loans, mortgages, their kids' college, and retirement."

During the first 2 years of the campaign, RAN met frequently with Citigroup to discuss the issues—the difficulty was getting any real response or action from Citigroup. RAN was clearly frustrated by the lack of progress.

## Response from Citigroup

Citigroup had assigned its vice president of community relations to interact with RAN, although she initially delegated day-to-day communications with RAN to others. Community relations typically dealt with issues like community reinvestment and partnering with Habitat for Humanity. As the campaign wore on, the vice president, who had a long tenure at Citigroup and was highly respected, began to develop expertise on project-finance and environmental issues.

After 2 years of campaign activity and regular meetings with RAN, Citigroup had to decide what to do about the RAN campaign.

SOURCE: This is an abridged version of a case written by Research Associate Erin Yurday, Cornell MBA 1998, under the supervision of David P. Baron. This case would not have been possible without the help of Mike Brune and Ilyse Hogue of Rainforest Action Network. Copyright © 2004 by the Board of Trustees of the Leland Stanford Junior University. All rights reserved. Reprinted with permission.

## PREPARATION QUESTIONS

1. Identify the issues, interests, institutions, and information characterizing this nonmarket situation.
2. Was it strategically wise for RAN to launch a campaign on project finance? Can RAN realistically expect to affect project finance, which is provided by banks around the world?
3. Was Citigroup a good or bad target for RAN? Why not focus on the project contractors themselves?
4. Is Citigroup vulnerable to such a campaign? What harm can RAN impose on Citigroup, and how serious is that harm?
5. What should RAN do next in its campaign? Should it abandon the campaign? Should it accept a symbolic agreement with Citigroup and turn its attention elsewhere?
6. What action, if any, should Citigroup take in light of the RAN campaign?

# CHAPTER 5

# Political Theory and Government Institutions

## Introduction

This chapter provides foundations for the study of nonmarket activity and public politics, that is, nonmarket activity in the arenas of government institutions. The institutional focus is legislatures, and in particular Congress, as arenas in which the nonmarket strategies of firms and other interests are implemented. Other public institutions, including regulatory agencies, antitrust agencies, and the courts, are considered in Part III of the book, and institutions in China, Japan, and Europe are considered in Part IV.

This chapter is both conceptual and institutional. The conceptual subjects include the relationship between markets and incentives for nonmarket action, collective action and the free-rider problem, social and political dilemmas, and characteristics of majority rule systems. The institutional focus is on the organization of Congress, the legislative process, committees, political behavior, parties, and the executive branch. The conceptual and institutional materials are brought together in an example involving the extension of daylight saving time.

## Markets

### The Role and Functioning of Markets

Markets are the principal institutions through which resources are allocated and firms interact with those in their environment. Goods and services are exchanged voluntarily in markets based on a system of property rights that entitles the participants to the benefits from their exchanges. Market transactions make those who transact better off, since otherwise they would refuse to make the transaction. That is, because they voluntarily exchange property rights, market participants have incentives to make their transactions to their advantage.

The focus in this section is on competitive markets for undifferentiated goods in which market participants transact at the market price. The equilibrium market price equates supply and demand, and since the supply function represents the cost of the resources expended to produce the marginal unit exchanged, the market price equals that cost. The market price thus informs buyers and sellers of the cost of society's resources expended in supplying the marginal unit. Given this price consumers decide how many units to buy and producers decide how much to produce. These individual decisions determine the allocation of society's resources.

The efficiency of the allocation of resources is evaluated using the concept of Pareto optimality. An allocation is Pareto optimal if there is no other feasible allocation such that all market participants are at least as well off and at least one is strictly better off, evaluated in terms of their preferences. Pareto optimality may be viewed as a necessary condition for market efficiency, and a fundamental theorem of economics is that every competitive market equilibrium is Pareto optimal. Thus, at the equilibrium price there are no remaining economic transactions that could make any individual better off without making another worse off.[1]

Pareto optimality pertains only to efficiency and not to the distributive consequences of market competition. An individual with a small endowment of human capital or other resources may fare poorly in a competitive market compared with a better endowed individual. Similarly, a firm with an inefficient production technology may fare poorly relative to a more efficient firm. The distributive consequences of market competition create incentives for nonmarket action, as considered in the following section.

Markets may be imperfectly competitive because of product differentiation, the technological characteristics of production, or barriers to entry that limit the number of firms in the industry. Markets may also temporally be imperfectly competitive as the dynamics of innovation and technological change create advantages for some firms and disadvantages for others. Continual technological improvement sustains the advantages garnered by companies such as Intel, Microsoft, and Pfizer. In these cases, firms can affect market prices, and hence they take into account the strategies of other firms in choosing their own strategies. The field of strategic management is concerned with the interactions between the strategies of firms in imperfectly competitive markets.[2]

## Consumer Surplus and Economic Rents

Distributive consequences result on both the demand and the supply sides of a market. A market, or industry, demand function represents the amount consumers are willing to pay for an incremental unit of a good. The willingness of consumers to pay is represented by the height of the demand curve $D$ in Figure 5-1, and the surplus on a unit of the good is the difference between the willingness to pay and the price $p^0$ that must be paid for that unit. The area labeled *consumer surplus* in Figure 5-1 is the aggregate surplus of consumers from the quantity $q^0$ they purchase. A decrease in the price increases the surplus, so consumers have an incentive to engage in nonmarket activity to lower prices or protect their surplus against a price increase.[3]

A supply function represents the incremental or marginal cost of producing an additional unit of a good. Supply functions can be short run or long run depending on whether the factors of production are fixed or variable. A long-run supply function pertains to a time period sufficiently long that all factors of production can be varied in the most efficient manner. A short-run supply function corresponds to a time period in which some factors, such as plant capacity, are fixed and other factors, such as labor, can be varied. If all factors of production can be varied and the markets for all factors

---

[1]The principal qualification to this conclusion is when externalities are present, as considered in Chapters 10 and 11.
[2]See Besanko, Dranove, Schaefer, and Shanley (2004), Oster (1999), Porter (1980, 1985), and Saloner, Shepard, and Podolny (2001).
[3]The measurement of changes in consumer surplus due to changes in the price is complex because of income effects and because prices of other goods may change. The presentation here abstracts from these considerations.

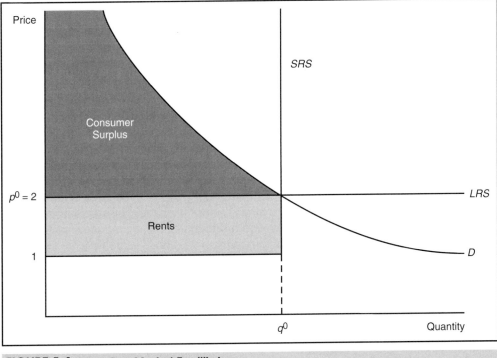

**FIGURE 5-1** Long-Run Market Equilibrium

of production are competitive, marginal and average costs are equal and the long-run supply curve (*LRS*) is horizontal, as illustrated in Figure 5-1. In a market equilibrium, the price equals marginal (and average) cost, so producers earn only normal profits—profits just sufficient to cover the cost of capital.

In the short run, firms earn economic *rents* on their fixed factors of production. An economic rent is the difference between the price at which a unit of a good can be sold and the price that is just sufficient to induce the producer to supply that unit.[4] The latter price is given by the height of the short-term supply function, which represents the marginal cost of those factors of production that can be varied. If the costs associated with the fixed factors are sunk, the rents equal the cash flow to the producers. The difference between economic rents and accounting profits is due to depreciation, amortization, and other expenses associated with the fixed factors.

As an example, consider the nonmarket issue of reducing sulfur dioxide emissions from coal-fired electric power plants, as addressed in the Chapter 6 case, *Scrubbers and Environmental Politics*. To meet the more stringent emissions standards, scrubbers can be used to remove sulfur dioxide from the emissions. The use of a scrubber would allow high-sulfur eastern coal to be burned in new power plants in the East and Midwest. If scrubbers were not mandated, many of those power plants would burn low-sulfur western coal instead. Mandating scrubbers thus reduces the demand for low-sulfur coal mined in the West and increases the demand for high-sulfur coal mined in the East. Suppose that in the absence of more stringent emissions standards the eastern coal industry was in long-run equilibrium. That is, price and output are determined by the

---

[4]In an imperfectly competitive market, there is no supply curve, and rents are defined in terms of cash flow, i.e., relative to the marginal costs of production.

intersection of the demand function and the long-run supply function. Suppose that the long-run supply function is horizontal, as illustrated in Figure 5-1. The equilibrium market price is $p^0$, and the quantity $q^0$ produced in equilibrium is equal to the capacity in the industry.

More stringent emissions standards and mandating scrubbers has consequences in both the long run and the short run. Consider first the long run. The eastern coal industry is labor-intensive and has sunk costs in terms of mine shafts and equipment. Suppose the technology in the industry involves only two factor inputs: labor and the mine itself (i.e., the shafts and equipment). Also, suppose that each represents half the total cost. More specifically, assume that it takes $1 of labor to produce 1 ton of coal and it takes $100 to open a mine with a capacity of 100 tons. The long-run supply function is thus located at $2, and $2 is also the industry price $p^0$ in Figure 5-1. Suppose that the cost of the mine itself is sunk and already paid for but labor is variable; that is, workers can be laid off or hired if demand decreases or increases, respectively. In the case of a coal company with one mine with 100 tons of capacity, operating at capacity yields revenue of $200 and labor costs of $100. The company thus has a rent, which equals its cash flow, of $100. The rents for the industry are identified in Figure 5-1.

To determine the short-run supply function (*SRS*), consider the question, "What price of coal would be required to bring an additional ton of coal into production?" Suppose that the mine is operating at less than capacity. The answer is $1, since only additional labor has to be hired to produce an additional ton. The short-run marginal cost is thus $1, and the short-run supply function for the industry is at $1, as illustrated in Figure 5-1. As indicated by the vertical line, an increase in output above the capacity of 100 is impossible in the short run, so the short-run marginal cost becomes infinite. That is, the SRS is vertical at a quantity of 100. Note that the short-run supply function intersects the long-run supply function and the demand function at the long-run equilibrium $(p^0, q^0)$.

The issue in the scrubbers case resulted from more stringent emissions standards that required reductions in sulfur dioxide emissions. If scrubbers were not mandated, the more stringent emissions standard would shift demand from eastern to low-sulfur western coal. Consider a shift in demand from $D$ to $D^1$ in the demand function for eastern coal due to a required reduction in emissions. As indicated in Figure 5-2, the price of eastern coal then falls to $p^1 = \$1$ and output falls to $q^1$. Workers are laid off, and eastern coal companies have lost all their rents, since the price of a ton of coal has fallen to the cost of the labor required to produce it. The revenue of a coal company that now produces 80 tons is $80 and its total labor costs are $80.[5] Consumer surplus increases because of the lower price.

If scrubbers were mandated to reduce emissions, the power plants in the East and Midwest would continue to burn eastern coal. Requiring scrubbers thus would prevent a shift in demand from $D$ to $D^1$ and would preserve the rents being earned by the eastern mines. The incentives to take nonmarket action in support of mandating scrubbers arise from these rents. The coal companies have an incentive to support mandating scrubbers to prevent the shift in demand and hence preserve their rents; and workers, represented by the United Mine Workers, also have an incentive to take nonmarket action to retain their jobs. Mandating scrubbers and burning eastern coal increases the cost of producing electricity, however, since burning western coal is lower cost. The surplus of consumers is thus lower.

---

[5]In the long run if demand remained at $D^1$, mines would be closed, and capacity would be reduced to $q^1$.

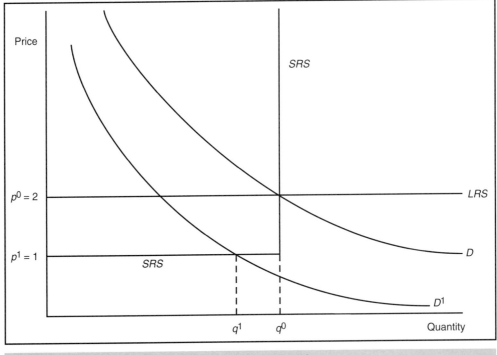

**FIGURE 5-2** Market Equilibrium and a Shift in Demand

# The Connection between the Market and Nonmarket Environments

## The Demand for Nonmarket Action

This section addresses the relation between the distributive consequences arising in the market environment and incentives for nonmarket action. Interest groups and firms act in the nonmarket environment to affect surpluses and rents. Their actions include lobbying, coalition building, grassroots campaigns, testimony in hearings, and electoral support. These actions affect the outcomes of nonmarket issues, such as whether to mandate scrubbers, and hence affect surpluses and rents. In the example considered at the end of the chapter, firms recognized that if daylight saving time were extended, the demand curve for their products would shift outwards, thereby increasing their rents. Not only would the rents of the firms increase, but the higher output would result in increased employment and, if the labor supply curve were upward-sloping, higher wages. The rents associated with shifting the demand function provided incentives to firms to take nonmarket action to obtain an extension of daylight saving time. The effects on surpluses and rents provide the incentives to bear the cost of nonmarket action.[6]

A demand for nonmarket action arises not only from shifting the demand function outward but also from preventing a shift to the left, as in the example in Figure 5-2. Pharmaceutical firms with patented drugs have incentives to slow the entry of generic drugs to prevent the demand function for patented drugs from shifting inward. A demand for nonmarket action can also arise on the supply side of a market. Pharmaceutical

---

[6]Baron (1997a, 1999) presents formal models of the relation between nonmarket action and rents in the contexts of the Chapter 17 case, The *Kodak–Fujifilm Trade Dispute,* and the Part II integrative case, *CAFE Standards 2002.*

firms worked to accelerate the FDA drug approval process so that their patented drugs would reach the market earlier. The incentives for nonmarket action thus can come from both the demand and supply sides of a market.

Consumers also have incentives for nonmarket action. Consumers have an incentive to oppose a scrubbers mandate that would raise electricity prices relative to the price of electricity produced from western coal. Similarly, protection from imports results in a loss to consumers that exceeds the gains to producers. These incentives, however, do not necessarily imply that consumers will take nonmarket action to oppose a scrubbers mandate or import protection, since consumers typically have high costs of taking nonmarket action. Because of these costs, the demand for nonmarket action need not translate into realized action.

## The Costs of Nonmarket Action

Pluralist theories predict that common interests, such as those that result from a potential decrease in consumer surplus, lead to nonmarket action consistent with those interests. These demand-side theories draw implications about nonmarket activity directly from the interests of individuals and firms, as measured by surpluses and rents. Olson (1965), however, argued that such theories ignore the costs of taking nonmarket and collective action. Those costs are an important determinant of the effectiveness of those with common interests.[7] The higher those costs, the lower is the nonmarket action taken and therefore the less effective are those with common interests. Consumers did not oppose mandating scrubbers, and they seldom oppose import protection because of the costs of nonmarket and collective action.

Taxpayers have a common interest in lower taxes, and consumers have a common interest in lower prices. With some exceptions neither taxpayers nor consumers have been particularly effective in nonmarket arenas, in part because their costs of organizing for collective action are high relative to the per capita benefits they would receive as a result of that action.[8] The (per-capita) benefits for an individual consumer from eliminating sugar import quotas are outweighed by the costs of taking nonmarket action.[9] Large groups thus may have a high demand for political action, but their costs of acting can also be high. Common or aligned interests therefore do not translate directly into action and nonmarket success but instead are mediated by the costs of nonmarket action.

## The Free-Rider Problem and Collective Action

The costs of nonmarket action can be reduced through *collective action*. On many nonmarket issues, a firm's interests are aligned with those of other firms, labor, or suppliers. With an alignment of interests, collective action is possible. Outcomes of nonmarket issues, however, often have the property of a public good in the sense that they pertain to everyone, regardless of whether they contributed to realizing the outcome. For example, preventing a shift in demand, as illustrated in Figure 5-2, benefits all firms in the industry regardless of whether they contributed to preventing the shift. When the benefits from nonmarket action accrue to those who do not contribute, a *free-rider problem* may be present.[10]

---

[7]See Moe (1980) and Hardin (1982).
[8]This does not mean that the interests of taxpayers and consumers are not reflected in political outcomes. Their interests can be represented by a government officeholder, who can claim credit for having done so.
[9]The costs and benefits from nonmarket action are considered in more detail in Chapter 6.
[10]See Shepsle and Boncheck (1997) for an introduction to collective action.

To illustrate the free-rider problem, consider the case of an industry such as steel that seeks protection from imports. Suppose that nonmarket action by any one firm costs that firm $c$ and yields benefits $b$ for each of the $n$ firms in the industry, for a total benefit of $nb$. That is, participation by an individual firm increases the likelihood of protection, which is a public good for the firms in the industry. Whenever $nb > c$, the firms in the industry are better off if an individual firm participates in the collective action. Consequently, it is collectively rational for all firms to contribute to the non-market action when $nb > c$. If all $n$ firms contributed, the total benefits would be $n^2b$, which may be interpreted as the increase in rents in the industry.

What is collectively rational, however, may not be individually rational. An individual firm has an incentive to contribute to the collective action only if the cost $c$ it incurs is less than the benefits it receives from its own participation, and those benefits are only $b$. Consequently, if $c > b$, an individual firm has no incentive to participate even though its participation produces collective benefits $nb$ to the industry that exceed its costs $c$. If $c > b$, the firm prefers to free ride on the efforts of the other firms, since doing so saves it the cost $c$ and it loses only the benefits $b$ from its own contribution. The temptation or incentive to free ride is thus $c - b$. Each firm has an incentive to free ride, and the possibility of collective action is in doubt. The free-rider problem thus is present when $b < c < nb$.[11]

The larger the number of potential participants, the more serious is the free-rider problem. Large groups such as consumers and taxpayers often have difficulty overcoming this problem. Large groups thus must develop other means to induce participation. Some groups form associations to reduce the cost of nonmarket action. Some groups encourage participation by providing selective benefits that can be denied to those who do not participate. The largest organized interest group in the United States is AARP (American Association of Retired Persons), which has a membership of over 30 million. AARP is politically active on a variety of issues of concern to its members, and it attracts members in part by providing selective benefits to them. AARP, for example, offers its members discount prices on pharmaceuticals and supplemental health insurance, as well as discounts on travel and accommodations.

Labor unions also face a free-rider problem in obtaining contributions from members to undertake nonmarket activities. The unions have solved this collective action problem by obtaining legislation that requires mandatory dues for everyone in a collective bargaining unit, and a portion of those dues is used for political action such as supporting candidates in federal and state elections.[12]

In summary, those with aligned interests on an issue have a collective incentive to take nonmarket action, and the stronger that incentive, the more action will be taken, other things being equal. Other things are not always equal, however. In particular, the costs of taking nonmarket action can exceed the benefits, resulting in little collective action. Interests may be able to organize to reduce those costs. Large groups have the greatest potential for collective nonmarket action but may be plagued by the free-rider problem. Large groups attempt to provide selective benefits to induce participation. Small groups have lower costs of organizing and often have an easier time punishing or excluding those who do not participate, as considered in the following section. The chapter case, *Repeal of the Luxury Tax*, provides an opportunity to consider which interests will be active on a nonmarket issue.

---

[11]If $c > b$, each individual firm benefits sufficiently from its own participation to act on its own, so there is no collective action problem.

[12]Union members can file a statement each year to take back the portion of their dues that would otherwise go to electoral support.

# Social and Political Dilemmas

As the free-rider problem suggests, certain dilemmas can be difficult to resolve. The characteristic of these dilemmas is that what is collectively rational may not be individually rational. This section examines the nature of these dilemmas and considers how repeated encounters can mitigate them.

## The Prisoners' Dilemma

The *prisoners' dilemma* is a situation in which each player individually has a dominant strategy, but if each used that strategy, each would be worse off than if they cooperated. An example of a prisoners' dilemma is presented in Figure 5-3. Players 1 and 2 each have two possible actions, A and B, and they choose their actions simultaneously and independently. The entries in the cells are the benefits to players 1 and 2, respectively. For example, if player 1 chooses A and player 2 chooses B, player 1 receives $-1$ and player 2 receives 3.

To determine which actions the players will choose, note that for whichever action player 2 chooses, player 1's benefit from action B is higher than that from action A. That is, if player 2 were to choose A, player 1 would receive 2 if she chose A and 3 if she chose B. If player 2 were to choose B, player 1 would receive $-1$ if she chose A and 0 if she chose B. Consequently, B is a dominant strategy for player 1 because it yields higher payoffs regardless of the action player 2 takes. The same reasoning implies that B is a dominant strategy for player 2. Each player thus chooses B. The outcome $(0, 0)$ from these strategies, however, is strictly worse than the outcome $(2, 2)$ if both players were to choose A. The dilemma is that it is individually rational for each player to choose B, but it is collectively rational for both to choose A.[13] Individual rationality and collective rationality are thus not the same. As long as this game is played only once and the two players independently take actions, not even communication between them can resolve the dilemma. For example, even if the players each promise to take A, each has an incentive to break the promise and take B. Promises are thus likely to be viewed with skepticism.

A variety of business and social situations have the characteristics of a prisoners' dilemma, including price wars, defection from certain agreements such as a cartel, the choice of protectionism or free trade by individual countries, the choice of subsidizing or not subsidizing exports, and the use of common natural resources. The free-rider

FIGURE 5-3  A Prisoners' Dilemma

|  |  | Player 2 | |
|---|---|---|---|
|  |  | A | B |
| Player 1 | A | 2, 2 | $-1, 3$ |
|  | B | 3, $-1$ | 0, 0 |

---

[13]The prisoners' dilemma received its name from describing the players as prisoners arrested for a crime the police know they committed together. The police, however, only have evidence to convict them on minor charges resulting in a short sentence. The police offer each prisoner a deal in which each can provide (B) or not provide (A) evidence against the other prisoner. If one prisoner provides evidence and the other does not, the former is offered the minimum sentence and the latter is given the maximum sentence. If both provide evidence, both receive a long sentence but shorter than the maximum. If neither provides evidence, both sentences are intermediate. It is then a dominant strategy for each to give evidence against the other, resulting in long sentences for both.

problem is a version of the prisoners' dilemma, where in Figure 5-3 each ($n = 2$) player's nonmarket action ($A$) costs $c = 4$ and provides benefits $b = 3$ to each player.

## Dilemmas, Repeated Encounters, and Cooperation

One possibility for resolving dilemmas is cooperation in which the parties take into account not only the consequences for themselves but for the other parties as well. Cooperation in this sense is mutual altruism. In the context of the prisoners' dilemma in Figure 5-3, cooperation would involve both players choosing $A$ rather than $B$ because they are better off by doing so. In this situation, however, there is no compelling reason to believe that the players would actually cooperate. Once they have agreed to do so, it remains a dominant strategy to choose $B$. That is, once they agree to take action $A$, each recognizes that there is an incentive to defect from the cooperative agreement. Recognizing that player 2 has a dominant strategy of choosing $B$, player 1 is likely to worry about whether player 2 will actually play $A$. Once player 1 harbors some doubt about whether player 2 will choose $A$, the choice of $B$ by player 1 becomes even more compelling. Such doubts can lead to the play of $B$ by each player.

This reasoning suggests that prisoners' dilemmas are difficult to resolve, yet many are resolved. Resolution often occurs because the prisoners' dilemma is repeated rather than encountered only once. In that case, players have a stake in the future, and the set of strategies that players can employ is much broader. A player can, for example, reward or punish the other player for the choice made in the previous round. Consider a "tit-for-tat" strategy in which player 1 plays $A$ in the first round and thereafter plays whatever player 2 played in the previous round. When the game is played repeatedly, the outcome $(2, 2)$ in Figure 5-3 can be attained. These strategies are self-enforcing—they constitute an equilibrium and do not require a contract enforceable by a third party such as a court.[14] The self-enforcement occurs because each player finds it in his or her interest to play $A$ in each round, as long as both played $A$ in the past. If one player chooses $B$, the other will play $B$ in the next round and the outcome $(0, 0)$ will result in every future round. This outcome serves as punishment that can deter playing $B$ in the first place. That is, the long-term loss exceeds the short-term gain from playing $B$, and hence each player has an individual incentive to play $A$.[15] In employing these strategies, the players do not take into account the interests of the other party in their reasoning about how to play, so altruism is not involved. This resolution of the prisoners' dilemma is thus noncooperative rather than cooperative.

Behavior generated by repeated play can be supported by the creation of an institution to punish deviations from the mutually beneficial actions. The World Trade Organization was created to lower trade barriers for the mutual benefit of its members and is equipped with a dispute resolution and punishment mechanism to deal with violations of the trading rules.[16] Similarly, firms that repeatedly take nonmarket action on issues on which their interests are aligned may be able to solve the free-rider problem by forming an association that acts on the behalf of its members on a series of issues and can monitor and punish free riding.

---

[14]See Dixit and Skeath (2004) for a discussion of such strategies in a repeated setting.
[15]This reasoning requires that the game be repeated infinitely often, since if it were repeated only a finite number of times, the equilibrium would unravel from the last round. That is, in the last round both players have dominant strategies of playing $B$, and that implies that each has a dominant strategy of playing $B$ in the next-to-last round, and so on.
[16]The World Trade Organization is considered in Chapter 17.

# Majority-Rule Institutions

## Properties of Majority Rule

A unanimity rule—a rule that requires the consent of all parties—governs exchanges in markets. This rule is used when property rights are well defined and it is reasonable to allow individuals to make voluntary decisions. In some cases, however, a unanimity rule is either impractical or impossible. For example, if everyone had to agree on tax rates before they could become law, reaching an agreement would be problematic. In such situations, the rules used to reach decisions require less than unanimous agreement. These rules include both the simple majority rule used in committees and New England town meetings and the complex set of rules that govern lawmaking in the federal government.

Although majority rule has desirable features, it can result in reductions in aggregate well-being and in outcomes contrary to majority preferences. Protection from imports, for example, generally results in higher prices and lower aggregate well-being, as measured by the sum of consumer surplus and producer rents. Yet the United States protects industries such as sugar and steel. If put to a vote in a public referendum, this protection would likely be rejected by voters because there are many more losers than winners from the protection. In majority-rule institutions such as Congress, however, the sugar and steel industries have, through collective action, obtained protection.

## Condorcet's Paradox and Arrow's Impossibility Theorem

In one of the most important accomplishments in the social sciences, Kenneth Arrow (1963) demonstrated that it is generally impossible to design institutions that aggregate the diverse preferences of individuals to make a social choice in a manner consistent with a set of reasonable conditions. This impossibility theorem has a variety of implications for public institutions and hence for strategies for addressing nonmarket issues.

Arrow asked whether it is possible to design institutions that, using the preferences of individuals, can select social alternatives or public policies in a manner consistent with a minimal set of conditions that any institution should possess. Those institutions include simple majority rule, a strong executive system in which an executive has veto power over a majority-rule legislature, and a parliamentary system in which a government continues in office until the next election or until it loses a vote of confidence. To illustrate this result, the institution of simple (50 percent) majority rule is used.

Suppose there are three individuals (1, 2, and 3) and three social alternatives (*A*, *B*, and *C*). Suppose also that the preferences of the individuals are as given in Figure 5-4, where, for example, individual 1 prefers *A* to *B*, *B* to *C*, and *C* to *A*. When each alternative is paired against each of the other alternatives under majority rule, *A* defeats *B* by a vote of 2 to 1, *B* defeats *C* by a vote of 2 to 1, and *C* defeats *A* by a vote of 2 to 1.

**FIGURE 5-4** Condorcet's Paradox

| *Individual's Preference Ordering* | | |
|:---:|:---:|:---:|
| *1* | *2* | *3* |
| *A* | *B* | *C* |
| *B* | *C* | *A* |
| *C* | *A* | *B* |

Each alternative thus defeats one alternative but is defeated by another. Majority rule thus is incapable of choosing an alternative. That is, majority rule cannot aggregate the preferences of these individuals to select a social alternative.

This paradox, due to Condorcet (1785), illustrates the fundamental problem Arrow examined. Arrow showed that for any institution satisfying certain reasonable conditions, there is some configuration of individual preferences such that the institution yields no consistent choice, as in the *Condorcet paradox*.[17]

## Agendas

One implication of Arrow's impossibility theorem is that in an actual institution there may be an opportunity to act strategically. For example, with the preferences in Figure 5-4, suppose that individual 1 is the agenda setter and can specify the order in which a legislature will vote on the three alternatives. Suppose individual 1 sets the agenda in Figure 5-5 in which *A* is first voted against *C* and then the winner is voted against *B*. In their voting, the three individuals will recognize that in the second stage the winner of the first vote will be voted against *B*, so the outcome will be *B* if *C* is the winner of the first vote and will be *A* if the winner of the first vote is *A*. These winners are denoted by the circled alternatives in Figure 5-5. Consequently, the first vote is actually a vote between an outcome of *A* and an outcome of *B*. Both individuals 1 and 3 prefer *A* to *B* and thus will vote for *A* rather than *C* on the first vote. Then, on the second vote, 1 and 3 will vote for *A* over *B*, yielding *A* as the winner. The agenda setter in this case obtains the alternative that he or she most prefers. It is straightforward to show that the other two possible agendas formed from the three alternatives yield *B* and *C* as the outcomes.

This example should not be interpreted as implying that agendas are regularly manipulated. An agenda setter who acts against the preferences of a majority can always be replaced. Instead, the example indicates that a simple institutional structure, in this case an agenda, can result in a social choice.[18] That choice depends on which agenda is used, and hence there are incentives for strategic behavior. This also implies that institutional positions with agenda-setting authority are important.

**FIGURE 5-5 A Voting Agenda**

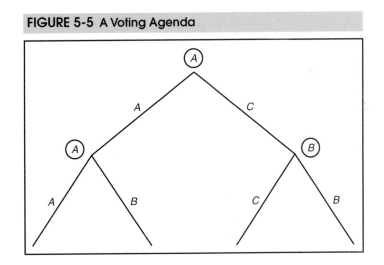

---

[17]Some of Arrow's conditions have been criticized, and alternative conditions have been proposed; however, they all yield the same conclusion as his impossibility theorem.
[18]Arrow's impossibility theorem, however, applies to the choice of an agenda. That is, there is no consistent method for choosing among the three possible agendas.

# Committees in Legislatures

In a legislature, committees are often the agenda setter. In Congress each committee has a jurisdiction and can bring to the floor of the legislature bills in its jurisdiction. Amendments can be offered but may be restricted by the rules under which a legislature operates. In the House of Representatives, a germaneness rule requires amendments to be germane to the policy issue addressed by the bill under consideration. The committee jurisdictions and amendment rules can structure the set of alternatives under consideration, which means that committees play a strategic role in the legislative process. Committees are thus a focus of nonmarket action.

# The Median Voter Theorem

The impossibility theorem implies that if there are to be consistent social choices, the social choice problem must satisfy more restrictive conditions than Arrow imposed. An agenda is one such condition, since it imposes a specific order in which votes are taken. Another condition is when the alternatives can be arrayed on one dimension. For example, the alternatives may be the spending on a government program, the stringency of an environmental standard, or the patent duration for pharmaceuticals. If (1) the alternatives are one-dimensional, (2) the decision-making process is open so that all alternatives can be considered, and (3) voters have a most-preferred alternative, or ideal point, and prefer alternatives closer to rather than farther from that ideal point, then the outcome is the median of the ideal points. The median ideal point will receive at least a majority of votes against any alternative to either its left or its right. That is, including the median, there is a majority of voters on one side or the other that will defeat any other alternative. The logic of this theorem is explored further in the daylight saving time example presented at the end of the chapter.

The *median voter theorem* is powerful because it is only necessary to know voters' ideal points and not their entire preference ordering. Moreover, if the median ideal point is known, it is not necessary to know the exact location of the other ideal points. Although the median voter theorem does not extend to alternatives with more than one dimension, related results suggest that outcomes are likely to be close to the intersection of the medians on each dimension.

The median voter theorem is an important tool for analyzing legislative outcomes in an open process, that is, a process in which any alternative can be proposed. If the issue under consideration is one-dimensional and the ideal points of the members of a legislature can be estimated, the outcome can be predicted. Members' ideal points are not directly observable, but information on them can be inferred from voting records. Interest groups analyze roll-call votes on issues on their agendas and provide scores for each member of Congress. The League of Conservation Voters provides ratings based on how members of Congress voted on environmental issues. Similarly, Americans for Democratic Action (ADA; a very liberal group), the Chamber of Commerce (COC) (a more conservative group), and the American Federation of State, County and Municipal Employees (AFSCME), a union with 1.3 million members, provide ratings based on issues important to them.[19] These ratings are used by analysts as an indicator

---

[19]For each member of Congress, the *Almanac of American Politics 2004* (Barone and Cohen, 2003) presents ratings by the following organizations: League of Conservation Voters, Americans for Democratic Action, Chamber of Commerce, AFSCME, Concord Coalition, Information Technology Industry Council, National Taxpayers Union, Christian Coalition, National Tax-Limitation Committee, American Civil Liberties Union, and American Conservative Union. Each group selects a different set of issues on which to score members, so the ratings are not necessarily comparable. Similarly, the issues differ from year to year, so intertemporal comparisons are problematic.

that in an open seat election voters select the candidate they like better, and in subsequent elections only lower quality challengers run because potential candidates recognize that the incumbent has attributes the voters like.

In 1994 a major change in Congress occurred as a result of voter anger with the Clinton administration and the Democrats, who had controlled both the House and Senate with substantial majorities. Republicans won a majority in both the House and the Senate and held that majority through the rest of the decade and most of the first half of the next decade.

## The Organization of Congress

The Congress is bicameral. The House of Representatives is composed of 435 voting members serving 2-year terms and elected from districts with approximately the same population.[22] The 10 largest states account for half the members, whereas Alaska, Delaware, Montana, North Dakota, South Dakota, Vermont, and Wyoming have only one representative each. House districts are reapportioned after each census, and as a result of the 2000 census, the West and the South gained seats at the expense of the Northeast and the Midwest. The Speaker is the presiding officer of the House and is selected by the majority party and elected by the entire House.

Each of the 50 states has two senators, serving staggered 6-year terms. States with a small population thus have relatively more weight in the Senate, and states with large populations have relatively more weight in the House. The vice president presides over the Senate and has a vote in case of a tie.

The Constitution specifies neither how the chambers are to be organized nor how they are to conduct their business. Over time, they have developed their own formal and informal organizational structures and procedures. The formal organization is found in the committee structure and the legislative process. The informal organization is found in the party organization within the chambers. Each party elects a leader, whips, a secretary of the party conference, and heads of policy and steering committees. The primary responsibility of the whips is to generate party discipline on those issues on which the party has taken a position. Although parties and the party organization of Congress are important, members have considerable latitude in their voting, and party discipline is not the rule.

## The Legislative Process

During the 107th Congress (2001–2002), 5,767 bills were introduced in the House and 3,190 in the Senate, yet the number of laws enacted was 377.[23] Many bills are introduced with little expectation that they will even be considered, and some are introduced to appeal to interest groups or particular constituents. When submitting a bill a member will often seek cosponsors, but cosponsorship does not commit a member to support the bill if it comes to the floor for a vote. The number of cosponsors also does not necessarily translate into votes because interest group activity often intensifies with the submission of a bill and can result in some members changing their positions. Only members of the Congress may introduce legislation, and the president's legislative proposals are introduced by a member of the president's party.

---

[22]Representatives from the District of Columbia, American Samoa, Guam, Puerto Rico, and the Virgin Islands are members of the House but do not have a vote.
[23]See Ornstein, Mann, and Malbin (1997) for longitudinal data. Any legislation pending at the end of a Congress dies.

Figure 5-6 illustrates the legislative process.[24] When a bill is introduced, it is referred to a committee. The committee can then consider the bill or, in the case of most bills, take no action on it. A bill is usually considered first by a subcommittee, which, by a majority vote, sends it to the full committee. A subcommittee cannot, however, effectively block a bill that a committee majority wishes to consider because the committee can consider the bill directly. Much of the substantive legislative work in Congress is done in committees, including amending and rewriting ("marking up") bills.

When a bill receives a majority vote in committee, it is ready to be scheduled for consideration on the floor of the chamber. In the House the bill goes to the Rules Committee, which assigns an amendment rule that governs floor consideration. The Rules Committee may assign a restrictive rule, which specifies or restricts the amendments that can be offered, or an open rule, which places no restrictions on the amendments that may be offered on the floor. Amendments on the floor, however, are governed by a standing rule of the House that prohibits nongermane amendments.[25] Special orders are used to schedule legislation and limit the time allocated to floor debate. Little true debate actually takes place, and many speeches on the floor are made to appeal to constituents.

The legislative process in the Senate is similar to that in the House except that all bills are technically considered on the floor under an open rule. In practice, however, the Senate operates under unanimous consent agreements (UCAs) specifying which amendments may be considered on the floor. These agreements are negotiated under the auspices of the Senate leadership. An objection to a UCA by any senator prevents it from taking effect.

Senate rules allow members to speak on the floor for an unlimited time, and senators opposed to a bill can speak continuously (a filibuster), thus preventing a vote on a bill. Cloture can be invoked by a vote of 60 senators, preventing any member from speaking for more than an hour and precluding nongermane amendments. The minority party in the Senate frequently uses a filibuster to extract concessions from the majority or at times to kill a bill. A filibuster thus makes it more difficult to change the status quo.[26]

Before a bill can be enacted, it must be passed by both chambers in identical language. The bills passed by each chamber seldom have the same language or substantive provisions and must be reconciled before they are sent to the president. Conference committees composed of representatives of each chamber and selected by the majority party leadership are usually used to reconcile major legislation.[27] Members of both parties from the committee that reported the bill plus the authors of principal amendments are typically appointed to the conference committee. Conference committees are important because the conferees have to bargain when the bills passed by the two chambers differ substantially. Thus, conference committees are often the focus of political activity. As an indication of the importance attached to conference committees, over 100 members of the House served as conferees on the 1990 amendments to the Clean Air Act. If the conferees from the two chambers agree on common language, the bill is returned to the floor of each chamber for a final passage vote. If approved by both chambers, it is sent to the president for signature or veto.

---

[24]Oleszek (2004) provides detailed information on the legislative process and on congressional procedures.
[25]On a majority vote, the House may waive any of its rules.
[26]See Krehbiel (1996) and Brady and Volden (1998) for theories of gridlock and Krehbiel (1998, 1999) for a theory in which filibusters and vetoes play an important role.
[27]Instead of convening a conference, Congress often uses the procedure of amendments between the chambers to reconcile differences between bills. As in the daylight saving time example, one chamber can simply adopt the language of the other's bill. A bill may go through several iterations of amendments between the chambers before common language is reached. This means of achieving reconciliation typically involves implicit bargaining.

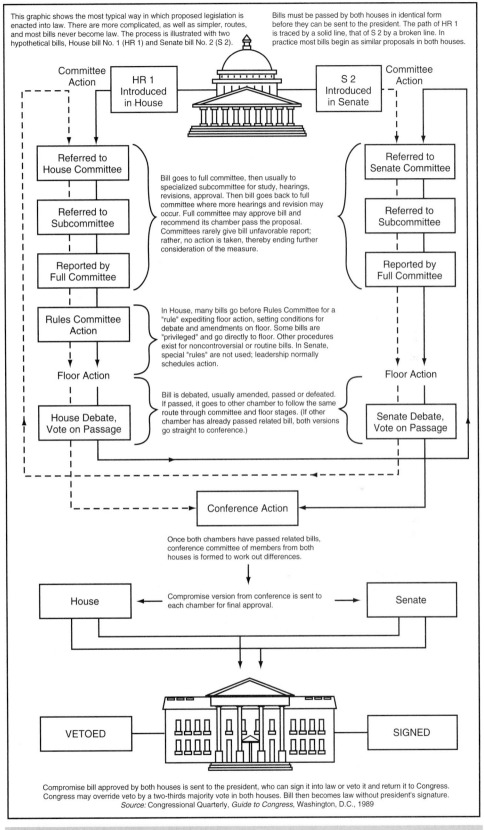

This graphic shows the most typical way in which proposed legislation is enacted into law. There are more complicated, as well as simpler, routes, and most bills never become law. The process is illustrated with two hypothetical bills, House bill No. 1 (HR 1) and Senate bill No. 2 (S 2).

Bills must be passed by both houses in identical form before they can be sent to the president. The path of HR 1 is traced by a solid line, that of S 2 by a broken line. In practice most bills begin as similar proposals in both houses.

Committee Action

HR 1 Introduced in House

S 2 Introduced in Senate

Committee Action

Referred to House Committee

Referred to Senate Committee

Bill goes to full committee, then usually to specialized subcommittee for study, hearings, revisions, approval. Then bill goes back to full committee where more hearings and revision may occur. Full committee may approve bill and recommend its chamber pass the proposal. Committees rarely give bill unfavorable report; rather, no action is taken, thereby ending further consideration of the measure.

Referred to Subcommittee

Referred to Subcommittee

Reported by Full Committee

Reported by Full Committee

Rules Committee Action

In House, many bills go before Rules Committee for a "rule" expediting floor action, setting conditions for debate and amendments on floor. Some bills are "privileged" and go directly to floor. Other procedures exist for noncontroversial or routine bills. In Senate, special "rules" are not used; leadership normally schedules action.

Floor Action

Floor Action

Bill is debated, usually amended, passed or defeated. If passed, it goes to other chamber to follow the same route through committee and floor stages. (If other chamber has already passed related bill, both versions go straight to conference.)

House Debate, Vote on Passage

Senate Debate, Vote on Passage

Conference Action

Once both chambers have passed related bills, conference committee of members from both houses is formed to work out differences.

House

Compromise version from conference is sent to each chamber for final approval.

Senate

VETOED

SIGNED

Compromise bill approved by both houses is sent to the president, who can sign it into law or veto it and return it to Congress. Congress may override veto by a two-thirds majority vote in both houses. Bill then becomes law without president's signature.
*Source:* Congressional Quarterly, *Guide to Congress*, Washington, D.C., 1989

**FIGURE 5-6 How a Bill Becomes a Law**

A bill passed by Congress becomes law when the president signs it or when Congress overrides a presidential veto on a vote of two-thirds of the members of each chamber. When a bill is passed while Congress is still in session, the president must act on the bill within 10 days or it automatically becomes law. If Congress is no longer in session, the president can choose not to act on the bill, and then it dies.[28] The authority to veto legislation gives the president considerable power.

Because legislation can be stopped at a number of points in the legislative process, it is more difficult to enact than to stop legislation. To be enacted, a bill must clear a number of hurdles. Committees represent an important hurdle, which gives power to the committees and their chairs. A majority of the members of the parent body can circumvent any hurdle that a chairperson or committee might erect, however.

## Committees

Most of the work of Congress is done in committees, and each chamber chooses its own committee structure. The standing committees of the 108th Congress are listed in Figure 5-7. The House has 19 and the Senate has 17 standing committees, each of which has several subcommittees. Each chamber may also have select and special committees, and there are five joint committees.

Committees have policy jurisdictions, but those jurisdictions can overlap when issues cut across formal boundaries. In the House, for example, an environmental protection issue such as regulation of an agricultural pesticide could be under the jurisdiction of the Agriculture Committee as well as committees with environmental jurisdictions. Committees thus often battle over jurisdictions and hence over influence on legislation.

Government expenditures are governed by a complex process requiring both an authorization and an appropriation. The House Agriculture Committee or the Armed

**FIGURE 5-7** Standing Committees of the 107th Congress

| House of Representatives | Senate |
|---|---|
| Agriculture | Aging (Special) |
| Appropriations | Agriculture, Nutrition and Forestry |
| Armed Services | Appropriations |
| Budget | Armed Services |
| Education and the Workforce | Banking, Housing and Urban Affairs |
| Energy and Commerce | Budget |
| Financial Services | Commerce, Science and Transportation |
| Government Reform | Energy and Natural Resources |
| Homeland Security | Environment and Public Works |
| House Administration | Ethics (Select) |
| International Relations | Finance |
| Intelligence (Select) | Foreign Relations |
| Judiciary | Governmental Affairs |
| Resources | Health, Education, Labor and Pensions |
| Rules | Indian Affairs |
| Science | Intelligence (Select) |
| Small Business | Judiciary |
| Standards of Official Conduct | Rules and Administration |
| Transportation and Infrastructure | Small Business and Entrepreneurship |
| Veterans' Affairs | Veterans' Affairs |
| Ways and Means | |

---

[28]This is called a pocket veto.

Services Committee may authorize expenditures for an agricultural subsidy program or a new weapons system, but the funds for those programs are provided by the Appropriations Committee. The process is designed to have the authorization committee act first, with the Appropriations Committee then providing funding no greater than the amount authorized. In recent Congresses authorization committees have begun to require program funding at particular levels. Beginning in the 1990s, the budget process has involved complex bargaining between the president and Congress over both the budget and the funding of individual programs.

Authorization committees have the responsibility for enacting legislation and reauthorizing programs with fixed expiration dates. In addition to their legislative roles, authorization committees have oversight responsibilities. Committees attempt to influence the policies of regulatory and administrative agencies by holding hearings and threatening legislative or budgetary action.

Committee membership is proportional to a party's representation in the chamber, and party conferences assign their members to committees. Newly elected legislators give a ranking of their committee preferences, and the party conferences do their best to assign members to the committees they have requested. Members of the House generally serve on two standing committees, and some also serve on select or joint committees. In the Senate, each member serves on several committees. Members accumulate committee-specific seniority, and the members of each committee are ranked by seniority within their party. Seniority is usually not transferable if the member changes committees. Because committee and subcommittee chairs are generally selected according to seniority and because chairpersons have strategic positions, members do not frequently change committees. Remaining with the same committee also gives members an incentive and an opportunity to develop expertise in its policy jurisdictions.

The chairs of committees and subcommittees are selected by the majority party. The 2000 election resulted in a Senate composed of 50 Democrats and 50 Republicans. Because of the tie-breaking vote of the vice president, the Republicans held all the chairs, and an equal number from each party served on each committee. A few months into the session Senator James Jeffords of Vermont left the Republican party to become an independent. The Democrats were then the majority party and took over the chairs of all committees and subcommittees. The Republicans regained the majority in the 2002 elections.

Approximately half of the House majority party and virtually all the Senate majority party are chairs of a committee or subcommittee. Committee chairs are selected by a party conference, and incumbents generally retain their chairs. Occasionally, however, a chair is replaced. When they became the majority party in the House in 1995, the Republicans passed over several more senior members in selecting committee chairs. In 2005 the Republicans replaced the chair of the Veterans Affairs Committee, and they passed over a more senior member in choosing the chair of the Appropriations Committee. The House Republicans also imposed a term limit of 6 years on all chairs. Committee chairs traditionally had chosen the chairs of their subcommittees, but the Republican Conference now chooses the chairs of the Appropriations subcommittees. In addition to their role as the first stage of legislative activity, subcommittees have the opportunity to hold hearings to direct public attention to issues and provide interest groups with a forum to advance their interests.

In 1974 in the wake of Watergate, a large number of new members were elected to the House. They pushed through reforms that gave a degree of autonomy to subcommittees, which previously had been under the control of the committee chair. This decentralization increased the number of strategic positions in the House by a factor of six, significantly changing House activity. As one congressman observed, a system of "wholesale politics" in which strong committee chairs controlled the legislative process was transformed into "retail politics" in which power was more diffuse.

## Committee and Individual Power

Members develop power based on their committee positions, seniority, expertise, hard work, and ability to form alliances and coalitions. The chair of a committee or subcommittee has a degree of power. The chair can initiate investigations and hold hearings, influence agenda, craft legislative bargains, and trade favors.

One source of committee power is its opportunity to draft, rewrite, and mark up bills. This allows a committee to set the legislative agenda in its jurisdiction. In recent years the House Republican leadership has exercised more control over the legislative process. Without majority support in the full chamber, however, a committee or a party has little ability to move legislation through the chamber. A principal activity is thus to write legislation that will command majority support. Because most legislation has consequences over several dimensions of a policy issue, a committee may have several different majorities from which it can seek support.

Committee power can also result from refusal to report a bill for floor consideration. The extent to which committees have this gatekeeping power is a matter of contention, as the parent body has ways to thwart it. In the House a discharge petition signed by a majority of members brings a bill out of committee to a vote on the floor even though the committee has not reported the bill. In the Senate there is no germaneness rule, and a senator can offer any bill as an amendment, as in the daylight saving time extension example considered later in this chapter. Nevertheless, committees do gain some leverage because of their opportunity to delay legislation.

Expertise is a source of power because members of Congress must deal with numerous complex issues, and information on the issues is necessarily imperfect. Members thus seek information from a variety of sources, including interest groups, policy analysts, committeess, and other members of Congress. A member who develops expertise in a policy domain thus has an opportunity to influence other members. On floor votes outside their areas of expertise, members often rely on the advice of another member who has similar preferences and is on the committee bringing the bill to the floor. Expertise also provides an opportunity to form and lead coalitions on legislation. Members may also obtain influence through their knowledge of congressional rules and procedures.

On issues about which information is imperfect, committees play an important role in developing new information and in shaping legislation.[29] The opportunity to craft bills to serve their own interests provides committee members with an incentive to acquire information and expertise that can be beneficial to themselves and their constituents as well as to the committee and the chamber. Members also obtain information from interest groups. An information provision strategy can be effective where information is imperfect.

## Bargaining in Political Institutions

Although legislatures act under majority rule, bargaining often takes place when disagreements arise among majorities on different aspects of an issue. Bargaining also takes place in conference committees, where House and Senate conferees reconcile differences between the chambers. Legislative bargaining can also take place outside Congress. For example, the Chapter 6 case, *Tobacco Politics,* considers the Tobacco

---

[29]See Gilligan and Krehbiel (1987) and Krehbiel (1991).

Resolution reached between tobacco companies, state attorneys general, and trial lawyers, which provided the basis for congressional legislation.

Because Congress is an institution whose members interact repeatedly, legislators can develop long-term patterns of behavior in which the failure to compromise on an issue today may be met by an unwillingness of others to compromise on future issues. Consequently, parties can establish patterns of behavior that give the minority party opportunities that its minority status does not require. On committees, for example, the chair often accommodates the interests of the ranking minority member. When bills are considered in committee, the chair offers the first amendment and the ranking minority member offers the second amendment.

## Delegation

Congress delegates the implementation of legislation to agencies, and the nature of that delegation can be important.[30] At times the delegation is designed to favor the interest groups that supported the initial legislation.[31] To promote the development of product safety standards through government regulation, supporters incorporated into the Consumer Product Safety Commission Act a provision that allowed anyone to petition for a safety standard for a product.[32] The act also required the CPSC to act on the petition within 6 months. Similarly, legislation provides for citizens' petitions that put issues on the Food and Drug Administration's agenda, as in the Part III integrative case, *Pharmaceutical Switching*.

Delegation is also used for the enforcement of legislation and regulations. Some environmental legislation allows individuals to file a lawsuit to enforce compliance by polluters and receive a portion of the penalties assessed. The Natural Resources Defense Council, for example, used these provisions to generate income to finance its activities.

Congress also delegates implementation to states. States implement certain provisions of the Clean Air Act, which puts them in potential conflict with the Environmental Protection Agency (EPA). In the case of motor vehicle carbon dioxide $(CO_2)$ emissions, California declared $CO_2$ a pollutant even though the EPA had ruled that it was not a pollutant.

## Legislators and Their Constituents

Whatever are their personal policy objectives, legislators must be reelected to have a continuing opportunity to achieve those objectives. Legislators thus vote on bills based on two considerations: their reelection incentives and their policy preferences.[33] Elected representatives thus are responsive to the preferences of their constituents not only because they have a duty to represent them but also because they want to be reelected. To enhance the reelection of incumbents, many states have gerrymandered their congressional (and state legislature) electoral districts so that few are competitive. For example, in the 2004 elections in California not a single congressional seat, state Assembly seat, or state Senate seat changed party.

An electoral constituency includes voters, campaign volunteers, and providers of campaign resources.[34] The reelection motive gives legislators an incentive to be attentive to the interests of those likely to vote. It also gives them an incentive to develop a personal

---

[30]See Epstein and O'Halloran (1999).
[31]See McCubbins, Noll, and Weingast (1987) for a theory of delegation with this feature.
[32]This opportunity was subsequently eliminated.
[33]See Fiorina (1989) and Mayhew (1974) for analyses of congressional behavior.
[34]Members may also have a policy constituency that includes those outside an electoral district whom the member chooses to represent, such as the elderly, environmentalists, labor, or business.

constituency by providing services to constituents. Mayhew (1974) refers to this as the *constituency connection.* The reelection motive also may provide an opportunity for interest groups with electorally important resources to influence the behavior of legislators.

Mayhew characterized members of Congress as exhibiting two types of behavior: *credit claiming* and *blame avoidance.* Credit claiming is the practice of claiming credit for legislative or oversight activity that is in the interest of constituents. Because it is difficult for most constituents to know the actual effectiveness, or in some cases even the position, of a legislator, credit claiming may go beyond actual accomplishments. Interest groups, however, monitor the behavior of legislators and often have a good idea of their effectiveness.

Blame avoidance involves distancing oneself from unpopular events, policies, or positions that might provide an opportunity for an electoral challenger. To avoid blame for the savings and loan crisis mentioned in Chapter 3, several members who had served on the important congressional banking committees chose to leave those committees.

## Committee and Personal Staffs

Members of Congress each have a personal staff that includes a chief, a press secretary, legislative assistants, and administrative assistants. The staff keeps the member informed about legislation, hearings, and other developments and also serves as an important link between members and their constituents and interest groups. A substantial portion of staff time is devoted to providing constituents with services such as assisting with lost social security checks, obtaining appointments to military academies, assisting with immigration problems, and interacting with government agencies. The staff also responds to constituents' letters on issues, often acknowledging the receipt of the letter, expressing concern for the issue, and stating that attention is being given to it. From 1960 to 1980 legislators' personal staffs expanded considerably; but since 1980 staff size has been relatively stable.

Committee staffs have shown a similar pattern. The committee staff is directed by the chair of the committee and, at quiet times, may serve as an adjunct to his or her personal staff. The committee staff is important in drafting legislation, marking up bills, and interacting with interest groups. For firms, trade associations, and other interest groups, the staff represents an important point of access to the legislative process and to information about the committee's activities. The majority party is allocated a substantially larger number of committee staff positions than the minority party. In 1995 the Republicans reduced the committee staff in the House by about one-third.

## Parties

Political parties are important in legislative politics, yet legislators have a considerable degree of independence from party positions and party leaders. In Congress, parties attempt to maintain discipline in voting within committees and on the floor. On issues important to their constituents, however, members often depart from the party position. One measure of the degree of party-line voting is the percent of roll-call votes in which a majority of one party voted contrary to a majority of the other party. In 2002 only 45 percent of the roll-call votes in the Senate and 43 percent of those in the House had this partisan characteristic. As these data indicate, party-line voting is not the rule. The more important an issue is to constituents, the more likely a legislator is to deviate from the party position. Sometimes, though, when the party has taken a position on an issue, strong constituent pressure must be present before members will deviate from that position.

Parties in the United States are relatively weak compared to parties in many other countries, particularly those countries with a parliamentary system of government.

One reason is that in the United States nominations for elected office are controlled locally rather than by a national party. In addition, issues important to voters are often local rather than national, which allows members to develop local, personal constituencies to improve their reelection prospects. This personal vote is developed through district work, directing federal funds to the district, and constituent service. Parties are also relatively weak in the United States because most campaign contributions are made directly to candidates rather than to parties, which gives members a further degree of independence.

## The Presidency and the Executive Branch

The president has a range of powers—some granted by the Constitution, some delegated by Congress, and some derived from public support.[35] The Constitution assigns to the president the right to veto legislation as well as certain powers in foreign affairs. Congress has delegated to the president the authority to negotiate treaties and trade agreements. The president also has authority in certain administrative areas, as granted by legislation. President Reagan had a substantial impact on regulatory rule making through his executive authority. In 1981 he issued an important executive order requiring a cost-benefit analysis of new regulations proposed by executive branch agencies. When President Clinton took office, he modified the order, requiring a review of costs and benefits only for major regulatory rule making. President Bush strengthened the role of the office that reviews regulations.

The president also appoints, with the consent of the Senate, the heads of cabinet departments, the members of regulatory and other commissions, and the top levels of executive branch agencies. The executive branch thus is responsive to the policy objectives of the president. (Cabinet departments are listed in Figure 5-8.) The executive branch agencies and cabinet departments have influence not only on the administration of laws but also on policy formation through their expertise and their ability to develop policy proposals.

The president submits an annual budget to Congress. Although Congress may make any changes it chooses, the president, through pressure, bargaining power, and the veto, has considerable influence over the final product. The budget process is typically characterized by intense bargaining between the Office of Management and Budget and the congressional leadership.

In reasoning about political behavior, it is important to recognize that the absence of certain behavior does not mean that it is not important. For example, presidents cast relatively few vetoes, even when the president and Congress are from different parties. The infrequency of vetoes does not, however, mean that the veto is unimportant. The

### FIGURE 5-8 Cabinet Departments

| | |
|---|---|
| State | Labor |
| Treasury | Education |
| Defense | Housing and Urban Development |
| Justice | Transportation |
| Homeland Security | Energy |
| Interior | Health and Human Services |
| Agriculture | Veterans Affairs |
| Commerce | |

---

[35]The president can be removed from office only through impeachment by the House and a trial in the Senate. Only Andrew Johnson and Bill Clinton have been impeached, and neither was convicted.

threat of a veto causes Congress not to pass some legislation that it would otherwise pass and causes it to modify legislation that it does pass so as to avoid a veto.

One of the most important powers of the president is the responsibility, with the consent of the Senate, to appoint members of the federal judiciary. In addition to deciding individual cases, the judiciary interprets the Constitution and federal statutes. The precedents established by court decisions have lasting effects. Through their appointments, the Reagan and (George H. W.) Bush administrations changed the Supreme Court from one with a liberal and judicial activist orientation to one with a more conservative orientation reflecting judicial restraint.

## State Governments

State governments are granted specific responsibilities by the Constitution, such as the right provided by the 21st Amendment to regulate the use of intoxicating liquors. The Constitution also limits the jurisdiction of the federal government to matters of interstate and not intrastate commerce, leaving major public policy areas largely to the states. State law governs liability standards, insurance and public utility regulation, occupational licensure, real estate, and some aspects of labor and securities law, incorporation law, and commercial law. States also have the authority to levy taxes and make expenditures and have the principal responsibility for education and the administration of some welfare programs such as Medicaid.

State government processes and structures are similar to those at the federal level, although most states elect more of their executive branch officials than at the federal level.[36] Also, 23 states have a referendum mechanism by which citizens can exercise direct democracy by enacting legislation or changing the state constitution.[37] The Chapter 8 case, *Proposition 211: Securities Litigation Referendum (A)*, is about a public referendum.

Because each state can enact its own laws, the multiplicity of state laws is a continuing source of problems for firms. Differences among state regulations force firms to meet a variety of standards, often at considerable expense, as in the case of automobile emissions standards. Firms and interest groups work in state capitals to address these differing regulations. On some issues, firms have sought uniform federal regulations and standards to replace or preempt different state regulations. For example, firms supported federal legislation on securities fraud litigation to avoid differences in state laws. Some firms supported a federal Internet privacy law to preempt the passage of a myriad of state privacy laws.

## Politics and the Public Interest

One approach to understanding political activity is to envision elected officials following a set of normative principles about what is good or right. This *public interest theory* of political behavior has two weaknesses. First, as Arrow's impossibility theorem suggests, there may be no general agreement about which principles to use to identify the public interest and, therefore, about which alternatives are in the public interest. Second, much observed political behavior appears to be motivated by private interests rather than by some concept of the public interest, although that behavior may be cloaked in the rhetoric of the public interest. These observations suggest that the public interest is identified not by consensus but from a *pluralism of competing interests*. That is, the public interest is revealed through the competing actions of individuals and the groups they form in pursuit of their interests.

---

[36]There are some exceptions, however. For example, Nebraska has only one chamber in its legislature.
[37]Nearly half the states have term limits for state legislators, and most have a term limit for the governor.

When public policies arise from a pluralism of interests and the political action those interests motivate, the study of individual interests and the manner in which they are transformed into political and collective action is fundamental to understanding political and other forms of nonmarket activity. The case analyzed next expands on this perspective.

# The Politics of the Extension of Daylight Saving Time

## The Nature of Political Explanations

Since the Uniform Time Act was enacted in 1966, daylight saving time had begun on the last Sunday in April and lasted 6 months until the last Sunday in October.[38] Bills to extend daylight saving time were introduced in Congress beginning in 1976, and the battle for an extension lasted for 10 years, concluding in 1986 with a 3-week extension to the first Sunday in April. The forces that led to the extension are representative of those present on many political issues affecting business.

Two contrasting approaches can be taken to explain the politics of the extension. The public interest perspective predicts that the alternative that best serves the public will be adopted. In this case, the public interest would select the extension that yielded the greatest differences between aggregate benefits and costs. This perspective was first advanced in 1784 when Benjamin Franklin argued to the French that they could save 96 million candles per year from an extra hour of daylight.[39] During World Wars I and II the United States adopted daylight saving time, and in World War II it lasted for $3\frac{1}{2}$ years. During the oil crisis in 1973–1974, the United States extended daylight saving time as a means of saving energy. The waning of the oil crisis and protests from parents who objected to their children having to walk to school in the early morning darkness led to the elimination of the extension. Subsequently, the Department of Transportation (DOT) estimated that the extension during the oil crisis saved 6 million barrels of oil and traffic accidents decreased 2 to 3 percent.

A second approach focuses on the political competition resulting from the actions of those whose interests are affected by the length of daylight saving time. For most nonmarket issues it is better to view political action as arising from the interests of individuals, firms, and groups than to view political outcomes as the result of the pursuit of the public interest. This does not mean that public policy analysis has no effect on the outcome of political activity. Often it does. Even in those cases, however, public policy analysis should not be viewed as the determinant of the outcome of political activity. Instead, public policy analysis is better viewed as providing information about the consequences of alternatives for interests.

## The Legislative History of the Extension

In 1976 the Senate passed a bill extending daylight saving time to 8 months and 1 week, but the House did not act. In 1981 the House passed a bill providing for a shorter extension, but the Senate did not act. In 1983 the House rejected an extension. Finally, in 1985 the light at the end of the tunnel began to appear. Representative Edward J. Markey (D-MA), chairman of the Subcommittee on Energy Conservation, introduced a bill that would extend daylight saving time to the third Sunday in March and to the first Sunday in November. The Subcommittee approved the bill by voice vote. The

---

[38]States retained the right not to adopt daylight saving time. The dates had been chosen because the weather was generally similar at the beginning and end of the period.
[39]*Fortune*, November 12, 1984, p. 147.

Energy and Commerce Committee, however, approved an amendment by Howard C. Nielson (R-UT) that moved the starting date back 2 weeks to the first Sunday in April. Approving the amended bill by voice vote, the committee sent it to the full House, which approved it by a 240 to 157 vote in October 1985.

In July 1985 Senator Slade Gorton (R-WA) introduced a bill extending daylight saving time, but opposition by senators from rural and Midwestern states led by Senators Wendell Ford (D-KY) and J. James Exon (D-NE) blocked the bill in the Commerce Committee. With the committee gates closed, Senator Gorton introduced his extension bill as a rider to an authorization bill for fire prevention and control programs. The amendment provided the same starting date as the House bill, but to recruit additional votes Gorton removed the 1-week extension in the fall. By a 36 to 58 vote the Senate defeated a motion to table the amendment and then by voice vote adopted the amendment and the bill. The House and Senate thus had both passed extensions of daylight saving time, but the measures were not identical. Rather than convene a conference to reconcile the bills, the House chose to enact the Senate bill. An authorization bill for fire prevention and control had been working its way through the House, and on June 24, 1986, the House, by unanimous consent, agreed to drop the 1-week extension in November and passed the Senate bill.

## The Politics of Daylight Saving Time

The politics of daylight saving time can be understood as a competition between those interests favoring and those opposed to an extension. Congress was the institutional arena for that competition. Senator Ford characterized the differences in interests as "any Kentucky mother who has sent a first-grader out to catch a bus on a dark, misty April morning takes a dim view about . . . electricity that might be saved on the East and West coasts and the number of afternoon tennis games that might be played here in Washington."[40]

The effects of an extension were broadly distributed, and at the beginning of the political competition in 1976 interest groups were poorly organized and their strategies only loosely coordinated. The status quo prevailed. The benefits to a number of groups, including recreation and business interests, were substantial, however, so interest groups had an incentive to form.

An extension of daylight saving time affected a wide array of economic activity. As James Benfield, a lobbyist who served as executive director of the Daylight Saving Time Coalition, explained, "Here's a way to increase economic activity by doing nothing more than changing the time on your wrist. . . . We are simply fine-tuning our use of time to adjust for daily life patterns and to translate those patterns into dollars for business."[41] In the context of Figure 5-2, an extension shifted the demand curve outward for a variety of goods. The Barbecue Industry Association estimated that an extension would increase the sales of briquettes by $56 million and starter fluid by $15 million. The Kingsford Company was an active supporter of the extension. Bob Lederer of the American Association of Nurserymen stated, "When daylight saving time comes, people think spring and they start buying plants. And if daylight saving comes earlier, people will buy a lot more plants."[42] The Sporting Goods Manufacturers Association estimated that golfers would spend $7 million more on clubs and balls and would play 4 million more rounds of golf a year. Expenditures for tennis balls and rackets could increase by $7 million per year. Hardee's estimated that an extension would increase sales by an average of

---

[40]*Congressional Quarterly Weekly Report,* May 24, 1986, p. 1177.
[41]*Fortune,* November 12, 1984, p. 150.
[42]*Fortune,* November 12, 1984, pp. 150–151.

$800 per week per store. The Southland Corporation estimated that daylight saving time could increase sales at its 7-Eleven stores by $30 million annually. Pamela Sederholm, a spokesperson for 7-Eleven, said, "Women shop in daylight hours at a 7-Eleven. They go to supermarkets when it's dark."

Benfield conceived the idea of including Halloween in the extension to bring the candy industry into the coalition.[43] Candy makers were interested in an additional hour of daylight on Halloween because some parents would allow their children to extend their trick-or-treating. Those candy companies were represented by the Chocolate Manufacturers Association, the National Candy Brokers Association, and the National Confectioners Association. Representative Markey said, "This small step could make trick-or-treating for young children a much safer experience."[44] The deletion of the fall extension by Senator Gorton was a substantial blow to the candy interests—as well as to children.

Firms measured the impact of an extension in terms of their sales and profits. Increased sales also mean that customers benefit. Similarly, increased sales mean an increase in employment. The difference between the incentives of a firm (or its shareholders) and the incentives of customers and employees is both in the magnitude of their benefits and the cost of taking nonmarket action. Firms have relatively low costs of taking nonmarket action and thus may act when those with higher costs would not act. Customers and future employees typically are widely dispersed and costly to organize, and thus their costs of taking nonmarket action are high. On the daylight saving time issue, they would not be expected to act. Their interests, however, were represented by the nonmarket actions of the firms that benefited from an extension. Thus, an important consequence of the participation of firms in nonmarket activity is that they often represent the interests of those who might otherwise not be represented due to high costs and low per-capita benefits. Firms regularly inform members of Congress of the jobs that would be created and other benefits that would accrue to their constituents.

An important factor in political competition is the alignment of interests among dissimilar groups. An interest group with a strong incentive to support the extension of daylight saving time was the RP Foundation Fighting Blindness, which had 400,000 members who suffered from retinitis pigmentosa and other eye diseases that caused night blindness. Although their interests were not directly economic, as were those of 7-Eleven and Kingsford, they had an incentive to support an extension just as business had. The fact that individuals with night blindness were disadvantaged could, however, be more compelling to some members of Congress than the economic interests of firms, customers, and employees.

On most issues, there are opposing interests, and one nonmarket strategy is to provide substitutes to reduce the adverse consequences to those opposed to the issue. The National Association of Broadcasters, for example, opposed the extension. Although most of the 2,450 AM radio stations licensed to operate only in the daytime had a PSA (presunrise authorization) that allowed them to begin broadcasting with reduced power at 6:00 A.M., nearly 450 did not have a PSA.[45] For many of these stations the most profitable advertising time was the morning commute hours, and profits would be reduced by an extension that would add an hour of broadcast time in the evening and eliminate an hour in the morning. This opposition was relatively easy to accommodate because adjustments in authorizations for AM radio stations were virtually costless to the supporters of the extension. As Benfield argued, the Federal Communications Commission (FCC) could extend the broadcast time in the morning. The amendment

---

[43]He was successful in expanding the coalition from 4 members in 1983 to 16 in 1985.
[44]*Congressional Quarterly Weekly Report,* May 4, 1985, p. 839.
[45]*Congressional Quarterly Weekly Report,* May 24, 1986, p. 1177.

offered by Senator Gorton contained a provision allowing the FCC to make appropriate adjustments in broadcasting authorizations.

In other instances there may be no means of satisfying opponents. Some Christian fundamentalists opposed the extension because they viewed it as contrary to God's will. Some Orthodox Jews opposed the extension because their morning prayers cannot begin earlier than 45 minutes before sunrise, and the length of the prayers might make them late for work. A number of other groups also opposed the extension.[46] Some parents opposed it because their children would have to go to school in the dark. This was more of a problem on the western edges of time zones.[47] Some farmers objected to the extension, and their interests were represented by a number of members of Congress. Representative Thomas A. Daschle (D-SD) said, "The time shift would hurt farmers, particularly the estimated thirty percent who hold second jobs and who would have less daylight to perform morning chores." Even more important, he said, was the safety threat to "children who would wait in the dark for school buses as early as 6:30 A.M."[48] These interests were represented by organizations such as the PTA and the American Farm Bureau.

## The Role of Information

One feature of political competition is the provision of information about the consequences of political alternatives. The DOT and the National Safety Council reported that the extension of daylight saving time would not significantly increase the risk to school children. Opponents of the extension attacked DOT's accident data from the 1974–1975 extension and argued that it was insufficient to warrant any conclusion. In 1986 the DOT countered when Secretary Elizabeth H. Dole wrote to Senate majority leader Robert Dole (R-KS) stating that its studies concluded that an extension "would reduce traffic deaths nationwide by a minimum of 22, injuries by a minimum of 1,525, and societal costs from auto accidents by a minimum of $28 million [annually] . . . with possible savings being as much as twice as large."[49]

The impact of such facts is difficult to determine, but whatever their significance, politics is not primarily a competition among facts. Politics is better viewed as a competition of interests, and information is important to the extent that it helps identify the relationship between political alternatives and their consequences for those interests. Through the efforts of the Daylight Saving Time Coalition, many legislators learned of the benefits to businesses and their constituents. Complaints from farmers, parents, and others provided information that led Representative Daschle and Senators Exon and Ford to oppose an extension.

## An Analytical Characterization of the Politics of Daylight Saving Time

The next step in the analysis is to move from interests to outcomes. In the case of daylight saving time, the median voter theorem provides that step. The alternatives before Congress can be summarized by the length of daylight saving time, as measured by the number of weeks constrained by beginning and ending on a Sunday. The principal alternatives in 1986 are displayed in Figure 5-9. The status quo *q* is farthest to the left, and Representative Markey's bill, denoted by *m,* is farthest to the right.

---

[46]Some opposition defied logic. Representative Thomas F. Hartnett (D-SC) asked "how big the mushrooms are going to be with that extra hour of daylight in the evening" (*Fortune,* November 12, 1984, p. 150).
[47]DOT estimated that dawn would be, on average, at 6:48 A.M. but would occur at 7:00 A.M. on the western edges of time zones.
[48]*Congressional Quarterly Weekly Report,* May 4, 1985, p. 839.
[49]*Congressional Quarterly Weekly Report,* May 24, 1986, p. 1177.

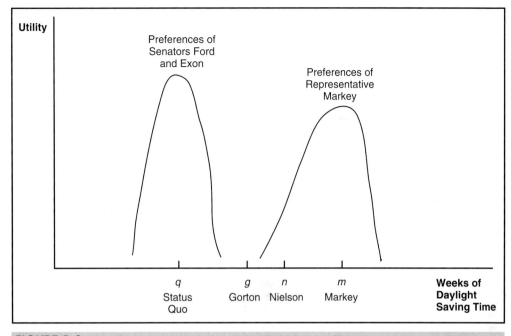

**FIGURE 5-9** Median Voter Theorem and Daylight Saving Time

Because of the constituency connection, members of Congress were concerned about the interests of their constituents. Particularly in states and districts at western edges of a time zone, pressure from farmers and parents of school-age children outweighed the pressure from the supporters of the extension. Senators Ford and Exon, then, can be thought of as preferring a length of daylight saving time at, or perhaps to the left of, the status quo. This is illustrated in Figure 5-9 by a preference function with a peak at their most preferred length, their ideal point, and declining the farther an alternative is from that point.[50] The preferences of Representative Markey, whose district was on the eastern edge of a time zone, are also illustrated in Figure 5-9. Indeed, each member of Congress can be thought of as having preferences of a similar form.

If the House had only two alternatives, *q* and *m,* representatives would simply vote for their preferred alternative. The alternatives were not restricted, however, because the legislative process was open and any number of weeks of daylight saving time could be proposed. Legislators could thus introduce alternatives they preferred to either *q* or *m.* For example, an alternative to the right of *q* and to the left of the median would be preferred to *q* by all those representatives with ideal points to the right of the median plus some of those to the left. It thus would defeat *q* on a majority vote. Indeed, the only alternative that could not be defeated in this manner by some other alternative is the median of the ideal points of the legislators. That is, any other alternative would receive fewer than half the votes against the median. Hence, the median is the majority-rule winner. In the House, Representative Nielson's amendment *n* to the Markey bill was closer to the median and was preferred by a majority to both *q* and *m.*

In the Senate Commerce Committee, Senators Ford and Exon were successful in preserving the status quo against Senator Gorton's bill *g.* Senator Gorton, however, was able to attach his bill as a rider to an authorization bill. A majority of the Senate preferred *g* to *q,* as reflected by the 36 to 58 vote defeating the motion to table *g.* The fact that Senator Gorton's proposal provided a week less of daylight saving time than

---

[50]Daschle's district was also at the western edge of a time zone, whereas Gorton's state was at the eastern edge.

the Nielson amendment may indicate that Gorton believed that *n* was farther from the median of the ideal points in the Senate.

The House and the Senate had thus passed extensions that were preferred to the status quo, but before an extension could become law, the two chambers had to reconcile the two bills. Bargaining between the chambers resulted in the House agreeing to *g,* which was enacted. The chapter case, *Summertime in the European Union,* examines the daylight saving time issue in the context of the institutions of the European Union.

## Summary

Understanding nonmarket activity in the arenas of government institutions requires both theories of behavior and knowledge of the structure and procedures of those institutions. Nonmarket activity often arises from the effects of political alternatives on markets. Those alternatives affect rents and surpluses, providing incentives for nonmarket action. Interests, however, do not translate directly into action because of the costs of collective action. In large groups the free-rider problem is likely to be more prevalent than in small groups.

The free-rider problem is a variant of the prisoners' dilemma. The dilemma is that what is individually rational is not collectively rational. Some dilemmas can be resolved through repeated encounters that allow individuals over time to reward and punish each other for their actions. Others are resolved through institutional mechanisms.

Majority rule is an institution for making collective decisions, but, as Arrow demonstrated, a fundamental problem with any collective decision-making institution is that coherent choice is not always possible. If the alternatives are one-dimensional and voters prefer alternatives closer to their ideal point, the median voter theorem predicts that the choice will be the median of the voters' ideal points. The length of daylight saving time is a one-dimensional issue, and the extension can be explained by the median voter theorem. Coherent choice also results because of institutional structures such as agendas, but institutional structures also create the possibility of strategic behavior on the part of officeholders.

In addition to agendas and committee structures, majority-rule institutions such as Congress are structured by procedures that govern amendments, the assignment of bills to committees, and reconciliation between the chambers. The work of Congress largely occurs in its committees, which hold hearings, draft and mark up legislation, and conduct oversight activities. Committees have a strategic position in the legislative process, but their ability to thwart the preferences of a majority of the parent body is limited. In the case of the extension of daylight saving time, Senator Gorton was able to circumvent a closed committee gate by attaching his bill as a rider to another bill. Committees have power, however, because of their ability to delay legislation, provide expertise, and facilitate bargaining to resolve disagreements.

Members of Congress are motivated by reelection considerations, their duty to constituents, and their policy preferences. Reelection is central to the concerns of most members. To improve their reelection prospects, they develop personal constituencies and serve the interests of groups that can provide votes and electoral resources. The success of these efforts, in addition to the other advantages of incumbency, is reflected in the incumbency advantage.

The president and the executive branch are important in both legislative and administrative activities. The president uses the power of the veto, public suasion, and executive branch expertise to influence legislation. The president also has a major impact through appointments to the courts, regulatory commissions and agencies, and administrative agencies.

# Summertime in the European Union

Summertime, or daylight saving time, began in Europe in 1916 when Ireland and the United Kingdom set their clocks ahead by an hour in the summer. Italy adopted summertime in 1966, and France introduced it in 1976. The other member states of the European Union (EU) then adopted summertime, with Germany and Denmark the last in 1980. Not all the member states, however, had adopted the same beginning and ending dates.

In 1980 the European Union began to harmonize the summertime period, but by the 1990s, harmonization had not been accomplished.[51] In the 1990s transportation and communications companies again sought harmonization. Opponents, however, viewed this as an opportunity to eliminate summertime.

The European Union encompassed three time zones: Greenwich Mean Time (GMT), GMT + 1 (Central European Time [CET]), and GMT + 2. The countries in the GMT time zone include the United Kingdom, Ireland, France, the Benelux countries, Spain, and Portugal. During World War II, however, the Germans imposed their time, and after the war France, Belgium, The Netherlands, Luxembourg, and Spain retained GMT + 1. Portugal also adopted GMT + 1. The adoption of summertime by these countries gave them a second hour of summertime for half the year.

Summertime began on the last Sunday of March at 1 A.M. GMT. The sixth EU Directive on summertime extended through 1994 and established that summertime would end on the last day of September on the continent, with the United Kingdom and Ireland retaining an ending date of the last Sunday of October. In 1994 the EU began considering a seventh Directive on summertime.

The principal issue in the seventh Directive was the ending date. Recreational and other interest groups supported an ending date of the last Sunday of October, but there was no pan-European confederation supporting the extension.[52] Most business organizations, and particularly the transportation and communications industries, were indifferent to the ending date but supported uniformity across the European Union. In the United Kingdom the interest group Daylight Extra supported an extension on the continent to the last Sunday of October.[53] A European barometer survey of public opinion showed strong public support for an extension.

The possible extension of double summertime in the CET led to opposition by interest groups in several countries and by some pan-European associations of national interest groups. Opposition was concentrated in the countries located in the western part of the European continent and in the southern part. The opposition included GASHE (Groupe d'Action pour une Heure Stable en Europe) with participating associations in Belgium, France, Germany, and Switzerland; COPA (Compagnie d'Organization Professionelle d'Agriculture) representing farmers; and COFACE, a consumer group concerned about children having to go to bed during daylight and get up in the dark. Some of the opposition referred to a "disturbance of the biological rhythm with emphasis on children and elderly people, negative effects on agriculture, and a possible increase in environmental pollution. In addition doubts have been expressed about the real benefits of summertime with particular reference to the energy savings issue, for which it is argued that the savings are not important."[54]

The European Commission, the body that initiated legislation, proposed harmonization to the last Sunday of October beginning in 1997. The harmonization of summertime in the European Union was

[51]Chapter 15 provides information on the institutions of the European Union.

[52]The Belgische Vereniging Pro Zomerur, composed of hotel and catering interests, supported an extension, for example.
[53]Daylight Extra's principal objective was to move the United Kingdom from GMT to CET.
[54]European Commission, "Report on the advantages and disadvantages of summertime," VII-A-2, p. 2.

governed by the co-decision procedure established by the Maastricht treaty.[55] Under this procedure the European Commission prepared a proposal that was then considered by the Council of Ministers and the European Parliament. All laws in the European Union must be enacted by the Council, which had as its members the countries in the European Union.

Under the co-decision procedure, the Council operated under qualified majority; that is, enactment of a law required 54 of the 76 votes in the Council.[56] A qualified majority in support of a proposal, which could be modified by the Council, resulted in a "common position." A key feature of the co-decision procedure was that the European Parliament could reject (veto) the common position of the Council. Rejection required an absolute (50 percent) majority. If the European Parliament did not reject the common position, it became law. ■

SOURCE: Copyright © 1997 by the Board of Trustees of the Leland Stanford Junior University. All rights reserved. Reprinted with permission.

---

## PREPARATION QUESTION

**1.** Using a figure similar to Figure 5-9 in the extension of daylight saving time example, what conditions are required for enactment of an extension to the last Sunday of October? Hint: In this framework, the countries repre-sented on the Council correspond to legisla-tors in the U.S. case, and rather than the median legislator being pivotal with simple (50 percent) majority rule, a qualified majority in the Council is required. If a qualified major-ity in the Council prefers an extension, where must the pivotal voter in the European Parliament be located relative to the prefer-ences of the countries in the Council for the common position to be adopted? Do not consider amendments.

---

[55]The co-decision procedure governs the harmonization of regulations for the completion of the single market.
[56]Each country had a number of votes based on its population. The inclusion of new member states in 1995 changed the qualified majority requirement to 62 of the 87 votes.

# Repeal of the Luxury Tax

In 1990 Congress, with the acquiescence of the Bush administration, enacted legislation imposing a 10 percent federal luxury tax on the sale of furs and jewelry costing more than $10,000, automo-biles costing more than $30,000, boats costing more than $100,000, and aircraft costing more than $250,000 (except for aircraft used at least 80 percent for business). Effective in 1991 the tax was applied to the difference between the price and the tax base, so the tax on a $1,000,000 yacht was $90,000. The luxury tax was a component of the Deficit Reduction Act of 1990 and was viewed not as a significant source of additional revenue but as a symbol that the rich should bear a larger share of the tax burden. The tax yielded $251 mil-lion in 1991 and $146 million in the first half of 1992 with the vast majority coming from the sale of automobiles.

As the economy slowed, sales of boats costing at least $100,000 began to decrease, falling from 16,000 in 1987 to 9,100 in 1990. In 1992 after the lux-ury tax was imposed, only 4,200 boats were sold. Sales of boats 35 feet or longer fell from 1,300 in 1989 to 400 in 1991, with sales revenue falling from $2.5 billion to $800 million. Employment in the industry decreased from 600,000 to 400,000 in 1993. Hatteras Yachts of New Bern, North Carolina, expe-rienced a 50 percent decrease in sales and was forced to lay off 1,000 of its 1,800 employees. Viking Yacht of New Gretna, New Jersey, was forced to cut its workforce to 65 people. Yacht manufacturers from Minnesota, Wisconsin, Maine, Connecticut, and Florida experienced similar declines. As one potential customer who decided to stick with his current yacht rather than purchase a new one said, "I don't care how much you spend for a boat,

$190,000 in taxes is ludicrous."[57] Some purchasers of yachts registered their boats in the Bahamas and the Cayman Islands to avoid the luxury and state sales taxes. The National Marine Manufacturers Association and its members blamed the collapse of the market on the luxury tax.

The light aircraft industry was also hard hit, as were the other industries subject to the tax. Jaguar auto sales fell by 55 percent, and the company decided to rebate the luxury tax of over $3,000 to customers.

The luxury tax had been enacted by inserting it in a large tax bill during conference committee deliberations, and opponents had little opportunity to oppose it. Once in place and its effects were realized, opposition mounted. "The purpose [of the tax] was to tax the rich and their toys," said Republican Senator John H. Chafee of Rhode Island, a big boat-building state. "What it really did was hurt the toymakers."[58] Senator Robert Dole (R-KS) of Kansas, where light aircraft manufacturers were located, said, "A lot of middle-class people are losing their jobs."[59]

Opponents of the tax pressured Congress and the Bush administration, and Senator Dole introduced a bill to repeal the tax. The repeal bill was included in a more comprehensive bill, but Congress was unable to reach agreement on the package. Opponents saw another opportunity in the spring of 1993 as President Clinton pushed for a deficit reduction package that would include increases in personal and corporate income taxes in addition to an energy tax. ■

---

**PREPARATION QUESTIONS**

1. Use supply-and-demand analysis to identify the incidence of the luxury tax for producer rents and consumer surplus.
2. Are the consumers or producers of luxury goods more likely to be politically active on this issue? Why?

3. Are the interests of U.S. automobile manufacturers aligned with those of yacht builders?
4. Are the opponents of the luxury tax likely to be successful?

---

[57]*Business Week*, August 3, 1993.

[58]*Business Week*, August 3, 1993.
[59]*The Wall Street Journal*, June 12, 1991.

# UPS and Multi-Employer Pension Plans

Nine-and-one-half million employees were covered by 1,600 multi-employer pension plans. The plans were widely used in the unionized sectors of the construction and trucking industries. Under the conditions of a 1980 law, if an employer were unable to meet its pension contribution obligations, other employers in the plan would have to increase their contributions to cover the shortfall. New firms in industries covered by multi-employer pension plans refused to join these plans and opposed unionization of their employees. Moreover, many incumbent firms with employees organized by unions had high costs, forcing some of them to exit the industry. In 2002 the bankruptcy of Consolidated Freightways resulted in 6,500 Teamsters losing their jobs. Both entry and exit thus put burdens on the remaining firms, since there were fewer firms in the multi-employer plans to bear the pension obligations.

Multi-employer pension plans were created through negotiations between a labor union, such as the Teamsters, and the firms in an industry. The Teamsters' pension plans were organized geographically, and the largest was the Central States pension fund. In 1980 there were four working union members for each retiree, but by 2002 the plan had 0.87 active workers for every retiree. By 2010 the plan was expected to have a ratio of 0.5. Payments into the fund were made by employees and employers under the terms of the labor agreement with the Teamsters. The benefits paid to retirees were determined by the trustees of the fund. A portion of the contributions of active participants in the Central States fund was used to pay the benefits of those already retired. The Consolidated Freightways bankruptcy reduced by 5% the active participants. At the end of 2002 the

Central States fund had assets of $18.5 billion and pension obligations of $31 billion. Such pension plans were covered by the government's Pension Benefit Guaranty Corporation (PBGC), but in 2003 the PBGC's multi-employer plan fund had a deficit of $7 billion—its first deficit in over 20 years. In 2003 the Central States fund was forced to reduce the benefits paid to retirees.

In the express industry United Parcel Service (UPS) participated in the multi-employer pension plan under a labor agreement with the Teamsters. UPS, the fourth largest private-sector employer in the United States, was concerned about its mounting pension obligations as a result of the failure of other firms in the industry. In 1997 UPS had attempted to negotiate with the Teamsters to limit its obligations for the workers of other companies. This resulted in the only strike in UPS history. Withdrawing from the pension plan was not a feasible option, since a company that withdrew was required to pay its share of any deficit in the fund.

UPS chose a nonmarket strategy to address its increasing obligations. Its strategy was to seek from the federal government an amendment to the Employee Retirement Income Security Act (ERISA). UPS pledged to cover the pension obligations of its own employees plus all of its present obligations for the employees of other firms, with the latter to be amortized over 30 years. UPS proposed only that the government cover obligations for employees of firms that failed in the future. UPS was a large employer in Ohio, Georgia, and Kentucky, and its congressional allies introduced legislation in Congress to change the pension laws. The Senate was scheduled to consider pension reform when it convened in 2004.

The Teamsters opposed any changes in the pension laws because they worried that more firms would drop out of the plans, causing the plans to unravel. In particular, the Teamsters strongly opposed the UPS proposal. Teamsters President James P. Hoffa stated, "The Teamsters Union does not intend to sit idly by as UPS attempts to use its political influence to push our funds into further crisis."[60] The UPS proposal would transfer future pension obligations for failing firms to the government, but the PBGC had insufficient funds to provide the pensions covered by the multi-employer plans.

The weak economy in 2003 and the precarious financial health of the airline and other industries brought congressional attention to the pension obligations of weak companies with defined-benefits pension plans. Congress sought to provide relief in the hope that fewer businesses would fail and turn their pension plans over to the PBGC. For example, in 2002 US Airways filed for bankruptcy and turned over its pension plan to the PBGC. The pension relief bill under consideration would provide relief for airlines, steel companies, and a few surface transportation companies, including Greyhound. The relief would take the form of reducing required contributions by 80 percent for 2 years. The relief was supported by both the companies and the unions covered by the plans. The unions feared that the companies would go bankrupt as US Airways had. Tom Buffenbarger of the International Association of Machinists and Aerospace Workers said, "Without this legislation, struggling airlines could be forced by investors to terminate employee pension plans to escape or avoid bankruptcy."[61] The Air Line Pilots Association and the Transport Workers Union also supported the bill. The provision was believed to be crucial to United Airlines' attempt to emerge from bankruptcy, since the revised basis for contributions were estimated to reduce United's pension contributions by $1.8 billion over the 2 years. American, Continental, Delta, and Northwest would also benefit. The bill was opposed by JetBlue, America West, and Frontier, which did not have defined-benefits plans but instead used 401k plans. No relief was provided for these plans.

The congressional action on pension funding provided an opportunity for UPS and the Teamsters to obtain relief for their multi-employer pension plans. The White House had stated its opposition to relief for multi-employer plans because of the potential cost, so specific provisions would have to be made for the Teamster pension funds. Allies within Congress were essential in such a situation.

---

[60]*Traffic World*, December 1, 2003.

[61]*The New York Times*, April 9, 2004.

Opposition in the Senate to the pension relief act came from Arizona Republicans McCain and Kyle, who argued that the Act helped airlines with defined-benefit plans but provided no relief for younger airlines with 401k plans. Senator Ted Kennedy (D-MA) also opposed the Act because it did not provide relief for all multi-employer plans, many of which covered union workers.

---

## PREPARATION QUESTIONS

1. Identify the stages through which an amendment to ERISA and the pension relief bill must progress to be enacted.
2. Which interests would be affected by the two legislative alternatives? Which will be active on this issue? On which political alternatives are the interests of UPS and the Teamsters aligned?
3. On which alternative, an amendment to ERISA or an amendment to the 2003 pension relief bill, is UPS more likely to have success?
4. What strategy should UPS adopt?

# Nonmarket Analysis for Business

## Introduction

This chapter presents frameworks for analyzing political and nonmarket action on issues characterized by opposing interests. The frameworks provide the foundation for strategy formulation and implementation in Chapters 7 and 8, respectively. Although the focus is on the competition among interests in the arenas of government institutions, the approach also applies to private politics as considered in Chapter 4. The approach is presented in the context of U.S. institutions, but, as indicated in Part IV of the book, it is also applicable to settings outside the United States. The approach is illustrated using a case involving Boeing and tax benefits on foreign leasing.

The perspective presented in Chapter 5 is that public policies result from the nonmarket action taken by pluralistic interests in the context of government institutions. The study of individual interests and the manner in which they are transformed into nonmarket action thus is one foundation for the analysis of nonmarket issues. In public politics nonmarket action is transformed into outcomes through government institutions—legislatures, administrative agencies, regulatory agencies, courts, and international accords. The characteristics of these institutions are the other foundation of nonmarket analysis. Because these institutions structure the nonmarket actions of individuals, firms, and interest groups, the approach presented here is referred to as *structured pluralism*.

Structured pluralism is illustrated in Figure 6-1 in the context of the issues, interests, institutions, and information that characterize the nonmarket environment. The nonmarket issue is the unit of analysis. The actions of the pluralistic private interests affected by the issue compete in the arenas of government institutions. Those institutions have structures and procedures under which their officeholders consider alternatives for resolving the issue. The officeholders have preferences derived from their policy interests and, through the constituency connection, the interests of their constituents. Information comes from two sources. First, research and public policy analysis provide technical information about the likely consequences of alternatives. Second, interests provide politically relevant information to institutional officeholders. The outcome of this process is a public policy to address the issue.

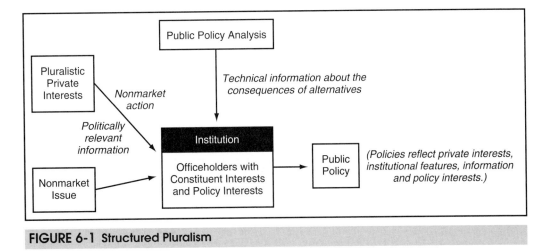

**FIGURE 6-1** Structured Pluralism

# A Framework for the Analysis of Nonmarket Action in Public Politics

## Interests and Interest Groups

The term "interests" has a dual use in nonmarket analysis and strategy formulation. One refers to those individuals, firms, and organizations with a stake in an issue. The other refers to the magnitudes of their stakes. Interests in the first usage are the actors (as in interest groups), and interests in the second usage are the incentives or motivation for the actors.

The framework begins with an assessment of the incentives. Stakes may be distributive or moral. Most issues have *distributive consequences*, as measured by benefits and costs, surpluses and rents, or profits and losses. In the example analyzed in Chapter 5, convenience stores, sporting goods manufacturers, and the charcoal and barbecue industries identified the effects of an extension of daylight saving time on their sales and profits. Issues may also involve *moral concerns*. In the chapter case, *Scrubbers and Environment Politics*, the motivation of some environmentalists were moral rather than distributive. The moral determinants of nonmarket action are often more difficult to assess than the distributive consequences, but on some issues they are as important.

Incentives, whether distributive or moral in origin, can cause an individual, firm, union, nonprofit organization, or activist group to become active on an issue. They may act on their own, but they may also form groups to organize, coordinate, and mobilize collective actions. Interest groups form among individuals and organizations with aligned interests. A necessary condition for formation of an interest group is that the benefits from collective action exceed the costs of organization. Interest groups may organize around a single issue, such as an extension of daylight saving time. High-tech companies, public accounting firms, and other firms formed an ad hoc coalition to coordinate their actions to obtain uniform national standards for securities fraud lawsuits. Interest groups may also be organized by a political entrepreneur who mobilizes the common interests of dispersed individuals, by a trade association that represents firms in an industry, or by a labor union that represents workers. Although interest groups form because of an alignment of interests, they are sustained by the fruits of their efforts. Once uniform national standards for securities fraud lawsuits had been enacted, the coalition disbanded.

Interest groups can also have aligned interests that lead them to act in parallel rather than jointly. The Daylight Saving Time Coalition and the RP Foundation Fighting Blindness both worked to extend daylight saving time, although the former represented business interests and the latter represented individuals afflicted with night blindness. Aligned interests also allow specialization. Environmental interest groups engage in a wide variety of nonmarket activities, and many focus on particular issues or strategies. The Sierra Club has a broad agenda, the Wilderness Society focuses on open lands, the Natural Resources Defense Council emphasizes litigation, and Greenpeace emphasizes confrontation to draw attention to environmental issues.

In some cases an interest group may be successful in having the government establish an agency through which its interests can be served. The Small Business Administration, the Department of Agriculture, and the Export-Import Bank are examples of such agencies. Environmental interest groups, however, repeatedly have sought without success a cabinet department for environmental protection. Members of Congress interact directly with interest groups and have established means of responding to their interests—the agriculture and small business committees of both chambers are examples.

The political system grants rights to individuals and organizations to pursue their interests and protect those interests from the actions of others. For example, U.S. trade law gives firms, labor unions, and communities rights to seek relief from imports. Similarly, wilderness groups exercise their rights before the courts to block the commercial development of public lands. Whatever their motivation, interest groups have become skillful in putting pressure on elected and administrative officeholders through direct action, their standing before the courts and regulatory agencies, and their rights to participate in governmental processes. The chapter case, *Tobacco Politics*, provides an opportunity to assess the interests involved in the tobacco issue.

## The Amount of Nonmarket Action

From the perspective of structured pluralism, a principal driver of public policies is the nonmarket action taken by interests. That nonmarket action includes activities such as lobbying, grassroots and other forms of constituent pressure, research and testimony, electoral support, and public advocacy. The extent of these activities is a function of their costs and benefits, and the optimal amount of nonmarket action maximizes the excess of benefits over costs.

To assess the nonmarket action of interests, the approach of supply-and-demand analysis from economics is used. The demand side pertains to the benefits, or incentives, associated with nonmarket action on an issue, and the supply side pertains to the cost of taking, or supplying, nonmarket action. An increase in the benefits results in more nonmarket action, and an incrase in the costs results in less nonmarket action. One component of nonmarket strategy is thus to work to increase the benefits for the interests on your side of the issue and decrease the incentives of the interests on the other side of the issue. Another component is to reduce the cost of nonmarket action for the interests on your side of the issue through, for example, the formation of an association or coalition to implement a nonmarket strategy.

The demand for nonmarket action can be characterized in terms of three factors. One is the aggregate benefits to the interests on a side of an issue. The second is the per capita benefits for an individual interest, such as a taxpayer, firm, or consumer. The third is whether there are any other means, such as substitutes, for achieving the benefits by, for example, turning to a different institutional arena.

The costs of nonmarket action have three components. The first includes the costs associated with organizing for collective action. The second includes the direct costs of undertaking nonmarket action, including the cost of lobbying, maintaining a

Washington office, and preparing testimony, as considered in Chapter 8. The third component is the effectiveness of nonmarket action, which depends, for example, on the size of the interest group and its coverage of legislative districts. The following sections consider the demand or benefits and the supply or costs and effectiveness of nonmarket action.

## The Demand for Nonmarket Action

The demand for nonmarket action is derived from the distributive consequences of an alternative, such as a bill before Congress. For firms, those consequences are reflected in sales, profits, and market value. Employee interests are measured in terms of jobs and wages. For consumers, the distributive consequences are measured in terms of the prices, qualities, and availability of goods and services.

The demand for nonmarket action depends on the *aggregate benefits* for an interest. In the Boeing example the aggregate benefits to taxpayers from eliminating the tax breaks on foreign leasing exceeded the aggregate benefits to Boeing from preserving the tax breaks. In the daylight saving time example the benefits to firms stemmed from the increase in demand for their products, and those benefits were greater the longer the extension. In the chapter case, *Scrubbers and Environmental Politics*, eastern coal interests would benefit from mandating scrubbers because the demand curve for high-sulfur eastern coal would be shifted outwards. Conversely, consumers of the electricity generated from eastern coal would be worse off because the combination of eastern coal and scrubbers was more costly than burning low-sulfur western coal.

Aggregate benefits are important indicators of the demand for nonmarket action. In many cases, however, the *per capita benefits* are a better indicator of the incentive to take nonmarket action, since individual interests must decide whether to participate. If the benefits are substantial and concentrated, the per capita benefits will be high, and those who benefit will have an incentive to act. The per capita benefits for Boeing as a company were $200 million a year from preserving the tax breaks on foreign leasing. The members of the Daylight Saving Time Coalition each anticipated substantial benefits from an increase in the demand for their products.

If the aggregate benefits are widely distributed, however, the per capita benefits can be small, providing little incentive for nonmarket action. Although the aggregate benefits to taxpayers from eliminating tax breaks on foreign leasing were larger than the benefits to Boeing, the per capita benefits for an individual taxpayer were very small. Individual taxpayers generally take little nonmarket action because their per capita benefits are typically small. In some cases nonmarket action can occur even when benefits are not large on a per capita basis. Proposition 13, a public referendum in California that reduced property taxes, resulted from political entrepreneurship that allowed individuals to lower their property taxes by simply casting a vote.

### Substitutes

On some issues the benefits from nonmarket action can be obtained through other means, referred to as *substitutes*. The benefits from nonmarket action are lower when there are other means of generating them, and the closer these substitutes come to replicating the benefits, the smaller are the incentives. Substitutes may be available in the market environment or in the nonmarket environment. On an issue such as unitary taxation—the taxation of corporate profits on a worldwide basis by a state—a foreign electronics firm considering where to locate a new U.S. subsidiary has an incentive to support the repeal of California's unitary taxation law. That firm, however, has available the market substitute of locating its subsidiary in Oregon, which already repealed its unitary taxation law. The alternative of avoiding unitary taxation by locating in Oregon reduces the benefits from, and hence lowers the firm's incentives for, nonmarket action to change the California law.[1]

An example of a public substitute is pursuing an objective in a different institutional arena. In the chapter case, *Tobacco Politics*, farmers had a substitute to opposing the tobacco settlement. They could seek government subsidies to compensate them for reducing their acreage in tobacco and transitioning to other crops. In the Internet Wine Sales example the wineries sought state legislation to allow direct interstate sales of wine to consumers. A substitute in the six states that allowed intrastate but not interstate direct sales was to file lawsuits seeking equal treatment for interstate direct sales. If a lawsuit were successful, the demand for new legislation in that state would be reduced.

## The Costs and Effectiveness of Nonmarket Action

The amount of nonmarket action also depends on cost, or supply, considerations. One cost is associated with identifying, contacting, motivating, and organizing those with aligned interests. If the number of affected individuals or groups is small, the *costs of organizing* are likely to be low. When the number is large, those costs can be high. Taxpayers are costly to organize because they are numerous and widely dispersed, whereas pharmaceutical companies are relatively easy to organize. The costs of organization can be reduced by associations and standing organizations. Labor unions, the Sierra Club, and business groups such as the National Federation of Independent Business reduce the cost of organizing for nonmarket action.

The cost of organizing is greater the more serious is the free-rider problem. If the number of potential members of a group is small, the importance of one additional participant can be significant enough to justify each member's participation. Furthermore, as indicated in Chapter 5, when groups are small, punishment and exclusion are easier to apply to those who free ride. If the group is large, a potential participant may conclude that joining in collective action will have little effect on the outcome and hence may decide to free ride. Interest groups attempt to reduce the free-rider problem by bundling together nonmarket action and services for their members. Many industry associations collect market data that they make available only to their members. The Sierra Club publishes a magazine and also arranges trips for its members. The free-rider problem also can be mitigated when interests expect to address a series of nonmarket issues, since they then have longer-run incentives.

Another component of the cost of organizing is mobilizing interest group members to deliver collective nonmarket action. Members may be mobilized on an ad hoc basis to address a particular issue. They may also be represented by a formal organization that can monitor issues and act when the interests of the group can be served. In addition to this readiness function, formal organizations monitor the progress of issues through their life cycles. Trade and professional associations, unions, the National Federation of Independent Business, and environmental groups provide these functions.

### Effectiveness

**Numbers** *Effectiveness* refers to the impact of a given level of nonmarket action on the outcome of an issue. Effectiveness depends on several factors, including the number of members of an interest group and their geographic distribution. Those members

---

[1]Under pressure from a number of countries, California revised its unitary taxation law. In 1994 the Supreme Court upheld the law taxing profits on a unitary basis.

are also constituents of legislators. For a firm, potentially relevant constituents are its stakeholders—shareholders, employees, suppliers, distributors, and in some cases customers. There are few automobile manufacturers, but they have many employees, extensive dealer organizations, many suppliers, and millions of customers.

The Sierra Club has 700,000 members, and the National Federation of Independent Business has 600,000 member firms. The greater the number of members of an interest group, the greater is its potential effectiveness, but the costs of organizing and mobilizing those members can be high. In addition, members may have an incentive to free ride.

**Coverage**   Particularly for issues addressed in legislative arenas, the geographic location of interest group members affects the effectiveness of nonmarket action. Nonmarket strategies based on the constituency connection are more effective the greater is the number of political jurisdictions covered by the group. Although small businesses do not have the resources of large businesses, they are politically effective because they are numerous and located in every political jurisdiction. Automobile assembly plants are concentrated in a relatively small number of congressional districts, but the *coverage* of the auto companies' dealer and supplier networks is extensive. The greater the number of districts covered by the members of an interest group, the more effective is its nonmarket action.

**Resources**   A nonmarket strategy must be financed, and the greater are the *resources* available to an interest group, the greater is the set of activities that can be funded. Financial resources fund research, lobbying, legal services, grassroots campaigns, and the group's administrative staff. The greater is a group's stake in an issue, the greater are the resources that potentially can be used to fund a nonmarket strategy. Pharmaceutical companies have ample resources, and when the stakes are high, as in the case of reimportation of drugs or Medicare coverage of prescription drugs, substantial resources are allocated to nonmarket action. The members of the Sierra Club also have ample resources, but their willingness to contribute to the Club's nonmarket campaigns is more limited.

**Supply Side Summary**   These supply side considerations indicate that the costs of organizing interests are higher when the costs of identifying and mobilizing those with common interests are higher. These costs are also higher when the free-rider problem is more prevalent and fewer means are available to mitigate it. Nonmarket action is more effective when the group has more members, their resources are greater, and it has more extensive coverage of legislative districts. A strategy that reduces the costs of collective action or increases its effectiveness will increase the impact of the interest group's nonmarket action.

The effectiveness of nonmarket action also depends on the actions others take on an issue. A grassroots political campaign in which members of an interest group contact their congressional representatives can be quite effective. If, however, an interest group on the other side of the issue responds by mounting its own grassroots campaign, the effectiveness of the first campaign will be reduced. Consequently, the assessment of the benefits from nonmarket action must take into account the likely actions of opposing interest groups. In many cases there are synergies between the actions of groups with aligned interests. In the daylight saving time case, the separate actions of the coalition of businesses and the RP Foundation Fighting Blindness increased the effectiveness of the other's nonmarket action.

## The Distributive Politics Spreadsheet

The analysis of the demand and supply sides can be summarized in a spreadsheet as presented in Figure 6-3 for the Boeing case. The distributive politics spreadsheet pertains to a specific alternative, such as a bill to revoke the tax benefits on foreign leasing, or equivalently to a particular change from the status quo. The spreadsheet is organized in terms of the interests that would benefit from the adoption of the alternative and hence support it, and the interest groups that would be harmed by the alternative and hence oppose it. The top panel of the spreadsheet pertains to the supporting interests and the bottom panel to the opposing interests. The spreadsheet is intended to summarize rather than substitute for the analysis of the benefits and costs of nonmarket action.

The demand side information summarized in the spreadsheet for each interest includes the available substitutes, the aggregate benefits, and the per capita benefits for individual members of the interest group. The supply side information includes the number of members, their coverage of political jurisdictions, their resources, and the costs of organizing, including the effects of the free-rider problem, for nonmarket action.

The information summarized in the spreadsheet provides the basis for a prediction of the nonmarket action likely to be generated by the interests. This prediction then is used in assessing the likely outcome of the issue and in formulating strategies to affect the outcome. The Boeing example illustrates the link between the analysis summarized by the spreadsheet and strategy formulation.

Institutions are not included in the spreadsheet because they are viewed as arenas in which the nonmarket actions of interests are deployed, as indicated in the next section. The institutional officeholders who decide the fate of the nonmarket alternative are also not included in the spreadsheet, since they are regarded as part of the institution.

## The Nature of Political Competition

When interests are opposed, their nonmarket actions may be viewed as competing in an institutional arena. The actions of these interests, coupled with the characteristics of the institution and its officeholders, determine the outcome of the competition. The outcome may be a win for one side and a loss for the other. In other cases, the outcome may be a nonmarket equilibrium influenced by all the competing interests. In the daylight saving time example, the outcome as characterized by the median voter theorem was in the center of the distribution of preferences of members of Congress. The ratification of the North American Free Trade Agreement (NAFTA) was a win for business and consumers and a loss for organized labor.

Building on the work of Lowi (1964), Wilson (1980) categorized the nature of political competition on an issue as a function of the concentration or dispersion of the benefits and costs from an alternative.[2] Although this categorization focuses on the nature of the politics and not on the outcome, it is useful for distinguishing among types of competition.

The Wilson-Lowi matrix presented in Figure 6-2 pertains to the benefits and harm of a nonmarket alternative, such as the enactment of a bill, relative to the status quo. The columns of the matrix are associated with those interests that would benefit from the alternative relative to the status quo. The rows of the matrix are associated with interests that would be harmed by the alternative relative to the status quo. The benefits or harm are said to be *concentrated* if the per capita effects are high. If the per capita benefits or harm are low, they are said to be to be *widely distributed*. Eliminating the tax breaks for foreign leasing would concentrate harm on Boeing and a few other exporters.

---

[2]Heckathorn and Maser (1990) provide a reformulation of Lowi's typology from a transactions cost perspective.

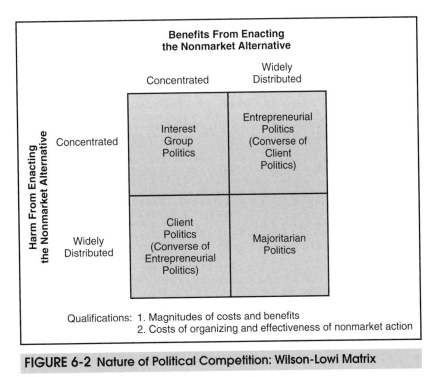

**Benefits From Enacting
the Nonmarket Alternative**

|  | Concentrated | Widely Distributed |
|---|---|---|
| **Concentrated** | Interest Group Politics | Entrepreneurial Politics (Converse of Client Politics) |
| **Widely Distributed** | Client Politics (Converse of Entrepreneurial Politics) | Majoritarian Politics |

*Harm From Enacting the Nonmarket Alternative*

Qualifications: 1. Magnitudes of costs and benefits
2. Costs of organizing and effectiveness of nonmarket action

**FIGURE 6-2 Nature of Political Competition: Wilson-Lowi Matrix**

The increased tax revenue was widely distributed among taxpayers. On some issues the benefits (or harm) may be widely distributed across interests, yet some benefits (or harm) may be concentrated for some specific interests. Interests with concentrated effects have a strong incentive to take nonmarket action, whereas interests with widely distributed effects have weaker incentives.

If both the benefits and the harm are concentrated, both supporters and opponents have incentives to take nonmarket action. If, in addition, their costs of nonmarket action are low, interest groups will be active on both sides of the issue. The resulting competition, according to the Wilson-Lowi matrix, takes the form of *interest group* politics. The outcome is then largely determined by the amounts and effectiveness of the nonmarket action generated by the interests on each side of the issue. Legislation that pits business against labor is typically characterized by interest group politics. International trade policy, which often finds business opposed by labor unions and environmentalists, is also characterized by interest group politics.

When the consequences from an alternative are widely distributed, the incentives to take nonmarket action are likely to be weak. When this is the case for both the interests who benefit and those who bear harm from the alternative, the political competition is said to be *majoritarian*. The outcome then is determined by the preferences of a majority. The politics of social security are majoritarian because each individual benefits from social security but is also taxed to support it, albeit by different amounts. The politics of the extension of daylight saving time were at one level majoritarian, since everyone was affected.

When the benefits from an alternative are concentrated and the harm is widely distributed, the interests that benefit have stronger incentives to take nonmarket action than do those who incur the harm. The competition then takes the form of *client* politics with the beneficiaries working to become the clients of the institutional officeholders—that is, to have the officeholders serve the beneficiaries. In client politics, officeholders can serve their clients with little risk of opposition from the other side. A firm seeking a subsidy for ethanol use in oxygenated fuels is engaged in client politics. The extension of daylight saving time had a component of client politics because some benefits were concentrated on businesses and the harm was widely distributed among individuals on the western edges of time zones.

When the benefits are widely distributed and the harm is concentrated, those bearing the harm have a stronger incentive to take nonmarket action than do the beneficiaries. Wilson refers to this situation as *entrepreneurial* politics, since if the alternative is to be adopted over the status quo, an entrepreneur is needed to mobilize or represent those with dispersed benefits. A member of Congress, an activist, or a business leader can be a nonmarket entrepreneur. The elimination of tax breaks in the Boeing in a Pickle case analysis was entrepreneurial politics, since the benefits were to taxpayers and the harm was borne by exporters.

In terms of the concentration and distribution of benefits and harm, entrepreneurial politics is the opposite side of the coin from client politics. On which side of the coin the political competition is located depends on the alternative in question relative to the status quo. In entrepreneurial politics, benefits from the alternative are widely distributed, whereas the harm from the alternative is concentrated. This favors the status quo, and for the alternative to be adopted a political entrepreneur is needed to mobilize the interests with widely distributed benefits. In client politics the benefits to the interest groups supporting the alternative are concentrated, and the harm to those supporting the status quo are widely distributed, so other things being equal, the alternative is favored over the status quo. The Chapter 5 case, *UPS and Multi-Employer Pension Plans*, is an example of client politics.

One strategy of interests is to attempt to change the nature of the politics of an issue. The politics of the extension of daylight saving time was basically majoritarian because everyone would be affected by an extension. Although a majority of people likely preferred the extension, their benefits were widely distributed. Some benefits, however, were concentrated, and those beneficiaries worked to change the politics from majoritarian to client through collective action. The Daylight Saving Time Coalition, representing business, and the RP Foundation Fighting Blindness, representing those suffering from night blindness, reduced the costs of nonmarket action for the beneficiaries. Those opposing the extension were unable to organize effectively and unable to prevail against the better organized supporters of an extension.

The Internet Wine Sales example considers the application of the Wilson-Lowi matrix.

---

### EXAMPLE

### Internet Wine Sales[1]

The 21st Amendment to the Constitution ended prohibition and also gave the states the right to regulate the sale of alcohol. All but three states adopted a three-tier system in which producers

(tier one) sold to distributors (tier two) who sold to retailers (tier three) and then to the consumer. This system made interstate direct sales of alcoholic beverages illegal.

Over the past few decades the number of wineries increased 500 percent to 2,700, most of

[1]This example is based on Wiseman and Ellig (2004).

*(Continued)*

*(Continued)*

which were family-owned "cottage businesses" shipping fewer than 25,000 cases a year. During the same period the number of distributors (wholesalers) decreased from 5,000 to 400.

The development of the Internet made possible an online market in wine with the potential to broaden the availability of wines, benefiting both consumers and wineries. Online retailers were quickly formed. Direct sales from wineries to consumers, however, would by-pass distributors, costing them significant business. The distributors sought a ban on direct sales, and the wineries sought specific permission for direct sales. By 2003, 26 states allowed direct sales, and 24 states banned direct sales, including five states in which a direct sale was a felony.[2] In Virginia rival bills backed by the two sides were introduced in the state legislature. This example considers the demand and supply of nonmarket action and the political competition in Virginia.

The principal interests were consumers, wineries, and distributors.[3] Consumers had large stakes, but their per capita stakes were small. Moreover, they were costly to organize, particularly in light of the free-rider problem. Consumers could not be expected to be active on this issue, although their interests could be represented by the wineries or by political entrepreneurs in the state government. The wineries were organized primarily through the Wine Institute from California and Wine America. The 50 largest wineries accounted for 95 percent of the wine sales in the United States, and their wines generally had broad distribution. The smaller wineries, however, had limited access to interstate markets, and their interests in direct sales were strong. Their per capita stake was high, and they were already organized, so they could take considerable nonmarket action. The effectiveness of that action, however, was plagued by the fact that most of the wineries

were out of state. Fortunately for the wineries, Virginia also had wineries, providing some direct coverage of state legislative districts. The out-of-state wineries had a degree of political effectiveness because they could represent the interests of Virginia consumers. Five wine industry associations and centers formed Free the Grapes to represent the interests of consumers and the wineries. The distributors were represented by the Wine and Spirit Wholesalers of America, and Southern Wine and Spirits played the lead role. The distributors had large stakes and were well organized, and their costs of acting were low.

In terms of the Wilson-Lowi matrix, consider first the bill to specifically allow direct sales. The harm would be borne by the distributors, and that harm was concentrated. Consequently, the nature of the politics was either interest group or entrepreneurial. The principal beneficiaries of direct sales would be consumers, and if they were the only interest benefiting, the politics would be entrepreneurial. The wineries could be viewed as representing the interests of consumers in entrepreneurial politics, but they had their own interests and were the ones to take nonmarket action. The politics thus were primarily interest group with some elements of entrepreneurial politics. Consider next the alternative of a ban on direct sales. The benefits would accrue to the distributors, so the politics were either client or interest group. Again, if only consumer interests were present, the politics would be client, but the presence of the organized wineries made it interest group politics, again with some elements of client politics.

The nature of the politics does not predict the outcome, which requires a more fine-grained analysis of the demand, supply, and effectiveness of nonmarket action. The Boeing in a Pickle case provides such an analysis. In Virginia consumers and the wineries won. Direct sales by out-of-state wineries were allowed with a permit, a requirement to remit taxes, and a requirement that the wine be shipped by a common carrier registered with the state.

---

[2]The legal strategies pertaining to direct shipments are considered in Chapter 12.
[3]In Virginia retail sales were through state Alcohol Beverage Control stores, so retailers were not an interest.

## Institutions and Institutional Officeholders

Although the Wilson-Lowi matrix is suggestive of some of the important characteristics of the politics of a nonmarket issue, it does not provide a complete theory of the outcome. For example, the free-rider problem and the coverage of political jurisdictions as well as the effectiveness of nonmarket strategies can affect the outcome. Outcomes also depend on the institutions that deal with the issue. The characteristics of legislative institutions considered in Chapter 5, such as the committee structure and the location of supporters and opponents on the relevant committees, can affect the outcome. The position taken by a cabinet agency or the president can also be important.

Since an institution is an arena in which interests deploy their nonmarket strategies, the preferences of those who hold offices in the institution can affect the outcome. Officeholders may support an interest group or may work to advance their own policy agendas. They may attempt to influence other officeholders or trade their vote on an issue of lesser importance for the vote of another officeholder on a more important issue. Legislators, however, are constrained by both their duty to represent their constituents and their desire to be reelected. The constituency connection thus constrains their behavior. One means of determining how legislators are likely to vote on a political alternative is to examine the interests of their constituents and how those interests would be affected by the alternative in question. The implications of this constituency connection for strategy formulation are developed further in Chapters 7 and 8.

## Moral Determinants of Collective Action

On some issues, moral concerns motivate individuals and interest groups to take nonmarket action. Moral concerns are the subject of Part V of this book, and only a brief discussion of these concepts is presented here. Assessing how individuals with various moral concerns view a nonmarket alternative can be difficult. The equally difficult task is determining how many people have a particular moral concern and how likely they are to act in the arenas of government institutions or through private politics.

Because moral concerns can differ among individuals, nonmarket competition can take place on moral dimensions, as in the cases of abortion and genetically modified foods. Just as one would not expect all physicians to perform abortions, neither would one expect all people of goodwill to agree on issues regarding genetically modified foods, working conditions in the factories of foreign suppliers, or drug testing of employees. The difficulty in predicting when moral concerns will lead to nonmarket action arises not only from the differences among individuals but also because the conviction with which those concerns are held can differ.

Despite these difficulties, managers must attempt to understand the moral motivations of individuals and interest groups and the strategies they are likely to employ. A church group concerned about a corporation's marketing activities in developing countries may use a private politics strategy that is quite different from exporters seeking a higher lending authorization for the Export-Import Bank. The exporters may use low-profile strategies such as lobbying and coalition building. The church group may initiate shareholder resolutions, pressure institutional investors, and demonstrate to attract the attention of the news media and government officeholders. These strategies are considered in Chapter 4 in the context of private politics, and similar strategies can be used in the arenas of government institutions.

# Boeing in a Pickle

Since 1962 the investment tax credit had provided incentives for capital investment through credits deducted from a firm's tax liability. By the 1980s, however, a number of companies were incurring operating losses and had no tax liability to which the credits could be applied. With the nation in a recession, Congress passed the Economic Recovery Tax Act (ERTA) of 1981 to stimulate economic activity. ERTA allowed companies with losses to purchase capital equipment and "sell" the investment tax credit to a profitable company that could use the credit to reduce its taxes. Thus, a steel company with operating losses could obtain a new rolling mill by having a lessor take title to the mill and then lease it back to the steel company. The lessor would receive the investment tax credit plus the tax benefits from accelerated depreciation, and the lease payments by the steel company would be lowered by the amount of those benefits.[3] ERTA thus restored the incentives for capital investment of those companies with operating losses.

Prior to ERTA many foreign sales were made under lease arrangements designed to capture the investment tax credit. A U.S. lessor would purchase capital equipment from a U.S. manufacturer, take the investment tax credit and the accelerated depreciation, and lease the equipment to a foreign customer. The tax benefits were then shared among the three participants in the transaction. Commercial aircraft had frequently been sold through these leasing arrangements. Investment tax credits were available for aircraft purchased by a U.S. lessor and leased to a foreign airline if the aircraft were used substantially in regular service to the United States. The "substantially" condition involved a modest number of landings on U.S. territory in a year.

Foreign leasing inadvertently became an issue because of the way ERTA was written. Its language allowed tax-exempt entities to make the same type of lease arrangements a steel company or a foreign airline could make. In addition, ERTA allowed the sale and leaseback of assets already owned by a firm or a tax-exempt entity. Tax-exempts thus could sell an existing asset to a lessor who would take the investment tax credit and the accelerated depreciation benefits and lease the asset back to the tax-exempt at a price reflecting the tax benefits.

The number of tax-exempt entities that could benefit from such leasing was enormous. Every municipality, museum, school district, university, library, nonprofit corporation, and government entity could use it. The pace of leasing by tax-exempts began to accelerate in 1983, and the federal government became alarmed about the potential loss of tax revenues, particularly because of the record federal budget deficit and the sluggish economy. In addition, several leasing plans attracted media attention. Bennington College announced plans to sell its campus to alumni and then lease it back, with the alumni passing back to the college the tax benefits allowed by ERTA. The Navy planned to lease 13 cargo ships instead of purchasing them, with the "purchaser" of the ships taking the investment tax credit and the depreciation benefits and passing back to the Navy a portion of the tax benefits in the form of a price reduction. Transactions such as the Navy's and sale-and-leaseback transactions such as that planned by Bennington College were clearly contrary to the intent of ERTA.

The House Ways and Means Committee had drafted ERTA, and members of that committee had a vested interest in its original intent. Representative J. J. (Jake) Pickle (D-TX), a ranking member of the committee, was determined to eliminate the abuses

---

[3]The economic efficiency rationale for this provision of ERTA was that it would equalize marginal tax rates across firms and thus lessen distortions in the pattern of capital investment. The political pressure from industries unable to use the investment tax credits was undoubtedly the impetus for the provision, however.

of ERTA. His idea was that those who were exempt from taxes should not receive tax benefits. This was expressed as, "People who don't pay taxes should not get tax breaks."[4] This slogan was quickly interpreted to include foreign lessees, since foreign firms do not pay U.S. taxes. U.S. exporters that had used leasing for foreign sales suddenly faced the risk of losing the tax benefits on which they had relied.

In May 1983 Representative Pickle introduced a bill, H.R. 3110, that would deny the investment tax credit and accelerated depreciation benefits to tax-exempts and to foreigners who leased assets from U.S. lessors.[5] Hearings were held 2 weeks later, and H.R. 3110 was passed by the Ways and Means Committee on July 27. Floor action in the House was scheduled for the end of October. Senators Robert Dole (R-KS) and Howard Metzenbaum (D-OH) introduced a similar bill in the Senate.

At the then-current volume of leasing, the Department of Treasury estimated that the bill would increase tax receipts by $1.65 billion per year, with foreign leasing accounting for $570 million. Approximately $300 million of the $570 million was attributable to Boeing, which used leasing for nearly half its foreign sales of 747s.[6] The other exporters affected included oil drilling rig manufacturers, producers of containers for ocean shipping, and other aircraft manufacturers.

In 1983 the 747's only competitors were the DC-10 and the Airbus A300. The A300's range did not allow it to make transoceanic flights, so many observers believed that the 747 had little foreign competition for flights to the United States. The DC-10 had a smaller capacity than the 747 but a similar range. McDonnell-Douglas was rumored to be phasing out the DC-10 because of lagging sales.

Boeing maintained that it was locked in a fierce competitive struggle with the highly subsidized Airbus, a consortium of four European companies supported by their home governments. According to Boeing, foreign airlines used their wide-bodied aircraft on many routes that involved a trade-off between long legs and short hops. For some foreign airlines, the A300 was a substitute for the 747, according to Boeing. An airline that operated routes in Asia as well as a route to the United States could fly 747s on the U.S. route and A300s on the Asian route, with a series of hops if necessary. Alternatively, it could use 747s on the Asian routes and fly each aircraft on the U.S. route often enough to qualify for the leasing tax benefits. Boeing thus argued that elimination of the tax benefits on foreign leasing would result in a loss of U.S. exports. Critics of foreign leasing, however, maintained that Boeing would not lose sales because it faced no competition. Furthermore, if sales would be lost, then U.S. taxpayers must be subsidizing foreigners. Representative Pickle wanted such subsidization stopped.

One means by which Airbus was subsidized was through government export financing at below-market interest rates. To compound Boeing's problem, the U.S. Export-Import Bank (Eximbank) had recently stopped providing subsidized export financing for 747s. This decision reflected the Eximbank's limited lending authorization and its conclusion, strongly criticized by Boeing, that the 747 faced no effective competition.[7]

---

[4]*Fortune*, September 19, 1983, p. 52.

[5]Straight-line depreciation would be allowed on foreign leasing.

[6]In 1983 the 747 was the only Boeing aircraft still in production that was certified for transoceanic flights. The 767 was not yet certified because of a Federal Aviation Administration's (FAA) administrative rule that permitted transoceanic crossings by twin-engine aircraft only if they remained no more than 60 minutes flying time from an acceptable airport. Approval was later granted, allowing the 767 to make transoceanic flights.

[7]The Eximbank had limited lending authority, requiring it to support those sales where its financing would have the greatest incremental effect on exports. See Baron (1983) for an analysis of Eximbank financing.

Hearings were scheduled before the Senate Finance Committee, chaired by Senator Dole, for the end of September. Neither senator from the state of Washington was a member of the Finance Committee, and Republican Slade Gorton was in his first term in the Senate. Longtime Senator Henry Jackson had died in August 1983 and had been replaced by the former Republican governor Daniel Evans, who was in the process of campaigning to retain his seat in the November special election.

Boeing's problem was how to deal with the challenge posed by Representative Pickle's bill.

# Analysis of Boeing in a Pickle

## The Nonmarket Issue

The issue of eliminating the tax benefits on leasing by tax-exempt and foreign entities arose suddenly as a result of the rapid increase in leasing by tax-exempts. The potential loss of tax revenue for the federal government was large, and the issue advanced quickly to the legislative stage of its life cycle. Although the politics of the issue were basically distributive, the sale-and-leaseback deals on existing assets by tax-exempts constituted abuse of ERTA's intent because those deals neither created jobs nor stimulated economic growth. The tax abuse coupled with the record federal budget deficit meant that the issue was likely to advance quickly through the rest of its life cycle. The dilemma for Boeing was that its leasing was threatened by the actions of the tax-exempts.

The following analysis illustrates the approach presented in this chapter.[8] The analysis is intended to develop an understanding of the politics of the issue and the relative strengths of the interests involved. This provides a basis for making judgments about the likely outcomes and therefore about strategy.

## Distributive Consequences

The demand for nonmarket action depends on the value of the associated tax benefits. The investment tax credit ranged up to 10 percent and represented a cash inflow for the entity holding title to the asset. The value of the accelerated depreciation was the present value of the difference in the tax liability between accelerated and straight-line depreciation. On a sale of a $100 million 747, the tax benefits threatened by Pickle's bill were approximately $20 million, composed of a $10 million investment tax credit and approximately $10 million due to accelerated depreciation. At a sales rate of ten 747s a year, Boeing's tax benefits at stake were approximately $200 million.[9]

Although the magnitude of the tax benefits from foreign leasing is straightforward to estimate, the distribution of those benefits is more complex. A foreign leasing transaction involves three parties: the aircraft manufacturer, the foreign lessee, and the U.S. lessor. The share of the tax benefits captured by each party depends on the competitiveness of the aircraft and leasing markets. The leasing industry includes large banks, some insurance companies, and several leasing companies. Because of the number of potential lessors, competition would be expected to leave them with

---

[8]This is not a description of Boeing's analysis.
[9]The difference between this figure and the Treasury estimate of $300 million is that the Treasury was reporting the tax collections reflecting the accelerated depreciation during the first years after the sale. The $200 million is a present value that takes into account the lower depreciation in later years.

competitive profits. The bulk of the benefits thus should accrue to the aircraft manufacturer and the foreign airline.[10]

The distribution of the tax benefits between the manufacturer and the airline depends on whether other aircraft are close substitutes for the 747 for the route configuration of the airline. Indeed, each airline can be considered individually, since sales result from negotiations between the airline and aircraft manufacturers. For an airline for which there is no substitute for the 747, Boeing is in the position of a monopolist and captures the tax benefits. For example, consider a foreign airline that is willing to pay no more than $100 million for a 747. With foreign leasing Boeing can make the following arrangement. It can sell the 747 to a lessor for $125 million, with the lessor taking the 20 percent tax benefits of $25 million and leasing the aircraft to the foreign airline for $100 million. If the Pickle bill were enacted, Boeing would reduce its price to $100 million, retain the sale, and no jobs would be lost. Boeing would, however, have lost $25 million as a result of the Pickle bill.

If there were some degree of competition from the A300, the tax benefits from leasing would be shared between the foreign airline and Boeing. If the A300 were a close substitute, the foreign airline might capture all the benefits. In that case, the elimination of the tax benefits would result in the loss of sales and jobs. U.S. taxpayers in that case are subsidizing the foreign airlines. In other cases Boeing and the airline could each capture a share of the tax benefits.

The Eximbank apparently concluded that the 747 faced little competition and that Boeing captured the bulk of the tax benefits from its financing. Representative Pickle and his staff came to the same conclusion. Even if there were a degree of competition, Representative Pickle and the other supporters of the bill had an attractive issue. If there was competition and foreign airlines captured a portion of the benefits, then U.S. taxpayers were subsidizing foreign airlines. If there was little competition and Boeing captured the benefits, U.S. taxpayers were subsidizing a large, profitable company. Boeing was in a pickle.

Boeing maintained that foreign leasing allowed it to make sales that would otherwise be lost to Airbus and that Pickle's bill would cost sales and jobs at both Boeing and its suppliers. In its testimony before the Senate Finance Committee, Boeing could expect to be asked why it could not lower its price to avoid losing sales if the tax benefits were eliminated. Boeing could also expect to be asked if the tax benefits on foreign leasing subsidized the foreign airlines that competed with U.S. international airlines.

To assess the impact of the Pickle bill, Boeing must determine if there are any public or private substitutes for the leasing. One obvious private substitute is to lower its price, which is possible, since Boeing is far down the learning curve on an aircraft that it had been producing for nearly 20 years. The other possible private substitute is to arrange for foreign lessors to make the lease arrangements, taking advantage of their own domestic tax laws. Other countries, however, did not have investment tax credits, so even if foreign lessors financed Boeing's exports, the tax benefits would be much lower. The Eximbank was unlikely to reverse its withdrawal of financing for 747s, so that public substitute was not a realistic alternative. The U.S. government was even less likely to subsidize a profitable company.

This analysis suggests that Boeing is likely to be capturing most, or at least a substantial share, of the tax benefits. If the tax benefits were lost through Pickle's initiative, except for some airlines for which the A300 was a close substitute, Boeing would retain

---

[10]If the lessors captured a substantial share of the tax benefits, Boeing could establish its own financing subsidiary as McDonnell-Douglas had done. That would permit Boeing to realize the depreciation tax benefits but not the investment tax credit.

the bulk of its sales by reducing its prices. Boeing thus stood to lose profits but probably few sales as a consequence of the Pickle bill—at least that was the conclusion reached by Representative Pickle, the Ways and Means Committee, and the Eximbank.

## Boeing's Nonmarket Agenda and Objectives

Boeing had several issues on its nonmarket issue agenda, including Eximbank policy, U.S. pressure on Airbus and its parent countries, antitrust concerns in the U.S. aircraft industry, the high value of the dollar, the Reagan administration's increased defense spending from which it expected to benefit, and the media and public attention being given to defense contractors. The foreign leasing issue had little direct relationship to these other issues, but the action the company took could affect its ability to deal with other issues.

Choosing an objective is a central component of a nonmarket strategy, and Boeing could pursue the following objectives:

1. Defeat of the Pickle bill
2. An exemption for job-creating leases consistent with the intent of ERTA
3. An exemption for job-creating export leases consistent with the intent of ERTA
4. An exemption for its own leases
5. Grandfathering of current orders
6. A phaseout of the tax benefits on foreign leasing

The best outcome for Boeing would be the defeat of Pickle's bill, but there was considerable support for the bill, and it was likely to pass in some form.[11] Objective 2 is consistent with the original intent of ERTA, but a substantial tax loss would remain because tax-exempts would still be able to use leasing for all but sale-and-leaseback deals. This objective is unlikely to be achievable. Objective 4 singles out Boeing without any particular justification, and so it, too, is unlikely. Therefore, Boeing's primary objective should be 3, with 5 and 6 as contingent objectives in the event that an exemption for job-creating export leases cannot be obtained. This objective means that the interests of other exporters are aligned with Boeing's interests, whereas the interests of tax-exempts are opposed.

## The Nature of the Politics

The principal beneficiaries of the Pickle bill are taxpayers and those who would benefit from lower interest rates if the federal budget deficit were reduced.[12] These benefits are widely distributed and small on a per capita basis. The harm resulting from Pickle's bill is concentrated among tax-exempts, exporters of capital goods that use lease financing, and lessors. In the framework of the Wilson-Lowi matrix, the politics of Pickle's bill are entrepreneurial, and Pickle is the entrepreneur. This issue is attractive to a politician because it involves good government—the elimination of a tax abuse—and the entrepreneur can claim credit for it. Boeing's objective, however, is not to defeat the Pickle bill, which was expected to pass, but instead is to obtain an exemption for job-creating export leases. The relevant alternative thus is the exemption, and using the Wilson-Lowi matrix again, Boeing, the other exporters, and lessors are clients with concentrated benefits from an exemption with widely distributed costs for taxpayers.

---

[11]One indication of this was that the Senate bill was introduced by Senators Dole and Metzenbaum, who were from different parties and had quite different positions on many issues. Their support signaled that this was not a partisan bill.
[12]U.S. airlines that compete with foreign airlines would also benefit to the extent that the foreign airlines currently capture some of the tax benefits.

## Interests and the Demand for Nonmarket Action

Boeing accounts for over half the tax benefits associated with foreign leasing, so the other exporters have smaller stakes in the issue than Boeing has. Employees, suppliers, shareholders, and local communities that depend on the exporters would also benefit from an exemption to the extent that sales would be lost. The lessors are likely to earn competitive profits on foreign leasing but still have an incentive to take action on the issue.[13] Since a relatively small number of firms is affected, general business associations such as the Chamber of Commerce and the National Association of Manufacturers are unlikely to be active on the issue.

The tax-exempts have a strong demand for nonmarket action in opposition to the Pickle bill. They also oppose an exemption for export leases because if the exemption fails, Boeing would then join them in opposing the Pickle bill. Although the impact on any one tax-exempt is small compared with the impact on Boeing, in the aggregate their demand is great. Many tax-exempts are already squeezed by federal budget reductions and the recession. Furthermore, they have few, if any, substitutes for replacing the tax benefits. Collectively, their demand is very high.

The interests of taxpayers are opposed to those of Boeing and the tax-exempts. The benefits to taxpayers from the Pickle bill correspond to the additional tax receipts, which would contribute to a lower federal budget deficit and hence lower interest rates and increased economic activity.

## The Supply Side

The affected exporters not only are few in number but also are geographically concentrated. Boeing's affected employment, if it loses sales, is in Seattle. Oil drilling rig exporters are concentrated on the Gulf Coast, and container manufacturers are few in number. The exporters thus have poor coverage of congressional districts, even though they have considerable resources. Boeing has a supplier network whose coverage is extensive, and it could attempt to organize its suppliers for nonmarket action. Boeing, however, may not want to mobilize its suppliers in a grassroots campaign because the overt use of political pressure by a defense contractor could attract media attention and result in a backlash.

The tax-exempts are numerous, their coverage of congressional districts is virtually complete, and many of their leaders and supporters have access to members of Congress. Although they have few resources, they have the ability to deliver considerable nonmarket pressure. To assess their strategy, it is useful to distinguish between those tax-exempts that already have a leasing deal in hand or in the planning stages and those that do not. The recipients of the benefits of leasing in the latter group are as yet unidentified, so it is difficult to mobilize them for nonmarket action. The former group, however, has identifiable benefits and a strong incentive to organize and act.[14] Their benefits, however, can be protected by simply grandfathering existing deals. Grandfathering would allow Pickle and Dole to avoid constituency pressure on them and their colleagues while preventing further drains on the Treasury.

Taxpayers are numerous, have complete coverage of congressional districts, and have large resources. They are costly to organize, however, and given their low per

---

[13]No lessor testified in the House hearings on the Pickle bill, although one association of lessors involved primarily in domestic leasing sent a letter that was entered into the hearing record.
[14]Some of the groups testifying were the National Housing Rehabilitation Association; American Federation of State, County, and Municipal Employees; YMCA; National Conference of Black Mayors; Municipal Finance Officers Association; Bennington College; and the Preservation Alliance of Louisville and Jefferson County.

capita benefits, cannot be expected to be active on this issue. Their interests are represented by a political entrepreneur, Representative Pickle.

Boeing's ability to generate effective nonmarket action on this issue is limited. It could attempt to mobilize its shareholders, but most are unlikely to contact their representatives on an issue such as this. Furthermore, a letter from Boeing stressing the urgency of this issue could cause some of them to sell their shares. Boeing employees have a demand for nonmarket action if sales would be lost, and their costs of organizing are low. Their coverage of congressional districts, however, is limited to the Seattle area. Consequently, their nonmarket action is likely to have only a limited effect, although their unions could represent them. Similarly, the communities potentially affected by the bill are geographically concentrated. Boeing could obtain coverage of congressional districts by mobilizing its suppliers. Their demand for nonmarket action varies considerably as a function of their volume of 747 subcontracts, but in all likelihood enough suppliers could be mobilized to supply a moderate amount of nonmarket pressure. As a defense contractor, however, Boeing is cautious about taking high-profile actions.

## The Distributive Politics Spreadsheet

Figure 6-3 presents a distributive politics spreadsheet summarizing this analysis. The conclusion from this analysis is that the supporters of an exemption for job-creating export leases are unlikely to be able to generate a great amount of nonmarket action. Attention should thus also be directed to the contingent objectives of grandfathering and a phaseout of the tax benefits.

## Institutions and Institutional Officeholders

Although Congress is the institutional arena in which this issue was contested, the executive branch was also interested in its budget consequences. A White House working group had begun meeting to develop measures to curb the leasing by tax-exempts.

Boeing might have been able to enlist the support of executive branch agencies concerned with exports. The Department of Commerce and the U.S. Trade Representative were potential supporters. The Department of the Treasury had stated that the additional tax receipts from eliminating the tax benefits on export leasing were not as important as the exports potentially at risk, but the Treasury could not be expected to work on Boeing's behalf.

Boeing's best hope was to have an exemption for job-creating export leases incorporated into the Senate Finance Committee's bill. Success in the Finance Committee would likely mean success on the Senate floor. If the committee did not provide an exemption, the chances of having an exemption amendment adopted on the Senate floor were not good, given the limited coverage of Boeing and the other exporters. Obtaining an exemption through a floor amendment in the House would be difficult because it would be necessary to obtain from the Rules Committee an open rule or a modified rule to allow the amendment. Ways and Means bills sometimes receive a closed rule, and Representative Pickle would certainly seek one. There was little hope of successfully introducing an amendment in the House.

The likelihood that the Pickle bill would pass in the House meant that if Boeing were successful in obtaining an exemption in the Senate, it would have to preserve that exemption in a conference committee. The contingent objective of grandfathering current orders might be a reasonable compromise to achieve in conference if the House were unwilling to concede more. Pickle would be among the House conferees.

*Alternative being analyzed: Exemption for job-creating exports*

**Supporting Interests**

| Interests | Demand Side — Benefits from Supporting an Exemption | | | Supply Side — Ability to Generate Nonmarket Action | | | | | Prediction |
|---|---|---|---|---|---|---|---|---|---|
| | | | | Effectiveness | | | | | |
| | Substitutes | Aggregate | Per Capita | Numbers | Coverage | Resources | Cost of Organizing | | Amount of Nonmarket Action |
| Boeing Company | | | | | | | | | |
| • shareholders | lower price | large | large | small | little | large | small | | moderate |
| • employees | sell shares | large | small | large | extensive | large | very high | | little |
| • suppliers | few | large | substantial | large | little | limited | very low | | little |
| Communities | other business | substantial | moderate | substantial | extensive | moderate | high | | moderate |
| • Boeing | few | substantial | considerable | small | little | small | low | | little |
| • suppliers | few | moderate | moderate | considerable | extensive | small | high | | limited |
| Oil rig mfgrs. | lower price | moderate | small | few | little | moderate | low | | little |
| Container mfgrs. | lower price | moderate | small | few | little | moderate | low | | little |
| Lessors | other loans | moderate | moderate | small | little | large | low | | little |

**Opposing Interests**

| Interests | Demand Side — Benefits from Opposing an Exemption | | | Supply Side — Ability to Generate Nonmarket Action | | | | | Prediction |
|---|---|---|---|---|---|---|---|---|---|
| | | | | Effectiveness | | | | | |
| | Substitutes | Aggregate | Per Capita | Numbers | Coverage | Resources | Cost of Organizing | | Amount of Nonmarket Action |
| Taxpayers | none | large | very small | huge | complete | huge | very high | | little |
| Tax-exempts | none | substantial | substantial | large | extensive | small | low | | large |

**FIGURE 6-3** Distributive Politics Spreadsheet

The key institutional actor was Senator Dole. Although Boeing had a major facility in Wichita, much of the work there in 1983 was on defense contracts. The Senator had won with nearly two-thirds of the vote in the last election and was electorally safe. His current policy interest was in reducing the federal deficit, and his personal objectives were to become Senate majority leader and position himself for a possible run for the presidency. To achieve the first objective, he had to avoid offending his Senate colleagues. They were under pressure from their constituents to preserve leasing deals for tax-exempts in their states. Dole could easily accommodate them and still be fiscally responsible simply by grandfathering their deals. The bill then would have clear sailing through the Senate.

The final opportunity for Boeing then would be the president. It was unlikely that he would veto this bill, which promoted fiscal responsibility, since he had been berating Congress for its unwillingness to cut spending. If a veto were likely, Congress had ways to protect the bill. One was to consolidate the Pickle bill with other pending tax legislation the president wanted passed. That could insulate the leasing provisions from a veto.

## Nonmarket Strategy Formulation

For a nonmarket strategy to be successful on an issue characterized by client politics, the client must demonstrate to enough members of Congress that either their constituents would benefit from an exemption or their own policy interests would be served. Given the belief that the 747 faced little competition, it would be difficult to demonstrate either that many jobs would be preserved by an exemption or that the trade deficit would be significantly affected. Indeed, the pressure on Congress came from the tax-exempts, and members were busy working to protect their constituents' deals. A client can attempt to build a coalition, but in this case there were only a few potential coalition members (the other exporters and the lessors), and their coverage of congressional districts was very limited.

Boeing's best strategy was to provide information indicating that export leases created jobs in a manner consistent with the objectives of ERTA. In doing so it could distinguish between its lease transactions and sale-and-leaseback transactions that did not create jobs. Boeing could also emphasize its importance in lowering the U.S. trade deficit. The trade deficit, however, was of much less concern to members of Congress than the budget deficit. Boeing also could challenge as inflated the Treasury estimate of the increase in tax revenues from eliminating the tax benefits on foreign leases.

Members of Congress were uncertain about Boeing's claims about the effects on sales and jobs, so Boeing could enlist the aid of some of its customers, such as Singapore Airlines, to attest to the impact of this legislation on their orders. In the upcoming hearings, senators, however, were likely to ask if Boeing could not lower its price to retain sales. This would reduce Boeing's profits, but few in Congress were concerned about lower profits for a quite profitable company.

Boeing could remind the members of the Finance Committee that it faced unfair competition from a highly subsidized Airbus and that eliminating the tax benefits on foreign leasing would place it at a further disadvantage. This argument, however, had not stopped the Eximbank from ending its financing of 747s. Moreover, Congress preferred to try to stop unfair competition than to subsidize U.S. firms. Furthermore, all U.S. exporters were complaining about losing sales because of the high value of the dollar.

In pursuing its objectives, Boeing could enlist the aid of the congressional delegation from the state of Washington. The House delegation was small, however, and the senators had little seniority. Senator Evans was spending much of his energy campaigning for election in November, and Senator Gorton was in his first term. Neither was on the Senate Finance Committee. Boeing thus had relatively weak representation in Congress, and few other members were likely to view Boeing as their client.

Because of the other issues on its nonmarket issue agenda and because of the sensitivity of overt political activity by a defense contractor, Boeing generally preferred to maintain a low profile. Using suppliers for a grassroots campaign had too high a profile for this issue.[15] A grassroots program involving employees would also be high profile and would likely have been insufficient to attain Boeing's primary objective given its coverage problem.

Boeing's best nonmarket strategies were lobbying and coalition building. Lobbying the Senate Finance Committee was essential. Boeing would be able to address the complexity of the issue in its discussions with key committee members and their staffs. It also could discuss its contingent objectives and the importance of protecting orders already in hand. In its lobbying, Boeing should stress the effects of lost sales on its suppliers and on its own operations and employees. The cost of lobbying was low compared with the potential consequences, and Boeing should use its executives in the lobbying.

Boeing could form a coalition with other firms that used leasing to finance exports, or it could coordinate its nonmarket activities with them. McDonnell-Douglas, oil drilling rig manufacturers, container manufacturers, engine manufacturers, and a few other exporters had incentives to act, although the aggregate effect on them was smaller than on Boeing. These companies were relatively few in number and had relatively poor coverage of congressional districts. The same was true of lessors, so there was a mismatch between their incentives and their ability to supply nonmarket pressure.

Boeing should, of course, modify its market strategy by developing alternative means of financing foreign sales.

## The Outcome

The Pickle bill had strong support from members of Congress who wanted to stop the tax abuse and the drain on tax revenues. As is clear from the previous analysis, exporters were unable to generate sufficient nonmarket pressure to stop the Pickle bill. The bill was eventually passed as part of the Deficit Reduction Act of 1984. The final provisions eliminated the tax benefits for both tax-exempts and foreign leases, but the current projects of many of the tax-exempts were grandfathered. Straight-line depreciation was allowed for foreign leases, and the depreciation period had to extend for the life of the asset or 125 percent of the lease term. The other tax benefits were phased out over several years. Grandfathering was provided for wide-body aircraft, containers, and drilling rigs. The provision for Boeing read: "The amendments in this section shall not apply with respect to any wide body, 4-engine commercial passenger aircraft used by a foreign person or entity if (i) on or before November 1, 1983 the foreign person or entity entered into a written binding contract to acquire such aircraft, and (ii) such aircraft is placed into service before January 1, 1986." Boeing thus achieved its contingent objectives.

The chapter case, *Leasebacks by Tax-Exempt Entities*, considers the second chapter in the foreign leasing saga.

---

[15]Boeing undoubtedly wanted to avoid media attention because the political entrepreneur had the better side of this issue. Furthermore, a large, profitable company seeking to preserve tax benefits—or subsidies, as its critics called them—had the potential for unfavorable media treatment.

# Summary

The analysis of nonmarket and political action has two foundations—interests and institutions. Interests can arise from distributive consequences and moral concerns. Distributive consequences can be assessed in terms of the benefits and costs from an alternative. The moral determinants of nonmarket action are based on considerations of well-being, rights, and social justice.

Interests give rise to a demand for nonmarket action, and that demand depends on the private and public substitutes available. The incentive to act depends on the per capita benefits, and if the aggregate benefits are high but the per capita benefits are low, incentives for nonmarket action can be weak.

The costs of nonmarket action are of three types. The first is the cost of organizing interests and joining together for collective action. The second is the direct cost of implementing a political strategy. The third is associated with the effectiveness of a given amount of nonmarket action. If the number of affected interests is small, the costs of organization are likely to be small. The larger the number of affected interests, the more likely they are to encounter the free-rider problem. The effectiveness of nonmarket action depends on the number of people affected, their resources, and their coverage of legislative districts. The paradox of collective action is that while effectiveness increases with the number of constituents affected and with their coverage of legislative districts, dispersed groups often have low per capita benefits and high costs of organization, resulting in little nonmarket action.

The analysis of the benefits and costs of taking nonmarket action can be summarized in the distributive politics spreadsheet. The chapter case, *Scrubbers and Environmental Politics*, provides an opportunity to apply nonmarket analysis and the distributive politics spreadsheet to a legislative issue.

The nature of political competition depends on the relative concentration and dispersion of the benefits and harm from enactment of a nonmarket alternative. The categories of interest group, client, entrepreneurial, and majoritarian politics characterize the nature of the political competition, but the outcome depends on additional factors, including the characteristics of the institutions in whose arena the competition takes place.

The Boeing case indicates the complexity of even a relatively straightforward issue. It also illustrates the difference between the demand for nonmarket action and its supply. Taxpayers have low per capita benefits relative to their costs of taking nonmarket action and thus were represented by a political entrepreneur. The tax-exempts had benefits that exceed their costs, so they were active. Boeing and other exporters had a high demand for nonmarket action and low costs of organizing, but their effectiveness was limited by a lack of coverage of congressional districts. As a defense contractor, Boeing preferred a low-profile strategy to avoid compromising its effectiveness on other issues. Boeing's best political strategy was to lobby using the message that sales and jobs would be lost. The best that Boeing was able to achieve, however, was a phaseout of the benefits and the grandfathering of orders in hand.

# Tobacco Politics

The tobacco industry has long been an economic juggernaut. By one estimate, as of 1998 tobacco accounted for 500,000 jobs and generated up to $170 billion in revenue annually in the United States—an amount approximately equal to the gross domestic product of Columbia.[16] Tobacco was grown in 20 states and was one of the most successful cash crops. Renewed efforts to regulate tobacco were fueled by new reports on the effects of secondhand smoke, such as one claiming that smoking accounted for as many as 400,000 deaths annually.

The federal government's efforts to control tobacco and cigarette advertising can be traced to 1954, when Representative John Dingell (D-MI) proposed a bill banning interstate advertising of tobacco products and alcoholic beverages. Although Representative Dingell's proposal did not succeed, in 1970 President Nixon signed a bill banning cigarette advertising on radio and television. In the 1980s several additional measures were passed that restricted smoking, including a ban on smoking on domestic airline flights. The 1990s saw further action taken against the tobacco industry, with legislation enacted to limit tobacco advertising and ban smoking in federal buildings.

Throughout this period, antismoking advocates portrayed the tobacco industry as an all-powerful, evil empire that held lawmakers in its hip pocket. Antismoking advertisements in the late 1990s claimed that tobacco companies consciously targeted teenagers in their advertising campaigns in the hope of recruiting and addicting the nation's youth. The threat to the tobacco industry and its beneficiaries increased significantly in November 1997, when S.1415, the National Tobacco Policy and Youth Smoking Reduction Act, was introduced by Senator John McCain (R-AZ).

## Provisions of the Act

S.1415 was an outgrowth of an agreement reached on June 20, 1997, known as the Tobacco Resolution. The agreement between the major tobacco companies, state attorneys general, and class action lawyers provided the tobacco industry with protection from future punitive damages lawsuits and set caps on damage payments in exchange for a substantial per-pack tax increase and lump-sum damages payments.[17] Overall, the bill would constitute a significant increase in the regulatory role of the federal government with respect to the tobacco industry. As proponents of the bill portrayed it, the bill required tobacco companies to pay $506 billion over 25 years to cover health care expenses related to smoking. The mechanism for funding this transfer was a $1.10 excise tax on the price of each pack of cigarettes. The bill also provided block grants to states to deal with medical costs stemming from tobacco use. In return for the tax increase, the liability of tobacco companies would be capped at $6.5 billion per year.

In addition to the monetary and legal provisions, the bill also restricted tobacco advertising and promotion. Tobacco companies would be prohibited from advertising on billboards, in public arenas, and on the Internet. In an attempt to reduce underage smoking, human or cartoon characters such as R. J. Reynolds's "Joe Camel" were to be banned from advertising campaigns. Companies also could not sell items of clothing bearing their brand name, provide gifts to customers, sponsor public events, or pay for product placements in television programs or movies. Advertisements could no longer use phrases such as "low tar" or "light" that would imply that a given cigarette brand was less dangerous than another brand.

Other provisions would affect the regulation and distribution of tobacco. The Food and Drug Administration (FDA) would have the power to regulate nicotine like a drug, including, with the

---

[16]The $170 billion estimate is from Alan Greenblat, "Growing Ranks of Cigarette Tax Critics Invigorate Big Tobacco's Lobbying Effort," *Congressional Quarterly Weekly Report*, May 16, 1998, p. 1306. Bulow and Klemperer (1998), however, report that retail sales of cigarettes were only $50 billion, which suggests that the $170 billion figure includes multiplier effects.

[17]Bulow and Klemperer (1998) provide an excellent overview of the provisions of the resolution.

consent of Congress, the power to ban it altogether. Retail stores would have to apply for licenses to sell tobacco, and tobacco companies would have to disclose all corporate documents about their product, which would then be placed in a national depository for public use.

## Interests

In addition to the tobacco companies, other interests would be affected. Trial lawyers for plaintiffs in individual and class action lawsuits would receive a financial windfall. To avoid the public fallout and demands for accountability associated with the payment of extremely large fees, the bill created a payment mechanism whereby three "arbitrators" representing lawyers and tobacco companies would determine the actual payment figures. In addition, tobacco companies agreed to provide the lawyers, who were instrumental in the agreement, an annuity of up to $500 million a year.[18]

State attorneys general who had filed state lawsuits wanted S.1415 to pass for two reasons. The first was to recover damages associated with smoking that could be used to cover state Medicaid expenses. The second and more subtle reason was the expectation of political gains from public sentiment for helping to pass what was being promoted as a major blow against the tobacco industry.

Foremost among the bill's supporters were dozens of antismoking groups, including the Coalition on Smoking OR Health, Americans for Nonsmokers' Rights, Action on Smoking and Health (ASH), Airspace, The BADvertising Institute, Smoke*Screen, the National Center for Tobacco-Free Kids, Effective National Action to Control Tobacco (ENACT), the American Heart Association, and the American Lung Association.

Wholesalers would be hurt by the per-pack excise tax provision because of the way the tax was to be collected. Wholesalers would have to extend credit to many retailers, and the book value of wholesalers' inventory would be higher, resulting in higher insurance costs and "shrinkage" (theft). In estimating the damage at $367 million over 5 years, the American Wholesalers Marketers Association's spokeswoman, Jacqueline Cohen, explained, "Your shrinkage will grow."[19]

Cigarette-only stores would benefit under the proposed legislation because they would be exempt from point-of-sale promotional restrictions that would affect other retailers. Some of these stores were "adult bookstores."

Convenience stores would be hurt by the excise tax and the registration requirements. Convenience store cigarette sales accounted for approximately 40 percent of U.S. cigarette sales, and cigarettes alone comprised 20 percent of the average convenience store's total business.[20] A 1997 Department of Agriculture study confirmed the suspicion that many of these stores would likely not survive price and distribution reforms such as those included in S.1415.

The National Association of Convenience Stores, an international trade association, represented almost 3,300 convenience store operators, petroleum marketers, and suppliers, with 63,000 convenience stores around the world. In 1996 the convenience store industry posted $151.9 billion in sales.[21]

Grocery chains would also be hurt, since tobacco companies currently paid $2 billion annually in slotting fees to obtain prime placement for their products. Grocery retailers were organized in a number of associations, including the Food Marketing Institute (FMI)—a trade organization of over 100 grocers, including Giant-Eagle, Dominick's, Piggly-Wiggly, Safeway, and Tom Thumb. The FMI's annual trade show hosted over 35,000 representatives from the supermarket industry. Additionally, the National Grocers Association has a membership of 2,060 and a budget of $5 million. It had food retailer members in 50 states and also included 60 wholesale food distributors.

The advertising industry would also be affected. By one account, tobacco advertisements and promotions totaled $5 billion, and the provisions of S.1415 chipped away at virtually every advertising approach used by firms.[22] Although print advertisements only generated $20 million in revenue, the prohibition on billboard advertising would eliminate $290 million in revenue. Point-of-purchase displays would also

---

[18]Bulow and Klemperer (1998).
[19]Greenblat (1998).

[20]Greenblat (1998).
[21]www.cstorecentral.com/public/nacs/rf05.htm.
[22]Greenblat (1998). Data provided by Bulow and Klemperer (1998), table 10, however, suggests that all tobacco marketing expenses are treated as advertising expenses in the $5 billion figure. Most marketing expenses are promotional allowances such as price cuts for distributors and coupon and retail value-added promotions, neither of which would be prohibited by the bill.

be prohibited and would reduce retailer revenues from slotting fees. The American Association of Advertising Agencies, with membership of 6 percent of the 13,000 U.S. agencies, accounted for 75 percent of advertising revenue in the United States.[23]

Tobacco farmers naturally opposed S.1415, but a 1997 Department of Agriculture study found that the preponderance of jobs attributed to tobacco were in the retail and wholesale trade—not in farming per se. Furthermore, the bill as drafted was sensitive to farmers' concerns, providing transition payments for them. Meanwhile, the foreign market for cigarettes continued to grow.

Concert promoters would be rocked by the expected loss of underwriting, which was dependent on prominent displays of advertisements. Likewise, organizers of golf tournaments would be driven to find alternative sources of underwriting revenue, while the net proceeds for tennis promoters would decline.

Not even universities escaped the reach of tobacco politics. By one estimate as many as 70 percent of university portfolios included tobacco stock, and some portfolio managers began to contemplate alternative investment strategies due to heightened public antitobacco sentiment and/or reduced profitability of tobacco firms. Harvard and Johns Hopkins had already divested, and Yale's board of trustees considered selling $16.9 million of tobacco stock from its $6 billion portfolio. ■

SOURCE: This case was prepared for class use by Professor Keith Krehbiel and Alan Wiseman using publicly available information. Copyright © 1998 by the Board of Trustees of the Leland Stanford Junior University. All rights reserved. Reprinted with permission.

### PREPARATION QUESTIONS

1. For each of the following groups, assess the likelihood that it will engage in nonmarket action on S.1415, and identify the specific cost and/or benefit characteristics underlying your assessment: smokers, tobacco companies, tobacco farmers, trial lawyers, antismoking groups, cigarette-only stores, grocery stores, convenience stores, advertising agencies, concert and event promoters, and universities.

2. Using the Wilson-Lowi matrix, what kind of politics best characterizes the activity surrounding McCain's bill?

3. Assess the prospects for coalition formation.

4. What outcome do you predict for the bill and why?

---

[23]Some legal scholars believed the advertising provisions in S.1415 would be subject to court challenges on grounds of violating the First Amendment.

# Scrubbers and Environmental Politics

In 1972 the Environmental Protection Agency (EPA) promulgated a "new source performance standard" (NSPS) for new coal-fired power plants, capping sulfur dioxide emissions at 1.2 pounds per million Btus (MBtus) of energy produced. As part of the stationary source emissions control section of the Clean Air Act Amendments of 1977, Congress had the task of implementing the NSPS for new power plants. The issue before Congress was not whether the NSPS would be attained but whether to specify how it would be achieved. More specifically, the issue was whether to require power companies to use a particular technology—a scrubber—to remove sulfur from their emissions.

Coal was produced both in the eastern and the western parts of the United States, but the technologies of extraction and the qualities of the coal differed greatly. Most of the coal in the East (West Virginia, Kentucky, Illinois, Indiana, Pennsylvania) was found in deep seams, requiring shaft mining. Shaft mining was labor intensive, and the coal miners were organized by the United Mine Workers (UMW). The wages earned by UMW members were high, and employee benefits were generous. Much of the coal mined in the East had a high sulfur content of up to 12 pounds per MBtus with an average of approximately 4 pounds. Sulfur dioxide emissions were a principal contributor to acid rain.

In Montana and Wyoming, coal lay just below the surface, and the extraction technology was strip mining, which was capital rather than labor intensive. Western coal was clean, with a sulfur content of approximately 1 pound per MBtus. Miners in the West generally were not unionized, and their wages and benefits were lower than those of the eastern UMW miners. The UMW had tried unsuccessfully to organize the western miners.

The EPA had concluded that scrubbers could remove approximately 90 percent of the sulfur oxides, although this determination was based on engineering data rather than actual applications. A scrubber was a large and very costly system that sprayed a water and limestone mixture inside a smokestack, causing a chemical reaction that removed sulfur from the smoke. Sludge was produced by the reaction and collected at the base of the scrubber, leaving a substantial waste disposal problem. A scrubber could require 400 tons of limestone and thousands of gallons of water a day to remove 200 tons of sulfur dioxide. When they worked, scrubbers were effective in sulfur removal but their initial reliability had been low, in part because of the corrosion caused by the chemical reaction and in part because the apparatus could become clogged by the sludge.[24] Scrubbers were thus often shut down while the power plant continued to operate. Not only were they quite expensive to build, they were also costly to operate.

The EPA concluded that the most efficient means—the lowest cost to society—of meeting emissions standards in the Midwest and certain parts of the East would be for new power plants to burn low-sulfur western coal. This would allow emissions standards to be met without having to build and use scrubbers. (Despite the difference in transportation costs, it was less expensive to use western coal in eastern power plants than to use eastern coal and scrubbers.) If scrubbers were mandated, however, it would be less expensive for power plants in the East to burn high-sulfur eastern coal than low-sulfur western coal, since scrubbers would have to be used with either type of coal.[25] Some experts warned, however, that unless significant advances were made in scrubber reliability, emissions in the East would actually be higher with mandated scrubbing and the burning of eastern coal than if scrubbers were not required and western coal were burned.

Environmental groups, which were particularly strong in the West, expressed little concern about the possibility of worsened air quality in the East if scrubbers were mandated and power companies used high-sulfur eastern coal. The western environmentalists were primarily interested in preventing air-quality degradation in the West, and they preferred lower emissions in the West than allowed by the 1.2 pounds per MBtus NSPS. The NSPS for the West could be achieved without using scrubbers, but the environmentalists preferred that scrubbers be mandated to reduce emissions below the NSPS. The environmentalists recognized that this would increase the cost of electricity in the West, but they preferred cleaner air. ∎

## PREPARATION QUESTIONS

1. From a social efficiency perspective, should Congress mandate scrubbers?
2. Which interests are affected by this issue? Which are likely to take nonmarket action?
3. Prepare a distributive politics spreadsheet and assess which interests will be active on this issue.
4. Are there any opportunities for coalition formation that would allow coalition members to achieve their primary objectives?
5. What do you predict Congress will do and why?

---

[24]By the mid-1980s scrubber technology had improved significantly.

[25]The effect of emissions standards on eastern coal interests is analyzed in Chapter 5.

# Leasebacks by Tax-Exempt Entities

The Tax Reform Act of 1984 ended the use of accelerated depreciation and the investment tax credit for sale-and-leaseback arrangements by tax-exempt entities, but straight-line depreciation continued to be allowed. In the 1990s financial services firms created new vehicles to obtain tax benefits from straight-line depreciation of the assets of tax-exempt entities. In a LILO (lease-in, lease-out) arrangement a tax-exempt entity leased an asset to a for-profit company, which then depreciated the asset, thereby reducing its tax liability. In exchange, the company leased the asset back to the tax-exempt entity and in most cases made an up-front, one-time payment to the tax-exempt of a portion of the tax benefits. Some officials in the federal government became concerned that the leasebacks were tax abusive and represented unwarranted corporate tax breaks.

In the United States the lease arrangements were used to extend the resources of state and municipal government agencies. Washington D.C.'s Metro system generated $100 million over a 6-year period through tax-advantaged leases. If a tax-exempt entity's assets had been purchased using federal funds, the Department of Transportation (DOT) was required to review the lease arrangements to ensure that the assets remained under the control of the tax-exempt entity. DOT had consistently approved the lease arrangements. Ray Friedman of the Washington Metro commented, "If in the future these monies are not available to us, that's a $16 to $17 million hit per year . . . We're going to [Capitol] Hill to argue [that] we have about $1.5 billion in unfunded capital needs over the next six years and to add this on the top . . . "[26]

The renewed use of leasebacks in the form of LILOs was the result of innovation by the leasing industry to avoid the sale of assets by tax-exempt entities, since some of those entities were unwilling to transfer title of their assets. These arrangements were described in testimony before the Senate Finance Committee by a witness seated behind a screen to avoid possible retaliation.[27] The witness described the widespread use of LILO transactions involving European tax-exempt entities. Leasing and financial-services companies made arrangements with European government-owned entities in which assets such as subways, water lines, and dams were "leased" on a long-term basis to a U.S. company that then leased the assets back to the tax-exempt entity. U.S. tax law treated the long-term leases in such a LILO arrangement like a sale for tax purposes, and hence the lessor was able to depreciate the asset. The cities of Dusseldorf, Dortmund, and Essen in Germany had leased their subway systems for between $60 to $80 million each. The city of Frankfurt sought to lease its subway system in a LILO transaction in exchange for an up-front payment of $100 million. Officials from Frankfurt traveled to New York to find a lessor to make the deal. These transactions benefited the tax-exempt entity and the lessors at the expense of U.S. taxpayers.

In addition to the criticism of LILO transactions as tax breaks, objections were raised to the valuation of the assets for depreciation purposes. For example, the North Hudson Sewage Authority sold its sewer line to the AmSouth Leasing Corporation in exchange for a $12 million cash payment and a leaseback. For depreciation purposes the company valued the sewer lines at $325 million, whereas the value of the sewer lines on the Authority's books was $48 million.[28]

The Internal Revenue Service (IRS) moved to eliminate LILO arrangements, but the leasing industry responded with transactions in which the lease arrangement was accompanied by a service contract. The leasing industry also developed SILO (sale-in, lease-out) arrangements in which a tax-exempt entity sold an asset to a lessor that took the tax deduction and leased the asset back to the tax-exempt entity. At the end of the lease term the asset reverted to the tax-exempt entity at the fair market value. This achieved the same tax savings as a LILO arrangement and circumvented IRS rules. Michael Geffrard, president of the Liati Group which arranged leases with tax-exempt entities, said,

[26]*The Washington Post*, January 14, 2004.
[27]Testimony of "Mr. Janet"—a Witness Pseudonym, U.S. Senate Committee on Finance, October 21, 2003.

[28]*The New York Times*, January 14, 2004.

"These are transactions that benefit the municipalities that allow them to raise needed capital for infrastructure. It allows them to raise money for capital improvements without raising taxes at the local level."[29] Pamela Olson, assistant secretary of the Treasury, said, "We find little financial activity going on in these transactions. There is very little to be said in support of these transactions."[30]

Abusive tax shelters became a concern to politicians and threatened to become an election issue in 2004. Senator Charles Grassley (R-IW), chairman of the Senate Finance Committee, held hearings on tax shelters. He and Senator Max Baucus (D-MT) introduced a bill to stop abusive leasing. Democrats attacked the Bush administration for tolerating the tax shelters. The Bush administration proposed banning a variety of abusive tax shelters, including the lease transactions used by tax-exempt entities. The proposal was estimated to generate $33 billion in additional tax revenue over a 10-year period.

Leasing was widely used in business and government with an estimated $208 billion of lease financing in 2003. The lessors were represented by the Equipment Leasing Association (ELA), which argued that the lease arrangements with tax-exempt entities met existing IRS rules.[31] The ELA's position was that the lease arrangements with tax-exempt entities equated the cost of assets to tax-exempts to the cost of the identical assets bought by a for-profit company. The ELA also argued that the proposed changes threatened "the future of public–private partnerships" in which private investors helped fund some public projects. "Unfortunately, this proposal will take away the ability for tax-exempt entities, such as hospitals, charities, and schools, already strapped for capital, to lease equipment and severely limit their financing options," said Michael Fleming, president of ELA.[32] The opposition to the Bush administration proposal was led by a group of ELA member companies referred to as the "Big-Ticket Leasing Group." ■

## PREPARATION QUESTIONS

1. Using the Wilson-Lowi matrix, what is the nature of the politics of the leasing issue?
2. Is there a political entrepreneur potentially available?
3. Analyze which interests are likely to be active on the leasing issue and how effective they are likely to be.
4. What is the likely outcome?
5. Are the lessors acting responsibly in making LILO and SILO deals?

[29]*The New York Times*, January 14, 2004.
[30]*The New York Times*, January 14, 2004.
[31]The ELA had 800 member companies and a staff of 25.
[32]Business Wire, January 14, 2004.

# CHAPTER 7

# Formulating Nonmarket Strategies for Government Arenas

## Introduction

For many firms and industries the rules of the game are established by legislation. For 65 years the Glass-Steagall Act imposed walls between the banking, insurance, and securities industries, and after decades of effort by industry members the Act was repealed in 1999 by the Gramm-Leach-Bliley Act. The Telecommunications Act of 1996 opened telecommunications markets but left some barriers to entry in certain segments of the market. Congress regularly passes legislaton imposing a moratorium on any new taxes on the Internet.

This chapter addresses the nonmarket strategies used by business and other interests to participate effectively and responsibly on nonmarket issues addressed in legislative arenas. The First Amendment to the Constitution grants to persons, including firms, the right to free speech and the right to petition government. Business and other interests thus have the right to participate in government processes, and that participation requires strategies. The chapter considers the strategy process, presents generic nonmarket strategies, and provides examples. The integration with market strategies is considered through the chapter cases. The context is U.S. institutions, but the approach is also applicable to other countries, as indicated in Part IV of the book.

Strategy formulation in the nonmarket environment differs in a number of ways from its counterpart in the market environment. First, nonmarket issues attract a broader set of participants than those involved in markets. Second, important components of nonmarket strategies are implemented in public view, which requires sensitivity to the concerns of that broader set of participants. Third, the logic of collective and individual nonmarket action is different from the logic of market action. Fourth, in the nonmarket environment issues are not resolved by voluntary agreements as in markets but in most cases by government institutions with the power to compel action, regulate, and set the rules of the game. These differences require firms and other interests to ensure that their strategies are responsible. In the framework for the analysis of nonmarket issues presented in Figure 2-5, nonmarket strategies must be evaluated for responsibility in both the screening and the choice stages.

This chapter first considers the issue of responsible nonmarket action and the legal basis for business participation in government policy processes. Then, the process of nonmarket strategy formulation is developed with a focus on strategic assets. Three basic strategies are then presented and illustrated with examples. A representation strategy is based on the constituency connection and involves directing constituent pressure to government officeholders. A majority building strategy involves building a majority to support or oppose legislation and focuses on pivotal legislators. Informational strategies focus on the strategic provision of technical and political information to officeholders. These generic strategies are then related to the nature of nonmarket competition as developed in Chapter 6. Implementation of nonmarket strategies is the subject of Chapter 8.

# Responsible Nonmarket Action

In the long run, a firm has influence on nonmarket issues to the extent that its interests are aligned with those of people. In the short run, however, firms and such other interests as labor unions and activists can have greater influence. An important issue thus is the appropriateness of interests attempting to influence public decisions. In addressing this issue, an analogy to markets is useful. In market competition, a firm that faces little competition has market power that enables it to restrict output and raise its price. Society has two responses to such a situation. First, it may rely on market forces. A high price attracts entrants to the industry and provides incentives for innovation that can reduce the market power of the incumbent firm. Second, society may use its constitutional powers to control the exercise of that market power through, for example, antitrust or regulation, considered in Chapters 9 and 10, respectively.

In nonmarket competition, society also has two responses to the exercise of nonmarket power. First, it can rely on countervailing influences from opposing interests to mitigate that power. The pluralism of competing interests can be effective in limiting power, but participation may be limited because of the free-rider problem and other costs of organizing and taking nonmarket action. In some cases, advocacy and watchdog groups can alert the public and government officeholders, thereby limiting the exercise of nonmarket power. Second, society can control the exercise of nonmarket power or require disclosure of nonmarket actions. For example, corporations are prohibited from making contributions to federal election campaigns, and contributions by a political action committee (PAC) are strictly limited and must be publicly reported. In addition, actions such as hiring a lobbyist and holding ex parte meetings with regulators require public disclosure. These responses to the exercise of nonmarket power, however, leave a substantial gray area in which firms must exercise judgment, and at times restraint, to ensure that nonmarket strategies are responsible and do not exceed the limits of public acceptability.

## Criticisms of Business Nonmarket Action
### Business Objectives and the Public Interest

One criticism of nonmarket action by business is that it can be contrary to the public interest. What is in the public interest, however, is often the subject of fundamental disagreement. For example, the antidumping laws that impose duties on imported goods sold at lower prices than in the exporting country are viewed by economists as harmful to consumers and the economy. Yet, antidumping laws have been in place for over 80 years in the United States and have been enacted by most countries. Firms, labor unions, interest groups, and governments use the antidumping laws against foreign imports, even though that may be contrary to some conceptions of the public interest.

From a pluralist perspective, the public interest is identified by the interests of individuals and groups in the context of political institutions. The public interest thus can be advanced by business participation, since the interests of firms are ultimately the interests of those who have a stake in their performance, including shareholders, employees, retirees, customers, suppliers, and the communities in which they operate.

Firms have the right to participate in political processes irrespective of the particular interests they represent. In *First National Bank of Boston v. Bellotti,* 435 U.S. 765 (1978), the Supreme Court held that the First Amendment protects the right of corporations to make expenditures and participate in the political competition on a state ballot proposition. The Bank of Boston had challenged a Massachusetts law prohibiting a corporation from making expenditures to influence the vote on public referenda that did not "materially" affect the corporation. The Supreme Court held that the Bank of Boston's right under the First Amendment derived less from its right to speak than from the public's right to hear what others have to say. The court stated that freedom of speech "embraces at least the liberty to discuss publicly and truthfully all matters of public concern without previous restraint or fear of subsequent punishment. . . ." In addition, the court ruled that a state could not single out a set of entities, such as corporations, because of the interests they represent. The court stated that the prohibition in the Massachusetts law was "an impermissible legislative prohibition of speech based on the identity of the interests that spokesmen may represent in public debate over controversial issues. . . ."

Two years later, the Supreme Court overturned a ruling by the Public Service Commission of New York that had prohibited Consolidated Edison from including messages about public issues in its billing envelopes.[1] The court held that the prohibition was an impermissible restriction on speech. In *Pacific Gas & Electric Co. v. Public Utilities Commission of California,* 475 U.S. 1 (1986), the Supreme Court ruled that a company cannot be compelled to include messages from other groups in its billing envelopes. The California Public Utilities Commission (PUC) had ordered Pacific Gas & Electric to include an insert from a consumer group with its bills. The Supreme Court held that a corporation cannot be forced to associate with ideas to which it objects any more than can an individual. The majority opinion stated that the PUC order "discriminates on the basis of the viewpoints of the selected speakers and also impermissibly requires appellant to associate with speech with which appellant may disagree . . . that kind of forced response is antithetical to the free discussion that the First Amendment seeks to foster."

The rights accorded corporations by the First Amendment can also override certain restrictions imposed by legislatures. In *Eastern Railroad Conference v. Noerr Motor Freight,* 365 U.S. 127 (1961), the Supreme Court ruled that collective nonmarket action, such as joint lobbying to influence government, does not violate antitrust laws against collusion because the First Amendment grants the right to petition government. Firms thus have the right to form and participate in coalitions and associations to conduct nonmarket activity.[2]

### Unwarranted Power

In *Austin v. Michigan Chamber of Commerce,* 494 U.S. 652 (1990), the Supreme Court upheld a Michigan law that prohibited corporations from making independent expenditures on behalf of a candidate.[3] Justice Thurgood Marshall, writing for the majority,

---

[1]*Consolidated Edison Company v. Public Service Commission of New York,* 199 S. Ct. 2326 (1980).
[2]The protection of the First Amendment does not extend to "sham" organizations. See also *Mine Workers v. Pennington,* 381 U. SU. 637 (1965), and *California Motor Transport Co. v. Trucking Unlimited,* 404 U.S. 508 (1972). The Noerr-Pennington doctrine may not apply to nongovernmental legislative bodies such as standard-setting bodies; see *Allied Tube & Conduit Corp. v. Indian Head,* 486 U.S. 492 (1988).
[3]An independent expenditure is made directly, for example, by taking out an advertisement supporting a candidate rather than through a candidate's campaign organization.

referred to "the corrosive and distorting effects of immense aggregations of wealth that are accumulated with the help of the corporate form." In his dissent, Justice Antonin Scalia wrote, "The fact that corporations amass large treasuries is not sufficient justification for the suppression of political speech unless one thinks it would be lawful to prohibit men and women whose net worth is above a certain figure from endorsing political candidates." These opinions reflect disagreement about whether a corporation has the same freedom of speech as a person and whether its resources pose a threat to democratic processes.

The criticism that business has unwarranted power also arises because some interests may not participate due to the costs of becoming informed and organizing. Other interests thus are necessarily "overrepresented." Corporate participation in political activities, however, can give voice to people whose interests might otherwise be unrepresented. Just as unions represent their members, corporations give voice to their stakeholders.[4] Firms represent the interests of their shareholders and pensioners when they act to increase shareholder value. Similarly, firms often represent the interests of employees and suppliers on issues affecting sales, which determine employment and purchases from suppliers. In the chapter case, *Wal-Mart and Its Urban Expansion Strategy,* the company's interests were aligned with those of the prospective employees who would be hired if its stores were approved by the Chicago city council. Firms may also represent the interests of customers. In the Part II integrative case, *CAFE Standards 2002,* the automakers represented the interests of SUV and truck buyers whose options could be sharply restricted by a major increase in fuel economy standards.

Often, the nonmarket power of business is controlled because it is naturally divided. Business differs from many single-interest groups because business interests are often fragmented, leaving firms on opposite sides of some issues. U.S. automobile manufacturers may support restrictions on automobile imports, but dealers who sell foreign automobiles oppose them. American exporters interested in opening foreign markets to domestic goods oppose protectionist measures because they are concerned about retaliation by other countries. Generic and brand-name pharmaceutical companies are on opposite sides of many issues, including patent enforcement and market exclusivity. In the telecommunications industry local service companies and long-distance companies are on opposite sides of many issues such as network access, as considered in the Chapter 10 case, *The FCC and Broadband Regulation.* Because business interests on many issues are fragmented, so is business power.

Business nonmarket power is also checked by the power of other interest groups. There are many well-funded environmental groups, and they have been effective in advancing their agendas through both public and private politics. Activist groups also serve as a check on business power. The news media plays an important role in monitoring the nonmarket activities of business and other interest groups.

Business interests can also be aligned with activist groups. Shaffer and Ostas (2001) studied the enactment of state automobile lemon laws. Prior to the enactment of the laws, car buyers could seek recourse in the case of a lemon by filing a lawsuit under warranty law. The defendant in a lawsuit was generally the auto dealer that sold the car, since the automobile manufacturer was shielded by a privity rule that limited a consumer's ability to sue down the supply chain to the producer. Lemon laws were pushed by consumer and activist groups, yet the enactment of these laws was due more to the support by automobile dealers. The lemon laws in most states shifted responsibility

---

[4]See Hirschman (1970) for an analysis of the voice issue.

from auto dealers to auto manufacturers, and the 25,000 dealerships located in every congressional district worked hard for the laws. On this issue auto dealers' interests were aligned with those of consumer and activist groups.

The abstract ability to exercise power is also not the same as its actual use. Business PACs could make their campaign contributions on a partisan basis, but instead they contribute to both Democrats and Republicans. In contrast, labor PACs contribute almost exclusively to Democrats. Business may also exercise self-restraint on the use of its power. In the example presented in Chapter 6, Boeing did not mobilize its supplier network to oppose restrictions on the tax treatment of leases to foreign customers. Similarly, an increasing number of companies do not make political contributions.

### The Possibility of Manipulation

A third criticism of business nonmarket activity goes beyond interests and power and focuses on manipulation. Manipulation can take two basic forms. One involves misrepresentation or activities that play on ignorance, fear, or biases. As considered in Chapter 8, providing false or misleading information rarely is beneficial in the long run. An example is the tobaco company CEOs swearing in a congressional hearing that they believed that cigarette smoking was not addictive. Under the Racketeer Influenced and Corrupt Organizations Act the Department of Justice filed a fraud case in 2004 seeking $280 billion in damages from five tobacco companies for "a half-century campaign of deception, half-truths and flat-out lies." Enron consistently misrepresented information about its financial condition and the propriety of its financing deals, as considered in the Chapter 18 case, *The Collapse of Enron.* In the framework for nonmarket analysis presented in Chapter 2, nonmarket strategies with these characteristics are to be rejected in the screening stage.

The second form involves exploiting institutional features. For example, a company may exploit a gray area or a loophole in the law that it knows will be closed by the government. In the Chapter 6 case, *Leasebacks by Tax-Exempt Entities,* lessors exploited opportunities provided by IRS rules to engage in lease-in, lease-out deals that were without "economic substance"—a requirement for tax deductibility. Similarly, Long-Term Capital, a darling of the financial-services industry until its collapse in the 1990s, was found by a federal court to have engaged in tax-beneficial deals that were without economic substance. In the Chapter 19 case, *Enron Power Marketing and the California Market,* the company exploited flaws in the design of the California electricity market and was accused of price manipulation.

As another example, to induce pharmaceutical companies to bring generic drugs to market quickly when a patent on a drug expired, Congress passed a law granting a 6-month exclusivity period to the first company to bring a generic drug to market. Pharmaceutical companies with drugs whose patents were about to expire responded with "authorized generics" in which the companies contracted with generic drug makers to bring authorized copies of the patented drugs to market, thereby effectively eliminating the incentives of other generic drug companies. In the context of the framework in Chapter 2, strategies that exploit institutional features are to be evaluated in the screening stage to determine whether they are responsible.

The distinction between participation in and manipulation of public processes can be a fine one. In 1984 Johnson & Johnson, the maker of Tylenol, the best-selling nonprescription pain reliever, faced a new competitive challenge when the Food and Drug Administration (FDA) allowed the nonprescription sale of the drug ibuprofen, an antiarthritis drug previously available only by prescription. Upjohn estimated that within 2 years ibuprofen would garner 10 to 15 percent of the $1.3 billion pain-reliever market. Bristol-Myers planned to market Upjohn's ibuprofen under the brand name Nuprin, and American Home Products planned to market its version under the brand name Advil.

To counter this competitive challenge, Johnson & Johnson filed a lawsuit against the FDA challenging the sufficiency of warnings on ibuprofen labels as well as the procedures under which it had approved the nonprescription sale. The suit alleged that the FDA had authority over the advertising only of prescription drugs, not over-the-counter drugs. Johnson & Johnson claimed injury by the alleged improper approval, stating that it would have a "direct and immediate impact" on Tylenol sales. Bristol-Myers responded, calling the suit "an arrogant and unconscionable effort by Johnson & Johnson to keep an important new drug off the nonprescription pain-relief market."[5]

By 1989 the tables had turned as American Home Products, which makes Anacin as well as Advil, asked the FDA to require drugs containing acetaminophen to include in their labels a warning about possible kidney damage from extended use.[6] The objective was to handicap the market leader, Tylenol, which has acetaminophen as its principal ingredient. The tables turned further in 1994 as American Home Products filed suit against Syntex and its marketing partner Procter & Gamble, charging that their FDA-approved advertising for their recently approved pain reliever Aleve involved "unwarranted and unsubstantiated claims." Were the Johnson & Johnson and American Home Products actions responsible uses of the companies' standing before the FDA and the courts, or did they involve manipulative use of institutional procedures? The Chapter 1 case, *The Nonmarket Environment of the Pharmaceutical Industry,* concerns these issues.

# Nonmarket Strategy Formulation

## Managers and Nonmarket Strategies

Because of the importance of nonmarket issues for the performance of firms, responsibility for formulating nonmarket strategies ultimately rests with management. From the lower levels of an organization, nonmarket issues often are seen as regrettable complications that reduce autonomy and create headaches. The higher managers are in an organization, the more likely they are to appreciate that the progress of these issues can be affected by the firm's participation. They are also more likely to be involved in the formulation and implementation of nonmarket strategies.

Most managers address nonmarket issues on an episodic rather than a continual basis. They thus need parsimonious frameworks for formulating effective and responsible strategies. Much of the task of strategy formulation involves bringing together the approach to political analysis presented in Chapter 6, the institutional knowledge and theories presented in Chapter 5, and the characteristics of the nonmarket environment developed in Part I of this book. The following sections present this approach and provide examples.

As indicated in Figure 7-1, the nonmarket strategy of a firm competes in institutional arenas against the strategies of other interests. The outcome of this competition often involves the delegation of administrative responsibility to an agency or a regulatory

---

[5]The suit failed, and ibuprofen was marketed on a nonprescription basis beginning in 1985.
[6]The basis for the submission was a May 1989 study by the National Institute of Environmental Health Sciences that suggested that daily use of drugs containing acetaminophen for over a year could cause kidney damage. This possibility was confirmed in a study reported in 1994 in the *New England Journal of Medicine.*

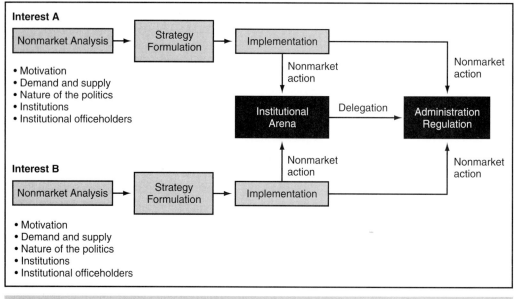

**Interest A**

Nonmarket Analysis → Strategy Formulation → Implementation

- Motivation
- Demand and supply
- Nature of the politics
- Institutions
- Institutional officeholders

Nonmarket action

Nonmarket action

Institutional Arena —Delegation→ Administration Regulation

**Interest B**

Nonmarket Analysis → Strategy Formulation → Implementation

- Motivation
- Demand and supply
- Nature of the politics
- Institutions
- Institutional officeholders

Nonmarket action

Nonmarket action

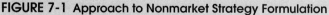

**FIGURE 7-1** Approach to Nonmarket Strategy Formulation

commission. Nonmarket strategies thus focus both on the initial institutional arena in which an issue is addressed and on subsequent delegation to administrative or regulatory agencies. The foundation for those strategies is nonmarket analysis.

# An Approach to Strategy Formulation
## Nonmarket Analysis

Nonmarket analysis forms the basis for effective strategies. Building on Chapter 6, nonmarket analysis includes the following components.

- assessing the characteristics of the issue and where it is in its life cycle
- identifying the interests affected by the issue
- assessing motivations and incentives
- analyzing the likely demand for and supply of nonmarket action
- assessing the nature of the politics of the issue
- identifying the institutional arenas in which the issue will be addressed
- assessing institutional characteristics
- identifying the relevant institutional officeholders and their constituent and policy interests

If the issue is primarily distributive, the Wilson-Lowi matrix (Figure 6-2) provides a first step in assessing the nature of the competition. To predict the likely outcome, the demand for and costs of generating nonmarket action must be assessed to determine which interests are likely to participate and their effectiveness. The distributive politics spreadsheet (Figure 6-3) provides a format for summarizing this analysis. If the issue has moral dimensions, the likelihood of morally motivated nonmarket action must be assessed. The following sections address the next stages in strategy formulation.

## Objectives

The specification of objectives is an essential component of a nonmarket strategy not only because objectives focus attention but also because they affect which interests will be aligned with and against a firm. In the case in Chapter 6, the objective of seeking an exemption for export leasing put Boeing on the opposite side of the issue from the tax-exempt organizations. Contingent objectives must also be specified and pursued in case the primary objectives cannot be achieved. The primary objective may be the defeat of a legislative proposal, but if the proposal is likely to pass in some form, a more realistic objective is to seek wording that lessens its impact, provides alternative means of compliance, or allows time to adjust. Boeing's secondary objectives were to grandfather orders in hand and obtain a gradual elimination of the tax benefits. The choice of objectives is a central feature of the Part II integrative case *CAFE Standards 2002.*

### Selection of Institutional Arenas

The institutional arenas in which most issues are addressed are typically determined by the forces that put the issues on the firm's agenda. Boeing had no alternative but to address the foreign leasing issue in Congress. In some cases, however, a firm has the opportunity to choose the institutional arena. A firm injured by unfair foreign competition can file a petition for relief under a number of sections of U.S. trade law. As considered in Chapter 17, the section selected determines the process and the institutions that will govern it. The processes differ—some are administrative, whereas others encourage negotiations with the other countries involved. In the Chapter 17 case, *Cemex and Antidumping,* Cemex, the Mexican company that has become the world's third largest cement producer, sought to overturn an antidumping order in the institutional arenas of the International Trade Commission, the International Trade Administration, the U.S. Court of International Trade, the General Agreement on Tariffs and Trade, the North American Free Trade Agreement, and finally Congress. Similarly, in the Chapter 8 case, *Proposition 211: Securities Litigation Referendum (A),* high-tech companies addressed the issue of frivolous securities fraud lawsuits first in the courts, then in Congress, then in a state referendum, and finally back in Congress.

Firms may also pursue an objective at either the federal or the state level. In the Chapter 8 case, *Internet Taxation,* opponents of Internet taxes worked at the state level to stop new taxes and worked at the federal level to impose a moratorium on all new taxes. Firms seeking protection from hostile takeovers had little success in Congress or with the Securities and Exchange Commission, so they turned their attention to the states. Pennsylvania enacted a law that made it more difficult to acquire firms incorporated there. Business has had only limited success at the federal level in its attempts to reform the liability system, but it has had some success at the state level. Firms can also switch institutional arenas at the local level. When Home Depot was stymied by the Mountain View, California, city council in its attempt to open a home-improvement center, it circulated a petition for a ballot initiative that would enact the zoning change needed to allow it to build its store.

### Nonmarket Strategy Choice

Strategies are the link between objectives and the specific actions taken to achieve them. When there is competition among interests, as in the case of interest group politics, the effectiveness of a strategy depends on the strategies of others active on the issue. Strategy formulation thus is not a linear process but instead involves adjustments as the issue progresses. One aspect of the strategy challenge therefore is to anticipate the strategies of other participants. The chapter case, *The Bermuda Triangle,* considers such a situation.

One basic principle underlying strategy formulation in interest group politics is that the weight of nonmarket action for and against an alternative affects the outcome.

Therefore, a strategy should increase the benefits to those with aligned interests and reduce their costs of taking nonmarket action. For example, a firm may reduce the costs of participation for its employees, suppliers, and customers. Conversely, a strategy could reduce the opposing side's incentives to take nonmarket action. Identifying substitutes, for example, can reduce the incentives to oppose the objective sought. The Daylight Saving Time Coalition effectively eliminated opposition by the National Association of Broadcasters by including in the legislation a provision asking the Federal Communications Commission to authorize AM radio stations to begin broadcasting before sunrise. In the Boeing case, opposition from the tax-exempt organizations was reduced by grandfathering those deals already underway. In the chapter case, *Wal-Mart and Its Urban Expansion Strategy,* Wal-Mart sought a way to reduce the opposition of unions.

The nonmarket strategies available to firms are the same as those available to other interest groups, but their appropriateness and effectiveness can differ. Activists often rely on high-profile campaigns to attract the attention of the media and the public. Such strategies are seldom effective for business and, if undertaken, may embroil the firm in a highly visible controversy that constrains its ability to act on other issues. The set of effective nonmarket strategies for firms thus is often smaller than the set of strategies used by other interests.

### Unilateral and Coalition Strategies

A firm may have the opportunity to form a coalition or act unilaterally to address an issue. If the issue could shift the industry demand curve, the firms in the industry are in a similar situation. Moreover, the success (or failure) of the nonmarket strategy produces a public good (or bad) for the industry members. Such issues are best addressed at the industry level through an ad hoc coalition or an association. Even if the firms in an industry address an issue collectively, an individual firm may choose to supplement the industry strategy. In the Part II integrative case, *CAFE Standards 2002,* the automobile industry primarily worked through the Alliance of Automobile Manufacturers, but individual companies such as Ford also took actions on their own to strengthen the industry effort.

An industry strategy potentially suffers from two problems: the incentive to free ride and the heterogeneity of interests. In the Chapter 2 case, *Exclusive Resorts: Entrepreneurial Positioning and Nonmarket Defense,* Exclusive Resorts was the clear market leader in the luxury residence club market and sought to form an industry association to address the nonmarket strategy of the timeshare industry. The smaller firms, however, could free ride, so Exclusive Resorts was forced to act unilaterally.

On many issues the interests of firms in an industry differ. The greater the heterogeneity of their interests, the more difficult it is to form a coalition. In addition, firms may have differences of opinions about the best strategy. As the AIDS pandemic grew, the pharmaceutical industry came under nonmarket pressure to increase the availability of AIDS drugs to developing countries that lacked the means to pay for them. An industry response was precluded by the fact that only a few companies had AIDS drugs. Those companies sought to address the issue jointly, but Pfizer objected to the preferential pricing approach of the other companies. Pfizer broke ranks and provided its drug for free.

### Nonmarket Assets

Firms and interest groups build their strategies on nonmarket assets. Access to institutional officeholders is an important asset to be developed and maintained. Access to members of Congress is a necessary condition for effective lobbying. That access can be based on the constituency connection, campaign contributions, or a reputation for providing reliable information. Some firms obtain access by hiring former government officials or retaining well-connected advisors and consultants. Some firms attempt to develop personal relationships between their managers and government officeholders.

The reputation of the firm and its top management is also an important asset. The success of Intel has been due both to its leading edge technology and respect for its leaders. Reputation also depends on how responsible are the nonmarket actions of the firm and its managers. Actions that are deceptive, manipulative, or represent an abuse of power can quickly damage a reputation and depreciate its value. Government officeholders as well as interest and activist groups can have long memories.

The costs of collective action are a significant obstacle to nonmarket action, so any means of lowering those costs represents an important asset. A trade association reduces the costs of collective action, particularly for industries with many firms and for issues on which it is important to present a common rather than a fragmented position. When seeking legislation, it is often effective for the firms in the industry to adopt a common position. When an industry seeks to defeat legislation, a fragmented position may be more effective by revealing to officeholders a wider set of contentious dimensions and adverse consequences of the legislation.

### The Rent Chain

An important nonmarket asset is an alignment of the firm's interests with those of constituents of government officeholders. The value of this asset depends on the number of people affected, their resources, and their coverage of political jurisdictions. A large employment base or an extensive supply or distribution network is a potentially important asset. Its value increases as its coverage of political jurisdictions broadens, since greater coverage provides a broader base for lobbying and grassroots activities. Automobile dealers represent an important political asset of the automobile industry because they are numerous, have substantial resources, and provide extensive coverage of congressional districts. This asset, however, can be a liability when interests are not aligned, as in the case of the enactment of lemon laws.

Porter (1985) introduced the concept of a value chain that identifies the stages of a firm's operations in which value is created for its owners. Nonmarket strategies are also directed at creating value, and the *rent chain* is the analogous concept.[7] The underlying principle of the rent chain is that the greater are the rents affected by a nonmarket issue, the greater are the incentives to take nonmarket action to protect or increase those rents. The rent chain represents a basis for influence in the nonmarket environment, particularly in the context of distributive politics.

As developed in Chapter 5, a rent is a surplus. In the long-run the rent of a firm equals its profit, but in the short run a rent can differ from profit because of sunk costs. Rents are also earned by the factors of production. Employees earn a rent if their wages and benefits are higher than what they could earn in alternative employment. When jobs are threatened by a nonmarket alternative, employees have an incentive to act to protect their rents. Labor unions are thus one of the strongest supporters of protectionist measures when the jobs of their members are threatened by imports. The United Steel Workers and steel producers joined to seek quotas on imports, as considered in Chapter 17. Rents can also be earned by distributors, retailers, and customers, which can motivate them to take nonmarket action. Rents are thus a fundamental source of incentives for nonmarket action.

---

[7]This concept is developed in more detail in Baron (1995a).

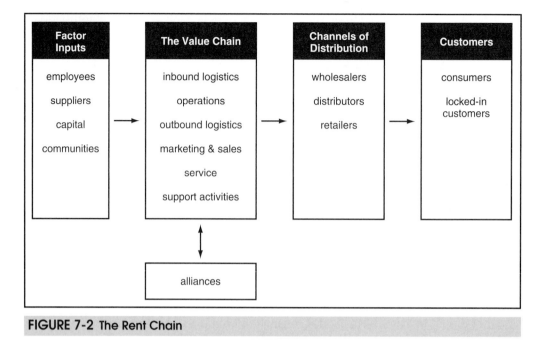

**FIGURE 7-2** The Rent Chain

A firm's rent chain includes those stakeholders that benefit from their interactions with the firm. When a nonmarket alternative, for example, increases the demand for a firm's products, the rents of the firm increase and employees and suppliers also benefit. Interests are then aligned along the rent chain, and hence there is the potential for collective action. Because rents are earned by the factors of production—in supply chains, in the channels of distribution, and by customers—the rent chain is larger than the value chain. The relationship between the rent chain and value chain is illustrated in Figure 7-2. To the extent that jobs, supply contracts, alliance relationships, and communities are affected, the firm has an additional basis for appealing to government officeholders. Grassroots strategies are based on the rent chain, and lobbying also draws strength from information about the effects on the rents of constituents.

The rent chain provides two types of strategic advantage. First, it can provide enfranchisement, giving the firm the right, or opportunity, to participate in public processes. Many U.S. pharmaceutical firms believed it was important to locate facilities in Japan in order to participate effectively in the regulatory and consultative processes that formulate policy and set drug prices. In a country where market opportunities are controlled by government regulation and where administrative directives are pervasive, locating a portion of the rent chain in that country can be important. Second, a rent chain can provide the basis for generating nonmarket action through the constituency connection. Toshiba's strategy considered later in the chapter included such a component.

The rent chain can also be mobilized on issues outside governmental institutions. In 1992 Wal-Mart was the subject of a critical story on NBC's *Dateline,* alleging that some of the company's Asian suppliers used child labor. The story also raised concerns about whether Wal-Mart's Buy America program for creating jobs by sourcing products in the United States was being compromised. In response to the allegations, several of Wal-Mart's suppliers, including large companies such as General Electric Lighting and smaller companies such as Brinkman Corporation and Cheyenne Lamps, took out advertisements in newspapers with headlines, "We Support Wal-Mart's Buy America Program."

### Implementation

Implementation pertains to the selection of specific actions and the assignment of tasks to organizational units and individual managers. This can involve undertaking a grassroots strategy, hiring a Washington law firm to provide technical advice on a legislative issue, assigning managers to lobby in Washington, or forming an ad hoc coalition. The specifics of strategy implementation are considered in Chapter 8.

Strategies are implemented over time, so contingent strategies should be developed. This is particularly important because the nonmarket competition on an issue may move from one institutional arena to another. Alternatively, in the context of Figure 7-1, a firm that fails to achieve its objective in a legislature may continue its nonmarket activity before the administrative agency to which responsibility has been delegated. If unsuccessful at that stage, the firm may take the issue to a judicial arena. In the Chapter 10 case, *Echelon and the Home Automation Standard (A),* Echelon turned to Congress after it failed in the regulatory arena.

# Generic Nonmarket Strategies

Three generic nonmarket strategies are *representation, majority building,* and *informational.* These strategies are not mutually exclusive but instead can be used together when there are synergies. Representation strategies are based on the consequences of alternatives for constituents. The Toshiba example, and the Chapter 8 case, *Drexel Burnham Lambert and Junk Bond Politics,* involve representation strategies. These strategies often involve the mobilization of a rent chain and may include a grassroots campaign, coalition building, and public advocacy, as considered in Chapter 8.

Majority building strategies focus on developing the needed votes in a legislature to enact or defeat a bill. A majority building strategy can build on a representation strategy, as when the rent chain is mobilized in districts of pivotal legislators. The chapter case, *Federal Express and Labor Organization,* and the Part II integrative case, *CAFE Standards 2002,* involve majority building strategies.

Informational strategies focus on providing to government officeholders information about consequences. Informational strategies can be coupled with representation and majority-building strategies, as when a firm lobbies to provide information in conjunction with a grassroots strategy involving the mobilization of its rent chain. Informational strategies are important in the *Drexel Burnham Lambert and Junk Bond Politics* and *CAFE Standards 2002* cases.

## Representation Strategies

A representation strategy is based on the connection between elected officeholders and their constituents. Since members of Congress are interested in reelection, they are interested in serving their constituents. A firm's stakeholders are constituents, so a firm has an opportunity to build support for its objectives by representing stakeholders' interests. It may go further by mobilizing them for nonmarket action. Automakers represent the buyers of SUVs and light trucks when they oppose higher fuel economy standards. Pharmaceutical companies represent the interests of patients who benefit from their drugs.

When its attempts to overturn the antidumping duties were unsuccessful, Cemex established a production base in the United States. In 1996 it acquired a cement plant in Texas and built ready-mix plants in the Southwest. This gave the company a rent chain and constituent base on which it could deploy a representation strategy to obtain relief from the duties. Its U.S. operations were geographically concentrated, however, limiting its coverage of congressional districts. To overcome its coverage deficit, Cemex formed an alliance with the 180,000 member National Association of Home Builders (NAHB). Their legislative objective was an amendment to U.S. trade law to allow the Department of Commerce to temporarily suspend antidumping duties in times of shortage of a good.[8] The coalition deployed a representation strategy, but it was countered by a representation strategy of the U.S. cement producers, and the status quo prevailed. In response, Cemex acquired the largest independent U.S. cement company, expanding both its value chain and its rent chain.

The formulation and implementation of a representation strategy are considered in the Toshiba example.

---

## EXAMPLE

## Toshiba and Trade Sanctions

The U.S. Department of Defense observed that Soviet Union submarines were operating more quietly than in the past, making tracking more difficult. A Pentagon investigation revealed that Soviet propeller technology had improved substantially, possibly due to the sale of highly sophisticated milling equipment to the Soviet Union by the Toshiba Machine Company of Japan. Any such sale would be in violation of the regulations of the Coordinating Committee for Multilateral Export Controls (CoCom), an international agreement that prohibited the export to communist countries of technology that could improve their military capability.

When a U.S. newspaper reported the Pentagon investigation in March 1987, the Japanese Ministry of International Trade and Industry (MITI) shrugged off the report. U.S. pressure, however, eventually led MITI to investigate. MITI found that the Toshiba Machine Company had twice sold milling machines to the Soviet Union in violation of both CoCom regulations and Japanese law. This machinery could have enabled the Soviets to improve their propeller technology. Toshiba Machine Company was 50.1 percent owned by the Toshiba Corporation (referred to as Toshiba hereafter), which report-edly was unaware of the illegal sales. The MITI investigation also revealed that Toshiba Machine had falsified export documents to qualify for export licenses and that the trading company Wako Koeki had illegally arranged for computer software for the milling machines to be supplied by Kongsberg Vaapenfabrik, a government-owned Norwegian defense contractor.

The uproar in the United States was immediate. Several consumer boycotts of Toshiba products were reported, and members of Congress smashed Toshiba products on the lawn of the Capitol. A $1 billion sale of Toshiba laptop computers to the U.S. Department of Defense came under fire. Some U.S. companies canceled purchase agreements with Toshiba, and others were noticeably nervous about dealing with it.

Political entrepreneurs were eager to represent constituents angry over the sale of the milling machines. In mid-June the House passed a nonbinding resolution calling on the Department of State to seek compensation from Japan for damages. Bills barring Toshiba sales to the Defense Department and banning all Toshiba imports to the United States for a period of 2 to 5 years were speeding through Congress. Legislatively imposed sanctions seemed a certainty.

---

[8]The European Union has such a provision in its international trade laws, and suspensions are allowed under GATT.

### Strategy Formulation

Toshiba's problem was characteristic of client politics. Because sanctions seemed inevitable, the relevant status quo was that sanctions would be imposed, and Toshiba's objective was to limit them. On the other side of the issue, the costs from opposing a reduction in the sanctions were widely distributed rather than concentrated on identifiable interest groups. Pressure for sanctions came from the public and from members of Congress, who wanted to prevent further illegal sales to the Soviet Union and claim credit for doing so.

To limit the sanctions, Toshiba adopted a multifaceted strategy that addressed the threat of sanctions and the concerns the incident had caused.[9] The facets included putting its house in order and directly addressing the political issue in the United States. In Japan, Toshiba's strategy had two components. The first was to ensure that no further illegal sales were made by any of its subsidiaries or affiliated companies. The second was to work with the government to ensure that other Japanese companies would also comply with CoCom regulations.

In the United States reaction to the sales did not distinguish between the Toshiba Machine Company and the Toshiba Corporation. Toshiba Machine had U.S. sales of $100 million. Toshiba, with U.S. sales of $2.6 billion, was a much more visible target. One component of Toshiba's strategy was to direct attention to the Toshiba Machine Company. This involved providing information about the relative independence of Toshiba Machine and the fact that Toshiba had been unaware of the sales. A second component of its strategy was to protect Toshiba Machine's business in the United States. The fact that Toshiba Machine had production plants and hence stakeholders in the United States allowed Toshiba to argue that sanctions would hurt constituents. A third component of its strategy was to attempt to place time limits on any sanctions and allow exceptions for certain exports such as spare parts and specialized products, particularly those used for defense purposes. Furthermore, Toshiba sought to grandfather sales agreements already signed. A final component of Toshiba's U.S. strategy was to focus attention on the future rather than on the past. Toshiba emphasized the measures it was taking to ensure that such violations would not happen again.

### Strategy Implementation

To implement its strategy, Toshiba took a number of steps in Japan and the United States. Both Toshiba and the Japanese government acted to put their own houses in order. In an act of contrition, the chairman as well as the president of Toshiba resigned their positions. Toshiba increased by 80 its staff responsible for verifying compliance with export regulations. MITI announced that it would increase its surveillance of exports, strengthen penalties for violations, and contribute more to the support of CoCom's secretariat in Paris. MITI also offered to provide the U.S. Department of Defense with the same milling machines that had been sold to the Soviet Union so that it could develop improved submarine detection devices. The Japanese government hurriedly prepared strengthened laws on CoCom compliance.

Toshiba's strategy in the United States was implemented on a broad scale, reportedly at a cost of $30 million. It took out full-page advertisements apologizing for its actions and pledged not to make any further illegal sales. In other quarters Toshiba attempted to assure its critics that it was taking steps to prevent further violations.

Toshiba mounted a major lobbying campaign. To obtain access to Congress and the executive branch, it hired several former government officials, including the former

---

[9]The account presented here is based on public sources and does not necessarily reflect the reasoning of Toshiba executives. Instead, the presentation is intended to analyze Toshiba's strategy and its implementation.

chairman of the House Budget Committee, a well-known Republican lawyer who had served in the Nixon administration, a lobbyist who had served in the Nixon White House, and a former deputy U.S. trade representative.

Toshiba used its rent chain in a grassroots strategy by bringing to Washington the managers of many of its U.S. operations. It also flew a number of its suppliers and customers to Washington to impress on Congress the harm to U.S. interests that harsh sanctions would cause. Toshiba's employment of 4,200 people in the United States provided a link between possible sanctions and constituents' jobs. For example, Toshiba had a microwave oven plant in Tennessee and was able to enlist the governor to write to each member of the state's congressional delegation warning that retaliatory measures directed at Toshiba could have a direct impact on over 600 employees in the state. Even potential employment provided a basis for generating political action. The governor of Indiana, who had been working to attract a Toshiba facility to his state, asked the Indiana congressional delegation to oppose sanctions.

Toshiba had little difficulty enlisting the support of its customers, many of whom relied on its products. The Electronic Industries Association argued that over 4,000 jobs held by employees of Toshiba's customers were threatened by the sanctions. Some 40 companies, including Apple Computer and Honeywell—importers of Toshiba printers and semiconductors, respectively—opposed the proposed sanctions. Toshiba suppliers also rallied to its defense. Toshiba was able to enlist other allies as well. In a letter to the House Armed Services committee chairman, an assistant secretary of defense wrote that Japan was "succeeding in punishing the guilty, establishing stronger controls, and funding antisubmarine warfare programs which will help the United States and Japanese navies."[10]

### The Outcome

The sanctions eventually imposed against Toshiba were considerably less severe than initially expected, and Toshiba's nonmarket strategy was given considerable credit for the outcome. The sanctions included a ban on imports by Toshiba Machine and Kongsberg for 3 years and a ban on any sales to the U.S. government for the same period. The parent company in Japan was also banned from sales to the U.S. government for the same period. However, exceptions were provided for products necessary for national security, spare parts, servicing and maintenance, and for those items under contract before June 30, 1987.

## Majority-Building Strategies

### Vote Recruiting

A majority is required to enact legislation, or in the case of a presidential veto, two-thirds of the members of both the House and the Senate are required to overturn the veto. Conversely, to defeat legislation a blocking majority of votes is required or, in conjunction with a veto, one-third of the members of the House or Senate is required. Strategies directed at legislatures focus on building a majority for or against an alternative.[11] The chapter case, *Wal-Mart and Its Urban Expansion Strategy,* concerns building a majority in the Chicago city council for permission to open two stores.

A key component of a majority-building strategy is *vote recruitment.* Votes are recruited by interest groups and by public officeholders. For example, the majority and minority leaders in the House and Senate recruit votes on some issues by providing

---

[10]*The New York Times,* March 14, 1988.
[11]Baron (1999) introduces the concepts of majority building and vote recruitment strategies for client and interest group politics.

favors to legislators. Similarly, the president frequently recruits votes by providing favors to members of Congress. President Clinton used this approach to recruit votes of congressional Democrats for the North American Free Trade Agreement.

Votes may be recruited by interest groups through a variety of means. One is in conjunction with a representation strategy based on the constituency connection. Votes can also be recruited through vote trading. A legislator who has strong preferences on issue A and does not care about issue B may be willing to trade her vote on issue B for a vote on issue A of another legislator who has strong preferences on B. Consequently, an interest group with allies in the legislature may be able to enlist them in vote trading and recruiting.

Votes are also recruited by providing politically valuable support for a legislator. This could involve electoral support pledges or endorsements by constituent groups such as those in a firm's rent chain. Other means are assisting in voter mobilization and supplying volunteers as practiced by labor unions, providing endorsements and advertisements as used by the Sierra Club and other environmental interest groups, and campaign contributions. There is little evidence that campaign contributions influence congressional voting, and the caps on contributions are very low. Campaign contributions are thus better thought of as developing access to members of Congress for the purpose of lobbying, as considered in Chapter 8.

Vote recruitment also occurs in nongovernmental settings. In 2003 Hewlett-Packard CEO Carly Fiorina faced a possible rejection by shareholders of the controversial acquisition of Compaq Computer. Deutsche Bank reportedly had decided to vote as many as 25 million shares against the acquisition, and Northern Trust was also believed to be against the acquisition. Fiorina left a voice mail message for the HP CEO stating, "So, if you would take Deutsche Bank, I'll take Northern Trust, get on the phone and see what we can get, but we may have to do something extraordinary for those two to bring 'em over the line here." The acquisition was narrowly approved.

### Pivotal Voters

A vote recruitment strategy focuses on *pivotal voters*—those most likely to switch the outcome between victory and defeat.[12] To identify the pivotal voters in a vote recruitment strategy, consider an issue for which the alternatives can be arrayed on a line. Consider a 101-member legislature that operates under simple (50 percent) majority rule and is considering two alternatives, $a = 60$ and $b = 30$, as depicted in Figure 7-3. Also suppose that the preferences of each legislator are represented by the distance of an alternative from her ideal point—the outcome she most prefers.[13] To simplify the exposition, assume that

**FIGURE 7-3 Majority Building and Pivotal Voters**

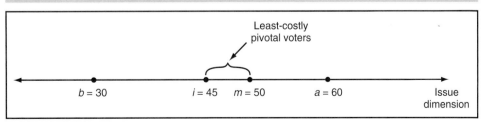

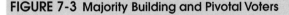

---

legislators' ideal points are uniformly distributed along the line in Figure 7-3 with the legislator the farthest to the left having ideal point 0 and the legislator farthest to the right having ideal point 100. The median legislator is denoted by $m$ and has an ideal point at 50. Since alternative $a$ is closer to $m$ than is alternative $b$, the median legislator prefers $a$.

Consider client politics in which an interest group prefers $b$ to $a$. The first step in a vote recruitment strategy is to identify the pivotal voters. The voter who is indifferent between $a$ and $b$ is the one with an ideal point at 45, which is the midpoint between $a$ and $b$, as illustrated in Figure 7-3. In the absence of a vote recruitment strategy by the interest group, alternative $a$ would be enacted on a vote of 56 to 45, assuming that the indifferent voter (45) votes with the majority. Consequently, for alternative $b$ to win, the interest group and those in the legislature who prefer $b$ to $a$ must recruit six votes. The 45 legislators with ideal points to the left of 45 will vote for $b$ if the interest group does not recruit them; that is, they are natural allies of the interest group on this issue. Consequently, only six additional votes are needed to form a majority for $b$.[14] Any six votes are pivotal, but the interest group prefers to recruit those votes that are least costly. The least-costly votes are of those legislators who only mildly prefer $a$ to $b$. These are the legislators with ideal points between (and including) 45 and 50. The focus of a vote recruitment strategy is thus on these six legislators.

There is no reason to recruit legislators with ideal points from 51 through 100. First, their votes are not needed to pass $b$. Second, recruiting their votes would be more costly because they prefer $a$ to $b$ more strongly than the legislators with ideal points between 45 and 50. Using the same logic, recruiting the vote of legislator $m = 50$ is more costly than recruiting the vote of legislator 45, since $m$ prefers $a$ to $b$ more strongly than does legislator 45. Consequently, greater support or a more valuable vote trade must be provided to $m$ than to legislator 45.

### Multiple Pivots

The U.S. legislative process is more complicated than the example just considered because it has multiple pivots. First, it is a bicameral system, which requires that both the House and Senate pass a bill in identical language before it can become law. To enact legislation, it may be necessary to recruit pivotal voters in both chambers. To defeat legislation, however, it is only necessary to build a majority in one of the two chambers. Second, senators can filibuster a bill, and cloture—stopping the filibuster and proceeding to a vote—requires a vote of 60 senators. Third, the president can veto a bill, and overriding the veto requires two-thirds of both the House and Senate.[15] Institutions in other countries also have multiple pivots. In Japan, a two-thirds vote in the lower house of the Diet can enact legislation without approval by the upper house. The Council of Ministers of the European Union operates with qualified majority rule, which requires 232 of the 321 votes to approve legislation. The Chapter 5 case, *Summertime in the European Union*, and the Chapter 15 case, *The European Union Carbon Tax*, involve a pivot at the qualified majority. The chapter case, *Federal Express and Labor Organization*, involves a pivot at the majority needed to overcome a filibuster.

### Competition and Majority Building

The vote recruitment strategy considered in the context of Figure 7-3 involves only one interest group and thus corresponds to client politics, where opposing interests

---

[14]If the interest group and its allies in the legislature are uncertain about the preferences of legislators, they may want to recruit more than six votes as insurance.
[15]Krehbiel (1998) (1999) provides a theory of legislation that considers these pivots.

have low per capita benefits or high costs of taking nonmarket action. This strategy is also used in interest group politics in which the opposing interest group has already implemented its strategy and the interest group supporting b has the last move. For example, in the chapter case, *Federal Express and Labor Organization*, organized labor deployed its strategy by enlisting its allies in the Senate to undertake a filibuster against a bill sought by Federal Express. Given that organized labor had already deployed its strategy, Federal Express was in the situation depicted in Figure 7-3.

When two interest groups are actively competing, majority building becomes more complicated. Suppose that interest group $G_a$ supports the status quo a and group $G_b$ supports alternative b. Because $G_b$ seeks to overturn the status quo, it naturally moves first. If it attempts to build a majority by recruiting votes, the opposing interest group can recruit any majority of votes to preserve the status quo. For example, if in Figure 7-3 $G_b$ were to recruit the votes of legislators 45 through 50, group $G_a$ could counter either by attempting to recruit those same legislators or by attempting to recruit voters to the left of 45 who only mildly prefer b to a. Consequently, group $G_b$ must employ a *majority protection* strategy that may require recruiting more than the minimal number of pivotal voters. That is, group $G_b$ may have to recruit a supermajority of voters and provide them with sufficient support to protect each majority against the strategy of the opposing interest group.[16]

### Agenda Setting

If the legislative process is open so that legislators can easily offer amendments, and if there is no vote recruitment, the winning alternative is typically centrally located among the preferences of legislators, as in the daylight saving time example in Chapter 5. That is, in an open process the median voter theorem provides the basic prediction of the outcome. If interests can recruit pivotal voters, the outcome can be moved, as considered in the context of Figure 7-3.

If the legislative process is relatively closed and a committee's bill is protected from amendments by a closed rule, strategic agenda setting is possible. In the European Union the Commission is the principal agenda setter, and under some legislative procedures amendments by the European Parliament are difficult to make. The committee in the first example and the Commission in the second are agenda setters. Nonmarket strategies are often directed at agenda setters.

Agenda-setting strategies focus first on recruiting the agenda setter and then on building support for the alternative on the agenda. Consider Figure 7-3, and suppose that the status quo is a. Also, initially assume that there are no interest groups attempting to recruit votes. If the agenda setter has an ideal point at 30, it can place the alternative $c = 41$ on the agenda and a majority will vote for it against the status quo a. To see this, note that the pivotal voter $m = 50$ just prefers $c = 41$ to $a = 60$. Consequently, an interest group on the left with an agenda-setter ally with ideal point 30 can obtain $c = 41$ without having to recruit any votes.[17]

The ability of an agenda setter to use the status quo to its advantage is mitigated to the extent that there is vote recruitment competition between interest groups. A strategy that involves agenda setting is thus more likely to be effective in client politics.

---

[16]Groseclose (1996) and Groseclose and Snyder (1996) present theories of competitive vote recruitment.
[17]Viewing the alternative placed on the agenda as a function of the status quo, note that a more extreme status quo allows the agenda setter to obtain an outcome closer to his ideal point. For example, if the status quo were 70, the agenda setter could place the alternative $c = 31$ on the agenda and it would pass. If the status quo were 80, however, the agenda setter would put the alternative $c = 30$ on the agenda, since that is its ideal point.

An agenda setter's power is also limited by the ability of others to offer amendments or counterproposals. When amendments are freely allowed, the median voter theorem is applicable, and in the absence of vote recruitment the outcome can be expected to be centrally located.

## Informational Strategies

Information is a politically valuable resource. Information enables officeholders to better serve their constituents and pursue their policy interests. Interest groups thus employ informational strategies in an attempt to influence outcomes. Informational strategies are based on the superior information an interest group has about, for example, the consequences of alternatives for constituents. Thus, a necessary condition for an informational strategy to be effective is that the interest group is better informed about some aspect of the issue than are government officeholders. Informational strategies typically involve providing information favorable to the firm or interest group. That is, firms advocate "their side of the case" as in a court where lawyers advocate the side of their clients. The recipients of the information understand this and take the advocacy into account in updating their beliefs. Even though information may be provided strategically, it can be beneficial to the officeholder.

The strategic provision of information is a, if not the, principal component of lobbying, testimony in legislative or regulatory proceedings, and public advocacy. To implement an informational strategy through lobbying, an interest group may invest in obtaining access to legislators or administrative officials. Influence thus often has two stages. The first involves obtaining access, and the second involves the strategic provision of information. In public processes such as those of many regulatory agencies, interests have due process rights to participate in the process and provide information. In legislative institutions, however, access is not guaranteed and may have to be developed. A firm's rent chain can provide access through the constituency connection.

Lobbying involves the strategic provision of two types of information—*technical* and *political*. Technical information pertains to the likely consequences of alternatives. Political information pertains to the effects of alternatives on the constituents of officeholders. Political information is often provided in conjunction with representation and majority building strategies. Both technical and political information may be provided strategically—to advocate the outcome sought by the interest. This may involve the strategic advocacy of a position, the choice of methodologies that generate data and conclusions favorable to an interest, or the emphasis on favorable, and deemphasis on unfavorable, information. Some informational strategies are counteractive—that is, they are undertaken to counter the information provided by an opposing interest.

Information must be credible to have an effect. Credibility can be established in several ways. First, the information may be verifiable in the sense that the officeholder or her staff can check its validity. Second, if it is not verifiable, information can be credible if the group's interest is aligned with the interests of the officeholder. That is, the officeholder can rely on the information the interest group provides because she knows that the interest group would not provide the information unless it wanted her to act on it. A member of Congress whose constituents have strong environmental preferences may rely on the information provided by the Sierra Club. Third, if an interest group and the officeholder have divergent preferences, the information provided can be credible if it is confirmed by information provided by a nonaligned or opposing interest. This confirmatory information need not be identical to provide corroboration.

Fourth, an interest may commission a study by an organization that has a degree of independence. Studies are frequently used to bolster advocacy. Credibility is considered in more detail in Chapter 8.

A concern about informational strategies is whether an interest is legally or morally obligated to provide information that it prefers not to disclose. Unless there is specific legislation or regulation compelling the provision of information, a firm is generally not legally obligated to provide information contrary to its interests. It would be illegal, however, for a pharmaceutical company to withhold data on the safety of an approved drug, and it would be immoral, and probably illegal, to make false claims about a product's performance. It is both allowed and commonplace, however, for interests to advocate their side of an issue or to provide estimates based on methodologies likely to provide answers favorable to their side. A common example is a trial in which the plaintiff and the defendant provide expert witnesses who reach different conclusions regarding an issue. In executive and legislative institutions, the same type of advocacy takes place. Pharmaceutical companies, however, have generally withheld negative clinical test results that did not demonstrate that a drug was an effective treatment for a health condition. This issue is the subject of the Chapter 21 case, *Reporting of Clinical Trial Results.*

## Public Officeholders as Targets of Nonmarket Strategies

In public politics, nonmarket strategies are ultimately directed at government officeholders, who as in a legislature are often in a collective decision setting. These officeholders have duties to their institution and to their constituents. The constituency connection provides a basis for developing allies among officeholders. Allies are legislators who see the firm's interests as consistent with their own. Some allies may support bills that benefit the firm, whereas others may simply be willing to listen to the firm's position on an issue.

The interests of officeholders may also depend on career concerns. Those career concerns include reelection, running for higher office, advancement in a bureaucracy, and employment after government service. Because of career concerns, most officeholders are risk averse and wary of taking actions that risk their advancement or jeopardize their electoral prospects.

When officeholders seek to avoid risk, the status quo is often favored. An interest group seeking to preserve the status quo can thus adopt a strategy emphasizing the uncertainty inherent in the issue. This may involve counteractive lobbying that calls into question the information provided by the proponents of change from the status quo. Another strategy that is often effective is raising new dimensions of the issue. Toshiba, for example, emphasized the importance of its products to U.S. defense contractors. Drexel Burnham Lambert emphasized the importance of junk bond financing to young, high-growth companies that provided much of the new employment in the economy. Through its informational lobbying Boeing attempted to emphasize the uncertainty about the consequences of failing to renew China's MFN status, as indicated in the example.

Conversely, an interest that seeks to change the status quo should focus on reducing uncertainty about the consequences of the change. In the Chapter 5 case, *Repeal of the Luxury Tax,* yacht builders provided specific information about the loss of jobs caused by the luxury tax. Such information must be credible, and its corroboration by other interests contributed to the repeal.

---

| EXAMPLE |
| :---: |

## China and Most Favored Nation Status

Prior to China's admission into the World Trade Organization (WTO), the United States had annually extended most favored nation (MFN) status to China. Congress had refused to grant permanent MFN status because of human rights concerns, disclosures that China had supplied missiles and chemical weapons technology to Iran, and revelation that it had attempted to gain influence in the United States through illegal campaign contributions. In 1997 the extension was in trouble in Congress.

In 1997 Boeing, the largest U.S. exporter, was involved in intense market competition with Airbus, based in France and three other countries, for a $4 billion sale to China. China was expected to purchase an estimated $140 billion of aircraft over the next 20 years. In early April at the United Nations human rights conference in Geneva, the United States voted for a resolution to condemn China, whereas France voted against the resolution, causing it to fail. With President Chirac of France scheduled to visit China in May, Boeing faced a considerable challenge to obtain the sale.

Larry S. Dickenson, vice president of international sales for Boeing, noted the advantage France had obtained through its vote on the human rights motion: "When President Chirac arrives in Beijing in a few weeks, I am sure he will be rewarded for that stance."[1] When President Chirac arrived in China, the government announced that it would purchase 30 Airbus aircraft valued at $1.5 billion. China's Premier Li Peng explained the decision to buy from Airbus: "They do not attach political strings to cooperation with China."[2]

Boeing and other U.S. firms, such as the Ford Motor Company, used informational and representation strategies in support of MFN and China's admission into the WTO. Representative Todd Tiahrt (R-KS), who had worked for Boeing for 14 years, said he talked with Boeing lobbyists "once a week, sometimes daily. They never fail to bring [MFN] up."[3] After President Chirac's visit, the president of Boeing's commercial aircraft business, Ronald Woodard, said, "The Chinese just bought 30 Airbus planes to reward Europe for not punishing human rights. The Europeans love the fight over MFN."[4]

The information provided by Boeing and other companies pertained to the effects on the companies and their stakeholders and to broader consequences. Dickenson identified the long-term seriousness of the matter: "If we lose the opportunity to get China into a rule-based organization like the W.T.O. now, it will take us another five years to get back to the spot we're in today."[5] He added, "I told [Congress] about Airbus, Chirac's visit, what was likely to happen. I told them the realities: that every time there's a blip in U.S.-China relations, it helps our foreign competitors."[6]

### ANALYSIS

In this case, Boeing could provide information on (1) the likelihood that sales would be lost, (2) the profits that would be affected if sales were lost, (3) the effects on its and its suppliers' stakeholders, (4) future sales that might be jeopardized, and (5) the effects on the competitive positions of Airbus and Boeing. Some of this information was soft in the sense that an officeholder was unable to verify its accuracy and completeness. In particular, the information in (1), (4), and (5) was to varying degrees soft and difficult to evaluate. Other information, such as that in (2) and (3), was hard in the sense that the officeholder could understand the data by inspection; for example, Boeing could identify the aircraft it was offering to China, the current subcontractors, and the possible lost sales. Because Boeing had superior information, it had an opportunity to advocate its position strategically. This could involve emphasizing favorable information and remaining silent on unfavorable information. It could also involve emphasizing worst-case scenarios or utilizing data that presented its side of the

---

[1]*The New York Times,* April 29, 1997.
[2]*Business Week,* June 16, 1997.
[3]*Business Week,* June 16, 1997.

[4]*Business Week,* June 16, 1997.
[5]*The New York Times,* April 29, 1997.
[6]*The Wall Street Journal,* June 24, 1997.

*(Continued)*

*(Continued)*

issue in a favorable manner. Boeing, however, had a lengthy nonmarket agenda and interacted regularly with Congress and the executive branch. It thus had an incentive to build a reputation for providing reliable information.

Informational strategies can be integrated with broader nonmarket strategies including those of other interests. The major companies with business at risk in China allocated lobbying responsibilities. Boeing lobbied representatives from Alabama, Kansas, and Washington, and General Motors lobbied representatives from Georgia, Michigan, and Texas. The companies also backed grassroots organizations that supported continuation of MFN status. Boeing backed the Kansas Alliance for U.S.-China Trade, which had grown to include 120 member companies that did business with China. Similarly, in California 350 companies participated in the Coalition for U.S.-China Trade. MFN was granted.

# Institutions, Interests, and Strategy Choice

## Institutions

The choice among the three generic nonmarket strategies depends on the interests involved with the issue and the institutions in whose arenas the issue will be contested. The significance of institutional arenas for strategy is illustrated in Figure 7-4. Institutions can be arrayed in terms of their political responsiveness to constituent interests. Institutions that are highly responsive to constituent interests are legislatures and the presidency, or more generally institutions whose officeholders are directly elected. In contrast, the courts are not very politically responsive but instead make their decisions based on the Constitution, statutes, and case law precedents. Regulatory and administrative agencies are somewhere in between, depending on their policy domain and mandate. The figure provides more detail on the responsiveness of the institutions.

In more politically responsive institutions success depends more on the ability of interests to supply nonmarket action, and in less politically responsive institutions success depends more on the provison of technical information. For judicial institutions informational strategies, and particularly strategies that provide technical information and legal argument, are most effective. In legislative arenas representation strategies are the more important, since they can be linked to the constituency connection.

**FIGURE 7-4 Institutions and Responsiveness**

| | *Institutions* | |
|---|---|---|
| *Courts* | *Regulatory Administrative* | *Congress Presidency* |
| *less* | | *more* |
| | *degree of political responsiveness* | |
| *To what are the institutions responsive?* | | |
| Constitution | statutes and mandate | constituents |
| due process | due process | interest groups |
| statutes | interests with standing | policy agenda (Administration) |
| the record | court review | |
| precedents | congressional and executive pressure | congressional committee agendas |
| ideology | | |

Informational strategies that provide political information, for example, about the impact of a bill on constituents, are often used in conjunction with representation strategies in politically responsive institutions.

The choice of a nonmarket strategy for issues addressed in regulatory or administrative agencies depends on their political responsiveness. An agency with a narrow mandate such as the International Trade Commission (ITC; see Chapter 17) is less politically responsive than is an agency with a broad mandate such as the Environmental Protection Agency (EPA). Representation strategies tend to be more effective in the EPA than in the ITC. Similarly, the Department of Justice and Federal Trade Commission are closer to the courts than are the Department of Commerce and United States Trade Representative.

## Interests: Client and Interest Group Politics

The choice among nonmarket strategies is related to the nature of the politics of an issue, as characterized in the Wilson-Lowi matrix presented in Chapter 6. In client politics the benefits are concentrated on the clients, whereas harm is widely distributed. Because the opposition is not active in client politics, the client interest group usually adopts a low-profile strategy outside the view of the public. Lobbying and information provision are typically the centerpieces of such a strategy. The information is often political—about the stakeholders who would benefit from the alternative sought by the client or about how that alternative would serve the policy interests of the officeholder. In a legislative arena the strategy frequently focuses on both majority building and agenda setting with a particular focus on committees. In conjunction with a majority building strategy, a firm may use a high-profile strategy of organizing and mobilizing its stakeholders and those of other interests into a coalition that can take coordinated action and improve the coverage of legislative districts. The Daylight Saving Time Coalition's strategy of adding candy manufacturers by including Halloween is an example.

The danger in a behind-the-scenes nonmarket strategy in client politics is that watchdog groups and opponents in the legislature will expose the activities of the client. The label often given to client relationships is "special-interest" politics, and many members of Congress seek to avoid such politics. Clients thus often wrap their objectives and messages in the rhetoric of the public interest.

Interest group politics usually involves more visible strategies. A high-profile strategy could include public advocacy and grassroots activities. Firms engaged in interest group politics also use lobbying and coalition building. The formation of the Daylight Saving Time Coalition was important in achieving an extension that had for many years been stalled in Congress. Informal alignments of interests can also be important, as in the case of the Coalition and the RP Foundation Fighting Blindness.

If a coalition seeks new legislation, its chances of success are enhanced if its allies are able to restrict the opportunities of others to amend the proposal in ways that could split the coalition. This can at times be accomplished by incorporating the desired legislation in a larger bill to give it a degree of protection. Representative Pickle incorporated his bill ending the tax benefits for tax-exempts and foreign leasing into a larger tax bill. In the chapter case *Federal Express and Labor Organization,* the company and its allies were successful in having a provision inserted in the bill in conference committee, after which no amendments were allowed.

Competition between interest groups gives more importance to pivotal legislators, often increasing the cost of vote recruitment in majority building strategies. Providing substitutes for opposing interests can be effective in reducing the incentives of the opposition and conserving the resources of the interest group and its allies. The Daylight Saving Time Coalition supported pre-sunrise authorization for radio stations to eliminate their opposition. The cost of a vote recruitment strategy can also be reduced by proposing compromises. In the foreign leasing case Boeing was able to attain its secondary objective of preserving its orders in hand and having the tax benefits phased out over several years.

When a firm is on the side of dispersed benefits in entrepreneurial or majoritarian politics, a number of strategies are available. One is to identify pockets of interests that can be organized and mobilized. The basic politics of the extension of daylight saving time was majoritarian, but there were pockets of interests—convenience stores, recreation and sports products firms, candy makers, and nursery firms—that could be organized. This transformed the politics from majoritarian to client politics. A second strategy is to identify other aligned interests, as in the case of the Daylight Saving Time Coalition and the RP Foundation Fighting Night Blindness. A third strategy is to seek a nonmarket entrepreneur who can either organize those with dispersed benefits or represent them in the government institution. To the extent that an entrepreneur is able to mobilize dispersed interests, the potential of collective action can be realized. Particularly when interests are not well informed about an issue, a nonmarket entrepreneur can alert those interests and provide information on the possible consequences of the issue. Pharmaceutical companies use this approach in mobilizing patient groups that benefit from particular drug therapies.

## Summary

Nonmarket action by firms as well as other interests must meet standards of responsibility. Firms have the constitutional right to speak on issues and to petition government, and those actions should be forthright and transparent. The nonmarket power of firms is often controlled by the differences in their interests. In addition, the power of business is often limited by the actions of groups such as organized labor, environmentalists, and health advocacy groups. Firms must avoid the temptation to manipulate public processes and should exercise restraint in the gray area between manipulation and the exercise of their rights.

The formulation of nonmarket strategies is the responsibility of managers, and the strategy process has as components:

- nonmarket analysis (Chapters 5 and 6)
- specification of primary and contingent objectives
- selection of institutional arenas
- choice among strategy alternatives
- development and utilization of nonmarket assets, including the rent chain
- implementation (Chapter 8)

The principal nonmarket strategies used by firms are representation, majority building, and informational. Representation strategies are based on the link between the firm's rent chain and an officeholder's constituents. Majority-building strategies involve building a majority in support of or opposition to a legislative alternative. These strategies focus on pivotal legislators and agenda setters. Informational strategies involve the strategic provision of technical and political information as in advocacy and are often used in conjunction with representation and majority building strategies.

The choice among strategies depends on institutions and interests. Institutions can be arrayed in terms of their political responsiveness. Representation strategies are used for politically responsive institutions such as Congress and the presidency. Strategies involving the provision of technical information are associated with less politically responsive institutions including the courts and some regulatory and administrative agencies. Strategies involving the provision of political information are often used in conjunction with representation strategies. In legislatures majority building strategies are often based on representation and informational strategies.

The nature of the politics also affects the strategy choice. In client politics firms face no direct opposition, and firms typically prefer low-profile strategies implemented through lobbying. In interest group politics firms may be forced to adopt a higher profile strategy to counter the opposition. In client politics majority-building strategies are relatively straightforward to formulate, but in interest group politics a firm may need not only to build a majority but also to protect that majority from the majority building strategies of those on the other side of the issue.

# Federal Express and Labor Organization

Historically, labor relations for the Federal Express Corporation had been governed by the Railway Labor Act (RLA), which required that unions attempting to organize the employees of a company must do so nationally. Federal Express had operated as an "express company" under the RLA. Organized labor, however, claimed that a bill enacted in 1995 subjected Federal Express to labor organization under a different law, the National Labor Relations Act (NLRA), which allowed unions to organize workers locally. Avoiding unionization was a key element of Federal Express's market strategy. Of its 110,000 domestic employees, only its 3,000 pilots were unionized.[18] Because local organization was usually easier for a union than national organization, Federal Express wanted Congress to pass new legislation that would clearly place its labor practices under the RLA.

Federal Express's nonmarket objective was to have a Senate ally attach a relatively small amendment (a "rider") to a much larger bill (a "vehicle"). The legislative vehicle in this instance was the annual authorization bill for the Federal Aviation Administration, which was regarded as a "must-pass" measure. The substantive aim of the rider was to remove the jurisdictional ambiguity associated with the status quo by clearly making Federal Express's labor relations subject to the RLA.[19] Although minor in comparison with the larger bill, the amendment would have attracted attention and opposition if offered outright on the Senate or House floors, so Federal Express deferred to the judgment of one of its Senate allies who successfully negotiated for insertion of the amendment in the conference committee. When the bill and rider came back to the Senate for a vote on final passage, however, senators aligned with organized labor decided to mount a fight. They sought to block the vote on final passage of the conference report (and hence the bill) unless and until the rider were dropped. They began a filibuster.

To stop the filibuster (i.e., to invoke cloture) and thereby move to certain passage of the bill and the rider, Federal Express and its supporters in the Senate had to build a majority of at least 60 votes. Suppose that supporters were willing to trade votes or other support of varying value to recruit the needed votes to stop the filibuster. Let the status quo $q$ denote the current ambiguous labor jurisdiction, and let the conference committee bill $b$ denote unambiguous RLA jurisdiction. Along with the filibuster pivot $f$ (the 41st ideal point) in the Senate, these points are identified in Figure 7-5.

Assume that each senator has a symmetric utility function, so that his or her preference for $q$ or $b$ is determined by the relative distances from his or

## FIGURE 7-5 Federal Express and Labor Organization

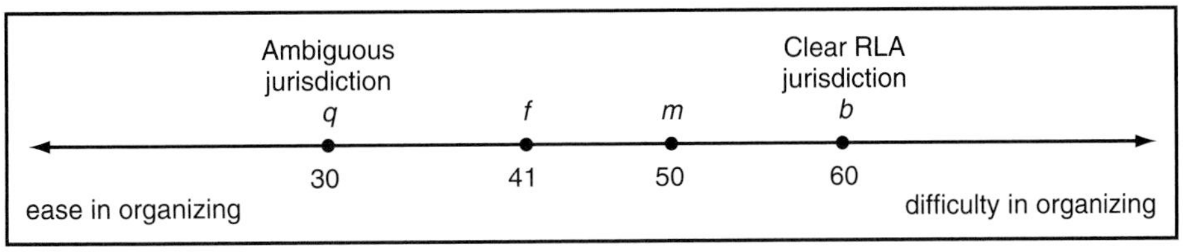

[18] "This Mr. Smith Gets His Way in Washington," *The New York Times*, October 10, 1996.

[19] Public laws cannot mention private companies explicitly. Therefore, the language that accomplished this task was necessarily opaque. The provision simply inserted the term "express company" into the Railway Labor Act of 1926. The term had been stricken—some claimed accidentally—from the law in 1995 when Congress eliminated the Interstate Commerce Commission, which had regulated surface transportation.

her ideal point to $q$ and $b$. For convenience, assume also that the shapes of senators' utility functions are symmetric and that their ideal points are uniformly distributed (equally spaced) over the line as shown. The median senator's ideal point is shown as $m$, and Federal Express's allies have ideal points on the right side of the spectrum. Finally, assume that if the support provided or votes traded are sufficiently valuable, a senator will vote for $b$. Remember, however, that Federal Express supporters do not want to trade more votes or provide more support than is necessary. ∎

SOURCE: This case was prepared by Professors David P. Baron and Keith Krehbiel for the purpose of illustrating theories of vote recruitment. Although it is based on an actual legislative history, it is not intended to suggest that Federal Express dealt with this nonmarket issue in this manner. Copyright © 1997 by the Board of Trustees of the Leland Stanford Junior University. All rights reserved. Reprinted with permission.

## PREPARATION QUESTIONS

1. Which senators will not receive support or vote trades and why not?
2. Which senators will receive support or vote trades and why?
3. Which senator will receive the most valuable support or vote trades and why?
4. Does it make a difference if an opposing group (say, the AFL-CIO) were working to offset the efforts of Federal Express and its legislative allies by implementing its own vote recruitment strategy?

# The Bermuda Triangle

In 1999 the ACE Group of Companies, a rapidly growing insurance and reinsurance company located in Bermuda, was considering an important extension of its market strategy. Cigna Corporation, a major U.S. insurance company, had decided to sell its property and casualty business and was searching for a buyer. ACE was one of the companies contacted. The acquisition would give ACE a substantial presence in the U.S. market. As importantly, under U.S. and international tax law ACE would realize a considerable tax advantage. The tax advantage would also give it a competitive advantage in the U.S. market, allowing it to expand Cigna's market share. The value to ACE of the property-casualty business thus was higher than to Cigna.

## The Ace Group of Companies

ACE was formed in 1985 to provide excess liability insurance and directors and officers liability insurance. During the 1990s ACE expanded its insurance offerings and began a series of acquisitions that would make it one of the world's largest property and casualty insurance companies. ACE acquired Tempest Reinsurance Company in 1996, CAT Limited and Westchester Specialty Group in 1998, and Capital Re in 1999. It also invested in Lloyds and expanded its Ireland-based company to increase its presence in the European Union. In 1999 ACE acquired the Insurance Company of North America (INA), which had written its first policy in 1792 insuring the cargo and hull of the ship *America* on a voyage from Philadelphia to Londonderry. Cigna's property and casualty business would be another addition to ACE's expanding set of companies.

## The Bermuda Insurance Industry

Bermuda was home to a large insurance industry. Bermuda companies engaged in a number of lines of insurance and participated in a variety of international markets. These companies had not directly participated in the U.S. property-casualty market, but they provided reinsurance to U.S. companies that sought to hedge their risks in the event of a catastrophe such as a major hurricane or flood.

Reinsurance allowed U.S. companies to avoid having to maintain large reserves for catastrophic losses. The Bermuda companies also provided coverage to U.S. corporations for major losses.

Bermuda was an attractive location for insurance companies because of its relatively loose regulations. Its attractiveness had increased over time as more companies located there, attracting insurance and risk experts to the island.

## The U.S. Property and Casualty Market

Premiums in the U.S. property-casualty market were $287 billion in 1999, but insurance companies earned little if any profits on the policies they sold. Competition drove insurance rates down to the level of operating expenses and claims paid. Property and casualty insurance companies earned their profits, estimated at $40 billion in 1999, from the investment of premiums paid in advance of claims. The earnings on those investments were subject to the U.S. corporate profits tax of 35 percent and state profits taxes, which averaged nearly 5 percent.

## The Tax Advantage

Bermuda did not tax corporate profits. ACE could thus operate Cigna's U.S. property-casualty business by keeping the insurance activities on the books of its U.S. company while having the earnings on that company's investments on the books of its headquarters in Bermuda.

To avoid U.S. and state corporate profits taxes, Cigna's U.S. property-casualty subsidiary would transfer the premiums from policyholders in the United States to its parent ACE in Bermuda. The transfer of the premiums would be treated as a business expense of the U.S. subsidiary, allowing it to avoid all profits taxes. The transfer of the premiums would be subject only to a U.S. excise tax of 1 percent. Under Bermuda law ACE would not be taxed on the earnings on the investment of the premiums.

To obtain the same tax advantage, U.S. property and casualty companies could move their headquarters to Bermuda, but doing so would be treated as a sale. This would require the company to pay a capital gains tax on the difference between the value of the company and its tax basis, where the latter was the book value of its assets less the depreciation taken for tax purposes. There would generally be a greater capital gain for older companies than newer insurance companies, which would not have accumulated as much depreciation. United States companies moving to Bermuda would also have the expense of moving personnel and setting up operations in Bermuda.

## The Opportunity

The opportunity for ACE was considerable. Suppose that the premiums from Cigna's property-casualty business were $4 billion a year, earnings before taxes were $280 million, and all the earnings were generated by investments. If the effective tax rate were 40 percent in the United States, after-tax earnings would be $168 million. Suppose that the market capitalization of this earnings stream was $2.4 billion. If ACE bought Cigna's property-casualty business, it would have the $280 million without having to pay corporate profits taxes. The tax on the premiums transferred would be $40 million. Even if there were additional costs of $10 million annually resulting from structuring the investments so that the earnings flowed to ACE in Bermuda, the increase in earnings would be $62 million annually. The market capitalization of this increased income stream could be $1 billion. The potential value of Cigna's business to ACE thus would be approximately $3.4 billion.

The tax advantage could also give ACE a potential competitive advantage in the U.S. property-casualty market. Since it would have lower costs than other companies, it could lower its rates for insurance and capture a larger market share. This could provide additional premiums for investment and greater earnings.

A number of U.S. insurance companies expressed concerns about the potential competitive effect of a sale of Cigna's business to a Bermuda company. A few weeks earlier in a speech to the Federal Bar Association, Treasury Secretary Lawrence Summers had spoken out against tax evasion by corporations that used what he referred to as abusive corporate tax shelters that were "devoid of economic substance." He said these transactions "undermine the integrity of the tax system" and announced that the Clinton administration would propose new legislation to give the Treasury additional authority to deal with abusive tax shelters.

The Bermuda tax advantage was legal both under U.S. and international tax law. As Learned Hand, a distinguished U.S. judge had written, "There is nothing sinister in arranging one's affairs as to keep taxes as low as possible. Everybody does so, rich or poor; for nobody owes any public duty to pay more than the law demands; to demand more in the name of morals is mere cant." ∎

SOURCE: This case was written by Professor David P. Baron based on information from public sources, including the article "Bermuda Move Allows Insurers to Avoid Taxes," *The New York Times,* March 6, 2000, and the ACE Web site. Copyright © 2000 by David P. Baron. All rights reserved. Reprinted with permission.

## PREPARATION QUESTIONS

### Market Strategy

1. As ACE, if you acquired Cigna's property-casualty business, would you maintain prices and capture only the value of the present tax advantage, or would you lower prices somewhat to gain additional market share yielding higher premiums and greater earnings from the investment of the premiums?
2. As ACE how much would you pay for Cigna's property-casualty business?
3. Would you expect U.S. property and casualty insurance companies to move to Bermuda? Would you expect other Bermuda insurance companies to follow ACE's lead and acquire U.S. companies?

### Nonmarket Strategy

1. How should ACE reason about the market and nonmarket environment of this situation? Is any action in the nonmarket environment likely? If so, which institutions might be involved?
2. As a U.S. property-casualty company what would you do in response to an acquisition by ACE?
3. Should ACE be prepared to mount a nonmarket strategy if needed? If so, what should it be prepared to do?
4. What do you predict is likely to happen in the nonmarket environment if ACE acquires Cigna's property and casualty business?

### Business Strategy

1. What should ACE do?

# Wal-Mart and Its Urban Expansion Strategy

Wal-Mart was the world's largest corporation with sales of $256 billion, a $9 billion profit, and 1.3 million associates, as it called its employees. Wal-Mart was the most admired company in *Fortune*'s annual survey. In addition to its traditional merchandise Wal-Mart had expanded to sell pharmaceuticals and groceries. In the United States its strategy had been to locate in small towns and suburban areas. Only 38 of its 3,000 stores were located in cities with populations of at least 1,000,000. With attractive sites in its traditional areas becoming scarce, Wal-Mart embarked on an urban expansion strategy. The company had 53 Wal-Mart and Sam's Club stores in the Chicago metropolitan area, but none in the city itself. In 2004 Wal-Mart sought approval to build two stores in Chicago.[20] The stores would employ 600 workers.

Wal-Mart's market strategy emphasized low prices, low costs, helpful sales people, an efficient distribution system, bargaining power over suppliers, and low wages compensated for by opportunities to advance as the company opened new stores. Although the company paid low wages, those wages were comparable to those paid by its competitors such as Target and K-Mart. Wal-Mart provided health insurance to its employees after 1,000 hours of employment. Wal-Mart also employed many elderly workers who were eligible for Medicare.

---

[20]Wal-Mart stated that it had no current plans to sell groceries in the proposed new stores.

Wal-Mart had experienced a host of labor incidents that generated criticism. In late 2003 Immigration and Customs Enforcement agents raided several Wal-Mart stores, taking into custody 200 undocumented workers employed by custodial service companies that cleaned the stores. It was also revealed that some Wal-Mart employees had been forced to punch out and continue working, and some minors had worked too many hours. Wal-Mart was also criticized for refusing to sell some magazines and CDs and concealing parts of the covers of some magazines. The media reported that in high crime areas Wal-Mart had a policy of locking night shift employees in the building to prevent "shrinkage" from theft. In many cases there was no one with a key to unlock the doors in the case of an emergency, and employees had to call a store manager to have the doors unlocked. Employees could use the emergency exits, but Wal-Mart had made it clear they were not to do so except in a true emergency such as a fire. Some employees said that they had been told that they would be fired if they used the emergency exits. Wal-Mart was also named in the largest-ever class-action lawsuit on behalf of 1.6 million women alleging job discrimination in promotions.

Activists and union leaders criticized Wal-Mart for its low wages and because its low prices put pressure on other companies, including small retailers. Wal-Mart became a political symbol as Democratic presidential primary candidates Howard Dean and Richard Gephardt criticized the company for its health benefits. Wal-Mart had become a symbol of low pay and was accused of driving down wages across the country.

Wal-Mart had a history of opposing unionization, and its employees had rejected unions on a number of occasions. John Bisio, a Wal-Mart spokesperson, explained that the reason "our associates haven't wanted third-party representation is because they have faith in the company, and it provides them with tremendous opportunity."[21]

In Southern California supermarkets faced increased competition from Wal-Mart superstores that sold groceries. To remain competitive, the supermarkets sought to require their employees to bear a share of their health care insurance costs. The United Food and Commercial Workers (UFCW) struck Kroger, Albertsons, and Safeway for 5 months before agreeing to have employees share in the insurance costs.

Earlier in the year Wal-Mart had sought to open a 60-acre shopping center in Inglewood, California, but local opposition led the city government to reject the changes in zoning rules needed for the project to go ahead. Wal-Mart then campaigned to put the matter before the voters, but in a public referendum voters rejected it by a 60–40 vote.

## The Chicago Stores

Wal-Mart planned to open stores on the sites of a closed Ryerson Tull steel facility on the south side and a recently closed Helene Curtis plant on the west side. Both communities were poor and largely African-American.

The opposition to Wal-Mart in Chicago was led by the Chicago Workers' Rights Board, which represented a coalition of labor, religious, and civic groups. At a rally an economist from the University of Illinois at Chicago predicted that Wal-Mart's entry would cost more jobs than it would create. He said, "As a rule, Wal-Mart squeezes more sales out of each man hour, so they can generate the same dollars out of fewer workers. So, you'll have a net loss."[22] The unions focused on the specific threat. "The Chicago Federation of Labor has made three demands of the retailing behemoth it called 'Public Enemy No. 1': that Wal-Mart agree not to sell groceries at any of its Chicago stores to avoid driving down the wages of its supermarket competitors, that the company remain neutral in any union-organizing campaign and that it pays its Chicago employees a 'living wage.'"[23]

Elizabeth Drea of the UFCW said, "Wal-Mart has a well-documented history of violating workers rights and devastating communities with its predatory practices."[24] She added, "Wal-Mart usually comes in and pays the minimum wage, which forces all other workers' wages downward. That means there's a long-term impact many people may not be willing to explore."[25]

---

[21] *The New York Times*, May 6, 2004.

[22] *The Columbia Chronicle* via U-Wire, May 17, 2004.
[23] *Chicago Sun-Times*, May 26, 2004.
[24] *USA Today*, May 26, 2004.
[25] *The Columbia Chronicle* via U-Wire, May 17, 2004.

The NGO Good Jobs First produced a study reporting that Wal-Mart had received over $1 billion in state and local tax subsidies during its decades-long expansion. The study was financed in part by the UFCW.[26] A Wal-Mart spokeswoman responded that in the past decade "Wal-Mart has collected $54 billion in sales taxes, paid $4 billion in local property taxes, and paid $192 million in income and unemployment taxes to local governments. 'It looks like offering tax incentives to Wal-Mart is a jackpot investment in local government,' she said."[27]

Mark Brown, writing in the *Chicago Sun-Times,* said "Of course, if Chicagoans prefer to keep their tax dollars closer to home, they can shop at Target or Lowe's or Home Depot or any of numerous other discount retail stores operated with non-union workers, all of which have opened new locations in the city in recent years without a peep from organized labor that I can recall. . . . Labor's main concern seems to be in protecting its workers in the grocery business, because some Wal-Mart stores operate full-service groceries, although the company says that's not part of its initial plan here."[28]

Alderwoman Emma Mitts, who represented the West Side ward, explained her support for the stores, "For a lot of people, this will be their first job of any kind. This is where they'll learn that in the world of work, you have to show up on time, you have to look good, you have to be helpful and courteous. Our young people are going to learn how to stock shelves, how to answer customers' questions, how to make change. Don't underestimate what it will mean to our community to have a place where young people can learn skills like these."[29] She estimated that the unemployment rate in her ward was 60 percent. In response to the criticisms of Wal-Mart, Mitts said, "We want to take the worst retailer in the world, the worst, as they say, and make it the best. But you know something? To make them the best, you've got to have them inside."[30]

Wal-Mart's average compensation for its associates in the Chicago area was $10.77, which it argued was not low relative to small retailers or large retailers, including Home Depot and Target. "A February 2004 report from U.S. Representative George Miller (D-Calif.), a senior member on the House Committee on Education and the Workforce, says that the average Wal-Mart employee nationally earns $8.23 an hour, below the average supermarket employee's wage of $10.35 an hour."[31] Bisio said, "As far as having an impact on the overall economy, if you talk to the Chambers of Commerce in any town where we're present, they'll tell you that we not only create jobs, but we also help attract revenues for ourselves and neighboring retailers, which generates taxes that pay for law enforcement jobs and roads and everything else."[32]

Alderman Howard Brookins, Jr., in whose South Side ward the Ryerson Tull facility was located, said, "I don't understand any opposition. Target and Home Depot aren't unionized and they're in the city."[33] Brookins added, "When [Wal-Mart] said they were interested in coming, there was interest from other businesses. Restaurants such as Red Lobster and Applebee's, that weren't interested in coming into the inner city before, signed onto the project."[34]

After Wal-Mart opened a store in Los Angeles, local merchants did not experience the disaster critics had predicted. "'The traffic is definitely there. We're seeing more folks,' says Harold Liecha, a cashier at Hot Looks, a nearby clothier. . . . But the larger picture is that many [shops] that were there before the big discounter arrived are still there. There are new jobs now where there were none. And a moribund mall is regaining vitality. In short, Wal-Mart came in—and nothing bad happened."[35]

Wal-Mart had worked to build support for the stores in both the communities and Chicago more generally. Approval of each store required 26 votes from the 50-member city council, and the council usually deferred to the wishes of the relevant alderman. This, however, was not business as usual, and despite support from Mayor Richard Daley, the city council postponed a vote on the stores.

Mr. Bisio observed, "In Chicago, you have to be willing to step out of your so-called comfort zone and what you're used to doing. We recognize that there are experiences there that are different from

[26]Good Jobs First also lobbied for a living wage.
[27]*The New York Times,* May 24, 2004.
[28]*Chicago Sun-Times,* May 6, 2004.
[29]*The New York Times,* July 6, 2004.
[30]*The New York Times,* May 6, 2004.
[31]*The Columbia Chronicle* via U-Wire, May 17, 2004.
[32]*The New York Times,* May 6, 2004.
[33]*Crain's Chicago Business,* April 5, 2004.
[34]*The Columbia Chronicle* via U-Wire, May 17, 2004.
[35]*Business Week,* May 10, 2004.

other places. Organized labor is very strong there. We know we're going to be subject to great scrutiny, and we really want to adhere or conform to the spirit of how things are done in Chicago."[36] ■

[36]*The New York Times,* July 6, 2004.

## PREPARATION QUESTIONS

1. Should Wal-Mart give up on entering Chicago?
2. If not, should it agree to the demands of the Chicago Federation of Labor?
3. What should it do to build a majority in the city council?
4. Formulate an integrated strategy for Wal-Mart's urban expansion.

# 8

# Implementing Nonmarket Strategies in Government Arenas

## Introduction

The three preceding chapters focused on political theory and institutions, nonmarket analysis, and nonmarket strategy formulation in government arenas. Strategies must be implemented effectively, and conversely, the effectiveness with which strategies can be implemented affects the choice among them. For example, implementing an informational strategy as considered in the previous chapter requires access to government officeholders, the development of politically relevant information, lobbying, and perhaps public advocacy. If access cannot be obtained or politically relevant data cannot be developed, an informational strategy is unlikely to be effective. Strategy formulation and implementation thus are necessarily intertwined. This chapter considers the following strategy implementation activities: (1) lobbying, (2) electoral support, (3) grassroots and constituency campaigns, (4) coalition building, (5) testimony, (6) public advocacy, and (7) judicial strategies. As the following PacifiCare example indicates, companies have a portfolio of activities in their nonmarket strategies.

Nonmarket issues often receive media and public attention, and that attention can shape and accelerate nonmarket activity. An important decision in any nonmarket strategy is whether a firm's actions should be high or low profile. A low-profile strategy emphasizes behind-the-scenes actions such as lobbying and is intended to reduce the chances of a reaction from the opposition. Defense contractors, for example, typically employ low-profile strategies. A high-profile strategy involves more visible activities, including grassroots campaigns, public advocacy, and broadscale lobbying. Whether a nonmarket strategy is implemented in a high- or low-profile manner depends on the nature of nonmarket competition, as considered in Chapters 6 and 7.

## PacifiCare's Nonmarket Portfolio

In the second half of the 1990s health maintenance organizations (HMOs) were under attack from patients, doctors, activists, and state and local governments. The health care industry had defeated President Clinton's earlier attempt to restructure the industry, and although HMOs and their managed care providers had been responsible for holding down the cost of health care, complaints mounted from patients who wanted both unrestricted access to care and the lower cost associated with managed care.

Individual HMOs conducted a wide variety of nonmarket activities to avoid more extensive regulation and additional restrictions on their operations. PacifiCare Health Systems, with 1997 revenue of $9 billion and profits of $107 million, was the fifth largest HMO in the country. It provided managed care for group plans and Medicare beneficiaries in nine states plus Guam. As with other health care providers, PacifiCare faced a series of government initiatives to expand the scope of regulation.

To address these challenges, PacifiCare developed a broad nonmarket portfolio and an infrastructure to support it.[1] PacifiCare had a vice president for public affairs, a vice president for government affairs, and a senior vice president who had been the head of a state Democratic Party and an unsuccessful senatorial candidate. PacifiCare had no Washington office and relied on a trade association, the American Association of Health Plans, for some lobbying and monitoring work. PacifiCare contributed $900,000 to the association. PacifiCare was also active at the state level and hired a public relations firm to help introduce it to state policymakers.

PacifiCare's political action committee (PAC), which received contributions from about 250 of its executives, contributed about $100,000 to Republican and Democratic candidates in the 1997–1998 election cycle. PacifiCare also provided an equivalent amount of soft money to Democratic and Republican House and Senate reelection organizations and the Democratic Leadership Council. These contributions helped provide access to members of Congress for informational lobbying about issues on the company's agenda. It planned to spend $130,000 in 1998 to collect data and prepare research reports for use in its lobbying.[2] It also retained two lobbying firms headed by former Democrat staffers.

To address specific issues such as the Clinton administration's Patient Bill of Rights, PacifiCare participated in the 1,000-member Health Benefits Coalition, which successfully portrayed the administration's campaign as a costly intrusion by government. PacifiCare also used its rent chain by hiring a grassroots lobbying firm, which prepared lists by congressional district of satisfied PacifiCare patients who were willing to write or call members of Congress.

To repair the tarnished image of HMOs, PacifiCare joined with Cigna Corporation, WellPoint Health Networks, and other providers to form the Coalition for Affordable Quality Healthcare. The coalition initially planned to spend $6 million on an advertising campaign. A spokesperson said, "We are concerned we're getting a bad deal with the media and the only way around this anecdote-a-day is to try to appeal directly to the public to make them aware of the benefits of HMOs."[3] The campaign was in response to congressional hearings in which people claimed to have been denied care for serious illnesses.

Despite the low public opinion of HMOs, the industry was able to block the Clinton administration's efforts in 1998. Health care issues retained considerable popular interest, however, and PacifiCare and other health care providers faced continuing threats at the federal and state levels.

---

[1]This section is based on the article "Capital Clout: A Buyer's Guide," *Fortune*, October 26, 1998, by Jeffrey H. Birnbaum and on other public sources.

[2]*Fortune*, October 26, 1998.
[3]*Dallas Morning News*, September 4, 1998.

# Lobbying

*Lobbying* is a central component of most representation and informational strategies. Lobbying is the strategic communication of *politically relevant information* to government officeholders. That information may be provided to the president, a governor, executive branch officials, members of Congress or state legislatures, their staff, and committee staff. Lobbying also occurs at regulatory and administrative agencies, where it often takes place in ex parte meetings. Lobbying requires access, and access may be obtained through the constituency connection, campaign contributions, and personal relationships. In contrast to public advocacy and testimony before congressional committees, lobbying typically takes place behind the scenes.

Firms and other interests spend much more on lobbying than on any other strategy implementation activity. According to data compiled by the Center for Responsive Politics, companies, unions, and other organizations spent $1.45 billion in 1999 on registered lobbying in Washington, DC.[1] In addition, these interests spent substantial amounts on lobbying not subject to reporting requirements.

Lobbying expenditures by sector are reported in Table 8-1, and not surprisingly, the largest expenditures are in sectors in which government policy and regulation are important. This is consistent with Figure 2-2, which relates the importance of nonmarket strategies to the control of opportunities by government versus markets. As discussed in a later section, the pattern of lobbying expenditures is quite different from the pattern of campaign contributions. The Center for Responsive Politics reported that the pharmaceutical and health products industry spent $90 million on registered lobbying in 1999, which was larger than its campaign contributions for the decade of the 1990s. In contrast, lawyers and law firms spent only $12 million on lobbying, but made campaign contributions of $108 million in the 1999–2000 election cycle. The lobbying expenditures by individual companies vary with their nonmarket agendas.

**TABLE 8-1 Business Lobbying Expenditures**

|                                     | 1999 *(millions)* |
|-------------------------------------|------------------:|
| Finance, Insurance & Real Estate    | $215              |
| Health                              | 197               |
|   Pharmaceuticals/Health Products | 91         |
|   Health Professionals    | 49                |
|   Hospitals/Nursing Homes | 36                |
|   Health Services/HMOs    | 17                |
|   Misc. Health            | 4                 |
| Misc. Business                      | 192               |
| Communications/Electronics          | 192               |
| Energy and Natural Resources        | 158               |
| Transportation                      | 117               |
| Agribusiness                        | 83                |
| Construction                        | 24                |
| Total                               | $1,178            |

*Source:* Center for Responsive Politics, www.opensecrets.org/lobbyists.

---

[1]www.opensecrets.org/lobbyists.

In 1999 Schering-Plough spent $9.2 million on lobbying in its unsuccessful attempt to extend the patent on its allergy drug Claritin.[2]

Lobbying takes place at both the state and federal levels. Lobbying expenditures in California totaled $109 million in the 1999–2000 period. The largest expenditures were by local governments ($16 million), the health care industry ($12 million), manufacturing/industrial companies ($9 million), and educational institutions and unions ($8 million).

## The Nature of Lobbying

Particularly in Congress, lobbying is important because of the large number of legislative proposals under consideration; for example, over 5,000 bills may be introduced in the House in a session. Members necessarily know little about many of the bills, so they have a demand for information. Conversely, in some cases members will check with lobbyists to determine whether the draft language of a bill is acceptable to them—that is, whether the interest group the lobbyist represents will support or at least not oppose it. This serves as a useful barometer of the political support or opposition a bill is likely to receive.

The scope of lobbying has broadened considerably over the past two decades. This broadening has had four components. First, managers have become more active participants in lobbying, just as they have become more deeply involved in formulating nonmarket strategies. Second, the professional lobbying industry has grown substantially as more interests participate in public policy processes. Third, the professional lobbying industry has become increasingly specialized with firms focusing on mobilizing constituents, grassroots lobbying, and research and technical services as well as the more traditional functions of monitoring government, providing access, and communicating information. Fourth, on majoritarian issues such as health care policy that affect large numbers of people, lobbying coordinated with communication directly to citizens through the mass media has become more common.

Lobbying is strategic in the sense of advocating one's position or counteracting the information provided by the other side. Analogous to a court trial, an interest advocates its side of an issue, and interests on the other side of the issue advocate their positions. Lobbying is also strategic in the sense that it is targeted to influential or pivotal office-holders and timed to the stages of the institutional process governing the issue. Lobbying does not involve threats or coercion and should not involve false information. Crying wolf and making false claims rarely is effective in the long run. Members of Congress and their staffs have heard such claims before and can have long memories.

Executives are often effective lobbyists because members of Congress and other government officials want to hear about a firm's concerns from the people in charge. A busy member of Congress will more often meet with a CEO or other high-ranking manager than with a representative of the firm's Washington office. High-level managers also have a better knowledge of the firm's activities than professional lobbyists and thus can be more specific. They also can make commitments that others cannot.

## Technical and Political Information

Lobbying conveys two types of information: technical and political. Technical information consists of data and predictions about the consequences of alternatives. In the Part II integrative case, *CAFE Standards 2002*, the automobile companies provided technical information about costs, available technologies for achieving higher fuel economy, and

---

[2]See the Part III Integrative case *Pharmaceutical Switching.*

the effect of downsizing of vehicles on traffic safety. In the chapter case, *Internet Taxation*, both supporters and opponents of Internet taxation provided technical information on the effects on the economy and lost revenue to states.

Political information pertains to the impact of an alternative on the constituents or policy interests of an officeholder. In the *CAFE Standards 2002* case the coalition formed by the automobile companies provided information on consumer preferences, which for many were for larger SUVs and light trucks. Since consumers are constituents, that information had an impact. To support their lobbying, many firms develop data on their rent chains, including the number of employees and the supply contracts in each congressional district. This enables the firm to tell members of Congress how much business in their districts could be affected by a legislative proposal. The task of the lobbyist is to provide information that links the interests of the firm with those of legislators.

As an example of political information, consider the 1986 attempt to eliminate the tax credit for employing disadvantaged youths. The Treasury had estimated that eliminating the credit would increase tax collections by nearly $500 million a year, helping to reduce the federal budget deficit. One of the largest employers of youth, and thus one of the largest recipients of the tax credit, was the fast-food industry. The lobbying message of Pizza Hut was that the tax credit was an employment program that served constituents and was consistent with the policy objective of providing opportunities for disadvantaged youth. The members of the tax-writing committee understood that Pizza Hut would benefit from retention of the tax credit, but they also understood that Pizza Hut's interests were aligned with those of the disadvantaged. The tax credits were retained.[3]

When lobbying Congress, information should be provided at several levels, as illustrated in Figure 8-1. The CEO or other high-ranking manager may directly lobby a member of Congress with access facilitated by a professional lobbyist or government affairs professional. In addition to lobbying at the top, lobbying also takes place at the level of the member's personal staff and the staff of the relevant committee. The staff is

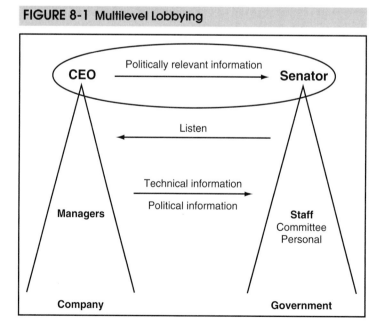

**FIGURE 8-1 Multilevel Lobbying**

---

the eyes and ears of the member, and providing information to a key staff member may be as effective as meeting with the member. Technical information and detailed policy studies are best presented to the staff rather than the member. Political information can also be presented to the staff, which is generally quite knowledgeable and well equipped to evaluate such information.

The following are principles of effective lobbying:

- Target key officeholders.
- Know the institutional arenas in which the issue is addressed (e.g., Congress works through committees).
- Know the officeholder's interests and goals and frame messages accordingly.[4]
- Respect the officeholder and staff; in most cases they are intelligent and savvy.
- Educate but don't just talk. Listen to the officeholder and staff for information about their interests and concerns and for strategic advice about process, the preferences of other officeholders, and so on.
- Make straightforward presentations. Members of Congress are busy, understand politics well, and can see beyond window dressing. (Managers and professional lobbyists often leave a detailed written statement with members or their staff.)
- Explore compromises or concessions that might help resolve officeholders' concerns.
- Give credit to the officeholder.
- Look for alignments of interests and explore opportunities to build coalitions.
- Time lobbying to the stages of the institutional decision-making process. (Lobby committee members, then pivotal floor members in advance of a floor vote.)
- Establish access and maintain continuing relationships for the future (e.g., meet with committee staff even if there is no pending issue). Don't wait until there is a crisis.

## Credibility of Information

Information provided through lobbying must be both credible and relevant. Credibility requires an established reputation, self-evident data and analysis, or corroboration by others with different interests. A firm may have developed a reputation for being a reliable predictor of the effects of legislative alternatives on the constituents of a government officeholder or for providing technical information. Lobbying information that is backed by data and studies is generally more effective. Even if information is only soft and cannot be backed by conclusive data, lobbying can be effective when the interests of the firm and of the government officeholder are aligned, as in the Pizza Hut example. Firms operating on the Internet used this alignment in conveying information about the possible effects of Internet taxes on growth, entrepreneurship, and employment. When interests are not aligned, information can be credible if it can be corroborated by information provided by a party with opposing or nonaligned interests. The automakers' information about the relation between safety and vehicle size was corroborated by studies by the Insurance Institute for Highway Safety and by universities and was supported by a report by the National Academy of Sciences.

Politically relevant information is something that is not known to the government officeholders and their staffs; that is, "Tell me something I don't already know." Consider an issue that threatens the business of a firm. Officeholders understand that firms are interested in their profits, and information about the effect on profits is

---

[4]Information on members of Congress and governors is provided in the *Almanac of American Politics 2004*, Barone and Cohen (2003).

unlikely to be helpful. For example, a regulatory issue that would lower the profits of all firms in an industry could still leave a level playing field. If a firm, however, can credibly demonstrate that firms will fail and jobs will be lost or new businesses not started, the message can be effective. The messages of the opponents of Internet taxation focused on this.

The provision of technical and political information through lobbying is consistent with the perspective of pluralism that public policies are determined by a competition of interests in the context of government institutions. Better information provided to officeholders then results in policies that better serve the interest of citizens. This process can be subverted by the provision of false or manipulated information. As considered in Chapter 7, providing such information is irresponsible. Moreover, false or manipulated information is often exposed, which can damage a reputation and reduce the effectiveness of future nonmarket strategies.

## Access

The congressional decentralization of the early 1970s gave additional autonomy to subcommittees and thereby increased the number of influential positions substantially. Successful lobbying thus demands much more than developing relationships with a few powerful committee chairpersons. A firm that deals with Congress on a variety of issues must maintain access to several committees and their relevant subcommittees. Lobbying typically focuses on members who hold strategic positions, such as a committee or subcommittee chair, and members who may enlist the support of others. On many issues, lobbying executive branch agencies can also be important. The Department of the Treasury, for example, can have a significant effect on the outcome of a tax issue through its expertise in predicting the tax revenue effect of alternatives. The Department of Commerce is often a willing advocate of business interests. On a trade issue, lobbying may target the Office of the U.S. Trade Representative in addition to members of Congress. These agencies do not have direct constituents as does a member of Congress, so technical information is relatively more important than political information.

Members of Congress and executive branch officials have only limited time to meet with lobbyists and must allocate access. Those who have access possess an important asset. The key to continued access is the ability to provide politically valuable resources. Those resources include information about the effects of political alternatives on constituents, technical information pertaining to the likely consequences of alternatives, and information about the support that can be mustered for or against an alternative. Those resources also include electoral support, endorsements, and campaign contributions. Former officeholders are frequently useful to provide contacts, access, and expertise. In 1999, 129 former members of Congress were registered lobbyists.

Federal Express, which faces a continuing set of issues involving Congress, has developed access through a variety of means. As Doyle Cloud, vice president of regulatory and government affairs, explained, "We have issues constantly in Washington that affect our ability to deliver the services our customers demand as efficiently as possible."[5] In 1999 Federal Express spent $3.3 million on lobbying, including outside lobbying firms. Using outside firms is a common tactic, particularly for their contacts and established relationships with government officials. Federal Express also had on its board of directors Howard H. Baker, Jr., former Republican Senate majority leader, and George J. Mitchell, former Democratic Senate majority leader. Federal Express and its managers also were the second largest corporate campaign contributor in the

---

[5]*The New York Times,* October 12, 1996.

1999–2000 election cycle, contributing $2.6 million. Federal Express also made its four corporate jets available to members of Congress on a regular basis.[6]

## Timing and Focus

Lobbying should be timed to the stages of the legislative process. Some interests begin early and work with members of Congress in drafting new legislation. At the subcommittee or committee stage, the appropriate focus is the committee members, particularly the chair and ranking majority and minority members. When legislation is being drafted or marked-up, lobbying often focuses on the committee staff who do the drafting. Because majority rule governs the committee process, lobbying is directed at those members who are likely to be pivotal, as considered in Chapter 7. Larry Whitt, vice president of Pizza Hut, explained, "We focus on those on the fence."[7] Lobbying for support on the floor requires a broader effort and again focuses on pivotal members.

On an issue in conference committee, the focus is on the conferees. In the case of the tax credit for employing disadvantaged youth, the House bill provided a 2-year extension, whereas the Senate bill provided a 3-year extension. Having been successful in both chambers, Pizza Hut turned its attention to the conference committee. Peyton George, a lobbyist for Pizza Hut, stated, "I've figured out my list of who will be the conferees, and I'm trying to maintain contact with every one of [them]."[8]

## Government Allies

The effectiveness of lobbying can be enhanced by developing allies in Congress. The Semiconductor Industry Association (SIA) encouraged the formation of the Congressional Support Group, a caucus composed of senators and representatives who worked to support the SIA's legislative agenda. Because many SIA members were headquartered in California, the California congressional delegation also represented its interests. Having allies in government can make a difference in the outcome of a political competition. Not all expressions of support by members of Congress, however, are credible. For example, in response to constituent or interest group pressure, members of Congress may introduce or cosponsor bills they know will not pass.

Executive branch officials may also act as allies if doing so will help them further their agency's policy objectives. The Departmernt of Commerce may support a firm seeking to open a foreign market to U.S. goods and may take a position opposing a bill supported by organized labor.

## Controls on Lobbying

The First Amendment to the Constitution establishes the right to petition government, so lobbying is a relatively unregulated activity. The principal law governing lobbying is the Lobbying Act of 1946. In *United States v. Harriss,* 347 U.S. 612 (1954) the Supreme Court interpreted the act as pertaining only to the direct lobbying of Congress by a hired lobbyist. Therefore, activities that involve a firm's own managers and Washington representatives are not considered lobbying under the law, although Washington representatives of firms may be required to register. The act also does not cover public relations and grassroots political activities or consultants and advisors.

---

[6]Although members are required to reimburse the company at the equivalent of first-class airfare, the corporate jets provide privacy and convenience to their passengers. In most cases, the flights take members of Congress to fundraising events. "Mr. Cloud said that during political seasons, Federal Express might fly a group of lawmakers about once a week." *The New York Times,* October 12, 1996.
[7]*Peninsula Times Tribune,* February 23, 1986.
[8]*The Wall Street Journal,* June 25, 1986.

Recent legislation has focused on disclosure. Lobbyists are required to register with the clerk of the House and the secretary of the Senate. They must file quarterly reports listing the issues and bills on which they are lobbying, the positions they support, how long the lobbying is likely to take, and details about how their efforts are funded.

In 1995 with unanimous votes by both the House and Senate, Congress passed the Lobbying Disclosure Act that requires lobbyists to report the fees they receive as well as their expenditures. The act also requires registration of those who lobby the executive branch and the staffs of Congress members. This provision was estimated to have increased the number of registered lobbyists by a factor of 3 to 10. In 1999 there were 12,113 active registered lobbyists in Washington, according to the Center for Responsive Politics.

Laws as well as House and Senate rules prohibit gifts to members of Congress, including dinners and privately paid travel to conventions and events.[9] Laws prohibiting gifts also cover executive branch officials. In 1997 Tyson Foods pleaded guilty to providing the secretary of agriculture in the Clinton administration with $12,000 of illegal gratuities. Tyson paid a criminal fine of $4 million and costs of $2 million. The Robert Mondavi winery had hosted a visit by the secretary that included some wine and a dinner. The $187 for the wine and $207 for the dinner for the secretary and his friend resulted in $150,000 in civil penalties for the winery, including paying for a public education program on bribery and gratuity laws.

The Ethics in Government Act of 1978 addressed the "revolving door" of officials who leave government service and then lobby their former employers.[10] The act restricts the contacts of former executive branch officials and regulators with their former agencies for a 2-year period and former members of Congress and congressional staff from lobbying Congress for 1 year after their terms in office end.[11] The law also prohibits officials who were involved in trade or other negotiations from lobbying their former offices for 1 year.

The interactions of business and other interest groups with regulatory agencies are also limited by ex parte requirements. Public notice of meetings with regulatory officials are required unless all interested parties are present.

# Electoral Strategies

*Electoral support* focuses on providing electorally important resources to candidates. Unions and some interest groups endorse candidates, provide volunteer workers, staff get-out-the-vote campaigns, align with political parties, contribute to campaigns, and fund political advertising for and against candidates. Firms provide a much narrower set of electoral support, and as the PacifiCare example indicates, electoral strategies are only one component of companies' nonmarket portfolios. Moreover, business spends vastly more on lobbying than on electoral resources, and its contributions to charities dwarf both. Corporate contributions are approximately $300 million, compared to lobbying expenditures of $3 billion, and charitable contributions of $35 billion.[12] This section

---

[9]Senate rules allow gifts or meals up to $50 and up to $100 from any individual.
[10]Not all ex-government employees take jobs in business. Joan Claybrook, former head of the NHTSA, heads Public Citizen, and David Pittle, a former commissioner of the Consumer Products Safety Commission, became the technical director of Consumers Union.
[11]The prohibition extends to 2 years in areas for which they had primary responsibility.
[12]Milyo, Primo, and Grosclose (2000).

considers the myths and realities of corporate campaign contributions, the legal context for campaign contributions, the pattern of contributions, and the role of contributions in corporate nonmarket strategies.

## Myths and Realities of Campaign Financing

A popular impression about campaign financing is that huge amounts of money are involved, contributions buy favor from officeholders, and corporations provide the bulk of the funding. These are largely myths. Ansolabehere, de Figueiredo, and Snyder (2003) studied campaign finance and were left with quite different conclusions. Despite the popular impression, campaign expenditures by all candidates for federal office have not grown relative to the size of the economy, although expenditures in real terms have increased. For the 1999–2000 election cycle, campaign spending in federal elections was approximately $3 billion. Expressed as a percent of GDP, expenditures decreased during the 20th century until the campaign financing reforms in the mid-1970s and have been essentially constant since then.[13] The bulk of the contributions are made by individuals. In the 1999–2000 election cycle 21 million individuals contributed $2.4 billion, whereas PACs contributed $600 million. Moreover, the number of PACs declined 12 percent since 1988, and only 60 percent of the Fortune 500 firms had a PAC.

In the 2003–2004 election cycle $1.4 billion was spent in federal elections. For the presidency, the Bush campaign spent $339 million and Democrats spent $465 million, including primaries. Republicans spent $579 million and Democrats $512 million on Congressional races. PAC contributions represented 34 percent, 14 percent, and 0.4 percent of contributions to House, Senate, and presidential races, respectively. Individuals contributed $1.34 billion, and PACs contributed $302 million. Fifty-six percent of the PAC contributions were to Republicans and 43 percent to Democrats.[14]

Empirical studies show little effect of campaign contributions on congressional voting, so despite examples suggesting the contrary, contributions seem to have little effect on policy. Moreover, if contributions did buy favor from elected officials, business would be expected to contribute up to the campaign limits. Average PAC contributions to campaigns, however, were $1,700 compared to a limit of $10,000 for primary and general election campaigns. Moreover, few corporate PACs contributed the maximum. Ansolabehere, de Figueiredo, and Snyder asked the rhetorical question, "Why is there so little money in politics?" Their conclusion is that there is not more money in campaigns because money has little direct effect on policy.

A second question then is why companies contribute at all. The conclusion of Ansolabehere, de Figueiredo, and Snyder was that contributions are a form of consumption or entertainment for the executives of the contributing companies. As indicated by the decline in the number of PACs, fewer companies are finding the entertainment worth the cost. Most companies make campaign contributions to gain access to members of Congress for lobbying.

Beginning in the 1990s soft money contributions to political parties and organizations set up by candidates began to increase. These funds could be used for campaign advertisements as long as the ads did not recommend voting for a candidate.[15] Most of the advertising was negative. The example addresses the response to the growth of soft money and the 2004 innovation in campaign finance.

---

[13]Spending for the 2000 presidential election increased, however.

[14]The data was through December 14, 2004.

[15]Interest groups can also make "independent expenditures" of their own funds in support or opposition to a candidate. The Christian Coalition and the Sierra Club make such expenditures.

---

**EXAMPLE**

## Campaign Finance Innovation or Abuse?

The campaign finance innovation of the 1990s was soft money, which reached approximately $250 million for each of the national parties in the 2001–2002 election cycle. Many companies and interest groups felt compelled to contribute to the national parties, which openly solicited contributions. Soft money contributions were unrestricted, and more importantly companies could contribute their own funds. Corporate contributions accounted for 40 percent of the soft money. Soft money contributions were widely criticized, and Congress passed the McCain-Feingold Act, which prohibited soft money contributions that were "coordinated" with campaigns or parties. The Act also increased the hard money caps for individuals.

In 2003 the Federal Election Commission issued a set of rules to implement McCain-Feingold, including a narrow interpretation of the term "coordinated," which allowed the next innovation. Opponents of President Bush innovated by forming 527 organizations, named after Section 527 of the Internal Revenue Service code. These organizations were unrestricted and unregulated, as were contributions to them. Inspired by the Internet fundraising success of the activist organization MoveOn.org, a variety of 527 organizations were formed. Some of these organizations were backed by billionaires Peter Lewis and George Soros, both of whom contributed approximately $23 million to anti-Bush 527s.[1] The Center for

Responsive Politics reported that $573 million was contributed to 527s in the 2003–2004 election cycle, of which $277 million was to "Democrat/liberal" 527s, $100 million to "Republican/conservative" 527s, and $90 million to 527s organized by unions. Although the 527s were required to be independent of candidate campaigns and parties, many were organized by party officials and partisans. For example, Howard Ickes, an official in the Clinton administration and a member of the executive committee of the Democratic National Committee, headed the Media Fund, the third largest 527, and then moved on to the largest 527, America Coming Together. Two members of the Bush campaign organization were forced to resign when it was disclosed that they were advising a 527.

The 527s came under criticism for the absence of regulation and for their controversial campaign advertisements. Calls for new legislation or a revised FEC interpretation of McCain-Feingold mounted. Senator McCain viewed the FEC's narrow interpretation of the Act as at fault. One legislative proposal was to allow only hard money contributions, which were tightly capped, to 527s. Six weeks before the 2004 elections a federal judge invalidated 15 of 19 contested rules issued by the FEC to implement McCain-Feingold. The FEC's interpretation of coordination was rejected as too narrow, as was its rule that the Internet and certain charitable groups were not covered by the Act.

---

[1] Source: Center for Responsive Politics, www.opensecrets.org.

---

The controversy over 527s provided an opportunity for firms to refuse to contribute soft money. Companies such as Verizon, International Paper, and Federal Express, which had been major soft money contributors, refused to contribute to 527s. None of the top 10 soft money contributors in 2000 contributed to 527s in the 2003–2004 election cycle.[16] This is consistent with the decline in PACs and the reluctance of many companies to make contributions to election campaigns.

---

[16] *The Wall Street Journal*, September 3, 2004.

## Election Financing Laws

Federal election financing is regulated by the Federal Election Commission (FEC) under the Federal Election Campaign Act (FECA), as amended in 1974. Corporations are prohibited by the Tillman Act of 1907 from making contributions to the federal election campaigns of candidates. Contributions by unions were prohibited in 1943. State campaign contribution laws can vary substantially from federal law. In California, corporations may make direct contributions to state election campaigns.

At the federal level, corporations, labor unions, trade and professional associations, and groups of individuals may form multicandidate PACs for the purpose of soliciting contributions and distributing them to candidates or expending them independently in election campaigns.[17] A major turning point for PAC activity was a 1976 FEC ruling that employees as well as shareholders could contribute to corporate PACs. Most contributions to corporate PACs are now made by employees, primarily management, and contributions must be voluntary.[18]

Unions collect funds for political contributions through dues, but members cannot be forced to contribute to the union's political activities. The Supreme Court has held that individuals may not be compelled to support political positions they oppose. Applied to unions, this means that members and covered nonmembers can be forced to pay only that fraction of the dues used for collective bargaining purposes.[19]

Campaign financing law distinguishes between expenditures in electoral campaigns and contributions to those campaigns. In *Buckley v. Valeo,* 424 U.S. 1 (1976), the Supreme Court ruled that any limit on campaign expenditures threatens the freedoms of speech and association and thus violates the First Amendment. This decision also overturned state laws limiting campaign spending.[20] As a result of this decision, candidates are not restricted in their personal expenditures. In 2000 Jon Corzine (D-NJ) spent $60.2 million of his own funds to win a Senate seat by 3 percent of the vote. Hillary Rodham Clinton (D-NY) raised $41.5 million to finance her 2000 New York senate race against Rick Lazio, who raised $40.5 million.

In contrast to limits on campaign expenditures, limits on contributions to candidates' campaigns have been upheld by the Supreme Court. The court reasoned that such limits represent less of an abridgment of First Amendment rights than limits on expenditures.[21] Contributions to a candidate's campaign are called *hard money* contributions and are strictly limited, as indicated in Table 8-2.

Violations of campaign contribution regulations can lead to substantial penalties. A prominent lobbyist was convicted of making illegal campaign contributions to the same secretary of agriculture mentioned previously and was fined $150,000 and ordered to write an essay on the election laws. The essay was distributed to the members of the American League of Lobbyists.[22]

---

[17]The FEC designates six categories of PACs: corporate, labor, nonconnected, trade/membership/health, cooperative, and corporation without stock. The organization and operation of PACs are discussed by Handler and Mulkern (1982).

[18]See Sabato (1984) for a study of PACs. See www.opensecrets.org and www.fec.gov for data on campaign contributions.

[19]In 1998 the Supreme Court held that federal labor law permitted dues collected from nonunion workers in the private sector only to be used for collective bargaining purposes. In 1986 it had made a similar ruling for public employees. In 1991 the Court extended this principle in ruling that public employee union members cannot be forced to support lobbying and other political activities.

[20]In 1998 the Supreme Court declined to review this decision.

[21]Independent expenditures on campaigns were held to be immune to restrictions in *FEC v. National Conservative Political Action Committee,* 470 U.S. 480 (1985), but in *FEC v. Massachusetts Citizens for Life,* 479 U.S. 238 (1986) the Supreme Court stated that restrictions on expenditures by for-profit corporations would be upheld.

[22]*The New York Times,* September 29, 1998.

**TABLE 8-2** Hard Money Contribution Limits

| Recipient ⟋ Contributor | To Candidate Committee (per election) | To National Party (per year) | To PAC or Other Committee | Aggregate Total |
|---|---|---|---|---|
| Individual | $2,000 | $25,000 | $10,000 | $95,000 |
| PAC | $5,000 | $15,000 | $5,000 | None |
| Other political committee | $1,000 | $20,000 | $5,000 | None |

## The Pattern of Campaign Contributions

Campaign contributions are an important aspect of electoral politics, if not of corporate political strategies. PAC contributions constitute, however, a relatively small percent of campaign financing. Corporations accounted for 35 percent of total PAC contributions in the 1997–1998 election cycle.[23]

PAC contributions are primarily made to incumbents, and because a substantial majority of incumbents were Democrats until 1995, a majority of PAC contributions had gone to Democrats. When the Republicans became the majority party in both the House and Senate in 1995, PAC contributions shifted to the Republicans. Corporate PACs contribute slightly more to Republicans than to Democrats. Labor PACs contribute almost exclusively to Democrats.[24] The largest PACs are not corporate but are formed by realtors, trial lawyers, unions, auto dealers, and doctors.

## Purposes of Campaign Contributions

Campaign contributions are made for three basic purposes. The first is to affect the outcomes of elections, the second is to obtain access to present or future officeholders, and the third is to obtain services. As indicated previously, studies have been unable to find any systematic effect on congressional voting. Most contributions by individuals are made for the first purpose, as are the contributions by labor unions. Business, however, takes a more pragmatic approach and tends to make contributions to those most likely to win, largely for the purpose of facilitating access. As former Senator Rudy Boschwitz (R-MN) commented, "All they're [corporate PACs] doing is buying a bunch of access and playing the damn thing like a horse race. They don't do it philosophically. They do it on who's going to win."[25] The role of campaign contributions in providing access was explained in a deposition by former Senator Alan Cranston (D-CA) in the "Keating five" ethics inquiry: "The only thing I will grant is that the person who makes a contribution has a better chance to get access than someone who does not. All senators know you may get ten, twenty, thirty, fifty phone calls a day, people trying to reach you, and you cannot answer all those phone calls. So you answer those from those whose names you recognize and who you think you have some obligation to at least hear out."[26] The Silicon Valley example illustrates developing access.

---

[23]Milyo, Primo, and Groseclose (2000).
[24]Organized labor also provides substantial in-kind support to Democrats in addition to campaign contributions. Unions provide volunteer workers who staff phone banks, ring doorbells, deliver campaign materials, and help register voters.
[25]*The New York Times,* September 26, 1988.
[26]*The New York Times,* November 30, 1990.

---

**EXAMPLE**

## Silicon Valley Goes to Washington

As they grew, Silicon Valley companies retained their entrepreneurial characteristics. In particular, their focus on opportunities provided by open markets, rapidly changing technologies, and constant formation of new firms and new markets stood in sharp contrast to the caution and deliberateness in Washington. The entrepreneurs' libertarian bent and "bristling self-confidence," as one observer put it, were in sharp contrast to the style in Washington. Many companies exhibited disdain for politics, and their record in Washington increasingly reflected this attitude. Prior to 1996 many companies did not have a lobbyist or a Washington representative. Microsoft, for example, did not hire its first lobbyist until 1996. Many companies did not have a political action committee, and for those that did, many executives refused to contribute.

High-technology industries, including computers, software, Internet service and content providers, and biotechnology, however, were becoming too important as a source of opportunity, jobs, and growth for politicians to ignore. The nonmarket issue agenda grew rapidly during the second half of the 1990s. Issues included securities fraud litigation, taxation of electronic commerce, patent policy, increases in visa limits for computer programmers and other specialists, software piracy, export controls of software with sophisticated encryption features, extension of the tax credit for research and development expenditures, and Internet privacy.

Because most nonmarket issues had differing effects on the companies, they often found themselves on different sides of issues. In 1996, however, a galvanizing event occurred. California trial lawyers placed on the November ballot an initiative that would make it easier to sue firms for alleged securities fraud. (See the chapter case, *Proposition 211: Securities Litigation Referendum (A).*) The Silicon Valley companies viewed securities fraud lawsuits as extortionary because they were filed whenever a share price fell by 10 percent or more and were intended to extract a settlement from the defendant to avoid a costly court battle. To file a lawsuit, the plaintiffs were not required to have any evidence of fraud but instead hoped to find evidence through the discovery process. Most of the companies had been sued or recognized that they could be sued at any moment.

The following year a group of Silicon Valley CEOs and venture capitalists gathered to establish a "political relationship" organization named the Technology Network (TechNet). TechNet was unique on several dimensions. First, it adopted a very narrow agenda on which its members could agree—education at the state level and federal legislation to take securities fraud cases out of the state courts and into the federal courts.[1] Second, it was explicitly bipartisan, striving for balance between Democrats and Republicans. For example, its PAC contributed $25,000 to both the Democratic and Republican gubernatorial candidates in California. Third, TechNet focused on developing relationships between executives and officeholders in Washington and Sacramento. Since members of Congress were eager to learn about high-tech companies and to raise contributions from them and their executives, TechNet hosted events for individual members. Those events included "meet and greets," fundraisers, and small meetings of a dozen or so executives with a senator or Congress member. The personal relationships developed through these gatherings were believed to have been an important factor in the success of the high-tech industry on many of its agenda items. TechNet subsequently broadened its agenda, and chapters were established in Southern California, New England, Texas, and the Pacific Northwest.

---

[1]TechNet subsequently substantially expanded its nonmarket agenda.

---

An access theory of campaign contributions predicts that the more valuable the services the candidate can provide, the more an interest group will be willing to contribute. This suggests that access to those members of Congress who hold strategic positions should be more valuable than access to those members who do not. In particular, it suggests that senior members, and particularly the chairs of committees and subcommittees, should receive more contributions than other members.[27] The data support this prediction. Similarly, members of the committees that deal with legislation affecting an industry may receive substantial contributions from the firms in those industries. In addition, this theory predicts that the bulk of contributions are made to incumbents. In the 1999–2000 election cycle incumbents received 87 percent of PAC contributions. In part this reflected the incumbency advantage, and in part it reinforced that advantage.

Studies by Hall and Wayman (1990) and Wu (1994) indicate that another purpose of campaign contributions is to develop allies and encourage them to work for legislation that both the member and the contributor support. Thus, campaign contributions could affect legislative outcomes by mobilizing congressional efforts on behalf of legislation rather than by directly affecting the votes of recipients.

Many firms would like not to make political contributions but believe that they are caught in a prisoners' dilemma. That is, if no other interest group were to make contributions, an interest group that made a contribution would be important to the candidate and might see benefits flow from its contribution. Conversely, if many firms and interest groups contribute, a noncontributor might be at a disadvantage, possibly suffering a loss of access. Contributing, then, is a dominant strategy, resulting in a situation in which interest groups contribute, with their contributions then yielding no benefits. All would be better off not contributing.

## Grassroots and Constituency Campaigns

*Grassroots campaigns* are based on the connection between constituents and their elected representatives. Grassroots campaigns are often a component of a broader representation strategy and are often tactical in nature. Labor unions, community interest groups, environmental groups, the National Rifle Association, and many other interest groups engage in grassroots nonmarket activity intended to demonstrate the breadth and intensity of their members' interests on issues.[28] Beginning in the 1980s, firms and industries adopted this strategy and applied it effectively to issues on their nonmarket agendas. The grassroots campaign by Toshiba (Chapter 7) was effective because it reflected the potential costs to employees, suppliers, and customers. Grassroots campaigns have become sufficiently pervasive that a grassroots lobbying industry has developed to organize the campaigns. The industry includes firms that, for example, translate data by postal zip codes into congressional districts. This allows shareholder, retiree, supplier, and customer lists to be organized by district to target members of Congress. In the PacifiCare example, the company organized its patients by congressional district. Grassroots activity has also become increasingly specialized. Some political consulting firms now provide "grass-tops" services: they recruit prominent citizens to lobby their representative or senator on an issue.

### Mobilization

Members of interest groups and stakeholders of firms must be mobilized for effective grassroots action. Mobilization involves providing information to stakeholders on the significance of an issue and helping to reduce their costs of participation. Letter-writing campaigns are the least expensive grassroots activity. They are also difficult to implement because constituents often are unwilling to spend the time to write a letter or send a telegram. Volume can be generated through the use of preprinted letters, postcards, or

---

[27]See Kroszner and Stratmann (1998) for a study of financial services PACs and their contributions to committees.
[28]See Fowler and Shaiko (1987) for an analysis of the grassroots activities of environmental organizations.

e-mail, but recipients know that postcards generally do not reflect the same intensity of preferences as handwritten letters. Although handwritten letters have a greater impact than postcards, there is a trade-off with volume. Some congressional offices sort and count mail by issue and distinguish between letters and postcards. Others, however, just weigh the postcards. In a survey of congressional staff Lord (2000) found that letter writing and telephone calls had the greatest effect and petitions and mass-mailing responses the least effect.

A more effective means of demonstrating grassroots preferences is to have constituents go to Washington or a state capital to lobby. Labor unions developed this tactic by organizing "bus-ins" in which busloads of union members converged on Washington to lobby and engage in other political activities. "Fly-ins" are the modern counterpart of bus-ins. For example, overseas U.S. firms participate in the American Chamber of Commerce (ACC). The Asian chapters meet annually to discuss a variety of governmental and nonmarket issues pertaining to international trade policy, government relations, and U.S. policy pertaining to foreign operations. Members of the ACC chapters then fly to Washington to conduct a "knock-around" in which they knock on as many doors as possible to explain their positions on issues.

Grassroots activities may be directed at government officeholders as in the case of a fly-in, or they may be directed at constituents. The former are components of informational strategies and are a form of lobbying. The latter are components of representation strategies and are intended to develop public support for an alternative. As the PacifiCare example indicates, the health care industry has used this strategy effectively. Constituent-based grassroots strategies are frequently accompanied by mass advertising, Internet, or e-mail campaigns to inform the public and officeholders and to recruit participants, often by giving a toll-free number they can call for more information. The Internet has become an important force in generating grassroots actions such as letter writing and e-mailing members of Congress. The activist organization MoveOn.org sent out an e-mail appeal for $25,000 to pay for an advertisement, and it received $400,000 in response. The Internet has become an important vehicle for raising funds for both public and private politics.

## Business Grassroots Campaigns

A business grassroots strategy involves corporate stakeholders as identified by the rent chain. These stakeholders can include employees, shareholders, retirees whose pensions depend on company performance, franchisees, suppliers, and in some cases customers. Not all constituencies are equally easy to organize and mobilize, however.[29] Shareholders and pensioners may be mobilized to some extent, but alerting them to a potentially serious issue may cause them to sell their shares.

To the extent that their interests on an issue are aligned with those of the firm, employees may be relatively easy to include in a grassroots program. Mobilizing employees can generate criticism, however. In the last days of the Clinton administration's attempt to restructure the U.S. health care system, IBM and General Mills asked their employees to oppose bills mandating employer-provided health insurance. Some IBM employees complained about the request, and IBM was publicly criticized for changing its practice of not involving employees in political issues.

More recently, however, companies have begun to embrace grassroots strategies involving employees. Companies such as International Paper and Sun Microsystems make information on policy issues and voting records of members of Congress available to their employees on company Web sites. International Paper then encourages employees to write their representatives on policy issues and may recommend a candidate to

---

[29]See Keim (1985) and Baysinger, Keim, and Zeithaml (1985) for an analysis of corporate grassroots programs.

employees requesting such information.[30] Cigna urged its employees to write members of Congress on tort reform legislation in 2004.

Some firms also take positions on ballot initiatives and referenda. In the chapter case, *Proposition 211: Securities Litigation Referendum (A),* Silicon Valley firms urged their employees to vote no on the proposition. In the same election a number of companies, including Atlantic Richfield, Hewlett-Packard, Pacific Gas & Electric, and Southern California Edison, publicly opposed Proposition 209, which would ban affirmative action in public contracts, education, and employment.

Suppliers and customers are frequently mobilized when their rents are affected. The grassroots campaign organized by Toshiba to weaken sanctions resulting from its illegal sales to the Soviet Union relied heavily on its U.S. production base, its suppliers, and its customers. Toshiba's U.S. production provided a link between possible sanctions and jobs at its suppliers. Similarly, Toshiba had little difficulty enlisting the support of its customers, many of whom depended on its products.

## The Effectiveness of Grassroots Programs

The effectiveness of a grassroots program depends on the supply-side factors considered in Chapter 6 as well as on the credibility of the program itself. The larger the number of participants in a grassroots program and the more extensive their coverage of political jurisdictions, the more effective it is likely to be. These factors determine the amount of pressure that can be transmitted through the constituency connection. This pressure, however, must be credible. The following two examples, both of which involved attempts to defeat legislation, illustrate the credibility dimension of a grassroots campaign.

Legislation was introduced in Congress to require financial institutions to withhold taxes on the interest and dividend income of savers and trust fund beneficiaries. Supporters of the proposal included Treasury officials and members of Congress concerned with the federal budget deficit. In addition to the considerable administrative expense to financial institutions, the legislation would reduce the short-term cash flow to savers and beneficiaries, who would receive lower quarterly payments as taxes were withheld. The financial institutions were in a position to mobilize a dispersed constituency of savers to oppose the bill. Their grassroots campaign generated over 22 million letters and postcards, and the interest withholding issue died.

In 1987 the Pharmaceutical Manufacturers Association (PMA) campaigned against the adoption of a catastrophic illness program for the elderly. Pharmaceutical companies were concerned that federal budget pressures would lead to the substitution of generic for brand-name drugs and perhaps to price controls, or reimbursement limits, on drugs. The PMA hired a political consulting firm to conduct a $3 million grassroots campaign opposing the program. Even though the campaign generated over 100,000 contacts between constituents and members of Congress, it was largely ineffective. Congress members knew that their constituents did not understand the program under consideration. Moreover, it may have worsened relations with members of Congress. As Senator Lloyd Bentsen (D-TX) said, "I know the difference between grassroots and Astroturf."

In his survey of congressional staff Lord (2000) found that corporate constituency activity was relatively more effective in influencing how members of Congress voted on legislation. Professional and executive lobbying was relatively more important in influencing the content of legislation. The effect of constituency actions was greater in the House than the Senate presumably because members of the House face elections every 2 years. Among the corporate constituents, employee contacts with staff and members had the largest effect.

---

[30]*The Wall Street Journal,* September 3, 2004.

# Coalition Building

*Coalition building* is an important component of many nonmarket strategies. Coalitions are the principal means of forging a majority from a collection of minorities. Business coalitions are of three types: peak organizations, trade associations, and ad hoc coalitions. Peak associations emphasize issues that affect more than one industry, trade associations represent a single industry, and ad hoc coalitions tend to be issue specific. Trade associations and individual firms also participate on issues addressed by peak organizations and trade associations, respectively.

Many of the most effective coalitions are ad hoc and issue specific, as in the case of the Daylight Saving Time Coalition. Some are not formal coalitions but instead are alignments of interests, as in the case of the Daylight Saving Time Coalition and the RP Foundation Fighting Blindness considered in Chapter 5.[31] At times, two interest groups may find themselves working on the same side of one issue and opposite sides of another. Automobile manufacturers, dealers, and the United Auto Workers (UAW) opposed increases in fuel economy standards, but the automakers and the UAW were on opposite sides of the North American Free Trade Agreement, and automakers and dealers were on opposite sides of the lemons law discussed in Chapter 7.

## Peak Associations

Peak, or umbrella, organizations include firms from a number of industries and thus represent a range of interests. In the United States these organizations include the U.S. Chamber of Commerce, the National Association of Manufacturers, the Business Roundtable, the American Business Conference, the National Federation of Independent Business, and the National Small Business Association, among others. These organizations support issues such as liability reform, tax reductions, trade liberalization, and regulatory reform. The heterogeneity of the interests of their members and their desire to maintain a reasonable consensus, however, limits the scope of the issues on which they act. Consequently, individual firms do not rely solely on peak organizations to represent their interests but instead participate in trade associations and often take independent nonmarket action.[32]

As an example of an umbrella organization, the Chamber of Commerce is the oldest general business organization in the United States and has a budget of over $70 million. The Chamber focuses on tax, labor, trade, and regulatory issues. An important source of strength for the chamber is its 3,000 state and local chambers, which give it complete coverage of congressional districts. To generate political pressure, it organized over 2,700 Congressional Action committees, composed of local businesspeople who have personal contacts with members of Congress. The chamber also had a public interest lobby, the Grassroots Action Information Network, that conducted grassroots campaigns. The Chamber's National Chamber Alliance for Politics provided electoral support to candidates.

The National Federation of Independent Business (NFIB) focuses on the concerns of small business. The influence of small business should not be underestimated. Although individual small businesses may have limited resources, collectively their resources are large. The NFIB, for example, has 600,000 members and offices in Washington and every state capital, which gives it comprehensive coverage of political jurisdictions. It has been effective in lobbying and mobilizing small firms by reducing their cost of participation in collective action. The NFIB worked effectively for President Bush's tax cut plan. About

---

[31]See Salisbury (1992) for an analysis of interest group alignments.
[32]Peak organizations are more important in a number of other countries than in the United States. The Keidanren in Japan and the peak organizations in Germany and other European countries are quite influential.

85 percent of NFIB members pay their business taxes through their individual tax returns, and the tax plan allowed the immediate expensing of an additional $75,000 of equipment. Small business has also been particularly effective in obtaining exemptions from certain regulations. Its effectiveness is strengthened by the access provided by the small business committees in the House and Senate.

## Trade Associations

Trade associations serve a variety of market and nonmarket functions.[33] Market functions include the collection of market and industry statistics, the development of technical standards, and in some cases research. Nonmarket functions center on reducing the cost of collective action, particularly by reducing the costs of information acquisition. Trade associations also monitor potential and current legislative activity, regulatory rule-making activities, and administrative actions. In the Chapter 2 case, *Exclusive Resorts: Entrepreneurial Positioning and Nonmarket Defense,* the American Resort Development Association worked at the state level for constructive re-regulation of the timeshare and vacation club industry. Trade associations also reduce the cost of lobbying, grassroots programs, and other political strategies.

The Pharmaceutical Research and Manufacturers Association (PhRMA) with a 2004 budget of $150 million allocated $72.7 million for lobbying Congress, $4.9 million for lobbying the FDA, and $48.7 million for advocacy aimed at state governments. Funds were also allocated to fight a union-led campaign for lower drug prices in Ohio, support policy research, hire economists to discuss pharmaceutical issues, oppose the Canadian discount drug system, fund public advocacy, and foster ties with minority congressional caucuses and medical organizations.[34] Small firms are more likely than large firms to rely on trade associations, as the Calgene example indicates.

---

**EXAMPLE**

### Calgene and Canola

Calgene, a small agricultural biotechnology company, had developed a strain of rapeseed that produced canola oil—used in a variety of products—and needed to induce farmers in the United States, where rapeseed was not grown, to begin to grow it.[1] One reason farmers did not grow rapeseed was that it was not included in the government's agricultural support system. Calgene initially sought approval for rapeseed to be grown on set-aside land under the USDA's crop stabilization program. That program required farmers to take land out of production. Since the land was not being used for any other crop, Calgene reasoned that farmers would be eager to grow rapeseed rather than let the land remain fallow.

After expending considerable effort lobbying members of Congress without success, Calgene abandoned its focus on set-aside land.

It decided instead to seek inclusion of rapeseed in the USDA's commodity support programs, and to accomplish this it worked to build a coalition. Calgene and companies such as Procter & Gamble, Archer-Daniels-Midland, Cargill, and Kraft formed the U.S. Canola Association. In the context of client politics the association was successful in having a bill introduced in Congress to include rapeseed in the commodity support program. To broaden support, the bill was written to include sunflower. Support from sunflower growers was important in obtaining inclusion of both canola and sunflower in the program. The bill was passed as part of a farm bill.

---

[1]Calgene was subsequently acquired by Monsanto.

---

[33]See Lynn and McKeown (1988) for an analysis of trade associations.
[34]*The New York Times,* June 1, 2003.

## Ad Hoc Coalitions

An ad hoc coalition is a group of interests that join together on a specific nonmarket issue. Subsequent to the events in the chapter case, *Proposition 211: Securities Litigation Referendum (A),* high-tech companies, public accounting firms, underwriters, and others that had been subjected to frivolous securities fraud lawsuits formed the Uniform Standards Coalition to work for federal legislation requiring security fraud lawsuits to be filed in federal rather than state courts. The Coalition was successful with legislation enacted in 1999, and the Coalition disbanded.

Although firms in the same industry are often aligned on issues, they may be opposed on some nonmarket issues. In 1992 British Airways announced it would invest $750 million in USAir, forming a global alliance. Robert L. Crandall, chairman of American Airlines, criticized the investment on the grounds that the arrangement provided the United Kingdom increased access to the U.S. market, while U.S. airlines remained restricted in their access to the U.K. market. Crandall was subsequently joined by the CEOs of United Airlines, Delta Air Lines, and Federal Express. USAir countered their lobbying with a grassroots letter-writing campaign by its employees, but the relentless lobbying by the four airlines caused British Airways to cancel the investment and alliance.[35]

The alignment of interests on some issues can be broad. The clean air legislation pending in Congress during the 1980s led to the formation of the Clean Air Working Group, which included 2,000 businesses and trade associations. Aligned with the group were labor unions representing auto, construction, and other workers. This allowed the opponents of stringent legislation to speak from a relatively unified position on the 1990 amendments to the Clean Air Act.

## Coalitions and Consensus

The heterogeneity or homogeneity of interests not only affects who participates in a coalition but also the bargaining within a coalition. When interests are homogeneous, as in the case of the Uniform Standards Coalition, bargaining is relatively easy because disagreements are likely to be small. On an issue where interests are heterogeneous, the bargaining can be more complex and lengthy. The SIA includes members as diverse as merchant-semiconductor producers such as Intel and Advanced Micro Devices, purchasers of semiconductors such as Hewlett-Packard, and firms such as IBM that are both producers and purchasers. The bargaining within the SIA on the issue of Japanese competition and market opening lasted nearly 2 years before an agreement was reached on a position its members could support. The SIA filed a petition for relief under Section 301 of the Trade Act, seeking the opening of the Japanese market to U.S. semiconductors. This objective appealed both to "free traders" who sought the opening of foreign markets and to those who wanted retaliation against Japan for its trade practices.[36]

On some issues, disagreements among members of a coalition may be irreconcilable. In 1999 eBay and eight other Internet service providers, including Amazon.com, America Online, DoubleClick, and Yahoo!, formed NetCoalition.com. The coalition's mission was to serve as "the collective public policy voice of the world's leading Internet companies. . . . " Within a few months, however, the collective voice split over the issue of database protection.[37] eBay backed legislation to protect its databases, and other

---

[35]The following year British Airways invested $340 million in USAir, but by 1996 the alliance had disintegrated.
[36]See Yoffie (1988a).
[37]See the Chapter 12 case, *eBay and Database Protection.*

members backed rival legislation that, according to eBay, would provide little if any protection. eBay withdrew from the coalition.

In the Chapter 2 case, *Personal Watercraft, aka Jet Skis,* personal watercraft (PWC) manufacturers faced a host of nonmarket issues relating to safety, pollution, noise, and disruption of fishing, canoeing, and other water sports. One strategy used by the PWC manufacturers was to argue that any new regulations on jet skis should also apply to boats. The purpose was to force boat manufacturers to oppose the new regulations. PWC manufacturers and boat producers belonged to the National Marine Manufacturers Association (NMMA), which worked against the proposed regulations. Genmar, the world's largest independent boat manufacturer, however, objected to being aligned with the PWC manufacturers and quit the NMMA in protest.[38]

Trade associations can be effective on those nonmarket issues that have similar impacts on their members. In those cases a trade association can effectively speak with one voice before congressional committees, regulatory agencies, and executive branch agencies. As the jet ski example indicates, however, on matters that affect members quite differently, consensus may not be possible. The pharmaceutical politics example illustrates this even in the case of an industry with relatively homogeneous interests.

---

### EXAMPLE

## Pharmaceutical Politics

The Food and Drug Administration (FDA) required extensive laboratory and clinical testing that could take from 5 to 10 years or more, and many millions of dollars, before a new drug was approved for sale. Since a drug was patented before testing began, a new drug might have only a few years of patent protection before generic drug manufacturers could introduce a chemically identical drug. The companies retained some protection because generic drugs had to undergo testing that could take up to 5 years to complete even though they were chemically the same as the already approved drugs. Furthermore, a federal appeals court had ruled that testing by a generic drug manufacturer could not begin until the patent on the original drug had expired.

In 1984 the Generic Pharmaceutical Industry Association (GPIA) sought legislation requiring the FDA to establish simplified approval procedures for generic drugs, requiring proof only that a generic drug was biochemically identical to an already approved drug. Legislation to expedite the approval of generic drugs was introduced in both the House and the Senate, and it received considerable support. Changes in the approval process would have a major impact on the brand-name drug companies because patents on over 150 drugs with sales of $4 billion either had recently expired or were about to expire.

The Pharmaceutical Manufacturers Association (PMA), representing the makers of brand-name patented drugs, opposed the legislation, arguing that the revisions in FDA testing requirements would reduce their incentives to develop new drugs. This, it was argued, would result in fewer drugs being discovered, which in turn would reduce the level of health care.

The PMA sought outright defeat of the legislation. Once it became apparent that this objective could not be realized, it reached a compromise in negotiations among the GPIA and the chairpersons of the cognizant congressional committees. The compromise would extend patent protection for certain brand-name drugs and speed the approval process for generic drugs.

*(Continued)*

---

[38]The Genmar chairman stated, "I am convinced the PWC industry will ultimately force new regulations and restrictions on the boating industry that will cause irreparable damage to us all due to their product's potential dangers and the abuse of our lakes and rivers." Genmar Press Release, November 19, 1997.

*(Continued)*

Consensus on the compromise could not be sustained within the PMA, however. Eleven companies were furious with the compromise and succeeded in having the head of the PMA and its chief lobbyist fired. The CEOs of the companies, including American Home Products, Hoffman-LaRoche, and Merck, then lobbied intensely over the next few weeks to strike from the compromise bill the provision that would speed the approval of generic drugs.[1] Their efforts failed, however, and they were only able to obtain a provision pertaining to exclusive-marketing rights for nonpatented drugs.

---

[1]*Dun's Business Month,* January 1986, p. 36.

## Testimony

Companies testify before regulatory agencies, congressional committees, administrative agencies, and courts. In a regulatory setting, *testimony* is important not only because the information presented can affect regulatory decisions, but also because it creates a record that may serve as a basis for judicial review. Many regulatory rulings are challenged in the courts, and the courts will at times consider both substantive and procedural challenges to a ruling. Testimony thus not only must stand up to cross-examination during the hearing, but it should also provide a basis for a possible court action.

Congressional hearings serve a variety of purposes ranging from issue identification to information provision. A hearing provides an opportunity to present a position that may be backed by a policy study conducted by a firm, association, or coalition. Testimony of firms and interest groups, however, is often preceded by lobbying, so for many members of Congress hearings provide little new information.

Hearings are not always held to obtain information. Some are held to generate publicity and mobilize support for a particular position. For example, trial lawyers and consumer groups have opposed liability reform, and one of their tactics is to bring accident victims to congressional hearings to testify against limits on liability awards. Hearings can also be managed to promote the side of the issue supported by the chair. Testimony on the chair's side of an issue may be scheduled in the morning so that television stations will be able to prepare the story and edit the tape in time for the evening news. Testimony on the other side may be scheduled for the afternoon, when it is too late for the evening news. By the next day, that testimony is often too old for television. Hearings thus can provide a stage on which a committee chair can play out a story to advance a policy interest or cater to constituents.

Stephen Breyer (1982, pp. 317–340), now a Supreme Court Justice, gave a detailed description of the 1974 oversight hearings on regulation of the airline industry. Breyer, who then served on the committee staff, characterized the hearings as "drama" to be orchestrated. In preparation for hearings, the committee staff prepared a script that included an opening statement for the chair and a set of questions to ask each witness. Because the chair already knew much of what the witness would say, the chair was able to direct the dialogue. Breyer also discussed the tactics used by members of Congress in their questioning of witnesses. One tactic was to ask a zinger—a question whose only possible answer would support the Congress member's own position. As an example, in the foreign leasing example in Chapter 6, Representative Pickle asked the general manager of Boeing, "Are we not subsidizing the competition of our own foreign carriers [international airlines]?"[39]

---

[39]Hearing, Committee on Ways and Means, House of Representatives, Washington, DC, June 8, 1983, p. 212.

# Public Advocacy

On some issues, particularly those characterized by majoritarian politics, firms use *public advocacy* to communicate directly with the public. The health care industry demonstrated the effectiveness of mass communication with its "Harry and Louise" advertisements, raising alarms about the Clinton administration's plans to restructure the health care industry. The ads turned the public against the administration's plan, contributing to its collapse. As indicated in the PacifiCare example, the industry continued with this approach in its criticism of the Clinton administration's patients' bill of rights.

During the political activity on the Clinton administration's health care restructuring proposal, pharmaceutical firms concerned about possible price controls and mandated rebates adopted a nonmarket strategy that included a communication component. The industry's basic strategy was to emphasize the discovery of new drugs and the incentives needed for research and development. The industry association added "Research" to its name and undertook lobbying and public advocacy with the message that the discovery of new drugs would be jeopardized by price controls.

Several major pharmaceutical companies also formed a coalition, Rx Partners, that conducted media tours in 65 cities and hosted a series of breakfasts for members of Congress. Individual firms also took action. Several companies conducted public education campaigns similar to those of Rx Partners. Bristol Myers held 350 meetings with community groups and lobbied extensively in Congress. Several companies conducted advertising campaigns that emphasized the discovery of new drugs. They also stressed the beneficial therapeutic value of existing drugs, which, invariably, some member of Congress or a relative had used. As the threat of price controls dissipated, the industry turned to advertisements containing personal testimony on the benefits of pharmaceuticals.

How a message is framed can be important when communicating with the public and government officeholders. An example is provided by the plan developed by AT&T and the Federal Communications Commission (FCC) to lower long-distance telephone rates toward the cost of service. The reduction was to be accomplished by introducing usage-independent access charges to be paid monthly by residential and business customers for long-distance service. The FCC and AT&T chose the term "access charge" because the monthly charge would cover the costs of the connection, or access, to the interstate telephone network. The reaction to the plan shocked the FCC and AT&T. Customers, consumer groups, and politicians complained about having to pay for access they might not use. The uproar nearly resulted in legislation barring the plan. As the FCC scaled back the plan, it renamed the charges "end-user charges." The new term implied "use" and did not serve as a lightning rod. The damage had already been done, however.

# Judicial Strategies

*Judicial strategies* pertain not only to those cases in which a firm finds itself the defendant but also to those in which it initiates legal action as a component of a nonmarket strategy. Judicial strategies are implemented in state and federal courts, which are governed by statutory and common law. Judicial strategies are also implemented in quasi-judicial arenas, such as those of regulatory and administrative agencies, which are governed by administrative law. Judicial strategies are used to enforce rights, obtain damages for breach of contract, and address unfair competitive practices under the antitrust laws. Many firms aggressively protect their intellectual property by filing patent and copyright infringement lawsuits.[40] Lawsuits are also used to deter competitors from taking certain actions and to caution the media or regulatory or administrative agencies. Firms frequently file lawsuits against regulatory agencies, alleging an inadequate basis in the record for their rule making. General Motors filed suit against the Department of Transportation because of its preliminary decision to recall GM pickup trucks with side-mounted gas tanks.[41] The secretary of transportation backed down and did not order a recall. On the other side, environmental and activist groups often file lawsuits against agencies for not adequately enforcing the laws.

A judicial strategy can also be used to open markets. The coalition working for the Internet sale of wine direct to consumers used litigation to overturn protectionism by states. Florida, Michigan, New York, North Carolina, Texas, and Virginia allowed intrastate direct sales by wineries within their states but prohibited interstate direct sales. The coalition filed lawsuits to overturn the ban on interstate direct sales, but the Court of Appeals upheld the ban.[42] The Supreme Court agreed to hear an appeal by the coalition in 2005.

Judicial action, particularly in the courts, can be costly. The Department of Justice's antitrust suit against AT&T took 8 years before it was settled out of court with the breakup of the Bell system. It is estimated to have cost AT&T $360 million and the government $15 million.[43] In arenas governed by administrative law, cases, such as petitions to the International Trade Commission for relief from injury by imports, often proceed more expeditiously and at lower cost because of legislatively imposed time limits. Although lawsuits can be extremely costly, awards can also be high. As a fledgling company, MCI successfully sued AT&T on antitrust grounds, and its award was used to finance its expansion. MCI also filed a number of other lawsuits against both AT&T and the FCC seeking the opportunity to provide expanded telecommunications services. The lawsuits helped open the telecommunications market to competition.

In 1998 PepsiCo filed an antitrust lawsuit against the Coca-Cola Company alleging that it used exclusionary practices and abused its dominant position in the fountain-dispensed segment of the soft drink market. Most restaurant chains had avoided carrying Pepsi because PepsiCo owned their competitors Pizza Hut, Taco Bell, and Kentucky Fried Chicken. In 1997, however, PepsiCo spun off its restaurants and began to aggressively pursue the fountain business, which accounted for 27 percent of soft drink sales. The lawsuit alleged that Coca-Cola's exclusive contracts with independent distributors hindered PepsiCo's efforts to win the accounts of restaurant chains, since those distributors would not distribute to restaurants that would like to carry Pepsi. Coca-Cola said that the lawsuit "smacks of desperation."[44]

Regulatory and administrative law channels may be used for a variety of purposes, including to protect rights, handicap a competitor, or gain a direct advantage. When the FDA attempted to streamline its rules for approving generic drugs, the brand-name pharmaceutical companies filed lawsuits challenging its authority to do so. Thwarted in this administrative channel, the generic drug companies subsequently took their cause to Congress, as the Pharmaceutical Politics example indicates.

---

[40]See Chapter 12.
[41]See the Chapter 3 case, *General Motors Like a Rock? (A)*.
[42]See Wiseman and Ellig (2004).
[43]Shipper and Jennings (1984, p. 115).
[44]The lawsuit was dismissed in 2000.

## Organizing for Nonmarket Effectiveness

Firms that expect to be involved in issues addressed in government arenas must anticipate rather than simply react to developments. Consequently, they need to organize and be prepared for action. It is essential to monitor issues, and for many firms this means full-time representation in Washington and in the capitals of key states. For other firms, associations can be a cost-effective means of providing intelligence, although this may not be sufficient if the firm's interests differ from those the association represents. Most large firms also have government affairs departments that provide expertise and monitor the development of issues. A department may include lawyers, communications experts, former government officials, lobbyists, and analysts.[45]

Washington offices serve as the eyes and ears of firms. They provide information on developing issues and are a locus of expertise about issues, institutions, and officeholders. Because nonmarket issues are often episodic in nature, many firms on occasion engage the services of political consulting firms, Washington law firms, or public relations firms. Similarly, lobbyists may be hired for a specific issue. The size of a firm's permanent staff thus is determined relative to the cost and effectiveness of outside alternatives.

Because lobbying is the centerpiece of most firms' interactions with government, most employ lobbyists who are either political professionals or experienced managers responsible for presenting the firm's concerns to government officials. Their responsibilities typically include maintaining relationships with members of Congress, executive branch officials, and government agencies. Access is a necessary condition for lobbying, so many firms make a practice of maintaining contact with those members of Congress in whose districts they have their operations and with the committees that regularly deal with issues on their nonmarket agendas. Firms also provide training for their managers who are involved in nonmarket issues. That training often emphasizes sensitivity to the possible public reaction to the firm's activities and the development of personal skills for participating effectively in government arenas.

## Summary

Firms and interest groups have broad nonmarket portfolios. Lobbying is essential in addressing issues in legislative and administrative arenas. Lobbying involves demonstrating to legislators that the interests of their constituents or their own policy interests are aligned with those of the firm and its stakeholders. Providing politically relevant information to officeholders is at the heart of effective lobbying. That information may be technical or political, relating to the constituents or policy interests of officeholders. Lobbying often focuses on committees and their staffs. Testimony in hearings is related to lobbying and can be coordinated with it. Access to policymakers is necessary for lobbying. It can be attained through the constituency connection, personal relationships, former government officials, and in some cases campaign contributions. Lobbying remains a relatively unregulated activity.

Corporate electoral support primarily involves campaign contributions. These contributions are typically made to obtain access to members of Congress and otherwise seldom play a major role in the nonmarket strategies of most firms.

---

[45]A detailed description of the organization of a Washington office in the heyday of the politics of the oil industry is provided in the case "Gulf Oil Corporation: Public Affairs and the Washington Office" in Fox (1982, pp. 287–306).

Grassroots campaigns are based on the rent chain and are designed to put pressure on legislators through the constituency connection. Firms and interest groups often organize and mobilize their constituents for grassroots activities, including letter-writing and visiting Washington for personal lobbying. The effectiveness of those activities depends on their credibility as well as on their scale. Grassroots campaigns are often coordinated with public advocacy programs. Public advocacy programs are used to inform both the public and those involved in policymaking processes.

Coalition building is an important component of many nonmarket strategies. Firms participate in peak organizations, trade associations, and ad hoc coalitions. Peak organizations address general business issues rather than industry-specific matters. Trade associations are important, particularly for issues that pertain to a specific industry. Ad hoc coalitions address specific issues and often bring together interests that may not be aligned on other issues. When members of a coalition have heterogeneous interests, the maintenance of the coalition requires effort, and its activities are determined through internal bargaining. Large firms often supplement coalition activities with their own individual nonmarket strategies.

Judicial strategies are implemented both in the courts and in regulatory arenas governed by administrative law. These strategies can be effective but can also be expensive.

Most large firms are organized to address nonmarket issues in government institutions. That organization may involve a Washington office, professional lobbyists, a government affairs department, associations and coalitions, and management training. This organization complements but does not substitute for management involvement in nonmarket strategy formulation and implementation.

The chapter cases, *Drexel Burnham Lambert and Junk Bond Politics, Internet Taxation,* and *Proposition 211: Securities Litigation Referendum (A),* and the Part II integrative case, *CAFE Standards 2002,* involve issues that require a nonmarket strategy and an implementation plan.

# Drexel Burnham Lambert and Junk Bond Politics

In early 1985 Drexel Burnham Lambert faced a nonmarket challenge to its lucrative market strategy of using high-yield debt instruments to facilitate acquisitions, restructure firms, and finance growing companies. These debt instruments were popularly called junk bonds, although Drexel preferred the term non-investment grade securities.

Throughout the 1970s virtually all junk bonds were "fallen angels"—bonds that had been investment grade when issued but had fallen because of the financial difficulties of the issuer. In the late 1970s Drexel pioneered the use of junk bonds to finance small firms and high-growth firms and to restructure firms through takeovers and leveraged buyouts (LBOs). Takeovers, restructurings, and LBOs provided the bulk of Drexel's profits and the bonuses paid to its employees. The securities issued by the high-growth firms, which had previously had to rely on venture capital and financing by banks and insurance companies, were typically below investment grade because the firms had often only recently gone public or because of the risk associated with their size. The distinctions between these three types of junk bonds—fallen angels, acquisition instruments, and bonds issued by high-growth firms—were not well understood by the public or Congress.

The pace of corporate acquisitions, particularly hostile takeovers, had aroused considerable opposition among many corporate executives. In early 1985, as a result of a variety of forces and with the support of activist groups and some business organizations such as the Business Roundtable, seven bills pertaining to junk bonds were introduced in Congress. Some of the bills would limit the tax deductibility of the interest on junk bonds used in hostile takeover attempts, others would limit the amount of acquisition junk bonds that federally insured institutions could hold, and others would impose a moratorium on hostile takeovers financed with junk bonds. For example, the Securities Safety and Soundness Act would impose a moratorium through December 31, 1985, on hostile takeovers in which at least 20 percent of the acquisition was financed by junk bonds. The Junk Bond Limitation Act would limit the amount of junk bonds that federally insured financial institutions could hold. As congressional committees began to consider these bills, the threat to the heart of Drexel's business and its reputation was enormous.

A number of commentators believed that corporations supported the bills because they feared being the targets of hostile takeover attempts. The size of some of the takeover attempts, and the fact that some of them succeeded, sent chills through many an executive suite. Andrew Sigler, CEO of Champion International and chairman of the Corporate Responsibility Task Force of the Business Roundtable, was one of the leading advocates of restrictions on hostile takeovers. He argued for "legislative approaches aimed at curbing the current destructive takeover frenzy and restoring some semblance of sanity to the tender offer process." He warned that increased leverage threatened the future of American corporations.

Opponents also claimed that acquisitions financed with junk bonds increased concentration in American industry, threatened local communities, diverted capital from new productive investment, and resulted in layoffs and increased unemployment. Drexel, however, maintained that the acquisitions promoted efficiency by replacing ineffective management and that capital was not diverted because it flowed to the shareholders of the acquired firm, who reinvested most of it. Drexel also cited studies by economists showing that even with the recent spate of acquisitions, industrial concentration had not increased, in part because of the growing number of spin-offs, divestments, and start-ups.

Drexel also pointed out that over 95 percent of U.S. public corporations with assets above $25 million would receive a rating below investment grade from Moody's or Standard & Poor's. Moreover, 12 states had no corporations that would receive an investment grade rating. A Drexel representative pointed out that debt instruments with ratings below investment grade were essential to many of the small, high-growth companies that accounted for a high percentage of the jobs created in the economy.

The investment banking industry was divided on the issue of restrictions on junk bonds. Many of the leading investment banks viewed Drexel, which had the bulk of the junk bond business, with hostility but also with admiration for its rapid growth. Some leading investment banks had refused to use junk bonds, and some refused to participate on the acquisition side of hostile takeovers. Felix G. Rohatyn, a senior partner of Lazard Freres & Company, spoke out against hostile takeovers and the way junk bonds were used to finance them. He called for laws to restrict their use. Morgan Stanley commissioned a study showing that the default rate on total debt was 0.08 percent, but the default rate on non-investment grade debt was 1.52 percent. Drexel refuted those data and cited studies showing that high-yield bonds outperformed Treasury bills by a wide margin during the late 1970s and the first half of the 1980s.[46]

In April 1985 Drexel was approached by David Aylward, until recently the general counsel of the House Subcommittee on Telecommunications, Consumer Protection and Finance, who proposed forming an association to oppose the bills. The association would solicit contributions of $25,000 each from high-growth companies, ranging from a day care center company to a computer leasing company to a steel company, all of which used high-yield, non-investment grade bonds to finance their growth. The association would then represent the interests of these and other companies before Congress. Aylward asked for Drexel's assistance in contacting potential members of the association. ■

---

## PREPARATION QUESTIONS

1. What are the relevant dimensions of the nonmarket threat to Drexel?
2. What is the nature of the politics of the issue and where is it in its life cycle?
3. Which interests are likely to be active on this issue?
4. What political strategy should Drexel adopt, and how should it be integrated with its market strategy? How should it be implemented?
5. Should Drexel assist Aylward with the formation of the association he has proposed? What name should be given to it if it were formed? Would the formation of the association be responsible?

---

[46]Frederick H. Joseph, "High-Yield Bonds Aren't Junk," *The Wall Street Journal*, May 31, 1985.

# Proposition 211: Securities Litigation Referendum (A)

*Our attitude was, "We don't like the way the political game is played so we're just not going to play it." But you know what? It's the only game there is. And if you don't play, you get what you deserve. We can't just bury our heads in the sand and assume that what we don't know won't hurt us.*[47]

— TOM PROULX

In late July 1996 business leaders in Silicon Valley were anxious. A statewide ballot initiative, Proposition 211, had been placed on California's November 5 ballot. The initiative had been sponsored by attorney Bill Lerach, whose firm, Milberg, Weiss, Bershad, Hynes & Lerach ("the Lerach firm"), had represented plaintiffs in lawsuits against 53 of the top 100 Silicon Valley companies since 1989. A typical lawsuit alleged that a company had committed securities fraud that had harmed shareholders. Executives generally viewed the allegations as meritless and designed to extract a settlement from the company. The trigger for a lawsuit was usually a drop in the company's share price. Said Intel chairman Gordon Moore, "There are only two kinds of companies in Silicon Valley, those that have been sued and those that are going to be sued."[48] Regardless of whether a company had been sued, nearly every Silicon Valley executive recognized the threat of being "Lerach-ed," the term used when a firm was served with such a lawsuit.

Proposition 211 would change state securities laws to make it easier for plaintiffs to prevail in shareholder securities litigation and would heighten the liability of a company's directors and officers as well as so-called "aiders and abettors," which could include accountants, underwriters, and other professional services firms.

Tom Proulx, a cofounder of software maker Intuit, was joined by several other business leaders who had volunteered to fight Prop 211— John Doerr, a venture capitalist with Kleiner Perkins Caufield & Byers; John Dean, CEO of Silicon Valley Bank; and John Young, former CEO and chairman of Hewlett-Packard. Silicon Valley had developed a reputation for political naiveté, preferring to avoid politics and focus on business and technology. Although Silicon Valley leaders had successfully lobbied some issues in the past, notably issues such as semiconductor trade and stock option accounting, they had never successfully waged a statewide electoral campaign. What strategy would be most successful against the seasoned political opponent they faced in Bill Lerach and the almost $4 million that proponents of the measure had already raised?

## Background

Shareholders had the right under the Securities Act of 1933 to file suit against public corporations for fraudulent or misleading statements made by management and directors of a company. For example, suppose management announced that it expected continued strong demand for a product line when in fact it knew of underlying factors that might significantly jeopardize sales. If the underlying factors materialized in the form of lower than expected sales, a company's stock price might fall. The drop in the share price could then be cited as damage to the shareholder—a loss of value resulting from the shareholder's purchase of the stock at a price "inflated" by management's fraudulent representations. Lerach had turned this logic around by using a drop in share price to allege fraudulent representations and then use the discovery process to look for evidence to support the allegations.

To recover damages shareholders had been required to both identify the specific fraudulent information they relied on in purchasing the company's stock and demonstrate that the losses they incurred resulted from their reliance on that information. A Supreme Court ruling in *Basic Inc. v. Levinson*, 485 U.S. 224, 108 S.Ct. 978 (1988) changed the reliance requirement by embracing the concept of "fraud on the market." Fraud on the market theory posited that

---

[47]*The Los Angeles Times,* November 4, 1996.
[48]Taxpayers Against Frivolous Lawsuits, "License to Destroy" videotape.

because financial analysts and intermediaries played a crucial role in gathering and interpreting company information, and because in an efficient market this information and its interpretation were incorporated into the price of a traded security, shareholders did not need to demonstrate reliance on specific corporate information to establish fraud. Instead, they could rely on the stock price as an indicator of the impact of such information. Consequently, shareholders could rely on a significant drop in the price of a company's stock as preliminary evidence that fraud had occurred.

Accountants, brokers, and insurers were often named as codefendants in securities class-action suits as so-called aiders and abettors. Plaintiffs could recover damages jointly and severally from all codefendants, regardless of the extent of their involvement in the alleged fraud. Thus, if a company became bankrupt or did not have sufficient funds to pay a proposed settlement, the professional services firms became liable for those amounts. Typically, a lawsuit also named as defendants the senior directors and officers who allegedly participated in the fraud. Companies usually purchased insurance for such claims against their directors and officers.

From April 1988 to September 1996, approximately 1,300 shareholder class-action lawsuits were filed under Rule 10(b)5 of the Securities Act of 1933.[49] Sometimes lawsuits were filed within hours of a precipitous drop in a stock's price, for example, of 10 percent or more, regardless of whether the plaintiff had any knowledge or evidence of fraud on the part of management. Shortly after a complaint was filed, a discovery process would begin in which plaintiffs' counsel requested documents and information from the company. Discovery often included depositions of key management personnel.

If management believed the lawsuit was without merit, it would file a motion for dismissal on the basis of insufficient evidence to support plaintiffs' claims. Only about 10 percent of the actions filed were dismissed, however. If the motion were unsuccessful, management could defend the case through trial or settle out of court. The settlement decision relied

on several factors, including an assessment of the evidence, the cost of defending a case through trial, the likelihood of winning a trial, and potential settlement costs. Many executives preferred settlement to the threat of overly burdensome judgments or the significant cost of discovery and defense through a trial. In one case litigated by Bill Lerach, a verdict of $100 million was ordered against Apple Computer and its officers after 8 years of legal proceedings. Apple appealed and the case was eventually settled for $16 million. Tom Proulx commented on the decision executives faced in defending against a shareholder suit:

> Someone accuses you of fraud. You know with absolute certainty it's a lie. You want to fight, but then you find out you really don't have the opportunity. You're a dumb businessman if you fight it. No matter how good your case, there's uncertainty in a jury trial. You don't think you're going to lose, but we all know that anything can happen in front of a jury. If you lose, it can mean you're literally out of business. So you settle.[50]

In a study of 952 shareholder suits, 88 percent were settled, whereas only 1 percent were tried (11 percent were dismissed). The average settlement was $7.3 million, and the highest was $250 million. Plaintiffs' counsel typically received one-third of the settlement or the damages ordered by the court.

A relatively small number of law firms filed a very high proportion of these class action claims. From 1988 to 1996, three firms were involved in the filing of over 50 percent of the cases, and the Lerach firm was involved in over 30 percent. These firms had developed reputations among some executives as indiscriminate filers of frivolous lawsuits with the objective of extracting a settlement from companies so as to collect attorney's fees. Law firms often competed to be named lead counsel for the class. Some firms were said to have "stables" of "professional plaintiffs" who owned a few shares in several companies and would lend their names to lawsuits—sometimes without their immediate knowledge. The Lerach firm was reported to have represented a single individual in 12 separate class-action lawsuits.

---

[49]Investors also had the right to form a "class" of shareholders who had been exposed to allegedly fraudulent information (or, alternatively, the omission of truthful information). The class of shareholders could unite their claim under a single court proceeding and be represented by a single team of attorneys, typically referred to as plaintiffs' counsel.

[50]*Upside,* November 1996.

## Industry Actions

Growing discontent with the securities litigation process led to pressure from the business community for reforms of the Securities Act of 1933. A loose coalition comprised of groups such as the National Association of Manufacturers, American Electronics Association, NASDAQ, American Stock Exchange, American Business Conference, National Venture Capital Association, and Biotechnology Industry Association formed to bring their concerns to the attention of Congress. In early 1994 Senators Christopher Dodd (D-CN) and Pete Domenici (R-NM) introduced a bipartisan bill on shareholder litigation reform, but the 103rd Congress ended without action beyond the committee stage. In the November 1994 elections Republicans gained a majority in both the House and Senate, campaigning on the "Contract with America." One plank of the contract called for shareholder litigation reform. On February 27, 1995, Representative Thomas Bliley (R-VA), chair of the House Commerce Committee, introduced H.R. 1058, the Private Securities Litigation Reform Act of 1995 (PSLRA). A similar measure was introduced in the Senate. The House bill passed on March 8, and a Senate bill on shareholder litigation reform passed on June 28. The major provisions of the reform were as follows:

- Heightened pleading standards that made it more difficult for plaintiffs to allege securities fraud without having solid information on which to base such a claim.
- A stay of discovery while a motion to dismiss was pending.
- Designation as the "lead plaintiff" the one with the largest financial interests at stake, giving it the right to control the course of litigation and select the lead counsel for the class. (The lead plaintiff would often be an institutional investor, such as a pension fund.)
- Creation of a limited "safe harbor" for the release of forward-looking information about a firm's prospects provided it is accompanied by "meaningful" cautionary language identifying factors that could cause actual results to differ materially from those projected. (This provision was intended to prevent companies from being subject to class action litigation simply because their forecasts proved inaccurate.)

- Modification of the "fair share" rule of proportionate liability to limit the exposure of accountants and underwriters named as codefendants in an action.
- A provision to limit attorney's fees to a "reasonable percentage of the amount of recovery awarded the class" as determined by the court.

Despite lobbying by the plaintiffs' bar, by early December the bills received conference committee approval, and by votes of 65 to 30 in the Senate and 320 to 102 in the House the bill was sent to President Clinton. The President, citing concerns that the heightened pleadings standards would make it too difficult for defrauded investors to recover losses, vetoed the bill.[51] Three days later both the House (by a margin of 319 to 100) and Senate (by a margin of 68 to 30) had overridden the President's veto, and PSLRA became law.

## State Venues

Securities class action cases were typically not filed in state courts, but the prospective passage of the PSLRA made state courts more attractive than federal courts. In particular, the new pleadings requirements, safe harbor provisions, discovery stays, and certain other provisions of PSLRA might be avoided in state courts.

The focus of litigation reform shifted from the federal to the state level, and both proponents and opponents were active in California. The first move was made by a group of technology business leaders who sought additional protection for companies from securities litigation. These firms were targets because the volatility of their stock led to more frequent large stock price changes.[52] Utilizing the California initiative process, an organization calling itself the Alliance to Revitalize California qualified Propositions 201 and 202 for the March 1996 California primary. The Alliance was chaired by Tom Proulx, who had taken leave from Intuit to pursue outside interests.

---

[51]The plaintiffs' bar and trial lawyers associations were major contributors to the Democratic Party and President Clinton's campaign.

[52]Together, companies from the high-technology and financial-services industries were named defendants in 53 percent of securities class action cases, and both industries watched litigation reform developments closely.

Al Shugart, CEO of disk-drive manufacturer Seagate, was also on the Alliance's board of directors.

Proposition 201 would change state securities laws to require the losing party in any securities class action to pay the winner's attorney's fees and other litigation expenses.[53] By imposing a cost on plaintiffs who filed and lost shareholder lawsuits, the measure was expected to discourage filings of questionable merit. Proposition 202 would limit attorney's fees in class action and other tort cases with the intent of increasing the incentives for plaintiffs to settle early and avoid the expense of drawn out procedures during which attorney's fees accumulate.

Propositions 201 and 202 were strongly opposed by plaintiffs' counsel. During the final weeks of the campaign, opponents utilized heavy television advertising with messages suggesting that business interests were attempting to build protection that would allow them to defraud investors and reap benefits by exercising personal stock options at prices inflated by their own fraudulent representations. In one television advertisement, the photographic image of Seagate CEO Al Shugart (whose management had been sued under securities laws) was "morphed" into the image of Charles Keating, who several years earlier had been convicted for defrauding bondholders of Lincoln Savings & Loan in a widely publicized case. Proponents of the measures were less successful than the opponents in raising funds early in the campaign, and when money became available for television advertising, only the less desirable media buys were available, such as cable channels and off-peak hours. On March 6, 1996, Prop 201 was defeated by a 59 to 41 percent margin. Prop 202 was more narrowly defeated, 51 to 49 percent.

## Drafting of Proposition 211

In May 1995 a group headed by Bill Lerach together with the Consumer Attorneys of California (formerly the California Trial Lawyers Association) drafted the preliminary text of a proposed ballot initiative, the Pension and Retirement Fund Protection Act. The act was drafted in response to Propositions 201 and 202 and concerns raised by plaintiffs' counsel over proposed federal reforms. Soon after Congress's override of President Clinton's veto of the PSLRA,

signature gathering began. The proposed law included the following provisions:

- Removal of "safe-harbor" protection for forward-looking statements by management.
- Prohibition of the indemnification of directors and officers. (Companies could not make insurance co-payments on behalf of directors and officers for settlements or judgments. This would leave directors and officers personally liable for damages.)
- Authorization of punitive damages, in addition to compensatory damages. (Federal law prohibited punitive damages.)
- Authorization of private action against "aiders and abettors," including stock brokers, accounting firms, legal firms, and investor relations firms. (Under current law only the Securities and Exchange Commission could bring such actions.)
- Establishment of full joint and several liability.
- Elimination of an automatic stay of discovery.
- Prohibition of any future regulation of attorney's fees in securities litigation or any other state action.

Unlike other state securities laws, the initiative was not expressly limited to securities offers or sales in California. It was envisioned that a company could be sued by injured California residents even if the company were based outside California and conducted the alleged fraud outside the state. While these provisions would be subject to tests of constitutionality, the initiative was potentially applicable to all public corporations in the United States.

In June 1996 the proposition was qualified for the November 1996 ballot as Proposition 211, popularly known as Prop 211.

## Proponent's Strategy

The Consumer Attorneys of California (CAOC) had long-established ties with leaders of the Democratic Party, and the Lerach firm in particular was a large donor. In the first half of 1996 Lerach and his firm gave over $465,000 to the Democratic National Committee. Lerach personally was the single largest trial-lawyer contributor in the country during the 1989 through 1995 time period, giving over $1.5 million, almost all to Democratic Party causes. A consultant's planning memorandum to leaders of the CAOC

---

[53]This is similar to the British system for assigning attorney's fees.

indicated that the proponents' strategy would rely heavily on its ties to the Democratic Party. Preliminary polls conducted by the consultants showed over 70 percent of those surveyed supported the measure.

Proponents of Prop 211 sought the support of two important voter groups: seniors and unions. Both groups had significant assets invested in securities through pension funds and retirement savings plans. Both groups also were well organized politically within the state. Seniors and union members were expected to support Prop 211 because it would give them stronger means of recovering retirement funds lost as a result of fraud on the part of management. An organization known as Citizens for Retirement Protection and Security was formed to support Prop 211. In addition, the Congress of California Seniors became a sponsor of Prop 211 and signatory to the arguments that would accompany the proposition on the ballot. Proponents hoped that by bringing together these three politically active constituencies (seniors, unions, and the Democratic Party), voter support would follow.

Proponents of Prop 211 argued that it would benefit Californians by

- making corporate officers' personal assets available to repay fraud victims
- making all parties fully liable for participating in a fraud
- restoring seniors' legal rights, which had been usurped by federal law
- punishing only those executives who committed fraud

To support these messages, campaign literature and publications reminded voters of Charles Keating and the Lincoln Savings scandal, arguing that Prop 211 was necessary to protect future Keating-type victims. In addition, the campaign suggested that fraud among corporations and executives was rampant. A 1990 survey by the National Association of Accountants was cited indicating that 87 percent of corporate executives were willing to commit fraud, and a *San Jose Mercury News* survey was cited indicating that 45 percent of Silicon Valley executives had said their officers, directors, and large investors had violated SEC reporting regulations. Reference was also made to $1.74 billion in payments by Big Six accounting firms to federal government agencies, states, corporations, and individual investors in class-

action lawsuits in the past 5 years. Jonathan Cunio, a congressional lobbyist for Lerach, explained, "This is not just about punishing, this is about deterrence. Generally, in these cases, it is the top executives themselves who are making misrepresentations to the marketplace while pocketing millions of dollars in insider sales."[54] Supporters of the initiative insisted that honest officers and directors had nothing to fear from the initiative.

Responding to criticism that he had sponsored Prop 211 to mitigate the effects of federal reforms on his law practice, Lerach replied, "We have plenty of lawsuits that we are litigating. The reason we are supporting the initiative is that we think it is high time that someone stood up to these big corporations and accounting firms. Is it not better public policy for the state of California to have more protections for victims of fraud?"[55]

Proponents of Prop 211 succeeded in gaining the early support of several senior and union groups, including the American Association of Retired Persons (AARP), the California State Employees Association, and several regional AFL-CIO councils. Proponents also secured the endorsement of the California Democratic Party.

By June 30, 1996, proponents had spent approximately $3.8 million on their organizational efforts to build support for the measure. No significant paid media campaigns had yet been undertaken. The proponents had retained political and media consulting services from several firms.

## Opponents' Response

In the fall of 1995, when proponents of Prop 211 began the drive to put an initiative before voters, a group calling itself Taxpayers Against Frivolous Lawsuits (TAFL) was formed to oppose the initiative. TAFL was initially led by Kirk West, president of the California Chamber of Commerce, and John Sullivan, president of the Association for California Tort Reform. With substantial financial support from the Big Six accounting firms, TAFL began conducting surveys and initiated campaign planning in December 1995. In a benchmark public opinion survey conducted for TAFL in December, 49 percent of respondents supported Prop 211 with 24 percent opposed and the rest undecided.

---

[54]*Wired,* November 1996.
[55]*Chicago Tribune,* June 23, 1996.

After the defeat of Propositions 201 and 202, the opponents' coalition broadened substantially as high-tech business interests became increasingly concerned about the potential impact of Prop 211. The TAFL steering committee was expanded to include Tom Proulx. TAFL also retained the professional campaign management firm Goddard*Claussen/ First Tuesday to help plan, manage, and implement the campaign. In July 1996 John Young, retired president and CEO of Hewlett-Packard, was named the national chairman of TAFL. Young was a particularly respected executive among technology business leaders. He said, "Every company in the country lives with the threat of these frivolous lawsuits that serve only to drain the resources for thousands of good jobs. Proposition 211 would impact virtually every public company, not just those in California."[56]

Many executives were concerned about the effect of Prop 211 on the willingness of individuals to serve as directors, since it would make directors personally liable for damages and preclude companies from insuring them. Intel CEO Andy Grove said, "It's a horrendous notion. Boards will either not be able to attract good board members or they have to restructure . . . All is inimical to the interests of shareholders."[57] Separately, he warned, "Passage of Prop 211 would destroy corporate governance as we know it."[58] Venture capitalist John Doerr added,

Three of the best CEOs I work with are resigning if Prop 211 passes. I can't pay them enough to take on that personal liability. Their vice presidents are resigning. And every one of my partners is resigning from the 40 boards on which we serve that are public. I am worried that if Prop 211 passes, it will be the undoing of the risk-taking, reward-gaining entrepreneurial system that we use to build new growth companies.[59]

Citizens for Retirement Protection and Security spokesman Sean Crowley responded to these assertions stating, "That's just a scare tactic to raise money. No director or company officer who is innocent of wrongdoing is at risk. This only punishes those who steal people's retirements savings and pensions."[60] Melvyn Weiss, a partner in the Lerach law firm, suggested, "Corporate America knows that if it beats us, then it is home free to do anything it wants."[61]

## Planning the Campaign

To help create momentum for a successful campaign, leadership of the campaign in Silicon Valley was broadened to include John Doerr and John Dean. In late July they met in their Silicon Valley campaign office. With the exception of Tom Proulx's experience in the March campaign, none had previously managed a political campaign. They noted the historic reluctance of the Silicon Valley business community to involve itself in nonmarket issues. Many of the business leaders had disdain for the political process, becoming involved only when immediately threatened by potential changes in the nonmarket environment.

As they met, they discussed the challenges before them:

- Proponents were well organized and appeared willing and able to raise significant funds for the campaign—initial estimates based on funds raised in opposition to Proposition 201 and 202 suggested up to $20 million.
- Proponents appeared likely to succeed in gaining the endorsements of seniors and union groups.
- Proponents had several "hot-button" messages that resonated well with potential voters, such as the Charles Keating scandal and the recent bankruptcy of Orange County in southern California.
- The initiative title and summary on the ballot were viewed by opponents as an unfair description of the actual initiative. Voters would need to be educated as to the potential effects of the initiative.[62]
- Opponents ran the risk of being perceived as protecting business interests at the expense of investors and retirees.

---

[56] *Eye on Global Management*, September 15, 1996.
[57] *The Washington Post*, September 24, 1996.
[58] *Forbes*, August 26, 1996.
[59] *Financial World*, October 21, 1996
[60] *San Francisco Chronicle*, September 13, 1996.

[61] *Business Week*, August 26, 1996.
[62] Proponents of Prop 211 had submitted the initiative as the Retirement Savings and Consumer Protection Act. California Attorney General Dan Lungren, a Republican, changed the initiative title to "Attorney-Client Fee Arrangements. Securities Fraud. Initiative Statute." Nonetheless, Prop 211 opponents did not view the title or proposition description as accurately describing the intent or potential effects of the initiative.

- Voters had rejected securities litigation reform sponsored by business interests in the March elections.

Campaign leaders also considered their strategic assets:

- History had shown that a "no" vote was easier to obtain on California ballot measures than a "yes" vote. Moreover, proponents would need to demonstrate to voters that there was a major problem with current securities laws—so dramatic that it required a ballot measure to fix. Preliminary research by opponents suggested this would be difficult.
- According to research studies, trial lawyers were in general not well liked in California. Both the Consumer Attorneys of California and California Trial Lawyers Association were at the very bottom of the credibility scale among nearly 80 individuals and g. recent study.
- Nearly 20 ballot measures had qualified for the November ballot. It was anticipated that voters would experience some confusion, which could encourage "no" votes.
- Opponents' support came from a broad base of industries representing significant financial, information, and communication resources—if they could be tapped.

Campaign leaders needed a strategy built on these assets that would prevail against the proponents of Prop 211. ■

SOURCE: Chris Watts prepared this case under the supervision of Professor David P. Baron as the basis for class discussion rather than to illustrate either effective or ineffective handling of an administrative situation. Copyright © 1997 by the Board of Trustees of the Leland Stanford Junior University. All rights reserved. Reprinted with permission.

## PREPARATION QUESTION

1. What strategy should the campaign leaders adopt, and how should it be implemented?

# Internet Taxation

On May 10, 2000, the House of Representatives passed H.R. 3709, the "Internet Non-Discrimination Act," by a resounding majority of 352–75. The bill provided a 5-year extension of an existing moratorium on new Internet taxes that was due to expire in 2001.[63] The bill had been embraced by a diverse coalition of consumer groups, Internet users, and high-tech companies that argued that the imposition of taxes on electronic commerce would slow both the development of the Internet and the growth in the U.S. economy.

In the Senate intense lobbying by a diverse set of interests led Senator John McCain (R-AZ), chairman of the Commerce Committee, to cancel a hearing on a bill to make the tax moratorium permanent. When questioned about the cancellation, McCain said the topic of Internet taxes was "incredibly complex [and had] not been nearly fleshed out enough."[64] At the same time the legislation stalled in the Senate, the solidarity of the high-tech community on the Internet taxation issue began to slip. In a June hearing before the Joint Economic Committee, Intel Chairman Andy Grove argued for applying sales taxes to transactions on the Web, saying that he felt there was no "justification" for the online tax advantage. At the

---

[63]The existing moratorium prohibited the imposition of "multiple and discriminatory" taxes on electronic commerce. These taxes included those that subjected buyers and sellers to taxation in multiple states and localities, as well as taxes on goods specifically sold over the Internet by companies that did not have brick-and-mortar counterparts in the state. Discriminatory taxes included taxes imposed on Internet sales but not on catalog sales. The moratorium also prohibited the federal government from imposing taxes on Internet access or electronic commerce generally. See www.house.gov/chriscox/nettax/.

[64]*The Wall Street Journal,* June 22, 2000.

same hearing, Hewlett-Packard CEO Carly Fiorina warned that "to apply the current system of taxation to the online world would be disastrous." She, however, criticized those opposed to any Internet taxes, saying that such a stance was "unrealistic."[65] A new report by the General Accounting Office (GAO) estimated that state and local governments stood to lose anywhere between $300 million and $3.8 billion in sales tax revenue in 2000.[66]

## Precedents and Mail-Order Sales

The controversy surrounding Internet taxation resulted from court decisions that exempted from taxes mail-order sales to out-of-state residents. In two landmark court cases, *National Bellas Hess v. Department of Revenue of the State of Illinois* (386 U.S. 753, 1967) and *Quill v. North Dakota* (504 U.S. 298, 1992), the U.S. Supreme Court concluded that requiring mail-order merchants to calculate, collect, and remit the appropriate tax to the appropriate authorities would constitute an undue burden because of the approximately 35,000 state and local tax rates in effect. The Court decided that merchants were only required to collect sales taxes from customers that resided in a state where the merchant had a "nexus." A nexus, loosely defined, was a physical presence, such as a warehouse or retail outlet.

The Supreme Court decisions effectively absolved merchants of their responsibility for tax collection on out-of-state sales, but responsibility for the remittance of the tax remained for consumers. Most states required the remittance of individual consumers to report to their state government how much tax they owed and pay accordingly. Use taxes provided governments with a legal basis to collect revenue on out-of-state purchases, but such collection rarely occurred. Compliance was very low, as most consumers were unaware that they were required to pay the use tax. Few states attempted to collect from individual consumers.[67] Although the inability to collect use taxes on catalog sales had not led to new tax legislation, the rise of the Internet significantly changed perceptions about the scale of purchases potentially free from state and local taxes. As more transactions migrated to the Web, state and local governments feared a substantial erosion of their tax bases.[68]

Fears of dwindling revenues were accompanied by the concerns of off-line main street merchants who felt that the tax advantage of online stores gave them a significant advantage. These issues led to the introduction of bills in several state legislatures, all of which were aimed at providing some form of tax collection on online sales, at least from their own residents. Online merchants, however, argued that they had to bear delivery costs, which, as with catalog sales, offset the tax exclusion. The online merchants also argued that they did not use state resources other than for delivery and hence should not be required to fund state services.

While state and local governments were clamoring for action, the federal government was effectively putting on the brakes. The Internet Tax Freedom Act (ITFA), introduced in Congress by Representative Christopher Cox (R-CA) and Senator Ron Wyden (D-OR), was passed as part of the Omnibus Appropriations Act of 1998. Placing a 3-year moratorium on new Internet taxes, the ITFA also created the Advisory Commission on Electronic Commerce to study issues related to the taxation of the Internet and to recommend to Congress by April 2000 an appropriate tax policy.[69]

The Advisory Commission consisted of 19 members, eight of whom were from industry and consumer groups, eight from state and local government, and three from the Clinton administration. Early in its deliberations the Commission separated

---

65 *The Atlanta Journal and Constitution,* June 8, 2000.

66 *Report to Congressional Requesters,* "Sales Taxes: Electronic Commerce Growth Presents Challenges; Revenue Losses Are Uncertain," United States General Accounting Office, June 2000.

67 States that took measures to collect use taxes met with little success. Several states, such as New Jersey, had a separate line for use taxes on residents' income tax forms. In 1997 less than 1 percent of New Jersey residents reported use taxes. (Robert J. Cline and Thomas S. Neubig, 1999. "Masters of Complexity and Bearers of Great Burden: The Sales Tax System and Compliance Costs for Multistate Retailers," Technical Report, Ernst and Young Economics Consulting and Quantitative Analysis.)

68 All states except Alaska, Delaware, Montana, New Hampshire, and Oregon had a sales tax.

69 www.ecommercecommission.org.

into three camps. One camp, including executives such as C. Michael Armstrong of AT&T and Theodore Waitt of Gateway, was in favor of taxing electronic commerce, provided that an equitable collection mechanism could be devised. A second group included representatives of state and local governments and was prepared to support any tax regime that would allow recovery of revenues lost to electronic commerce. A third group, represented by Governor James Gilmore (R-VA) and Grover Norquist of the Americans for Tax Reform, opposed any taxes on online commerce.[70]

The Commission considered a variety of alternatives ranging from no taxes to a flat tax on all electronic transactions. One alternative considered would keep the current tax system intact but would require credit card companies to act as trusted third parties in collecting use taxes from consumers and remitting them to the relevant governments.[71] While the Commission was studying the tax question, new measures were being introduced in Congress to address the Internet tax question. Wyden and Cox introduced new legislation asking the World Trade Organization to consider a permanent global moratorium on Internet taxes. Senator McCain introduced legislation to make the ITFA tax moratorium permanent. On the other side of the aisle Senator Ernest Hollings (D-SC) introduced legislation mandating a uniform 5 percent tax on all remote sales, including Internet and mail-order transactions.

As the April deadline approached, the Advisory Commission was unable to reach a consensus for "official" recommendations, which required the agreement of a supermajority of 13 members. A supermajority could not be achieved because the members representing the Clinton administration and state and local governments abstained on necessary votes, arguing that the Commission had been subverted by industry interests and was not operating with the consensus of the relevant stakeholders.[72] Congressional leaders urged the Advisory Commission to make unofficial policy recommendations nonetheless. Among the unofficial recommendations was an additional 5-year extension on the existing tax moratorium, which was quickly incorporated into the pending Internet Non-Discrimination Act.

## Interests and their Stakes

Online consumers were, not surprisingly, opposed to the Internet taxes. According to one poll, 57 percent of Internet users took tax rates into account when making purchasing decisions.[73] Similarly, 75 percent of online consumers reported that they would be less likely to purchase goods online if they were required to remit taxes for their purchases. Furthermore, large-sample statistical studies indicated that taxing online sales could reduce online purchases by as much as 30 percent.[74]

Many members of the high-tech community opposed online taxes, arguing that instituting taxes on the Web would chill the growth of the Internet in at least two ways. First, if taxes were imposed, consumers might choose not to shop online, constricting the Web's expansion. The demand for many companies' products and services was directly proportional to how many people were using the Web. Second, given the high costs associated with collecting and remitting use taxes under the current system, executives argued that the costs of implementing the taxes would lead to the death of many online firms. The possibility of chilling the Internet's expansion and the high compliance costs led most high-tech companies to support an extended moratorium. They argued that given time more consumers would experiment with, and gain confidence in, online commerce, and during the moratorium some solution might be developed to handle the burdensome compliance costs. Recent research had supported this infant industry argument for an extension of the tax moratorium.[75] Many high-tech leaders viewed the Internet as an essential component of the infrastructure of both business and society, and its public goods characteristics warranted as extensive an expansion of the Internet as possible.

Among the groups that voiced opposition to "discriminatory" taxes (i.e., taxes that targeted online products but had no catalog or telephone-order counterparts) was the Information Technology

---

[70]*The New York Times*, September 13, 2000.
[71]*The Washington Post*, October 4, 1999.
[72]*The Washington Post*, March 22, 2000.
[73]*The Atlanta Journal and Constitution*, July 2, 2000.
[74]Austan Goolsbee, 2000, "In a World Without Borders: The Impact of Taxes on Internet Commerce," *Quarterly Journal of Economics*, 115(2):561–76. Goolsbee also argued that the implementation of online current use taxes would lead approximately 20 to 25 percent of the current consumer base not to shop online.
[75]Goolsbee, *ibid*. For a discussion of other research on these topics, see Wiseman (2000).

Association of America (ITAA), which represented over 26,000 companies, including Compaq, IBM, MCI-Worldcom, and Microsoft. The American Electronics Association represented over 3,000 companies in the high-tech and electronics industry and also opposed new Internet taxes.

To counter the advocates of online taxes, companies formed several ad hoc coalitions. The Global Business Dialogue on Electronic Commerce was a consortium of several major companies, including Disney, Hewlett-Packard, and IBM, and was co-chaired by America Online CEO Steven Case and Time-Warner CEO Gerald M. Levin.

Another ad hoc coalition, the Internet Tax Fairness Coalition (ITFC), was formed by 11 companies and associations. ITFC was "committed to ensuring that any taxation imposed on electronic commerce not thwart the development of the Internet marketplace."[76] Mark Nebergall of the ITFC also stressed fairness: "In order to achieve a true 'level playing field,' remote merchants must enjoy the simplicity and predictability of sales tax collection and remittance enjoyed by brick-and-mortar stores. Otherwise, the burden on remote sellers amounts to a competitive advantage for merchants deciding to stay out of electronic commerce."[77] The ITFC also argued that virtually all sectors of the U.S. economy, including state and municipal governments and main street businesses, had benefited from the growth of the Internet. Furthermore, there was currently no efficient technology to collect taxes under the present tax system. The ITFC argued that any hasty decision on Internet taxation could hinder the country's economic growth.

Opposing the tax moratorium were conventional brick-and-mortar businesses that viewed the tax advantage to online retailers as unfair competition and injurious to their business. The National Retail Federation (NRF) represented retailers ranging from small independent shops to major department stores. Representing shopping centers was the International Council of Shopping Centers, which had 38,000 members. An ad hoc coalition was

formed specifically to address the Internet tax question. The E-Fairness Coalition, composed of several interest groups and major retail firms, including the International Council of Shopping Centers, the American Booksellers Association, Tandy/Radio Shack, and Wal-Mart, claimed to represent over 350,000 retail outlets. It consistently argued for a "level playing field" where "customers [were] treated fairly regardless of where they [chose] to shop."[78]

State and local governments strongly favored some form of Internet sales taxation. Arguing that online commerce would lower their tax revenues by as much as $20 billion a year by 2002, state governors had begun pressuring their representatives in Washington. The governors were represented by the National Governors Association (NGA), a national lobbying organization representing the interests of the 50 states. A counterpart to the NGA was the National Council of State Legislatures (NCSL), which represented state legislatures.

City and county governments had voiced their opposition to any tax-moratorium extension.[79] City governments were organized primarily through the U.S. Conference of Mayors, which represented approximately 1,100 cities with populations of at least 30,000. Eighteen thousand smaller cities and towns were represented by the National League of Cities. In legislative matters the National Association of Counties represented over 1,800 counties, covering almost 75 percent of the U.S. population.

The June report by the GAO added to the concerns of state and local governments. The GAO estimated that they would lose sales tax revenue up to $3.8 billion in 2000 and up to $12.4 billion in 2003. A University of Tennessee study estimated the sales tax loss at $20.1 billion in 2003. The GAO also estimated that the losses in 2003 would be $20.4 billion if the taxes not collected on mail-order catalog and telephone sales were included.

## Congressional Activity

Any legislation on Internet taxation implicitly dealt with interstate commerce and hence was referred to the cognizant committee in each chamber of Congress. Under the Rules of the House, the Judiciary Committee, chaired by Henry Hyde

76The members were America Online, Charles Schwab, Cisco Systems, First Data Corporation, and Microsoft, as well as the American Electronics Association, Information Technology Association, Investment Company Institute, Securities Industry Association, and Software and Information Industry Association. www.nettaxfairness.org.
77www.nettaxfairness.org.

78www.e-fairness.org.
79*Chicago Sun Times*, July 24, 2000.

(R-IL), had jurisdiction over all legislation dealing with "interstate compacts generally," which included Internet taxation. The Standing Rules of the Senate assigned matters dealing with interstate commerce to the Commerce, Science and Transportation Committee, chaired by Senator McCain. During his bid for the Republican presidential nomination McCain had come out in favor of a permanent moratorium on all Internet sales taxes.

Congress faced other vexing taxation issues created by technological change. State and local governments imposed taxes of between $4 and $7 billion on telephone usage, but with the growth of cellular telephone usage the state and local governments faced the question of which tax rates applied to cellphones. In July 2000 Congress resolved the issue by enacting legislation specifying that the applicable taxes were those for the address to which the bill was sent. Exceptions were made for corporations that provided cellular telephones to their employees, allowing the company to designate the area code in which the phone was registered as the location for taxation. Lisa Cowell, executive director of the E-Fairness Coalition, commented, "A lot of politicians have stopped hiding behind this bogeyman of 'it can't be done' because no one knows where the customer is."[80]

While the Internet Non-Discrimination Act had sailed through the House without serious complications, the procedural differences between the House and the Senate raised possible problems for the moratorium extension. Any senator could filibuster the bill, which if cloture were not invoked, would likely kill the bill, since the Senate had important pending legislation remaining. One senator, in particular, had voiced opposition to an extended moratorium and had proposed an alternative scheme to remedy the problem of multiple and conflicting tax jurisdictions. Senator Byron Dorgan (D-ND) proposed that online sellers be required to collect and remit use taxes at point of sale, and states could join a "compact" to collect and distribute tax revenues. To join the compact, states would have to adopt uniform definitions of taxable products and have a flat use-tax rate for the entire state. As of June 2000, several states had announced their participation in this "streamlined sales tax project,"

an NGA initiative to create uniformity in tax laws so as to facilitate online collection.[81] Working with the NGA, the NCSL organized a tax project to simplify state sales taxes. Wal-Mart was one of five retailers that volunteered to test a pilot program technology to distinguish among the myriad of state and local tax laws. If successful, the program would be a major step toward making taxation of online sales practical.

## State Activity: California

Legislative activity at the state level complicated the movement toward a uniform federal solution for the tax issue. In August 2000 the California state legislature passed legislation requiring Internet merchants with brick-and-mortar stores in California to collect sales taxes on purchases made online by California residents. If enacted, Barnesandnoble.com and Borders.com would have to collect taxes on purchases made by California consumers, since they had retail outlets in California even though their Internet businesses were housed outside California.[82] Barnesandnoble.com and Borders.com claimed that their online companies were separate from their brick-and-mortar companies and hence were not affected by the nexus principle. Borders.com, however, directed customers to a Borders store if they wanted to return a book. While proponents of the bill hailed it as a "fair and square measure," other parties, such as the American Electronics Association, argued that California was trying to "shoehorn e-commerce business into an old tax system that doesn't make any sense."[83] As the legislation arrived on Governor Gray Davis's desk, observers wondered what its enactment might mean for the future of electronic commerce and state tax autonomy.

## International Activity

International developments were also complicating U.S. attempts to resolve the Internet taxation issue. The 1999 Human Development Report of the

---

[80]*The New York Times*, July 19, 2000.

[81]Senator Dorgan's proposal would extend the current moratorium on Internet use and access taxes for an additional 4 years.
[82]Amazon.com did not have a nexus in California and thus did not collect taxes from California residents. It collected state sales taxes in its home state of Washington.
[83]*The San Francisco Chronicle*, August 31, 2000.

United Nations made a formal recommendation to impose a $0.01 "bit tax" for every 100 e-mails sent between users. The tax would raise an estimated $70 billion a year for underdeveloped countries. Both the Clinton administration and Congress urged the WTO to impose bans on the bit tax and similar Internet-specific taxes. Embracing the sentiments of the Clinton administration, at its Seattle meeting in December 1999 the WTO decided to extend for 2 years an existing moratorium on Internet taxes, effectively striking down the bit tax proposal.

Other international organizations were also weighing in on the tax question. In October 1998 the 29-nation Organization for Economic Cooperation and Development (OECD) proposed the Ottawa Taxation Framework Conditions. In the hope of developing a uniform taxation scheme for online commerce, the Ottawa Conditions envisioned a tax plan that was economically neutral, efficient, simple, fair, and flexible.[84] The conferees agreed that any taxation scheme should levy taxes on goods based on where they were consumed rather than where they were produced. The flexible nature of Internet commerce, however, raised difficult questions about how to determine where, precisely, goods purchased online were consumed.[85] The OECD established several industry and government working groups to examine these issues in more detail. The United States and the European Union (EU) used the OECD as a forum for their negotiations on Internet taxation.

Most member states of the European Union imposed a value-added tax (VAT) on electronically delivered goods and services supplied by EU companies to EU residents. In June 2000 the EU Commission proposed extending the VAT to non-EU companies, despite the existing WTO moratorium. Specifically, the proposal required any firm selling more than €100,000 worth of electronic goods into the European Union to be registered with one of the 15 member states' tax authorities and charge that state's rate. The VAT rates of the EU member states varied from 15 percent in Luxembourg to 25 percent in Denmark and Sweden. The VAT accounted for approximately 40 percent of the tax revenue of the EU member states and financed the entire EU budget.[86]

The Commission was heavily criticized by the United States for acting unilaterally despite continued negotiations within the OECD. Stuart Eizenstat, Undersecretary of the Treasury Department, argued that the proposal "if implemented, could well hinder the development of [the] global medium of [electronic] commerce." Similarly, Andy Grove came out against the VAT, calling it "e-protectionism."[87] Implementation issues also arose as to how such taxes would be collected, as well as whether the necessary unanimous endorsement of all member states of the European Union could be expected. Mark Bohannon of the U.S.-based Software and Information Industry Association called the Commission report "fatally flawed" because it was impossible to determine where a customer in cyberspace resided.[88]

## Companies

A variety of companies would be directly affected by an Internet tax, and others would be indirectly affected. A tax would have a major impact on Amazon.com, the largest online retailer. A sale to a customer in California saved the customer the sales tax of approximately 8 percent, and a sale to a Texas customer saved 8.5 percent.[89] The tax savings helped compensate for delivery costs, which were paid by the customer. Despite not facing sales taxes, Amazon.com lost $207 million before special equity arrangements on sales of $578 million in the quarter ending June 20, 2000.

Amazon.com had worked behind the scenes to oppose any Internet taxes. Its perspective was revealed in its commentary on the California bill to impose taxes on sales by those online companies that claimed that their Internet companies were separate from their brick-and-mortar stores. "Paul Misener, vice president for global public policy at Amazon.com, said he does not see any need to tax Internet sales in general since so many state and

[84]OECD Committee on Fiscal Affairs, "Implementing the Ottawa Taxation Framework Conditions," June.
[85]*Financial Times*, "Plan for Taxing Internet Commerce Outlined," October 9, 2000.

[86]In contrast, sales taxes accounted for approximately 25 percent of the tax revenue of U.S. states and none of the federal government's tax revenue. The VAT systems in Europe were less complicated than the sales tax systems across the U.S. states.
[87]*Business Week*, June 26, 2000.
[88]*The New York Times*, September 30, 2000.
[89]Customers in the State of Washington were required to pay the sales tax.

local governments are running surpluses right now. 'We really have to see the problem first,' he said. 'This is almost a solution in search of a problem.' Misener added that if online sales are taxed, it should be at a lower rate than off-line transactions because sales made over the Internet 'use fewer state and local resources.' Amazon opposes the . . . bill because it does not recognize this principle, even though the bill would affect one of the company's biggest competitors: Barnesandnoble.com."[90]

Cisco Systems, the leading suppler of servers for the Internet, supported the Internet Non-Discrimination Act because state governments were running surpluses and "the often-confusing tax rules of 7,500 separate jurisdictions could severely impede development of this rapidly expanding medium for global trade, investment, and communication. State and local governments should use an extended moratorium period to simplify their existing, complex tax structures."[91]

Cisco worked on the Internet taxation issue primarily through the Internet Tax Fairness Coalition and the American Electronics Association. Katrina Doerfler of Cisco Systems, testifying on behalf of the American Electronics Association, articulated five principles for any legislation on Internet taxation. "One, impose no greater tax burden on electronic commerce than other traditional means of commerce. Two, support simplicity in administration. Three, retain and clarify nexus standards. Four, avoid new access taxes on the Internet. And, five, consider tax issues in a global context."[92] ∎

SOURCE: This case was written by Alan Wiseman under the supervision of Professor David P. Baron. Copyright © 2000 by the Board of Trustees of the Leland Stanford Junior University. All rights reserved. Reprinted with permission.

## PREPARATION QUESTIONS

1. How would the market strategy of Amazon.com be affected by the application of state and local sales taxes to online sales?
2. How would the market strategy of Cisco Systems be affected by the application of state and local sales taxes to online sales?
3. How much influence are the various interests identified in the case likely to have on the issue of Internet taxation?
4. Are there any interests not identified in the case that are likely to be active on this issue? Will they be able to overcome the free-rider problem?
5. What is likely to happen with the Internet Non-Discrimination Act?

---

[90]*San Jose Mercury News*, September 12, 2000.
[91]www.cisco.com/warp/public.
[92]Hearings, House Committee on the Judiciary, Subcommittee on Commercial and Administrative Law, June 29, 2000.

# CAFE Standards 2002

In March 2002 the U.S. automobile industry faced its greatest threat in over a decade as the Senate approached a vote on a major increase in fuel economy standards. The momentum for an increase stemmed from three developments. First, the global climate change issue remained unaddressed by the U.S. government, and environmentalists had turned their attention to higher fuel economy standards. Burning a gallon of gasoline added 20 pounds of carbon dioxide to the atmosphere, and passenger cars and light trucks accounted for 17 percent of human-caused $CO_2$ emissions in the United States. Second, the fuel economy of the U.S. new vehicle fleet had declined as the market share of light trucks and SUVs neared 50 percent. Third, the September 11 terrorist attacks heightened concerns about security and the dependence on foreign sources of oil.

The 13 members of the Alliance of Automobile Manufacturers (AAM) employed 620,000 people in the United States and operated 250 manufacturing facilities in 35 states.[1] The automobile industry accounted for 6.6 million direct and indirect jobs with a payroll of $243 billion. The automobile industry had been hurt hard by the slowdown in the economy, and Ford had a loss of $5.5 billion in 2001.

## CAFE Standards History

In the aftermath of the 1973–1974 oil embargo Congress enacted the Energy Policy and Conservation Act (EPCA), EPCA provided for corporate average fuel economy (CAFE) standards for new automobiles with a 27.5 mpg standard set for

model year (MY) 1985, compared to the actual average of 14.2 mpg in 1974. The principal objective of EPCA was to reduce the dependence on unreliable foreign sources of oil. In response to the second oil embargo in 1978–1979 Congress imposed a gas guzzler tax on low-mileage cars, and the National Highway Transportation Safety Agency (NHTSA), an agency of the Department of Transportation, set light truck CAFE standards with an MY1985 standard of 21.0 mpg.[2] The auto industry met the MY1985 standards, and the Reagan administration blocked any further increases in CAFE standards.

Once the CAFE goal was reached, NHTSA had the authority to change the standard but not increase it above 27.5 mpg. As low gasoline prices led consumers to buy larger cars, NHTSA lowered the standards to 26.0 mpg. In 1989 the Bush administration returned the standard to 27.5 mpg for passenger cars, where it remained. The standard for light trucks has been 20.7 mpg since 1996.

Concern about global climate change increased in the 1980s, and in 1990 Senator Richard Bryan (D-NV) introduced a bill to increase the CAFE standard for passenger cars by 40 percent by MY2001. The percent would be applied to a manufacturer's actual average fuel economy for the 1988 base year, so automakers would face different standards. For example, the CAFE standards for Toyota and Ford would be 45.0 and 37.0, respectively.

In response to approval of the bill by the Senate Commerce Committee, the auto industry and others opposed to higher CAFE standards formed

---

[1] The members were BMW, DaimlerChrysler, Fiat, Ford, General Motors, Isuzu Motors of North America, Mazda, Mitsubishi Motors, Nissan North America, Porsche, Toyota Motors North America, Volkswagen of America, and Volvo.

[2] Congress directed NHTSA to set light truck standards at the "maximal feasible level." Trucks and SUVs over 6,000 pounds were classified as medium trucks for which there was no fuel economy standard. The Hummer H2 was classified as a medium truck.

the Coalition for Vehicle Choice.[3] The Coalition mounted an intense public advocacy campaign against the Bryan bill emphasizing the twin themes of vehicle choice and safety. The Coalition's advertising campaign repeated the theme, "Who should choose your next automobile? You or Congress?" Two research studies indicated that during the 1970s and 1980s the downsizing of automobiles to meet the CAFE standards had substantially increased traffic fatalities. The Bush administration joined in the opposition to the Bryan bill, and the Departments of Energy and Transportation along with the EPA opposed it. The United Automobile Workers (UAW) was sympathetic to the concerns of the environmentalists who backed the Bryan bill, but it opposed the major increases provided in the bill. U.S. automakers preferred the percent approach to the current system but opposed any increase in the standards. General Motors (GM) opposed the CAFE system itself, arguing that the system failed to provide incentives for consumers to buy higher fuel economy vehicles. The top 10 vehicles in fuel economy accounted for only 2 percent of sales in the United States. The Bryan bill ultimately was defeated.

## The CAFE System

The CAFE was the number of fleet miles driven divided by the number of gallons of fuel consumed, under the assumption that all vehicles were driven the same number of miles under the same mix of city and highway driving. The CAFE system included a two-fleet rule. Automakers had to meet the CAFE standard in both their domestic and import fleets. A domestic vehicle was defined as having at least 75 percent of its components manufactured in the United States or Canada. To improve its domestic CAFE in the 1990s, Ford increased its use of foreign components to reduce the domestic content of its Ford LTD Crown Victoria and Mercury Marquis models from 94 to 74 percent. Those autos then were included in Ford's imported fleet along with its Korean-made Festiva.

[3]In 2002 the Coalition had 40,000 members, including 120 associations and companies, among them the American Farm Bureau, the International Association of Chiefs of Police, the National Alliance of Senior Citizens, the National Association of Home Builders, the National Center for Handicapped Rights, the Seniors Coalition, the National Automobile Dealers Association, and the National Motorists Association, Kampgrounds of America, the International Professional Rodeo Association, and the National Muscle Car Association.

Failure to meet the CAFE standard resulted in a civil penalty of $5.50 per tenth of a mile per gallon shortfall multiplied by the number of vehicles in the fleet. For MY2001 several automakers were expected to miss the standard. For MY2000 BMW, Porsche, Volkswagen, and Fiat paid penalties of $27.4, $3.7, $0.3, and $0.7 million, respectively. No U.S. or Asian automobile manufacturer had yet been assessed a penalty.

Automakers could use credits to cover shortfalls. If in a year an automaker exceeded the CAFE standard, it could carry the excess over for use during the following 3 years. Automakers also could carry back credits expected to be earned during the upcoming 3 years. Ford filed a carry-back plan in 2001 to cover the impact on its import fleet caused by the acquisition of Volvo.

Environmentalists and agricultural interests backed the use of ethanol as a motor fuel as a means of reducing pollution. Legislation granted automakers credits for producing vehicles that could operate on both gasoline and alternative fuels such as ethanol, and the credits were used to meet CAFE standards. These multifuel credits were granted for the vehicle and did not require that it actually use an alternative fuel. The availability of such fuels was very limited, and only 1 percent of the fuel used in the multifuel vehicles was an alternative fuel. These credits enabled DaimlerChrysler and Ford to meet the MY2001 CAFE standards.

A gas guzzler tax was imposed on very low-mileage passenger cars. A tax of $500 was imposed on a car that did not achieve 22.5 mpg, and it increased to a maximum of $3,850 if the car did not achieve 12.5 mpg. The gas guzzler tax did not apply to light trucks.

GM, along with some environmental groups and some members of Congress, argued that a broad-scale carbon tax was a better means of reducing $CO_2$ emissions than CAFE standards. In 1993 the Clinton administration attempted to pass a closely related Btu tax, but political pressure from those who would bear the distributive consequences of the tax caused the plan to fail in Congress.

## Fuel Economy and Fuel Efficiency

The fuel economy of the U.S. light vehicle fleet had increased steadily as newer vehicles replaced older vehicles, despite a major shift in demand to light trucks and SUVs. After 1998, however, the new fleet fuel economy declined by 1.9 mpg as the market share of light trucks and SUVs reached 46.7 percent in 2001. In 2001 the fuel economy of the combined new vehicle fleet was 24 mpg, the lowest in 20 years. Table 1 presents the actual fuel economy for MY2000 and MY2001 by manufacturer.

Although fuel economy had not improved, fuel efficiency had improved substantially as the industry introduced new and improved technologies. (Fuel efficiency refers to how efficiently a vehicle used the energy from fuel. Fuel economy is how many miles a vehicle travels on a gallon of fuel.) Those gains, however, were consumed by increases in the weight of cars and the horsepower of engines as automakers responded to consumer preferences for larger and more powerful vehicles.

Honda quantified the effects of technological improvements. Edward B. Cohen, vice president of Honda North America, stated, "If the current car fleet were still at 1981 performance, weight and transmission levels, the passenger car CAFE would be almost 36 mpg instead of the current level of 28.1 mpg. The trend is particularly pronounced since 1987. Based on EPA's data, technology has gone into the fleet from 1987 to 2000 at a rate that could have increased fuel economy by about 1.5 percent per year, if it had not instead focused on other vehicle attributes demanded by the market. There is no reason why this technology trend of improved efficiency (as opposed to fuel economy) should not continue."[4] He indicated that average vehicle weight had increased by 12 percent from 1987 to 2000, and average horsepower increased by 70 percent.

## Technology

DaimlerChrysler, Ford, and General Motors participated in the European Automobile Manufacturers Association, which reached a voluntary agreement with the Commission of the European Union to reduce vehicle CO$_2$ emissions 25 percent by 2008 from a 1995 baseline. Ford had already reduced its emissions by 9 percent and expected to meet the 2008 goal. One means of meeting the goal was to increase the use of diesel engines, which were approximately

20 percent more efficient than gasoline engines. Diesel engines accounted for nearly 40 percent of sales in Europe, but despite technological advances those engines did not meet the new U.S. emissions standards for particulates and nitrogen oxides. The auto industry sought more stringent EPA regulations to force the oil industry to reduce the sulfur content of diesel fuel so that existing diesel engines could be used.

The Honda Insight and Toyota Prius employed hybrid-electric technology with both a gasoline engine and an electric motor that provided a boost at low speeds and during acceleration. In contrast to electric vehicles that had to be charged, hybrids ran solely on gasoline with the electric motor charged by the gasoline engine. During braking the electric motor acted as a generator, and the electricity generated was stored in batteries. The Insight and Prius used high voltage electric motors (274 and 144 volts, respectively), whereas the big-three U.S. automakers favored low-voltage motors. Ford planned to use a 42-volt system in the hybrid version of its Escape SUV.

Although the Insight and the Prius had found favor with some consumers, the cars were far from broad market acceptance. James Olson, senior vice president of Toyota Motor North America, explained, "The typical Prius buyer is very different from the typical buyer. Prius purchasers are older, wealthier, more educated and more interested in technology than typical compact buyers. Therefore, to reach the typical buyer of a vehicle in the compact or any other high-volume market segment, something must be provided to encourage buyers to purchase an advanced-technology vehicle or the most fuel-efficient vehicle in that segment."[5]

Hybrids were significantly more costly than conventional gasoline-powered cars. Honda planned to introduce a hybrid Civic that would attain 50 mpg, an increase of 35 percent over the standard Civic. The price was expected to be $3,000 higher than the gasoline version. A hybrid was eligible for a $2,000 tax deduction.

The Clinton administration in conjunction with the big-three U.S. automakers established the Partnership for a New Generation of Vehicles to develop an 80 mpg family car. A review of the

[4]Statement of Edward B. Cohen, vice president, Honda North America, before the Senate Committee on Commerce, Science and Transportation, December 6, 2001.

[5]Statement of James Olson, Toyota Motors North America, before the Senate Committee on Commerce, Science, and Transportation, December 6, 2001.

**TABLE 1 Actual Fuel Economy**

| Company | MY2000 | MY2001 |
|---|---|---|
| | *mpg* | *mpg* |
| **Passenger Cars** | | |
| BMW (I) | 24.8 | 25.1 |
| Daewoo (I) | 28.6 | 29.7 |
| DaimlerChrysler (D) | 27.9 | 27.7 |
| DaimlerChrysler (I) | 25.3 | 27.1 |
| Fiat (I) | 13.6 | 13.7 |
| Ford (D) | 28.3 | 27.5 |
| Ford (I) | 27.4 | 27.8 |
| General Motors (D) | 27.9 | 28.1 |
| General Motors (I) | 25.4 | 26.5 |
| Honda (D) | 31.4 | 36.3 |
| Honda (I) | 29.3 | 29.3 |
| Hyundai (I) | 30.7 | 31.4 |
| Kia (I) | 30.0 | 30.4 |
| Lotus (I) | 20.7 | 20.6 |
| Mitsubishi (I) | 29.4 | * |
| Nissan (D) | 28.1 | 27.2 |
| Nissan (I) | 28.3 | 28.3 |
| Porsche (I) | 24.3 | 24.2 |
| Subaru (I) | 28.0 | 27.8 |
| Suzuki (I) | 35.0 | 35.2 |
| Toyota (D) | 33.3 | 34.2 |
| Toyota (I) | 28.9 | 28.9 |
| Volkswagen (I) | 28.8 | 28.1 |
| Average (D) | 28.7 | 28.8 |
| Average (I) | 28.3 | 28.4 |
| **Light Trucks** | | |
| BMW | 17.5 | 19.2 |
| DaimlerChrysler | 21.0 | 20.7 |
| Ford | 21.0 | 20.5 |
| General Motors | 21.0 | 20.5 |
| Honda | 25.4 | 24.9 |
| Hyundai | ... | 25.2 |
| Isuzu | 20.9 | 21.1 |
| Kia | 23.5 | 22.9 |
| Land Rover | 16.8 | ** |
| Mitsubishi | 21.5 | * |
| Nissan | 20.8 | 20.7 |
| Suzuki | 23.0 | 22.0 |
| Toyota | 21.8 | 22.1 |
| Volkswagen | 18.9 | 20.5 |
| Average | 21.3 | 20.9 |

Note: (D) = Domestic; (I) = Import. No distinction is made
between domestic and import light trucks.
\* Included in DaimlerChrysler.
\*\* Included in Ford.

*Source:* National Highway Traffic Safety Administration, "Automobile
Fuel Economy Program, Annual Update Calendar Year 2001."

program early in the Bush administration indicated that there was little hope of achieving an 80 mpg vehicle that anyone would want to purchase. Consensus supported dropping the program and focusing research on other technologies. The Bush administration and the big-three U.S. automakers established the FreedomCAR research program with emphasis on fuel cell technology. An affordable vehicle with fuel cell technology, however, was at least a decade in the future.

## Safety

Opponents of substantially higher CAFE standards argued that vehicles would have to be downsized, which would increase fatalities and injuries. A number of studies concluded that the increase in CAFE standards to 27.5 mpg had resulted in the loss of thousands of lives a year. A 1990 study by NTHSA estimated that the downsizing of vehicles from 1978 to 1986 resulted in an additional 2,000 deaths a year. A 1997 NHTSA study concluded that further downsizing could result in additional deaths. The number of miles driven increased 80 percent between 1979 and 1999, and the fatalities per mile driven had fallen nearly 50 percent. In 2000 motor vehicle accidents resulted in 41,821 fatalities, 5.3 million nonfatal injuries, and 28 million damaged vehicles. NHTSA estimated that the social cost of the crashes was $230.6 billion.[6]

Environmentalists and safety activists argued that the relation between vehicle weight and safety was unclear. They argued for stronger safety standards as a means of reducing fatalities and injuries.

In January 2002 Honda broke ranks with the rest of the industry. Honda had hired Dynamic Research to study the relation between fuel economy and safety "using more recent accident data with newer vehicles." The study concluded that reducing the weight of an average vehicle by 100 pounds would have a "very small and not statistically significant" effect on the number of fatalities. The consultant had updated the 1997 NHTSA study by taking into account the safety features, such as dual air bags, incorporated in new vehicles. Honda argued that vehicle size was more important than weight and that new lightweight materials could reduce weight without reducing size. John German of Honda concluded, "The updated analysis indicates that weight reduction across the entire vehicle fleet may not have a negative safety effect."[7] Honda forwarded the report to NHTSA.

## The National Academy of Sciences Report

In early 2001 Congress and the Bush administration asked the National Academy of Sciences (NAS) to study the fuel economy issue. The NAS report concluded that currently available technologies were capable of improving fuel economy from 12 to 42 percent over the next 15 years, "although at a significantly higher cost." The technologies included "direct-injection, lean-burn engines; direct-injection compression-ignition (diesel) engines; and hybrid electric vehicles." The report noted that diesel engines faced significant technological challenges because they did not meet the 2007 Tier 2 emissions standards for nitrogen oxides and particulates. The report also concluded that "Hybrid electric vehicles face significant cost hurdles, and fuel-cell vehicles face significant technological, economic, and fueling infrastructure barriers."

The study also indicated that the increase in fuel economy standards had contributed to thousands of additional deaths because of downsizing. The estimate was "an additional 1,300 to 2,600 traffic fatalities in 1993." The NAS report called on NHTSA to conduct further research on the relation between fuel economy and safety.

The NAS also concluded that the multifuel rule had resulted in decreases in fuel economy. The report recommended that the multifuel credit as well as the two-fleet system be eliminated. The study also recommended allowing the trading of fuel economy credits to improve the efficiency of the CAFE system.

## CAFE Standards Legislation

Three events in 2001 increased the pressure for higher CAFE standards. First, environmentalists increased their pressure on the Bush administration to increase standards. Second, the 2000 elections produced a Senate split 50–50, but subsequently

---

[6]NHTSA, "The Economic Impact of Motor Vehicle Crashes 2000," Washington, DC (www.nhtsa.dot.gov).

[7]Statement of John German, Manager Honda Motor Company, before the Senate Committee on Commerce, Science and Transportation, January 24, 2002.

Senator James M. Jeffords of Vermont changed from Republican to Independent, giving the Democrats a 50–49–1 majority. Democrats then assumed the chairs of all committees and subcommittees. This allowed them to control the hearings agenda, and the Commerce Committee held pro-increase hearings that added to the pressure for higher CAFE standards. Moreover, several Republican senators, including Olympia Snowe (R-ME), supported higher standards. Third, the September 11, 2001, terrorist attack heightened concerns about security and the dependence on imported oil. One response was a renewed effort to increase CAFE standards.

The chances of enacting higher fuel economy standards increased when in February 2002 Senators John Kerry (D-MA) and John McCain (R-AZ) each introduced bills to substantially increase standards. Senator Kerry's bill would increase the combined passenger car and light truck CAFE standard to at least 35 mpg by MY2013. McCain's bill would increase the combined CAFE standard to 35 mpg by MY2016 and would eliminate the two-fleet system and the multifuel credit. Senators Kerry and McCain were expected to reach agreement on a bill they could both support. Their agreement would be included in an energy bill that was nearing completion in the Senate. That bill covered other controversial issues, including oil drilling in the Arctic National Wildlife Refuge.

The Sierra Club, Public Citizen, and the Union of Concerned Scientists supported a combined CAFE standard of 40 mpg to be phased in over 10 years. In her Senate testimony Ann R. Mesnikoff of the Sierra Club argued that current technologies could achieve a 40 mpg combined standard for passenger cars and light trucks at a modest cost. "For the $1000–$1500 investment—the average cost across all vehicle types—in technology, consumers would save several times that at the gas pump."[8] The Union of Concerned Scientists identified four categories of currently available technologies: vehicle load reduction (e.g., aerodynamics), efficient engines (e.g., stoichiometric burn gasoline direct injection engines), integrated starter generators, and improved transmissions (e.g., continuously variable transmissions). Mesnikoff also

argued for extending the gas guzzler tax to light trucks and eliminating the multifuel credit, and she opposed allowing automakers to trade fuel economy credits. She argued that the safety issue could be addressed through design and by imposing stronger vehicle safety standards, such as a rollover standard for SUVs. She also cited broad support for higher fuel economy among the American people. "A CBS/*New York Times* poll released in June [2001] revealed that 81% of Americans 'Approve of the government requiring car manufacturers to meet higher fuel efficiency standards than they do now.' And 66% supported higher standards if it would increase the cost of the car (66% GOP and 70% Dem). Similarly, an ABC/*Washington Post* poll also released in June showed that 81% of Americans strongly support more fuel efficient vehicles."[9]

The AAM, however, cited the 2000 Consumer Preference Survey by MARITZ Marketing Research that found that consumers ranked safety sixth in importance and fuel economy 25th in importance when purchasing a new vehicle. One automobile executive commented, "Car buyers care little about safety and less about fuel economy."

The AAM opposed any increase in CAFE standards, particularly because of the weak economy and the losses being incurred by the U.S. auto companies. As a compromise the AAM supported delegating the decision to NHTSA, which could weigh the safety, cost, and fuel economy effects. The Alliance also sought increased subsidies for consumers who purchased new technology vehicles. The basic argument of the automakers was that consumers simply preferred larger and more powerful vehicles and these market forces were inconsistent with CAFE standards. Senator Barbara A. Mikulski (D-MD) said, "American women love SUVs. When you are a soccer mom and you are picking up kids or you are car-pooling or have kids with gear, you need large capacity."[10] Moreover, studies indicated that car owners drove more when the cost per mile fell, so critics argued that the dependence on imported oil had not been lessened as a result of CAFE standards.

The UAW generally supported the CAFE program but adamantly opposed increases in standards

[8]Statement of Ann R. Mesnikoff, Sierra Club, before the Senate Committee on Commerce, Science and Transportation, December 6, 2001.

[9]Statement of Ann R. Mesnikoff, Sierra Club, before the Senate Committee on Commerce, Science and Transportation, December 6, 2001.
[10]*The New York Times*, March 14, 2002.

that would jeopardize the jobs of union members. The UAW pointed to the slowdown in the U.S. economy and to the layoffs in the auto industry. "Given these conditions, it is important that any changes to CAFE not aggravate the challenging economic circumstances facing automakers and their suppliers and result in additional job losses for American workers . . . ."[11] "It is particularly important that any future changes in the CAFE standards should ensure that full-line manufacturers are not placed at a competitive disadvantage relative to companies that historically have specialized more in the production and sale of small vehicles."[12] The U.S. plants of Asian and European auto companies were generally not unionized.

The UAW was particularly opposed to the provision in Senator McCain's bill to eliminate the two-fleet system. UAW vice president Richard Shoemaker said, "The Big Three would be able to outsource their small car production to foreign countries. Why? Because they would no longer be required to average the fuel economy of more efficient, domestically built cars with less efficient large cars produced here."[13] The UAW preferred the percentage approach to any increase in CAFE standards and opposed a fuel economy credit-trading system.

In February 2002 the UAW along with General Motors and political representatives held a "fuel economy town hall" at the GM plant in Pontiac, Michigan, where Chevrolet Silverado and GMC Sierra pickup trucks were produced. The purpose was to protest the Kerry and McCain bills. UAW vice president Richard Shoemaker told the assembly, "The UAW submits now is not the time to impose onerous, excessive and discriminatory standards on General Motors, Ford and DaimlerChrysler that will lead to job loss, which will of course have an adverse effect on the economy."[14] Senator Carl Levin (D-MI) said, "The proposal . . . will do little or nothing for the environment, but do . . . a lot to endanger American jobs."[15] GM vice president Guy Briggs added, "No pickup, van or SUV GM builds today could survive the higher requirements."[16]

The Bush administration supported efforts to improve fuel economy but opposed increases in CAFE standards. Concerned about the possibility of Senate action, the Bush administration proposed transferring to the Department of Transportation the authority for setting fuel economy standards. This would include the possibility of redesigning the CAFE system.

The auto industry was interested not only in the CAFE standards, but also in the multifuel credits that had become important in meeting existing standards. The credit system was scheduled to end in 2004, and the industry sought an extension to 2008. Ethanol producers strongly supported an extension.

Honda was the only auto company operating in the United States that had not joined the AAM, and it broke ranks with the other automakers and supported an increase in CAFE standards. Honda quietly lobbied through "under-the-radar activities like bringing our engineers in and having talks with both sides of the aisle."[17] A Senate staffer commented, "Honda came in, they were willing to talk about things. They didn't just say no. Imagine what a difference that makes." This "gave us confidence in the numbers we ultimately picked. That's not to say they endorsed those numbers. But they made us comfortable we weren't crazy."[18] James Olson, the top lobbyist for Toyota, said, "Honda is a superb technical company, they have very strong principles, and they're very honest." He added, "They've always been a maverick."[19] Although it supported higher fuel economy standards, Honda strongly opposed the percent approach.[20] Whether Honda would support a combined standard of 35 mpg was not clear.

## The Ford Motor Company

In October 2001 Ford fired CEO Jacques Nasser, and Chairman Bill Ford assumed the CEO position. Bill Ford had a reputation for supporting the environment, and environmentalists were optimistic that Ford would provide environmental leadership in the industry. In the summer of 2000 Ford had pledged to improve the fuel economy of its SUVs by 25 percent by the end of the 2005 model year. In

[11] www.uaw.org/cap/issue/issue07.html.
[12] Statement of Alan Reuther, UAW before the Senate Committee on Commerce, Science and Transportation, December 6, 2001.
[13] Speech at a town hall meeting, UAW Local 2166, Shreveport, LA, no date.
[14] *San Jose Mercury News,* February 26, 2002.
[15] *San Jose Mercury News,* February 26, 2002.
[16] *San Jose Mercury News,* February 26, 2002.

[17] *The Wall Street Journal,* March 11, 2002.
[18] *The Wall Street Journal,* March 11, 2002.
[19] *The New York Times,* June 12, 2002.
[20] The NAS study also opposed the percentage approach.

addition, Bill Ford pledged to introduce a hybrid version of its Escape SUV and make its Rouge plant an "earth-friendly manufacturing facility." The company, however, lagged behind several other auto companies in hybrid and other new technologies.

Ford's competitive situation had been deteriorating for several years, and in 2001 it lost $5.5 billion.[21] Ford undertook a major cost-cutting program and began to act more cautiously on its environmental commitments. Deborah Zemke, director of corporate governance, explained, "Because of the announcements we've made in the past, there was an expectation about how fast Ford was going to be rolling out new technologies. What we're saying is, let's get real in the near term. We're going to focus on what we've already committed to, and not making new commitments in the near term."[22]

As Ford struggled to turn around its situation, Bill Ford began to appear in television commercials discussing the company. In one commercial he stated, "A lot of people have accused me of having gasoline in my veins." In another he emphasized Ford's commitment to producing powerful vehicles. At a press conference he said, "We were against CAFE. I know that disappointed some people, but we've always been against CAFE."[23]

## The Sierra Club and Private Politics

The Sierra Club, the oldest and largest U.S. environmental interest group with 700,000 members, advocated a combined CAFE standard of 40 mpg by 2012 and 55 mpg by 2020. It argued that reaching 40 mpg would save consumers between $3,000 and $5,000 over the life of a vehicle and by 2012 would avert 374 million tons of global warming pollution annually.[24] The Sierra Club promoted its Freedom Option Package of technologies that it argued could be implemented immediately. The three technologies were continuously variable automatic transmission, the variable-valve-control engine, and the integrated starter-generator.

The Sierra Club had praised Ford when it made its pro-environment pledges, stating, "The Sierra Club applauds Ford for recognizing the seriousness

of global warming, acknowledging that its vehicles create a large part of the problem and committing to cut that pollution."[25] When Ford began to back away from its pledges because of financial problems, the applause turned to criticism. Executive director Carl Pope commented on Ford's 2002 environmental report, "It moves the ball backwards by refusing to set firm goals for the future, and raises troubling questions about Ford's commitment to improving its environmental performance."[26] The Sierra Club asked the company to "walk their talk."

When opposition to increased CAFE standards mounted in Congress, the Sierra Club turned to private politics. It began a 3-year campaign to put public pressure on the big-three auto manufacturers to increase the fuel economy of their light vehicles. As Carl Pope explained, "We're going now to the customers." The Sierra Club conducted an advertising campaign challenging the automobile companies.[27] Television spots focused on security and featured former Nebraska senator Bob Kerrey and retired Navy vice admiral Jack Shanahan. In one ad Kerrey said, "It's time for us to tell the auto industry that we want to break the grip of oil-producing countries and reduce our oil use." In another Kerrey stated, "We ask our young men and women to sacrifice their safety and perhaps their lives to fight the war against terrorism. We all know that our dependency on imported oil is part of the problem and we know that increasing the fuel economy of the cars we drive is part of the solution."

Radio ads specifically called on Bill Ford "to do his part" to improve fuel economy. An ad stated, "Now more than ever, America needs cars that get better gas mileage. That's why we're asking Bill Ford, head of the Ford Motor Company, to do his part and to produce more fuel efficient, SUV's and pickup trucks."[28]

In addition to the ad campaign, the Sierra Club planned to organize grassroots actions against auto dealers. It also sent a delegation to Detroit to meet with UAW officials. ■

SOURCE: This case was written from public sources by David P. Baron. Copyright © 2002 by David P. Baron. All rights reserved. Reprinted by permission.

---

[21] Ford operated 48 manufacturing facilities in North America and employed 163,000 people in the United States and 370,000 worldwide.

[22] *The Wall Street Journal*, August 20, 2002.

[23] *The New York Times*, June 12, 2002.

[24] Sierra Club press release, June 20, 2001.

[25] Sierra Club press release, May 3, 2001.

[26] *The Wall Street Journal*, August 20, 2002.

[27] The Sierra Club had earlier campaigned against the Ford Excursion, which it dubbed the Ford Valdez.

[28] *The New York Times*, June 13, 2002.

## PREPARATION QUESTIONS

1. Identify the issues, interests, institutions, and information in the case. What are the various components of the fuel economy issue—for example, two-fleet system, multifuel credit, percent approach?

2. Assess the significance for Ford of a sharply higher CAFE standard.

3. Where is the issue in its life cycle?

4. What is the nature of the politics of the Kerry and McCain bills?

5. Prepare a distributive politics spreadsheet for the alternative of a Kerry-McCain bill

that would set a combined CAFE standard of 35 mpg.

6. Based on the spreadsheet what is your prediction of the outcome of the congressional action on fuel economy standards?

7. What should Ford do about the Sierra Club campaign?

8. What integrated strategy should Ford adopt for the fuel economy issue for both its market and nonmarket environments?

CHAPTER 9

# Antitrust: Economics, Law, and Politics

*People of the same trade seldom meet together, even for merriment and diversion, but the conversation ends in a conspiracy against the public or in some contrivance to raise prices.*

—ADAM SMITH, 1776

## Introduction

Antitrust policy is an amalgam of social policy, economics, law, administrative practice, and schools of thought.[1] Antitrust policy had its origins in the populist movement of the 1870s when a number of states enacted statutes to regulate economic activity and control the exercise of economic power. At the federal level, this movement led to the Interstate Commerce Act of 1887, which provided for federal regulation of interstate commerce, and the Sherman Act of 1890, the first federal antitrust statute. These acts resulted from political pressure by farmers and others concerned about railroad cartels, the railroads' pricing practices, and the distribution of power between farmers and railroads. The laws thus represent both social and economic policy.

As social policy, the antitrust laws express concern about concentrations of economic power and the potential for abuse inherent in that concentration. This parallels the concern about the concentration of political power and the preference for its dispersion in the electorate and among the institutions of government. Just as the Constitution controls political power through checks and balances among the branches of government and through popular elections, antitrust policy has focused on controlling economic power.

Antitrust policy also reflects economic policy. The basic objective is to protect competition and by doing so to benefit consumers. Antitrust is thus concerned with the structure of markets, the conduct of market participants, and the resulting performance of those markets. Protecting competition does not mean protecting competitors; vigorous competition can result in firms being driven from the market. Moreover, practices that may appear to be anticompetitive must be evaluated in terms of their effects on consumers. Antitrust economics has both a theoretical and an empirical component. Theory has been an indispensable guide for reasoning about the relationships among structure, conduct, and performance. Empirical research has provided evidence about those relationships.

---

[1]The antitrust policies of Japan and the European Union are considered in Chapters 14 and 15, respectively.

Antitrust law includes statutes and the court decisions interpreting those statutes. The principal federal statutes are the Sherman Act, the Clayton Act of 1914, and the Federal Trade Commission Act of 1914. These acts are broadly worded, employing such terms as monopolize, restraint of trade, and unfair practices. This has required the courts to interpret the acts in the context of the specifics of individual cases.[2] Antitrust law is thus both statutory and interpretive. It is also the subject of politics as interest groups, politicians, and public policy specialists attempt to influence the law.

Although there have been few major changes in the antitrust statutes in recent years, antitrust has not been static. Change results from its administration and enforcement. At the federal level, public enforcement is provided by the Antitrust Division of the Department of Justice (DOJ) and the Federal Trade Commission (FTC). During the 1980s the DOJ and the FTC made significant changes in antitrust policy through their merger guidelines, which revised the policies governing federal enforcement. Similarly, enforcement policies on vertical restraints of trade changed considerably. During the 1990s the pace of antitrust enforcement increased substantially. The antitrust laws, however, are enforced less by government than by private litigants—often by one firm filing a lawsuit against another. Over 90 percent of the lawsuits filed under the federal antitrust laws are brought by private litigants. Consequently, decisions made by courts on cases brought by private litigants cause antitrust law to evolve, even when there is no legislative or government enforcement activity.

Much of the recent evolution of antitrust law, and of antitrust policy more broadly, has resulted from changing economic and legal thought about markets, business strategies, and performance. This thought has a coherence and perspective not necessarily found in the historical record of court decisions, and it has shaped a number of recent decisions. Three approaches, or schools of thought, to reasoning about antitrust law are considered in this chapter.

The traditional or structure-conduct-performance school focuses on the structure of industries and on conduct that may foreclose opportunities or diminish competition. In the 1970s new understandings of the functioning of markets and the nature of competition were developed by the Chicago school of economics; these understandings had a major impact on antitrust enforcement and court decisions.[3] More recently, industrial organization economists have challenged some conclusions of the Chicago school by considering more closely the implications of informational asymmetries, network externalities, and strategic interactions among market participants. This perspective has qualified a number of the conclusions of the Chicago school.

These understandings of the purpose of antitrust policy and its appropriate application are particularly important in the United States because of the adversarial nature of judicial proceedings. Both plaintiffs and defendants have incentives to make the best cases they can and to use whatever new understandings support their sides. Consequently, new theories and empirical evidence quickly find their way into court proceedings. Hearing these arguments, judges make decisions that can be influenced by how compelling the theories are, in addition to the facts of the case, empirical evidence, and legal precedents. Antitrust law thus is shaped by economic thought.

---

[2] See Carp and Stidham (2001) and Chapter 12 for information on the U.S. federal courts.
[3] Much of the theory was developed by economists and legal scholars at the University of Chicago.

Antitrust policy has broad implications for management. Firms must conform to the law, but in many cases and for many practices, there is a considerable gray area in which the requirements of the law are unclear or untested. Similarly, because antitrust law evolves, a practice that once was allowable under the law may no longer be allowable. Practices that were once illegal may now be legal. Legal counsel is thus essential when issues or practices may have antitrust implications. Managers, however, must have an understanding of antitrust law, enforcement practices, and antitrust thought, since they must recognize when a policy or practice may raise antitrust concerns.

The purpose of this chapter is to provide an introduction to antitrust law and thought, the forces that have shaped antitrust policy in recent years, and the forces that may shape its future development. The next section introduces the principal antitrust laws and discusses their enforcement both by the government and private litigants. The following section considers the two rules under which antitrust lawsuits are tried: a rule of reason and a per se violation. The three schools of antitrust thought are then introduced and applied to vertical arrangements, predatory pricing, and collusion and price-fixing. The antitrust guidelines used by the DOJ and FTC to review mergers are then considered. The effects of antitrust decisions on market opening are discussed, and the politics of antitrust is considered.

# Antitrust Law

## The Antitrust Statutes

The principal antitrust statutes, excerpts from which are presented in Figure 9-1, have remained largely intact for over 90 years. Section 1 of the Sherman Act pertains to unreasonable restraints of trade with a focus on joint conduct. Section 2 focuses on unilateral conduct and proscribes *monopoly* and attempts to monopolize and to maintain a monopoly. The Sherman Act thus pertains to the reality of monopoly and *restraints of trade* and to the process of obtaining or maintaining a monopoly.

The Clayton Act goes further by addressing potentially anticompetitive actions. The Clayton Act contains terms such as "may be" and "tend to," which address monopolization and restraints in their incipiency. The Federal Trade Commission Act goes beyond the other two acts by prohibiting unfair methods of competition and *unfair or deceptive acts*. The broad language employed leaves considerable room for interpretation and thus a substantial role for the courts.[4]

The Sherman Act does not provide for private lawsuits, but Section 4 of the Clayton Act states "that any person who shall be injured in his business or property by reason of anything forbidden in the antitrust laws may sue therefore in any district court of the United States. . . ." This allows private parties to bring lawsuits for practices that are illegal under either the Sherman Act or the Clayton Act. Section 4 also provides for treble damages. Section 7 of the Clayton Act prohibits mergers that may substantially lessen competition or create a monopoly.

The Robinson-Patman Act of 1934 strengthened Section 2 of the Clayton Act's prohibition of price discrimination. The Robinson-Patman Act was intended to protect small businesses and merchants from their larger competitors, which were able to obtain lower prices on their supplies. Small grocers, for example, sought protection

[4]See Areeda and Kaplow (1997) and Gavil, Kovacic, and Baker (2002) for comprehensive treatments of antitrust law and Spulber (1989) and Viscusi, Vernon, and Harrington (2000) for the economics of antitrust.

## Sherman Act

Section 1. Every contract, combination in the form of trust or otherwise, or conspiracy, in restraint of trade or commerce among the several States, or with foreign nations, is hereby declared to be illegal. . . . Every person who shall make any contract or engage in any combination or conspiracy hereby declared to be illegal shall be deemed guilty of a felony. . . .

Section 2. Every person who shall monopolize, or attempt to monopolize, or combine or conspire with any other person or persons, to monopolize any part of the trade or commerce among the several States, or with foreign nations, shall be deemed guilty of a felony. . . .

## Clayton Act

Section 2. (a) That it shall be unlawful for any person engaged in commerce . . . to discriminate in the price between different purchasers . . . where the effect of such discrimination may be substantially to lessen competition or tend to create a monopoly in any line of commerce, or to injure, destroy or prevent competition . . . nothing herein contained shall prevent differentials which make only due allowance for differences in the cost of manufacture, sale, or delivery. . . .

Section 3. That it shall be illegal for any person [to enter an arrangement] . . . on the condition . . . that the lessee or purchaser thereof shall not use or deal in the goods . . . of a competitor or competitors, where the effect . . . may be to substantially lessen the competition or tend to create a monopoly in any line of commerce.

Section 7. That no corporation engaged in commerce shall acquire, directly or indirectly, the whole or any part of the stock or other share capital . . . where in any line of commerce in any section of the country, the effect of such acquisition may be substantially to lessen competition, or tend to create a monopoly.*

## Federal Trade Commission Act

Section 5. (a)(1) Unfair methods of competition in commerce, and unfair or deceptive acts or practices in commerce, are hereby declared unlawful.**

*As amended by the Celler-Kefeauver Act of 1950.
**As amended by the Wheeler-Lea Act of 1938.

**FIGURE 9-1 Excerpts from the Antitrust Statutes**

from supermarkets, which used their greater buying power to obtain lower prices. Critics of the Robinson-Patman Act claim that it causes firms to be wary of price competition, resulting in higher prices for consumers. Proponents, however, contend that it is necessary to prevent small firms from being driven out of business, thereby increasing concentration and lessening competition.

Practices that come under the antitrust laws are classified as horizontal or vertical. A *horizontal* practice is one that involves activities in the same industry. A merger, for example, is horizontal if the two firms operate in the same industry. Horizontal arrangements include monopolization, predatory pricing, price fixing, bid rigging, the allocation of customers, and group boycotts. The concern with horizontal arrangements is that they may increase market power, leading to lessened competition and higher prices.

*Vertical* practices are those involving firms in a supply arrangement or a channel of distribution. Vertical practices include the allocation of territories by a manufacturer among distributors or retailers, refusals to deal, exclusive dealing arrangements, retail price maintenance, reciprocal arrangements, and tying. Vertical practices also include the merger of a manufacturer and a supplier or distributor. Figure 9-2 provides brief definitions of the principal practices of concern under the antitrust laws.

## Horizontal

**Horizontal merger** — A merger is horizontal if it involves two firms in the same industry. A horizontal merger comes under Section 7 of the Clayton Act and under Section 2 of the Sherman Act, if it would create a monopoly.

**Horizontal price fixing (collusion)** — Horizontal price fixing includes explicit or implicit agreements to control prices in an industry or with respect to a product. Horizontal price fixing comes under Section 1 of the Sherman Act.

**Monopoly** — Concerted efforts to monopolize come under the purview of Section 1 of the Sherman Act, and the unilateral attempt to monopolize comes under Section 2 of the Sherman Act.

**Price discrimination** — Price discrimination involves charging customers different prices that are not justified by cost differences of serving those customers. Price discrimination comes under Section 2 of the Clayton Act, as amended by the Robinson-Patman Act.

## Vertical

**Boycotts and refusals to deal** — A manufacturer refuses to sell to a distributor or a retailer. If two or more parties agree to refuse to deal with another party, it is a boycott. These practices are considered under Section 1 of the Sherman Act.

**Exclusive dealing** — A manufacturer grants another firm an exclusive right to distribute or market a particular product. Exclusive dealing comes under Section 3 of the Clayton Act.

**Exclusive territory** — A manufacturer grants an exclusive territory to a seller, and no other seller is permitted to sell in the territory. Exclusive territories come under Section 1 of the Sherman Act.

**Resale price maintenance** — A manufacturer requires a retailer to sell only at a price at least as high as a price it specifies. Such cases come under Section 1 of the Sherman Act.

**Tying** — Tying is the practice of bundling one product with another. For example, Mercedes-Benz requires its dealers to carry only Mercedes-Benz parts. * Tying arrangements come under Section 3 of the Clayton Act and Section 1 of the Sherman Act.

**Vertical integration** — Vertical integration involves the joining together, in terms of a merger or venture, of firms at various stages of a production process or channel or distribution. A vertical merger comes under Section 7 of the Clayton Act. ** A vertical contract that forecloses or restrains competition comes under Section 3 of the Clayton Act.

## Conglomerate

**Conglomerate merger** — A conglomerate merger involves two firms that do not operate in the same industries either as competitors or as part of a channel of distribution or supply. Conglomerate mergers come under Section 7 of the Clayton Act. The concern in the case of a conglomerate merger is the elimination of a potential competitor.***

*The DOJ dropped its antitrust suit against Mercedes-Benz because it concluded that a tying arrangement could only be anti-competitive if it is based on horizontal market power.
**See *Brown Shoe Co. v. U.S.*, 294 (1962), in which the Supreme Court invalidated the merger between Brown Shoe and the G. R. Kinney retail chain.
***See *Federal Trade Commission v. Procter & Gamble Co.*, 368 U.S. 568 (1967).

**FIGURE 9-2 Arrangements and Practices Subject to Antitrust Scrutiny**

# Exemptions

A number of exemptions from the antitrust laws are provided. The Norris-LaGuardia Act of 1932 strengthened the statutory exemption the Clayton Act provided to unions. The economic activities of labor unions taken in their own interest, such as strikes, are protected. Exemptions are also provided for agricultural cooperatives and for certain activities of industries, such as insurance, that are regulated by government.[5] Exemptions for joint export trading activities are also provided under the Webb-Pomerene Act of

---

[5]The exemption for the insurance industry is provided in the McCarron-Ferguson Act, and the exemption for agricultural cooperatives is provided by the Capper-Volstad Act of 1922.

**EXAMPLE**

## Monopoly

In basic economic theory a monopoly is present when a firm has a dominant position in a market and can restrict its output to increase the price consumers pay. In some markets, however, a monopoly may be the inevitable result of competition. For example, if there are benefits from standardization, competition can drive the market to concentrate on a single standard. If that standard is proprietary, as in the case of Microsoft's Windows operating system, a monopoly results. A monopoly achieved as a result of market forces combined with a superior product is not illegal, since consumers can benefit from the competition to become the standard and from the development of a superior product.

Monopoly is the subject of Section 2 of the Sherman Act. In *United States v. Aluminum Co. of America*, 148 F2d 416 (2d Cir 1945), Judge Learned Hand formulated a two-step procedure for deciding monopolization cases under Section 2.[1] The first step is to determine if the defendant has a monopoly. The second step is to determine if the monopoly was willfully acquired or unreasonably maintained or if it was the result of "superior skill, foresight and industry."

[t]he offense of monopoly . . . has two elements: (1) the possession of monopoly power in the relevant market and (2) the willful acquisition or maintenance of that power as distinguished from growth or development as a consequence of a superior product, business acumen, or historical accident.

Having a monopoly thus is not illegal, as in the case of a firm that becomes a monopoly through a superior product with which others are unable to compete. Willful monopolization or maintenance of a monopoly through anticompetitive practices is illegal.

For example, the online person-to-person auction market tipped to eBay, which has over 80 percent of the market. Similarly, Microsoft has over 90 percent of the personal computer operating system market. Having such monopolies is not illegal if they were achieved through superior performance and characteristics of the market, such as the characteristics of information technologies considered in Chapter 13. Maintaining a monopoly using anticompetitive practices is illegal, as is using a monopoly position in one market to attempt to monopolize another related market. In the chapter case, *The Microsoft Antitrust Case*, the Department of Justice alleged that Microsoft used anticompetitive practices to maintain its monopoly in the PC operating system market and used that monopoly to attempt to monopolize the Internet browser market.[2]

[1] Early cases broke up the oil [*Standard Oil Co. v. United States*, 221 U.S. 1 (1911)] and tobacco [*United States v. American Tobacco Co.*, 221 U.S. 106 (1911)] monopolies.

[2] Monopolization cases are rarely filed. The most recent case prior to the Microsoft case was against IBM for monopolization of the computer industry. That case was filed on the last day of the Johnson administration in 1969 and dropped by the Reagan administration.

1918 and the Export Trading Company Act of 1982. A partial antitrust exemption was established for joint research and development ventures such as Sematech and for certain insurance pools. Exemptions can also be provided by specific legislation, as in the Soft Drink Interbrand Competition Act considered later in the chapter.

Baseball never had a statutory exemption from the antitrust laws but was protected by a 1922 Supreme Court decision, which had been upheld in subsequent decisions because the courts believed that it was the role of Congress, not the court, to change the antitrust status of baseball.[6] In 1998 Congress modified the antitrust exemption by no longer exempting labor agreements, but a partial exemption continues.

[6] See *Federal Baseball Club of Baltimore v. National League of Professional Baseball Clubs*, 259 U.S. 200 (1991), *Toolson v. New York Yankees, Inc.*, 346 U.S. 356 (1953), and *Flood v. Kuhn*, 407 U.S. 258 (1972).

# Enforcement of the Antitrust Laws

## Government Enforcement

Both the DOJ and the FTC have the authority to enforce the Sherman and Clayton Acts, but only the FTC can enforce the Federal Trade Commission Act.[7] Their dual enforcement responsibilities led the DOJ and the FTC to reach an interagency liaison agreement in 1948. As a result of the agreement, cases are allocated primarily by industry and secondarily by the nature of the complaint.[8] For example, the DOJ has enforcement responsibility for computer software and the FTC for semiconductors, so the DOJ filed the antitrust lawsuits against Microsoft and the FTC filed an antitrust lawsuit against Intel. Most enforcement activities are civil rather than criminal, and only the DOJ can bring criminal charges under the antitrust laws. Bringing criminal charges requires a grand jury indictment, and the standards of proof are higher than in a civil case.

In criminal cases the available penalties are fines and imprisonment. In civil cases injunctive relief can be granted, contracts dissolved, and business units ordered divested. Fines cannot be imposed in civil cases except to compensate the government for actual damages when it is a purchaser of goods and services. The courts not only decide cases but also approve consent decrees, such as that which split AT&T into seven regional operating companies and a residual AT&T. The DOJ can enforce the antitrust laws only through lawsuits filed in federal courts, but the FTC has authority to issue orders directly. The FTC can also seek injunctions in federal court, for example, to block a proposed merger, as in the chapter case, *The Staples–Office Depot Merger*?[9]

The FTC is an independent commission with five commissioners appointed, subject to Senate confirmation, by the president to 7-year terms. It can initiate its own investigations of practices it believes may violate the antitrust laws. As a consequence of an investigation, the FTC may negotiate a consent decree with a firm. If a firm refuses to agree to a consent decree, the FTC can continue the case through an administrative law procedure. A hearing is held before an administrative law judge, who issues an opinion and recommendations for action. The case is then decided by a majority vote of the commission. As penalties, the FTC can issue cease and desist orders that have the effect of injunctions against the activity in question. If a firm violates an order, the FTC can impose fines. Both the orders issued by the FTC and the court decisions in cases brought by the DOJ can be appealed to the U.S. Court of Appeals.

A consent decree is an agreement reached by the litigants under the sanction of a court. It does not involve a judicial determination and hence does not signify a violation of the law. A consent decree generally involves restrictions on the actions of the defendant. It binds only the consenting parties and does not set a precedent for other cases. A consent decree may remain in effect indefinitely and requires the agreement of both the plaintiff and the defendant and the court to lift or modify it. In 1997 a federal court lifted, effective in 2001, a 1956 consent decree that had restricted IBM's sales and service practices on its mainframe and mid-range computers. The judge concluded that IBM's market power "has substantially diminished."

The 1974 Antitrust Procedures and Penalties Act classified as felonies violations such as price fixing and increased the allowable fines. Fines against corporations can be as high as $10 million per count in criminal cases. Individuals, including managers of

---

[7]Technically the FTC has no authority to enforce the Sherman Act, but in practice, it does. The courts have held that practices violating the Sherman Act constitute "unfair" methods of competition under Section 5 of the Federal Trade Commission Act.

[8]See Shugart (1990, p. 947).

[9]See Clarkson and Muris (1981) for an analysis of FTC policy and enforcement. See Weaver (1977) for a study of FTC enforcement policy and Elzinga and Briet (1976) for a study of antitrust policies.

corporations, can be fined up to $350,000 and can be imprisoned for up to 3 years. Since 1990 the federal government has been able to collect treble damages. Federal sentencing guidelines enacted in 1991 allow fines to be based on the amount of business affected in addition to other factors. In 1999 Roche Holdings, BASF, and Rhone-Poulenc (now Aventis) pleaded guilty to criminal price fixing in vitamins, and Roche paid $500 million in fines and BASF $225 million. Rhone-Poulenc paid no fine in exchange for cooperating with the government.

The Hart-Scott-Rodino Antitrust Improvements Act of 1976 amended Section 7 of the Clayton Act to enhance the enforcement of the antitrust laws pertaining to monopolization and restraint of trade through mergers.[10] Hart-Scott-Rodino requires pre-merger notification to the DOJ and the FTC of plans to merge.[11] In 2000, 4,926 mergers were reported to the DOJ and FTC under Hart-Scott-Rodino. The DOJ and FTC decide which agency will review a merger based on "expertise and experience." A merger cannot be completed for 30 days, and during this period the agencies can require the firms to submit information about the market effects of their merger. For example, the firms may be required to submit information about their market shares in the market segments in which they both participate. In 2001 the Hearst Corporation agreed to pay a $4 million fine for failure to produce key documents as required by Hart-Scott-Rodino. If the DOJ or FTC decides that there are grounds to challenge the merger, it seeks a preliminary injunction. In most cases, this convinces the firms to abandon their plans to merge. The chapter case, *The Staples–Office Depot Merger?*, concerns an FTC action to obtain a preliminary injunction against a merger.

The Robinson-Patman Act prohibits price discrimination not justified by cost differences in serving customers. In addition to a cost difference defense, a firm can defend itself by arguing that the price discrimination was necessary to meet competition. The Clayton Act assigns the burden of proof in a price discrimination case to the plaintiff to show that there has been discrimination. Given a prima facie case, the defendant has the burden to show that the discrimination was justified by, for example, cost differences.[12]

During the past 25 years the DOJ and the FTC have effectively stopped enforcing the Robinson-Patman Act because of their view that it stifles competition. The DOJ and the FTC have also stopped enforcing the prohibition against resale price maintenance, although private enforcement continues. Resale price maintenance pertains to restrictions imposed by manufacturers on the prices that can be charged by retailers. In the 1930s small retailers sought protection from price competition by having manufacturers establish minimum resale prices. States passed "fair trade laws" that required retailers to sell at the prices specified by contracts signed with manufacturers. The Miller-Tydings Act of 1937 allowed states to exempt price maintenance agreements from coverage under Section 1 of the Sherman Act as long as there was competition from other brands. The McGuire Act extended this to nonsigners of resale price contracts. In 1975 Congress repealed the Miller-Tydings and the McGuire Acts and withdrew the states' authority for fair trade laws.

The explanation for the lack of government enforcement of the resale price maintenance and price discrimination provisions of the antitrust laws is found in the changing schools of antitrust thought considered later in the chapter. To indicate the

---

[10]See Federal Trade Commission (1990).
[11]Notification is required if the acquirer will have a 15 percent stake or a $15 million investment in the acquired firm and the acquirer has either sales or assets of $100 million or the acquired firm has assets of at least $10 million. If the acquired firm is a manufacturer, the asset figure is replaced by sales of $10 million.
[12]A prima facie case is one that needs no further demonstration.

type of case to which the DOJ and the FTC object, Cuisinart was found to have violated the antitrust laws by requiring sellers of its food processors to maintain a minimum retail price. Cuisinart held a dominant share of the market for food processors at the time the lawsuit was filed, but its share was largely due to its having developed the original product. Cuisinart had no fundamental horizontal market power, as entry into the food processor market was easy. Furthermore, the high minimum price established by Cuisinart stimulated entry, which quickly eroded its market share. Prices fell substantially when entry occurred. The resale price agreement, if it had continued, would likely have had little effect on the market for food processors. To clarify its policy, in 1985 the Antitrust Division of the DOJ issued revised guidelines indicating that it would not investigate vertical accords when a firm has less than a 10 percent market share. A market share above 10 percent could lead to an investigation.

In spite of the lack of enforcement against certain vertical arrangements, federal enforcement of the antitrust laws is active. During the 1990s the pace of federal antitrust enforcement accelerated considerably. In part this was due to the increase in merger activity, but vigorous enforcement of price fixing and other antitrust violations also occurred. In 1998 three former Archers-Daniel-Midland executives, including the son of the chairman of the board, were sentenced to from 2 to 3 years in prison for price-fixing of lysine and citric acid.

The growth in new industries also generates new antitrust activity. The dietary supplements industry reached $12 billion in sales in 1997, and the FTC turned its attention to the advertising claims made for the supplements. The FTC took legal action against seven supplements manufacturers, sent e-mail warnings to 1,100 Web sites that made "incredible claims," and issued advertising guidelines.[13]

In 1998 the DOJ filed an antitrust case against Visa and MasterCard alleging that their prohibitions preventing banks from issuing other credit cards such as Discovery and American Express was exclusionary. The district court found against Visa and MasterCard and ordered them to allow banks to issue other cards. The companies appealed, but the Court of Appeals upheld the lower court decision. The companies then appealed to the Supreme Court, which rejected the appeal, opening a $1.3 trillion market to American Express and Morgan Stanley's Discover card.

The DOJ also became more active in another area. It filed a price fixing suit against the 23 colleges in the "overlap" group that met annually to exchange financial aid information for admitted undergraduate students. The DOJ reached a consent decree with the eight Ivy League schools, but the Massachusetts Institute of Technology (MIT) decided to go to trial, losing in district court. Upon appeal the U.S. Court of Appeals reversed the lower court decision. The DOJ and MIT then reached a settlement in which colleges may discuss general guidelines for financial aid and compare data on financial need but may not exchange information on individual students or their aid packages.[14]

Although the federal antitrust agencies are usually successful in obtaining at least a consent decree in the cases they bring, companies do win cases. In 1994 in a case brought by the DOJ alleging that General Electric had engaged in price fixing for industrial diamonds, the judge ruled that the DOJ had presented insufficient evidence and dismissed the case without requiring the company to present a defense.

---

[13]*The Wall Street Journal*, November 18, 1998.
[14]See Bamberger and Carlton (1999). The only schools allowed to participate in the system are those that practiced need-blind admissions and provided full-need financial aid.

# Private Enforcement

Most antitrust cases are the result of private lawsuits.[15] The number of private antitrust suits increased beginning in the early 1960s and peaked at over 1,600 in 1977, declining to 570 in 1997. The decline was a function of a variety of factors, including Supreme Court decisions that made it more difficult for some plaintiffs to prevail in cases involving vertical restraints and predatory pricing. Firms also instituted compliance programs that contributed to the decrease.

Most antitrust suits are brought against a firm, and cases pertaining to vertical arrangements represent a somewhat higher percent of the total than those pertaining to horizontal practices. Of the total cases in their study, Salop and White (1988) found that 36.5 percent were filed by competitors and 27.3 percent by dealers. Of the cases filed before 1980, 71 percent were settled out of court and 11 percent were dismissed. Of the 12 percent of the cases that continued, plaintiffs prevailed in approximately 30 percent. Only 5.4 percent of the cases went to trial.

The treble damages provision of the Clayton Act provides strong incentives for a private party to file an antitrust lawsuit. If a suit is filed against a firm by the DOJ, private parties often follow with private lawsuits. A court decision for the government is interpreted by the courts as providing a prima facie case against the defendant, greatly increasing the likelihood that private cases will be decided in favor of the plaintiffs. In the vitamin price-fixing case, private class action lawsuits were filed against seven drug companies. The companies settled the lawsuits for $1.1 billion. The companies also reached a $340 million settlement with state attorneys general, bringing the total fines in the United States to $2.2 billion.

In 1996 Wal-Mart and other retailers filed an antitrust lawsuit against Visa and MasterCard, which had imposed an "honor-all-cards" policy on merchants, requiring them to accept debit cards if they accepted Visa and MasterCard credit cards. The merchants alleged that this was illegal tying under Section 1 of the Sherman Act and also that Visa and MasterCard were attempting to monopolize the debit card market in violation of Section 2 of the Sherman Act. As the case was going to trial in 2003 a settlement was reached in which Visa paid $2 billion and MasterCard $1 billion to the merchants and agreed to revise their policies and reduce their charges for debit cards.[16]

Treble damages are understandably controversial. Their proponents argue that they provide an important incentive for private enforcement. Critics contend that treble damages provide an incentive to challenge the practices of competitors, thereby making firms reluctant to compete on a number of dimensions, including price.

Private suits can have significance beyond their impact on the parties involved. When a private antitrust case is tried and appealed, higher court decisions can establish a precedent that is then followed by courts in similar cases. Many of the important interpretations of the antitrust statutes and the precedents followed by the courts have come from private lawsuits.

# Per Se Violations and the Rule of Reason

The courts have held that there are some sufficiently egregious acts that on the face of it violate the antitrust laws. These acts are said to be *per se* illegal, and the only defense allowed is that the defendant did not commit the act. The Supreme Court established this rule in *Northern Pacific Railroad Co. v. U.S.*, 356 U.S. 1 (1958), stating, "There are

15Viscusi, Vernon, and Harrington (2000, p. 68) report that approximately 90 percent of antitrust lawsuits filed in U.S. courts during the 1970s and 1980s were private. See also White (1988).
16The lawyers for the plaintiffs asked for fees of $600 million, but the judge reduced the amount to $220 million.

certain agreements or practices which because of their pernicious effect on competition and lack of any redeeming virtue are conclusively presumed to be unreasonable and therefore illegal without elaborate inquiry as to the precise harm they have caused or the business excuse for their use."

In contrast, other cases are considered by the courts under a *rule of reason*.[17] Under this rule, a restraint of trade, for example, is illegal if it is unreasonable. Per se violations are presumed to be unreasonable. The rule of reason was needed because much of the language of the antitrust laws is too sweeping and a literal interpretation would be harmful to competition and efficiency. Section 1 of the Sherman Act, for example, might be interpreted as prohibiting supply contracts because they restrain the opportunities for others. Similarly, combinations such as partnerships might otherwise be held to be in violation of the Sherman Act. The DOJ case against Visa and MasterCard for exclusionary practices was tried under a rule of reason.

A defendant has two defenses under a rule of reason. The first is the same as under a per se rule—the defendant did not commit the act in question. The second is that, although the defendant committed the act, it was not unreasonable. In evaluating whether an act is unreasonable, courts look to its purpose and effect. In the case of vertical arrangements, the stimulation of interbrand competition is a purpose the courts recognize. In evaluating the effect of an act, the courts examine whether it restrains or promotes competition and whether it is the least restrictive means of achieving the purpose. A court may hold for the plaintiff if either the purpose or the effect is unreasonable.

The courts do not decide which rule is applicable on a case-by-case basis but instead hold that certain practices are per se illegal and others are not. Presently, price-fixing, output restraints, minimum resale price maintenance, and the allocation of customers among competitors are per se violations of the antitrust laws. Some practices that in the past were considered per se offenses are now considered under the rule of reason. For example, in 1997 the Supreme Court ruled that maximum price resale maintenance, where a manufacturer sets a maximum price that retailers may charge, is not per se illegal and is to be considered under a rule of reason.[18]

A variety of arrangements and practices have come under the scrutiny of the antitrust laws, as indicated in Figure 9-2. A treatment of each of these requires more space than is available, so the following sections focus instead on antitrust thought and on the application of that thought in the areas of vertical restraints, predatory pricing, collusion, and mergers.

# Antitrust Thought

Antitrust policy, enforcement practices, and court decisions are influenced by the prevailing schools of thought about the purposes of antitrust policy and the likely consequences of specific practices. The *structural* or *structure-conduct-performance school* of thought prevailed into the 1970s, when it was confronted with the understandings of the *Chicago school*. The Chicago, or law and economics, school viewed the objectives and principles of antitrust policy differently, particularly with regard to vertical arrangements. It has had considerable influence on legal education, the courts, and the enforcement activities of the DOJ and FTC beginning with the Reagan administration.

[17]The rule of reason was first articulated by the Supreme Court in *Standard Oil Co. of New Jersey v. United States*, 221 U.S. 1 (1911), which broke up the Standard Oil Trust. A judicial rule is a standard of interpretation for a law that is ambiguous in the absence of that interpretation.
[18]*State Oil Company v. Khan*, 522 U.S. 3; 118 S.Ct. 27 S.

In addition, the courts have adopted many understandings of the Chicago school, and several Chicago school scholars have been appointed to the federal judiciary.

In the 1990s antitrust practice and policy were influenced by the work of industrial organization (IO) economists, who focused on new considerations such as network externalities and compatibility and on theories of oligopoly that take into account the strategic interactions among market participants in imperfectly competitive markets. This *new IO* approach challenges some of the understandings of both the structural and the Chicago schools. The new IO approach is a collection of theories rather than a unified perspective from which broad conclusions can be drawn. Furthermore, courts have only cautiously embraced its theories, in part because of the complexity and subtle reasoning involved. Nevertheless, it represents an important force in antitrust.

These three approaches agree on many points but differ on others. Figure 9-3 contrasts the approaches.

## The Structural Approach

From the perspective of social and economic policy, government intervention in markets is intended to improve economic performance and further the social objectives of limiting economic power. From this perspective, concentrations of economic power should be checked, just as is political power. Because economic power can result in the unfair treatment of competitors and consumers, government has a responsibility to protect citizens and society from the presence, and the abuse, of economic power. Antitrust policy and regulation are the principal public instruments for checking that power.

The structural approach views the performance of markets as determined by the conduct of market participants, which is largely determined by the structure of the market, such as the number of competitors. This approach takes as its starting point the economic theories of monopoly and perfect competition. Perfect competition serves as the standard for evaluating an industry, and monopoly is its antithesis. Monopolistic pricing can be characterized by the generalized Lerner index, given by

$$\frac{p - mc}{p} = \frac{1}{n\varepsilon},$$

where *p* is price, *mc* is marginal cost, *n* is the number of firms in the industry, and $\varepsilon$ is the price elasticity of demand.[19] The left side of the index is the percentage markup on price; for a monopoly ($n = 1$), the markup set by the firm equals one divided by the elasticity of demand. As the number of firms increases, the markup decreases and price approaches marginal cost, which is the case of perfect competition. Market power is thus the ability to command a price above marginal cost and that power is greater the smaller the number of firms in an industry, other things equal. In the chapter case, *The Staples–Office Depot Merger?*, the FTC and the court concluded that prices were higher in markets with only one office supply superstore than in markets with two or three superstores.

The structural approach thus views economic power as a function of the number of firms in the industry or, correspondingly, their market shares. The smaller the number of firms, the more likely they are to restrict output to raise prices and worsen the performance of a market. The focus of antitrust policy thus should be on the structure of the industry, and industries with substantial *concentration*—a substantial market share held by a small number of firms—should be regarded with suspicion. The structural approach finds support for this conclusion in empirical studies that show a positive correlation between industry concentration and profitability, as predicted by the Lerner index.

---

[19]This relation is derived from a Cournot model of oligopoly.

| Dimension | Structural | Chicago School | New IO |
|---|---|---|---|
| • Purpose of antitrust policy | Social and political as well as economic objectives. | Economic objectives — efficiency with a focus on prices. | Economic objectives; static and dynamic efficiency. |
| • View of markets | Markets are fragile and prone to failure. | Markets are resilient; market imperfections can be addressed through incentives. | Most markets are resilient, but some have imperfections such as network externalities; strategic behavior can limit efficiency. |
| • What is needed | Government to protect society from economic power. | Competition is the best protector of consumers and economic efficiency. | Competition is the best protector of consumers, but government intervention can be required. |
| • Perspective on consumers | Need to protect consumers from others and from themselves; e.g., unfair practices. | Consumers are responsible for their own decisions and will protect themselves. | Consumers can protect themselves when they have choices. |
| • Requirements for markets to function efficiently | Protect competitors to prevent monopoly; avoid foreclosing opportunities for competitors. | Conditions for perfect competition are sufficient but not necessary. | Both innovation and competition are required for efficiency; dynamic efficiency is important. |
| • Relationship between the number of competitors and market performance | More competitors means more competition. | Competition can be effective with only a few competitors. | Competition can be effective with a small number of competitors. |
| • Entry | High barriers to entry reduce efficiency; potential entry may not limit the power of incumbent firms. | Few barriers to entry; barriers are due to the efficiency of incumbent firms; potential entry limits the economic power of incumbents. | Barriers to entry can be present; e.g., from the economies of standardization. |
| • Sources of economic power | Market power derives from horizontal power and from vertical arrangements. | Market power can only arise from horizontal power. | Market power derives from horizontal factors but can be extended through vertical arrangements and strategic behavior. |
| • Collusion | Increases profits, so firms can be expected to collude. | Is difficult for firms to enforce and thus is unlikely. | Is possible with repeated encounters. |
| • Where is collusion most likely | In concentrated markets. | In industries with government regulation or protection. | In industries with repeated encounters and easy monitoring, as well as in regulated and protected industries. |
| • Interpretation of the relationship between concentration and profits | Positive correlation indicates that more concentration reduces market efficiency and increases profits. | Positive correlation is more likely due to lower costs of larger firms. | Positive correlation can be due to lower costs, market power, or strategic opportunities. |
| • Relevant market for antitrust scrutiny should be | Defined narrowly so that pockets of concentration can be detected and addressed. | Defined broadly to include substitutes and imports. | Defined broadly to include substitutes and imports. |
| • Conclusion about antitrust | Proscribe many practices as per se offenses. | Judge business practices in terms of their effects on efficiency and prices; use the rule of reason. | Judge business practices in terms of impact on present and future competition; use rule of reason except for egregious practices such as price fixing. |
| • Values underlying the perspective | Efficiency and fairness; government protection. | Economic efficiency; individual choice and responsibility. | Economic efficiency; individual and collective responsibility. |

**FIGURE 9-3 Structural, Chicago School, New IO Perspectives**

Improving performance in the market requires dealing with industry structure as well as the conduct of market participants. Remedies for antitrust violations should include breaking up monopolies, ordering the divestiture of business units, requiring tight standards for mergers, and requiring the licensing of technologies. Because a larger number of firms correlates with more competition and lower prices, the more firms in the industry the better. To ensure that there are enough firms for vigorous competition, it may be desirable to protect firms from their rivals, particularly from predatory behavior or from unfair advantages such as not being able to purchase inputs at low prices (as reflected in the Robinson-Patman Act).

The Lerner index implies that market power arises from horizontal considerations. Market power can also occur from vertical arrangements in channels of distribution, as when a manufacturer requires a distributor or retailer to maintain a minimum price, carry only the manufacturer's replacement parts, or sell only within a specified territory. From the perspective of the structural approach, it is important to avoid foreclosing opportunities for competitors, since competition would then be less vigorous. Vertical arrangements thus should be viewed with suspicion because they can foreclose opportunities for competitors and increase economic power.

The economic power of the incumbent firms in an industry can be checked by entry into the industry. The structural approach, however, is concerned about possible barriers to entry. *Barriers to entry* are said to include such factors as technological advantages, advertising and brand names, and capital requirements. Because of barriers to entry and economic concentration, this approach often views markets as fragile. Government thus has a role in helping markets function more efficiently.

When there are barriers to entry and economic power is concentrated in a relatively small number of firms, incumbent firms may have an opportunity to collude. The structural approach views collusion as more likely the more concentrated the industry. Collusion can take the form of price fixing among firms in an industry or in a channel of distribution. The empirical research finding a positive correlation between concentration and profitability could reflect this collusion. This provides another rationale for focusing on concentrated markets.

Because economic power harms consumers through higher prices, the structural approach holds that markets should be viewed narrowly to identify market segments in which economic concentration is present. Similarly, it is important to keep market opportunities open. Consequently, restraints of trade and market foreclosures should be limited to those that are absolutely necessary, and antitrust should proscribe practices that foreclose opportunities or restrain competition. Many of those practices should be per se illegal.

In summary, the structure-conduct-performance paradigm views performance as following from conduct, which follows from the structure of markets. Antitrust policy thus should be concerned about concentration, barriers to entry, possible collusion, and exclusionary practices. Antitrust enforcers should closely scrutinize market structure for economic concentration, market foreclosures, and restraints of trade. Antitrust remedies should include structural as well as conduct remedies.

## The Chicago School

The Chicago school views the objective of antitrust policy as economic efficiency, which may be understood in its simplest form as the maximization of producers' plus consumers' surplus. Since economic efficiency depends on the level of prices, the focus is on the prices consumers pay. Thus, a price equal to marginal cost is efficient, whether it results from a perfectly competitive market or a monopolistic industry in which price is held down by the threat of entry. The focus of the Chicago school is on performance—the prices in markets—rather than on the structure of markets.[20] The Chicago school recognizes the potential for horizontal market power and its abuse but believes that competition, not government, is the best protector of consumers and the best promoter of economic efficiency.

Perfect competition is the ideal, but the conditions for perfect competition—many firms, a homogeneous product, technologies available to all firms, and complete information—are viewed as sufficient but not necessary for economic efficiency. Competition can be efficient even with few firms in an industry since, given the opportunity, firms will compete vigorously.

The Chicago school is skeptical about the nature and scope of barriers to entry. Claimed barriers such as advertising, brand-name advantages, and capital requirements are unlikely to be true barriers. Capital markets are viewed as efficient, so investors will provide capital for ventures that have prospects for at least a market rate of return. Barriers to entry are likely to be due to the cost advantages of incumbent firms, and the inability of a potential entrant to raise capital could be due to efficiency advantages of incumbent firms. Thus entry may be limited not by structural barriers but by economic efficiency. Indeed, incumbent firms are those that have already survived competition.

The positive correlation between industry concentration and profitability that the structural approach views as reflecting the exercise of economic power could, according to the Chicago school, result from the greater efficiency of those firms that have survived the competitive process. Furthermore, larger firms may have lower costs because of economies of scale. Their markups thus could be higher but their prices lower than if the firms in the industry were smaller. That is, if as firms become larger their costs decrease and competition is present to force prices down, consumers benefit. The firms could also benefit because of their lower costs and greater market shares. Consequently, both markups and profits could increase with concentration, yet higher concentration could result in lower prices for consumers.

The Chicago school also views collusion among firms as unsustainable because of the difficulties in monitoring and enforcing collusive agreements. Colluding firms have a strong incentive to cheat on an agreement by, for example, making secret discounts to customers to increase sales. A collusive agreement may have the structure of a prisoners' dilemma in which each firm finds it in its interest to cheat on the agreement. Unless there is a clear mechanism for monitoring the agreement, collusion is unlikely to be sustained.

From the Chicago school's perspective, collusion is most likely to be sustainable when there is government protection or regulation. Government regulation that precluded entry into the airline and trucking industries is viewed as having resulted in implicit collusion, with much of the rents captured by labor rather than by firms. Consistent with this perspective, during the Reagan administration the DOJ pressed its antitrust case against AT&T because it believed that regulation was inhibiting competition and technological progress. The DOJ, however, dropped its antitrust case against IBM because whatever market power IBM might have had was being dissipated by the rapid technological change in the computer industry.

Because barriers to entry are low and collusion is difficult to sustain, competition—both existing and potential—can be expected. Because it is the performance of the market that is important, the rule of reason should be used by courts in judging practices under the antitrust laws. Correspondingly, few practices should be per se illegal. In particular, vertical restraints are harmful only if the firm has horizontal market power, which should be assessed for its consequences for prices.

---

[20]See Posner (1976) for an analysis of antitrust policy from the Chicago school perspective.

In assessing horizontal power the relevant market should be defined broadly. Both present and potential competition should be considered because either can hold prices down. The relevant market thus includes not only the product in question but also close substitutes for that product. The definition of the relevant market should also include imported as well as domestic products. In the case of capital goods, the relevant market should include the market for used goods. In the case of a commodity such as aluminum, it should include the scrap and recycling markets as well as aluminum produced directly from bauxite. As an example of this perspective, Eastman Kodak has a 70 percent share of the U.S. color film market, 60 percent of the color paper market, and 70 percent of the wholesale photofinishing market. Its market dominance and practices had twice resulted in antitrust consent decrees. In 1994, however, the courts lifted both consent decrees. The courts concluded that Kodak did not have substantial market power because it had only a 36 percent market share worldwide. The courts concluded that if Kodak were to exercise market power by restricting output to obtain high prices, imported film would quickly rush into the U.S. market, forcing prices down.

In summary, the Chicago school views the objective of antitrust as economic efficiency and competition as the best means of achieving efficiency. Perfect competition is not the only means of achieving efficiency, however, as competition among a few firms can be sufficient to drive prices down to marginal costs. Barriers to entry are viewed with skepticism and collusion as difficult to sustain, so market forces should correct most attempts to restrain trade. Furthermore, the relation between profitability and concentration may be due to costs that decrease with the size of firms rather than to the exploitation of market power. Because the objective is economic efficiency, the focus of antitrust policy should be on performance, and the market in which that performance is assessed should be viewed broadly.

The Chicago school does not conclude that conduct such as vertical arrangements should be legal. Instead, it concludes that vertical arrangements could be pro-competitive rather than anticompetitive. Hence, they should not be per se illegal but rather should be considered under a rule of reason. This allows firms to adopt those practices that enhance efficiency but also allows successful prosecution of practices that harm efficiency.

## The New IO Approach

The new IO approach to antitrust is derived from the economics of modern industrial organization. This approach rejects the static equilibrium approach taken by the Chicago school and focuses on the opportunities for strategic behavior not initially considered by the Chicago school.[21] For example, even when firms act in a noncooperative manner, implicit collusion could result from repeated interactions among market participants and be sustained by expectations that cheating would be met by punishment by other market participants. Similarly, interactions over time may allow firms to develop a reputation for a particular mode of behavior, such as price cutting in response to entry into a market, that can deter potential entrants.

The possibilities for such strategic behavior are greater when there is incomplete information about factors important to the strategy choices of firms. A potential entrant may have incomplete information about the costs of incumbent firms and thus may be reluctant to commit the capital required for entry, since it could turn out that the incumbent firms actually had costs lower than anticipated. Furthermore, incumbent firms may be able to deter entry by signaling that they have low costs even when they have high costs.

---

[21]See Holt and Scheffman (1989) for a discussion of this approach and its implications for antitrust.

The new IO approach is also concerned with the potential for anticompetitive behavior in markets characterized by network externalities and where compatibility and standardization are required. For example, the benefits from standardizing software development on a small number of platforms, such as Microsoft's Windows operating system, can result in the development of market power for the suppliers of the platforms. Similarly, network effects are important in businesses ranging from Internet commerce to credit cards to commercial real estate. In addition to supply-side economies of larger networks, there may also be demand-side increasing returns, as considered in Chapter 13. This generates incentives to compete to develop the largest network, and the winner then has an "essential facility" and hence market power. Moreover, the owner of an essential facility may be able to use it to thwart innovation or block alternative technologies that provide the potential for competition. The threat to Microsoft's dominance of the desktop operating systems market from the Internet and the Java programming language were alleged by the DOJ to have led to anticompetitive practices.

As summarized in Figure 9-3, the new IO perspective on antitrust focuses on the objective of static and dynamic efficiency; thus, it is concerned not only about the performance of markets at a point in time but also about innovation and incentives to develop new products and processes. Most markets are viewed as resilient, although some markets have imperfections such as those due to network externalities. Therefore, although competition and ensuring choice among products are the best protectors of consumers, government intervention may be warranted to ensure that standardization on a particular technology does not lead to market abuse and that incentives and opportunities for innovation are not thwarted. Most markets can be efficient even if there is only a small number of competitors, provided that barriers to entry are low, but other markets may require scrutiny. For example, switching costs and the efficiencies from standardization can make it virtually impossible for a firm with a new technology to enter a market dominated by an incumbent. Easy entry thus cannot be assumed.

The new IO perspective agrees with the Chicago school that market power derives from horizontal considerations but holds that it can be extended through vertical arrangements. For example, the DOJ alleged that Microsoft attempted to extend its market power to the Internet by bundling its Internet browser with its operating system and giving its browser away for free.

The new IO perspective acknowledges that competition with only a few firms can be efficient in a one-time encounter, but it also recognizes that repeated encounters provide an opportunity for implicit collusion. Collusion is more likely the better is the monitoring of the actions of firms. The price fixing cartels in vitamins, lysine, and citric acid are evidence of the ability of firms to collude. The positive empirical relationship between concentration and profits thus could be due to lower costs or to collusion and market power. In examining the likelihood that market power will impair static and dynamic efficiency, the new IO perspective agrees with the Chicago school that the relevant market should be broadly defined.

With respect to antitrust enforcement and policy, the new IO perspective concludes that business practices should be evaluated in terms of their effects on static and dynamic efficiency under the rule of reason except in egregious situations such as price fixing. Individuals can protect themselves when choice is available in the market, but government intervention can be warranted when choice and innovation are stifled through exclusive practices and the exercise of market power.

The new IO approach concludes that there are situations in which firms can employ anticompetitive strategies, as in the case of products that exhibit network externalities or have compatibility and standardization characteristics as well as when implicit collusion can be supported by repeated encounters. The new IO approach has not at this point presented a comprehensive theory of antitrust economics, however. Instead, the approach is a collection of theories about behavior under particular structural and informational conditions.

# Examples of the Differences in Antitrust Thought

## Vertical Arrangements

The principal area in which the structural and Chicago schools have differed is in regard to vertical arrangements. These arrangements take a variety of forms, but most involve restrictions imposed by a manufacturer on the sale or distribution of its products. Because most of these arrangements involve the foreclosure of a market opportunity or a restraint of trade, a number of vertical practices had been held by the courts to be per se illegal. Economic understandings developed by the Chicago school, along with a changed the law on vertical arrangements. Many of the vertical arrangements that had been per se illegal during the 1970s are now considered under a rule of reason. Furthermore, the courts have upheld the use of many of the previously illegal vertical arrangements. These changes have occurred in the absence of new legislation.

Vertical price restrictions had been per se illegal since the Supreme Court decision in *Dr. Miles Medical Co. v. John D. Park & Sons*, 220 U.S. 373 (1911). Nonprice vertical restrictions were not per se illegal, however, until the decision in *U.S. v. Arnold Schwinn & Co.*, 388 U.S. 365 (1967). In Schwinn, the Supreme Court decided that vertical nonprice restrictions on the resale of goods, such as territorial restrictions, restrictions on customers served, refusals to deal, and exclusive dealerships, were per se illegal.

The Chicago school found little logic in the court's reasoning, since from its perspective a vertical arrangement could be harmful to competition only if there were horizontal market power. That is, vertical arrangements do not create market power but can extend market power resulting, for example, from a dominant market position. Indeed, vertical arrangements generally are viewed as tolerable unless there is horizontal market power. When that power is present, vertical arrangements should be judged under a rule of reason.

In reasoning about vertical arrangements, the Chicago school distinguished between *interbrand* and *intrabrand* competition. Intrabrand competition refers to competition between sellers of the same brand, as in the case of two Toyota dealers competing against each other. Those dealers also compete against the sellers of other makes of automobiles—interbrand competition. If interbrand competition is vigorous so that a manufacturer does not have horizontal market power, restrictions on intrabrand competition will have little impact on the efficiency of the market.

Moreover, vertical arrangements that restrict intrabrand competition can make interbrand competition more efficient by, for example, strengthening dealer networks. Competition among stronger networks holds down prices, and stronger dealer networks can reduce costs and better serve consumers on the nonprice dimensions of sales. Restrictions on intrabrand competition can also reduce transaction costs in a firm's channels of distribution, as Williamson (1975) has emphasized.

In addition, the Chicago school argued that competition does not take place only on price. Many products require the provision of information to enable consumers to use the product effectively. Also, many products must be supported with service, both at the time of purchase and later. To provide information and customer service, manufacturers establish dealer networks. The networks, however, are often plagued by the free-rider problem. Customers can visit a dealer to obtain information and then buy from a discount store that offers neither information nor service. Customers then are free riding on the information provided by the licensed dealers. This weakens the dealer network, resulting in less information being provided to consumers. Consumers then may make less-informed decisions, reducing economic efficiency. Indeed, one reason dealers charge a higher price than discount stores is that they must have a margin adequate to cover the costs of a well-trained sales staff and a service facility.

In *Continental TV v. GTE Sylvania*, 433 U.S. 36 (1977), the Supreme Court, influenced by this reasoning, changed the precedent established in *Schwinn*. The court held that nonprice vertical restraints should be considered under a rule of reason. GTE Sylvania, a producer of television sets, had experienced declining sales. By the beginning of the 1960s it had only 1 to 2 percent of the U.S. market. Sylvania distributed its television sets through both company-owned and independent distributors, which supplied retailers. In an attempt to increase its sales, Sylvania changed its method of distribution by eliminating its distributors and selling directly to franchised retailers. Sylvania also required its retailers to sell only from a specified location. This provision allowed Sylvania to control the number of retail outlets in an area. The objective of the changes was to attract a stronger but smaller group of retailers that would have the incentive to promote Sylvania TV sets. The franchised dealers could sell other brands and were not restricted in the prices they could charge.

The change proved successful. Dealers promoted Sylvania sets, increasing its market share to 5 percent by 1965. In 1965 Sylvania decided to authorize a new retailer in San Francisco. Continental TV, a Sylvania dealer there, protested and asked permission to sell Sylvania TVs in Sacramento. Sylvania refused, and Continental decided to sell them there anyway. Sylvania then refused to sell to Continental. Continental sued, and the federal district court, following *Schwinn*, held in its favor. The Court of Appeals reversed the decision and ordered a retrial on the grounds that it did not believe that *Schwinn* was applicable in this case. Continental appealed, and the Supreme Court took the case as an opportunity to reconsider whether vertical arrangements such as the one in question should be per se illegal.

The Supreme Court concluded that "Per se rules of illegality are appropriate only when they relate to conduct that is manifestly anticompetitive." As indicated in *Northern Pacific*, such conduct must have a "pernicious effect on competition" and have no "redeeming virtue." In considering whether this was true of the practice in Sylvania, the court found that "The market impact of vertical restrictions is complex because of their potential for a simultaneous reduction in intrabrand competition and stimulation of interbrand competition. . . ."The court then held that a vertical restriction could not be said a priori to have a pernicious effect on competition or to have no redeeming virtue. Hence, nonprice vertical arrangements were not per se illegal. The court pointed to the possible redeeming virtues stating:

new manufacturers and manufacturers entering new markets can use the restrictions in order to induce competent and aggressive retailers to make the kind of investment of capital and labor that is often required in the distribution of products unknown to the consumer. Established manufacturers can use them to induce retailers to engage in promotional activities or to provide service and repair facilities necessary to the efficient marketing of their products. Service and repair are vital for many products, such as automobiles and major household appliances. The availability and quality of such services affect a manufacturer's good will and the competitiveness of his product. Because of market imperfections such as the so-called "free rider" effect, these services might not be provided by retailers in a purely competitive situation. . . .

The Supreme Court affirmed the decision of the Court of Appeals and thus changed the per se rule of illegality for vertical practices to a rule of reason, reversing what had served as law for the previous 10 years. Since *Sylvania*, most nonprice vertical restrictions have been considered under a rule of reason. The new IO perspective generally agrees with this result, as does the structural perspective.

The Supreme Court followed the *Sylvania* decision with two decisions extending the applicability of the rule of reason in nonprice vertical arrangements. In *Monsanto Co. v. Spray-Rite Service Co.*, 465 U.S. 752 (1984), the court held that terminating a price-cutting dealer after complaints from several other dealers was not a per se violation. In *Business Electronics Corp. v. Sharp Electronics Corp.*, 485 U.S. 717 (1988), the court held that terminating a dealer relationship because another dealer had complained about its price-cutting was not a per se violation unless there had been an agreement between the manufacturer and the complaining retailer. The rationale for these decisions was again that the practices could have the redeeming virtue of strengthening the dealer networks and stimulating interbrand competition and thus should be tried under a rule of reason.

The chapter case, *Apple Computer and Mail-Order Sales*, raises related issues about a nonprice vertical arrangement.

## Predatory Pricing and Entry Deterrence

The traditional perspective on predatory pricing is that a firm can drive a competitor out of a market by cutting prices below costs. A firm with deep pockets can bear the short-term losses from the price cutting, and once the weaker rival is forced from the market, it can set higher prices to recoup its losses. The standard used to determine if a firm is engaging in predatory pricing is whether price is below marginal cost. Marginal cost is not easy for a court to measure, however, so a standard such as average variable cost is often used as the proxy.[22]

The Chicago school's criticism of this view of predatory pricing focuses on its aftermath. Suppose a firm were to engage in predatory pricing and successfully drive a competitor out of the market. Could it then set a higher price than prior to the predation? The answer depends on whether there are barriers to entry in the industry. If there are not, and the Chicago school is skeptical about the presence of barriers to entry, then raising the price will simply attract new entrants. This will force the price down, and the predation will have been for naught. Recognizing this, a firm will not engage in predatory pricing in the first place.

If there were high barriers to entry, a firm could exercise market power. The principal barrier to entry recognized by the Chicago school is due to the sunk costs of incumbent firms. Even those sunk costs, however, are not a long-run deterrent to entry because once an entrant has entered the market, the incumbent firm no longer has a reason to price below long-run costs. The entrant will anticipate this and not be deterred from entering. Also, if an incumbent firm has sunk costs, a competitor already in the market also is likely to have sunk costs. Prices thus would have to be cut below short-run marginal costs to drive out the competitor.[23]

Even if predatory pricing were possible, it may not be desirable to drive a smaller competitor from the market. An industry leader would have to incur losses on a larger volume of sales. Predation in this case might not be in the interest of an industry leader, even though the industry had barriers to entry.

---

22 See Areeda and Turner (1975).

23 This argument would not hold if an incumbent had a cost advantage over a competitor or a potential entrant. The incumbent then could set a price just low enough that the potential entrant would stay out of the market. In this case, the threat of potential entry limits the incumbent firm's ability to increase its price but does not necessarily force the price down to the costs of the most efficient producer.

The conclusion of the Chicago school is that predation is unlikely to be successful, so it will not be attempted. The price cutting observed in markets is instead likely to be the result of competition rather than of predation. Applying antitrust law to alleged predation thus would discourage firms from competing on price, resulting in higher prices.

Research from the new IO perspective, however, casts some doubt on these conclusions. One theory of potential entry is based on the recognition that a potential entrant may not know whether an incumbent firm has a cost advantage. Because of this incomplete information about the incumbent's costs, the incumbent may be able to signal that it has low costs, even though its costs are actually high. The incumbent can do this by setting a price equal to the average of what a low-cost and a high-cost incumbent firm would choose. This pricing strategy can deter some entry that would be desirable from the perspective of economic efficiency.[24]

Another theory developed from the new IO perspective indicates that an incumbent firm may have an incentive to engage in predatory pricing in several geographic or product markets so as to develop a reputation as a "tough" competitor, thus discouraging entry by new firms.[25] The development of such a reputation hinges on the incomplete information of potential entrants about, for example, the costs of the incumbent firm. A reputation for toughness, then, may deter entry into a market even if no real barriers to entry are present. In the supermarket industry Safeway developed a reputation as a tough competitor, which, according to some economists, deters entry.

Whatever the appropriate economic theory of predatory behavior, antitrust scrutiny of price cutting poses a serious concern. In practice it is difficult to distinguish between vigorous price competition and predatory pricing. Even in a competitive industry, prices can rise and fall in response to shifts in demand, and when entry occurs, prices will adjust as other firms change their outputs or exit the industry. Applying antitrust law in situations in which prices are being cut could stifle price competition. For example, new entrants may set low prices to build market share and utilize their capacity efficiently. Precluding an incumbent firm from responding to those prices would restrain competition and possibly prevent output from being produced at the lowest possible industry cost.

As an example, in 1992 American Airlines revamped its pricing by grouping fares into four classes, and it then cut full-fare prices substantially. Continental and Northwest filed an antitrust suit under the Sherman Act charging that American was trying to drive them out of the market with predatory prices and then use its increased market power to raise prices. The plaintiffs asked for damages of $1 billion, which would be trebled in the event of a guilty verdict. Robert Crandall, CEO of American, said that Continental and Northwest were "hoping to accomplish in the courtroom what they couldn't accomplish in the marketplace." A jury acquitted American.

As another example, in the chapter case, *The Microsoft Antitrust Case*, the court did not conclude that Microsoft's decision to give away its Internet Explorer (IE) browser for free was anticompetitive, even though that decision was a major blow to its rival Netscape. Its Navigator browser was selling at $15 to $20 a copy to licensees, and Netscape was forced to set its price to zero. Pricing IE at zero, which is its marginal cost, is economically efficient. The court concluded that a price of zero benefited consumers, and the competition to win in the browser market stimulated substantial improvements in browser quality, also benefiting consumers. Pricing at zero in this case was not predatory.

---

[24]See Milgrom and Roberts (1982) for a development of this theory.
[25]See Kreps and Wilson (1982) for a development of this theory.

# Collusion and Price-Fixing

All schools of thought agree that collusion and horizontal price fixing are anticompetitive, and the DOJ has vigorously prosecuted price fixing and obtained large fines, criminal convictions, and prison sentences for those found guilty. The schools, however, disagree about how likely it is that collusive arrangements can be sustained.

The structural perspective on collusion and price fixing is that firms will collude when possible, so tight antitrust supervision is necessary. The Chicago school, however, points to historical evidence indicating that cartels broke down as a result of cheating by their own members. Furthermore, the larger the number of firms that are required to collude, the more difficult it is to prevent cheating and defection. For collusion to be sustained, the colluders must have a means of detecting cheating, as in the case of bidding on government contracts when the bids are publicly reported.

The new IO approach, however, reaches a different conclusion. Because firms in the same industry will be in competition over time, firms have a broad set of strategies that could sustain implicit collusion.[26] A firm that believes that another firm is cheating on an implicit agreement to maintain high prices can punish that firm by lowering its own price. If the second firm is confident that the first firm indeed has an incentive to punish any perceived cheating, the second firm will have no incentive to cheat in the first place. The threat of punishment in repeated encounters thus can, in principle, enforce high prices even when there is neither an explicit agreement nor communication among the firms. Price-cutting thus could be a means of punishing deviations from implicit collusion rather than an indication of either vigorous competition or predation.

## Mergers and Merger Guidelines

Mergers can create horizontal market power or restrain competition in supply or distribution channels. The passage of the Celler-Kefauver Act in 1950 decreased the number of mergers, but when the Reagan administration took office in 1981 it signaled that it did not view mergers with the same hostility as had prior administrations. Indeed, mergers were viewed as potentially beneficial to efficiency and competition. Mergers can yield cost efficiencies and synergies that benefit consumers. Mergers can also remove bad management and eliminate inefficient cross-subsidization of one line of business by another.

To provide guidance to firms about when it was likely to initiate an antitrust investigation, the DOJ issued revised merger guidelines in 1982.[27] The FTC issued similar guidelines, and in 1992 the agencies jointly issued updated guidelines.[28] The guidelines reflect both structural and Chicago school perspectives by identifying where market power may be present and whether it can be exercised. The guidelines also reflect the new IO perspective with respect to the dynamics of competition. In contrast to the structural perspective, the guidelines do not assume that market power automatically will be exercised. Market power is viewed as a horizontal concept, and nonhorizontal mergers, either vertical or conglomerate, do not affect market concentration and so are not necessarily a threat to competition. Nonhorizontal mergers are a concern only to the extent that they have horizontal consequences, such as eliminating a potential entrant.

The merger guidelines identify collusion as the means to the exercise of market power. The exercise of market power requires a restriction of output to increase prices

[26] See Green and Porter (1984) for a presentation and empirical test of this theory.
[27] See Ordover and Willig (1983) for an evaluation of the DOJ merger guidelines.
[28] Department of Justice and Federal Trade Commission, Horizontal Merger Guidelines, Washington, DC, April 2, 1992.

and profits. Since the smaller is a firm's market share, the more it has to restrict output to achieve a given price increase, unless a firm has a dominant market position collusion must be the means to the exercise of market power. In accord with the Chicago school's perspective, the greater the number of firms that would have to collude to restrict output, the more likely collusion is to break down. Collusion is easier the more homogeneous the product, since then there is only one dimension of competition that must be monitored under an explicit or implicit collusive arrangement. Collusion is more difficult when substitutes are available in the relevant markets and is easier when repeated encounters provide an opportunity to punish cheating on the collusive arrangement.

In its definition of the relevant market, the DOJ and FTC focus on "economically meaningful" markets. These are defined in terms of products and geographic areas in which a firm could restrict output and thereby increase price above prevailing levels. To do so, a firm would have to have horizontal market power. Assessing market power involves consideration of substitute products, since an attempt to raise prices may cause consumers to switch to a substitute. It also takes into account imports and the resale market for durable goods.

To assess the potential for achieving price increases in the case of horizontal mergers, the DOJ and FTC use the Herfindahl-Hirschman index (HHI) to measure concentration in an industry. The HHI is defined as the sum of the squares of the market shares of firms, or

$$HHI = \sum_{i=1}^{n} s_i^2,$$

where $n$ is the number of firms in the industry and $s_i$ is the market share of the $i^{th}$ firm expressed as a percent. The HHI is zero for a perfectly competitive industry and is 10,000 for a monopoly. If two firms with 10 percent market shares merge, the HHI increases by 200. For an industry with 10 firms with equal market shares, the HHI is 1,000, and for an industry with two firms with 30 percent shares and eight firms with 5 percent shares, the HHI is 2,000.

The merger guidelines state that the agencies will not challenge a merger in which the postmerger HHI is below 1,000. They are unlikely to challenge a merger in which the postmerger HHI is between 1,000 and 1,800 (six equal-sized firms) unless the merger would increase the HHI by more than 100. In the case of an industry with an HHI above 1,800, they are unlikely to investigate if the merger increases the HHI by less than 50, and are likely to investigate if the HHI increases by at least 100. The agencies, however, will take into account other factors that affect market power or its exercise.

In 2004 the FTC reported on its merger enforcement actions in industries other than grocery, oil, chemicals, and pharmaceuticals. Table 9-1 reports the enforcement data, where "Closed" means that

**TABLE 9-1  Horizontal Merger Enforcement 1996–2003**

|  | Increase in HHI 0–299 | Increase in HHI 300 or more |
|---|---|---|
| Postmerger HHI 0–2399 | Enforced: 0  Closed: 6 | Enforced: 3  Closed: 16 |
| Postmerger HHI 2400 or more | Enforced: 2  Closed: 7 | Enforced: 183  Closed: 45 |

Kovacic, and Baker (2004) reports the enforcement data, where "Closed" means that no action was taken by the FTC and "Enforced" means that some antitrust action was taken. The data indicate that concentration, and particularly the increase in concentration, plays a central role in enforcement decisions.

The use of the HHI requires identification of the relevant market for determining shares. One approach is to identify the scope of substitutes for the product. Another approach is to use data to identify which products compete with others. This approach was used by the FTC in the chapter case, *The Staples–Office Depot Merger?*[29] Using product price data, the court defined the relevant market as office supply superstores, and since there were only three superstores, the HHI was high. Moreover, the HHI would increase substantially if two superstores merged.

A merger, however, can result in greater efficiency, and in 1997 the FTC issued a revision to the merger guidelines. The FTC identified the potential efficiencies from a merger and stated that the efficiencies considered should be net of the efficiencies that would have been realized in the absence of a merger. The FTC also stated that any efficiency claims must be verifiable and substantiated. It also stated that efficiencies would likely carry little weight if the merger were to create a monopoly or near-monopoly. The efficiency considerations played an important role in *The Staples–Office Depot* case.

In addition to the structural factors involving market concentration, the antitrust agencies take into account technological change and the rate of innovation in an industry. In an industry that experiences rapid technological change, a large market share of merging companies may be of little concern because market share can be won or lost relatively quickly. Similar reasoning led to dropping the government's antitrust suit against IBM.

The antitrust enforcement agencies frequently negotiate with merging companies under the "fix-it-first" approach in which areas of antitrust concern are fixed prior to a merger being consummated. For example, in 2004 after initially opposing it, the FTC approved the merger between Nestlé and Dreyer's Grand Ice Cream after potentially anticompetitive features had been fixed. Dreyer's sold three of its brands, and Nestlé sold its U.S. distribution assets. Similarly, in 1996 the FTC required Ciba-Geigy and Sandoz to sell part of their gene-therapy technology as a condition for their merger to form Novartis.

In 2000 AOL and Time Warner announced a merger that the FTC delayed because of concerns about anticompetitive effects. After nearly a year of negotiations to fix the concerns, the companies and the FTC agreed to a consent order that allowed the merger to be completed. AOL Time Warner agreed to make Earthlink's ISP service available to subscribers on Time Warner's cable system before AOL could offer its broadband ISP service. AOL Time Warner also agreed not to discriminate against independent ISPs and not to price discriminate on DSL service provided to subscribers and competing services unless there were cost differences.

Mergers often come under the jurisdictions of other countries. The European Union approved the AOL Time Warner merger with the stipulation that Bertelsmann AG withdraw from a joint venture in Europe in which AOL's CompuServe and Vivendi SA participated. In 2001 the United States also approved a merger between General Electric and Honeywell after the companies agreed to some minor fixes. The European Union, however, rejected the merger, causing the companies to abandon their merger plans. This decision is considered in more detail in Chapter 15.

Antitrust enforcement has also been active in health care industries. The FTC blocked the four largest pharmaceutical wholesalers from merging into two companies. The FTC also blocked several mergers of hospitals in small towns where the merger would have reduced competition substantially, even though cost reductions would have been realized through the consolidations.

[29]See also Baker (1997) and Dalkir and Warren-Boulton (1999) for analyses of the Staples–Office Depot case.

## Compliance

Compliance with the antitrust laws involves both procedures and policy. Firms provide training and guidance to employees who may encounter situations in which antitrust concerns are present. For example, in its Standards of Business Conduct, Hewlett-Packard provides guidance on trade practices (vertical arrangements), price discrimination, unfair practices, and competitor relations (horizontal practices). Cisco Systems requires employees to watch an antitrust primer on its Web site. Companies with dominant market positions restrain their competitive practices and language. Cisco and Intel do not use the term *leveraging,* as in leveraging from a dominant position.

A firm may find itself in a situation in which a contemplated practice falls in an area in which the antitrust laws and the court decisions interpreting them are unclear or changing. In addition to seeking the advice of counsel, the firm should examine whether the purpose of its practice is anticompetitive. In *Sylvania* the court held that the policy of territorial restrictions served the purpose of stimulating interbrand competition. In such a case a firm should use a practice that is the least restrictive in achieving the desired purpose. On retrial the court acquitted GTE-Sylvania because it concluded that the practice of terminating a dealer that violated its policy was the least restrictive means of achieving the intended purpose of strengthening its dealer network. Hewlett-Packard's policy on terminating relationships reflects the decisions in *Sylvania, Monsanto,* and *Sharp* as well as the remaining ambiguity: "Terminating relationships with customers can lead to litigation. It is therefore important that the decision to terminate be made carefully and for valid business reasons. HP's Legal Department should be consulted before terminating any such relationship without the customer's consent. Possible termination of one customer's contract should not be discussed with another customer."[30]

## The Politics of Antitrust

Antitrust policy has important distributive as well as efficiency consequences for firms and consumers, so it is the subject of nonmarket action.[31] In the 1970s the FTC adopted an aggressive posture and initiated several new investigations, some of which were directed at such politically influential industries as insurance and funeral homes. The resulting political pressure on Congress led it to pass the Federal Trade Commission Improvements Act of 1980, which reined in the FTC.[32] The framework for nonmarket analysis presented in Part II of this book provides the basis for analyzing the politics of antitrust policy.

Most proposed changes in the antitrust laws fail because of the intensity of the ensuing politics and the complexity of the issues. In 1986 the Reagan administration proposed amending Section 7 of the Clayton Act (which deals with mergers) by replacing "may be" and "tend to" with "significant probability." It also proposed relaxing merger standards for firms that had been injured by foreign competition. Because of a concern that private antitrust lawsuits were being used to stifle competition, the administration proposed eliminating treble damages except for price-fixing violations. The FTC and the Reagan administration also proposed that the FTC

---

[30]Hewlett-Packard Company, "Standards of Business Conduct," Palo Alto, CA, 1989.
[31]See Shugart (1990) for a perspective on antitrust and interest group politics.
[32]See Weingast and Moran (1983), Moe (1985), and Wilson (1989, Chap. 13) for differing perspectives on the relationship between the FTC and Congress.

authority over unfair advertising be eliminated, because the term *unfair* was too vague to be enforced. None of these initiatives was successful.

Democrats in Congress have also sought revisions in the antitrust laws, attempting to counter DOJ and FTC decisions to stop bringing suits for certain vertical restraints. They also attempted to revise the standards established by the Supreme Court in *Monsanto* and *Sharp* involving nonprice vertical arrangements. In 1991, for example, the Senate passed a bill that would make it easier to win cases against retail price maintenance practices. Both activist groups and discounters who had been cut off by manufacturers backed the bill, arguing that consumers were injured by the nonprice arrangements. They were opposed by manufacturers and specialty retailers, who viewed vertical arrangements as promoting interbrand competition. The bill failed.

In 1998, 25 state attorneys general threatened antitrust actions against major airlines for predatory pricing and launched an investigation of three alliances formed by the six largest airlines.[33] The Clinton administration had proposed guidelines that specified when action would be taken against a major airline for driving a low-cost competitor out of a market by lowering prices and providing more seats on routes. The administration reported that fares for last-minute travel had skyrocketed and that the number of cities served by more than two airlines had fallen by 41 percent in less than 10 years. The airlines countered with a lobbying and public advocacy campaign charging that the Clinton administration was attempting to re-regulate the airline industry. One airline hired a former Clinton administration official who argued there was no basis for intervention in the industry. The airlines increased their political contributions by 66 percent in the 1997–1998 election cycle and backed a bill in Congress that would have delayed for at least a year the implementation of any guidelines. The House Transportation Committee rejected the bill in favor of requiring notification by the Clinton administration before any guidelines were implemented. No guidelines were issued.

The politics of antitrust also manifests itself in legislative action seeking exemptions or providing for affirmative defenses in antitrust suits. For decades the soft drink industry had been organized around exclusive territories for its distributors. Soft drink manufacturers produced syrup, which was sold to bottlers that were allowed to distribute the soft drink only in a specified geographic area. In 1971 the FTC issued complaints against seven national-brand soft drink syrup manufacturers, including Coca-Cola, PepsiCo, Seven-Up, and Canada Dry. The complaints charged that exclusive territorial distributorships were illegal vertical restraints of trade. With the strong support of the National Soft Drink Association, in 1972 a bill was introduced in the Senate to permit exclusive territorial arrangements for soft drink manufacturers.

The FTC complaint was resolved in 1978 when the FTC ruled that the exclusive distributorships were anticompetitive. The decision was appealed and was still before the courts when Congress finally acted. After 10 years of effort, the soft drink manufacturers and their bottlers succeeded in 1980 in obtaining an effective antitrust exemption. The Soft Drink Interbrand Competition Act provided protection from antitrust suits if soft drinks were in "substantial and effective competition." Despite opposition by the DOJ, the bill passed the Senate on an 86 to 6 vote, passed the House on a voice vote, and was signed by President Carter.[34]

[33] *The New York Times*, July 25, 1998.
[34] The case, *The Malt Beverage Interbrand Competition Act*, in Baron (1996) considers the beer industry's unsuccessful attempt to obtain similar protection.

# Summary

The principal antitrust laws are the Sherman Act, the Clayton Act, and the Federal Trade Commission Act. The Sherman Act pertains to monopolization and restraints of trade. The Clayton Act addresses monopolization and restraints of trade in their incipiency and provides the basis for government authority over mergers. The act also restricts price discrimination. The Federal Trade Commission Act prohibits unfair competition and unfair and deceptive acts.

Both the DOJ and the FTC have enforcement responsibilities for the Sherman and Clayton Acts, but only the FTC can enforce the FTC Act. Considerable enforcement of the antitrust laws occurs through private lawsuits, most of which are filed by one firm against another. Private lawsuits are encouraged by the prospect of treble damages.

Antitrust enforcement and court decisions are influenced by schools of thought about the role of antitrust policy and the likelihood of adverse economic consequences from business practices. The structural approach is based on the structure-conduct-performance paradigm and focuses on the structure of industries and on practices that may foreclose opportunities for competitors. The Chicago school focuses on economic efficiency and consumer prices and views markets as both resilient and the consumer's best protection. Both the structural approach and the Chicago school view horizontal market power as a concern but differ about how likely collusion is and how substantial are barriers to entry. The Chicago school concludes that most practices should be considered under a rule of reason, whereas the structural approach supports a broader application of the per se standard. The new industrial organization perspective emphasizes the strategic interactions among competitors that can result from repeated interactions and incomplete information. These strategic interactions have the potential to sustain implicit collusion and limit entry into industries. This perspective also focuses on factors such as network externalities and standardization that can provide the basis for anticompetitive practices.

These schools of thought have influenced the thinking of government antitrust officials and judges. In the case of vertical arrangements and maximum price restrictions, the courts reversed earlier decisions in holding that those practices are no longer per se illegal but are to be considered under a rule of reason. Certain arrangements that enhance interbrand competition but harm intrabrand competition have been held by the courts to be legal under the antitrust laws.

The DOJ and FTC have applied revised guidelines to the surveillance of mergers. The guidelines are based both on industry structure and on the likelihood that market power can be exercised. The government has used a fix-it-first approach to reduce the anticompetitive effects of mergers that otherwise would produce efficiencies.

Antitrust policy has important distributive consequences and so is the subject of considerable political activity. The complexity of the issues, however, makes significant legislative changes in the antitrust laws difficult to achieve.

# Apple Computer and Mail-Order Sales

Apple Computer Corporation started the personal computer industry. At first most of its sales were to hobbyists. As the market began to develop, Apple shifted its emphasis to home computers. By 1981, however, the market changed again as business and professional demand began to grow. The personal computer industry had been born, and in 1981 Apple was the market leader. Apple faced competition from several firms, including Compaq, Radio Shack, Sinclair, and Commodore. IBM was expected to enter the market with its own personal computer in the near future.

The distribution channel had become increasingly important as the market evolved to the personal computer phase. Apple computers were sold primarily through its 1,100 dealers, and dealers sold both over the counter and by mail order. Mail-order sales were generally made to knowledgeable buyers who did not need point-of-purchase information about the selection of a computer and to customers located in areas with no Apple dealers.

At the end of 1981 Apple decided to emphasize personal service. It changed its distribution policy, no longer allowing sales that could not be supported with both maintenance and personal service. The policy change meant that telephone and mail-order sales would no longer be permitted. Apple sent out amended contracts to its dealers and included a letter explaining its new policy. In the letter, Apple Vice President Fred Hoar wrote, "Mail-order sales are neither suited to providing the consumer education that emerging markets require, nor are they structured to provide the customer satisfaction that has become associated with the Apple name." Hoar added that no exceptions would be made.

Most Apple dealers reacted favorably to the policy. They faced the problem of customers coming in to their stores, obtaining the information needed to make an educated choice, and then buying by mail order to save money. The suggested list price for an Apple III computer was $3,495, and

Apple dealers could sell it at any price they wished. Some mail-order houses sold it for $2,800. Apple sold the computer to dealers for $2,325 when they made multiple-unit purchases. Edward E. Faber, president of the 182-store ComputerLand system, which sold Apple computers at the suggested list price, welcomed the change in policy. "It's discouraging to do all the presale education and support of a prospective customer, and then have him buy the equipment somewhere else." Faber said that it cost about $150,000 to open a store that provided sales support and maintenance. "If the dealer makes that kind of investment, he must get a return on the sale of the product," he explained. Losing sales to mail-order houses reduced the incentive to provide the service that Apple desired.

Joseph Sidney, owner of Micro Business World of Tarzana, California, said Apple's new policy "stinks" and was "an outright effort to fix prices." He maintained that the mail-order houses adequately educated customers about the choice of a computer and provided sufficient service. Joseph Monroe of Consumer Computers of San Diego said that 75 percent of his $6 million sales were by mail order and Apple's new policy would put him out of business. The mail-order houses argued that Apple was adopting the policy because its dealers were pressuring it to do so.

Mail-order sales of Apple computers were also made by nondealers such as New York's 47th Street Photo, which sold 3,000 Apples a year. Nondealers would not reveal where they obtained their computers, but it was generally understood that they purchased them from Apple dealers that had over-purchased.

One of the most vocal critics of Apple's policy was Francis Ravel, owner of Olympic Sales Company of Los Angeles. "There are about 150 black sheep like us. All we want to do is buy and sell and be left alone . . . They can't tell us not to ship from our store. Hewlett-Packard wouldn't dare do that." Ravel filed a suit in federal district court in

Los Angeles charging that Apple's policy violated federal antitrust law. Ravel asked for a preliminary injunction. Apple described the suit as "completely without merit."

Steve Jobs, cofounder and chairman of Apple, said, "What we're doing is the state of the art in antitrust law. We could go all the way to the Supreme Court." He added, "It's not discounting that bothers us. It's the smile—or rather, the lack of it—on our customer's face when service isn't adequate."  ∎

### PREPARATION QUESTIONS

1. What sections of the antitrust laws pertain to Apple's new policy? What case law is applicable? Is this a per se offense, or will the case be governed by a rule of reason?
2. On whom is the burden of proof, and what does that party have to show?
3. What defense should Apple use?
4. What decision should the court make?

# The Staples–Office Depot Merger?

On September 4, 1996, Staples, the fast-growing No. 2 office supply retailer, agreed to buy Office Depot, the industry leader, in a transaction valued at $3.36 billion. Staples and Office Depot were among the pioneers that a decade earlier developed the successful concept of office supply superstores. By pursuing aggressive marketing strategies, charging low prices, and leveraging their buying power and efficient mass supply channels to cut costs, the companies created a profitable, rapidly growing industry. Staples had the second largest superstore chain in the United States with approximately 550 stores in 28 states, $3 billion annual revenues, and net income of $74 million. With more than 500 stores in 38 states, Office Depot had the largest sales, approximately $5.3 billion, and net income of $132 million. The only other office supply superstore chain was OfficeMax.

The companies identified significant cost reductions as the main reason for the merger. Thomas Stemberg, chairman and CEO of Staples, said, for example, that the two companies bought envelopes from three separate vendors. "We'd entertain proposals from all three," he said, "and we'd say, you can have all of the business or none of it."[35] Stemberg also commented on the combined entity's ability to pass through the savings to customers: "Both Staples and Office Depot were founded a decade ago to bring savings to purchasers of office products. The combined company, with over $10 billion in revenues, will be able to offer even greater value to our customers through increasing operating efficiency and purchasing scale."[36]

The companies, as well as commentators, anticipated from the outset that the transaction would raise antitrust concerns: "The merged organization—with 1,100 stores in 96 percent of the country's largest metropolitan areas—will reduce the number of distributors for manufacturers, giving them less bargaining power. The deal is also likely to draw close scrutiny from the U.S. antitrust regulators."[37] David Fuente, chairman and CEO of Office Depot, stressed both that the companies did not compete with each other in many geographical areas and that the market was much larger than the merged companies. Fuente said, "The reality today is that there's very little overlap in our store base and geographical locations, and two or three years from now that might not be the case if both companies continue to grow at the pace that we were predicting."[38] Fuente also stated, "Our new company operates in an office products industry which is very large, highly fragmented

[35]*The Wall Street Journal*, September 5, 1996.

[36]*Business Wire*, September 4, 1996.
[37]*The Wall Street Journal*, September 5, 1996.
[38]*The Wall Street Journal*, September 5, 1996.

and growing rapidly. As a result of this strategic combination, we will be better positioned to participate fully in the enormous growth opportunities that exist in our industry."[39] Juris Pagrabs, vice president of Investor Relations of OfficeMax, the third largest office supply superstore chain, offered a positive view on the announced merger: "We think the merger is quite good for the industry. It's better to have two players instead of three."[40]

The Federal Trade Commission (FTC) did not share this view. The FTC contended that the overall expected effect of the proposed merger on customers would be negative, since it expected the merger to reduce competition significantly in many markets. Underlying this contention was a claim that the expected pass-through to customers of the efficiencies created by the merger would not be large enough to offset the effect of the reduction in competition. The issue thus revolved around the assessment of the expected economic consequences of the planned merger. To assess these effects, verbal pronouncements such as "reduction in competition," "respective market," and "efficiencies that pass-through to customers" had to be reduced to quantifiable measures.

## The Antitrust Review

Following the procedure required by Hart-Scott-Rodino, Staples and Office Depot filed a Premerger Notification and Report Form with the FTC and the Department of Justice on October 2, 1996. This was followed by a 7-month investigation by the FTC, in which additional information was requested from the companies, hundreds of boxes of documents were examined, depositions of 18 officers and employees of both Staples and Office Depot were taken, and (ex parte) discovery of third-party information was made. The FTC voted 4 to 1 to challenge the merger.

In an attempt to satisfy the FTC's objections, Staples and Office Depot negotiated a consent decree with the FTC staff that would allow the merger if the companies would sell 63 stores to OfficeMax for $109 million to reduce the concentration in those local markets. The FTC, however, in a shock to the companies, rejected the negotiated consent decree by a vote of 3 to 2, and in a revision of its merger guidelines it expressed skepticism about projected cost efficiencies from mergers that

cannot "be verified by reasonable means." The FTC then filed a motion with the District Court of the District of Columbia on April 9, 1997, seeking a preliminary injunction to block the merger. The matter thus was for the court to decide.

## The Court's Review

In deciding whether to issue a preliminary injunction, the court required the FTC to show (1) that its challenge was likely to succeed on the merits after complete consideration of the facts, and (2) that in "balancing the equities" it was of greater harm to let the transaction proceed and later try to reverse it than to enjoin it until the review process reached its final conclusion. Since the preliminary proceedings raised the key issues that would be raised in the complete review process, the hearing on the preliminary injunction would in effect resolve the entire case. The findings of fact by the court would determine whether those conditions were satisfied.[41]

## Likelihood of Success on the Merits

### The Geographic Market

There was no dispute that the appropriate geographic market was 42 metropolitan areas in which Staples and Office Depot competed with each other prior to the merger agreement, as well as several areas in which they planned to begin competing in the near future.

### The Product Market

The court defined the product market for antitrust purposes as "the sale of consumable office supplies through office superstores," thereby accepting the FTC's claim that although the products Staples and Office Depot sold had perfect functional substitutes sold at other stores such as Wal-Mart, the market should be viewed as office superstores only. The court based its conclusion on pricing data.

The FTC compared Staples' prices in geographic markets in which Staples was the only office superstore (termed one-firm markets) with markets in which it competed with Office Depot or OfficeMax (two-firm markets), or both (three-firm markets).

---

[39] *Business Wire*, September 4, 1996.
[40] *The Wall Street Journal*, September 5, 1996.

[41] These findings were based on the public version of the decision. The court examined specific price data submitted by the parties in classified documents. The public version of these documents, as well as the decision, withheld all these data.

Prices in one-firm markets were, on average, 13 percent higher than in three-firm markets.[42] Prices were compared at one point in time (January 1997), and they were based on a sample accounting for 90 percent of Staples's sales. Additional, less comprehensive data showed that average prices were well over 5 percent higher in one-firm markets than in two-firm markets. Based on the merger guidelines, price differences of 5 percent or more were viewed by the court as indirect evidence that office supply superstores were a distinct product market for antitrust purposes. The FTC presented similar evidence regarding Office Depot's prices based on a sample of 500 items (also from January 1997). Prices in Office Depot–only markets were on average well over 5 percent higher than they were in three-firm markets. Additional data showed that on average Office Depot's prices were highest in its one-firm markets and lowest in its three-firm markets.

The FTC also had to determine if the office superstores represented a largely independent market or were part of a much broader office supply market of which the companies had only a 5.5 percent market share. To do this, the FTC considered the cross elasticity of demand between products in the superstore market and their functional substitutes in the broader markets. (The cross elasticity of demand is the percentage change in the demand for one product divided by the percentage change in the price of another product.)

Retail and discount chains other than office superstores carried consumable office supplies (functional substitutes), and the court identified the set of other sellers as Wal-Mart, Kmart, and Target; wholesale clubs such as BJ's and Price Costco; computer and electronic stores such as Computer City and Best Buy; independent retail office supply stores; mail-order firms; and contract stationers. The court concluded that "these competitors, albeit present in every one of [the superstores' markets]." Despite this fact, Staples and Office Depot were able to charge higher prices in their one-firm markets than they did in their two- and three-firm markets. The court found a lower price sensitivity to the existence of other superstore competitors. For example, Staples maintained a "warehouse-club-only" price zone, which was a zone where it competed with a warehouse club but not with other

superstores. The data the FTC presented showed average variation in prices of only 1 to 2 percent between warehouse-club-only zones and one-firm markets; that is, the cross-elasticity of demand was low, suggesting that the stores were not competing in the same market. These findings led the court to conclude that the office superstore market was distinguishable from other markets for consumable office supplies and should thus be considered the relevant market for antitrust purposes.

### Perceptions and Behavior of Market Participants

The court also based its definition of the product market on several additional considerations. First, in all of their internal documents and communications, both Staples and Office Depot viewed the relevant competitive market as comprised of office superstores only. For example, when determining whether to enter a new metropolitan area, both companies repeatedly referred to markets without office superstores as "noncompetitive," regardless of the existence of other sellers of office supplies. Staples used the phrase "office superstore industry" in strategic planning documents. In a monthly report entitled "Competitor Store Opening/Closing Report," which it circulated to its Executive Committee, Office Depot reported all competitor store closings and openings, but the only competitors referred to were Staples and OfficeMax.

Also, both companies price checked the other superstores much more frequently and extensively than they price checked other retail outlets. Executives of nonsuperstore competitors, who were summoned to testify by the FTC, were aware of the distinct nature of the superstore market. The court concluded that Staples and Office Depot considered the other superstores as their primary competition.

### Cost Differentials

Staples and Office Depot offered two cost explanations for the average price differentials between one-, two-, and three-firm markets. The first explanation was that there were differences in wages and rents across localities. These differences, however, were not correlated with the price differences across localities, so the court rejected this explanation.

The second explanation was related to differences in advertising and marketing costs. Indeed, these costs were higher, on average, in one-firm markets than in two- and three-firm markets. Yet, the court found that the differences in costs were

---

[42]These price data had been submitted by the companies.

too small to account for the significant price differentials shown by the FTC. The court rejected the second explanation as well.

### Distinctive Features

The court also distinguished between the superstores and other distribution channels in terms of appearance, physical size, format, variety of items offered, and the type and character of targeted and served customers. The court concluded that "office supply superstores look far different from other sellers of office supplies . . . No one entering a Wal-Mart would mistake it for an office superstore."

## The Probable Effect on Competition

### Concentration

Once the relevant product market had been defined, the concentration analysis was straightforward. The court examined the concentration within each identified geographic market. The HHIs in many of the geographic markets were at "problematic levels" even before the merger. The least concentrated market had an HHI of 3,597, and the most concentrated had 6,944. In contrast, if the merger were completed, the least concentrated market would have an HHI of 5,003, and many areas would have an HHI of 10,000 (i.e., monopoly). The merger guidelines stated that unless mitigated by other factors, an increase in the HHI in excess of 50 in a postmerger, highly concentrated market raised significant competitive concerns. The average increase in the HHI caused by the Staples–Office Depot merger would have been 2,715 points. The court also examined concentration statistics. The merged Staples–Office Depot was expected to hold a dominant market share in 42 geographic markets across the country. In 15 markets the combined market share would be 100 percent.

The court's definition of the relevant product market had, in effect, determined the concentration issue. If the product market had been defined more broadly as, for example, "consumable office supplies," the concentration figures would have been much lower. The product market definition had a similar effect on the consideration of entry.

### Entry

The court assessed the existence and significance of barriers to entry with respect to the relevant market. Staples and Office Depot claimed that the rapid growth in overall office supply sales had encour-

aged, and would continue to encourage, expansion and entry. They pointed to the fact that all office superstore entrants had entered within the last 11 years. They also offered testimony regarding the general ability of mass merchandisers of various types to change store configurations and shift shelf space to accommodate new demands. Yet, the FTC showed that new superstore entrants did not survive as self-sustaining businesses. The number of office superstore chains dropped from 23 to 3 over the few years preceding 1997. All but Staples, Office Depot, and OfficeMax had either closed or been acquired. The failed office superstore entrants included large, well-known retailers such as Kmart, Montgomery Ward, Ames, and Zayles.

The court determined that a "new office superstore would need to open a large number of stores nationally to achieve the purchasing and distribution economies of scale enjoyed by the three existing firms." The court thus found that it would be extremely unlikely that a new office superstore would enter the market and thereby lessen the anticompetitive effects of the proposed merger.

The court also concluded that even in one-firm markets no retailer had successfully expanded its consumable office supplies to the extent that it constrained superstore pricing increases to less than 5 percent. Entry into the relevant market was therefore rejected as a factor likely to offset the merger's expected anticompetitive effects.

### Efficiencies

Staples and Office Depot submitted an Efficiencies Analysis that predicted that the combined business would achieve savings of between $4.9 and $6.5 billion over the first 5 years. The companies also claimed that additional dynamic efficiencies would result because the superstores' suppliers would become more efficient as a result of the increase in their sales to the combined business. Staples and Office Depot argued that two-thirds of the cost savings would be passed along to consumers.

The court, however, found these figures to be inflated and unreliable and preferred the evidence and expert testimony the FTC provided. First, the court noted that the estimates provided by the companies exceeded by almost 500 percent the figures that were presented to the two boards of directors in September 1996, when they approved the transaction, and which had been disclosed to the companies' shareholders and the SEC in the Joint Proxy Statement/Prospectus of January 1997. Second, the companies estimated only the overall savings that the merger was expected to yield and did not deduct the savings both companies would generate as standalone entities if the merger did not materialize. Third, large parts of the argued savings were unverifiable—the companies' experts could not provide figures and explicit methods of calculation to justify the projections.

The court also found the companies' projected pass-through of savings to customers in the form of lower prices to be unrealistic. The court did not find a convincing argument for the combined business to increase significantly its pass-through rate to two-thirds from the historical pass-through rate of 15 to 17 percent established by the evidence.[43]

### Pricing Practices

The court used the historical pass-through rate as an indication of the likely future rate. In a similar manner, as an indication of the likely future behavior and practices of the combined entity, the court used the historical pricing practices of the two companies, which had been established in identifying the relevant product market. This further supported the likely anti-competitive effects of the merger: "The evidence of the defendants' own current pricing practices, for example, shows that an office superstore chain facing no competition from other superstores has the ability to profitably raise prices for consumable office supplies above competitive levels . . . Since prices are significantly lower in markets where Staples and Office Depot compete, eliminating this competition with one another would free the parties to charge higher prices in those markets, especially those in

which the combined entity would be the sole office superstore." The court concluded that the FTC had shown that its case was likely to succeed on its merits. The court then considered the equities.

### Balance of Equities

The court concluded that "Unscrambling the eggs' after the fact is not a realistic option in this case." The combined company's postmerger plans included consolidation of warehouse and supply facilities, closing 40 to 70 superstores, changing the name of Office Depot stores to Staples, renegotiating contracts with manufacturers and suppliers, and consolidating management, which was likely to lead to layoffs of many Office Depot key personnel.

The court then turned to consider the possible private equities. Staples and Office Depot argued that the principal private equity at stake was the loss to Office Depot shareholders, who would likely lose a substantial portion of their investments if the merger were enjoined. While acknowledging this possible harm to Office Depot shareholders "at least in the short term," the court concluded that such private equity alone did not justify a denial of preliminary injunction where the public equity clearly supported it.

The court issued the preliminary injunction requested by the FTC. Shortly thereafter, Staples and Office Depot terminated their merger agreement. ∎

SOURCE: This case was written by Professor David P. Baron and Chen Lichtenstein based on public sources. Copyright © 1998 by the Board of Trustees of the Leland Stanford Junior University. All rights reserved. Reproduced with permission.

### PREPARATION QUESTIONS

1. What was the key finding by the court that effectively decided the case for a preliminary injunction?
2. Was the court's analysis of the pricing data appropriate for determining the likely effects of the merger?
3. Could Staples and Office Depot be reasonably expected to pass two-thirds of any cost efficiencies through to consumers?
4. Since Staples and Office Depot and their attorneys understood the antitrust laws and the facts that the FTC and the courts would examine, why did they believe that the FTC and the courts would not block the merger?
5. As a commissioner of the FTC how would you have voted on the consent decree negotiated by your staff?

---

[43]One of the FTC's expert witnesses presented uncontroverted evidence that Staples had historically passed through 15 to 17 percent of firm-specific cost savings in the form of lower prices to consumers.

# The Microsoft Antitrust Case

*At a 1995 meeting with Intel, Microsoft's Chairman and CEO Bill Gates said, according to an Intel executive, "This antitrust thing will blow over. We haven't changed our business practices at all."*

On May 18, 1998, the U.S. Department of Justice (DOJ) together with 19 state attorneys general filed an antitrust action against Microsoft Corporation. The DOJ compliant was filed under Sections 1 and 2 of the Sherman Act (the Act) to restrain anticompetitive conduct by Microsoft, the world's largest supplier of computer software for personal computers (PCs), and to remedy the effects of its alleged past unlawful conduct.

The DOJ specifically alleged four violations of the Act:

1. **Microsoft engaged in "unlawful exclusive dealing and other exclusionary agreements"** (Section 1 of the Act). The DOJ contended that Microsoft's agreements requiring other companies not to license, distribute, or promote non-Microsoft products, or to do so only on terms that materially disadvantage such products, and its agreements with PC manufacturers restricting modification or customization of the PC boot-up sequence and screens "unreasonably restrict competition." These agreements allegedly restricted the access of Microsoft's software competitors to significant segments of the market. The DOJ claimed that "the purpose and effect of these agreements are to restrain trade and competition in the Internet browser and PC operating system markets."

2. **Microsoft engaged in "unlawful tying"** (Section 1 of the Act). The DOJ viewed the Windows operating systems and Microsoft's Internet Explorer browser as separate products—they were sold in different markets, their functions were different, there was separate demand for them, and they were treated by Microsoft and other industry participants as separate products. The DOJ claimed that it was socially "efficient for Microsoft not to tie them and/or to permit [PC manufacturers] to distribute Windows 95 and Windows 98 without

Microsoft's Internet browser software." The DOJ argued that "Microsoft had tied and plans again to tie its Internet browser to its separate Windows operating system, which has monopoly power." The "purpose and the effect of this tying are to prevent customers from choosing among Internet browsers on their merits and to foreclose competing browsers from an important channel of distribution."

3. **Microsoft illegally maintained its monopoly of the PC operating systems market** (Section 2 of the Act). The DOJ contended that Microsoft "possesses monopoly power in the market for PC operating systems" and claimed that Microsoft had maintained that power through anticompetitive conduct.

4. **Microsoft attempted to monopolize the Internet** (Section 2 of the Act). The DOJ claimed that Microsoft had targeted Internet browsers because they had the potential to facilitate the development of products to compete with its Windows operating system and thereby "erode Microsoft's Windows operating system monopoly." Microsoft allegedly engaged in a "course of conduct, including tying and unreasonably exclusionary agreements," for the purpose of obtaining a "monopoly in the Internet browser market."

## The 1995 Consent Decree

The DOJ also sought to show that Microsoft remained dismissive of a long-running antitrust investigation, even after Microsoft had signed a consent decree with the DOJ in 1995. The DOJ had filed an action against Microsoft under Section 2 of the Sherman Act for "unlawfully maintaining its monopoly in the market for PC operating systems." The complaint alleged, among other things, that Microsoft had engaged in anticompetitive agreements and marketing practices directed at PC manufacturers, and the consent decree restricted those practices.

In 1997 the DOJ filed a complaint against Microsoft alleging that it had violated the consent decree. In response, Judge Thomas Penfield Jackson, in whose court the 1998 antitrust case was also tried, issued a preliminary injunction requiring Microsoft to offer Windows independently of Internet Explorer. In July 1998 a federal Court of Appeals overturned Judge Jackson's order, stating that the courts should not be "second guessing the claimed benefits of a particular product design." This ruling gave Microsoft an argument to use in the 1998 case. It could argue that consumers benefited from the integration of Internet Explorer and the Windows operating system.

## Microsoft's Position

Microsoft maintained that because of the nature of the industry it did not have a monopoly in the PC operating systems market nor could it become a monopoly in the Internet browser market, despite its market shares in these markets. According to Microsoft the rapid change in technology and in the business environment did not allow a single company to establish and maintain a monopoly. Microsoft also argued that antitrust law definitions, such as a monopoly identified by market share, did not apply to the software market as they did to traditional markets. Since it could not be categorized as a monopoly, Microsoft contended that its business conduct, even if as depicted by the DOJ, did not amount to unlawful conduct. Microsoft also rejected many of the DOJ's factual claims regarding its actual conduct and intent. For example, Microsoft argued that Windows and Internet Explorer were integrated to provide consumers with a superior product.

Microsoft also argued that its competitors employed strategies similar to its own. Moreover, the fact that firms with little market power used the same competitive strategies suggested that there were efficiencies associated with those practices. Although competitive strategies identical to those of a dominant firm were likely to be harmless when used by firms with little or no market power, when used by a firm with substantial market power, the efficiency benefits of those strategies could be outweighed by their anticompetitive effects.

## The Trial

An industry's economics are key in any antitrust case and in particular in the Microsoft case. The

DOJ proved at least some of its alleged "course of conduct" factual claims with credible clarity, so the court's decision focused on fundamental economic issues rather than on factual controversies. The trial consisted of two phases. The first was a decision by Judge Jackson on the facts of the case and the specific allegations made by the DOJ. If Judge Jackson found for the DOJ, the second phase would focus on remedies for the illegalities.

## The DOJ's Case

The DOJ's complaint was based on a set of factual claims, which together were intended to establish Microsoft's "unlawful course of conduct." The first determination by the court was the relevant market. The judge ruled that Intel-based desktop operating systems constituted the relevant market.

The DOJ sought to demonstrate the following:

- Microsoft possessed monopoly power in the market for PC operating systems (OS). Its Windows operating system was used on over 80 percent of all Intel-based PCs, the dominant type of PC in the United States. More than 90 percent of all new Intel-based PCs were shipped with a pre-installed version of Windows. PC manufacturers had no commercially reasonable alternative to Microsoft's operating systems for their PCs.

- Barriers to entry in the market for PC operating systems were high. One of the most important barriers stemmed from network effects and was due to the number of software applications that must run on an operating system to make it attractive to end users. End users wanted a large number of applications, and since it was the dominant operating system, most applications were written to run on Windows. It would be prohibitively expensive to create an alternative operating system to run the programs that ran on Windows.

- Consequently, the most significant potential threat to Microsoft's operating system monopoly was not from existing or new operating systems but from new software products that could support, or themselves become, "platforms" to which applications could be written and which could be used on multiple operating systems. The specific threat to

Windows was from Internet browsers and the Java programming language.

### The Threat of Internet Browsers and Java

The DOJ cited Microsoft CEO Bill Gates as saying in May 1995 that the Internet posed a serious potential threat to Microsoft's Windows operating system. Mr. Gates warned his executives:

A new competitor "born" on the Internet is Netscape. Their browser is dominant, with a 70 percent usage share, allowing them to determine which network extensions will catch on. They are pursing a multi-platform strategy where they move the key API [applications programming interface] into the client [the browser] to commoditize the underlying operating system.

James Barksdale, president and chairman of Netscape, described a June 1995 meeting with Microsoft as exceptional. He said, "I have never been in a meeting in my 35-year business career in which a competitor had so blatantly implied that we would either stop competing with it or the competitor would kill us."[44]

The DOJ asserted that Internet browsers posed a competitive threat to Microsoft's operating system monopoly in two basic ways.

- If application programs could easily be written to run on multiple operating systems, competition in the market for operating systems could be revitalized. The combination of browser technology and the Java programming language developed by Sun Microsystems for writing software that would run on any operating system threatened one of the key barriers to entry protecting Microsoft's operating system monopoly. Browsers represented the most significant vehicle for the distribution of Java technology to end users. Microsoft recognized that the widespread use of browsers could increase the distribution and use of Java and hence threaten Microsoft's operating system monopoly.
- A browser was itself a "platform" to which many applications were being written. Instead of writing software to run on Windows, software developers could write to the browser platform. Since the browser would run on any

operating system, software applications would be decoupled from the operating system. PC companies thus could use other operating systems on their computers.

The DOJ presented documents and e-mail messages indicating that Microsoft regarded Java as a key threat. A Microsoft document said that it was a "strategic objective" for Microsoft to "kill cross-platform Java" by expanding the "polluted Java market."—Microsoft's altered version of Java. A senior Microsoft executive identified Java as "our major threat" in an e-mail and added that Netscape's Internet browser was Java's "major distribution vehicle."

### Microsoft's Alleged Response to the Threat

Microsoft embarked on an extensive campaign to market and distribute its own browser, Internet Explorer (IE). Microsoft executives had described this campaign as a "jihad" to win the "browser war." The DOJ acknowledged that continued competition on the merits between Navigator and Internet Explorer would result in greater innovation and the development of better products at lower prices. The DOJ alleged, however, that Microsoft was unwilling to compete on the merits. The DOJ cited Microsoft's Christian Wildfeuer writing in February 1997 that Microsoft concluded that it would "be very hard to increase browser share on the merits of IE 4 alone. It will be more important to leverage the OS asset to make people use IE instead of navigator."

The DOJ alleged that Microsoft engaged in anticompetitive conduct to halt this threat.

- One measure was to develop a polluted version of Java that would run on the Windows OS but not on other operating systems. This could force a recoupling of software applications to Windows.
- A second step was to bundle IE with Windows and provide it free. To bundle IE with Windows, Microsoft removed IE from the Add/Delete menu so that neither PC manufacturers nor users could delete it.
- The DOJ argued that providing IE at no additional cost to PC manufacturers that preloaded Windows or to users who purchased Windows constituted predatory pricing. The alleged intent was to drive Netscape, which charged $10 to $15 to PC manufacturers who preloaded

---

[44]See Cusamano and Yoffie (1998) for an analysis of Netscape and its competition with Microsoft.

it, out of the market. Netscape was forced to provide Navigator for free, eliminating much of its revenue.

- The DOJ also alleged that giving away IE for free represented illegal leveraging from its operating system monopoly in an attempt to monopolize the browser market.

- The DOJ alleged that Microsoft provided discounts to PC manufacturers that agreed not to preload Navigator. Microsoft was said to "take $7.50 off the unit price of Windows if PC makers agree to carry a 'Windows' logo on their machines and submit to certification by Microsoft's labs."[45] Microsoft maintained that price discounts to PC makers were not favoritism to reward them for not carrying rival products but instead were volume discounts.

- Microsoft's contracts with PC manufacturers were alleged to be exclusionary. While not prohibiting PC manufacturers from preloading Navigator, the contracts were written to discourage the use of rival products. Contracts restricted the ability of PC manufacturers to modify the start-up sequence and desktop. Microsoft also allegedly required PC manufacturers to favor its products and threatened to terminate their license to use Windows if they failed to do so. The DOJ produced documents from Compaq and depositions of its executives indicating that Compaq may have taken the Netscape Navigator icon off its desktops and chosen Internet Explorer because of fear of retaliation by Microsoft. Microsoft pointed to depositions by Compaq executives stating that Microsoft had never objected to the Navigator icon appearing on the desktop. Microsoft had objected when Compaq planned to delete the Internet Explorer icon.

- Microsoft was alleged to have illegally tied IE to Windows by not giving original equipment manufacturers (OEMs) and consumers the opportunity to purchase one without the other. Tying occurs when a firm conditions the purchase (or license) of one product on the purchase (or license) of another product. Pro-competitive reasons for tying include cost savings and quality control (it could be easier to identify the source of quality problems with a tied sale than if the products were sold sepa-

rately). Tying could, however, be an anticompetitive leveraging practice if it foreclosed competition in network markets.

- Microsoft allegedly withheld APIs from software developers that threatened its products.

- Microsoft built incompatibility into its products. For example, when Microsoft's Real Media player was installed, RealNetwork's media player would not work.[46]

### Microsoft's Defense

Microsoft challenged the government's witnesses and sought to support its fundamental line of argument. Microsoft argued that it did not have monopoly power, any apparent monopoly power could quickly be dissipated in a dynamic industry, its behavior and practices were not abusive and were similar to standard practices in the industry, and consumers were not harmed but instead benefited from its practices. As the defendant Microsoft did not have to prove its arguments but instead needed only to raise substantial doubt about the DOJ's allegations.

Microsoft witnesses argued that the relevant market was not operating systems but was much broader and included the Internet and handheld computers, for neither of which Microsoft had a dominant position. Microsoft argued, for example, that it was not a monopolist, since it faced competition from Sun's Java programming language and Internet browsers.

Microsoft argued that if it had monopoly power in operating systems, it would have charged a much higher price for Windows. A government witness countered that all that the price charged for Windows indicated was "that Microsoft is not maximizing its short-run profits."

Many economists viewed pricing IE at zero as economically efficient, since the marginal cost of producing an additional copy of IE was essentially zero. Moreover, consumers benefited from competition in browsers, since improvements in browser quality resulted from the competition. A government witness, however, testified that it would be difficult to determine the exact standard for concluding that a price for Internet Explorer was predatory, but the fact was that Microsoft charged a "zero price," and had spent $100 million a year since 1995 developing IE.

Microsoft executives denied allegations of coercive behavior and argued that consumers benefited

---

45 *The Wall Street Journal*, March 1, 1999.

46 Microsoft was able to eliminate the source of the incompatibility.

from its innovations. Paul Maritz, senior group vice president, testified, "Ironically, the very thing that makes Windows valuable to computer manufacturers, software publishers and customers . . . is now under attack in this lawsuit. The popularity of Windows, owing entirely to Microsoft's efforts to innovate, evangelize and license the software cheaply to promote wide distribution, is derided as monopoly."

Much of Microsoft's defense was directed at countering the testimony of government witnesses. A considerable portion of that testimony centered on recollections of and notes taken at private meetings between Microsoft and companies such as Apple, Intel, and Netscape. Microsoft witnesses provided different interpretations of what had transpired at the meetings than had the government's witnesses. Paul Maritz, for example, testified that Microsoft opposed Intel's development of software because that software was second-rate and that Microsoft had withheld software support for Intel's MMX microprocessor because of overzealous intellectual property claims by Intel. Maritz also denied that he had ever told an Intel executive that Microsoft would "cut off Netscape's air supply." He also said that Microsoft's reluctance to continue producing software for Apple's Macintosh was due to concerns that Apple might fold.

Microsoft also denied that it had harmed Netscape through exclusive arrangements with and financial incentives to PC makers and Internet service providers. A Microsoft attorney stated, "Whatever those arrangements were, whatever measure of exclusivity they created for a period of time, Netscape was able to gain a substantial number of new users. There was no foreclosure of consumer choice."[47]

A Microsoft executive testified that it had not attempted to undermine Java. The DOJ, however, produced a memo from Bill Gates stating that he was "hardcore about NOT supporting" Java. When the executive tried to explain what Gates meant, the judge abruptly cut him off, stating that it was abundantly clear what Gates meant.

Microsoft's direct testimony was attacked effectively by DOJ lead attorney David Boies. *The Wall Street Journal* wrote, "Microsoft's defense is in disarray and its executives and economist have been battered so badly on the witness stand that the judge

[47] *The New York Times*, February 28, 1999.

has questioned key elements of the Redmond, Wash., software giant's case."[48] *The New York Times* referred to the trial as "a humbling courtroom experience" for Microsoft.[49] *Fortune* said, "We're seeing Microsoft's defense go down in flames."[50] Microsoft countered that the DOJ's attacks amounted to showmanship and that the case would be decided on the facts and the law.

One major faux pas for Microsoft occurred in Senior Vice President James Allchin's testimony. Allchin showed a videotape produced by Microsoft that purported to show "performance degradations" in the Windows 98 operating system when Internet Explorer was removed from the system. The videotape had been produced to challenge the testimony of a government witness that Internet Explorer could be removed from the Windows operating system without any significant performance degradation. The government consultants who reviewed the videotape noticed that the title bar displayed the words "Internet Explorer" even though the Microsoft narrator said it had been removed. Allchin maintained that the computer shown was the one from which its browser had been removed. Two days later Microsoft admitted that the videotape was prepared in a studio and showed a number of different computers to simulate its claims about performance degradation. Microsoft then prepared a new videotape that observers said showed that the system without Internet Explorer performed well, although applications requiring a browser, of course, did not work.

## Developments Outside the Courtroom

Two developments occurred during the trial that lent support to Microsoft's argument that the market was constantly changing and monopoly power was a transient phenomenon at most. In November 1998 AOL announced that it would acquire Netscape for $4.2 billion and form an alliance with Sun Microsystems. Microsoft asserted that the deal fundamentally changed the industry's landscape and that it therefore was sufficient grounds for the DOJ to drop the lawsuit. DOJ witnesses such as William Harris, chairman and CEO of Intuit Corporation, stated that they did not view the new

[48] *The Wall Street Journal*, February 18, 1999.
[49] *The New York Times*, February 28, 1999.
[50] *Fortune*, March 1, 1999.

alliance as an industry shift that would diminish Microsoft's dominance.

Microsoft also asserted that Linux, a free UNIX operating system, posed a potential threat to Windows because several of Microsoft's chief competitors were writing software to run on it. In fact, on March 1, 1999, Oracle, Intel, Dell, and Hewlett-Packard all announced substantial investments in Linux, and IBM announced greater offerings of computers using Linux. Although Linux had several million devotees around the world, it held an insignificant share of the operating system market. A DOJ expert witness firmly rejected the proposition that it threatened Windows: "Whatever role Linux may have, it is not expected to constrain the monopoly power of Microsoft . . . If you truly believe this product is going to constrain Microsoft's market share, then run, don't walk, to your broker and sell Microsoft stock short."

## Remedies

If the court found against Microsoft, the next issue would be which remedies to impose. Many companies in the industry, including rivals of Microsoft, were fearful that the cure imposed could be worse than the disease. The principal fear was that some form of government supervision or oversight of the industry would be imposed that would impede innovation and technological change.

Possible remedies were generally classified as behavioral or structural. Behavioral remedies sought to eliminate the abusive conduct and exclusionary practices without altering Microsoft's control of the Windows operating system. Structural remedies focused on eliminating Microsoft's Windows operating system monopoly either by breaking up the company or by replicating the source of its power through the creation of clones. Behavioral remedies were favored by those who worried that breaking up Microsoft's monopoly could lead to multiple industry standards that would impede the development of software applications. Many commentators and industry members, however, were skeptical that behavioral remedies would be sufficient to curb Microsoft's alleged monopoly power and abusive conduct. Opposition to behavioral remedies resulted not only from skepticism about their effectiveness but also because such remedies would require supervision or regulatory oversight of the industry. Most industry members

and economists feared any supervision or oversight of a dynamic industry with rapid product development and obsolescence.

Most behavioral remedies under discussion focused on breaking Microsoft's hold on PC manufacturers that resulted from its licensing agreements for Windows. A number of PC manufacturers had sought more flexible licensing agreements, and under antitrust scrutiny Microsoft had recently granted some leeway.

Behavioral remedies could include stopping Microsoft from using exclusive contracts prohibiting PC manufacturers from offering other Internet browsers. Another behavioral remedy would be to require Microsoft to publish its "most-favored customer" prices and make those prices available to all OEMs. This would reduce the likelihood that Microsoft could punish an OEM by not offering it a discount available to other OEMs. More generally the court could impose a pricing "transparency" policy under which Microsoft would set fixed prices for its products. A third behavioral remedy would require Microsoft to publish the APIs, or software hooks, required to write software for the Windows operating system. This would address the alleged strategy of releasing APIs in stages or selectively to favored software developers.

In February 1999 the 1,400 member Information Industry Association (IIA), of which Microsoft was a member, presented a report to the DOJ urging it to "seriously consider" structural remedies.[51] The structural remedy preferred by the IIA was to break Microsoft into three standalone companies. One would have the Windows operating system, including the CE and NT systems. Another would have Microsoft's software business, and the third would have its Internet and electronic commerce businesses.

An alternative structural remedy was to break Microsoft into three to five clones, referred to as "Baby Bills," each of which would have Microsoft's source codes for Windows and its other products. A related proposal was to auction the Windows code and brand name to several companies. These remedies would introduce competition and break the alleged monopoly power of Microsoft. The IIA report, however, concluded that this type of

---

[51]The initial draft reportedly recommended structural remedies, but lobbying by Microsoft led to the wording "seriously consider."

remedy could be harmful if it led to multiple technical standards.

## The Trial Court: Conclusions of Law and Findings of Fact

On April 3, 2000, Judge Jackson ruled that Microsoft had violated the Sherman Act. Microsoft's conduct was found to have violated the Sherman Act not because of the practices themselves, many of which were standard in the industry, but because they were used by a monopolist to maintain its monopoly. As conclusions of law, he found that the relevant market was "Intel-based PC operating systems" and that Microsoft had a monopoly. The judge concluded that Microsoft's conduct had a "significant exclusionary impact." He also concluded that "middleware [Navigator and Java] threatened to demolish Microsoft's coveted monopoly power" and that Microsoft engaged in a "deliberate assault upon entrepreneurial efforts . . ." He cited Microsoft's efforts in the OEM channel to stifle innovation, including tactics such as requiring the installation of IE and bundling proprietary software. The former constituted illegal tying of one product with a monopoly product, which he concluded was in effect a per se violation of the Sherman Act. The latter constituted "exclusionary behavior in the IAP [Internet access provider] channel," which also constituted a violation of Section 1 of the Sherman Act.

The judge also concluded that Microsoft's behavior was as a whole "predacious" and cited providing IE for free and offering promotional inducements to bundle it with other offerings. In addition, he concluded that Microsoft used its control of technical information (APIs) to induce Internet service vendors to distribute the so-called "polluted" version of Java. Judge Jackson also found that although Microsoft had used exclusionary contracts, such as inducing Compaq not to distribute Navigator, those contracts "did not ultimately deprive Netscape of the ability to have access to every PC worldwide to offer an opportunity to install Navigator." These exclusive contracts thus were not themselves sufficient to constitute a violation of Section 1.

## Judge Jackson's Remedies

At the conclusion of the trial Judge Jackson urged the DOJ and Microsoft to reach a settlement of the case. In a highly unusual move he appointed a distinguished U.S. Court of Appeals judge, Richard Posner, to convene the parties and seek a settlement. Efforts to reach a settlement failed.

On June 7, 2000, Judge Jackson ordered both structural and behavioral remedies in response to his findings that Microsoft had violated the Sherman Act. The remedies largely followed those recommended by the DOJ and the 19 state attorneys general. Jackson's decision was notable in that it took an arguably hostile tone toward the company. He stated that Microsoft was "unwilling to accept the notion that it broke the law" and that it had "proved untrustworthy in the past."

The structural remedy involved breaking Microsoft into two separate companies. One, referred to as "ops," would have Microsoft's operating systems business, including Windows 2000, Windows ME, and Windows CE. The other, referred to as "apps," would have all other lines of business, including software applications (e.g., Microsoft Office, Exchange, IE) and Internet services (e.g., MSN, Hotmail, Expedia, CarPoint). Microsoft was ordered to submit to the court a plan for creating the two companies. The breakup would be complete at the management level with a "firewall" between the two companies.

In addition to the structural remedy, Judge Jackson's ruling included a set of behavioral remedies intended to restore viable competition in the operating system and applications markets. The behavioral remedies were to last for 10 years and pertained to Microsoft's conduct with respect to customers and rivals. In response to allegations that Microsoft had illegally tied IE to the Windows operating system, Judge Jackson ruled that Microsoft must allow OEMs to remove any applications from the operating system. OEMs could modify the start-up sequence and desktop, including removing Microsoft icons, and would be given 30 days' notice before Microsoft could terminate a Windows license. Microsoft would have to license operating systems products under uniform conditions with the exceptions of volume discounts. Microsoft would be prohibited from interfering with any non-Microsoft middleware, discriminating against a hardware or software company for using non-Microsoft products, favoring Microsoft over non-Microsoft products, or linking licenses to the use of Microsoft products. Microsoft would also be required to continue to offer the previous version of its Windows OS when it introduced a new version. This was intended to limit Microsoft's ability to force migration.

To ensure the "interoperability" of software and hardware, Judge Jackson ordered Microsoft to allow hardware, software, and computer makers access to technical information and developers to view the "relevant necessary portions" of code. This included all APIs and portions of the OS code. The APIs and code would be available only in a "secure facility."

## The Court of Appeals Decision

Microsoft appealed the decision and in its appeal attacked the conduct of Judge Jackson for statements made outside of the courtroom. Microsoft asked that he be removed from the case. On June 28, 2001, the U.S. Court of Appeals issued a unanimous decision affirming some of the trial court's conclusions, vacating some of its orders, and remanding some to a different district court for resolution.

In its most important ruling the Court of Appeals vacated the order breaking Microsoft into two separate companies. In doing so the Court observed that divestiture had traditionally been reserved for firms that had grown through acquisition and merger, but the Court left the door open for a divestiture order. The District Court was ordered to reconsider the appropriateness of divestiture and whether there was a sufficient relationship between the maintenance of monopoly and the illegal conduct to warrant the full structural remedy of divestiture. The Court of Appeals also ordered the district court to hold full evidentiary hearings on appropriate remedies.

The Court of Appeals concurred with Judge Jackson's conclusion about monopoly power: "We uphold the District Court's finding of monopoly power in its entirety." This conclusion was important not only for the present case, but also because in private antitrust cases the plaintiffs would not have the burden of proving that Microsoft had monopoly power.

The Court of Appeals concurred that Microsoft's conduct violated the Sherman Act. First, its license restrictions on OEMs were found to be anticompetitive. Second, the exclusion of IE from the Add/Remove program of Windows so that a user could not remove IE was found to be a violation of Section 2. The Court stated, "Microsoft failed to meet its burden of showing that its conduct serves a purpose other than protecting its operating system

monopoly." The Court also held that Microsoft developed a polluted version of Java that would run only on Windows, and this "conduct is exclusionary, in violation of Sec. 2 of the Sherman Act."

The Court of Appeals reversed without remand Judge Jackson's conclusion that Microsoft attempted to monopolize the browser market. The Court stated that the Department of Justice had not properly defined the relevant market nor established that there were barriers to entry.

Judge Jackson had concluded that the tying or bundling of IE with Windows was in effect a per se violation of Section 1 of the Sherman Act. The Court of Appeals, however, concluded that per se analysis was inappropriate and remanded the issue to the District Court to be considered under a rule of reason.

The Court of Appeals also strongly criticized the conduct of Judge Jackson and disqualified him from the case. The court found "no evidence of actual bias" but concluded that "the trial judge engaged in impermissible ex parte contacts by holding secret interviews with members of the media and made numerous offensive comments about Microsoft officials in public statements outside the courtroom, giving rise to an appearance of partiality." Consequently, the court vacated the remedies ordered by Judge Jackson and on remand assigned the case to a different trial judge to be assigned by random draw. The new judge would determine the remedies.

The headline of the front page article of *The Wall Street Journal* on the day after the Court of Appeals decision was "With Its Old Playbook, Microsoft Is Muscling Into New Web Markets: Using Aggressive Bundling, It Roils High-Tech World With Windows Overhaul."

## The Settlement and Next Stage

Claiming victory, the DOJ did not appeal the decision. Microsoft, however, appealed the decision and Judge Jackson's findings of fact, but the Supreme Court refused to consider the appeal. Faced with a complex and potentially lengthy case dealing both with tying and remedies, District Court Judge Colleen Kollar-Kotelly appointed a mediator to attempt to settle the case. In November the DOJ and Microsoft reached a settlement. The state attorneys general engaged in brief negotiations with Microsoft, obtaining some potentially important changes in the settlement. In a highly unusual development, however, nine state attorneys general refused to accept the settlement. Thomas F. Reilly, attorney general of Massachusetts, said, "There is no question in my mind that Microsoft will use this agreement to crush the competition, and they will have the imprimatur of the U.S. government to do it."[52] Kelly Jo MacArthur, general counsel for RealNetworks, said, "This is a reward, not a remedy. This agreement allows a declared illegal monopolist to determine, at its sole discretion, what goes into the monopoly operating system in the future."[53] She was referring to Microsoft integrating its Media Player into Windows XP, in effect giving it away for free just as IE had been integrated into Windows without charge. Scott McNealy, CEO of Sun Microsystems, asked, "Does anyone think this settlement is going to change Microsoft's behavior? These guys are unfettered."[54] Michael Morris, senior vice president and general counsel of Sun Microsystems said, "I think everybody who isn't a Microsoft vassal understands, and has been saying, this is the most bizarre, pointless, ridiculous antitrust settlement that anyone could have possibly imagined. It doesn't even pass the red face test."[55] In a more dispassionate statement professor David Yoffie and research associate Mary Kwak, co-authors of *Judo Strategy*, referred to the settlement as "a spectacular victory for Microsoft."

Microsoft chairman Bill Gates said the case had "a profound impact on me personally and on our company" and "we will focus more on how our activities affect other companies." He added, "While the settlement goes farther than we might have wanted, we believe that settling this case now is the right thing to do to help the industry, and the economy, to move forward."[56] CEO Steve Ballmer observed that during the lawsuit "our industry didn't rise to support us the way we might have supposed as an industry leader."[57] Bill Gates said that Microsoft was "committed to becoming a better industry leader."

U.S. assistant attorney general Charles A. James, who headed the antitrust division of the DOJ and negotiated the settlement, said, "The settlement will promote innovation, give consumers choice and provide computer manufacturers and the industry

with more certainty as they go forward in marketing their products. This consent decree will remedy the problems that were caused by Microsoft's unlawful conduct, prevent the recurrence of those problems and restore competition in the software industry."[58] Observers speculated that Mr. James was eager to settle the case to remove uncertainty from the economy in the wake of the September 11 terrorist attacks.

The terms of the settlement were as follows:

- Microsoft can integrate any product into Windows.
- PC makers can hide any Microsoft feature, and Microsoft cannot restrict or retaliate against any PC maker that installs non-Microsoft software.
- Microsoft must license Windows on the same terms to all PC makers and must publish its prices on a Web site.
- Microsoft must share certain technical information for middleware, both for desktop systems and server software for the Internet, with software developers. Microsoft retains all intellectual property rights but must license that property to allow PC makers and software developers to exercise their rights under the agreement. Microsoft cannot retaliate against any software developer.
- Microsoft must appoint an internal compliance officer to ensure that its executives and board members understand the terms of the settlement.
- A three-person technical committee, with one member appointed by Microsoft, one by the DOJ, and one by agreement of both parties, was established to determine which parts of the software code need to be released to competitors, to monitor compliance, and to hear complaints. The committee has no enforcement authority but can inform Microsoft and the courts of serious complaints, possibly leading to a court enforcement hearing.
- The consent decree extended for 5 years, and if Microsoft willfully and systematically violated the terms, it would extend for an additional 2 years.

Judge Kollar-Kotelly set two tracks for the case. On the first track, under the Tunney Act a 90-day review period began in which the judge must decide if the settlement is in the public interest. The public and the parties in the case could make comments.

---

[52]*The New York Times*, November 6, 2001.
[53]*The Wall Street Journal*, November 5, 2001.
[54]*The New York Times*, November 5, 2001.
[55]*San Jose Mercury News*, November 3, 2001.
[56]*The New York Times*, November 3, 2001.
[57]*The Wall Street Journal*, November 5, 2001.

[58]*The New York Times*, November 5, 2001.

In this track the DOJ and Microsoft would be on the same side in defending the settlement. On the second track to resolve the case pursued by the nine remaining states, the judge scheduled hearings on remedies to begin March 11, 2002.

In 2002 both Sun Microsystems and Netscape/AOL filed private antitrust lawsuits against Microsoft. ∎

## PREPARATION QUESTIONS

1. Should the DOJ have brought an antitrust case against Microsoft?
2. Does the evidence indicate that Microsoft violated the Sherman Act?
3. Did Microsoft's conduct benefit consumers?
4. Were Judge Jackson's remedies appropriate? Should a structural remedy be used?
5. Were the terms of the settlement appropriate? Sufficient?
6. What, if anything, should be done with Microsoft's operating system monopoly and its growing dominance in other software applications?

# CHAPTER 10

# Regulation: Law, Economics, and Politics

## Introduction

Markets and property rights are the centerpieces of the free enterprise system. Markets allow people to exchange goods and services, and property rights allow them to gain from trade. Markets also provide information by establishing prices that reflect the cost of society's resources used to produce goods and services. Under some conditions, however, markets may not function efficiently, inhibiting gains from trade. When there are market imperfections, government intervention in markets could improve their efficiency. This intervention can be the responsibility of the judiciary, as in the case of antitrust law enforced through the courts, or it can be the responsibility of specialized regulatory agencies responsible for particular markets or imperfections. Regulation is government intervention in economic activity using commands, controls, and incentives. Both regulation and judicial enforcement are based on legislatively enacted statutes. This means that regulation can be used for purposes other than making markets more efficient. Regulation is thus a political as well as an economic instrument.

Regulation takes place through a public process that is open and allows participation by interested parties. In contrast to antitrust, regulation is not implemented through judicial institutions but instead by independent commissions and agencies of the executive branch. The courts, however, have played an important role in interpreting regulatory statutes, determining their constitutionality, and ensuring that regulatory decisions satisfy due process requirements.

Regulatory decisions and rule-making proceedings are extremely important to many firms, industries, and interest groups. Kerwin (1994, p. 194) reported a survey of 180 interest groups that found that two-thirds of the groups saw participation in regulatory rule making as at least as important as lobbying Congress and conducting grassroots activities.

Regulation includes a broad set of interventions:

- controlling prices (electric power, local telephone service)
- setting price floors (crops, minimum wages)
- ensuring equal opportunity (banning discrimination in employment)
- regularizing employment practices (overtime)
- specifying qualifications (occupational licensure)
- providing for solvency (financial institutions, insurance, pension plans)
- controlling the number of market participants (broadcast licenses, taxi medallions)

- limiting ownership (media, airlines)
- requiring premarketing approval (toxic chemicals, pharmaceuticals)
- ensuring product safety (pharmaceuticals, toys, food)
- mandating product characteristics and technology (automobile safety standards)
- establishing service territories (local telephone service)
- establishing performance standards (automobile emissions standards)
- controlling toxic emissions and other pollutants (sulfur dioxide emissions trading)
- specifying industry boundaries (insurance, banking, and stock brokerage boundaries)
- allocating public resources (spectrum allocations)
- establishing standards (telecommunications interconnections)
- controlling unfair international trade practices (antidumping)
- providing information (labeling)
- rationing common pool resources (fisheries)

As this list indicates, regulation is a broad subject and often specific to particular industries, products, and conditions. The focus of this chapter is the nature of regulation. Two principal perspectives are considered—one based on the correction of market imperfections and the other based on the political economy of regulation. The institutional focus is on regulation administered by government agencies and commissions with applications to telecommunications and electric power. Environmental regulation is considered in Chapter 11, and the regulation of international trade is considered in Chapter 17.

The next section identifies periods of regulatory activity in the United States, and the following section considers the constitutional basis for regulation. Regulatory agencies and the regulatory process are then discussed. The nonmarket environment of regulatory agencies is considered with an emphasis on the external influences on agencies. The economic rationale for correcting market imperfections is presented, including natural monopoly, externalities, public goods, asymmetric information, and moral hazard. The broader political economy of regulation is then considered along with the distributive objectives of regulation. The chapter concludes with an analysis of deregulation in the telecommunications and electric power industries.

## Periods of Regulatory Change

The United States has experienced four major periods of regulatory change. The first occurred during the populist era of the late 1800s as a result of nonmarket action by interest groups. Farmers succeeded in establishing regulatory bodies at the state level to control the market power of grain elevators and railroads. This was extended to the federal level with the passage of the Interstate Commerce Act in 1887, which established the Interstate Commerce Commission (ICC) with the authority to regulate railroad rates. In the same tradition, additional legislation was enacted early in the 20th century to shore up regulatory and antitrust powers that had been narrowly construed by the courts.[1]

The second period was the progressive era and the New Deal. Regulation was extended to labor markets and industries, including electric power, food, pharmaceuticals, trucking, air transport, securities, and communications. Much of this regulation was industry specific and focused on pricing, entry, and conditions of service.

The third period, which began in the 1960s and accelerated in the 1970s, brought social regulation. In contrast to the earlier regulation that focused on the economic regulation of industries, social regulation addressed externalities and hazards. Regulation was extended to consumer products, the environment, and the workplace. The new social

---

[1]See McCraw (1981) for the history of regulation. The Sherman Antitrust Act was enacted in the same era.

regulation differed dramatically from the regulation of earlier periods. The new regulation cut across industries by focusing on issues such as safety, health, and the environment. This changed the nature of the politics of regulation. In the past, the politics had been dominated by industry interests, as when the railroads used ICC regulation to limit competition from the emerging interstate trucking industry. The new social regulation brought to the politics of regulation a new set of interest groups, including safety and health activists and environmentalists.

The fourth period brought economic deregulation to several industries, including electric power, natural gas transmission, telecommunications, air transport, and surface transportation. Public policy analysts, regulators, and executive branch officials recognized that regulation, which had been intended to keep prices down, seemed instead to lead to higher costs and higher prices. Beginning in the 1970s several regulatory systems were dismantled, and market forces were substituted to improve economic efficiency. In some industries, such as electric power and telecommunications, economic regulation is steadily being replaced by market competition. The deregulation movement also led to the substitution of marketlike mechanisms, such as auctions and the trading of pollution allowances, for regulatory control and allocation procedures. On January 1, 1996, the first regulatory agency, the Interstate Commerce Commission, closed its doors.

The past four decades have witnessed two quite different regulatory movements. The social regulation that began during the 1960s has expanded at the same time as deregulation has occurred in a number of industries. Although new regulatory agencies have not been created in recent years, the authority of some existing social regulatory agencies such as the Environmental Protection Agency has been expanded. Economic regulation has moved in the other direction as markets and competition have been substituted for government controls. These two movements have come together as marketlike mechanisms have been substituted for some social regulation, as in the case of the trading of sulfur dioxide allowances considered in Chapter 11.

## The Constitutional Basis for Regulation

Government regulation can be traced to the 1100s when the English monarchy began to contract with private parties for the provision of services. The monarchy granted rights-of-way to stage lines and in return retained the authority to regulate services and prices. Private property committed to a public use thus became subject to government controls. This contractual relationship between the state and a firm provided the basis for the evolution of regulatory authority through the common law.[2]

The U.S. Constitution provides the authority for regulation but also limits its application. Section 8 of Article I of the Constitution gives Congress the power "To regulate Commerce . . . among the several States . . ." The Fifth Amendment to the Constitution limits this power by stating, "No person shall be deprived of life, liberty, or property, without due process of law; nor shall private property be taken for public use without just compensation." The Fourteenth Amendment extends the due process protection to actions taken by the states.

Many of the legal principles of regulation in the United States have come from court decisions that draw on the common law. The common law doctrine that private property committed to a public use could be regulated was extended to property that was "affected with a public interest." In *Munn v. Illinois*, 94 U.S. 113 (1877), the Supreme Court upheld an Illinois statute regulating the prices charged by grain elevators, which in the state constitution had been declared "public warehouses." The court cited the

[2]The common law is considered in Chapter 12.

English common law principle that when "affected with a public interest, [private property] ceases to be *juris privati* only. . . . Property does become clothed with a public interest when used in a manner to make it of public consequence, and affect the community at large. When, therefore, one devotes his property to a use in which the public has an interest, he, in effect, grants to the public an interest in that use, and must submit to be controlled by the public for the common good. . . ." In this sweeping statement, the court established the government's right to regulate private property. However, the court went on to warn: "We know that this is a power which may be abused; but there is no argument against its existence. For protection against abuses by the legislatures the people must resort to the polls, not to the courts." In upholding minimum price regulation of milk sold in grocery stores, the Supreme Court ruled in *Nebbia v. New York*, 291 U.S. 502 (1934), that the same principle applied to enterprises not affected with a public interest. The government's authority to regulate is thus extremely broad.

The Fifth and Fourteenth amendments, however, place limits on regulation.[3] In *Smith v. Ames*, 169 U.S. 466 (1898), the Supreme Court held that "What a company is entitled to ask is a fair return upon the value of that which it employs for the public convenience."[4] This established the right of public utilities to obtain a fair return on their capital and led to cost-of-service regulation. The due process provisions of the Constitution are also important factors in structuring regulatory processes, as considered later in the chapter.

# Regulatory Commissions and Agencies

The principal federal regulatory agencies are listed in Figure 10-1. Regulatory agencies are of two basic forms—independent commissions and executive branch agencies. Independent commissions include the Federal Communications Commission, Federal Trade Commission, Federal Reserve System, International Trade Commission, Federal Energy Regulatory Commission, Securities and Exchange Commission, National Labor Relations Board, Consumer Products Safety Commission, and Nuclear Regulatory Commission. The Federal Communications Commission, for example, has five commissioners appointed by the president and confirmed by the Senate. They serve 7-year terms, and no more than three commissioners may be from the same political party. Most commissions make decisions through majority-rule voting and formal rule-making procedures.

Agencies typically have a single administrator appointed by the president or a cabinet secretary. Most executive branch regulatory agencies are located in a cabinet department, as in the case of the Federal Aviation Administration, National Highway Traffic Safety Administration, Occupational Health and Safety Administration, and Food and Drug Administration. The Environmental Protection Agency is an independent executive branch agency not housed in a cabinet department.[5]

Most states also have regulatory commissions and agencies. Considerable economic activity such as local telephone and electricity service is regulated by the states and not the federal government. Most states also have regulatory agencies to deal with environmental, occupational safety, and health issues. As indicated in Chapter 11, federal law delegates the implementation of certain federal regulations to the states. States, for example, are responsible for developing implementation plans for achieving clean air standards.

---

[3]The "takings" clause in the Fifth Amendment has been the subject of political and legal activity intended to require public compensation for the loss of value due to regulations such as zoning and environmental protection.

[4]See also *Federal Power Commission et al. v. Hope Natural Gas Co.*, 320 U.S. 591 (1944).

[5]For a description of the regulatory agencies, see *Congressional Quarterly* (1994).

Federal Reserve System (1913)
Federal Trade Commission (1914)
International Trade Commission (1916) (formerly the Tariff Commission)—considered in Chapter 17
Federal Energy Regulatory Commission (1930) (formerly the Federal Power Commission)
Food and Drug Administration (1931) [HHS]
Securities and Exchange Commission (1934)
Federal Communications Commission (1934)
National Labor Relations Board (1935)
Federal Aviation Administration (1948) [DOT]
Federal Maritime Commission [1961]
Equal Employment Opportunity Commission (1965)—considered in Chapter 20
Environmental Protection Agency (1970)—considered in Chapter 11
National Highway Traffic Safety Administration (1970) [DOT]
Consumer Product Safety Commission (1972)
Occupational Safety and Health Administration (1973) [DOL]
Nuclear Regulatory Commission (1975) (formerly the Atomic Energy Commission)

**FIGURE 10-1** **Principal Federal Regulatory Agencies and Commissions**

*Note:* The cabinet departments in which agencies are located are shown in brackets.
*Source: Congressional Quarterly, Federal Regulatory Directory,* 7th ed., Washington DC, 1994.

## Delegation, Rule Making, Due Process, and Discretion

Article I, Section 1 of the Constitution grants Congress the sole power to enact laws. It does not authorize Congress to delegate policymaking to agencies. Yet regulatory agencies promulgate rules, establish policies, and resolve disputes. Prior to 1935 courts held that the delegatee was simply making a determination in the implementation of a law enacted by Congress. In 1935 the Supreme Court overturned as unconstitutional two delegation provisions of the National Industrial Recovery Act. Subsequently, the courts have not overturned a congressional delegation.[6] Instead, the courts have sought to ensure that the exercise of any delegated authority is consistent with the constitutional protections of the Fifth and Fourteenth Amendments and the common law doctrine of consistency.

Congress also was concerned about the exercise of agency powers and enacted the Administrative Procedure Act (APA) of 1946 to provide for public notice and comment prior to agency action. Agencies also adopt their own rule-making procedures in a manner consistent with the APA. Under the APA, agencies can use either a formal or an informal rule-making process.[7] The informal model of rule-making requires publishing in the *Federal Register* a Notice of Proposed Rule Making (NPRM) and a request for the submission of comments. The agency may also hold a public hearing on the proposed rule. The agency next reviews the comments received, revises the rule, and publishes it in the *Federal Register* with an effective date at least 30 days in the future. Under the formal model, the agency employs a quasi-judicial process involving hearings conducted by an administrative law judge, the presentation of evidence, and

_____
[6]See Mashaw and Merrill (1985, pp. 2–5).
[7]See Kerwin (1999), Breyer (1982, pp. 378–381), and Howell, Allison, and Henley (1987, pp. 179–188). Magat, Krupnick, and Harrington (1986) and Owen and Braeutigam (1978) consider the administrative processes of regulation.

the cross-examination of witnesses. A formal record of the proceedings is kept and may be reviewed by the courts. Appearances may be made and testimony given by any interested party. The authorizing statutes of some agencies also prescribe public hearings for certain types of actions. Under this model, the agencies are restricted by ex parte rules against having contacts with interested parties outside the proceedings.[8]

The APA grants parties the right to sue for judicial review of an agency action. One basis for that review is the failure to follow the procedures required for an action. This is review under the framework of *procedural due process.* The APA [Section 706(2) (A)] requires that agency actions not be "arbitrary, capricious, an abuse of discretion, or otherwise not in accordance with law." Because of the right to judicial review, agencies are careful to follow procedures and base their decisions on the record. Nevertheless, in 2003 the Court of Appeals overturned as "arbitrary and capricious" an NHTSA rule allowing automakers to choose one of two tire-pressure monitoring systems when the record showed that one system was clearly superior in the court's view. NHTSA announced a new NPRM, and the process began again.

An important procedural due process decision pertained to the bases for changing a regulatory rule. NHTSA began rule-making proceedings on air bags in 1967. In 1977, the first year of the Carter administration, it promulgated a rule requiring new automobiles to be equipped with a passive restraint system—either an air bag or automatic seat belts. The Reagan administration opposed the rule, and the new administrator of NHTSA revoked it in October 1981. The revocation was based not on new information but rather on a reevaluation of the previous record. The administrator concluded that because auto manufacturers planned to use seat belt systems that were easily detachable, the benefits from the rule would not justify the costs. The insurance industry, one of the principal interest groups that had worked for the passive restraint rule, filed a lawsuit challenging the revocation, and the case reached the Supreme Court.[9] The court ruled that the revocation was arbitrary and capricious because NHTSA had failed to develop new evidence to justify a change in the rule.[10]

The courts also review regulatory actions based on *substantive due process.* The basic concern under substantive due process is whether an action exceeds the scope of the mandate of the regulatory agency.[11] Regulatory decisions thus are required to bear a relationship to a proper public purpose. In *Nebbia,* the Supreme Court stated: "So far as the requirement of due process is concerned, and in the absence of other constitutional restriction, a state is free to adopt whatever economic policy may reasonably be deemed to promote public welfare, and to enforce that policy by legislation adapted to its purpose. . . . If the laws passed are seen to have a reasonable relation to a proper legislative purpose, and are neither arbitrary nor discriminatory, the requirements of due process are satisfied. . . . With the wisdom of the policy adopted, with the adequacy or practicality of the law enacted to forward it, the courts are both incompetent and unauthorized to deal." The courts have traditionally been reluctant to substitute their judgments for those of a legislature.[12] The Court of Appeals overturned telecommunications regulations "for failure to give fair weight to Congress's directive that the Commission unbundle only those elements that would impair the viability of entry . . . ," leading to the chapter case, *The FCC and Broadband Regulation.* The Court of Appeals also overturned an FCC rule

---

[8]See Mashaw and Merrill (1985, pp. 470–476).

[9]*Motor Vehicles Manufacturers Assn. v. State Farm Insurance Co,* 463 U.S. 29 (1983).

[10]For the majority, Justice Byron R. White wrote, "We have frequently reiterated that an agency must cogently explain why it has exercised its discretion in a given manner, and we affirm this principle again today." See Mashaw and Merrill (1985, pp. 343–354).

[11]See Mashaw and Merrill (1985, pp. 318–385).

[12]See Edley (1990) for a treatment of administrative law and judicial review.

prohibiting ownership of a local television station by a cable company and expressed skepticism about the FCC's national television ownership rule, leading to the chapter case, *The FCC Media Ownership Rules.*

Rule making is the most important activity of most regulatory agencies. Agencies must follow the procedures specified in their authorizing statutes. Interested parties participate in both formal and informal rule-making procedures, but they also attempt to influence agency actions outside those procedures. Contacts with firms and other interests are generally required to be disclosed in advance through ex parte notification requirements, which contribute to the relative openness of regulatory processes. Lobbying and other forms of information provision are the principal approaches to influencing agency decisions in addition to participation in formal rule-making procedures. The chapter case, *Echelon and the Home Automation Standard (A)*, considers a company that faced a challenge because it failed to participate in a rule-making procedure.

# The Nonmarket Environment of Regulatory Agencies

Regulatory agencies operate in a complex environment, and even "independent" regulatory commissions are subject to a variety of influences, as illustrated in Figure 10-2. Commissioners and administrators of regulatory agencies are appointed by the president, and most require Senate confirmation. The appointment of regulators can have an important impact on regulatory policy and practice, as the discussion of the deregulation of the airline industry in Chapter 1 indicates. When President Carter sought to deregulate the surface transportation industries, he needed a majority of pro-deregulation commissioners on the ICC. When his appointment of the chairman gave the pro-deregulation side a four-to-three majority, with four seats vacant, he chose not to fill the vacancies. The ICC then began to deregulate. The executive branch can also influence regulatory commissions through the policy expertise of cabinet agencies.

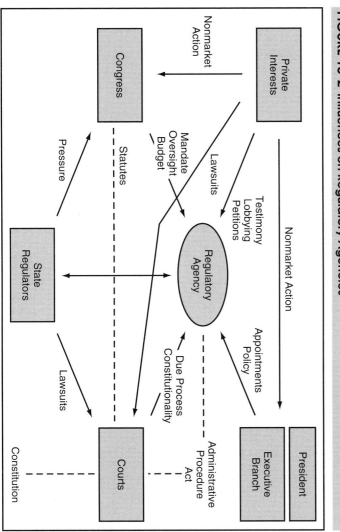

**FIGURE 10-2 Influences on Regulatory Agencies**

The president thus has a number of instruments to influence regulatory agencies, particularly those in the executive branch.

The president also exercises considerable influence through his ability to direct the review of regulations. President Carter issued an executive order requiring analysis of all new regulations and established the Regulatory Analysis Review Group to review those analyses. Shortly after taking office, President Reagan issued Executive Order 12291, which required that "regulatory action shall not be undertaken unless the potential benefits to society from the regulation outweigh the potential costs to society." The order required regulatory agencies to prepare a Regulatory Impact Analysis for any proposed rule.[13] The Office of Management and Budget (OMB) reviewed the agencies' analyses and could request changes. The order was an important tool in the Reagan and George H. W. Bush administrations' efforts to limit regulation. When he took office, President Clinton modified President Reagan's order by restricting the reviews by OMB's Office of Information and Regulatory Affairs (OIRA) to "significant" regulations and by requiring that OMB take into account "qualitative" as well as quantitative measures of costs and benefits. OMB estimated that the cost in 1997 of the rules reviewed under these orders was $198 billion.[14] The influence of the president on specific rules is indicated by the example.

## Regulatory Rule Making in the Bush Administration

The George W. Bush administration set out to make regulation less burdensome and to apply better data and science to the analysis of regulatory rules. The Data Quality Act required regulatory agencies to set standards for the quality of their scientific studies, including the quality not only of the data but also of the analysis of the data. OIRA played the lead role in the evaluation of proposed new rules and modification of existing rules.

As examples of the changes, the Bush administration relaxed costly requirements for hospital emergency rooms that had led a number of hospitals to close their emergency rooms. At the urging of the U.S. Conference of Mayors, the EPA revised brownfields regulations to allow the sale of contaminated sites to private parties that would assume clean-up responsibilities. In response to a surge in lawsuits pertaining to eligibility for overtime pay, the administration put into place new rules under the Fair Labor Standards Act that required mandatory overtime for an additional

1.3 million workers but allowed employers to decide whether employees earning between $23,660 and $100,000 were administrators and hence not eligible for overtime. Unions claimed that this threatened the overtime pay for 6 million workers. Under the Clean Air Act the EPA proposed a system of tradable mercury permits to achieve reductions in mercury pollution.[1] New rules issued under the Endangered Species Act counted hatchery-raised salmon as well as wild salmon in determining whether a species was endangered. Following complaints by the governors of western states, the administration revised rules issued in the final days of the Clinton administration prohibiting logging and other activities in "roadless areas" of national forests. Under the new rules governors of states could ask the Forest Service for permission to authorize logging.

---

[1]Tradable permit systems are considered in Chapter 11.

---

[13]See Weidenbaum (2004, p. 171).
[14]OMB, Report to Congress on the Costs and Benefits of Federal Regulations, Chapter II, http://www.whitehouse.gov/omb/inforeg/chap2.html.

Congress exercises considerable influence over regulatory agencies through its budgetary and oversight authorities. Congressional influence also comes from its ability to revise and block changes in statutes. The Reagan administration attempted to deregulate in the area of social regulation, but the congressional oversight committees with responsibilities over the regulatory agencies joined with interest groups to oppose those efforts. For example, the Reagan administration sought to eliminate the Consumer Products Safety Commission (CPSC), but Congress refused.

Congress has power over regulatory agencies because it writes their legislative mandates and reauthorizes those agencies whose statutes require it. The CPSC requires reauthorization every 3 years, yet from 1981 to 1990, threatened by a possible presidential veto, Congress could not agree on reauthorization legislation. The difficulty in reauthorization resulted in part because, in contrast to the statutes establishing economic regulation that use broad terms such as "the public interest," the statutes establishing social regulation often have very detailed language. For example, the reauthorization bill passed in 1990 required the CPSC to establish safety standards for automatic garage door openers.[15] Congress also can include provisions in budget appropriations bills that prevent regulatory agencies from spending any funds on particular programs or regulatory initiatives. For example, in the 1990s Congress prohibited the Department of Energy from spending on any new rule making on energy efficiency standards.

Congress and its committees also provide oversight of regulatory agencies and can pressure regulators through oversight hearings in which regulators can be called to task for their actions. Members of Congress also frequently call or write regulatory agencies asking for explanations of agency actions. The agencies always answer.

Federal regulatory agencies can also be influenced by state regulatory agencies. The National Association of [state] Regulatory Utility Commissions strongly criticized Congress for imposing a moratorium on new energy efficiency standards. State regulatory commissions also may file lawsuits against federal regulatory agencies and make their interests known to their state's congressional delegation.

Private interests affect regulatory agencies directly through their participation in hearings and other regulatory proceedings and indirectly through pressure on Congress and the executive branch. The statutes for some regulatory agencies give citizens rights to petition for action. In the Part III integrative case, *Pharmaceutical Switching*, a citizen's petition was filed asking the FDA to switch Claritin to the over-the-counter market. Private interests also lobby regulatory agencies, although ex parte contracts with regulators must be disclosed in advance. Activists file lawsuits to force regulators to enforce what the activists see as the agency's mandate. Firms frequently appeal regulatory decisions. Fox Television successfully appealed an FCC rule and order blocking the acquisition of local television stations. The chapter case, *The FCC Media Ownership Rules*, considers the FCC review of those rules.

The courts have a considerable influence on regulation, reviewing regulatory actions for constitutionality and for consistency with statutes. In both the Broadband and Media Ownership Rules chapter cases the FCC decisions were appealed to the courts. As considered in Chapter 11, many of the rules promulgated by the EPA are appealed.

At times regulatory agencies also face pressures from within. Mary Cheila Gall, a Republican appointed by President Clinton to the CPSC, criticized the Commission as promoting "a federal nanny state." She also said, "The Commission strives to be a data-driven agency and one committed to sound science in its activities. In this case, however, the commission requested reformulation [of crayons] in the absence of adequate data. This 'science' more closely resembled 'political' science than traditional scientific inquiry."[16] Senate Democrats retaliated by rejecting on a party line vote her nomination by President Bush to be chair of the CPSC.

## Explanations for Regulation

Two theories have been offered to explain where regulation is and is not imposed. The first is the theory of market imperfections, which predicts that regulation will be instituted to correct market imperfections. The second theory is political and predicts that interest groups seek regulation to serve their interests. The regulation of the prices charged by grain elevators that gave rise to *Munn v. Illinois* allowed farmers, rather than grain elevators, to capture the profits from the sale of their crops. The same interests were important in the passage of the Interstate Commerce Act and the Sherman Antitrust Act. The market imperfections perspective is grounded in economic theory, and the next section examines five types of market imperfections: natural monopoly, externalities, public goods, asymmetric information, and moral hazard.[17] The following section then considers political explanations for regulation.

## Market Imperfections

### Natural Monopoly

A monopoly is natural if one firm can produce a given set of goods at lower cost than can any larger number of firms. A *natural monopoly* results when costs are decreasing in the scale of output or in the scope of the set of goods a firm produces. The classical theory of natural monopoly predicts that a monopolist will restrict its output, raising its price above marginal cost. The restriction of output causes economic inefficiency because some consumers who are willing to pay the cost of the resources expended to satisfy their demand are prevented from doing so by the restricted output. This inefficiency is referred to as a *deadweight loss* (DWL), since an opportunity to achieve economic gains is forgone.

The case of a monopoly is illustrated in Figure 10-3, which presents a demand curve ($D$) and the monopolist's average cost ($AC$) and marginal cost ($MC$) curves. The marginal and average cost curves are decreasing because of economies of scale. A monopolist exercises its market power by restricting its output to the point $q_2$ at which marginal revenue (not shown) equals marginal cost, resulting in a price $p_2$ that is above average and marginal costs. The profit of the firm is the difference between the price $p_2$ and average cost multiplied by the quantity $q_2$; that is, profit is the area FAHG. Consumer surplus is the area under the demand curve above the price $p_2$. A deadweight loss results because there are consumers who are willing to purchase the product at a price above the marginal cost of producing it. These units are the difference between $q_0$ and $q_2$, and the deadweight loss is the shaded area ABC.

In the case of a natural monopoly, economic theory recommends that government set price equal to marginal cost, or $p_0$, so that all consumers who are willing to pay the

[16]*The New York Times*, May 23, 2001.
[17]See Breyer (1982, Ch. 1), Spulber (1989), and Viscusi, Vernon, and Harrington (2000) for discussions of the nature of market imperfections.

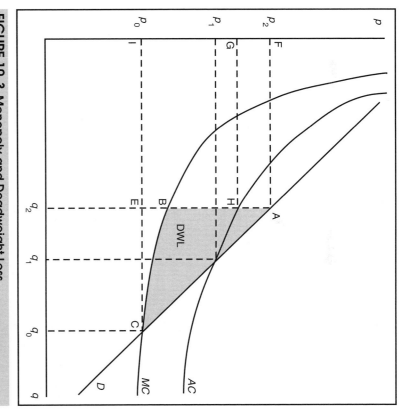

**FIGURE 10-3 Monopoly and Deadweight Loss**

incremental cost of the resources expended to satisfy their demand will purchase the good. Lowering the price to $p_0$ has two effects. The first is the elimination of the deadweight loss because output expands from $q_2$ to $q_0$. The second is a pure transfer from the firm to consumers consisting of the profit FAHG and the area GHEI, which represents a gain in consumer surplus and a loss of profit from lowering the price from $p_2$ to $p_0$.

In the presence of decreasing costs, however, pricing at marginal cost does not provide sufficient revenue to cover the total cost of the firm. Total costs could be covered by a government subsidy financed by taxes. This alternative is generally opposed, however, because taxes distort the activity on which they are levied and subsidies weaken the incentives of the monopolist to be responsive to consumer demands. Consequently, either regulated prices are set equal to average costs, denoted $p_1$ in Figure 10-3, or costs are covered through fixed charges, such as monthly charges. For example, under cost of service regulation consumers pay monthly charges to cover the fixed costs of electric power plants, including a fair rate of return on capital.

Before concluding that regulation is warranted in the case of a natural monopoly, two questions must be answered. The first is whether there are any natural monopolies. If there are, the second is whether significant economic efficiency would be gained by regulation. With respect to the first question economies of scale and scope certainly exist over some sets of goods and services, but these economies may be exhausted at output levels that allow more than one supplier to persist in the market. Empirical studies indicate, for example, that the large electric power plants in the United States have exhausted the achievable economies of scale. Moreover, advancements in gas turbine generators have resulted in highly efficient power generation at much smaller scales. A natural monopoly can also result if having more than one supplier would result in an uneconomical duplication of facilities. Local electricity distribution systems within cities may remain a monopoly to avoid duplicate sets of distribution wires. This rationale does not apply in telecommunications, however, since cable television and wireless communications systems provide alternatives to the local wire connections. A monopoly could also result from network effects and standardization as considered in Chapter 13 and as found in the Chapter 9 case, *The Microsoft Antitrust Case*, with respect to computer operating systems.

If there is a natural monopoly, it does not necessarily follow that there is substantial economic inefficiency. First, if entry into the industry is easy, the threat of potential competition may limit the extent to which an incumbent monopolist will restrict its output. Second, a monopolist may choose to use nonlinear pricing, involving fixed charges and a low unit price; that is, a price near $p_0$. This can both increase profits and benefit consumers. Third, if there are a number of possible suppliers of a monopoly service, competitive bidding for the right to be the monopolist can be used to lower the supply price and increase economic efficiency. Similarly, an alternative to the regulation of the electric power industry is for communities to own the local distribution system and solicit bids from power companies for the supply of electricity.[18] As considered in the section on deregulation, industries such as electric power and telecommunications had been subject to price regulation based on a natural monopoly rationale. Competition, however, is replacing regulation in these industries and not only improving pricing but also inducing more efficient production.

## Externalities

*Externalities* are of two types. A pecuniary externality is present when the actions of one economic agent affect other economic agents through changes in the prices of goods and services. When a firm builds a plant, its demand for labor drives up the wage rate unless labor is perfectly elastically supplied. This pecuniary externality does not result in economic inefficiency because the wage rate in the labor market is determined by the forces of supply and demand. Thus, a pecuniary externality does not provide a rationale for regulation.

Pecuniary externalities do, however, affect rents and hence may motivate nonmarket action. The oil shocks of the 1970s increased prices dramatically, and politicians responded by enacting a complex regulatory system to lower the price of oil so as to reduce the rents of the owners of U.S. crude oil reserves. The price controls, however, both dampened the incentive to find new domestic crude oil and stimulated the demand for oil, resulting in increased oil imports. The resulting inefficiency was sufficiently costly that crude oil price regulation was eliminated by the early 1980s.[19]

The second type of externality is nonpecuniary and occurs when an action of one economic agent directly affects the preferences or production opportunities of another economic agent. An individual who drives an automobile generates pollution that both is unhealthy and affects visibility. Similarly, one firm's waste disposal site may pollute another's water supply. These externalities result in a divergence of private costs from social costs. Economic inefficiency results unless agents take into account the full social

[18]See Joskow and Schmalensee (1983) and White (1997) for an assessment of the potential for competition in electric power.
[19]See Breyer (1982, pp. 164–171) and Kalt (1981) for analyses of the inefficiency resulting from crude oil price regulation.

costs of their activities. Externalities provide an efficiency rationale for regulation that aligns private and social costs as considered in detail in Chapter 11 on environmental protection. Energy-efficiency regulation of household appliances may be warranted because burning carbon-based fuels to generate electricity causes externalities in the form of pollution and the release of gases that contribute to global climate change. Energy-efficiency regulation is, however, only a second-best form of regulation, as considered in Chapter 11 in the context of incentive-based systems for environmental protection.

## Public Goods

A *public good* is one whose consumption by one person does not reduce its availability for others. When a person consumes a private good such as an apple, it is not available for consumption by others. When a person consumes a good such as national defense or a radio broadcast, however, the amount of the good available for consumption by others is not diminished. For a private good, economic efficiency requires that the marginal utility from consumption equals the price of the good, or, more correctly, that the marginal rate of substitution of one private good for another equals the ratio of their prices. Since a public good is available to all economic agents in a quantity undiminished by their consumption, economic efficiency requires that the sum of the marginal utilities of all individuals equal the price of the public good.[20] Many public goods are "local" in the sense that at some point adding more consumers diminishes the amount of the good available for others due to congestion, as in the case of a bridge at rush hour.

For some public goods, such as national defense, bridges, and roads, government provision is customary. Government provision, however, does not imply that a good has the characteristics of a public good. Many goods, such as public housing, food stamps, and soil-bank programs, are provided by government to redistribute income rather than because they are public goods. Also, public goods can be supplied by the private sector. Radio and television broadcasts are provided by private enterprises subject only to noneconomic regulation. Similarly, the government privatized its Landsat satellite system, which provides data and photographs of the earth's surface.

A fundamental problem with either private or public provision of public goods centers on the "revelation of preferences." If those who benefit from a public good are asked to pay for it based on how much they value it, people may understate their valuations and free ride on the payments of others. Because of the free-rider problem, public provision may be warranted. This, however, does not resolve the problem of determining the public's aggregate valuation of the good and thus whether it should be supplied in the first place. If individuals could be excluded from consuming the public good, the revelation and free-rider problems could be resolved—at least in principle. For example, preventing satellite-dish owners from obtaining free television programming induces customers to pay for Direct TV and Dish Network.

## Asymmetric Information

A market imperfection can also result from *asymmetric information*. If people have different (private) information at the time they act, markets may not perform efficiently, even when there are advantageous trades that could be made. Akerlof (1970) considered the case of a used car market in which each seller knows the true value of

[20]In this sense, an externality is also a public good (or bad), since the efficient provision of goods involving externalities requires that the sum of the marginal utilities and disutilities from its supply be equated to its marginal cost.

the car she wants to sell, but the buyers know only the probability distribution of the values of the cars that might be offered for sale. For each used car there is a potential buyer who is willing to buy it, but a buyer cannot through casual inspection determine the true value of any particular used car offered for sale. All he knows is that a car might be a lemon, might be high quality, or might be somewhere in between.

Because a potential buyer does not know the true value of any particular car, the maximum amount he is willing to pay is the average of the values of those cars that will be offered for sale. Potential sellers with high-quality cars find that the amount buyers are willing to pay is less than the value of their cars. They thus will not offer their cars for sale. Buyers recognize this and understand that the only cars that will be offered for sale will be those of low quality. The average value of those low-quality cars is low, however, so buyers will be willing to pay only a low amount. The low amount buyers are willing to pay again means that the potential sellers of cars at the high end of the remaining range will not offer their cars for sale. Buyers will then be willing to pay even less for any car offered for sale. The market thus may collapse with no sales being made. This is clearly inefficient, because for every used car there is a buyer who is willing to buy it if he only knew its true value.

This phenomenon, known as *adverse selection*, also occurs when sellers have incomplete information about customers. Insurance, in principle, is to provide coverage for individuals with similar risk characteristics. When those characteristics cannot be readily observed, people with quite different risks can be placed in the same pool. High-risk individuals have an incentive to buy insurance, which can drive up the price of insurance and cause some low-risk individuals not to buy insurance. Insurance companies respond to this adverse selection by requiring a physical examination for life insurance and basing auto insurance rates on observables such as accident and traffic citation histories and the number of years of driving experience.

When market participants have incomplete information and acquiring information is costly, the mandated provision of information through regulation may be warranted. Regulation may not be warranted in all situations involving asymmetric information, however. Information has value, so there is a demand for it. In the used car example, a potential buyer may take the car to a mechanic for inspection. More generally, individuals may invest in information acquisition or hire agents who are more knowledgeable than they are. On the supply side, manufacturers can offer warranties to signal to consumers that their products are of high quality.[21] Some dealers, for example, offer warranties on their used or pre-owned cars.

Information, however, can remain undersupplied when it is in the self-interest of its possessor not to supply it. Manufacturers are understandably reluctant to release negative information about potential hazards associated with their products because doing so may reduce demand. The Chapter 21 case, *Reporting of Clinical Trial Results*, concerns the practices of pharmaceutical companies in releasing the results of clinical trials. Consequently, consumers may be inadequately informed about hazards. Similarly, an employee may be incompletely informed about possible health and safety hazards in the workplace. In such situations, regulation could be warranted, but the liability system, considered in Chapter 12, is an alternative to regulation.

## Moral Hazard

*Moral hazard* refers to inefficient actions induced by policy instruments that cause people not to bear the full consequences of their actions. In the case of medical care, fully-insured individuals have an effectively unlimited demand for medical care, since

---

[21]See Spence (1973) for the seminal work on signaling.

they bear none of the cost of the care they receive. In addition, individuals may not have the proper incentive to take socially efficient preventive measures because they know that the cost of any illness or accident will be covered by insurance. For example, federally funded flood insurance encourages people to live in areas prone to flooding and can lead to socially inefficient location decisions.

Regulation is one response to moral hazard problems, but regulation can also cause moral hazard problems, making the regulation itself less effective. In a controversial article Peltzman (1975) argued that automobile safety regulation induced drivers to take more risks, thus reducing the effectiveness of mandatory safety standards. Peterson and Hoffer (1994) studied data on automobile personal injury and collision insurance claims from 1989 to 1991 and for each model compared data for those vehicles with an airbag to those with no air bag. Their data indicated that the number of accident claims were systematically higher for the identical automobile model with air bags than those without an airbag. The authors concluded that although these results were consistent with Peltzman's argument, they could be due to higher-risk drivers being more likely than lower-risk drivers to choose automobiles with air bags.

As an example of moral hazard, the 1986 Emergency Medical Treatment and Labor Act (EMTLA) requires all hospitals that participate in Medicaid and have an emergency room to provide a medical screening evaluation to anyone who comes to the emergency room and to stabilize a patient's condition if there is a medical emergency. The rules implementing EMTLA also require that physicians be on call to treat a wide variety of conditions in emergency rooms. Patients were also granted the right to sue the hospital. Uninsured individuals who could not pay began using emergency rooms for their health care, imposing a heavy cost burden on hospitals. Moreover, doctors began to refuse to be on call because they could be exposed to fines or a lawsuit. The response of an increasing number of hospitals, particularly those in low income areas, was to close their emergency rooms. In 2003 and 2004 six hospitals in the Los Angeles area closed their emergency rooms to avoid the costs of EMTLA. The regulation had induced behavior that reduced rather than expanded the availability of emergency care.

Moral hazard can also occur within a firm. To increase the incentives for individuals to report corporate wrongdoing, federal laws allow a whistle-blower to receive 10 to 30 percent of any judgment won in court. In response to such laws, companies have instituted internal disclosure and ethics systems to reduce the likelihood of wrongdoing and encourage the reporting of suspected wrongdoing at an early stage. Moral hazard results because the reward provided by the federal law encourages employees to avoid companies' internal control systems, wait for evidence to accumulate, and then go directly to the public authorities. This makes the internal systems less effective in stopping wrongdoing.

In industries in which cost-of-service pricing and rate-of-return regulation are used, cost increases are passed on to consumers. The incentive for the firm to hold down costs is thus weakened. This is a form of moral hazard because the firm does not bear the full consequences of the higher costs that result from its own decisions.

The principal means of dealing with this market imperfection is to structure incentives so that the moral hazard is taken into account in decision making. In the case of medical insurance, copayments can be required and reimbursement limits imposed. Moral hazard can also be addressed by monitoring the behavior of individuals to increase the likelihood that they take proper care. Imposing fines for not wearing a seat belt is an example of monitoring. In cost-of-service regulated industries, the problem of moral hazard is reduced by the delay between the time at which the cost increase occurs and the time at which the regulators approve higher prices. Moral hazard is also reduced by breaking the link between cost increases and the prices charged for services, as in price cap regulation used in some states for telecommunications.

Markets can also resolve some potential moral hazard problems. A common problem in markets is the incentive for sellers to shirk on the quality of the goods or services they sell. For example, if quality can be observed only through use, a seller may have an incentive to shirk. If, however, consumers can sully the reputation of the firm by informing other consumers that the firm shirked on quality, shirking can be reduced or eliminated. Consumers can follow the strategy of purchasing from the firm as long as its reputation for producing high-quality products is unsullied and not purchasing from it if its reputation is ever sullied. If the potential gain from future sales is sufficiently great, the firm will have no incentive to shirk on quality.[22]

## Government Imperfections

Market imperfections in many cases warrant government regulation. In some cases, however, regulation may be a cure that is worse than the disease. Wolf (1979, p. 138) argues that government intervention to deal with a market imperfection or failure may itself be subject to a "nonmarket failure."[23] He argues that the market failure "rationale provides only a necessary, not a sufficient, justification for public policy interventions. Sufficiency requires that specifically identified market failures be compared with potential nonmarket failure associated with the implementation of public policies. . . ."

Market imperfections are thus only a necessary condition for regulation to improve economic efficiency. Regulation is not perfect, and even well-intentioned regulation can in some instances worsen the performance of markets. In addition, regulation is not always intended to correct market imperfections but instead can be the result of political forces that serve objectives other than economic efficiency. The next section considers the political economy of regulation.

# The Political Economy of Regulation

## Capture and Rent-Seeking Theories

One theory of economic regulation is that it is initially imposed to address a market imperfection, but through interaction with the firms they regulate, regulators begin to see the firms' problems as their own. Regulation then evolves over time to serve the interests of regulated firms in addition to, or instead of, the goal of economic efficiency.[24] This *capture* theory predicts that regulation initially will be found where there are market imperfections and over time will evolve to serve the interests of the regulated industry.

Observing that much of the economic regulation of industries increased costs and generated rents, Chicago school economists provided a different explanation for where regulation would be expected. Their focus was not on market imperfections but on the ability of interest groups to obtain regulation through political pressure. From this perspective, regulation is demanded by interest groups and supplied through the political process.[25] Regulation thus was not established to address market imperfections and then captured but instead was established to benefit politically effective interests. Once established, regulation continued to serve those interests. From this *rent-seeking* perspective, the railroads in the 19th century sought regulation to support their cartel agreements, which were plagued by defections and cheating. Similarly, regulation in the airline and trucking industries was sought in part to serve the interests of incumbent

---

[22]See Kreps (1990) for an exposition of this theory.
[23]See also Wolf (1988).
[24]See Bernstein (1955) and Quirk (1981).
[25]See Stigler (1971), Posner (1974), and Peltzman (1976).

firms by limiting entry and passing on cost increases through higher regulated prices. This perspective and the supporting empirical evidence provided impetus for the deregulation of a number of industries.

Regulation is also supplied in response to the demands of interest groups other than business. This is clearest in the context of social regulation where, for example, environmental groups successfully overcame agricultural interests in obtaining the regulation of pesticides and where organized labor succeeded in obtaining workplace safety and health regulation. During the early 1990s consumer complaints about basic cable television prices led Congress to establish price regulation over the veto of President Bush.

Firms also seek federal regulations to avoid individual states imposing different regulations. Appliance manufacturers sought uniform energy-efficiency standards across the states to avoid having to produce different models for different states. Some Internet service and content providers supported federal Internet privacy standards to preclude the enactment of disparate state standards. Companies also seek regulation to level the playing field by requiring competitors to meet the same standards they meet. When McDonald's decided to implement a no-smoking policy in its company-owned restaurants, it sought uniform federal regulation to impose a no-smoking policy on all restaurants.

## A Nonmarket Theory of Regulation

Although the capture and rent-seeking theories are insightful, they give insufficient attention to market imperfections, as is most apparent in the regulation of externalities such as pollution. These theories also give insufficient attention to the role of institutions in structuring the competition among interest groups, and they lack an account of the organization, strategies, and effectiveness of those interest groups. As indicated in Figure 10-2, regulation takes place in a complex institutional and political environment, and the mandates and procedures of those institutions, as well as the policy objectives of the executive branch, can be important. In the case of the regulation of basic cable television prices, members of Congress saw the issue as sufficiently popular with constituents that it was worthwhile for them to enact the Cable Television Act of 1992 and claim credit for it.[26]

Regulation and regulatory change can be more fully understood through the frameworks presented in parts I and II of this book combined with the characteristics of the regulatory environment, as illustrated in Figure 10-2, and the analysis of market imperfections. This *political economy* theory views regulation as shaped by market imperfections, institutions and their officeholders, and the nonmarket action of private interests. The impact of nonmarket action on regulatory agencies is direct, as well as indirect through Congress and the executive branch. In addition, regulation has procedural requirements imposed by both legislation and due process rights. The economic efficiency objective of addressing market imperfections also influences the policymaking process, particularly if that objective is embraced by the presidential administration. The civil service personnel of the agencies and the nature of bureaucracy also play a role.[27] Interest group politics represents a strong force for change in some cases and for preservation of the status quo in others.[28] Regulatory change in the telecommunications and electric power industries considered later in the chapter illustrates the importance of institutions as well as of interests.

[26]Price regulation was eliminated during the Clinton administration.
[27]See Wilson (1989).
[28]See Noll and Owen (1983), Wilson (1980), and Francis (1993) for studies of the politics of regulation.

Regulation is also shaped by the efficiency consequences of policy alternatives and the policy responses to those consequences. The impetus for deregulation in the transportation industries came from information provided by public policy analysts, the staff of regulatory commissions, and policymakers in the executive branch.[29] Regulatory policy is thus a product of both interest group actions and institutions and their officeholders.[30]

To illustrate the perspective, consider the case of social regulation and small business. One distinctive feature of much of the social regulation enacted over the past 35 years is the regularity of special provisions for small businesses. Many regulations provide small businesses with exemptions, streamlined reporting procedures, reduced compliance burdens, smaller penalties, or less stringent standards. Brock and Evans (1986, Table 4.2) list 29 federal regulatory programs that provide "tiers" of regulation based on the size of firms. For example, the Family Leave Act of 1993 exempts firms with fewer than 50 employees. Furthermore, the Regulatory Flexibility Act of 1980 encourages regulators not to burden small businesses unduly.

Small business receives these exemptions in part because the compliance costs, and particularly their administrative components, are disproportionately burdensome for small business. Exemptions, however, are also due to the effective political organization of small businesses. As indicated in Chapter 8, small businesses are numerous, have complete coverage of legislative districts, and in the aggregate have substantial resources. Small business is also well organized for nonmarket purposes, with the National Federation of Independent Business and the National Small Business Association having considerable influence in Washington and in state capitols.

## Redistribution and Cross-Subsidization

In addition to addressing market imperfections, regulation can be used to redistribute income. Rent control in the housing market is an example, and cable television price regulation is another. Regulation can also be used to redistribute income through cross-subsidization of one customer class by another. Because of distributive concerns, state regulatory agencies have instituted lifeline rates for low-income consumers. In California, at the end of 2001 the number of low-income individuals receiving lifeline rates for basic telephone services reached 3.7 million. Lifeline rates require cross-subsidization by other customers, which in California took the form of a 4 percent surcharge on basic telephone service.

Cross-subsidization occurs when one group of customers pays more and another group pays less than the cost of providing their service. Inefficiency results on both sides of the cross-subsidization. When a price is below costs, some consumers receive service even though the cost of satisfying their demand is greater than their willingness to pay for it. When a price is above costs, some consumers who are willing to pay the cost of the resources required to produce their service are denied the opportunity to do so.

Cross-subsidization is a common feature of the economic regulation of industries. Long-distance and business telephone services have been used to cross-subsidize basic residential service. When airline fares and routes were regulated, long-distance flights cross-subsidized shorter flights, and high-density airline routes cross-subsidized low-density routes. Cross-subsidization is unsustainable when entry into the industry is possible, since customers who are paying more than the cost of their service have an

---

[29] See Derthick and Quirk (1985) for a study of the influence of policy analysts on regulatory policy.
[30] Harris and Milkis (1989) provide an analysis of regulatory change at the FTC and EPA.

incentive to seek alternative suppliers. Much of the deregulation movement in the United States has been the result of forces created by cross-subsidization. The entry of MCI into the long-distance telecommunications market occurred because AT&T's long-distance rates were used to cross-subsidize other services. MCI offered services at prices that did not include the cross-subsidization, and customers switched to it. Similarly, as the airline industry was being deregulated, entry occurred first on high-density, long-distance routes.

## Cost-of-Service Regulation

Regulation in a number of industries has centered on cost-of-service pricing. In industries such as airlines and trucking, entry was controlled and industry-wide prices were set with cost increases passed on to consumers in the form of higher prices. This allowed inefficiencies to creep into the industries. Because industry-wide wage increases affected all firms similarly and the increased costs could be passed through to consumers, firms had weak incentives to resist wage demands. This moral hazard feature of cost-of-service regulation allowed organized labor, such as the Teamsters, to capture substantially higher wages than would otherwise have been possible.[31] When deregulation occurred in those industries and entry was permitted, wage rates and union membership began to fall. Similarly, in the airline industry pilots and machinists captured high wages, and with deregulation the growth of nonunion carriers threatened the existence of airlines such as United, US Airways, Delta, and American.

In the electric power, natural gas transmission, and telecommunications industries prices were set on a firm-by-firm basis to yield the revenue required to cover the firm's actual costs plus an allowed return on equity capital. Price changes occurred only with regulatory approval, and the approval process was similar to formal adjudication. Data and analyses were presented by the firm in support of the price changes, comments were requested from interested parties, hearings were held, witnesses testified and were cross-examined, and the commission issued an order specifying the prices. Much of the contention in this process centered on the rate of return the firm was allowed. In some cases, the emphasis on rate of return caused regulation to focus more on the profits earned by firms than on efficient pricing or cost efficiencies.

Cost-of-service regulation of telecommunications service focused on the rate of return in part because neither the regulators nor the firms had reliable data on the costs of providing individual services. The cost structure of telecommunications involves large common costs of facilities, such as network and switching equipment, used for a variety of services. In addition, network externalities complicate the determination of costs. Moreover, the firms' accounting and information systems were not designed to identify costs of individual services, making it virtually impossible to base prices for individual services on their actual costs.

This cost-of-service regulatory system has been blamed for inducing high costs and slowing the introduction of new technology in telecommunications. Firms were said to invest in excess capacity and higher-quality equipment than needed because that increased their asset base. Since profits were determined by applying the allowed rate of return to the asset base, higher profits resulted. This also caused other inefficiencies. AT&T was said to have inhibited the rate at which new technology was introduced because it did not want to write off existing assets and lose the return allowed on those assets. These inefficiencies coupled with cross-subsidization led to deregulation.

---

[31]See Rose (1987).

# Deregulation

## Telecommunications

Over the past 50 years, interstate telecommunications regulation has evolved from strict cost-of-service regulation of a monopoly (AT&T and the Bell system) to reliance on competition with only limited supervision by regulators. Intrastate telecommunications service was also tightly regulated by state public utility commissions, and competition is slowly emerging at the local level. Regulation of interstate long-distance service traditionally focused on who was permitted to provide service and what prices could be charged for those services. After World War II a series of technological advances changed the cost structure of the industry with microwave transmission technology reducing costs dramatically. In the 1950s state police departments and oil and gas pipeline companies received permission to build microwave systems tailored to their specific needs and dedicated to their own use.[32] Entry into the industry had begun.

Technological progress continued, and for several decades both real and nominal prices for telecommunications services decreased. Despite the lower prices, the price structure in telecommunications resulted in considerable economic inefficiency. Because of the early public policy objective of achieving universal service, basic residential service was cross-subsidized by business and long-distance service. This cross-subsidization continued as a result of nonmarket pressure from consumers and from politicians who sought to represent their interests. Technological change in the form of microwave and satellite systems and electronic switching equipment, however, made it possible for large business customers to bypass the Bell network by establishing their own private telecommunications systems. Bypass was sufficiently attractive that the system of cross-subsidization was in jeopardy.

Entry of new service providers had been blocked by the FCC, but as a result of court decisions overturning several FCC decisions, competitors such as MCI and Sprint were allowed to enter increasingly broad segments of the interstate telecommunications market. The breakup of the Bell system further complicated the practice of cost-of-service and rate-of-return regulation.[33] The FCC faced the problem of restructuring the rates for long-distance and local service in light of bypass, entry, and competitive pressures.

Telecommunications deregulation thus was spurred by technological change and cross-subsidization, which provided opportunities for new entrants to offer selected services at prices substantially below regulated prices. Technological change essentially eliminated any remaining vestiges of natural monopoly in the industry. For example, local connections could be provided by cable television connections and wireless communications systems in addition to copper wire. Deregulation proceeded most rapidly at the federal level with more modest steps taken by states.

State regulation had also been rampant with cross-subsidization, with intrastate long-distance service subsidizing local service and business service subsidizing residential service. State deregulation has focused less on cross-subsidization and instead on incentive regulation intended to provide firms with flexibility to operate more efficiently and to pass on some of the efficiency to customers. Kridel, Sappington, and Weisman (1996) reviewed the empirical literature on state deregulation and concluded that the evidence on the effects of the regulatory initiatives was mixed; that is, it is "premature to conclude that incentive regulation has been an overwhelming success." They noted, "There is no evidence that incentive regulation has led to streamlined regulatory proceedings."

[32]Pipeline companies already had rights of way and thus could readily construct microwave systems.
[33]See Temin (1987) for a history of the Bell system and its change. See Fisher, McGowan, and Greenwood (1983) for an analysis of the breakup.

At the federal level Congress had attempted for 20 years to amend the Communications Act of 1934, which had remained largely as originally written despite dramatic technological change. Finally, a compromise among the three principal sets of companies—long-distance carriers, regional Bell operating companies, and cable television providers—was reached in the Telecommunications Act of 1996. This complex act sought to open both local service and long-distance markets to entry provided that the entrant's market was open to competition.

The Telecommunications Act of 1996 was a milestone in the transformation of virtually all segments of the telecommunications market from tight regulation to competition. The Act and continued technological change resulted in restructuring of the industry. Through mergers and acquisitions the seven regional Bell operating companies plus GTE have consolidated leaving four companies: SBC, Verizon, Bell South, and Qwest. AT&T and its former research and manufacturing unit Lucent Technologies stumbled badly in the new competitive environment.

Harris and Kraft (1997) examined the act and evaluated the compromises it reflected.[34] A local-service company is permitted to provide long-distance service, which it had been prohibited from providing by the settlement in the AT&T antitrust case, but only if it provided all potential competitors access to its local network. Thus, the quid pro quo for local exchange companies to provide integrated local and long-distance service is that they open their local service market to competition. Similarly, cable television companies were freed from the price controls imposed in the Cable Television Act of 1992 when local-exchange companies were ready to provide video services.[35] To spur competition, local-exchange companies were required to provide interconnections to their networks, which stimulated entry.

Entry occurred in fits and starts in the local and interstate telecommunications and cable television markets. In 2001 SBC won approval to offer long-distance service to Texas residents, marking the next step in competition in the interstate long-distance market. Verizon subsequently entered the interstate long-distance market, becoming one of the largest providers.

The Telecommunications Act required the incumbent local-exchange carriers (ILECs) to lease elements of their networks to other companies entering their markets. The entrants, referred to as competitive local exchange carriers (CLECs), sought low prices for the network elements, and the state regulators provided discounted prices to spur entry and drive down prices for consumers. Some 300 CLECs entered, but many failed when the technology bubble burst in 2001 and 2002. The FCC was responsible for determining which network elements should be provided to the CLECs, but the courts overturned the FCC's decisions because they went beyond the courts' interpretation of Congress's directive to provide "only those network elements that would impair the viability of entry. . . ." The FCC's decisions affected not only voice communications but also the provision of broadband. The chapter case, *The FCC and Broadband Regulation*, concerns the FCC's attempt to determine which network elements were necessary to avoid impairing entry.

## Electric Power

The electric power industry represents approximately 3 percent of GDP and is nearly the size of the telephone and airline industries combined. Electricity prices vary greatly across the states with average 1999 retail prices of 11.75 and 9.3 cents per kilowatt hour

---

[34] They also provide a brief history of deregulation at the federal level.
[35] The Act deregulated prices of small cable systems and phased out price controls for large systems over 3 years.

in New Hampshire and California, respectively, at the high end, and 4.0 and 4.2 cents per kilowatt hour in Idaho and Kentucky, respectively. The price differences are in large part due to historical factors including the high costs of nuclear power plants still in the rate base. Technological change in electric power has also had an important effect as improvements in gas turbine generators have lowered costs and greatly reduced the minimum efficient scale in the industry. Moreover, legislation required electric utilities to purchase electricity, often at high prices, from qualified facilities such as cogeneration plants and renewable energy sources.[36] In addition, line losses from electricity transmission have been reduced.

These technological changes have made it both feasible and economical to transmit cheap electricity to distant customers. For example, the lower cost of power in adjacent states provided incentives for California's customers to import electricity. In 1992 Congress passed the Energy Policy Act, which required a transmission company to "wheel" electricity from a producer in one state through its lines to a customer in a third state. This, in effect, made wholesale electricity a competitive market. Brokers and trading companies such as Dynegy and Enron made a market in electricity, where industrial customers bought electricity on the spot market in 15-minute blocks. The potential for competition led a majority of states to deregulate their electric power markets.[37] The actions taken by the states varied considerably, and only the most extensive deregulation effort, that in California, is considered here.[38]

Electricity prices in California were nearly double the prices in neighboring states. This had two effects. First, the price gap plus nonmarket forces, including stringent environmental regulation and NIMBY protests, led to no additions of electric power generation capacity during the 1990s. This also meant that California power plants were older and required considerable maintenance. Second, industrial customers in the state sought access to the cheaper power available just across the border. If power were imported and the market opened to competition, however, the California utilities would have stranded investments—investments in generating plants that were no longer economical to operate. This stranded investment was estimated at $28 billion.[39] Opening the market would cause the California electricity producers to default on their bond obligations. Default could undermine the credit rating of the state government, forcing it to pay higher interest rates on its bonds, since the investments in generating plants had been made with the approval of state regulators.

The state government and the electric utilities essentially struck a bargain in which the stranded investments were addressed and the market opened to competition. Any California customer was free to purchase electricity from any supplier. An industrial customer or a municipality with its own local distribution system thus could purchase electricity from the lowest bidder in a deregulated retail market. The wholesale market was also opened, and California began to import electricity from neighboring states. California utilities were not permitted to sign long-term supply contracts, so they bought power on the spot market. Consumers received an immediate 10 percent reduction in their electricity rates, and those rates were frozen for 4 years to provide income to electricity producers to cover a portion of their stranded investments. Also, government agencies issued $7.4 billion in bonds, the proceeds from which were used to pay off a portion of the stranded investments. Taking the $7.4 billion off the electricity companies' books allowed the 10 percent price reduction. Consumers, however, were

[36]The high-price contracts with qualifying facilities began expiring at the end of the 1990s.
[37]Wilson (2001) analyzed in detail the market for electricity and the management of that market.
[38]White (1997) analyzed the political economy of electric power deregulation across the states.
[39]Moody's Investor's Service estimated the stranded investment of U.S. electricity producers at $135 billion.

billed for the debt service on the state bonds and thus received little benefit during the 4-year price freeze, scheduled to expire in 2002.[40]

Strong economic growth in California during the 1990s and the failure to build new generating capacity reduced the peak-load reserve capacity in the state to almost zero. During the summer of 2000 a drought in the Northwest reduced the supply of hydroelectric power and reduced electricity exports to California. California utilities were forced to increase their purchases of electricity on the wholesale market, and the wholesale price skyrocketed. California utilities could not increase prices to their customers and were obliged to meet demand, so they purchased electricity on credit. When the utilities were unable to pay for the electricity, some qualifying facilities, some of which had not been paid for 6 months, refused to generate electricity. Power shortages developed in Northern California leading to occasional rolling blackouts. Pacific Gas & Electric, the utility in Northern California, declared bankruptcy. Southern California Edison also ran out of credit and sought relief from the state government.

In January 2001 the California governor, using executive authority, signed secret $43 billion long-term electric power contracts, many at very high prices. Prices to retail customers were increased only slightly, so the demand for electricity did not drop. The crisis ended in May 2001 as a result of several factors. First, substantial retail price increases were finally adopted, which reduced demand. The higher prices, however, would pay only for future purchases of electricity. Second, cool weather throughout the summer reduced peak demand by approximately 10 percent. Third, the Federal Energy Regulatory Commission instituted a price monitoring system for the western United States and a price mitigation plan for California. Within 2 months wholesale prices in the West fell by 80 percent.

The power crisis was over, but the California deregulation effort had been crippled. Moreover, the state of California was stuck with long-term power supply contracts at high prices and volumes that at times forced it to resell power at substantial losses. To pay for the power the state was forced to issue bonds for past electricity purchases that ultimately would be paid by California residents. California voters recalled the governor in 2003.

The failure of the California power market was due to several factors. First, risks, such as the drought in the Northwest, were larger than had been contemplated. Second, nonmarket pressures had prevented construction of new power plants in California. Third, the prohibition against utilities signing long-term contracts forced them to pay spot prices on the wholesale market. Fourth, the fixed retail prices meant that consumers did not curtail their demand when the wholesale price of electricity skyrocketed. Fifth, the refusal of the California Public Utility Commission to raise retail prices caused the utilities to bear all the risk, and they quickly became insolvent. The rules governing the electricity market were revised, and the market began to operate more efficiently.

Part of the volatility of wholesale prices was due to the trading strategies of companies such as Enron that exploited flaws in the design of the California electricity market. The Chapter 19 case, *Enron Power Marketing and the California Market*, concerns these trading strategies.

## Auctions

The FCC has innovated by substituting auctions for its comparative license award system for allocating the radio spectrum. The FCC had traditionally allocated broadcast licenses, for free, by evaluating applications using a set of noneconomic

---

[40]Consumer activists attempted to rescind the California deregulation plan by qualifying a ballot initiative for the November 1998 election, but voters rejected the initiative by a 2-to-1 vote.

standards.[41] With the development of cellular telephones, the FCC had to allocate portions of the radio spectrum for that service, and it initially turned to the same system it used to allocate broadcast licenses.

It became clear, however, that the traditional allocation system was cumbersome and inefficient and, with a major segment of the radio spectrum to be allocated in 1995 for personal communications services, the FCC needed a better mechanism. For decades economists had urged the use of auctions to allocate scarce public resources such as the radio spectrum. Auctions award resources to the highest bidders—the ones with the highest-valued uses for the resource. In a competitive market the highest-valued uses are determined by how effectively the bidders can compete to serve customers. Auctions thus yield economically efficient outcomes; that is, resources (the spectrum) are allocated to their highest-valued use. Moreover, auctions capture for the government the rents that previously went as gifts to the selected applicants. The 1995 auction for spectrum licenses suitable for personal communications systems attracted 70 bidders and raised $7 billion for the federal Treasury—$7 billion that under the previous system would have been a windfall gain to those receiving the licenses. The total amount generated by spectrum auctions in the United States has been approximately $25 billion.

The FCC continued to use auctions to allocate the radio spectrum. A 1996 auction restricted to small bidders for a 30-MHz block of the broadcast spectrum generated $10.2 billion in proceeds. Cramton (1997) provides a detailed analysis of the first four FCC auctions and concluded that they were well designed and effective in both allocating the spectrum efficiently and in extracting the rents from bidders and for the public treasury.[42] Other countries began to use auctions to allocate licenses. In Europe spectrum auctions brought in over $100 billion, but overbidding weakened many of the successful bidders.

# Summary

Government regulation has a long history in the United States, beginning in the populist era, expanding during the New Deal, and taking new directions during the period of social regulation. Although considerable deregulation has occurred, particularly at the federal level, there is still considerable economic regulation in many industries.

The government's right to regulate is unquestioned and broad but limited by due process and the constitutional protections against the taking of property without compensation. Regulation is conducted by commissions and agencies located at both the federal and the state levels. To implement their guiding statutes, regulatory agencies issue rules through formal and informal procedures.

Regulatory commissions and agencies are embedded in a complex institutional environment. They are influenced by the executive branch, Congress, private interests, and the courts. The president has considerable influence through both the appointment process and the policies advocated by executive branch agencies. Agencies have a considerable range of discretion, which allows the president to modify existing rules. In addition to writing the authorizing statutes for a regulatory agency, Congress controls the agency's budget and has oversight responsibility. Private interests affect the regulatory agency directly through testimony and lobbying and through their influence with Congress and the executive branch. In response to lawsuits filed by private interests, the

---

[41]See Breyer (1982, pp. 71–95) for a description and critique of this system.
[42]See the special issue of the *Journal of Economics & Management Strategy*, Vol. 6, Fall 1997, for additional analysis of auctions for spectrum allocations.

nature and scope of regulation are also shaped by the courts, which review statutes, policies, and individual rules.

Regulation is provided in response to both market imperfections and nonmarket forces. Market imperfections include natural monopoly, externalities, public goods, asymmetric information, and moral hazard. One role of regulation is to correct these market imperfections, but regulation itself is imperfect and can be worse than the imperfection it is intended to correct. In some cases regulation is intended to protect incumbent firms and in other cases to redistribute income through cross-subsidization. The political economy perspective on the locus and form of regulation emphasizes the role of private interests in shaping regulation. Institutions and the regulatory agencies themselves have an important impact, and regulators at the federal level have actively worked for deregulation in the airline, electric power, natural gas transmission, surface transportation, and telecommunications industries.

# The FCC and Broadband Regulation

*Broadband deployment is the central communications policy objective in America today.*

—Michael Powell, FCC Chairman

*Broadband should be a national imperative for this country in the 21st century, just like putting a man on the moon was an imperative in the last century. To stay competitive, educate the workforce and increase productivity, the United States must have ubiquitous broadband.*

—John Chambers, President and CEO of Cisco Systems

## Introduction

The Telecommunications Act of 1996 provided a structure for the deregulation of the telecommunications industry from long distance to local service. The Act allowed the remaining regional Bell operating companies, referred to as incumbent local exchange carriers (ILECs), to provide interstate long-distance service once their local service areas were open to competition from other carriers, including AT&T, MCI, and Sprint, as well as from resellers. Verizon was the first ILEC to offer long-distance service, and within 2 years it had become the third largest provider. The Act delegated authority to the Federal Communications Commission (FCC) to spur local competition by requiring the ILECs to provide access to their network by providing unbundled network elements (UNEs) to competing carriers. Some 300 companies, referred to as competitive local exchange carriers (CLECs), began to offer telecommunications services, including broadband. Some built their own fiber optics networks but most leased UNEs from the ILECs and rebundled them to provide UNE-Platforms (UNE-Ps) for their services. UNE-Ps were used by the CLECs for both voice and DSL broadband service. Although voice was by far the bigger revenue source, broadband was crucial to many business opportunities.

The CLECs included not only newly formed companies such as DSL providers NorthPoint and Rhythms NetConnections but also AT&T, MCI, and Sprint. The CLECs were able to compete against the ILECs because they leased the UNEs at theoretically calculated costs referred to as TELRIC prices. In addition, some state regulatory commissions ordered discounts of up to 50 percent from those prices. The ILECs referred to this as false competition and argued that the UNE discount eliminated their incentives to invest in new facilities. Under current regulations any upgraded DSL equipment and technology would have to be made available to CLECs at the prices set by state regulatory commissions.

During the late 1990s the telecommunications industry embarked on an aggressive build out of fiber optics capacity based on what turned out to be major overestimates of demand. The telecommunications meltdown left many of the CLECs bankrupt and the ILECs in precarious financial conditions.

Internet broadband service was provided by ILECs and CLECs through the DSL technology and by cable companies using cable television lines. Cable modem service was available nearly 2 years before DSL service was offered, and cable had captured two-thirds of the broadband market. The ILECs claimed that the false competition dampened their incentives to the point that they had little reason to expand their DSL capacity. Moreover, in March 2002 the FCC declared that cable modem service was an information service, so cable companies were not required to share their facilities or provide open access for competing carriers and ISPs.

President Bush appointed Michael Powell as chairman of the FCC, and Republicans became a majority on the Commission. In 2002 the FCC began its Triennial Review of the UNE requirement for both voice and broadband services. The FCC was required to make its decision by February 20, 2003.

## The Federal Communications Commission

The five FCC commissioners were three Republicans—Kathleen Abernathy, Kevin Martin, and Michael Powell—and two Democrats—Jonathan Adelstein and Michael Copps. The FCC made decisions using majority rule.

Chairman Powell advocated quick deregulation of voice and broadband services and argued that deregulation should not be "a reward for competition" but instead should be an instrument to spur competition. In particular, he wanted to stimulate new investments in digital technology.

In contrast, Commissioner Copps, a liberal Democrat and former aide to Senator Fritz Hollings (D-SC), opposed rapid deregulation and supported a major, continuing role for state public utility commissions (PUCs) in telecommunications regulation. Copps had informally organized the opponents of deregulation in the telecommunications industry.

Commissioner Martin had a position between those of Powell and Copps. Martin had been a senior White House adviser to President Bush. He favored a longer transition to deregulation so that orderly competition could be developed. In a speech on December 12, 2002, Martin stated, "ILECs should receive the benefits of making investments in new infrastructure deployment, but competitors should maintain the ability to receive access to end-user customers at the service capacity levels that they currently receive."[43] He believed in states rights and advocated devolving regulatory responsibility to state regulatory commissions where possible.

Commissioner Abernathy had served as a staff member in the FCC and as legal advisor to former FCC chairman James Quello. In the private sector she had practiced law and served as vice president of AirTouch Communications, U.S. West, and Broad-Band Office Communications.

Commissioner Adelstein had been a Senate committee staff member and aide to Senator Tom Daschel (D-SD). He joined the Commission in December 2002.

### The FCC UNE Triennial Review

In 1996 the FCC had ordered the unbundling of seven network elements. In response to a U.S. Supreme

Court decision, in 1999 the FCC reconsidered the unbundling decision and required that six elements be unbundled:[44]

1. Loops, including loops used to provide high-capacity and advanced telecommunications services
2. Network interface devices
3. Local circuit switching (except for large customers in major urban markets)
4. Dedicated and shared transport
5. Signaling and call-related databases
6. Operations support systems

The DC Circuit Court of Appeals overturned the 1999 FCC decision and ordered that the UNE Triennial Review be more "fine-grained" and "identify more precisely how incumbent local-exchange carriers must provide competitors access to their ubiquitous networks."[45] On December 12, 2001, the FCC issued a Notice of Proposed Rule Making (NPRM) with the principal objective of determining how to apply the statutory standards, as well as whether and how the Commission should take into account other goals of the Act, such as encouraging broadband deployment, investment in facilities, and technological innovation. The NPRM requested comments on whether new facilities should be exempt from the unbundling requirement and whether certain facilities, such as fiber optic cable, with advanced telecommunications capabilities should be exempted.[46]

### Broadband Technology

The principal technologies for residential broadband service were DSL (digital subscriber line) and cable modems. DSL operated at higher frequencies than voice service and came in a variety of flavors. Asymmetric DSL, for example, had a maximum download speed of 1.5 to 8 megabits per second but a maximum upload speed of only 640 kilobits. DSL service was limited because users had to be within

---

44The Supreme Court had required the FCC to reexamine the "necessary" and "impair" standards of the Act. *AT&T Corp. v Iowa Utilities Board*, 525 U.S. 366 (1999).
45FCC, Notice of Proposed Rulemaking, FCC 01-361. *Verizon Inc. v. FCC*, 122 S.Ct. 1646 (2002).
46FCC, Notice of Proposed Rulemaking, FCC 01-361, paragraph 24.

3 miles of a provider's central switching office. In addition, DSL was costly due to the costs of order taking, installation, and support and maintenance services. DSL service could be provided at substantially higher speeds if fiber ran close to a residence and the copper wire pair to the residence was short. DSL also required dedicated switches in the central office and hence was costly to provide, as was fiber to the curb of residences that were not in high-density locations.

Cable generally operated at a higher speed than DSL and had the capacity to provide the very high-speed service needed for advanced applications.[47] The actual speed at which cable modems operated, however, could be lower because of congestion resulting from many customers using the Internet at the same time. Congestion could be relieved by laying additional fiber optic cable to a node and increasing switching capacity at the cable system head end, but providing that capacity was costly.

## Catch 22: The Broadband/Content Dilemma

Cisco Systems pointed to the existing benefits of broadband, including entertainment, e-learning, national security, teleworking, and telehealth.[48] But, the next killer application was over the horizon, and without it many consumers were reluctant to subscribe to broadband service. Without substantial penetration of broadband many content providers were hesitant to commit the major investments to provide new, innovative services. And, without new, innovative content many consumers were unwilling to pay $40 to $50 or more a month for broadband service. Moreover, the technology to provide some applications was limited by the current speed of DSL and cable modems, which content providers believed prevented them from reaching their capabilities.

"Everyone understands that getting some serious movement in broadband is critical to restoring growth in our industry," said Cisco lobbyist Jeff Campbell. "Right now, the tech sector is in a vicious cycle. Content-rich applications aren't being developed because few people have the high-speed connections needed to use

them. Yet, consumers aren't signing up for broadband because of the lack of new applications."[49]

## Perspectives on Voice and Broadband Regulation and the Triennial Review

### ILECs

Commenting on the Telecommunications Act of 1996 and the unbundling requirement, Verizon CEO Ivan G. Seidenberg said, "The deal was we would make our network open to competitors on a nondiscriminatory basis. Nobody ever said we'd give it away at below market prices." The ILECs not only complained about the UNE discounts but also accused the CLECs of cream skimming by entering the most attractive markets and serving the most profitable customers. The ILECs sought to limit the role of state commissions in regulating broadband.

The FCC had set Total Element Long Run Incremental Cost (TELRIC) pricing rules for UNEs, but state PUCs were responsible for specific pricing orders. The ILECs complained that TELRIC understated the cost of capital by failing adequately to take risk into account. In addition, some state commissions had ordered price discounts to stimulate competition from the CLECs to force consumer rates down. "In Massachusetts, the straight 'resale' discount is 29 percent, or 25 percent if competitors use Verizon for operator and directory-assistance services. But competitors can exploit UNE-P to get a 46 percent discount, according to Michael Glover, the Verizon senior vice president and deputy general counsel. On high-end residential and business lines, Glover said, the discount can be as much as 70 percent off Verizon's retail cost."[50]

SBC claimed that UNE discounts forced it to provide 4 million lines below cost, which it said was a major reason it had to lay off 11,000 employees in 2002. The discounts on voice services eroded profits, reducing the funds available to invest in digital and other voice capacity, and the discounts on UNEs for broadband service dampened incentives to invest in DSL capacity. SBC's senior vice president for the FCC explained, "The wholesale business is important to us—we'd rather have competitors use our lines. We are willing to offer our network to competitors as long as the prices are compensatory."

---

[47]Cable systems used coaxial cable to the customer premises in conjunction with fiber optic trunks.
[48]Cisco's Broadband Primer (www.cisco.com/gov) identified the bandwidth required for various services. For example, movies on demand required from 1 to 7 megabits per second.
[49]*San Jose Mercury News,* November 3, 2002.
[50]*Boston Globe,* October 14, 2002.

One objective of the ILECs was to eliminate the UNE requirement on new fiber optics facilities and UNE capacity. "For the old wire, old rules should apply. For any new fiber that's laid, the new rules should apply," said Business Software Alliance President Robert Holleyman.[51]

## CLECs

CLECs served approximately 11 percent of the switched telephone lines. Some 11.9 million lines were provided by CLECs that used none of their own facilities, and an additional 4 million were provided by CLECs that used a combination of owned facilities and UNEs. All CLECs used the "last mile"—the ILEC copper wire twisted-pair connection to a customer premise. Some CLECs provided their own switching, whereas others leased switching capacity from the ILECs. Some CLECs argued that their use of UNEs was a temporary step leading to their own facilities build out. Developing their own facilities would free them from their dependence on the ILECs, but all CLECs sought to preserve access to the last mile. The CLECs were represented by the Competitive Telecommunications Association (CompTel) and the Association for Local Telecommunications Services (ALTS).

The number of CLECs had fallen from 300 to approximately 70, according to ALTS. A number of CLECs, such as NorthPoint Communications and Winstar Communications, had attempted to build their own fiber optics networks but had gone out of business.[52] Covad Communications had emerged from Chapter 11 bankruptcy and was a major DSL provider. Covad relied on line sharing, access to the unused high-frequency band on the copper pair to the customer premises, for its services.

In response to the ILECs' attempts to convince the FCC to eliminate the current UNE discounts, MCI Mass Markets President Wayne Huyard wrote to the 50 state utility commissions asserting that the ILEC efforts were "characterized by threats, distortion and political manipulation.... It's classic monopolistic maneuvering. Pressure regulators to change the rules, eliminate the competition, and re-monopolize the market."[53]

A number of smaller CLECs formed PACE (Promoting Active Competition Everywhere) to support access to UNE-P CEOs of the participating companies set out for Washington in January 2003 to carry their message to the FCC and the Bush administration.

CLECs, CompTel, and PACE urged the FCC to maintain a major role for state regulatory commissions in promoting local competition based on UNEs. The group wrote, "In the *Triennial Review*, the Commission must ... conduct a refined and fact-specific analysis of factors previously identified by the Commission. Most, if not all, of these factors are highly fact-specific and may vary from geographic region to geographic region, and accordingly, state commissions are, no doubt, best situated to conduct these analyses."[54]

## Cable Companies

The largest multiservice operator (MSO) was Comcast, which acquired AT&T Broadband in November 2002. Comcast had 21.6 million subscribers, followed by Time Warner Cable with 10.9 million subscribers and Charter Communications, Cox Communications, and Adelphia Communications with approximately 6 million each. The 25 largest MSOs served over 63 million cable television subscribers. In addition to cable television the MSOs provided broadband cable modem service to over 9 million subscribers. Compared to cable television service, broadband did not require paying for content, as with television programming. Brian Roberts, CEO of Comcast, explained that subscribers were "sending Comcast about $45 a month without significant programming costs."[55] The cable industry was represented by the National Cable Television Association (NCTA).

Because of the FCC ruling that cable access to the Internet was an information service, cable broadband services were not subject to the UNE requirements. The ILECs complained that this gave the cable companies an unfair competitive advantage and diminished their incentives to expand their broadband facilities. The cable companies, however, argued that over half the new customers dropped their second telephone line when they subscribed to broadband service, which explained why ILECs had been slow to deploy DSL.

[51] *San Jose Mercury News*, November 3, 2002.
[52] Some commentators believed these companies were victims of unfair squeeze tactics by the ILECs.
[53] *Rocky Mountain News*, October 18, 2002.
[54] Ex parte letter, www.comptel.org/press/oct24_2002.html.
[55] *The Wall Street Journal*, January 8, 2003.

## Equipment Suppliers and High-Tech Companies

High-tech equipment suppliers wanted rapid expansion of broadband service and competition between DSL and cable modem broadband. In November, CEOs of companies in the High Tech Broadband Coalition (HTBC) held a press conference prior to calling on FCC commissioners and National Telecommunications and Information Administration (NTIA) officials.[56] The CEOs argued that the UNE requirement discouraged the ILECs from expanding their broadband networks and that renewed capital expenditures for broadband deployment were essential for generating the demand for the next generation of Internet services. Cisco Systems commissioned a broadband study, "Customers at the Gate: Mounting Demand for Broadband-enabled Services," based on a survey of U.S. households. The report concluded that even the most conservative estimates put the demand for Internet-delivered services for the home at $25 billion a year.

Equipment suppliers had been hurt by the slump in the telecommunications industry. Catena Networks CEO Jim Hjartarson pointed to the dramatic drop in equipment demand. He said that Catena had laid off 55 percent of its employees and that "North America's technical prowess is being jeopardized."[57] Michael Norris, CEO of NextLevel Communications, which had laid off 70 percent of its staff, said, "We're losing a great resource. I don't come to Washington often but the issues here are incredibly important."

### Consumer and Activist Groups

The American Civil Liberties Union, the Center for Digital Democracy, and the Consumer Federation of America argued that the threat of only a few monopoly Internet service providers meant that the FCC should require cable and telecommunications companies to allow other Internet service providers, such as EarthLink and United Online, onto their systems. Companies including Amazon.com and Microsoft were concerned about the control of content availability. Content providers were concerned

that the cable companies would increase their share of the broadband market and become monopoly gatekeepers to the Internet and a bottleneck to the provision of content and variety. The consumer groups and the concerned companies advocated "open access" to cable systems.

In November representatives of the Media Access Project, ABC Disney, and other content providers met with commissioner Abernathy seeking a "nondiscrimination" rule that would allow broadband users to connect to any Web site of their choosing. "[Y]our electric company doesn't care if you use their service to hook up a hair dryer or a sex toy. Your Internet service should not be able to control where you go, either," said Andrew Schwartzman, head of the Media Access Project.[58]

The Media Access Project and the Alliance for Community Media joined with companies including Microsoft, eBay, Apple, RadioShack, Disney, and Yahoo! to form the Coalition of Broadband Users and Innovators. The Coalition urged the FCC to "ensure that transmission network operators do not encumber relationships between their customers and destinations on the network." The Coalition was concerned that broadband network operators would impose restrictions that would inhibit "innovative content, services, and devices on the broadband network."[59]

State regulators were also concerned about possible FCC actions. The National Association of Regulatory Utility Commissioners (NARUC) weighed in by meeting with FCC Commissioner Martin to urge him to stop major changes in the regulatory system and preserve their role in setting discounts for competitive carriers.

## The Competitive Landscape in Broadband

High-speed Internet connections by cable or DSL were estimated to be available to approximately 70 percent of U.S. households, but only 17 percent had subscribed. According to Morgan Stanley, cable served 11.7 million households and telecommunications companies served 6.4 million. Broadband subscriptions were projected by InStat/MDR to increase by 38 percent in 2003, 23 percent in 2004, and less than 20 percent in 2005.

[56]The HTBC was formed in April 2002 by six trade associations, the Business Software Alliance, Consumer Electronics Association (CEA), Information Technology Industry Council, National Association of Manufacturers, Semiconductor Industry Association, and Telecommunications Industry Association (TIA).
[57]Washington Telecom Newsletter, November 14, 2002.

[58]Cable World. November 25, 2002.
[59]Coalition of Broadband Users and Innovators, Press Release, November 18, 2002.

The competitive situation in telecommunications was that CLECs leased UNEs at discount rates and resold those lines to customers in competition with the ILECs. Herschel Abbott of BellSouth referred to it as "false competition." Chairman Powell also viewed the current system as not providing real competition. Real competition required rival networks, he argued. CLECs, however, could not be expected to build their own networks quickly, since the estimate for the capital required for each telephone line was $2,000, or $360 billion for the nation. Fiber optic cable to the curb or home would be costly.

The "false competition" had several effects. First, the ability to obtain lines at discounted rates enabled AT&T and WorldCom to enter the local service voice telecommunications market and garner an 11 percent share. For those companies local service was viewed as more profitable than

long-distance service. Second, prices for local service had been pushed down, benefiting consumers and pleasing state regulators. Moreover, some state regulators had increased the UNE discounts to encourage competition. Third, consumers were being offered a greater variety of plans.

The elimination of UNE discounts could have a dramatic effect on the industry. As AT&T vice president Len Cali said, "Without the wholesale rates, this is an unsustainable business."[60] Doug Allen, writing in *Network Magazine*, argued that without the discounts the interexchange carriers (AT&T, Sprint, MCI) were "business-wise, toast" and that most CLECs that resold services were "dead."[61]

SOURCE: Copyright © 2003 by David P. Baron. All rights reserved. Reprinted with permission.

## PREPARATION QUESTIONS

1. Are there any market imperfections in broadband that require correction through regulation?
2. What are the likely consequences in the voice and broadband marketplaces of reducing the set of network elements that must be unbundled?
3. What are the likely consequences of requiring "just and reasonable" rates for UNEs?
4. As an equipment manufacturer such as Cisco Systems, what would you urge the FCC to do with regard to UNEs and broadband?
5. What considerations will the FCC take into account in its decision making on UNEs and broadband?

6. What are the principal dimensions of disagreement among the interests?
7. What theory could be used to predict the likely FCC decision on UNEs and broadband?
8. What strategies should the ILECs, CLECs, and cable companies use to advance their perspectives before the FCC?

---

[60] *The Wall Street Journal*, January 6, 2003.
[61] *Network Magazine*, November 1, 2002.

# Echelon and the Home Automation Standard (A)

Chris Stanfield, vice president and CFO of Echelon Corporation, learned much to his surprise that the Federal Communications Commission (FCC) had begun a rule-making proceeding to establish a compatibility standard for the television set, VCR, and cable television interface that would severely disadvantage Echelon in the home

automation market. The FCC's rule making was mandated by the Cable Television Act of 1992 in response to consumer complaints about difficulties in using advanced features of televisions and in operating VCRs in conjunction with cable television service (e.g., taping one channel while viewing another).

The compatibility standard being considered by the FCC was advocated by the manufacturers of televisions and by cable television providers and included a particular communications protocol called CEBus. The proposed CEBus-based standard would change the way consumers interacted with their televisions. Televisions would no longer be slaves to the cable box or VCR but instead would serve as the gateway to control systems for other consumer electronic devices. These devices would be connected to the television through the television to control other electronic systems in a home, including security systems, timer-operated appliances, heating and cooling systems, and personal computers. The threat to Echelon was that the CEBus protocol conflicted with its LonTalk communications protocol, and thus its adoption would severely limit the use of Echelon's control networks in the emerging home automation market. Echelon's objective was not to have its protocol mandated by the FCC but to preserve its opportunities and let the marketplace decide which products, and hence which protocols, would succeed and which would not. The concern was that the FCC would foreclose its opportunities.

## Company Background

Echelon was a privately held company based in Palo Alto, California, with subsidiaries in London, Paris, Munich, and Tokyo and offices in Amsterdam and Beijing. Its president and CEO since its founding in 1988 was M. Kenneth Oshman, cofounder and former president of ROLM Corporation. Echelon was initially backed by venture capital firms, and subsequently a number of companies, including Motorola with a 21 percent stake, invested in Echelon. Echelon held over 50 patents and had hardware licensing agreements with Motorola and Toshiba.

Echelon's primary market was control networks—communications systems that integrated disparate pieces of electronic hardware over some distance. These systems enabled administrators to monitor and control remotely the environment under their jurisdiction. Building-wide security systems commonly used such networks, as did automated assembly lines. Hospitals could use control networks for monitoring patients, and home automation could be based on such networks. Demand for control networks had grown rapidly in the last decade, and

Echelon expected the market to continue to grow for the foreseeable future.

The analogy between control network architectures and computer operating systems is helpful for understanding Echelon's business. Echelon did not make the actual "nodes" of a control network—thermostats and alarms that actually interacted with the physical environment. Like an operating system, control network architecture was the "infrastructure" that tied together the various pieces of hardware and software in the network. Echelon provided "open architecture" systems that allowed equipment of different manufacturers to work together. The open architecture also allowed systems designers great flexibility in developing a broad array of applications.

Echelon's main product, the LonWorks network, was a family of hardware and software systems that provided off-the-shelf foundations for customers to build complete control networks. Since its introduction in 1991, the LonWorks network had been adopted as a standard by several industries. In addition, Echelon had established the LonMark Interoperability Association, which established technical guidelines and promoted LonWorks. There were over 100 members from more than 10 countries, including Ameritech, Honeywell, Hewlett-Packard, IBM, Microsoft, Motorola, Philips, Toshiba, and Yokogawa.

In 1996 there were over 2,500 developers of LonWorks network technology, accounting for about 2 million installed nodes. Building automation accounted for roughly 30 percent of LonWorks's market. Users of LonWorks included Honeywell, Schlumberger Industries, Trans-Lite, Inc., and NASA. The NASA application demonstrated that in addition to factories, office buildings, hospitals, and homes, satellites could also be monitored using control network technology.

## Technology and Compatibility

Applications of LonWorks networks fell into four categories: building, home, industrial, and utilities. The home automation category was the application threatened by the FCC's rule making. A home automation network allowed a single network to control heating, air conditioning, lighting, watering, energy management, security systems, and consumer electronics devices. LonWorks allowed nodes on these systems to be linked using a wide range of network options, from twisted-pair to coaxial cable to wireless RF (radio frequency) and IR (infrared). For older homes without preexisting networks, LonWorks included hardware that used power lines for communications, thus avoiding costly retrofitting.

Other forms of home control networks were feasible. In particular, the Cable Consumer Equipment Compatibility Advisory Committee (C3AG), a group composed of members of the Electronics Industries Association (EIA) and National Cable Television Association (NCTA), had proposed a Decoder Interface standard to the FCC in August 1994.[62] The EIA's Consumer Electronics Group, which represented a wide spectrum of electronics manufacturers, including television manufacturers, favored this standard because it could transform televisions from a commodity product to a high-margin electronic control system.[63] Cable providers favored the standard because it positioned them as the primary providers of the next generation of value-added home electronic services, such as online shopping and video entertainment.[64] Although the Decoder Interface standard was aimed primarily at television-related equipment such as cable descramblers and VCRs, it contained the CEBus communications protocol.

Echelon's concern was that the inclusion of the CEBus protocol into the next generation of televisions would effectively establish CEBus as the dominant protocol for home automation services. Indeed, the C3AG proposal to the FCC made explicit mention of the CEBus protocol as a "home automation standard" for a "wide spectrum of consumer products."[65]

The operating principle behind the CEBus protocol was quite different from that of LonWorks. Its primary technical innovation was to transform televisions from monitors into intelligent devices. Many consumers used a cable converter and/or a VCR as an intermediary between the television signal and the physical screen. In effect, televisions were "slaves" of these set-top devices. Televisions with the CEBus-based Decoder Interface, however, would have the ability to communicate with a setback box, which was essentially an elaborate cable converter. Under this system, the user would interact with the television directly, which then would give instructions to the setback box. The setback box could be made to serve as the gateway to the home control network.

In contrast, a LonWorks network placed no restriction on the control center of a home control network. In principle, one could use a television with a setback box, a set-top box, a computer, or a custom controller to operate the nodes of the control network. In addition, these nodes could be connected using any means available—wireless or not. The CEBus-based Decoder Interface, however, would specifically require designers to tailor devices to communicate with the setback box and receive only those instructions that could be transmitted through the television. In addition, innovation would be far more centralized with television manufacturers having a favored position if the CEBus protocol were the standard. Wide consumer adoption of home automation technology would then be dependent on a massive replacement of televisions, costing as much as $150 billion.[66] This was the ultimate objective of the television manufacturers. Not only would the CEBus-based Decoder Interface standard handicap Echelon's LonWorks network, but since television life cycles were typically 10 to 15 years, the development of the home control network market itself could slow considerably.

Echelon's problem was that the FCC could preempt the judgment of the marketplace and force standardization around the CEBus protocol. From Echelon's perspective, just as there was no reason for the government to select a standard computer operating system, there was no reason for the FCC to set a standard for home automation networks. A wide variety of companies agreed with this view.

---

[62] The C3AG was not an official advisory group to the FCC but had been working for several years on a standard.

[63] Founded in 1924, the EIA was the principal association of the $381 billion U.S. electronics manufacturing industry. The EIA had a staff of 200, a budget of $26 million, and a new 110,000-square-foot office building in Arlington, Virginia. Some of Echelon's investors were also active members of the EIA. For example, Motorola senior vice president John Major was elected EIA treasurer for 1996. The EIA was organized into divisions and groups. The Consumer Electronics Manufacturers Association was one of its principal components, and its members constituted the Consumer Electronics Group. Another association of the EIA was the Telecommunications Industry Association, which included 600 companies providing telecommunications systems, products, distribution services, and professional services.

[64] The NCTA had 3,073 members, a staff of 92, and a budget of over $5 million. Members included cable operators, cable networks, and suppliers and distributors.

[65] EIA submission to FCC, August 15, 1994, p. 8, cited in "Cable Equipment Compatibility Standards," ET Docket 93-7, p. 1.

[66] Reply Comments of Echelon Corporation," CS Docket No. 95-184, April 17, 1996, p. 8.

For example, home computers were an equally plausible candidate for running control networks, as were set-top boxes. Thus, industry rivals Apple and Intel both opposed a mandated CEBus-based Decoder Interface standard.

## The FCC and the Cable Act of 1992

In 1992 the cable industry was under attack by consumers complaining of high prices, abusive market tactics, and problems operating their VCRs and televisions with cable systems. Congress responded with legislation to regulate the industry and addressed the incompatibility problem in Section 17 of the 1992 Cable Act.[67] This section directed the FCC to consult with industry representatives and issue regulations "to ensure compatibility between cable systems and consumer TV receivers and video cassette recorders (VCRs), consistent with the need to prevent theft of cable service."[68] The FCC was to report to Congress in April 1994 with a means for resolving the compatibility issue.

The C3AG had proposed to the FCC the development and adoption of a Decoder Interface connector that would work with an associated setback decoder box and would establish standards ensuring long-term compatibility between cable technologies and consumer equipment.[69] Having received little in the way of objections, the FCC tentatively endorsed the as-yet incomplete standard on April 4, 1994, and gave the C3AG 90 days to submit a completed proposal.[70] In August 1994 the C3AG submitted a proposal for IS-105, its "interim" Decoder Interface standard. This standard incorporated both a physical interconnection specification as well as the CEBus communications protocol.

## The FCC's Rule Making

Neither Echelon nor its supporters had been heavily involved in the FCC's initial consideration of the Decoder Interface standard, and Echelon had not filed comments for the FCC's May 1994 "First Report and Order" on the implementation of Section 17. Most of the disagreements in the comments filed had pertained to the extent to which third parties could provide the hardware associated with the Decoder Interface. For example, some parties, such as Circuit City Stores of Richmond, Virginia, understandably wanted to prevent cable companies from having a monopoly on the sale of decoder equipment.

The FCC saw Section 17 of the Cable Act as a mandate for using its standard-setting authority to resolve once and for all a host of cable interoperability problems. Part of the disagreement turned on the meaning of the term *interoperability*, as used in the Cable Act. As Glenn Manishin, an experienced technology lawyer and partner in Blumefeld & Cohen, Washington, D.C. pointed out:

[I]nteroperability means different things to different industries. In telecommunications parlance, it generally connotes the ability of systems to communicate and exchange information; in the computer industry, it often has more limited scope, confined largely to the physical interconnectivity of equipment.[71]

From this perspective, the Cable Act required the FCC to regulate interconnectivity, but mandating the CEBus-based Decoder Interface would be a considerable step toward interoperability.

The Consumer Electronics Group of the EIA and the cable industry, however, had bigger objectives than just compatibility among televisions, VCRs, and cable systems. They saw an opportunity to secure an important future market by influencing the FCC's standard setting.

## Echelon and the FCC

Echelon had been told by an employee of the EIA that there was nothing in the C3AG proposed standard that would affect home automation. However, in late 1994 Chris Stanfield heard that

---

[67] Cable Television Consumer Protection and Competition Act of 1992. Pub. L. No. 102–385, 106 Stat. 1460, (1992) 17 (codified at 47 U.S.C. 544a).

[68] "Implementation of Section 17 of the Cable Television Consumer Protection and Competition Act of 1992, Compatibility Between Cable Systems and Consumer Electronics Equipment," First Report and Order 9, FCC Rcd 1981 (1981).

[69] "Report to Congress on Means of Assuring Compatibility Between Cable Systems and Consumer Electronics Equipment," Federal Communications Commission, October 5, 1993.

[70] "Implementation of Section 17 of the Cable Television Consumer Protection and Competition Act of 1992, Compatibility Between Cable Systems and Consumer Electronics Equipment," First Report and Order, 9 FCC Rcd 1981 (1987).

[71] G. B. Manishin, "Learning to (Tele)communicate Together," *Legal Times*, November 6, 1995, p. 45.

## Echelon and the Communications Act of 1996

When its attempts to stop the FCC from mandating CEBus failed, Echelon's only remaining avenue was through Congress. In early 1995 the Republican leadership in Congress was committed to enacting legislation that would reshape the future of telecommunications. The Senate Commerce Committee had recently reported a bill that would rewrite the Communications Act of 1934, and the House Commerce Committee was preparing to consider a similar bill. The CEBus-based Decoder Interface standard had already built a significant constituency of television manufacturers, cable companies, and electronics retailers, so whatever strategy Echelon deployed would meet with considerable resistance. Furthermore, the battle would be a protracted one, since each chamber was expected to pass its own version of the bill, requiring reconciliation of the two versions in a conference committee. ∎

one of the companies supporting the Decoder Interface standard had bragged about the FCC mandating the CEBus protocol. The threat was imminent.

Echelon's first step was to address the standards issue in the arena of the FCC. Echelon was at a disadvantage in the FCC for three reasons. First, it was starting late, since the EIA and NCTA had been working for several years on a compatibility standard. Second, computer companies were not the natural clients of the FCC—the television and cable companies were. Third, Echelon viewed the regulators' mindset as quite different from that of high-tech entrepreneurs with regulators preferring certainty and order and entrepreneurs preferring opportunity and the judgment of the marketplace. In November 1994 Echelon initiated a series of ex parte meetings with the FCC's Office of Engineering and Technology and Competition Division. The FCC's Office of Engineering and Technology, however, had been working with C3AG, and its influence led the FCC to continue with its rule making and with the proposed standard incorporating the CEBus protocol.

### PREPARATION QUESTIONS

1. Why were Echelon's efforts with the FCC unsuccessful?
2. Why did the FCC continue with the C3AG standard?
3. In which institutional arena should Echelon pursue its objective of achieving an open standard?
4. What strategy should Echelon formulate to achieve its objectives?
5. How should that strategy be implemented; that is, what specifically should Oshman and Stanfield do?

---

# The FCC Media Ownership Rules

Media ownership had been regulated for decades, but in a little-noticed section of the Telecommunications Act of 1996 Congress required the Federal Communications Commission (FCC) to review the justifications for its regulations every 2 years. In addition, the D.C. Court of Appeals had remanded several FCC decisions requiring better justifications for its rulings and orders.[72] In the *Fox* decision the court

stated, "Section 202(h) carries with it a presumption in favor of repealing or modifying the ownership rules.... [T]he Commission may retain a rule only if it reasonably determines that the rule is 'necessary in the public interest.'" The FCC emphasized "diversity, localism, and competition," and its restrictions on media ownership were justified by concerns that viewpoints could be restricted by dominant companies and that a diversity of views should be encouraged.

As required by the Telecommunications Act, the FCC issued a Notice of Proposed Rule Making (NPRM) in 2001 on two broadcast ownership

[72]*Sinclair Broadcasting Group, Inc. v. FCC,* 284 F.3d 148, 168–69 (D.C. Cir. 2002) and *Fox Television Stations, Inc. v. FCC,* 280 F.3d 1027, 1048 (D.C. Cir. 2002).

rules—the Broadcast-Newspaper Cross-Ownership Rule and the Local Radio Ownership Rule. In September 2002 the Commission issued a NPRM for the biennial review required by the Telecommunications Act. The review included the Local Television-Radio Cross-Ownership Rule, the Dual Network Rule, the Local Television Multiple Ownership Rule, and the National Television Ownership Rule. The focus of this case is the National Television Ownership Rule and the Local Television Multiple Ownership Rule.

## The FCC

The five FCC commissioners were three Republicans—Kathleen Abernathy, Kevin Martin, and Michael Powell—and two Democrats—Jonathan Adelstein and Michael Copps. The FCC made its decisions using majority rule.

FCC chairman Powell expressed three objectives for the Commission's review of the media ownership rules. The first was to promote "diversity, localism, and competition" in the broadcast media and to do so in a manner that would withstand court scrutiny. Diversity referred to the number of "voices" available to the public. Localism referred to the local ownership of media organizations, which was valued because it promoted local programming. Competition was the preferred means of promoting progress in the media. The second was to recognize "the explosion of new media outlets for news information and entertainment." The third was to formulate rules that would allow ownership changes "while ensuring that no company can monopolize the medium."[73] The FCC scheduled a vote on revised media ownership rules for June 2, 2003. Three weeks before the scheduled vote, Powell circulated a draft set of rules.

Powell contended that free broadcast television was in jeopardy from cable and satellite TV. He and Commissioner Martin argued that the economics of the news business had changed and that the traditional concern with providing a diverse set of views was of less concern now due to the rise of cable and satellite systems and the Internet. Martin was viewed as the strongest supporter of media ownership deregulation among the commissioners.

Commissioners Copps and Adelstein argued that there was little evidence that mergers led to

better or expanded news programming. As a result of the Telecommunications Act the FCC had relaxed rules on radio ownership, and Copps argued that the number of station owners had decreased by 34 percent as a result of the change and the number of minority owners had decreased by 14 percent. Michael Bracy of the Future of Music Coalition said, "Radio clearly is the coal mine canary" and claimed that radio listeners had declined to the lowest level in the past 27 years.[74] Adelstein commented, "Radio is a very sick canary in the coal mine, and we're about to infect television with the same disease." Copps pointed to Clear Channel Communication, which owned 1,200 radio stations, and criticized it for its homogenized programming.[75] Andrew Levin of Clear Channel responded, "Deregulation revived local radio."

## The Media Ownership Rules

The National Television Ownership Rule prohibited a company from owning television stations that reached more than 35 percent of the national audience.[76] However, as a result of acquisitions that the FCC was unable to block because of court decisions, both CBS, a unit of Viacom, and Fox, a unit of the News Corporation, owned stations reaching 39 percent of the households. The FCC reported that of the 1,340 commercial stations Viacom owned 39, Fox 37, NBC 29, and ABC 10. Powell had initially questioned whether any cap was required, given the growth in cable systems and the Internet as sources of news. The networks sought a much higher cap and expected to benefit by attracting more advertising and having greater power in buying programming. Jay Ireland, president of the NBC television stations, said, "To leave these rules in place would subject television broadcasters to unfair and burdensome constraints that prevent them from competing against other forms of media."[77]

Local affiliates strongly opposed relaxation of the regulation, fearing that greater size would increase the power of the networks. Independent programmers also opposed relaxation of the rule. They had been hurt by changes in 1996 that allowed

---

[73]*The New York Times*, June 3, 2003.

[74]*The New York Times*, May 28, 2003.
[75]The United States had approximately 10,800 commercial radio stations.
[76]The 35 percent limit was based on potential rather than actual viewers; i.e., on the number of people who could watch a channel.
[77]*The Seattle Times*, February 28, 2003.

the networks to produce their own programming, and relaxation of the 35 percent rule would give the networks greater control over programming. Affiliated stations not owned by the networks also opposed relaxation so as to preserve their independence.

Powell's draft would raise the cap to 45 percent and retain the UHF viewer rule, which for the purposes of the National Television Ownership Rule counted two viewers of UHF stations as one viewer. The UHF "discount" allowed media companies to reach more than 35 percent of the national audience. Powell argued that the UHF discount had spurred the growth of new networks, such as UPN (owned by Viacom), Paxson Communications (32 percent owned by NBC), WB (owned by AOL Time Warner), and Fox.

Since almost all UHF viewers received their signal by cable, there was little reason to continue the discount, according to Commissioner Copps. Gene Kimmelman of the Consumers Union referred to the UHF discount as "total hypocrisy" and said, "If the theory behind changing the rules is that the FCC needs to keep up with market conditions, to preserve a significant discount for UHF stations is simply a fraud on the regulatory process." Andrew Schwartzman, head of the Media Action Project, said that the UHF discount "eviscerates the cap."[78]

The Local Television Multiple Ownership Rule pertained to the ownership of television stations in local markets and was based on the "eight-voices test." Before a company could own two stations in a local market, eight separate voices (television stations) were required. The networks would benefit from relaxation of the eight-voices rule, as would media companies such as the Tribune Company, Gannett, Belo, E.W. Scripps, and Sinclair Broadcasting.[79] The FCC's eight-voices test effectively precluded a duopoly in small markets, but television stations in small markets argued that they could provide better news coverage if they were allowed to merge. Moreover, consolidation would ease the burden of providing digital broadcast capability for HDTV as the FCC required by 2007. A digital antenna capable of transmitting HDTV signals cost between $3 and $5 million. Powell's draft would allow a company to own two stations in a market with at least five stations and three in a market with at least 18 stations, provided that only one was among the four largest. In markets

[78] *The New York Times*, May 13, 2003.
[79] *The New York Times*, May 11, 2003.

with 11 or more stations, the FCC would consider on a case-by-case basis the merger of two of the top four stations.

## Perspectives and Preferences

The disagreement between the Republican and the Democrat commissioners resulted from a difference in perspectives. The Democrats focused on the fear of greater media concentration and the corresponding reduction in the diversity of views available to the public. The Republicans focused on the increase in the number of media outlets over the past 50 years, the emergence of cable and the Internet as sources of news and entertainment, and the lack of evidence that mergers and the growth of media conglomerates had resulted in any harm to the public. Commenting on the predominance of the networks in prime time, Abernathy said, "Four companies air the programming that is chosen by approximately 75 percent of viewers during prime time. To me, the critical fact is that these providers control no more than 25 percent of the broadcast and cable channels in the average home, even apart from the Internet and other pipelines. Given these other viewing options, I can only presume that this means that Americans are watching these providers because they prefer their content, not because they lack alternatives."[80] Commissioner Martin commented,

I recall having extremely limited choices on our family television set when I was growing up. There was no cable. There was no satellite. Even with our roof antenna, we received just five channels—the three major networks, one independent, and one public television station....

While my parents still live in the same house, they now have access to seven broadcast networks, hundreds of digital cable channels (including a local cable news channel), many more radio stations, and thousands of sites on the Internet. Indeed, people today have access to more information from more diverse sources than at any time in our history.[81]

Commissioner Abernathy chided the Democrats for focusing on "fear and speculation about hypothetical media monopolies." She argued that with

[80] Separate Statement of Commissioner Kevin J. Martin on Biennial Review of Broadcast Ownership Rules, June 2, 2003.
[81] Statement of Commissioner Kathleen Q. Abernathy, June 2, 2003.

"the breakneck pace of technological development, and the ever-increasing number of pipelines into consumers' homes, it is simply not possible to monopolize the flow of information in today's world. Indeed, the fall of Communism in the 1990s and of military dictatorships in the 1980s shows that diverse viewpoints cannot be suppressed even by authoritarian governments, much less by private media companies."[82]

To build public opposition to changes in the media ownership rules, Commissioners Copps and Adelstein held hearings around the country to provide a forum where critics could voice their opposition.[83] Copps argued that diversity had not increased despite the increase in the number of media sources. He claimed that 90 percent of the leading cable channels were owned by the companies that owned the major networks and the cable systems. A Nielsen survey revealed that 80 percent of Americans obtained their news from television or newspapers and only 6 percent from the Internet. Moreover, the 20 most-visited Internet news sites were owned by 16 large media companies, and the top five sites had more visits than the next 15.

The organized opponents of possible changes in the media ownership rules included the National Organization of Women (NOW), Leadership Conference on Civil Rights, Writers Guild of America, United States Conference of Catholic Bishops, Parent Teachers Association, and National Rifle Association (NRA). The critics warned of media monopolies that could control the information the public received. Wade Henderson of the Leadership Conference said, "Diversity of voices, not merely the variety of programming, is what matters."[84] NOW organized a protest outside the FCC building demanding that it "halt further media consolidation and act to preserve the openness and diversity of the Internet." The FCC hearings attracted 750,000 communications, by far the largest number ever received by the FCC.

The NRA opposed revisions in the ownership rules for quite different reasons. It opposed allowing the large media companies to become larger, since those companies were opposed to the right to bear arms. The NRA message to its 4 million members was that the "gun-hating media giants like AOL Time Warner, Viacom/CBS and Disney/ABC . . . could literally silence your NRA and prevent us from communicating with your fellow Americans by refusing to sells us television, radio or newspaper advertising at any price."[85] Nearly half the 750,000 communications were generated by the NRA.[86]

The opposition on the left was led by advocacy and activist groups. MoveOn.org, Common Cause, and the Free Press financed television and newspaper advertisements criticizing any relaxation of the rules. Some of the ads showed the face of Rupert Murdock, head of the News Corporation, with the caption "This Man Wants to Control the News in America. The FCC Wants to Help Him."

The opposition to relaxation of the ownership rules was informally coordinated by four people. Gene Kimmelman of the Consumers Union focused on building support in Congress for legislation to preserve the 35 percent cap. Andrew Schwartzman of the Media Access Project focused on lobbying the FCC. Mark Cooper, research director of the Consumer Federation of America, provided economic analysis on the extent of diversity in media markets. Jeff Chester of the Center for Digital Democracy focused on providing information to the news media.

In a joint press release by the Consumers Union and the Consumer Federation of America, Cooper stated, "Encouraging further concentration by relaxing the current rules on media ownership, . . . would reduce the prospects of competition in local markets, diminish the provision of local news and information and limit the diversity of local perspectives." Kimmelman said, "Merging the dominant local newspaper with a major local TV station is dangerous to our democracy because it combines the key watchdogs who keep an eye on each other, and point out each other's abuses in the market or in their reporting."[87]

The Center for Digital Democracy joined with the Writers Guild of America and independent producers to protest the impending FCC decision. Award-winning writers and producers urged Senators John McCain (R-AZ) and Fritz Hollings

---

82 Separate Statement of Commissioner Kathleen Q. Abernathy, June 2, 2003.
83 They held over a dozen hearings but had to fund the hearings from their own office budgets because the FCC provided funding for only one hearing outside Washington.
84 *The New York Times*, May 28, 2003.
85 Some media organizations refused NRA ads.
86 Many of the other communications were from an online petition circulated by MoveOn.org.
87 Joint press release, May 12, 2003.

(D-SC), chair and ranking minority member, respectively, of the Commerce Committee, to stop the FCC from relaxing the media ownership rules. Norman Lear wrote, "We built these companies in the seventies and eighties under the watchful eye of an FCC that was committed to keeping the playing field even, protecting against the vertical integration of the major broadcasting networks that would, if they had been allowed, have forced independent companies such as ours to take a minority interest in the very shows we had created, giving majority ownership to the network in order to get on the air."[88]

The supporters of relaxation of the media ownership rules were generally well-organized industry groups with aligned preferences. In the case of the National Media Ownership Rule, however, the networks were pitted against their local affiliate stations. On the other rules the media companies were aligned, well organized, and represented by high-powered lobbying firms. The broadcast companies reportedly had 70 meetings with FCC officials, whereas public interest groups had only five meetings.[89]

## Congressional Action

As details of Powell's draft were revealed, members of Congress swung into action. Bills were introduced in both the House and Senate. Senators Hollings and

Ted Stevens (R-AK) introduced a bill to preserve the 35 percent cap. Senator Byron Dorgan (D-ND) commented, "There has been galloping concentration in virtually every area of the media industry. It's hard to argue that we need more."[90] Senator McCain had agreed to hold hearings on the bill despite his view that "the FCC was set up to be an independent agency and should be so." Senator Hollings threatened to attach a rider to an appropriations bill to prohibit the FCC from spending funds to implement its decision. The House was believed to be more sympathetic to the FCC's perspective than was the Senate. Representative David R. Obey (D-WI) announced his intention to attach a provision to an appropriations bill to preserve the 35 percent cap. The Bush administration supported the relaxation of the media ownership rules, and the president threatened to veto any measure overturning the FCC decision. Whatever rules the FCC chose were certain to be challenged in the courts.

The proponents of the bills in Congress along with the two Democrat commissioners called for a postponement of the FCC vote so that further consideration could be given to the alternatives. Powell responded, "This isn't like wine. It doesn't get better with age." He refused to postpone the vote. ∎

---

## PREPARATION QUESTIONS

1. To what extent does Powell's draft respond to the changes in the media industries?
2. How closely aligned are the preferences of the commissioners?
3. What theories could be used to predict which majority will prevail in the FCC?
4. As the CEO of a major television network, what strategy would you adopt to advance

relaxation of the ownership rules? As the owner of an affiliated local television station, what strategy would you adopt to oppose relaxation of the media ownership rules?
5. What is the FCC likely to decide? Why?
6. What is likely to happen in Congress? Why?

---

[88] Center for Digital Democracy, May 12, 2003.
[89] The number of meetings was identified in a study by the Center for Public Integrity. (*The Wall Street Journal*, June 2, 2003.)

[90] *The Wall Street Journal*, May 14, 2003.

# 11

# Environmental Protection: Economics, Politics, and Management

## Introduction

The public, government, and business recognize the importance of environmental protection and the benefits it yields. Those benefits include improved human health, a more vibrant natural environment, the preservation of ecosystems, and a more sustainable relationship with the natural environment. Environmental protection is also expensive. Compliance with existing environmental regulation cost each person in the United States nearly $900 a year in 2004—or a total of $250 billion annually, representing 2.1 percent of GDP. Any new programs to meet other environmental goals, such as addressing global climate change, would add to that cost. The cost of environmental protection has raised concerns ranging from who should bear that cost to its effect on the economy and the international competitiveness of firms. It is thus imperative not only that the environment be protected but that it be accomplished as efficiently as possible. Although there is widespread agreement about protecting the environment, there remains considerable disagreement about how much protection is appropriate and about the distribution of the burden of that protection. These disagreements generate the politics of environmental protection.

This chapter focuses on public and managerial policies for environmental protection. The following section considers pollution externalities from the social efficiency perspective and examines marketlike incentive approaches for dealing with them, with an emphasis on tradable permits systems. Environmental regulation is considered next with a focus on the policies of the Environmental Protection Agency (EPA). The politics of environmental protection are then addressed. The management of environmental and regulatory issues from a firm's perspective is then considered. Examples include BP's internal emissions trading system, Intel's participation in the EPA's XL program, the Responsible Care program in the chemical industry, and McDonald's and Dow Chemicals' cooperative programs with environmental groups.

# Socially Efficient Regulation of Pollution Externalities

Social efficiency is attained when aggregate well-being is maximal. Aggregate well-being takes into account the harm from pollution and the social costs of reducing that harm. Just as it is not socially efficient to prevent all accidents, it is not socially efficient to prevent all pollution. Instead, that pollution which is not too costly to prevent should be prevented. The control of pollution externalities, however, has often taken the form of *command-and-control* regulation in which regulators order engineering controls, such as scrubbers for electric power plants, or require the best available technology for pollution abatement. This approach deals with the source of the harm, but it takes into account neither the benefits of the avoided harm nor the cost of abatement. Command-and-control is a blunt instrument that imposes uniform controls and standards on dissimilar sources of pollution, resulting in excessive abatement costs. In contrast, social efficiency requires that the polluter and those affected by the pollution externality take into account both the harm and the costs of abatement. For each source of pollution, social efficiency requires that costs and benefits be considered and that reductions in pollution be attained at the least cost. The lower the cost of reducing pollution, the larger are the reductions that can be made.

*Incentive approaches* take into account the benefits and costs of attaining environmental objectives and achieve those objectives by aligning the social and private costs of pollution and its abatement. These approaches attain social efficiency by requiring polluters to internalize the social costs of their pollution externalities. These approaches also decentralize pollution-control decisions because the generators of pollution rather than regulators have the responsibility for evaluating alternative abatement strategies and technologies. Rather than dictating how environmental goals should be achieved, incentive-based approaches impose a cost on pollution-causing activities, leaving it to individual polluters to decide how best to respond. Incentives then drive these decisions toward the least-cost means of attaining environmental objectives. The incentives to reduce costs also provide incentives to redesign production processes to reduce pollutants, eliminate harmful components of products, and develop better pollution control technologies.

The underlying principles of incentive approaches to achieving social efficiency in the presence of externalities are provided by the Coase theorem. It addresses the private attainment of social efficiency and its limitations.

## The Coase Theorem

The *Coase theorem* pertains to market imperfections, including externalities and public goods. It focuses on the standard of social efficiency and provides a conceptual foundation for both regulation and the liability system considered in Chapter 12. The theorem does not address other standards, such as distributive objectives and social justice, that could be used in evaluating alternative social arrangements and public policies. The Coase theorem has gained influence in the economics of externalities and public goods and in the law through applications to issues such as breach of contracts, nuisance law, and torts.[1] Coase's (1960) original exposition focused on externalities.

Coase observed that an externality is reciprocal in the sense that at least two parties are required. In the case of noise pollution, there would be no externality without the polluter nor in the absence of anyone to hear the noise. In the case of a toxic risk from an oil refinery, an externality exists because of both the refinery and the presence of

---

[1]See Polinsky (2003) for an exposition of the role of the Coase theorem in the law.

homes and businesses near it. When an externality is recognized to be reciprocal, it is clear that there is more than one means of achieving social efficiency. Coase's analysis began with an entitlement protected by a *property rule*. A property rule prohibits other parties from infringing the entitlement without the consent of the party holding it. Homeowners are protected by a property rule that prohibits other persons from taking their home without consent or forcing them to sell it at a price they deem inadequate.

As an example of Coase's analysis, suppose firm A discharges pollutants into a river whose water is used as an input to a production process by a downstream firm B. In principle, the two firms can voluntarily reach an agreement to internalize the externality regardless of which firm has the entitlement. That is, social efficiency can be achieved whether A has the entitlement to pollute or B has the entitlement to be free from pollution. If A has the entitlement to pollute, B has an incentive to bargain with A to reduce the pollution. B would be willing to pay A to the point at which the marginal damage done to B's production equals the marginal cost of reducing pollution at A. This minimizes the total cost of abatement and harm from pollution, resulting in social efficiency.

If B has the entitlement not to have its production harmed by the pollution, A has an incentive to bargain with B to allow A to discharge some amount of pollutants into the river. A is willing to pay B up to A's marginal cost of abatement. B would require a payment equal to the marginal damage it would incur from the pollution, so in an agreement the marginal cost of abatement would equal the marginal damage. The assignment of the entitlement to B thus also results in the socially efficient level of pollution. The Coase theorem example illustrates this logic in more detail and extends the analysis to include abatement alternatives.

The Coase theorem states that, in the absence of transactions costs that would impede the bargaining over these private agreements, the socially efficient outcome can be realized if the entitlement is assigned to either party. The role of government thus is to assign entitlements to the parties and allow them to reach private agreements that internalize the externality. Although social efficiency is attained with either assignment of the entitlement, the assignment affects the distribution of the social costs of the externality. The Coase theorem example illustrates this in more detail.

Since an externality is reciprocal, one approach to dealing with an externality is to remove one side of the reciprocal relationship between polluter and those harmed by the pollution. Many plants have closed because of the costs they would have to bear to reduce their pollution. Conversely, to reduce the harm to local residents, the American Electric Power Company bought for $20 million the town of Chesire, Ohio, where one of its coal-fired power plants was located. The amount paid was three times the value of their homes, and the residents quickly accepted the offer.[2] Similarly, Exxon paid $4 million to purchase 110 homes and businesses to create a safety zone around its Baton Rouge, Louisiana, refinery. From the perspective of the Coase theorem, the entitlements in these two cases were assigned to the homeowners and were protected by a property rule. The firms bargained to purchase those entitlements, thereby bearing the cost of reducing the risk of harm.

As the Coase theorem indicates, social efficiency can be achieved given any assignment of entitlements, but the distributive consequences can differ substantially. Environmental politics often arises from the existing assignment of entitlements and its implications for the distribution of the benefits and burden of environmental protection. As an example, residents of the Old Diamond neighborhood of

Norco, Louisiana, conducted a 12 year private and public politics campaign against Shell. The neighborhood was located between a Shell chemical plant and an oil refinery owned by a Shell joint venture. The plants met EPA emissions standards, and Shell had reduced its emissions. The residents, however, wanted further reductions or a higher price for their homes. The entitlement rested with Shell, but the pressure of the campaign finally forced Shell to buy the residents' homes.[3]

## EXAMPLE

## The Coase Theorem

To illustrate the concept of social efficiency, suppose company A produces apple cider up river from a brewery B. Company A can produce 0, 100, or 200 gallons of apple cider, and its corresponding profit is 0, 40, and 70. The company's plant also pollutes the river, and the pollution causes harm to the brewery's product of 0, 20, and 60, respectively. These data are summarized in Table 11-1. Social well-being or social value is the aggregate of the profit of company A and the harm to company B. As indicated in the table, the social value is maximized at a production level of 100, which yields profit of 40 and harm of 20 for a social value of 20.

Identifying the social optimum is one thing; attaining it is another matter. Company A has an incentive to maximize its profit by producing 200 gallons, which yields a profit of 70. The harm, however, of 60 results in a social value of 10. One means of achieving social efficiency is through bargaining between A and B.

For bargaining to take place, entitlements must be clearly assigned and their protection specified. Suppose that B has the entitlement not to be harmed by pollution, and the entitlement is

**TABLE 11-1 Production, Harm, and Social Value**

| | A | A | B | B | |
|---|---|---|---|---|---|
| Production | Emissions | Profit | Harm | Social Value | |
| 0 | 0 | 0 | 0 | 0 | |
| 100 | 10 | 40 | −20 | 20 | |
| 200 | 20 | 70 | −60 | 10 | |

protected by a property rule. B thus will not allow A to produce at all unless it is compensated for the harm it incurs. A is willing to pay up to 40 to be able to produce 100 units, and B requires compensation of at least 20 for the harm. Suppose that as a result of their bargaining they split the difference, with A paying 30 to B to be allowed to produce 100 units accompanied by the pollution. Next, consider whether A wants to increase its production from 100 to 200. If it does, its profit increases by 30, but B requires at least 40 more to compensate for the additional harm. A thus is not willing to pay enough to induce B to bear the additional harm. Consequently, the bargaining between A and B results in the socially optimal output of 100 and a social value of 20. Through bargaining the two parties have *internalized the externality.*

Coase considered such situations and asked whether social efficiency would be obtained regardless of how the entitlement was assigned. That is, suppose that A is assigned the entitlement to produce, and pollute, as much as it chooses and the entitlement is protected by a property rule. A would then want to produce 200 units. B, however, would incur harm of 60, so it is willing to offer A up to 40 if A will reduce its production from 200 to 100. Since A loses only 30 in profit from cutting back its production to 100, the two parties can strike a bargain (at 35 if they split the difference). It is straightforward to verify that B will not be willing to compensate A enough to induce it to cut its production to zero. The socially efficient outcome has again been

(Continued)

*(Continued)*

obtained. The Coase theorem states that social efficiency can be achieved regardless of which party has the entitlement.

Although social efficiency is achieved with either assignment of entitlements, the distributive consequences of the assignments are quite different. If the entitlement is assigned to B, A has profit of 10 (= 40 − 30) and B has 10 (= 30 − 20). If the entitlement is assigned to A, A has a profit of 75 (= 40 + 35) and B has −55 (= −20 − 35). (Note that B's profit is not included here.) These distributive consequences are the source of politics as people seek to have the entitlement assigned to them.

The Coase theorem is more general than indicated by the analysis of a property rule. A property rule is distinguished from a *liability rule*. A liability rule does not prohibit a party from interfering with another party, but if harm is done, compensation must be paid to the injured party. In the example, suppose that the entitlement is assigned to B and is protected by a liability rule. Then A will produce 100 units and compensate B for the actual harm of 20. A will not increase its production to 200 because its profit would increase by only 30, but additional compensation of 40 would be required. Similarly, A would not reduce its output to 0. Social efficiency is again achieved. The same is true if the entitlement is assigned to A and protected by a liability rule. In this case, B would enjoin A from producing 200 and would be required to compensate A for the loss of profits of 30. B is willing to do so since it avoids harm of 40, so A will produce 100, again achieving social efficiency.

As in the case of a property rule the distributive consequences of the assignment of the entitlement protected by a liability rule differ. When the entitlement is assigned to B and protected by a liability rule, A has 20 and B has 0. When the entitlement is assigned to A, A has 70 and B has −50.

This analysis can be extended to include an abatement alternative. Suppose that, as indicated in Table 11-2, A and B each have an abatement alternative. Each can reduce the pollution by 50 or 100 percent at different costs. A can reduce the pollution by 50 and 100 percent at costs of 15 and 30 respectively, and the corresponding costs for B are 20 and 40 respectively. The socially efficient outcome is then for A to produce 200 and to pay 30 to reduce pollution by 100 percent. The social value is 40. This outcome is achieved regardless of to whom the entitlement is assigned and whether it is protected by a property or a liability rule. For example, if the entitlement is assigned to B and protected by a liability rule, A will produce 200 and, rather than compensate B by 60 for the harm, will install the 100 percent abatement technology at a cost of 30. A's profit is then 40, and B incurs no harm.

**TABLE 11-2 Abatement and Social Value**

| Reduction in Emissions, % | Cost of Abatement | | Social Value* | |
|---|---|---|---|---|
| | A | B | A Abates | B Abates |
| 0 | 0 | 0 | 10 | 10 |
| 50 | 15 | 20 | 25 | 20 |
| 100 | 30 | 40 | 40 | 30 |

*Based on production of 200.

## Transactions Costs and the Limits of the Coase Theorem

The Coase theorem implies that when bargaining between the parties to an externality is possible, social efficiency can be achieved. Consequently, from the Coasean perspective social efficiency is a problem only when there are impediments to bargaining. These impediments are referred to as *transactions costs* because they are associated with the process of arriving at a transaction or agreement. When the parties involved are identifiable and their number is small, transactions costs are likely to be low and private agreements can be reached, as in the case of the power plant in Ohio and the oil refineries and checimal plant in Louisiana. When the parties are difficult to identify or are large in number, however, transactions costs can be prohibitively high, preventing private arrangements.

Consider air pollution from automobile emissions. Millions of automobiles generate pollution, and many more people are affected by that pollution. The costs would be exorbitant if all these individuals attempted to reach agreements about measures to reduce emissions or the amount of driving allowed. Because of the very high transactions costs associated with private bargaining, automobile emissions are controlled through government regulation.

In the case of an externality such as automobile emissions with high transactions costs of bargaining, either a command-and-control approach specifying particular controls can be used or performance standards can be set. Performance standards are preferred because they allow firms to choose the most cost-effective means of achieving those standards based on their superior information about the costs of alternatives. This approach is decentralized with localized information being used to achieve abatement at the lowest cost.

A market is the logical extension of a decentralized system in which entitlements are assigned and can be traded. Markets, or incentive-based systems, have become an effective means of achieving environmental goals at the least cost to society. These systems are considered next.

# Tradable Permits System

A *tradable permits system*, or *cap-and-trade* system, caps the total allowed emissions of a particular pollutant, issues permits (entitlements) for that amount, and allows the permits to be traded.[4] Cap-and-trade systems are used for sulfur dioxide emissions and nitrogen dioxides, and several systems are in operation regionally, as in Southern California. A tradable permits system has been adopted to reduce greenhouse gasses emissions in conjunction with the Kyoto Protocol on global climate change. Although the United States did not ratify the Kyoto Protocol, a voluntary compliance system has been established and permits are traded on the Chicago Climate Exchange in a pilot program. Members have committed to reducing their greenhouse gasses emissions by 4 percent by 2006 based on a 1998–2001 baseline. BP has established an internal tradable permits market for greenhouse gasses.

The Coase theorem applies to this type of system. That is, the permits can be allocated to polluters for no charge, can be allocated to the public, or can be auctioned to the highest bidder. With any of these allocations, social efficiency can be achieved provided the permits can be traded. The allocation of the permits, however, affects the distribution of the burden of the emissions reduction and hence motivates politics. The politics of a tradable permits system are considered in the scrubbers example later in the chapter. The focus in this section is on the social efficiency of a tradable permits system.

The control of an externality in a market-based system has three components. The first is providing incentives for abatement by internalizing the cost of the harm done by the pollutants. The second is allowing parties to respond to those incentives by choosing the most efficient means of abatement. These means include reducing output, installing pollution-control equipment, redesigning products and production processes to reduce the pollutants generated, and reducing the harm from emissions, as when oil refineries create safety zones around their facilities. The third component involves reflecting in the prices of goods and services, the costs of abatement, and the social

[4]The Chapter 20 case, *Environmental Justice and Pollution Credits Trading Systems*, provides another example of a tradable permit system.

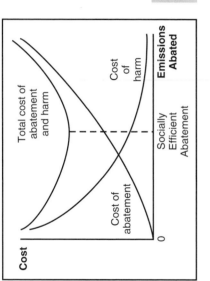

**Cost**

Total cost of abatement and harm

Cost of harm

Cost of abatement

0        Socially Efficient Abatement       **Emissions Abated**

**FIGURE 11-1A** Socially Efficient Regulation and Total Costs

costs of the harm from the remaining pollution. This allows consumers to take into account the full social cost of the goods they consume. These three components operate simultaneously. An equilibrium results when (1) all advantageous trades have been made, (2) emitters have taken the abatement measures they prefer given the market price of permits, and (3) the quantities of products consumers purchase result in total emissions equal to the number of permits issued.

The optimal number of permits to issue minimizes the sum of the social costs of the harm from the emissions and the costs of abatement. This is illustrated in Figure 11-1A, where the horizontal axis corresponds to the emissions abated. The cost of abatement is increasing in the emissions abated. The cost of the harm is decreasing in the emissions abated. Social efficiency requires that the number of permits issued minimize the sum of these costs, as illustrated in the figure. Figure 11-1B presents the marginal social costs of harm and marginal cost of abatement that correspond to the cost curves in Figure 11-1A. At the socially efficient amount of abatement, the marginal cost of abatement equals the marginal cost of harm.

The emissions remaining after the socially efficient level of trading equals the number of permits issued, and this equating of supply and demand establishes the price $t$ of a permit. As illustrated in Figure 11-1B, with a competitive market for permits, the price is equal to the marginal cost of abatement and the marginal cost of harm.

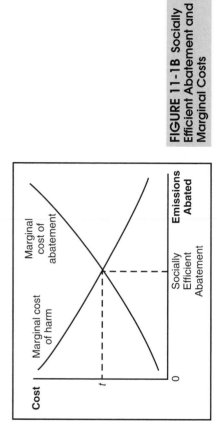

**Cost**

Marginal cost of abatement

Marginal cost of harm

$t$

0        Socially Efficient Abatement       **Emissions Abated**

**FIGURE 11-1B** Socially Efficient Abatement and Marginal Costs

Consider a firm A whose production process generates one pound of pollution per unit of the product produced. The firm could purchase a permit at a cost $t$ for each unit of the product it produces. Instead of purchasing permits, the firm could install abatement equipment or change the design of the product or the production process to reduce the pollution generated. The firm will use these alternatives in the combination that minimizes its cost of abatement plus the cost of permits for any remaining pollution. Suppose, for example, that a firm can install pollution-abatement equipment to reduce emissions and that the marginal cost of abatement increases with the amount of abatement, as illustrated in Figure 11-2. The firm will install pollution-abatement equipment as long as doing so is less costly than the cost $t$ of purchasing a permit. Consequently, firm A will abate to the level indicated in the figure. Using the same reasoning, a firm B that has higher marginal costs of abatement will abate less than firm A, as illustrated in the figure.[5] The high cost abater thus abates less than the low cost abater.

Next consider the market for permits. Suppose that the initial allocation of permits were made to polluters as in the sulfur dioxide permits system discussed in the next section. If firms A and B in Figure 11-2 each had permits that required abatement to the point $x$ on the horizontal axis, B would have to abate more than the efficient amount, incurring a high cost. In contrast A would abate less than the efficient amount, incurring a low cost. With a market for permits B would purchase permits and A would sell permits. An equilibrium in the market for permits occurs at a price $t^*$ such that no firm prefers to either buy or sell additional permits at that price. This equilibrium has the feature that each firm abates to the point at which its marginal cost of abatement equals the price $t^*$ of a permit, as indicated in Figure 11-2. All firms thus have the same marginal cost of abatement in equilibrium, and firms that have low marginal costs abate more than those that have higher marginal abatement costs.

The final feature of a tradable permits system is reflecting the costs of abatement in the prices of products. As illustrated in Figure 11-3, the marginal costs of abatement are added to the marginal cost of production, which shifts upward the supply curve in the industry from $S$ to $S^*$. This reduces the quantity demanded by consumers of the

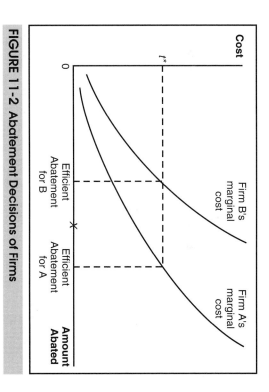

**FIGURE 11-2 Abatement Decisions of Firms**

---

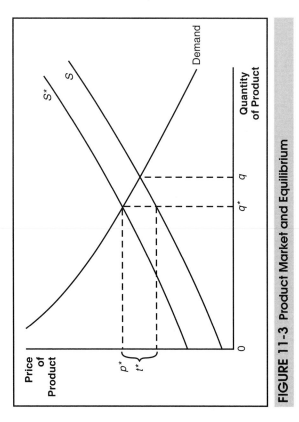

**FIGURE 11-3  Product Market and Equilibrium**

product from $q$ to $q^*$, as illustrated in the figure. At the quantity $q^*$ the supply curve $S^*$ is above the supply curve $S$ by exactly the price $t^*$ of a permit. In the market equilibrium consumers pay the marginal cost of abatement, and the industry produces less than it would have if pollution had not been capped.

Finally, the equilibria in Figures 11-2 and 11-3 must be consistent with Figure 11-1. That is, the regulator must issue permits that equal the emissions corresponding to the quantity $q^*$ of the product produced in Figure 11-3 when the firms make abatement decisions as in Figure 11-2. When the price of a permit in Figure 11-1B is $t^*$, the equilibria in the permits market and the product market have the property that the marginal social harm from the emissions and the marginal cost of abatement of each firm equal $t^*$. This condition is necessary for social efficiency.

A tradable permits system is equivalent to a system in which an emissions tax $t^*$ is imposed on each unit of pollution omitted. A tradable permits system is said to be superior to an emissions tax because the amount of abatement is known in advance with a permits system, whereas with an emissions tax the amount is known only after firms have responded to the tax. Emissions taxes or fees are used in Southern California for organic gasses, nitrogen oxides, carbon monoxide, sulfur oxides, and particulate matter. Maine uses an emissions fee that increases from \$3.28 per ton for emissions up to 1,000 tons to \$15.85 per ton for emissions over 4,000 tons. Fees or taxes are used for landfills, grazing on public lands, and hazardous waste disposal. The Chapter 15 case, *The European Union Carbon Tax*, considers such a system.

A permits system has another advantage over an emissions tax system in that it allows people with different preferences to express them in the market for permits. If people have a preference for lower levels of pollution, they can purchase permits and retire them, thereby reducing emissions. Some people have purchased permits and given them as gifts. The Cleaner and Greener Green Energy program facilitates the donation of permits.[6]

---

[6]www.cleanerandgreener.org. In a related expression of preferences, The Nature Conservancy has purchased 117 million acres, including 14.3 million in the United States, and has total assets of \$3.7 billion. As an example, The Nature Conservancy purchased a 1,711 acre ranch in northern California and transferred it to the Bureau of Land Management for stewardship.

Both emissions tax and tradable permits systems involve complications when abatement costs or damages change. When the change does not affect the socially efficient level of emissions, a tradable permit system has an advantage over an emissions tax system because the price adjusts automatically as permits are bought and sold. Changing an emissions tax would require a legislative or regulatory decision, which would involve a lengthy process. If the socially efficient level of emissions changes, however, the number of permits issued would have to be changed.

Tradable permits and emissions tax approaches to environmental protection also provide incentives for dynamic efficiency. Firms have incentives to invest in research and development to find more efficient means of reducing their emissions. If they can do so, they can sell their permits. Similarly, the pollution-control technology industry has an incentive to develop new abatement technologies because firms have a continuing demand for emissions reduction rather than a demand that arises only when more stringent engineering controls are mandated, as in a command-and-control system.

Despite the efficiency advantages, some people believe that controlling a social bad, such as pollution, through marketlike mechanisms demeans the objectives of environmental protection.[7] Objections have been made that marketlike mechanisms such as a tradable permits system amount to a right to pollute—and no one should have such a right.[8] Objections also arise because under incentive approaches some firms will reduce emissions considerably whereas others will reduce them less. Some people who view pollution as a social wrong rather than as an external cost of production believe that all firms should be forced to reduce their emissions by the same amount so that, for example, neighboring residents all receive the same reduction in pollution. The Chapter 20 case, *Environmental Justice and Pollution Credits Trading Systems*, addresses this issue and the politics it generated.

## Acid Rain and Tradable Permits

The bulk of the sulfur dioxide emissions that cause acid rain come from coal-fired electric power plants in six states: Indiana, Illinois, West Virginia, Pennsylvania, Ohio, and New York. New power plants are subject to New Source Performance Standards (NSPS), but existing power plants had not been subject to emission limits. These six states, and others as well, had lower electricity prices because their plants did not have to meet stringent controls. Adding a scrubber to remove the sulfur dioxide, for example, could increase the cost of electricity by 15 percent. Since the damage from acid rain occurred primarily in Canada and the northeastern states, addressing the issue involved benefits for one region and costs to another. Bargaining thus focused on both efficiency and the distributive consequences of policy alternatives. The political competition over acid rain went on for a decade, culminating with the Clean Air Act Amendments of 1990, which provided for an 87 million pounds, or 45 percent, reduction in sulfur dioxide emissions from the 1980 level and a 2 million pounds reduction in nitrogen oxide emissions.

The amendments addressed efficiency through a tradable permits system and the distributive consequences through a number of special provisions. Called "allowances" rather than permits, the system reduced the cost of abatement by allowing electric power companies to use the most efficient means of achieving emissions standards. They could choose low-sulfur coal, coal washing to remove sulfur before burning, new technologies such as fluidized bed combustion, or a scrubber. More importantly, the

[7]Kelman (1981) makes this and related arguments.
[8]See Stewart (1988) for responses to the criticisms of incentive systems for environmental protection.

system permitted firms to trade allowances in a market, providing incentives for the efficient distribution of abatement across firms. The value of the sulfur dioxide allowances issued in 2004 was estimated at $3.6 billion, and the price in 2004 had skyrocketed from $200 a ton to $650 a ton. The economic harm from a ton of sulfur dioxide emissions is estimated to be $4,000.[9] A total of 21.4 million allowances were traded in 2003.[10] The tradable allowances system has been estimated to reduce costs by 50 percent, or $2.5 billion per year, compared with a uniform command-and-control approach.[11] An Office of Management and Budget study concluded that the acid rain program yielded benefits of $70 billion for a benefit-cost ratio of 40 to 1. With a tradable permits system, emissions must be monitored to ensure that they do not exceed the permits held by the firm. The sulfur dioxide cap-and-trade system uses continuous monitoring by sources and is verified by the EPA and posted on the Internet for public inspection.[12] If a source emits more sulfur dioxide than the allowances it has, a fine of $2,900 per ton of excess emissions is imposed (in 2003).

In the initial phase of the program the EPA administrator annually allocated allowances to 110 coal-fired power plants in 21 states in the Midwest, South, and East according to formulas specified in the legislation.[13] Unused allowances could be carried forward to the next year and transferred or sold to other companies. Power companies were also allowed to transfer allowances among their own plants. New power plants completed after enactment of the amendments were not allocated any allowances and had to purchase them from existing plants. New power plants were already subject to the NSPS of 1.2 pounds of $SO_2$ per MBtu, so their emissions were substantially below the emissions levels of existing plants. In 2000 the emissions cap under the Clean Air Act Amendments was extended to cover all power-generating units above 25 megawatts and all new units.

Wary of the transferable allowances approach, Congress declared that the allowances were not property rights of the power companies but instead were grants that could be revoked or changed at the discretion of the EPA administrator.[14] No administrator has done so. The EPA administrator conducts an annual auction of allowances from a reserve formed by taking a percentage of the allowances allocated to the plants.[15]

The distributive consequences of the tradable allowances system depend in large part on how the allowances are allocated. Since regulated electricity prices are cost-of-service based, the full costs of both allowances and abatement are borne by the customers of the electric power plants. If the allowances were initially allocated to the EPA and auctioned, the power companies and their customers would bear the costs of abatement plus the payments for the allowances. Taxpayers across the nation would be the beneficiaries. If the allowances were initially allocated to the power companies, taxpayers would receive nothing, and the power companies and their customers would bear only the costs of abatement. As the Coase theorem indicates, the efficiency consequences of assigning the allowances to the EPA or the power companies

[9] The value of the nitrogen dioxide credits was estimated at $1.4 billion.
[10] Cantor Environmental Brokerage reports market prices for allowances traded in over 30 markets (www.emissionstrading.com).
[11] Joskow, Schmalensee, and Bailey (1998); Schmalensee et al. (1998); and Stavins (1998) evaluated the market for $SO_2$ allowances and concluded that by 1994 it was functioning relatively efficiently.
[12] www.epa.gov/airmarkets.
[13] See Joskow and Schmalensee (1998) for a study of the political economy of the allocation of allowances.
[14] One reason for not using the term "right" was that some environmentalists criticized transferable allowance systems because they believed that the systems involved trading the right to pollute.
[15] The proceeds are distributed back to the plants from which the allowances were originally obtained.

are identical, so the choice between the two methods is a distributive matter. Assigning the allowances to the power companies would produce concentrated benefits in the 21 states and particularly in the six states that emit the most sulfur dioxide. The loss to taxpayers would be widely distributed. Client politics prevailed, and the allowances were assigned to the power companies, resulting in lower costs for the power plants and their customers.

The EPA also established an emissions trading system for nitrogen oxide similar to the one for sulfur dioxide. The program reduces by 28 percent the emissions in 22 states and the District of Columbia and covers coal-fired and oil-fired power plants and industrial boilers. Nitrogen oxide is a major component of smog and can flow to down-wind states. In 2002 nitrogen oxide emissions were 60 percent below 1990 levels.

## Global Climate Change and Emissions Trading Systems

In 1998 the Clinton administration signed the Kyoto Protocol on global climate change, which called for country-specific reductions in carbon dioxide emissions by 2010. The U.S. target was a 7 percent reduction from 1990 levels. The Protocol had strong opposition in the Senate, which in 1997 adopted a resolution opposing the protocol unless developing countries made firm commitments to reduce their emissions. President Clinton chose not to submit the protocol to the Senate for ratification. The Clinton administration argued that the Kyoto agreement would have little effect on costs, but the Department of Energy predicted that gasoline prices would increase by nearly 40 percent and electricity prices between 20 and 86 percent in real terms by 2010. President Bush announced that the United States would not ratify the Kyoto Protocol. The president believed the cost to the U.S. economy was too high and objected to the absence of targets for developing countries and for China and India in particular. Australia also rejected the Kyoto Protocol. Russia approved the Protocol in late 2004, enabling it to go into effect.

The signatories to the Kyoto Protocol agreed to use an emissions permits trading system to reduce the cost of achieving their commitments. Countries can earn credits toward their Kyoto goals by investing in emissions reduction programs in developing countries. The European Union took the lead on multination emission trading with the European Trading System (ETS) commencing in 2005. The ETS is a cap-and-trade system that covers 12,000 facilities in 15 EU member states. The EU goal is an 8 percent reduction by 2012 from a 1990 base. Skeptics believed that the goal would not be reached. National trading systems have been established in the United Kingdom and Denmark, and in 2001 DuPont and MIECO, a subsidiary of Japan's Marubeni, made the first trade of allowances under the United Kingdom.

The United States under the Bush administration has adopted a voluntary approach to greenhouse gasses reductions with a 2012 goal of an 18 percent reduction in emission per unit of GDP. Greenhouse gasses are traded on the Chicago Climate Exchange under a voluntary cap-and-trade system. U.S. power companies formed the Power Tree Carbon Company to plant trees, and American Electric Power reported that it had planted 22 million trees, sequestering 9.1 million tons of $CO_2$, at a cost of $12 million.[16] Excelon reported eliminating 24.8 million tons of $CO_2$ by upgrading its nuclear power plants to increase their capacity. Power and coal companies formed the FutureGen Project with funding of $1 billion to develop a coal-fired electricity and hydrogen plant with 100 percent $CO_2$ sequestration. States in the northwest and in the northeast began work on regional trading systems for greenhouse gasses.

## Emissions Trading Within BP plc (British Petroleum)

Emissions trading can occur not only among firms and nations, but also within firms. To address the global climate change issue, in 1998 BP plc committed by 2010 to reduce its emissions of greenhouse gasses (GHGs) by 10 percent from 1990 levels.[17] BP's greenhouse gasses policy is guided by a target for the earth of 500 to 550 parts per million (ppm) of GHGs compared to the present level of 370 ppm and 280 ppm before the industrial revolution.

To achieve its goal, BP worked with Environmental Defense to develop an internal GHGs trading system for the company. Each BP business unit is given an annual cap that it must meet either through reduction projects or by purchasing allowances (permits) on the internal company market. No additional allowances are given for growth, although the baseline is adjusted in the case of an acquisition. A central broker within the company administers the market. In the first year of the market 2.7 million tons of allowances were traded, and the average price was $7.60 per ton. Trading operates as it does in the basic theory of tradable permits systems. A chemicals unit that installs a new furnace that improves combustion frees up allowances that it can sell to a business unit whose cost of $CO_2$ reduction is greater than the price of an allowance.

BP's internal trading system was instrumental in enabling the company to achieve its 2010 goal in 2001. Having achieved its goal, BP set a new goal of no increase in GHG emissions through 2012. BP also participated in the UK emissions trading scheme and the sulfur dioxide and nitrogen oxides trading systems in the United States.

## The Environmental Protection Agency

The EPA, an independent agency located in the executive branch, is headed by an administrator appointed by the president and confirmed by the Senate.[18] The EPA was created by an executive order of President Nixon in 1970 to bring together in a single agency a number of environmental regulation programs then housed in different federal agencies. Congress quickly passed several measures expanding the new agency's responsibilities.[19] The EPA is now responsible for administering the major acts listed in Figure 11-4. As was characteristic of the new social regulation, the acts were written in the fear that they would not be enforced because the agencies would be captured by industry. The acts thus are often highly detailed and frequently include timetables intended to force the agency to act.[20] Many of these measures established specific goals for environmental protection without reference to costs. The goals in some cases were unrealistic and served more as symbols than as commitment.[21] The Federal Water Pollution Control Act of 1972, for example, established the goal of eliminating all discharges of pollutants into navigable waters by 1985.

Federal environmental regulation is a major undertaking. The EPA had a budget of $7.8 billion in 2005 and nearly 18,000 employees. The EPA has responsibility for air

---

[17]BP's response to the global climate change issue is considered in more detail in Chapter 21.
[18]See *Congressional Quarterly* (1994) for a description of the EPA and its powers.
[19]Marcus (1980) discusses the political forces that shaped the EPA in its first decade.
[20]Vogel (1986) provides a comparison of U.S. and UK environmental policy.
[21]See Kneese and Schultze (1975) for an early critique of environmental legislation.

and water quality, drinking water safety, waste treatment and disposal, toxic substances, and pesticides. The Department of the Interior has responsibilities for some conservation programs, and the Department of Agriculture has responsibilities for some pesticide control programs.

A number of the statutes assign to the states the responsibility for formulating implementation plans for attaining federal environmental standards. Under the Clean Air Act, states are responsible for developing State Implementation Plans to meet air quality standards. This gives the states a considerable role in environmental protection. States have their own environmental laws and regulatory agencies as well, and some enforcement is delegated to those agencies.

Federal Insecticide, Fungicide and Rodenticide Act of 1947 (amended in 1972, 1988)
Clean Air Act of 1963 (amended in 1970, 1977, 1990)
Solid Waste Disposal Act of 1965
Air Quality Act of 1967
National Environmental Policy Act of 1969
Water Quality Improvement Act of 1970
Federal Environmental Pesticide Control Act of 1970
Federal Water Pollution Control Act (Clean Water Act) of 1972 (amended in 1987)
Marine Protection, Research and Sanctuaries Act of 1972
Noise Control Act of 1972
Endangered Species Act of 1973
Safe Drinking Water Act of 1974 (amended in 1997)
Toxic Substances Control Act of 1976 (amended in 1988)
Resource Conservation and Recovery Act of 1976
Clean Water Act of 1977
Comprehensive Environmental Response, Compensation, and Liability Act of 1980 (amended in 1986) [Superfund]
Emergency Planning and Community Right-to-Know Act (1986)
Water Quality Act of 1987
Ocean Pollution Dumping Act of 1990
Pollution Prevention Act of 1990
Oil Pollution Act of 1990
Reclamation Projects Act of 1992
Food Quality Protection Act of 1996

**FIGURE 11-4 Principal Environmental Acts**

## Enforcement

The EPA enforcement process requires the filing of a notice of a complaint and a hearing before an administrative law judge (ALJ). The ALJ's decision can be appealed to the agency's administrator and to the courts. Under some statutes the EPA has the authority to forward cases to the Department of Justice, which can file a civil proceeding in federal district court. Typically, however, the EPA seeks voluntary compliance with environmental standards. Some environmental laws also allow lawsuits by private citizens against polluters who violate regulations.

The federal government can seek both civil and criminal convictions of polluters, both of firms and individual managers. In 1997 the EPA referred for prosecution 278 criminal cases and 425 civil cases with total fines of $264.4 million. In the wake of the

Alaskan oil spill by the *Exxon Valdez*, felony and misdemeanor criminal charges were brought against Exxon and the captain of the tanker. The captain was acquitted of three of the four charges, including the felony charges, and convicted on one charge of misdemeanor negligence. In 1991 Exxon agreed to a settlement with the federal and Alaska state governments in which it pleaded guilty to three misdemeanor charges and agreed to pay $1.15 billion in civil and criminal fines and restitution, of which $287 million was for actual damages. In addition, Exxon spent over $2 billion on the cleanup. In 1994 a federal court jury found that Exxon had acted in a negligent and reckless manner and ordered it to pay $5 billion in punitive damages to Alaskans. In 2001 the Court of Appeals ruled that the punitive damages award was excessive and ordered the district court to reduce the award. The trial judge reduced the punitive damages to $4 billion, and in 2003 the Court of Appeals again overturned the award as excessive in light of a recent Supreme Court decision limiting punitive damages.[22]

## Standards Setting and Engineering Controls

EPA regulation has largely been command and control, in which uniform rules or standards are ordered and then enforced. This type of regulation is often a blunt instrument, imposing uniform rules in dissimilar circumstances. Under this approach the EPA, for example, sets emissions limits for each pollution source, where a source may be as specific as an individual piece of equipment in a chemical plant. Uniform stationary-source pollution standards that ignore differences in abatement costs and achievable benefits across emissions sources have created both economic inefficiency and administrative nightmares. This experience contributed to the decision to use tradable permits systems.

The EPA both establishes overall standards, such as for ambient air quality, and specifies engineering controls to reduce emissions. The engineering controls, in order of increasing stringency, are the "best practicable technology," "best conventional technology," "best available technology," and "maximum achievable control technology." The use of engineering controls has been criticized on efficiency grounds, but its advocates believe it is necessary to force polluters to comply. The Chapter 6 case, *Scrubbers and Environmental Politics*, illustrates the politics of mandated controls.

One advantage of the standards-setting approach is that it can be used to force the development of new pollution-control technologies. Emissions standards for automobiles, for example, were set beyond what available technology could achieve, forcing automakers and suppliers to develop new technologies. These standards had to be changed at times because of the difficulty in achieving the needed technological advancements, but overall, technology-forcing regulation has been effective in reducing auto emissions.

Not only is the command-and-control approach a blunt instrument, but it often imposes high administrative costs on firms and limits their flexibility in responding quickly to market changes and product developments. For example, an Intel semiconductor plant may have 35 to 40 chemical process changes a year, and each change can require EPA approval. For a company like Intel that introduces a new generation of microprocessors every year or two, the delay caused by the required process approvals can be more costly than the administrative and compliance costs. To deal with such problems Intel and the EPA reached an agreement on simplifying the permit and compliance process in the context of the EPA's Project XL. The following example describes the Intel project.

---

[22]See Chapter 12.

---

**EXAMPLE**

## Intel and the Project XL

The objective of the EPA's Project XL is to "provide a forum for companies to test new technologies and alternative regulatory approaches that eventually might be used by more companies to boost efficiency and achieve better environmental protection." In 1996 Intel and the EPA reached an agreement on the first XL project at its Chandler, Arizona, semiconductor plant.[1] The plant was subject to regulations under four principal statutes administered by five different EPA offices:

- Clean Air Act administered by the Office of Air Quality Planning and Standards
- Clean Water Act administered by the Office of Wastewater Management and the Office of Wetlands, Oceans, and Watersheds
- Resource Conservation and Recovery Act administered by the Office of Solid Waste
- Pollution Prevention Act administered by the Office of Prevention, Pesticides, and Toxic Substances

In addition, the Intel plant was subject to regulation by the Arizona Department of Environmental Quality, the Maricopa County Bureau of Air Pollution Control, and the City of Chandler.

The Intel project had two principal features: (1) elimination of case-by-case process change reviews by the EPA, provided that Intel emissions remained below a capped amount, and (2) preapproval of major plant expansions, provided that

[1] EPA, "Project XL Progress Report: Intel Corporation," 100-R-00-031, January 2001.

emissions remain below a cap for the entire site. Environmental groups initially criticized the agreement. The National Resources Defense Council (NRDC) said, "We are disappointed with the environmental performance required by this agreement."[2] Local environmental and labor groups also criticized the agreement, charging that it "allows Intel to expose its employees and the communities of Chandler and Phoenix to increased toxic chemical hazards."[3] Intel has remained well below the emissions caps.

According to the EPA, "Intel also has avoided millions of dollars in production delays by eliminating 30 to 50 new source permit reviews a year. The company has found the emissions caps so successful that it will invest $2 billion to build a new wafer fabrication facility (Fab 22) at the site. Under the existing cap, Intel can proceed with expansion without first going through regulatory review." The Project XL was one of the factors that led Intel to build its Fab 22 at the Chandler site.

The project also included an informational component. The project allowed Intel to use a consolidated reporting system for all the regulatory statutes, with the exception of the Toxic Release Inventory. Intel invited local stakeholders to participate in designing environmental reports, and those reports were made available on Intel's Web site. Intel also participated in an emergency preparedness program with the City of Chandler.

[2] *The New York Times*, November 20, 1996.
[3] *The New York Times*, November 20, 1996.

---

## Incentive Approaches

In addition to imposing engineering controls and establishing standards, the EPA has increasingly used incentive approaches.[23] One approach used in local air quality regulation under the Clean Air Act is the "bubble" program. Under the command-and-control approach, engineering controls are specified for each individual processing unit in an oil refinery, chemical plant, or steel mill. Under the bubble policy, the EPA sets permitted

[23] Ellerman, Joskow, and Harrison (2003) provide an introduction to incentive approaches in the United States.

emissions levels for the entire plant—imagine a bubble around the plant—and allows the producer to achieve those levels in the most efficient manner. The plant, for example, may achieve the required reduction on a single processing unit or through controls on several units.

Another program to improve the efficiency of air quality regulation in nonattainment areas—those that do not meet federal air quality standards—uses *credits and offsets*. For example, under the Clean Air Act Amendments of 1990, the EPA allocates credits to states for implementing enhanced auto emissions testing and maintenance programs.[24] The EPA allocates more credits for centralized testing programs than for decentralized programs because of their greater effectiveness. The credits are used to cover the emissions of new plants to be built in the area.

Under the offset program, to construct a new plant in a nonattainment area a firm must reduce pollutants elsewhere in the area by the amount to be released by the new plant. The firm can reduce emissions at another of its facilities or may purchase credits from another firm. In 1995 the California Institute of Technology and the Pacific Stock Exchange created an electronic market for trading credits in four Southern California counties. The Regional Clean Air Incentives Market (RECLAIM) hosts trades of credits in sulfur dioxide and nitrogen oxides. Trading has been active, and a state review concluded that the program was efficient and effective.[25]

The EPA does not have the authority to tax pollution, but Congress has taken an interest in pollution taxes. In 1989 a federal law imposed a tax on chlorofluorocarbons (CFCs) as a means of reducing the use of the ozone-depleting chemicals while production was being phased out. To address the global climate change issue, some firms, members of Congress, and environmentalists have urged the use of a broadscale carbon tax on fuels. In 1993 the Clinton administration attempted to have a closely related Btu tax enacted by Congress, but the political pressure from those who would bear the distributive consequences of the tax caused the plan to fail. The Chapter 15 case, *The European Union Carbon Tax,* concerns a similar measure.

The EPA reported that in 2003 the aggregate total emissions of the six pollutants identified in the Clean Air Act had been reduced by 51 percent since 1970 and 7.8 percent since 2000. Much of the reduction was achieved by the cap-and-trade systems for sulfur dioxide and nitrogen oxides. The Bush administration established the Clean Air Interstate Rule that will use a cap-and-trade system for power plants in 29 eastern states to reduce sulfur dioxide emissions by an additional 40 percent and nitrogen oxides by 50 percent by 2010 and by 70 percent and 60 percent respectively when fully implemented.

## Superfund

The EPA administers the Superfund for the cleanup of existing toxic waste disposal sites. Estimates placed the number of sites requiring Superfund cleanups as high as 20,000, and cost estimates were as high as $600 billion. Under the Superfund program the EPA attempts to identify the source of the dumping and force it to clean the site. If the EPA does the cleanup, it can go to court to recover the costs. As of 2003 the EPA had completed work on 58 percent of the over 1,500 sites on the National Priorities List. The Superfund program has been criticized both for moving too slowly and for spending funds where there was little hope of a successful cleanup. In recent years the pace of cleanup of toxic waste sites has increased. Of the $30 billion spent by business and government on the Superfund program, however, a third is estimated to have gone

[24]See the Chapter 2 case, *Envirotest Systems Corporation (A),* for the management and politics of an auto emissions testing program.
[25]Each trade is listed at www.aqmd.gas/reclaim/reclaim/html.

to lawyers in litigation over who is liable for the costs. Another criticism of the program is that it requires the same cleanup level of all sites, regardless of their future use or the costs of cleanup.

In addition to the litigation costs the Superfund has been criticized for its "retrospective liability" feature that requires companies to pay for the cleanup of wastes that had been disposed of legally. The Clinton administration responded to this criticism by proposing to exempt small firms. The criticisms and disagreements over the Superfund caused its congressional reauthorization to be mired in politics for most of the 1990s, and the taxes imposed on firms to fund the program expired in 1995. The Superfund is now financed by the federal budget and by fees imposed on identified polluters. Approximately 70 percent of the cleanup costs are paid by the party held responsible for the pollution with the rest paid by the government.

# The Politics of Environmental Protection

## The Nature of Environmental Politics

Environmental issues are of concern to most people, and hence to interest groups and the news media, and often advance rapidly in their life cycles. Since most of the costs of environmental protection are borne by private parties, government budget considerations have imposed few limits on the advance of environmental issues.[26] The costs of environmental protection are borne by firms, their stakeholders, and consumers, and those costs generate opposition to more stringent regulation. Similarly, the benefits of environmental protection are both widespread and concentrated on those with strong interests in particular issues such as health impairment from pollution, air quality at the Grand Canyon, wetlands, logging in national forests, or cattle grazing on Bureau of Land Management lands. Environmental issues thus are the subject of intense public politics, as evidenced by the 1990 amendments to the Clean Air Act, considered later in the chapter, over which Congress struggled for a decade.[27] Environmental issues are also the subject of private politics led by environmental and activist groups, as considered in Chapter 4 and in the Chapter 4 case, *Strategic Activism: The Rainforest Action Network*, and the Part I integrative case, *Anatomy of a Corporate Campaign: Rainforest Action Network and Citigroup*.

Environmental issues are complex, in part because of scientific uncertainty about the consequences of pollution, incomplete information about the costs and benefits of environmental protection, and disagreements about alternative approaches, such as liability versus regulation. Environmental issues are also complex because of differing perspectives about the protection of entitlements. From the social efficiency perspective, the entitlement to be free from the hazards of pollution should be protected by a liability rule because the transactions costs associated with a property rule would be prohibitive. Yet many individuals treat the environment and their health as if they were protected by a property rule. They seek to prohibit activities that may pose a risk to their health or to the environment. In one instance, Congress responded to these sentiments by enacting the Delaney amendment, which prohibited the use of any food additive found to be a carcinogen in laboratory animals. Environmental politics—including the NIMBY movement—thus is motivated both by distributive consequences and normative perspectives about the protection of the environment and health.

---

[26] Some regulation does have budget effects. For example, municipalities are one of the largest water polluters, and the federal government provides subsidies to municipalities for the construction of waste treatment plants.
[27] See Greve and Smith (1992) and Rosenbaum (1995) for treatments of environmental politics.

## Judicial Politics

The politics of environmental protection often moves into judicial arenas. The NRDC sued the EPA, seeking enforcement of the Delaney amendment for pesticides used in the production of foods. As a practical means of dealing with potential risks, the EPA had followed a practice of allowing pesticide use if the risk to human health was "negligible." The courts held for the NRDC, requiring the EPA to enforce the Delaney amendment. This decision required the banning of dozens of widely used pesticides. The court decision added to the pressure for congressional action to repeal the Delaney amendment, which occurred in 1996.

Environmental groups have succeeded in inserting citizen provisions in environmental statutes. Under the citizen provision of the Clean Water Act the environmental group Water Keeper Alliance sued Smithfield Foods, the nation's largest hog producer, alleging that runoff from its hog farm in North Carolina polluted the state's rivers. Such lawsuits are not uncommon, but this one was potentially important because it was financed by the trial lawyers who had successfully filed class action lawsuits against the tobacco companies. Such litigation can also be backed by interests seeking to preserve their rents. Some populist farm groups backed the lawsuit because the efficiency of Southfield's operations threatened many family-style hog farms.

## Advocacy Science

Much remains unknown about environmental hazards and their control, and this scientific uncertainty is a source of contention in environmental politics. For example, the EPA estimated that 8 million homes were contaminated by dangerous levels of radon, a naturally occurring radioactive gas formed as radium decays in the ground. The EPA projected that the exposure to radon over a lifetime could cause 20,000 lung cancer deaths a year. In 1986 the EPA issued an Indoor Radon Health Advisory that said, "Radon causes thousands of deaths each year." Other scientists placed the number of households with radon concentrations at the EPA's action level as low as 100,000. In one study, the lung cancer rate of people exposed to radon was found to be no different from that of people who were not exposed.[28] In 1993 the EPA issued voluntary guidelines for new homes and an information pamphlet for homeowners.

The scientific uncertainty about the harm to the environment caused by pollution and about the risks to people's health, as in the case of radon, provides an opportunity to use advocacy science—proclaiming dangers to health and the environment—as a component of a private politics strategy. The Alar episode considered in Chapter 3 provides an example of the effectiveness of such a strategy. Because the media sees health and environmental risks as having societal significance and considerable audience interest, environmental issues quickly find their way to the public's attention and are frequently contested in full view of the public. These issues often arise from data provided in epidemiological studies. Feinstein (1988) characterized the pattern: "The episodes have now developed a familiar pattern. A report appears in a prominent medical journal; the conclusions receive wide publicity by newspapers, television, and other media; and another common entity of daily life becomes indicted as a menace to health—possibly causing strokes, heart attacks, birth defects, cancer. . . . The reported evidence is almost always a statistical analysis of epidemiological data, and the scientific tactics that produced the evidence are almost always difficult to understand and evaluate." He criticized the studies because "the research methods seldom have the precautions, calibrations, and relative simplicity that are taken for granted in other branches of science."

---

[28]*The New York Times*, January 8, 1991.

Another source of contention in environmental politics results from laboratory studies. Studies of health risks are often conducted on laboratory animals, which are exposed to pollutants at concentrations higher than human beings would ever encounter.[29] The laboratory results then must be extrapolated to the size and weight of people. Whether such results bear a reasonable relationship to the health risks to human beings can be a matter of disagreement.

## Distributive Politics

In addition to concerns about hazards, environmental politics is motivated by the distributive consequences of environmental policy, the costs of environmental protection, and the benefits from the reduction in pollution and hazards. Much of the battle over the Clean Air Act Amendments was between "clean" and "dirty" states. The clean states wanted credit for their accomplishments and wanted to avoid having to pay the dirty states' cleanup costs. The dirty states were primarily in the Midwest, and many of them also mined high-sulfur coal. Their representatives in Congress sought both to hold down electricity prices and preserve jobs for miners. The dirty states also sought cost sharing through federal tax subsidies for scrubbers and sought compensation for jobs lost. The example considers the politics of these two issues.

Although the immediate costs of reducing pollution are concentrated on the generators of the pollutants, most environmental protection costs are ultimately borne

---

[29]This is often because of the short life span of some laboratory animals and the desire to reduce the cost of experiments and speed completion of the research.

---

**EXAMPLE**

## Environmental Politics: Scrubbers and the Clean Air Act Amendments

The NSPS adopted by the EPA set allowable emissions standards for all new coal-fired power plants at 1.2 pounds of sulfur per million Btus. As a result, the demand for low-sulfur coal, most of which was mined in Montana and Wyoming, skyrocketed. Coal production in Wyoming increased from less than 10 million tons in 1970 to 171.4 million tons in 1989. The coal mined in the Powder River Basin of Wyoming contained at most 0.5 percent sulfur, whereas much of the eastern coal has a sulfur content of 4 to 5 percent.[1] Much of the eastern coal was extracted in shaft mines, whereas more efficient strip mining was used for western coal.

Demand for high-sulfur eastern coal had been maintained in part by the Clean Air Act

Amendments of 1977, which required scrubbing of flue gasses for all new power plants.[2] Existing power plants had not been subject to these regulations, and by 1990 less than one quarter of the coal-fired power plant capacity had scrubbers. The acid rain problem focused attention on those existing power plants that continued to burn high-sulfur eastern coal. The proposed Clean Air Act Amendments threatened the eastern coal industry, but the combination of strong pressure from environmentalists and the George H.W. Bush administration's commitment made adoption of stringent acid rain provisions likely.

Power plants had three principal means of reducing emissions: using low-sulfur western coal, installing scrubbers, and retrofitting plants

---

[1]Some eastern coal had a low sulfur content.

[2]See the Chapter 6 case, *Scrubbers and Environmental Politics.*

(Continued)

*(Continued)*

with new technology. Retrofitting was usually expensive, so many power plants were expected to switch to low-sulfur coal. Thousands of coal miners in the Ohio River Valley and Appalachia would lose their jobs, and a number of small towns that depended on coal mining would be wiped out.

In the Senate, supporters pushed two measures to aid the miners. Senator Robert C. Byrd (D-WV), former majority leader and then-chairman of the Appropriations Committee, offered a bill to provide $500 million in job-loss benefits and retraining programs for displaced miners. The program would provide 90, 80, and 70 percent of their wages and benefits for 3 years respectively. In the first year, each miner on average would receive $41,000.[3] Senator Byrd called in past IOUs to gain votes, but the Bush administration opposed the measure, and the opposition in the Senate was intense. Senator Phil Gramm (R-TX) said, "People in other states are not going to be treated better than the people in Texas."[4] Bringing one senator from a hospital to the Senate floor, Senator Byrd lost on a 49 to 50 vote as one of his supporters returning from a funeral was delayed by bad weather.

The other measure would provide a 20 percent tax credit for any utility installing a scrubber or other pollution-control device. This would reduce the cost of scrubbing, causing some power plants to choose scrubbing and high-sulfur eastern coal over low-sulfur western coal. Between 3,000 and 5,000 miners' jobs would be saved by the measure, but it was estimated to cost $3.3 billion. The measure was tabled on a 71 to 26 vote.

In the House, representatives from the Midwest were better represented on the Commerce Committee than were Midwestern senators on the Senate Energy Committee. Supporters of eastern coal sought a subsidy for scrubbers, and representatives from clean states sought special allowances to enable their states to grow without being blocked by emissions limits. After lengthy bargaining in the Commerce Committee an agreement was reached providing additional emissions allowances to clean states and to plants that installed scrubbers.

The fight for job-loss benefits in the House was led by Representative Bob Wise (D-WV), who was successful in obtaining a 5-year, $250 million program to provide 26 additional weeks of unemployment benefits plus retraining. In the conference committee, support for the job-loss benefits was strong, and the Bush administration recognized that it would have to accept some form of benefits for the miners. The administration obtained concessions, putting the benefits under an existing retraining program. Authorized funding was left at $250 million.

The supporters of eastern miners were able to incorporate two provisions in the amendments to encourage scrubbing. The acid rain provisions allowed a 2-year extension in achieving emissions standards, but only if the power plant had a scrubber. More importantly, power plants that reduced sulfur dioxide emissions below the NSPS, by using scrubbers, for example, received two allowances per ton of reduction. A total of 3.5 million allowances were earmarked for this during the 1997 to 1999 period. The market price for an allowance was approximately $150 a ton.

The failure of the proposed tax subsidy for scrubbers was due to its cost. A subsidy would benefit eastern coal miners and consumers in the states in which the scrubbers would be installed, but these beneficiaries covered only a relatively small number of congressional districts. The tax burden would be widely borne across the country, which normally provides the beneficiaries an advantage in client politics. However, the price tag of up to $1 million per job saved was more than many members of Congress were prepared to accept. The alternative of job-loss benefits for coal miners was an effective substitute that contributed to the failure of the scrubber subsidy tax credit. The additional allowances did not affect the federal budget and hence were a politically useful currency.

[3] *Congressional Quarterly Weekly Report*, March 31, 1990.
[4] *Congressional Quarterly Weekly Report*, March 31, 1990, p. 984.

by consumers in the form of higher prices. The EPA estimated that the price of a new automobile would increase by $600 because of the auto emissions standards contained in the 1990 amendments to the Clean Air Act. The costs of environmental protection are a principal motivation for environmental politics, as indicated by the opposition of many businesses to strong measures to reduce carbon dioxide emissions.

At the federal level, attention had focused primarily on major sources of pollution, often exempting small business. The 1990 amendments to the Clean Air Act, however, addressed emissions not only by automobiles and electric power plants but also by dry cleaners, furniture manufacturers, and printers. In spite of their claims of hardship, these firms were required to install costly pollution-control systems. Joe Gerard, vice president of the American Furniture Manufacturers, stated, "What's unnerving for our industry is that the law would affect the application of [wood] finishing materials, and that's what gives us our competitive edge over imports." Linda Greed of the NRDC responded: "Everything that comes down the pike, we're told it'll put them out of business. . . . When they come up with the data to show it costs too much, they usually do get some relief. But when it's just arm waving, they don't. We hear it too often to be credible."[30]

The benefits from environmental protection accrue to people quite broadly, as in the case of the air quality improvements. The basic structure of environmental politics thus is entrepreneurial. The broad public sensitivity to environmental and health issues has meant that there are many political entrepreneurs seeking to represent the dispersed beneficiaries. Particularly when the costs of environmental protection are paid through prices rather than taxes, the government has often been responsive to environmental political entrepreneurship. The growth and sophistication of environmental interest groups, however, have transformed the politics of environmental protection into interest group politics.

## Private and Public Politics

There are many environmental organizations active in public politics at the federal, state, and local levels. Environmental groups testify regularly in legislative and regulatory hearings, and some demonstrate to attract media coverage to their side of the issue. Environmental groups are also active in private politics, as considered in Chapter 4 and in the Chapter 4 cases, *Strategic Activism: The Rainforest Action Network and Shell, Greenpeace, and Brent Spar,* and the Part I integrative case, *Anatomy of a Corporate Campaign: Rainforest Action Network and Citigroup.* Some environmental groups have been active participants in the antiglobalization protests against the World Trade Organization and other international economic organizations such as the World Bank and the International Monetary Fund. Environmental groups also monitor the activities of government officials. The League of Conservation Voters annually rates members of Congress based on their votes on a set of environmental bills. The Sierra Club and some other environmental groups endorse candidates in federal and state elections. The example on the Equator Principles illustrates the role of environmental groups and private politics at the global level.

The politics of environmental protection also involves the market and nonmarket strategies of individual companies, as indicated in the chapter case, *Philips and the Low-Mercury Fluorescent Lamp.* The environmental politics of light bulbs continued in 2001 when General Electric introduced its new bulb Reveal, which produces truer colors. Philips criticized GE for producing energy inefficient bulbs that produce less light per watt than standard incandescent bulbs.

## The Equator Principles

Project finance provides the funding for dams, pipelines, transportation systems, mines, power plants, and other infrastructure projects. The financing was typically secured by the anticipated revenue from the project. Many of these projects were in developing countries, and environmentalists complained that some of the projects caused environmental damage and disrupted the lives of indigenous peoples. For example, the Three Gorges dam in China displaced many thousands of people and resulted in considerable environmental damage in addition to the power it provided for the country. In 1996 the Export-Import Bank (Eximbank) of the United States refused to provide financing for the dam because of concerns about potential environmental damage. Within the Organization for Economic Cooperation and Development (OECD) the Eximbank began to promote better environmental standards, but as chairman James Harmon observed, "To my amazement, opposition to our proposal was not only intense, but came from virtually every OECD member."[1]

The campaign for higher standards was subsequently led by NGOs. Environmental groups advocated stronger guidelines for projects and targeted individual lenders as well as the construction companies. WestLB of Germany had been targeted because of a pipeline project in Ecuador. The Rainforest Action Network (RAN) targeted Citigroup because of its major role in project financing. RAN blamed Citigroup for contributing to "rainforest destruction, climate change and the disruption of the lives of indigenous peoples." RAN's tactics included hanging a large banner across Citigroup's headquarters "accusing it of 'banking on' global warming and deforestation." RAN also urged college students not to accept Citigroup credit cards and for those with cards to cut them and mail the pieces to the bank.[2] In addition to targeting by individual environmental activist groups, a group of 100 advocacy groups signed the Colleveccio Declaration calling for financial institutions to adopt more responsible lending practices.

Under pressure from the NGOs four banks, ABN Amro, Barclays, Citigroup, and WestLB, began discussions under the auspices of the International Finance Corporation (IFC), the private-sector financing unit of the World Bank.[3] The IFC hosted negotiations involving the four banks and environmental groups, and the result was the Equator Principles, a set of voluntary principles for project financing. In addition to the initial four banks, Credit Lyonnais, Credit Suisse, HVB Group, Rabobank, Royal Bank of Scotland, and Westpac joined in signing the Principles. By late 2004, 27 banks had subscribed to the Principles. These banks arranged 75 percent of the $73.5 billion in project finance in 2003.

The Equator Principles applied to all projects of $50 million or more and categorized projects as A, B, or C (high, medium, and low) for their environmental or social impact. For A and B projects an Environmental Assessment was required, and the loan contracts from subscribing banks included a covenant stipulating that the borrower must comply with the Environmental Assessment. If a borrower did not fulfill its commitments, the bank could declare the loan in default. The Principles are available at www.equator-principles.com.

Citigroup proclaimed, "We are extremely proud to be part of this voluntary, private-sector initiative and we are confident that we will see more and more banks active in project finance adopt these principles in the coming months." Peter Woicke of the IFC said, "The adoption of these principles by the private sector marks a profound victory for sustainable development. . . . some of the banks came under pressure from NGOs. They also realized without the best graduates they cannot compete, and the best people

---

[1]*Financial Times*, April 9, 2003.
[2]*The Wall Street Journal*, June 4, 2003.
[3]The IFC had 175 member countries and authorized capital of $2.45 billion. The IFC provided loans and equity capital for projects to improve the lives of people in developing countries.

*(Continued)*

*(Continued)*

want to work for companies which pay attention to environmental and social issues."[4]

Fred Krupp of Environmental Defense praised the actions of the banks: "This is a major step forward in trying to achieve environmental standards for the global economy."[5] He added, "It is remarkable to have a private bank committing to this even ahead of supposedly green governmental institutions like the European public export credit agencies."[6]

Those sentiments were not widely shared within the environmental activist community. Ilyse Hogue of RAN said, "We're glad to see banks responding to pressure that's been brought on them. But I think that you'll find broad consensus around the NGO (nongovernmental organization) community that the Equator Principles don't go far enough. The loopholes are wide enough for bulldozers to move through."[7] Michelle Chan-Fishel of Friends of the Earth commented, "We are pleased that banks are responding to public pressure and are trying to address the environmental and social impact of their transactions. But one of the key weaknesses of most corporate-led voluntary initiatives is the lack of accountability in implementation mechanisms. This may be the fatal flaw of the Equator Principles."[8]

In July 2004 the participating banks met with the NGOs, including Environmental Defense, Friends of the Earth, and RAN, to discuss progress and implementation of the Equator Principles.

[4] *Financial Times*, June 4, 2003.
[5] *Financial Times*, April 7, 2003.
[6] *Financial Times*, April 9, 2003.
[7] *The Wall Street Journal*, June 4, 2003.
[8] *Financial Times*, June 4, 2003.

## NIMBY and Private Politics

In 1989 William Ruckelshaus, former EPA administrator and CEO of Browning-Ferris industries, a worldwide waste disposal company, wrote of the coming solid waste disposal crisis, "More than a third of the nation's landfills will be full within the next decade. New York will exhaust its capacity in nine years, Los Angeles in six, and Philadelphia is out of capacity now, and must engage in continuous negotiations to dispose of its 800,000 tons per year. Why? Nobody wants garbage put down anywhere near where he lives, the 'not-in-my-backyard' syndrome—the dreaded NIMBY."[31] The NIMBY movement focuses on local environmental concerns, particularly as they involve possible risks to person or property. The movement is often directed toward refuse disposal sites, toxic waste sites, chemical and oil plants, and other facilities that may emit toxins. Hamilton (1993) studied the location decisions and expansion plans of hazardous waste disposal and incineration facilities and found that companies take into account the anticipated opposition by local groups in making their site decisions for capacity expansion.

The NIMBY movement has been energized by information provided by the federal government's Toxics Release Inventory (TRI), which provides detailed information on the emissions by 22,000 plants of over 300 chemicals believed to have health consequences.[32] The TRI is a result of the "right-to-know" amendment to a 1985 Superfund reauthorization bill. The amendment was passed by the House on a 212 to 211 vote.[33] The TRI has become the focus of considerable nonmarket activity with some industries seeking to have chemicals they emit dropped from the TRI and industries such as agriculture, forestry, and mining working to preserve their exemptions. Environmentalists have sought to eliminate exemptions and expand the list of chemicals. The release of

[31] *The Wall Street Journal*, September 5, 1989.
[32] Firms are required to notify the federal, state, and local governments of any emission of the chemicals.
[33] See Hamilton (1997) for a study of the voting on the amendment.

the TRI has become a strategic event for environmentalists. The NRDC uses the data in the TRI to release the names of the largest emitters of those chemicals listed by the EPA as "probable human carcinogens."

In addition to allowing national organizations to take action, the TRI facilitates private politics in the form of local NIMBY action. The data in the TRI are presented for each plant, so emissions can be identified for individual communities. This allows local citizens to take nonmarket action against the plants. As an example, in 1989 the NRDC released an analysis of the TRI data listing Shendahl of Northfield, Minnesota, as the 45th largest emitter of the 11 chemicals analyzed by the NRDC. Shendahl had been legally emitting 400 tons a year of methylene chloride, a chemical whose emission was unregulated at both the federal and state level. The firm had no visible chemical emissions and had routinely been issued a permit for the discharges.[34]

When residents of Northfield learned of the emissions, their reaction was immediate. Within a week of the revelation, Shendahl announced that it would reduce emissions by 90 percent by 1993 and eliminate them entirely by 2000, switching to flammable solvents. Residents and activists formed Clean Air Northfield to continue the pressure. The activists charged that the company had withheld information on its emissions from the public, knowing in 1985 that the EPA had listed methylene chloride as a probable carcinogen. One activist group sought closure of the plant, but employees, arguing that the plant was the largest employer in town, sought an orderly reduction in emissions to save their jobs. The Amalgamated Clothing and Textile Workers Union, which represented the employees, was concerned that reducing emissions by the planned 90 percent might cause a hazardous accumulation of methylene chloride inside the plant, threatening employees. The union sought and won contract rights to monitor the emissions reduction program. The activists and the union also took action at the state level, persuading the state to include in Shendahl's emissions permit a required 93 percent reduction by 1995. Clean Air Northfield then lobbied the state government for the elimination of all methylene chloride emissions.

Empirical studies by Hamilton (1995) and Konar and Cohen (1997) found that the market value of companies included in the TRI fell upon release of the TRI, and those with the greatest decreases subsequently had the largest reduction in their toxic releases. Maxwell, Lyon, and Hackett (2000) studied voluntary reductions in TRI releases and concluded that reductions were larger the higher the local membership in the Sierra Club and the NRDC. Since the toxic chemicals released were within the levels permitted by environmental regulations, the identified effects were likely due to local environmental pressures and private politics that caused firms to reduce their emissions.

---

# EPA Activism and Cost-Benefit Analysis

With Republican majorities in both houses of Congress beginning in 1995, major new environmental legislation seemed unlikely. Environmentalist and government activists needed a strategy to achieve their objectives without going through Congress or through the traditional procedures required by administrative due process, such as a public notification and comment period and publication of new regulations in the *Federal Register.* The strategy adopted by the EPA had three principal components. The first was suggested by the success of the TRI in generating local nonmarket action to force greater reductions in emissions. The Internet provided a powerful new vehicle for disseminating information to citizens and local groups. The second component was

---

[34]This account is based on an article in *The New York Times*, January 2, 1991.

to focus on possible health risks rather than environmental protection, with particular emphasis on health risks to children. The third component was to use other laws to expand the scope of the EPA's programs.

The first component of the strategy was implemented in several ways. In 1994 the EPA added 152 additional chemicals to the TRI, and in 1996 it took an additional step in announcing a major expansion in the number of companies to be included in the TRI. The industries added included coal mining, electric utilities, and commercial hazardous waste treatment facilities. The EPA also quietly launched an internal project to grade the pollution risks at 661 plants and put the information on the Internet. The EPA did not go through the standard public notice and comment process nor did it take the grading project to its Science Advisory Board. When they learned of the EPA project, companies demanded to see the data on which the grading was based. They found serious errors in the data. Some worked with the EPA to correct the errors, and others simply refused to help correct the data, calling the project "irresponsible." Nineteen state environmental agencies also objected to the project, calling it a "premature undertaking of questionable value." Under pressure from companies and states, the EPA shelved its grading project but did put on the Internet detailed records of environmental inspection and infraction reports for 653 industrial facilities. In 1998 the EPA extended the right-to-know initiative to include mercury emissions from coal-fired electric generating plants. EPA Administrator Carol Browner said, "Putting information about toxic chemical pollution directly into the hands of citizens helps them make informed decisions about how to best protect the health of their families and work in their communities to prevent the pollution in the first place."[35] This approach encourages environmental protection through private politics.

To implement the second component of the strategy, Browner established an Office of Children's Health Protection in the EPA. She also announced that all new standards would take into account the risks for children. The new emphasis on risks for children provided a rationale for the review of existing standards, giving the EPA the opportunity to set more stringent standards without new congressional authorization. For example, the standards set under the Clean Air Act had not been based on the risks to children. Asthma is a chronic childhood illness, and the EPA justified stringent new rules for small particles (dust and soot) and ozone on this basis.

A third component of the EPA's environmental strategy was to use civil rights law to take into account the effects of pollution and toxics on minorities and women. President Clinton and Administrator Browner invoked Title VI of the Civil Rights Act of 1964 to launch a program on environmental justice without going through Congress for authorization. The EPA program focused on the disparate effect of toxic waste disposal sites and industrial emissions on minorities and women. Local interest groups also began to file environmental lawsuits under Title VI. The Chapter 20 case, *Environmental Justice and Pollution Credits Trading Systems,* addresses the ethical and political dimensions of claims about environmental justice.

When the Bush administration took office in 2001, the president suspended for further review a number of the recent actions by the EPA. Upon review the EPA administrator approved many of those actions, including the controversial small particles rules. The Bush administration, however, curbed further regulatory activism by applying a more consistent and refined cost-benefit analysis on new regulations issued by agencies including the EPA. One controversial aspect of the cost-benefit analysis was use of life-expectancy analysis, which estimates benefits based not on the number of deaths prevented by a regulation but the number of years that life expectancy would be increased. This meant that the benefits from preventing a death of an elderly person were lower than from preventing a death of a younger person. This approach was used in medical research and had been used for years by the Food and Drug Administration. When environmentalists learned in a footnote in a report that the EPA used it as a secondary method in estimating benefits, they labeled it a "senior citizen death discount" and ran an advertisement showing an elderly person with a price tag hanging from her glasses. On the tag was written "37% off." Fearing that the method would lead to less stringent regulation, environmentalists and health care advocates created a firestorm of criticism that led the EPA to end use of the method.[36]

## Management of Environmental Protection Issues

The management of environmental issues involves both external and internal activities. Externally, firms and their managers must address a set of issues that arise in their market and nonmarket environments. These issues may be addressed in government institutional arenas such as Congress, state legislatures, courts, and regulatory agencies; or outside those institutions, as with NIMBY activities and direct interactions with environmentalists. The chapter case, *Procter & Gamble and Disposable Diapers*, brings together a number of these issues.

Environmental issues have become so important, pervasive, and costly that high-level attention must be given to them. Some firms have established committees of their boards of directors to assume oversight responsibility on environmental matters. Some CEOs have personally declared a commitment to environmental protection. When DuPont Chairman Edgar S. Woolard, Jr., assumed the role of the company's chief environmentalist, the level of awareness rose. DuPont's vice president for safety, health, and environmental affairs commented on the difference: "I used to have to do a real selling job to line up people. . . . Then suddenly it wasn't just me trying to get the organization to do things, it was Ed. Now they call all the time."[37] Some firms established corporate environmental groups and audit units. IBM created the position of vice president for environmental health and safety in its corporate office and gave that office responsibility for ensuring compliance with environmental regulations and company policies. Home Depot has been aggressive in its environmental policies, particularly in its wood procurement, as considered in the chapter case, *Environmental Activism at Home Depot.*

A commitment from top management may be necessary for successful management of environmental matters, but it is not sufficient, since compliance takes place at the level of the individual facility. Sensitivity to environmental issues and compliance responsibility must be distributed throughout the firm. Furthermore, ideas for waste reduction and pollution control often are generated at the plant level. The Carrier Corporation, for example, was able to eliminate through engineering redesign its degreasing operation in the manufacture of air conditioners.

Many companies attempt to instill the attitude that environmental matters are the responsibility of all employees. Many companies have established Environment, Health, and Safety (EHS) programs with explicit goals and public reporting on the progress made on those goals. BP reports publicly on its EHS performance, which is independently reviewed as part of its sustainability reporting.

Managers must interact with a host of regulatory officials, ranging from those who grant permits and inspect facilities to those who write implementation regulations. Managers should deal with regulators on the basis of trust and mutual respect but must

---

[36]The life-expectancy approach is considered in more detail in Chapter 19.
[37]*The New York Times*, March 3, 1991.

also be prepared to suggest new means for achieving environmental goals and to oppose rules that may be overly burdensome. Managers should recognize that just as they face competing pressures for profits and for environmental goals, regulators face competing pressures from environmental groups and their political allies and from those who bear the cost of regulation. Recognizing the pressures regulators face can be important in developing workable relationships.

Many firms have extended their internal environmental management programs to include external advice and consultations with local communities. Dow Chemical formed a Corporate Environmental Advisory Council to advise the company on its environmental stewardship policies and programs. Dow also encouraged its plant managers to form community advisory councils to address local issues and assure the community that its activities met environmental standards. Dow's emphasis was on pollution prevention through the four Rs: reduce, reuse, recycle, and recover. Source reduction was the preferred method followed by recycling and recovery.[38] The example illustrates the importance of source reduction in pollution. King and Lennox (2002) found that source reduction reduces total production and pollution control costs as argued by Porter and van der Linde (1995).

---

[38]See Popoff (1992).

---

## Dow Chemical and Local Environmentalists

In 1996 Dow Chemical, in conjunction with the NRDC, invited five local activists to join in a project at its Midland, Michigan, plant complex to make environmental improvements that would also save money.[1] Despite concerns about the possible release of proprietary information and the possibility of public criticism, Dow agreed to reduce toxic chemicals by 35 percent and to reduce emissions into the air and water by the same amount. These reductions were beyond any required by government regulations and were to be achieved only through pollution prevention approaches. More strikingly, Dow allowed the environmentalists to choose which toxic chemicals to be included, and it accepted without challenge the 26 selected.

Dow and the environmentalists agreed to use an outside environmental engineering expert to provide recommendations for how to achieve the reductions. Often the reductions were for small changes in processes or equipment settings that reduced the production and release of the

toxic chemicals. Many of these changes had been overlooked by Dow engineers, whose focus had been on satisfying regulations rather than going beyond those requirements. Dow reported that it spent $3.1 million on process changes yielding cost savings of $5.4 million a year. A major part of the savings occurred in its waste treatment facilities, which no longer had to treat certain toxics. Moreover, the company exceeded the targeted 35 percent reductions.[2]

The project also had less tangible benefits. Samuel Smolnik, vice president for global EHS, commented on a practical benefit of the project, "When you reduce waste and emissions, a community is a lot more willing to issue permits for other operations down the road."[3]

The NRDC offered to cooperate with other companies and expressed disappointment that it had no takers. Part of the explanation may be due to its other stances, such as its criticism of Intel's Project XL program with the EPA, discussed earlier in the chapter.

---

[1]This example is based on an article in *The New York Times,* July 18, 1999.

[2]The final project report is available from the NRDC.

[3]*The New York Times,* September 9, 2001.

With increasing frequency companies are joining with environmental groups to discuss issues and solve particular environmental problems. As indicated in Chapter 4, most companies prefer moderate science-based groups such as Conservation International and Environmental Defense. Environmental Defense (ED) has embraced the objective of efficiency in pollution control and advocates the use of incentive approaches to achieve that end. This earned ED a role in the development of the provisions of the Clean Air Act Amendments of 1990 and in the design of the emissions permits trading system for the Kyoto Protocol. As indicated previously, ED also joined with BP to develop an internal tradable permits system for $CO_2$ emissions. ED has also developed a working relationship with McDonald's, resulting in over 20 joint projects. Their first project, a waste reduction program, is discussed in the example.

**EXAMPLE**

## McDonald's and Waste Reduction

McDonald's is the largest restaurant system in the world and also one of the world's largest generators of solid waste. For a number of years McDonald's had been reducing its use of packaging materials. The packaging weight for a Big Mac, fries, and a shake had been reduced from 46 grams in the early 1970s to 25 grams by the 1990s. McDonald's had also conducted a number of waste reduction experiments, including a test program in 800 restaurants to recycle polystyrene containers. Environmental groups, however, pressured the company to make further reductions in its solid waste.[1] The Citizens' Clearinghouse for Hazardous Waste worked for 3 years, pressuring McDonald's to replace its polystyrene clamshell sandwich container. McDonald's replaced it with paper in 1990.

In 1990 McDonald's decided to work with ED on the solid waste reduction issue. ED had a staff of over 110, including scientists, engineers, economists, and attorneys. It also had both a moderate stance on environmental protection and considerable experience in dealing with solid waste issues. The relationship began when Ed Rensi, president of McDonald's U.S.A., accepted ED President Fred Krupp's invitation to discuss the waste issue. After a

number of joint staff meetings, McDonald's and ED established a joint task force project to study options for reducing solid wastes. The task force studied McDonald's operations and its 39 regional distribution centers and visited suppliers and disposal and recycling facilities. Each ED member also worked for a day in a McDonald's restaurant to gain an appreciation for its operations.

In 1991 the task force released its final report, identifying 40 steps that could reduce McDonald's solid wastes by 80 percent.[2] An important part of the task force study was a detailed investigation of McDonald's solid waste generation. The study revealed, for example, that 79 percent by weight of on-premise waste was generated behind the counter. "The results of the task force far exceed all of our expectations and original goals,' said Keith Magnuson, McDonald's director of operations development and a task force member. 'We started out to study waste reduction options. Instead, we developed a comprehensive waste reduction plan that is already being implemented.' ... 'The task force has set forth a long-term vision bolstered by concrete actions to be taken in the short term,' said Dr. Richard

---

[1]See the Chapter 1 case, *The Nonmarket Environment of McDonald's*.

[2]The McDonald's Corporation–Environmental Defense Fund Waste Reduction Task Force report is available at www.environmentaldefense.org.

*(Continued)*

*(Continued)*

Denison, a senior scientist with ED and a task force member."[3]

The task force study also resulted in changes in McDonald's decision-making criteria. In its purchasing decisions on disposable packaging, McDonald's had considered three factors: availability, functionality, and cost. As a result of the task force study, it added a fourth: waste reduction.

In addition to the specific measures, the task force emphasized instilling a commitment to waste reduction throughout the McDonald's system. Three-quarters of McDonald's 8,500 U.S. restaurants were owned and operated by independent franchisees. In addition, McDonald's had over 100 packaging suppliers. McDonald's had a tradition of standardization and strict enforcement of policies, so institutionalizing the waste reduction commitment was not difficult. Overall compliance assurance rested with the Environmental Affairs Department, but the commitment was lodged in all areas of its operations, including with suppliers and franchisees. McDonald's senior environmental officer reported directly to the board of directors on progress in implementing the task force recommendations.

---

[3]McDonald's Corporation press release, April 16, 1991. In contrast to these statements, the original agreement between McDonald's and ED sought agreement rather than an action plan and contained language allowing for separate opinions to be issued and for either side to withdraw from the project.

# Voluntary Collective Environmental Programs

A number of voluntary self-regulation programs have been established. These programs are relatively new, and their effectiveness has only begun to be evaluated. The International Organization for Standards has established ISO 14001, a worldwide voluntary environmental program for improved environmental management systems. In contrast to government regulation, ISO 14001 does not establish environmental standards or specify pollution-control practices. Instead, it emphasizes managerial processes to improve environmental performance. Over 36,000 companies have obtained ISO 14001 certification, with over 1,500 in the United States. Delmas (2000, 2001) studied the participation of firms in ISO 14001. Potoski and Prakash (2005) studied participation of U.S. facilities in ISO 14001 and concluded that, although it is costly, participation provides reputational benefits for participants. They, however, were not able to determine how effective it was in achieving improved environmental performance beyond that required by government and induced by private politics.

The Responsible Care program is a worldwide EHS voluntary regulation program operated by the chemical industry. Initiated in Canada in 1985, Responsible Care was established in the United States in 1989 following the accident at the Bhopal chemical facility that killed thousands. Responsible Care programs are now conducted by chemical industry associations in 47 countries that account for over 90 percent of chemicals production. Responsible Care focuses on improved practices for human and environmental protection. In addition to the direct benefits from improved practices, the program provides reputational benefits to the industry. Participation is voluntary, and many chemical companies do not participate. Among the participants, companies with public images and brand names are overrepresented.

King and Lennox (2002) evaluated the Responsible Care program in the United States and found that companies with poor performance were disproportionately represented in the program. They also found that participants did not improve their performance at a faster rate than companies not participating in the program. The former is consistent with the hypothesis that companies with the worst performance have the most to gain from an improvement in the collective reputation of the industry, and the latter is consistent with the hypothesis that some participants shirk on their commitments to improve performance.

# Summary

Environmental protection has broad support among the public, government, and the business community. Environmental protection is costly, however, and the more efficient the approach taken to the reduction of pollution, the more reduction can be attained for any given expenditure. Conversely, for a given level of pollution reduction, the approach used to achieve that reduction affects the costs that society must bear. The social efficiency approach to environmental protection seeks to minimize the sum of the harm from pollution and the cost of reducing it.

An emissions tax system imposes a charge on pollutants emitted, which increases the costs of emissions and provides incentives to reduce them. A tradable permits system caps emissions, issues permits equal to the cap, and allows the permits to be traded. A polluter with relatively low costs of reducing emissions has an incentive to reduce emissions by more than its permits require and sell the unused permits to another firm that has higher costs of reducing emissions. Both systems provide incentives to achieve social efficiency. The EPA has also used other incentive approaches in its bubble, offset, and credits programs, but the largest system in operation is the transferable allowances program for controlling sulfur dioxide emissions that cause acid rain. The transferable allowances system has substantially reduced pollution control costs, benefiting companies and their customers and also benefiting the environment. Tradable permits are also used in implementing the Kyoto Protocol and internally by BP.

Environmental policies such as the transferable allowances system are the product of a political competition in which distributive consequences and efficiency considerations weigh large. The Clean Air Act Amendments of 1990 involved bargaining on several specific measures affecting those distributive consequences. On the acid rain provisions, bargaining occurred on the distribution of the allowances and on provisions to protect eastern coal miners.

Environmental issues spark a wide range of private politics in addition to public politics at the federal and state levels. At the local level, environmental groups have been increasingly active in addressing environmental issues. The NIMBY movement and private politics have grown in importance.

Environmental protection and compliance are important components of management responsibility. Firms and their managers must address a variety of nonmarket issues that involve local communities, environmental groups, legislators, and regulators. A number of firms and environmental groups have developed relationships that allow them to address issues in a nonconfrontational manner. Some firms have worked directly with environmentalists, as in the case of the McDonald's–Environmental Defense project on reducing the company's solid wastes.

# Philips and the Low-Mercury Fluorescent Lamp

In June 1997 the Philips Lighting Company, a division of Philips Electronics North America Corporation, a subsidiary of Philips Electronics N.V., held an unusual news conference in Washington, D.C. Philips announced that it would share with its competitors its technology for producing fluorescent lamps with low-mercury content. Mercury, which was an essential component of fluorescent lamps, was a highly toxic metal that affects the central nervous system and kidneys and, like lead, could cause brain damage in children and fetuses.[39] Philips was supported by several environmental groups that participated in the news conference and praised Philips's action. Velma Smith, executive director of Friends of the Earth, said, "We thank Philips for, once again, taking a leadership role in an area that will lead to significant, meaningful source reductions of mercury in our environment." Robert K. Musil, Ph.D., executive director of Physicians for Social Responsibility, said, "Residual mercury in the environment poses a clear health risk, especially to pregnant women and young children." Michael Bender, executive director of the Coalition of Lamp Recyclers, added, "We strongly support the efforts of Philips to promote lamp recycling, and to keep hazardous fluorescent lamps out of municipal incinerators and landfills." Senator John D. Rockefeller IV (D-WV) also participated in the news conference, stating that Philips's development of the low-mercury lamp was "a case history of how the system is supposed to work."

## The Mercury Issue

An EPA-commissioned study had identified electric light bulbs as the second largest source (behind batteries) of mercury in the solid waste disposal system. Between 500 and 600 million fluorescent lamps containing an estimated 34 tons of mercury were disposed of each year. Larry Wilton, president and CEO of Philips Lighting, stated, "If all the lamps were replaced with low-mercury types, nine tons of mercury would be removed from the hazardous waste stream annually."

In 1990 the EPA prescribed a stringent Toxicity Characteristic Leaching Procedure (TCLP) that was designed to simulate disposal in a landfill to determine whether mercury leached out from a fluorescent lamp. A fluorescent bulb that did not pass the TCLP was classified as hazardous waste under the Resource Conservation and Recovery Act and had to be disposed of in an approved hazardous waste facility rather than in a municipal landfill.[40] At the time the TCLP was introduced, Philips scientists in West Virginia had succeeded in removing cadmium from its lamps and had begun working on reducing the mercury content. Philips succeeded in developing a new technology that combined a precise amount of mercury with a chemical buffering mechanism. After considerable testing, in June 1995 Philips introduced its ALTO lamp, which contained less than 10 milligrams of mercury. Philips's lamp was the only one that had passed the EPA's TCLP test at all stages of its life, making it the only lamp

---

[39]The presence of mercury is essential for fluorescent lamp operation. Electricity must pass through mercury gas in order to produce the ultraviolet energy that is converted to visible light by the phosphor coating." ("Alto Lamp Technology," Philips Lighting Company).

[40]Exemptions were provided for homes and businesses, which were classified as "conditionally exempt small-quantity generators" if they disposed of less than 100 kilograms of hazardous waste a month.

that could be disposed of in municipal landfills. Conventional fluorescent lamps had to be disposed of in hazardous waste facilities. Philips distinguished its ALTO lamps with bright green end caps and projected that Alto technology would be used in 80 percent of its bulbs by the end of 1997.

A study by the National Electrical Manufacturers Association reported that the mercury content of a 4-foot fluorescent lamp had decreased from 45.2 milligrams in 1985 to 38.4 milligrams in 1990 to 22.8 milligrams at the end of 1994. The association estimated that by the year 2000 the content would be below 15 milligrams.

## Recycling

Recycling of electric lamps was spurred by the EPA's 1995 Universal Waste Rule, which provided a platform for states to develop regulations for recycling lamps. By mid-1997, 10 states had adopted such regulations and 17 were in the process of formulating regulations.

Recycling had also been stimulated by the disposal cost of fluorescent lamps. Disposal in a hazardous waste landfill could cost up to $1 for a 4-foot lamp, and recycling costs were between 30 and 50 cents. Mercury Technologies of Minnesota charged hardware stores 55 cents for lamps up to 4 feet and 90 cents for longer lamps. Other estimates, however, placed recycling costs at $2 a lamp. Recycling was estimated to account for approximately 5 percent of the lamps disposed of annually. Philips purchased retorted mercury from recyclers.

## The Nonmarket Competition

Philips's principal competitors in fluorescent lamps were General Electric and Osram Sylvania, a unit of Osram GmbH of Germany. The three companies each had approximately one-third of the market. Although Philips's competitors had recently announced low-mercury lamps, their lamps had not passed the TCLP test at all stages of a lamp's life, which required extensive testing data and several years before the bulbs reached the end of their lives.[41] Philips thus had a considerable competitive advantage relative to its competitors.

In 1995 General Electric and Osram Sylvania went to Congress seeking a "conditional exclusion" from the EPA rules to allow their high-mercury bulbs to be disposed of in state-approved municipal landfills. By 1997 their lobbying was believed to be nearing success as congressional pressure on the EPA had led the agency to reconsider its fluorescent lamp rules. At the news conference, Philips's Larry Wilton said, "It's time to play by the rules. Providing an exemption for waste that is defined as hazardous by the Environmental Protection Agency's own standards sends exactly the wrong message. It suggests that uncontrolled release of mercury into the environment is not a problem. And it is a disincentive for manufacturers to produce and market products with low-mercury content. We've met the challenge. Other companies should have no excuse for not doing the same." He also said, "There is no need to make high-mercury tubes when America can benefit from low-mercury technology. Exempting traditional high-mercury tubes from hazardous waste rules would send the wrong signal." Senator Rockefeller added, "It would be unfair to penalize a company like Philips that invested and innovated to meet EPA requirements. Now that Philips is sharing its technology, there is no reason to have the EPA set aside or waive the standards." Philips produced most of its fluorescent lamps in West Virginia.

In response to the nonmarket strategy of General Electric and Osram Sylvania, Philips developed a counteractive nonmarket strategy. Its objective was to preserve its current market advantage by blocking the efforts of its competitors to obtain a conditional exclusion. The centerpiece of Philips's strategy was to switch the institutional arena in which the fluorescent lamp disposal issue was addressed. Rather than leave the issue in the arena of the behind-the-scenes congressional–agency relationship, Philips sought to bring the issue into the arena of public sentiment. Philips's strategy was to make the issue public by drawing the attention of politicians, environmental interest groups, and the public to the disposal issue and the strategy of its competitors. At the news conference Larry Wilton directly addressed the strategies of its competitors: "Two years ago, General Electric and Sylvania went begging to Congress for a special break from this mandate. If they take this route again, and if they

---

[41]Fluorescent lamps sold in the United States had a life of approximately 20,000 hours.

succeed, they will have no reason to ever market environmentally responsible, low-mercury fluorescent lamps."

Philips had three objectives in making the issue public. First, making the issue public made it more difficult for some members of Congress to support a conditional exclusion. Second, Philips sought to enlist the aid of environmental groups in opposing a government affairs of the association, said, "The position of the industry now is that we have no position."

In addition to making the issue public, Philips also had a regulatory objective. It sought to place fluorescent bulbs under the EPA's 1994 Universal Waste Rule, which would simplify reporting requirements but would require continued special handling of fluorescent lamps.

Sharing its technology would weaken Philips's current competitive advantage but perhaps not as much as suggested by the news conference. Philips estimated that it would take its competitors at least 3 years and several million dollars to catch up with its technology. However, General Electric and Philips had a cross-licensing agreement that already gave General Electric access to Philips's low-mercury technology, and Osram Sylvania had recently introduced a low-mercury lamp.

One risk in its strategy was that it could be transparent and characterized as such. *The New York Times* in a June 19, 1997, article referred to Philips's strategy as "enviro-politics" and to the news conference as a "media event." The article characterized its offer to share its technology as "the gimmick of seeming to give away its technology."

relaxation, and the presence of several environmental groups at the news conference was testimony to the success of this aspect of its strategy. For example, Robert Musil of Physicians for Social Responsibility stated, "EPA's proposed exemption is a setback for pollution prevention and public health." Their involvement and pressure on members of Congress and on the EPA would counteract to some extent the pressure from General Electric and Osram Sylvania and their supporters. The environmental groups also had better means of communicating with components of the public than did Philips. By raising health and safety issues in addition to environmental concerns, some members of the public might decide to act. Third, making the issue public could have a positive impact on its sales if environmentally sensitive consumers switched to Philips's low-mercury lamps.

In addition to changing the institutional arena, Philips sought to enlist as allies those in its extended rent chain who benefited from the low-mercury lamps. Those beneficiaries included environmentalists whose objectives were served by Philips's nonmarket strategy. The benefits to its conventional rent chain were attested to by the participation of Senator Rockefeller in the news conference. Philips also sought and received the support of the Coalition of Lamp Recyclers.

Another component of Philips's nonmarket strategy was to reduce the pressure coming from its

competitors. One means of doing so was to limit their use of industry associations in their pursuit of a conditional exclusion. The National Electrical Manufacturers Association had lobbied for a conditional exclusion from the EPA for General Electric and Osram Sylvania, but Philips broke ranks and the association went silent. Eric Erdheim, senior manager for

SOURCE: This case was prepared by Professor David P. Baron from public sources and materials provided by Philips Lighting Company. Copyright © 1997 by the Board of Trustees of the Leland Stanford Junior University. All rights reserved. Reproduced with permission.

---

## PREPARATION QUESTIONS

**1.** How effective was Philips's nonmarket strategy likely to be?

**2.** Was Philips's nonmarket strategy responsible?

**3.** Were General Electric and Osram Sylvania acting responsibly in seeking a conditional exclusion?

# Environmental Activism at Home Depot

Home Depot was founded in 1978 and became the world's largest home improvement specialty retailer with 1,707 stores in all 50 states. Its sales reached $64.8 billion in 2003 and earnings were $4.3 billion. Home Depot was the world's second largest retailer and had 300,000 associates. It had frequently been ranked as one of the nation's most-admired companies.

After Earth Day in 1990 Home Depot established its Environmental Principles and initially focused on recycling and offering some green products. In 1992 the company faced its first challenge from environmental groups. The Rainforest Action Network (RAN) challenged the company to eliminate its use of old growth tropical timber. Home Depot phased out its line of teak furniture and pledged to buy wood from sustainable sources. Environmental activists, including RAN, again targeted Home Depot and other companies in 1997 to stop their use of old growth redwood, and Home Depot and the other companies did so. RAN then launched its old growth market campaign in 1998, again targeting Home Depot. RAN hung a banner on Home Depot's headquarters and held protests at hundreds of stores.[42] Concerned about the public criticism of its timber sourcing, Home Depot agreed to stop buying old growth products. It also agreed to give preference to Forest Stewardship Council (FSC) certified wood.[43]

Home Depot's environmental practices were recharged when in 2000 Ron Jarvis was appointed as merchandising vice president with authority to terminate timber supply contracts. When Jarvis learned that an Indonesian supplier was using slash-and-burn harvesting, he cancelled the contract. Subsequently, Home Depot reduced by 90 percent its sourcing from Indonesia, where illegal logging was commonplace. The remaining purchases were from sources with sustainable practices. Rewarding those sources for their practices, however, did not cause other loggers in Indonesia to change their practices.[44] Jarvis also cancelled all purchases from Gabon when suppliers refused to change their practices.

When it was targeted by the activists, Home Depot realized that it had no means of identifying the sources of the wood products it sold nor how much wood it purchased from that forests. It began a major tracking effort that bore fruit in 2002. Home Depot now knows the source of every wood product it sells. In 1999 it issued its first Wood Purchasing Policy, and in 2002 it issued its current Policy. Ninety-four percent of its wood products now comes from North American timber, where forest land has increased by 1.5 percent during the past decade.[45] Home Depot pledged to purchase wood only from "forests managed in a responsible way and to eliminate wood purchases from endangered regions of the world . . ."

Home Depot went beyond its own practices and began corporate environmental activism. Along with Lowe's and other companies, it joined with environmentalists to convince the Canadian government to stop logging in the Great Bear Rainforest in British Columbia. Home Depot joined with The Nature Conservancy and a British agency to put bar codes on timber from Borneo. Home Depot had reduced its purchases of Indonesian lauan by 70 percent and worked with The Nature Conservancy, Tropical Forest Foundation, Tropical Forest Trust, and the World Wildlife Fund to improve practices in Indonesia. RAN executive director Michael Brune, however, criticized any purchasing from Indonesia. "This is not a time to establish small toeholds of good production."[46] RAN wanted all purchases from Indonesia halted.

Home Depot recognized only FSC certification, but the supply was too small to satisfy its demand, let alone other retailers and home builders. Home Depot decided to increase the supply. It worked with Tembec, a large Canadian lumber producer, to increase FSC lumber. Tembec agreed to obtain FSC

[42]See the Chapter 4 case *Strategic Activism: The Rainforest Action Network*.
[43]FSC was backed by environmental groups including RAN and Greenpeace.
[44]*The Wall Street Journal,* August 6, 2004.
[45]www.homedepot.com.
[46]*Business Week,* November 24, 2003.

certification for all its lumber by 2005, compared with 25 percent in 2003.[47]

After a call from the environmental activist group Forest Ethics claiming that tree farms were wiping out the natural forests in Chile, where Home Depot purchased 10 percent of the country's timber production, Jarvis called the heads of the two timber suppliers in Chile that had been targeted by a boycott by U.S. and Chilean activists. The timber executives disputed the activists' claim, stating that they had in the past cleared less than a million acres of forests but had discontinued the practice. The companies now planted their tree farms on agricultural and ranch land. Jarvis invited the activists and the Chilean timber producers to Home Depot's headquarters in Atlanta to discuss the matter. The next meeting was in Chile, where the timber companies gave the activists a tour of their farms. Jarvis said, "I basically told both sides, 'If you want to win on this, you have to give.'"[48] The timber companies agreed not to buy recently cleared land for their tree farms and made some changes in their practices. The activists agreed to call off the boycott and praised the companies. Randy Hayes, president of RAN, observed, "If you've got Home Depot carrying your water, you're going to get a lot farther than as just an environmental group."[49] The environmentalists stopped targeting Home Depot.

Ron Jarvis commented, "I think that maybe this is a template we can use in other countries."[50] ∎

## PREPARATION QUESTIONS

1. Why is Home Depot being so aggressive in its timber sourcing?
2. Will Home Depot be rewarded in the marketplace for its environmental policies?
3. Will it be rewarded in its nonmarket environment?

# Procter & Gamble and Disposable Diapers

Disposable diapers were a great product success. American consumers preferred disposable diapers by at least a 4-to-1 ratio over cloth diapers. With an infant using 7,800 diapers during the first 130 weeks, total disposable diaper use was estimated at 18 billion in 1989.

Procter & Gamble (P&G) had approximately half the U.S. disposable diaper market, with its Pampers brand slightly outselling its Luvs brand. Disposable diaper sales in the United States represented nearly $2 billion of P&G's $24 billion in revenue. Kimberly-Clark's Huggies brand had increased its market share substantially at P&G's expense, however, and had over 30 percent of the market.

Disposable diapers offered convenience that appealed to dual-career couples in particular. Priscilla Flattery of the Environmental Protection Agency said, "Disposable diapers are just too convenient and too easy. . . . I've never even bought any cloth diapers."[51] Disposable diapers were also said to be superior because their greater absorbency reduced discomfort and diaper rash.

Environmentalists had attacked disposable diapers because of the solid waste disposal issue. A Media General–Associated Press poll found that a ban on disposable diapers was favored by 71 percent of the respondents, and a *Wall Street Journal/NBC News* poll found a ban supported by a 3-to-1 ratio. A Gallup Poll found 43 percent favoring a ban and

47 Canada News Wire, December 3, 2003.

48 *The Wall Street Journal*, August 6, 2004.
49 *The Wall Street Journal*, August 6, 2004.
50 *The Wall Street Journal*, August 6, 2004.
51 *The Wall Street Journal*, December 26, 1989.

38 percent favoring a tax on disposable diapers.[52] Only about 9 percent of households had a diaper-age child.

Disposable diapers represented between 3.6 and 5 billion pounds, or between 1 and 2 percent, of the solid waste disposal in landfills. Calling attention to the contribution of disposable diapers to the solid waste disposal problem, activists both raised awareness among consumers and stimulated nonmarket activity to limit the use of disposable diapers.

The disposable diaper issue was on the legislative agenda in several states, but as of 1990 only Nebraska had enacted a law requiring that by 1993 disposable diapers be "biodegradable." (The biodegradable disposable diapers on the market used corn starch in the plastic, and Nebraska was a leading corn-producing state.) P&G had been successful in defeating bills in California and New York that would have required environmental warning labels on disposable diapers. Wisconsin had proposed a tax on disposable diapers, but Kimberly-Clark, which had operations there, mobilized Wisconsin parents to defeat the bill. Many day care centers would not accept children in cloth diapers, but a law passed in Maine required day care centers to accept them.[53]

As part of its strategy for addressing the disposable diaper issue, P&G produced two six-page pamphlets that it mailed to 14 million households.[54] The pamphlets were titled "Answers to Your Questions about the Environment" and "Diapers and the Environment." The latter, written in patient, junior-high science text prose, seeks to put the environmental uproar in perspective: 'In repeated studies, experts have discovered diapers make up less than two percent of total solid waste in municipal landfills. This means, in the life of a landfill, diapers represent seven weeks of a 10-year lifetime.' Attached to the brochure: discount coupons for Pampers and Luvs."[55] The brochures stated that disposable diapers kept babies drier than cloth diapers and reduced diaper rash. The brochures also pointed out that cloth diapers harmed the environment.

In the market, some consumers turned to cloth diapers and others to "biodegradable" disposables. The National Association of Diaper Services estimated that 750,000 households used cloth diaper services, representing a 38.5 percent increase over the previous year.[56] In some areas, demand outstripped capacity and waiting lists for diaper service grew rapidly.

P&G expressed confidence about the continued market success of disposable diapers. "We don't think mothers are willing to give up one of the greatest new products of the postwar era,' said Richard R. Nicolusi, the 42-year-old group vice president in charge of P&G's worldwide paper operations. . . . Why should they?''[57]

Some consumers responded to environmental concerns, however. Some turned to biodegradable disposable diapers. Disposable diapers were mainly wood pulp with plastic inner and outer wrappers. Biodegradable diapers used plastic mixed with corn-starch. When put in landfills, microorganisms, in principle, would consume the cornstarch, causing the plastic to break into small pieces. Those pieces did not decompose, however.

Waste disposal experts pointed out that in most landfills there was not enough moisture or oxygen to allow diapers or other solid waste to decompose. The Environmental Marketing Task Force, formed by the attorneys general of eight states, was investigating the marketing claims of one disposable diaper manufacturer and had earlier sued Mobil Oil, forcing it to withdraw its photodegradable claims for its Hefty brand trash bags. Asked about the biodegradability claims for disposable diapers, Hubert H. Humphrey III, attorney general of Minnesota, said, "We have the possibility of having something that makes the oat bran craze look like a Sunday-school picnic."[58]

P&G joined the biodegradability claim issue. "There simply is no data to support the claim of biodegradability," said Scott Stewart, a Procter & Gamble spokesman. "There's no question that this is a deception to consumers."[59] P&G took its contention to the public in the form of a test advertisement in the *Boston Globe* attacking the biodegradability claims. The ad said, "Almost nothing biodegrades in a landfill. That includes every diaper currently on the shelf. Even the ones calling themselves biodegradable." Neither P&G nor Kimberly-Clark had plans to introduce a "biodegradable" diaper.

---

[52] *Peninsula Times Tribune*, June 14, 1990.
[53] *The Wall Street Journal*, June 15, 1990.
[54] *The New York Times Magazine*, September 23, 1990, p. 27.
[55] *The New York Times Magazine*, September 23, 1990, p. 27.
[56] *Peninsula Times Tribune*, June 14, 1990.
[57] *The New York Times Magazine*, September 23, 1990.
[58] *The New York Times*, February 17, 1990.
[59] *The Wall Street Journal*, February 7, 1990.

Environmentalists were also skeptical of the claims. "Biodegradable plastics are perpetuating the myth that it's okay to produce plastic in great quantity and not worry about its effect on the environment," said Richard Denison, senior scientist for Environmental Defense.[60] In a column in *Newsweek* Robert J. Samuelson responded to the critics who complained about his declaration that he used disposable diapers for his child. "What my critics really resent is that I've denied their moral superiority. Using cloth diapers is an environmental badge, and I've said the badge isn't worth much."[61]

In response to the biodegradability issue P&G hired Arthur D. Little, Inc., to conduct a study of the overall environmental impact of disposable versus cloth diapers. The study reported that disposables used 25.3 pounds of raw materials and generated 22.18 pounds of solid waste, compared with 3.6 pounds and 0.24 pounds for cloth diapers. Cloth diapers used 144 gallons of water compared with 23.6 gallons for disposables, emitted 0.860 pounds of air pollutants versus 0.093 pounds for disposables, and produced 0.117 pounds of water pollutants compared with 0.012 pounds for disposables.[62] The study concluded, "Neither disposable nor reusable diapers are clearly superior in the various resource and environmental impact categories considered in this analysis."[63]

The Natural Resources Defense Council (NRDC) was also unable to conclude that disposables were better or worse than cloth diapers. Allen Hershkowitz of the NRDC wrote, "We simply can't say that disposables are terrible and reusable diapers are great for the environment, or vice versa. Whatever the choice, there are environmental costs."[64] He added, "People are wrong to think that simply using cloth diapers puts them on a higher moral plateau."[65] Edward Groth III of the Consumers Union conducted a study similar to that of Arthur D. Little and said, "I came to the same conclusion [NRDC] did, i.e., that there is no clear winner and each poses its own set of environmental problems."[66]

The Arthur D. Little study was criticized for some of its methodological assumptions. "We have a lot of questions about the assumptions in the Little study," said Ann Beaudry, a consultant to National Association of Diaper Services. "The study assumes an average of 1.9 cloth diapers per change compared with 1.0 for disposables. . . . People don't routinely double diaper. Those assumptions can have a big impact on the outcome."[67] Hershkowitz also criticized the study for not taking into account the pesticides used in cotton fields.

"The Environmental Protection Agency has endorsed none of the various comparative studies. The E.P.A. 'generally supports the use of cloth diapers because disposables cause so much solid waste,' said Lynda Wynn, a senior staffer on the Municipal Solid Waste Project at the E.P.A. in Washington. But, Wynn continued, 'the E.P.A. believes that until a scientifically valid "product life assessment" methodology is devised, no study can be considered definitive. Toward this end, the E.P.A. will assemble an advisory group of industry representatives, ecologists and government experts to work out methods for evaluating the environmental impact of various types of solid waste.'"[68]

In its strategy P&G sought to relieve what Chairman Edwin L. Artzt called "the guilt people feel about using products they think contribute to the solid-waste problem."[69] P&G announced that it would spend $20 million on research to develop a disposable diaper that would completely decompose into humus when composted. Artzt said, "We're hoping this will help people really understand the solid-waste issue and convince them that something can be done before we're awash in our own garbage."[70]

Rather than individual composting, P&G advocated industrial composting. Ten industrial composting plants were in operation in the United States, but they accounted for a negligible share of the solid waste disposed of annually. Environmentalists remained skeptical about composting, observing that most solid waste disposal was done by municipalities,

60 *The Wall Street Journal*, February 7, 1990.
61 *Newsweek*, April 16, 1990.
62 *The New York Times*, July 14, 1990.
63 *The New York Times*, July 14, 1990.
64 Quoted in "Diapers: The Sequel," by Robert J. Samuelson, *Newsweek*, April 16, 1990.
65 *The New York Times*, July 14, 1990.
66 *The New York Times*, July 14, 1990.
67 *The New York Times*, July 14, 1990.
68 *The New York Times Magazine*, September 23, 1990, p. 62.
69 *Business Week*, October 22, 1990.
70 *Business Week*, October 22, 1990.

and they were likely to skimp on composting by not sorting the waste enough to produce a product that could be sold.

As part of its study of industrial composting, P&G helped finance a contract between the city of Seattle and Baby Diaper Service Company to recycle disposable diapers. The company collected used disposable diapers from 722 households and 33 day care centers and delivered them to an experimental recycling plant. The plant turned the diapers into paper pulp and recycled plastic. Although the output

of the plant was not yet being sold, the pulp could be used by paper mills. "Highgrade pulp is the 'cash crop' of disposable diaper recycling" said Nancy Eddy, a microbiologist for P&G. "Though it can be used for flower pots, garbage bags and a host of other uses, the prices for recycled plastic—when you can sell it at all—are still way below the costs of recovery."[71] ■

## PREPARATION QUESTIONS

**1.** Are disposable diapers better or worse than cloth diapers on environmental dimensions?

**2.** Evaluate the components of P&G's strategy for addressing the disposable diaper issue. What is its overall strategy?

**3.** What is the nature of the politics of disposable diapers? What should P&G do about the private and public politics of disposable diapers?

**4.** What should P&G do about its diapers? In Europe, P&G marketed a "biodegradable" diaper using cornstarch. Should it introduce that diaper in the United States?

[71] *The New York Times Magazine*, September 23, 1990, p. 64.

## Introduction

Markets are the cornerstone of a free enterprise system. For markets to function efficiently individuals must be confident that the terms of their exchanges will be fulfilled. An exchange may be supported by a contract that establishes mutual expectations about terms such as the quality and quantity of an item, delivery, and payment. An exchange may also carry with it some residual obligations not explicitly included in the contract. For example, a party may be responsible for harm to the other party or to third parties caused by the item exchanged. That harm could involve environmental damage, personal injury during use, or adverse health consequences. An exchange may also involve other risks for the parties. For example, does a party actually have a property right to the item to be exchanged? Can the item be easily appropriated by a third party without payment? Does the contract cover the possible events that could affect its execution? What if there is an extenuating circumstance, such as an act of nature or human intervention, that leads one party to breach the contract? Is compensation due? What if there is an accident or injury associated with the item exchanged? These uncertainties can impair the functioning of markets and the realization of the gains from trade. The law plays a principal role in reducing such uncertainties and in supporting exchange in markets.

Laws are established by constitutions, statutes enacted by legislatures, and decisions made by judges. Statutory law, for example, specifies the length of a patent and the statute of limitations on filings of lawsuits. The common law, or judge-made law, is a body of law that has evolved through cases brought before the courts by private parties. The decisions made by judges serve as precedents for future cases, and the set of precedents establishes a body of law. Judges also interpret statutes, and their interpretations become part of the law. This chapter addresses aspects of the law that support the functioning of markets. The objective is to illustrate the role of the law in improving the workings of markets and private agreements. The subjects considered are property (with a focus on intellectual property), contracts, and torts (with an emphasis on products liability).

Despite its importance the law is not the principal means of reducing uncertainty and resolving disputes. The alternative to the public order provided by the law is private order based on private assurances among trading partners. Private means of assurance include trust, honesty, the development of reputations for fulfilling promises, and the use of bargaining to resolve disputes. Anyone who has ever purchased a mail-order item relies on the reputation of L.L. Bean or Lands' End rather than the law. Similarly, buyers on eBay pay in advance for items, relying on the descriptions and pictures of items offered and on the reputations of sellers established through feedback from other buyers. For high-value items buyers and sellers may use a private escrow service. Disputes are also resolved between a company and a customer through return and refund policies. On eBay the parties to a dispute can use an online dispute resolution mechanism, and if that does not work, an online mediator can be engaged for a modest fee.[1]

In some instances the law plays even less of a role in resolving disputes. A private ordering could be established through face-to-face and repeated interactions that allows norms to develop and be sustained. Ellickson (1991) studied the norms of ranchers and homeowners in Shasta County, California, and found that they settled disputes based on norms largely without reliance on the law and often in a manner contrary to the law. The ranchers and homeowners were able to rely on norms and punishments, primarily through gossip, because they had repeated interactions and were proximate. Repetition and proximity allowed norms to be respected.

Private orderings, however, function in the shadow of the law, which provides a final recourse for disputes. The homeowners at times resorted to lawsuits when the norms failed to resolve recurring violations. Similarly, cases of suspected fraud on eBay are turned over to law enforcement authorities. In areas where the stakes are high, the law remains the principal basis for supporting expectations about future performance. The cost of developing a new drug is over $1 billion, and a pharmaceutical company wants assurance that when it discovers a new drug, other companies will not simply copy its discovery. Patent law and its enforcement provide the assurance, and the decisions of judges have refined the law of patents to address new issues that arise.

This chapter first considers the common law and contrasts it with civil law. The concept of property is then introduced, and the establishment of incentives to develop property are analyzed. The focus is on intellectual property and its protection through patents and copyrights. Contracts are then considered along with principles governing their enforceability and efficient breach. Torts and the liability system are considered next with a focus on establishing incentives to guide the actions of buyers and sellers to reduce accidents associated with a product. Products liability is considered both because of its importance and because it illustrates the evolution of the common law. The chapter cases deal with product safety, possible liability for a health problem, and the protection of databases on the Internet.

# The Common Law

One perspective on the law is that it is imposed from above by a legislature or, in earlier times, by a ruler. In issuing decrees even a ruler may look for guidance to how the people have organized their activities. For example, people privately developed practices for the control and management of land, and in England the king often looked to those practices as the basis for the king's law.[2] That law then evolved both as the practices of people evolved and through the precedents set by the king's court. The resulting body of law is referred to as the *common law*. It is used in the United Kingdom, the United States, and most of the other former English colonies. Common law countries typically have an adversarial system of litigation in which each party

---

[1]See the Chapter 13 case *eBay: Private Ordering for on Online Community*.
[2]See Cooter and Ulen (1997. Ch. 3).

advocates its side of the dispute and judges and juries render decisions based on the evidence, the arguments provided, and precedents.[3]

The role of the common law is to help people accomplish what they want to accomplish. The advantage of the common law is that it can adjust to changing circumstances without having to rely on new statutes established by legislatures. The common law evolves through lawsuits filed by people in response to the problems they need addressed. As considered in a later section, the evolution from a law of warranty to the law of products liability occurred as a result of the changing nature of products.

In contrast, on the European continent, in Latin America, and elsewhere, *civil law* is used rather than common law. Civil law was developed by the Romans and served as the basis for the Napoleonic Code written after the French revolution by legal scholars commissioned by Napoleon. The Napoleonic code spread through the European continent and to the colonies of those countries. Civil law is also used in Louisiana and Puerto Rico in the United States, Quebec in Canada, and Scotland in the United Kingdom. Japan has a civil law system developed from German civil law. Civil law is written in codes based on legal principles, and judges decide cases based on those codes and the principles expressed in them. Civil law thus does not evolve in as flexible a manner as does the common law. Civil law countries typically do not use an adversarial system, and in many cases a judge is as much a fact finder as an adjudicator. Civil law countries also generally do not use juries as widely as in the United States, where the Constitution grants persons the right to a jury trial in both criminal and civil cases.

The origins of commercial law are similar to those of common law. The origins were in the medieval Merchants Law and in institutions such as the law merchant that developed to facilitate long-distance trade. Trade centered around fairs, such as the Champagne fair, to which merchants would travel great distances to arrange the exchange of goods. The trades often involved future delivery, with merchants agreeing to deliver goods of a particular quality in the future. The traders themselves were often from different regions and relied on their reputations for fulfilling promises. Disputes naturally arose even when merchants sought to fulfill their promises. The law merchant was an office established by merchants to resolve disputes. Moreover, over time merchants developed understandings about how particular uncertainties were to be handled. These understandings formed the basis for the development and evolution of commercial law.

In the United States the common law governs a number of important domains, including property, contracts, torts, products liability, and some aspects of labor contracting. The decisions of judges and the precedents established have been codified in a number of areas. On some matters statutes have been enacted to address specific issues in the domain of the common law.

# Property

*Property* is a set of rights to control a tangible or intangible thing. In the terminology of the Coase theorem introduced in Chapter 11, a property rule protects an entitlement by allowing the holder to use the entitlement, transfer it to another person, or prevent others from unwanted infringement of that entitlement. That is, a property right is the right to do whatever one chooses with the entitlement. Some property is well defined, whereas others are more difficult to define. Real property in the form of land, buildings, and physical assets is well defined. Ideas, inventions, and expressions are more difficult to define. The former are easier to protect than the latter, and their protections

---

[3]See Carp and Stidham (2001) for information on the courts.

may differ. Real property is generally protected indefinitely, whereas intellectual property is protected for a limited time.

The economic efficiency rationale for property is twofold. First, property rules can facilitate bargaining, allowing economic transactions to be made and gains from trade to be realized. Second, property rules provide incentives to create assets, as in the case of intellectual property.

## Bargaining

Bargaining can be illustrated using the classic Coasean example involving a rancher and a farmer. Each has real property, and the problem is that the rancher's cattle can go onto the farm and cause damage to crops. If the farm were protected by a property rule, the farmer could exclude the cattle by obtaining an injunction. Suppose, however, that their properties are in an open range territory where cattle are not prevented from roaming. An open range assigns the entitlement to the rancher and protects it with a property rule. The entitlement is that the cattle may roam, and it is protected by a property rule because the farmer cannot force the rancher, for example, to build a fence to prevent the cattle from roaming.

On his property the farmer grows alfalfa, and since alfalfa is used to make hay that is sold to ranchers for winter feeding, the cattle have a strong incentive to go onto the farmer's property. If they do, suppose they cause damage of 100 and suppose the value to the rancher of the alfalfa the cattle eat is only 40. A fence that will keep the cattle out can be built around the farm at an annual cost of 30. Because of the topography of the ranch, the rancher could build a fence to keep the cattle away from the farm for only 10. To resolve the conflict, the farmer and the rancher can bargain, and absent transactions costs the two will reach an agreement under which the rancher builds the fence. Their bargaining and the open range property rule determine who pays for the fence. For example, if they split the difference, the farmer will pay 20 to the rancher in exchange for the rancher's building the fence.[4] The farmer saves 10, and the rancher gains 10.

## Incentives and Appropriability

The second efficiency role of property is to provide incentives to create assets. The incentives are clear in the case of physical assets such as a house. The incentive to build a house results from a property rule that allows the holder to exclude others from the use of the house, with enforcement provided by public authorities. In the case of intellectual property, exclusion can be considerably more difficult. A music recording company that releases a recording can have thousands of copies distributed instantaneously over the Internet. Similarly, a pharmaceutical company can develop a new drug, but once developed it is easy to copy. The same is true for inventions whose technology can be copied at low cost. Many intellectual creations have low costs of replication, making exclusion difficult. It thus can be hard for the creator to appropriate the returns from the creation. When those returns are not appropriable, the incentives to create are weakened. Since innovation and discovery are engines of economic growth, means are needed to strengthen those incentives.

Some means of establishing appropriability are private.[5] Firms may keep their intellectual assets proprietary. Microsoft keeps its Windows XP code proprietary. The

---

[4]Note that the threat point of the farmer is to build the fence, which leaves the rancher with 0.
[5]Some incentives to develop information can be provided by the opportunity to take financial positions in the information. For example, some private equity investment firms appropriate returns from their investment in information by acquiring companies that they identify as undervalued.

formula for Coca-Cola is kept secret. Similarly, some production technologies are kept within the company. The private protection of intellectual assets is often incomplete or expensive, however. Recording companies may be able to encrypt their products, but people may crack the code.

## Intellectual Property

The characteristics of intellectual assets and the difficulty in excluding others from their use implies that those assets can be undersupplied in markets. To address this undersupply, protection is publicly provided. Article I of the Constitution states, "Congress shall have the Power . . . to promote the Progress of Science and useful Arts, by securing for limited times to . . . Inventors the exclusive Right to their respective writing and Discoveries." The issues for Congress and the courts are then what can be protected, what type of protection should be provided, and the duration of that protection.

The basic trade-off in the protection of intellectual property is between the benefits to society from the use of ideas and inventions and the incentives for their creation. Consider the issue of the duration of a patent. A patent grants a monopoly on use of the invention, and the longer the duration, the greater are the returns that may be appropriated, and hence the greater are the incentives to invent. The longer the duration of the monopoly, however, the lower are the benefits to society, since the holder of the patent restricts use so as to appropriate the monopoly returns. This is illustrated in Figure 12-1. The optimal duration of a patent maximizes the sum of the benefits to society and to the inventor. The same principle applies to the breadth of protection for an invention or idea.

The appropriability of the returns from a discovery thus depends on two principal factors. The first is how easy it is for others to replicate the discovery. The second is the strength of the public protection for the discovery. Figure 12-2 is adapted from Teece (2000, p. 19) and relates these factors to appropriability. The cost of replicating a CD is very low, whereas the cost of replicating an oil refining process may be high. The protection given to pharmaceutical patents in the United States is generally tight, whereas the protection in India is loose because Indian patent law grants a patent if the method of production of a product is different. Hence, one company's patented drug can be produced in India by another company that uses a different manufacturing process. Returns to pharmaceuticals in India are weakly appropriable, whereas in the United States they are more strongly appropriable.[6]

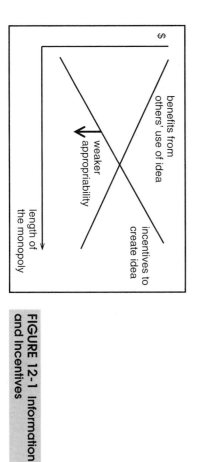

**FIGURE 12-1 Information and Incentives**

---

[6] In 2005 India changed its patent law to allow patents on products and discoveries, including drugs. The change was required by the World Trade Organization and will be phased in over time.

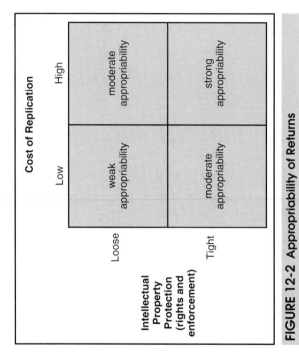

**FIGURE 12-2 Appropriability of Returns**

Changing technology can dramatically alter the costs of replication of intellectual creations. The Internet and MP3 technology made it possible to exchange digital music and video files with little degradation in quality. Napster seized the opportunity provided by the technological developments to launch a peer-to-peer file sharing service. This lowered the costs of replicating music to close to zero, reducing the appropriability of returns to recording companies, music publishers, and film studios. Appropriability also depends on intellectual property protection accorded to recordings and films and whether peer-to-peer services infringe copyrights. Moreover, enforcing intellectual property rights is costly because legal proceedings are expensive and it is difficult to identify the persons copying files. As illustrated in Figure 12-3, the high cost of enforcement means that protection is loose rather than tight, and technological change reduced the cost of replication. The appropriability of returns in the music and film industries was weakened, and the remaining question was how far it would go. The example reviews the issues and the next round of the intellectual property dispute involving digital piracy.

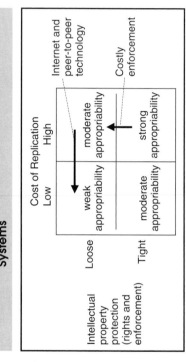

**FIGURE 12-3 Appropriability of Returns and Peer-to-Peer Systems**

## Intellectual Property Enforcement and Digital Piracy

Napster began with software written by 19-year-old Shawn Fanning that allowed people to exchange digital music files on the Internet. A user downloaded Napster's software and registered with the service, receiving a user name and a password. Users could upload and download MP3 files with ease. Napster operated central severs to maintain a "hotlist" of where to find requested music and routed users to the locations. Napster was so successful that the number of registered users reached 62 million.

Venture capitalists were reluctant to invest in Napster, however, for two reasons. One was the concern about how it would generate revenue. The other was whether its service was legal. Music publishers and record companies quickly filed a copyright infringement lawsuit charging that Napster facilitated digital piracy. The courts concluded that Napster had contributorily and vicariously infringed copyrights.[1] The court issued an injunction against Napster and required it to put in place software to block 100 percent of the copyrighted material before it could reopen. Napster appealed, and the Court of Appeals rejected its appeal [*A&M Music, Inc. v. Napster, Inc.*, 2001 WL 115033 (9th Cir., February 12, 2001)].[2]

Napster closed, and the user bases skyrocketed at Morpheus, KaZaA, and Grokster. In addition, Gnutella networks allowed peer-to-peer exchanges of music files. In contrast to Napster, these peer-to-peer services had no central computers but instead coordinated file sharing from the computers of users. These free services threatened the appropriability of returns to the recording companies, music publishers, and film companies.

The companies developed a three-pronged nonmarket strategy to increase the appropriability of returns. First, they filed lawsuits against several thousand individuals using peer-to-peer systems. Second, they filed copyright infringement lawsuits against the services providing the peer-to-peer services. Third, they sought federal legislation to strengthen appropriability.

For the second prong, the legal issues were similar to those in the Napster case, but the peer-to-peer systems had attempted to position themselves in a manner that gave them a stronger defense. These systems described their software as a general technology for sharing any kind of file. Although their systems could be used for sharing files that violated copyright, their software had other noninfringing uses. The rationale for this positioning derived from *Sony Corp. of America v. Universal City Studios*, 464 U.S. 417 (1984), in which Sony successfully defended its VCR, which could be used to violate copyright by sharing or reproducing television programs and movies. The court concluded that a VCR had substantial noninfringing uses, such as time-shifting programs, that did not violate copyrights. The court ruled in favor of Sony. In 2003 the Court of Appeals concluded that Grokster and StreamCast, which made Morpheus, had not violated copyrights because they did not operate central computers and had no means to prevent piracy. The entertainment industry appealed to the Supreme Court, which agreed to hear the appeal with a decision expected in 2005.[3]

In response to the entertainment industry's efforts to restrict file sharing on open networks such as KaZaA, new ventures were formed to

---

[1] In 2000 a federal court ruled that the Digital Millennium Copyright Act did not protect Napster.

[2] For an analysis of the decision, see Matthew Antonelli, C. Raj Kumar, Bernadette McCann-Ezring, Chad Peterman, and Jeffrey Steck, "Unanimous Ninth Circuit substantially affirms lower court injunction against Napster," *Intellectual Property & Technology Law Journal*, May 2001.

[3] *Metro-Goldwyn-Mayer Studios v. Grokster Ltd.* No. 04-480. The plaintiffs included the Motion Picture Association, the Recording Industry Association, and 27,000 music publishers and songwriters. The state attorneys general of 40 states, individual recording artists, and other organizations, including professional sports leagues, joined the plaintiffs in friend-of-the-court briefs. *The New York Times*, December 11, 2004.

*(Continued)*

*(Continued)*

facilitate sharing among a designated group of people. Grouper Networks provided software that allowed groups up to 30 to share movies, music, and photos. For example, a family could form a group to share home videos. The company was positioned to lessen the risk of copyright infringement. For example, instead of exchanging music files, the software allowed a group member to stream music from another member's computer. Movies, however, were shared by exchanging files. The new venture had some of the virtures identified in the *Sony* decision, but the Internet enforcement director of the Motion Picture Association of America said, "We do think it's a problem. It's something we're watching."

The third prong of the rights holders' nonmarket strategy focused on the Induce Act under consideration in Congress. The bill would make companies that create peer-to-peer software liable for copyright infringement. The bill was backed by the entertainment industry and opposed by Silicon Valley firms that feared that the bill would impede the development of new technology. The Consumer Electronics Association sought to narrow the scope of the bill, and the U.S. Copyright Office sought to widen the scope. A quick resolution of the issues was unlikely.

As fate would have it, in 2004 Shawn Fanning launched a new venture, Snocap Inc., that would allow copyright holders to set a price and terms of use on copyrighted files that could be exchanged on peer-to-peer systems. This time the venture was supported by recording companies such as Vivendi's Universal Music Group, and the first peer-to-peer system to participate with the venture was Mashboxx, which was headed by the former president of Grokster

## Intellectual Property Protection

The four principal types of protection for intellectual assets are *patents, licensing, copyright,* and *trade secrets* and *trademarks.*

### Patents

A patent may be granted for an invention of "any new and useful process, machine, manufacture, or composition of matter, or any new and useful improvement thereof." A patent establishes a property right that allows the holder to exclude others from using the invention; that is, a patent grants a monopoly to the inventor. A patent does not allow the holder to use the invention, because its use could infringe other patents. As a result of a 1981 Supreme Court decision computer software may be patented, but software patents are not easily obtained. The principal type of patent is a utility patent, which has a duration of 20 years beginning with the filing of the patent application with the Patent and Trademark Office. Patents are also granted for designs and for plants. Patents are enforced by the courts, which may enjoin others from infringing the patent or may order compensatory damages.[7]

As an indication of the importance of intellectual property protection, Rambus, a memory chip designer, claimed its patents covered some of the components of standard memory chip designs and sought license fees from memory chip producers.

---

[7]Treble damages can be awarded but seldom are, unless there is intentional and continuing infringement. See Bouchoux (2001).

It went to the courts to enforce its claims, but in a countersuit the court found Rambus guilty of fraud for not informing a standards board of its patents. Rambus appealed, and the Court of Appeals reversed the lower court decision and upheld Rambus's claims. Rambus's share price increased by 400 percent that day. The defendant in the original case appealed to the Supreme Court, and Rambus's share price increased by another 37 percent when the Court refused to hear the appeal.

In addition to the duration of a patent, the breadth of the patent is important. Breadth pertains to issues such as whether a patent for a discovery also covers closely related applications and improvements thereon. Inventors seek as broad a patent as possible, whereas competitors and potential users of the invention want a narrow patent. The appropriate breadth of patents is a source of contention both within the courts and among legal scholars.

Patents are the driving force in the pharmaceutical industry, providing strong incentives for research, development, and testing of new chemical entities. A patent on a new drug and approval for marketing by the Food and Drug Administration gives the innovating company a monopoly on the sale of the drug. Reflecting this monopoly, the company appropriates returns by charging a high price. When a patent expires, generic versions of the drug can be marketed. This typically drives the price down significantly and widens the use of the drug. This increases the benefits to society of the drug. Not only do pharmaceutical companies have strong incentives to innovate, but they also have strong incentives to enforce their patent rights and to obtain extensions of their patents through congressional and other actions. The Chapter 1 case, *The Nonmarket Environment of the Pharmaceutical Industry*, addresses these issues.

Licensing makes an invention available to others and hence increases the benefits to society from the invention. Licensing also allows the discoverer to appropriate returns. Licensing is attractive when there are complementary goods whose value is enhanced by the intellectual asset.[8] A biotechnology company that develops a gene may license it to another company that can use it to develop a noncompeting pharmaceutical. Similarly, to appropriate returns an engineering company may license a refining technology to oil companies rather than go into the oil refining business. In some cases an intellectual asset may be given to the producers of complementary products. Microsoft provided its application programming interfaces (APIs) to software developers because the more software written for Windows, the greater the demand for its operating system and other proprietary software.

Licensing can also provide other benefits. In the Chapter 10 case, *Echelon and the Home Automation Standard (A)*, Echelon organized the licensees of its LonWorks control technology into an association with the potential for nonmarket action to back its technology as a standard.

## Copyright

Works of original expression may receive a copyright allowing the recipient to restrict use, reproduction, and distribution of the work. A copyright can be claimed even without a filing with the government. The first copyright law in 1790 established a maximum duration of 28 years. Since then Congress has extended the duration 11 times. The most recent extension in 1998 was stimulated by the imminent expiration of the copyright on early Mickey Mouse cartoons, as considered in the example. The duration of a copyright is now the life of the author plus 70 years, or in the case of a disguised authorship it is the minimum of 75 years or 100 years after creation. The

---

[8]See Teece (2000, Ch. 8) for strategic considerations in licensing.

breadth of a copyright pertains to which uses are allowed without authorization by the author. The fair use doctrine allows limited unauthorized use for research, scholarship, and literary criticism.

## Mickey Mouse Politics and Law

The copyrights on the early Mickey Mouse cartoons (e.g., *Steamboat Willy*) were due to expire in 2003, and Pluto, Goofy, and Donald Duck would lose their protection in 2009. Disney and other entertainment and media companies saw this as an opportunity to extend the duration of copyright. The European Union had issued a directive in 1993 to set the copyright duration at 70 years, and the U.S. interests, arguing for harmonization, sought a 20-year extension to 70 years. The issue was characterized by relatively quiet client politics, and in 1998 Congress provided the extension by passing the Sonny Bono Copyright Term Extension Act.

The opponents of the extension soon challenged the Act in the courts. The opponents included individuals and companies that relied on public access to materials. They made two arguments. First, they argued that the extension violated Article I of the Constitution by essentially giving nearly unlimited rights to creations. Second, they argued that the law stifled free speech in violation of the First Amendment. The district court, the Court of Appeals, and in 2003 the Supreme Court upheld the law. In the majority opinion Justice Ruth Bader Ginsburg wrote that Congress had acted within its authority as granted by the Constitution and that copyright was intended to "promote the creation and publication of free expression." With respect to the wisdom and the public policy effects of the extension, Ginsburg wrote "that it is generally for Congress, not the courts, to decide how best to pursue the copyright clause's objectives,. . . ."

An important issue in information technology and information services industries is whether the "look and feel" of software or a Web site can be protected by copyright. This is an unsettled matter. In an important case Apple Computer filed a copyright lawsuit against Microsoft arguing that the user interface of its Windows operating system copied the look and feel of Apple's system. The court held in favor of Microsoft.

The issue of what may be copyrighted has required both legislation and court interpretation. Consider the issue of whether compilations of facts can be protected by copyright. A 1991 Supreme Court decision (*Feist Publications, Inc. v. Rural Telephone Service Co.,* 499 U.S., 340) held that "facts," even if collected through "sweat and effort," remained in the public domain. Earlier court decisions had held that databases were protected by copyright under the "sweat of the brow" doctrine. This doctrine prevailed despite 1976 amendments to the Copyright Act that required a degree of creativity or originality for compilations of data to be protected. In *Feist* the court affirmed the originality and creativity requirement and stated that "all facts—scientific, historical, biographical and news of the day . . . are part of the public domain available to every person." For example, the telephone white pages cannot be copyrighted because they are simply an alphabetical list of names and numbers, whereas the Yellow Pages can be copyrighted because the information is arranged by category, which has a degree of originality. eBay had been concerned about whether auction aggregators could copy its database of online auctions and provide listings to their users, as considered in the chapter case, *eBay and Database Protection.*

## Trademarks and Trade Secrets

A trademark provides social and private value. The social value results from reducing search costs for consumers by allowing branding of products. Branding can also support a reputation for quality, uniformity, or service. The word Coke is a trademark, as are eBay and Intel. Trademarks can be registered at the federal or state levels and if maintained can be perpetual. Remedies for infringement can take the form of injunctions and compensatory damages. The requirement for a trademark is distinctiveness. Generic terms such as "online auction" cannot be protected by a trademark, but the name eBay can be protected. As mentioned in Chapter 2 a new entrant into the online auction market used a front page that closely resembled eBay's homepage. The most defensible trademarks are those that are "arbitrary and fanciful," and an eBay attorney explained, "eBay is a completely coined name. It means nothing."[9] eBay filed a successful trademark infringement lawsuit against the entrant.

A trade secret is almost anything that is unique and of value or potential value to a company. This includes process information, operating methods, programs, and business plans. To receive protection the information must be adequately protected by the company on a continual basis. Trade secret protection can be perpetual, and the secrets do not have to be registered. Remedies for violations of trade secrets include injunctions and compensatory damages. Trade secret law has been used to prohibit employees who move from one company to another to take along information from their former employer.

# Contracts

Contracts are governed both by the common law and by statutes pertaining to particular types of contracts and transactions. This section focuses on the principles of contract law derived from the common law, which developed over time to resolve economic problems associated with noncontemporaneous trades. People benefit from the exchange of goods and services, and because of their knowledge of the specific circumstances, people know best how to realize the gains from trade. The objective of the law is to support people in what they want to do by addressing impediments to those trades. In this sense the common law looks to what people do and want to do to arrange and complete exchanges. Contracts are one means by which people arrange mutually advantageous trades.[10]

In a contract both parties seek assurances. A mortgage lender wants assurance that the borrower will repay the loan with interest. To make it costly for the borrower to fail to repay the loan, the house is pledged as collateral. The borrower wants to induce the lender to provide funds, and without a contract no lender would extend funds with a repayment period that extends over 25 to 30 years. Contracts make the mortgage lending market possible. Contracts thus are mutually advantageous to the participating parties.

Contracts are also entered into to induce *reliance*. Reliance refers to a change in behavior by a party. For example, an electric power plant wants a steady source of coal, and rather than develop a mine itself, it prefers to have a coal company with the required expertise develop the mine. Opening a mine requires major expenditures that the coal company is unwilling to make without assurances that the coal will have a buyer. To induce the coal company to make the investment, a reliance expenditure, the

[9]*San Jose Mercury News,* July 31, 2001.
[10]Other means include contemporaneous exchange (at the grocery store), relational contracts built on longterm relationships (as in supply chains), and reputation (as in online auctions).

power company must provide assurances to the coal company. The power company may agree to build a generating plant at the mine mouth and to purchase at market prices specific quantities of coal for an extended period such as 50 years. With such an assurance, the coal company is willing to make reliance expenditures. In the event of default on the contract by the power company, the reliance expenditures provide a basis for damages.

A contract is an agreement over which parties are to have bargained. The contract then is mutually advantageous, making each party better off than it would be in its absence. As in the case of mortgage lending, some markets would not exist if it were not for contracts. Contracts cover promises to take particular actions in the future. Contracts commit the parties to those actions, and the commitments are credible because the failure to follow through on them is costly. For example, a lender may foreclose on the house provided as collateral for a mortgage.

Contracts are seldom complete in the sense of providing for all the possible contingencies that could arise. The transactions costs associated with completely specifying the responsibilities of the parties in every conceivable circumstance are typically too high, so contracts have a degree of incompleteness. When one of those contingencies arises, the courts may be called upon to resolve the ambiguity or resulting conflict. The Genentech and City of Hope example illustrates this in the case in which a long-term licensing contract containing sections that appeared to have conflicting implications.

Contracts can be either written or oral and generally involve an offer, acceptance, and consideration. Consideration is what a promisee gives to a promisor to induce the latter to make the promise, and mutual consideration is usually given. In the purchase of an automobile, the seller gives the automobile as consideration to the buyer to elicit a promise to pay for the car. To induce the seller to provide the car, the buyer gives the seller a down payment and a promise to pay as well as recourse to the car in the event of breach of the contract. In the case of financing the purchase of a house, the buyer provides as consideration a lien or deed of trust on the house to induce the lender to provide the funds. The lender provides the funds to induce the borrower to agree to the lien or deed of trust.

---

**EXAMPLE**

## Genentech and City of Hope

In 1976, as a fledgling company, Genentech entered into a contract with the City of Hope Medical Center (COH) under which two COH researchers agreed to splice a human gene into bacteria to synthesize the DNA for human insulin.[1] In 1978 the scientists were successful, resulting in the first

genetically engineered pharmaceutical and the birth of the biotechnology industry. The contract provided that all research findings and resulting patents were the property of Genentech, and Genentech obtained 127 patents related to the COH research. Upon the discovery Genentech licensed the DNA patent for human insulin to Eli Lilly & Co. Under the license Lilly agreed to pay a 6 percent royalty to Genentech and a 2 percent royalty to COH. COH had received $285 million in royalties from human insulin and also the human growth hormone.

*(Continued)*

---

[1]COH is a world renowned nonprofit cancer research center that in addition to giving birth to the first genetically engineered pharmaceutical also pioneered bone marrow transplants and opened a facility to produce experimental drugs for untreatable diseases.

*(Continued)*

In the mid-1990s COH began inquiring into Genentech's licensing of the DNA patents to pharmaceutical companies in addition to Lilly. Genentech had licensed the patents to 22 companies, and COH filed a breach of contract lawsuit, claiming that Genentech owed it $445 million in additional royalties. COH also claimed that Genentech intentionally concealed the licensing, which opened the possibility of punitive damages. COH based its lawsuit on a paragraph of the 16-page contract that stated, "Should Genentech license any third party under any patent acquired by it hereunder, then Genentech shall secure from that party and pay to City of Hope the same royalty City of Hope would have received had Genentech itself carried out the licensed activity."

Genentech rejected COH's claim and argued that the governing section of the contract was the section that stated, "Genentech shall pay to City of Hope a royalty of 2 percent of the net sales of all polypeptides (proteins) sold by it or its affiliates, provided only that manufacture of the polypeptide employs DNA synthesized by City of Hope under this agreement."[2] Genentech stated that the term "provided only" meant that royalties were due only on products that used the DNA developed by the COH scientists. Genentech not only argued that it had not violated the contract but that the case was actually about patent law and hence should be tried in federal, not state, court.

The case was tried in state court in 2001 and the jury split 7 in favor of Genentech and 5 in favor of COH. Since nine votes were required to decide the case, the judge was forced to declare a mistrial. The case was retried and the jury voted 9 to 3 that Genentech had breached the contract and 10 to 2 that it had done so with fraud or malice. The jury awarded COH $300 million in compensatory damages and $200 million in punitive damages.

[2]*San Francisco Chronicle*, September 10, 2001.

## Enforceability

The central issues in contracts are which contracts are enforceable, when can they be breached, and what damages are due in the event of a breach. A contract may be voided if an individual, such as a minor, does not have the authority to enter into it. Similarly, a contract to sell one's vote in an election is voidable because the right to vote is inalienable; that is, it is not transferable. A contract is generally not enforceable if it is illegal or unconscionable and is voidable under certain conditions such as fraud or a mistake. These conditions may be augmented by statute. In California individuals have 3 days during which they can cancel certain contracts. Unconscionability may be either procedural or substantive. The former pertains to contracts entered into under duress or unfair circumstances such as when one party has no bargaining power. The latter pertains to contracts that, for example, may obligate a person to pay a penalty that has no relation to the value of the item purchased.

Duress and unconscionability are ex ante concepts in the sense that the conditions are present when the parties agree to the contract. Circumstances may develop after signing a contract that make it unenforceable. One such circumstance is impossibility, where a party is unable to fulfill a contractual promise. For example, an act of nature such as a fire may destroy a company's plant, making it impossible to fulfill a supply contract. The responsibility in such a case should be assigned to the party that is able to cope with the situation at the least cost. For example, if the buyer can obtain the contracted supplies from another producer, the factory owner may have no remaining obligation. If the buyer had made reliance expenditures, however, for a unique product produced by the destroyed plant, the factory owner may be responsible for damages. In the case in which reliance expenditures are made by the buyer, the factory can take out insurance against the risk of both the fire and the inability to fulfill the contract.

Another situation that can make a contract unenforceable is frustration of purpose. If an event occurs that causes the purpose of the contract to disappear, the courts have held that the contract is unenforceable, since there is no point to its fulfillment. As with impossibility, damages may be awarded. From the perspective of economic efficiency, responsibility for the risk that the purpose of the contract could vanish should be assigned to the party that can best avoid the risk or, if that is not possible, deal with it ex post at the least cost. This principle of the least-cost avoider is considered in more detail in the following section on torts.

## Breach

Contracts and their enforcement provide credible commitments about the actions of parties. These contracts, however, cannot be complete, so circumstances can arise under which one or both parties prefer not to fulfill its commitment. In such circumstances the parties could mutually agree, perhaps with the payment of compensation, to terminate a contract. A party may also unilaterally *breach* a contract. Breaches are allowed because under some circumstances it is economically efficient not to fulfill the conditions of the contract. For example, if a change in the market makes a necessary input to the production process prohibitively expensive, it may be better to breach a purchase contract and allow the buyer to contract for a product made with different inputs.

If the circumstances can be anticipated under which it may be economically inefficient to fulfill the commitments, the contract can be written to specify the obligation each party has to the other in those circumstances. There may be disagreement, however, about whether the circumstances are as claimed by the breaching party. One purpose of contracts is to reduce transactions costs associated with circumstances that develop during fulfillment of the agreement. When contract terms do not specify the obligations of the parties, the rules followed by courts for remedies allow the contracting parties to anticipate the consequences of broken promises.

## Remedies

Courts use two basic types of remedies in the event of breach: damages and specific performance. Damages can be compensatory for the harm caused or punitive, as in the Genentech and City of Hope example. Compensation for foreseeable damages depends on the baseline used by the courts.[11] One baseline is to leave the plaintiff as well off as she expected to be if the contract terms had been fulfilled. These *expectations damages* can differ from the amount required to allow the plaintiff to contract with someone else for the provision of the product or service. For example, in the case of an antique a promisee may have expected to pay a certain amount for the item, but finding another identical item may be considerably more expensive because of search costs, transportation costs and special handling. In such a case the court could order *consequential damages* based on the opportunity cost of the next

---

[11]In *Hadley v. Baxendale, Restatement (Second) of Contracts,* § 351(1) 1979, the court held that the defendant was not responsible for damages that could not be reasonably foreseen. This decision is consistent with the notion that the common law provides incentives for actions to increase economic efficiency, and if something cannot be foreseen, no action can be based on it. Hence, there is no efficiency rational for awarding damages.

best alternative. Another rule for awarding damages is to put the promisee in the same position she had been in prior to signing the contract. This rule corresponds to *reliance damages*, since it compensates the promisee only for reliance expenditures made as a result of the contract. In some cases the courts may simply require the defendant to return the item provided by the promisee. For example, an auto dealer may repossess an automobile when a purchaser defaults on payments.

Court awards of damages take place ex post, and anticipation of those awards provides ex ante incentives to fulfill promises, while leaving the flexibility to breach contracts when it is efficient to do so. The parties to a contract may also write into the contract contingencies in the event of breach. This *liquidated damages* approach is ex ante and is based on the principle that more complete contracts can be more efficient. Liquidated damages are limited to compensation for harm and are not intended as penalties for particular actions.

In cases in which it is difficult to determine the actual damages incurred as a consequence of a breach, the courts may provide relief in the form of *specific performance*. This generally involves an order directing the promisor to take the action called for in the contract. The court could, for example, order the antiques dealer to deliver the item to the buyer.

Many contracts contain mandatory arbitration clauses that require disputes to be resolved outside the courts. The purpose of these clauses, which have been used for credit card and brokerage accounts for years, are intended to avoid the legal and administrative costs associated with a court case. Arbitration clauses are being used more broadly by a wider set of industries. Arbitration itself can be costly, so some companies have turned to jury waivers. In signing a contract such as a residential lease or an automobile loan agreement, an individual may waive the right to trial by jury. The purpose of the waiver is to avoid what some companies view as unreasonable awards by juries. Such waivers, however, have been held to be in violation of a state constitution, as in California.

# Torts

*Torts* are civil wrongs—wrongs done by one person to another.[12] The law of torts is common law that evolves through decisions made by judges in cases brought by private plaintiffs. The common law of torts evolves as innovative cases are brought before the courts. Obesity has become a health concern, and trial lawyers have brought lawsuits against restaurants for their alleged contribution to obesity and the associated health risks. The chapter case, *Obesity and McLawsuits*, concerns the litigation against McDonald's. Tort claims also are laid to rest. In 2002 the claims of 1,900 plaintiffs who said their health was damaged by radiation from the 1979 Three Mile Island nuclear plant accident were finally resolved when the Court of Appeals upheld the district court's summary dismissal of the claims. The court concluded that not enough radiation leaked to cause adverse health effects. The plaintiffs decided not to appeal the decision to the Supreme Court.

The law of torts is applied in situations in which people are unable to bargain over the compensation that will be due in the event of a wrong such as an injury. Accidents that involve damage to real property or injury to a person are one subject of torts.

The basic elements of a tort case are an injury, an action that caused the harm, and the breach of a duty owed to the injured party. In the case of an automobile accident, the injury may have been caused by a brake failure, and if the brake failure was due to

[12]See Franklin and Rabin (1987) and Cooter and Ulen (2004) for treatments of the law of torts.

a faulty design or a failure of a part, the injured party may be able to recover damages from the automaker. If, however, the injured party was at fault as a result of negligence, the court may find for the defendant and not award damages. For example, if the owner of an older car had an inspection that revealed that the brake pads and rotors needed replacement and brake fluid was leaking but the owner did not have repairs made, the court could find that the owner had acted negligently. This could relieve the automaker of liability or reduce the damages awarded.

To identify the role of the law of torts in markets, the issue of product safety is used. The next section introduces the product safety problem and the concept of social efficiency. The following sections introduce the role of the liability system in achieving social efficiency, the development of the law of products liability, and the performance of the products liability system.

# The Product Safety Problem and Social Efficiency

Safety is a primary concern for responsible management and occupies a prominent place on the nonmarket agendas of most firms. No firm wants injuries in its workplaces or associated with one of its products, yet preventing all injuries could be prohibitively costly if not impossible. The issue thus is the extent of care to take in reducing the number and severity of injuries. The principal and most comprehensive source of institutional guidance on safety is the law of torts. Lawsuits filed by injured persons bring both a specific case and broader issues of responsibility into the institutional arena of the courts. The law of products liability, for example, has developed from these cases, and the awards courts make and the costs of litigation and liability insurance provide firms with incentives to take care in manufacturing and in the incorporation of safety features, instructions, and warnings.[13]

The product safety problem can be conceptualized as shown in Figure 12-4. The producer makes a number of ex ante decisions including product conception, research and development, design, manufacturing, and marketing. Once the product is put on the market, it becomes the property of the consumer. Ex post some consumers may be injured or incur property damage through their use of the product. From the perspective of social efficiency, decisions by both the producer and consumers should take into account the social cost of possible injuries to persons and property as well as the costs of preventing those injuries.

Both producers and consumers should also take into account the social costs of the care they take to reduce injuries. The producer can make design change, improve manufacturing quality, add safety features, and provide instructions and warnings. The consumer can develop skill in using the product and take precautions against accidents. In the case of a chain saw the producer can add safety features such as a safety tip, provide warnings about the hazard of kickback, and provide instructions on proper use, including a videotape. The consumer can purchase goggles, a hard hat, and steel-tipped boots. The costs of these measures constitute the cost of care by the producer and the consumer. The cost of care also includes any loss of benefits, for example, from the product because of safety features or additional costs from use. In the case of a chain

---

[13]The law of torts served as the principal source of institutional guidance on a broad range of safety issues until the 1970s, when the wave of social regulation led to the creation of regulatory agencies, such as the National Highway Traffic Safety Administration (NHTSA), the Consumer Product Safety Commission (CPSC), and the Occupational Safety and Health Administration (OSHA), to address particular safety issues. These agencies focused on specific hazards and mandating controls and safety standards.

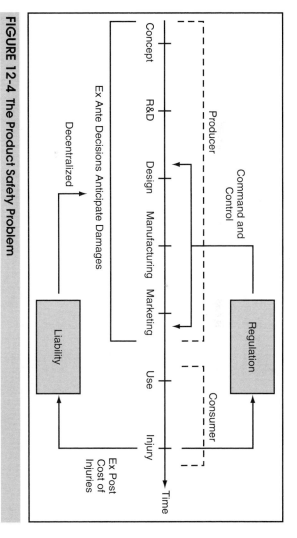

**FIGURE 12-4** The Product Safety Problem

saw a safety tip reduces the cutting length of the blade and increases the weight of the saw, contributing to fatigue of the user. Similarly, using a chain saw safely can lengthen the time required to complete a job.

Social efficiency requires balancing the costs of injuries and the costs of care. This perspective is illustrated in Figure 12-5, which graphs costs as a function of injuries prevented. The social cost of injuries decreases as more injuries are prevented. If all injuries were prevented, however, the cost of care—the cost of injury avoidance— would be very high. In the case of a chain saw, this would require not producing the

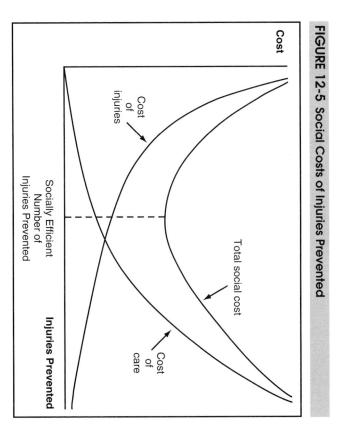

**FIGURE 12-5** Social Costs of Injuries Prevented

product. Total social costs are the sum of the costs of care and the costs of injuries, as illustrated in the figure. The socially efficient number of injuries prevented, or equivalently the optimal amount of care, minimizes total social costs and is determined by a trade-off between the cost of injuries and the cost of preventing them.[14] As shown in the figure, society tolerates some injuries because preventing them is too costly. That is, society prevents those injuries that are not too costly to prevent. Society allows chain saws to be produced and used despite the resulting injuries.

The cost of care curve in Figure 12-5 reflects the most efficient, or least cost, combination of care taken by producers and consumers. Thus, for any given level of injuries prevented, the socially efficient allocation of care between the producer and consumers is that which minimizes the total costs of care. This is referred to as the principle of the *least-cost avoider*; that is, efficiency requires care by the producer or the consumer or both, depending on which has the lower cost of preventing injury.

The social costs of injuries and the cost of care taken by producers are reflected in the prices consumers pay for products. The higher price required to cover these costs reduces the demand for a product and thus the injuries resulting from it. Consumers will not purchase a product whose price and the associated cost of taking care during use exceed the benefits anticipated from its use. Those who value the product more highly than those costs will purchase it. Over 1.5 million chain saws are sold every year.

As illustrated in the lower part of Figure 12-4, the institution of liability is intended to assign the ex post social costs of injuries to producers and consumers so that each takes the efficient level of care. The prices of products demanded and supplied then fully reflect those costs. This then results in the socially efficient number of injuries prevented, as illustrated in Figure 12-5.

In the United States and in many other countries, the institution of liability is the principal institution that guides producers and consumers in product safety decisions. Liability operates through the courts, which assign the social costs of injuries to consumers and producers through the damages assessed in cases brought by injured consumers. These assignments of costs are intended to induce consumers and producers to take the socially efficient level of care. By aligning private and social costs, the liability system not only provides incentives for the socially efficient level of care, but also allows decentralized decision making on the part of producers and consumers rather than relying on government regulation through command and control.

The actual institution of liability, however, differs from this ideal. Distributive considerations influence courts, which can focus on compensating the injured as well as on aligning private and social costs. The distributive consequences of the liability system also motivate nonmarket action. Products liability law and measures to reform it are considered in more detail after the distinction between liability and property rules is developed.

# Entitlements, Liability, and Social Efficiency

## Entitlements and Their Protection

Starting from the perspective of the Coase theorem, Calabresi and Melamed (1972) defined an entitlement, or right, as the ability of an individual to control a particular resource or to take an action, with the state protecting that control or action from infringement. The nature of the protection given to entitlements is important. Calabresi

---

[14]The socially efficient number of injuries prevented is identified by the point at which the marginal social cost of injuries equals the marginal cost of care.

and Melamed distinguished between two types of rules for protecting entitlements—property rules and liability rules.[15]

A *property rule* prohibits other parties from infringing the entitlement without the consent of the party holding it. Homeowners are protected by a property rule that prohibits a person from either taking their home without consent or forcing them to sell it at a price they deem inadequate.

A *liability rule* protects an entitlement in quite a different manner. When an entitlement is protected by a liability rule, a person may infringe the entitlement but must compensate its holder for the objectively assessed loss resulting from that infringement. Although a home is protected by a property rule against infringement by a person, it is protected only by a liability rule that permits the state to take a home for a public purpose and requires the state to compensate the owner for its objectively assessed value. Even if owners would prefer to hold out for greater compensation, as would be their right under a property rule, eminent domain does not allow them to do so. A person injured in an accident associated with a product is protected only by a liability rule.

The remarkable feature of the Coase theorem is that social efficiency is achieved when entitlements are protected with either a property rule or a liability rule.[16] To illustrate the concept of a liability rule, consider again the rancher and farmer example from earlier in the chapter. Suppose that instead of an open range the range is closed.[17] By the year 1353 English common law had established the principle of a closed range, under which an owner of livestock was strictly liable in tort for any damage done by his animals.[18] A closed range assigns the entitlement to the farmer and protects it with a liability rule. The rancher then must compensate the farmer for any crop damage.

A liability rule also provides the proper incentive for the construction of a fence, even when the farmer can build a fence at a lower cost than can the rancher. To illustrate this, suppose that the topography is such that the rancher would have to spend 50 annually to fence in her cattle, whereas the farmer can build a fence around his property to keep the cattle out at an annual cost of 30. The efficient solution is to build the fence around the farm with the rancher paying the cost of 30.

As another example, consider the case of a swimming pool in a person's backyard. An externality is present because of the swimming pool and the presence of neighbors. Because the greatest likelihood of injury centers on neighborhood children, they will be the focus here. If the swimming pool owner posts a clear and obvious warning not to trespass, anyone who trespasses and is injured in the pool is in some sense "at fault." From the perspective of fault, the swimming pool owner should be protected so that people neither trespass nor use the pool without the owner's consent. The costs of avoiding harm then would be assigned to the neighborhood children and their parents. Parents then would take care in supervising their children and take measures such as building a fence around their own yards to prevent their children from going to the pool. Is this assignment likely to result in social efficiency; that is, is it likely to result in actions that minimize the sum of the costs of harm and the costs of the care by the pool owner and the neighbors? No, it would be more efficient for the pool owner to build

---

15 Calabresi and Melamed also consider inalienability rules. When an entitlement is protected by an inalienability rule, an individual is not allowed to give up or transfer the entitlement even voluntarily. An individual's entitlement to vote in a public election is governed by an inalienability rule, since a person is not permitted to transfer that entitlement to another person.

16 This feature is also considered in Chapter 11 in the context of the control of externalities.

17 For example, in California the five northern-most counties are open range, and Shasta County has a mixture of open and closed range. The rest of the state is closed range.

18 See Ellickson (1991, pp. 42–45).

a fence around the pool than for all the neighbors to build fences to keep their children away from the pool. This suggests that the swimming pool owner should be assigned the costs of injuries—that is, be liable for injuries associated with the pool. That assignment then creates incentives to build a fence around the pool.

Protecting certain entitlements with a liability rule is believed to involve fewer transactions costs than protecting them with a property rule. For example, it would be prohibitively expensive to negotiate agreements between each motorist and every other motorist and all pedestrians regarding compensation for injuries. Consequently, injuries are governed by liability rules rather than by property rules. The next section addresses the issue of transactions costs and their implications for the use of property and liability rules.

## The Assignment of Social Costs and the Choice Between Liability and Regulation

The Coase theorem pertains to situations in which entitlements can be clearly assigned and private agreements can be reached without substantial transactions costs. When entitlements are not well defined or there are transactions costs, the assignment of responsibility for the social costs of injuries is a task for government.

Calabresi and Melamed provide five principles for the assignment of costs and the choice between the institutions of liability and regulation.

1. The assignment of entitlements should favor knowledgeable choices between social benefits (e.g., preventing injuries) and the social costs of obtaining them.
2. When it is unclear whether the social benefits exceed the social costs, "the cost should be put on the party that is best located to make such a cost-benefit analysis."
3. When there are alternative means of achieving social benefits (or of avoiding social costs), the costs of achieving them (or avoiding social costs from accidents) should be assigned to the party that can do so at the lowest cost.
4. When it is not clear who that party is, "the costs should be put on the party or activity which can with the lowest transactions costs act in the market to correct an error in entitlements by inducing the party who can avoid social costs most cheaply to do so."
5. Given principles one through four, protect the assignment with a liability rule or government regulation depending on which is more likely to lead to social efficiency.

Breyer (1982) gives examples of the application of the *Calabresi and Melamed principles* to safety and pollution:

When it is uncertain whether a benefit (such as a lawnmower with a certain risk) is worth the potential costs (such as the harm of related accidents), one should construct liability rules such that the costs (of the harm) are placed on the party best able to weigh the costs against the benefits. This principle is likely to place costs upon the party best able to avoid them, or, where this is unknown, on the party best able to induce others to act more safely. This principle seems to argue for making the lawnmower manufacturer strictly liable if he is best able to weigh the benefits, risks, and avoidance costs involved. Similarly, in the case of pollution, the rule would place liability on the factory owner, for he is in the best position to determine whether it is more efficient to curtail pollution or to compensate the victims of his noisome emissions.

In the case of lawnmower safety, the fifth principle pertains to the choice among government regulation, voluntary standards, and reliance on the liability system. Principles three and four call for placing social costs on those who can most efficiently reduce them or induce others to take care to reduce them. In many cases, this means that the producer and the consumer should each bear some portion of the social costs of injuries, so as to induce each to take the efficient level of care.[19]

In the case of a chain saw, the producer is better located than is the consumer to determine whether, for example, the social benefits of a safety feature exceed its costs. If accidents can be reduced either by a safety feature or by care taken by the consumer, the producer is likely better located to determine which can do so at lower cost. For example, the producer is better located to determine if a safety tip is more effective in reducing the risk from kickback than are warnings to the consumer not to bore with the tip. If it were not clear which would reduce the risk at lower cost, the costs should be put on the party best able to correct an error in the assignment of the cost. Surely the producer is better located to induce the consumer to change his actions than is the consumer able to induce the firm to change its actions. In the case of a chain saw, liability rather than regulation is used to govern the provision of safety, although the industry has adopted some voluntary standards to lessen the risk that some producer would free ride on the safety reputation generated by other producers.

## Products Liability

### The Development of Products Liability Law

Products liability is a branch of the common law of torts. Products liability cases that are litigated—particularly those that reach a state or the U.S. Supreme Court—establish legal precedents under which future cases are decided. Those precedents also provide the basis for plaintiffs' and defendants' expectations about likely court decisions in their own cases and so provide the basis for settlements.

The issues brought before the courts change over time, and the common law evolves to address those changes. Technological progress has changed the nature of many consumer products, particularly as electronics replaced mechanical functions. It is now often more difficult to determine a product's likely hazards through casual inspection. The Calabresi and Melamed principles suggest shifting the cost of injury prevention toward the producer because the producer is likely to have a lower relative cost of preventing injuries through design and manufacture than the consumer has in inspecting the products and taking precautions. The producer is also better placed to take actions in the market, such as providing warnings and instructions, that can induce consumers to take care. Court decisions have followed a similar logic, resulting in evolving legal standards on which cases are decided.[20]

The common law of products liability has evolved considerably since the 1950s, with legal standards originating in the law of contracts evolving into a standard of *strict liability* under which a producer may be held fully responsible even if it was not at fault and could not have prevented the injury. Some activists and legal scholars

---

[19]These principles also provide the basis for the choice among remedies for breach of contract, as discussed earlier in the chapter.

[20]Some legal scholars, such as Posner (1981), argue that social efficiency is the cornerstone of legal justice and that court decisions will in the long run produce a common law that supports efficiency. Rubin (1983) and Priest (1977) have argued that the natural incentives for parties to bring lawsuits when social efficiency gains can be realized will lead to new legal precedents that promote social efficiency.

have advocated going further to a system of absolute, or total, liability. Under such a system a producer would be held liable for any injury associated with a product. Such a system would be equivalent to a producer attaching to each product it sells an insurance policy with no deductible or copayment.

This section provides an introduction to some of the principal changes in and central principles of products liability. One reason for the complexity is that products liability is largely state law, and not all states have adopted the same legal standards. Nearly all states have adopted the standard of strict liability, but some allow certain defenses that others do not allow. For example, a number of states now allow state-of-the-art design defenses which have made liability less strict. Thus, a problem for firms is dealing with dissimilar laws across the states. This has led some business groups and some lawyers to advocate a uniform federal code for products liability.

The law pertaining to product safety developed from the laws of contracts and *warranties*, which focus on economic well-being. The law of warranties is codified in the Uniform Commercial Code, which has been adopted for commercial transactions by all the states. In addition, the Magnuson-Moss Warranty Act of 1975 regulates the content and clarity of written warranties. Warranties include those expressly made by the producer and those implied by, for example, the fact that the product was put on the market for sale. *Express* warranties are made in writing by the producer and, as part of the sales agreement, represent obligations binding on the producer. If the manufacturer states that a chain saw will cut at a particular speed and it does not, the consumer may sue for damages under the law of warranty.

*Implied* warranties are not made by producers but are held by the courts to be associated with a product put on the market. Products are held to have an implied *warranty of merchantability.* A chain saw is supposed to cut wood—if it does not, the consumer may sue. However, a chain saw is not supposed to cut cement blocks or metal pipe. A product also has an implied warranty for fitness for a particular purpose. A food or drink carries an implied warranty of *fitness for human consumption.*

The legal foundations provided by the law of contracts and warranties were transformed through two steps into the current law of products liability. The first step was a movement away from the rules of contract law by expanding the concept of who has standing to sue whom. In addition, certain principles of tort law were applied to injuries associated with products. The second was the replacement of the standard of negligence by strict liability. A negligence standard is still used in many parts of tort law, but the standard of strict liability is used in most jurisdictions in cases of products liability.

At the turn of the 20th century, state laws had generally required *privity of contract* in which a party incurring a loss of property associated with the use of a product could sue only the party from whom the product had been purchased. A producer who sold a product through a retailer could not be sued by a consumer because the consumer had privity of contract only with the retailer. This standard changed when the State Appeals Court of New York in *MacPherson v. Buick Motor Company,* NY Court of Appeals, 111 N.E. 1050 (1916), held that an injured consumer could sue the manufacturer when the manufacturer had been negligent in failing to detect a defect in a product. The court stated, "If the nature of a thing is such that it is reasonably certain to place life and limb in danger when negligently made, it is then a thing of danger. . . . If he is negligent, where danger is foreseen, a liability will follow." This decision not only eliminated the privity requirement but also led to injuries associated with products being treated as torts. This began the development of products liability.

The limits of privity of contract were further eroded by a court decision that extended the implied warranty of merchantability to cover an automobile driver, in this case the spouse of the purchaser, who was not in privity with the seller.[21] These two cases extended the reach of tort law to users other than the purchaser and back through the channel of distribution to the manufacturer. In most jurisdictions, a consumer is now able to sue the producer as well as virtually all those in the channel of distribution through which the product passed. In addition, other people, including injured bystanders, can sue the producer for damages.

The *MacPherson* decision applied to cases in which negligence was shown. *Negligence* is defined as "the omission to do something which a reasonable man, guided by those ordinary considerations which ordinarily regulate human affairs, would do, or the doing of something which a reasonable and prudent man would not do."[22] The second phase of the evolution of products liability was the abandonment of the negligence standard and its replacement by the standard of strict liability in tort. Under a negligence standard, the burden of proof was on the plaintiff to show that the producer was at fault. Fault was determined by whether the producer had taken *due care* in the manufacture of the product and whether adequate warnings had been given. Cases often focused on showing that the product had a defect that caused an injury that would not have occurred had the manufacturer exercised due care.

Under strict liability the concept of fault is irrelevant and negligence is not required.[23] The courts do not inquire into who was at fault but instead are concerned only with whether the product in question was associated with the injury.[24] The courts also do not allow due care defenses, so a producer may be held liable even if everything possible had been done to prevent the defect that caused the injury.

The transformation to strict liability was the result of a set of cases decided in state courts. In *Escola v. Coca-Cola Bottling Co.,* 24 Cal. 2d 453, 150 P.2d 436 (1944), a case involving a person injured by an exploding Coca-Cola bottle, California Supreme Court Judge Traynor stated in a dissenting opinion: "I believe the manufacturer's negligence should no longer be singled out as the basis of a plaintiff's right to recover in cases like the present one. In my opinion it should now be recognized that a manufacturer incurs an absolute liability when an article that he has placed on the market, knowing that it is to be used without inspection, proves to have a defect that causes injury to human beings." Judge Traynor provided two rationales for his conclusion: one based on ex ante social efficiency and one based on which party can best bear the distributive consequences of the injuries. "Even if there is no negligence, however, public policy demands that responsibility be fixed wherever it will most effectively reduce the hazards to life and health inherent in defective products that reach the market. It is evident that the manufacturer can anticipate some hazards and guard against the recurrence of others, as the public cannot. Those who suffer injury from defective products are unprepared to meet its consequences. The cost of an injury and the loss of time or health may be an overwhelming misfortune to the person injured and a needless one, for the risk of injury can be insured by the manufacturer and distributed among the public as a cost of doing business."

Judge Traynor's call for a system of absolute liability has not prevailed, but his opinion influenced later court decisions that established the somewhat narrower standard of strict liability. In *Greenman v. Yuba Power Products,* 59 Cal. 2d 57 (1963), a person injured by a piece of wood when using a shop tool was awarded damages

[21]*Henningsen v. Bloomfield Motors,* 32 N.J. 358, 161 A.2d 69 (1960).
[22]*Black's Law Dictionary* (1983, p. 538).
[23]Negligence due, for example, to careless manufacturing may expose a company to punitive damages.
[24]Even proof of direct causation need not be given, as indicated by the DES decision considered later in the chapter.

under the principle that "a manufacturer is strictly liable in tort when an article he places on the market, knowing that it is to be used without inspection for defects, proves to have a defect that causes injury to a human being." The explanation given for strict liability was "to insure that the costs of injuries resulting from defective products are borne by the manufacturers that put such products on the market rather than by the injured persons who are powerless to protect themselves." The definition of strict liability given in the *Restatement (Second) of Torts (1965)* is presented in Figure 12-6.[25]

The courts have adopted a broad interpretation of what constitutes a defect in a product. Defects include those that come from manufacturing, as for example, a defective Coca-Cola bottle. It is often difficult to prove whether a product had a manufacturing defect, so many courts assume that if a person was injured by a product, the product was defective. Defects can also result from the design of the product. If a shop tool were designed in such a manner that a piece of wood could fly out of it during use, the product may be said to have a defect. Defects also can be associated with the instructions provided with a product or with the warnings given. Producers thus have a *duty to warn*. A defect in a warning is complicated because it involves both the warning given by the producer and the consumer's understanding of it. Many firms tailor their warnings to the lowest common denominator, and some use pictographs because some consumers cannot read. The adequacy of warnings and instructions is evaluated by the courts.

*Design defects* include both those that are knowable and in some cases those that are unknowable — for example, because of the limitations of science at the time the product was manufactured. Manville was held liable for some asbestos-related injuries because of a failure to warn even though the court concluded that the danger was unknown to science at the time and thus the company could not have warned against it.[26] A defense that a firm used *state-of-the-art design* may not prevail when a standard of strict liability is applicable.[27] Producers have thus been held liable for injuries from "defects" that were neither knowable nor preventable.

Warnings about the product's proper and intended use may not protect producers from liability. Proper and intended use is an imprecise concept. Is the proper and intended use of a screwdriver only to turn screws, or does it include opening paint cans and serving as a chisel? Because a product such as a screwdriver can be anticipated to

---

**FIGURE 12-6  Strict Liability Section 402A of the *Second Restatement of Torts* (1965)**

(1) One who sells any product in a defective condition unreasonably dangerous to the user or consumer or to his property is subject to liability for physical harm thereby caused to ultimate user or consumer, or to his property, if (a) the seller is engaged in the business of selling such a product, and (b) it is expected to and does reach the user or consumer without substantial change in the condition in which it was sold.

(2) The rule in Subsection (1) applies though (a) the seller has exercised all possible care in the preparation and sale of his product, and (b) the user or consumer has not bought the product from or entered into any contractual relation with the seller.

---

[25]A restatement is a collection of the rules established through court decisions, prepared by the American Law Institute, an association of legal scholars. A restatement is intended to reflect the case law in a majority of the states. A restatement is not itself the law but instead provides guidance to plaintiffs, defendants, and the court in reasoning about particular cases.
[26]*Beshuda v. JohnsManville Prods. Corp.,* 90 N.J. 191, 447 A.2d 539 (1982).
[27]Some states allow state-of-the-art defenses.

be used for a variety of purposes, courts have assigned to producers the duty to *anticipate misuse.* A manufacturer of a pickup truck, for example, was held liable for an injury caused by a rollover when a user attached a camper that exceeded the truck's stated carrying capacity.[28]

Since the *Restatement (Second),* products liability has become both more important and increasingly controversial as courts have addressed a variety of difficult issues. In 1998 the American Law Institute issued the *Restatement (Third) of Torts: Product Liability* to reflect changes in the law as developed in the states. The *Restatement (Third)* is itself controversial; for example, it does not reflect the law in California and Oregon, and the Supreme Court in Connecticut has rejected the restatement as it pertains to design defects. How influential it will eventually be is unclear.

The *Restatement (Third)* distinguishes between manufacturing defects, design defects, and inadequate instructions and warnings defects. Strict liability applies only to manufacturing defects and applies "even though all possible care was exercised." A design is defective if a "reasonable alternative design" is available to reduce or avoid a foreseeable risk. The burden is assigned to the plaintiff to show that there is a reasonable alternative design. This assignment represents a departure from the law in many if not most states and makes establishing liability considerably more difficult for the plaintiff. The *Restatement (Third)* also requires that an improved design be used rather than a warning to reduce or avoid a foreseeable risk. It also states that a manufacturer has a duty to warn if a risk is identified after the sale.

## Allowable Defenses Under Strict Liability

Some defenses are allowed under strict liability, but they vary among the states. In all of these defenses, the burden of proof is on the defendant. The only absolute defense is that the product was not associated with the injury or was not the *proximate cause of* the injury. The concept of proximate cause was broadened considerably in the DES case to that of probabilistic causation. A woman whose mother had taken the drug DES during her pregnancy developed cancer over 20 years later.[29] The woman did not know which of several manufacturers had produced the DES her mother had taken, but the court held for her and apportioned damages among the producers according to their market share.[30] By the 1990s, third-generation DES lawsuits were being filed as granddaughters of women who had taken DES sought compensation.

The other defenses are not absolute. One is based on the *assumption of risk* by the consumer. If a consumer voluntarily and knowingly assumes a risk, a producer may be protected. Such assumptions are routine for surgery and certain medications, but they may provide little protection if the patient did not understand the risk. The burden of proof is on the defendant to prove that the assumption was both voluntary and understood. A producer may also have a defense if the consumer accepted a known and avoidable danger.

As indicated in the statement of strict liability in Figure 12-6, a producer may have a defense if a product had been altered by someone other than the producer in a manner

---

[28] In recent years companies have substantially increased their warnings. After an award to a woman scalded when she spilled a cup of its coffee, McDonald's added the warning on its cup, "Caution: Contents Hot." A manufacturer of a Batman costume warned, "Parents: Please exercise caution . . . cape does not enable user to fly."

[29] The FDA banned DES in 1971 as a result of an abnormal cancer rate in the daughters of women who had used the drug.

[30] *Sindell v. Abbott Laboratories,* 26 Cal. 3d 588, 607 P.2d 924 (1980). In 1989 the Supreme Court let stand a New York court verdict holding DES manufacturers liable.

that caused injury to the plaintiff. A *correction of a defect* may also provide a degree of protection in some instances.

In some jurisdictions a defense of *contributory negligence* on the part of the plaintiff is allowed. The burden of proof is on the defendant to show that the plaintiff was negligent in the use of the product; if proven, the defendant may avoid damages or have the assessed damages reduced by the plaintiff's share of responsibility.[31] Producers are generally held responsible for anticipating misuse, however.

A producer may be able to use *disclaimers* to limit liability, but the courts have held some disclaimers to be invalid. The Magnuson-Moss Act prohibits producers from disclaiming express warranties and any implied warranties that go with it. Disclaiming is a concept from contract law and as such is intended to be a factor over which the parties bargain. Otherwise the courts may hold that it is invalid. One type of disclaimer that is upheld by courts is that associated with an assumption of risk in which a consumer voluntarily and knowledgeably agrees to bear the risk. Courts, however, typically examine closely whether the consumer actually understood the disclaimer. Disclaimers that limit the remedies available to parties, such as the right to sue, may not be upheld.

Compliance with government safety standards can in some cases be used as a defense, although such standards may be viewed by the courts as providing only the minimum level of safety. In a potentially important decision in 1993, the Court of Appeals ruled that FDA approval of a medical device and its subsequent monitoring of the device precluded state lawsuits alleging negligence and breach of warranty.[32]

In most jurisdictions, products liability cases are covered by a *statute of limitations*, which is often 4 years. For capital equipment, a *statute of repose* serves the same function as a statute of limitations, but the time allowed is much longer.

## Damages

The principal form of damages awarded in products liability cases is *compensatory*—compensation for the loss incurred. The determination of compensation is straightforward in the case of property that has a readily established value. In other cases measurement is more difficult. It is possible to determine the cost of medical care for an injury, but measuring pain and suffering or the loss of a limb or a life is more difficult. Juries do make such decisions, however. Moreover, trial lawyers have available detailed data on the damages awarded in personal injury lawsuits. For example, Jury Verdict Research (2001) annually publishes its *Personal Injury Valuation Handbook*, which provides data on awards in a variety of categories such as vehicular liabilities and products liability with breakdowns by type of injury. In 1999 the median jury award in products liability cases was $1.8 million compared to $500,000 six years earlier. Awards ranged from $11,000 to $285 million. Part of the explanation for the higher awards is that trial lawyers have shied away from cases they expect will yield only modest awards. Jury Verdict Research conducts statistical analysis of cases and awards and provides probabilities of a plaintiff victory and predictions of awards for particular types of cases. For example, the median jury awards for burns and leg fractures were $891,000 and $500,000 respectively. Most cases do not reach trial, and out-of-court settlements are substantially lower than awards in litigated cases, presumably because stronger cases are more likely to be litigated than weaker cases.

---

[31]See Cooter and Ulen (1988, pp. 354–360) for an analysis of the efficiency consequences of a contributory negligence defense. Negligence is not the same as misuse but is better understood as gross misuse.
[32]*King v. Collagen Corp.*, First U.S. Circuit Court of Appeals, No. 921278. The Supreme Court refused to grant *certiorari*.

In cases in which both the producer and the consumer are responsible for the injury, some courts assess *comparative damages*. If the consumer is found to be 30 percent at fault for an accident and the producer 70 percent at fault, the producer is assessed damages equal to 70 percent of the consumer's loss. *The Restatement (Third) of Torts: Product Liability* requires comparative damages.

Defendants often complain about the magnitude of some awards. The awards may reflect the sympathy jurors feel for accident victims and the deep pockets they see in firms. The awards in many of these cases are reduced by the trial judges or on appeal. Most cases are settled out of court with the settlement amounts not revealed. The largest settlement was in 1998 when a class action suit against Dow Corning involving silicone breast implants was settled for $3.2 billion.

The number of personal injury lawsuits of all types have declined in recent years, although class action lawsuits and "mass torts," such as those involving tobacco and asbestos, have increased. The overall decline in the number of cases in California, for example, has been attributed to several factors, including declines in accident rates, trial attorneys pursuing fewer but larger award cases, the use of alternative dispute resolution mechanisms such as arbitration, court decisions making certain types of cases more difficult to win, and tort reform. The size of awards and settlements has continued to increase. Settlements, awards, and court costs in asbestos cases have totaled nearly $54 billion, and projections are that the total will be over $200 billion. Eighty-five corporations have gone bankrupt as a result of the litigation.[33]

In most jurisdictions *punitive* damages can be assessed. The legal standard for imposing punitive damages is higher than that for compensatory damages and generally requires a finding of negligence and fault. This allows defendants to use defenses, such as state-of-the-art design, that may not be allowable under strict liability. Jury Verdict Research reported that in 1995 and 1996 punitive damages were awarded in 12 percent and 6 percent, respectively, of the products liability cases litigated. The median awards were $1.25 million and $2.5 million, respectively. In 1999 punitive damage awards increased substantially. The magnitude of some of the punitive damages awards has attracted considerable attention. In a case in which a Pinto's gas tank caught fire and caused injury, a jury awarded $3.5 million in compensatory damages and $125 million in punitive damages. The judge reduced the punitive damages to $3.5 million.[34] In 1994 the Georgia Court of Appeals struck down the award of $105 million in punitive damages mentioned in the Chapter 3 case, *General Motors Like a Rock (A)?*, involving an accidental death in a GM pickup truck with gas tanks mounted outside the frame walls.

## Imperfections in the Liability System

The products liability system has been criticized on equity, distributive, and efficiency grounds.[35] The equity arguments often express a belief that cases should be decided on the basis of fault and negligence. In particular, firms consider it inequitable to be assessed damages when there was nothing they could have done to prevent the injury. Objections have been made to the inability to use state-of-the-art design as a defense in cases governed by strict liability. In the absence of a statute of repose for capital equipment, this means that an injured party may be able to sue successfully for an injury caused by a product manufactured many years earlier when technological capabilities were more limited. The *Restatement (Third) of Torts* addresses this issue.

[33]See White (2004).
[34]See Cooter and Ulen (1988, pp. 403–407) for an analysis of Pinto cases.
[35]See Viscusi (1991) for an analysis of products liability and recommendations for reform.

The distributive objection is that the awards in many cases are too large and seem to provide a prize, as in a lottery, rather than providing compensation for actual losses. The deep pockets of producers are seen by some jurors as a means of helping those who were unfortunate enough to have been injured. Criticism has centered on damages awarded for pain and suffering, which some argue are often unreasonable and unguided by legal standards. Whether awards are too large is unclear, however, and limits on awards remain the subject of considerable disagreement.

Most products liability cases are filed in state courts, and trial lawyers shop for the state venue most likely to favor their cases. The state of Mississippi earned a national reputation for large jury awards to consumers, and many trial lawyers attempt to have their cases tried there. Venue shopping focuses on Mississippi's 22nd Judicial Circuit, which the American Tort Reform Association designated a "Judicial Hellhole."[36] The governor of Mississippi has pushed for state tort reform, citing not only the bad reputation the state has earned but also the business opportunities the state has lost. In explaining why Toyota had decided not to build a plant in the state, the company stated that "the litigation climate in Mississippi is unfavorable...." Similarly, the CEO of Caterpillar explained why the company was not expanding operations in the state: "Unfortunately, Mississippi's current lawsuit environment makes us very reluctant to consider expanding our activities in the state."[37] Mississippi took the first steps toward reform by eliminating joint and several liability, reducing the liability of retailers, and capping awards for noneconomic damages at $1 million except for medical liability, which was capped at $500,000.

As the Coase theorem indicates, the distributive consequences of a legal standard can be independent of their efficiency consequences. However, liability awards can force firms into bankruptcy or dissuade them from producing certain desirable products. Because a number of pharmaceutical companies had stopped producing certain vaccines as a result of liability costs, Congress passed the Childhood Vaccine Act of 1986, which established a no-fault compensation system and capped pain and suffering awards. Similarly, there might be no nuclear power plants in the United States were it not for the Price-Anderson Act, which limits liability in the case of an accident. In the aftermath of the September 11 terrorist attacks, President Bush issued an executive order that indemnified makers of smallpox and anthrax vaccines that contracted with the government in its effort to fight terrorism.

Some critics argue that the development of drugs to treat conditions associated with pregnancy has been chilled by lawsuits such as those involving Bendectin, a drug used to treat morning sickness. Congenital abnormalities occur naturally in about 3 percent of newborns, and pharmaceutical companies can face lawsuits if a mother used one of their products. As the silicone breast implants example indicates, liability cases can result in large settlements even when there is no scientific evidence linking a product to a disease.

In addition to concerns about the standards on which cases are decided and awards based, the liability system is costly to operate. Court costs and legal expenses for defendants are high, and under the contingent fee system, attorneys for plaintiffs typically receive one-third of any award or settlement. Of the $54 billion cost of asbestos litigation, approximately $34 billion has gone to lawyers (White 2004). Investigating the facts in a case can also be expensive. Products liability cases are frequently consolidated into class action lawsuits, which generally reduces the costs of litigation. The high cost of taking a case to trial encourages settlements, but it can also encourage frivolous suits that seek to extract a settlement from defendants who prefer to avoid the legal fees and court costs.

---

[36] Madison County, Illinois has also been called a Judicial hellhole.
[37] *Associated Press State & Local Wire*, April 28, 2004.

## EXAMPLE

## Silicone Breast Implants

In the 1970s and 1980s, 600,000 women received silicone breast implants in the United States. In 1982 a woman claimed that she became seriously ill when her breast implants leaked into her body. She sued and received an award of over $1 million. The Dow Corning Company subsequently was sued by 170,000 women, filing bankruptcy in 1995 as a result of a proposed settlement that collapsed shortly thereafter. Three other manufacturers settled the claims against them later in 1995. In 1998 Dow Corning reached an agreement with the plaintiffs in which it agreed to pay $3.2 billion over 15 years.

The litigation was coordinated by trial lawyers and was well orchestrated. The trial lawyers hired Fenton Communications to conduct a public relations campaign to highlight the claims of serious illness resulting from the implants.[1] The settlements reached were in spite of consistent scientific evidence that there was no link between the leaks and serious illness. The American College of Rheumatology stated that the scientific evidence was "compelling" that there was no link between implants and systemic disease. The Council on Scientific Affairs of the American Medical Association stated, "To date, there is no conclusive or compelling evidence that relates silicon breast implants to human auto-immune disease." The American Academy of Neurology stated that "existing research shows no link between silicon breast implants and neurological disease." Dr. Marcia Angell, executive editor of the *New England Journal of Medicine* and author of a book on breast implants, said that 15 scientifically valid epidemiological studies had been conducted and none showed any higher rate of illnesses among women with breast implants than women without them. She referred to the systemic diseases reported by women as "coincidental." Dr. David Kessler, who in 1992 as head

of the Food and Drug Administration banned the sale of silicone-gel implants and later became dean of the Yale University School of Medicine, said, "There's no evidence that they cause systemic disease."[2]

Citing a Supreme Court decision calling on judges to act as "gatekeepers" to rule out unscientific testimony and speculation in favor of "pertinent evidence based on scientifically valid principles," a federal district court judge hearing implant cases barred plaintiffs' expert witnesses from testifying that the implants can cause systemic diseases.[3] A special panel of independent experts appointed by the judge studied the issue for 2 years and in December 1998 issued its report concluding that there was no evidence that implants induce systemic diseases. The plaintiffs vowed to continue to press their cases.

The evidence continued to accumulate. A 1999 Institute of Medicine study found no increase in risk of cancer, autoimmune diseases, or neurological problems. A National Cancer Institute (NCI) study published in 2001 concluded there was no increased risk of cancer. Louise Brinton, an NCI researcher said, "[The study] helps lay to rest much of the concern."[4] Dr. Stuart Bondurant, chair of the Institute of Medicine committee, said, "We could find no evidence to support a causal relationship between the breast implants and any systemic disease. As far as I know there has been no information since the report was written that would naturally change that conclusion."[5]

In 2005 an FDA advisory panel voted in favor of the sale of the silicone breast implants of one firm and recommended further study of the implants of another manufacturer.

[1]Fenton Communications was the firm that orchestrated the nonmarket campaign against the apple-ripening chemical Alar discussed in Chapter 3.

[2]*The New York Times,* July 11, 1998. The European Union did not ban the implants, but in 2001 required that recipients be at least 18 years of age.

[3]Some women did suffer some scarring and hardening of tissue from leaks.

[4]*Milwaukee Journal Sentinel,* April 27, 2001.

[5]*The New York Times,* October 11, 2003.

A particular concern of business is *joint and several liability*. In a case in which several parties have a role in an injury, such as a manufacturer and a distributor or a manufacturer and a government, all may be held liable. A motorist who hits a pothole, loses control of the car, hits a telephone pole, and is injured may sue both the city government and the telephone company under the principle that the harm to the victim is indivisible.[38] In such a case, the damages awarded are allocated among the defendants in proportion to their responsibility for the injury. Comparative liability is used in all but six states and the District of Columbia. But if one of the defendants is unable to pay its share of the damages, the defendant with "deeper pockets" can be required to pay the entire award. This standard focuses on compensating the injured party rather than providing appropriate incentives for care.

Another criticism is that punitive damages awards are governed neither by statute nor clear constitutional guidelines. Instead, juries have been largely free to assess punitive damages as they see fit. The imposition of punitive damages without standards to guide their award has been a source of concern to both firms and jurists. In a concurring opinion, Supreme Court Justices Sandra Day O'Connor and Antonin Scalia, discussing punitive damages, wrote, "The impact of these windfall recoveries is unpredictable and potentially substantial . . . this grant of wholly standardless discretion to determine the severity of punishment appears inconsistent with due process."[39]

Although there are no explicit constitutional limits on punitive damages, in 1996 the Supreme Court threw out as constitutionally excessive a decision against BMW of North America in a case in which a jury awarded $4,000 in compensatory damages and $4 million in punitive damages because the paint on a new car had been retouched.[40] In an important decision in 2003 the Supreme Court overturned a punitive damages award that exceeded the compensatory damages award by a ratio of 145 to 1.[41] The court stated that the award was an "irrational and arbitrary deprivation of the property of the defendant." The court also stated that an award with a double-digit ratio was unlikely to be constitutional and that when compensatory damages are substantial an award "at or near the amount of compensatory damages" would likely be justified. The decision quickly had effects as the Court of Appeals ruled that punitive damages of $4.0 billion against ExxonMobil for the *Exxon Valdez* oil spill were excessive.

From the perspective of producers, damage awards are difficult to predict, complicating the estimation of the ex post consequences of their ex ante decisions. The insurance system allows firms to insure against that risk, but the insurance system itself is imperfect and costly to operate. Also, many firms are unable to purchase liability insurance. In response, Congress passed the Risk Retention Act of 1981, which allows firms in the same industry to form their own insurance pool.

The standard of strict liability is said by some to assign too much of the cost of injuries to firms and too little to consumers, distorting the incentives for care. This can cause firms to take more care and consumers to take less care than is efficient. The *Restatement (Third) of Torts* reflects this concern by allowing defenses in design defect cases. Efficiency is improved by allowing a defense of contributory negligence and assigning damages on a comparative basis. In an imperfect world, however, the Calabresi and Melamed principles indicate that liability should be assigned to that party who is best placed to evaluate costs and benefits and to induce the other party to take appropriate care. Producers are generally better placed than consumers for these

[38]See Cooter and Ulen (2004, pp. 362–64, 429–431).
[39]*Bankers Life & Casualty v. Crenshaw*, 486 U.S. 71 (1988). Quoted in Mahoney and Littlejohn (1989).
[40]*BMW of North America v. Gore*, U.S. Supreme Court, 116 S.Ct.1589 (1996).
[41]*State Farm Mutual Automobile Insurance Co. v. Campbell*, No. 01-1284, 2003 WL 1791206 (2003).

purposes, so efficiency may be served by assigning liability to producers rather than to consumers.[42]

The chapter case, *California Space Heaters, Inc.*, provides an opportunity to consider decisions on safety features in light of the products liability system.

## The Politics of Products Liability

The costs and consequences of liability cases, and the proportion of awards that go to trial lawyers, provide strong incentives to take liability issues into the legislative arena. Liability costs not only affect safety decisions, but they also affect the prices of products and in some cases whether products are produced. In part because of soaring liability costs, production in the small aircraft industry fell from 17,811 aircraft in 1978 to 964 in 1993. Cessna Aircraft stopped producing single-engine, piston-powered aircraft in 1986 because of liability costs. The plight of the industry led to enactment of the General Aviation Revitalization Act, which prevents lawsuits against manufacturers for accidents associated with aircraft more than 18 years old. When the law went into effect in 1994, Cessna announced that it would resume producing single-engine, piston-powered aircraft.

Producers of medical implants such as heart valves have been subject to numerous liability lawsuits. Fearing that they would be included as defendants, the suppliers of biomaterials began to stop supplying implant makers. The amount of biomaterials used in an implant is small and represented little loss of revenue to the suppliers. Implant makers and patient advocacy groups feared that a shortage would develop and worked for federal legislation shielding suppliers from liability. The Biomaterials Access Assurance Act was enacted in 1998.

Business has worked for over two decades for federal products liability legislation.[43] With Republican majorities in both houses of Congress as a result of the 1994 elections, business hopes for reform were buoyed. The American Tort Reform Association—which includes 300 nonprofit organizations, professional societies, trade associations, and businesses—has actively worked for tort reform. The 60,000-member Association of Trial Lawyers and its consumer advocate allies, such as Public Citizen, renewed their opposition to reforms and geared for another battle.

The foci of the federal efforts were (1) caps on punitive damages for small companies, (2) limits on the liability of wholesalers and retailers in products liability lawsuits unless they altered a product, (3) heightened standards for punitive damages by requiring evidence of "conscious, flagrant disregard" for safety, (4) restrictions on damage awards if the plaintiff misused a product or was under the influence of alcohol or drugs, and (5) a cap on noneconomic (pain and suffering) damages. Federal tort reform, however, succumbed to filibusters in the Senate and a presidential veto during the Clinton administration. In 2004 the House passed bills to cap pain and suffering awards at $250,000 and penalize lawyers who file frivolous lawsuits and engage in venue shopping. The Senate, however, did not act on the measures. Also, a filibuster in the Senate stopped a bipartisan compromise to move class action lawsuits from state to federal courts.

After the 2004 elections President Bush pledged to try again on tort reform. At an economic conference attended by the president, selected economists, and business executives, Home Depot CEO Robert Nardelli described the concerns of business: "What you have today is business on one side, and you've got the trial lawyers on the other side. . . . You've got deep pockets colliding with shallow principles." Todd Smith, president of the Association of Trial Lawyers of America, responded in referring to

---

[42]See Epstein (1980) for an argument supporting strict liability.
[43]See Cohen (1990) for a review of the early legislative efforts.

the president and his tort reform objectives, "He [unashamedly] advocates legislation that would protect insurance-industry profits and prohibit any punishment for the makers of dangerous drugs like Vioxx, while penalizing your mother for being abused in a nursing home or your daughter for having her baby killed by medical malpractice."[44]

In 2005 the Bush administration prevailed and congress passed a law requiring most class action lawsuits to be tried in federal rather than state courts. The law was intended to stop venue shopping. Tort reform at the state level has been more successful than federal efforts. Many states have acted to cap and otherwise limit damage awards. In addition to the limits imposed by recent Supreme Court decisions, 36 states have adopted some limits on punitive damages. In addition, many states have capped awards in medical malpractice cases in an attempt to slow the increases in the cost of insurance for doctors. Severals states have also abolished or otherwise restricted joint and several liability. The American Tort Reform Association (www.atra.org) tracks changes in tort law in each state. One proposal for reform is to have punitive damage awards paid to the government rather than the plaintiffs. This would preserve the deterrence effects of punitive damages without providing additional incentives for trial lawyers to file lawsuits.

In a study of the effects of changes in state liability laws over the 1970 to 1990 period, Campbell, Kessler, and Shepherd (1998) found that states that decreased their levels of liability awards experienced statistically significant gains in productivity of approximately 1 to 2 percent. Other studies have indicated that high levels of awards in liability cases reduce innovations.[45] As indicated above, businesses have shied away from Mississippi because of its litigation record.

Reform can also come from private litigants. A class action lawsuit filed in 2000 against DuPont alleged that perfluoractanoc acid (PFOA) used in making Teflon was harmful to humans. No evidence existed showing that PFOA was harmful, and DuPont maintained that it was harmless. In a settlement of the lawsuit, DuPont agreed to pay $22 million for attorney's fees and $85 million to the plaintiff and $5 million for a study to assess whether there is a link between PFOA and diseases. If a probable link is found, additional payments of up to $225 million will be made by DuPont.

## Summary

The law is an important institution for improving the efficiency of markets and private agreements. The United States has three basic types of laws. The first are those enacted by Congress, state legislatures, and local government bodies. The second includes rule making and decisions of administrative agencies, frequently involving an administrative law judge, as considered in Chapter 10. The third is the common law, which is law developed from the rulings of judges on cases brought by plaintiffs. Common law consists of the precedents established by those decisions and forms the basis for important branches of the law including the law of property, torts, and contracts. The common law evolves as courts address new issues brought before them by private parties.

The fundamental efficiency perspective on the law is provided by the Coase theorem, which identifies two basic principles. The first is that when transactions costs are low, efficiency can be attained by assigning the entitlement to either party to a transaction, agreement, or injury. The second is that efficiency can be attained with either a property

---

[44] *San Jose Mercury News*, December 16, 2004.
[45] See Viscusi and Moore (1993) and Huber and Litan (1991).

rule or a liability rule. When transactions costs are high as in the case of accidents, a liability rule is more efficient. In some cases regulation may be used to address a market failure.

In the case of real property a property rule is natural, since the parties can reasonably be expected to bargain to an efficient outcome. In the case of an idea or invention, an intellectual property rule is required to allow the creator to appropriate the returns from the creation. Appropriability is stronger the tighter is intellectual property protection and the higher the cost of replicating the creation. Intellectual property is protected by patents, copyright, trademarks, and trade secrets.

The law of contracts allows parties to make credible commitments to future actions. This can provide the needed assurances for noncontemporaneous trades and for reliance expenditures. Contracts may be unenforceable if they are made under duress, violate statutes, or are unconscionable. Breach of a contract can be efficient, and courts award damages for both efficient and inefficient breach and may order specific performance such as fulfillment of the contract. Damages may be awarded based on expectations, reliance, or opportunity costs, and the parties to a contract may stipulate liquidated damages. Contracts may be judged unenforceable ex post or damages may be reduced because of impossibility or a frustration of purpose.

Torts are civil wrongs, and strict liability in torts applies to manufacturing defects and in most states to many other types of defects. Under strict liability a producer may be held liable even if it has exercised all possible care. The social efficiency role of products liability is to provide incentives to producers and consumers to take appropriate care to avoid those injuries that are not too costly to avoid. The assignment of the entitlement to consumers is generally supported by the Calabresi and Melamed principles. In practice, courts have also assigned the entitlement to consumers to compensate them for the losses they incur. Under strict liability that compensation can be independent of fault. The defenses allowed under strict liability vary among the states and include the absence of proximate cause, the assumption of risks, product alteration, and contributory negligence.

Products liability law continues to evolve as courts consider cases involving new issues. This has led to a broadening of the definition of products liability and at the same time a narrowing of the grounds for lawsuits as reflected in the *Restatement (Third) of Torts*. The Supreme Court has also limited punitive damages. Tort reform has occurred in many states, and to a limited extent at the federal level. Business has sought federal legislation to limit liability awards and expand the allowable defenses, but the political competition over this legislation has been intense.

# California Space Heaters, Inc.

California Space Heaters had developed a line of unvented, convection kerosene space heaters using a new technology and was making preparations to sell them. For a modest purchase price the heaters could heat a room economically, without requiring a central heating system. A particular advantage of the heaters was that they allowed the consumer to focus the heat where and when it was needed. Because of high energy prices in the early 1980s, the demand for the heaters was expected to be brisk. Demand was anticipated to be particularly strong among low-income consumers and homeowners who had electric heating systems, especially in the East where electricity prices were very high. The heaters would also inevitably be used by people whose electricity had been cut off.

Although the heaters were very economical, there were safety hazards associated with their use, ranging from the risk of fire to adverse health effects from their emissions. The hazards were functions of the heater's design, its maintenance, and the conditions of use, including the fuel used. The company could incorporate a variety of safety features in the heaters, but safer heaters had a significantly higher cost and somewhat lower efficiency, requiring more fuel for the "effective warmth" produced.

In terms of hazards, a heater could cause a fire if it were placed too near curtains or furniture. The heaters could be designed so that the temperature could be as low as 320 degrees or as high as 500 degrees. The higher the temperature, the more efficient the heating but the greater the fire hazard, and the greater the risk that small children and others could be burned by touching the heater. The temperature in the heater depended in part on the wick adjustment, which could be controlled manually or by a thermostat. Fires could also occur from "flare up." Should that happen, closing the shutoff valve would extinguish the flame.

Ignition also posed a fire hazard. Electric spark ignition of the wick was safer than match ignition. Fires were a risk each time the fuel tank was refilled, particularly if the unit was already hot. This risk

could be reduced by incorporating a removable fuel tank that could be filled outside the house. A siphon could also be incorporated into the tank to lessen the risk of spills when using a funnel. Because kerosene expands when warmed, the tank should never be completely filled; instead, some air space should be maintained to allow for expansion. Kerosene itself was difficult to burn without a wick, but if spilled, a carpet or curtains could act as a wick. The units with electric spark ignition—a battery-operated ignition device—could be equipped with an automatic cutoff system that instantly stopped combustion if the heater were tipped over or jarred. These units could also be equipped with a power-loss shutoff system that stopped combustion if the batteries lost power.

In addition to the risk of fire, toxic emissions from the heaters posed a potential hazard because the heaters were not vented to the outside as were central heating systems and fireplaces. Inhaling noxious fumes could be harmful, particularly if substandard kerosene were burned or combustion were incomplete. Kerosene came in two grades: 1K, which had a low sulfur content and was appropriate for the heaters, and 2K, which had a higher sulfur content and was inappropriate. Grade 2K kerosene was used in diesel automobiles and trucks and was available at many gasoline stations, whereas 1K kerosene usually had to be purchased at a hardware or specialty store. Since the two grades of kerosene could not be distinguished without conducting a chemical test, consumers could not easily verify which grade they had purchased and had to rely on the supplier. Gasoline should never be used in the heater, nor should fuel oil, which has a significantly higher sulfur content than kerosene.

Proper ignition involved raising the wick, igniting it, and lowering it until the flame burned cleanly. Some consumers might attempt to regulate the heat by adjusting the height of the wick. If the wick were set too low, combustion was less complete and emissions were increased. A wick stop could be incorporated into the heater to prevent the wick from being lowered too far. Because the heater rested on the floor, it could be difficult to adjust the wick properly, requiring the consumer to bend low to see the flame.

The hazard from improper combustion and the burning of the wrong kerosene centered on carbon monoxide and nitrogen dioxide emissions, which posed particular problems for asthmatics, children, the elderly, and pregnant women. EPA standards for outside air were 9 parts per million (ppm) for carbon monoxide and 0.05 ppm for nitrogen dioxide.[46] U.S. Navy standards for submarines were 15 and 0.5 ppm respectively, and NASA's standards for the space shuttle were 25 and 0.5 ppm. The company's studies indicated that its heaters would not meet the EPA standards but would meet the Navy and NASA standards by a comfortable margin. The EPA had not issued standards for indoor air nor was it expected to do so within the next few years.

The risk associated with emissions could be reduced by using a kerosene additive that improved clean burning. The wick should be replaced each year, since the cleanliness of the burn depended on wick quality. Even if combustion were complete and the proper grade of kerosene were used, however, injury or asphyxiation could occur if the room were inadequately ventilated and the heater consumed too much of the oxygen in the room. A window should be left open to prevent oxygen depletion.

Kerosene heaters using old technologies had been banned by several states and municipalities, but most state legislatures had decided to allow the new-technology heaters because of the savings in fuel costs they provided. No federal safety standards for kerosene heaters had been promulgated, but such standards could be forthcoming if injuries resulted from the heaters. The cognizant regulatory agency was the Consumer Products Safety Commission (CPSC), but the CPSC had been immobilized recently and was unlikely to mandate standards, at least for several years.

The design alternatives available to California Space Heaters centered on the safety features that could be incorporated into the heaters. Table 12-1 lists the potential hazards and the design steps, beyond the least expensive model, the company could take to respond to the hazards. Each safety feature was expected to be effective in reducing the specific hazard. The production process for the heaters involved standard technologies and methods, so the chance of a manufacturing defect was slight.

**TABLE 12-1  Heater Hazards and Remedies**

| Potential Hazard | Design Remedy | Cost |
| --- | --- | --- |
| temperature adjustment | thermostat | $ 7.50 |
| overheating due to flare-up | automatic temperature shutoff | 22.00 |
| tank overflow | tank level gauge | 3.00 |
| tip-over fire | automatic cutoff | 8.00 |
| contact fire | low burn temperature | * |
| spill during filling | siphon filling system | 12.00 |
| ignition fire | electric spark ignition | 19.50 |
| fire during refilling | large tank | 12.00 |
| noxious emissions | removable tank** | 6.00 |
| substandard kerosene | none | |
| incomplete combustion | a) wick stop | 6.50 |
|  | b) electric wick adjustment | 32.00 |
| oxygen depletion | none | — |

\* Estimated loss in efficiency of $40 per year.
\*\* Only effective if tank is removed and taken outside.

---

46The EPA standard was set to protect individuals with angina while they exercised.

Consumers could also take care to reduce the likelihood of accidents and injury, such as making sure to always have the room properly ventilated. They could purchase the proper grade of kerosene and could use the "clean burn" additive that sold for $3.99 per 12-ounce bottle. The heater should be cleaned and the wick changed at least at the beginning of each heating season. The consumer should, of course, purchase the appropriate wick.

The least expensive model of kerosene space heater with match ignition could be manufactured for $44, and the standard markup was 100 percent for a discount store and slightly higher in an appliance store. With proper use, the least expensive model was safe. The demand for the low-end heaters was expected to be strong and price elastic. At a price of $88 sales could reach 2 million units per year. The safest and most expensive model the company could make would include all the safety features listed in Table 12-1. It could be manufactured for $189. The demand for the safest heater was expected to be limited. The venture capitalist backing the company commented, only partly in jest, that at a price of $378 the only sales would be to the wealthy for use in their ski cabins.

To indicate the savings attainable from use of the heaters, a marketing analyst compared the cost of heating a house to 68 degrees with heating it to 55 degrees and using a kerosene space heater to bring the living room up to 68 degrees. The estimated savings was $470 a year for a house in New England that used fuel oil; if the house had electric heat, the savings would be $685 per year. Smaller savings could be attained with a portable electric heater, which cost less than a kerosene heater.

The heaters could be marketed through various channels of distribution, ranging from discount stores to appliance stores to heating and air-conditioning shops. Appliance stores might be interested in carrying a full line of heaters, but discount stores were expected to be interested in only the least expensive model. Heating and air-conditioning stores were not

expected to stock the heaters but would order them for customers. Their customers were likely to be interested in the more expensive models. The channels of distribution differed significantly in their ability to provide consumers with information on safety features and proper use.

The company consulted a lawyer who indicated that products liability lawsuits were probable should there be injuries or adverse health consequences associated with the use of the heaters. Strict liability in tort would in all likelihood be the applicable liability standard, so the company could be held liable even if an injury were due to foreseeable misuse by a consumer. The costs to the company included the cost of liability insurance, legal and court costs, and the management time required by the cases. These costs could be reduced by adding more safety features to the model. The lawyer had investigated the cost of insurance and roughly estimated that insurance costs plus legal fees might be as much as $55 per unit for the lowest priced model and $10 per unit for the safest model given the estimated sales. The lawyer also estimated that the purchasers of the lowest-cost heaters were less likely to file lawsuits in the event of an injury because they were less familiar with the legal process.

The likelihood of an injury associated with a heater was difficult to estimate, but the company's engineers gave a ballpark estimate of one in a million of a manufacturing defect resulting in a death or a permanent disability from a fire. They estimated that the likelihood of a fire death from misuse was approximately five in one hundred thousand with the least expensive model over the life of the heater and four in a million with the most expensive model. The lawyer asked the engineers for estimates associated with each safety feature, but so far they had provided only two estimates. They estimated that adding electric spark ignition to the least expensive model would reduce the probability of a death by 50 percent, whereas electric wick adjustment would reduce the probability of a death by less than 2.5 percent. ∎

## PREPARATION QUESTIONS

1. How should California Space Heaters reason about its responsibility for the safety of its heaters and their use?

2. What safety features should be incorporated into the heaters? Should electric spark ignition be incorporated? Electric wick adjustment? What criteria should be used for those decisions?

3. What other actions should be taken in the design or marketing of the heaters?

4. How should prices be set; that is, on what cost basis?

# eBay and Database Protection

*I don't want to sound flip, but when people tell me, "The Internet's like the Wild West," I like to remind them we used to hang cattle rustlers in the Wild West.[47]*

—Edward Miller

The popularity of online auctions pioneered by eBay led not only to rival Internet auction sites for items ranging from antiques to automobiles and from real estate to time with celebrities, but it also spawned a group of "auction aggregators." Companies such as Bidder's Edge, AuctionRover.com, and ultimatebid.com searched Internet auction sites, extracted data, and provided it to their users. Bidder's Edge, for example, provided information on auctions in a variety of categories corresponding to those on eBay's front page. A person searching for a Roman coin on Bidder's Edge received information on coins available on eBay, Yahoo!, and Amazon.com. This provided comparative information and convenience to users, but it was based on information extracted from eBay's site. One of eBay's most important strategic assets was its database and the information it gained from conducting auctions. This information was invaluable for the design of auctions and for identifying service enhancements and other business opportunities, including partnering with other service providers. The aggregators threatened the value of that asset.

## eBay and Online Auctions

Pierre Omidyar founded eBay in September 1995 with the business concept of providing an Internet site, Auction Web, where person-to-person trading could take place. Buyers and sellers flocked to the site, and AuctionWeb became eBay in September 1997. eBay recruited Meg Whitman, who had been a general manager of Hasbro and president and CEO of FTD, to serve as president and CEO, and Pierre Omidyar continued as chairman. eBay's growth was spectacular. By mid-2000 eBay had over 15.8 million registered users who traded items in more than 4,320 categories. On any day approximately 4.3 million auctions were active on eBay's

site, with 500,000 new items listed every day. Nearly 1.8 million visits were made to its site on an average day, and the average visit was 20 minutes.

An online auction involved listing an item for sale with a closing date and time. The seller provided a description of the item, and most provided pictures. The seller could specify a minimum opening bid, a bid increment, and a reserve price that was not disclosed to bidders, although bidders were told whether the reserve had been met. A bid consisted of an initial bid and a maximum bid, which authorized eBay to increase the bid to the maximum if forced by another bidder. Often, there was a flurry of bidding just before the closing. Transactions between the seller and the high bidder were executed without charged small fees for listings and sales. eBay strove for a high level of user satisfaction, and its reputation helped maintain its leadership among the online auction sites that had followed in its footsteps. eBay also sought to ensure the privacy of its users. Its privacy policy was TRUSTe-approved, and eBay was a founding member of the Online Privacy Association.

eBay's revenue in 1999 was $224.7 million, and its net income was $11 million. The first half of 2000 saw a doubling of revenue from the previous year and net income increased by nearly 400 percent to $17.9 million. In 2000 its market capitalization reached $30 billion, reflecting its leading position in the online auction market and its seemingly unlimited potential. In spring 2000, however, its market capitalization fell to $16 billion with the market decline in high-tech stocks.

eBay's rivals ranged from small niche Web sites to Yahoo! and Amazon.com. eBay, however, was estimated to host nearly 90 percent of the online

eBay's principal asset was its ability to aggregate buyers and sellers on its Web site, for which it fied by their account names or e-mail addresses, and they earned reputations through feedback from their trading partners. The feedback was summarized and available to buyers and sellers.

eBay's involvement. Sellers and buyers were identi-

auctions in the United States and to have 85 percent of the market. eBay had expanded into international markets and was a leading online auction site in Canada, Germany, Australia, and the United Kingdom. It planned to expand into France and Italy. In February 2000 eBay entered the Japanese market, where Yahoo! Japan Auctions was the leader.

## Auction Aggregators and Database Protection

Bidder's Edge and two dozen other auction aggregators, or "auction portals" as some preferred to be called, searched across auction sites to provide listings and price information for their users. The opportunity for auction aggregators was provided by a 1991 U.S. Supreme Court decision (*Feist Publications, Inc. v. Rural Telephone Service Co.*, 499 U.S., 340) in which the Court held that "facts," even if collected through "sweat and effort," remained in the public domain. In *Feist* the court stated that "all facts—scientific, historical, biographical and news of the day ... are part of the public domain available to every person." This ruling gave auction aggregators a legal defense for extracting "facts" from eBay and other online auction sites.

The first auction aggregator appeared in the Spring of 1999, and in September eBay declared that the listings on its Internet site were its "property" and prohibited auction aggregators from searching its site. Bidder's Edge stopped its searches and took out a full page ad in *The New York Times* protesting eBay's move. Undaunted, other auction aggregators resumed listing eBay items on their sites, and seeing itself at a competitive disadvantage, Bidder's Edge did also.

eBay attempted to work with the auction aggregators and offered a license for free and a small bounty for each user directed to eBay's site. Five aggregators took licenses, allowing them to query in real time eBay's system as a user would. The license, however, prohibited copying data. eBay entered into negotiations with Bidder's Edge on a license, but little progress was made. As Kevin Pursglove of eBay explained, "This is a clear-cut example of one business trying to get a free ride off eBay's success. What we've been trying to do is reach out to these third parties and establish some appropriate business guidelines." AuctionRover, for example, had agreed to eBay's conditions and had a separate eBay tab on its Web site. Scot Wingo, CEO of AuctionRover, said, "We've taken a more pro-eBay approach. Our

competitors have taken a more, if you pardon the vernacular, 'screw eBay!' approach."[48]

Bidder's Edge obtained data from nearly 100 online person-to-person and merchant auction sites, providing users with an overview of available items, comparison information, and tracking services of items available for auction. Items available on eBay, however, accounted for 69 percent of Bidder's Edge's database. Instead of querying eBay's system to fulfill a user's search request, Bidder's Edge used a robotic program that daily copied approximately 80,000 pages, which were stored on Bidder's Edge's computers and updated recursively. A query by a visitor to the Bidder's Edge Web site was then answered by searching its rather than eBay's database. Since Bidder's Edge searched recursively, the information it provided to its users was necessarily stale and could be inaccurate. Bidder's Edge accounted for between 1.1 and 1.53 percent of the queries received by eBay and imposed a heavy load on eBay's computers. More importantly, eBay believed that those using Bidder's Edge and other auction aggregators' sites were not receiving the full value of its Web site and the eBay community.

eBay used a Robot Exclusion Standard and a robots.txt file that notified those searching its site that robotic searches were prohibited. Compliance was voluntary, and search sites such as Yahoo! and Google respected the Standard. Bidder's Edge, however, did not. eBay also had a security unit that detected any unusual number of queries from an IP number and blocked those suspected of violating its policies. Bidder's Edge used proxy servers to avoid eBay's IP blocks.

In addition to eBay there were other Internet service providers that sought to protect their databases. Reed Elsevier PLC and Thomson Corporation provided a comprehensive database of court cases and decisions. Reed Elsevier's Lexis unit was locked in a legal battle with Jurisline.com, whose founders had leased Lexis's 160 CD-ROMs for $2,365, copied them, and provided the data free on its Internet site. Jurisline contended that the data were developed from court records, which were public information and hence could not be copyrighted.

Other Internet service providers were concerned about database protection and access but had quite different interests. Virtually all companies that searched across Internet sites to bring information

---

[48]*MSNBC*, November 2, 1999.

to users wanted to maintain access to information on Web sites. These companies included America Online, Yahoo!, and other portals and search engines. In addition, shopping bots feared that they would be shut out of the information they used to provide price and other comparisons for consumers.

## Intellectual Property Law and Databases

Intellectual property law provided protection for information through patents, trademarks, copyrights, and trade secrets. The Coalition Against Database Piracy (CADP), however, argued that existing intellectual property laws provided little protection for databases. According to the CADP, "copyright law only protects a database to the extent that it is creative in the selection, arrangement or coordination of the facts it contains. Copyright law does not shield the database's factual content from thievery. Very few databases meet this 'creativity' requirement because all the things that make a database valuable and user-friendly—its comprehensiveness and its logical order (whether alphabetical in print products or random in electronic products)—are deemed to involve no 'creative' selection, arrangement or coordination."[49]

CADP also argued that the U.S. Anti-Hacking Statute as well as state contract and misappropriation laws provided inadequate protection. The Anti-Hacking Statute has "never been held to apply to a published database at all—no matter what its format. Nor would the statute apply in a situation where a database producer—like eBay—makes information available over the Web without a password or firewall protecting it." State contract law applied only to signed agreements. Moreover, "[m]isappropriation is an ill-defined state law doctrine and it does not provide database creators with uniform, nationwide protection."[50]

## Strategy Alternatives

One alternative available to eBay was to attempt to establish through the courts intellectual property rights to the data on its auctions. If successful this would allow it to block the auction aggregators. The *Feist* decision, however, placed a heavy burden on

[49]CADP Web site, www.gooddata.org.
[50]CADP Web site, www.gooddata.org.

eBay to demonstrate creativity. Another possibility was to use the Computer Fraud and Abuse Act to claim that the aggregators were committing fraud. If eBay decided to take legal action, it could direct its action against Bidder's Edge or it could name additional auction aggregators as defendants.

eBay could also seek a preliminary and ultimately a permanent injunction against Bidder's Edge and other auction aggregators. To obtain a preliminary injunction, eBay would have to demonstrate probable success in a trial and convincingly show that the absence of an injunction would cause irreparable injury. Although eBay believed it would prevail, it recognized that pursuing a court resolution could be both costly and time consuming. Moreover, decisions could be appealed, and in the rapidly changing field of Internet law, legal innovation could thwart what appeared to be the current law. In addition, since eBay was by far the largest online auction site, legal action might attract the attention of federal or state antitrust authorities and possibly raise issues of unfair business practices, the exercise of market power, or the use of the courts to stifle competition.

For several years companies, including Reed Elsevier and other publishers, had backed the Collections of Information Antipiracy Act to protect their databases. In 1998 the bill had passed the House of Representatives but the Senate had not acted. Another alternative for eBay was to actively to support the bill when it was reintroduced.

The World Intellectual Property Organization (WIPO) also sought stronger protection of intellectual property in light of the *Feist* decision.[51] A treaty negotiated under the auspices of WIPO provided additional protection for creative works and limited protection for online information that could be protected by copyright. Each signatory was to enact legislation to bring its laws into accord with the treaty, and the United States did so in the Digital Millennium Copyright Act of 1998. The Act established liability for online copyright infringement and protected ISPs from liability from material posted on their services, but it did not overturn *Feist*.

eBay could also attempt to use technology to thwart attempts to extract information from its database. A technology fix in the form of a firewall, however, could make its site less convenient for consumers. It could also lead to a technology race

[51]WIPO is one of 16 specialized agencies of the United Nations system of organizations.

as aggregators developed software to overcome the barriers erected by eBay.

## eBay and Public Policy

As with many high-tech companies, eBay had begun to address public issues. In the past 2 years it had established a Washington office and hired professionals to represent it. It had also established a PAC, the eBay Committee for Responsible Internet Commerce, which had contributed to members of Congress. eBay executives began to make Washington one of their regular stops on the East Coast.

In July 1999 eBay and eight other Internet service providers, Amazon.com, America Online, DoubleClick, Excite@Home, Inktomi, Lycos, theglobe.com, and Yahoo!, formed NetCoalition.com The coalition's mission statement read, "As the collective public policy voice of the world's leading Internet companies, NetCoalition.com is committed to building user confidence in the Internet through responsible market-driven policies; preserving the open and competitive environment that has allowed the Internet to flourish; and ensuring the continued vitality of the Internet through active dialogue with policymakers." Meg Whitman explained, "We want to be active participants in the dialogue that is addressing the critical issues facing the burgeoning Internet industry. As a group we can be a valuable resource and a powerful educational tool for policymakers and the public."

Within a few months, however, the "collective voice" split over the issue of database protection. eBay backed legislation to protect its databases, and other members backed rival legislation that, according to eBay, would provide little if any protection.

## Legislation

The Collections of Information Antipiracy Act was reintroduced in February 1999 as H.R. 354 by Representative Howard Coble (R-NC), chair of the Subcommittee on Courts and Intellectual Property of the Judiciary Committee. Seventy-five other House members co-sponsored the bill. The bill had been redrafted to address concerns with earlier versions, and the Judiciary Committee reported it in October 1999. The bill would provide substantial protection to those who collected information, including those that did so on the Internet. Facts were not protected by the bill and remained in the public domain, but the effect of the bill would be to overturn *Feist.*

The bill had not yet been introduced in the Senate, since Senator Orrin Hatch (R-UT), Chairman of the Judiciary Committee, had decided to wait until the House acted before taking up the issue.

The Judiciary Committee expressed the basic principle underlying H.R. 354.

Developing, compiling, distributing and maintaining commercially significant collections requires substantial investments of time, personnel, and effort and money. Information companies, small and large, must dedicate massive resources to gathering and verifying factual material, presenting it in a user-friendly way, and keeping it current and useful to customers. . . . But several recent legal and technological developments threaten to derail this progress by eroding the incentives for continued investment needed to maintain and build upon the U.S. lead in world markets for electronic information resources.[52]

H.R. 354 allowed an injured party to bring a civil action in U.S. court for actual damages as well as for any profits earned by the defendant and attributable to the action in question. An award for actual damages could be trebled by the court. Any person who violated the Act "for purposes of direct or indirect commercial advantage or financial gain" could be subject to a fine not to exceed $250,000 and imprisonment of not more than 5 years or both.

Interests benefiting from the status quo countered with a rival bill, H.R. 1858, the Consumer and Investor Access to Information Act of 1999, introduced in May under the sponsorship of Representative Tom Bliley (R-VA), chairman of the Commerce Committee. The bill was referred to the Commerce Committee and reported in October.

H.R. 1858 focused on the value of information to consumers and the benefits to Internet users from being able to obtain comparisons of information from different databases. The bill would proscribe "the sale or distribution to the public of any database that: (1) is a duplicate of another database collected and organized by another person or entity; and (2) is sold or distributed in commerce in competition with that other database."[53] Enforcement

---

[52]House Report 106-349, September 1999.
[53]The Act provided certain exclusions for certain news and sports activities, law enforcement activities, scientific and educational activities, government databases, databases related to Internet communications, computer programs, subscriber lists, certain legal materials, and certain securities market data.

responsibility would be assigned to the Federal Trade Commission. The bill also prohibited the misappropriation of real-time securities market information but restricted the ability of market information providers to control that information. This would protect the access of online brokers to financial market information. Yahoo!, America Online, research librarians, telecommunications companies, the U.S. Chamber of Commerce, Consumers Union, Charles Schwab, and Bloomberg L.P. backed H.R. 1858.

eBay viewed H.R. 1858 as worse than the current state of the law. Joining eBay in supporting H.R. 354 were Reed Elsevier, Thomson, the American Medical Association, the New York Stock Exchange, and the National Association of Realtors (NAR).

## Interests

The e-Commerce Coalition, with nearly 300 members, was formed to support database protection and H.R. 354 in particular. eBay was a principal member of the Coalition, which argued that H.R. 354 "would strike a balance between protecting the huge investments of e-Commerce database developers and maintainers and recognizing the need for continued open access to information. Thus, it is aimed at the misappropriation of collections of information, not at uses that do not effect marketability or competitiveness. Its goals are to stimulate the creation of even more collections of information and to encourage more competition among those collections."[54]

Online auction companies, Internet service providers, and publishers were not the only ones concerned about their databases. One of the largest and most valuable databases was the Multiple Listing Service of real estate properties. Dennis R. Cronk, president of NAR, stated, "The piracy of online data poses a threat to everyone who is using the Internet to gain real estate information."[55] The NAR was capable of generating considerable grassroots support for, or opposition to, pending legislation.

Companies providing print databases also sought protection. Fifteen companies and associations formed the CADP to work in support of H.R. 354 and against H.R. 1858. The CADP argued that H.R. 354 was pro-Internet and pro-consumer, and it established an Internet site gooddata.org to provide

[54] www.theecommercecoalition.org.
[55] The NAR had 750,000 members.

information on the issue. The CADP argued that "H.R. 1858 only bars thefts that result in duplicative databases (i.e., those substantially similar to the original database). This allowed 'free riders' to avoid liability by the simple contrivance of cutting and pasting the stolen data so that the 'new database' is not a 'duplicate' of the original—a simple task today for anyone with a computer."[56]

In February 2000 the CADP released a public opinion poll in support of H.R. 354. Gail Littlejohn of Reed Elsevier stated, "This data confirms what we have known all along—the American people share the view that database piracy is a serious problem and that there is an urgent need to enact antipiracy legislation this Congress. . . . Consumer access to accurate information is being compromised when anyone can copy and steal a privately owned database with no fear of penalty. Without protection, databases are in jeopardy, and consumers will lose access to trusted information."[57] Harvard law professor William Fisher, however, said, "There are huge advantages to enabling people when navigating the Internet to have as much information as possible."[58]

The opponents of H.R. 354 argued that it would give too much protection to databases, effectively creating data monopolies. Brokerage companies, for example, were concerned about their ability to obtain and provide their customers with real-time stock quotes. Bloomberg feared that it would be prevented from providing stock price analysis: "The bill would mean that they would have absolute ownership right over something as basic as stock quotes." A spokesperson for the Chamber of Commerce said, "Factual data is the nuts and bolts of the information age. If you try to control its use, you're going to stifle commerce."[59]

NetCoalition.com also weighed into the battle. "As Congress considers the database issue, it must balance the objective of preventing database piracy with the equally important objective of preserving legitimate access to information, that does not conflict with the principles [in *Feist*]. Accordingly, additional database protection should be narrowly crafted to address specific, defined problems. NetCoalition.com believes that H.R. 1858 meets this test and, against the background of the many existing forms of protection,

[56] www.gooddata.org.
[57] Coalition Against Database Piracy, February 3, 2000.
[58] *Fortune*, June 26, 2000, p. 200.
[59] *The New York Times*, June 6, 2000.

achieves the necessary balance between protection and access."[60] In February, 2000, NetCoalition.com wrote to every member of the House urging them to support H.R. 1858 and to oppose H.R. 354.

Matthew Rightmire, director of business development of Yahoo!, argued, "H.R. 1858 has a critical provision which protects Yahoo! and other search engines against liability for linking to or listing categories of data. Absent such a provision, Yahoo! and others could be liable simply for acting like a card catalogue for facts and information available on the Internet."[61] He added, "Yahoo! is somewhat uniquely positioned to comment on this issue. We have spent and continue to spend a great deal of effort developing our own databases. At the same time, we aggregate and disseminate large amounts of information. In our view, legislating on the availability of information is not unlike two porcupines making love: it must be done very carefully. And, in both cases, there are significant unintended consequences which must be avoided."

## Database Protection in the European Union

The European Union (EU) adopted a Directive on the Legal Protection of Databases, effective January 1998.[62] For EU citizens and firms the Directive established copyright protection for "the intellectual creation involved in the selection and arrangement of materials" and established a 15-year *sui generis* (specific to the investment) right for an investment "in the offering, verification or presentation of the contents of a data base." This *sui generis* right effectively established the sweat of the brow doctrine for databases developed within the EU.

Henry Horbaczewski, testifying on behalf of the CADP, stated, "CADP does not advocate

adopting a database protection law that mirrors the EU Directive but ignores traditionally accepted U.S. concepts of protecting intellectual property. Nonetheless, the United States database industry cannot endorse enactment of a law [H.R. 1858] whose deficiencies in regard to domestic protection also increase the discrepancies between U.S. and EU law." He also stated, "Without comparable U.S. legislation, U.S. databases will not be protected from piracy in Europe, thereby placing the U.S. database industry at a significant competitive disadvantage in the huge EU market. Each day that passes without fair, balanced and comparable U.S. legislation gives the EU database-producing industry another leg up on its U.S. competitors."[63]

## The Challenge

Its database and the community it had developed were important strategic assets for eBay, and its challenge was to protect those assets while allowing information to flow freely on the Internet. James Carney, CEO of Bidder's Edge, however, argued, "We're no different from any other search engine. Yahoo! and Lycos garner lots of information every day from sites without exclusive permission. If eBay is right and the courts agree, that would rip the guts out of the Web itself."[64]

Edward Miller, representing the NAR, recognized the reluctance of most members of Congress to regulate the Internet. He said, however, "I don't want to sound flip, but when people tell me, 'The Internet's like the Wild West,' I like to remind them we used to hang cattle rustlers in the Wild West."[65] ∎

SOURCE: This case was written by Professor David P. Baron based on public sources and interviews with eBay personnel. Copyright © 2001 by David P. Baron. All rights reserved. Reprinted with permission.

### PREPARATION QUESTIONS

**1.** How important to eBay is the protection of its database from auction aggregators and other search engines? In what ways do the auction aggregators harm eBay?

**2.** What strategy should eBay adopt to protect its intellectual property?

**3.** Should eBay take legal action against Bidder's Edge? If so, on what grounds should it file?

[60]NetCoalition.com.
[61]Testimony on H.R. 1858, House Commerce Committee, June 15, 1999.
[62]Parliament and Council Directive 96/9/EC.
[63]Testimony before the House Commerce Subcommittee on Telecommunications, Trade, and Consumer Protection. July 15, 1999 on H.R. 1858, the Consumer and Investor Access to Information Act of 1999.
[64]*Mass High Tech*, November 8–14, 1999.
[65]*The Wall Street Journal*, April 10, 2000.

4. Should eBay use technology to attempt to thwart the aggregators?
5. What are the possible consequences for the Internet and electronic commerce of H.R. 354 and H.R. 1858?
6. Would enactment of H.R. 354 establish monopoly rights to information and limit the availability of information to Internet users?
7. What specifically should eBay do to move H.R. 354 through the House? Should it attempt to mobilize the eBay community in support of H.R. 354?

# Obesity and McLawsuits

In 2001 New York trial lawyer Samuel Hirsch filed a liability lawsuit against McDonald's alleging that his 5 feet 10 inch, 272-pound client had become obese from eating at McDonald's and other fast-food restaurants. The man had continued to eat at fast-food restaurants despite two heart attacks. After dropping that lawsuit, Hirsch represented two obese teenagers who claimed to have eaten at McDonald's regularly for several years and to have developed obesity-related illnesses.

Hirsch was advised by professor John Banzhaf of the George Washington University Law School, whose students had earlier filed a lawsuit against McDonald's for claiming that its french fries were fried in vegetable oil when they were also par-fried in beef fat at the potato processing plant.[66] The case was settled in 2002 for $12.5 million. Banzhaf "teaches a unique world-famous courses—'Legal Activism' [Law 637], which has been dubbed 'suing for credit' and 'Sue the Bastards'—where his law students, which the press dubbed 'Banzhaf's Bandits,' learn to become public interest lawyers by bringing their own legal actions. . . . He and his students are widely known for bringing hundreds of innovative public interest legal actions. . . ."[67]

After their success in litigation against tobacco companies, trial lawyers sought a new mass tort, and obesity was their next campaign. Banzhaf said, "A fast-food company like McDonald's may not be responsible for the entire obesity epidemic, but let's say they're 5% responsible. Five percent of $117 billion is still an enormous amount of money."[68] The

Public Health Advocacy Institute of Boston held a seminar at Northeastern University on "Legal Approaches to the Obesity Epidemic." Brian Murphy, an attendee and a recent graduate of the Rutgers Law School, said, "It's a very important and pressing issue, and its outcome will be with us for years to come. I'm hoping to be able to build a career out of this."[69]

Lisa A. Rickard, president of the U.S. Chamber Institute for Legal Reform, stated, "Lawyers hungry for more money should resist the temptation to take a bite out of the fast-food industry. Overweight Americans will not find the solution to obesity in the courtroom but in making wise choices to eat smaller portions and healthier foods wherever they go."[70] Brendan Flanagan of the National Restaurant Association commented that "people who are filing these suits are trying to legislate via the court system."[71]

## Obesity

Interest in the obesity issue intensified after a government study revealed that Americans had become heavier and that obesity had become a serious health problem. A study released in February 2004 by the Centers for Disease Control and Prevention (CDC) stated that in 2000, 400,000 deaths were caused by obesity-released illnesses compared to 435,000 deaths caused by tobacco.[72] The Surgeon

---

[66]The Daily Buzz, www.foodservice.com, March 12, 2004.
[67]http:banzhaf.net
[68]*Time*, August 3, 2003.

[69]*Time*, August 3, 2003.
[70]Press Release, U.S. Chamber of Commerce, July 2, 2003.
[71]Associated Press Online, March 10, 2004.
[72]Obesity is associated with greater risk of developing type 2 diabetes, chronic lower back pain and joint disorientation, cardiovascular diseases, certain cancers, respiratory problems, and depression.

General estimated that health care costs resulting from obesity were $117 billion annually, and the Department of Health and Human Services began an advertising campaign promoting personal responsibility and urging more exercise and less eating. The U.S. government and the World Health Organization urged food manufacturers and restaurants to offer healthier foods.

The body mass index (BMI), defined as a person's weight in kilograms divided by height in meters squared, was used to measure obesity. A BMI in the 19 to 25 range was considered healthy, 26 to 30 was overweight, and over 31 was obese. The BMI had increased by 0.9 from 1971–75 to 1988–94, and the proportion of people considered obese increased from 15 to 31 percent from 1980 to 2000.[73] Sixty-four percent of American adults were overweight or obese. The average weight of an adult male had increased from 168 pounds in the early 1960s to 180 pounds at the beginning of the 21st century. The average weight for an adult female increased from 143 to 155.

Substantial increases in weight occurred throughout the 20th century with the BMI for people in their 40s increasing by 4 units.[74] This increase was accompanied by only a modest increase in calorie intake. During the last century, however, technological change reduced the strenuousness of work both in the home and in the marketplace. Another long-term factor was a substantial decline in the relative price of food as a result of technological progress in agriculture. Lakdawalla and Philipson estimated that in the post-WWII period approximately 40 percent of the increase in BMI was due to the expansion in the supply of food, and 60 percent was due to demand-side factors such as a decrease in physical activity.[75]

From 1977–78 to 1994–96 the average intake of calories increased from 1826 to 2002. Surveys based on food diaries indicated that the increase did not come from meals but instead from snacks between meals. Cutler, Glaeser, and Shapiro concluded. "Fast food has certainly increased, from about 60 calories per day to over 200 calories per day. But this increase is largely at formal meals, where it has been offset by reduced home consumption."[76] They concluded that "the evidence also rules out the view that fattening meals at fast-food restaurants have made America obese." Their explanation for the increase in obesity was that technological change had led Americans to switch from home-prepared food to mass-produced food. For example, the total potato consumption in the United States increased by 30 percent from 1977 to 1995 as a result of improved technologies for producing potato chips and french fries. The lower cost of mass-produced food also led to greater consumption.

In a report prepared for the U.S. Chamber of Commerce, Todd Buchholz argued that the increase in obesity was caused by a variety of factors, including the lower real price of food, changes in the nature of work, and the failure to exercise more as the calorie intake increased.[77] Buchholz reported that in 1961 consumers spent 17 percent of their income on food and in 2001 spent 10 percent. He also cited U.S. Department of Agriculture (USDA) data indicating that the ratio of the prices of restaurant meals to supermarket prices had declined from 1.82 in 1986 to 1.73 in 2001. Moreover, a smaller percent of people were employed in jobs requiring physical work than in the past. Buchholz also argued that fast food meals derived fewer of their calories from fat than "a typical home meal from 1977–78."

Buchholz argued that the greatest increase in BMI from 1971–75 to 1988–94 was accounted for by college educated people rather than those who had a high school education or less. On average Americans were consuming 200 more calories a day and not compensating for it with exercise. The USDA's "Continuing Survey of Food Intakes by Individuals" indicated that Americans were not eating larger meals but instead were eating more between meals.

[73]Cutler, Glaeser, and Shapiro concluded that demographic changes did not explain the increase in obesity. David M. Cutler, Edward L. Glaeser, and Jesse M. Shapiro, "Why Have Americans Become More Obese?" Working paper, National Bureau of Economic Research, nd.
[74]Dora Costa and R. Steckel. "Long-Term Trends in Health, Welfare, and Economic Growth in the United States." NBER Historical Working Paper No. 76. National Bureau of Economic Research, Cambridge, MA. 1995.
[75]Darius Lakdawalla and Tomas Philipson. "The Growth of Obesity and Technological Change: A Theoretical and Empirical Examination." Working Paper 8946, National Bureau of Economic Research, Cambridge, MA, May 2002.

[76]Cutler, Glaeser, and Shapiro, op. cit.
[77]Buchholz, Todd G. "Burger, Fries and Lawyers: The Beef Behind Obesity Lawsuits," U.S. Chamber of Commerce and the U.S. Chamber Institute for Legal Reform, July 2, 2003.

## McDonald's Market Response to the Obesity Issue

For nearly 20 years McDonald's had provided nutrition information in each of its restaurants, but it did not provide information for individual menu items. After the government reports on obesity, McDonald's announced that it was discontinuing its supersize meals to simplify its menus. It also introduced the "Go Active" meal with a salad, water, a pedometer, and an activity log, an all-white-meat chicken McNugget, and other healthier items. McDonald's, the International Olympic Committee, and the American College of Sports Medicine opened a Web site, www.goactive.com. McDonald's also introduced an educational campaign, Real Life Choices, about how to track diets and put menu items into three categories: Watching Calories, Watching Fat, and Watching Carbohydrates.[78] McDonald's also provided nutritional information on its Web site. Chuck Horton of Virginia commented, "If I want to eat healthy, I'll eat at home. I come to McDonald's for one reason: the fries. . . . I think this healthy eating thing has gone too far."[79]

## Obesity Lawsuits

In dismissing the case brought by Hirsch on behalf of the two teenagers, U.S. District Court Judge Robert W. Sweet wrote "that the dangers of over-consumption of . . . high-in-fat foods, such as butter, are well-known. Thus any liability based on over-consumption is doomed if the consequences of such over-consumption are common knowledge. . . . Thus, in order to state a claim, the Complaint must allege either that the attributes of McDonald's products are so extraordinarily unhealthy that they are outside the reasonable contemplation of the consuming public or that the products are so extraordinarily unhealthy as to be dangerous in their intended use. The Complaint—which merely alleges that the foods contain high levels of cholesterol, fat, salt and sugar, and that the foods are therefore unhealthy—fails to reach this bar."[80] He also wrote that under New York law, "The standard for whether an act or practice is misleading is objective, requiring a showing that a reasonable consumer would have been misled by the defendant's conduct."[81]

Judge Sweet, however, left the door open for a lawsuit based on showing that fast food was addictive or that it was deceptive because it contained more harmful content than consumers anticipated. He wrote that "Chicken McNuggets, rather than being merely chicken fried in a pan, are a McFrankenstein creation of various elements not utilized by the home cook." Judge Sweet also stated that this lawsuit could "spawn thousands of similar 'McLawsuits' against restaurants."

## Strategy Alternatives

To deal with the McLawsuits, McDonald's and other restaurants could continue to defend themselves in court on a case-by-case basis. Cases could be brought in both state and federal courts, and the incentive for trial lawyers was to attempt to qualify for a class action lawsuit.

Some state courts were believed to be friendlier than federal courts to plaintiffs. Mississippi in particular had been a favorite venue for trial lawyers, who would shop in the state for plaintiffs whom they could represent. A study by Harris Interactive for the U.S. Chamber of Commerce and the U.S. Chamber Institute for Legal Reform concluded that Mississippi had the worst, most unfair liability system among the 50 states.[82] The new governor of Mississippi had campaigned on the theme that the state had earned a reputation as hostile to business, which discouraged companies from locating in the state. The governor sought legislation to limit and cap tort awards. Many states had placed caps on medical malpractice awards, and in tort cases states had imposed limits on punitive awards. A number of states also adopted liability standards based on comparative liability and had narrowed and limited joint and several liability.

McDonald's could also seek legislation to shield restaurants and food processors from liability. Legislation could be pursued in federal or state legislatures. The House of Representatives, whose

[78] PRNewswire, January 6, 2004.
[79] Associated Press Online, April 16, 2004.
[80] Pelman v. McDonald's Corporation, 2003 U.S. Dist. Lexis 707, 13.

[81] Second Opinion in Pelman v. McDonald's, September 3, 2003.
[82] Harris Interactive, Inc. "State Liability Ranking Study." U.S. Chamber of Commerce and the U.S. Chamber Institute for Legal Reform, March 8, 2004.

members faced reelection every 2 years, were often responsive to issues that appeared to be popular with voters. The House quickly passed the Personal Responsibility in Food Consumption Act, dubbed the cheeseburger bill, on a 276–139 vote. The bill provided protection from obesity and weight-based lawsuits unless the weight gain had been due to the violation of a state or federal law. Author of the bill Ric Keller (R-FL) said, "We need to get back to the old-fashioned principles of common sense and personal responsibility and get away from this new culture where everybody plays the victim and blames other people for their problems."[83] James Sensenbrenner (R-WI) was more direct, stating that "fat people should 'look in the mirror' and that parents need to monitor children's eating habits to make sure that 'little Johnny' doesn't become 'big Johnny.'"[84] House Speaker Dennis Hastert (R-IL) commented, "We as Americans need to realize that suing your way to better health is not the answer. Trial lawyers need to stop encouraging consumers to blame others for the consequences of their actions just so they can profit from frivolous lawsuits against restaurants."[85] The White House added, "Food manufacturers and sellers should not be held liable for injury because of a person's consumption of legal, unadulterated food and a person's weight gain or obesity."[86] During floor debate on the bill representatives cited a Gallup poll indicating that 89 percent of those surveyed "oppose the idea of holding fast food companies legally responsible for the diet-related health problems of fast food junkies." The bill had also been introduced in the Senate, but the Senate was often less willing to go along with such measures than was the House.

Commenting on the cheeseburger bill, Representative James McGovern (D-MA) said, "It protects an industry that doesn't need to be protected at this particular point and we're dealing with a problem that doesn't exist. The problem that does exist is that we have an obesity problem in this country."[87] Neil Barnard, president of the Physicians Committee for Responsible Medicine, commented, "[The bill] is an unsavory attempt to protect corporate profits at the expense of

American health. The bill strips the public of its right to seek any redress against food manufacturers for their contribution to the obesity crisis, and the related epidemics of heart disease and diabetes. Given that we are just now beginning to discover the industry's involvement, granting them sweeping immunity is, at best, dangerously short-sighted."[88] Ben Cohen of the Center for Science in the Public Interest (CSPI) argued, "If Congress really believed in personal responsibility, it would help them make more responsible choices by passing legislation that would require fast food chains to post signs showing the calorie count for each item on their menu."[89]

The restaurant industry backed the Commonsense Consumption Act, the state version of the cheeseburger bill, which would shield restaurants and food processors from liability. As of mid-2004 the cheeseburger bill had been introduced in 23 state legislatures, and 12 had enacted it.

The public attention to the obesity issue led to the introduction of the Menu Education and Labeling Act (MEAL) in the House and the Senate in November 2003.[90] The so-called McMenu bills applied to chains with 20 or more locations operating under one trade name. The Senate bill required disclosure "in a statement adjacent to the name of the food on any menu listing the food for sale, or by any other means approved by the Secretary [of Health and Human Services], the number of calories, grams of saturated fat plus trans fat, and milligrams of sodium contained in a serving of the food, offered for sale, in a clear and conspicuous manner" and "information, specified by the Secretary by regulation, designed to enable the public to understand, in the context of a total daily diet, the significance of the nutrition information that is provided."

In April 2004 Ruby Tuesday, Inc. began providing nutritional information on its menus for every item served. The nutrition analysis cost the 750-restaurant chain $650 per menu item, and whenever the chain changed a portion size for an item, it would have to determine the nutritional information and reprint the menus. Moreover, the company found that customers' ordering was unaffected by the information. After 4 months the company stopped providing

---

83 The Daily Buzz, www.foodservice.com, March 11, 2004.
84 The Daily Buzz, www.foodservice.com, March 11, 2004.
85 Associated Press Online, March 10, 2004.
86 Associated Press Online, March 10, 2004.
87 Associated Press Online, March 10, 2004.

88 The Daily Buzz, www.foodservice.com, March 9, 2004.
89 The Daily Buzz, www.foodservice.com, March 11, 2004.
90 The CSPI supported the MEAL bill.

nutritional information on its menus and substituted cards at every table with the information. For years McDonald's had provided nutritional information on a placard in each restaurant, and in 2004 began to provide that information on tray liners.[91]

The fast-food industry also faced the possibility that state attorneys general would use the same strategy they used against the tobacco industry by filing lawsuits seeking reimbursement for Medicare costs of obese people.

Later in the year the CDC concluded that its estimate of the number of deaths from obesity contained errors and stated that it would substantially revise downward its estimate. Other researchers were also concerned about the CDC's estimates and criticized the assumptions on which the estimates were prepared, suggesting that the actual number of deaths was far lower. For example, the death rates used by the CDC were based on people who became obese early in their life, whereas many people became obese later in life. Their death rates from obesity were believed to be considerably lower. ∎

SOURCE: This case was written by Professor David P. Baron based on public sources. Copyright © 2004 by David P. Baron. All rights reserved. Reprinted with permission.

## PREPARATION QUESTIONS

1. Given the *Restatement (Second) of Torts*, assess the likelihood of a plaintiff prevailing against McDonald's on an obesity lawsuit.
2. How would the doctrine of comparative liability address the obesity issue?
3. Is McDonald's likely to prevail in the courts?
4. Should McDonald's portray the lawsuits as being led by trial lawyers eager for large fees?
5. What market and nonmarket strategies should McDonald's use to address the obesity issue?
6. Should McDonald's fund research on a possible obesity–fast food link, such as addiction? If so, should it pledge in advance to release the results of the research regardless of the results? Should it instead require the researchers to sign a nondisclosure agreement so that it could keep the results secret in the event that they supported a possible link?
7. In which institutional arenas is McDonald's most likely to be successful?

# CHAPTER 13

# Information Industries and Nonmarket Issues

## Introduction

Information has become an important product, and the information industries have been a major source of growth in the past two decades. The Internet is a powerful information network that has had major economic and social impacts. The Internet allows communication of information among remote users, serves as a platform for online markets, and provides opportunity to individuals and businesses. Despite the bursting of the dotcom bubble, the potential for commercial activity on the Internet remains enormous. What has proven to be difficult is how to capture value from that potential. One fundamental problem stems from the public goods nature of information. Information is costly to produce, but once it has been produced it is cheap to reproduce and transmit.

Associated with the promise and reality of the Internet are nonmarket issues that pose challenges for business, government, and individuals. The Internet is a network, and associated with networks are economics quite different from that in markets for physical goods. A number of lines of business, both online and off-line, are characterized by network externalities, and complementary goods make compatibility and standardization important. This can mean that a market tips, leaving one firm with the bulk of the market; that is, the market is winner-take-all or at least winner-take-most. The market for desktop computer operating systems tipped to Microsoft, the online auction market tipped to eBay, and the microprocessor market tipped to Intel. Winner-take-most markets pose a set of nonmarket issues including antitrust concerns such as those addressed in *The Microsoft Antitrust Case* in Chapter 9.

As considered in Chapter 12 the Internet allows the sharing of files, which has hurt the recording, music publishing and movie industries and threatens the fee-based services. This has raised intellectual property issues for both online and off-line companies. More fundamentally, the public goods nature of information raises the issue of the appropriability of the returns from the investment in developing information.

Substantial commercial activity has migrated to the Internet. Some of it consists of online versions of off-line mail-order and catalog sales and brick-and-mortar retailers, but much represents new business activity such as the online sale of books by Amazon.com and other companies. Some of the online revenue is taken from brick-and-mortar merchants, creating nonmarket opposition to online business. In particular, online transactions escape most of the sales taxes that would be paid on off-line transactions. The lost tax revenue to state and local governments has resulted in efforts to tax online transactions, as considered in the Chapter 8 case, *Internet Taxation.*

Online transactions require providing personal information to the seller, and that information can be valuable for a variety of uses. Moreover, browsing on the Internet is tracked via cookies deposited on a user's personal computer and by spyware and adware. In some cases that anonymous browsing data can be matched with personal information, as when users identify themselves by participating in a sweepstakes, a drawing, or an online poll. Online searches are monitored, as is some e-mail, to provide users with advertisements relevant to the interests revealed by the searches. Online privacy concerns have been raised about the use of both personal and anonymous information. These concerns can reduce commercial activity on the Internet, and the information industries have attempted to deal with these concerns through self-regulation in lieu of government regulation.

Hosting online auctions has proven to be a profitable business model, giving eBay a market capitalization of $30 billion. eBay has developed a huge online community of traders in the United States and many other countries, and that community is eBay's principal business asset. The community is composed of remote and largely anonymous individuals, and payments are made by buyers before they have an opportunity to physically inspect the items. These features would normally impede trade, but from the potential gains from trade and the development of trust among members of the eBay community and between community members and eBay as a company. The development and nurturing of a community are fundamental components of the success of Yahoo!, Amazon.com, AOL, and other online business, yet what allows those communities to function effectively?

This chapter is concerned with this set of nonmarket issues arising from the Internet and information industries, and the cases in this chapter and in several other chapters provide more detailed settings for these issues. The economics of the Internet and winner-take-most markets is considered in the next section, and the following section introduces the online privacy issue and the concept of self-regulation. The public policy issue of whether transactions on the Internet should be taxed is then considered. The chapter concludes by considering an online community and the provision of order for that community by hosts such as eBay. The chapter cases address the protection of online privacy, online communities, and e-mail advertising. Other cases about the information industries include the following:

- *Internet Taxation* (Chapter 8)
- *The Microsoft Antitrust Case* (Chapter 9)
- *Echelon and the Home Automation Standard (A)* (Chapter 10)
- *eBay and Database Protection* (Chapter 12)
- *The European Union Data Privacy Directive* (Chapter 15)
- *Sophis Networks and Encryption Export Controls (A)* (Chapter 17)
- *RFID Tags* (Chapter 20)

# The Economics of Winner-Take-Most Markets

In describing Microsoft's business strategy, CEO Bill Gates said, "We look for opportunities with network externalities—where there are advantages to the vast majority of consumers to share a common standard. We look for businesses where we can garner large market shares, not just 30% to 35%."[1] Gates was referring to properties of Microsoft's software products that yield increasing returns for users. This and additional features of the economics of software were central issues in the Chapter 9 case, *The Microsoft Antitrust Case.* Some of these features are also present in the chapter case, *eBay: Private Ordering for an Online Community.*

A product such as an apple or an automobile is said to have rivalry in consumption in the sense that if one person consumes or uses it, others cannot. One person's consumption thus precludes another person's consumption. One person's use of Microsoft's Windows, however, does not preclude another person from using it, since the cost of producing another copy is essentially zero. Although it is extremely costly to develop, it is cheap to reproduce once developed.

Software such as Windows often has another important property.[2] When an additional person uses Windows, the first user is actually better off because, for example, the two users can swap files. A third person using Windows provides even more benefits because that person can swap files with each of the first two people. The number of ways that two people can swap files is two, since one person can give a file to the other and the other can give a file to the first person. With three people there are six ways—or links—that files can be shared. With four people the number is 12. When there are $n$ users the general formula for the number $N$ of possible links is $N = n(n-1)$. For example, if $n = 4$, there are 12 possible combinations.[3] The value of Windows to any person increases when there are others who use it, and the more users, the more valuable is the product to all users. That is, the average number ($N/n = n - 1$) of links is increasing in $n$.

The property that the value of the product to each user increases the more people who use it is what Gates meant by *network externalities.* The term *network* applies to the underlying economics of a product, not to the hardware or software associated with the product. Network effects, or network externalities, are present when an individual's demand for a product is positively related to the use by other individuals.[4] Network externalities yield increasing returns on the demand side of the market. Network effects are also present in more traditional industries, such as transportation, but the development of industries such as computers, telecommunications, software, and online markets has been driven by these effects.

Many products such as software have another important property. Their value to a consumer is greater if there are *complementary products.* Windows is more valuable to a consumer if there is a word processor or e-mail program that works with it. Complementary products thus also create increasing returns on the demand side, since the greater the number of complementary products, the greater is the value of Windows. Both network externalities and complementary products yield *demand-side increasing returns.*

Complementary products require *compatibility* so that they may operate together in a seamless manner. Compatibility is facilitated by *standardization.* A common standard allows developers of software and other complementary products to write to a single platform. Although multiple standards could exist, in industries with network effects and demand-side increasing returns consumers have incentives to use products

[1] "Microsoft, 1995," HBS Case 9-795-147, Tarun Khanna and David Yoffie, Harvard Business School.
[2] See Saloner, Shepard, and Podolny (2001. Ch. 12) for a discussion of the economics of industries with demand-side increasing returns. Shapiro and Varian (1999) provide a comprehensive analysis of the market for information and the network economy. Saloner and Spence (2002) examine electronic commerce and provide a set of cases on e-commerce companies.
[3] This is known as Metcalfe's law.
[4] See Besanko, Dranove, and Shanley (2000), pp. 554–557, for an introduction to network effects. See also Shapiro and Varian (1999) for a treatment of competitive strategy in information and network industries.

compatible with those used by others. A common standard allows all the products to work together.

A standard can be *open* or *proprietary*. The advantage of an open standard is that software developers are more willing to write for an open standard because they face less risk of developing a product that cannot be used elsewhere. Linux is an open source system based on the UNIX operating system, and the number of users preferring it as an alternative to Windows has grown. The advantage of a proprietary standard is that it is easier to appropriate returns. Windows has become the standard to which software developers write, and Microsoft maintains it as a proprietary standard. Microsoft, however, makes its APIs (application programming interfaces) available to software writers to encourage the development of complementary products.

In 2000 eBay adopted a strategy to attract complementary products. It announced that it would make public its APIs written in XML so that Web sites could link to its online auction site. For example, sports Web sites could provide a link to eBay auctions for sports memorabilia, and Topps could provide access to eBay baseball card auctions from its site. Releasing its APIs also allowed independent software developers to write programs that benefited its community. More importantly, eBay hoped that its architecture would become the (open) standard and serve as an operating system or platform for electronic commerce. eBay planned to charge a licensing fee for its architecture as a means of appropriating returns.

Although it is more efficient to write software applications for one rather than multiple operating systems and although network effects are strongest with a single standard, this does not imply that the winning standard must be owned or controlled by a single firm. For example, technologies that become standards can be licensed by their owner. Even when standards are proprietary, competition to become the standard can be intense, and competition among multiple standards can persist when network effects are sufficiently limited, or offsetting factors sufficiently strong, to permit multiple networks to survive in the marketplace. AOL's and Yahoo!'s networks and Microsoft's MSN have survived, and Google has developed a network.

The presence of demand-side increasing returns means that the company wants as large a *user base* as possible, and as soon as possible, since the product then is more valuable to all. Moreover, the greater the user base, the greater the incentive for software developers to write to Windows. Microsoft could, for example, set a low price for Windows so as to gain rapid adoption and hence expansion of its user base. It could even be desirable for Microsoft to develop a browser and give it away for free to increase the number of users of Windows. And, since the cost of producing another copy of Internet Explorer (IE) is zero and a browser increases the demand for PCs and hence Windows, a negative price for the IE could be justified.

The threat to a user base is that users may switch to another competing product. If there are costs of switching, however, the user base may be *locked in*. For example, when databases are written for Windows, it can be costly to switch them to a Linux format. Similarly, if employees are trained on Windows and its complementary products, it can be costly to retrain them for a Linux system. Thus Windows is protected from competing operating systems by high switching costs. Even if Linux were the better operating system, it would be difficult to take users away once Windows established its user base. Linux has the advantage, however, of not being tied to a dominant firm.

These factors interact and may result in *positive feedback*. Software developers prefer to write to an operating system used by many people, and conversely the greater the number of popular software applications written for it, the greater the demand for the operating system. Thus, the larger installed base attracts software developers. The more compatible software is available, the greater is the value to consumers, and network externalities further increase the value to consumers. New consumers thus choose the operating systems, further increasing the user base, and the cycle of incentives continues.

This positive feedback may cause the market to *tip* in favor of one product. The classic example is the competition between alternative formats for videotape recorders. Sony introduced its Betamax format, and Matsushita introduced its VHS format. Content producers had a strong incentive to put their movies on a single format to reduce production and distribution costs. Similarly, videotape rental stores had an incentive to stock only one format, since that would allow them to hold less inventory. Consumers had an incentive to coordinate on the format for which more content was produced. They also benefited from demand-side increasing returns when more content providers and retailers chose a single format. In such a situation the market can tip in favor of one of the products. Videotape rental stores and content producers wanted to standardize on the format that would ultimately have the larger market share. As soon as they suspected that one format would win, they concentrated on that format. The VHS format appeared to be winning in the marketplace, and content producers, retailers, and consumers all focused on VHS. The market tipped. Betamax was then shut out and disappeared from the market, even though it may have been the better technology.

The possibility of tipping means there is a strong *first-mover advantage*. The first-mover has the opportunity to build an *installed base* of users before competition appears and may be able to attract complementary products and generate demand-side increasing returns. The first mover often has the best chance of having the market tip in its favor. For example, the online auction market in the United States tipped to eBay, which was the first online auction service. In Japan, however, Yahoo! Auctions was the first mover, and the market tipped to it.

A tipped market means that a single winner takes most of the market. Moreover, once a market has tipped, it may be difficult to unseat the incumbent. One possible means of doing so is to leverage from the installed base of users for a complementary product. For example, RealNetworks was the first mover in audio and video streaming on the Internet, and the market tipped in its favor. Microsoft attempted to change that by introducing its MediaPlayer, but the market remained tipped in favor of RealNetworks. Microsoft's next attempt to unseat RealNetworks was to integrate MediaPlayer with its Windows XP operating system, in effect giving away MediaPlayer for free. Microsoft thus was leveraging from its Windows operating system monopoly in an attempt to dominate another market. eBay entered the Japanese market late, and its hope of unseating Yahoo! Auctions was to leverage off its dominant market position in the United States and other countries where it was by far the largest online auction service. Its efforts were unsuccessful, and eBay withdrew from Japan.

In some markets, tipping may be irreversible due to lock-in or to a product becoming a de facto standard. A new operating system such as open source Linux, for example, has a considerable challenge in attempting to unseat Windows. Linux has a large number of ardent users, and some large users are concerned about being dependent on a monopolist Microsoft. Moreover, a number of foreign governments have been concerned that Windows has a secret "back door" that could allow the U.S. government access to their computer systems. Microsoft responded by offering discounts to governments and by establishing a Government Security Program. Participating governments are given access to much of the Windows source code and the code for its Office suite. The Chapter 17 case, *Sophis Networks and Encryption Export Controls (A)*, is concerned with security.

The economics of information markets has important implications for competitive strategy, and it also raises a host of nonmarket issues. Many of those issues revolve around antitrust concerns. For example, the practices used to compete for a user base could ultimately be anticompetitive. A firm could, for example, use predatory pricing, although when the marginal cost of production is zero it is not clear that giving away a product is predatory, particularly if the product is complementary to a proprietary product. Once a market has tipped, the winner has strong incentives to fend off new technologies that may threaten its dominant position. Microsoft belatedly recognized that the Internet and the Java programming language threatened its Windows monopoly by allowing software to be written for any operating system. Microsoft then engaged in a set of anticompetitive practices to stop the distribution of Java. This included producing the so-called polluted version of Java that would run only on Windows. *The Microsoft Antitrust Case* in Chapter 9 considers these issues in more detail.

## Internet Privacy

Privacy, both online and off-line, is like motherhood and apple pie. When asked in surveys if they want privacy, respondents invariably answer yes. When asked to list the issues they are concerned about, however, privacy is seldom mentioned by respondents. A survey of 150,000 Web sites by WebSideStory in 2001 found that fewer than 1 percent of Internet users blocked cookies when visiting a Web site. Zero-Knowledge Systems, whose software package Freedom allowed individuals to block cookies and protect personal information, found little demand for its product and shut down its Freedom Network because of a lack of revenue. In a survey of online purchasers, 43 percent responded that they would sell their personal data for a $100 gift certificate.

Many online customers, however, remain concerned about how their personal information might be used. Some of these individuals are reluctant to purchase online or to conduct Internet activities that require personal information. Yet catalog and mail-order companies thrive, and few people are reluctant to use a credit card at brick-and-mortar establishments. Moreover, a 2003 survey showed that 60 percent of adults believed that the posting of a privacy policy by a Web site meant that the site was not gathering or sharing personal or other information. Many sites share that information with business partners and others, as their privacy policies state.

In the United States Internet privacy has largely been governed by self-regulation by Internet companies, as companies have formulated privacy policies and established independent organizations to certify those policies. Moreover, government has been reluctant to regulate a rapidly evolving industry and technology. Perhaps the importance of the Internet privacy and broader privacy issues is indicated by the growing number of companies that have established the position of chief privacy officer. Some 40 percent of the *Fortune* 500 companies have a chief privacy officer. This section introduces the Internet privacy issue and the self-regulation efforts of companies and identifies a number of current problems. The chapter case, *DoubleClick and Internet Privacy,* concerns a company that planned to merge anonymous data on Internet browsing with personal information obtained online and off-line. The chapter case, *Google: Gmail and Privacy,* involves the design of an e-mail advertising service about which privacy concerns were raised.

Technologies other than the Internet also raise privacy issues. The Global Positioning System (GPS) can pinpoint the location of an object within 3 feet. This can be invaluable when a motorist seeks directions, but it also has the potential to provide the information to others. Similarly, antitheft tracking systems and telematics on rental cars provide location and tracking information and can detect if a renter has been speeding. Cellular telephone use allows location to be identified, and telephone caller ID provides information that could be used for a variety of purposes. The development of radio frequency tags and their use in products provide a myriad of privacy concerns, as considered in the Chapter 20 case, *RFID Tags.* The rapid development of information technologies will continue to generate a host of new privacy concerns.

Privacy issues associated with the Internet range from the use of personal information provided to electronic commerce sites by customers to the use of Web bugs that record who visits personal Web pages. DoubleClick used the banner ads it placed on a Web site to deposit a cookie, a text file with a unique ID number, on a user's computer. The cookie allowed DoubleClick to identify when that computer visited a Web site in its network. DoubleClick collected click-stream data and used that information to develop profiles of the visitors to a Web site, target advertisements on Web sites, and personalize advertisements to the ID numbers.

Spyware and adware are the second generation of monitoring technology. Adware programs are deposited on a user's computer, and in contrast to DoubleClick, which tracked visits to Internet sites that participated in its network, these programs can track each click a user makes when browsing anywhere on the Internet. Using these data the programs provide pop-up advertisements with messages tailored to the user's browsing. The programs of Gator Corporation and Claria Corporation are downloaded along with free Internet programs and record browsing activity that, like DoubleClick's system, is associated only with an ID number of the program deposited on the user's computer. The pop-up ads are popular with advertisers because the ads can appear on any Web site. Some companies objected to ads for others appearing while users browsed on their Web sites, and Hertz and Dow Jones filed lawsuits charging that the ads violated copyright and trademark laws. Gator and Claria programs were each deposited on over 30 million computers.

Whereas Gator and Claria are downloaded with a user's consent, spyware is a secret program that goes beyond adware and collects personal information such as passwords and credit card information. Privacy watchdog organizations along with many users have complained about the programs, and several companies have developed software to remove adware and software from computers. Privacy on the Internet involves a technology race, and adware and spyware companies have responded by better hiding their programs. CoolWebSearch adware can change its name and location on a user's computer several times a day, making it difficult to find and eliminate.[5]

Businesses are necessarily customer oriented and focus on the value or benefits they provide to customers, clients, and Internet users. Focusing on benefits, however, can cause one to overlook rights. Privacy advocates focus on rights rather than benefits. Those rights need not be established by government but instead can be established by moral principles. Some privacy advocates argue that an individual's privacy is protected by a property rule, using the terminology of Chapter 12. This would mean that an individual's privacy cannot be infringed without that person's consent.

Why a person has a privacy right and the nature of that right are moral questions. Conceptions of moral rights are developed in Chapter 20, and only some basic concepts are introduced here. Minimal conditions for establishing rights require that individuals be able to make knowledgeable choices for themselves regarding privacy. In the case of the Internet a basic principle is the *right to know*, and this right imposes duties on companies using the Internet. A right to know could pertain to what data would be collected, how it would be used, whether it would be shared, how long it would be stored, and how secure it would be. A second basic principle is *choice*; that is, choice of whether to have data collected. This could be based on either an opt-out or opt-in policy. A third basic principle is to be *free from arbitrary treatment*. For example, an individual could have the right to inspect the data collected and to correct any incorrect information. The chapter cases, *DoubleClick and Internet Privacy*, and

---

[5]*The New York Times*, September 19, 2004.

*Google: Gmail and Privacy*, and the Chapter 20 case, *RFID Tags*, provide opportunities to apply these principles.

Privacy has been the subject of considerable legislation, although none has established specific Internet privacy rights. The Privacy Act of 1974 restricted information gathered for one government purpose to be used for another purpose or shared with another government agency. For example, the Internal Revenue Service was prohibited from sharing income tax information with other agencies. In 1988 Congress enacted the Video Privacy Protection Act that prohibited videotape rental companies and service providers from disclosing information about rentals or requests by individuals. The 1994 Driver's License Privacy Protection Act prohibited states from selling drivers license information. The Fair Credit Reporting Act regulated the disclosure of credit application data and credit histories. The Electronic Communications Privacy Act prohibited unauthorized access to e-mail, and other statutes prohibited unauthorized wiretaps. In 1998 Congress passed the Children's Online Privacy Protection Act, which prohibits collecting information from children under the age of 13 unless authorized by their parents. In 1999 Congress passed the Financial Services Modernization Act, which limited disclosure of nonpublic personal information to nonaffiliated third parties unless disclosure and opt-out requirements were met.

Although there has been no legislation establishing basic Internet privacy rights, a variety of bills have been introduced in Congress and in state legislatures. Business has generally opposed these measures as unneeded and potentially harmful to the development of the Internet. A number of companies, however, would support federal legislation if it were needed to block states from enacting a set of dissimilar Internet privacy laws. Individual states have been hesitant to enact laws, however, because of concerns that they may be branded as hostile to the information industries. As an example of possible federal legislation, the McCain-Kerry bill introduced after the DoubleClick episode would have required clear, conspicuous, and easily understood notice and full disclosure of how personal information would be used. Internet users would be given an easy opt-out of any data collection. The bill also would grant a safe harbor to companies that complied with a seal program such as TRUSTe. Enforcement would be by the Federal Trade Commission (FTC), which could act if a company violated its privacy policy. The bill would also require state attorneys general to file privacy lawsuits in federal rather than state courts. The bill was never enacted.

The principal reason government has not enacted legislation to require privacy protection is self-regulation by companies. Companies argued that self-regulation was working and that improvements in technology were providing more ways for Internet users to choose the level of protection they preferred. Self-regulation generally has the following components:

- Policies and practices of companies
- Certification by independent, nongovernmental organizations; for example, the seal programs of TRUSTe and others
- Compliance through self-assessment, including in some cases public release of the assessment, and organizational arrangements such as having a chief privacy officer
- Complaint resolution
- Backstopping by the FTC authority over unfair and deceptive practices (e.g., stating a privacy policy and then violating it)
- Education and outreach regarding privacy protection alternatives
- Providing technology alternatives
- Monitoring of company practices by activist and watchdog groups
- Personal protection by individuals (e.g., setting a browser to reject cookies)

Self-regulation has so far been relatively successful in forestalling government action, although incidents, such as those involving DoubleClick, and certain programs, such as adware and spyware, provide motivation for government actions. In 2004 the FTC took the first public action against spyware by filing a lawsuit against the owner of two spyware companies charging "unfair or deceptive acts or practices in or affecting commerce."

As an example of a privacy policy consider the case of eBay.[6] To participate in an auction, either as a buyer or seller, a person had to become a member of eBay. The member agreed to abide by the eBay User Agreement and related policies and to provide personal information, such as name, address, e-mail address, and a credit card. A Privacy Policy posted on the eBay Web site governed the use of the information. The policy was a long, legal statement, but embodied the following core privacy values:

- We do not sell or rent your information to third parties.
- We do not give your personally identifiable information to advertisers.
- We let you select how you may be contacted by us when you join our community.
- We use safe, secure encryption technology to protect your personally identifiable information.
- We have no tolerance for spam (unsolicited, commercial e-mail).[7]

To ensure that the privacy policy could be understood by those who were not lawyers, the company developed a simple chart. For each piece of personal information collected during the member's registration, such as name or e-mail address, the chart described how the information could be used by each of five classes of organizations: advertisers, internal service providers, external service providers, eBay community representatives, and in response to legal requests. The information might be provided

- not at all,
- only in aggregate form with no personal identification,
- with the member's agreement,
- to fulfill an eBay service requirement,
- if the member was involved in a transaction, or
- in response to a subpoena.

Even companies with policies and security systems can have problems. Victoria's Secret reached a settlement with the New York state attorney general agreeing to pay a fine and improve its security. A customer discovered that the company left a hole in its security system that gave access to customer accounts.

Some companies believe that their privacy protection policies can be a competitive advantage. Earthlink attempted to use privacy as an instrument in its competition with other ISPs. To attract users, Earthlink gave away tens of thousands of bags of chocolate chip cookies with the label "Do you know where your cookies come from?" and the caption "Earthlink protects your privacy."[8] The company also communicated with its subscribers on how they could control the use of cookies and provided them with software to accept or reject cookies. Earthlink found that its name recall increased significantly, but whether an increase in subscribers resulted was unclear.

An important source of contention centers on the type of choice given to Internet users. Most companies prefer opt-out, where a user must affirmatively choose not to have data collected or browsing tracked. Privacy advocates argue that opt-out places

[6]This material is from the case "eBay: Private Ordering for an Online Community," P-37, Graduate School of Business, Stanford University, August 2001.
[7]pages.eBay.com/help/privacycentral1.html.
[8]*The New York Times*, September 5, 2001.

too great a burden on individuals and that most will not bother to read the notice explaining the data collection and hence will not exercise choice. Privacy activists support opt-in, where an Internet company would not be allowed to collect or share data without the individual affirmatively agreeing to have the data collected and used. The difference in participation rates is believed to be enormous between these two alternatives. The prevalent practice in the United States is opt-out, whereas in the European Union opt-in is required for personally identifiable information (PII).

The European Union (EU) has taken a different approach to Internet privacy. It enacted a directive (law) providing strong privacy protection for PII. In addition, companies are not allowed to transfer PII outside the European Union unless the recipient country provides "adequate" protection. A credit card company may want to transfer PII to its headquarters in the United States for billing and other purposes. Since self-regulation is the basic policy of the United States, the issue is whether U.S. policy satisfies the EU requirement of adequate protection. This issue is considered in more detail in Chapter 15 and in the case, *The European Union Data Privacy Directive*, in that chapter. To update its electronic company telephone directory, General Motors was required to obtain permission from employees in the European Union to include their office telephone numbers, which were viewed as personal information by the European Union. Sending the numbers outside the European Union could be a criminal offense in some EU countries. GM had 200 of its affiliates sign contracts stating that they would not misuse the telephone numbers.

Confidence in the Internet is a public good, but the provision of that public good is subject to a free-rider problem. Some Internet companies infringe on the privacy of users who anticipated that the information they provided would remain private. To address this problem independently of government, a group of firms took private collective action to form an independent organization, TRUSTe, to establish privacy standards, monitor compliance, and grant a seal to Web sites that met the standards. TRUSTe has evolved into a private government in which Web sites voluntarily participate. TRUSTe legislates standards such as opt-out requirements for the transfer of personal information, regulates participating Web sites by requiring TRUSTe approval for any changes in consumer privacy notices, and enforces standards by reviewing privacy policies of participants and submitting unique user information to a site and monitoring where that information turns up. TRUSTe also has established a judiciary. It provides a dispute resolution program for Internet users, makes decisions on individual complaints, and has an appeals panel for users and participating Internet sites. TRUSTe was selected by the Department of Commerce to provide a seal for compliance with the Safe Harbor Provisions for ensuring privacy of PII transmitted from the European Union to the United States.

When the dotcom bubble burst, many companies found themselves in the position of toysmart.com in the example. Webvan, eToys, Wine.com, Garden.com, and Egghead.com all sought to sell their databases. The question was how to accomplish the sales. Although the companies had pledged not to sell or share the data without their users' permission, as David Steer of TRUSTe explained, "When a company declares bankruptcy, all bets are off. The bankruptcy judge can declare all previous contracts null and void to help raise as much money as possible in a liquidation."[9] For example, the judge supervising the Egghead.com bankruptcy approved the sale of its database to Fry's Electronics.[10] The FTC announced it would continue to monitor sales and was prepared to attempt to block them.

[9]*San Jose Mercury News*, October 29, 2001.
[10]The sale collapsed due to other factors.

## Bankruptcy and Internet Privacy: Toysmart.com

Toysmart.com was an e-commerce toy retailer backed by the Walt Disney Company, which held a 60 percent stake in the venture. Because of continuing losses Disney pulled the plug on toysmart.com in 2000, and the company filed for bankruptcy under Chapter 11. Under Chapter 11 the bankruptcy court has jurisdiction, and its responsibility was to obtain as much as possible for the creditors of the bankrupt company. One asset of the company was its database of customer information, and the bankruptcy court sought to sell that database. Toysmart.com was one of the most visited sites during the Christmas season, so its database was extensive. Information about the attempted sale was leaked to TRUSTe, which condemned the sale as "an invasion of privacy," and called it "ethically wrong." TRUSTe notified the FTC, calling the sale an "information Valdez."

Toysmart.com had assured customers about the information they provided. Its Web site

stated: "When you register with toysmart.com, you can rest assured that your information will never be shared with a third party." Once in bankruptcy the toysmart.com CEO said he would not sell the data to "inappropriate organizations." Nevertheless, the FTC filed a lawsuit seeking a preliminary injunction against the sale. The FTC reached a settlement with the bankruptcy court that restricted the sale to a buyer in a family-related commerce market and required that the company obtain permission from individuals before their data could be sold. A federal court, however, threw out the settlement as premature; that is, there was no actual sale of the data pending. The news media followed the saga of toysmart.com with extensive coverage. The criticism of the sale by privacy advocates as well as members of Congress continued, and Disney decided to buy the database for $50,000 and destroy it.

## The Internet and Tax Policy

In 1998 Congress passed the Internet Tax Freedom Act, which imposed a 3-year tax moratorium prohibiting states from enacting any new tax on Internet access and any tax that singled out the Internet. Nine states had already enacted Internet access taxes, but the big issue was a tax on sales transacted on the Internet. No state had enacted such a tax. The moratorium did not ban the collection of the sales tax on Internet transactions, but if such collection were required, it would have to apply as well to mail-order and telephone sales. Amazon.com, based in the state of Washington, for example, collected the state sales tax from Washington residents but not from customers in other states.

Customers are obliged to pay the sales tax, but because of a Supreme Court decision states are prohibited from ordering out-of-state mail-order companies to collect the taxes unless they had a physical location (nexus) in the state. The "singled-out" language of the moratorium had been supported by electronic commerce companies that sought as allies the mail-order and telephone sales companies. Internet sales represented less than 2 percent of U.S. retail sales, whereas catalog and telephone sales represented 3.4 percent.

The potential growth of electronic commerce, however, was the concern. Texas estimated that it received $45 million on its Internet access tax in 2001 but would lose $1.2 billion in uncollected sales taxes on Internet purchases. The General Accounting Office estimated that states would lose $12.5 billion in uncollected sales taxes in 2003. The Center for Business and Research at the University of Tennessee, however, estimated that the tax loss on Internet sales in 2001 would be between $9.4 and $13.3 billion and by 2011 would be $54 billion. States were concerned about their ability to provide public services if that much tax revenue were lost.

In addition to the lost tax revenue by states, brick-and-mortar retailers lost sales. They viewed Internet retailers as having an unfair advantage because they did not collect taxes, and that advantage loomed larger each year. The retailers were also concerned about the advantage of mail-order and telephone sales companies. Those concerned about the tax advantage included not only the major retail chains such as Wal-Mart but also the small, main street retailers.

Online retailers argued that they did not utilize state services and that collecting taxes due would be prohibitively costly. In the United States not only do states, counties, and municipalities impose taxes, but so do school, library, and mosquito abatement districts. The United States has approximately 7,600 state and local tax jurisdictions, and electronic commerce companies argued that it would be too costly to have to determine and collect the taxes due in each of those jurisdictions. Electronic commerce companies were also concerned about having to undergo multiple tax audits. In response, 30 states launched a tax simplification project with the objective of dramatically reducing the number of different tax rates and jurisdictions. The challenge was substantial, since, for example, clothing was not taxed in 13 states and in six of the other states a handkerchief was not considered clothing.

In addition, many online retailers believed that they could be forced into bankruptcy if they had to collect taxes on their sales. Avoiding sales taxes was an important factor in their survival. The Direct Marketing Association's chairman said, "It literally will put a lot of small and medium-sized businesses out of business."[11]

Some public policy analysts argued that the Internet was a public good and part of a nation's infrastructure. They favored the current moratorium on Internet taxation because it would lead to greater use of the Internet and hence more investment in infrastructure capacity. The infrastructure included not only the Internet and the servers on which Web sites operated but also connections to the Internet. Bill Gates had called for more rapid deployment of DSL lines as a part of infrastructure investment. The telecommunications and cable companies that provided access generally supported the moratorium, as did equipment manufacturers.

The moratorium on taxes on Internet transactions was temporary, and Congress was the institutional arena in which the issue was considered. Three basic alternatives were available. The first was to let the moratorium expire, allowing the states to take their own actions. The second was to extend the moratorium while the states attempted to simplify their tax structures. The third was to make the moratorium permanent. The Chapter 8 case, *Internet Taxation*, addresses these issues in more detail.

## Online Communities

The business model of some Internet companies centers on developing a community of users who interact with each other as well as with the company. The interactions may center on trades, as in the case of online auctions, or the sharing of information through community bulletin boards or instant messaging. The purpose of developing a community is to allow members to benefit from interactions that may have the characteristics of demand-side increasing returns due to network externalities. For example, eBay has the largest community of online buyers, and this means that sellers are attracted to its site. The fact that more sellers list their items on eBay than on any other online auction site means that buyers prefer to look for items on eBay first. The incentives for buyers and sellers are reinforcing and generate positive feedback. Moreover, users may become locked into eBay. A seller might have an interest in switching to Yahoo! Auctions, which had been free, but unless buyers also switched, the seller would face a thin market. Buyers would not switch because the other sellers remained on eBay, and the sellers remained there because the buyers were there. Buyers and sellers who traded in a particular class of items could collectively switch to another online auction site, but they would incur high costs, since coordinating their switching would be extremely difficult.[12] Collective switching was attempted once and failed. These collective switching costs meant that it was difficult for groups of traders to be taken away from the eBay community.[13] The eBay community reached 114 million registered members in 2004.

To illustrate the role of community, it is useful to consider the traders and their interactions. eBay's online community was composed of anonymous and remote individuals who were unlikely to have repeat dealings. Trade was impersonal with, for example, a seller knowing only the eBay user name of bidders until the winner of the auction provided a shipping address. Buyers did not have an opportunity to inspect the goods on which they bid, and the winning bidder paid for the item prior to shipment. Moreover, since public enforcement was costly, trades were neither supported by explicit contracts nor in most cases by public enforcement of implicit contracts. Unlike an off-line auction house eBay never saw the items offered for sale nor certified their authenticity or quality or the accuracy of the descriptions provided by the sellers. Furthermore, eBay did not act as an agent of the seller or the buyer, certify the creditworthiness of buyers, nor play a role in settling the transaction.[14] Despite the inherent opportunities for abuse in such a setting, the unenforceability of implicit contracts among traders, and eBay's very limited role, trade flourished with over 332 million auction items offered in 2003.

On its Web site eBay explained, "The key to eBay's success is trust. Trust between the buyers and sellers who make up the eBay community. And trust between the user and eBay, the company." Trust among the members of the eBay community was supported by a multilateral online *reputation mechanism* based on feedback provided voluntarily by the transacting members. The reputation mechanism not only provided information to traders but also established a target for punishment, since members could simply not trade with a member with a bad reputation. The reputation mechanism was supplemented by rules designed by eBay to govern who could be a member, which items members could trade, and how they were to conduct themselves on its Web site. The mechanism was also supported by programs, such as eBay-provided insurance against fraud, designed to reduce the cost of trust.

The multilateral online reputation mechanism, the rules, and eBay's programs provided a *private ordering* for eBay's community. This was in contrast to off-line markets. Off-line markets were supported by the public order—that is, laws and their enforcement. This public order was supplemented by the reputation of the seller and by the

---

[12]See Saloner, Shepard, and Podolny (2001, p. 313).
[13]This section is based on Baron (2003b).
[14]eBay thus differed from other venues such as the New York Stock Exchange, where in its early years members (brokers) acted as agents of investors, provided information about creditworthiness, used their information about prices, and helped enforce contracts through a "miniature legal system" (Banner, 1998).

use of contemporaneous transactions. For noncontemporaneous off-line trades, order was supported by reputation and enforceable contracts.

eBay's private ordering existed in the shadow of the public order. Public order in the form of policing for activities such as fraud or the breach of implicit contracts was costly for a community of dispersed individuals whose only interaction was through a Web site. Because fraud was a threat to its community, eBay established an enforcement group to investigate allegations, spot shill bidding, and monitor its site. When illegal activity was spotted, eBay put the victims in contact with law enforcement officials and cooperated in their investigations. The public order also led eBay to position itself to avoid regulations and liabilities such as those associated with the sale of items that infringed copyrights, as considered in Chapters 2 and 12. The public order also impacted the scope of its activities as well as the relations between the company and its members.

In the early days of eBay, order occurred spontaneously among the members of the community. Members established informal standards, provided feedback on other members' performance, and policed the site. Some traders formed neighborhood watch groups to police their trading areas—that is, the items in which they traded. One group of six members that called itself "The Posse" actively monitored activity on the eBay site. Traders who violated implicit standards could quickly have their reputations damaged by The Posse. Spontaneous order was facilitated by the relatively small number of traders and listings (in the thousands) and by the communication they exchanged through e-mail and on bulletin boards. As the listings and membership grew, private policing became more difficult.

Early in its existence eBay established its Feedback Forum where members could provide feedback on other members, enabling them to establish an online reputation. The spontaneous private ordering that developed was supported by the basic honesty of people and by a set of norms that continued to guide eBay. The company hoped they would guide its members as well:

eBay is a community where we encourage **open and honest communication** between all of our members. We believe in the following five basic values.

We believe people are basically good.
We believe everyone has something to contribute.
We believe that an honest, open environment can bring out the
    best in people.
We recognize and respect everyone as a unique individual.
We encourage you to treat others the way that you want to be treated.[15]

eBay's principal objective was to achieve order for its community so that buyers and sellers could trust each other and realize the gains from trade. Since participation was voluntary, the size and composition of the community itself was a function of the efficacy of the private ordering. That is, the community was endogenous to the private ordering it sustained. The product of its private ordering was trust. Trust among remote and anonymous traders who interacted infrequently and then only through impersonal trading could be sustained through reputations carried by the traders and made available to trading partners.

The establishment and updating of an online reputation required information and communication. Those with the best information were the traders themselves, since

---

[15]Emphasis in the original.

they knew whether the quality of the good was as described in the auction listing, payment had been timely, and the good was delivered as promised. Within the broader eBay community of users were a number of communities of traders in particular items, such as in particular collectibles. These communities had repeated transactions with the same traders, which allowed bilateral reputations to be established. Most members, however, would transact with many different members rather than have repeat dealings with the same person, so bilateral reputation formation was insufficient to establish trust.

Although bilateral reputation formation could not be relied on to engender widespread trust, a multilateral reputation mechanism, where a seller's reputation was based on the experiences of all those who traded with her, could generate trust. A multilateral reputation mechanism also provided for uncoordinated, multilateral punishment of a seller who violated the trust of other traders. Punishment was administered by not bidding on items offered by a seller with a bad reputation or bidding less for those items or, in the case of sellers, by refusing to sell to a buyer with a bad reputation. eBay could also administer punishment by suspending or banning a user or by providing information to public law enforcement authorities in the case of fraud. This multilateral reputation mechanism generated incentives similar to those in a long-term relationship between a buyer and a seller.

The Internet enabled the collection and transmission of transactions and reputation information with little organization or coordination. eBay did not participate in the reputation and information systems other than to establish rules such as whether feedback could be retracted. Punishment was voluntary and uncoordinated and occurred because individuals feared that they would have a bad experience with a member with a bad reputation, as others had in the past. The effectiveness of this system was indicated by the importance members placed on their online reputations and on the feedback they received.

In eBay's reputation mechanism, feedback could be negative, neutral, or positive, and written comments also could be given. Positive feedback received +1 points, neutral feedback 0 points, and negative feedback −1 points. The aggregate score was reported as the "seller's rating" on an auction listing and the "buyer's rating" when a bid was made. A score that reached certain levels earned a star of one of nine different colors. In addition, written feedback was available on members.

One potential problem with a reputation mechanism is that a reputation can be exploited. For example, a member who had developed a good reputation could begin to harvest short-term benefits by taking advantage of his trading partners, who were relying on that reputation. This would result in negative feedback weakening the member's reputation somewhat, but a prior high rating would decrease slowly. To deal with these problems, eBay summarized in a convenient table the number of positives, neutrals, and negatives for the past week, month, and 6 months. This allowed a potential trader to check whether the other member's behavior had changed.

A private ordering can be supplemented through design to increase its efficacy. Over time eBay developed a set of rules for its community to reduce the cost of trust and provided a set of services to reduce the risks of trading. In some cases, the rules were a response to incidents that identified weaknesses in the private ordering. For example, as the community grew and became more anonymous, eBay required members who were not otherwise identifiable to provide credit card information to establish their identity.

The chapter case, *eBay: Private Ordering for an Online Community*, considers these aspects of community in more detail.

# Summary

The economics of some information markets are quite different from the economics of the markets for consumption goods. Network externalities or complementary products can generate demand-side increasing returns. The increasing returns provide incentives to develop an installed base of users as quickly as possible, so the first mover has an advantage. A firm also has an incentive to build a user base by charging low initial prices. If the firm can lock in the user base, positive feedback can result and the market may tip. In such cases, the winner takes most of the market. This raises a number of antitrust concerns not about being a monopoly but about the practices used to become the winner and to maintain the monopoly.

Privacy on the Internet is of concern to users and to legislators and regulators. Privacy pertains to both personal information such as that provided to complete a purchase and anonymous data such as browsing information. The FTC has authority to take enforcement actions against Web sites that state privacy policies but then violate them. Other than that authority, privacy on the Internet is a matter of self-regulation by Web sites and self-protection by users. Self-regulation has a variety of components, the most controversial of which is opt-out versus opt-in. Most electronic commerce companies use opt-out, which critics argue places too great a burden on Internet users. Opt-in, however, would greatly reduce the data available to Internet companies. The bankruptcy of dotcom companies presents a host of privacy issues, since bankruptcy puts the company under the supervision of a bankruptcy court whose responsibility is to obtain as much as possible from the assets. For some companies databases are one of their more valuable assets. The courts have allowed considerable discretion in the sale of the databases, raising concerns about privacy.

The collection and remittance of sales taxes on Internet transactions is not required unless the seller has a physical nexus in the state. States and brick-and-mortar retailers have pressed for requiring collection of the taxes. The loss of tax revenue and sales provided incentives for political action, but opposition was strong from the electronic commerce companies and from mail-order and telephone sales companies that feared that they might be subject to the same requirements. The opponents of Internet taxation argued that with 7,600 tax jurisdictions collection and remittance of the taxes would be prohibitively costly. Congress had passed a moratorium against Internet-only taxes, but a permanent resolution of the issue remained elusive.

A number of Internet companies develop online communities. These communities can benefit from demand-side increasing returns, but they are composed of remote and anonymous individuals. In the case of online auctions, this provides members with opportunities to take advantage of other members. Web sites thus must provide order for their communities. That order can be private in the sense that it does not rely on the law, or public. Trust is the centerpiece of eBay's online community, and reputation is the basis for trust. Reputations on eBay are based on feedback from trading partners and are the foundation for the private ordering of its community. eBay supplements the reputation mechanism with a set of policies and rules intended to support trust by reducing the likelihood of opportunistic behavior.

# DoubleClick and Internet Privacy

*It is clear from these discussions that I made a mistake by planning to merge names with anonymous user activity across Web sites in the absence of government and industry privacy standards.*

—Kevin O'Conner, CEO of DoubleClick

## Introduction

DoubleClick, the industry leader in Internet advertising services, saw its $1.7 billion strategic investment in Abacus Direct dissolve in the face of a privacy firestorm over the merger of the Abacus data on off-line purchasing with information gleaned from the browsing of Internet users. DoubleClick tracked Web activity on its DoubleClick Network of 1,500 Web sites and placed banner advertisements on 11,000 sites. The information it collected was identified only by an ID number assigned to a cookie deposited on the user's computer by the banner advertisements. DoubleClick's DART software technology processed the anonymous information to generate user profiles for tailoring advertisements for Web sites. Abacus Direct was the leader in collecting information from catalog purchases and using that data to target advertising and catalog configurations to consumers. Abacus had 5-year buying profiles on 88 million households, including name, address, demographic information, estimated income, and purchases.

DoubleClick recognized that the value of targeted online advertising would be substantially increased if information from consumers' online browsing activities could be linked with their off-line purchase activities. Rates for targeted advertising based on anonymous profiling were 50 to 100 percent higher than for untargeted bulk advertising, and rates for targeted ads based on the merged databases would be even higher.

DoubleClick's plans were interrupted in February 2000 when *USA Today* disclosed its plan to merge its anonymous online data with Abacus Direct's database. A firestorm erupted, and DoubleClick quickly suspended its plan to merge the databases. It then faced the problems of developing a strategy for regaining public confidence

and for the collection and use of information going forward.

## DoubleClick

Kevin O'Conner founded DoubleClick in 1996 to serve advertisers on the Internet. By early 2000 DoubleClick had 1,800 employees, 7,000 customers, offices in 30 countries, and a market capitalization of $10 billion. Its revenue for the first quarter of 2000 was $110 million, an increase of 179 percent over the year-earlier quarter. Its gross profit was $53 million, but heavy marketing expenses resulted in a loss of $18 million. Forrester Research projected that online advertising would increase from $3.3 billion in 1999 to $33 billion in 2004.

Shortly after founding DoubleClick, O'Conner stated in an interview that the company would not collect and keep information that identified a person. He said that linking data to names and addresses "would be voluntary on the user's part, and used in strict confidence. We are not going to trick people or match information from other sources."[16] In accord with this policy DoubleClick allowed Internet users to opt out of its data collection system. Its opt-out policy was available on its own Web site at the end of a lengthy legal notice and a description of cookies.

To target advertisements to Internet users' interests, DoubleClick tracked their click-stream data. The technology for tracking click-stream data began with cookies. A cookie is a small text file deposited on a user's hard drive and containing an ID number associated with the computer but not the user. Cookies were a major convenience to many users. They enabled a portal such as Yahoo! to remember

[16]*Forbes,* November 4, 1996.

a user's password and immediately bring up personalized pages and information. They also allowed advertising and other content to be targeted by ID number. When a user visited a Web site that had deposited a cookie on the user's hard drive, the visit and ID number were recorded. DoubleClick collected the visit information through its network of Web sites, which included popular sites such as AltaVista and Travelocity. Since the ID number was associated with a computer and DoubleClick had no information on who owned or used the computer, the information remained anonymous. Abacus Online, however, was different.

## DoubleClick's Abacus Online Strategy

DoubleClick's market strategy was to integrate the two databases to offer advertising better tailored to Internet users' actual purchasing behavior as well as their browsing. To implement its strategy DoubleClick formed Abacus Online. Participating Web sites identified users by name but were required to post a notice explaining the information to be collected and giving users the opportunity to opt out. Participating users could also choose whether to receive targeted advertisements. DoubleClick was actively recruiting companies and Web sites to join Abacus Online. AltaVista and Travelocity had not yet decided whether to join.

Sites participating in Abacus Online would not only allow click-stream data to be collected, but they also would collect personal information when individuals identified themselves to the site—for example, when they made a purchase, completed a survey, or signed up for a drawing. With that personal information the ID number assigned to the cookie could be associated with the user. The click-stream data then could be combined with Abacus Direct's database of off-line information. DoubleClick operated one such site, Netdeals.com, where users could sign up for drawings for prizes, giving their name, age, and street and e-mail addresses. Users who agreed to receive "valuable offers" were added to its database.

DoubleClick explained its objective: "This is about getting the right ad to the right person at the right time. It's important for users to understand that the only time DoubleClick will actually have personally identifiable information attached to a browser is when the user has volunteered [it] and

been given notice and choice."[17] DoubleClick had no intention of selling or disclosing information on individuals' Internet use to any third party. The information would only be used internally to enhance the value of its services to advertisers. DoubleClick also pledged that it would not collect data on medical, financial, or sexual transactions or browsing or on children's browsing.

DoubleClick argued that the information would benefit consumers because advertisements would be tailored to their interests and purchasing behavior. Just as consumers using Amazon.com received messages about books that might be of interest based on their past purchases, DoubleClick would provide advertisements of interest to users of a Web site based on the purchasing and browsing behavior of those who visited the site. Similarly, just as a consumer could design a personalized page on a portal such as Yahoo!, DoubleClick would provide personalized information for the consumer. Because advertisements were provided on virtually all Web sites, a consumer would benefit from receiving advertisements of interest rather than blanket ads.

Kevin O'Conner said, "There are some people on the Internet who want to go back to the old days when there was no advertising and it was government controlled. We believe that [the Internet] is a tremendous thing and that it should be free. That means it is going to be funded by advertising."[18] O'Conner pointed to recent polls indicating that 70 percent of Internet users understood that the Internet was free because of advertising and that two-thirds liked the personalization of information.[19] Broadcast television and radio were also funded by advertisements, and magazines and newspapers were largely funded by ads.

Dana Serman of Lazard Freres predicted, "Over time, people will realize it's not Big Brother who's going to show up at your door in a black ski mask and take your kids away or dig deep into your medical history. This is a situation where you are essentially dropped in a bucket with 40 million people who look and feel a lot like you do to the advertising community."[20]

---

[17] *USA Today*, February 2, 2000.
[18] *The Guardian*, February 25, 2000.
[19] *The Wall Street Journal*, March 7, 2000.
[20] *The Washington Post*, February 18, 2000.

## Internet Privacy

The U.S. Constitution does not have an explicit privacy provision other than the Fourth Amendment's restrictions on searches and seizures by government. A number of court decisions, however, established certain privacy rights supported by constitutional interpretation.[21] A right to privacy was also established in a number of state constitutions, including that of California. Although there was no legislation specifying Internet privacy rights, other legislation reflected the sensitivity of privacy issues, as indicated earlier in the chapter.

The Federal Trade Commission (FTC) had jurisdiction over unfair and deceptive practices, and in 1999 the FTC reached a decision not to regulate Internet privacy. One commissioner, however, dissented and advocated immediate action on privacy. The FTC established an Advisory Committee on Online Access and Security.

## Self-Regulation and the Activist Landscape

The e-commerce industry had taken steps to provide better security and privacy and to stop theft and fraud on the Internet. Two industry groups, the Online Privacy Alliance and the Electronic Commerce and Consumer Protection Group, advocated continued self-regulation by Internet companies.[22] A number of Internet companies had established TRUSTe to certify the privacy policies of Web sites, and other organizations also provided certification.[23] This self-regulation and the complexities of the privacy issue had led the U.S. government to go slowly in establishing explicit consumer privacy rights for the Internet. Not everyone, however, was satisfied with self-regulation. Marc Rotenberg of the Electronic Privacy Information Center (EPIC) said, "Self-regulation is inviting a race to the bottom."

When it acquired Abacus Direct in 1999, DoubleClick was criticized by privacy activists who feared that it would integrate the information it collected online with the personalized information in Abacus Direct's database. Some activists drew analogies to George Orwell's *1984*, and Jason Catlett, head of JunkBusters, a for-profit consulting company, said, "Abacus is now becoming part of a company that will be despised by anyone who values privacy."[24] In response to the criticism, DoubleClick and nine other Internet advertising and online profiling companies formed the Network Advertising Initiative to develop privacy protection guidelines.

JunkBusters and EPIC had earlier created a storm when they revealed that Intel planned to put a serial number on its Pentium III processor, allowing identification of the computer on which it was installed. EPIC threatened a boycott, and Intel quickly backed down and abandoned its plan. A number of other companies had also had privacy incidents and were forced to change their policies. Lexis-Nexis was forced to abandon its plans to provide personal information to other companies. Similarly, in 1997 America Online (AOL) planned to release its subscribers list to telephone marketers despite an earlier pledge not to do so.[25] Referring to Marc Rotenberg of EPIC, Steve Case, chairman of AOL, said, "The guy can create a privacy uproar at the click of a mouse."[26]

Privacy activists were also suspicious of companies' stated privacy policies. First, policies could be changed at any time. For example, in August 1999 Amazon.com changed its policy and introduced "purchase circles" that used personal data and purchase data to identify publicly the best-selling products by geography, employer, university, or organization. Second, companies could violate their policies and escape detection. In November 1999 RealNetworks was revealed to be collecting information on user's Internet activity without disclosure and in violation of its own privacy policy.[27] The company apologized and stopped the practice.

[21]See *Griswold v. Connecticut*, 383 U.S. 479 (1965).

[22]The Online Privacy Alliance had 85 corporate and association members. The members of the Electronic Commerce and Consumer Protection Group were AOL, AT&T, Dell, IBM, Microsoft, Network Solutions, Time Warner, and Visa U.S.A.

[23]TRUSTe was established in 1996 based on the principles that users have a right to informed consent and that "no single privacy principle is adequate for all situations." TRUSTe granted a site a "trademark" if it met the tests of (1) adoption and implementation of a privacy policy, (2) notice and disclosure, (3) choice and consent, and (4) data security and quality and access (to personal information). By mid-2000 approximately 2000 Web sites had received TRUSTe approval.

[24]*Forbes*, November 24, 1999.

[25]Peter P. Swire, and Robert E. Litan, *None of Your Business.* 1998, Brookings Institution: Washington, DC, p. 10, AOL continued to sell its subscribers list but notified its subscribers of the practice.

[26]*Business Week*, May 15, 2000.

[27]Its free RealJukebox allowed users to convert music to a digital format and play it on a personal computer. People downloading the software were required to give their e-mail address and zip code and were assigned a Globally Unique Identifier. The software transmitted daily information to RealNetworks on songs downloaded by users. RealNetworks was TRUSTe approved.

A basic objection to the collection of click-stream data was that it was invisible to users. Activists argued that average consumers did not know their activity was being tracked let alone how the informa-tion was being used. Another objection was that the identifiers of consumers were persistent and the user did not have a relationship with the company doing the tracking, as when a consumer made a purchase using a credit card.

Some activists opposed the transformation of the Internet from an anonymous environment to one in which individuals were identified and their Internet use monitored. As one commentator put it, "You can escape your surroundings through the Internet, but your actions can easily catch up with you."[28]

## The Reaction to Abacus Online

Shortly after Abacus Online was revealed, the Center for Democracy and Technology (CDT) launched a consumer education campaign to alert Internet users.[29] CDT provided an Operation Opt-out Web site allowing consumers to opt out of DoubleClick's system and urging them to write letters to DoubleClick protesting its policies. Several thousand letters were also sent to Web sites that participated in the DoubleClick Network.

Jason Catlett of JunkBusters described Abacus Online as, "Thousands of sites are ratting on you, so as soon as one gives you away, you're exposed on all of them. For four years, [DoubleClick] has said [the services] don't identify you personally, and now they're admitting they are going to identify you."[30] He added, "If you don't like Yahoo!'s privacy policy, you don't have to use its site. But it's very difficult for con-sumers to avoid DoubleClick because most don't know when it is collecting information."[31] Richard Smith, a privacy advocate, added, "Computers are like elephants: they never forget. And they are watching us all the time."[32] Other critics likened DoubleClick to the computer HAL in the movie *2001* and referred to the company as "Doublecross." Jonathon Shapiro, senior vice president of DoubleClick, said, "We are

good actors. We've been leaders in protecting con-sumer privacy for the past four years, and we think our commitment to providing notice and choice to consumers puts us ahead of the curve."[33]

DoubleClick pointed out that since its founding 50,000 people had opted out of its tracking. Tom Maddox, editor of *Privacyplace*, argued, "People don't know they have to opt out."[34] David Banisar of Privacy International said, "This is not permission. That is fraudulent on its face."[35] Barry Steinhardt of the American Civil Liberties Union said, "The onus should be on the data collector to get your affirma-tive consent, in a knowing way. You shouldn't have to bargain for your privacy."[36]

Privacy advocates argued that consumers should have access to the data collected so that they could correct errors and decide whether to continue allow-ing the data to be collected. They also argued for an opt-in policy under which consumers would have to give their express permission before any information could be collected on them. In June 2000 the Supreme Court let stand a Court of Appeals deci-sion voiding part of a statute that had required local telephone companies to obtain opt-in permission before using billing records to sell new services to customers. US West had filed the lawsuit so that it could use an opt-out policy instead.

## Personal Assurance of Internet Privacy

Most people seemed willing to give personal infor-mation and credit card numbers to catalog compa-nies such as L.L. Bean and Lands' End. Information on credit card transactions was routinely collected, and financial services companies had for many years used data that passed through their systems to target consumers. Moreover, the growth of the Internet and electronic commerce had been very rapid under the self-regulation approach without explicit Internet privacy rights. A Forrester Research poll of 10,000 Internet users revealed that two-thirds were willing to provide personal information, but 90 percent wanted control over how that information was used.

Users had a growing array of direct means of assuring privacy, including both those taken by ISPs

[28]Esther Dyson, *The Los Angeles Times*, March 20, 2000.
[29]Members of CDT included America Online, AT&T, Business Software Alliance, Disney WorldWide, Ford Foundation, Markle Foundation, Microsoft, the Newspaper Association of America, the Open Society Institute, and Time Warner.
[30]*USA Today*, January 26, 2000.
[31]*U.S. News & World Report*, March 6, 2000.
[32]*Financial Times*, January 29, 2000.

[33]*Los Angeles Times*, February 3, 2000.
[34]*The San Francisco Chronicle*, January 27, 2000.
[35]*USA Today*, January 26, 2000.
[36]*Financial Times*, January 29, 2000.

and those taken individually. ISPs had privacy policies and published those policies on their Web sites. A growing number had their policies and practices certified by independent companies and organizations, such as TRUSTe, BBBOnline, and SecureAssure. SecureAssure affixed a seal to a Web site that pledged not to sell personal information about a user to a third party without express permission.[37] In contrast, sites with BBBOnline and TRUSTe approval could sell data.

Another means of avoiding online profiling was to block cookies from being deposited on a computer. Cookies could be blocked by simply configuring Internet Explorer (IE) or Netscape Navigator to reject them. On IE go to Tools, Internet Options, Security, and choose high. On Navigator go to Edit, Preferences, Advanced, and select the option.

Economic theory predicted that if there were a demand for Internet privacy the marketplace would supply the means of achieving it. Webroot.com's Windows Washer allowed a user to cleanse certain areas of Windows of cookies. Some companies, including TopClick International, Anonymizer.com, and Zero-Knowledge, provided anonymous surfing of the Internet using technologies that masked a user's identity. Zero-Knowledge's Freedom program gave users digital pseudonyms and routed their surfing through a variety of servers to cloak their activity. Anonymizer acted as an intermediary and encrypted a user's inquiries. Hundreds of re-mailers removed revealing information from e-mail messages. Earth Proxy provided free downloadable software intended to inhibit tracking software.

Purchasing items on the Internet, however, required a billing record, which gave sellers information on purchasers. Infomediaries such as PrivaSeek offered subscribers downloadable software that allowed them to decide what information was made available when they purchased online. In May 2000 at a weekend privacy retreat organized by the U.S. Chamber of Commerce, Microsoft and a number of other companies displayed technologies to protect consumers. One technology demonstrated by DataTreasury Corporation allowed transactions to be made within its secure system.

In 1998 the World Wide Web Consortium, backed by a group of companies including America

Online, AT&T, IBM, and Microsoft, formed P3P, the Platform for Privacy Preferences Protection, along with the Massachusetts Institute of Technology and universities in France and Japan. P3P was unveiled in June 2000, and Microsoft announced that it would incorporate it in its next version of Windows. Both Microsoft and America Online said they would offer it as a plug-in to their browsers. P3P software allowed Internet users to specify the personal data they wanted to divulge to a Web site, and P3P technology notified them when a site requested additional information. The participants in P3P were reported to have been unable to agree on more than a notification procedure. Marc Rotenberg of EPIC referred to P3P as "pretty poor privacy," criticizing it for being an opt-out rather than an opt-in procedure and requiring too much initiative by Internet users. He said, "It is not a technology to protect personal privacy. It's a means to enable the disclosure of personal information."[38] Dr. Horst Joepen, CEO of Webwasher.com, a German software privacy company affiliated with Siemens, characterized P3P as "too little, too late."

## Government Action

As a result of the privacy concerns raised about Abacus Online, the Center for Democracy and Technology filed a complaint with the FTC, which began an inquiry into DoubleClick's data collection and advertising practices. CDT, the Privacy Rights Clearinghouse, Consumer Action, the Gay and Lesbian Alliance Against Defamation, and the American Civil Liberties Union subsequently filed a "Statement of Additional Facts and Grounds for Relief" with the FTC.

In addition to the FTC inquiry the New York State attorney general initiated an informal inquiry. The attorney general of Michigan referred to DoubleClick's plan as "a secret wiretap" and announced that she would file suit against the practice. "The average consumer has no idea that they are being spied upon," she said, and the lack of warning constituted "a deceitful practice under our consumer-protection act."[39] She said that DoubleClick's policy was like putting a "bar code" on a consumer's back. A California woman filed a lawsuit alleging that DoubleClick violated her state constitutional right to privacy.

[37]The fee charged by SecureAssure ranged from $200 to $2,500 a year.

[38]*The New York Times*, June 22, 2000.
[39]*The Washington Post*, February 17, 2000.

Legislation on Internet privacy had been introduced in Congress by Senators Burns and Wyden, Senator Leahy offered another bill, and Representative Markey introduced another. A number of members of Congress supported a federal Internet privacy agency. The Clinton administration was also concerned about online privacy but favored self-regulation. The administration backed the P3P technology and installed it on the White House Internet site.

In May 2000 the FTC reversed its position and voted 3 to 2 to ask Congress for new legislation granting it rule-making authority to regulate privacy on the Internet. The FTC sought required notice of privacy policies, including telling Internet users how the data would be used and allowing them to inspect and correct their information. Companies would also be required to implement security measures to prevent unauthorized disclosure. In a statement FTC chairman Robert Pitofsky said, "This is not a report that comes to the conclusion that self-regulation has failed. On the contrary, self-regulation has made considerable progress. But in certain respects it looks as if self-regulation would be more successful if there was some backup legislation."[40] In his dissent commissioner Orson Swindle called the FTC request "breathtakingly broad."

The FTC's survey of Internet sites revealed that only 41 percent posted a privacy policy that told users how data was used and only 20 percent of the major Internet sites had adequate privacy policies. Commissioner Swindle said the survey was "embarrassingly flawed." The Direct Marketing Institute countered with a survey showing that 93 percent of major Internet sites had privacy policies and most of them told users how their data would be used.

Industry generally supported self-regulation and opposed government regulation, but some companies feared that states would enact their own Internet privacy laws. Internet privacy legislation had been introduced in 17 states. A number of companies believed that some federal regulation was an acceptable price if it would preempt state regulation. Tod Cohen of eBay said, "We would work with the FTC, Congress and the administration to develop a national standard." Robert Levitan, CEO of Flooz.com, commented, "I would like to think that industry could self-regulate, but I think we all have accepted the fact that there will be some regulation. We're not jumping up and down complaining about regulation. We're just saying, let's do it wisely."[41] Andy Grove, Chairman of Intel, stated, "I would prefer to recognize this trend and get ahead of the possibility that . . . states are going to take matters in their own hands."[42]

## Doubleclick's Challenge

In putting Abacus Online on hold, Kevin Ryan, president of DoubleClick, said, "I think we could have done a better job of communicating. Because we are the largest and most successful Internet company in our space, we certainly attract more attacks than other people."[43] He observed, "There are always going to be controversies when people start using new technologies. When credit cards were introduced, people wouldn't use them because they were worried that the credit card companies would be tracking them. And when people first started using the Internet, they wouldn't buy anything because they were worried about credit card fraud. But they got over it."[44]

■

## PREPARATION QUESTIONS

1. How important is the privacy issue to Internet users? Is Kevin Ryan correct in his belief that users will get over their concern about privacy?
2. Why was there an uproar over DoubleClick's strategy when there was little concern about Abacus Direct's off-line data collection?

3. Should DoubleClick have anticipated the reaction to Abacus Online and the merger of the databases?
4. Is anonymous click-stream tracking and profiling objectionable? Is sending targeted

[41]*The New York Times,* May 22, 2000.
[42]*The National Journal,* June 17, 2000, p. 1924.
[43]*The Washington Post,* February 18, 2000.
[44]*U.S. News & World Report,* March 6, 2000.

advertising messages to a computer using cookie ID numbers objectionable?

5. How can DoubleClick restore consumer and public confidence in its business? Should it institute an opt-in policy?

6. What type of Internet privacy rights should individuals have? Is self-regulation adequate

to protect those rights? Is legislation needed? Is consumer ignorance of privacy protection issues and alternatives a sufficient rationale for government regulation of Internet privacy?

7. What should DoubleClick do about the FTC inquiry and request for new legislation?

# eBay: Private Ordering for an Online Community

*By providing a safe trading place on the Internet, the eBay community has flourished. Not only does eBay provide an efficient medium for people to buy or sell items directly from or to a large number of people, it's a forum where buyers and sellers develop reputations and, in some cases, it can change people's lives.*

*—eBay Web site[45]*

By the end of 2000 eBay hosted the world's largest online trading community of 22 million buyers and sellers. When it started in 1995, the eBay community consisted of a small group of people trading Pez dispensers. It grew dramatically in the next few years, and millions of items in thousands of categories were offered for sale at any given moment. eBay was used by people selling a few items from their attics and as a primary distribution method for personal businesses. Buyers included collectors and hobbyists, carpenters buying tools, and people searching for homes or automobiles.

This community of buyers and sellers was the core of eBay's business. Many were passionate, avid defenders of the community. eBay worked to nurture, develop, and grow its community. It sought to make the experience of buying and selling on its site both pleasant and safe. Since community members remained anonymous, trust among traders was essential. The principal instrument of trust was the reputation members developed based on feedback from their trading partners. As its community grew in size and diversity, eBay established rules of conduct to supplement the reputation mechanism. The reputation mechanism and the rules of conduct provided order for eBay's

community. As the community grew, that private ordering was both extended and broadened.

In addition, new issues arose on a regular basis, and old ones had to be revisited. By late 2000, some of these issues included

- the availability of contact information to facilitate communication between members while protecting the community from spam and privacy violations,
- members conducting their transactions outside the eBay marketplace,
- the sale of controversial items such as those associated with hate crimes,
- the sale of banned and regulated items.

## Background

In 1995 Pierre Omidyar founded eBay, Inc., which operated an Internet site AuctionWeb for person-to-person trading, inspired by his girlfriend's desire to find other collectors with whom to trade Pez dispensers. The initial participants were people with similar hobbies, but the number of buyers and sellers grew by word of mouth, and soon many different items were being traded. The growth continued and became difficult to manage, and Omidyar tried to slow it by charging fees. The growth continued unabated, however, and AuctionWeb was inundated

[45]pages.eBay.com/community/abouteBay/community/profiles.html.

with small checks. The person-to-person Internet auction industry had begun.

In the fall of 1997 Omidyar eliminated the AuctionWeb brand and the site began operating under the name of eBay. In May 1998 Meg Whitman joined the company as president and CEO, after serving as general manager of Hasbro and president and CEO of FTD. Omidyar continued as chairman. In 2000 more than 256 million items were listed for sale on eBay, in a wide range of categories, including antiques, collectibles, computer hardware, musical instruments, camera equipment, fine art, coins, stamps, cars, and real estate. By the end of 2000 eBay had local sites in 60 cities in the United States and country-specific sites in Austria, Australia, Canada, France, Germany, Ireland, Italy, Japan, Korea, New Zealand, Switzerland, and the United Kingdom.

In 2000 the company had $431 million in revenue, almost double the previous year, and $59 million in net income, an increase of more than three times over 1999. Market capitalization was over $8 billion at the end of 2000. In July 2000 eBay acquired Half.com, an online marketplace for sales at fixed prices. This provided an online outlet for sellers of discounted mass-market items, as well as a way for companies to sell overstocked or used merchandise.

eBay operated as an online venue for buyers and sellers. Sellers listed items and provided descriptions, often including photographs. An auction was then conducted in which potential buyers could bid on the item until a fixed time. The seller specified the conditions of the auction (such as the minimum opening bid, bid increments, and the reserve price, if any), as well as the time the auction would close. Potential buyers could place an initial bid and a maximum bid and authorize eBay to increase the bid to the maximum if forced by another bidder. Bidding was often active as the auction neared its closing time, sometimes driven by automated "sniping" programs that some buyers used to get their bid in just before the auction closed. After the auction ended, the sales transaction was completed between the seller and high bidder without eBay's involvement. eBay charged a small fee for listing an item for sale plus a fee based on the final sales price.[46]

In creating an online marketplace, eBay operated much like a newspaper classified section. It facilitated person-to-person transactions but did not take

[46]For items whose sales process was regulated, such as real estate and automobiles, the eBay fee was fixed rather than a percentage of the final sale price.

possession of the items being sold. It had no information about an item beyond the description provided by the seller, did not certify the items sold, did not handle the exchange, and assumed no liability for the sale. It exercised control over buying and selling only in restricting which items could be listed on its site (for instance, illegal items could not be listed) and on the configuration of the auctions. Even then eBay could not control listings before they were placed, and only whether a listing could remain on the site.

Traditional auction houses differed from eBay in many ways. Some auction houses served as the agent of the seller and were responsible for obtaining the best price for the items sold. They also served the buyer by authenticating the items. eBay performed neither of these roles. Some auction houses served as the bailee of the seller, took possession of the items, and provided a guarantee to either sell or return the items. eBay did not serve these functions either.

## Community Development

The foundation of eBay's business was its community of buyers and sellers. The size, growth, happiness, and loyalty of the community was its principal competitive advantage. For the eBay community to flourish, members had to be secure and confident in their interactions with one another. The eBay community was analogous to a real-world society in which people interacted with each other under a set of shared rules and expectations. In small, isolated communities in which everyone knew each other and had a strong sense of shared values, little regulation was required. However, as the community grew, became more diverse, and individuals felt more anonymous, trust could become problematic.

## Trust Among Members

eBay's fundamental challenge was to establish trust among remote and anonymous traders who might never interact again. Reputation served to establish trust. If a remote trader reneged on a sale or delivered an item different than its description, the other party could sully the reputation of the seller. Similarly, if a trader lived up to her promises, the trading partner could bolster her reputation. Such a reputation mechanism could engender trust but required an information system to report reputations to new trading partners and allow those reputations to be updated. Almost from its inception, eBay used a feedback system involving the posting of comments on a trade and a scoring rule to aggregate the feedback.

## Feedback

The most important vehicle for establishing trust was feedback, which allowed buyers and sellers to evaluate each other based on their experiences in eBay transactions. They could rate the transaction experience as positive, negative, or neutral and could also provide a written evaluation. Members obtained points when they received positive feedback and lost them when they received negative feedback. The feedback record, both the total points or score and the comments, established a community member's online reputation. The score and comments were automatically available to potential trading partners whenever an item was listed for sale or a bid was made. Reputation represented an asset for a trader and was jealously guarded, since negative feedback could ruin a seller's business. The feedback system also allowed sellers to determine if bidders had paid promptly in the past.

Initially, community members could provide feedback even if they had not been involved in a specific transaction. For instance, a member might provide comments on how a seller had handled a listed item. This "nontransactional" feedback was listed but was not reflected in the seller's numerical score. While this kind of feedback provided information, it also made the system vulnerable to "feedback bombing," an unhappy person flooding the system with feedback messages. Eventually, nontransactional feedback was eliminated. By late 2000 the system allowed only the parties to a transaction to provide feedback about each other.

Another issue was feedback removal. This was important because of the potential for feedback extortion. If feedback could be retracted, a buyer could give negative feedback and make a demand on the seller in exchange for removing the feedback. The importance of a member's online reputation made such threats serious. eBay's rules thus allowed removal of feedback only in specific situations, such as when it had been sent to the wrong address or when it contained personal information that was prohibited by another eBay policy. In cases not covered by the written policy, feedback was removed only by court order.

Although unwarranted feedback could not be removed, members could respond to the feedback given them, and the response was listed along with the original comment. For instance, a buyer might provide

feedback stating that the seller was late in delivering. The seller might reply that he was waiting for the buyer's check to clear and report how long it had taken from receipt of the check to the shipment of the item. Potential bidders could evaluate the situation for themselves before deciding if they wanted to bid on an item offered by that seller.

## Rules of Operation

The eBay community was subject to the laws that governed society as a whole ("public law," which creates a "public order") as well as to rules that eBay developed to supplement the feedback mechanism creating "private order" for its community. The rules eBay developed were intended to further the interests of the community, and of eBay, within the overall constraints of public law. Those rules were based on a guiding principle—do what is good for the community and what is good for the enterprise. eBay's community was subject to the public laws regulating sales. Sales of illegal goods, such as controlled substances, were prohibited, as were sales of counterfeit goods or sales of items such as software or music in violation of copyright laws.

Public law also prohibited fraud, such as failure to deliver the purchased item, listing an item with a misleading description, and manipulating auctions (for example, "shill" bidding in which the seller engaged accomplices to place bids intended to drive the price higher, which is illegal in some jurisdictions). eBay worked with law enforcement officials to assist victimized members and help ensure that community members could deal with each other in an atmosphere of trust. eBay's view of fraud was realistic. It believed that it could stop the amateur, but stopping the determined professional would be very difficult. To combat fraud, the company employed two former federal law enforcement officers and in both San Jose and Salt Lake City maintained support staff dedicated to fraud and piracy issues.

In addition to protecting the community from illegal activity, eBay's rules supported trust among members. Those rules were stated in the User Agreement that each member agreed to when registering to join the eBay community. Violations of the agreement were punishable by warnings and temporary or permanent suspension from eBay. The agreement was supplemented by policies, such as a detailed privacy policy, and processes, such as the feedback mechanism. These rules, policies, and processes constituted the private ordering of eBay.

## Tools for Assisting Safe Transactions

In addition to the feedback system for building reputations, community members could use a number of tools to make their transactions more secure or to resolve disputes. Some of these were developed by eBay, while others were provided by third parties that contracted with eBay.

**Insurance**  Most purchases on eBay were protected by a free insurance policy administered by Lloyd's of London as part of the standard eBay service. The policy protected against items that were purchased but not delivered or those that were of substantially less value than described (such as bidding on a gold item and receiving a copper one). The policy provided coverage up to $200, with a $25 deductible.

**Escrow**  To protect buyers and sellers in high-value transactions, eBay contracted with Tradenable, a third-party escrow service company. The service was available with the agreement of both buyer and seller and was generally used for purchases of over $500. When using the service, the buyer paid the purchase price to Tradenable, which notified the seller. The seller shipped the item to the buyer. When the buyer received and accepted the item, Tradenable paid the seller. The escrow service fees were paid as agreed between the buyer and seller.

**Payment Methods**  Transactions took place directly between the buyer and seller; eBay was not a party to any transaction. Payment for an item was made in a manner agreeable to both buyer and seller. This might be by credit card, check, or through an Internet payment system. eBay established one such system, called Billpoint, through which buyers could establish an account that would be used to pay sellers. Similar systems, such as PayPal, were provided by third-party companies and were available to eBay traders.[47]

**Dispute Resolution**  Disputes between buyers and sellers occasionally arose. eBay believed that a respected, independent third party could assist in resolving these disputes. The company contracted with SquareTrade to provide a free online dispute resolution service for eBay members. When a member filed a complaint, it notified the other party, and the two could use online negotiation tools within a secure portion of the SquareTrade Web site to resolve the disagreement. Most conflicts were resolved using this system. If a dispute were not resolved using the online system, for a $15 fee the parties could request a SquareTrade mediator, who would mediate the dispute online.

Sellers could obtain a SquareTrade Seal if they agreed to participate in dispute resolution in the event of a problem, committed to SquareTrade's standards for online selling, and had their identity verified. The SquareTrade Seal then was displayed when they listed items for sale, providing additional information to buyers in evaluating the seller's trustworthiness.

**Authentication**  For many items, confirmation of authenticity of items was important. eBay did not authenticate, as it never saw the items offered on its site. However, it did refer sellers to experts who could provide authentication services. Referrals were made for authenticating art works, stamps, coins, sports memorabilia, Beanie Babies, comics, and trading cards. Some buyers also hired their own experts to authenticate items before purchasing.

## Trust in eBay

Trust between community members and eBay was also important. Three primary issues—privacy, community support, and fraud prevention—were central to that trust.

### Community Support

As eBay grew, it learned that many users felt that it was their community and objected strenuously to unilateral changes by eBay. In one early case, eBay changed the system by which feedback scores were graphically displayed. That system used stars shown after the member's user name. The eBay employee charged with revising the system changed the colors of the stars, implementing the change without consulting the community. Two weeks of flaming e-mails, angry phone calls, and upset chatboard postings ensued. Finally, the employee rescinded the changes and asked the community members what they wanted. For two weeks she received input, leading to extensive dialog with the users. eBay learned that its community was powerful and wanted to be consulted on issues affecting it.

In 1997 there were only 40 categories of items for sale, but the postings increased dramatically and additional categories were needed. eBay evaluated the items listed and developed new listing categories, again without consulting the community. The result was 4 weeks of angry e-mails and phone calls. Not only were users passionate about their community, but they were also much more knowledgeable about the items traded than eBay employees could ever hope to be. Categories that made sense to a generalist were viewed as inappropriate by those with detailed knowledge of the items and how people collected them. For instance, there were many types of buttons of interest to different groups of traders. Eventually, four categories were created for buttons, three in the collectibles part of the site and one in the hobbies and crafts section.

**Voices** These experiences led eBay to solicit user input in decisions affecting the community—primarily the features and functionality of the site. eBay customer service representatives were open with users and were required by the company to respond to user e-mails as quickly as possible. Ideas for changes were discussed with users, and their comments were considered when making changes. eBay was uncertain whether the users participating were a vocal minority or if they represented the majority opinion. However, they were passionate, and passionate people were evangelists, accessible to anyone interested in the company, including competitors and investors. It was important for them to be committed to eBay.

When eBay went public in an IPO in 1998, communications had to be more controlled. The company was subject to SEC disclosure regulations and to intense scrutiny by the press. To continue communications with its community and at the same time exercise control over disclosures, a mechanism was needed to interact with its community while keeping pending changes confidential.

The company decided to form a group called "Voices," consisting of 12 people from the eBay community. eBay defined the types of people it wanted for Voices—initially a broad spectrum of buyers and sellers—and the community suggested candidates. Those selected agreed to participate for 1 year, without compensation, and to sign a nondisclosure agreement. They were brought to eBay for 2 days of meetings with key eBay personnel. eBay discussed its plans with the group but spent significant time listening to the group. After returning home, the group continued to discuss issues with eBay by e-mail and telephone.

New Voices groups were started each quarter, and occasionally a Voices group would be constituted for a shorter period to focus on a particular issue, such as how to improve the way in which eBay dealt with a specific item category. More generally, Voices helped eBay make better decisions on issues affecting the community.

In some cases, decisions were made without Voices input, as in the case of a legal requirement.

Sometimes even these were discussed with one or more Voices groups before implementation or a public announcement. This allowed eBay to better understand the likely reaction of the community, implement the change more effectively, address anticipated concerns in the announcement, and prepare responses (FAQs) to concerns raised by the announcement.

### Enforcement and Fraud Prevention

Members remained concerned about the potential for fraud even though the fraud rate was very low.[48] eBay actively supported law enforcement efforts to identify and prosecute fraud. When a member contacted eBay regarding potential illegal activity, eBay identified the appropriate law enforcement official and in some cases assisted in the investigation. In some cases the scope of illegal activity was not apparent based on an initial complaint. eBay frequently was able to identify additional victims and put them in contact with the appropriate law enforcement officials.

Two cases illustrate eBay's involvement in detecting and prosecuting fraud. In one case, a seller offered a wide variety of items for sale, including sunglasses, Rolex watches, diamonds, rare coins, and computer equipment. However, the items did not exist. Buyers made their payments and received no goods. The buyers had no way of knowing the true identity of the person who had defrauded them. When eBay received complaints, it had the information needed to identify the seller and connect the victims with the appropriate law enforcement officials. eBay also determined who had "won" auctions from the fraudulent seller, notified them of the suspected fraud, and gave them the contact information. Without eBay's involvement, law enforcement could not have determined the full extent of the fraud or identified all the victims.

In another case, an unusual coin, described as an "1879c Morgan Hill Silver Dollar," was offered for sale. A photograph was included in the listing, showing the coin encased in a plastic container with a serial number from a grading service (an independent firm that authenticates coins). The bidding was heavy,

---

[48] The fraud rate on eBay was low, at approximately one case per 40,000 listings, in part due to eBay's efforts to prevent fraud and the community's vigilant policing efforts. However, the large number of listings on its site required continual diligence in identifying and eliminating fraud.

reaching well over $100,000. A community member, who was a coin expert, contacted eBay to express his concern about the coin's authenticity. The member had never heard of the coin and suggested that eBay investigate. eBay's lawyers contacted the grading service. The service had never heard of such a coin, and the serial number in the listing corresponded to a Lincoln penny. Apparently, the seller had digitally created the photograph in the listing and was attempting to defraud buyers. eBay contacted the Secret Service, which investigated and arrested the seller.[49]

eBay also formed a group to detect fraud by screening for suspicious activity using a profile. When it found potentially fraudulent behavior, it investigated further, and if necessary contacted potential victims and law enforcement officials.

## Issues Facing eBay and Its Community

Many issues faced eBay and its rapidly growing community at the end of 2000. Addressing them in a manner that sustained trust among community members and between the community and eBay was essential to an increasingly diverse and dispersed community of traders. Four issues illustrate the challenges: communication between members, off-site transactions, the sale of controversial items, and recalled and regulated items.

### Communication Between Members

Originally, members had access to all other members' e-mail addresses and thus could communicate directly with each other. When an item was listed for sale, the seller's e-mail address and the addresses of each bidder were also displayed. This was done to facilitate communication in the belief that visibility would encourage good conduct. It was a natural consequence of eBay's philosophy that "people are generally good."

As the community grew and more people became aware of eBay, problems arose. One problem was that outsiders could collect members' e-mail addresses ("e-mail harvesting") and use them for their own purposes, such as sending unsolicited e-mail ("spam").

eBay's competitors could also collect e-mail addresses and solicit business. In 1997 OnSale, Inc. sent unsolicited e-mail to eBay members announcing its competitive auction service. OnSale had used software to gather e-mail addresses from eBay's site.[50] OnSale had registered as an eBay member and thus agreed to the eBay User Agreement. Violation of the agreement was sufficient for eBay to force a halt to this practice.

In 1999 using information it had taken from the eBay database, another competitor, ReverseAuction, sent e-mail messages to eBay users, stating incorrectly that their eBay user IDs would soon expire and suggesting that they join ReverseAuction. In this case, the Federal Trade Commission intervened, resulting in a consent decree that forced ReverseAuction to notify eBay users who had registered with its site, prohibiting it from making further misrepresentations, and imposing other sanctions.[51] eBay later sued ReverseAuction and obtained a monetary award.

In addition to e-mail harvesting and spamming, privacy was a concern, as members did not want their e-mail addresses broadly publicized. However, it was still important for members to be able to communicate regarding transactions. A potential buyer needed to be able to ask questions of the seller. Buyers and sellers also needed to communicate after the auction was completed to finalize the payment and shipping arrangements and deal with any post-sale issues.

Some companies requested e-mail addresses from eBay. A manufacturer of crystal collectibles, for instance, would benefit from a list of all people who bid on items it had made, as well as those who bid on competitors' products. Such requests identified a potential business opportunity for eBay. It could partner with companies that were interested in selling to a highly targeted audience. Members with specialized interests might also see such partnerships as beneficial. However, providing member contact information to other companies or organizations was not possible within eBay's existing privacy policy.

---

[49]In this case, the member who first informed eBay worked undercover with the Secret Service by placing a high bid on the item to prevent others from bidding. When he won, the seller told him where to send the payment, and he forwarded the information to the Secret Service.

[50]"Internet Spam," EDGE: Work-Group Computing Report, EDGE Publishing, November 10, 1997.

[51]Daniel R. Valente, "Database Protection in the Next Century," *Information Today*, June 1, 2000. The consent decree, filed in federal court on January 6, 2000, can be found at www.ftc.gov/os/2000/01/reverseconsent.htm.

The ability of users to communicate with each other for legitimate purposes, while protecting privacy and preventing spam, continued to pose problems. The eBay legal staff and community relations personnel were constantly assessing the balance between protecting the company and community versus the benefits of open communication. Should they place new restrictions on the community? How should they handle requests by manufacturers to partner and provide targeted e-mail lists?

### Off-Site Transactions

Sales outside the eBay marketplace were a concern to eBay as an enterprise, since it did not receive fees for off-site transactions. The company was also concerned that off-site transactions deprived the participants of eBay's services in case of problems. The number of these transactions was unknown, but eBay believed that it was significant.

In one type of off-site transaction, the seller, after the auction, would note the e-mail addresses of losing bidders and contact them directly, offering to sell them the same or a similar item without going though eBay. The initial auction thus served as an advertisement for off-site sales. In another type, a buyer and seller that had a successful transaction using eBay might conduct additional business off-site in the future. Off-site transactions also occurred when sellers included hyperlinks in their listings that directed potential bidders to their own Web sites, where they could make purchases without going through eBay.

Off-site transactions were a difficult issue for eBay and its community. On the one hand, if off-site transactions were successful, its members would be happy and likely to continue to use eBay for other transactions. On the other hand, eBay lost revenue from off-site transactions, and members lost the protections eBay offered, such as feedback, insurance, payment options, and dispute resolution services. Moreover, if the off-site transactions were bad experiences for buyers, trust between eBay and the community could be weakened. In some cases, the buyer might be confused, thinking that the eBay protections applied to a purchase that had not been made on the eBay site.

In one case, a member sold a Rolex watch on eBay. The seller then contacted the second-highest bidder and offered to sell another Rolex. The person agreed, sending several thousand dollars to the seller. When he received the watch, he found that it was a fake. The member sued eBay (unsuccessfully),

even though it had been an off-site transaction, not covered by the User Agreement.

eBay advised its members not to participate in off-site transactions because of the potential risks. The User Agreement and Listing Policy prohibited practices that circumvented eBay's fee structure, such as the sale of catalogs that offered items for sale outside the eBay venue.[52] eBay believed that off-site transactions still caused a serious loss of business and potentially placed members in jeopardy. Was this something they should give high priority? What could eBay do to prevent off-site transactions?

### Controversial Items

Items that were legal to buy and sell but were offensive to members of the eBay community were a concern. Three obvious examples were Nazi memorabilia, material from hate groups such as the Ku Klux Klan, and items associated with heinous crimes, sometimes called "murderabilia." While such items could be objectionable, they were legal to sell in the United States. Also, prohibiting their sale would represent a form of editorial censorship.

eBay's basic policy was that as long as the sale of an item was legal, it could be sold on the site. Exceptions were items subject to a myriad of local laws and regulations that made sale on eBay impractical, such as alcohol, tobacco, and firearms.

**Items Related to Hate Groups** This issue was contentious but not clear-cut. On the one hand, Nazi-related items might be offered for sale by a World War II veteran who had obtained them during the war. Such items might be of interest to museums, academic institutions, or history enthusiasts. On the other hand, a neo-Nazi group might try to use eBay to sell its paraphernalia. The seller could also try to express his or her philosophy and include hyperlinks to the group's Web site. The eBay listing policy prohibited hate speech and required that the listing be limited to things relevant to the sale of the item. The potential for abuse, however, existed.

eBay did not want to become, or be perceived as, a platform for the expression of hate. Such a perception might damage the company's reputation and cause people to avoid the site. Moreover, eBay recognized that just the knowledge that hate-related items were listed would disturb some members, weakening its community.

---

[52]pages.ebay.com/help/community/png-list.html.

eBay was expanding internationally, and some countries, such as France and Germany, prohibited the sale of Nazi-related items. These items were not allowed on the Web sites serving France and Germany, but eBay's reputation could be harmed in those countries if the items were sold in the United States.

**Items Related to Crimes** There were several classes of items associated with notorious criminals and crimes. For instance, items associated with the assassination of President Lincoln were likely to be of historical interest and probably not widely objectionable. However, items associated with a recent mass murderer were likely to be objectionable to large segments of the eBay community and extremely traumatic to the families of the victims. If objectionable items should be prohibited, could this be done in an objective, fair manner?

**Recalled and Regulated Items**

Problems with the sale of recalled items first surfaced in early 2000, when a community member complained about a listing for "Jarts." eBay investigated and learned that a "Jart" was a lawn dart that

had been recalled by the Consumer Products Safety Commission. They further learned that there were several such listings on its site.

eBay realized that members might be cleaning out their attics, selling old toys and other items without knowing that the items had been recalled. This was possible in a variety of categories, such as baby toys, cribs, and power tools. In addition, some people might be unwittingly selling items made from endangered species or trading items internationally that were prohibited by import/export regulations. How could the company address the innocent sale of recalled products and other items that were prohibited by law without inhibiting the sale of other similar items that were legal?

---

**PREPARATION QUESTIONS**

1. How did eBay's position as a venue affect the development of its community policies?

2. What are the fundamental problems eBay addressed in building trust among its members and between its members and the company? Are its policies and practices appropriate for building trust?

3. How do eBay's policies regarding communication between members affect the community? How might they hurt eBay? What should eBay

do to optimize communication between members without negative results?

4. How do off-site transactions affect eBay and its community? What should the company do to address the issue of off-site transactions?

5. How should eBay address the sale of items associated with hate groups and crimes? How does the company's statement of values affect this issue?

6. What should eBay do regarding the potential sale of recalled products and other problem items?

---

# Google: Gmail and Privacy

*Consumers really need to look this gift horse in the mouth because it has rotten teeth and bad breath.*

—Beth Givens, Privacy Rights Clearinghouse[53]

*That's why I'm a little baffled by this. We take people's trust in us very seriously. If we were to violate that trust, that would hurt our business seriously.*

—Larry Page, President-Products, Google[54]

*We are not going over to the dark side. Consumers can expect us to treat their e-mail as private and with a great deal of respect. I don't think we are doing anything unreasonable.*

— Wayne Rosing, Vice-President, Google[55]

## Google

In 1996 two Stanford University PhD students, Sergey Brin and Larry Page, wrote as a project a search engine that counted the links to a Web site. The search engine became popular at Stanford, and observing its popularity, the pair left school and launched Google from a rented garage.[57] In a little over a year the company had raised $25 million in venture capital and had millions of users. By 2004 Google handled 138,000 queries a minute in over 100 languages in searching 6 billion Web pages. Google was so successful that the word "Google" had become a verb.

The founders sought to build a company with a culture consistent with their personal styles. The company's motto was "Don't be evil." The 1,000 employees at its Googleplex campus in Mountain View, California, enjoyed free food and unlimited ice cream, and engineers were allowed to spend 20 percent of their time on projects of interest to them. Scientists, however, were not allowed to publish their results.

Google's 2003 revenue was $962 million, 96 percent of which came from advertising based on its AdSense service that provided advertising based on the search words entered by a user. Profits were $106 million. In the first quarter 2004 revenue was $390 million and profits were $64 million. Web advertising was estimated at $4 billion annually and was projected to triple over the following 4 years.

In the early spring of 2004 investment bankers expected Google, Inc. to soon file papers for an initial public offering (IPO), which they anticipated could result in a record IPO valuation of $20 to $30 billion. On April Fools Day 2004 Google launched a beta version of a free e-mail service—Gmail—with one gigabyte of memory provided for each user. In exchange a user agreed to allow Google to search its e-mail messages for keywords and receive targeted advertisements displayed with the message. Google requested volunteers, and hundreds of thousands of Internet users applied for the service.[56] The response from privacy advocates was quite different, however. Privacy groups strongly criticized Google and Gmail and warned consumers of the dangers associated with the service. Politicians joined in the criticism with a California state legislator introducing a bill to stop the service. Google was dismayed by the response to its offering, since Gmail was accompanied by a strong privacy policy. Google had to decide whether to make any changes to its service before it offered Gmail to the general public.

## Gmail

Gmail provided free e-mail service with 1 gigabyte of memory, which was up to 500 times greater than that of the free e-mail services offered by Yahoo! and Microsoft's Hotmail. Gmail also allowed the user to organize messages in a variety of convenient ways. A user who subscribed to Gmail agreed to have messages searched for keywords and receive advertisements associated with those words. Google provided a Gmail Privacy Policy, which stated, "By using Gmail, you agree to the collection and use of your personal information as described in this policy."

The only personal information required from a Gmail user was a first and a last name. Gmail did not use cookies to identify a user but instead identified the user's location by the service hub where the user logged on. The Gmail system searched incoming e-mail messages for keywords selected by advertisers, and when found, a text advertising message appeared along with the message. Ads were placed via Google's widely used AdSense.

Advertisers received information on Gmail users when they clicked on an advertisement. Google's Gmail Privacy Policy stated, "Advertisers receive a record of the total number of impressions and clicks for each ad. They do not receive any personal information about the person who viewed the ad. If you click on an ad, Google will send a referring URL to the advertiser's site identifying that you are visiting from Gmail. Google does not send personally

[55]*Financial News,* April 7, 2004.
[56]Part of the explanation of the rush to the new e-mail service was believed to be people who sought to obtain their favorite e-mail name. Google subsequently invited individuals to join the beta version of Gmail.
[57]The name Google is a based on the word googol, which is 1 followed by 100 zeroes.

identifiable information to advertisers with the referring URL. Once you are on the advertiser's site, however, the advertiser may collect personal information about you. Google does not control or take responsibility for the privacy policies of other sites."[58] Sergey Brin commented, "We wouldn't store anything related to what ads show up in your e-mail messages. That is one of the misconceptions."[59]

## The Privacy Issue

The privacy concerns stemmed from the user's understanding of Gmail, the possibility that Gmail information could be combined with the possibility that Gmail information could be combined with tracking data from other Google searches, possible access to the data from outside Google, and more general considerations about privacy in society. As the privacy policy stated, when a user closed his or her Gmail account, the data could be retained for an indefinite period. Google used cookies with its search engine to provide convenience to users. The cookies allowed Google to keep track of the Web pages visited by its users.

California state senator Liz Figueroa introduced a bill to block the service. She stated, "I cannot urge you strongly enough to abandon this misbegotten idea. I believe you are embarking on a disaster of enormous proportions, for yourself, and for all your customers. The proposal is little different from asking people to let the phone company listen in on their calls and butt in at any time to say, 'This call is brought to you by...'"[60] She called Gmail a Faustian bargain.

Twenty-eight privacy organizations, including the Consumer Federation of America, the Electronic Privacy Information Center (EPIC), and Privacy International, wrote to Google urging that Gmail be suspended. The organizations wrote that Gmail "sets potentially dangerous precedents and establishes reduced expectations of privacy in e-mail communications. These precedents may be adopted by other companies and governments and may persist long after Google is gone."

Google responded that the searches of e-mail messages would be done solely by computers with no human involvement. Pam Dixon of the World Privacy Forum countered, "The fact that it's machines is

irrelevant. Machines are much more efficient than humans and far more able to be privacy invasive than humans because they can read so much more. We're concerned that users of Gmail, who must give Google their names to sign up, may have their names correlated with the search terms they type in when searching. This can be done through cookies and IP addresses."[61] Wayne Rosing responded, "We do not keep that data in correlated form, it's separated in various ways and we have policies inside the company that do not allow that kind of correlation to happen. We consider any program or programming that correlates user data with user identity to be a violation of trust and we do not do that."[62] Google was cautious in its response, since it knew that it could be forced under subpoena to supply both Gmail and search data. Rosing pointed out that antispam and antivirus filters also searched e-mail messages.

Simon Davies of Privacy International filed complaints with 17 countries in Europe as well as in Canada and Australia. Davies stated, "We will be filing simultaneous complaints with the data privacy regulations of every other European nation on April 22 should we not receive a satisfactory response from the ICO [UK's information commission]. Germany, for example, has much stricter policies regarding privacy and they would not blink at taking severe action. Sweden, as well, has shown a willingness to address similar issues."[63] Davies suggested that the privacy policy could violate Article 7(a) of the European Union's Data Protection Directive, which requires that a consumer give informed and unambiguous consent to the use of personal information. Davies said, "The service is fundamentally unlawful, under EU law, under the Data Protection Act. EU law is explicit on this point. There's a sanctity in communications that must be protected."[64] Davies warned, "If millions of people have their communication history kept on Google computers, then that storehouse becomes a very valuable source of information for a range of unintended consequences."[65] Michael Allison, of the Internet Crimes Group in New Jersey, said, "Google could create a potential monster—people with wicked ways could use it for everything from

---

58 www.google.com/gmail/help/help/privacy.html.
59 *The Washington Post*, May 13, 2004.
60 A web user checked Figueroa's Web site and reported that not only did it collect personal information but it did not have a privacy policy. (*Washington Internet Daily*, April 15, 2004.)

61 ClickZ News, www.clickz.com, April 2, 2004.
62 ClickZ News, www.clickz.com, April 2, 2004.
63 IDG News Service, www.infoworld.com, April 15, 2004.
64 Marketplace Morning Report, April 20, 2004.
65 www.cbsnews.com, April 7, 2004.

extortion to harassment."[66] In the United States the Electronic Communications Privacy Act prohibited persons from intercepting and reading e-mail.

A spokesperson for the UK's ICO stated, "As long as Google makes it clear that it is monitoring e-mail usage and passing that information on for marketing purposes, there shouldn't be a problem. But I want to make it clear that Google has not even launched the service yet, and has agreed to work with us to make sure that its notification process is very clear."[67]

A Google spokesperson said, "We are confident that Gmail is fully compliant with data protection laws worldwide. Google actively solicits user feedback on our privacy policies. If they can be made clearer or otherwise improved, we want to hear about it. We look forward to a detailed dialogue with data protection authorities across Europe to insure their concerns are heard and resolved."[68]

Kevin Bankston of the Electronic Frontier Foundation said, "Google is in a de facto manner creating incredibly detailed dossiers on every one of us that the government would never be allowed to create. And by creating them, they become available to the government."[69] Ari Schwartz of the Center for Democracy and Technology (CDT) said Gmail has a "definite creepiness factor." CDT, however, did not join the 28 other organizations in a letter to Google because notice and disclosure were adequately provided.

Chris Hoofnagle of EPIC said, "Individuals would be throwing away the protections of their communications for a few dollars. We don't see this as any different than letting a company listen in on your phone conversations and letting the Postal Service

open your mail."[70] He also said, "It's an interference into an area where people have enjoyed a great deal of privacy. It's like a telemarketer listening in to your phone call and then trying to sell you something."[71]

Harrison Rainie, director of the Pew Institute and American Life Project, commented, "You tell people the trade-off you're making is you're letting yourself be followed significantly in exchange for some convenience. Most people say, that's fine."[72] Matthew Berk, an Internet analyst, said, "At the end of the day, consumer behavior will defer to convenience. When it comes to privacy concerns the bark is always far worse than the bite."[73] In 1999 Scott McNealy, CEO of Sun Microsystems, had said, "You have zero privacy anyway. Get over it."[74]

## The Challenge

Google had planned to offer Gmail to the public in 3 to 6 months after reviewing experience with the beta version. The initial reaction to Gmail was both gratifying and troubling. The number of users applying for the beta version suggested strong demand for the service, but the privacy criticism had surprised the company. In spite of the privacy criticism, Sergey Brin said, "I'm not seeing any rash changes to make off the bat. I'm nervous about making a change based on feedback from people who haven't had a chance to try it out yet."[75] Wayne Rosing said that Gmail was "entirely an opt-in service and anyone who reads our privacy policy can make their own decision."[76]

## PREPARATION QUESTIONS

1. Why is there any privacy objection to Gmail if no one is forced to use it and all users must opt-in?
2. Is the concern about what machines could do rather than what they actually do?
3. What changes if any would you make before the full launch of Gmail?
4. If you allow Gmail users to opt out of the advertising, how much memory should Google

provide them, or what should it charge them for Gmail?
5. Are your competitors likely to match Gmail with a similar service of their own? And offer stronger privacy?

[66]*The Daily Telegraph*, April 14, 2004.
[67]www.infoworld.com. nd.
[68]IDG News Service, www.infoworld.com, April 15, 2004.
[69]*The Wall Street Journal*, April 6, 2004.
[70]www.cbsnews.com, April 7, 2004.
[71]*San Jose Mercury News*, April 2, 2004.
[72]*The Wall Street Journal*, April 6, 2004.
[73]*The Wall Street Journal*, April 6, 2004.
[74]*The Wall Street Journal*, April 6, 2004.
[75]*USA Today*, April 15, 2004.
[76]*The Wall Street Journal*, April 6, 2004.

# Pharmaceutical Switching

*If the FDA agrees to these switches, the changes discussed today will be the tip of the iceberg. It is likely that many products will be proposed for such changes of status on a very frequent basis by those who have a strong self-interest in the change.*[1]

—Bert Spilker of the Pharmaceutical Research and Manufacturers Association

U.S. spending on prescription pharmaceuticals increased by 19 percent to $131.9 billion in 2000, the fifth consecutive year of increases above 13 percent. One factor contributing to the increased spending was direct-to-consumer advertising of prescription drugs, which was allowed under relaxed Food and Drug Administration (FDA) guidelines in 1997. Pharmaceutical companies responded aggressively to the opportunity. In 1999 Schering-Plough spent $137.4 million on advertising for Claritin, an antihistamine used to treat allergies.[2] Sales of Claritin reached $2.5 billion in the United States in 2000.

Prescription pharmaceuticals were covered by insurance programs, whereas over-the-counter (OTC) drugs were not. The increased spending on prescription drugs imposed a substantial burden on insurance companies. In an unprecedented action on July 22, 1998, Robert C. Seidman, vice president and chief pharmacy officer of Blue Cross of California, a unit of WellPoint Health Networks, Inc., filed a Citizen Petition with the FDA seeking an exemption for three second-generation antihistamines, Allegra (fexofenadine), Claritin (loratadine), and Zyrtec (cetirizine), used to treat allergic rhinitis. The exemption would in effect switch the drugs from prescription to OTC status. The petition noted that over 100 antihistamines were already sold over the counter, and those first-generation drugs were more "dangerous" than the second-generation nonsedating drugs. The petition stated that prescription status "deprives a majority of patients ready access to quality pharmaceutical care" and places an undue burden on patients. The petition also noted, "Patients are seeking greater ownership of their health care and often prefer to self-medicate when feasible."

A switch would not only put the second-generation antihistamines under considerable price pressure but would also disrupt the product planning of their manufacturers. Moreover, a switch initiated by an insurance company could lead to future petitions for switches of other prescription drugs.

On May 11, 2001, an FDA advisory committee composed of doctors and researchers voted overwhelmingly that the three second-generation antihistamines could safely be marketed over the counter. Although the vote was not binding, the FDA usually acted in accord with the judgments of its advisory committees. The pharmaceutical companies strongly objected to the committee's vote and faced the challenge of developing a strategy for dealing with the threat.

## The Petition

Claritin (loratadine) was first marketed in Belgium and Canada in 1988, and in 1989 Canada switched it to the OTC market. In 2001 loratadine was sold on a prescription-only basis in approximately 80 countries, and in 17 countries it was sold "behind the counter," requiring supervision of a pharmacist. In four countries, Canada, Australia, New Zealand, and the Philippines, it was sold over the counter.[3] Allegra

[1] *San Jose Mercury News,* May 12, 2001.

[2] In 1999 AstraZeneca and Pfizer each spent $79.5 million on Prilosec and Viagra respectively. In the first half of 2000 Merck spent $94.6 million on Vioxx.

[3] Schering-Plough, "Briefing Book," April 12, 2001, p. 7.

was produced by Aventis Pharmaceutical, and Zyrtec was produced by UCB SA and marketed in the United States by Pfizer. In 2000 U.S. sales of the three drugs were nearly $4.5 billion with Claritin accounting for $2.5 billion, Allegra $1.1 billion, and Zyrtec $800 million.

Making the three nonsedating antihistamines available on a prescription-only basis was part of the conservative approach used by the FDA. Two other nonsedating antihistamines, terfenadine (Seldane) and astemizole, had been approved on a prescription-only basis and after a few years of marketing were withdrawn from the U.S. market because of a serious safety concern associated with cardiac arrhythmias.

The petition by Blue Cross was unprecedented. The only other switch petitions had been filed by pharmaceutical companies seeking approval to move their drugs to the OTC market. A number of widely used OTC drugs, including Actifed, Bactine, Dimetapp, Pepcid, Sominex, and Tagamet, had been switched by their makers to the OTC market. In 1982 the FDA had initiated a switch of metaproterenol, but criticism by physicians led it to return the drug to prescription status.

In January 1999 the FDA indicated that it needed more time to evaluate the petition. In June 2000 it held a hearing to review the process of switching a drug from prescription to OTC status. The FDA also established an OTC Switch Review Team in the Center for Drug Evaluation and Research (CDER) and scheduled the May 11 meeting. The staff noted that Canadian regulators had studied the post-marketing experience with Claritin and had taken no significant regulatory action since it was first sold on the OTC market. A review of the safety and scientific evidence by the FDA staff concluded that the second-generation antihistamines had "certain safety advantages" as well as cognition advantages relative to first-generation antihistamines, many of which were marketed as OTC sleep aids. The Federal Aviation Administration allowed pilots to fly while taking Claritin and Allegra but not first-generation antihistamines.

The FDA had earlier ruled in a separate docket that antihistamines as a class could be sold on the OTC market and that consumers could diagnose allergies and treat them without consulting a doctor. Paradoxically, the sedating antihistamines were available over the counter, whereas the nonsedating antihistamines were available only by prescription. Referring to the Claritin advertisements that proclaimed that the drug was safe like "a sugar pill," Blue Cross's Seidman said, "If they are marketing these like candy, then they should be sold like candy."

The joint advisory committee composed of the Pulmonary-Allergy Drug Advisory Committee and the Nonprescription Drugs (OTC) Advisory Committee met on May 11 to review evidence on whether the three antihistamines could be used safely by consumers without the intervention of a doctor. The Food, Drug and Cosmetics Act stated that drugs were to be sold on a prescription-only status only if a "learned intermediary" was required for proper use. The question to be answered for each of the three drugs by the joint committee was, Does loratadine (fexofenadine, cetirizine) have a safety profile acceptable for OTC marketing; that is, can it be used safely without a learned intermediary? The Durham-Humphrey Amendment to the Food, Drug and Cosmetic Act added, "A drug is expected to be made available without a prescription if, by following the labeling, consumers can use it safely and effectively without professional guidance." The FDA had implemented that requirement by asking three questions: Can the condition be adequately self-diagnosed? Can the condition be successfully self-treated? Is the self-treatment product safe and effective for consumer use under conditions of actual use?

After reviewing safety data and hearing presentations from WellPoint, Aventis, and Schering-Plough, the committee voted 19–4 in the cases of Claritin and Zyrtec and 18–5 in the case of Allegra that a learned intermediary was not required for safe and proper use. If the FDA followed the advice of the joint committee, the implications would be profound. "This is a new paradigm," said John Jenkins, director of the FDA's office of drug evaluation."[4]

## Opposition to a Switch

In its presentation at the May 11 meeting Schering-Plough made three broad points: "1. Prescription status may be necessary to protect and optimize public health. 2. The safety profiles of the second-generation antihistamines in an OTC setting are not fully known. 3. Allergies are frequently chronic, complex diseases with serious co-morbidities."[5]

[4] *San Jose Mercury News*, May 12, 2001.
[5] Robert J. Spiegel, Schering-Plough, Presentation to FDA Advisory Committee, May 11, 2001.

The principal co-morbidities were asthma, sinusitis, and otitis media. The principal concern cited by Schering-Plough was that allergies occurred with more serious conditions such as asthma. The company stated that 78 percent of asthma patients have nasal symptoms, and 38 percent of allergic rhinitis patients have asthma. This resulted in 3 million Claritin prescriptions being co-prescribed with asthma medications.

Schering-Plough argued that OTC sales of Claritin would lead consumers not to visit their doctors when they had allergy symptoms, leaving many of the co-morbid conditions such as asthma undiagnosed and untreated. Dr. Robert J. Spiegel, chief medical officer for Schering-Plough, noted that asthma cases had increased by 75 percent from 1980 to 1994, and deaths increased from 11.5 to 18.0 per million people.[6] Schering-Plough concluded that the FDA should make a decision on the switch only after a "robust assessment," which would require evidence on the following:[7]

- Ability to accurately self-diagnose the condition
- Assessment of risk of initial misdiagnosis
- Assessment of label comprehension under conditions of use
- Assessment of risk of disease exacerbation or common co-morbid conditions due to subsequent misdiagnosis
- Assessment of risk of incorrect dosing (voluntary and/or inadvertent)
- Assessment of potential outcomes of OTC use

In a filing in conjunction with the May 11 hearing, the American Academy of Otolaryngology—Head and Neck Surgery wrote, "We believe that it is critical for patients with severe allergy problems to see a physician.... There is great public health risk in inappropriate and/or over utilization of these potent second generation drugs owing to inaccurate self-diagnosis and potential overmedication. In addition, we believe that pharmacists provide important patient education on adverse interactions of drugs."[8] Dr. Hari Sachs, a member of the Nonprescription Drugs Advisory Committee, said, "The bottom line for all of us is the asthma question, which is a big red

flag. As a pediatrician, I am always surprised at the kids who come into my office wheezing—and their parents think it's a cold or an allergy."[9]

Similarly, the American Academy of Allergy, Asthma and Immunology wrote that "OTC availability will eliminate the physician from the care process of patients taking antihistamines.... Allergies are not necessarily a self-diagnosable condition."[10] The Academy also stated that "the cost of these drugs will likely make them unavailable to those patients who received them through insurance covered formularies."[11] That is, the OTC price of the drugs would be higher than the current insurance copayment. During the Advisory Committee meeting, "Andrea Apter, a panel member and associate professor at the Hospital of the University of Pennsylvania, expressed concern about access to the drugs for the low- and moderate-income clients who now rely on insurance coverage." "That situation applies to everything we review" for over-the-counter switches, said Charles Ganley, director of the FDA's division of over-the-counter drugs. If that were the criteria, 'nothing will ever get taken to over the counter.'"[12]

In its presentation to the advisory committee Aventis argued that the FDA should follow the practice used in past switches, which included a comprehensive New Drug Application (NDA) supplement that presented new safety data based on post-approval clinical trials or post-marketing data. Aventis pointed to the same issues raised by Schering-Plough, arguing that OTC status would make the patient responsible for diagnosis, selection of the medication, and dosage. At the May 11 meeting Dr. François Nader of Aventis Pharmaceutical argued that Allegra was undergoing ongoing clinical development, post-approval and effectiveness trials, and extensive safety monitoring.[13] Nader reminded the committee of the experience with Seldane and argued that once a drug was sold over the counter the collection of post-marketing data became more difficult. Dr. Nader added, "The patients would be playing a costly trial-and-error game with their health, their quality of life and their money."[14] During the meeting, however,

[6] Robert J. Spiegel, Schering-Plough, Presentation to FDA Advisory Committee, May 11, 2001.
[7] Schering-Plough, "Briefing Book," April 12, 2001, p. 9.
[8] Letter from G. Richard Holt to CDER, April 20, 2001.

[9] *Los Angeles Times*, May 12, 2001.
[10] Letter from Emil J. Bardana, Jr. to FDA, April 19, 2001.
[11] Letter from Emil J. Bardana, Jr. to FDA, April 19, 2001.
[12] *San Jose Mercury News*, May 12, 2001.
[13] François Nader, "Non-Sedating Antihistamines Rx-to-OTC Switch," May 11, 2001.
[14] François Nader, "Non-Sedating Antihistamines Rx-to-OTC Switch," May 11, 2001.

advisory committee member Alastair Wood of the School of Medicine of Vanderbilt University asked the drug companies, "Can you give me an example of a specific safety concern you are pursuing?"[15]

As Ira A. Loss, an analyst for Washington Analysis, said, "The drug companies are against it. And the doctors don't like the idea that the number of office visits might fall. It's hard to find an honest broker in the whole deal."[16]

## Reactions to the Committee Vote

Robert Seidman of WellPoint celebrated the committee's vote stating, "Patients can readily self-diagnose and patients can safely use these drugs. This goes to a societal need—it's in society's best interest for these safe and effective drugs to be made available without a prescription."[17] WellPoint also argued that if the costs of pharmaceuticals were not controlled, insurance companies could withdraw their coverage for pharmaceuticals. Seidman explained, "One of the reasons we filed the petition was to protect consumers from out-of-control drug costs. I'm afraid if we do nothing we'll get to the point where there will be no prescription drug benefits at all."[18] Uwe Reinhardt, a health economist at Princeton University, said, "My message to the American people is: 'Get used to it.' Every year for the next decade you will see your benefit package cut."[19]

Larry Sasich of Public Citizen, a public-interest activist group, said, "It's purely self-serving on the part of (WellPoint) to shift cost from their bottom line to the pockets of consumers."[20] Public Citizen had long campaigned against high pharmaceutical prices, yet it did not support the switch to the OTC market where the price would be substantially lower. Several consumer groups, including Families USA, the National Consumers League, and American Association of Retired Persons (AARP), had not taken a position on the issue. Ronald Pollack of Families USA said that although most consumers would benefit from a switch, it "could result in making drugs less available to a very vulnerable part of the population [low-income consumers with prescription-drug coverage]...."[21]

After the vote Dr. Spiegel of Schering-Plough stated, "We don't believe this would be in patients' best interest. We're concerned that the insurance company is trivializing the importance of the patient–physician relationship."[22] He explained, "The second-generation antihistamines tend to be used for long-duration use," and he cited company data indicating an average duration of use of over 60 days.[23]

Commenting on the positions of the drug companies, Stephen W. Schondelmeyer, an economist at the University of Minnesota, asked, "Is the industry saying that American consumers are not as wise in using medicine as consumers in Canada or Mexico or England?"[24]

Dr. Robert Brook, professor of medicine at UCLA and director of the Rand Corporation's health practice program, stated, "This [committee vote] is consistent with the movement we're seeing in medicine, which is to give consumers more control over their lives. I suspect that, as we get more sophisticated with drugs and their safety margins, we're going to see more of this."[25]

The patient-advocacy group Allergy and Asthma Network/Mothers of Asthmatics (AAN/MA) spoke in favor of prescription-only status. President Nancy Sander said, "The average consumer does not possess the knowledge and skills necessary to safely self-diagnose and treat allergy symptoms without medical guidance. At best, their efforts are experimental. Stand in the cold and cough section of the grocery store and you'll witness confused consumers seeking medical advice from stocking clerks as to which medications they should take home to try. . . . The health insurers say nonsedating antihistamines are safe. And I agree. But only when used as prescribed by a physician."[26]

## Blue Cross of California, WellPoint Health Networks Inc.

WellPoint Health Networks was a leading managed care company serving 9.7 million medical members and over 40 million specialty members. WellPoint

[15] *San Jose Mercury News,* May 12, 2001.
[16] *The New York Times,* May 12, 2001.
[17] *Los Angeles Times,* May 12, 2001.
[18] *The Sacramento Bee,* May 11, 2001.
[19] *The Washington Post,* May 10, 2001.
[20] *The Wall Street Journal,* May 11, 2001.
[21] *The Wall Street Journal,* May 11, 2001.
[22] *The New York Times,* May 11, 2001.
[23] *The Pink Sheet,* May 21, 2001.
[24] *The New York Times,* May 12, 2001.
[25] *Los Angeles Times,* May 12, 2001.
[26] Letter to FDA Advisory Committee, May 11, 2001, www.aanma.org.

Pharmacy Management was the nation's leading health-plan-owned pharmacy benefit management company serving 27.8 million people.[27] WellPoint was formed in 1992 to operate Blue Cross of California's managed care business. WellPoint subsequently acquired the group life and health businesses of Massachusetts Mutual Life Insurance and John Hancock Mutual Life Insurance companies. WellPoint also acquired Rush Prudential Health Plans of Illinois and Blue Cross and Blue Shield of Georgia.[28] Total revenue for 2000 was $9.2 billion, and net income was $342.3 million, a 21 percent increase over the previous year. For 3 consecutive years WellPoint had been voted the most-admired health care company in *Fortune* magazine's annual survey. "Our success in attracting customers is a result of our focus on offering products that deliver choice and flexibility," said Leonard D. Schaeffer, WellPoint's chairman and chief executive officer.[29]

Blue Cross of California estimated that it would save $45 million annually if the three drugs were switched to the OTC market. In addition, the company would not have to pay for physician visits for patients who chose to self-diagnose.

27www.wellpoint.com.
28Blue Cross is a national trade association.
29www.wellpoint.com.

## Schering-Plough Corporation

Schering-Plough was a research-based, worldwide pharmaceutical company with four major therapeutic areas: allergy/respiratory, anti-infective/anticancer, dermatology, and cardiovascular. Its products were sold in 125 world markets. In 2000 the company had net income of $2.4 billion on sales of $9.8 billion and total assets of $10.8 billion. Spending on research and development was 13.6 percent of sales in 2000, and its gross margin was 80.6 percent. Sales for the first quarter of 2001 were down 3 percent from the year-earlier quarter, and net income was down 10 percent. The company's leading product was Claritin (and Claritin D), and Claritin sales were up 8 percent over the year-earlier quarter. Over 85 percent of the $3 billion Claritin revenue came from the United States. The company's OTC products included Dr. Scholl's foot care products, Lotrimin, Tinactin, Chlor-Trimetron, Coricidin, Di-Gel, St. Joseph's aspirin, Solarcaine, and Coppertone sun care products.

## Schering-Plough's Market Strategy

Claritin received FDA approval in 1993 as a prescription drug and as such was promoted primarily through doctors. In 1997 the FDA revised its regulations, making possible direct-to-consumer (DTC) advertising of prescription drugs in the broadcast media. Schering-Plough and other pharmaceutical companies then began to directly advertise to consumers on television, radio, and through other media. The advertisements gave a toll-free number to call for information, referred to magazine advertisements where warnings were required, and instructed viewers to "ask your doctor." The marketing strategy was to induce consumers to ask their doctors for the drug by brand name. This strategy proved to be quite successful. Schering-Plough reportedly spent $322 million on advertisements for Claritin in 1998 and 1999, and U.S. sales reached $2.5 billion.[30] A 2001 survey by *Prevention Magazine* found that 72 percent of the respondents recalled an advertisement for Claritin.

The Pharmaceutical Research and Manufacturers of America explained the rationale and success of DTC advertising.[31]

Advertising allows the pharmaceutical companies to educate consumers directly about possible treatment options. A study released by *Prevention Magazine* found consumers give high marks to pharmaceutical advertising because it "allows people to be more involved with their health." Further, the study found DTC advertising "is an extremely effective means of promoting both the public health and prescription medicines," and concluded that "the benefits of DTC [direct-to-consumer] advertising could go far beyond simply selling pharmaceutical medicines: these advertisements play a very real role in enhancing the public health." More importantly, the survey found that DTC advertising prompted an estimated 21.2 million Americans to talk to their doctors about a medical condition or illness they had never discussed with their physicians before. In other words, millions of people who had previously suffered in silence were encouraged to seek help.

An Ohio State University study of 246 North Carolina patients taking Allegra, Claritin, or Zyrtec

30Stephen S. Hall, "Prescription for Profit," *The New York Times Magazine*, March 11, 2001.
31www.pharma.org.

revealed that 65 percent did not have allergies. The study, however, was funded by a company that was marketing a blood test for allergies. Dr. Steven D. Shaefer of the New York Eye and Ear Infirmary said, "It's hard to separate those people who have sinusitis from those who have allergic disease."[32]

The U.S. Senate took an interest in DTC advertising. The Consumer Affairs Subcommittee of the Commerce Committee scheduled hearings for May 22 but decided to postpone them.

A second component of the market strategy for Claritin was to set a high price. Drug prices in the United States were considerably higher than in most other countries. The price of Claritin averaged $2.13 a tablet in the United States, whereas in Canada the price was $0.70 before taxes. WellPoint estimated that Claritin might sell in the OTC market for $15 for a month's supply compared to $60 to $80 as a prescription drug. Part of the increase in U.S. spending on pharmaceuticals was due to high prices, and some critics of the industry pointed to DTC advertising, which allowed pharmaceutical companies to establish market power and obtain higher prices.

A third component of the market strategy was driven by the length of the patent. Because of the unusually long review process for Claritin, Schering-Plough had succeeded in having the patent extended to December 2002. The company subsequently mounted a formidable campaign to extend the patent beyond its 2002 expiration date. "To press its case in Washington, the company has paid millions of dollars in political contributions and assembled a high-powered, strange-bedfellows team of lobbyists (including former senators Howard Baker and Dennis DeConcini, the Gore-confidant Peter Knight, and Linda Daschle, wife of the Senate minority leader Tom Daschle); it has also encouraged repeated attempts by Congressional supporters to insert language favorable to Schering into legislation at the last instant."[33]

Once the patent expired, a generic version of loratadine produced by Geneva Pharmaceuticals, a unit of Novartis, could be marketed with a 180-day period of exclusivity.[34] After that period other generics could enter once FDA approval had been granted. Teva Pharmaceuticals had received tentative FDA approval for its generic version of loratadine. Six other companies had also filed to sell generic versions of loratadine, including two that planned to sell on the OTC market.[35]

Schering-Plough had two basic alternatives for dealing with the generics. It could leave Claritin as a prescription-only drug using DTC marketing and its brand name to maintain a price premium over the generics. Second, it could voluntarily move Claritin to the OTC market, which would take the generics with it, since FDA regulations prohibited selling the same drug on both the prescription and OTC markets. The company had employed this strategy in 1991 with Gyne-Lotrimin, used in the treatment of vaginal yeast infections.

To replace Claritin, Schering-Plough had developed a third-generation antihistamine Clarinex (desloratadine) and filed an NDA in October 1999.[36] Clarinex would be sold as a prescription drug and heavily advertised, as was Claritin. Schering-Plough's strategy was to try to migrate prescription demand from Claritin to Clarinex, but to do so in a manner that would leave Claritin in a strong position when switched to the OTC market. Schering-Plough recognized that migrating prescriptive demand to Clarinex would be easier if Claritin were still on a prescription-only basis.

In January 2001 Clarinex was approved for sale in the European Union, and the FDA issued an "approvable" letter for the drug indicating that there were no outstanding clinical or scientific issues.[37] The FDA, however, withheld approval because of quality control problems in Schering-Plough's New Jersey and Puerto Rico manufacturing facilities. The company temporarily shut down its production facilities and embarked on an extensive Good Manufacturing Practices program. CEO Richard Jay Kogan stated, "I am taking full responsibility for resolving these matters in a timely manner and securing FDA confidence in the quality and reliability of our manufacturing systems and controls."

[32]*The Wall Street Journal*, May 18, 2001.
[33]Stephen S. Hall, "Prescription for Profit," *The New York Times Magazine*, March 11, 2001.
[34]Schering-Plough had sued Geneva Pharmaceuticals alleging patent infringement.
[35]Stephen S. Hall, "Prescription for Profit," *The New York Times Magazine*, March 11, 2001.
[36]Desloratadine was developed for Schering-Plough by Sepracor, Inc. Separately, Sepracor had developed a new antihistamine with the brand name Zoltara, and it hoped for FDA approval in 2001.
[37]Desloratadine was marketed in Europe under the brand names Aerius and Neoclarityn.

The Clarinex strategy would be put at risk by an FDA decision to switch Claritin to the OTC market, since Schering-Plough would not have an opportunity to migrate demand to Clarinex. Moreover, if Claritin were given OTC status, the FDA might at some point do the same with Clarinex. Bert Spilker of the Pharmaceutical Research and Manufacturers Association said a switch "would chill many areas of research and development...."

## Schering-Plough's Nonmarket Strategy

Schering-Plough had advertised Claritin as safer than the non-prescription antihistamines and having side-effects like "taking a sugar pill," so it could not argue that Claritin was not safe when sold over the counter. The company instead took the position that more post-marketing studies should be conducted. With regard to the switching process the FDA Review Team had concluded, "The switch of a prescription drug to OTC marketing requires a review of the post-marketing safety data and a determination that a consumer can adequately use the product in an OTC setting". Schering-Plough used this statement to argue that insufficient data on post-marketing safety were available. "It took about 10 years to realize the cardiac toxicity of the once-popular antihistamine Seldane,' said Chandler May, a researcher funded by the drug companies. 'The science needs five or 10 years to say if Claritin is safe at this level or Allegra is safe at that level.'"[38]

Schering-Plough argued that it was better positioned to monitor consumer use and safety data. Spiegel said, "What we don't know is as you move away from [prescription status], how might the benefit decrease and the risk increase."[39]

One alternative for Schering-Plough was to fight the FDA on a step-by-step basis as the FDA decision-making process progressed. One possible focus was on the OTC label for the drug. Some members of the advisory committee argued that the labels should include warnings about use by the elderly and young children. In its presentation to the advisory committee WellPoint had anticipated this and provided a draft label with the following warnings:

If you are pregnant or nursing a baby seek the advice of a health care professional before using this product. KEEP THIS AND ALL OTHER DRUGS OUT OF THE REACH OF CHILDREN. In case of accidental overdose, seek professional assistance or contact a Poison Control Center immediately.

Schering-Plough could also file a lawsuit to challenge an FDA-mandated switch. William O'Donnell of Schering-Plough said, "We think this (move) raises many legal and policy issues. Any switch would be considered an unprecedented departure from past agency policy and would implicate the sponsor's statutory and constitutional rights."

Another alternative was to attempt to enlist congressional and White House support for prescription-only status. One natural opportunity was the appointment of a new commissioner for the FDA.

## Aventis and UCB/Pfizer

Aventis and Pfizer were both much larger companies than Schering-Plough, and Allegra and Zyrtec respectively accounted for a much smaller percent of their sales. In 2000 Aventis had sales of €22.3 billion and net income of €1.1 billion.[40] In the first quarter of 2001 sales were €5.865 billion, and net income was €317 million. Allegra sales reached €384 million in the first quarter, and U.S. sales accounted for one-third of the sales of Aventis Pharma. Allegra and Zyrtec had longer remaining patent lives than Claritin.

Pfizer had sales of $29.6 billion and net income of $3.7 billion, which was down 25 percent from the previous year because of merger expenses. In the first quarter of 2001 Pfizer earned $1.9 billion. UCB had sales of €2.204 billion, and net income of €269 million. Zyrtec was one of the two principal drugs of UCB's Pharma Group.

Pfizer declined to participate in the May 11 panel meeting and immediately after the vote presented the FDA with a 49-page legal brief stating grounds on which it was prepared to sue the FDA. The brief argued that a switch would infringe Pfizer's proprietary information, since a public hearing was required and the FDA would be forced to disclose proprietary information that would deprive it of its property. Lisa Kennedy of Aventis Pharmaceuticals also said the company would file suit. She said, "Decisions about the product should be made in

[38] *The Washington Post*, May 10, 2001.
[39] *The Wall Street Journal*, May 11, 2001.
[40] Aventis was formed in December 1999 by the merger of Hoechst AG and Rhone-Poulenc SA.

agreement with us and health care professionals."[41] "If the agency goes forward, we would definitely challenge it."[42]

## The FDA Decision

For its final decision the FDA had to follow administrative procedures established in the Food, Drug and Cosmetics Act and the Administrative Practices Act. The procedures could include a public hearing, notice of proposed decisions in the *Federal Register*, and a comment period. Any decision by the FDA could be appealed to the federal courts, but preventing a decision from taking effect would require a preliminary injunction by a federal judge.

Whether the FDA had the authority to force the drugs to be sold over the counter was unclear.

David A. Kessler, former commissioner of the FDA and dean of the Yale University School of Medicine, said, "It appears the FDA has the authority." Ira Loss observed, "The statute does not prevent them from doing this, but it doesn't say they can either."[43] David F. Weeda, a former FDA attorney who now represented pharmaceutical companies, said, "It's a legal question that has not been answered in court. In my gut, I think that it is going to be a close case."[44]

The Bush administration had yet to appoint a commissioner for the FDA, and the switching issue was certain to be raised in the Senate confirmation hearing on the appointee.

SOURCE: This case was prepared from public sources by Professor David P. Baron. Copyright © 2001 by David P. Baron. All rights reserved. Reprinted with permission.

## PREPARATION QUESTIONS

1. Assess the significance of an FDA-mandated switch on Schering-Plough, Aventis, UCB, and Pfizer.
2. How would a possible switch affect Schering-Plough's market strategy and product planning process?
3. What are the implications of a possible switch for the pharmaceutical and health care insurance industries?
4. Formulate an integrated market and nonmarket strategy for Schering-Plough.
5. Formulate an integrated market and nonmarket strategy for WellPoint.

[41]*Saint-Louis Post Dispatch*, May 11, 2001.
[42]*The New York Times*, May 16, 2001.
[43]*The New York Times*, May 16, 2001.
[44]*The New York Times*, May 11, 2001.

# CHAPTER 14

# The Political Economy of Japan

## Introduction

The characteristics of the market and nonmarket environments of business differ across countries. These characteristics are important to the formulation of both market and nonmarket strategies. Market strategies are typically adapted to the tastes of local consumers even in the case of a global brand such as McDonald's or Honda. In a similar manner nonmarket strategies must be tailored to the issues, interests, institutions, and information in individual countries. This chapter provides an approach to nonmarket strategy using as the context the nonmarket environment of Japan. The emphasis is on political economy—the interaction between government and interests—and on strategies for addressing nonmarket issues. Chapters 15 and 16 present similar analyses for the European Union and China, respectively.

Culturally, Japan is relatively homogeneous, which facilitates the structuring of political and social activity. Cultural homogeneity is a consequence of a variety of factors, including Japanese isolation prior to 1853, its resistance to immigration, the absence of fundamental religious differences, relatively small regional differences, and a uniform national education system. This relative homogeneity combines with tradition to generate a system in which consultation and consensus are easier to achieve and sustain than they are in many western nations. Nevertheless, interests are often in conflict, and the willingness to sacrifice for the sake of tradition or for the good of the nation has diminished. The pluralism of interests in Japan is sufficiently diverse that interests are increasingly difficult to bring into agreement, and change is continual if not rapid.

A conventional perspective on understanding political and social structures in a country is based on cultural and historical explanations. For managing effectively in the nonmarket environment and addressing specific nonmarket issues, however, cultural and historical explanations operate at too aggregate a level. On specific issues, interests are the primary driving force, and they and their actions must be the focus of analysis. Moreover, interests are diverse and change much more rapidly than do culture and history. Culture and history remain important, but their role is in providing structure and continuity to political and social relationships. The pluralism of interests implies that the framework of structured pluralism introduced in Chapter 6 is the starting point for understanding the environment of business in a country.[1] That framework—modified

---

[1] Curtis (1975, pp. 60–61) provides an early discussion on the pluralism of interests in the business community in Japan. See also Muramatsu and Krauss (1987).

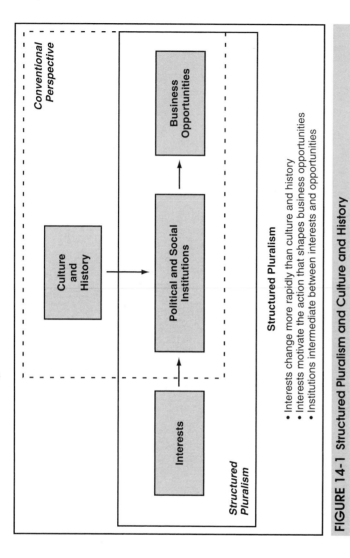

*Conventional Perspective*

Culture and History → Political and Social Institutions → Business Opportunities

Interests → Political and Social Institutions

*Structured Pluralism*

**Structured Pluralism**

- Interests change more rapidly than culture and history
- Interests motivate the action that shapes business opportunities
- Institutions intermediate between interests and opportunities

**FIGURE 14-1 Structured Pluralism and Culture and History**

to fit Japan by including the influence of culture and history—provides a basis for understanding the nonmarket environment and how firms address nonmarket issues in the context of Japanese political and social institutions. This perspective is illustrated in Figure 14-1.

The political economy of Japan is complex and requires a more complete treatment than can be given here. The focus thus is on a characterization of the nonmarket environment in terms of the four I's—issues, interests, institutions, and information— and the cultural underpinnings of the interactions between interests and government. The organization of business in Japan differs from that in the United States due to long-term relationships, many of which are supported by patterns of interlocking ownership among firms in a *keiretsu*. Because of the importance of government in the national economy and the extensive regulation and administrative guidance of many industries, firms in Japan develop a set of relationships with political officeholders and the bureaucracy. Some of these relationships are formalized by a system of advisory committees and consultation processes. Others are developed and maintained through political contributions, the hiring of retired bureaucrats, and personal connections. Firms not only develop relationships but also develop the ability to monitor government activities to obtain the information needed to interact effectively with the political parties, the Diet, and the bureaucracy. These relationships provide the foundations for lobbying, electoral, and coalition-building strategies and for their integration with market strategies.

The chapter begins with a characterization of the nonmarket environment, with an emphasis on issues involving government. The institutional focus is on the Diet and the legislative process, the political parties, and the bureaucracy. The judicial system and the antimonopoly law are then considered. Cultural foundations are then identified, and a framework for political exchange is presented to tie together these components. The organization of business is then considered with an emphasis on business–government

# Issues

interactions. Nonmarket strategies based on information, lobbying, and interactions with the bureaucracy are then discussed. The chapter concludes with a consideration of corporate political styles. The chapter cases, *The Breakup of Nippon Telephone and Telegraph?*, *The Privatization of Japan Post*, and *Uniqlo: Success Breeds Nonmarket Challenges*, provide opportunities to consider strategy formulation in the context of the structural pluralism framework.

The principal systemic-level issues in the political economy of Japan have centered on deregulation of the economy, a massive financial crisis, a stagnant economy, a large government budget deficit, Japan's large trade surplus, and political reform and stability. The Japanese economic miracle ended at the beginning of the 1990s with the bursting of the real estate bubble that had driven prices to astronomical levels. Land prices in the business districts of six major cities fell by over 80 percent between 1990 and 1999. Growth was sluggish during the 1990s and worsened with a recession commencing in 2001. The Nikkei stock average reached a 16-year low, and unemployment reached a postwar high of 5.4 percent in 2001. Most of the large banks had huge nonperforming loans from earlier real estate lending and continued to carry the loans on their books.

Japan also faced serious demographic problems. Its population was aging; by 2020, 27.4 percent of the population would be 65 and older. Their retirement and health care costs would have to be borne by a shrinking workforce. Moreover, the birth rate was low, and if it did not increase, the population could dwindle dramatically, according to one government forecast.

Government efforts to resuscitate the economy were having little success. The government lowered to zero the discount rate—the interest rate at which the Bank of Japan lends to banks—but the principal instrument used to attempt to stimulate the economy was fiscal policy. The government had increased public spending to the point at which the budget deficit reached 8 percent of GDP and public debt reached 130 percent of GDP. The economy not only was stagnant but deflation was occurring. Consumer and producer prices in 2001 were below 1995 price levels because cheap imports from East Asia poured into the country as consumers sought lower priced goods and firms sought to reduce their costs to avoid losses. The trade surplus was still large as a result of exports to the United States, but Japan was running a large and growing trade deficit with China. Corporate profits had plunged, and 15 major banks had approximately $145 billion of bad loans. Despite Japan's economic woes, personal income remained high and Japanese exports were strong.

Japan also faced a set of specific issues including the further opening of domestic markets to international competition, the evolution of antitrust policy, and specific legislative and deregulation measures pertaining to particular industries. Managers in Japan faced the challenge of developing strategies to address the proposed deregulation measures in the context of a sluggish economy and pressure for more rapid economic reforms.

As an example, the financial-services industry in Japan was heavily regulated by the Ministry of Finance (MOF). The industry faced a set of issues arising from within the industry and outside the country. Japan's foreign trade surplus and the difficulty foreign firms had in entering the Japanese market had generated continuing pressure for change. Under pressure from the United States and the European Union, the financial-services markets were gradually being opened. Some liberalization of the insurance industry, for instance, had resulted from external pressure that led the government to allow entry into the auto and commercial fire insurance markets. In 1995 Japan and the United States reached an agreement that allowed a broader set of foreign firms to compete for the management of Japan's $1 trillion pension fund market—a market in which only trust banks and insurance companies had been allowed to operate. By 1999 other insurance markets were deregulated, and insurers were no longer required to use the rates set by the national rating agency.

Reform in financial services was complicated by a financial crisis that required a massive government bailout. The MOF was blamed for not having dealt with the source of the crisis—speculative real estate investments during the 1980s financed by loans from financial institutions. Moreover, a scandal involving MOF personnel had undermined its credibility and its ability to implement reforms, such as making the Bank of Japan independent of the ministry. In addition to the bad real estate loans, the financial situation of major banks remained precarious because of continuing loans to prop up "zombie" companies that were unlikely to be able to repay the loans.

The government took measures to force the banks to write off a portion of their nonperforming loans, and the major banks consolidated into four large banks. The government reduced the budget deficit and undertook a program of privatizing government-owned companies. The economy began to grow in 2003, and deflation stopped. Optimism slowly returned.

A major issue facing the financial services industry was the government's huge postal savings system, which was the world's largest bank and largest life insurance company. The postal savings system offered high interest rates on deposits, providing what the banks viewed as unfair competition. The postal savings system had $12 trillion in deposits and insurance policies. Since the early 1990s deposits in the postal savings system had increased 73 percent, and deposits in banks had decreased 15 percent. The banking and insurance industries urged privatization of the postal savings system, and economists argued the system was distorting the capital markets by funneling funds into quasi-government companies, providing public projects to maintain voter support for the government. The chapter case, _The Privatization of Japan Post_, considers the issues in more detail.

## Interests

Interests in Japan are pluralistic, as they are in the United States. In the United States, however, coalitions are fluid and frequently issue-specific, and interactions with the government are often episodic. In Japan, interests are also varied, but coalitions in Japan are less fluid, and patterns of interaction with government are structured by formal and informal long-term relationships. If Japanese businesses disagree on a trade issue, they are more likely to seek consensus within industry and general business associations and then consensus with the government. They are less likely to contest the issue in public. Business, however, is not a unified interest group in its interactions with government. Interactions with government are conducted by peak organizations, such as the Keidanren (Federation of Economic Organizations), _keiretsu_ (business groups), industry associations, and individual firms. In the business sector, the cross-shareholdings in _keiretsu_ result in complex aggregations of interests that cannot be as issue-specific as they are in the United States.

The interactions among firms, the governing political parties, and the bureaucracy are complex and intermediated by a set of formal and informal arrangements. Advisory committees established by government ministries facilitate communication, policy formulation, and consensus between the bureaucracy and interest groups. The career path links between the political parties and the bureaucracy facilitate interactions between them. Also, many high-ranking bureaucrats take positions in business or seek elected office after they retire, which facilitates the coordination of nonmarket activity.

Japan does not have an encompassing labor movement as do countries such as Sweden and Germany. In Japan, employees of large corporations are unionized, but those unions tend to represent workers at a single enterprise. These enterprise unions are linked in federations and associations, but union members in Japan identify with both their employer and their union.[2] Enterprise unions are not required by law but evolved in the 1950s as a result of conflict between business and national unions, which had adopted a radical posture. Business defeated the national unions, and most workers organized into enterprise unions and focused on employment-specific matters, although some radical elements remained. The movement of jobs offshore and the decline in some unionized industries resulted in a decline in union membership with only 19.6 percent of the workforce belonging to a union.

Japan has activist and public interest groups, but in contrast to the United States they are fewer in number, less active, and more cautious. Dispersed groups, such as consumers and urban residents, are neither well organized nor broadly represented. Their direct influence in the nonmarket environment is thus limited, but political parties attempt to anticipate the interests of these "floating voters" to garner their electoral support.

The Japanese government was modeled after the British parliamentary system, but it has uniquely Japanese characteristics and an overlay of American-style institutions. The country has 47 prefectures, each headed by a governor, and each has its own government—as do cities and municipalities. The powers of the prefecture governments, however, are considerably less extensive than those of state governments in the United States.[3] The principal institutions of Japanese government are the Diet, the electoral and party systems, and the bureaucracy. In addition to its parliamentary structure, Japan has a constitution that guarantees individual rights and a supreme court with the power to declare laws unconstitutional.

## The Diet (Parliament)

The government is parliamentary, so the executive and the legislature are aligned. The Diet is composed of two houses with unequal powers.[4] The lower house, the House of Representatives, elects the prime minister and is the more powerful and the focus of most legislative activity. For example, it can enact legislation by a two-thirds vote even if the upper house disapproves it. The upper house, the House of Councillors, can block legislation unless overridden by a two-thirds vote in the lower house. The lower house can vote no confidence in the prime minister, which requires him to either resign or dissolve the lower house and call new elections. The Liberal Democratic Party (LDP) had been in continuous control of the lower house since 1955, but as a result of scandals and its failure to enact electoral reforms, it lost its majority in 1993. Several groups of dissident LDP members split from the party, resulting in party fragmentation and

---

[2] In spite of the system of enterprise unions, basic wages for workers at large companies have been negotiated in the annual spring *shunto* (spring fight) involving unions and companies in four major industries. The negotiations are seldom a fight, and in recent years the unions have not sought increases in base wages due to deflation in the economy.
[3] See Reed (1986).
[4] See Baerwald (1974).

shifting government coalitions. The LDP, however, remained the largest party and returned to office shortly thereafter, leading coalition governments. In 2004 the LDP had a small majority in the lower house and 40 percent of the seats in the upper house.

The lower house has 480 members. Electoral reform enacted in 1994 replaced multimember districts by a system in which the majority of members are elected from single-member districts and the rest are elected under a proportional representation system. Elections are scheduled every 4 years, but under the parliamentary system the prime minister may call an early election. The upper house has 252 members who serve 6-year terms, with half elected every 3 years. One hundred "national constituency" members of the upper house are elected at large through a proportional representation system. The rest are elected by prefectures, each of which has at least two seats.

In a parliamentary system, a government—the prime minister and the cabinet—serves with the consent of the parliament—the support of a majority of the members of the lower house. A majority party can thus form a government, but in the absence of a majority party, a coalition is required. In forming a coalition government, parties bargain over the allocation of ministries among the parties, the selection of the prime minister, and the principal policies the government will implement. The prime minister is elected by the lower house, but in practice the prime minister is chosen by the LDP. In 2005 reformer Junichiro Koizumi was prime minister and president of the LDP.

The government is of the cabinet form, with the cabinet assuming collective responsibility for policy. The cabinet consists of the ministers who head the principal ministries plus the heads of a few other agencies, such as the Economic Planning Agency. The prime minister does not have formal powers with regard to legislation, as the U.S. president has through the veto. The prime minister, however, has a number of crucial roles, including convener of the cabinet, spokesman for the government, and representative of the nation in international affairs. The prime minister consults with coalition parties and key interest groups and at times with opposition leaders before taking major initiatives. Decisions often await the development of consensus. On some issues the prime minister must build majorities to support policy reforms, as in the chapter case, *The Privatization of Japan Post.*

The houses of the Diet have a committee structure. The lower house has 17 standing committees, most of which corresponded to the principal ministries and agencies. In addition to dealing with the budget, the Budget Committee serves as a forum for questioning the cabinet about policies. Diet committees have relatively small staffs, and many staff members are provided by the ministries themselves. Since much of the major legislation is written in the ministries, the Diet committees have traditionally been weak compared with the bureaucracy. During the past decade, however, the Diet has exercised more power, and committees have begun to play a more significant role.

## Political Parties and the Electoral System

The 1994 electoral reforms replaced multimember districts with a majority of single-member, plurality-winner districts with proportional representation used for the rest of the seats. A single-member district system typically leads to a two-party system, whereas proportional representation results in many parties.[5] In 2004 the number and composition of parties were still in flux. Existing parties had splintered, new parties

[5]Duverger's (1954) law predicts that single-member, plurality-winner districts will result in two-party competition, since with three or more parties some votes will be wasted. A proportional representation system can sustain more parties.

had formed and many dissolved, and coalitions had come and gone.[6] Several members had left the LDP to form new parties, and those parties formed the opposition. The opposition was led by the Democratic Party of Japan (DPJ), which had merged with the Liberal Party. The DPJ won more seats in the 2004 upper house elections than did the LDP. Prime Minister Koizumi continued economic reform but faced resistance primarily from within the LDP.

Electoral reform was spurred by scandals involving large contributions by businesses to the LDP and other political parties. One of the rationales for establishing single-member districts was to eliminate the competition for votes and funds among members of the same party, which was prevalent in the previous system of multimember districts. The reforms included public financing of parties based on the number of votes received.

Contributions to parties and candidates in Japan have been important not only for electoral purposes but because members of the Diet seek to develop personal relationships with constituents. Among other things this involves holding parties, attending weddings and funerals at which gifts are typically given, and organizing excursions for constituents. To maintain constituency support, many Diet members have a *koenkai*, a local organization that serves to organize and mobilize support for the member. Because of restrictions on electoral campaigns, a *koenkai* is officially a cultural organization, and as Reischauer (1988, pp. 264–265) indicates, it conducts constituency activities on a year-round basis. Curtis (1999) argues that *koenkai* have become more important with the fragmentation of the political parties.

One function of a Diet member is to represent constituents' interests not only in the Diet but also before the bureaucracy. For example, Asao Mihara, an LDP member of the lower house from Fukuoka, "has to spend nearly all his time and most of the funds he can collect from supporters acting as a middleman between his constituents and the central government in Tokyo. This includes submitting petitions to bureaucrats on behalf of local businessmen and steering central government-funded public works projects in the general direction of Fukuoka."[7] This is referred to as a "pipe."

Members of the Diet also participate in groups, known as *zoku*, that intermediate between interest groups and the bureaucracy. *Zoku* are important to a ministry because they can represent the ministry's interests in the Diet and the LDP when there are interministerial disputes. In exchange for this support, the ministry may serve the interests that provide the political support for the *zoku* members. In addition to the *zoku*, Diet members have formed caucuses that support policies that cut across both factions and *zoku*. The principal function of the *zoku*, however, is to represent interest groups. The agriculture *zoku* succeeded in obtaining $60 billion over 6 years for relief for rice farmers who had been hurt by the opening of the Japanese market to imports. The construction *zoku* supports the construction industry before both the ministry for construction and the political parties.

## Party Organization

Parties play an important role in governing in a parliamentary system. A majority party resolves a variety of matters internally, including proposed legislation, before they go to the legislature. Because the LDP has been the largest party in Japan, its structure and functioning are considered here.

---

[6]For example, in the mid-1990s dissident LDP members formed Sakigake, but it failed in the 1998 elections and dissolved shortly thereafter. In 1996 the Democratic Party of Japan was formed by socialists and former LDP members and became the principal opposition to the LDP. See Curtis (1999) for an analysis of the parties through the 1990s.

[7]*Far Eastern Economic Review*, March 9, 1989.

Although it is conservative in its orientation, the LDP is neither strongly ideological nor homogeneous, nor does it have a well-defined legislative program. Instead, its program arises out of the work of the party, the Diet, and the bureaucracy. The LDP is a flexible collection of interests and politicians who have mutual incentives in governing.

The LDP has been composed of factions. The factions are not ideological but form around leaders and provide a base from which the leader can seek top ministerial positions.[8] Because the size of the factions is important in intraparty bargaining and the subsequent distribution of rewards, LDP leaders attempt to increase the size of their factions by attracting junior Diet members. For a member of the Diet, a faction provides a vehicle for reaching higher office and a means of participating in legislative activity. LDP members have an incentive to join a faction because the success of the faction and its leader could be important to their personal advancement in the party and appointments to positions in the government.[9]

The LDP developed an extensive internal decision-making process formalized in the Policy Affairs Research Committee (PARC).[10] PARC has 15 sections, or divisions, the policy jurisdictions of which correspond to the ministries and Diet committees. PARC takes positions on issues before the government. For example, the posts and communications section of PARC opposed the privatization of Japan Post.

## The Legislative Process

The policy formation and legislative process is illustrated in Figure 14-2. The top portion of the figure represents the bureaucratic component of the legislative process, as considered in the following section. The lower portion represents the components of the process that take place within the governing party or coalition. In both portions, interest groups are consulted early in the development of policies. Interest group activity thus begins before the Diet considers legislation.

In the lower portion of the figure, PARC committees formulate policies and at times draft legislation, although most legislation is written by the bureaucracy. The draft legislation is reviewed by the party in the government's executive committee, which includes representatives of all the parties in the governing coalition. Once the proposal is approved by the executive committee, it is forwarded to the appropriate ministry. Next, it goes to the cabinet for approval; if it is approved there is it submitted to the Diet. Legislation drafted by a ministry passes through a similar process.

By the time a bill is introduced in the Diet, consensus has been developed within the policymaking apparatus of the governing coalition, support has been obtained from the bureaucracy, and the cabinet has given its approval. In addition, the government may have negotiated with the opposition parties on the legislative process for a bill.[11] Thus, most of the legislative work has been completed before the bill is introduced in the Diet. In many cases, Diet consideration involves going through the formalities—the outcome has been determined long before a vote is taken. Interest groups thus have a strong incentive to be involved early in this process and to develop relationships with the bureaucracy and the parties to obtain access to the policymaking process. Because Diet action comes at the end of the policymaking process, much of the interest group activity and nonmarket competition takes place out of the public view.

---

[8]In 2004 the LDP had five factions: Hashimoto, Mori, Kamei, Horiuchi, and Komura.
[9]Prior to the public funding of elections, factions were used to raise campaign funds for their members.
[10]See Reischauer (1988, pp. 273–274) and Fukui (1970, pp. 83–89).
[11]See Curtis (1999, pp. 118–120).

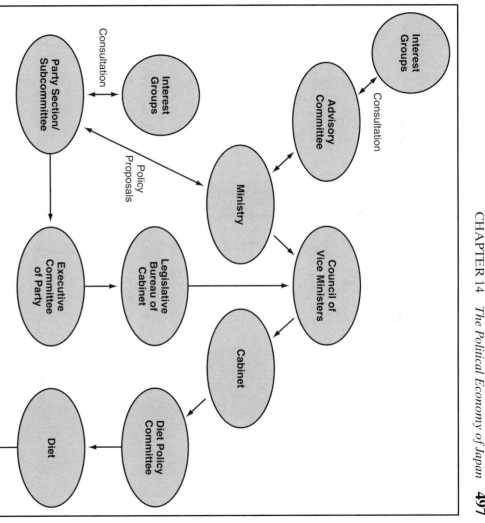

**FIGURE 14-2 Policy Formulation and Legislative Process**

# The Bureaucracy

## Structure and Power

The bureaucracy in Japan has traditionally been viewed as the central force in government, and interactions with the bureaucracy have been essential to many businesses. Japanese culture confers respect on the bureaucracy, but its status has also been due to its expertise, dedication to the national interest, the innovativeness and leadership some ministries have demonstrated, and the economic prosperity Japan has enjoyed. The bureaucracy has also developed exchange relationships with interest groups that give it the political strength needed to develop and administer policies in its jurisdiction. In the 1990s, however, scandals and poor economic performance reduced public confidence in the bureaucracy.[12]

---

[12] As an example of a scandal that reduced the respect for the bureaucracy, to benefit certain pharmaceutical companies the Ministry of Health and Welfare delayed the introduction of heated blood products that reduce the risk of HIV infection. Hundreds of people unnecessarily contracted AIDS because of the delay. As another example, in 2001 the Ministry of Foreign Affairs revealed a kickback and entertainment slush fund system that led to the firing of two senior bureaucrats and the disciplining of 326 other civil servants.

The ministries differ significantly in their functions and their importance. The Ministry of International Trade and Industry (MITI), now the Ministry of Economy, Trade and Industry, has a planning and economic rationalization function and is the lead ministry in international trade negotiations. The posts and telecommunications ministry has a substantial regulatory role, and the construction ministry plays an important role in the expenditure of government funds. Japan does not have a system of separate regulatory commissions, so many ministries have regulatory as well as policy and administrative responsibilities.

A ministry is generally headed by a politician from one of the government parties. The ministry is administered by two vice ministers. The parliamentary, or political, vice minister is a member of the lower house of the Diet, who typically is rotated through a position in the bureaucracy. The day-to-day affairs of the ministry are supervised by the administrative vice minister, who is a career civil servant.

A ministry has influence as a function of several factors. The two most important are (1) its expertise in resolving problems and devising effective policies and (2) its authority to direct resources or control economic activity through guidance, regulation, and the allocation of government funds.[13] One source of the power of the bureaucracy is its ability to act without having to enact new laws. The ministries have considerable discretion within their jurisdictions and often use informal administrative guidance to implement their policies.

Ministries such as MITI have in some cases been effective in encouraging the development of certain industries, but the power of the ministries is found less in their industrial policies than in their regulatory, licensing, resource allocation, and supervisory functions. Many regulatory requirements are nontransparent, causing particular difficulty for foreign and other firms unfamiliar with the system. This requires firms subject to the requirements to maintain relationships with the bureaucrats to obtain information.

Ministries in Japan also have been powerful because of the absence of separate regulatory commissions. The MOF, for example, had formal authority over tax collection, the government budget, financial market regulation, tax policy, and the regulation of financial institutions. In the United States these are the responsibility of, respectively, the Internal Revenue Service, the Office of Management and Budget, the Securities and Exchange Commission, the Department of the Treasury, and for the regulation of financial institutions the Federal Reserve System, the Comptroller of the Currency, the FDIC, and the Office of Thrift Supervision. Although an independent agency, the Bank of Japan (the central bank) has been informally controlled by the MOF. The administrative vice ministers and senior bureaucrats at a number of agencies also came from the MOF.

In the mid-1990s the bureaucracy came under criticism from business, the public, and politicians who argued that it was impeding the deregulation needed to improve the efficiency of a number of sectors of the economy in which regulation served to protect firms and the status quo. Shoichiro Toyoda, chairman of Toyota, argued, "Japan must shift from an economy burdened by regulations and bureaucracy to one in which the private sector can operate unfettered. We must also downsize the public sector and create a small, efficient government."[14] Such criticism led to a restructuring of the ministries in 2001, as considered in the next section.

---

[13]The expertise of the bureaucracy was accentuated because the prime minister, Diet members, and the Diet committees had very small staffs, requiring the politicians to rely on the ministries for information and expertise.

[14]*The New York Times*, April 17, 1997.

## Career Bureaucrats

The bureaucracy attracts some of the best university graduates in Japan, which adds to its expertise and contributes to its influence. In 1997, 45,000 applicants from universities took the advanced civil service examination for 780 positions in the senior civil service. The ministries choose from among the successful candidates. The MOF chooses first, and the Ministry of Local Autonomy and MITI choose next. These new bureaucrats become members of the career *gumi*, or career team. At the Ministry of Finance approximately 800 of the 80,000 employees are career bureaucrats. Graduates of Tokyo University (Todai) dominate the highest ranks of the ministries; its graduates held the administrative vice minister post in 11 of the 12 ministries in 1994. In 1994, 90.5 percent and 78 percent of new MOF and MITI classes, respectively, were composed of Todai graduates.

The class that enters a ministry constitutes a cohort that moves up, and eventually out of, the ministry hierarchy together.[15] Throughout this process, no member of a cohort will be in a position of hierarchical superiority to another member of the same cohort.

Job rotation is an important part of the career path of a bureaucrat, and a shuffle of positions occurs every June. Job rotation develops the breadth and human capital needed for a consensual system in which conflicts are resolved through bargaining and accommodation. It also reduces the likelihood that a bureaucrat will become too closely allied with interest groups that could exert unwarranted influence and divert the ministry from its mission.

The links between ministries and business are facilitated by the *amakudari* ("descent from heaven") system.[16] After 30 years in a ministry, one member of the cohort will become a vice minister. During this period others will resign and "descend" to careers in universities, business, public enterprises, or a government-owned financial institution such as the Export-Import Bank. Others will run for political office; approximately one-third of the LDP Diet members in 1994 were former bureaucrats. Post-retirement employment tends to be easiest for bureaucrats from ministries that have regulatory authority over industries, since those industries are most in need of the relationships and information channels the ex-bureaucrats can provide. One factor in the chapter case, *The Breakup of Nippon Telephone and Telegraph?*, was a ministry's concern for the placement of its career bureaucrats.[17]

## Advisory Committees

The links between the bureaucracy and business are strengthened by over 200 ministerial advisory committees composed of bureaucrats, Diet members, representatives of relevant business and labor organizations, academics, and others. The explicit purpose of the advisory committees is to develop consensus on policies, regulations, or standards before they are proposed as legislation or implemented by the bureaucracy. The ministries also use advisory committees to persuade business and other interest groups to support—or at least not to oppose—the policy directives the ministry seeks to implement. The advisory committees also serve as communication channels that keep

[15]See Atsuyuki (1978) for a description of a bureaucrat's career. Bronte (1982, p. 137) describes the cohort process in some detail. See "Inside MOF: The Men from the Ministry," *Tokyo Business Today*, January 1995, for a description of the career path in the MOF.

[16]*Amakudari* bureaucrats are to wait 2 years before joining a firm that deals with their ministry, but they can obtain a waiver of the requirement from the National Personnel Authority (*Japan Economic Journal*, May 26, 1990).

[17]See Yayama (1998, pp. 109–111) for a discussion of NTT and the interests of bureaucrats.

the bureaucracy informed about issues of concern to interest groups and keep the interest groups informed about the activities of the ministry.

# Economic and Political Reform

## Economic Reform

The slumping economy and old-style politics provided an opportunity for economic and political reform. Reform was popular with the public and brought Prime Minister Koizumi into office. One reform objective was to rein in the soaring budget deficit. Japan had attempted to spend its way out of its economic slump, but critics argued that this strategy resulted only in high deficits and a soaring public debt. The new government pledged not to use government spending to stimulate the economy. One benefit of controlling the government budget deficit was to reduce pork barrel spending, which was one of the foundations for the "pipe" through which public expenditures flowed to the local level.

Part of the old-style politics centered on the public and quasi-public corporations, many of which had close connections with the LDP. Japan had 77 public corporations supported by government financing and another 86 quasi-public corporations. The Japan National Oil Corporation, for example, had losses totaling $3.5 billion in recent years. The Japan Highway Public Corporation had been criticized for waste and its pork barrel spending. Privatizing these companies would both improve economic efficiency and eliminate their use for political purposes. Many of these companies, however, had considerable support from within the LDP and the ministries. The government planned to privatize the public highway corporations, expressway corporations, and a bridge authority. In 2004 Japan began the privatization process for two companies, Impes, an oil and gas producer, and the Electric Power Development Company.

An important component of the government's economic reform program was to privatize the postal savings system. Its $2 trillion of deposits made it the largest savings system in the world, and it was also the world's largest life insurer. Japan Post was said to have an unfair competitive advantage over banks and insurance companies. It was also used to funnel funds to support political objectives. The postmasters, an important support group for the LDP, opposed privatization. The privatization of Japan Post posed a major challenge for the government, as indicated in the chapter case.

The banking system was saddled with huge bad debts and had difficulty dealing with the problem because of the economic slump and the requirement of keeping an array of failing companies afloat through continued lending. With unemployment at a postwar high the government had been reluctant to let companies fail. Reform, however, required letting them fail. The major banks also had large shareholdings in Japanese companies, and with the stock market depressed, the value of those holdings had decreased, further weakening the banks. Banks began to sell some of those shares and also merged to strengthen their balance sheets. The MOF forced the banks to shed some of their nonperforming loans by writing off bad debts, which in 2 years decreased from $400 billion to $242 billion.

Some progress had been made in deregulation, but more remained to be accomplished. Economic reform efforts were threatened by the same two forces that had hindered real reform over the past dozen years. First, the sluggish economy made it difficult to control the government budget deficit and to deal with financial crises such as in banking. Second, opposition to dismantling the pork barrel system was strong within the LDP, whose strength derived from the benefits provided to local constituencies.

## Political Reform

Criticism of the government, continuing scandals, a stagnant economy, and weakening electoral support led the LDP to reform the government. The reform, implemented in 2001, had three components: (1) increase the power of the cabinet relative to the bureaucracy, (2) restructure the bureaucracy, and (3) streamline the government. To increase the power of the prime minister and the cabinet, a Cabinet Office was established with a staff and administrative responsibilities. For example, the Financial Services Agency (FSA) became part of the Cabinet Office and had regulatory, planning, and inspection responsibilities formerly held by the MOF. In 2004 the FSA ordered Citigroup to close its private banking operations in Japan after finding a series of violations of regulations.[18] The Cabinet Office formally has greater power than any of the ministries.

**FIGURE 14-3** Ministries

- Cabinet Office
- Public Management, Home Affairs, Posts, and Telecommunications
- Justice
- Foreign Affairs
- Finance
- Education, Culture, Sports, Science, and Technology
- Health, Labour, and Welfare
- Agriculture, Forestry, and Fisheries
- Economy, Trade, and Industry
- Land, Infrastructure, and Transport
- Environment

The bureaucracy was reformed by merging some of the ministries and establishing a new Ministry of the Environment. The ministries are listed in Figure 14-3. Their number was reduced from 12 to 10, and some of their implementation responsibilities were separated from their policymaking responsibilities. A set of Independent Administrative Institutions (IAIs) were established to assume implementation responsibilities. The IAIs are autonomous institutions associated with ministries and responsible for implementing policies. They are subject to external, independent ex post evaluation of their performance. The establishment of the IAIs was intended to reduce the influence of interests on the administration of policies and regulations.

The reform was also intended to streamline the national government and downsize the personnel by 25 percent. This involved the elimination and consolidation of bureaus and divisions within the ministries. For example, the Pearl Inspection Station was eliminated. The streamlining also involved delegating some responsibilities to local governments.

# The Judicial System and the Antimonopoly Law

The Japanese judicial system is patterned after the civil code systems of continental Europe rather than the adversarial system found in the United Kingdom and the United States. Japan has no common law but has antitrust, labor, and securities laws patterned after those in the United States. A striking feature of the Japanese legal system has been the reliance on conciliation of disputes. The Japanese people place great value on harmony and the absence of confrontation and conflict. They seek to

---
[18]Citigroup also closed another subsidiary in Japan as a result of compliance problems.

resolve disputes "within the family" without recourse to the courts, and hence there has been a low demand for the resolution of disputes in the courts. Van Wolfren (1989, p. 214) reported that Japan had one lawyer for every 9,294 citizens, compared with 1 for every 360 in the United States and 1 for every 1,486 in Germany.

Japan has an Anti-Monopoly Law (AML), which is enforced by the Fair Trade Commission (FTC). Enforcement is different from that in the United States for cultural reasons, say its proponents—or by intention, say its critics. Frequently, when the FTC concludes that a company has violated the AML, it issues a warning.[19] This administrative sanction is said to be a mark of shame that both causes the practice to end and serves as a deterrent to others. In 2003 the FTC ordered Intel to stop tying discounts on microprocessors to promises not to purchase microprocessors from rivals. Fines are also used and have been increased to bring them closer to those in the European Union and the United States. Criminal charges are rarely brought against executives found to have violated the AML. The Chapter 17 case, *The Kodak–Fujifilm Trade Dispute*, involves antitrust as well as trade issues.[20]

Critics contend that the FTC does more to sanction collusion than to deter it. On approval by the appropriate ministry and the FTC, cartels are legal in Japan for the purpose of rationalizing an industry. There are approximately 270 approved cartels, some of which were responses to voluntary restrictions on Japanese imports to the United States. Cartels were believed by many to insulate industries from certain market forces. As mentioned previously, automobile insurance companies had been required to charge prices established by a rating agency, which critics argued created a cartel.[21]

Some segments of the construction industry operated under an illegal system of bid rigging, price fixing, and market allocation known as *dango*. In the *dango* system, construction companies met in private to decide what bids to make and which company would win the contract.[22] In 1988 the FTC ruled that 140 construction companies had colluded on bids for work at the U.S. naval base at Yokosuka. The FTC issued a warning but imposed small fines totaling $2 million. The U.S. Department of Justice then hired a Japanese law firm to represent the United States, and within a year 99 construction companies agreed to pay $32.6 million to settle the bid-rigging claims. The settlement represented approximately 25 percent of the value of the contracts in question. Under pressure from within Japan and from the United States, the FTC issued new guidelines for the construction industry defining an additional set of illegal practices.

## Cultural Foundations

Japanese culture emphasizes harmony and the role of formal and informal hierarchical relationships, such as that between a superior and a subordinate. At the same time, Japanese business practices emphasize horizontal relationships, flexibility, and consensus. The cultural explanation for these practices lies in part in the importance of groups in Japanese society and the relationship between the individual and the group and between groups and society.

---

[19]See Upham (1987, Ch. 5) for a discussion of litigation and industrial policy.
[20]Private antitrust suits are allowed in Japan but are rarely filed because of limits on discovery, the absence of class actions, high filing costs, and the requirement that the FTC issue a finding of a probable violation before a case can proceed.
[21]See Lake (1998, p. 129).
[22]McMillan (1991) estimated that *dango* increased the price of public works contracts by 16 to 33 percent. In addition, *dango* represents a barrier to trade.

A cultural explanation for the societal value of harmony can be found in the religious tradition in which a person progresses toward a closer relationship with or deeper understanding of the "universe."[23] Work is also a path to a closer or deeper relationship with the universe, which has led to an ethic of diligence and a desire for harmony with other individuals and with groups in the work environment. Employment practices such as lifetime employment and a seniority system sustain this ethic.[24] A group, including a business group, thus is to be nourished and its members to act in harmony so that the group can progress, thereby allowing its members to progress. Groups balance a need to adapt to their environment, and hence for their members to act in a concerted manner, with a desire for individuals to express their individual intentions and interests. This may require leaders to modify their expectations toward their subordinates and may require subordinates to suppress their own interests. Doi (1988, pp. 22–23) argued that this consensus building through accommodation by both leaders and subordinates resolves the fundamental tension in groups. The desire to build consensus for government actions and the extensive consultation processes of the bureaucracy are consistent with this perspective.

Taka (1994) characterized the social environment in which individuals and groups are located in four concentric circles of "family, fellows, Japan, and the world." Appropriate behavior depends on the principal relationships in each circle. The notion that appropriate behavior differs among the circles, and the relationships in them, derives from early Confucianism, which held that although all persons are equal, a person is "to treat others in proportion to the intimacy of their relations."[25] A fundamental cultural value that characterizes these relationships is *on*, which refers to obligation and its fulfillment. *On* "is the indebtedness of subordinate to superior for the superior's benevolence in supplying resources to the subordinate."[26] In a fundamental sense, *on* can never be fully repaid and the remaining obligation serves to perpetuate the relationship.

The first circle centers on the *ie*, or family, which is viewed as a group that continues through time. In a business context the second, or "fellows," circle focuses on relationships with friends and colleagues. Viewing a company as analogous to a family, the principal relationship within the work environment is the hierarchical superior–subordinate relationship. This circle also includes the relationships among individual businesses and the ministries relevant to their industry. The fellows circle also includes the businesses in a *keiretsu*, which are expected to contribute to and draw assistance from other fellow members, but each is expected to have a positive balance of benefits over obligations remaining.

Taka characterizes the Japan circle as functioning under the principle of free competition. This is consistent with the notion of Confucian capitalism, the term given to the organization of the economy in terms of markets and groups, including *keiretsu*, supply networks, and long-term relationships among companies.[27] The bureaucracy in Japan may also be viewed from this perspective. In Japan a *samurai* was both a military and a civil officer—a bureaucrat. Morishima (1988, p. 38) states, "In Confucian political thought, those who play the most important roles in society are the bureaucrats."

[23]The Confucian support for this perspective is found in the concept of persons having within them a microcosm of the universe that is connected with the outer universe. The Buddhist underpinning of this perspective is the view that all human beings are the same.
[24]A seniority system also is consistent with the Confucian value of respect for elders.
[25]The five basic Confucian relationships are parent and child, husband and wife, older sibling and younger sibling, friend and friend, and superior and subordinate (ruler and subject). Confucianism is considered in more detail in Chapter 16.
[26]Hamilton and Sanders (1992, p. 24).
[27]Morishima (1988, pp. 36–38) addresses the Confucian bases for capitalism.

In the Japan circle, businesses have mutual interests supported by reciprocal behavior, including that with government, that maintain harmony within the country through the accommodation and subordination of interests. This occurs among businesses and business groups in the context of a larger group—the business community—or the business community in relation to government. An economic phenomenon consistent with this value is the rescue of failing firms. When a firm is failing, a group or an industry rescues the firm. The rescuer is not always a Japanese firm—in 1994 creditors asked Ford Motor Company to assume managerial control of the failing Mazda, in which Ford had an ownership share.[28] In 2005 three companies in the Mitsubishi *keiretsu* rescued Mitsubishi Motors, as they had in 2004.

The outer, or world, circle requires an outward orientation, but order is maintained among those who share the understandings of the inner three circles. Reciprocal relationships are less important in this circle, and business relies more on law to resolve conflicts.

## Tying the Components Together: A Framework of Political Exchange

The framework of political exchange brings together the components of government and their interactions with interests. Interests have incentives for nonmarket action, and culture and institutions structure those actions, as indicated in Figure 14–1. The outcome of a nonmarket issue affecting business depends on the alignment and strategies of interests and the relevant institutions—the Diet, the governing parties, and the bureaucracy. Because of the powerful bureaucracy and the cultural values of harmony and consensus, political competition is not as freewheeling as in the United States. Much of the action takes place within the governing coalition or in behind-the-scenes consensus-building activities involving the government coalition, the bureaucracy, and interest groups. This nonmarket action is less visible than it is in the United States.

One path of influence for interests has been through parties and their leaders, but interests have often sought assistance from a broader set of officeholders. *Zoku* and caucuses give Diet members an opportunity to respond to the needs of interest groups. From the perspective of interest groups, *zoku* provide another access point to the government and are an important link between interest groups, the governing parties, and the Diet.

The bureaucracy plays a central role in the maintenance of interest group relationships, and to some extent ministries have been politicized. The most politicized ministries are those whose actions have a direct impact on industry, professional groups, and other organized interests through expenditure programs and regulation.

## Political Exchange

The interactions between interest groups and the government can be viewed as political exchange in which interests provide political support and the government provides policies that benefit the interests. This takes place through a set of relationships, referred to as an iron triangle, formed by interest groups, political parties, and the bureaucracy. During the 1990s the importance of these iron triangles diminished somewhat, but they remain important for many businesses and interest groups. Okimoto (1989) classifies these exchanges into four categories: (1) clientistic exchange, (2) reciprocal (pork barrel) exchange, (3) untied financial support, and (4) generalized voter support. Only reciprocal exchange is considered here.

---

[28]In 1996 Ford increased its stake in Mazda to 33.4 percent, and a Westerner assumed its presidency.

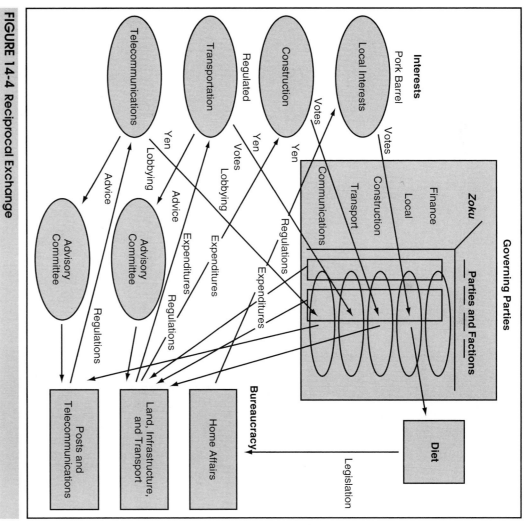

**FIGURE 14-4 Reciprocal Exchange**

## Reciprocal Exchange

Reciprocal exchange, illustrated in Figure 14-4, involves government regulatory policies, licensing, and expenditures that benefit particular interest groups. In turn, those interest groups provide support for the governing parties. The parties and the interests recognize that future benefits depend on maintaining the system. Reciprocal exchange occurs in regulated industries such as electric power, telecommunications, and transportation. In these sectors the ministries, which are the regulators, again serve as intermediaries.[29] Expenditure programs primarily affect the construction, transportation, and defense industries. The businesses in these industries are generally not heavily involved in international trade and seek benefits from government programs. In the context of Figure 2-2, the regulation and expenditure programs of the ministries make nonmarket strategies essential.

[29] Aoki (1984) characterizes this as administrative pluralism in which the bureaucracy acts as a referee among competing pluralist interests.

The governing coalition may be thought of as a matrix with Diet members belonging to a party, and also to a faction, as well as to a *zoku* or caucus. The points of access for an interest group, then, may be through a party, particularly those in the governing coalition, a *zoku*, or a caucus. The points of access to the bureaucracy include direct relationships and the advisory committee system.

The Ministry of Land, Infrastructure, and Transport is one of the most important participants in reciprocal exchange. Construction accounts for nearly 15 percent of GDP, and every project must be licensed by the ministry. In addition, as Yayama (1998, pp. 105–107) indicates, the Ministry benefits selected contractors through the "designated bidders" system in which only certain companies are allowed to bid on certain contracts. Because of the magnitude of the funds allocated by the ministry and its licensing function, construction companies have been strong supporters of the traditional system and are important participants in the *koenkai* of many LDP Diet members. The ministry provides the bureaucratic support for this exchange. The creation of IAIs should lessen this politicization and reduce the influence of the ministry.

The nature of political concessions to interest groups is illustrated by the case of small enterprises. Small enterprises have been one of the traditional support groups for the LDP, and in exchange the LDP provided a set of specific benefits, such as preferential tax treatment and favorable regulation, as a means of protecting them. To protect small retailers, the government restricted the growth of large stores, and this restriction was in part responsible for Japan's large retail and wholesale sector. To strengthen the reciprocal relationship among small merchants, the bureaucracy, and the LDP, the government enacted the Large-Scale Retail Store Law, which required any store that sought to expand beyond 1,500 square meters to obtain approval from the Small and Medium Enterprise Agency of MITI. When approval was sought, other stores in the neighborhood were consulted. Their protests often delayed an opening for years. In exchange for this regulatory protection, small merchants and wholesalers typically supported the LDP.

When some large stores began to build stores smaller than 1,500 square meters side by side, local retailers pressured municipal and prefecture governments seeking additional protection. Those governments began to enact regulations that placed additional restrictions on large stores. These regulations were "illegal" because they conflicted with the national law, and MITI sought to void them. The municipal and prefecture governments sought and received support from the Ministry of Home Affairs (MHA), which opposed MITI on this issue. The bureaucratic battle was arbitrated by the Cabinet, which eventually decided in favor of the MHA and the local merchants. Regulations were established requiring notice to the prefecture government of any plan to open a store with more than 500 square meters. These regulations along with subsequent legislation provided a role for local government in the protest process, strengthened the role of the local merchants, and allowed the merchants to appeal decisions to the ministries.[30] The Part IV integrative case, *Toys 'Я' Us and Globalization*, involves a retailer seeking to enter the Japanese market and facing this set of restrictions and the underlying reciprocal exchange relationship.

## Characteristics of Business

Many of the most prominent Japanese companies are part of a network or group intended to provide mutual benefits to its members. In the United States, corporations tend to have wholly owned subsidiaries, and cross-shareholding of publicly traded

---

[30]These regulations were subsequently largely eliminated.

companies is atypical. In Japan, business groups are supported by interlocking owner-ship, which serves both to facilitate coordination and insulate the group from outside forces. As Sonji Noguchi, a general manager at the Industrial Bank of Japan (IBJ), which had the largest shareholdings of any bank, explained: "When we issue stock, friendly companies hold it. When they issue stock, we hold it. . . . If I own 1,000 shares of IBJ, I don't feel I own the company. It's just an investment. It's the relationship."[31] The groups typically have no more than one firm in any industry, so cooperation rather than rivalry characterizes behavior within a group. Groups compete vigorously against each other, however. The companies in a group remain independent and serve their own interests first.

The interlocking networks, called *keiretsu*, are of three types: (1) the three groups, Mitsui, Mitsubishi, and Sumitomo, formed from the prewar, family-controlled *zaibatsu*, (2) groups formed around major banks, and (3) groups formed around major industrial companies. Members of the first two groups are referred to as horizontal *keiretsu*, whereas those in the third are called vertical *keiretsu*.[32] The firms in a *keiretsu* are independently managed, but each *keiretsu* has a "presidents' club" that meets regularly and focuses on group maintenance activities, the exchange of information, and, when necessary, the resolution of conflicts among members.

The stagnant economy in recent years has meant financial hardship for many com-panies. Many *keiretsu* companies have raised funds by selling some of the shares they held, reducing the extent of cross-shareholdings. These sales and the weak economy depressed stock prices, which caused a considerable problem for the major banks. Not only did they have huge bad debts on their books, but one of the principal assets—their shareholdings in Japanese companies—had lost much of its value.

Vertical *keiretsu* are centered around a major manufacturing company such as Toyota or Matsushita Electric and involve supply and distribution networks. These groups may include wholly owned subsidiaries, partially owned subsidiaries, and inde-pendent suppliers. The form of the relationship varies with some subsidiaries supplying other companies in addition to their parent and the parent purchasing from competitors of a subsidiary. Toyota directly controls 13 suppliers with ownership shares in 1990 rang-ing from 8.9 to 49 percent, and another 178 companies, organized into three societies, supply Toyota. Matsushita maintains a distribution network of 25,000 small "National shops" that account for much of its sales in Japan.

Maintenance of the network relationships in a vertical *keiretsu* involves implicit or relational contracting. As practiced in Japan, relational contracting is characterized not only by the absence of formal contracts but also by mutual adjustment to changing cir-cumstances. Within a *keiretsu*, long-term supply relationships are frequently augmented by a market allocation system in which suppliers receive fixed shares of the purchase orders of a company, but the quantity purchased varies with the level of demand. The relationship between NTT and a group of its suppliers had been so stable that the suppliers were referred to as the NTT "family." (See the chapter case, *The Breakup of Nippon Telephone and Telegraph?*) Market allocation and long-term relationships made it difficult for new firms, both Japanese and foreign, to enter certain Japanese supply markets.

Implicit contracts also govern the employment relationship in most large firms. The compensation system in Japanese firms typically has three principal components: (1) an annual bonus, (2) pay graduated by seniority, and (3) a contingent retirement

[31] *The New York Times*, June 27, 1989.
[32] Gerlach (1992) provides an analysis of the *keiretsu* and other alliances in Japan and of the implications of these networks for corporate business strategy.

payment. Many Japanese employees receive a significant part of their income in the form of an annual bonus, which can be reduced along with hours worked when the firm has to improve its profits. Consistent with the cultural analogy to a family, most firms had based wages on seniority. These firms hired young employees directly from high schools and universities and offered them lifetime employment, so workers looked forward to a rising income stream.[33] These features of the compensation system provided strong incentives for employees to remain with the company, and they also aligned the interests of employees with those of the company.

Although lifetime employment and seniority systems continue to be used by many companies, pressure for improved efficiency and lower costs as well as the economic slump in Japan have generated change. Layoffs have occurred, and some companies have skirted the lifetime employment policies by hiring temporary workers. Compensation systems also have changed. As Osamu Sakuri, president of the Sumitomo Trust Bank, explained: "Under the lifetime employment system we could not offer appropriately high salaries to obtain top talent. Nor could we hire on a short-term basis."[34] Merit-based, rather than seniority-based, pay has become much more common, and companies such as Fujitsu put all employees on merit pay. In addition, companies such as Matsushita are giving employees more control over their retirement programs rather than providing all the funds at the time of retirement.

# Business–Government Interactions

## The Organization of Business for Nonmarket Action

Mutual gains, such as those from long-term relationships among businesses, also result from relationships with the government. Japanese firms cultivate relationships with politicians and bureaucrats that provide the foundation for participation and influence. When a Japanese firm faces a nonmarket issue that involves the government, it already has well-established relationships that provide it access. Firms participate in ministerial advisory committees and develop relationships with the relevant ministries and their career bureaucrats. They may employ *amakudari* bureaucrats or use them as advisors and counselors. Firms develop contacts with the relevant Diet committees and with the *zoku* and caucuses concerned with policy in their industries. Firms also participate in industry associations and Keidanren committees. These relationships represent major assets to a firm, and considerable effort and resources are expended to maintain them.

These relationships do not guarantee success on nonmarket issues, but they can be important for effective participation in the Japanese system. The success of a nonmarket strategy in Japan depends on the strength of the interests and the nature of the exchange relationship between business and government. The opposition to entry into an industry, for example, is naturally weakest for those products that have no Japanese competitor. A company such as McDonald's was able to enter the Japanese market with relative ease because the fast-food market segment was unoccupied. The same was true for Blockbuster.

A firm seeking access to an industry in which the relationship between interest groups and the government is characterized by clientistic or reciprocal exchange may,



[33]Lifetime employment was available only to a small proportion of the workforce. Tachibanaki (1984) estimates that in the late 1970s approximately 9.7 percent of males and less than 2 percent of females had lifetime employment. He argued that this was quite similar to the United States, except that in the United States a much higher percent of young employees engaged in job shopping.
[34]Quoted in Mroczkowski and Hanaoka (1989, p. 50).

however, find the opposition formidable. In industries such as agriculture, construction, and financial services, the U.S. government has played a major role in opening the markets. In other cases long-term arrangements through *keiretsu* limit the ability of foreign as well as new Japanese firms to break into some markets. For example, a principal impediment to increased sales by foreign semiconductor manufacturers was the long-standing supply relationships and market allocation policies of both *keiretsu* and independent firms.[35]

## Nonmarket Strategies

### Electoral Strategies

The principal nonmarket strategies used in Japan are electoral, coalition building, relationship building, and lobbying. Electoral strategies had been a central component of the nonmarket strategies of most large firms, and political contributions had been a part of those strategies. Those contributions took place in the context of clientistic, reciprocal, and less-structured exchange relationships.[36] Scandals and electoral reforms reduced their importance, however. Shoichiro Toyoda, chairman of Toyota and chairman of the Keidanren, stated, "In the future one hopes that public financing and donations from individuals will be sufficient to cover political parties' expenses, but we can't expect to reach that position overnight."[37]

### Coalition Building

Coalition building often takes place through industry associations and peak associations that represent business interests on broad public issues. The principal peak organization is the Keidanren, which includes the 1,200 or so largest firms, both Japanese and foreign, plus the major trade associations. The other three principal peak organizations are the Nickering (Federation of Employers Association), the Japan Chamber of Commerce and Industry, and Keizai Doyukai (Japan Committee for Economic Development).[38] The principal business organization for political participation is the Keidanren, which advocates policies that support the general climate for business. It seldom supports particular industries or individual companies.[39] The Keidanren's approach is to attempt to build consensus on policies affecting the economy and business in general. It has supported deregulation and the opening of Japanese markets to imports as a means of improving economic efficiency, reducing Japan's trade surplus, and lessening the pressure for market opening from the United States and the European Union.

Because of the extensive set of long-term relationships among firms and between business and government in Japan, coalitions in Japan are less fluid and issue-specific than in the United States. Thus, many of the interactions with the government take place through standing associations rather than ad hoc coalitions. In Japan, associations are numerous and politically active. Lynn and McKeown (1988) provide an analysis of industry associations in the steel and machine tool industries. The Japan Machine Tool Builders Association represented 112 companies, and the Japan Metal Forming

---

[35]Mason (1992) documents the difficulties encountered by firms such as Coca-Cola and Texas Instruments in entering the Japanese market in the early part of the post–World War II period.
[36]Foreign firms, particularly U.S. firms, have been more hesitant to make campaign contributions in light of the Lockheed scandal, considered in Chapter 22, which involved large, illegal contributions to the office of Prime Minister Tanaka and others.
[37]*Tokyo Business Today,* September 1994.
[38]See Lynn and McKeown (1988, pp. 78–81).
[39]The Keidanren does not deal with labor issues, which are the domain of the Nickering.

Machine Builders Association represented another 115. The associations addressed issues of industrial standards and provided information on foreign markets and competitors. These associations were linked through a hierarchical network with other associations, including the Japan Machinery Federation, the Machine Tool and Related Products Committee, and the Japan Society for the Promotion of the Machinery Industry, which provided subsidies to machinery companies from funds raised through motorcycle and small car racing.[40]

The extent to which companies act on their own outside their industry associations and the Keidanren and whether their participation in *keiretsu* causes them to restrain the pursuit of their own interests is not well documented. Most companies, however, maintain their own relationships with bureaucrats in the relevant ministries and with important politicians rather than relying solely on the activities of the associations to which they belong.

## Relationships with the Bureaucracy

In the context of Figure 2-2, the importance of nonmarket strategies is greater the greater the control of opportunities by government. Interactions with ministries and agencies are crucial for many companies because the government has been heavily involved in the economy. Extensive regulation and the administrative allocation of government resources such as public works contracts has made nonmarket strategies important. In addition, the bureaucracy has considerable discretion under existing laws, and it plays an important role in writing new legislation. Companies develop relationships with the bureaucracy and bureaucrats, and these relationships are reciprocal. Schaede (1998, pp. 165–166) indicates that administrative guidance represents the bulk of the regulation in industries. Moreover, "Administrative guidance is not transparent and often involves delicate conversations between ministry officials and firm management. Rules can be implemented or revoked at the discretion of the ministry in charge and without any prior notice."

Bureaucrats also seek close relationships with companies for their own purposes. Okimoto (1989, p. 158) wrote:

> Deputy division directors in MITI's vertical divisions have significant leeway to structure their relationships with corporate executives in ways that fulfill their notion of what their job should entail. Usually, there is a fairly well defined hierarchy of companies with which deputy directors must deal. The three deputy directors of the information industry divisions—Electronic Policy, Data Processing Promotion, and Industrial Electronics—are expected to establish close working relations with representatives from the big, blue-chip electronics corporations that dominate their fields—Hitachi, NEC, Toshiba, Mitsubishi Electronics, and Fujitsu. Working with industrial associations like the Electronics Industry Association of Japan (EIAJ) is also essential, especially when the association is strong or when there are too many large corporations for one or two MITI officials to handle.[41]

Ministries may also provide assistance to business through regulation and licensing. When the telecommunication industry was first opened to limited entry, the Public Highway Corporation encouraged a group of major companies, including Toyota,

---

[40]Lynn and McKeown (1988, pp. 71–73).
[41]Okimoto (1989, p. 158).

Mitsubishi, Mitsui, Mitsui & Company, and Sumitomo Corporation, to form a common carrier in the Tokyo-Nagoya-Osaka corridor. The company, Telway-Japan, was formed shortly before the filing deadline, and one purpose of the company was to compete with a joint venture formed by Daini Denden (DDI) and Motorola to provide cellular telephone service.[42] The Ministry of Posts and Telecommunications (MPT) had the responsibility for deciding which territories Telway-Japan and the Daini Denden–Motorola joint venture could serve. Telway-Japan was allocated the territory constituting the largest potential market for cellular service. The resulting conflict between Motorola and the bureaucracy was a source of considerable discord between the United States and Japan in international trade negotiations. That discord is considered in more detail in Baron (1996).

## Lobbying and Points of Access

Lobbying is extensive in Japan and involves presenting information and representing interests before the bureaucracy, political parties, and the Diet. As shown in Figure 14-2, the policy formulation process begins before legislation is considered by the Diet or actions are taken by a ministry. It is thus essential that a firm or interest group be able to learn when an issue is being considered by a ministry or the policymaking apparatus of the governing parties. This requires developing relationships and points of access. Although there are many points of access, because of the close interactions among the governing parties' policymaking apparatus, the bureaucracy, *zoku,* and Diet committees, these points of access are not independent.

The appropriate points of access depend on the issue and the nature of the exchange relationship between business and government. An issue involving telecommunications necessarily involves the Ministry of Public Management, Home Affairs, Post and Telecommunications (MPMHAPT) and the Ministry of Economy, Trade, and Industry (METI) and their advisory committees. Policy committees of the governing parties will also be involved, as will the Diet committees for telecommunications and for commerce and industry. Access to the MPMHAPT may be provided both through its advisory committees and by *amakudari* bureaucrats who have maintained personal relationships with current vice ministers and bureau heads. Those high-ranking bureaucrats had been responsible for the careers of those in the junior cohorts who now run the ministry, so there can be a personal as well as a professional relationship. A number of *amakudari* bureaucrats hold positions in firms with which their former ministries had dealt.

The rise of the *zoku,* in terms of both expertise and political power, makes them an important point of access on many issues. Former Prime Minister Tanaka was the most important politician when NTT was privatized and the telecommunications industry was opened to competition, but he did not hold any formal position in the government other than his seat in the Diet—however, he headed both of the relevant *zoku.*

Access to political parties and members of the Diet is also important, particularly on issues requiring bureaucratic action, since parties can act as intermediaries between firms and ministries. The need for access had led many Japanese companies to make campaign contributions to parties and their leaders.

Access is often facilitated by personal relationships between business executives and government officials. For example, the American Chamber of Commerce in Japan (ACCJ) held a 3-day series of meetings with key members of the Diet, including the prime minister and cabinet ministers. Rather than focusing on policy issues, the purpose of the meetings was for the U.S. executives from companies such as Boeing and

[42]Harris (1989, p. 125).

AT&T to develop personal contacts with Diet members. As the organizer explained, "This is an attempt to go directly to people at the political level who make policy."[43]

Foreign firms have developed their capacity for lobbying the Japanese government and maintaining ties with the relevant ministries, the governing parties, and the Diet. AT&T hired a former U.S. trade negotiator to be its full-time lobbyist in Tokyo, and Nippon Motorola hired a former U.S. embassy official in Tokyo and a former congressional staffer as full-time lobbyists. Motorola retained former officials of METI and MPMHAPT as advisors.[44] These two ministries were the most important to the industries in which Motorola was engaged and were involved in the agreements granting the company access to the cellular telephone market.

## Information

Because legislative activity in Japan is often near completion when a bill is introduced in the Diet and because legislation is written within the bureaucracy and the government parties, advance information on potential legislative activity is essential for effective participation in the process. Similarly, since bureaucratic decisions are not made in public and regulations and other administrative practices are often not transparent, advance notice of possible bureaucratic action is important. Thus an important activity of business is gathering information about government activities, plans, and proposals. Many firms employ *amakudari* bureaucrats to provide information; others hire them as advisors. Schaede (1998) reported that 1,111 *amakudari* bureaucrats held positions in companies and many more were in public corporations and associations. *Amakudari* bureaucrats have by the time of their descent developed extensive personal communications networks called *jinmyaku* that can be valuable to their new employers or clients.

Johnson indicates the scope of the information that Japanese companies routinely develop about the government and its activities.[45]

The potential lobbyist must know which ministry or ministries has jurisdiction over his or her problem and then find out everything it is possible to know about that organization, including its history, personnel cliques, post retirement patterns, scandals, and so forth. This is precisely the kind of information that any Japanese manufacturer or marketing organization compiles all the time. The major Japanese daily newspapers, for example, routinely print on page 2 details of personnel shifts within the ministries and agencies of the central government. It would be unheard of to read such information in *The New York Times* or the *Washington Post* on, say, the Department of Commerce, but in Tokyo it is important news. The Japanese press reports on who is in charge of what section throughout the Japanese executive branch because its readers need and want that information.

Government officials also need information, and firms are an important source of it. Homare Takenaka, managing director for external affairs of IBM Japan, explained: "If they think we have good intelligence and information, they rely on us. By doing this we can strengthen and expand our position. . . . I can call on director generals of ministries anytime. I know them personally."[46] Companies also participate on advisory committees for the purposes of obtaining information and influencing outcomes.

[43]*The Wall Street Journal*, October 19, 1994.
[44]Motorola follows a similar strategy in the United States, where it employed a number of former government officials.
[45]See Johnson in Johnson, Tyson, and Zysman (1989, p. 231).
[46]*The Japan Economic Journal*, May 19, 1990.

## Corporate Nonmarket Styles

Some U.S. firms have adopted a strategy of acting aggressively, both in Japan and in the United States, to pressure the Japanese government to open its markets to the company's products. Other firms have adopted the Japanese style of patience both in markets and in their political and governmental interactions. Two U.S. semiconductor manufacturers, Texas Instruments and Motorola, opened production facilities in Japan, and they followed quite different nonmarket strategies. Texas Instruments, which has operated in Japan for over 30 years, maintained a low profile. In contrast, Motorola adopted a demonstrative style, using U.S. trade laws and political sentiment in Washington as levers to open Japanese markets for its telecommunications and semiconductor products. This caused resentment in Japan. Robert Orr, director of government relations for Motorola, explained: "We've got good friends in the U.S. government. And we have good friends in the Japanese government. That's the way it's played. There is resentment because they feel we ignited the trade issue, but it has been here a long, long, long, long time."

Johnson & Johnson has operated in a more traditional style. It had been unable to market Tylenol in Japan because the Ministry of Health, Labor, and Welfare (MHLW) restricted the dosage of acetaminophen, the active ingredient in Tylenol, to less than half the amount needed to make the pain reliever effective. Instead of taking aggressive action in Washington or Tokyo as Motorola had done, Johnson & Johnson adopted the Japanese style. President Masami Atarashi of Johnson & Johnson Japan attempted to persuade MHLW officials to increase the permitted dosage. He explained, "We believe in being an insider, wherever we are."[47] This approach can be very slow, particularly in a regulatory system known for keeping out many drugs available to consumers in other countries. Johnson & Johnson finally applied for formal approval in 1995, and after forming a partnership with a Japanese company to market the drug, Tylenol was approved and marketed in 2000, some 45 years after being introduced in the United States.

In choosing its strategy, a firm attempting to penetrate the Japanese market must determine whether it should pursue an aggressive strategy or adopt the Japanese style of patience. For a company such as Motorola that required government licenses to sell some of its products in Japan, a strategy of patience may have been infeasible because of rapid technological change and the lengthy process required to gain access to the bureaucracy and to markets. The Part IV integrative case, *Toys 'Я' Us and Globalization*, and the Chapter 17 case, *The Kodak–Fujifilm Trade Dispute*, provide opportunities to consider market opening strategies in the context of the market and nonmarket environments in Japan.

## Summary

The nonmarket environment in a country may be characterized in terms of issues, interests, institutions, and information. Culture and history are also important in shaping the behavior of institutions and the pattern of social interactions. Because of culture and the distinctive characteristics of the nonmarket environments in countries, nonmarket strategies must be tailored to the environment in a country. The framework of structured pluralism provides the foundation for both nonmarket analysis and strategy formulation.

Japan's parliamentary system of government was dominated by the LDP for 38 years, but scandals and defections resulted in a period of party reorganization, consolidation, and intensified competition. The LDP regained a majority in the lower house of the Diet and governed with a coalition. The bureaucracy remained powerful and provided stability, but it was criticized for failing to deregulate the economy more quickly. Criticism of the bureaucracy led to political reform that reorganized several ministries and increased the power of the cabinet. The parliamentary system results in much of the legislative and policymaking work being done within the ministries and the party structure of the governing coalition. Consensus on policy is sought, although not always attained.

The bureaucracy has multiple roles as policymaker, regulator, and administrator. The ministries differ in the degree of politicization and power. One source of power is their expertise, often supported by a record of past successes. The bureaucracy attracts some of the most able Japanese college graduates, who enter and remain as a cohort until they retire. Many "descend" to positions in business, politics, or quasi-governmental organizations. Bureaucratic power is also due to regulatory authority, the allocation of public resources, and the use of administrative guidance. These activities often lack transparency. One aspect of governmental reform was to separate the implementation of policies from ministerial policymaking by creating Independent Administrative Institutions. The bureaucracy interacts with interests both directly and through a set of advisory committees that provide a mechanism for sharing information and developing consensus. Much of the important interaction between interest groups and the bureaucracy takes place outside the view of the public.

In Japan, complex networks of political exchange interconnect business and other interest groups with the three principal components of the government: the governing parties, the bureaucracy, and the Diet. The interaction between interests and the government may be understood in the framework of exchange. Reciprocal exchange, for example, involves support for the government in exchange for licensing, regulatory, and legislative policies that serve particular interests such as the construction and transportation industries. These interactions are both formal (party and ministerial advisory committees) and less formal (*zoku*). Some are visible, whereas others, such as the system of political donations and the personal relationships between *amakudari* bureaucrats and those who remain in the ministry, are largely invisible. Participating effectively in this system requires understanding both the pattern of these relationships and Japanese history and culture. Understanding is not enough, however. Firms invest in networks and in personal relationships between their executives and the appropriate members of government.

The principal nonmarket strategies of firms in Japan are electoral, relationship building, lobbying, and coalition building. Electoral strategies have been important, but they have diminished in importance due to electoral reform and the public financing of elections. Lobbying focuses on the bureaucracy, the governing parties, and Diet members. Access is important, and firms develop relationships with government officials to provide that access. Peak organizations and trade associations are important in business-government relations, and most firms participate in these associations.

In Japan much of the legislative activity is largely over once a bill is introduced in the Diet. Moreover, much economic activity is regulated or subject to the administrative guidance by the ministries. Firms thus develop information about government ministries, Diet activities, and the governing parties' policy processes. Some engage the services of "advisors" or *amakudari* bureaucrats who know the organizational and decision-making structure of the ministries and have personal contacts with high-ranking bureaucrats.

# The Breakup of Nippon Telephone and Telegraph?

In 1990 the Japanese government considered breaking up Nippon Telephone and Telegraph (NTT) but postponed a decision until April 1996. During the ensuing 5 years much changed, yet much remained the same. The Ministry of Posts and Telecommunications (MPT) continued to press for breaking up NTT, and NTT continued to oppose a breakup. As 1996 approached, the political and economic situation remained complex and contentious.

Despite the "privatization" of NTT in 1985, the Ministry of Finance (MOF) still held 66 percent of NTT's shares. Several planned sales of shares by the MOF had been postponed because of the depressed price of NTT's shares. NTT continued to provide only domestic telecommunications services, and Kokusai Denshin Denwa (KDD) remained the country's dominant international carrier. NTT was prohibited by law from providing international telecommunications services, but it was allowed to invest overseas. NTT began investing offshore in 1992, but only 0.3 percent of its assets were outside Japan. NTT did not manufacture telecommunications equipment but instead relied on suppliers with which it maintained long-term relationships. NTT's principal suppliers were Fujitsu, Hitachi, NEC, and Oki, which were referred to as the "NTT family." NTT had begun to purchase from foreign suppliers, but the amounts were a much smaller percent of NTT's total equipment purchases compared with the equipment purchases from foreign suppliers by other Japanese telecommunications companies.

## The Telecommunications Industry

On the surface the Japanese telecommunications industry was structurally competitive with over 100 common carriers. In addition to NTT and KDD, there were three domestic long-distance carriers, 32 cellular companies, and international carriers, 32 cellular companies, and

28 personal handheld system providers. As a result of the competition, NTT's long-distance market share had declined to 69 percent, but it still held 99 percent of the local service market and 80 percent of the total domestic telecommunications market. NTT practiced cross-subsidization with long-distance rates subsidizing local service, but it planned to reduce the current 340 yen charge for a 3-minute daytime long-distance call to 100 yen by the year 2000.

Most of its competitors were dependent on NTT's local network for access to customers, and some companies paid up to 50 percent of their revenues as access charges. Long-distance competitors such as DDI complained that interconnections with NTT required lengthy negotiations. DDI President Yusai Okuyama said, "We have to spend years on interconnection negotiations [with NTT] and that has obstructed the speedy development of our business plan."[48] Jupiter TeleCommunications, a joint venture between Sumitomo Corporation and TeleCommunications International of the United States, sought access to NTT subscribers in its cable franchise area so that it could offer telephone and other services. If approved by NTT, Jupiter would then file for a license with the MPT. In the past NTT had refused to provide interconnections to cable companies.

As a virtual local service monopoly NTT's prices were high. The MPT reported that NTT's basic subscription rate for telephone service had risen by more than 15 percent during the past 10 years, and the initial subscription (hookup) charge of over $700 was four times that in the United Kingdom and 13 times the charge in France.[49] Moreover, subscribers had to purchase a long-term telephone bond that helped finance NTT's capital expenditures.

[48]*Financial Times*, August 7, 1996.
[49]*Financial Times*, August 7, 1996.

NTT's access charges were sufficiently high that they limited entry.

The MPT maintained that not only did high access charges limit competition, but NTT also discriminated against competitors in interconnections and obtained commercially sensitive information on competitors through the negotiations on access and interconnection.

## Regulation

The MPT had taken some steps to deregulate the long-distance, cellular, and CATV industries, and some politicians and economists believed that further deregulation would stimulate economic activity and create jobs. In 1994 the MPT allowed customers to own their own cellular terminals, which was credited with spurring growth in cellular telecommunications. This significantly reduced the market shares of existing carriers, including NTT and DDI.

## Bureaucratic Influence

Critics of the MPT argued that it had allowed entry into the industry to give it more firms to regulate, more places to which its bureaucrats could descend, and more influence over the firms. These critics claimed that the MPT's push to break up NTT had the same motivation. As an example of the MPT's strategy for maintaining its influence and providing opportunities for *amakudari* bureaucrats, four members of NTT's board of directors were former MPT officials, including Shigeo Sawada, a former administrative vice minister of the MPT who joined NTT in 1990 as senior vice president. Eighteen other former bureaucrats were in NTT-affiliated companies. As another example, the paging industry was divided into 32 regional operators, and according to a senior official at one Tokyo-based paging company, this division was "'only to give all the regional heads of the ministry places to enjoy their retired life.'"[50] Private companies such as the long-distance and cellular provider DDI also had *amakudari* bureaucrats. DDI President Okuyama was a former MPT administrative vice minister, and three other MPT officials were employed by DDI.

In 1994 the MPT had pushed for Sawada to be appointed president of NTT, but NTT opposed the appointment and supported Junichiro Miyazu, a

career NTT employee. A stalemate resulted, and the current president, Masahi Kojima, remained in office. The MPT then turned its attention to preventing NTT from naming Kojima chairman and Miyazu president. The MPT enlisted the aid of the telecommunications *zoku*, members of the Diet who maintained an interest in telecommunications, in support of Sawada, but the financial community preferred Miyazu. Recognizing that Miyazu would likely become president, the MPT then sought to block Kojima from being appointed chairman. It blocked the appointment using a 1986 executive directive intended to restrict the influence of *amakudari* bureaucrats in special corporations, such as NTT. In 1996 an agreement was reached between NTT and its backers, the MPT and its backers, the telecommunications *zoku*, and politicians. In the agreement Sawada was appointed chairman, Miyazu was appointed president, and Kojima was named special advisor.[51]

## The Government Coalition

After scandals resulted in the resignation of two prime ministers from the opposition parties in 1994, the government was formed by a coalition among the Liberal Democratic Party (LDP), the Social Democratic Party (SDP), and the small New Party Harbinger (Sakigake). To establish the coalition, the president of the SDP was given the position of prime minister. A poor performance in upper house elections and defections from the SDP, however, weakened the prime minister and resulted in a change in the government. Mr. Ryutaro Hashimoto, a long-standing member of the LDP, was elected head of the LDP and became prime minister in 1995. Hashimoto had entered politics at age 25 when he inherited his father's constituency and was elected to the Diet. He joined the Tanaka faction of the LDP and served as Minister of Finance and Minister of International Trade and Industry in previous governments. Hashimoto was popular with the Japanese public in part because he had stood up to the United States in trade negotiations. His popularity gave the LDP hope that it might return to power by winning a majority of the seats in the lower house in the April 1997 election. The prime minister could dissolve the Diet and call an early election, and the speculation was that he would do so.

[50]*The Nikkei Weekly*, February 26, 1996.

[51]*Mainichi Daily News*, May 28, 1996.

The Minister of Posts and Telecommunication in Hashimoto's cabinet was Ichiro Hino, a member of the SDP. The SDP was backed by labor unions, including *Zen Dentsu*, which represented 185,000 NTT employees. *Zen Dentsu* believed that a breakup of NTT would result in a substantial loss of jobs. NTT had already reduced its employment from 314,000 in 1985 to 197,000 in 1994, although some of those job losses represented transfers to affiliated companies.

## NTT's Strategy

NTT deployed an integrated strategy to avoid a breakup. In its market environment it announced in September 1995 that it planned to spin off its two software divisions. In the same month it announced that it would open its local service network to competitors. The high access charges, however, would prevent competitors from taking advantage of the opening. NTT subsequently announced that it would reduce its access fees. NTT also announced that it would eliminate 45,000 jobs over the next 5 years to improve its efficiency.[52]

In the nonmarket environment NTT used a representation strategy, rallying its suppliers and its union. Within the Keidanren, NTT's principal suppliers opposed a breakup, leading the Keidanren to take no position on the issue. *Zen Dentsu* used its relationships with the SDP to encourage it to oppose a breakup in the cabinet. NTT also argued that size was increasingly important in the global telecommunications industry and that a breakup would threaten its future international competitiveness.

## Policy Analysis

A number of possible ways to break up NTT had been considered. One was to break it geographically into a set of regional companies, but as Japan is approximately the size of California, regional companies might not make economic sense. Another possibility was to break NTT vertically into a long-distance company and a local service company. A third possibility was to break it into a long-distance company and as many as 11 local service companies.

[52]The *Nikkei Weekly* reported, however, that over half the employees would be loaned to NTT subsidiaries.

In late 1995 some policy analysts had come to believe that deregulating the telecommunications industry and allowing increased competition was more important than breaking up NTT. This, however, was contrary to the MPT's plans. Any substantial deregulation would thus have to come from the governing parties through new legislation.

The Keidanren supported deregulation of the Japanese economy, and its Telecommunications Council studied the issue of the breakup of NTT. The council, however, chose not to issue a report due to internal disagreement with NTT's family of suppliers opposing a breakup and NTT's competitors and customers supporting a breakup. A Keidanren spokesperson stated that deregulation should take place before a breakup. The absence of Keidanren support for a breakup weakened the MPT's position.

The National Institute for Research Advancement also studied the issue and concluded that the AT&T breakup model was no longer valid and could weaken research and development and harm rural areas by reducing cross-subsidization. The Institute, however, did not make a recommendation.

## The Decision-Making Process

In traditional fashion, the MPT issued a report in 1994 supporting greater competition in telecommunications. An Administrative Reform Council studied the issue and recommended a breakup, but did not specify how it should be done. That decision was referred to the Telecommunications Council, a deliberation council (advisory panel) of the MPT. Deliberation councils rely on the resources of the ministry and had been criticized as supporting the outcome the ministry wanted. The council was asked to make a recommendation regarding a breakup by early 1996.

At the end of February 1996, the Telecommunications Council recommended that by 1999 NTT be split into a long-distance carrier and two local service companies, one serving the western part of Japan including Osaka and one serving the eastern part including Tokyo.[53] In addition, the council recommended that NTT be allowed to provide international services, and KDD and International

[53]Ministry of Posts and Telecommunications, "The Status of Nippon Telegraph and Telephone Corporation: Toward the Creation of Dynamism in the Info-Communications Industry," February 29, 1996.

Digital Communications be allowed to provide domestic services. In an unusual failure of consensus, 3 of 22 members of the Telecommunications Council dissented, arguing that global competition required large companies.

NTT argued that the western region would be unprofitable because it would not serve the main business centers. It projected that the eastern region would have profits of ¥70 billion and the western region a deficit of ¥80 billion. The MPT countered with its own estimates. It forecasted a profit of ¥217.4 billion for the western region.

MITI had traditionally backed NTT because it believed that NTT was Japan's only realistic hope in the international telecommunications industry. MITI believed that preserving NTT's economies of scale and its investments in research and development was necessary to ensure its international competitiveness. Both MITI and the MOF, however, remained largely neutral in the current conflict. ∎

## PREPARATION QUESTIONS

1. How will the decision regarding breaking up NTT be made? That is, who will have influence in the decision making and why?
2. How effective is NTT's strategy likely to be?
3. What outcome do you predict and why?

# The Privatization of Japan Post

The postal service in Japan was much more than its 24,000 post offices and 270,000 employees. Japan Post was also the world's largest bank and largest provider of life insurance. Japan Post operated the postal savings system which had deposits of $2 trillion in yucho savings accounts, much more than Japan's four largest banks and about half the total amount in savings accounts in Japan. In addition to the postal savings system Japan Post operated Kampo, which provided life insurance. Kampo received $150 billion of premiums in 2003. In total Japan Post held $3.2 trillion in assets, which represented 25 percent of Japan's household assets. Japan Post also held approximately 25 percent of the total outstanding government bonds.

The post office system was established during the Meiji period (1868–1912). The Postal Life Insurance Service began providing life insurance in 1916 to serve rural and poor parts of the country. Its successor Kampo had 40 percent of the market in Japan, which was the world's second largest, representing 22.8 percent of the world's life insurance market. Both the postal savings system and Kampo were obligated to provide universal service throughout Japan.

Economists complained that Japan Post funneled funds into quasi-government companies to fund public projects of questionable value. This distorted capital markets, resulting in economic inefficiency. The savings deposits received by Japan Post were funneled into the Fiscal Investment and Loan Program, which financed government-affiliated special corporations that provided public works projects. "The program has been criticized for using repayable postal savings for policy objectives like tax revenue, and for serving merely to perpetuate the franchises of politicians and bureaucrats, while accumulating latent delinquent assets."[54] *The International Herald Tribune* referred to the Program as a "murky slush fund." The projects funded were important to the constituency exchange relationships of the Liberal Democratic Party.

The banking and insurance industries complained about unfair competition, since Japan Post was not subject to regulation. For example, it was not required to pay premiums to the government-backed Deposit Insurance Corporation. Kampo also benefited from large tax benefits as a government entity.

A survey by the *Nihon Keizai Shimbun* found 47 percent of respondents in favor of privatization and 34 percent opposed.

---

[54] *Financial Times Information*, July 1, 2004.

## The Privatization Plan

The government was a coalition of the Liberal Democratic Party and the New Komeito party, which was backed by the Soka Gakkai Buddist organization. Prime Minister Junichiro Koizumi had been postal minister in 1993 and became convinced that the postal system had to be privatized. He made privatization a core feature of his reform policy. He reshuffled his cabinet in 2003 and reportedly made support of privatization a condition for inclusion in the cabinet.

The privatization plan was to break Japan Post into four separate business entities: mail delivery, postal savings, insurance, and over-the-counter services. The split would occur in April 2007, and the entities operating the postal savings and the insurance services would be under private management at that time. The entities would be owned by a holding company, and the government would retain a one-third stake in the holding company even after the 10-year transition period was completed in 2017. In 2007 the pre-existing Kampo insurance policies would be transferred to a new entity, the Public Successor Corporation. A remaining issue was whether any of the privatized companies should be broken up regionally. This would be left up to the management of the companies.

The privatization policy was to be formalized in a bill to be submitted to the Diet in the session commencing in January 2005. The Council on Economic and Fiscal Policy, chaired by the prime minister and located in the Cabinet Office, was responsible for developing the privatization policy. The Council issued its "Basic Policy on Postal Privatization," which was submitted for review and approval by the cabinet. To prepare the details for a bill to be submitted to the Diet, the government established the Preparatory Office for the Privatization of Postal Services, composed of members of the relevant ministries, agencies, and the Cabinet Office as well as private sector representatives.

As privatized companies, the savings bank and Kampo would be required to pay corporate profits taxes and deposit insurance premiums and would be required to meet reserve requirements rather than be supported by government guarantees. A privatized Kampo would be subject to the Insurance Business Law, although the government's Basic Policy mentioned "certain exemptions" during the 10-year transition period.

## Interests

The interests supporting privatization had two objectives. The first was to make certain that the privatization process was not derailed. The second was to prevent Japan Post from using the time until 2007 to favorably position the entities to be privatized.

The Japanese Bankers Association argued that a privatized savings company should not offer fixed-rate savings instruments, and the Life Insurance Association of Japan argued that the privatized life insurance company should not be required to provide universal service. They were concerned that if universal service were required, which under the current law meant the same rates and prices throughout the country, the company would have to be subsidized to support loss-making services in some parts of the country. Yamato Transport Company, the largest parcel-delivery company, took out an advertisement in newspapers to protest the plan to require the privatized mail-delivery company to provide universal service. Yamato believed that a universal service mandate would require subsidies that would give the privatized company an unfair advantage.

With respect to the second objective the business interests wanted assurances that Japan Post would not use the time until 2007 to expand the scope of its services. Under the current law the postal savings system was prohibited from making loans, and Kampo could only provide life insurance. Kampo, however, had already begun offering a whole life insurance policy with a health care rider. Moreover, Japan Post had entered into an arrangement with Lawson Inc. to handle parcels delivered by Japan Post. Yamato Transport filed a lawsuit against Japan Post complaining that the arrangement could force it out of the parcel-delivery business. Yamato had a similar arrangement with Lawson, which it felt compelled to cancel as a result of the Japan Post-Lawson arrangement. Heizo Takenaka, Minister for Economic and Fiscal Policy and Minister for Privatization of Postal Services, commented, "The biggest message from the [Yamato] lawsuit is that Japan Post should be privatized as speedily as possible. If it is privatized under the same terms as other businesses, problems like these would not take place."[55]

55 *Kyodo News International,* October 4, 2004. Takenaka had been responsible for ordering Japan's largest banks to cut their bad loans by 50 percent by March 2005.

The American Council of Life Insurers (ACLI) prepared a study showing that Kampo had received over $20 billion of tax breaks during the past 10 years. Allen Smith, chairman of the privatization task force at the American Chamber of Commerce in Japan, said, "This is an opportunity to introduce market principles, and if done well could be very good for the Japanese economy. The big issue is, at what point will it come under the same regulations as applied to the private sector?"[56] Along with the ACLI, the U.S. Chamber of Commerce and the Life Insurance Association of Japan supported privatization of Kampo.

Since 1994 the United States and Japan had been holding bilateral discussions on the insurance industry. In 2004 the United States Trade Representative (USTR) initiated talks about the sale of life insurance by Kampo. Kampo was said to be offering new life insurance products to position itself favorably prior to the possible privatization. The USTR called on Japan to apply the same regulations to Kampo as applied to other insurance companies. The USTR also asked that no new postal services be offered until a level playing field had been established.

Masaharu Ikuta, president of Japan Post, argued that breaking up the system would lose the synergies among its services. He also said, "It may not make sense if (a new organizational plan) would weaken the services. It should be a great loss as (Japan Post) runs quite a few number of jobs. We want (the government) to bear these points in mind and make a plan under a certain timeframe."[57] The Ministry of Public Management, Home Affairs, Posts and Telecommunications agreed with Ikuta.

Japan Post also argued that it would be impossible to restructure its computer systems by April 2007. The government assigned a team of technical experts to evaluate whether the computer systems could be ready.

The workers at Japan Post were represented by two unions. The Japan Postal Workers Union represented 142,000 employees, and the All Japan Postal Labour Union represented 87,000 employees. In addition to its 270,000 employees, Japan Post had 100,000 temporary and part-time workers. Japan

Post employees would no longer be public servants beginning with the privatization in 2007.

Some critics of privatization were concerned that universal service for postal savings and life insurance could be jeopardized by privatization. Economists also warned that interest rates could rise, slowing the growth in the economy, if Japan Post were privatized in a manner that required the sale of a substantial number of government bonds.

## The Road to Privatization

To advance its privatization objectives, the Koizumi government had to go through a series of stages. The privatization policy required approval of the cabinet. The cabinet was composed of ministers from the LDP and its government partner the New Komeito party. Before seeking approval from the cabinet, Koizumi sought approval from the LDP, which could attempt to block the privatization policy in the cabinet. Opposition to privatization came from within the LDP.

The government decided to meet with both the LDP and the cabinet on the same day. In the morning the government went before the LDP and New Komeito Diet members to present its privatization policy. Two hundred and fifty of the 360 LDP members in the Diet signed a petition opposing privatization, and the members put "reservations" on any policy that they said should be taken into account in the privatization bill to be put before the Diet. The opponents in the LDP, however, did not attempt to block the plan in the cabinet. Referring to the customary practice of obtaining party approval before a bill could be submitted to the Diet, Tamisuke Watanuki, chair of the LDP's committee on postal business, said, "Without party procedures, no bills can be passed."[58] Koizumi was successful in obtaining cabinet approval in the afternoon. He said, "We are unable to win agreement with the party but we have finally reached cabinet approval."[59] He added, "This is the biggest reform since the Meiji Restoration. Although the party's approval was not obtained, it has great significance that the Cabinet approved it."[60] He said the government would "closely coordinate" with the party in drafting the bill to be submitted to the Diet.

[56]*The Wall Street Journal*, September 13, 2004.
[57]AFX Europe, July 21, 2004.
[58]Agence France Presse-English, September 12, 2004.
[59]Agence France Presse-English, September 12, 2004.
[60]Japan Economic Newswire, September 10, 2004.

Privatization was supported by the Democratic Party of Japan (DPJ), the largest opposition party. The challenge for the Koizumi government was how it could win the support of a majority of the LDP. The poor showing by the LDP and the success of the DPJ in the upper house elections in July provided an opportunity for the prime minister. Robert Feldman, chief economist of Morgan Stanley Japan, commented, "Koizumi has a strong opposition party that he can use to threaten the LDP."[61] ■

SOURCE: This case was prepared from public sources by Professor David P. Baron. Copyright © 2004 by David P. Baron. All rights reserved. Reprinted with permission.

## PREPARATION QUESTIONS

1. Identify the interests that will attempt to influence the road to privatization.
2. Which institutions in the Japanese government will play a role on the road to privatization?
3. What strategy should a Japanese bank or insurance company adopt to influence the privatization plan?
4. What strategy should a U.S. bank or insurance company adopt to influence the privatization plan?

# Uniqlo: Success Breeds Nonmarket Challenges

The Uniqlo brand burst onto the Japanese retail clothing scene in 1998 and was an instant success. By 2000 the Uniqlo chain had nearly 500 stores in Japan with sales of $5 billion for its parent company Fast Retailing. Its flagship items were fleece jackets for men and women, with sales of 8.5 million jackets in 2000. Uniqlo offered good quality clothing at attractive prices. Its fleece jackets sold for $16.50 compared to prices nearly three times as high at other retailers such as the Gap. Uniqlo sold 300 million items of clothing in Japan, an average of nearly three per person in the country. Its profit for the first half of 2001 was $600 million.

Uniqlo's success was as much due to its cachet as to its prices. Tadashi Yanai began Uniqlo with stores in Tokyo suburbs. By late 1998 he was ready to take the Uniqlo brand nationwide.[62] Launched with a stylish TV advertising campaign featuring pop singer Masayoshi Yamazaki, Yanai opened a store in Tokyo's Harajuku district, where Japanese fashion trends originate. Suddenly, Uniqlo's low-priced goods became chic and, as customers recognized the quality of the goods, sales skyrocketed.

In contrast to other Japanese retailers, Uniqlo's strategy was to design items in Japan and directly contract with factories in China for their production. In addition to low-cost production in China, Uniqlo bypassed the inefficient Japanese distribution system by supplying its stores directly. A number of other major retailers responded to Uniqlo's success by lowering their prices 25 to 30 percent, but their cost structure made it difficult for them to sustain the price cuts.

Yanai planned to take Uniqlo to Europe where he announced plans to open 50 stores in Great Britain. He explained the choice, "France is too conservative and the American market too competitive. Britain is quite conservative, like the Japanese. We both live on islands and are common-sense countries. We both like to be a bit different, but not too different."[63]

Uniqlo's growth contributed to a dramatic increase in imports from China, led by textiles and

---

61 *The International Herald Tribune*, September 28, 2004.
62 Uniqlo is a combination of "unique" and "clothing."
63 *Sunday Times*, February 4, 2001.

agricultural products. By 2000 Japan purchased more goods from China than from either Europe or the United States, and its trade deficit with China reached $25 billion. The impact on Japan's textile market was severe. Domestic production of textiles fell 31 percent from 1990 levels. Imports had surged 16.9 percent in 2000, and most of the growth was due to imports from China. The heart of Japan's textile industry was Ehime and Osaka prefectures, which were particularly hard hit.

In response to the surge in textile imports from China and other East Asian countries, the Japan Towel Industrial Association, with 457 domestic manufacturers, filed a petition with the Ministry of International Trade and Industry (MITI) asking the government to invoke a World Trade Organization safeguard provision allowing import restrictions for 3 years to give domestic manufacturers time to adjust to international competitive pressures. Association president Yoshihide Yoshihara said, "Compared with two years ago, imports have increased 34.5 percent and domestic production has decreased 25.9 percent. Towel-producing areas have been hard hit and jobs have been lost in them."[64] The market share of imported towels had reached 57.7 percent, and the association predicted that imports would increase to 70 percent by 2003. In the first half of 2000 textile imports from China increased 36 percent. Some Japanese commentators drew an analogy to the 1970s when U.S. textile manufacturers sought protection from lower-priced goods from Japan. In 2001 Japan was on the verge of taking the position it had so vigorously criticized.

The economic conditions in the Japanese textile industry were shared to a lesser extent by the Japanese economy. As of November 2000 consumer spending in Japan had fallen for 44 consecutive months. Consumer prices had fallen for over a year. Many Japanese companies followed Uniqlo's strategy of sourcing in China as a means of lowering costs so that they could cut prices to increase demand. For example, Yamaha Motor Company sourced parts in China and was able to reduce the price of a motorized bicycle by 30 percent. One observer commented, "There still are a lot of consumer durables with price gaps between domestic

and overseas markets. Price decreases will spread into many other fields."[65]

Despite the filing by the Japan Towel Industrial Association, a number of towel manufacturers objected to the petition. Seven towel manufacturers from Ehime Prefecture filed a petition opposing invoking the safeguard provision. The seven companies had already moved much of their sourcing of products to China because of competitive pressures. Their petition stated, "If the safeguard is imposed, firms that have made efforts to survive by moving their factories overseas will be critically damaged." The companies explained, "The petition to invoke the safeguard was decided by a majority vote (of the national association) that we did not support."[66] More Japanese firms were expected to move their production to other countries in an attempt to achieve competitiveness and avoid bankruptcy.

Opposition to invoking the safeguard provision also came from consumers. "Yoriko Inubushi, vice president of the Consumption Science Federation, said: 'Consumers want low-priced, high-quality goods. If the safeguard is imposed while domestic makers have not shown they are making an effort to meet demand, even consumers who advocate the importance of buying Japanese will not do so."[67]

Yoshihisa Kitai, chief economist for Shinsei Bank said, "I call it the Uniqlo effect. The import of textiles and vegetables and home appliances from the rest of Asia is rising rapidly. Therefore, manufacturers of textiles and farmers will inevitably have to go out of business because they can't compete."[68] Tadashi Yanai was fond of saying, "Those who can't swim should drown."[69]

The Liberal Democratic Party continued to be rocked by scandals, and Prime Minister Mori was expected to resign soon. The appeal by the textile companies to invoke the WTO safeguard provision put the LDP and MITI in a difficult position. In the past the LDP and MITI might have sided with the manufacturers, but with the LDP's fragile electoral support, the government was nervous about acting

[65]*The Daily Yomiuri*, August 7, 2001.
[66]*The Daily Yomiuri*, March 10, 2001.
[67]*The Daily Yomiuri*, February 18, 2001.
[68]*San Jose Mercury News*, March 17, 2001.
[69]*The Scotsman*, January 3, 2001.

[64]*The Daily Yomiuri*, February 18, 2001.

against the interests of consumers. The Japanese government hoped that China would voluntarily limit its exports to Japan.[70] ■

## PREPARATION QUESTIONS

1. What are the causes of the surge in imports from China? Are imports from China and other East Asian countries likely to continue to grow?

2. What are the likely ramifications of invoking the safeguard provision?

3. What if anything should Uniqlo do in response to the strategy of the domestic manufacturers?

[70] *The Daily Yomiuri*, February 21, 2001.

# CHAPTER 15

# The Political Economy of the European Union

## Introduction

The European Union (EU) has taken landmark steps toward economic and political integration. It has established a single market with 455 million consumers that allows the free movement of people, goods, services, and capital. It has also established a commonality in defense and foreign policy. The eventual breadth of the union remains open with at least four other nations seeking to join the European Union. In addition, the eventual depth of that integration, particularly with respect to political union, remains unclear.

The European Union is scheduled to admit Bulgaria and Romania, and possibly Croatia, in 2007. In 2004 the European Union agreed to begin negotiations with Turkey, which first applied for membership in 1987. Norway was approved to join the Union, but in 1994 Norwegian voters rejected membership as they had done in 1972. The member states differ considerably with populations ranging from 436,000 to 82 million, a ratio of more than 5 to 1 in per capita incomes among the members, and unemployment rates ranging from 3.7 to 19.2 percent. The 10 new countries that became members in 2004 increased the differences among the member states. For example, the median corporate tax in the European Union was 33 percent, but the rate in Estonia was zero. The average price-level index in the 10 new members was 52 percent of that in the other 15 member states. The average wage and benefits of an autoworker in Germany were over $40 an hour, whereas the average in Poland was only $8.63. Yet remarkable progress toward economic integration has been made, and the commitment to deeper integration remains strong in most of the member states.

This chapter considers the nonmarket environment in the European Union using the structured pluralism framework illustrated in Figure 14-1. The next section traces the history of the European Union and considers the two principal instruments for economic integration. The principal institutions are then considered along with the legislative procedures used by the European Union. The monetary union, fiscal harmonization, competition policy, state aid, market opening, and social democracy are then discussed. Issues and interests are then considered, and these foundations are used to identify effective nonmarket strategies in the European Union.

# The European Union

In the aftermath of World War II Europeans recognized the need to increase trade and encourage political cooperation. In 1951 six nations—Belgium, France, Italy, Luxembourg, the Netherlands, and West Germany—signed the Treaty of Paris, which established the European Coal and Steel Community (ECSC). The ECSC's goal was to improve the efficiency of its member states' coal and steel industries through the reduction of trade barriers.

In 1957 those same nations signed the Treaty of Rome, which provided the basic framework for the European Union of today. The Treaty of Rome established the European Economic Community (EEC), or the common market, with the objectives of opening domestic markets to the members and rationalizing their industries.[1] The 1965 Treaty of Brussels represented an important step toward European integration by unifying the administration of the EEC, ECSC, and EURATOM. This provided an administrative structure upon which further steps toward economic and political integration could be built. The European Monetary System was established in 1979 to provide fixed, but adjustable, exchange rate bands for the currencies of the member states. In 1973 Denmark, Ireland, and the United Kingdom joined the EEC. Greece joined in 1981, Portugal and Spain in 1986, and Austria, Finland, and Sweden joined in 1995. The 2000 Treaty of Nice provided a road map for enlargement of the Union, and in 2004 the European Union admitted 10 new members: Cyprus, Latvia, Lithuania, the Czech Republic, Estonia, Hungary, Malta, Slovakia, Poland, and Slovenia.[2]

In addition to the broadening of the EU through the admission of new member states, the member states and their citizens faced the issue of the depth of political integration. Some supported a deeper union in which more authority would be transferred from the member states to the EU government. This could involve substantial changes in the institutions and the representation in those institutions. One possibility was a federal system such as the one in Germany or the United States. In contrast to those who sought a deeper union, a growing number of EU citizens began asking whether political union had already gone too far. This Euroskepticism stemmed from the view that once economic integration has been achieved, a deeper political union would provide little in the way of benefits.[3]

The two most recent major steps toward economic and political union have been the Single European Act and the Maastricht Treaty on European Union, considered next.[4]

## The Single European Act

Economic growth in the common market was strong during the 1960s, but beginning in the 1970s and particularly in the early 1980s growth slowed markedly, unemployment rolls swelled to over 10 percent, and job creation came to a crawl. The slow growth, the high cost of labor, and the difficulties and costs involved in workforce reductions made many firms reluctant to hire. Europeans called their economic disease "Eurosclerosis" and worried about worsening competitiveness relative to the United States and Japan.

---

[1] The six nations also formed the European Atomic Energy Community (EURATOM).
[2] Cyprus is partitioned, and only the Greek portion of the island has become a member.
[3] See, for example, Alesina and Wacziarg (1999).
[4] The 1997 Treaty of Amsterdam strengthened the human rights provisions of the European Union, committed the Union to take steps to increase employment, adopted the objective of sustainable development, strengthened the Common Foreign and Security Policy, elevated the formal powers of the European Parliament, and prepared for institutional change when new members were admitted.

Many business leaders recognized that competitiveness was also inhibited by a set of barriers that limited trade and increased costs. Progress in reducing many of the barriers had been slow because each state reserved the right to veto changes it believed were contrary to its interests. To document the potential gains from further market integration, the European Commission sponsored the Cecchini study, which concluded that the formation of a single market could increase GDP by 4.3 to 6.4 percent.[5]

The Single European Act (SEA), which took effect in 1987, addressed several impediments to trade and provided measures to facilitate access to national markets.[6] The SEA also increased the power of the EU government relative to the governments of the member states, particularly by limiting the use of the unanimity rule for decision making. The SEA mandated the realization of a single market by the beginning of 1993. The program to realize market integration involved the removal of three types of barriers: physical, technical, and fiscal. The removal of physical barriers pertained to the movement of both goods and people, eliminating customs and other goods inspections, removing restrictions on the entry of people, and allowing individuals to work in any member state.

The European Union took two approaches—harmonization and mutual recognition—to the removal of internal barriers to trade. Harmonization refers to the development of a common set of policies for all member states. Because of the complexity of the bargaining, progress on technical issues such as product standards, product certification, and the licensing of professional services had become tediously slow as nationalistic considerations complicated negotiations. To avoid the roadblocks of the past, the principle of mutual recognition, first articulated by the European Court of Justice in the Cassis de Dijon case, was adopted.[7] The EU member states were able to agree on mutual recognition, whereas they had been unable to agree on a common set of standards. The principle of mutual recognition represented a major change in EU policy and increased the speed with which internal barriers were removed.

Fiscal harmonization pertains to tax policy, particularly value-added taxes (VAT), excise and profits taxes, government fiscal policy, and subsidization or "state aids." The member states differed substantially in their tax and other fiscal policies, and those differences distorted trade, the location of facilities, and the movement of people.[8] For example, VAT rates were as high as 38 percent on some goods and as low as zero on others. Furthermore, some countries had multiple tiers of VAT rates, whereas others had a single rate. Progress on fiscal harmonization has been slow. One tax harmonization measure that was implemented abolished duty free sales for intra-EU travel, but the industry attempted to overturn the abolition, as considered in the chapter case, *Aldeasa and the EU Duty Free Abolition.*

With the entry of 10 new member states in 2004 the disparity in tax rate increased. The countries of Eastern Europe generally had low corporate tax rates, and several of them had reduced their tax rates prior to joining the EU. The average corporate tax rate of the 10 new entrants was 21.3 percent, whereas the average for the 15 prior members was 31.3 percent. Tax harmonization was even farther in the future.

Harmonization is also the approach taken to the sensitive and important issues of public health, safety, and the environment. The approach was to reach agreement on

---

[5]See Cecchini et al. (1988) and Emerson et al. (1988).
[6]European Commission (1986). See Overturf (1986) for an analysis of the benefits from economic integration.
[7]In 1979 the court ruled that a German regulation on the alcohol content of liqueurs could not be used to block the sale of the French liqueur Cassis de Dijon.
[8]European Commission (1985, para. 189).

a set of basic standards and then allow the individual member states to go beyond those basics as they choose.

## The Maastricht Treaty

In 1992 the member states agreed to the Maastricht Treaty on European Union. The Treaty ran into immediate problems as the United Kingdom opted out of part of it, Denmark first rejected and then narrowly accepted it, and French voters only narrowly approved it.

The treaty established a timetable for a common European currency and an independent European Central Bank.[9] Twelve member states that had met targets on inflation rates, government budget deficits, and interest rates formed a monetary union with a common currency—the euro, €—and a European Central Bank. Denmark, Sweden, and the United Kingdom met the targets but opted not to join.

Political integration was considerably more difficult than monetary union, but some steps toward political union were taken. The member states entered into a protocol to establish a joint social policy. Additional proposals included strengthening the European Parliament, establishing a European citizenship, and changing the unanimity rule still in effect for certain decisions. To advance the cause of political union, a constitutional convention was convened and developed a constitution, as considered in the next section, that awaited ratification by the 25 member states.

## The Institutions of the European Union

The four principal institutions of the European Union are the European Commission, the Council of Ministers, the European Parliament, and the European Court of Justice. The following sections consider the institutions in more detail and the changes that would result from the ratification of the EU constitution. Figure 15-1 highlights the roles of the three institutions involved in legislation and administration.

### The European Commission

The European Commission, located in Brussels, is the executive and administrative body of the European Union. The commission administers EU policies and enforces the various treaties. It is responsible for monitoring the implementation of EU legislation and ensuring that the member states comply with EU law. The commission is responsible for trade negotiations and manages the EU budget. The commission is the only body with the power to initiate legislation. The European Parliament and the Council of Ministers, however, can ask the commission to review proposals and consider issues. The European Commission's role in initiating legislation and administering policies makes it a target for lobbying. Moreover, the commission is obligated to consult with interests and to notify the Council of Ministers and the parliament that it has done so. The commission has a relatively small staff (21,750), so it needs information and expertise, and its consultations with interest groups are a means of obtaining that information.

Each member state has one commissioner, who is obliged to serve the interests of the European Union and not those of their own countries. Commission terms are

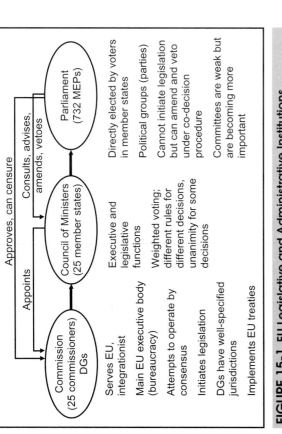

Approves, can censure

Appoints

Consults, advises, amends, vetoes

**Commission (25 commissioners) DGs**

Serves EU, integrationist

Main EU executive body (bureaucracy)

Attempts to operate by consensus

Initiates legislation

DGs have well-specified jurisdictions

Implements EU treaties

**Council of Ministers (25 member states)**

Executive and legislative functions

Weighted voting; different rules for different decisions, unanimity for some decisions

**Parliament (732 MEPs)**

Directly elected by voters in member states

Political groups (parties)

Cannot initiate legislation but can amend and veto under co-decision procedure

Committees are weak but are becoming more important

**FIGURE 15-1 EU Legislative and Administrative Institutions**

5 years, and commissioners are nominated by the individual member states. The commissioners must be approved as a whole by the European Parliament, and the parliament can dismiss the commission on a vote of no confidence. In an unprecedented event in 1999 all the commissioners resigned under a threat from the European Parliament stemming from allegations of corruption and mismanagement. In 2004 the incoming president of the commission withdrew his nominees for commissioners because of certain rejection by the parliament.

One commissioner serves as president and five as vice presidnets, and the others have responsibility for one or more of the 23 Directorates-General (DGs). A DG is a bureau, with a particular policy or administrative jurisdiction. For example, one DG has responsibility for economic and financial affairs, and the competition DG has responsibility for antitrust, mergers, and state aid. The commission also has several services.

The conflict between national and EU laws creates a tension within the community. EU law takes precedence over national law when a conflict arises, but not all national laws have been harmonized with EU law. In a number of cases member states have not complied with EU law, and the commission attempts to obtain compliance. In 2003 the commission initiated 1,552 infringement proceedings against member states for violating treaties or failing to implement directives. For example, the commission filed complaints against a number of countries for delays in implementing the Directive on Data Protection, as considered in the chapter case, *The European Union Data Protection Directive.*

The commission formally makes decisions by majority rule, but in practice it operates on a collegial basis, and no public reports of its deliberations or votes are issued. Conflict within the commission, however, can develop over policies, particularly those that have impacts across more than one DG. For example, the commissioner for industry proposed the elimination of price controls on pharmaceuticals as a means of encouraging firms to invest more in the development of innovative drugs. The commission, however, rejected the proposal in favor of asking the member states to bring their divergent pharmaceutical pricing policies into alignment.

# The Council of Ministers

The Council of Ministers, based in Brussels, is the principal legislative body of the European Union.[10] In contrast to the commission, whose members are obliged to serve the European Union, council members are the individual member states. The council consists of one minister from each state, but the nations have different numbers of votes as indicated in Figure 15-2. The presidency rotates among the member states every 6 months, and which ministers belong to the council depends on the issue under consideration. On an issue involving economics and finance, the cognizant ministers of the member states meet as the Economic and Financial Affairs Council (ECOFIN). The council operates in private, but since 1995 its votes have been reported publicly. Twice a year, the heads of state or government of the member states meet as the European Council, which sets the general directions for the European Union.

Associated with the council is the Committee of Permanent Representatives (COREPER), composed of ambassadors, or "permanent representatives," of the member states. COREPER represents the member states before the commission and serves as the secretariat of the Council of Ministers. It prepares the agenda, forms working parties, and negotiates informal agreements prior to council deliberations. Before the council considers proposals, COREPER appoints an ad hoc working party composed of government officials from the member states. Members of the commission may also participate. The working party gives its opinion on a legislative proposal to COREPER. If COREPER agrees with the opinion, it forwards the proposal to the council. COREPER is said to resolve 90 percent of the issues before they come to the council, leaving only the most politically sensitive for council deliberations.

Council decisions had been governed by a unanimity rule, which gave a veto to the member states. Because this created long delays on some issues, the SEA provided for decisions by majority rule. On most procedural matters the council acts under simple majority rule. Most of its substantive actions, however, require a "qualified" majority of 232 of 321 votes. A qualified majority also requires approval by a majority of the member states, and a member state can request "verification," which requires approval by member states comprising at least 62 percent of the population of the European Union. The Treaty of Nice replaced unanimity with qualified majority on 27 treaty provisions, including negotiated agreements on trade in services and intellectual property protection. Decisions involving foreign and security policy, justice and home affairs, some aspects of fiscal policy, and enlargement of the community, however, require unanimity.

**FIGURE 15-2  Council of Ministers Voting Weights**

| | |
|---|---|
| Germany, France, Italy, United Kingdom | 29 |
| Spain, Poland | 27 |
| Netherlands | 13 |
| Belgium, Czech Rep., Greece, Hungary, Portugal | 12 |
| Austria, Sweden | 10 |
| Denmark, Ireland, Lithuania, Slovakia, Finland | 7 |
| Cyprus, Estonia, Latvia, Luxembourg, Slovenia | 4 |
| Malta | 3 |
| TOTAL | 321 |

[10]See Hoscheit and Wessels (1988) and Nugent (2003) for an analysis of the Council of Ministers.

The council can take four types of actions, which differ in the extent to which they are binding on the member states.[11]

1. Regulations are legally binding on the member states and are enforced by the commission.
2. Directives are legally binding with respect to the result sought, but national governments are responsible for how the result is achieved.
3. Decisions are legally binding but pertain only to the parties identified in the decision.
4. Recommendations and opinions are not legally binding but may provide guidance and indicate future action on issues.

EU law becomes effective in a member state when that state accepts it as its law.

The Union operates under the principle of subsidiarity, meaning the intention to accomplish as much as possible at the level of the member states.[12] Article 35 of the Consolidated Treaty states that the Union can act "only if and in so far as the objectives of the proposed action cannot be sufficiently achieved by the Member States and can therefore, by reason of the scale or effects of the proposed action, be better achieved by the Community." This statement has been clarified by guidelines developed by the council. Any conflict over the application of the principle can be taken to the Court of Justice.

# The European Parliament

The European Parliament (EP) has 732 members directly elected for 5-year terms under proportional representation by voters in the member states. Although the European Parliament's power has increased over time, the turnout in the elections has decreased over time. Parliament members organize by parties or political groupings. In 2004 the European People's Party (Christian Democrats) and the European Democrats held 268 seats and the Socialists Group held 200 seats. The EP meets in Brussels and Strasbourg.

As the only popularly elected institution in the European Union, the EP has powers of "democratic supervision."[13] The EP approves of and can dismiss the commission and can ask questions of commissioners in writing or during "Question Time" when the EP is in session. Through the co-decision procedure, the EP and the council share legislative authority. Parliament cannot initiate or enact laws but plays a significant role in the legislative process. That role has expanded over time, and the SEA and the Maastricht Treaty gave it new legislative power, as described later in the chapter. Parliament also has budgetary authority.

The EP elects a president, who serves a 2 1/2-year term, and vice presidents from the other member states. It has 20 standing committees to which proposals are referred for consideration, and they are a focus of lobbying. Neither the committees nor the EP has the ability to delay a proposal, since action must be taken within a specified period. The EP operates under simple majority rule.

Individual citizens and firms may petition the EP on issues arising from either EU actions or conflicts between EU law and national laws. Petitions are reviewed by a Petition Committee; if accepted for consideration, the Petition Committee evaluates the petition and may hold a hearing. Interest groups often work through their national representatives in the petition process.

---

[11]See Nugent (2003).
[12]The pledge to abide by the principle of subsidiarity was important in obtaining Denmark's support for the Maastricht Treaty.
[13]The term *democratic deficit* refers to the fact that the council is not elected.

# The Court of Justice

The Court of Justice, located in Luxembourg, is the supreme judicial body of the Union and has the authority to overturn decisions that conflict with the EU treaties.[14] The court has one judge from each member state, with one judge elected as president for a 3-year term.[15] The Court makes decisions by majority vote in 13-judge chambers, and other cases are decided in three- and five-judge chambers. Dissenting opinions are not issued. The judges serve 6-year terms and are assisted by eight advocates general who provide independent and impartial opinions. The court hears cases pertaining to the various treaties of the European Union and other cases involving disputes between the community's institutions. Some of the cases brought to the court involve complaints by the European Commission against the member states. Actions can also be brought directly to the court by individuals and legal entities of the member states. Although the court has the final word on EU law, treaties give the courts of the member states some responsibilities for implementing EU law. The court also hears cases from member states when the states' own courts are uncertain about EU law.[16] Because of the court's workload, the Council of Ministers, under the SEA, established the Court of First Instance (CFI). The CFI applies the law established by the Court of Justice, and its decisions may be appealed to the higher court.

The Court of Justice also hears appeals of commission decisions. For example, cases involving the competitive practices of firms are usually decided by the commission's DG for competition. Firms can appeal its decisions and the penalties assessed. As indicated later in the chapter, European airlines appealed the commission's decision to allow France to subsidize Air France, and Microsoft appealed a competition case.

# The European Economic and Social Committee

The European Economic and Social Committee (EESC), based in Brussels, is an advisory body whose 317 members represent employees, employers, farmers, trades, and other interests. The EESC has six sections, or committees, which provide forums to express opinions on commission proposals and suggest changes in them. Interest groups interact with the EESC through the representatives of their home countries in the relevant sections. The final opinions of the EESC can be important because they reflect the concerns of interest groups.

# The EU Legislative Process

The European Union has three basic procedures—consultation, co-decision, and assent—for developing directives and regulations.[17] Under the consultation procedure that was used for nearly all important issues prior to the SEA, the European Commission, through one of its DGs, formulates a proposal that is sent to the Council of Ministers, which seeks opinions from both the EP and the EESC. The council weighs those opinions and returns the proposal to the commission for revision. The commission then sends the revised proposal to the council, which may amend, approve, or not act on it. If approved, the proposal becomes EU law, and the member states are required to abide by it.

---

[14]See Nugent (2003).
[15]Europe also has a Council of Europe that has a European Court of Human Rights, which hears cases under the European Convention on Human Rights.
[16]A major difference between the United States and European countries results from the due process requirements of the U.S. Constitution. As discussed in Chapter 10, due process imposes a complex set of requirements on government processes intended to ensure individuals the right to participate in governmental decision-making processes. Unless provided for by specific legislation, the European countries and the European Union do not have the same requirements.
[17]See Nugent (2003).

The SEA established the assent procedure, which gives the EP a veto over council action. The assent procedure is used for decisions about admission of new member states, international agreements, and the structure of the European Central Bank.

The Maastricht Treaty established the co-decision procedure, and the scope of its use was expanded in the Treaty of Amsterdam and the Treaty of Nice. This procedure, as illustrated in Figure 15-3, gives the EP a greater role and more power relative to the

**FIGURE 15-3 The European Union Co-Decision Legislative Procedure**

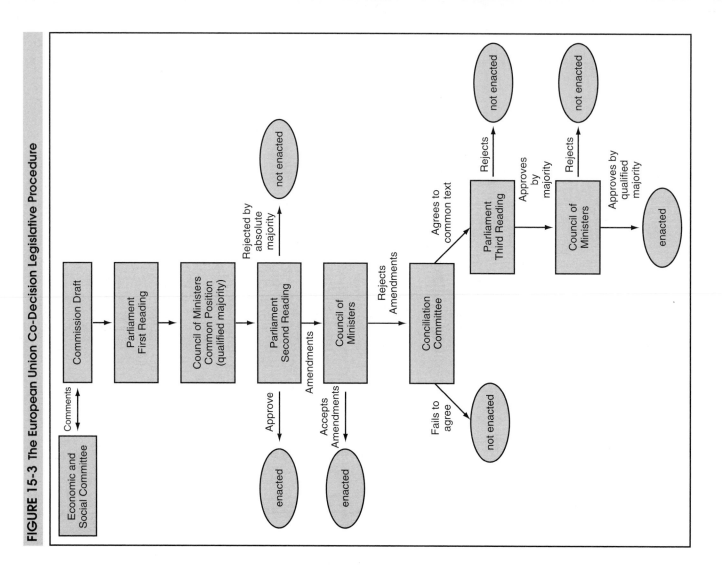

commission and the council. This procedure begins as in the consultation procedure, but once the opinions of the EP and the EESC have been obtained, the Council of Ministers develops by qualified majority a "common position" on the proposal. It is then sent to the EP for a second reading. If the EP approves the proposal, it is enacted. If an absolute majority of the EP votes against the common position, it is defeated and the process ends. If the EP amends the common position, the council can accept the amendments, thereby enacting the proposal. If the council rejects the amendments, a conciliation committee composed of members of the council and the EP is formed. If they reach agreement, the amended proposal is enacted by qualified majority of the council and a simple majority of the Parliament at the third reading. If no agreement is reached, or if either the council or the Parliament fails to approve the amended proposal, the proposal fails.[18]

The co-decision procedure is said to be bicameral, since approval by both the council and Parliament is required. The procedure is not fully "democratic," however, because the popularly elected Parliament cannot enact laws itself. The co-decision procedure is thus best viewed as a legislative process in which both institutions have a veto.

## Economic and Monetary Union

The European Union's interest in a monetary union officially began in 1989 when the Council of Ministers endorsed a series of steps to realize an Economic and Monetary Union (EMU). The EMU commenced in 1998 with the formation of the European System of Central Banks and the European Central Bank (ECB) to conduct a single monetary policy for its members. In 1999 the euro became the common currency of the EMU, and euro notes and coins replaced national currencies in 2002.[19] The ECB is an independent central bank patterned after Germany's central bank (the Bundesbank). The stated primary objective of the ECB is "to maintain price stability."

The European Union estimated that the savings on transactions costs associated with currency exchange would be 0.4 percent of GDP. The euro would become the second-most important currency after the U.S. dollar and could provide some benefits to the European Union as a reserve currency. Some countries such as Italy saw another advantage in the EMU. It would serve as a commitment device that would provide price stability to which its governments had had difficulty committing.

Not everyone shared the same enthusiasm for the EMU. Feldstein (1997, pp. 32–33) warned that the EMU may have costs that outweigh its benefits. He pointed to the loss of flexibility for a country to use discretionary monetary policy to offset temporary shocks to its economy. This could make it more difficult to reduce long-term unemployment.

One concern about monetary union is whether the member states will attempt to use the EMU for political purposes rather than price stability. The Treaty establishing the ECB stated that "without prejudice to the objective of price stability, the ECSB shall support the general economic policies in the Community. . . ." The ECB is independent of the governments of the member states, but some governments sought to influence the policies of the ECB to stimulate economic growth and create jobs.

[18]The stages of the process each have timetables; for example, the conciliation committee has 6 weeks to reach an agreement.
[19]The European Union had a long history of coordinating exchange rate policies. In the 1970s European countries maintained the "snake" with fixed exchange rates, and subsequently a stable Deutschmark zone developed. The European Monetary System (EMS) was established to band exchange rates together. The EMS also used a weighted average of exchange rates, the ECU, that was a forerunner of the euro.

## The EU Constitutional Treaty

The European Union convened a convention that wrote a treaty establishing a Constitution for Europe, which consolidates the seven EU treaties and revises the institutional structure of the Union. To take effect, the Constitutional Treaty had to be ratified by all member states, some of which used a popular referendum. The voters in both France and the Netherlands rejected it in 2005, reflecting a gulf between voters and political leaders. The next step was not clear.

The Constitutional Treaty incorporates the Charter for Fundamental Rights, making human and civil rights enforceable by the European Union. The Treaty extends the co-decision procedure to cover 95 percent of the lawmaking, so laws require approval of both the Council of Ministers and the EP. Matters of taxation, social policy, and foreign and defense policy continue to require unanimity. The Treaty establishes the positions of foreign minister and EU prosecutor for law enforcement. The Treaty establishes the European Council composed of the heads of states of the member states as a separate institution with a president with a 2 1/2-year term. The size of the EP is capped at 750, and after 2014 the number of commissioners will be two-thirds of the number of member states.

The most contentious aspect of the Constitutional Treaty was the voting rule for the Council of Ministers. A qualified majority is specified as a double majority of 55 percent of the member states and 65 percent of the population. To avoid a situation in which three large countries could stop an action, four countries are required for a blocking minority.

The Constitutional Treaty makes the institutions more transparent and democratic, although the EP remains the only popularly elected body. The Council of Ministers' legislative proceedings are to be open to the public. Citizens are given the opportunity to initiate legislation by collecting 1 million signatures on a proposal inviting the Commission to initiate legislation. To strengthen the role of national governments, the Commission is required to review a legislative proposal if one-third of the national parliaments believe the proposal is not in accord with the principle of subsidiarity. The Treaty also allows for enhanced cooperation in which groups of member states form agreements to go beyond basic EU law in policy areas such as environmental protection where that is permitted.

## Competition Policy

Competition policy includes EU policies involving the structure, conduct, and support of industries, including state aid. Antitrust policy is the centerpiece of competition policy, and this section addresses EU antitrust law and its administration. The member states also have their own competition laws. In 1998 France rejected Coca-Cola's planned acquisition of Orangina, after objections by PepsiCo and Orangina employees who feared layoffs.

The basic antitrust law of the European Union is found in Articles 81 and 82 of the Treaty Establishing the European Community, the principal components of which are presented in Figure 15-4.[20] The articles have two antecedents. The first is the Treaty of Rome goal of market integration. The second is U.S. antitrust law. Articles 81 and 82 correspond to Sections 1 and 2 of the Sherman Act, but EU antitrust law differs somewhat from U.S. law. Both aim at promoting competition, but EU antitrust law allows defenses, such as economic consequences, not provided for under U.S. law. Hence, EU law does not have per se offenses.

As with Section 1 of the Sherman Act, Article 81 refers to group activities that may limit competition or constitute a barrier to trade among member states. Much of the

---

[20]Article 82 is presented in its entirety.

**Article 81:**

(1) The following practices shall be prohibited as incompatible with the Common Market: all agreements between undertakings and all concerted practices which are liable to affect trade between Member States and which are designed to prevent, restrict or distort competition within the Common Market or which have this effect. This shall, in particular, include:

a) the direct or indirect fixing of purchase or selling prices or of any other trading conditions;

b) the limitation or control of production, markets, technical development or investment;

c) market-sharing or the sharing of sources of supply;

d) the application of unequal conditions on parties undertaking equivalent engagements in commercial transactions, thereby placing them at a competitive disadvantage;

e) making the conclusion of a contract subject to the acceptance by the other party to the contract of additional obligations which, by their nature or according to commercial practice, have no connection with the subject of such contract.

(2) Any agreement or decisions prohibited pursuant to this article shall automatically be null and void.

(3) The provisions of paragraph (1) may, however, be declared inapplicable in the case of

   -any agreement or type of agreement between undertakings

   -any decision or type of agreement between undertakings

   -any concerted practice or type of concerted practice

which helps to improve the production or distribution of goods or to promote technical or economic progress, whilst allowing consumers a fair share of the resulting profit and which does not: a) subject the concerns in question a any restrictions which are not indispensable to the achievement of the above objectives; b) enable such concerns to eliminate competition in respect to a substantial part of the goods concerned.

**Article 82:**

Any improper exploitation by one or more undertakings of a dominant position within the Common Market or within a substantial part of it shall be deemed to be incompatible with the Common Market and shall be prohibited, in so far as trade between Member States could be affected by it. The following practices, in particular, shall be deemed to amount to improper exploitation:

a) the direct or indirect imposition of any unfair purchase or selling prices or of any other unfair trading conditions;

b) the limitation of production, markets or technical development to the prejudice of consumers;

c) the application of unequal conditions to parties undertaking equivalent engagements in commercial transactions, thereby placing them at a commercial disadvantage;

d) making the conclusion of a contract to the acceptance by the other party to the contract of additional obligations which by their nature or according to commercial practice have no connection with the subject of such contract.

**FIGURE 15-4　European Union Antitrust Law Articles 81 and 82 of the Treaty Establishing the European Community**

text addresses vertical restraints, which were a concern at the time of establishment of the economic community because of the possibility that firms would use such arrangements in their channels of distribution to preserve national markets for themselves. Parts a, b, and c of Article 81, paragraph 1, pertain to vertical arrangements that might foreclose markets, and part d deals with price discrimination. Part e pertains to tying arrangements or reciprocal deals that might foreclose markets. The feature of Article 81 that distinguishes it most from Section 1 of the Sherman Act is the allowable defenses provided in paragraph 3. A firm may make the affirmative defense that an arrangement improves efficiency. The firm is obligated to use the least restrictive means to achieve that efficiency, and some of the efficiency gains must be passed on to consumers. The United States has adopted a similar perspective by considering whether a practice benefits consumers. Paragraph 3 virtually grants block exemptions for a variety of agreements—exclusive distributorships, exclusive purchase arrangements, patent licensing, motor vehicle distribution, specialization, research and development, franchises, and know-how licensing.

Article 82 deals with unilateral actions and differs from Section 2 of the Sherman Act. The article is not concerned with how a dominant position was obtained but rather with whether that position is abused. Article 82 thus does not provide a blanket prohibition of monopoly. Its specific provisions apply to unfair practices, monopoly restriction of output, price discrimination, and tying.

## Enforcement

Antitrust enforcement is by the DG for Competition, which investigates practices, initiates proceedings, serves as prosecutor, decides cases, and imposes fines. In contrast to the United States where antitrust cases are decided by judges or by an independent commission in the case of the Federal Trade Commission, the DG serves as both prosecutor and judge. The courts play no role unless there is an appeal of an action. Appeals are heard by the Court of First Instance and then by the Court of Justice if necessary. Private parties may file complaints with the European Commission, but private lawsuits are not permitted by Articles 81 and 82.[21] The DG is also required to consult with national competition officials before initiating proceedings. Those officials participate in the Advisory Committee on Restrictive Practices and Monopolies. In terms of remedies, the European Commission is limited to imposing fines and supervising conduct. Criminal penalties are not allowed. In 2004 the DG for Competition was given additional investigatory authority, and responsibility for certain merger approvals was devolved to the member states to allow the DG to concentrate on breaking up cartels. The commission has proposed that it be allowed to use structural remedies, such as ordering the divestiture of business units. The example on Microsoft includes a range of remedies.

Fines of up to 10 percent of a company's sales are the principal enforcement instrument. In 2000 the commission imposed fines of €110 million on ArcherDaniels Midland, two Japanese companies and one Korean company, for cartel price fixing of lysine used in animal foodstuffs. In 2001 the commission fined eight companies €855 million for cartel price fixing of vitamins. Roche Holding AG was fined €462 million as the ringleader of the price-fixing cartel.[22]

In 2004 the DG for Competition reached a settlement with Coca-Cola after a 5-year investigation. In member states in which its market share exceeds 40 percent and its sales are double those of the next largest company, Coca-Cola agreed to end restrictive practices, including offering large discounts on its popular brands in exchange for stocking its less popular brands. Coca-Cola also agreed to stop offering rebates for reserving shelf space as well as "target" and "growth" rebates. In addition, Coca-Cola agreed to make up to 20 percent of the space in its branded refrigerators available to competitors, including Pepsi, which had complained to the European Union about Coca-Cola's practices. The settlement avoided fines and years of appeals.

---

[21]Private lawsuits may be filed under the antitrust laws of the member states.
[22]See Chapter 9 for U.S. actions against the cartel members.

**EXAMPLE**

## Microsoft and EU Competition Policy

Microsoft's competitive practices and dominance of the operating system and desktop software markets have been a concern of the DG for Competition for more than a decade. In 1991 the U.S. Department of Justice (DOJ) and the European Commission signed an agreement to cooperate on antitrust investigations. The DOJ and the commission, acting under a complaint from Novell, Inc. cooperated in an antitrust case against Microsoft with both agencies pressuring the company to enter into a consent decree to change its software licensing practices. At the end of the 1990s the DG for Competition prevented Microsoft from exercising joint control over the United Kingdom's Telewest Communications, in which Microsoft had invested $3 billion.

Sun Microsystems filed a complaint with the DG for Competition (and not with U.S. antitrust authorities) alleging that Microsoft withheld interface (API) information for connecting servers to PCs in a network. Sun hoped to benefit from a precedent in which the commission had ordered IBM to share certain interface information with Amdahl. A similar complaint was filed pertaining to interface information for Windows 2000. The commission combined these two cases and added new allegations about the bundling of Microsoft's music and video-streaming software with Windows XP. In 2003 a group of global telecommunications, electronics, and software companies joined the case as intervenors, alleging

that Windows XP incorporated broader bundling, exclusion practices, and screen bias favoring Microsoft software.

After 5 years of investigation and several attempts to reach a settlement, in 2004 the DG for Competition found Microsoft guilty of abusing its dominant position in computer operating systems in violation of Articles 81 and 92. As remedies, the DG fined Microsoft €497 million and ordered it to offer a version of Windows without Media Player. The court also ordered Microsoft to disclose substantive portions of its Windows code to allow server manufacturers to develop software that works with Windows. The DG and Microsoft again attempted but failed to reach a settlement, and Microsoft appealed the decision to the European Court of First Instance and sought a suspension of the remedies order. The president of the Computer and Communications Industry Association (CCIA), which was among the intervenors said, "Their history is to appeal everything so as to delay."[1]

Microsoft subsequently settled with Novell for $536 million and with the CCIA for an undisclosed amount. Microsoft had earlier settled with AOLTimeWarner and Sun Microsystems, leaving Real Networks as the only remaining intervenor. The Court of First Instance rejected Microsoft's appeals.

[1]*The New York Times*, October 2, 2004.

## Mergers

The Treaty of Rome did not address mergers because they were viewed as a desirable means of enabling small-scale European firms to attain the scale needed to compete globally. In 1989 the Council of Ministers adopted a Merger Control Regulation, assigning the commission responsibility for reviewing large mergers, those in which the combined unit has sales of over €2.5 billion and the individual firms have sales of over €250 million.[23] Companies registered outside the European Union must submit a merger notification if they have sales in the European Union of €100 million. Merger review by the commission is based solely on the effect on competition. The member states have authority to review smaller mergers and can seek permission from the

[23]See Fishwick (1993) and Cini and McGowan (1998) for analyses of EU competition policy.

commission to conduct their own review of large mergers. If two-thirds of the revenues of each of two merging firms are from a single member state, that state rather than the commission has authority over the review. This allows a country to permit the merger of two of its major companies.

The European Union has been active in the review of mergers, and its decisions have generally been consistent with those of the United States. In 2000 both the European Union and the United States blocked the merger of MCI (then WorldCom) and Sprint Communications. Also in 2000 the United States approved the merger of AOL and TimeWarner after requiring the companies to provide rival Internet access through TimeWarner's cable systems. The European Union also approved the $118 billion merger with the requirements that AOL TimeWarner scrap joint ventures with Bertelsmann AG, Vivendi SA, and EMI Group that threatened competition in the music business.

In 2001, however, the European Union blocked the merger of General Electric and Honeywell International after the United States and 15 other countries had approved it. The DG for Competition was concerned about General Electric's dominant position in aircraft leasing and the portfolio effect if combined with Honeywell's avionics business. Critics charged that the decision was intended to protect Airbus Industrie from stronger competition. General Electric and Honeywell dropped the merger, but the companies decided to appeal the decision to the European Court of Justice so that the case would not set a precedent for future acquisitions. The previous year MCI appealed the EU decision to block its merger with Sprint for the same reason.

In 2003 the Court of First Instance overturned a DG decision to block the merger of two UK travel agencies. The court used unusually harsh language in its decision, stating that the DG had been guilty of "manifest error" and "exceeded the bounds of its discretion." The court added that the DG's analysis was "vitiated by errors" and that it was necessary to show a "direct and immediate effect" on creating or maintaining a dominant position. The DG for Competition subsequently announced that greater oversight and additional reviews, including a peer review panel, would be applied before making merger decisions.

## State Aids and the Common Agriculture Policy

State aids are subsidies paid by member state governments to industries or government-owned companies.[24] Compared with the United States and Japan, EU states provide considerably more subsidization for their firms. In 2002 the EU member states provided €49 billion in state aids, with Germany providing €13 billion, France €10 billion, and Italy €6 billion. Much of the subsidization has gone to declining industries in an attempt to protect labor and capital.

The European Commission monitors state aids and, for example, directed Italy to obtain a refund for a subsidy given to Fiat and ordered France to stop the large-scale sub-sidization of Renault. Private parties can file complaints with the DG for Competition to stop state aid. For example, the European Banking Federation complained about German loan guarantees to state-owned savings banks and regional banks, and the DG began an investigation. The DG for Competition had over 560 state aid cases in 1999 and in 2000—nearly the number of antitrust and merger cases combined.

EU member states also provide subsidies to failing companies. In 2004 France pro-vided a €2.2 billion bailout of Alstom, an engineering conglomorate, to avoid having the company broken up and the parts purchased by foreign companies. Such bailouts

---

[24]State aids are governed by Article 92 of the Treaty of Rome.

must be approved by the DG for Competition. To stem the declining prospects for a number of their companies, France and Germany sought to create globally competitive industrial champions by consolidating firms in some industries. Germany began with the consolidation of its shipbuilding industry.

In addition to state aid to agriculture and fisheries, the EU's Common Agriculture Policy (CAP) provides subsidies to farmers totaling €44 billion. The European Union sought to rein in CAP and made some progress, although opposition from farmers and some member states remained intense. The CAP, along with agricultural subsidization in the United States and Japan, has been the source of considerable international trade tension, as considered in Chapter 17. CAP also complicated enlargement negotiations with applicant countries. France, for example, sought to avoid any diversion of payments from its farmers to the new EU members.

## The Social Charter, Social Democracy, and Labor Markets

The European Union adopted a Social Charter as part of the Treaty Establishing the European Community. The charter provides a vision for the free circulation of labor and the rights to fair wages, improvement of living and working conditions; social security; free association and collective bargaining; vocational training and education; equal treatment for men and women; information; consultation and participation for workers; health protection and safety in the workplace; protection for children, adolescents, and the elderly; and protection of the disabled.[25] Translating the vision of the Social Charter into law has been marked by several disagreements between business and labor and by the reality of national policy differences.[26] This led to the practice of an open method of coordination for implementation. Many of the actions under the Social Charter have been directed to increasing employment.

The SEA and other EU laws reflect the objectives of empowering labor and protecting individuals from risk and hardship through extensive social programs.[27] The European Union requires works councils or a consultative process between management and workers, or "social partners" in the terminology of European Union. At the plant level in Germany, workers have both representation and a set of rights to participation.[28] Those participation rights are in the areas of personnel policy, working conditions, and information, such as required notification of business plans that affect workers. Works councils can effectively prohibit weekend and overtime work and have powers over dismissals and reassignments.[29] Works councils use their rights to influence management, and management thus has an interest in accommodating council interests. Management, however, controls most decision making.

Much of the European labor force is well educated and highly skilled, and labor costs in many EU member states are high. Workweeks are shorter and vacations longer in Europe than they are in the United States and Asia. The OECD reported that on average Americans worked 1,815 hours in 2002, whereas the French and Germans worked less than 1,500 hours and the Dutch 1,340 hours.[30] Edward Prescott, the 2004 Nobel laureate in economics, attributed the difference in hours worked between the United States and Europe to differences in the tax rates on income. During the

---

[25]See Nugent (2003, pp. 313–315) and Pierson (1999).
[26]See Wise and Gibb (1993).
[27]See European Commission (1988).
[28]See Streeck (1984, Ch. 3).
[29]See Streeck (1984, Ch. 7).
[30]The hours worked for Australia, Japan, and New Zealand were about the same as in the United States.

1970–1974 period the hours worked in France exceeded those in the United States, and tax increases in France and tax decreases in the United States led to the divergence, he argued.[31]

The short work hours led one German industrial relations manager to observe that "the German worker doesn't work very often, but when he does work, he works very, very hard."[32] Hard work was not enough, however, and the high labor costs led German companies to move jobs to the new, low-wage-rate members of the European Union. Some German unions began to accept longer work hours to retain jobs in Germany. France reduced its workweek to 35 hours in 2000 in an effort to reduce its unemployment rate. By 2004 President Jacques Chirac said, "I feel it's been a brake on economic development and therefore a brake on overall employment."[33]

With labor costs in the new EU member states far lower than those in the other member states, two threats faced the high-wage countries. One was that jobs could flow east to take advantage of both low wages and low taxes. This would increase unemployment and force wage concessions in the west. The other was that workers would flow west seeking higher wages. Anticipating this, the 15 existing EU member states reserved the right to restrict for up to 7 years the right of workers from the new member states to work in the west. Restrictions were imposed by several of the 15, including Austria, Denmark, Germany, the Netherlands, and the United Kingdom.

Economic growth in the Netherlands far outstripped that in other European countries during the 1990s, and by 2003 unemployment was less than 3 percent in contrast to over 9 percent in Germany and France. The economic performance of the Netherlands was credited to moderate wage growth and allowing labor market flexibility, including temporary and part-time work. In addition, the country cut unemployment benefits, which increased the incentives to find work. The country also shifted the burden of sick pay from the government to employers, which reduced significantly the number of employees calling in sick. Many of these reforms came under the leadership of a prime minister who was a former labor leader.

## Nonmarket Issues

Nonmarket issues in the European Union may be categorized by the level at which they are addressed, the EU level versus that of a member state, and whether they are specific to an industry or to an individual firm. At the EU level, important issues include deeper political integration, the economic integration of the 10 new member states, the administration of competition policy, persistent high unemployment, further reforms of the common agriculture policy, trade policy, defense, harmonization of fiscal policies, the continued opening to competition of industries such as energy and financial services, and takeover policy. As an example, the governments of several member states held golden shares in companies, which in effect gave the governments a veto over any takeover attempt. Some member states had voting rights caps that were intended to protect companies such as Volkswagen, a 20 percent cap, and the United Kingdom's BAA, a 15 percent cap. The DG for Competition sought to eliminate both golden shares and voting rights caps because they impeded the free flow of capital within the European Union.

At the national level an issue is the overall tax burden. Countries including Denmark, France, and Sweden have a taxes-to-GDP ratio over 50 percent, compared

[31]*The Wall Street Journal*, October 21, 2004.
[32]*The New York Times*, January 25, 1985.
[33]*The New York Times*, July 7, 2004.

to 31 percent in the United States and 33 percent in Japan. Citizens receive important services, such as health care, for the taxes, but many firms are concerned about the effect of taxes on global competitiveness. Moreover, as mentioned above, the tax rates in the 10 new member states are low, making them attractive locations for new plants and enterprises.

An important difference between the European Union and the United States is the nature of regulation. The European Union more readily uses what may be called "precautionary regulation" than does the United States. One example is the policy restricting the use of genetically modified organisms (GMOs) in food on the grounds that there might be health risks. This approach generated a major trade conflict between the European Union and the United States, as considered in Chapter 17. The United States tends to regulate known, as opposed to unknown, hazards, and GMO foods are widely available in the United States and other countries. Another difference is that the United States more frequently relies on voluntary approaches to regulation, as in the case of Internet privacy. The policies of the European Union and the United States diverge substantially on the protection of personally identifiable information on the Internet, as described in the example and explored in more detail in the chapter case, *The European Union Data Protection Directive*.

The European Union and most of its member states have strong environmental regulations. As indicated in Chapter 1 the European Union and the European automobile industry agreed to voluntary $CO_2$ reduction goals, and the industry initially made substantial progress toward the goals in part because of the shift to diesel engines led by the lower price of diesel fuel. As demand shifted to larger vehicles the industry quietly began to explore the possibility of revising the goals.

Some firms are directly involved in issues at the EU level, and more are involved in the issues at the level of member states. For example, Philips Electronics worked for the creation of a center to conduct research on semiconductors. Much of the nonmarket activity at the EU level is conducted by peak associations that represent businesses within the member states. The role of these associations is addressed in more detail in the next section.

At the level of the member states, issues affecting business include pharmaceutical approvals and price controls, tax policies to attract business, harmonization of financial-services regulation, the convergence of products liability laws, Internet taxation, and the opening of government procurement to competition among the member states. Issues also pertain to individual firms, including the privatization of government-owned firms and the subsidization of firms through state aids. Many of the issues at the level of the member states involve the implementation of EU regulations and directives.

Nonmarket issues at the industry and firm levels are abundant. Two examples at the industry level involve pharmaceutical pricing and data privacy. The pharmaceutical industry had sought the decontrol of pharmaceutical prices, which have been kept low in countries such as France to relieve the government's health care budget. Much of the nonmarket action at the industry level has been conducted by EU-wide associations representing the industry associations in the member states. For example, issues involving the pharmaceutical industry are addressed by the European Federation of Pharmaceutical Industries' Associations. In some cases ad hoc groups of firms from various member states join together to seek support, as when Philips, Siemens, Thomson, and General Electric (UK) sought support for the European computer and semiconductor industries.

Many nonmarket issues are firm-specific and result from actions taken by activists. Activist groups, for example, protested a Benetton advertisement showing a bloody uniform of a fallen Croat soldier in the Yugoslav civil war. The ad was intended as a plea for peace, but Benetton was accused of exploiting the war. A German court banned Benetton ads, and the French minister for humanitarian affairs called for a boycott of Benetton and urged people to "pull [Benetton sweaters] off the people who are going to wear them."[34]

## Data Privacy

Many Europeans are quite concerned with privacy issues, and these concerns have led to strong EU measures to protect personal information. These concerns range from information on credit card use to the use of cookies to track Internet site browsing. Some countries ban telephone marketing and unsolicited sales attempts by e-mail or fax. Germany and the Netherlands have strong national laws and enforcement agencies governing information. For example, in allowing Citibank to offer a credit card in Germany, the government obtained the right to supervise the data Citibank stores on cardholders. Inspectors from the Datenschutz regularly visit Citibank's Sioux Falls, South Dakota, data center "to make sure that the data are being handled according to [German] law."[1] American Express reached a similar agreement with several countries. An official with the Data Protection Agency of the Netherlands commented, "We are at the beginning of a new information society, and no one really knows the outcome. But privacy and trust are important parts of this society."[2]

At the EU level the Directive on Data Protection (95/46/EC) took effect in 1998 and required that a person grant explicit permission to a company before it could obtain personal information. In preparing its in-house telephone directory, General Motors had to obtain permission from each of its employees in the European Union to include their work telephone numbers, which were considered personal information.[3] Individuals also have the right to inspect any files

maintained and to correct any errors. Furthermore, an individual must be notified in advance if any personal information is to be sold. According to a spokesperson for Oracle, "Your business is essentially tubed until you get this resolved. It can be a life-or-death situation for some businesses."[4]

The European Data Protection Supervisor is responsible for enforcing the Directive and for working with the Data Protection Officers in each member state. In 2000 the Spanish data protection agency fined Microsoft $60,000 for using a U.S. Web site to collect data from its employees in Europe. In 2002 the Commission began an investigation of Microsoft's Passport system for possible violation of the Directive.

The Directive also required countries outside the European Union to provide adequate data protection before any personal data could be transferred from the European Union. To address the differences in the standards for data privacy between the European Union and the United States, the Commission and the U.S. Department of Commerce entered into negotiations seeking an arrangement under which companies that agreed to follow specific data protection policies would be held harmless by the European Union. The European Union said it had no current plans to stop data flows or to police the Internet and would decide specific issues on a case-by-case basis. The chapter case, *The European Union Data Protection Directive*, expands on these issues.

---

[1]*Business Week*, November 2, 1998.
[2]*The New York Times*, October 26, 1998.
[3]See Chapter 13 for General Motors' compliance steps for the Directive.

[4]*San Jose Mercury News*, October 26, 1998.

---

[34]See the Chapter 14 case *Benetton, Advertising Protests, and Franchising* in Baron (2000).

# Interests and Their Organization

Interests are pluralistic in the European Union as they are in the United States and other countries, but their organization is different, in part because the governments of the member states are parliamentary. Several European countries, such as Germany and Sweden and others to a lesser extent, have a strong corporatist organization in which interests are represented by national associations that interact directly, and often with formal sanction, with government. In a corporatist structure, unions and businesses have peak organizations that advise government and negotiate on policy. In Germany, for example, manufacturing enterprises, agricultural interests, service companies, and professionals are organized by law into "chambers," which exercise self-regulatory authority over members and represent their members' interests before the government. The Federation of German Employers' Associations (BDA) is composed of 56 employer associations and represents business on social and labor issues. The Federation of German Industry (BDI), whose members are 39 national federations that include 40,000 businesses and 85 percent of German industry, is more active politically.[35] It provides expert testimony on legislation, lobbies government institutions, and consults with government leaders. The peak business organizations cooperate both formally and informally. Informally, their leaders consult on issues, and formally the BDA and the BDI interact through organizations such as the Joint Committee of German Trade and Industry.

In many industries the national associations join to form EU-wide associations that implement nonmarket strategies directed at the EU institutions. The largest of these associations is the Union of Industrial and Employers Confederations of Europe (UNICE). The European Roundtable of Industrialists represents large companies in Brussels and in the member states. These peak associations take much of the nonmarket action that individual firms and ad hoc coalitions take in the United States. For example, the European Confederation of Retail Trade represents retail interests in the European Union, and CEFIC includes as members the national associations of chemical companies. A peak organization such as CEFIC represents relatively homogeneous interests, whereas the Confederation of Food and Drink Industries represents relatively heterogeneous interests including soft drinks, beer, beef, and cheese. CEFIC was active as are considered in the chapter case, *The European Union Carbon Tax*.

Foreign firms are organized in a similar manner. The EU Committee of the American Chamber of Commerce (Amcham) represents over 100 U.S. companies in Brussels and is highly regarded.[36] In addition, several U.S. associations formed the U.S. Industry Coordinating Group.[37] Some industry associations, such as the Pharmaceutical Research and Manufacturers Association, maintain offices in Brussels.

Unionization in the European Union is more extensive than in the United States, and unions are also organized in national federations and in EU-wide umbrella associations. For example, German unions typically are organized by industry and bargain with associations of employers in those industries. Seventeen German unions are members of the federation Deutscher Gewerkschaftsbund (DGB). The unions have considerable power because of the high rate of unionization and also because of their links to political parties, particularly socialist parties. For example, in Germany the DGB exercises political power both through the political parties and through its interactions with the executive branch and the legislature. Many Social Democrat members of the Bundestag are union members.

35A third, less active, peak organization is the Diet of German Industry and Commerce.
36See, for example, Coen (1999).
37See Calingaert (1993).

Activists and interest groups representing consumers and environmental concerns are active in the European Union, particularly in northern Europe. Consumer groups such as Consumentenbond in the Netherlands are linked to consumer groups in other countries. Some interest groups, such as the greens, have formed political parties. Green activists have vigorously opposed biotechnology and have had considerable success in slowing the growth of the industry. The Chapter 4 case, *Shell, Greenpeace, and Brent Spar,* concerns an activist protest in Europe against a company's actions.

## Nonmarket Strategies in the European Union

The EU government and its institutions have evolved over time along with the relationships among the expanded member states and the Community. If the Constitutional Treaty is ratified, additional changes will take place. The nonmarket strategies for addressing issues in the European Union thus will continue to evolve. Nonmarket strategies are implemented at the levels of the member states and the institutions of the European Union.

To illustrate the multiple levels of nonmarket strategies, the European Union committed to achieving the goals established in the Kyoto Protocol on global climate change and worked for a tradable permits system (see Chapter 11) among the signatories. Opposition occurred at both the EU and member state levels. A spokesperson for the Federation of German Industries said, "What we are against is the exaggerated ecological leadership which . . . the European Union wants to administer."[38] The commission was forced to delay the proposal because of complaints by pan-European associations and industry associations, such as those for autos and chemicals, concerned about the effect on their international competitiveness. The European Trading System finally began in 2005. The United Kingdom implemented a tradable permits system, and Blue Circle, a UK cement company owned by Lafarge Coppée of France, successfully lobbied to have its emissions goal stated in terms of $CO_2$ emissions per ton of cement produced. In contrast to an absolute cap, this allowed the company to expand its output.

The member states have parliamentary governments, but they differ considerably in terms of their governmental institutions, their party organization, and the strength and organization of various interests. Van Schendelen (1993) presents an analysis of interests and lobbying in 12 EU countries, and the Part IV integrative case *Toys 'R' Us and Globalization* considers strategies for individual countries. The focus here is on nonmarket activities and strategies at the EU level. Calingaert (1993) provides a description of the organization for nonmarket action at the EU level.

In the terminology of Chapter 7, both representation and informational strategies are important in the European Union. Representation strategies are based on the constituency for each of the principal EU institutions, as indicated in Figure 15-5. For example, the constituency of the Council of Ministers is the member states, and hence representation strategies are implemented primarily through the national governments. Because those governments are parliamentary and controlled by governing coalitions, political parties are an important focus of these strategies. The national ministries are a locus of expertise and play prominent roles in how a member state votes in the Council of Ministers. Important points of access to the council are COREPER and the working groups it forms to address issues.

[38]*The Wall Street Journal,* July 13, 2001.

| Institution | Constituency | Access |
|---|---|---|
| European Commission | EU-wide constituency—member states, citizens, interests | DGs, commissioners, staff |
| Council of Ministers | Member states | Member states, political parties, COREPER, working groups |
| European Parliament | Voters | Committees, political parties, members of Parliament |
| Economic and Social Committee | Interests | Representatives, Associations |

**FIGURE 15-5 EU Institutions, Constituencies, and Access**

Much of the nonmarket action in the European Union takes place behind the scenes, and most businesses avoid taking public action that might be subjected to criticism. In addition, because of the pervasive influence of government in most EU countries, firms seldom engage in open confrontation with government, as is more often the case in the United States. The chapter case, *Aldeasa and EU Duty Free Abolition (A)*, provides an opportunity to consider whether a behind-the-scenes approach is sufficient or whether a more public nonmarket strategy is needed.

Lobbying is the principal political activity for implementing both representation and informational strategies in the European Union. A lobbyist's strategy is to demonstrate that the interests of a firm or industry are aligned with those of the person or office being lobbied. In the case of the European Union, those interests are a mixture of economic efficiency and social objectives at the EU level; sectoral interests in the case of agriculture, steel, or computers; and local interests in the case of some members of the EP and the Council of Ministers. EU officials face pressures from their home country constituents and from their mandate of economic and political integration.

According to a 1994 study, some 3,000 organizations employed 10,000 lobbyists in Brussels, double the number in 1990. In addition, former EU and national government officials have formed lobbying firms to represent interests. EU lobbyists have backgrounds similar to those of lobbyists in the United States. Firms hire former EU officials, trade negotiators, ambassadors, and former officials of national governments as lobbyists. Lobbying services are also provided by law firms and consultants. Firms have been opening offices in Brussels to be close to the European Union and to track its activities. Managers frequently participate in lobbying along with heads of industry associations and peak organizations. In addition, in a number of countries business leaders have close personal relationships with government officials. In some countries, such as France, these relationships may have been formed through attendance at the same *grande écoles*. In Germany top government officials consult with business leaders because of the status and strength of business in the country.[39]

Peak associations play a number of roles including the monitoring of government activities, the funneling of information and expertise from their members to the government, and lobbying. Lobbying, for example, is pervasive in German politics, but because of the omnipresence of associations it tends to be collective in its nature. Much

[39]See Calingaert (1993).

of the political influence takes place through the executive branch and the interactions of high-ranking government officials, particularly bureaucrats, with the leaders of the peak associations. Seventy percent of the BDI's contacts were with the bureaucracy and only 5 percent with the Bundestag (parliament).[40] As a result of the SEA and the increasing importance of the EU government, German associations increased their presence and lobbying in Brussels.

Informational strategies center on the strategic provision of information to EU officeholders, and the nature and content of these strategies is the same as characterized in Chapter 7. The key to successful lobbying is the provision of information useful to the institutional officeholders. Successful lobbying requires an understanding of their interests, the relationship between policy alternatives and consequences, and the procedures and practices of EU institutions. Lobbying also takes place within each member state in attempts to convince politicians and bureaucrats of the importance of the interests affected. Figure 15-5 identifies the points of access.

The form that lobbying takes depends on the institution in question. The European Commission is perhaps the most important body because it is the agenda setter for legislation and also administers policies. The commission is the focus of interactions and consultations with member governments, and interest groups seeking to influence EU policy and its administration lobby the commission extensively. Because the commission has a relatively small staff, it needs information and expertise for its legislative and regulatory actions. The commission stated, "The Commission has always been open to ideas from the outside world. It believes that openness is crucial for developing its polices. This dialogue has proved valuable to both the commission and interested outside parties . . . The Commission will remain very accessible to the interest groups."[41] The commission has established a set of informal and formal consultation procedures, including the formation of advisory committees and policy forums.

The respect garnered by the American Chamber of Commerce in Brussels is due in part to the detailed information it provides on issues and its accurate representation of American concerns. As Coen (1999, p. 35) characterized the situation in the mid-1990s, "U.S. firms demonstrated to their European rivals the importance of direct, regular, and reliable representation at the European Commission . . . Amcham and its EU committee demonstrated the importance of both direct firm membership (at the collective European level) and the participation of senior executives with expertise in the policy debate. By adapting the organizational structure around 12 specialized technical committees on issues such as competition, trade, social affairs, and the environment, Amcham was able to complement the new European Commission's issue based forums . . ."

Interests contact the European Commission directly through its DGs, but interests can also be represented by members of either the EP or the Economic and Social Committee. Also, member governments intervene on behalf of interest groups in their own countries. The targets of lobbying are the commissioners and their cabinets. Because the DGs are the repositories of expertise and deal with the specifics of issues, access to members of the relevant DGs is important. Participation in working parties and advisory committees can be an important means of access as well as a source of information. The commission initiates legislation in the

---

[40]See Kohler-Koch (1998).
[41]europa.eu.int/secretariat/general/sgc/lobbies/approche/apercu_en.htm.

form of drafts that are circulated for comments before the legislative process begins (see Figure 15-3). Lobbying thus begins early in the process and is directed at the formulation of the initial draft as well as the subsequent legislative process. Affecting the agenda can be an effective means of laying a path to be followed with subsequent lobbying.

The Council of Ministers is the principal legislative institution, but it is difficult to influence directly because it operates in private. The principal route to influencing the council is through member state governments and their relevant ministries. National interests also are represented by a country's permanent representatives (COREPER) to the union. COREPER is required by law to consult directly with interests, and industry and labor organizations maintain close contacts with it. COREPER is expected to resolve political issues on behalf of the council.

As a result of the Maastricht Treaty and the increased use of the co-decision legislative procedure, the EP has become more important with its powers to amend and veto commission proposals. If the Constitutional Treaty is ratified, the scope of the EP's role will broaden. The EP's constituencies are voters and the political parties that represent them, and the principal points of access are the party organizations, individual members, and committees. The EP members are both issue oriented and concerned about the effects of issues on constituents. Members represent a variety of interests and may be willing to act as allies in advancing the interests of firms and industries. Although the EP has committees that formulate amendments, most of the lobbying takes place outside the formal committee structure. In addition, the party organization of the EP means that a path to influence is through the party system in the firm's home country. In practice, the attention given to lobbying the EP is smaller but growing relative to that given the commission, COREPER, and member state governments.

The custom in Europe has been to use peak organizations, such as UNICE and the Roundtable of European Industrialists, for political and other nonmarket actions. Issues involving the single market and international trade, however, are often industry-specific and may affect firms in different ways. Consequently, coalitions are formed that cut across the lines of peak associations. These coalitions may include firms domiciled in different member states acting together on a trade issue or a firm and a union joining together to advance their joint interests.

As an example of an ad hoc coalition formed to address a specific issue, in 1996 the EP proposed amendments to a commission policy on the media industry. France, backed by socialist members of the EP, pushed for tighter quotas on the foreign content on television and multimedia outlets. According to one report, American companies produced 80 percent of the programming shown on European television. Opposition to the proposed amendments included not only American interests and private broadcasters, but also a broad set of other interests. Advertisers opposed the amendments because they would restrict advertising on home shopping channels. Retailers opposed the amendments because they would restrict the number of hours regular TV channels could devote to teleshopping. The prospect of quotas on Internet content led one Bertelsmann lobbyist to comment, "It's very silly what they want to do. It won't work in an Internet, online environment."[42] The chapter case, *The European Union Carbon Tax*, concerns another issue involving a broad set of interests.

Some firms undertake independent political action or form ad hoc coalitions to advance their agenda. Philips Electronics has been one of the most active. It was an early advocate of the creation of a single market and also worked to limit competition from outside the European Union. For example, it lobbied successfully for protection against Japanese compact disc systems. In addition to its extensive lobbying, Van Schendelen (1993) reports that Philips was successful in "parachuting" one of its technology experts into the DG responsible for subsidies for technology programs. Philips obtained R&D subsidies for 150 projects. Philips was also one of the principal forces behind the EU subsidies for the development of a European HDTV system, which ultimately was a failure. Working with the European Information Technology Roundtable, Philips also led the effort to obtain $4 billion for semiconductor research.

Philips Chairman Cornelis van der Klugt was personally active, lobbying in Brussels to obtain import protection for Philips. He argued that free trade with the European Union required "real reciprocity." To protect its VCR business, Philips pushed through the European Union a 30 percent levy on Japanese and South Korean VCRs. He worked to have the European Union investigate dumping charges against Asian producers of small televisions and compact disc players and to have semiconductors assembled by Japanese firms in Europe classified as imports so they would be subject to tariffs.[43] An antidumping complaint against six Japanese semiconductor manufacturers led to an agreement between the European Union and Japan that set a price floor on imported semiconductors. Van der Klugt defended his efforts: "It's not necessary for the Japanese to export unemployment to Europe. We have enough unemployment."[44] At the same time that he worked for protection, van der Klugt pushed the European Union to scrap its internal trade barriers as quickly as possible.

Nonmarket issues and strategies are often complicated by national concerns. Pharmaceuticals is far from a single market. Under the principle of subsidiarity the member states are responsible for health care and may institute their own price controls. The European Commission has expressed concern that very stringent price controls were driving pharmaceutical innovation out of the European Union.[45] France, for example, required pharmaceutical companies to sign broad conventions that covered not only prices but also commitments to create jobs in France and to support state-owned research institutes. To hold down the cost of its national health care system, pharmaceutical prices were set at very low levels. This in part led the three largest French pharmaceutical companies to either merge or spin off their pharmaceutical operations into a jointly-owned affiliate. The French Parliament also enacted a law that made pharmaceutical companies responsible for any costs above ceilings set by parliament for the national health service. Industry members challenged the new law in France and before the European Commission and the European Court of Justice.[46]

Specific nonmarket issues can also arise in the normal course of EU activities. An example of such an issue, a German court decision about wedding dresses that had important implications for franchising, is considered in the example.

[43]Upon complaints by Philips and Bang & Olufsen of Denmark, the European Union imposed provisional duties of from 6.4 to 40 percent on Japanese and South Korean compact disc players. Sony expressed little concern because it planned to supply three-quarters of its European demand from its plant in France.
[44]*The New York Times*, June 4, 1989.
[45]European Commission press release, November 25, 1998.
[46]*The Wall Street Journal*, December 7, 1998.

## Pronuptia and Franchising

In 1984 a German court invalidated a franchise agreement that required a German retailer, Pronuptia, to sell only the wedding dresses of its French franchiser and only in specific territories. The French franchiser appealed the decision to the Court of Justice. U.S. franchisers saw the decision as crucial to their use of U.S.-style franchise arrangements in the European Union. They launched a lobbying campaign directed at the European Commission, which was to file an opinion on the case with the court. The lobbyist engaged by the U.S. franchisers conducted a "teach in" about U.S. franchising practices for officials of the DG for Competition. The commission subsequently argued before the court that the franchise restrictions were necessary to maintain product quality, among other things. In 1986 the court overruled the German court and upheld the rights of franchisers to restrict the actions of their franchisees on several dimensions.[1]

U.S. franchisers were still concerned that the franchising arrangements allowed by the court might be challenged under the antitrust provisions in Article 81. Some franchisers, including

Pronuptia, sought and received exemptions from the commission. They also encouraged the commission to grant a broader exemption from antitrust rules for franchise arrangements. The U.S. interests, including McDonald's, Pizza Hut, Kentucky Fried Chicken, Midas Muffler, Coca-Cola, Holiday Inns, and others, were represented by the International Franchising Association (IFA), which was active in Brussels. The IFA met with a variety of officials including the competition commissioner, who was also lobbied when he visited the United States.

The lobbyist for the U.S. franchisers said, "The most important lessons we've learned so far are for American interests to get in early; in a European, not American, way; and demonstrate from the start that American interests are compatible with European interests." From the other side, an official with the DG for Competition said the IFA "made their points forcefully, but also gave us a lot of useful information about how the U.S. system works."[2]

U.S. franchisers obtained "96.5 percent" of what they sought, but they were prohibited from requiring franchisees to purchase one brand exclusively. A fast-food chain thus cannot force its franchisees to carry only one soft drink brand.

---
[1] *Pronuptia de Paris GmbH v. Pronuptia de Paris Irmgard Schillgalis* (case 161/84), January 28, 1986, Common Market Report (CCH) para. 14,245 (1986). See Rosenthal (1990) for a discussion of this case. Also see Hawk (1988).

[2] *The Wall Street Journal,* May 17, 1989.

## Summary

The Single European Act represented a major step toward economic integration within the Union. It also increased the political power of the EU institutions relative to the governments of the member states. The Maastricht Treaty provided for a monetary

Firms also employ judicial strategies in the European Union. A German environmental law favored reusable materials such as glass bottles over recyclable materials such as plastic and cans. Since glass bottles were much more costly to transport than other containers, beverage firms were effectively excluded from the German market. French mineral-water companies complained that it was prohibitively costly to collect and truck the empty bottles back to their springs for refilling. The 50-member packaging association Europen, whose members included Coca-Cola and Nestlé, successfully lobbied the commission to file a lawsuit against Germany. In 2004 the Court of Justice ruled that the German law discriminated against foreign companies.

union and for steps toward a political union. The European Union has also broadened with 10 additional countries joining the Union in 2004 and others scheduled to join in 2007. The Maastricht Treaty also increased the power of the European Parliament, which exercises democratic supervision. The principal institutions of the European Union are the European Commission, the Council of Ministers, and the European Parliament. The Economic and Monetary Union established both an independent European Central Bank and a common currency among 12 of the member states, with others likely to join in the future. Considerable progress has been made in eliminating internal barriers to trade, but several difficult issues, including fiscal harmonization, remain. Rigid labor markets, high wages and taxes, and the high costs of laying off workers have resulted in an unemployment rate over 9 percent for the European Union.

Interests take action both individually and through associations and peak organizations, which play an important role at the EU level. The pattern of interest group activity and the nature of nonmarket action have evolved as firms, unions, and other organizations adapt their strategies to institutional changes. The growth in lobbying is a sign of both the increased importance of the EU government and the stakes involved in its actions. Lobbying is the principal nonmarket strategy for influencing the EU institutions. Since much of the legislative and regulatory activity takes place outside the view of the public and prior to the formal procedures beginning, it is important to participate both early and continuously in the EU governmental processes.

Although the power of the EU institutions has increased, the governments of the member states continue to be the focus of considerable nonmarket activity. Those governments are parliamentary but differ in their institutional structures and their politics. The organization of interests in the European Union is characterized by peak associations that are active in nonmarket and governmental matters. Individual firms, however, also engage in their own nonmarket activities and form alliances with firms in other EU member states.

# The European Union Carbon Tax

Whether and to what extent global warming was occurring remained the subject of considerable scientific uncertainty, disagreement, and debate during the early 1990s, but the scientific evidence increasingly supported the global warming hypothesis. The principal contributor to global warming was believed to be the burning of carbon-based fuels, principally coal, petroleum, and natural gas.

A European Union (EU) Joint Council of Energy and Environment Ministers declared in 1990 that the member states would by the year 2000 stabilize $CO_2$ emissions at the 1990 level. Because of projected economic growth, stabilization would require a reduction in emissions of approximately 10 percent from the unstabilized level. Some of the reductions required to stabilize emissions were anticipated to come from improved energy efficiency induced by the current prices of fossil fuels. These "no regrets" conservation measures were estimated to reduce emissions by 5.5 percent by 2000, leaving reductions of 5 percent to be accomplished by other measures. In October 1991 the European Commission issued a draft directive informing the member states of its plans to propose a variety of measures to reduce $CO_2$ emissions. These measures included R&D programs and a carbon/energy tax to achieve the remaining reduction of 5 percent. The proposed carbon/energy tax was intended to reduce carbon emissions by making fuels, particularly carbon-based fuels, more costly, thereby inducing conservation and the substitution of less carbon-intensive fuels.

The European Commission operated under collective responsibility but frequently deferred to the commissioner with policy jurisdiction if the issue was not controversial. This was not an uncontroversial issue. The lead commissions for this issue were DG XI (environment) and DG XVII (energy). Mr. Carlo Ripa di Meana, EU commissioner for the environment, pushed for a formal proposal by June 1992 in time for the Rio Earth Summit. Mr. Jacques Delors,

president of the commission, also supported the tax and the leadership position it would give the European Union in Rio. Mr. Antonio Cardoso e Cunha, EU commissioner for energy, supported the taxes because they would promote energy efficiency.

The European Commission proposal involved specific (per unit) taxes that would impose half the burden on carbon-based fuels and the other half on energy. The commission estimated that the full tax would increase the price of natural gas for industry by 33 percent, hard coal by 60 percent, and gasoline by 6 percent.[47] Because emissions of $CO_2$ were difficult to measure by source, the taxes would be applied to inputs rather than emissions. The proposed carbon tax would begin at $3 per barrel of oil and increase by $1 per year for the next 7 years, reaching $10 per barrel. (The $10 per barrel tax was equivalent to a tax of $75 per ton of carbon.) An equivalent tax would be applied to coal and natural gas. The energy tax would apply to all energy sources except renewable sources. The energy tax was included to satisfy environmentalists who opposed a pure carbon tax because it would provide incentives for the expansion of nuclear power. Countries such as Germany, Greece, and the United Kingdom, with carbon-intensive energy supplies, also favored an energy tax. Denmark and the Netherlands and two European Free Trade Association (EFTA) countries, Finland and Sweden, already had imposed a carbon tax.[48] Denmark's carbon tax averaged $16 per ton of carbon for industry, carbon tax averaged $16 per ton of carbon for individuals' consumption and $8 per ton for industry. Energy-intensive industries, however, could be granted an exemption of up to 100 percent of the tax. The Netherlands' carbon tax was $12.50 per ton. The tax in Sweden was $62 per ton of carbon, and in Finland the tax was $6.50 per ton.[49]

[47] The percent increase for gasoline was low because gasoline was already heavily taxed.
[48] In 1995 Austria, Finland, and Sweden joined the European Union.
[49] See Poterba (1991, pp. 71–98).

Neither Japan nor the United States had a carbon tax in 1992. The Japanese government argued that its regulations already set standards that were at least as strong as those the EU tax would achieve. Presidential candidate Bill Clinton had pledged during his campaign to address the global warming issue using efficient means, including taxes on carbon and/or energy. The Congressional Budget Office estimated that to stabilize $CO_2$ emissions a tax of $100 per ton of carbon would be required.[50] Representative Pete Stark (D-CA) introduced a bill to impose a tax of $15 per ton on coal, $3.25 per barrel of oil, and $0.40 per MCF of natural gas. The European Commission urged the member states to make every effort to ensure that other OECD countries, in particular Japan and the United States, adopted measures similar to its proposed carbon/energy tax.

The carbon/energy tax would affect production and consumption decisions throughout the European Union. It would also affect the competitiveness of EU businesses, particularly those that used energy-intensive technologies. Mr. Ripa di Meana, however, argued, "This is a chance to update European industry and make it a leader in a green-oriented market." To lessen the impact on the international competitiveness of European companies, the commission proposed to at least partially exempt from the tax those industries that had energy-intensive production processes.

The tax would ultimately be borne in large part by individuals and would have the greatest impact on those who intensively used energy, and particularly carbon-based fuels. Because lower-income individuals spent a higher portion of their income on energy, the tax would be regressive.

A carbon/energy tax also would generate substantial revenue for governments. For example, a tax of $100 per ton of carbon was estimated to generate revenue equal to 1.99 percent of GDP based on consumption in 1988. For France the revenue would be 1.28 percent of GDP, and for Germany and the United Kingdom it would be approximately 2.3 percent. The commission suggested that the carbon tax should be "fiscally neutral" for each country, although Mr. Ripa di Meana argued that a portion of the tax revenue should go to developing countries

to prevent deforestation. Fiscal neutrality would require that any additional revenue generated by the tax be offset by fiscal incentives or reductions in other taxes. Because the individual member states rather than the European Union would receive the revenue from the tax, each member state would determine its own use of the revenue. Under EU law the member states would be responsible for the implementation of the tax.

The EU legislative process required that the imposition of a carbon/energy tax be decided under a unanimity rule. Some bargaining among the member states would likely be involved with compensation given to certain countries that otherwise would be substantially impacted by the tax. As part of its annual budget, the European Union provided grants of structural funds for economic development to countries and to regions within countries. In 1992 these funds were approximately 19 million ECUs ($25 billion). The budget and thus the amount and allocation of structural funds were decided by a qualified majority of the Council of Finance Ministers. In 1992 a qualified majority required 54 of the 76 votes. The number of votes for each member state is presented in Table 15-1.

In December 1991 the EU Joint Council of Environment and Energy Ministers unanimously endorsed the European Commission's draft directive. Denmark, Germany, Italy, Belgium, and the Netherlands came out clearly in favor of the proposal, whereas the lower-income southern

**TABLE 15-1 Votes of Member States in the Council of Ministers, 1992**

| Member States | Votes |
|---|---|
| Belgium | 5 |
| Denmark | 3 |
| France | 10 |
| Germany | 10 |
| Greece | 5 |
| Ireland | 3 |
| Italy | 10 |
| Luxembourg | 2 |
| Netherlands | 5 |
| Portugal | 5 |
| Spain | 8 |
| United Kingdom | 10 |
| Total | 76 |

---

[50]The United States had imposed a tax on CFCs as a means of speeding the elimination of their production. In addition to contributing to ozone depletion, CFCs were greenhouse gasses and contributed to global warming.

## The Economics of Emissions Control in the European Union

Before the European Commission presented its proposal for meeting the EU-wide stabilization target, it commissioned a study of the costs and benefits of $CO_2$ emissions reduction. Although emissions were to be stabilized by the year 2000, the Council of Ministers requested that the study analyze the effects in the year 2010, since the stabilization target was to hold indefinitely and some investments in energy conservation would take several years before they were fully implemented. Table 15-2 outlines the "base-case" scenario that was predicted to occur in 2010 if no EU-wide emissions control took place. Column 1 of Table 15-2 presents 1988 $CO_2$ emissions for 10 EU countries for comparison

**TABLE 15-2** $CO_2$ Emissions (million tons) with No Further Abatement: 10 EU Countries

|  | 1988 | Projected, 2010 |
|---|---|---|
| Belgium | 109 | 110 |
| Denmark | 61 | 60 |
| France | 374 | 370 |
| Germany | 718 | 677 |
| Greece | 84 | 127 |
| Italy | 399 | 489 |
| Netherlands | 146 | 165 |
| Portugal | 28 | 51 |
| Spain | 196 | 265 |
| United Kingdom | 561 | 505 |
| Total | 2,676 | 2,819 |

*Source:* Coherence (1991). "Cost-effectiveness analysis of $CO_2$ reduction options," Synthesis report and country reports for the Commission of the European Communities, DG XII. May 1991.

countries led by Spain, along with Luxembourg, were concerned about how the abatement burden would be divided among the countries. The United Kingdom agreed in principle but was hesitant about the additional taxes. France, which generated much of its electricity from nuclear power, supported the proposed taxes but wanted to tilt the taxes more toward fossil fuels. Both endorsed the report. A few days later the EU finance ministers took note of the proposal and asked for a detailed study on the practical details of the tax.

purposes (Ireland and Luxembourg are omitted from the analysis because they had the lowest $CO_2$ emissions in the European Union and because important data were not available). Not surprisingly, the largest and wealthiest countries—France, Germany, Italy, and the United Kingdom—had the highest levels of $CO_2$ emissions in 1988. However, the projected growth in emissions for 1988 to 2010 exhibited a very different pattern. The lowest-income countries—Greece, Portugal, and Spain—were predicted, respectively, to emit 52, 82, and 35 percent more $CO_2$ by 2010 if no additional measures were taken, compared with decreases in emissions in France, Germany, and the United Kingdom. The declines were projected to result from increased energy efficiency.[51]

If emissions were to be stabilized in 2000 and beyond, the European Commission had to make a proposal that achieved a 143 million ton reduction in $CO_2$ by the year 2010. A uniform tax would induce efficient emissions control across countries by giving polluters in each country the incentive to abate up to the point at which the marginal cost of abatement equaled the emissions tax. As a result, the marginal cost of reducing pollution in any one country would equal the marginal cost of reducing pollution in every other country. The tax required to achieve the target reduction of 143 million tons of $CO_2$ was calculated by researchers to be approximately $75 per ton of carbon at an exchange rate of $1.30/ECU.[52]

## Costs and Benefits of a Carbon/Energy Tax

The relative impact of a carbon tax would be greatest on the lower-income countries. The tax would reduce their growth rate in addition to imposing high costs of abatement. The countries that would be most severely affected were Greece, Italy, Portugal, and Spain. A reduction in $CO_2$ emissions by the European Union would constitute a public

[51] For example, $CO_2$ emissions in the United Kingdom in 1992 were below the emissions levels in 1972.

[52] See "Reaching a $CO_2$-Emission Limitation Agreement for the Community: Implications for Equity and Cost Effectiveness," *European Economy*, Special Edition No. 1, *The Economics of Limiting $CO_2$ Emissions*, Directorate-General for Economics and Financial Affairs, Commission of the European Communities, 1992.

good for other countries, since all countries would benefit from the reductions. The benefits for individual EU member states would be roughly proportional to their populations.

The reactions to the proposed tax by industry were predictable. The trade association Euroelectric, representing the EU electricity industry, opposed the tax and argued for voluntary conservation measures. Electric power generators—Electrabel (Belgium), Endesa (Spain), PowerGen (United Kingdom), RWE (Germany), Scottish Power (United Kingdom), Union Fenosa (Spain), and VEAG (Germany)—pointed to the uncertain effects of the imposition of a tax and proposed a series of conservation measures as well as the export of energy-efficient technologies to Eastern Europe. In addition to the efforts of the coalition and the trade association, individual power generation companies lobbied to prevent the adoption of the tax.

The European Coal and Steel Council Consultative Committee also opposed the tax and argued for voluntary programs and payments to developing countries to stop deforestation. Opposition also developed within countries. For example, in France 14 major companies, including Electricité de France, Renault, Rhone Polenc, Total, Elf Aquitaine, Pécincy, and Unisor Sacilor, organized "Business for the Environment" to oppose the tax. In exchange, the coalition offered help in cleaning up toxic waste sites.

Chemicals was one of the premier industries in Europe. The industry was energy intensive, and the petrochemical component of the industry used petroleum feedstocks. The global competitiveness of the industry thus would be significantly impacted by the proposed taxes. The industry estimated that the impact of the taxes when fully implemented would be $4.45 billion per year. The chemical industry pointed to the success of voluntary measures undertaken by individual companies. The managing director of Montedison Primary Chemicals stated that since 1974 the European chemicals industry had reduced by 35 percent the energy usage per unit of output and that another 15 percent reduction would be achieved by the year 2000.[53]

As was the case in many European industries, the chemical industry in each country was represented by an association that included most of the companies operating in that country. These national associations acted on behalf of their members within their countries. The associations in the individual countries were organized into the European Chemical Industry Council (CEFIC) that acted at the level of the European Union. As the importance of the EU governmental institutions had grown, individual companies had begun to take actions in addition to those of their national and pan-European associations. ∎

SOURCE: This case was prepared by Professors David P. Baron, Daniel Kessler, and Daniel Diermeier. Copyright © 1996 by the Board of Trustees of the Leland Stanford Junior University. All rights reserved. Reproduced with permission.

## PREPARATION QUESTIONS

### Economics

1. Identify the efficiency and distributive consequences of a carbon/energy tax.
2. What are the effects of a carbon tax for the global competitiveness of EU companies?

### Government

1. What types of politics should be anticipated in the consideration of a carbon/energy tax in the European Union? Which EU institutions will be involved in the decision?
2. If structural funds could be provided to countries through the EU budget, what outcome would you expect? Assume for the purposes of this question that the European Union makes its decision on structural funds by a qualified majority of the Council of Finance Ministers.

### Nonmarket Strategy

1. As a European chemicals company dependent on petroleum feedstocks, what effects do you anticipate from the proposed carbon/energy tax?
2. What objectives and strategy should the company adopt to address the carbon/energy tax? How should that strategy be implemented? Which institutions should be targeted?

---

[53]*The Economist*, May 9, 1992.

# The European Union Data Protection Directive

Concerns about privacy led the European Union (EU) to harmonize the Internet privacy policies of its member states. The Directive on Data Protection, often referred to as the Privacy Directive, took effect in 1998 and prohibited the processing of personally identifiable information (PII) unless "the data subject has unambiguously given his consent" or the processing was necessary for the performance of a contract or government order.[54] Data could also be processed if it were in the vital interests of the individual, as in the case of a medical emergency. Individuals had the right to inspect any personal data maintained and to correct any errors. Furthermore, an individual had to be notified in advance if any personal information were to be transferred to a third party.

The Directive sought a "reasonable balance" between "the fundamental rights of the data subject, particularly the right to privacy" and "the business interest of the data controllers . . ."[55] To implement and enforce the Directive, each member of the EU established a data protection (privacy) agency, and the privacy commissioners served as a continuing body to monitor progress on the Directive. The European activist group Privacy International said it was investigating the practices of 25 companies, including

Microsoft and United Airlines, and planned to file lawsuits if it identified any violations of the EU directive.

The Directive also protected EU citizens from processors of information in other countries. Article 25 permitted data transfers only if the other country had an "adequate level of protection." The United States had no Internet privacy law or regulations to govern the Internet and relied on voluntary measures. Processing by U.S. companies of personal information on Europeans outside the European Union thus was problematic. Figure 15-6 summarizes features of data protection in the European Union and compares those features with the practice in the United States in 2001.

Critics of Article 25 argued that it was an unwarranted extraterritorial application of EU law. The U.S. National Business Coalition on E-Commerce and Privacy, which included such financial services companies as General Electric, Fidelity, and Aflac, in addition to Home Depot, Deere, and Seagrams, said, "The EU privacy principles that would effectively be imposed on American business . . . far exceed any privacy requirements that have ever been imposed in the U.S., thus raising a very real question of national sovereignty."[56] The European Union responded by stating that it had no

---

**FIGURE 15-6 Data Protection Practices for Personally Identifiable Information (PII)**

| *EU Data Protection* | *U.S. Practices* |
|---|---|
| • Strong notice | • Limited notice |
| • Strong opt in | • Opt out |
| • Access to PII | • Access not required |
| • Limited if any secondary use of data | • Secondary use allowed |
| • Data storage no longer than necessary for primary purpose; e.g., billing | • No limits on storage |
| • Privacy regulatory agency | • Self-regulation |
| • Notice if cookie deposited | • No notice of cookie |
| • Anonymous profiling (?) | • Anonymous profiling OK |
| • Security and data integrity | • Security and data integrity |
| • Privacy regulatory agency | |

---

[54]Directive 95/46/EC of the European Parliament and Council.
[55]"Data Protection: Background Information," The European Commission. www.europa.eu.int.

[56]*The Wall Street Journal*, April 6, 2000. The financial-services companies were concerned about their ability to use and sell information about customers.

interest in "exporting" its laws to other countries, but it also emphasized that it had to protect the privacy of its citizens and would block the transfer of information to countries with inadequate protection. It invited non-EU countries "to express their views." Jim Murray, director of the European Consumers' Organization, said, "We want anyone doing business with the EU to respect the rights that we have built up here."[57] The U.S. and EU governments initiated discussions about what U.S. policy would meet the adequacy standard.

The discussions had two tracks. The first was for nonfinancial institutions, and the second was for financial institutions. On the first track the Department of Commerce represented the United States, and the Commission represented the European Union. The European Parliament remained concerned that any agreement be operational before adequacy would be certified.

Financial institutions were treated separately because the United States had enacted the Financial Services Modernization Act, also known as the Gramm-Leach-Bliley Act, of 1999, which took effect in mid-2001. The act limited disclosure of nonpublic personal information to nonaffiliated third parties unless disclosure and opt-out requirements were met. In addition, the Fair Credit Reporting Act of 1970 restricted the reporting of personal information. The United States maintained that these laws provided adequate protection. An industry study by Ernst & Young commissioned by the Financial Services Coordinating Council estimated that full compliance with the Privacy Directive would cost U.S. consumers $16 billion a year in financial-services benefits. EU financial institutions supported the U.S. position.

The European Union viewed the Gramm-Leach-Bliley Act as inadequate. First, it did not provide individuals with access to their personal data. Second, the Act did not have an adequate enforcement mechanism. As a consequence of these shortcomings, the European Union sent privacy contracts to U.S. firms for them to sign. The financial-services industry was dead set against the contracts, in part because they would be legally binding and therefore establish a liability for the improper handling of personal data. The European Parliament in particular wanted companies to be liable for

violations of the Directive. The Parliament wanted "compensation for individual damage suffered as a result of possible violations . . ."The Parliament also stated that the commission should "draw up . . . standard contractual clauses that EU citizens could invoke in the courts of a third country."[58]

President George W. Bush personally announced that the United States rejected the privacy contracts, and he insisted that U.S. laws pertaining to financial institutions provided adequate protection. The Bush administration said that the contracts would "impose unduly burdensome requirements that are incompatible with real-world operations."The United States expressed a willingness to enter into discussions with the European Union on the issue, and asked the European Union to delay implementing the Directive. The European Union refused to do so.

In commenting on the difference in perspectives in Europe and the United States, Peter Swire and Robert Litan wrote, "It is roughly accurate to say that America does not have the general presumption that data should be used only for the purpose for which they were collected."[59] A spokesperson for TimeWarner in Brussels observed, "In Europe, people don't trust companies, they trust government. In the U.S., it's the opposite way around: Citizens must be protected from actions of the government."[60]

While establishing broad privacy rights, the EU Directive failed to address a number of issues. One was whether cookies and other devices could be used in the anonymous tracking of click-stream data. The Data Protection Working Party issued a draft report stating that "users must be informed before any cookie used in [online] profiling is placed" and that users have a right to object to the profiling.[61] Another was whether companies could internally transfer personnel information from the European Union to their offices in other countries. Microsoft had been fined $60,000 for obtaining information from its European employees using a Web site in the United States. Another issue was

[57]*San Jose Mercury News*, June 5, 2000.

[58]European Parliament, "Report on the Draft Commission Decision," A5–0177/2000, June 22, 2000.
[59]Swire and Litan (1998, p. 178).
[60]*Business Week*, November 2, 1998.
[61]Data Protection Working Party (Article 29), "Privacy on the Internet—An Integrated EU Approach to On-line Data Protection," WP 37, November 21, 2000.

unsolicited e-mail used for marketing purposes. The European Parliament voted to allow each member state to decide whether to use an opt-out or an opt-in approach but required opt-out for inclusion of information in electronic directories. The commis-

sion had proposed a uniform approach to both issues. ∎

SOURCE: Copyright © 2001 by David P. Baron. All rights reserved. Reproduced with permission.

## PREPARATION QUESTIONS

1. Do the regulations in the European Union go too far in protecting PII? Do they limit the services businesses can provide?
2. Is protection in the United States for PII adequate? Is any protection needed beyond providing clear and conspicuous warning and an easy opt-out?
3. Is opt-out different from opt-in?
4. The United States and the European Union entered into negotiations to stipulate practices for the United States that would satisfy the European Union's "adequate protection" requirement. Predict the outcome of those negotiations for both tracks. Does the European Union or the United States have the stronger bargaining position?

# Aldeasa and the EU Duty Free Abolition (A)

In 1985 the Single European Act paved the way for a complete integration of markets within the European Community by setting the stage for the free circulation of goods, capital, and people by January 1, 1993. One component of this drive toward economic integration was tax harmonization, especially on consumption taxes such as the value-added tax (VAT). Differences in tax rates across member states were considered important sources of distortions and impediments to full market integration, but most attempts by the European Commission to foster tax harmonization had been met with skepticism on the part of member states. One proposal that garnered support was to abolish duty free sales for intra-European travel.

In 1991 the European Union Council of Ministers (ECOFIN – Economy and Finance Ministers) decided under a unanimity rule to abolish duty free sales for travel within the European Union as part of a broader set of taxation and excise measures aimed at making the Single Market a reality. A lengthy transitional period, until June 30, 1999, was granted to allow duty free shop operators and suppliers to adapt to this drastic change in their nonmarket environment.

Aldeasa was a Spanish company whose core business was the operation of duty free shops in airports in Spain and abroad under exclusive concession contracts. At the end of 1995 Aldeasa ranked 11th by sales among the duty free operators in the world, with sales of $322

million and net profits of $35 million. As of November 1996 Aldeasa was still a state-owned company. The new conservative government elected in March 1996 announced that the company would be privatized, although no specific date was set. In July 1996 a new management team, headed by José Fernández Olano, was appointed by the Minister of Finance to design the privatization process and lead the company through it.

## The Duty Free Industry

The origin of the duty free industry was the traditional exemption from local and national taxes granted to travelers on international routes, rooted in the concept of "international waters."[62] Over the last 50 years the bulk of duty free trade had progressively shifted from seaports to airports. At the end of 1995 there were 662 airports, 227 airlines, and 82 ferry lines operating duty free shops, with an unknown number of duty free shops in border zones. Over 650 million travelers walked into duty free shops in 1995.[63]

---

[62]Since there was no national sovereignty on international waters, passengers and crew members on ships were entitled to purchase goods for personal use without being subject to customs. Thus "ship chandlers" (suppliers of goods to ships) became the first duty free merchants, and some of them still operated modern duty free stores at international airports and ports.
[63]*Source:* "The Best 'n' Most Duty Free," 1996.

Between 1990 and 1995 worldwide sales grew at an average rate of 6.5 percent and represented 2.7 percent of world exports. Airport stores accounted for 41.9 percent of total sales, followed by ferries (13.5 percent) and airlines (8.6 percent). Other channels (diplomatic stores, border shops, and free zones) represented the remaining 36 percent.

Goods sold in duty free shops were exempt only from certain duties and taxes. Those waived generally included the VAT, the luxury tax, local taxes, and import tariffs. In most countries duty free stores sold two different types of products: local products (tax free) and imported products (duty and tax free).[64] Price savings was not the only reason for duty free sales. In fact, in countries with relatively low taxes and import duties, many goods had higher prices at duty free stores than at local shops. This was because duty free retailers passed on to customers a portion of the higher operating costs they faced. Those costs resulted from special taxes on margins imposed on duty free retailers and the concession fees and rent paid to ports, airports, and customs offices for the right to operate the stores. Higher operating costs also resulted from the use of more qualified labor (e.g., shop assistants fluent in several languages), longer hours associated with flight schedules, special passenger control systems required by the customs authorities, and costs associated with sales in different currencies.

Most passengers were "captive" customers; they had time to kill either at the airport or on a ferry or aircraft. They tended to have high purchasing power and were intrinsically more receptive to commercial offers associated with their travel experience. Duty free customers could be classified into two groups: business travelers, who had a higher disposable income but usually not much time to shop, and tourists, who saw the opportunity to buy in duty free shops as another component of their travel experience. In fact, passengers on charter flights spent more on average than those on regular flights. There were also two types of duty free

products: heavily taxed products in the customer's country, such as perfumes or "socially disapproved" products like tobacco or alcoholic drinks; and gifts, such as watches, games, electronic items, and products associated with the local market (crafts, guides, local apparel and food, souvenirs). Many upscale products were heavily dependent on this channel.[65]

Passengers and retailers (whether airlines, ferries, or store operators) were not the only beneficiaries from duty free commercial activity. Owners of the facilities also extracted substantial revenue from the industry. For example, airports worldwide generated on average 19 percent of their total income in fees from retailers.[66] Moreover, as the European airline industry was liberalized in the late 1980s and early 1990s, competition intensified. Carriers faced increasing pressures to cut costs to maintain competitive fares. In turn, they passed those pressures on to airport operators, and the landing fees charged by airports fell. In parallel, new airport facilities were required to cope with the rapid growth in traffic, so most airports had entered into ambitious investment plans. Many countries had decided to alleviate the burden on public sector budgets by privatizing airport facilities. As a result airport retailing and duty free stores in particular had become an essential source of income for airports, and many of them were expanding their commercial areas.

In 1995 private companies operated most duty free stores with concessions granted by airports or ferry lines. However, in a number of countries the duty free business was controlled, totally or partially, by state-owned companies or directly operated by state airports. For instance, whereas all duty free shops in the United States belonged to private groups, in Greece and Spain state-owned companies operated them. In some countries such as Portugal, Austria, Finland, Denmark, France and Japan, local airlines owned a stake in the duty free operator. In spite of this, the industry had experienced a profound transformation in its ownership structure. As the attractiveness of the sector became more evident, the number of companies involved increased. At the end of 1995 there were 1,550 companies operating duty free businesses. Table 15-3 presents the ranking of the 15 largest world operators by sales in 1995.[67]

---

[64]The right to export tax-free products was granted to the passenger or traveler by the country of origin (and was normally unlimited), whereas the right to import duty free was granted by the country of destination and was subject to quantity and value limitations. Duty free shops thus were not concerned about quantity or value limitations, which were the responsibility of the traveler and the custom authorities at the destination. The exceptions to this rule were those stores where the "vendor control" system was applied. Under this system the store was responsible for enforcing the limitations.

[65]For example, 75 percent of cognac sales in the European Union occurred in duty free stores.

[66]*The Future of Duty Free Retailing, Volume 1*, Financial Times Business Limited, 1998.

[67]Nuance and Weitnauer were Swiss companies, but a large share of their operations was in EU countries.

**TABLE 15-3 Major World Operators (1995)**

| Ranking | Company/Operator | Country | DF Sales (US$ m) | Market Share (%) |
|---|---|---|---|---|
| 1 | DFS | USA | 2,800 | 13.7 |
| 2 | Nuance | Switzerland | 1,205 | 5.9 |
| 3 | Gebr Heinemann | Germany | 800 | 3.9 |
| 4 | Weitnauer | Switzerland | 744 | 3.6 |
| 5 | Duty Free International | USA | 515 | 2.5 |
| 6 | Stena Line | Sweden | 493 | 2.4 |
| 7 | Alpha Retail Trading | UK | 481 | 2.3 |
| 8 | Silja Line | Finland | 402 | 2.0 |
| 9 | Aer Rianta | Ireland | 355 | 1.7 |
| 10 | Duty Free Philippines | Philippines | 336 | 1.6 |
| 11 | Aldeasa | Spain | 322 | 1.6 |
| 12 | Viking Line | Finland | 314 | 1.5 |
| 13 | King Power | Hong Kong/Thailand | 307 | 1.5 |
| 14 | Lotte Group | South Korea | 307 | 1.5 |
| 15 | Brasif | Brazil | 306 | 1.5 |

*Source*: Santander Investment, The Best 'n' Most Duty Free, 1996

## The Impact of Abolition

According to estimates from the European Travel Research Foundation, 71 percent of total duty free sales in airports, airlines, and ferries in the European Union in 1995 were intra-EU sales. This amounted to $5.1 billion and was the portion of sales that was at risk from the proposed abolition of intra-EU duty free sales. However, the potential impact differed across channels and products (Table 15-4). The estimated potential impact of the announced abolition by country is shown in Table 15-5. Scandinavian countries (Finland, Sweden, and Denmark), where ferry companies operated flourishing duty free operations, would be potentially most adversely affected, together with Ireland and Luxembourg, with percentages at risk of over 80 percent.[68] The Netherlands and Italy would be the least impacted with percentages between 50 percent and 55 percent. An underestimated share of these sales would still take place after the abolition under a duty paid scheme essentially identical to that at ordinary retail outlets.

**TABLE 15-4 Intra-EU Duty Free Sales by Channel and Product Category (1995)**

| Channel | Total Sales US$ bn | Intra-EU Sales US$ bn | % Sales at risk | Product | Total Sales US$ bn | Intra-EU Sales US$ bn | % Sales at risk |
|---|---|---|---|---|---|---|---|
| Airports | 3.5 | 1.9 | 55 | Wine & Spirits | 1.7 | 1.2 | 71 |
| Ferries | 2.7 | 2.6 | 98 | Perfumes | 1.7 | 1.2 | 71 |
| Airlines | 1.0 | 0.6 | 57 | Tobacco | 1.3 | 1.1 | 85 |
| | | | | Others | 2.5 | 1.5 | 60 |
| EU | 7.2 | 5.1 | 71 | EU | 7.2 | 5.1 | 71 |

*Source*: Santander Investment, The Best 'n' Most Duty Free, 1996
*Source*: European Travel Research Foundation, 1996

[68]These were partly fueled by the weekend trips of young Scandinavians taking advantage of low prices to consume large quantities of alcohol, often without leaving the ferries for the duration of the weekend.

**TABLE 15-5 Intra-EU Duty Free Sales by Country (1995)**

| Sales by Channel | % Airports | % Airlines | % Ferries | Intra-EU Sales | Total Sales US$ m | Intra-EU Sales US$ m | % Sales at risk |
|---|---|---|---|---|---|---|---|
| Austria | 80 | 20 | 0 | Austria | 67.2 | 37.6 | 56 |
| Belgium | 66 | 15 | 19 | Belgium | 179.4 | 132.5 | 74 |
| Denmark | 25 | 20 | 55 | Denmark | 740.4 | 590.9 | 80 |
| Finland | 9 | 4 | 86 | Finland | 924.2 | 829.2 | 90 |
| France | 68 | 8 | 24 | France | 613.0 | 359.3 | 59 |
| Germany | 48 | 24 | 28 | Germany | 808.8 | 528.7 | 65 |
| Greece | 75 | 7 | 18 | Greece | 181.7 | 139.5 | 77 |
| Ireland | 72 | 10 | 19 | Ireland | 168.2 | 143.3 | 85 |
| Italy | 86 | 12 | 2 | Italy | 314.1 | 169.0 | 54 |
| Luxembourg | 95 | 5 | 0 | Luxembourg | 15.2 | 13.9 | 91 |
| Netherlands | 86 | 15 | 0 | Netherlands | 389.1 | 195.0 | 50 |
| Portugal | 82 | 18 | 0 | Portugal | 75.8 | 49.0 | 65 |
| Spain | 81 | 17 | 2 | Spain | 331.1 | 201.3 | 61 |
| Sweden | 22 | 17 | 62 | Sweden | 485.0 | 429.2 | 88 |
| United Kingdom | 52 | 12 | 36 | United Kingdom | 1,919.5 | 1,309.9 | 68 |
| **EUROPEAN UNION** | 51% | 14% | 35% | **EUROPEAN UNION** | 7,212.7 | 5,128.3 | 71% |

*Source:* European Travel Research Foundation, 1996

## The European Union Decision

After the publication of the White Book on the European Single Market in 1985, the official position of the European Commission was that duty and tax-free sales for travelers within the European Community would end by January 1, 1993. The commission's basic argument was that tax-free shopping was not compatible with a single internal market. Also, duty free operators benefited from privileged locations and from "captive" customers, which gave them a natural competitive advantage vis-à-vis other retailers and other transport operators. The implicit subsidy also favored international air and sea travel operators over domestic route operators. Finally, within the retail industry the subsidy for duty free sales adversely affected ordinary retailers who did not benefit from the duty free status.

Some studies of duty free operations had shown that the tax advantage was reflected in higher retail margins and was not significantly passed on to consumers. This happened even in products subject to special consumption taxes (alcohol and tobacco), where the exemptions presented a greater potential for retail price reductions. The European Commission argued that the tax exemption was an indirect subsidy to duty free retailers rather than a subsidy to demand. Moreover, many of the goods sold in duty free shops were taxed, since goods priced at more than €90 were subject to taxes on the full value of the good.

In 1987 the European Commission, and most specifically its Directorate-General XXI (Taxation and Customs Union), in its role as initiator of legislation within the European Union, presented a proposal for a directive on fiscal measures needed to establish the internal market on January 1, 1993. The proposal did not mention specific measures regarding duty free and tax-free sales, so it raised doubts as to whether the creation of the Single Market implied the end of duty free sales. In 1990 Commissioner Scrivener made her position clear by answering a question at the European Parliament (EP). In her opinion, the exemption would automatically end on January 1, 1993, under the legal dispositions abolishing the concepts of import and export in intra-EU exchanges.

The commission's position was increasingly contested, especially by the International Duty Free

Confederation (IDFC), created in 1988, which orchestrated an intense campaign aimed at maintaining the tax and duty free status. The IDFC argued that it would be impossible to achieve a completely integrated Single Market by December 31, 1992, since the drive toward the harmonization of indirect taxes had not gathered enough momentum. In June 1991 the European Parliament expressed its views on a projected directive concerning the "general framework for ownership and transport of products subjected to excise duties." One of the adopted amendments proposed postponing the abolition until December 31, 1995, to allow the industry to adapt and give time for the commission to prepare a detailed impact study.

In September the ECOFIN Council, after consulting with the European Parliament and the commission, decided to grant a transitional period to the duty free industry until June 30, 1999. The decision to grant such a long delay was received with surprise by some interested parties, for example, in the Parliament. It was difficult to know exactly what had happened in the council, but according to *The European* newspaper, Germany and Belgium stressed the contradiction between the Single Market and duty free sales.[69] In contrast, the British minister supported a 15-year exemption period, and Portugal defended an 8-year period. France remained neutral initially but finally supported postponement. A common view among commentators was that Ireland and Greece supported the longest possible delay; the Netherlands and Denmark supported Germany and Belgium; Spain supported Portugal; and Italy was aligned with France. The position of Luxembourg was not known.

The arrangement for VAT and excise duties, allowing for tax and duty free sales until June 30, 1999, was finally established in two separate directives (91/680/EEC of December 1991 and 92/12/EEC of February 1992). These directives set the rules for taxes and duties for intra-Community travelers after January 1, 1993. The legislation stipulated that member states may exempt from taxes and duties products sold in duty free stores located in ports or airports, in intra-Community flights and maritime routes, and in the two Eurotunnel terminals, until June 30, 1999. Although the commission's

[69]See *The European*, October 1995 supplement on duty free commerce.

fiscal proposals had been adopted after the Single European Act, both directives were approved under the consultation procedure and adopted by the council under the unanimity rule (as required for all issues pertaining to tax harmonization). The same rule governed future amendments or changes in the decisions.

## Aldeasa

Aldeasa was founded in 1974 by the Direccion General de Patrimonio del Estado (Patrimonio), a unit of the Spanish Ministry of Finance. The company was originally created to operate duty free shops in Spanish airports as well as customs warehouses and related logistical services. Like most companies owned by Patrimonio, Aldeasa operated as a monopolist under an exclusive concession granted by AENA (Aeropuertos Españoles y Navegación Aerea), another state-owned company that owned and operated all the airports in Spain. During the 1980s Aldeasa's duty free operations showed impressive growth, and the company opened duty free shops in virtually all the main tourist airports in Spain. In 1986 Spain became a member of the European Community. This caused a dramatic change in the company's regulatory environment, as Aldeasa's business became automatically subject to legislation and decisions adopted at the EU level.

After the European Commission initially proposed the abolition of intra-EU duty free sales with effect on January 1, 1993, Aldeasa started to implement a diversification strategy. The company created a Palaces and Museums division in 1990, operating souvenir shops located in museums, palaces, cathedrals, and other cultural or recreational sites. These shops were subject to the ordinary tax regime (duty paid as opposed to duty free). Aldeasa also created a Logistical Services division, where the company provided noncustoms warehousing, airport handling, and distribution. Simultaneously, it began expanding internationally, primarily in Latin America. In 1991 Aldeasa opened its first duty free shops outside Spain in the Dominican Republic. In 1993 the company won a contest to operate duty free shops at several airports in Peru. New concessions in Portugal, Chile (1995), Madeira, and Venezuela (1996) followed.

Other important changes in Aldeasa's operations came from its regulatory environment. Aside from abolition, new EU regulations impacted the company's business and forced it to react quickly to maintain its profitability. First, the implementation of the "vendor control" system in the European Union in 1993 had a direct negative effect on passengers' average spending at duty free shops and forced Aldeasa to reorganize its in-store operations, payment, and control technologies.[70] Second, the application of the Schengen agreements had a profound impact on the industry landscape. In the case of airports, passengers on EU-bound flights departing from airports located within the so-called "Schengen Zone" no longer had to go through passport control. In application of the new agreements, airports created two differentiated areas: Schengen and non-Schengen. This significantly altered passenger flows within airports, so Aldeasa had to relocate several stores or open new ones.

Despite the diversification initiatives, the Airports Division (duty free and duty paid shops, urban shops, and the wholesale business) still accounted for 89 percent of total sales and 96 percent of operating cash flow in 1995 (versus 95 and 90 percent, respectively, in 1990). Palaces and Museums contributed 5 percent to total sales and 2 percent to operating cash flow, whereas the Logistical Services Division contributed 6 and 2 percent, respectively. Fifty-six percent of Aldeasa's headcount, or 1,209 employees at the end of 1995, worked in the Airport Division. Revenues from this division had been growing since 1990 at a 17.6 percent compounded annual rate. Even after the implementation of vendor control in 1993, annual growth rates were well above 20 percent. The 67 duty free shops Aldeasa operated in Spain were located in the 14 most important Spanish airports. Madrid (27 shops), Barcelona (12 shops), Málaga (9 shops), and Palma de Mallorca (6 shops) were the main locations. Madrid was ranked 10th in the world by duty free sales in 1995. Palma and Málaga, two of the most popular tourist destinations in Europe, were also among the top 20 airports.

The high growth was impressive considering that the number of passengers on international departure flights in airports where Aldeasa operated had risen at an annual rate of only 7.6 percent between 1990 and 1995. The 20.2 million passengers spent an average of $11.6 shopping at Aldeasa's duty free shops in 1995. The average was higher in the case of nontourist airports: $14 versus $10. The sales breakdown by product category was essentially similar to the industry average (Table 15-4), although there were some differences between tourist and nontourist airports. The company estimated that between 75 and 80 percent of its duty free sales in Spanish airports corresponded to passengers on intra-EU flights and were therefore at risk in 1999. Tobacco and alcoholic beverages were likely to be more sensitive to the abolition, since unlike perfumes and miscellaneous items, they were subject to excise duties in addition to ad-valorem taxes and would therefore register a higher price increase. The actual impact, however, ultimately depended on Aldeasa's marketing and pricing strategies.

Aldeasa could follow a volume strategy (maintain pre-abolition prices to protect sales volume, absorbing the taxes as a margin reduction) or a margin strategy (raise prices to pass the taxes on to customers). The company's gross margins were estimated to be around 25 percent for duty paid compared to 32 percent for duty free sales.

The exclusive concession agreement between Aldeasa and AENA, which acquired a 20 percent stake in Aldeasa in 1992, was due to expire in July 1999. Under this agreement, Aldeasa paid AENA an annual fee of approximately 25 percent of sales on average (the actual fee on sales was calculated by product and airport). AENA generated 30 percent of its total revenue from retailing fees, with 50 percent coming from the Aldeasa exclusive concession contract.

## Privatization and Abolition

In November 1996 Fernández Olano, a friend of several Spanish cabinet members including the Finance Minister, had to preside over the privatization process. Investors and financial analysts regarded Aldeasa as a "jewel" among the state-owned companies. Indeed, it had always shown an extremely high and consistent profitability: a gross margin exceeding 30 percent of sales, an operating margin close to 15 percent of sales, and a net margin

---

[70] Under the vendor control system, compliance with the limits on duty free purchases (the so-called "duty free allowances") were controlled by the vendor as opposed to the country of destination. Passengers in intra-EU flights were allowed to purchase duty free goods up to certain limits (e.g., 1 liter of alcoholic beverages or 200 cigarettes). The limits did not apply to passengers on flights to destinations outside the European Union.

of approximately 10 percent of sales. Sales and operating profits had increased at an annual rate of approximately 20 percent, while net profits grew 15 percent per year in the period 1990 to 1995. Aldeasa also had a healthy balance sheet, with a net cash position of ESP 2.218 million ($15 million) at the end of 1995. The main challenge facing the new management team came from the upcoming aboli-

tion of the intra-EU duty free sales in 1999. The success of the upcoming privatization and the future of the company were dependent on the company's market and nonmarket strategies. ■

SOURCE: This case was prepared for class use by Gonçalo Cadete, Antonio Varas, and Professor Romain Wacziarg. Copyright © 1999 by the Leland Stanford Junior University. All rights reserved. Reproduced with permission.

## PREPARATION QUESTIONS

1. What nonmarket objective, if any, should Aldeasa pursue? Which institutions should it target?
2. How are the institutional rules for enacting legislation within the European Union significant from Aldeasa's point of view? How do they affect the industry's chances of success in the nonmarket arena?
3. Formulate an integrated strategy for Aldeasa.
4. Evaluate the likelihood of success of the nonmarket component of your proposed strategy.
5. How are prospects for Aldeasa's privatization affected by the abolition of duty free for intra-EU travel? What conditions should Aldeasa seek in renegotiating its contract with AENA?

# CHAPTER 16

# China: History, Culture, and Political Economy

## Introduction

China is an ancient country that since 1978 has embarked on a remarkable economic path in which markets and foreign direct investment have been encouraged and economic reforms have been frequent if not always successful. Yet China remains a country under the domination of the Chinese Communist Party (CCP) with little popular participation in political activity and continuing restrictions on civil and human rights. The importance of a country with 1.3 billion people cannot be underestimated for both foreign businesses and governments, but the absence of democratic institutions and weak legal protections present challenges. Economic reforms have led thousands of companies to set up operations in China and, combined with the liberalization of business opportunities for Chinese citizens, have resulted in spectacular economic growth. Real growth in GDP has averaged over 9 percent annually since the open-door policy began in 1978. The remnants of the planned economy era, however, posed a particular challenge for China as it attempted to make its state-owned enterprises (SOEs) more efficient while replacing the social services they provided for workers and retirees. Economic growth was not led by the SOEs but by private enterprises and enterprises supported by provincial and village governments. Continued economic liberalization had to be accomplished while preserving the supremacy of the CCP.

In 2001 China joined the World Trade Organization, which brought both opportunity and new challenges. Membership provided additional access to foreign markets, but it also required China to open major industries to imports and foreign investment. This put additional pressure on SOEs and on the country to strengthen legal protections.

This chapter provides background on the history and culture of China and briefly characterizes the four I's with an emphasis on government institutions and business issues. The next section provides a historical background on China beginning with the pre-republican era and concluding with the current era. The following section considers Confucianism and its implications for business, society, and politics. The nonmarket environment is then discussed with an emphasis on the institutions of government. Business in China is considered with a focus on SOEs, foreign direct investment, and international trade. Several current issues, including human rights, piracy, and corruption, are then considered. The chapter cases provide an opportunity to address particular managerial challenges in the context of China's political economy.

# Historical Background[1]

## Pre-Republican

Ethnic Chinese, also known as Han people, originated in the Yellow River Valley in North-Central China. Organized rural society has existed in this region for over 10,000 years, and political control was typically divided by rival dynastic kingdoms. Invasion by barbarians resulted in centuries (c. 771–221 B.C.) of political fragmentation, during which much of China's most impressive philosophy was developed. Three important schools of Chinese philosophical thought emerged in this period: Daoism, Confucianism, and Legalism.[2] These laid the basis for much of China's future political thought and made the unification of China a paramount ideal. Confucianism, considered later in the chapter, had a profound impact on the organization of Chinese government, as it advocated the concept of government by meritocracy. This provided the intellectual foundation for the imperial bureaucracy.

Many historians regard the victory of the Qin kingdom after a period of prolonged conflicts known as the Warring States Period (403–221 B.C.) as the beginning of China's existence as a unified nation. The resulting state controlled an area roughly half the size of today's People's Republic of China. Technology played a central role in the Qin's success, as it had mastered iron-working in advance of most of its rivals. The Qin Dynasty played an important role in shaping the institutions and practices of imperial China. It eliminated the remnants of China's ancient feudal society and established the beginnings of a central bureaucracy based on Confucian principles. It also standardized the currency, weights, and measures; built some of China's first extensive irrigation projects; introduced a uniform system of writing; and consolidated many of the nation's defensive walls.

## Bureaucracy in Imperial China

Despite the immense political changes made by the Qin, China's society and politics were dominated by regional aristocracies for almost another millennium. Each succeeding dynasty, however, expanded and strengthened the bureaucratic system, and by the Tang Dynasty (A.D. 618–907) the imperial bureaucracy was considered the preeminent political authority.[3]

Since the Early Han Dynasty (206 B.C.–A.D. 8), membership in the bureaucracy was attained through highly competitive national examinations that in theory were open to all. The wealth, power, and prestige afforded by passing the examinations were so great that families often invested handsomely in educating their young men. Successful examinees spent their entire youth studying the Confucian classics in preparation for the examinations and often were in their mid-30s when they passed. The bureaucracy played an important role in ensuring social stability by preventing the rise of rival sources of political power while still permitting the accumulation of family wealth.[4]

## Foreign Relations

Imperial China faced external military threats for much of its history. The Ming Dynasty (1368–1644) constructed the Great Wall of China to ward off northern

---

[1] This section is based on a note prepared by Michael M. Ting under the supervision of Professor David P. Baron. Copyright © 1998 by the Board of Trustees of the Leland Stanford Junior University. All rights reserved. Reprinted with permission.
[2] See Pye (1978, pp. 32–59; 1985) for an introduction to the early Chinese schools of thought.
[3] See Shue (1988, pp. 84–85) and Moore (1966, p. 164).
[4] Fairbank (1992, pp. 179–182).

barbarians, but it proved to be a military failure, as it could not stop a Manchurian invasion that resulted in the last dynasty, the Qing (1644–1911). In general, however, the pre-Ming Chinese welcomed foreign commerce. Trade with the Middle East and European nations flourished, and in the early 1400s a fleet of Chinese vessels successfully completed a trade and diplomatic mission to Africa. During the 15th century, however, Chinese leaders began to view foreign interactions with a peculiar contempt. Costly border wars and fiscal crises caused the Ming to pull back on their efforts to establish foreign relations and build a navy. Convinced that foreigners could offer little of value to China, conservative Confucian scholars of the period increasingly advocated xenophobic foreign policies.[5]

Notwithstanding the Qing's hostility, the British, led by the British East India Company, vigorously attempted to maintain trade ties in southern China. With the end of the Napoleonic Wars in 1815, England gradually increased its commercial interest in China. China's defeat in the Opium War at the hands of Britain's vastly superior military technology resulted in the 1842 Treaty of Nanjing. The terms of the treaty were widely regarded as humiliating to the Chinese, as they required massive reparations to Britain, the turnover of Hong Kong, and the opening of five coastal cities to British residents and commerce. Many of the Western powers also insisted on reciprocal "most favored nation" agreements that automatically granted to every foreign country the concessions made to any one country, thus hastening the pace and extent of economic concessions.

## Collapse of Imperial China

The latter half of the 19th century was marked by numerous large-scale revolts that reflected the inability of the Qing to maintain domestic peace and contain foreign influence. The imperial bureaucracy was increasingly perceived as an incompetent and backwards institution, incapable of performing even its traditional duties of maintaining China's important waterways. As the 19th century drew to a close, internal calls for reform became increasingly prevalent, and the Qing initiated many ambitious reforms. They attempted to copy several Western-style government institutions and abolished the centuries-old examination system in 1905. Their drive toward modernization resulted in the outfitting of a Western-style military and plans for a new national rail network.

## The Republican Era

By the first decade of the 20th century, local warlords had ascended to political prominence in China. Many raised their own armies, collected their own taxes, and showed questionable loyalty to the Qing. In addition, revolutionary societies and fraternities, many loosely organized into a group called the Revolutionary Alliance, were increasingly active in China's major urban centers. The Revolutionary Alliance, led by Dr. Sun Yat-sen, had relatively strong popular backing, but lacked an army. By early 1912, a large military faction led by former Qing general Yuan Shikai gained the upper hand, and the last Qing abdicated his throne in 1912.

While many credit Sun Yat-sen with the founding of the Republic of China in 1911, China at the time was hardly a coherent political entity. Yuan proved incapable of ruling China, as he insisted on central control over proposed modernizations but lacked substantial authority over local governments. He also actively attempted to undermine his Revolutionary Alliance allies, many of whom had organized themselves into the Guomindang (GMD), or Nationalist Party, under Sun.

[5]Fairbank (1992, pp. 138–140).

Sun's death in 1925 cleared the way for the ascendancy of Chiang Kai-shek as the new GMD leader. Capitalizing on both the strength of his National Revolutionary Army and a wave of nationalist sentiment in the mid-1920s, Chiang launched military offensives in 1926 and 1928 that established a new capital in Nanjing and brought most of China under GMD rule. His sudden success convinced many that the GMD was China's best hope for modernizing its economy and political system. This hope proved to be illusory, however, as the Nanjing leaders lacked sufficient control over many regions to execute their policies. The GMD's support base was primarily urban, but since China's urban-industrial sector was still very small, its base and resources were limited.

The main unifying force for the GMD was the threat from the Chinese Communist Party (CCP), formed in 1921. Chiang continually harassed the CCP and, in response, several communist uprisings took place, only to be crushed by GMD armies. The CCP did not recover until 1933, by which time it had transformed itself into a rural party largely independent of the international communist party. Headed by Mao Zedong, an early revolutionary leader who had carefully studied the rural economy, the CCP was once again strong enough to be of concern to the GMD. Chiang's continuous attacks drove the CCP to seek a new base, and in late 1934, 100,000 soldiers and party members began their famous Long March.

### War and Civil War

In 1937 Japan invaded and Chinese armies were quickly routed by superior Japanese tactics and technology. Chinese resistance to Japan was highly fragmented in spite of the initial promise of a united front between the GMD and CCP. During the war and occupation Mao was able to consolidate his leadership and develop his own distinctive brand of Marxism. As part of his program the CCP began to institute land reform in friendly areas, thus enlisting peasant support and swelling the ranks of CCP troops.

As World War II drew to a close, both sides prepared for a civil war. In 1945 the CCP was stronger than at any point in its history, but its army had little foreign support and was only half the size of Chiang's American-equipped army. American support, however, could not forestall the subsequent rout of the GMD in the 1946 to 1949 civil war. By mid-1949 the communist victory was nearly complete, and on October 1, 1949, Mao proclaimed the founding of the People's Republic of China.

As Chiang's losses mounted in 1948, he transferred the remains of the Republic of China to Taiwan, which as part of the Yalta agreements in World War II had been formally returned to the Republic of China after 50 years of Japanese colonization. The GMD instituted comprehensive land reform and compensated landlords with government bonds. With American economic aid it embarked on vigorous industrialization by attracting foreign investment and targeting export markets.[6]

## The Communist Era

Although the communist victory had been complete, Mao and his followers still faced a daunting task that had eluded Chinese rulers for centuries: establishing a state with unquestioned control over the entire nation. The CCP's assumption of power took two distinct tracks. First, in the countryside, it sought to complete the process of land reform that had begun in Northern China earlier in the decade. Because peasants benefiting from land redistribution overwhelmingly outnumbered landlords, the process was quickly and enthusiastically embraced.[7] Second, in keeping with Marxist

---

[6]See Deyo (1987) and Haggard (1990) for a comparative perspective on Taiwanese industrial policy.
[7]Vogel (1980, pp. 91–124) discusses policy debates during the early years of land reform.

philosophy, the party sought to control all commerce, but again the magnitude of the task demanded considerable flexibility. Only the largest companies came under state control in the early years, and most urban professionals were allowed to continue working regardless of their political background. Meanwhile, governments at all levels gradually asserted control over prices, the banking system, and the allocation of various important goods.

The end of the Korean War allowed policymakers to concentrate on their next task: the transformation of the Chinese economy into a socialist system. Following the early Soviet model, planners in Beijing hoped to stimulate the development of heavy industry by taxing the agricultural sector. They also believed that greater productivity could be best achieved by wiping out the remnants of capitalism and developing huge, self-contained production units in agriculture and industry.

A central feature of the First Five Year Plan was the collectivization of agriculture. Shortly after land reform was completed, the CCP began to organize peasant households into ever-larger cooperative associations. A similar process was underway in the industrial sector. State takeovers of large enterprises accelerated throughout the 1950s, until only the smallest street merchants were allowed to remain independent. With the aid of Soviet loans, CCP industrial policy emphasized sectors such as steel, petroleum, and chemicals at the expense of consumer goods. In addition to their economic importance, these enterprises also served a vital social role. Labor was furnished through the *danwei* ("work unit") system, under which workers were permanently assigned to enterprises upon completing their education. The *danwei* provided its members with housing, child care, schooling, health care, shops, post offices, and other social services. It was also an instrument of social control. Because there was no welfare system, urban residents had no access to even the most basic social services outside of their *danwei*, and opportunities for changing enterprises were rare.

Convinced that China's lagging production could be blamed not on poor economic reasoning but on a lack of mobilization, the CCP unleashed a flurry of production efforts to spur the economy. Many of these projects launched in the Great Leap Forward in 1958 were at best ill conceived, and at worst destructive.[8] Agricultural cooperatives were rapidly combined into even larger county-size communes, but in 1959 poor weather highlighted the inefficiency of the communes. Production plummeted and China suffered a famine that claimed over 20 million lives through 1962.

The clear failure of the large communes prompted authority to devolve back to smaller production units, so that individual households were once again held responsible for meeting production quotas. More importantly, the government legalized private plots on which peasants were allowed to raise and market their own vegetables and animals while their communes produced grain. On a larger scale, leaders also began to question the Soviet-inspired strategy of developing heavy industry first.

Mao's allies—notably his wife Jiang Qing and army chief Lin Biao—insisted that China's problems were the result of insufficient dedication to the CCP's revolutionary principles. Mao's gambit to reassert power combined this message with his still considerable populist appeal in launching the Great Proletarian Cultural Revolution in 1966. Mao and Lin organized thousands of Red Guard units, consisting largely of fanatical students who were directed to purge their jurisdictions of the four "olds"—old ideas, old customs, old cultures, and old habits. Their campaigns destroyed many of China's most valuable cultural artifacts and degenerated into destructive excess and mob rule

---

[8]See the chapter case, *Wugang and the Reform of State-Owned Enterprises*, for a description of one of these projects.

in the name of Mao. Finally in 1967 the army stepped in to control the chaos, often by imposing martial law. The cultural revolution had decimated much of the party's organization, especially at the provincial and lower levels. It had also elevated the army's status within the party hierarchy.

As a result of the split of the Sino-Soviet alliance in 1958, successive American administrations expressed interest in renewing relations with China, and these efforts culminated in President Nixon's historic visit to China in 1972. As a result of improved relations both nations gained a powerful ally against the Soviet Union.

## The Reform Era

The deaths of Mao and foreign minister Zhou Enlai in 1976 led to Deng Xiaoping assuming the leadership of China. Deng's rise occurred during a period of tremendous foreign and domestic ferment. The United States formally switched its recognition of China from Taiwan to the People's Republic on January 1, 1979, after which Deng made historic visits to America and Japan. Inspired by the beginnings of political liberalization, many Chinese began to express their bitterness toward the communist party with large posters on various city walls, the most famous of which became known as the Democracy Wall in Beijing. The party, which was ready to commit itself to many reforms, had little intention of sharing its authority, and to emphasize its control, Deng consolidated power.

Deng's economic reforms were headlined by the "Four Modernizations"—agriculture, industry, defense, and science and technology. Recognizing that China needed more exposure to Western products, ideas, and capital, Beijing lifted import restrictions in 1978 under its open-door policy. Four Special Economic Zones were opened in Southern China, where foreign investors could take advantage of low-wage labor and preferential tax rates. Small, household-run enterprises were once again legalized. Finally, larger enterprises such as agricultural production teams and many SOEs were subjected to a new fiscal regime under which some profits from above-quota production could be retained for the enterprise's use. This exposure to market forces resulted in a dramatic increase in nationwide investment in 1979 and 1980.[9]

A second, more intensive wave of reforms occurred between 1983 and 1985. In the agricultural sector, the government replaced mandatory grain purchases with a contracting system known as the Household Responsibility System, and prices for many goods were allowed to "float" to market levels. In the cities, SOEs were given increased discretion over their profits, and individual managers were made more accountable for their performance. Beijing also granted 14 additional coastal cities and Hainan Island a Special Economic Zone status. The sudden changes and influx of wealth, however, created economic and social backlashes. Economic crime and corruption were rampant, and leaders often voiced concerns about excessive Western cultural influence.

Another period of retrenchment occurred in 1986, as restrictions were placed on investments and imports in an attempt to cool the economy. More ominously, however, large-scale social unrest had become evident throughout the country, and students and intellectuals grew increasingly disappointed that the nation's rapid economic change was not accompanied by changes in the authoritarian political system. For many students, Hu Yaobang personified many of the disappointments they faced. An outspoken progressive, Hu was forced to resign as party general secretary in January 1987 after other party leaders blamed him for not stopping student protests. His sudden death in 1989 set off a wave of nationwide student demonstrations, the most prominent of

---

[9]Harding (1987, p. 4).

which attracted as many as a million demonstrators to Beijing's Tiananmen Square. For weeks the demonstrators and sympathetic civilians successfully resisted attempts to impose martial law, but in a move that was condemned worldwide, crack army units crushed the protests.

The repercussions of the Tiananmen massacre showed that China's efforts to join the world community were imposing constraints on the CCP and the government. China's desire to realize an international role commensurate with its growing economic strength had generated numerous frictions. Foremost among these were China's foreign economic relations. Both the United States, one of China's largest trading partners, and the GATT/World Trade Organization, which China hoped to join, insisted that China adhere more closely to international norms in its economy.

One foreign policy success was the 1984 agreement with the United Kingdom, returning Hong Kong to China in 1997. Under China's "One Country, Two Systems" policy, Hong Kong was to retain its autonomy, including a separate currency, for 50 years. Shortly before the return, the British government attempted to bolster the colony's legislative body as a popular institution, but Beijing ensured that only its own hand-picked representatives were permitted to sit. In 1999 Macao was returned to China by Portugal.

A potentially more serious sovereignty issue was the status of Taiwan. In their claims to sovereignty over both the mainland and Taiwan, both the CCP and GMD agreed that there was only a single Chinese nation. Because of their disparate political systems, however, movement toward reunification has been virtually nonexistent. Beijing originally proposed the One Country, Two Systems policy for Taiwan, but it was quickly rejected by the GMD government, which refused to unite with a communist regime. Beijing made clear that it would not tolerate a declaration of Taiwanese independence.

## Domestic Reform in an Authoritarian Framework

Domestically, China resumed its economic reforms shortly after the furor over Tiananmen subsided. The 1990s saw the increasing autonomy of SOEs, reforms of the nation's financial system, as well as a fully convertible currency. The government also handled the political transition of Deng's death in 1997 with few problems. The country, however, faced challenges that were as formidable as ever. One of the most urgent was the reform of over 300,000 obsolete SOEs. Few of these enterprises were profitable because they had functioned too long in the absence of competitive pressures. Many were hopelessly inefficient, saddled with old technology and employing up to 15 million excess workers nationwide. Moreover, these enterprises had accumulated combined debts approaching $120 billion (almost 20 percent of GDP), while absorbing most of China's domestic credit.[10] The problem was tightly linked with a crisis in the national banking system, whose long-standing practice of granting loans on the basis of political connections rather than commercial merit had resulted in high levels of bad debt. Transforming these enterprises into profitable entities would inevitably require the dismantling of the *danwei* system, but there was no social welfare system to replace it.

Beijing also faced a host of long-term economic and political issues. The central government's finances, along with the country's labor and housing markets, all required serious revamping. Corruption and cronyism were prevalent at all levels of government. The growing demand by an increasingly affluent population for energy and consumer goods was exacerbating China's already dire environmental problems. As SOEs were

---

[10]See Tomlinson (1997) for an example of the privatization of a state-owned enterprise.

restructured, millions of workers lost their jobs, and they and millions of rural workers moved to the cities in search of work. Finally, the CCP faced the daunting task of addressing these issues without once again raising demands for political liberalization.

# Confucianism and Social Explanations

An important factor in understanding Chinese social and economic organization is its rich cultural heritage. This section considers Confucianism, which has had a significant influence not only in China but also in several other Asian nations.[11] With its emphasis on hierarchy, deference, moral rectitude, and behavioral norms, Confucianism was well suited to the needs of social stability. Indeed, many historians have credited China's long existence as a unified nation to its Confucian heritage. Yet the attribution of highly complex social phenomena to a single body of philosophical work would be unwarranted. Over more than 2,000 years of development, a wide variety of theories have worked their way under the Confucian umbrella. Thus, the general framework of Confucian thought displays considerable flexibility. On the one hand, as Confucius might suggest, a degree of modesty is warranted in drawing conclusions about social and economic organization from this highly complex Chinese ethics system.[12] On the other hand, attempting to understand Chinese groups, organizations, and behavior without sensitivity to the Confucian heritage would be incomplete at best.

During the political turmoil following the fall of the Zhou Dynasty, Confucius (551–479 B.C.) recorded and organized the extant body of ethical thought and extended it by de-emphasizing religious aspects and giving priority to the human condition instead (De Bary, 1991). Under this humanistic reorientation, virtue figured prominently in personal and political affairs, and individuals were to possess virtue and follow rules of behavior just as emperors did. Thus, Confucius was responsible for initiating the central preoccupation of Chinese philosophical thought: moral self-cultivation (Ivanhoe, 1993).

Perhaps the fundamental distinction between Confucianism and many Western systems of thought lies in its orientation toward the fundamental problem of social organization. As Yang (1959, p. 172) explained:

Self-cultivation, the basic theme of Confucian ethics . . . did not seek a solution to social conflict in defining, limiting, and guaranteeing the rights and interests of the individual or in the balance of power and interests between individuals. It sought the solution from the self-sacrifice of the individual for the preservation of the group.

Confucianism links self-cultivation and social harmony through the development of group relations because it views the family as the ideal setting for moral self-cultivation. According to the Zhongyong, "Five Relationships" (*Wu lun*) must be perfected before social harmony is achieved: father and son, husband and wife, sibling and sibling, friend

---

[11]This section is adapted from a note prepared by Michael M. Ting under the supervision of Professor David P. Baron. Copyright © 1998 by the Board of Trustees of the Leland Stanford Junior University. All rights reserved. Reprinted with permission.

[12]Although the best exposition of Confucian thought is the *Analects*, over the centuries *Rujia* philosophers added dozens of major variations and extensions to this work. Zhu Xi grouped its existing strands into a two-tiered program of study that is regarded as the Confucian canon. First came the "Four Books": the *Analects*, *Mencius*, *Daxue* (*The Great Learning*), and *Zhongyong* (*Doctrine of Man*). Next were the "Five Classics": *Shujing* (*Book of History*), *Liji* (*Book of Rites*), *Shijing* (*Book of Odes*), *Spring and Autumn Annals*, and *Yijing* (*Book of Changes*). Thus, while Confucianism lacks a single, comprehensive statement, a commonly accepted body of tenets emerges from these works.

and friend, and ruler and subject. Taking a pragmatic view of human nature, Confucius felt that most people could achieve perfection only in their intrafamily relationships. By extension, if virtue and harmony could be found most readily in family relationships, the process by which virtue is acquired must be present there as well (Schwartz, 1985, p. 99). As the individuals most responsible for this process, the leaders of such groups—family elders or bureaucrats—were accorded a high degree of deference and respect. Groups were therefore a vital part of the Confucian ethical system, as the individual goal of moral self-cultivation was in some sense an achievement of a larger group, be it a family or a nation.

The objectives of self-cultivation are two interrelated concepts: *ren*, or humanity, and *li*, or propriety. Loosely speaking, the former refers to one's internal discipline, whereas the latter concerns one's social relations. Confucius regarded *ren* as the more fundamental of the two concepts and considered it the ultimate object of moral self-cultivation. In its most abstract sense, the concept refers to the love of all human beings, and all people were thought to have an innate capacity for it.

*Li* is the external, or social, manifestation of *ren*. Although *li* is most commonly interpreted as "propriety," the term is also synonymous with "ceremony," "ritual," "decorum," and "good form," since it addresses all aspects of human behavior, including personal, familial, social, religious, and political conduct (Tu, 1979, pp. 20–21, 29). The Confucian tradition places a strong emphasis on behavioral minutiae because of its belief that self-cultivation is not a solitary endeavor, but rather occurs in a social context.

Confucian behavioral norms display a strongly particularistic, as opposed to universal, inclination. In contrast with ethics systems that require equal treatment of all individuals, Confucianism explicitly condoned behavior differentiated on the basis of social relationships. That is, differing standards could be applied to different social relationships, such as within a group to which a person belonged versus with regard to strangers. Appropriate behavior in a group could also differ depending on the person's position. For example, within a family a parent follows a particular form of proper behavior with regard to a child, whereas within a work group the same parent may be in the position of the "child" in relation to his or her employer.

The notion that appropriate behavior is specific to particular social relationships is largely attributable to the group foundations of moral self-cultivation, which forces numerous concessions out of necessity. Self-cultivation ideally encompasses relations with all people, but in practice most individuals can achieve only a limited degree of success in perfecting relationships. A family bond, for instance, creates opportunities for developing *ren* and *li* that may elude those outside the family. Thus, self-cultivation is seen as a process of gradual inclusion, beginning with the individual, then progressing to relations with family, nation, and the world. In this framework, universalism exists as an ideal, but discrimination and favoritism within groups should be expected because Confucians would find the notion of universalistic humanity incoherent without the prior achievement of harmony within smaller groups (Tu, 1979, p. 28).

Another feature of *li* in Confucian ethics is its distinctive conception of reciprocity. Many cultures have some variation of the Golden Rule: "Do unto others as you would have them do unto you." Beginning with the *Analects*, Confucians have devoted a great deal of attention to the idea of *shu*, or consideration. Confucius's classic statement of the rule is:

Tzu-kung asked saying, Is there any single saying that one can act upon all day and every day? The Master said, Perhaps the saying about consideration: "Never do to others what you would not like them to do to you."

(Analects 15.23)

Numerous variations and extensions on the Golden Rule exist in the Confucian canon. Taken together, they share the characteristic of emphasizing hierarchy. Nivison (1996, p. 73) constructs the following synthesis of the idealized version of *shu:*

What I do to you, if I am in a superior position, should be what I would find it acceptable for you to do to me, if our positions were reversed. I should be kind, lenient, considerate. . . . What I do for you, if I am in an inferior position, should be what I would expect you to do for me, if our positions were reversed. I should be "loyal," and so should be strict with myself even when what I am doing might hurt me. . . .

Western variants of the Golden Rule typically make no allusions to the social status of the actors.

Confucianism does not include an independent notion of individual rights. As considered in Chapter 20, Western concepts of rights involve liberty, choice, and autonomy. These rights impose duties on others not to interfere with those rights. Chang (1998, p. 133) argues that "although the Confucians did not talk about 'human rights,' they maintained that people should treat each other as fellow human beings and help one another to live a good, human way of life. This idea is clearly comparable with the concept of 'human rights.'" Cheng (1998) explains the nature of rights in terms of the relationship between a person and a ruler and their duties within that relationship. A ruler, or government, has a duty to help develop virtue in subjects, and the "rights" of those subjects are to consideration by the ruler. Cheng (1998, p. 145) writes, "we can see how a Chinese might see his rights as his duties and define his own self in terms of his consciousness." That is, instead of independently identified rights, Confucianism focuses more on duties required by a relationship, and those duties give expectations of certain types of treatment for the others in the relationship.

# Applications in Society, Politics, and Business

## Political Institutions

The Confucian ideal of hierarchical relations within the family also extends to the political realm. Whereas family heads could exercise near-absolute authority over other family members, households were expected to defer to the state on nonhousehold matters. The promotion of one's self-interest in society was considered just as inappropriate as a child's selfishness before her parents (Pye, 1985). The analogy helped to justify the Confucians' advocacy of authoritarian rule by a meritocratic elite. It also identified some of the highest political priorities of the state: security, cohesion, loyalty, and stability. Confucius wrote extensively on the behavior expected of a ruler. The following passage touches on some important aspects of a ruler's behavior:

The Master said, Govern the people by regulations, keep order among them by chastisements, and they will flee from you, and lose all self-respect. Govern them by moral force, keep order among them by ritual and they will keep their self-respect and come to you of their own accord.

(ANALECTS 2.3)

Confucius saw the ruler as a moral exemplar, but the primary purpose of governing by moral force was not divine reward but the moral development of the people. To achieve this, the ruler could use formal rules or coercion, but setting a virtuous example was both necessary and sufficient for improving society's moral character and inducing social harmony.

One of the most striking differences between Confucian and Western political thought is that the former does not conceive of a role for "civil society," or the collection of intermediate organizations between the family and state (Shils, 1996).[13] Because households were to show the same loyalty to the state that children showed to their parents, allegiance to other organizations had the potential for destabilizing society. Remarkably, imperial Chinese society mirrored these priorities for over two millennia, as merchants never achieved any substantial social status and social advancement was secured exclusively through advancement in the state bureaucracy (Pye, 1985, p. 57). The lack of recognition of legitimate interests outside the state and the deference expected of citizens also rendered Confucianism inconsistent with modern conceptions of democracy.

## Firms and Bureaucracies

In more modern settings, Confucian paternalism may be seen in the context of other organizations, such as firms and bureaucracies (Abegglen and Stalk, 1985; Dollinger, 1988; Durlabhji, 1990; Taka, 1994). Because of the imperative of maintaining group harmony, decision making is typically achieved through consensus building. This process requires the cooperation of leaders and subordinates. Leaders must demonstrate decision-making ability commensurate with their position, treat subordinates fairly, and set a good example for all. Personal negotiation may be used to resolve disputes among peers. In return, subordinates are to recognize a leader's authoritarian prerogatives and subsume personal desires to the attainment of group goals. Little emphasis is placed on formal rules, and quiet suasion and deference are often sufficient for making decisions and maintaining organizational unity.

This familistic orientation can exert a powerful influence outside the boundaries of formal organizations. Informal personal ties in Chinese society are often referred to as *guanxi*. These relationships may be either vertical (e.g., between teacher and student) or horizontal (e.g., between residents of the same village). *Guanxi* ties create a form of diffuse reciprocity, allowing individuals to exchange favors even years after a formal relationship has been dissolved. Their importance in Chinese society should not be underestimated. Throughout history, decisions ranging from hiring to the sale of scarce goods have gone in favor of those possessing good *guanxi*. Such practices have persisted despite the increased bureaucratization of Chinese society during the communist era. Because these relationships are usually not reflected in formal laws, *guanxi* often makes Chinese organizational behavior appear nontransparent and at times resemble cronyism to outsiders. The strength of such ties in China frequently has frustrated Westerners, who are more accustomed to legally circumscribed contracts or quid pro quo arrangements (Pye, 1988).

The importance of *guanxi* is such that individuals must concern themselves with acquiring it. Some ties arise in the course of normal social interaction, for instance through school or family. Others require investment and must be cultivated directly through the giving of gifts and favors, for which an elaborate set of norms has evolved. Gift giving in China frequently serves the instrumental goal of initiating a relationship. Whereas gifts may sometimes be used to secure specific favors, the diffuse nature of *guanxi* requires that exchanges occur in private some time before the desired favor to avoid the public appearance of a quid pro quo (Yang, 1994, p. 144).

Confucianism's strong focus on group cohesion and solidarity has implications for other relationships. Because intragroup relations are so important, relationships of

---

[13]Gold (1996) argues that large family networks serve as the functional equivalent of civil society.

subordinates within a group with individuals outside the group are often frowned upon. Such relationships are the responsibility of the group leader, who may require the outsiders to acknowledge his or her moral authority (Pye, 1985, p. 63). As a result, outsiders hoping to influence a group must simultaneously respect the group leader's appearance of control while also exerting effort toward establishing trustworthiness and becoming more of an insider. The latter may entail a significant investment in the establishment of *guanxi* relationships prior to the execution of any significant interaction.

## Business Relationships

Confucianism often has been linked with the development and operation of capitalism in China and other Asian countries.[14] In particular, the Chinese tendency toward small, family-owned businesses that operate within tight networks shows many traces of the Confucian heritage (Hamilton, 1996). The high status associated with public office, which required tremendous investment in education, and the traditional practice of dividing inheritances equally among children, mitigated the concentration of wealth in large firms.[15] Instead, wealthy merchant families would establish multiple small businesses that could be distributed evenly to the next generation. These multiple businesses relied on sometimes vast *guanxi* networks to conduct their affairs. The success of such businesses depended critically on the level of trust, and *guanxi*-based ties proved to be extremely successful in this regard.[16] Over the past century during which Chinese have migrated throughout the Pacific Rim, these ties have proven to be invaluable to the success of Chinese business communities throughout the region. In China's reform era, these ties have also been credited with aiding overseas Chinese who sought to do business in China.

Commercial and political success were closely linked in imperial China, as successful businessmen could more easily afford to invest in education, and bureaucrats used their political influence to favor family businesses. Thus, relationships between businesses and government traditionally have been close, often to the point of inappropriateness by Western standards. *Guanxi*-based influence networks remain pervasive throughout Asia, and while they can play an important role in facilitating business, today they are increasingly criticized for inducing favoritism, poor economic decisions by political institutions, and corruption. The state banking system in China, for instance, faced a bad debt crisis as a result of loans given on the basis of cronyism instead of merit.

Li (2004) described another purpose of *guanxi*:

In China's relation-based system, personal connections are used to circumvent the legal and regulatory system to obtain public goods and to protect one's property rights when the legal system fails. The formal legal system in China tends to be opaque, unfair, and particularistic. This is the fundamental reason why circumventing laws and regulations by using personal connections is widely practiced in China and thus viewed as ethical by some investors as well as scholars. Furthermore, investors should realize that when they use their *guanxi* to protect their interest, their local partners or competitors may use their *guanxi* to the advantage of the foreign investors—and very often the local partners and competitors tend to have stronger *guanxi*.

[14]See Weidenbaum (1996).
[15]By contrast, *primogeniture*, or the granting of the entire inheritance to the first son, was practiced in Japan, which encouraged the concentration of capital.
[16]See Redding (1996) for a discussion and comparison of trust networks in other cultures.

# The Nonmarket Environment and the Four I's

The framework of structured pluralism illustrated in Figure 14-1 is relevant to China, but the importance of the components differs from that in other countries. With regard to culture and history, China has a long history as a relatively unified nation, but it has no democratic tradition. Instead, institutions have been dominated by the bureaucracy and in the postwar period by the CCP. Culturally, China has a rich tradition, and only one aspect of that culture, Confucianism, has been considered here. This section briefly considers the other components of the structured pluralism perspective, the four I's—issues, interests, institutions, and information—and pertains only to the current period.

A host of contentious market and nonmarket issues faced business and government in China. Externally, the European Union and the United States criticized China's policy of pegging the yuan to the dollar at a low exchange rate. This kept its export prices low, and the prices of imports high, resulting in a huge trade surplus with the United States. The International Monetary Fund and the Group of 7 nations urged China to float the yuan. China pledged to act, but some observers believed that inclusion in the G-7 was China's price for floating or revaluing the yuan. In late 2004 China's central bank raised its lending rate for the first time in 9 years to slow inflation.

Internally, China had the problem of reforming or closing a large number of inefficient SOEs, as considered later in the chapter. Many of the SOEs had close ties to the CCP and the ministries that controlled them. China's inclusion in the World Trade Organization (WTO) resolved one issue, but compliance with WTO requirements was difficult. China had to address commercial piracy, quotas on imports, and restrictions on entry in many markets. A variety of human rights complaints had been lodged against China, ranging from the absence of civil rights to the enforcement of the one-child-per-family law. Nonmarket issues stemmed from the weak protection of intellectual and other property rights in China and the widespread corruption stemming in part from the government's extensive involvement in and regulation of business.

Interests in China are pluralistic, but because of the domination of the CCP there is little interest group activity and collective nonmarket action is rare. Moreover, independent labor unions are not permitted. Instead, interests manifest themselves through client politics narrowly tailored to specific interests. This implies that interests do not drive outcomes in the same manner as in a democracy such as Japan, the European Union, or the United States. The government, however, is sensitive to the possibility of popular unrest and attempts to anticipate problems. Riots and demonstrations break out in China as a result of local issues. For example, as inflation increased retirees protested that their pensions were not indexed to inflation. Farmers rioted against some local governments that had taken their land for development purposes without adequate compensation. Ethnic clashes between the Han and Muslin Hui broke out in western China. Unrest and violent protests were increasingly frequent, particularly in China's rural areas and smaller cities.

The institutions in China are dominated by the CCP and include a strong and encompassing bureaucracy and a relatively weak legislature and judiciary. Despite the tight political control exercised by the CCP, China has devolved considerable authority to the provinces and local governments.

Information is important in China in part because of the presence of a dominant political party and a hierarchical government. It also is important because government rules and regulations are not transparent and can be changed without due process or electoral sanction. This situation is exacerbated by the dominance of both business and the administration of laws by a closed political party. *Guanxi* relationships between business and government facilitate obtaining information, but this also makes it difficult for those who do not have *guanxi*. The chapter case, *Direct Selling in China*, illustrates some of these features.

## Institutions and Government

China's government is characterized by close ties between the CCP and state institutions. In practice a government body wields power to the extent that its leadership is influential within the CCP. The constitution of the PRC places the party in the highest position of authority and requires that government policies and civil liberties conform to its direction. As a result, the informal configuration of power within the party leadership is usually more informative than the government's organization charts for determining where policies are made.

Since the ascendance of Deng Xiaoping, three general trends have developed. First, political power has steadily devolved to local governments, thus shifting the locus of a considerable body of policymaking away from Beijing. Second, the relationship between party and state has been weakened by new restrictions on joint appointments in the leaderships of both bodies. This has been coupled with significant advances in administrative law and an increasing professionalization of the bureaucracy. Third, although their influence remains small, democratic procedures, such as elections to local People's Congresses that were once considered mere formalities, have become more important.

### Party Organization

The CCP claims to represent the Chinese working people and is the highest source of political power in China. Moreover, the People's Liberation Army, which historically has been closely linked with the CCP, is sworn to defend the party rather than the state. In 1997 CCP membership stood at 58 million, or less than 5 percent of the population. At the local level, the party is represented in virtually all significant societal organizations, including townships, factories, and rural collectives. At higher levels, party organizations mirror the hierarchy of the national government. Decisions at all levels are made by a process known as democratic centralism, whereby party units may set their own policies in a democratic manner but may not contradict the directives of a higher level. This system of representation and centralization of authority guarantees significant party influence over potentially all aspects of political and economic activity.

**National Party Congress** Nominally the highest authority of the CCP, Party Congresses meet every 5 years. The 15th Party Congress in 1997 had 2,047 delegates, elected from local party organizations, the central party, and the military. Because meetings are brief (usually a few days) and the number of delegates is large, the Congress usually does little more than rubber-stamp the decisions of its delegated bodies.

**Central Committee** When the Party Congress is not in session, authority passes to the 198-member Central Committee, which convenes at least twice annually. The Central Committee is elected by the National Party Congress, but until 1987 ballots were not secret and the number of candidates did not exceed the number of seats. Members represent the central party, local party organizations, the government, and the military. The committee makes decisions by majority rule and has veto authority over many party decisions. Many of Deng's reforms catered to local governments to avoid a Central Committee veto.[17] The Central Committee also supervises many of the party's internal functions, such as propaganda and party organization.

[17]Shirk (1993, Ch. 4).

**Politburo** The Politburo is responsible for the ongoing administration of the party. This body meets regularly and makes decisions by majority rule. It holds a veto over many of the decisions of the Standing Committee and supervises the policy branches of the party organization (e.g., military, foreign affairs, finance). Much of the Politburo's authority comes from its personnel powers.

**Standing Committee of the Politburo** In 2002 the Standing Committee consisted of nine members. This group handles the day-to-day affairs of the party and like other CCP bodies makes decisions by majority rule. Much of its leverage comes from its ability to convene Politburo meetings and set their agendas.[18]

## The CCP and Policymaking

The prevalence of majority rule in CCP decision making may seem surprising, but in accordance with the principles of democratic centralism, the procedure is taken seriously. However, CCP decision making has an authoritarian character because delegated groups such as the Standing Committee of the Politburo exercise tremendous agenda control over their parent groups. The CCP's appointments process also contributes to intraparty unity. Because career advancement within the party is typically achieved through patronage, intraparty factions tend to be highly cohesive.

As a given policy's importance increases, the number of veto bodies it must pass through also increases. For example, Five-Year Plans must be approved all the way down through the National Party Congress. Because the Congress and the Central Committee are composed of very diverse groups (including geographically based representatives), major policies must satisfy some particularistic interests.

Virtually all high-ranking party officials belong to an "entrance" (*kou*) that covers a major policy area. The most important *kous*, such as Party Affairs and Military Affairs, are led by members of the Standing Committee of the Politburo, while other Politburo members lead less important or subordinate *kous*. *Kous* often form the basis of intraparty factions, and their members typically hold positions both within the party leadership as well as the state institutions that carry out the policies associated with the *kou*.[19]

## State Institutions
### The Legislative Branch

The National People's Congress (NPC) is both the highest legislative body and formally the highest institution of the central state. One of its duties is the election of a premier, who serves as the PRC's head of state. The premier, however, has only limited formal authority. The PRC constitution grants the NPC authority to pass legislation and to appoint and remove most executive branch officials. Membership selection has a reciprocal character similar to that of the upper echelons of the CCP: The plenum elects a Standing Committee which in turn selects representatives to the plenum. The NPC's 3,000 delegates are elected to 5-year terms, but the plenum meets for only 2 weeks annually, leaving most day-to-day activities to the 135-member Standing Committee. Representation is both geographical and functional (or corporatist). Large social interests such as the People's Liberation Army, ethnic minority groups, and peasants, among others, are granted fixed proportions of representatives. Non-CCP members account for 20 to 30 percent of NPC delegates.

---

[18]Christiansen and Rai (1996, pp. 110–111).
[19]See Lieberthal (1995).

Historically, the divergence between the NPC's formal and actual powers has been large due to the domination by the CCP elite of all aspects of statecraft. Since the early 1980s, however, the NPC has with increasing frequency defeated or forced the rewriting of bills submitted by the State Council. Additionally, the NPC has established specialized committees, such as an environmental committee founded in 1990, that have given it some leverage in policy debates.[20] Public appreciation for this trend is evidenced by the increased volume of constituent letters written to NPC delegates.[21]

## The Executive Branch

The three principal positions in the Chinese government are the chairman of the CCP, the prime minister of the country, and the head of the Chinese Army. These positions are frequently held by the same person. Jiang Zemin held the positions into the early 2000s. In 2002 Hu Jintao replaced Jiang as head of the CCP and in 2003 replaced him as prime minister. Jiang remained as chairman of the Central Military Commission, that is, head of the Chinese Army, a position he had held since the Tiananmen Square massacre. Hu replaced him as chairman of the Central Military Commission in 2004.

China's paramount executive body is the State Council, which is headed by the prime minister and serves as China's cabinet. The State Council is composed of about 100 people, including the prime minister, several vice presidents, and ministers and vice ministers of all major ministries and commissions. Like most deliberative groups in Chinese government, much of the State Council's day-to-day responsibilities are delegated to a Standing Committee. This committee consists of about 15 of the council's highest-ranking members and meets roughly every 2 weeks.

The State Council presides over dozens of commissions, which coordinate policies functionally across specific ministries. Commissions correspond roughly to departments in the U.S. executive branch; the National Defense Commission, for example, is analogous to the Department of Defense. Sometimes referred to as the "little State Council," the State Planning Commission (SPC) is perhaps the most powerful commission in the PRC. As its name suggests, the SPC is charged with overseeing China's vast planned economy. The magnitude of that task has resulted in SPC alumni being well represented in the Politburo. The decline of the planned sector relative to the private sector has reduced the SPC's authority, and the State Council's current formal delineation of its responsibilities reflects this. Nevertheless, the commission's ability to formulate plans; set macroeconomic targets and prices; regulate finance, credit, and currencies; and approve major capital construction projects makes it extremely powerful.[22]

Below the commissions stand the provinces and ministries. Each of the 22 provinces holds ministerial rank, as do some of China's largest cities (Beijing, Tianjin, Shanghai, and Chongqing). Ministries have more specific jurisdictions than commissions and often find themselves subject to oversight from many commissions. An important exception is the Ministry of Finance, which is the most powerful ministry and informally holds commission rank in the State Council hierarchy. Ministers are typically high-ranking party officials, and departments within ministries are staffed by contingents of party cadres to ensure compliance with CCP directives.

Each national-level commission or ministry is the head of a hierarchy, or *xitong*, of local offices that perform the same role for the corresponding local government. A *xitong* generally is under the informal control of a *kou*. A provincial government's Education Commission is therefore a branch of the State Education Commission.

[20]Christiansen and Rai (1996, pp. 106–107).
[21]See Pei (1997).
[22]See Wang and Fewsmith (1995) for a discussion of the SPC's political strategies.

*Xitongs* are known for protecting institutional turf. Very little information is shared across hierarchies, and the incentives for vertical integration are strong. Many *xitongs* own companies and operate colleges to satisfy funding and personnel needs. In response, the reform-era CCP leadership has become increasingly active in reorganizing and abolishing ministries, as well as strengthening interdepartmental professional organizations. For example, the Ministry of Power and Water Conservancy was broken up to fragment opposition to the Three Gorges Dam project.[23]

### The Judicial Branch

China has no tradition of an independent judiciary, and its highest court, the Supreme People's Court, has long been little more than a reflection of the CCP. There is no judicial review process in China. Likewise, the Supreme People's Procurator has little ability to pursue cases on its own initiative. Nevertheless, the emphasis of Deng's reforms on a stable and predictable legal environment has resulted in a growing role for the national judiciary. Citizens have increasingly turned to the courts to resolve disputes.

## Provincial and Local Governments

The governments and party organizations at the provincial, county, and city levels essentially mirror those at the national level. The highest state institution at each level is the People's Congress, a legislative body that has formal, but often weak, authority over the executive branch, the People's Government. Many representatives to People's Congresses are elected by popular vote at the county and township levels. The general devolution of fiscal authority to the provinces (as well as lower levels of the state hierarchy) has made local governments more attractive as targets of interest group activity.

Most provinces share their revenues with the central government according to a fixed formula that is renegotiated periodically. These formulas typically allow the provinces to keep a certain proportion of the earnings of provincial enterprises. Across China, lower levels of government also work under similar financial arrangements. As a result, local governments exercise a large amount of budget and taxation authority and frequently are the locus of bargaining with private interests. Village governments, for example, can offer a prospective enterprise favorable tax treatment in exchange for taking on extra workers to alleviate local unemployment.[24]

## Business: State-Owned Enterprises, Investment, and International Trade

### State-Owned Enterprises

The SOE is a unique entity that represents the single most important type of company in China in terms of employment as well as in problems for the country. The SOEs are not the future of the Chinese economy, however, nor have they been responsible for China's growth in the reform era. Economic growth has been fueled on the demand side by both domestic and export demand and on the supply side by foreign direct investment and local companies formed by entrepreneurs and local governments. Strong economic growth has been essential for China, since growth absorbed the

[23]Christiansen and Rai (1996, pp. 111–114).
[24]Christiansen and Rai (1996, pp. 232–233).

unemployed as SOEs were forced to improve their efficiency, China has privatized many of the SOEs, but the government still owns an average of 60 percent of all the companies listed on the Shanghi and Shenghen stock exchanges.

Most of China's largest firms are SOEs, and these enterprises employed over 112 million people, or 65 percent of the urban workforce. SOEs accounted for a third of industrial output in 1996, down from 55 percent in 1990 as other types of firms have steadily gained prominence in the economy.[25] Private enterprises have flourished in the reform era, although their role in industrial production remains relatively small. In between the SOEs and private enterprises are the urban collectives, which employed 33 million in 1994. Large urban collectives resemble SOEs in most respects, whereas small ones are run as local profit-sharing firms. Finally, joint ventures between SOEs and private or foreign firms are common. SOEs technically do not exist in rural areas, where private and collective firms have thrived in response to agricultural policy liberalization and a general lack of regulation. Although they tend to be individually quite small, rural enterprises were estimated to employ well over 100 million in 1994.

The labor policies of the SOEs were the heart of the socialist economic system and gave SOEs a distinctive dual purpose. In addition to production, SOEs were the primary providers of social services in the urban economy. They provided virtually all the major social services required by employees, their families, and retirees, including education, health care, and housing. Moreover, because many goods such as housing and food staples were rationed, workers could only receive necessities through enterprise-issued coupons. This set of services essentially served as China's social welfare system and became known as the "iron rice bowl." A major constraint on the Chinese government's willingness to take strong measures to reform SOEs has been the lack of social security and welfare systems for its citizens.

National plans promulgated by the State Planning Commission specified prices and production targets for national-level SOEs as well as for each province. In their rush to develop industry, planners set artificially low prices for inputs, including investment capital, and artificially high prices for outputs. In effect, agriculture subsidized industry, but instead of spurring industrial development, the subsidy became a permanent entitlement to the SOEs.[26] As a result, SOEs were inefficient and had little incentive to invest and innovate. Moreover, the social welfare role of SOEs made it difficult for managers to dismiss poorly performing employees.

Since the late 1970s, SOE reform has been a constant priority for Chinese leaders. Managers have been given more authority to evaluate employees, and the emergence of the private sector has allowed many SOEs to shed some excess labor.[27] Enterprises were permitted to retain profits, which were taxed by the state. The deregulation of prices and increasing competition from private, foreign, and rural industries increasingly exposed SOEs to market discipline. Subsidies provided to SOEs accounted for 21 percent of China's budget in 1989, but by 1996 subsidies accounted for only 4 percent of the budget as the state reduced its support.

Despite these changes, much of the system, and its dual role and chronic inefficiencies, remained intact at the beginning of the new century. SOEs were still losing money, underutilizing capacity, and consuming much of the country's available capital. The Chinese government ceased using its budget to subsidize SOEs, but in its place the state-run banks made "policy loans" to many of the SOEs. These, however, were more

[25]See Lardy (1998) for an analysis of SOEs.
[26]Christiansen and Rai (1996, p. 199). This phenomenon was commonly known as "price scissors," or the "scissor's gap."
[27]See Groves et al. (1994, 1995) for studies of incentives and the managerial labor market in SOEs.

in the form of subsidy than loans, and expectations were that the loans would never be repaid. These loans were in large part the cause of the financial difficulties of the state banks. The government planned to retain many of the larger and more competitive SOEs, but the remainder were to be sold, merged, privatized, or closed. The chapter case, *Wugang and the Reform of State-Owned Enterprises*, provides an example of the reform challenge.

# Foreign Direct Investment
## Joint Venture Policy

One cornerstone of Deng's liberalizations was the Central Committee's July 1979 decision to establish four Special Economic Zones (SEZs).[28] As a result of this liberalization, foreign direct investment (FDI) and joint ventures in the PRC skyrocketed, with over 100,000 in operation in the mid-1990s.[29] For example, in the chapter case, *Direct Selling in China*, Amway's plant in Guangzhou was a joint venture with a government development agency. Express companies such as UPS, FedEx, and DHL were required to have a Chinese partner.

Among the several forms of joint ventures, the most important is the equity joint venture (EJV). EJVs are limited liability companies in which the Chinese and foreign partners both manage day-to-day operations and divide the risk in direct proportion to their capital contributions to the project. Contractual (or cooperative) joint ventures (CJVs) divide risks by contract rather than by capital contribution. These arrangements permit greater flexibility for parties in allocating responsibilities. Such ventures are often riskier, however, because China's legal system is not well equipped to deal with contractual disputes between partners. CJVs were once quite popular but have declined in importance.

The third joint venture type is the wholly foreign-owned enterprise (WFOE). These give the foreign firm the greatest control and the greatest risk. The 1990 Law on Wholly Foreign-Owned Enterprises prohibited them from operating in markets such as media, insurance, and communications and restricted their activities in public utilities and real estate. Article 3 of the law permits WFOEs if they (1) are technologically advanced and (2) export most of their production. Large Western firms such as Motorola, 3M, and Shell have entered China as WFOEs because they provided the best protection from being forced to share sensitive technology.[30] Beijing realized that the autonomy offered to such enterprises was necessary for attracting export-oriented, high-technology firms that could help develop the Chinese economy, and as a result WFOEs have been the fastest-growing segment of the FDI.

As China joined the WTO, FDI was expected to reach $60 billion in 2004. WTO membership required China to open its markets to foreign firms, although the opening was gradual. Major industries including banking, insurance, telecommunication, and agriculture were to be opened.

## Government Institutions Involved in Joint Ventures

Foreign companies interested in investing in China must deal with progressively higher levels of government as the size of the project increases. The largest projects must receive national-level approval from the Leading Group on Foreign Investment (LGFI), a State Council body that creates FDI legislation and coordinates the foreign

[28]Grub and Lin (1991, p. 65).
[29]See Urata (2001) for a study of European FDI in China.
[30]Grub and Lin (1991, Chs. 4–5, Appendix 3).

investment policies of 11 national ministries. Additionally, state-run corporations, such as the China International Trust and Investment Corporation and other trust and investment corporations, play important roles through financial guarantees, financing, and currency swaps.

Local governments, both provincial and city, have parallel institutions (Foreign Economic Relations and Trade Commissions, or FERTCs) that have varying degrees of authority in approving projects. The largest cities, such as Beijing and Shanghai, which hold provincial rank in the national hierarchy, can approve large projects on their own, and after the 1983 Implementing Regulations small cities were allowed to approve projects valued at less than $5 million.[31] Like the LGFI and its associated agencies, FERTCs examine proposals for legality and feasibility as well as conformance with policies of the local government's other agencies. FERTCs are still responsible for most of the day-to-day regulation of joint ventures in their geographical jurisdiction, regardless of their size.[32]

## Regulation

Regulation in China is established through the ministries and commissions and through agencies associated with the State Council. Many of the regulations pertain to the same issues as in more developed countries. An example is fuel economy standards. China's automobile market boomed in the 2000s and became the third largest in the world behind the United States and Japan. As incomes grew Chinese consumers bought larger vehicles, and SUVs became popular. Economic growth and increased driving made China more dependent on imported oil and also pushed up the price of oil. To address the dependence on foreign oil, China issued fuel economy standards.

The standards were developed over more than 2 years and did not involve public inputs, although Volkswagen, which had a quarter of the market in China, was consulted. The standards, which had been developed by the Automotive Technology and Research Center, were issued by the State Council. A fuel tax, which would be the most effective means of reducing fuel use, was considered but rejected because of concerns about public anger and adding to inflation. Three basic types of fuel economy standards were used in other countries. The European Union had a voluntary program, Japan had standards for each model, and the United States had a corporate average system.[33] China chose a weight-based system for automobiles, vans, and SUVs. The standards did not apply to pickup trucks, which are primarily used by business in China. The standards, which were somewhat higher than in the United States, took effect in 2005 and were scheduled to increase in 2008. Automakers complained that the substandard gasoline sold throughout the country interfered with new technologies for achieving higher fuel economy.

## International Trade Policy and WTO Membership

In the pre-reform era trade increased substantially, but trade policies remained essentially the same. All trade had to be approved by the Ministry of Foreign Economic Relations and Trade (MOFERT), and imported items were marketed directly by the

[31]Pearson (1991, p. 109).
[32]Grub and Lin (1991, Ch. 6).
[33]See the Part II integrative case *CAFE Standards 2002*.

cognizant state-owned firm. Deng's reforms and the open-door policy allowed China a wide range of international finance arrangements, including direct loans, export credits, and development assistance from foreign governments. In 1980 China joined the International Monetary Fund and World Bank, which gave it access to loans and other development aid.

During the 1980s MOFERT's institutional monopoly was broken, and much of its authority was delegated to provincial and municipal governments, other ministries, and SOEs. In many cases these entities were also allowed to "profit" from the trade. This devolution of authority substantially lowered the obstacles faced by foreign importers and exporters, who could now negotiate with local officials instead of working through a large, monopolistic national bureaucracy.

Trade policy became one of the primary concerns of China's international relations in the 1990s. The PRC's application for membership in the WTO was a protracted and contentious issue. Many advanced industrialized nations, particularly the European Union and the United States, insisted that China open its markets further to foreign businesses as a condition for membership. Beijing resisted many market-opening initiatives because of worries about social instability caused by workers laid off from uncompetitive SOEs.

The United States is China's second-largest trading partner after Japan. The large U.S. trade deficit with China aroused animosity from some American policymakers and drew attention to PRC trade practices, including inadequate protection of intellectual property rights. Concerns over Chinese domestic policies and human rights abuses blocked WTO membership. After nearly 15 years of negotiations China was admitted to the WTO at the end of 2001.[34] During that period China made many domestic reforms to qualify for membership, and it was forced to make important changes in its foreign trade policies. It pledged to lower tariffs, reduce import quotas, open markets to imports, and open industries such as telecommunications and banking to FDI. In addition, companies, such as the express companies, were no longer required to operate through joint ventures with a Chinese company. China also agreed to reduce by 40 percent its tariffs, which averaged 15 percent. Foreign banks would be allowed to have wholly-owned subsidiaries and branches and to accept deposits. China was also required to improve its legal system, which in the late 1990s had become independent of the other parts of the government.

Market opening resulted in continuing nonmarket issues at the level of industries as well as a set of societal-level problems. Domestic firms resisted the opening of their markets to imports and FDI. Retailers had been restricted to selling only products made in China, but as a result of WTO membership they were, after a transition period, allowed to sell imported goods. At the societal level reductions in tariffs on agricultural imports threatened farmers, and those imports were expected to increase the already high unemployment in rural provinces. More than 100 million migrant workers had moved to cities seeking employment, and millions more would follow. Coupled with the competitive pressures on SOEs, China faced the challenge of developing social welfare programs to meet the needs of the unemployed and those harmed by the reforms.

China began to train judges to handle trade cases and established a WTO Department to develop policies for implementing WTO requirements. The *Direct Selling in China* case involves an opportunity to use WTO membership to overcome a directive barring the principal component of the direct sellers' business model.

---

[34]Two days later Taiwan was admitted to the WTO.

# Continuing Issues

## Human Rights and Political Reform

The issue of human rights in China became internationalized in the 1990s. Foreign governments as well as human rights groups targeted China as a major abuser of human rights. International concern focused on four areas.[35] First, China's criminal justice system was said to allow arbitrary imposition of the death penalty, the torture of prisoners, detention without trial, and the use of prison labor in industrial production. Second, China was accused of persecution of ethnic (primarily Tibetan) and religious (primarily Christian) minorities. Third, Beijing had little tolerance for political dissidents and held many political prisoners. Finally, critics argued that the condition of Chinese women had deteriorated despite the advances in gender equality made during the communist era. Beijing often dismissed these complaints as interference in domestic affairs.

China was alleged to engage in the harvesting of human organs primarily from executed prisoners. Surgery was often coordinated with executions, and a number of military and other hospitals were said to run a business of providing transplants to foreigners.[36] The chapter case, *Fresenius Medical Care in China*, considers a company that suspected that its dialysis center in China was used in the transplant business.

Several long-standing practices continued to provoke complaints and posed problems for companies. To control its population growth, China unofficially adopted a one-child-per-family policy with birth targets for each province. The average number of children per woman decreased from nearly six in 1970 to less than two in 2000. Responsibility for administering the policy rested with employers and local governments. To have a child, an employee of an SOE had to obtain permission in advance from the enterprise's family planning office as well as from the neighborhood family planning committee. Women who had more that one child were fined and in some cases a relative's house would be torn down as punishment. Forced sterilization was used in some cases. These measures were a continuing source of conflict between citizens and the government. Because of the problems associated with administering the policy, some local governments relaxed the policy, allowing two children or allowing a second child if the first was a girl. Beijing began studying population issues to determine if it would have enough workers to support an aging population.

Some Chinese preferred male to female children. The national ratio of male to female births was 117 to 100 and was believed to be due to selective abortions made possible by advances in ultrasound technology. The one-child-per-family policy along with the preference for boys was blamed for both the selective abortions and for female infanticide. The Chapter 18 case, *Advanced Technology Laboratories, Inc.*, addresses this issue in India.

In 1997 the U.S. Department of State prepared a report on the persecution of Christians in 78 countries and criticized China for the suppression of religious freedom. A year later Chinese police cracked down on "house churches" run by evangelical Protestants who refused to register with the government and worship in state-sponsored churches. China also cracked down on the spiritual Falun Gong movement.

In 1998 China signed the International Covenant on Civil and Political Rights and released the imprisoned leader of the Tiananmen Square democracy demonstrations. Although some elections have been held at the local level, the CCP has maintained

---

[35]See Levine (1997) for a summary of human rights concerns in China. The U.S. State Department's *Annual Country Reports on Human Rights Practices* identifies specific abuses and discusses trends in their occurrence.
[36]See *The New York Times*, October 18, 2001.

itself as the sole political party in China. When a group of democracy supporters formed the China Democratic Party in November 1998, the government arrested party leaders, including three of the most prominent dissidents remaining in the country. The three were sentenced to between 11 and 13 years in prison. Some observers feared that since he had consolidated his political power, Prime Minister Hu was beginning to suppress political criticism of the government and social conditions in China.

Despite the human rights abuses and political restrictions, Chinese citizens enjoyed greater freedoms than at any time since the communists gained control of the country. Much of the improvement resulted from growing economic prosperity that had given people the means to exercise more control over their lives. In addition, the accumulation of personal property led people to attempt to protect it, resulting in greater use of the courts. Moreover, with the widespread use of computers, faxes, and mobile telephones, information was more readily available and actions could be coordinated. This inevitably led to pressure for greater freedoms and a more responsive government, but democracy was not on the immediate horizon. International pressure on China decreased because of both its economic prowess and its role in dealing with the nuclear weapons crisis in North Korea.

## Piracy of Intellectual Property

A major concern of firms has been the piracy of intellectual property. Copies of compact discs, videotapes, and books often appeared on Chinese street corners before they were available in stores in the United States. Even the CCP had been a victim of piracy. The party sponsored production of an anticorruption movie, and prior to its release pirated copies were being shown in Chinese state-owned cinemas.[37] The U.S.-based Business Software Alliance estimated that in 2000, 91 percent of the software in China was pirated. One reason it was difficult to stop the pirating of intellectual property was that local officials were said to support it. The pirating companies paid local taxes and more importantly provided badly needed jobs.

Chinese joint venture partners have set up competing companies with technology taken from their foreign partners.[38] Many foreign joint venture partners complained to their home countries and began to take their cases to China's courts. The earlier excerpt from Li provides one perspective on the role of the courts in such matters. The example illustrates a case of piracy taken to the U.S. courts.

In some cases the piracy appeared to be legal. For example, patents and proprietary pharmaceutical formulas can receive administrative protection in China, but first an open and lengthy public comment period was required in which drug patents were available for inspection. Chinese pharmaceutical companies could inspect the patent filings and immediately file for permission to produce and market the drug. If the application was approved before the patent received administrative protection, the local company could sell its knockoff drug. For example, a Chinese pharmaceutical company received approval to produce Eli Lilly's Prozac before the patent had been protected. The company beat Eli Lilly to market with its drug. Eli Lilly sued in court, but lost at the lower court level. The deputy director of the Chinese company said, "Eli Lilly's effort against us can't possibly lead to any positive result, as any resolution must have a legal basis. And everything we have done is in perfect conformity with the law."[39] China's patent office also overrode Pfizer's patent on Viagra.

[37]*The New York Times*, October 5, 2000.
[38]See *Business Week*, October 6, 1997, for examples.
[39]*The Wall Street Journal*, March 25, 1998.

**EXAMPLE**

## An Intellectual Property Challenge

Huawei Technologies, located in Shenzhen, was founded in 1988 and by 2004 had 22,000 employees and sales of over $4 billion. Huawei manufactured telecommunications equipment and had begun producing routers and servers. Huawei told customers that the commands for its router were similar to those for routers made by Cisco Systems, and Cisco believed that Huawei had copied its software. Cisco engineers found many lines of Huawei code identical to its code, including spelling errors and other Cisco glitches. Huawei's manual also included paragraphs copied from Cisco's manual.[1]

Cisco wrote to Huawei, which immediately withdrew its router from the U.S. market, but continued to sell it outside the United States. Cisco followed with a lawsuit alleging copyright violation. This was the first intellectual property lawsuit ever filed by Cisco, which commented, "We don't go around suing people."[2] Huawei stated in court filings that it had copied the code but stated that it was unintentional and had not believed it was copyrighted. A federal court issued a preliminary injunction against Huawei ordering it to stop immediately "using, importing, exporting or selling" any software system using the Cisco code. A Huawei spokesperson stated, "Before Cisco initiated its legal action against Huawei, the company had already taken good-faith, voluntary action to proactively remove from the U.S. market the obsolete products outlined in the injunction." Huawei commented that the court order was immaterial because it was unenforceable outside the United States.

[1] Cisco also believed that Huawei had copied source code from its network operating system.

[2] *San Jose Mercury News*, January 24, 2003.

---

In 2004 the United States began a Strategy Targeting Organized Piracy (STOP) initiative. STOP was the result of increasing complaints by business about piracy, particularly in China. The U.S. Chamber of Commerce stated that there was no enforcement of intellectual property and warned that investor confidence in China could be threatened by piracy and counterfeiting, which had worsened in part due to the Internet. One strategy to be used was "name and shame." The United States planned to name publicly foreign companies that produced fake goods. The United States joined with the European Union and Japan in pressing China to stop the piracy.

### Corruption

Corruption increased during the 1990s as economic activity grew. Transparency International ranked China tied for 66 among 133 countries in its 2003 corruption perception index. Citizens protested the corruption, and the evident corruption reached the point at which the CCP became concerned that it would undermine confidence in the government and the party. One form of corruption was smuggling.

In the face of cutbacks in military spending during the 1980s, Prime Minister Deng Xiaoping encouraged the People's Liberation Army (PLA) to establish businesses to provide it with earnings to offset the budget cuts. By the end of the 1990s the PLA operated an estimated 15,000 businesses providing several billion dollars annually to the PLA. The PLA was also heavily involved in smuggling, particularly through naval ports, which allowed it to bring in large items such as automobiles and steel. China estimated it lost $10 billion a year in tariff revenues due to smuggling. More than 100,000 automobiles were believed to have been smuggled into the country in 1997. In 1998

Prime Minister Jiang Zemin, who as head of the CCP's Central Military Command was the Commander in Chief of the PLA, ordered the military to cease commercial activity and focus on military preparedness.

Smuggling was more widespread, however. In 2000 a major smuggling ring involving government and party officials and a private company was exposed in the port of Xiamen. The ring was believed to have smuggled $10 billion of goods into the country. Fourteen people in the ring were sentenced to death.[40] As a result of the crackdown on smuggling, tariff revenue was said to have increased substantially.

Corruption was present at all levels of the government. For example, farmers protested that local governments took their land for industrial development. The farmers complained that the government paid too little, promised jobs that never materialized, and sold the land at a large profit. Local governments also took independently owned oil wells and paid only a fifth the value, according to the former owners. The Chinese central government sought to stop corruption, but uprooting it proved difficult.

## Commitment

One concern in a nondemocratic country such as China has been commitment to policies. In democracies, changes in policy are often difficult to achieve because of due process, institutional checks and balances, and the effects of changes on future elections. In a country in which the only political party dominates all the government institutions, policies can be quickly changed. In the last months of 1998, for example, China acted to shore up its weakening domestic economy. It ordered its state-owned telecommunications companies to buy domestic rather than imported equipment. It also put off indefinitely its stated intention to break up its national telecommunications monopoly China Telecom and prohibited Chinese-Chinese-foreign joint ventures such as that used by Sprint to invest in the telecommunications industry. When the government decided to sell shares in China Unicom, a mobile phone company, it dissolved 40 partnerships including one with Sprint. The chapter case, *Direct Selling in China,* concerns companies attempting to deal with a sudden policy change.

During the Asian financial crisis China promised not to devalue its currency to compete with the devaluations of other Asian countries. It authorized, however, rebates of export taxes on goods that competed with those of its neighbors. To curb deflation China imposed price floors in an attempt to stabilize 21 industries. Smuggling and overcapacity were blamed for the deflation. The State Economic and Trade Commission imposed minimum prices on the 13 largest automobile manufacturers in China. The U.S. undersecretary of commerce commented, "The list of [trade] barriers is just getting bigger and we're not crossing anything off the list."[41] WTO membership required China to stop such arbitrary changes in its policies. At the end of 2004, however, it suspended foreign joint ventures in the tobacco industry because of "surplus cigarette-producing capacity."

## Summary

China provides tremendous business opportunities yet poses a host of problems, particularly in the nonmarket environment. China has no democratic tradition, and its Confucian heritage provides a degree of deference for hierarchical authority. It also has a long history as a unified nation and a willingness to assert and defend its independence. China has been building a modern economy that requires foreign direct

---

[40]See *The Wall Street Journal,* November 23, 2001.
[41]*The New York Times,* September 23, 1998.

investment and reform of its state-owned enterprises. Economic progress enabled people to have better control over their lives and generated pressure for political and economic liberalization. The Chinese Communist Party, however, dominated government at every level. Political competition was not tolerated, and human rights were restricted. The government was thus not responsive to interests in the same sense as in a Western democracy. In some ways this simplified the nonmarket environment because of the lack of activist and organized interest groups to monitor business activity. The government was sensitive to the possibility of popular dissent arising from economic dislocations and dissatisfaction with government performance, as in the case of corruption. Despite the limitations, Chinese citizens enjoyed greater liberty than at any time in the postwar period.

The nonmarket environment was important not only because of the government and party involvement in business but also because of issues pertaining to human rights, trade policy, and civil liberties. The nonmarket environment was structured by the hierarchical nature of government that persisted despite the devolution of authority to provincial and local governments. Since the government was not checked by opposition parties, elections, or interest or activist groups, some policies could be changed quickly, raising concerns about the credibility of commitments. Furthermore, the judicial system did not provide the protection available in other countries. The importance of *guanxi* networks, not only between companies but also between business and government, complicated strategies of those companies new to China. Joint ventures with domestic companies, most of which were enterprises owned by national, provincial, or local government units, could also provide the *guanxi* networks and access needed to address nonmarket issues. Joint ventures, however, posed their own set of problems.

# Wugang and the Reform of State-Owned Enterprises

The Wuhan Iron and Steel Company, also known as Wugang, was typical of Chinese state-owned enterprises (SOEs) and the problems surrounding their reform. Located in the large industrial city of Wuhan nearly 400 miles up the Yangtze River from Shanghai, Wugang was the first of many massive ironworks built after the Chinese revolution. The $2 billion enterprise had many of the characteristics of a medium-size city. The facility occupied 6.5 square miles and employed 120,000 workers. Most of the employees, plus their families and 30,000 retirees, lived in company-provided housing. The company also operated 31 schools, three polytechnic institutes, three universities, and two hospitals.

Built with Soviet technology, Wugang opened in September 1958 at the beginning of Mao's "Great Leap Forward," a crash effort that was to have brought China's industrial output up to par with Western Europe. As a national-level SOE, all inputs and outputs were determined by economic plans. The State Planning Commission and Ministry of Metallurgical Industry specified its prices and production targets, and the Labor Administration Bureau assigned workers to the enterprise, most of whom were guaranteed by the *danwei* system to remain there for life. Like other national-level SOEs, Wugang played a crucial dual role in the socialist economy. In addition to industrial production, Wugang was the exclusive provider of housing, food, medicine, and other social services to its employees, their families, and retirees. This system, known as the "iron rice bowl," resulted in a high level of vertical integration within the enterprise.

The Chinese steel industry began with high expectations, but three factors combined to undermine its productivity during the 1960s and 1970s. First, the social welfare role of the enterprise robbed its management of labor flexibility. In the 1960s

SOEs generally became overstaffed as central planners reacted to the oversupply of urban youths by assigning them to SOEs, and managers were unable to dismiss poorly performing employees. Second, in their rush to industrialize, planners had set artificially low prices for inputs and artificially high prices for outputs, effectively creating an industry-wide subsidy that led to inefficiency and weak incentives to invest and innovate. Individual plant managers also had little discretion in investments because profits were taxed at high rates and redistributed by government authorities.[42] Finally, the international isolation that China faced between 1960 and 1980 had cut off foreign investment, technology, and expertise, as well as potential export markets.

By the end of the 1990s the steel industry employed 2 million workers and accounted for 3 percent of China's industrial output by value. Wugang was one of the nation's four largest steel companies, with an annual production capacity of 6 million tons. These four companies accounted for about a third of China's steel production in 1996.[43] After the Baoshan Iron and Steel Corporation (Baogang), Wugang was the second-most profitable steel company in China, earning an $84 million profit in 1996. Although this was expected to drop to $24 million in 1997, Wugang's performance had been fairly good compared with most SOEs. By comparison, Angang, China's largest steel firm, was suffering huge losses.

[42]Because prices were centrally set, profits were in some sense illusory. A ministry in charge of an industry could redistribute funds from profitable to unprofitable enterprises, and it could also require expenditures on items not directly related to the enterprise's production (for instance, social services).

[43]These four companies each produced over 5 million tons per year. There were also 25 companies that produced between 1 and 5 million tons annually. Because many smaller companies were expected to close as a result of restructuring, the four largest SOEs were expected to account for 40 percent of total production by 2005. Sources: *South China Morning Post*, September 19, 1997, and *China Economic Review*, April 1998.

Wugang's primary asset was its specialization in high value-added products. The company manufactured extra-wide and heavy carbon structural plate, alloy structural plate, low-alloy high-strength plate, boiler and vessel plate, ship and offshore oil platform plate, and mould-making plate. It was also the only Chinese supplier of international-quality, cold rolled silicon steel sheets—a highly ductile type of plate. Its production processes had received certification from numerous international bodies, and its quality assurance system met ISO 9000 standards. Yet the company faced serious challenges.

Wugang's productivity, measured by tons of output per employee, was less than a fifth of those of the leading Asian firms.[44] Steel prices in China were declining, partially in response to imports from the former Soviet republics and South Korea, whose currency suffered a steep devaluation in 1997. At the same time, the cost of domestic inputs, such as energy and transportation, had risen substantially in 1997.

## SOE Reform: National and Local Strategies

As China's economic reforms progressed in the 1990s, the leadership in Beijing realized that despite their valuable social welfare role, SOEs were increasingly becoming an obstacle to the creation of a modern economy. The SOE sector employed 100 million people and accounted for nearly half of China's industrial output in the early 1990s, yet few enterprises were profitable, and even successful SOEs were often hopelessly inefficient by international standards. Since the inception of market-based reforms in the 1970s, Beijing had cautiously increased the discretion of SOE managers while also increasing their exposure to market forces. However, party leaders at the Fifteenth Party Congress in September 1997 agreed that more radical reforms would be necessary to prevent the financial collapse of such a large part of the Chinese economy.

While the government did not specify many details, it intended to privatize the vast majority of the over 300,000 SOEs by selling shares in the companies. These changes were expected to affect over 10,000 of the 13,000 largest SOEs, but Beijing would continue to own and support many of the largest enterprises, such as Wugang. There were three principal reasons for continuing to support large SOEs.

First, since privatization was expected to result in widespread plant closings and layoffs, Beijing wanted to avoid broad social unrest. Because of the SOE system, China had never developed a social welfare system, and despite a few pilot programs for worker retraining and social pensions, a comprehensive safety net was still years away. Second, Beijing hoped that its larger enterprises could duplicate the past success of large, government-favored industrial conglomerates such as the South Korean chaebol. This analogy proved worrisome as it had become increasingly evident that the chaebol were responsible in part for serious structural deficiencies in Korea's economy. Finally, the retention of some central control was necessary to placate conservatives within the Communist party.[45]

Unfortunately for Wugang's president, Liu Benren, continued government intervention deprived him of the autonomy to undertake cost-cutting methods that were commonly available to firms in other countries. Liu had little authority to reduce his vastly oversized labor force because the Wuhan city government would not permit the city's largest corporate employer to add to the growing unemployment problem. Like other official unemployment statistics across China, Wuhan's official unemployment rate was modest but unofficially was estimated to be as high as 26 percent. Many of the company's activities remained constrained by Beijing, even though in early 1998 steel was removed from the list of products subject to state-planned production targets. As part of the program adopted by the Fifteenth Party Congress, Beijing aided Wugang by facilitating its effort to go public and list its stock on domestic stock exchanges, but it also required the company to merge with smaller steel companies as a condition for doing so.[46] Wugang complied by announcing a merger with two smaller firms, the Daye Steel Group and the Ercheng Iron & Steel Group, in November 1997.[47] In 1998 it acquired the financially troubled Xiangfan Iron and Steel Group.

Liu was able to take some initiatives on his own to address Wugang's problems. For a number of years, he had pursued a foreign listing on the Hong Kong Stock Exchange. Despite the fact that the company was only listing its relatively profitable, cold rolled silicon steel unit, the offering was continually

---

[44] *China Economic Review*, April 1998.

[45] *The New York Times*, September 12, 1997, and *Business Week*, September 29, 1997.
[46] *South China Morning Post*, September 19, 1997.
[47] *South China Morning Post*, November 26, 1997.

delayed due to the lack of investor interest in the weak Chinese steel market as well as to the Asian financial crisis.[48] The $200 million listing, underwritten by Merrill Lynch, was finally approved in February 1998 but postponed indefinitely 2 months later due to poor investor response.[49] Beijing was partly responsible for the failure. One reason for the lack of interest was a Chinese law prohibiting companies from pricing shares below the company's net asset value per share.[50]

Wugang's failure in the stock market had not prevented it from exploring other avenues. Liu had aggressively invested in new technology, adding billions of dollars worth of American and Austrian equipment since 1993. With the improved physical plant, the company hoped to increase capacity to 8 million tons by 2000 and expand sales to foreign markets, which accounted for 800,000 tons of its output in 1997. In March 1998 Wugang proposed a merger with Baogang in the hope of creating a single advanced, profitable entity that would reduce overproduction in the Chinese steel market.[51] The combined entity would have been one of the world's 10 largest steel firms, but concerns were raised about the efficiency gains from merging facilities 400 miles apart.[52]

Because of the economic crises in Asia and Russia, China was flooded with cheap steel imports. In response, Wugang initiated antidumping proceedings with the Ministry of Foreign Trade and Economic Cooperation against Russian silicon steel plate exporters.[53] The flood of imports along with overcapacity in China continued to drive steel prices down, and the government responded by banning the construction of any new steel plants until 2000.

Wugang also sought support from the government for more radical reforms. With the support of the State Council, it secured permission to pare its workforce and reduce its dependence on subsidiary workshops that were not part of its core steel business. These "ancillary companies" would be forced to seek outside customers and turn a profit independently of Wugang. Liu hoped that after this process was completed, Wugang would be a leaner, more focused company of only 27,000 employees.[54] This reorganization had helped some of the company's former subunits, such as the Metal Structures Company, which manufactured boilers and furnaces, to become profitable. However, in many cases it had only shifted the tension between social welfare and company efficiency from Wugang to its former subsidiaries.

Some analysts were cautiously optimistic about Wugang's long-term prospects. Part of the optimism, however, stemmed from the strong support the enterprise had received from Beijing. The favorable restructuring plan and technological investments were facilitated by Beijing's unwillingness to allow Wugang—considered one of China's most prestigious steel firms—to fail. It was a measure of the magnitude of the challenges faced by all SOEs that Wugang's viability seemed so uncertain despite this support. ■

SOURCE: This case was written by Michael Ting under the supervision of Professor David P. Baron based on public sources and in part on R. Tomlinson, "A Chinese Giant Forges a Capitalist Soul," *Fortune* (September 29, 1997), pp. 184–192. Copyright © 1998 by the Board of Trustees of the Leland Stanford Junior University. All rights reserved. Reproduced with permission.

## PREPARATION QUESTIONS

1. What social and institutional factors limit Liu Benren's efforts to reform Wugang?
2. What should Wugang do about its social services responsibilities?
3. Should Liu Benren seek complete independence from the Chinese government?

[48]*South China Morning Post*, October 21, 1997, and March 19, 1998.
[49]*South China Morning Post*, February 21, 1998.
[50]*South China Morning Post*, April 1, 1998.
[51]*The New York Times*, March 12, 1998.
[52]*The Wall Street Journal*, March 11, 1998.
[53]*South China Morning Post*, July 14, 1998.
[54]Employment across the industry was scheduled to drop to 500,000 by 2000 and 300,000 by 2005 with many reductions achieved through reorganizations. *China Economic Review*, April 1998.

# Direct Selling in China

With over 1.2 billion people China represented an extremely attractive market for direct sellers such as Amway, Avon Products, Mary Kay Cosmetics, Sara Lee, and Tupperware. Also, in the 1990s the restructuring of state-owned enterprises had reduced workforces, providing an ample supply of people interested in becoming direct sellers, many of whom made door-to-door sales calls. With the Asian and Russian financial crises beginning in 1997 the supply of potential direct sales personnel increased further. In 1995 Amway opened a factory in Guangzhou and began sales in China. By 1997 it had 70,000 independent sales agents in China producing revenue of $178 million.[55] Avon's revenue in China was $75 million.

Companies such as Amway and Avon operated by enlisting independent sales agents who bought product from the company and sold it door-to-door. Amway used its standard business model in China with the exception that all other markets were supplied from U.S. plants. Its sales agents were compensated by their own sales and also were paid for the number of new sales agents they recruited. They also received a commission on the sales of those they recruited as well as those their recruits recruited. The companies operated distribution centers and provided training for their sales agents in both sales techniques and in the company's culture, which emphasized empowerment. Amway had a policy of buying back all unsold product, providing a full refund.

The success of U.S. direct sales companies led to a boom in home-grown direct sales companies selling everything from foot massagers to water beds to elixirs. By 1998 some 20 million Chinese were estimated to be working in direct selling.[56] It was said that 50,000 people had come to Wuhan seeking jobs selling Xingtian Company's foot massaging machine. Some of these companies operated pyramid and Ponzi schemes in which they profited by recruiting sellers and selling them products rather than making sure that products were being purchased by consumers. Other companies duped unsuspecting consumers. In a

---

[55] Amway had 667,000 independent sales representatives worldwide.
[56] In the United States 8.5 million people were engaged in direct selling.

front-page article the *China Daily* said that these companies "have been behaving badly, getting involved in underworld crimes and preying on innocent people through their superstitions."

On April 21, 1998, the State Council published a directive banning all direct sales in the country. The directive stated, "Criminals have used direct selling to set up sects and cults, spread superstition and carry out illegal activities, affecting the country's social stability." The directive expressed concern about the massive sales meetings of direct sellers in which they clapped and chanted to build enthusiasm. The directive also stated that direct selling had attracted people, including teachers, members of the military, and officials of the Chinese Communist Party, who were legally prohibited from such sales activity. The *People's Daily*, the official newspaper of the Chinese Communist Party, justified the State Council's decision: "Due to immature market conditions, inadequate legislation and immature consumer psychology, direct sales have proved unsuitable for China and thus must be resolutely banned." The newspaper also referred to "excessive hugging" at the mass sales meetings held by the direct selling companies.

The State Administration for Industry and Commerce, which was responsible for the distribution industry, asked local officials to enforce the ban and avoid civil disorder. Its director Wang Zhongfu said, "It's necessary to stop the operation of pyramid sales since it has begun to hurt social stability and economic development."[57] Government officials said that if the U.S. direct selling companies established normal retail shops they could stay.

This was not the first time China had addressed direct selling. In 1995 it had suspended all direct sales activity for several months over concerns about the "revival meeting atmosphere" used by some of the companies. Avon was forced to change its credo from "God first" to "Faith first."

Once the State Council had banned direct selling, many independent sales representatives were left with goods they could not sell. Protests occurred when they were unable to obtain refunds from

---

[57] China Business Information Network, May 12, 1998.

companies. According to press reports, 10,000 disgruntled door-to-door salesmen came to the town of Zhangjiajie seeking refunds from a company that made foot massagers, but it had closed its doors. "'It has left me worse than bankrupt,' says Chen, an unemployed steelworker, who has been left with 60 mechanized foot massagers and, now barred from selling them, losses of roughly $4,830."[58] Riots broke out leaving four people dead and 100 injured.

The directive issued by the State Council came as U.S. Trade Representative Charlene Barshefsky was in Beijing making preparations for President Bill Clinton's upcoming state visit. In a news conference in Beijing she stated, "The ban has effectively shut down the legitimate operations of these and other U.S. companies in China. These companies have invested over $120 million in China and provide income to more that 2 million Chinese." She added, "It is a serious matter when the [Chinese] government simply bans the legitimate business of foreign-invested companies. . . . [the ban] goes well beyond China's legitimate need to pursue consumer protection." Wu Yi, China's minister for trade and foreign investment, told her that in addition to consumer protection concerns the direct selling companies were breaking the rule requiring them to sell only goods manufactured in China.

Steve Van Andel, chairman of Amway Asia Pacific, said, "We understand and respect the Chinese government's decision to take additional steps to protect consumers from illegal scams, which have become a more serious social problem in recent months. . . . We have invested over $100 million in China over the past five years and we continue to believe in the long-term business opportunities of this enormous market. . . . While management of Amway China has established strong government relations and is hopeful that discussions with government officials will be successful, it is too early to project the short-term and long-term impact of the directive on our business."[59] Amway and other direct sellers began to evaluate alternatives for restructuring the way they conducted their sales activities.

Richard Holwill, Amway's director of international relations, said, "We're frustrated that this sledgehammer approach gets rid of ours as well as the ones they're really trying to get rid of. 'Shut it down and sort it out later' seems to be the attitude."[60] Holwill also stated, "We don't want to be part of the problem, we want to be part of the solution."

Holwill served as co-chairman of the Asia Task Force of the U.S. Chamber of Commerce and discussed the ban in testimony before the House Ways and Means Committee in June during hearings on renewal of most favored nation status for China. China was also in the process of negotiating entry into the World Trade Organization (WTO). This involved negotiations with the European Union and the United States regarding specific reforms and market openings in China. ∎

SOURCE: This case was written by Professor David P. Baron. Copyright © 1998 by the Board of Trustees of the Leland Stanford Junior University. All rights reserved. Reproduced with permission.

## PREPARATION QUESTIONS

1. Why did China ban direct selling?
2. How might the U.S. direct sales companies restructure their sales activities to satisfy the concerns of the Chinese government? Should they establish retail stores?
3. Should U.S. direct marketers form a coalition or act independently to address this challenge?
4. Should the U.S. companies attempt to enlist the aid of the U.S. government?
5. What nonmarket strategy should the U.S. direct sellers in China adopt?

[58] *The Financial Times*, May 5, 1998.

[59] Amway press release, April 21, 1998.
[60] *Los Angeles Times*, April 24, 1998.

# Fresenius Medical Care in China

Fresenius Medical Care with headquarters in Bad Homburg, Germany, was established in 1996 through the combination of the Dialysis Systems Division of Fresenius AG, a major German pharmaceutical and medical systems producer and distributor, and National Medical Care, a subsidiary of W. R. Grace. Fresenius Medical Care provided dialysis and renal services, dialysis products, and home care. In 1997 it had revenue of $3.3 billion, compared with $3.1 billion in 1996, and profits were $90 million. Fresenius Medical Care's core businesses were dialysis care and sales of dialysis products, representing a total market of $29 billion for dialysis treatment and products. Fresenius Medical Products treated 53,400 patients in the United States and 13,800 outside the United States. "As a result of our focused acquisition programs in the U.S, Europe and Latin America we dramatically improved our strategic position during the last year, and enhanced our continued leadership of the dialysis care industry," said CEO Udo Werlé.

Fresenius Medical Care operated or supplied products in 100 countries. The company had worked to strengthen its market position in the rapidly growing Asian-Pacific and Latin American markets by establishing additional subsidiaries and joint ventures. Fresenius Medical Care viewed Southeast Asia as its next major market for investment. China represented a major market opportunity, and Fresenius had a foothold through a joint venture, the Guangzhou Nanfang NMC Hemodialysis Center, established in 1994 between National Medical Care and a military hospital complex in Guangzhou.

Advanced chronic kidney failure was the irreversible loss of kidney function and required either regular dialysis treatment or a kidney transplant. Dialysis had to be continued indefinitely, whereas a transplant was typically a permanent solution. In the United States in 1995, 200,000 patients received regular dialysis treatment, but only 12,000 received regular kidney transplants. In the absence of a transplant, dialysis was required for the rest of the patient's life. Dialysis had two modes: hemodialysis and peritoneal dialysis. Hemodialysis involved taking the blood outside the body and through a filter or dialyzer to remove waste products and excess water and then returning the blood to the patient. The treatments lasted 3 to 6 hours each, and three treatments a week were typically required. The treatment was often exhausting and difficult. Peritoneal dialysis used a surgically implanted catheter through which a sterile solution was introduced and used the peritoneal, the membrane in the abdominal cavity covering the intestinal organs, as the dialysis membrane. Peritoneal dialysis involved less disruption of daily life than hemodialysis but required a patient to have some residual renal function. Only 15 percent of the worldwide patient population used peritoneal dialysis.

Human rights groups and activists had regularly charged that China sold human organs harvested from executed prisoners, many of whom were sentenced to death for political crimes or for theft or corruption. In fall 1997 ABC *Primetime Live* broadcast a report that a Chinese doctor was advertising human organs in a Chinese-language newspaper in New York with a price of $30,000 for a kidney. The organs were believed to have been harvested from executed prisoners. The FBI sting was arranged by Harry Wu, a woman from Thailand who had received a kidney transplant at the military hospital and had received kidney dialysis at the Nanfang dialysis facility.

In February 1998 in New York the FBI arrested two Chinese government officials who were attempting to sell human organs harvested from executed prisoners. The FBI sting was arranged by Harry Wu, a controversial Chinese dissident living in the United States, who had previously exposed a number of human rights violations. In February 1998 the German magazine *Stern* published an article consistent with the information in the *Primetime Live* report. The Chinese embassy in Washington issued a statement that organs were rarely harvested from executed prisoners and only with their written consent.

Fresenius Medical Care's Nanfang facility was operated by Chinese doctors, and Fresenius had one employee in Hong Kong who monitored the facility. The Nanfang dialysis center was located adjacent to a military organ transplant hospital, and Fresenius's investigation revealed that foreign patients were receiving dialysis treatment at Nanfang for relatively short periods. Patients awaiting transplants required ongoing dialysis. *Stern* quoted a Thai kidney specialist to the effect that no consent forms existed and that prisoners were "simply shot in the head and then disemboweled." *Stern* quoted another Thai kidney specialist, who said, "There would be no kidney transplants in Nanfang Hospital without Fresenius." *Stern* also had information on patients in Asia and the United States who were notified about upcoming executions so that they could travel to China. *Stern* referred to this as "patient tourism" and reported that the going price for a kidney transplant was $40,000. ■

SOURCE: This case was written by Professor David P. Baron. Copyright © 1998 by the Board of Trustees of the Leland Stanford Junior University. All rights reserved. Reproduced with permission.

## PREPARATION QUESTIONS

1. What should Fresenius Medical Care do with regard to the ABC and *Stern* reports?
2. Suppose that the reports were true. What should Fresenius Medical Care do?
3. Should Fresenius Medical Care and Fresenius AG sell medical equipment and supplies to the transplant hospital complex in Guangzhou?

C H A P T E R 17

# The Political Economy of International Trade Policy

## Introduction

International trade policy is the result of economic and political forces. The principal economic force is the gains from trade, which provide the economic rationale for free trade. The principal political force is the benefits that firms, consumers, employees, and suppliers can obtain through favorable trade policies. The present and potential beneficiaries have incentives to adapt nonmarket strategies to protect and increase those benefits.

Since the Smoot-Hawley Act of 1930, which raised tariffs dramatically and contributed to the depth and duration of the depression, the United States and other developed countries have supported reductions in tariffs and other barriers to international trade. In the aftermath of World War II, the reductions in trade barriers were largely the result of U.S. hegemony. As other countries recovered from the war and the U.S. share of international trade declined, the principal mechanism for reductions in trade barriers has been multilateral trade negotiations, most of which have been conducted in the context of the General Agreement on Tariffs and Trade (GATT). In 1995 the World Trade Organization (WTO) was established to encompass GATT and other multilateral agreements. The WTO also provided a continuing forum for addressing trade issues and resolving disputes among nations. In addition, a number of regional trade agreements, such as the North American Free Trade Agreement (NAFTA) and the treaties that established the single market in the European Union, have reduced barriers and increased trade. The United States and other countries also have concluded bilateral agreements to spur trade in services such as air transportation. The result has been a steady, if not uniform, reduction in trade barriers, and the resulting increase in international trade has been dramatic.

Trade policy consists of agreements among countries, domestic laws pertaining to international trade, and procedures for administering those laws and resolving disputes. International trade agreements are the result of bargaining among countries, but the positions from which countries bargain depend on domestic economic considerations and hence on domestic politics. The interactions between international trade

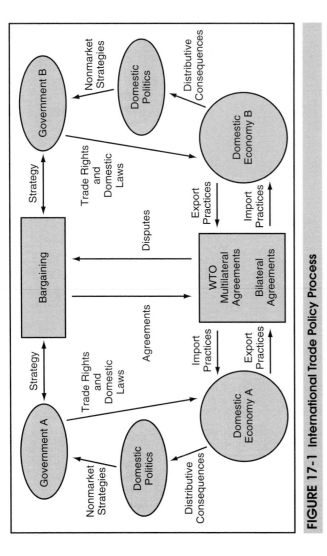

**FIGURE 17-1** International Trade Policy Process

policy and domestic politics are illustrated in Figure 17-1. The international negotiations, shown at the top of the figure, and the agreements reached, shown at the bottom, determine the rules of the game for the export and import practices of firms. The competition between imports and domestic production and the opportunities to trade in world markets provide incentives for interests—firms, employees, suppliers, and consumers—to seek support for exports and/or protection from imports. The opportunities to engage in domestic politics and the rights granted under domestic trade laws allow interests to affect trade policy directly by filing trade petitions as well as indirectly through the bargaining positions of their governments in bilateral and multilateral negotiations. Trade policy thus depends not only on government action but also on the market and nonmarket strategies of private interests. Conversely, international trade policy has important consequences for the market and nonmarket environments of business.

This chapter addresses the political economy of international trade policy, its connection to domestic politics, and the role of business and other interests in those politics. The perspective taken is that the system depicted in Figure 17-1 is animated by the incentives generated in domestic and international markets. Those incentives give rise to nonmarket strategies, implemented in both domestic and international institutional arenas, that shape trade policy. The next section considers the economics of international trade with an emphasis on competitive theory and strategic trade theory. Economic theory does not predict well the actual trade practices of countries, so the following section considers the political economy of international trade policy using the perspective developed in Chapter 6. The chapter also discusses the WTO and the agreements under its purview. The international trade policy of the United States is considered, including an analysis of the political economy of market opening and protectionism, including U.S. efforts to protect the steel industry. Current trade issues are considered, including the agenda for the current Doha Round of WTO multilateral trade negotiations.

# The Economics of International Trade

## Competitive Theory

The competitive theory of international trade is based on the *gains from trade*. Those gains are evident in the case of a country that cannot produce a product that its citizens wish to consume. Gains from trade are also evident when one country can produce a good more efficiently than another country, and the latter country can produce another good more efficiently than can the former country. There are also gains from trade when one country is absolutely more efficient than the other in the production of both goods. That is, even though a country has an absolute disadvantage, gains from trade can be achieved if it produces the good for which it is relatively more efficient and the other country produces the good for which it is relatively more efficient. This result, known as the law of *comparative advantage*, provides the basic rationale for free trade—all countries can gain from trade.

The gains from trade can be demonstrated when two countries either determine the terms of their trade through bargaining or trade goods in a competitive market. Consider two countries, each of which can produce two goods, A and B. The production possibilities of each country are characterized by its resources and the technology it uses to produce the goods. To simplify the analysis, suppose that each country has one resource: 12 units of labor. Country I has a technology that requires 2 units of labor to produce 1 unit of A and 1 unit of labor to produce 1 unit of B. Country II can produce 1 unit of A with 1 unit of labor and 1 unit of B with 2 units of labor. These production possibilities are illustrated in Figure 17-2. As the figure illustrates, Country I is more efficient in the production of good B, and Country II is more efficient in the production of good A.

In the absence of trade, the consumption possibilities of each country are its own production possibilities. That is, Country I can produce and consume 12 units of B and none of A, 6 units of A and none of B, or any linear combination of those two outputs. Each country will produce and consume at the point on its production possibility frontier

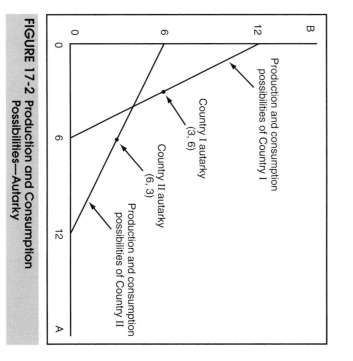

**FIGURE 17-2  Production and Consumption Possibilities—Autarky**

that yields the greatest aggregate well-being of its citizens. To be precise, suppose that the preferences of citizens in each country are identical and that their well-being is measured by the product of the quantities consumed of the two goods. For example, the goods could be bread and butter, and well-being is greatest when there is butter for each loaf of bread. The best combination of consumption is thus an equal amount of each good.

In the absence of trade, referred to as autarky, Country I can do no better than to produce and consume 3 units of A and 6 units of B. Analogously, under autarky Country II will produce and consume 6 units of A and 3 units of B. These autarky points are indicated in Figure 17-2 and correspond to levels of well-being of 18 for each country.

Trade benefits a country by allowing consumption to diverge from production. To illustrate this, Figure 17-3 presents the production and consumption possibilities of Countries I and II when they are able to trade. Gains from trade are possible because trade expands the consumption possibilities of each country beyond those of its own production. That is, both countries can benefit if Country I produces more of good B, for which it has an absolute advantage, and Country II produces more of good A, for which it has an advantage. In this example, Country I will specialize in producing 12 units of good B and none of good A, whereas Country II will produce 12 units of A and none of B. Country I then will export 6 units of B and import 6 units of A. Country II's imports and exports will be the opposite of those of Country I. With the trades indicated in the figures, the resulting consumption in each country is 6 units of A and 6 units of B. The well-being of each country is 36, so both are better off with trade.[1] Both countries gain from trade.

This example illustrates the gains from trade for the case in which Country I is more efficient (has an absolute advantage) in the production of good B and Country II is more efficient (has an absolute advantage) in the production of good A. Even if

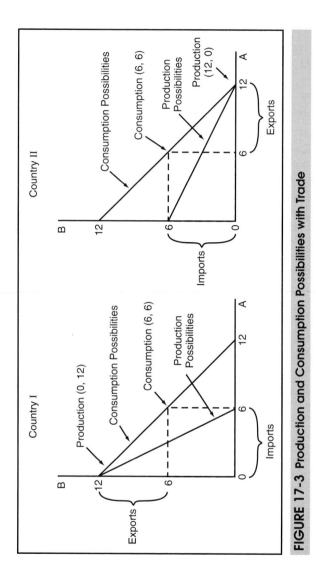

**FIGURE 17-3 Production and Consumption Possibilities with Trade**

[1]This outcome is a competitive market equilibrium in the sense that each country, taking prices as given, produces the quantities of the two goods that maximize its well-being, and each country consumes the quantities it prefers given the prices for the goods. In this example, the price, or rate of exchange, is one unit of A per unit of B. The value of imports thus equals the value of exports for each country.

Country I is absolutely more efficient in the production of both goods, there are gains from trade. To illustrate this, suppose that Country I's technology is the same as above, but Country II's technology requires 3 units of labor to produce 1 unit of A and 4 units of labor to produce 1 unit of B. In the absence of trade, Country II would produce 2 units of A and 1.5 units of B for a level of well-being of 3. Both countries can gain, however, if, for example, Country II produces 4 units of A and no units of B and Country I produces 2 units of A and 8 units of B. Country II then can trade 2 units of A to Country I for 3 units of B.[2] The well-beings of the two countries are then 20 and 6, respectively, compared with 18 and 3 in the absence of trade. This gain is possible because Country II is relatively more efficient in the production of good A than is Country I. That is, the ratio of the number of units of labor required to produce a unit of A and a unit of B is $3 \div 4 = 0.75$ for Country II, whereas the corresponding ratio for Country I is $2 \div 1 = 2$. Country II thus has a comparative advantage in the production of A even though it has an absolute disadvantage in the production of both goods. Gains from trade thus result from comparative advantage.

Gains from trade are also present if there are differences in the relative prices of untraded factor inputs such as labor. That is, if one country has lower wage rates than another, gains can be achieved from trade. The high-wage country can gain by importing labor-intensive goods from the low-wage country and allocating its high-wage labor to the production of goods for which it has a comparative advantage. Consequently, a country such as the United States, with high labor costs, and a country such as China, with low labor costs, can gain by China producing labor-intensive textiles and apparel for export to the United States and the United States producing capital-intensive machinery for export to China. The United States, however, has for decades restricted textile and apparel imports to protect employment in its domestic industries. The gains from trade thus is not a sufficient theory to explain the trade policies of countries. That is, politics can intervene in international trade, as indicated in Figure 17-1. The political dimensions of international trade and trade policy are considered in more detail in a later section.

## Strategic Trade Theory

The theory of comparative advantage is based on the assumption of perfectly competitive markets. Information is assumed to be complete, consumers and producers act as price takers, goods are undifferentiated, and production is characterized by constant returns to scale or by decreasing returns to scale with costless entry and exit. From these assumptions, theories such as the law of comparative advantage demonstrate the gains from trade among open economies. The theory also implies that intervention by governments in perfectly competitive domestic or international markets will reduce aggregate well-being. Competitive theory thus provides a compelling rationale for free trade, and the role of government is thus to join in international efforts to reduce tariff and nontariff barriers to trade.

Economists have also considered whether a nation can gain from a strategic trade policy—that is, intervention to protect domestic industries, subsidize exports, or stimulate demand for domestic goods.[3] These interventions can be beneficial for a country only if one or more of the conditions for perfect competition is not satisfied. Theories of strategic trade policy thus are set in the context of imperfect competition.

[2] Other mutually beneficial trades are also possible. For example, Country I could trade 2 units of A for 2 units of B.

[3] For a nontechnical exposition of these theories, see Krugman (1986, 1990).

As an example, consider the case of an undifferentiated good that is produced by only two firms, one domestic and the other foreign. Suppose they engage in Cournot competition where each firm chooses the quantity it will produce and both sell their quantities in the world market. Because there are only two firms, they each restrict output. Suppose one government subsidizes the production of its domestic firm, thus lowering that firm's marginal cost. This has two effects. First, the lower marginal cost induces the firm to expand its output. Second, as it expands its output, the foreign firm will react by reducing its output. This then allows the subsidized domestic firm to increase its output even more. This second effect is said to be strategic because the subsidization has altered the strategic relationship between the two firms by lowering the cost of one firm. In the new equilibrium, the subsidized firm makes greater profits than it did in the absence of the subsidy. Moreover, even taking into account the cost of the subsidy, subsidization can increase the aggregate well-being of the subsidizing country by expanding output.[4] The European subsidization of Airbus Industrie may be an example of this strategy. Although the subsidization of domestic firms in certain industries could increase well-being, it often does not. For example, the subsidization by the European Union of agricultural exports resulted in large reductions in well-being because agricultural markets generally satisfy the conditions for perfect competition.

The gains from strategic trade practices can turn to losses if other governments retaliate. If one country adopts a strategic trade policy, other countries can retaliate either by adopting the same policy or by taking measures to offset the effect of the other country's strategy. For example, the United States retaliated against the European Union's subsidization of agricultural exports with its own export subsidies, resulting in large losses to both. Once both are subsidizing exports, they are in a dilemma, since neither has an incentive unilaterally to stop the subsidization. To resolve the dilemma, countries negotiate agreements prohibiting such policies and establish institutions to enforce the agreements. This approach, represented by the WTO, is favored by most countries. Before considering international trade agreements, the nature of the politics of international trade is considered.

# The Political Economy of International Trade Policy
## The Dual Nature of the Politics of International Trade

As illustrated in Figure 17-1, the politics of international trade policy is driven by domestic politics, which arises from the interactions between international trade policy and the domestic economy. Trade policy has differentiated distributive consequences with some interests benefiting from trade liberalization and others harmed by it. Trade politics thus has two components—measures to liberalize trade and measures to support domestic interests harmed by liberalization.

According to the typology of political competition presented in Figure 6-2, the politics of international trade policy is at one level majoritarian. That is, everyone is affected by international trade. Because liberalized trade policy is beneficial in the aggregate, countries generally gain from reductions in tariff and nontariff barriers. The benefits, however, are often widely distributed, so preferences for trade liberalization may not be transformed into policy. In the United States, as in most countries, the politics of trade

---

[4]Indeed, worldwide aggregate surplus is increased because the total quantity produced is greater than it would be without the subsidy. This results because the subsidization leads to a price that is closer to marginal cost. These conclusions, however, are not completely robust and may be reversed if firms compete in a manner different from that assumed in Cournot competition.

liberalization are basically entrepreneurial. In the United States, Congress has delegated the role of entrepreneur to the president. Congress is willing to delegate because the aggregate benefits of trade liberalization exceed the aggregate costs, and the benefits are sufficiently widely distributed that leadership must be exercised. Since the constituency of the president is the nation as a whole, as opposed to a congressional district or a state, presidents generally support trade liberalization.

The distributive consequences of a liberalized trade policy, however, are not uniform. Instead, liberalization has concentrated effects on particular interests, and those interests have an incentive to take nonmarket action to increase the benefits they receive or reduce the costs they bear.[5] In the case of trade policies that reduce domestic barriers to trade and thereby increase imports, the benefits typically are distributed broadly among consumers, whereas the costs are concentrated on import-competing industries. For example, in the United States steel companies and the United Steel Workers (USW) have been hurt by imports and have strong incentives to seek protection. Protectionism is thus characterized by client politics. In most countries, interests, including companies and unions, can seek protection and relief from injury due to imports. For example, countries have antidumping laws that allow domestic firms to petition to have duties placed on imports sold at "less than fair value."

The benefits from protection are concentrated on those interests that compete against imports, whereas the costs of protection are widely distributed among consumers and other users of the protected goods. Although consumers are harmed by these policies, the harm is typically small on a per capita basis, and hence consumers seldom take nonmarket action to oppose protection. Importers, however, are often harmed and have incentives to oppose protectionism. The steel companies and the USW sought protection from imports, but General Motors and Caterpillar opposed it because it would raise the price of the steel they use. Interest group politics can thus develop. Interest group politics can also result in political competition between import-competing industries and exporters as in the case of the ratification of broad trade liberalizations, such as NAFTA, that require reciprocity.

The politics of international trade policy is summarized in Figure 17-4. In the aggregate, trade policy is characterized by majoritarian politics. At a disaggregated level, the nature of the politics depends on the specific policy alternative in question. Trade liberalization and market opening are basically characterized by entrepreneurial politics. Client politics characterizes protectionism, since the benefits from supporting protectionism are concentrated and the costs are typically widely distributed. Protectionist policies may generate a response by importers, and reciprocity in market opening policies may generate a response by import-competing industries, so the number of interest groups involved can expand. The politics of protectionism and the politics of market opening thus can lead to interest group politics.

## Asymmetries in the Politics

Although trade policy liberalization creates opportunities for exporters and threats for import-competing industries, the domestic politics of international trade are asymmetric. The asymmetry is due to sunk resources and the rents on those resources. Consider the case of a firm that would construct a new plant dedicated to exports, provided that foreign barriers to trade were lowered. The incentive to undertake political action to open the foreign market depends on the profit it can earn, which is given by the export

---

[5]Magee, Brock, and Young (1989) provide a theory of rent-seeking to explain aspects of international trade policy.

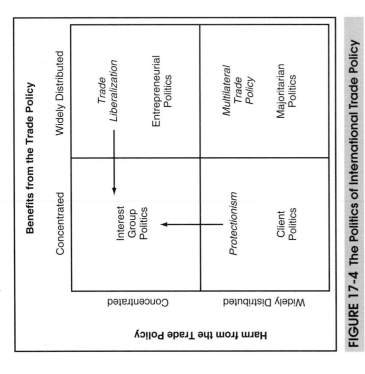

**Benefits from the Trade Policy**

|  | Concentrated | Widely Distributed |
|---|---|---|
| **Concentrated** | Interest Group Politics ← *Protectionism* | *Trade Liberalization* ↓ Entrepreneurial Politics |
| **Widely Distributed** | Client Politics | *Multilateral Trade Policy* Majoritarian Politics |

**Harm from the Trade Policy**

**FIGURE 17-4 The Politics of International Trade Policy**

revenue less the full cost of the resources required to produce the exports. In contrast, domestic firms faced with import competition typically have sunk resources. Because of sunk and nonfungible resources, the short-run supply curve is below the long-run supply curve, as illustrated in Figure 5-1, so the domestic firms earn rents on those sunk resources. When there are sunk resources, the import-competing industry can have more to lose than the exporting industry has to gain, so in the short-run the incentives for protection can be stronger than the incentives for market opening.

To illustrate this, consider the case of labor. Trade liberalization creates new jobs in exporting industries, but at the time at which the trade policy is chosen those new jobs are not yet identified, let alone occupied. Those jobs might be filled by many people, and hence the probability that any one person would obtain one is small. The incentive for an individual to take nonmarket action thus is weak. As the managing director of one of the largest U.S. investment banks commented on organized labor's opposition to NAFTA, "The jobs that will be lost are identifiable; the jobs that will be created are as yet unidentified." Cisco Systems projected that its increased exports to Mexico would create 200 additional U.S. jobs at its suppliers, but who would hold those jobs was as yet unidentified. Thus, Cisco had clear incentives to support NAFTA, but those unidentified individuals who would hold those new jobs could not support it.

In contrast, workers in import-competing industries are often earning rents in their jobs; that is, their wages are higher than the wages they could obtain elsewhere. Rents are thus concentrated on identified individuals, and their incentives to oppose trade liberalization and seek protection from imports can be strong. This is the case for organized labor, where, for example, the wages of USW members are higher than the wages most of them could earn in other employment. Not surprisingly, the USW and similarly the United Automobile Workers have sought protection for the U.S. steel and auto industries, respectively, and have opposed liberalized trade. Organized labor vigorously, but unsuccessfully, opposed NAFTA and the Uruguay Round accord that established the WTO.

Global firms often have mixed incentives. As with any import-competing firm earning rents, a global firm would benefit from protection of its domestic markets. A global firm also would benefit from opening foreign markets for its products. The simultaneous protection of domestic markets and the opening of foreign markets is not sustainable, however, since protectionism can generate retaliation by other countries and market opening may require reciprocity. Consequently, most global firms support liberalized trade because of the aggregate gains from trade and because liberalized trade gives them greater opportunity to pursue their competitive advantages.

# International Trade Agreements
## The World Trade Organization

At the conclusion of World War II, a group of countries led by the United States established the International Trade Organization (ITO). They hoped the ITO would allow them to avoid the disastrous trade policies that had contributed to the depression and the pressures for war. When the U.S. Senate failed to provide the two-thirds majority to ratify the organization's treaty, the ITO disbanded. However, a set of principles for international trade in goods had been drafted in conjunction with the ITO, and in 1948, 23 countries formalized those principles as the GATT. Seven subsequent rounds of multilateral trade negotiations among the signatories have resulted in major reductions in tariffs and nontariff barriers to trade.

The focus of international trade policy through the 1960s was on tariffs. Because tariffs limit the gains from trade, the United States and other countries sought in the Kennedy Round (1964–1967) of GATT negotiations to reduce tariffs on a more or less uniform basis among all signatories. The result was an average reduction of 36 percent in tariffs, and the volume of international trade increased substantially as a result.

After reducing tariffs to the point at which they no longer constituted a major barrier to trade, the focus of GATT turned in the Tokyo Round (1974–1979) to nontariff barriers to trade. Nontariff barriers were more complex and difficult to address and were often deeply rooted in both domestic politics and business practices that protected rents and surpluses.[6] Trade in agricultural products, for example, has been distorted by a variety of policies such as import quotas, domestic subsidies, and export subsidies. Although the Tokyo Round focused on nontariff barriers, it also resulted in an average reduction of 34 percent in tariffs. As a result of the Tokyo Round agreements, the average tariff in developed countries was 6.3 percent. Thirty-two percent of U.S. imports were duty free, and the average duty on the rest was 5.5 percent.[7]

The Tokyo Round left several sectors, such as agriculture, unaddressed, and several others, such as services, became more salient. The Uruguay Round (1986–1993) was intended to improve GATT provisions on trade in goods and expand the multilateral trade agreements to include trade in services, agriculture, intellectual property protection, government procurement, and other issues. After nearly 8 years of negotiations an agreement was concluded that made major improvements in international trade policies and, in addition, reduced tariffs by 38 percent to an average of 3.9 percent in developed countries. To encompass this broader set of agreements, the WTO was established. The WTO agreements include GATT, GATS, TRIPS, dispute settlement,

---

[6]Grieco (1990) provides an analysis of the compliance with Tokyo Round nontariff barrier agreements.
[7]See Lande and VanGrasstek (1986, p. 4).

and trade policy reviews. The WTO also encompasses the Agricultural Agreement and an agreement on government procurement.

The WTO has 148 member countries and over 20 others, including Russia, have applied for membership. The WTO has three principal roles. First, it provides a system of agreements that helps trade move more freely. Second, it provides a forum for trade negotiations such as the telecommunications agreement achieved in 1997. Third, it provides a dispute settlement mechanism to resolve trade disputes in a timely manner.

The central principle of the WTO agreements is embodied in the most favored nation (MFN) requirement that each signatory accord all other signatories the most favorable terms for trade provided to any country; that is, trade policies are to be nondiscriminatory.[8] A second principle is national treatment; that is, domestic and foreign goods are to be treated the same. For example, Canada imposed higher postage rates on U.S. magazines than for Canadian magazines, and a WTO dispute resolution panel held that the Canadian practice violated the national treatment principle.

GATT covers a variety of practices and policies governing trade in goods.[9] Article VI covers antidumping and countervailing duties and requires a finding of less than fair value sales or subsidization, respectively, and a finding of material injury. Article XI sets a framework for the elimination of quantitative restrictions on trade, but Article XVIII allows exceptions for balance of payments problems of developing countries. Article XIX allows for temporary safeguard relief from imports. Article XVI is the subsidies code, and Articles XX and XXI provide exceptions to the free trade provisions of the other articles. For example, a country may impose trade restrictions if they are required by national security considerations.[10]

## General Agreement on Trade in Services (GATS)

U.S. service industries had complained that their international expansion was hindered by the protection many countries provided for their domestic industries. The effort to reduce barriers to trade in services was led by a number of CEOs, including James Robinson of American Express, who for years personally campaigned to open foreign markets. In 1982 the Coalition of Service Industries was formed and was successful in including trade in services in the Uruguay Round agenda.

The result was the General Agreement on Trade in Services (GATS), which covers all services and provides for MFN and national treatment. The agreement also requires countries to make transparent all regulations and conditions of service. Since the services markets of many countries were largely closed to foreign firms, GATS allowed countries temporarily not to apply MFN treatment.

Two services, telecommunications and finance, posed particular problems because of government ownership of firms and heavy regulation. The Uruguay Round and GATS agreements were signed while negotiations on telecommunications and financial services continued. In 1997 over 68 countries agreed to open their telecommunications market to various degrees. Later in 1997, 102 countries reached agreement to open banking, insurance, investments, and other financial services to international

---

[8]Exceptions to the equal treatment principle include colonial preference arrangements in effect when GATT was established, preferences for developing countries, and certain multilateral agreements such as the Multi-Fiber Arrangement. The quotas established in the Multi-Fiber Arrangement were phased out by 2005.

[9]Prior to 1995 GATT was not a single agreement but instead a set of agreements, each of which countries could choose to sign. For example, GATT included a subsidies code intended to limit the domestic subsidization of export industries, but the signatories were largely the members of the Organization for Economic Cooperation and Development (OECD), an association of industrial democracies.

[10]With the exception of Article II, the GATT articles have counterparts in U.S. trade law.

competition. Some countries, however, limited foreign ownership stakes in their financial-services companies. GATS now covers all international trade in services.

## Trade-Related Aspects of Intellectual Property Rights (TRIPS)

Intellectual property rights include copyrights, patents, trademarks, brand names and logos, industrial designs, semiconductor circuit designs, and trade secrets. Such rights allow individuals and firms to capture the benefits from their efforts to creating new concepts and products; infringement of these rights reduces the incentives to create.[11] TRIPS provides broad protection and was included in the WTO dispute settlement system, allowing trade sanctions to be imposed in the event of violations. Because many countries had weak domestic laws for protecting intellectual property rights, developing countries were given 5 years to comply and the least developed countries were given 11 years.

Intellectual property is a contentious issue between developed and developing countries. Many developing countries believe that intellectual property rights allow companies to unfairly preclude their countries from obtaining important products such as pharmaceuticals that are priced too high for the countries to afford. TRIPS includes sections that allow a country to invoke compulsory licensing and to parallel import generic versions of drugs in the event of a public health emergency. Drug pricing, compulsory licensing, and parallel imports are considered in the Part V integrative case, *GlaxoSmithKline and AIDS Drugs Policy*. As an example of the contentious nature of intellectual property rights policy, under the auspices of the World Intellectual Property Organization, a unit of the United Nations, a treaty providing protection for intellectual property was negotiated. Developing nations, however, refused to sign it, leaving fewer than 10 signatories.

## Agriculture

Agriculture has been the sector with the greatest distortions in trade. An OECD report concluded that farm subsidies and import controls cost consumers and taxpayers $361 billion in 1999. The European Union accounted for the largest distortions, followed by the United States and Japan. The principal roadblock to an agreement on agricultural trade was the European Union's Common Agriculture Policy (CAP). CAP was intended to maintain farmers' incomes and did so by establishing prices high enough to yield a reasonable income for high-cost farms. The high prices, however, induced efficient farms to expand their output, resulting in huge crop surpluses, some of which were exported at subsidized prices. The European Union's export subsidization resulted in retaliatory subsidization of agricultural exports by the United States.

The Uruguay Round produced the Agricultural Agreement to reduce tariffs, domestic support, and export subsidies in agriculture. By 2000 developed countries were to reduce their tariffs by an average of 36 percent with a minimum reduction of 15 percent. Domestic support was to be reduced by 20 percent and export subsidies by 36 percent. The reductions required for developing countries were lower, and they were given until 2004 to comply. Because many countries used quotas to restrict imports, the agreement adopted a "tariffs only" policy in which quotas were replaced by equivalent tariffs, which were then subjected to the required reductions. The agreement on agriculture also addressed health and safety issues. It required that regulations be based on science and that they "be applied only to the extent necessary to protect human, animal, or plant life or health."

The Agricultural Agreement, however, left unresolved many issues. The European Union reformed CAP by decoupling the subsidies received by farmers from the amount they produced. A WTO trade policy review, however, concluded that "the reform of the Common Agricultural Policy (CAP) falls short of liberalizing EU's agriculture."[12] To advance negotiations on reducing distortions in trade in agriculture, the European Union pledged to eliminate all subsidies if the other WTO members agreed to eliminate their subsidies.

Developing countries complained that the agricultural subsidies and protection provided by the European Union, Japan, United States, and other countries impeded their economic development in two ways. Domestic subsidies and import barriers reduced export opportunities for the developing countries, and export subsidies unfairly competed with their exports. NGOs such as Oxam America called attention to the subsidies and lobbied for their elimination.

## Government Procurement

The Uruguay Round negotiators reached a new Government Procurement Agreement (GPA) that extended the existing agreement to include construction and services and some procurement by subcentral governments and government-owned firms. The GPA is a "pluralateral" agreement among a subset of WTO countries. Developing countries were given special conditions. In a bilateral agreement with the European Union, the procurement of 15 U.S. states and seven major cities was opened to EU firms in exchange for opening the European Union's $28 billion heavy electric equipment market.

## Antidumping, Countervailing Duties, and Safeguards

The Kennedy Round of GATT negotiations incorporated provisions in Article VI allowing domestic laws to include antidumping measures. From the perspective of economic theory, dumping occurs when a company sells a good at a price below the cost of producing it. As applied in international trade, however, antidumping pertains to sales at "less than fair value" that materially injure domestic industries. In response a duty on imports can be imposed to bring their price up to fair value. Antidumping provisions are thus intended to provide for "fair trade" rather than free or efficient trade. Antidumping provisions have been criticized as being protectionist because they can result in the imposition of duties on imports even when prices are above costs. Antidumping basically compares the domestic price of a product in the exporting country with the price in the importing country, so antidumping actually pertains to price discrimination rather than to dumping. In addition to a price less than fair value, the imports must cause material injury to domestic interests. The chapter case, *Cemex and Antidumping*, centers on this issue.

The Uruguay Round agreement standardized the procedures for calculating the dumping duty and for conducting investigations. It also imposed a 5-year sunset limit on any antidumping duty, unless ending the duty would result in imminent material injury.

Antidumping had been used almost exclusively by developed countries with the number of actions initiated averaging about 200 per year in the early 1990s.[13] The

[12]WTO press release, October 27, 2004.
[13]Bellis (1989) and Schuknecht (1992) provide analyses of the European Union's antidumping policies and procedures.

number of actions initiated by developed nations decreased to 120 in 1997. Since 1985 developing countries have become active in using antidumping, and by 1997 they initiated more actions than developed countries. India has become the largest user of antidumping, and China is the most frequent target. During the first half of 2004, 18 countries imposed 52 antidumping duties, with India, the European Union, and the United States imposing six each. Despite the protectionist nature of antidumping, most countries prefer to retain the provisions as a safety valve to relieve pressure for broader protectionist measures.

Countervailing duties are allowed by the WTO agreements to offset the effects of subsidies provided by another country. These duties are subject to the same standards for antidumping duties. Special provisions are provided for developing countries.

Temporary safeguards against a surge of imports can be taken to avoid "serious injury" to a country. The United States invoked the safeguards provision to protect its steel industry, as indicated in the example presented later in the chapter.

## Dispute Settlement

Under GATT, disputes between countries could be brought before a panel that investigated and issued a recommendation. The recommendation became binding, however, only if all countries agreed to it, and countries including the United States frequently withheld their agreement. A major achievement of the Uruguay Round was to establish the WTO Dispute Settlement Body (DSB) to hear disputes and issue binding orders to resolve them.[14] The DSB encourages the parties to resolve disputes through negotiation and compromise; if that is unsuccessful, a country may request a special panel be established to hear the dispute. The entire process, from the filing of the initial complaint to the issuance of a final report by the panel, is to be completed within 1 year, and any appeal is to be resolved in 3 months. Correction of a violation, however, can take considerable time.

If the DSB finds against a practice of a country, the country is required to correct the fault.[15] Failure to comply can be brought to the attention of the DSB, which can authorize the petitioner to impose trade sanctions against the violator. Thus, countries need not change their laws or practices to comply with the decision of the DSB, but if they fail to do so, sanctions can be authorized by the WTO. The sanctions typically take the form of a suspension of previously granted trade concessions accorded to the violator. The violator is to accept the sanctions. The United States and other countries have complied with the decisions of the DSB.

### Trade Disputes

The first case decided by the DSB involved a complaint by Venezuela, later joined by Brazil, that rules issued by the U.S. Environmental Protection Agency (EPA) for reformulated gasoline violated the WTO national treatment principle. The EPA had written its rules based on data that were readily available for U.S. refiners. Because foreign refiners had not kept the same data, the EPA required them to meet a more stringent standard. The DSB decided in favor of Venezuela, and the United States complied by rewriting the EPA rules to provide for national treatment.

Disputes typically center on specific protectionist practices. The European Union maintains a set of preferences for the overseas territories and former colonies of its

---

[14]The DSB is not an organization, but instead is the General Council of the WTO. It is better thought of as a procedure for resolving disputes.
[15]A DSB finding can be overcome by a majority of the WTO members.

member states. The United States and Latin American countries filed a complaint against EU rules issued in 1994 for preferential treatment for bananas from the overseas territories and former colonies, particularly in Africa.[16] Banana exports from Honduras to the European Union fell by 90 percent as a result of the rule. The DSB decided against the European Union and rejected an appeal. The European Union then revised its rule under contentious internal bargaining, pitting Germany and other countries that opposed the preferences against France and other countries that favored them. The United States and Latin American countries, however, contended that the revised rule did little to remove the barriers to Latin American banana imports. The United States proposed that the new rule be taken to the WTO for an expedited DSB process, but the European Union refused. When the DSB failed to authorize sanctions by the required deadline, the United States announced 100 percent punitive tariffs against $500 million of imports of wine, cheese, and other products. The DSB subsequently reached a decision authorizing the United States to impose punitive tariffs on $191 million of imports. Finally, the United States and the European Union reached a settlement in which the United States lifted the punitive tariffs on July 1, 2001, and the European Union agreed to phase out the preferences over 5 years.

The largest case to date involved profits taxes on exports. In 1971 Congress allowed U.S. exporters to establish offshore foreign sales corporations through which the paper transactions on exports were funneled, saving U.S. exporters several billion dollars in profits taxes. The European Union filed a complaint against the U.S. practice, and the WTO ruled in favor of the European Union. Congress responded in 2000 by revoking the foreign sales corporation law and enacting a law that actually expanded the tax breaks by allowing additional U.S. exporters, such as Boeing and Caterpillar, to receive the tax benefits. The European Union was incensed and complained to the WTO that the United States had not complied with the initial ruling. The WTO agreed, and the United States appealed the ruling. The appeal was denied as expected, and the European Union was authorized to impose punitive tariffs on as much as $4 billion of U.S. exports. The European Union phased in the punitive tariffs, and Congress passed a bill that phased out the foreign sales corporation provision and granted other business tax breaks that were not trade distorting. The European Union complained about the phaseout but withdrew its punitive tariffs.

In addition to the foreign sales corporation case, the United States lost a series of DSB cases in the 2000s. The DSB ruled against temporary safeguards for steel, as considered in the example, subsidies for cotton production, and antidumping procedures.

The trade conflicts between the European Union and the United States continued as the United States filed a trade complaint claiming that the European Union provided billions of dollars of subsidies in the form of low-interest loans to Airbus Industries. The European Union countered with a trade complaint claiming that the United States subsidized Boeing through military research and development grants. Negotiations to resolve the dispute collapsed.

A controversial case was brought by the United States against the European Union on its ban of beef from cattle treated with growth-enhancing hormones. The European ban did not violate the national treatment principle, because it applied to any hormone-treated beef, nor was it intended to protect European beef producers. Instead, the ban was enacted because of consumer health concerns about the beef. The DSB concluded that the European Union had no scientific basis for concluding that

---

[16]The United States was a petitioner because Chiquita Brands and Dole Food Company export Latin American bananas to the European Union.

the hormone-treated beef might be a health hazard. The European Union, however, was given a period of time to conduct its own safety tests on the hormone-treated beef. After 2 years of inaction by the European Union, the WTO authorized the United States to impose 100 percent punitive tariffs on $117 million of imports of European goods. The European Union subsequently reviewed the scientific literature and concluded that the hormone-treated beef constituted a health risk because some hormone residue could cause cancer. The European Union then enacted new legislation banning six beef hormones. The United States replied that the review provided no new scientific evidence. A spokesperson for the office of the U.S. trade representative said, "The hormone levels they are concerned about—represent a tiny fraction of what occurs naturally in an egg or one glass of milk."[17]

The beef dispute was part of a broader U.S. complaint against the EU ban on imports of foods with genetically modified organisms (GMOs). In 1998 the European Union and the United States had agreed to an EU moratorium on new approvals of imports of GMO foods and animal feed. The European Union lifted the ban in 2003, replacing it with regulations requiring documentation of the genetic history with a comprehensive paper trail for all food imports. U.S. exporters of agricultural products claimed that it would be impossible to provide such documentation. The European Union had substituted a regulatory ban for its explicit ban, and agricultural exporters turned to the WTO. Since the EU ban on GMO foods was seen as a violation of the WTO agreements, the United States filed a trade complaint with a decision due in 2005.

The EU ban and documentation requirement were based on the "precautionary principle" under which temporary bans could be imposed on products that might pose risks. A member of the EU trade delegation explained, that "in a democracy you have to take into account fears of the people, and the people in many European countries are concerned about genetically modified food."[18] In a case in which Monsanto claimed that Italy had illegally banned imports of GMO corn, the European Court of Justice upheld temporary bans under the precautionary principle "without having to wait until the reality and seriousness of risks become fully apparent, even if a full risk assessment becomes impossible because of the inadequate nature of scientific data available." The court, however, also said that the risks "must not be purely hypothetical or founded on mere suppositions which are not yet verified."[19] The court remanded the case to Italy to determine if there was any evidence of risks. Monsanto stated that it was pleased with the court decision.

The beef and GMO foods cases are important because they pertain to the question of whether countries can respond to consumer preferences whatever might be the basis for those preferences. Another example involves environmental protection. A U.S. law banned the sale of shrimp caught with nets from which sea turtles were unable to escape. The DSB upheld a complaint by India, Malaysia, Pakistan, and Thailand against the U.S. law on the grounds that the WTO agreements did not permit discrimination against products on the basis of how they were produced. Prior to the establishment of the WTO, a GATT panel had on the same grounds ruled against the U.S. Marine Mammal Protection Act ban of tuna caught in purse seine nets in which dolphins could become caught and drown. In the case of the dolphin decision, the United States withheld its consent and the panel decision did not take effect. Under the WTO DSB procedures, the sea turtle decision was binding. Environmental issues

17*The Wall Street Journal,* November 9, 2004. The European Union took its evidence to the WTO in an attempt to have the sanctions lifted.
18*The New York Times,* January 10, 2003.
19*The Wall Street Journal,* September 9, 2003.

such as these and health issues such as the EU ban on hormone-treated beef and GMO foods spurred calls for a new round of WTO negotiations.

## The Doha Round of WTO Negotiations

The Uruguay Round and follow-up agreements were generally successful, and the WTO dispute settlement process has been effective. Nevertheless, many trade issues remained unresolved. The members of the WTO had planned to adopt an agenda for a new round of multilateral trade negotiation at the 1999 Seattle ministerial meeting, but demonstrations by activist groups disrupted the meetings.[20] Finally, in 2001 after tense negotiations, particularly between developing and developed countries, the members agreed to a broad agenda for the Doha Round.[21]

Despite intense political pressure from the pharmaceutical industry, developing countries, led by India, received a pledge that TRIPS "does not and should not prevent Members from taking measures to protect public health." This would allow developing countries to violate pharmaceutical patents and produce or import generic drugs to protect public health without being subject to trade penalties.[22] Despite the opposition of France, the European Union agreed to negotiate the phaseout of agricultural subsidies. Market access is to be improved and domestic subsidization is to be reduced. The European Union obtained a pledge to support sustainable development and discussions on the relationship between trade and multilateral environmental agreements, but more specific environmental objectives were not specified. The United States agreed to negotiations on the clarification of antidumping procedures, much to the anger of U.S. industries that had used antidumping for protection from imports. The WTO members also agreed to reduce or eliminate tariffs on industrial goods. Activist groups failed to obtain commitments to labor protections due to objections by developing nations. The negotiations in the Doha Agenda were to pay special attention to the situations of developing countries. For example, developing countries were given until 2016 to bring their patent laws into accord with TRIPS.

Negotiations also were scheduled for competition (antitrust) policy and trade, intellectual property protection under TRIPS, and services under GATS. The members also committed to a review of DSB procedures, discussions on rules pertaining to investments, and negotiations on transparency in government procurement.

The U.S. agreement to negotiations on antidumping and pharmaceutical patents created opposition from U.S. interest groups and jeopardized U.S. Trade Promotion Authority, or fast track, for the ratification of the Doha Round agreement. Congress had routinely granted fast track authority to the president to negotiate trade agreements subject to an up or down vote without the possibility of amendment. This authority had been important in allowing the United States to commit to negotiated agreements.[23] Congress members aligned with labor unions and environmental interest groups opposed fast track authority because they wanted labor and environmental protection to which developing nations had objected because the protections would limit their growth.[24] The developing nations had refused to open new trade negotiations without assurances that the United States negotiate under fast track authority.

---

[20]See Prakash (2001) for an analysis of the Seattle meeting. The principal effect of the demonstrations in Seattle was to delay the next round of negotiations 2 years rather than to affect the agenda significantly.

[21]Esty (2001) analyzes the trade and environment issues.

[22]These are important issues in the Part V Integrative case, *GlaxoSmithKline and AIDS Drugs Policy.*

[23]See Destler (1997) for an analysis of fast track authorizations.

[24]See Destler and Balint (1999) for a perspective on the environment and labor dimensions of the politics of U.S. trade policy.

The politics of fast track began again in 2001, and the House voted 215 to 214 to grant fast track, and the Senate concurred.

## Other Trade Agreements

A number of regional free trade agreements have been concluded, and those agreements have broadened the set of countries participating. The largest of these free trade areas are NAFTA and the Common Market of the European Union. In Latin America there are four regional trading areas: the Central American Common Market, the Andean Community, Caricom, and Mercosur. Mercosur members are Argentina, Brazil, Paraguay, and Uruguay with Bolivia and Chile as associates. Mercosur and the European Union attempted to reach a free trade agreement, but negotiations broke down over the issue of trade in agriculture. In 1994 the 16 countries participating in the Asia-Pacific Economic Cooperation (APEC) forum agreed to work toward removing all barriers to trade by the year 2020. The developed countries in APEC established a goal of eliminating trade barriers by 2010. Progress has been slow.

In addition to WTO trade agreements, a large number of bilateral and multilateral agreements are in force. For example, in 2004 the United States concluded a free trade agreement with Chile, which already had such an agreement with Canada and the European Union. Also, the United States has worked to deregulate international air transportation, which had been governed by a cartel supported by countries with state-owned airlines. The U.S. strategy had been to negotiate bilateral agreements deregulating air fares and schedules with other countries. This increased competition and brought prices down, although restrictions remained in some markets because landing slots were limited.

# U.S. Trade Policy

## The Structure of U.S. Trade Policy

Article 1, Section 8 of the Constitution gives Congress the power "to regulate commerce with foreign nations" and to "lay and collect duties." In 1934 in the aftermath of the disastrous Smoot-Hawley tariff, Congress passed the Reciprocal Trade Agreement Act, which delegated to the president the authority to negotiate trade agreements. The authority for U.S. trade negotiations has remained largely with the president. The Office of the U.S. Trade Representative (USTR), located in the Executive Office of the President, serves as the president's representative in trade negotiations. The United States has supported trade liberalization through the multilateral policies embodied in the WTO agreements, regional free trade agreements including NAFTA and APEC, and bilateral arrangements such as those promoting competition in international air transport. U.S. membership in the WTO must be renewed by Congress in 2005.

In the late 1980s Congress began to assert its constitutional authority. The USTR is now required to consult with Congress on both trade policy and specific actions that implement that policy.[25] Being closer to constituents than the president, members of Congress have been concerned with protecting their constituents' interests. The result has been a series of amendments to the trade laws that make it easier for industries both to obtain protection and to initiate action to open foreign markets to their products. U.S. trade laws establish rights of private parties to initiate trade

[25]See O'Halloran (1994) for a study of the development of U.S. policy and the choice of trade institutions.

actions to further their interests, so U.S. trade actions have both public and private initiation.

The politics of international trade takes place in four institutional arenas—cabinet departments, regulatory agencies, Congress, and the Office of the President. The administration of trade policy has been placed with executive branch agencies, primarily the Departments of the Treasury, State, and Commerce. The International Trade Agency (ITA) of the Department of Commerce and the International Trade Commission (ITC), an independent regulatory commission, have administrative responsibilities for certain sections of U.S. trade law. Cabinet departments participate in international trade policy, both administratively and politically, and regularly conduct policy research, provide congressional testimony, lobby for their policy objectives and the interests they represent, and interact with business in other countries.

## U.S. Trade Law and Its Administration

The major components of U.S. trade law are embodied in the Trade Act of 1974 and the Tariff Act of 1930. The principal sections and their purposes are as follows:[26]

- Section 201 (temporary safeguards) provides for temporary relief for domestic industries seriously injured by increased imports; no unfair trade practice is required.
- Section 301 (presidential retaliation) provides for action against countries that restrict imports of U.S. goods or subsidize exports to the United States.
- Section 731 (antidumping) provides authority for the imposition of duties on goods imported to the United States at a price that is less than fair value (LTFV).
- Section 303 (countervailing duties) provides authority for the imposition of duties against those countries that subsidize their domestic industries.
- Section 337 (intellectual property) allows retaliation against countries that violate U.S. patents, copyrights, or protected trade secrets.
- Trade Adjustment Assistance provides assistance for those injured by imports.

These laws establish rights that private interests may exercise either directly or indirectly through administrative channels. For example, firms, unions, and other interests may file antidumping petitions to initiate a complex administrative process that can result in duties assessed on imports. Antidumping and countervailing duty petitions are considered by the ITA and the ITC. In Section 201 and 301 cases, the president has final authority, as illustrated in the steel imports example in this chapter. Decisions by the ITC can be appealed to the U.S. Court of International Trade and the Court of Appeals (Federal Circuit), and many of the decisions are appealed. The chapter case, *Cemex and Antidumping*, provides details on the ITC and ITA administration of an antidumping case and considers a firm's market and nonmarket strategies for addressing a dumping complaint.

The United States also imposes controls on the export to certain countries of sensitive items, including high-speed computers, encryption software, and computers with high-powered encryption software. These controls are mostly holdovers from the cold war, and high-tech firms have argued that the controls should be relaxed. The chapter case, *Sophis Networks and Encryption Export Controls (A)*, involves one such issue.

[26]See Trebilcock and York (1990) for studies of the administration of trade laws in a number of countries.

# The Political Economy of Protectionism

## Formal Policies

The politics of protectionism are clientistic and, in the case of WTO negotiations and NAFTA, are embedded in majoritarian politics. This section is concerned with nonmajoritarian issues in which private parties pursue their interests through political and administrative channels. Although official U.S. trade policy has promoted free and fair trade, the client politics arising from import competition has been important since the 18th century. Protection may extend indefinitely, have a specified duration, or be extendable. Protection for coastal shipping has continued since 1789, but most of the recent protectionist measures are intended to be temporary to give an industry time to improve its competitiveness.

Protection applies to two kinds of conditions. The first involves a predatory trade practice, such as export subsidization or predatory dumping, where a foreign firm sells in the United States at a price below its cost. The second involves relative efficiency—when foreign firms have lower costs than U.S. firms and sell in the United States at prices above their costs yet below the prices of domestic goods. Economic efficiency requires allowing nonpredatory imports and calls for blocking predatory practices if they will lead to long-run inefficiency. The political process, however, has not drawn the same line as economists and instead focuses on fair trade and protection from injury.

Predatory and discriminatory trade practices are addressed by the antidumping provisions of Section 731 and countervailing duties under Section 303. From 1990 through 2003, 99 countervailing duty reviews were completed under Section 303, and duties were ordered in 60 cases. Under Section 731, 451 antidumping reviews were completed and duties were ordered in 267 cases; few of these cases involved predatory practices.

The duties in antidumping cases had been paid to the U.S. government, but in 2000 Congress enacted a provision, the Byrd Amendment, under which the duties were paid to the companies that brought the case. The European Union and eight other countries filed a complaint with the WTO against the practice. As expected, the WTO ruled against the United States and authorized $150 million in duties on U.S. goods.

The United States also established sector-specific retaliation mechanisms to respond to subsidization by other countries. A 1985 act provided for subsidization of exports of agricultural commodities through the Export Enhancement Program in retaliation for agriculture export subsidization by the European Union.[27] This retaliatory program was important in the Uruguay Round negotiations on trade in agriculture that resulted in an agreement to reduce export subsidies and other distortions to trade.

The relative inefficiency of domestic industries is addressed in four ways. First, those injured may be compensated under the Trade Adjustment Assistance Act, which is intended to help a domestic industry adjust by improving its efficiency. Trade adjustment assistance also compensates those, such as workers, who are injured, thereby reducing their political opposition to liberalized trade. The assistance is generally restricted to workers and has focused on retraining programs. Trade adjustment assistance has been

---

[27]Although the program was directed at the European Union, it affected countries such as Australia that do not subsidize their agricultural exports. In response to complaints by Australia and other countries, the procedure for determining whether subsidies will be provided must include consideration of the effects on those countries.

provided sparingly because of concerns that it might become an entitlement for workers or used as a pork barrel program.

Second, safeguards relief can be granted under Section 201 in the form of temporary tariffs, import quotas, the suspension of previously granted trade concessions, or trade adjustment assistance. Relief under Section 201 is infrequently requested and seldom granted. Relief for the steel industry, considered in the example, was the first Section 201 case in 17 years.

Third, relief is granted under Section 731 when a petitioner's dumping complaint is affirmed by the ITC and the ITA. A finding of dumping requires only that the imported good is sold at LTFV and that the petitioner has been materially injured by the imports. Antidumping thus is not restricted to predatory practices but instead can be used to protect domestic firms from imports.

Fourth, protection is provided by measures ranging from tariffs to voluntary agreements to limit imports. The United States imposes a 2.5 percent duty on passenger cars but imposes a 25 percent duty on light trucks. Textile and apparel exports to developed countries had been restricted by quotas specified in the Multi-Fiber Arrangement (MFA). The Uruguay Round accord eliminated the MFA and its quotas beginning in 2005. In anticipation of the end of the quotas, the U.S. textile and apparel industries sought help from what was expected to be a huge increase in imports from China and India. U.S. manufacturers and textile unions petitioned the Bush administration for temporary safeguards protection under Section 201, and one week before the 2004 elections the president agreed to consider the petition. As the same time a group of the least-developed countries sought protection from the WTO for their domestic industries, which were expected to lose export markets to China. Under a provision in the agreement allowing China to join the WTO, the United States imposed quotas on some clothing imports. Under pressure from both developed and developing countries, China announced that it would impose a tariff on its textile exports.

## The Cost of Protectionism

Ultimately, the cost of protectionism is borne by consumers. Hufbauer and Elliott (1994) estimated that in 1990 special trade protection cost consumers over $70 billion, or approximately $280 per capita. U.S. producers were estimated to have captured approximately 45 percent of that amount as additional profits. Of the 21 cases of protection they studied, the annual cost per job saved ranged from $3,000 to $256,000, with an average of $54,000 for the 192,000 jobs saved by the protection. Over 152,000 of those jobs were in the apparel industry, and the cost to consumers per job was over $50,000 per year. Hufbauer, Berliner, and Elliott (1986) estimated that in the early 1980s the voluntary export restrictions (VER) on Japanese automobiles resulted in a 4.4 percent increase in automobile prices in the United States and an increase in employment of 55,000 jobs, at a cost to the economy of $105,000 per job saved in 1984. As a result of the higher prices resulting from the VER, domestic automakers captured profits of $2.6 billion per year, and foreign automakers captured profits of $2.2 billion.

Although they bear the cost of protectionism, consumers are costly to organize, and individual consumers are likely to remain politically inactive on protection issues. Furthermore, organized consumer groups have largely been inactive in cases involving protection of domestic industries. This leaves the political arena open to domestic industries, with political opposition coming primarily from importers, U.S. exporters, and those in government who support free trade and economic efficiency. For example, in the Section 201 petition the U.S. textile manufacturers and unions were opposed by the United States Association of Importers of Textiles and Apparel.

# Channels of Protection

Firms, labor unions, and industries can seek protection from imports through political and/or administrative channels. The political channel is through Congress and is directed either at specific legislation, such as a quota on sugar imports, or at the criteria used in the administrative channel. In addition to enacting new legislation, the political channel represents a threat that may strengthen the U.S. bargaining position with other countries. The protection obtained by an industry through the political channel depends on its ability to generate nonmarket pressure, as considered in Chapter 6, and on the opposing pressure. Industries such as automobiles, steel, dairy farming, sugar, and textiles with large numbers of employees have been able to generate considerable nonmarket pressure.

The administrative channel involves regulatory and executive branch agencies and is accessed by a petition filed pursuant to the U.S. trade laws. Much of the administration of trade policy is delegated to the ITC, the ITA, and the president. In the chapter case, *Cemex and Antidumping*, labor unions and U.S. cement producers filed an antidumping petition against Mexican cement imports. The administrative process imposes a series of gates through which a case must pass before relief is granted, and a petition may fail at any of several points in the process. In some cases, the threat of action is used to negotiate a voluntary settlement or suspension of the complaint. The steel imports example illustrates the use of both political and administrative channels.

## Steel Imports and the Nonmarket Campaign

Overcapacity in the steel industry worldwide caused employment in the U.S. steel industry to drop by 325,000 during the 1980s, much of it at the hands of imported steel. Employment at Bethlehem Steel fell from 130,000 in the 1960s to 16,400 in 1998. To improve its competitiveness, the industry invested $50 billion in modernization and new technology. Despite the investment, a number of inefficient plants were still in production, and the United States remained a high-cost producer. By the second half of the 1990s strong demand returned the U.S. industry to health, and prices and profits were up. The situation changed quickly, however, in 1997 as a result of the financial and economic crises in Asia and Russia and to a lesser extent in Latin America. Steel imports increased dramatically as foreign producers looked for markets for their excess capacity, and the robust U.S. economy with open markets was by far the most attractive opportunity. The imports drove prices down sharply and resulted in layoffs and the bankruptcy of one small steel company. The price of hot rolled steel fell by 18 percent in 1998 to the lowest level during the 1990s.

In response, the United Steel Workers (USW) and 12 leading steel producers joined in a broad client politics campaign to limit what they viewed as unfairly dumped steel. Curtis Barnette, CEO of Bethlehem Steel, said, "We're sometimes viewed as protectionist and rust belt in our thinking when we are a high-tech, low-cost, world-class industry. We believe in open markets. But when the rules are breached, they should be enforced. . . ."[1] Barnette was referring to U.S. laws against unfair competition resulting from dumping and the subsidization of foreign producers. To implement its nonmarket strategy the industry began the "Stand Up For Steel" campaign to bring the issue to the attention of the public, Congress, and the president.

Four producers of stainless steel and the USW filed antidumping petitions against eight countries and countervailing duty petitions

---
[1]*The New York Times*, December 10, 1998.

*(Continued)*

against Belgium, France, Italy, and South Korea for subsidizing their steel makers. Stainless sheet steel prices had fallen from $2,700 a metric ton in 1996 to $1,800 in 1998. Industry profits on stainless sheet steel fell from $466 million in 1995 to $141 million in 1997. In September the industry filed antidumping and countervailing duty petitions against Brazil, Japan, and Russia for dumping hot rolled steel and against Brazil for subsidizing its steel producers. With the downturn in the U.S. industry reflected in layoffs and lower prices and profits, the material injury standard was expected to be met.

In addition to pursuing its case in administrative channels, the industry pursued relief through political channels, deploying a nonmarket strategy intended to pressure the U.S. government to act. The industry lobbied Congress, and the House passed a nonbinding resolution calling for a ban on steel imports for a year. The industry also succeeded in inserting a provision in an appropriations bill requiring the Clinton administration to produce a plan for aiding the industry by January 5, 1999. Barnette and others lobbied in the Senate and convinced the Senate Steel Caucus to call on the administration to restrict imports.

The Stand Up For Steel campaign spent $3 million on a public advocacy campaign, including full-page newspaper advertisements presenting a letter calling on President Clinton to act.[2] George Becker, president of the USW, said, "We're fighting for the heartland of America. All the blood is gone from our industry; we can't bleed anymore."[3]

The ITA found in favor of the steel industry and announced duties ranging from 3.44 percent to 67.68 percent. Overall, however, only about half the petitions were approved. The industry also sent a message to the president and the Democratic Party. In the 1997–1998 election cycle the USW and the steel companies provided $1.2 million in campaign contributions, most of which came from the USW, with over 80 percent

[2] The New York Times, September 10, 1998.
[3] The New York Times, December 10, 1998.

going to Democrats. More importantly, the USW had been very effective in "get out the vote" efforts on behalf of Democrats. The president and vice president were not only concerned with rewarding their important political backers but also feared having unemployed steel workers when the 2000 elections arrived.

The campaign by the steel industry was not unopposed. Steel purchasers formed the Consuming Trade Action Coalition, which argued that any restraints on steel imports would result in higher prices for consumers. Both General Motors and Caterpillar criticized the antidumping and countervailing duty petitions. Caterpillar stated, "We strongly object to suggestions that steel trade should be subject to 'special' protection. The quotas used to protect the steel industry in each of the last four decades hurt American industries that use steel and rewarded foreign steel traders with a guaranteed share of a restricted market."[4]

Under the threat of action, Brazil and Russia agreed to quotas on imports of their steel products. The Clinton administration's report on the steel industry recommended that the administrative processes of U.S. trade law be accelerated, but the administration took no formal action under U.S. trade law. Some commentators believed that the failure to take action cost Vice President Gore the state of West Virginia and the election.

In 2001 President George W. Bush ordered a review of the state of the steel industry. Employment in the industry had dropped from 800,000 in 1980 to 160,000 in 2001. Imports accounted for 27 percent of U.S. steel consumption, down from 30 percent during the Asian crisis, but prices for some steel products had fallen to their lowest levels in 20 years. In addition, 18 steel companies including LTV—one of the largest—had filed for bankruptcy.[5] The situation in the industry was due in part to the inefficiency of U.S. integrated steel producers, which had lost market share not only to imports but also to

[4] The New York Times, December 10, 1998.
[5] Bethlehem filed for bankruptcy later in the year.

(Continued)

*(Continued)*

domestic mini mills. The market value of all U.S. steel producers was $10 billion, approximately the value of eBay and 3 percent of the value of Microsoft.

As a result of its review the Bush administration took the rare action of filing a Section 201 petition for relief of the industry, the first such petition since 1985. The Emergency Committee for American Trade, a business organization that supported free trade, criticized the Bush administration's decision to pursue a Section 201 case.

Later in the year the ITC concluded that the industry had been "seriously injured" by imports in 12 product categories representing 74 percent of the imports under investigation.[6] The ITC recommended duties of from 5 to 40 percent on products representing 80 percent of imported steel. Hufbauer estimated that the cost to consumers for each steelworker job saved by the steel. duties would be $326,000.[7]

The European Union and South Korea announced that they would file a complaint with the WTO if any new restrictions were imposed as a result of the Section 201 case. Pascal Lamy, the EU trade commissioner, said, "The cost of restructuring in the U.S. steel sector should not be shifted to the rest of the world."[8]

The steel industry and the USW mounted an intense political campaign along with their allies in Congress. Under pressure the Bush administration imposed temporary, 3-year tariffs on certain steel imports under Section 201. The ostensible purpose of the tariffs was to allow the steel companies to consolidate and improve their efficiency. The tariffs began at 30 percent and decreased to 24 percent the next year and to 18 percent in the third year. Developing countries were exempted, and the tariffs were primarily applied to industrialized countries and advanced developing countries. The Bush administration stated that the temporary tariffs were permitted under the WTO's safeguard provision, which allowed temporary relief in the event of a surge of imports.

Part of the assistance sought by the steel industry and USW was to cover the cost of health and pension benefits for 600,000 retired workers. The estimate of the cost over the next 10 years was more than $10 billion. The Bush administration refused to assume the pension obligations.

In response to the Section 201 action, the European Union took immediate action by filing two petitions with the WTO. First, it filed a complaint under the WTO dispute resolution process and identified U.S. imports to be targeted if the WTO ruled in its favor. Second, it filed a complaint that the United States had improperly imposed tariffs selectively under the "safeguards" procedures.

The direct effect of the tariffs on EU steel producers was small, since only 2.5 percent of EU production was affected. The principal concern was that low-cost steel that had been exported to the United States would now be diverted to the European Union, forcing prices down. The European Union announced that it would impose temporary tariffs on steel imports from any country that exceeded 2001 import levels. Canada also considered imposing temporary tariffs.

In late 2003 the WTO ruled that the U.S. tariffs were illegal and authorized punitive tariffs on $2.1 billion of U.S. exports to the European Union. In 2004 President Bush withdrew the safeguards tariffs. During the 2 years the tariffs were in effect, the U.S. steel industry consolidated and efficiency improved. As the tariffs were being withdrawn, U.S. demand for steel increased, raw material and energy costs increased, and the U.S. dollar fell, making steel imports more expensive. Steel prices in the United States rose sharply, and the industry returned to profitability.

6 The ITC found no serious injury in 17 product categories.
7 *The New York Times*, December 8, 2001.
8 *The New York Times*, June 7, 2001.

# The Political Economy of Market Opening

Market opening occurs through majoritarian policies such as those embodied in the WTO and NAFTA and through entrepreneurial politics, with the president attempting through multilateral and bilateral negotiations to reduce foreign tariff and nontariff barriers to trade. In some cases, market opening is characterized by client politics as interest groups pressure the government to take action to open specific foreign markets. This section considers the political economy of NAFTA and market opening under the threat of retaliation.

## The North American Free Trade Agreement

The North American Free Trade Agreement established, subject to certain exceptions, free trade among Canada, Mexico, and the United States. NAFTA was an expansion of the United States–Canada Free Trade Agreement that had been in effect since 1988, and it adopted many of the features of that agreement. NAFTA is a free trade agreement and not a market integration agreement as is the Single Market Act in the European Union. The agreement thus does not cover the movement of people or the harmonization of domestic laws.

NAFTA provided for the elimination of tariff and nontariff barriers over a 10-year period, although some barriers were to be phased out over 15 years. To the extent that external trade barriers remained in effect, the elimination of trade barriers within North America gave foreign firms an incentive to locate operations in the NAFTA countries. Because of both market and nonmarket considerations, Japanese automobile manufacturers had incentives to shift light-truck production to North America. The principal market factor was the lower wages in Mexico. The principal nonmarket factor was to avoid the 25 percent U.S. tariff on imports from outside the NAFTA countries.

Despite the expected economic gains, political opposition to the agreement was strong in Canada and the United States. In the United States, opposition was led by organized labor, which feared the loss of jobs to Mexico, and by environmentalists. To overcome the opposition, the Bush administration, which negotiated the agreement, and the Clinton administration, which obtained congressional passage, made a number of deals and provided safeguards to obtain the agreement, and it passed as a result of strong Republican support. Nevertheless, 60 percent of the House Democrats voted against the agreement, and it passed as a result of strong Republican support.

The politics of NAFTA were similar to those of other trade liberalization measures. The weight of majoritarian interests was in favor of liberalized trade, and the opposition came from concentrated interests that were likely to be injured. Without concessions those interests and the client politics they generated might have defeated the agreement. Three types of measures were taken to reduce opposition. First, NAFTA included transition provisions for a gradual phaseout of trade barriers to give industries time to adjust. Moreover, to reduce opposition from agricultural interests that feared a flood of low-priced Mexican produce, NAFTA included safeguards that would take effect if there were large surges of imports that depressed agricultural prices. Second, to obtain congressional votes, the Clinton administration made a number of side deals outside the trade area, including approval of public works projects in members' districts. Third, side agreements were concluded to reduce the opposition of environmental groups concerned about higher pollution as production expanded in Mexico and of organized labor that feared that high-paying jobs would be lost to Mexico.

The elimination of tariff and nontariff barriers did not mean that trade disputes disappeared. NAFTA left domestic trade laws in place, so antidumping and countervailing duty cases continued. The Canada–U.S. bilateral free trade agreement had established a dispute settlement mechanism to avoid use of the courts, NAFTA incorporated this feature by establishing a trilateral Trade Commission, composed of cabinet level officials, to hear complaints and resolve disputes on issues such as the application of antidumping laws. When the United States refused to allow Mexican trucks unrestricted access to U.S. roads, Mexico filed a complaint. A dispute settlement panel ruled in favor of Mexico, and fines could be imposed if the United States failed to grant access. The opposition in the United States was led by the Teamsters Union and by activists concerned that the trucks met U.S. safety standards. President Clinton refused to allow Mexican trucks into the United States, but President Bush announced that the United States would comply with the panel decision. Mexican trucks were allowed into the United States in 2004.

NAFTA established the Commission on Environmental Cooperation and the Commission on Labor Cooperation to monitor environmental and labor developments, promote compliance, receive complaints, and resolve disputes.[28] The first petition on environmental protection was filed in 1998 by local environmental groups in Mexico and the United States.[29] In 1998 the Canadian office of the USW filed a complaint against Mexico for failure to protect the rights of Mexican workers to choose which union represented them. The U.S. Department of Labor filed a supporting complaint to be addressed by the labor ministries of the three countries. To address environmental concerns, Mexico and the United States established the North American Development Bank to fund environmental projects along their 2,000 mile border.

## Market Opening Under the Threat of Retaliation

The most effective means of addressing foreign barriers to trade is through negotiations, but countries, and particularly the United States, have used retaliation and its threat to provide leverage in negotiations. In the 1980s the Semiconductor Industry Association filed a Section 301 petition to pry open the Japanese market to foreign-made semiconductors. Pressure from the United States and the threat of success in the administrative channel resulted in an agreement in which Japanese semiconductor manufacturers pledged not to sell in the United States at less than fair value, to open the Japanese market, and to increase the market share of foreign semiconductors to 20 percent by 1991.

More often, however, bilateral negotiations were lengthy and only moderately successful. Increasingly frustrated by what it viewed as inadequate action and by a process that placed much of the power in the hands of the president, Congress sought to increase its influence over both the relief and the retaliation processes. In 1988 Congress enacted the Omnibus Trade and Competitiveness Act, which established a mechanism for retaliation under a strengthened Section 301, referred to as Super 301.

Super 301 provided for mandatory sanctions against countries that engaged in unfair trade practices that injured U.S. industries. The USTR prepared the National Trade Estimate Report (NTER) listing the countries with which the United States had a large trade deficit and the policies and practices that inhibited U.S. exports. The

[28] Rugman, Kirton, and Soloway (1999) present an analysis of the implications for corporate strategy of environmental regulation under NAFTA.
[29] Hufbauer et al. (2000) provide a review of the first 7 years of the effect of NAFTA on the environment.

threat of mandatory retaliation under Super 301 contributed to an agreement under which Japan pledged to open its markets for wood products, communications satellites, and supercomputers.

Super 301 was sharply criticized by other countries, and both the European Union and Japan retaliated by issuing reports identifying specific U.S. tariff and nontariff barriers. Authorization for Super 301 expired at the end of 1990, but President Clinton issued an executive order reinstating a revised version of Super 301 under which sanctions were not mandatory. The rancor caused by Super 301 and the responses to it have convinced most countries to pursue market opening through multilateral negotiations under the WTO. The most recent major Section 301 action is considered in the chapter case, *The Kodak–Fujifilm Trade Dispute.*

# Summary

The gains from trade and the law of comparative advantage provide a compelling rationale for free trade. Under certain conditions, however, a nation can benefit from a strategic trade policy that restricts imports or subsidizes exports. In such situations countries may be in a prisoners' dilemma in which each has an incentive to adopt a strategic trade policy, but all are worse off when they do so. International trade agreements are intended to avoid these dilemmas and allow gains from trade to be realized.

International trade policy is driven by economic incentives but governed by the politics that stem from those incentives. The politics of international trade are basically majoritarian, but because of rents associated with sunk resources, the politics of protectionism are often strong. Protectionism is characterized by client politics, whereas the politics of trade liberalization are entrepreneurial. Opposition to protectionism can develop from importers and their customers and from exporters concerned about retaliation by other countries. Interest group politics can be the result.

Multilateral trade liberalization policies are incorporated in the agreements that govern trade and dispute resolution. The WTO agreements cover trade in goods, services, and agricultural products and provide for intellectual property protection. Several regional free trade agreements, including NAFTA, the Common Market of the European Union, and Mercosur, have been established to eliminate internal barriers to trade.

The political economy of international trade is best understood by focusing on domestic politics and the negotiations among countries on trade policy. Trade negotiations reflect the desire to open foreign markets while avoiding injury to domestic interests. The political forces supporting protectionism are naturally strong because of the rents that accrue to sunk resources, but the long-run gains from trade are greater than the rents that would be dissipated by trade liberalization. In the United States the president usually advocates trade liberalization, and protectionism manifests itself primarily in Congress and administrative agencies.

Whereas the United States has generally supported free trade, it provides both administrative and political channels for relief of industries injured by imports. Because protectionism is costly to an economy, the administrative channel has been designed to provide easy access but to make relief relatively hard to obtain. Success for an industry seeking relief in the political channel requires an ability to generate nonmarket pressure, and this requires numbers, resources, and coverage of political districts.

The Part IV integrative case, *Toys 'Я' Us and Globalization,* considers a firm that takes its domestic market strategy to other countries and encounters a variety of trade and other barriers.

# Cemex and Antidumping

Lorenzo Zambrano was accustomed to making tough decisions. During his 6-year tenure as chief executive officer of Cementos Mexicanos, S.A. (Cemex), he had transformed Cemex from a small Mexican cement manufacturer to an industry superpower. In the fall of 1990, however, Zambrano faced perhaps his most difficult challenge. In August the U.S. International Trade Commission ruled that Cemex had unfairly depressed cement prices in the southern and southwestern United States by dumping cement and cement clinker. As a result, a duty of 58 percent was levied on all subsequent Cemex exports from Mexico into the region. The ruling threatened Cemex's expansion and its access to the lucrative U.S. market. Cemex needed a strategy to address the threat.

In early 1989 cement producers in the southern portion of the United States were concerned about the erosion of their domestic market share due to increased imports from Mexico. Imports of gray portland cement and cement clinker, two principal cement products, had been increasing steadily over the previous 5 years. At the same time the lackluster performance of the economy in the region, and in particular the depressed level of new construction, was reducing the demand for cement.

Historically, the cement industry was a very regionalized business with high overland transportation costs preventing the commodity from freely flowing between regional markets. This insulation helped cement producers ride out hard times in the highly cyclical industry. Throughout the 1980s, however, Mexican producers were able to transport their cement across the border and still remain competitive on price, sometimes undercutting domestic producers. The majority of Mexican cement imported into the United States came from one producer, Cemex.

U.S. cement companies in the South and Southwest realized that imports from Cemex and other Mexican companies presented a threat to their profitability and perhaps to their survival. They

believed that with high transportation costs, Mexican producers must be selling their cement at less than fair value, which would constitute dumping under Section 731 of U.S. trade law. Cement producers in Arizona, New Mexico, Texas, and Florida filed an antidumping petition claiming that Cemex and the Mexican cement industry were dumping cement and clinker in their markets.

## The Mexican Cement Industry

Portland cement was used predominantly in the production of concrete, and cement clinker was the primary component in the production of portland cement. Demand for cement was cyclical and followed the general economic climate, demographic trends, and construction expenditures. In Mexico approximately 60 percent of cement expenditures were in residential construction, 20 percent in public works, and 20 percent in commercial construction.

A principal input to cement production was oil, with energy costs accounting for 40 to 50 percent of cement production expenses. Mexican cement firms had benefited from governmental policies. Mexico's vast oil resources allowed it to implement targeted domestic industrial policies, and in 1986 the government provided its domestic producers with oil for as little as $4 a barrel, compared with a weighted-average world price ranging from $14 to $16 a barrel.[30] In 1990, however, Mexican oil prices were raised to world levels.

The Mexican cement industry was dominated by Cemex, which by the early 1990s was the largest cement company in North America and the fourth largest in the world. By the end of 1991 its capacity had grown to 24 million tons, which was 63 percent of Mexican capacity. Cemex's primary Mexican competitor was Grupo Cementos Apasco, S.A. de

30"Cement Makers Fight, Yet Buy From, Importers," *Business Marketing*, August 1986, and *Energy Statistics Sourcebook*, 1987.

C.V. (Apasco), which was 60 percent owned by Holderbank Financère Glaris Ltd. (Holderbank), a Swiss company that was the largest cement company in the world.[31] Apasco had 17 percent of the Mexican market in 1991. The next largest competitor was Cruz Azul, which had 13 percent of the market.

Part of Cemex's rapid growth had come through acquisitions. Cemex had spent nearly $1 billion on acquisitions acquiring Cementos Anahuac, then Mexico's third-largest cement producer, in 1987 and in 1989 acquiring Empresas Tolteca, Mexico's second-largest producer and Cemex's chief competitor. Geographic diversification in addition to locating plants close to major markets rationalized production. Cemex also spent $950 million on new plant and environmental control equipment. This made the plants more energy efficient, raised labor productivity, and added 4.8 million tons of new capacity. Another $330 million was spent to develop international operations, including U.S. distribution facilities in Arizona, Texas, and California. Cemex subsequently acquired for $1.8 billion the two largest Spanish cement producers, giving it a presence in the European Union.

In 1991 Cemex's sales were approximately $1.7 billion with exports accounting for 15 percent of the total. The combination of its plant modernization and capital expenditure programs and its management and engineering know-how had given Cemex very low costs. Cemex had outstanding plant management practices and had been able to reduce plant downtime substantially, which increased its effective capacity and reduced costs.

Cemex had high brand loyalty in Mexico. In most countries, cement was a commodity purchased primarily by industrial and commercial buyers. In Mexico, however, about 78 percent of cement sold was through retailers in bags under brand names. In 1991 Cemex's bagged cement was sold through 4,500 exclusive retail distributors. Cemex provided technical and marketing assistance to its dealers and maintained long-term relationships with them.

Cemex had several plants located close to the U.S. border. Cemex's headquarters in Monterrey was only 130 miles from Texas, and the rapid economic growth in Mexico along the U.S. border provided an attractive location for new cement plants. Since cement production involved economies of scale, large plants were desirable, leaving some capacity for exports to the United States.

## The U.S. Cement Industry

As in Mexico, the U.S. industry was highly cyclical, depending on the general state of the economy and the construction industry in particular. Because of high overland transportation costs 95 percent of all gray portland cement shipments were made to customers located within 300 miles of the production site.

The U.S. industry was not nearly as concentrated as the Mexican industry. The leading U.S. cement producer in 1990 was Holnam, which was owned by Holderbank and had 11.8 percent of the domestic market.[32] Holnam was followed by Lafarge (6.7 percent), Southdown (6.1 percent), Lone Star Industries (5.5 percent), Ash Grove Cement (4.9 percent), and numerous other companies, at least five of which each had a domestic market share of over 3 percent. During the 1980s European companies began buying U.S. cement companies, and by 1989, 60 percent of the U.S. industry was owned by foreign companies. For example, Lafarge was owned by Lafarge Coppée of France, which was the world's second largest cement producer.

Cement imports accounted for 22 percent of the approximately 90 million tons of annual U.S. cement consumption, and imports had somewhat higher shares in the southern tier states. The Portland Cement Association estimated that in 1986 U.S. producers bought and resold approximately two-thirds of the cement imported into the country. The rationale provided by U.S. producers was that import prices were attractive, and since cement was a commodity, they were forced to serve their customers from the lowest-cost source.

The U.S. construction industry was weak at the end of the 1980s. The growth of the U.S. cement market was 1.3 percent in 1989 and 2.9 percent in 1990, whereas the growth rates of the Mexican cement market for the same years were 3.7 percent and 7.3 percent, respectively. In the southern and southwestern United States in particular, the success of Mexican cement importers contrasted sharply with the decline of local cement firms. In 1988, Mexican imports accounted for 14 percent of the

---

[31]Holderbank subsequently changed its name to Holcim.

[32]Holnam was formed by the merger of Dundee Cement and Ideal Basic, and in 2001 was renamed Holcim.

Arizona–New Mexico–Texas market and 22 percent of the Florida market. In addition, since 1983 seven domestic cement plants had closed in the Arizona–New Mexico–Texas region and two had closed in Florida.

Domestic firms believed that Mexican firms were dumping cement in the United States by selling their exports at less than fair value (LTFV). The antidumping petitioners included two unions and eight companies, which formed the Ad Hoc Committee of AZ-NM-TX-FL Producers of Gray Portland Cement. The committee was led by Southdown, the largest U.S.-owned cement manufacturer. "Our investigation to date . . . convinces us that the Mexicans' success in U.S. markets is due to dumping and not to any other factor," stated Clarence Comer, chief executive of Houston-based Southdown and chairman of the committee.[33]

The petitioners claimed that they had been materially injured by Mexican cement producers. The petition alleged that the dumping of cement depressed prices in the United States, caused investors to abandon the industry, and threatened their markets, production, and jobs. Comer summarized the allegation: "U.S. cement producers should not have to accept declining returns, declining employment, and declining capital investment. We should not have to cede U.S. markets and U.S. jobs to unfairly priced imports from Mexico. If we lose out to fair competition from Mexico, so be it."[34] Comer surmised that additional injury to the cement industry in the southern and southwestern United States was imminent. "Mexican producers continue to build export oriented capacity aimed at American markets."[35]

The petitioners identified two principal reasons the U.S. cement producers were vulnerable to imports from Mexico. First, because cement was a commodity, a small price change could result in large shifts in market shares. Thus, even a small price difference would cause a large loss of volume for domestic producers if they did not meet the lower import price. Second, cement imports displaced domestic production ton for ton because aggregate demand for cement was derived from the demand

33"U.S. Cement Companies Charge Mexican Producers With Dumping Cement in U.S. Markets," *Business Wire*, September 27, 1989.
34Ibid.
35Ibid.

for construction, and cement represented a small share of construction costs. Consequently, the aggregate demand for cement did not vary appreciably with price, so lower prices did not create additional demand.[36]

A similar but unsuccessful antidumping petition had been filed in 1986 by all U.S. cement producers against Mexico, Colombia, Venezuela, France, Greece, Japan, South Korea, and Spain.[37] In that case, the International Trade Commission (ITC) determined that there was no material injury to the U.S. cement industry because it had begun its recovery from the recession. The 1989 case, however, was different in three key respects: the petition was more narrowly focused; demand for cement in Arizona, New Mexico, and Texas was depressed; and Mexican imports were rising while U.S. cement prices were falling.

## U.S. Antidumping Law

The antidumping laws codified in Section 731 allowed either a private party or the International Trade Administration (ITA), an arm of the Department of Commerce (DOC), to file a petition for redress. The executive branch agencies charged with the administration of trade law in dumping cases were the ITC and the ITA. The ITC conducted a preliminary investigation to determine if there was a "reasonable indication" of material injury, or the threat of such injury, to the industry. Typically, the investigation covered the previous 3 years of activity. If no indication of injury were found, the petition was dismissed.

With a positive preliminary determination from the ITC, the ITA investigated whether there was a "reasonable likelihood" that imports were being sold at LTFV and calculated a preliminary estimate of the dumping margin. With an affirmative finding that a reasonable likelihood existed, the importer was required to make a cash deposit or post a bond or other security to guarantee the potential dumping liability. Upon concluding its investigation, the ITA announced its final determination of whether dumping was found. A positive finding included the final estimate of the dumping margin. A negative finding resulted in the petition being dismissed. Following an affirmative finding by the ITA, the

36Ibid.
37In contrast to shipping by land, shipping by sea is low cost.

ITC began the industry analysis stage. Here, the ITC investigated whether the imports in question caused or threatened to cause injury to the domestic industry. Unless the ITC found material injury, the case was dismissed. If the ITC found material injury, the case returned to the ITA for the negotiation of settlements and/or the imposition of duties.

## The ITC and ITA Determinations

To find material injury or the threat of material injury, the ITC had to first determine the "like product" and the "domestic industry." The petitioners and respondents agreed that gray portland cement and cement clinker comprised a single like product. On November 8, 1989, the ITC issued a unanimous affirmative preliminary determination in favor of the petitioners. The DOC then formally notified the Mexican cement producers that they had to submit to and fully cooperate with an administrative review if they wished to continue exporting to the United States. Questionnaires sent to Cemex requested general information on Cemex's strategy, production capacity, and number of plants. They also requested specific information on the Mexican and U.S. markets, including Cemex's costs, prices, pricing policies, market share, and customer information for the different markets.

The ITA concluded that Type II gray portland cement was the "like product" and that the bulk cement market was the relevant market for the basis of comparison. To test for dumping or the selling of a product at LTFV, the ITA considered the weighted-average price (for all the different plants from which U.S. sales were made) of the product as sold by the foreign firm to the first unrelated party in the importing country. This price was then compared with the

price at which the same or a similar product was sold in the home country. Since data for the price comparisons were limited, the ITA "constructed" prices at the mill gate using an administrative provision in its procedures that subtracted transportation and other costs. The price comparison thus was of mill net prices, determined by taking the sale price and deducting all costs other than those incurred in the mill. Dumping would be found if the price at which a ton of cement left the mill to a U.S. customer was lower than the price at which a ton of cement left the mill to a Mexican customer. The dumping margin was then the average of all the margins for those comparison sales for which dumping was found. Figure 17-5 presents a sample calculation.

The ITA set the dumping margin for Cemex at 58.38 percent and for Apasco, Cementos Hidalgo, and all others at 53.26 percent, 3.69 percent, and 58.05 percent, respectively. Thus, if the ITC were to find injury, Cemex would be assessed a duty of 58 percent of the dollar value of each ton of cement leaving the mill for the U.S. market.

To determine whether there was "material injury" or the "threat of material injury" from imports of Mexican cement, the ITC assessed the effects of Mexican cement imports on U.S. prices, production, capacity, capacity utilization, shipments, inventories, employment, wages, financial performance, capital investments, and research and development expenditures. The data showed that from 1986 to 1989 the total quantity of cement shipped by U.S. producers had increased by 4.7 percent, but declining prices caused the total value to decrease by 3.7 percent. Capacity for cement and clinker production changed little, and capacity utilization decreased slightly. Additionally, the employment, wages, and hours worked of production workers fell

| | Matched Pair of Sales in | |
|---|---|---|
| | *Mexico* | *United States* |
| Price | $85 | $80 |
| Transportation to terminal | 10 | 30 |
| Customs | 0 | 2 |
| Terminal and distribution | 11 | 7 |
| Other expenses | 12 | 10 |
| Mill net price | $52 | $31 |
| Dumping margin = 100 (52 − 31)/31 = 68 percent | | |

**FIGURE 17-5 Example of the Antidumping Margin**

by 19 percent, 13.8 percent, and 14 percent, respectively. Productivity rose by 23 percent. The financial performance of southern tier producers deteriorated, as gross profit fell by 18.1 percent and operating income dropped by 36.7 percent. Some firms had curtailed planned investment. The data also indicated that the volume of Mexican imports had increased 24 percent.

In August 1990 the ITC issued an affirmative final determination in favor of the petitioners. To continue importing cement and clinker, Mexican importers were required to tender cash deposits to the U.S. Customs Service equal to the estimated dumping margins. For Cemex and Apasco, those margins were 58 percent and 53 percent of their mill net prices, respectively. The antidumping order had an unlimited duration, so the duties would remain in effect until the dumping ceased. The duties, however, were to be recalculated every year based on updated data. As a result of the duties, all the Mexican producers except Cemex left the U.S. market.

## Cemex's Strategy

From the beginning of the process, Cemex complied fully with the requests for data. Cemex also opened its operations to the DOC as much as possible to expedite the administrative process and to demonstrate that the company was confident that it would prevail.

Cemex assigned the dumping issue top priority and created a new department to oversee the implementation of a multipronged strategy to address the issue. First, a U.S. law firm specializing in dumping cases was hired to provide advice. Second, Cemex sought to use the media in Mexico to build support and call the attention of the Mexican people to the alleged "unfair" treatment. Cemex also sought coverage from the US media, including *The Wall Street Journal*, to educate the American people about Cemex and its overall strategy and performance both in Mexico and in the United States. Third, a presentation was made to the Mexican Commerce Department to demonstrate the importance of the petition and the effect it would have on Cemex and Mexico. The goal was to obtain the Mexican government's support against the U.S. action. The Mexican government, however, was concerned about possibly jeopardizing the ongoing North American Free Trade Agreement (NAFTA) negotiations and decided not to pressure the U.S. DOC.

The opportunity for lobbying in Washington was limited because the issue was in the jurisdiction of regulatory rather than legislative institutions. As a result, little lobbying was done, although certain government leaders (including senators and governors in states where Cemex had operations) were contacted to explain the antidumping petition and Cemex's position.

Cemex believed that in reaching their conclusion that dumping had occurred the U.S. agencies had ignored Cemex's actual price and shipping costs. For example, Cemex sold its cement in the United States at market prices, but nearly a third of that went to the cost of transporting the cement from its plants south of the border. Zambrano noted that the ITC deducted the transportation costs and thus concluded there was dumping.[38]

Cemex argued that the antidumping petition was nothing more than an attempt by its competitors to halt its expansion in the United States. "Some of our competitors thought we were a rather weak neighbor," stated Zambrano. "And it just so happens that we grew, and they didn't like it."[39]

The ITC ruling had potentially devastating ramifications for Cemex's expansion drive into the U.S. market, and Zambrano implemented an integrated strategy, combining both market and nonmarket components. The market component consisted of a revamped short-term business strategy in response to the duty assessed. The nonmarket component focused on lowering the duty and reversing the ruling. It was designed to seek redress through three institutional arenas: administrative, judicial, and international.

### Cemex's Market Strategy[40]

First, Zambrano decided to reduce substantially Cemex's exports to the United States. This was offset to some extent by growth in Cemex's home market, which had become much more attractive because Mexico initiated a number of public works projects that caused demand for cement to grow by about 10 percent.

Second, the 58 percent duty made shipments unprofitable in states where cement prices were low, so Zambrano withdrew completely from some

---

38 "Cement Wars," *Forbes*, October 1, 1990.
39 Ibid.
40 Ibid.

U.S. states and focused only on those with higher prices. Cemex abandoned Florida outright after the ITC ruling and was content with breaking even in the higher-priced markets. Selling only in regions with high prices had the advantage of reducing the difference between U.S. and Mexican mill net prices, which would result in a lower dumping margin at the next annual review.

Third, Cemex maintained a substantial Type II (bulk) cement market in Mexico so that the ITA would compare the product sold in the U.S. market with the Mexican Type II (bulk) cement market. Cemex wanted to avoid the ITA concluding that the like product was its branded bagged cement in Mexico, which would substantially increase the dumping margin.

## Cemex's Nonmarket Strategy

As part of its nonmarket strategy Cemex requested administrative reviews of the duty, and in the first review the petitioners alleged that Cemex had created a fictitious bulk market in its home country to reduce the duties. The ITA found that no fictitious market had been created, and as a result of Cemex's new market strategy of limiting exports to regions with high prices, the duty was reduced to 30.74 percent.

Zambrano also attempted to have the ITC's ruling reversed in judicial arenas. Cemex appealed the ITC determination of material injury to the U.S. Court of International Trade (CIT), arguing that the ITC had not followed proper procedures. The CIT rejected Cemex's argument, and Cemex appealed, using the same argument, to the U.S. Court of Appeals, but was also unsuccessful. Cemex also appealed to the CIT the duties imposed by the ITA, arguing that the ITA had followed neither statutory requirements nor precedents in determining the dumping margin. The CIT, however, ruled that the overall weight of precedent was in favor of the approach used in the Cemex case. The CIT upheld the dumping duty.

After failing in the U.S. judicial arenas, the Mexican government petitioned the General Agreement on Tariffs and Trade (GATT) requesting that a panel be established to review the antidumping dispute. In July 1992 the GATT panel found that the United States had improperly imposed duties on the Mexican cement industry and recommended that $30 million in duties already collected be returned. The order to refund duties was rarely made by GATT, so the decision was considered severe. The panel did not address whether the Mexican companies had sold at less than fair value. Rather, the panel concluded that the U.S. Department of Commerce had not verified that the ad hoc committee of petitioners that brought the action was sufficiently representative of the industry. The committee represented only 61.7 percent of all U.S. cement producers in the region, but under GATT antidumping rules, the petitioner in a regional dispute must represent all or almost all of the production in the region.

Since all GATT member nations had to adopt the panel's recommendation for it to take effect, any single member could effectively block action. Concluding that the basis for the GATT panel's determination was contrary to U.S. law, the United States withheld its approval and the duties and findings imposed under U.S. trade law remained in effect.

Frustrated by the U.S. rejection of the GATT panel's decision, Cemex faced four immediate problems. First, the antidumping duty remained in effect on Cemex's remaining exports to the United States, and the U.S. producers were sure to argue at each annual administrative review that the bulk cement market in Mexico was fictitious and that bagged rather than bulk cement was the relevant like product. This posed the threat of an even higher duty. Second, Cemex had some stranded assets in terminal and distribution facilities in the United States. Third, the reduction in exports to the United States left Cemex with excess capacity in Mexico. Fortunately, domestic demand for cement had grown somewhat. Fourth, Cemex had to decide what to do about the U.S. market.

U.S. demand continued to exceed domestic capacity, creating a demand for imports. Cemex could import cement from Spain, but this left the risk of another antidumping petition. Cemex could also directly invest in the United States by building new plants. This would meet some of the shortfall in domestic supply but would reduce the need for imports and Cemex continued to want to export to the United States. Cemex could also attempt to purchase existing capacity from a U.S. producer. This would be advantageous if Cemex were confident that it could operate the plants more efficiently than the seller. Purchasing capacity would not reduce the demand for imports, leaving export opportunities if the antidumping problem could somehow be resolved. ∎

## PREPARATION QUESTIONS

1. Why might the price of cement be higher in Mexico than in the United States?
2. Is the dumping of cement likely to be harmful to the U.S. economy?
3. What was the motivation of the U.S. producers in filing the antidumping petition? Is this protectionism?
4. Evaluate Cemex's strategy for addressing the antidumping ruling. How well were its market and nonmarket components integrated?
5. After the United States withheld its approval of the GATT decision, what should Cemex do about the four problems?

# The Kodak–Fujifilm Trade Dispute

The Eastman Kodak Company (Kodak) and Fuji Photo Film Company (Fujifilm) were the dominant companies in their domestic markets and the worldwide leaders in film and photographic paper. Each had approximately 70 percent of its home market, and outside Japan and the United States Kodak had 36 percent of the market and Fujifilm had 33 percent. Kodak had long been the worldwide market leader, but in the past few decades Fujifilm had achieved major gains in market share as Kodak struggled to overcome a series of strategic mistakes outside its core lines of business. Fujifilm's dominance of the Japanese market provided it with a profit base for its expansion in the Asian, U.S., and European markets. Digital imaging technology represented a major opportunity, but it also posed a substantial threat to the core businesses of both companies.

Fujifilm and Kodak had been intense rivals for nearly 50 years, but the rivalry took a different direction in May 1995 as Kodak filed a Section 301 petition under U.S. trade law, supported by a 252-page report, charging that Japanese market practices, aided by government policies, prevented Kodak from capturing more than 7 to 10 percent of the Japanese market.[41]

Kodak charged that the principal impediment was Fujifilm's exclusive distribution arrangements with the four principal wholesalers for color film and photographic paper and that the Japanese antitrust authority, the Japan Fair Trade Commission (JFTC), was tolerating pervasive anticompetitive practices. Kodak claimed that Fujifilm controlled the four primary wholesalers that in turn controlled 70 percent of the color film market, resulting in Kodak film being available in only 15 percent of the retail outlets in Japan.[42]

In a 588-page rebuttal, Fujifilm denied both allegations and asserted that both companies had a home country advantage that had given them dominant positions in their home markets.[43] Fujifilm argued that Kodak's market share in Japan was due to consumer preferences and a series of strategic mistakes by Kodak regarding distribution and the introduction of new products. It also charged that Kodak dominated the U.S. market as a result of practices that were more egregious than those alleged to be used by Fujifilm in Japan. The conflict between the two companies turned acrimonious as George Fisher, CEO of Kodak, vowed to press on with the Section 301 petition and Fujifilm President

[41] Dewey Ballantine for Eastman Kodak Company, "Privatizing Protection: Japanese Market Barriers in Consumer Photographic Film and Consumer Photographic Paper," Memorandum in Support of a Petition Filed Pursuant to Section 301 of the Trade Act of 1974, As Amended, Rochester, NY, and Washington, DC, May 1995. (Referred to as Kodak hereafter.)

[42] Those retail outlets accounted for approximately 30 percent of film sales in Japan.

[43] Fujifilm, "Rewriting History: Kodak's Revisionist Account of the Japanese Consumer Photographic Market," Tokyo and New York, July 31, 1995. (Referred to as Fujifilm hereafter.)

Minoru Ohinishi called Kodak's allegations a violation of business ethics and said that Kodak "shamelessly made false allegations" against Fujifilm.[44]

Section 301 petitions typically led to negotiations between the countries involved, but the Minister of International Trade and Industry (MITI) vowed that Japan would not cooperate with the U.S. investigation of the allegations made by Kodak. In a news conference in Tokyo in July, Kodak's Ira Wolf said "to expect a long, drawn-out series of government-level negotiations between Japan and the United States. . . ."[45] He added, "We understand the risks inherent in going ahead with a 301 case, especially given the feelings of the average Japanese consumer about 301. But we decided there was no alternative. . . . The Office of the Trade and Investment Ombudsman [Japan] is too weak and Geneva-based World Trade Organization does not cover competition policy."[46]

### The Fuji Photo Film Co., LTD

In 1994 Fujifilm had sales of ¥1.067 trillion and net income of ¥1.142 trillion in 1992 at ¥63.771 billion. Sales peaked in 1992 at ¥1.142 trillion, and profits peaked at ¥94.778 billion in 1991. In response to its weaker economic performance and the appreciation of the yen, Fujifilm had embarked on a strategy of "localizing production." For example, in 1995 it opened a plant to produce one-time-use cameras in Greenwood, South Carolina, where it had videotape and presensitized plate manufacturing facilities. Kodak had filed an antidumping petition against Japanese producers of color photographic paper, and in 1994 Fujifilm and Konica agreed to raise their prices for imports into the United States. Fujifilm then decided to build a color photographic paper plant in South Carolina, which was scheduled to open in 1997.

### The Eastman Kodak Company

The Eastman Kodak Company was a global producer of consumer, professional, and business imaging products. Kodak had been besieged by bad investments, burdened by high costs, and had been criticized for not having done enough to counter the growth of Fujifilm from a modest domestic company to a powerful, worldwide competitor. In response to

sluggish economic performance, in 1993 Kodak's board of directors fired the CEO and recruited George Fisher, chairman of Motorola, to be CEO. Fisher's aggressive management style contrasted with Kodak's customary style and pace. He embarked on a restructuring program that included cost reduction programs, head count reductions, and the sale of its clinical diagnostics business, home products division, and pharmaceuticals business. As a result of the restructuring and new leadership, Kodak hoped that its troubles were behind it and that it was prepared to strengthen its leadership in the imaging industry.

Fisher focused Kodak on a single line of business—imaging—and began to invest heavily in digital imaging capability. He also assessed Kodak's worldwide position in all the markets in which it operated. The market that stood out was Japan. In Japan Kodak had a high share of the professional market and in sensitized plates, x-ray film, and movie film, but its share of the consumer film market stood at 8 percent with its share of the photographic paper market only slightly higher.

Fisher decided to adopt a new strategy for the Japanese market. That strategy had four components. The first was to achieve and maintain product leadership through innovation, including more rapid introduction of new products. Kodak also planned to advertise heavily in its role as official sponsor of the winter Olympics to be held in Nagano. The second was to leverage its brand name by, for example, supplying co-branded film. The third was to build a more effective organization in Japan. For example, Kodak opened a new distribution facility that significantly improved efficiency. Kodak hired as its director of Japan relations Ira Wolf, who had headed the United States Trade Representative's (USTR's) Japan office and had negotiated frequently with Japan. Kodak appointed a Japanese president of Kodak (Japan). The fourth component was to obtain greater access to the market. Fisher hired the Washington office of the law firm Dewey Ballantine to conduct a study of the Japanese market.

### Liberalization Countermeasures

Direct investment in many industries had been prohibited after World War II, but when Japan joined the OECD in 1964 it was required to eliminate its restrictions on foreign investment. The photographic supplies industry was one of the last to be liberalized, and Fujifilm was able to capture most of the growth

---

[44]This case does not attempt to assess the merits of the arguments of Kodak and Fujifilm.

[45]*Daily Yomiuri*, July 27, 1995.

[46]*Kyodo News Service*, July 26, 1995.

in the market during this period. The 1964 GATT Kennedy Round agreement required reductions in tariffs, but it was not until 1971 that the tariffs on color film and color paper were reduced to 26 percent. The 1979 Tokyo Round of GATT negotiations required countries to reduce nontariff barriers to trade in addition to tariffs.[47] According to Kodak, the tariffs and slow liberalization were one component of a set of "liberalization countermeasures" instituted by the MITI. Makoto Yokota, deputy director of MITI's chemical products division, explained, "We were afraid that Kodak would use its own capital structure to control the market with huge incentives like low prices, or attach some kind of gift to the films, and then, after ruling the market, they would raise the price. There was this worry, so we issued guidelines so that the competition would be fair."[48]

## Kodak in Japan

Kodak entered the Japanese market in 1889 and, operating through the Japanese distribution system, developed a substantial business. After World War II the Japanese government restricted the entry of foreign firms by limiting direct investment and by imposing tariffs and quotas on imports. In 1960 Kodak was told by the Japanese government that it would be required to import through a single importer, forcing Kodak to stop supplying wholesalers directly. Kodak chose the trading company Nagase & Co.

Kodak was frequently criticized for its reliance on Nagase. Abegglen and Stalk commented, "Nor does [Kodak] have control over its sales in Japan. It continues to sell through an agent, maintaining a liaison office with no direct sales force or sales management, and only indirect influence on pricing and promotion."[49] According to Huddleston, "One simply has to control the distribution to control one's destiny. This was Kodak's problem."[50]

In 1984 Kodak revised its strategy for the Japanese market, sending American managers to run its business in Japan. It formed a joint venture in

Japan to take over Nagase's Kodak division, and Kodak's shares were listed on the Tokyo stock exchange.[51] Because Japanese consumers preferred a sharper image than the softer image preferred by American consumers, Kodak reformulated its film for the Japanese market, introducing its Ektar 100 film for that market. Kodak also developed and introduced other new products for the Japanese market and advertised heavily in Japan, including sponsoring athletic events. Kodak took its campaign to the skies where its blimp, carrying the figure of a carp, which is a symbol of strength, dueled with Fuji's blimp.

Kodak imported all its consumer film and photographic paper sold in Japan. Because of economies of scale in film production and low transportation costs, it was efficient to manufacture in a relatively small number of locations. A modern machine that produced both film and photographic paper was nearly 1,000 feet long and 100 feet high.

Kodak invested $750 million in Japan and built its own distribution system with over 3,000 employees by 1992, yet its market share remained under 10 percent. Kodak believed that its sales were limited by the tight control Fuji held over the distribution system for film and photographic paper. It had thought that aggressive advertising, a strengthened sales organization, and price discounting would penetrate the Japanese market. By the 1990s, however, it was clear that its efforts were bearing little fruit.

The Japanese film and photographic paper market was the third-largest in the world with sales of $9 billion, close behind the markets in the United States and Europe. In film Fujifilm's only domestic competitor was Konica, and its only other major competitors were Kodak and Agfa.

## The Distribution System

The Japanese retail and wholesale sectors differed substantially from those of most other developed economies. Japan had substantially more retail establishments per capita, and to service them the Japanese distribution system had more layers than found in other developed countries. For many products, the distribution system included primary wholesalers that sold to secondary wholesalers that in some cases sold to tertiary wholesalers, which then

[47]In 1995 Japan had no tariffs on imported film, whereas the U.S. tariff on imported color film was 3.7 percent. Japan was the only industrialized country without a tariff on color film and photographic paper.

[48]*The New York Times*, July 5, 1995.

[49]Abegglen and Stalk (1985, p. 240).

[50]Huddleston (1990, p. 218).

[51]The acquisition of Nagase is discussed in Sieg (1994, pp. 101–108).

supplied the retailers. Manufacturers maintained close, long-term relationships with distributors, including making equity investments in them. Their relationships were said to result in implicit agreements to maintain prices. Ito referred to this pricing practice as *tatene*, or suggested pricing.[52]

Which means that the manufacturer sets the price at each level of wholesale and at retail. . . . Retailers go along with this rigid pricing structure in part because of a carrot and in part because of a stick. The carrot is that manufacturers agree to buy back all unsold inventory at the price retailers bought it for and pay rebates based on the volume sold. They also pick up promotional expenses, provide employees and accept IOUs from retailers. The stick is that retailers who object to this system find themselves subject to boycotts.[53]

The expansion of retail store chains, supermarket chains, and discount houses had increased their share of film sales to 30 percent, whereas the share held by small camera stores, photo shops, and kiosks had decreased to 50 percent. Kodak had a 25 percent share of the discount house and retail chain segment of the market in the major cities but only a very small share of the market served by small retailers.

Kodak maintained that the photographic film distribution system in Japan was dominated by four primary wholesalers—Asanuma, Misuzu, Kashimura, and Ohmiya. In the immediate postwar period they carried competing products such as Konica and Kodak film. Fujifilm, however, formed exclusive distribution arrangements under which the four wholesalers became "special contract agents," or *tokuyakuten*. Asanuma carried Fujifilm and Nikon products, and Fujifilm accounted for between 40 percent and 80 percent of the revenues of the other three. Fujifilm owned 17.8 percent of Misuzu and 15 percent of Kashimura. The *tokuyakuten* supplied Fuji film directly to large retail customers and to 300 secondary wholesalers, which in turn supplied 280,000 retail outlets.

Kodak argued that the distribution system was an "essential facility" for reaching the market segment consisting of 280,000 smaller photo shops, kiosks, and retail outlets. In addition to the exclusive

arrangements with the four primary wholesalers, control was said to be exercised through formal means including rebates used throughout the tiers of the distribution system, shareholdings of some wholesalers, and the holding by Fujifilm of security deposits made by wholesalers. Control was also said to be exercised through long-term relationships among Fujifilm, wholesalers, and retailers, as well as through their dependence on Fujifilm for most of their revenue. For fear of upsetting Fujifilm, wholesalers and retailers were said to be reluctant to discount prices of Fuji film or to sell Kodak film at significant discount from the price of Fuji film. Kodak alleged that the *tokuyakuten* maintained tight control over many retailers by threatening to cut them off from supplies if they did not comply with a wholesaler's directive. In addition, associations of retailers and wholesalers participated in the enforcement of fair trade codes, which Kodak maintained discouraged nonprice promotions as well as price discounting.

Kodak argued that the *tokuyakuten* were controlled through a rebate system constructed to promote the sale of Fuji film and discourage the sale of competitors' film. In addition to the rebates, the profit of the *tokuyakuten* depended on the price Fuji charged for film. According to Kodak, the price and the rebates were set so that the *tokuyakuten* were only marginally profitable and hence dependent on year-end rebates.

Fujifilm called Kodak's assertions about its rebates "a fantasy." In 1991 Fujifilm had revised its rebate system for the *tokuyakuten* and the progressivity was less than 0.6 percent. Fujifilm also provided rebates to retailers, but after 1990 it offered retailers rebates only to increase their sales of higher valued products, and these rebates were not progressive. The primary wholesalers also provided rebates to retailers and secondary wholesalers. The Nihon Jumbo company, an independent processor operating through 40,000 outlets, reported that Fujifilm had replaced its retail rebates with supplementary payments to share promotional expenses.

Small retailers were important in Japan, and Kodak had had difficulty selling to them. Fujifilm argued that the small retailers (e.g., kiosks) had space enough to display only one brand, and since consumers preferred Fuji film, the small retailers chose that brand. Carrying one brand also reduced the administrative costs of the small retailers. Kiosks accounted for approximately 10 percent of film sales in Japan.

[52]Ito (1992). *Tatene* is defined as "a price to be used as a standard in sales transaction." "Iwanami Japanese Dictionary, vol 4, p. 609.
[53]"Adam Smith in Tokyo," *Financial World*, 4 January 1994, p. 22. Quoted in Kodak, *op cit*, p. 49.

Albert Sieg, president of Eastman Kodak (Japan), characterized the significance of the kiosks:[54]

In fact, these tiny outlets are often replenished a number of times throughout the day by small trucks or motorbikes that deliver "just-in-time inventory": a small number of magazines, packs of cigarettes, pieces of candy, and say 10 rolls of film. Fuji film, that is, and that was the rub for us, especially the kiosks ... we spoke with many kiosk people who informed us that they had no objection to selling Kodak film but that they could sell only what the "guy on the motorcycle brings us. We don't want to upset that system in any way."

Walter Stork, president of Agfa-Gevaert Japan, commented on the difficulty of competing with a distribution system organized in this manner:

When you have one film maker that is so strong it has 70 percent of the market, the consumer tends to identify film with that brand. Getting consumers to think of another brand when buying film requires tremendous investment in advertising. However, consumer recognition is only part of the battle. Unless retailers are willing to stock the film so that consumers can buy it, expensive advertising is wasted. ... As soon as competitors found our products on the shelves, they would come and move it to the corner.[55]

In 1993 Agfa revised its strategy and began supplying private-label film to Daiei, Japan's largest retail chain; Lawson, an affiliated convenience chain; Shashimya-san 45; and Yodobashi Camera, a discount chain. Agfa's market share increased from 1 to 5 percent in 1994, but its share withered thereafter. In February 1995 Kodak began supplying at a 30 to 40 percent discount a private-label brand "CO-OP" to the Japanese Consumer Cooperative, which had 2,500 retail stores. The introduction of private-label film contributed to an estimated 10 to 15 percent retail price decline during 1994 and early 1995. Later in 1995 Kodak introduced co-branded film, which carried both the Kodak name and the retailer's name. The market for private-label and co-branded film was believed to be quite limited, however.

In addition to the vertical arrangements in the distribution system, Kodak argued that the wholesalers and retailers were organized horizontally through associations that served to limit competition. Fujifilm, Konica, and two producers of photographic paper constituted the Kanzai Kogyokai (Photo Sensitized Materials Manufacturing Association), which collected trade data. The retailers affiliated with Fujifilm and Konica constituted the Zenren (All Japan Federation of Photo Dealers), which Kodak maintained served to discourage price competition.[56] Kodak reported that "in 1995, when Kodak began selling film under private label with the Cooperative Stores the Zenren decided that 'we will ask them to consider our position.'"[57] The 19 principal wholesalers, including the *tokuyakuten*, constituted the Shashoren, and the Zenraboren was composed of the color finishing laboratories, including discounters and Kodak-affiliated laboratories. In 1982 these associations and the Camera Manufacturers Association joined to form the Kosei Torihiki Suishin Kyogikai (Fair Trade Promotion Council) to promulgate fair competition codes for industry members as a means of limiting certain types of promotional activities. These codes had been approved by the JFTC under the authority of the Premiums Law.

## Antitrust Issues

Japan's Anti-Monopoly Law (AML) was enforced by the JFTC, an Extra Ministerial Agency attached to the office of the prime minister. In practice, it was an independent commission.[58] Japanese antitrust law was in many ways similar to that in the United States, but it was more oriented toward enabling fair competition that was neither destructive nor excessive. Consequently, Japanese antitrust enforcement tended to focus on establishing guidelines for the practices of industry members. This could involve approving policies promulgated by industry members and delegating to the industry their enforcement, as in the case of the Fair Trade Promotion Council. The JFTC had rule-making authority to approve retail price maintenance cartels and to define unfair business practices. It also had

54 Sieg (1994, pp. 156–157).
55 *Financial Times*, June 1, 1995.

56 Fujifilm reported that *Zenren* has only 7,000 members of the 280,000 film retailers. Fujifilm, *op cit.*, Appendix, p 23, rejected the assertion that *Zenren* was a force for horizontal price stabilization.
57 Kodak, *op cit.*, p. 45. See also Fujifilm, *op cit.*, Appendix, p. 25.
58 See Iyori and Uesuji (1983).

quasi-judicial powers to enforce the AML through consent agreements and civil and criminal penalties.

The JFTC emphasized stopping illegal practices rather than punishing those involved as a means of deterrence. This led to relatively few formal cases.[59] When it found practices inconsistent with the AML, it typically asked the parties involved to cease the practices. Because of its dominant market position, the JFTC had classified Fujifilm as an "influential company" and monitored the film market for anticompetitive practices. Fujifilm had a code of practices intended to ensure that it did not violate the AML.[60]

Private parties with a permanent establishment in Japan could file antitrust suits under the AML, but such suits were rare for several reasons. First, no private party had ever won an antitrust suit. Second, for a private antitrust suit to be successful, the JFTC had to find a probable violation of the AML before the suit could proceed. Third, the filing fee for antitrust suits was 1 percent of the claimed damages, which discouraged lawsuits. Fourth, discovery was limited in the Japanese legal system, making it difficult for plaintiffs to substantiate charges. Fifth, the Japanese legal system did not provide for class action suits.

As a result of the Structural Impediments Initiative trade negotiations, the Japanese government agreed to adopt several new measures to strengthen its antitrust policies and enforcement activities. One such measure was the promulgation by the JFTC in 1991 of Antimonopoly Act Guidelines Concerning Distribution Systems and Business Practices. The guidelines for the distribution system pertained to "resale price maintenance, vertical nonprice restraints, providing rebates and allowances, interference in distributors' management, and abuse of dominant bargaining position by retailers."[61] The guidelines prohibited manufacturers and distributors from threatening to cut off the supply of products if distributors or retailers, for example, dealt in imported products. The guidelines also prohibited manufacturers or wholesalers from refusing to supply products to a distributor that discounted prices and from joining with manufacturers or other distributors to refuse to supply products to new entrants. As a result of his analysis of the 1991 guidelines, Richards

concluded, however, that "the nature of the Japanese legal system and the Japanese marketplace will prevent the new measures from making significant changes in the Japanese marketplace. Furthermore, it is highly questionable whether stricter antitrust enforcement measures, in general, will do anything to significantly change the Japanese marketplace."[62]

The JFTC had the authority to set Fair Competition Codes, as drafted by Fair Trade Councils. The codes were enforced by the JFTC and Prefecture Governors and monitored by the industry. These codes were authorized under Article 10 of the Law Against Unjustifiable Premiums and Misleading Representations (Premiums Law). The Premiums Law governed the use of promotional contributions and misrepresentations (e.g., misleading practices). Retailers and wholesalers were involved in enforcing the codes, such as those of the Fair Trade Promotion Council. Kodak argued that the Premium Law allowed wholesalers and retailers to limit both price and nonprice competition.

Kodak concluded that the JFTC was part of the problem. "The JFTC was itself actively engaged in, and had extended its legal authority to, a systematic campaign to stamp out a broad range of innocuous discount and promotional activity. In effect, the JFTC itself had become part of the problem."[63]

## The Trade Complaint

The Dewey Ballantine study of the Japanese market was headed by Alan W. Wolff, a former deputy USTR who was one of the nation's leading trade lawyers.[64] The completion of the study coincided with tense negotiations between Japan and the United States on access to the Japanese automobile and parts markets. In May 1995 President Clinton announced that he planned to impose 100 percent punitive tariffs on Japanese luxury car imports, and many observers believed that the threat of punitive measures was credible.

Later that month Kodak filed its Section 301 petition. The petition alleged that "The Government of Japan has also engaged in 'unreasonable' tolerance of systematic anticompetitive practices which restrict the sale of U.S. consumer film and paper in

[59]Until 1991 there had been only one criminal prosecution under the AML.
[60]Fujifilm, Legal Department, "Antimonopoly Law Don'ts," July 1992, Fujifilm, *op cit*, Exhibit 15.
[61]Richards (1993, p. 942).
[62]Richards (1993, p. 947).
[63]Kodak, p. 135.
[64]Mr. Wolff is the subject of an article "Wolff at the Door," by Ben Wildavsky, *National Journal*, August 5, 1995, pp. 1994–1997.

Japan. The Fuji distribution system and its associated conduct are inconsistent with at least Articles 3, 8(1), and 19 of the AML [Anti-Monopoly Law]. The Japanese government tolerated the anticompetitive practices systematically by not vigorously enforcing the AML, by aggressively supporting the so-called industry 'Fair Competition Codes,'..."[65] Kodak concluded that "Japanese market barriers in [color film and photographic paper] have cost Kodak an estimated $5.6 billion in foregone export sales since the mid-1970s, have enabled Fuji to amass a cash surplus of $10 billion in its home market sanctuary, have fostered dumping in the U.S. market, and are fundamentally altering the global competitive balance between the two companies."[66] The Section 301 petition was a key element of the market access component of Kodak's Japan strategy. Kodak also hoped to pry open the distribution system by inducing secondary wholesalers and perhaps one of the *tokuyakuten* to carry its products.[67]

In filing a Section 301 petition, Kodak chose a relatively political channel for market opening, but it believed that without a formal petition its complaints would not receive attention. In conjunction with the release of the Dewey Ballantine study and the filing of the Section 301 petition, Kodak and Dewey Ballantine conducted a high-profile public relations and lobbying campaign designed to build public and political support for its action. Fisher and Wolff held press conferences and lobbied in Washington. In a major coup for Kodak, *The New York Times* in an editorial entitled "Tokyo's Trade Hypocrisy" stated, "The upshot is that Kodak's sales are limited despite the high quality and competitive prices of its products. Japanese officials blatantly violated bilateral commerce accords, international trade accords and Japan's own antitrust laws to keep Fuji atop the market."[68] Kodak also lobbied in Congress, and Fisher obtained a letter of support

from Senate Majority Leader Robert Dole.[69] Fisher explained, "I've never lost to a good Japanese company in my life.... When you are sitting down with less than 10 percent market share and in the rest of the world you're sitting around 40 percent or higher, something is funny some place."[70]

Kodak's nonmarket strategy was presaged by the nonmarket strategies of Motorola and the Semiconductor Industry Association (SIA). In 1983 when he represented the SIA, Wolff pioneered the strategy of preparing a detailed industry study in support of a Section 301 petition. While at Motorola Fisher had been involved in trade disputes with Japan, as Motorola sought to unlock the Japanese markets for its pagers, semiconductors, and cellular telephone equipment. Fisher was the head of Motorola's pager division and was able to enlist the aid of the U.S. government in opening the Japanese market to Motorola pagers, and he was later involved in the cellular telephone dispute.[71]

Motorola's strategy had two objectives. One was to obtain access to the potentially lucrative Japanese market. The other was to make certain that its Japanese rival did not have a protected sanctuary from which it could generate profits to fund its worldwide competition and expansion. Motorola Chairman Robert W. Galvin referred to this as the "Principle of Sanctuary."[72]

You cannot allow any competitor to have sanctuary in his or her native market and be allowed to roam in your market in a way that would both cultivate customers and undermine your strengths. Simply put, you must find your way effectively into his native sanctuary.... We simply knew we could not leave Japanese competitors the isolation in Japan, while they prospected in our home market.

Fisher said, "While Fuji competes with Kodak on a global basis, it makes virtually all of its profits

---

65 Kodak, pp. 19-20.

66 Kodak, p. i.

67 For example, in 1995 Oriental, one of the producers and distributors of color photographic paper, began to distribute Kodak paper.

68 *The New York Times*, June 1, 1995. The editorial also stated, "To be fair, Fuji has not had the opportunity to respond fully to charges. But Kodak's case will be tough to refute." Bill Barringer, counsel to Fujifilm, was astounded by the *Times* editorial. "It's incredible to me that *The Times* did that. Any lawyer can put together a petition that makes their case look good. How can you write an editorial like that before getting the facts from the other side?" (*National Journal*, August 5, 1995, p. 1995.)

---

69 As Wolff characterized the perspective in the *National Law Journal* in 1987, "In a large trade case, the interaction of legislative activity, litigation and public policy-making in the executive branch can provide the solution. It's absolutely necessary to lobby."

70 *The Wall Street Journal*, May 19, 1995.

71 See Baron (1996), pp. 492–493, 505–575 for a discussion of the cellular telephone dispute.

72 Robert W. Galvin, "International Business and the Changing Nature of Global Competition," Miami University, Oxford, OH, October 1992.

in Japan, using those proceeds to finance low-price sales outside Japan."[73] He also said, "The Japan market, a large percentage, maybe 70 percent, is closed to us. And as a result, Fuji is allowed to have a profit sanctuary and amass a great deal of money, which they use to buy market share in Europe and in the United States."[74]

Fisher added, "All we are seeking is the opportunity to compete in an open market. We want resolution, not retaliation. Nor do we want market share targets. We want an end to illegal market barriers. . . . Kodak sells world class products. If given the chance, we believe that our products can compete successfully in any market. We have not had that chance in Japan."[75] Wolff explained, "This is not a spat between the companies. There is illegal activity taking place—it is not an industry-to-industry matter but a U.S. government concern over whether the government of Japan is behaving properly, reasonably."[76]

## Fujifilm's Response

Immediately upon Kodak's filing of the Section 301 petition, Fujifilm responded by sending to the media and the South Carolina congressional delegation a 16-page letter rejecting Kodak's allegations. Fujifilm hired the U.S. law firm Wilkie Farr & Gallagher to prepare a rebuttal and hired Edelman Communications to handle the public relations associated with the response. Its 588-page rebuttal to Kodak's claims was issued on July 31, 1995.

Fujifilm was infuriated by Kodak's filing and its timing. President Minouri Ohnishi characterized Kodak's actions as follows:[77]

Kodak has violated all the standards of business ethics. It has shamelessly made false allegations against Fujifilm in a self-serving attempt to use political pressure to accomplish what its own lack of managerial effort and failed marketing strategies have not been able to accomplish. What is most troubling about Kodak's action is not that it attempts to tarnish Fujifilm with false allegations of anticompetitive practices, but that it attempts to exploit growing tensions between the U.S. and Japan on trade issues to the detriment of

a crucial bilateral relationship. . . . Kodak's management, however, seems to view the bilateral tensions as an opportunity for Kodak to gain through the political process what it has been unable to gain through the competitive process.

Fujifilm argued that the Section 301 petition was without merit and that such petitions must be addressed to present and not past practices, stating that "any alleged violations [of treaties] ended some 20 years ago."[78] Moreover, Fujifilm argued that Kodak should exhaust domestic remedies in Japan before resorting to a Section 301 petition. Fujifilm stated that Kodak

1. has never complained to the Japan Fair Trade Commission (JFTC) about Fujifilm's alleged anticompetitive practices;

2. has never taken its case to the Office of Trade and Investments, an ombudsman system created to mediate market opening disputes; and

3. has made no attempt to introduce the issue onto the agenda of the U.S.–Japanese bilateral negotiations under the Framework Agreement.

Bill Barringer, senior partner of Wilkie Farr & Gallagher, stated that there were three primary ways Kodak could increase its market share in Japan—by competing on price, through innovation, and with massive advertising. Barringer said that Kodak failed on all three accounts.

- **Price**—With the exception of a brief period in the early 1980s, Kodak has maintained a relatively small discount off of Fujifilm's prices. It has never seriously attempted to gain market share by pricing aggressively relative to Fujifilm, and Kodak executives have been quoted as saying that they have no intention of doing so in the future.

- **Innovation**—Fujifilm has consistently beaten Kodak to market with new and popular products. When Fujifilm introduced the first one-time-use camera and high-resolution ISO 400 film in Japan, it took Kodak more than 2 years to introduce similar products.

[73]*International Trade Reporter*, BNA, Inc., June 7, 1995.
[74]*Moneyline*, August 2, 1995.
[75]Eastman Kodak Company press release, July 27, 1995.
[76]*The Christian Science Monitor*, August 2, 1995.
[77]Fuji Film Photo Co. press release, Tokyo, July 31, 1995.
[78]Wilkie Farr & Gallagher, "Comments of Fujifilm Regarding Legal Issues," filed in conjunction with USTR Docket No. 301–99, August 8, 1995, p. 2.

These products account for almost two-thirds of the total color film market in Japan.

• **Advertising**—In relative terms, Kodak has not spent enough on advertising in Japan, a prerequisite for improving brand awareness and capturing additional market share. Kodak makes much of the fact that it spent 5.3 billion yen on advertising between 1986 and 1988. However, over the same period Konica spent 8 times this amount on advertising, and Fujifilm spent 10 times this amount.

Kodak countered that it had been an innovator in the Japanese market, introducing "Ektar 1000 film, the Weekend 35 single-use camera, and the Panorama single-use camera—all tailored for Japanese consumers. Recently, Kodak's Snap Kids EX has won favorable reviews from the Japanese press."[79] Kodak also said that when it had sharply discounted prices, many of the retailers refused to pass along the discounts to consumers for fear of upsetting Fujifilm. Kodak provided data indicating that it had lowered its wholesale price of ISO 400 film by over 50 percent since 1986, but retailers continued to price its film in the same proportion to the price of Fuji film.

## Fujifilm's Allegations About the U.S. Market

In its rebuttal Fujifilm argued that Kodak's practices and dominance of the U.S. market were worse than Kodak's allegations about the Japanese market and Fujifilm's practices. The U.S. market differed in several ways from the Japanese market. First, retail chains, such as Wal-Mart, Kmart, Eckerd Drugs, Walgreens, and Rite Aide, accounted for a large share of film sales, whereas in Japan chains accounted for only a third of sales. Second, the chains bargained with and sought bids from film suppliers for exclusive supply of photographic paper and for placement of film in checkout lanes and other high-traffic areas. Third, manufacturers supplied the chains and other retailers directly without going through wholesalers.

Decades earlier Kodak's anticompetitive practices had resulted in two antitrust consent decrees, but those decrees were lifted by the courts in 1994. The standard used in cases alleging horizontal market power was whether a restriction in output would result in higher prices. In judging this issue, the courts looked to the availability of substitutes, including imports, that could offset any reduction in output. Antitrust authorities also looked to the relevant market. In lifting the two consent decrees, the court concluded that the relevant market was worldwide and that given Kodak's 40 percent market share, it did not have the market power to restrict output and force prices higher. The court concluded that imports and private-label film would rush in to offset any restriction of output by Kodak.

Fujifilm maintained that if this standard were applied to Japan, a court would conclude that it did not exercise market power in Japan. Kodak disagreed, however, arguing that imports and private-label film could not reach most of the retail outlets because Fujifilm had locked up the distribution system, which was the only means of reaching those outlets.

Fujifilm stated that Kodak had exclusive arrangements for color film with several major retail chains, including Eckerd Drugs, Caldor, Publix Supermarkets, Bradlees, Kmart, the Army and Air Force Exchange Service, and several major theme parks. Kodak's exclusive contracts with retailers were alleged to have been won through bids providing lump-sum, up-front payments. Kodak was reported to have paid Kmart $25 million up front to win all its photofinishing.[80] Competitors such as Fujifilm, with smaller market shares, argued that they could not match such payments. In 1996, however, Fujifilm outbid Kodak for a 10-year exclusive contract with Wal-Mart for the supply of photographic paper.

George Fisher responded to Fujifilm's allegations, stating, "For Fuji or the Japanese government to claim that what Kodak faces in Japan is the 'mirror image' of what Fuji faces in the United States is absurd. What Fuji is trying to do is take the focus off the facts."[81] ■

[79] Eastman Kodak, "Kodak Answers: Counter Points to Fuji's Assertions Regarding Kodak's Market Access Case," Rochester, NY, July 24, 1995.

[80] Fujifilm, p. 253.
[81] *The Wall Street Journal*, July 31, 1995.

## PREPARATION QUESTIONS

1. Why is the Japanese market so important to Kodak? Does Fujifilm have a profit sanctuary? Where is it?
2. Assess Kodak's market strategy in Japan prior to George Fisher becoming CEO. What were the causes of Kodak's problems in the Japanese market?
3. Evaluate Kodak's market and nonmarket alternatives for penetrating the Japanese market.
4. How well integrated were Kodak's market and nonmarket strategies? What other steps, if any, should Fisher take? In its discussions with the USTR, what specific concessions should Kodak press for?
5. Assess Fujifilm's strategy in response to the petition.
6. Was Kodak acting responsibly in filing a Section 301 petition?

# Sophis Networks and Encryption Export Controls (A)

On September 24, 1999, Joanne Mercer, vice president of Sophis Networks and head of the Security Products Division, faced a frustrating situation. She and the Government Affairs Group at Sophis Networks had spent the last 2½ years working closely with Congress and the Clinton administration to relax U.S. export restrictions on encryption products. Mercer had worked for passage of the Security and Freedom through Encryption Act (SAFE), but President Clinton had just pledged to veto it, and he announced his own legislative proposal. Sophis and other technology companies were dismayed by the proposal, which they believed would impair their competitiveness and cost them sales. The Clinton administration was concerned that the export of encryption products would impede the Federal Bureau of Investigation's (FBI) and the National Security Agency's (NSA) abilities to fight terrorists, spies, and criminals, who could conceal their plans using encryption products.

Encryption or cryptography is the science of designing code techniques that protect computer files and communications from eavesdroppers, hackers, spies, and other criminals. Encryption products allow employees confidential access to corporate data from remote locations using a public network. Encryption products protect medical records, corporate trade secrets, data on personal buying habits, air-traffic control centers, legal documents, credit histories, hospital databases, credit card transactions, and e-mail. Many companies, including Microsoft, Network Associates, Sun Microsystems, Lucent, Dell, IBM, Cisco Systems, and Sophis Networks, incorporated encryption and security technology into their products.

The United States restricted exports of encryption products and systems requiring encryption, allowing exports only of low-strength encryption products, whereas companies outside the U.S. could sell any type and strength of encryption products worldwide. The U.S. government worried that U.S. companies, including Sophis Networks, had sophisticated encryption products that were practically impenetrable, allowing terrorists and criminals to use encryption to conceal their activities. The export controls, however, meant lost sales for U.S. companies, since their customers outside the United States demanded products with the highest level of encryption available. Not only was encryption software affected by the controls, but more importantly, servers, computer systems, and other hardware systems incorporating encryption software were affected. A 1996 study estimated that the restrictions on encryption technology could cost the U.S.

information industry $30 to $60 billion in sales by the year 2000 and cost 200,000 high-skill, high-wage jobs.[82]

## Encryption

Cryptography dates back nearly 3,000 years to early Egypt. Between 50 and 60 B.C., Julius Caesar sent messages to Rome's distant forces using an encryption method that shifted and transposed the letters of their alphabet in a secret manner.[83] During the American Revolution, Benedict Arnold, while arranging his betrayal of West Point, passed secret correspondence to the British by using a code based on the legal classic "Commentaries on the Laws of England."[84] The use of cryptography flourished during World War II, and the United States succeeded in cracking the German "Ultra" codes and the Japanese "Purple" codes. In the postwar period cryptography increasingly involved computers to break codes, and the U.S. government began to view encryption as an important part of its national security system. The transfer of confidential data, messages, and information over communications networks and subsequently over the Internet dramatically increased the need for strong encryption products.

Cryptography involves making a "message incomprehensible to anyone who is not in possession of secret information needed to restore the message (ciphertext) to its normal plaintext form. The secret information is called the key, and its function is very similar to the function of a door key in a lock: it unlocks the message so that the recipient can read it."[85] Encryption converts a plain message to a secret message, and decryption is the process of converting the ciphertext back to its plaintext format.

Symmetric cryptography uses the same key for both encrypting and decrypting the coded message. To send a message about the time and location of a meeting at 3:25 P.M. on December 30, 2002, at the corner of 1st Avenue and 44th Street, the sender's message takes the following form:

| Year | Date | Time | Street |
| --- | --- | --- | --- |
| 2002 | 12 30 | 15 25 | 01 44 |

To encrypt the message, the sender and the receiver must agree on a key to transform the string of 14 digits into another string of 14 digits. Suppose the key was

*64 25 83 09 76 23 55 12*

The first agent would add the two strings and send the encrypted result

*84 27 95 39 91 48 56 56*

which would then be decrypted using the same (symmetric) key.

Symmetric cryptographic systems used in the mid-1990s usually involved an electronic machine that would encrypt and decrypt information by looking up data or letters in tables and adding them together using an arithmetic operation.[86] These systems, however, had an inherent vulnerability—finding a secure method to distribute the key among senders and receivers and protect it while in the custody of the recipients.

In the mid-1970s two Stanford University scientists, Whitfield Diffie and Martin Hellman, invented asymmetric encryption, or public key encryption, which sought to eliminate the symmetric key vulnerabilities. In public key encryption, the key used for encryption is different from the key used for decryption. Each person receives both a public and a private key.

1. A public key is used to encrypt a message that can only be decrypted using the mathematically linked private key. The public key is publicly available and can be transmitted and stored on unsecured networks, whereas the private key must be secured and is not transmitted. To send a message to person B, Person A looks up in a directory B's public key and uses that to encrypt the message so that it can only be decrypted with B's private key.

2. To ensure that a particular encrypted message is genuine, A uses her private key at encryption time to create a digital signature attached to the message. B then uses A's public key and the message to verify A's signature.[87]

Although the public and private keys are mathematically related, it is difficult or computationally

---

[82]Computer Systems Policy Project (CSPP), *Perspectives on Security in the Information Age.* (Washington, DC: CSPP, January 1996), p. 10. The members of CSPP are the CEOs of Compaq, Dell, Hewlett-Packard, IBM, Intel, Lucent Technologies, NCR, SGI, Sun Microsystems, and Unisys.

[83]Kahn (1967, p. 83).

[84]Stender (1998).

[85]Diffie and Landau (1998, p. 13).

[86]Diffie and Landau (1998, p. 25).

[87]www.rsasecurity.com/rsalabs/faq/2-1-1.html.

infeasible to derive one key from the other, thus making public key cryptography more secure than symmetric cryptography. The level of security provided by public key cryptography depends on the length (measured in "bits") of the public and private keys.[88] The more bits a key has, the more possible combinations a potential code-breaker would have to test and hence the stronger the encryption. For example, 56-bit symmetric encryption has 72,057,594,037,927,900 possible keys, and 128-bit symmetric encryption has 340,282,366,920,938,000,000,000,000,000,000,000 possible keys.

## Everyday Uses of Cryptography

Many Web sites encrypt incoming and outgoing data so that consumers can securely use online banking, trading, and shopping. When consumers enter their credit card information on a Web site, the information and often the entire online session is encrypted. The Web server, or computer where the site's data are stored, receives the encrypted information and decrypts it, authenticates the card and the user (proves the user is who he or she claims to be), and authorizes the transaction. When investors trade securities online, they authenticate themselves (give the site access to their credentials) and obtain authorization. As their transaction begins, the data are encrypted.

E-mail security products automatically encrypt e-mail messages and attachments, authenticate senders, and verify that the contents have not changed in transit. Software such as Lotus Notes, Netscape's browser, and the Eudora e-mail program require encryption technology. Cryptography is also used to regulate satellite and cable television services. Cable companies use encryption technology to give consumers the regular and upgraded cable packages they order. They also use encryption with pay-per-view movies, which are decoded when the cable company sends a signal to the subscriber's cable box.[89]

Virtually all companies use encryption technology to protect their data from potential intruders. As end users, employees have user profiles, allowing them access to various authorized levels of company information. Encryption technology enables the

authentication of machines (PCs, remote devices, and other hardware used to access corporate data) and users (individuals who must enter personal codes and passwords to gain entry).

## Key Recovery

Key recovery is used to provide access to encrypted information, whether for intelligence or law enforcement purposes or merely because an encryption key was lost, forgotten, or misplaced. One key recovery method is escrowed encryption, where a trusted third party keeps "in escrow" part or all of a key. Government agencies such as the FBI could then recover the key when necessary. The FBI sought a "back door" into computer systems by requiring escrowed keys to be integrated into encryption and computer systems, giving it access to private information. However, giving the government access to private information (even through a trusted third party) raised privacy issues.[90] Sophis Networks had refused to include key recovery in its products.

When raw data or information was created and stored on a computer or device, they were in a form that could be accessed without a key. In the case of a message, this would be the case prior to the data being encrypted on the sender's machine or after it was decrypted on the receiver's machine. Companies such as Sophis Networks could pinpoint where the raw data was located on the receiver's machine, providing three points at which to access the new data, similar to a "digital wiretap."

## How Secure Is Encrypted Information?

Until the mid-1990s the U.S. government believed that 56-bit symmetric encryption was effectively impenetrable to even sophisticated data hackers. Then, in 1997 a team of technology professionals proved the government wrong. Granted a budget of approximately $1 million, the team cracked a 512-bit RSA Security asymmetric encryption code after 8 months of effort (roughly equivalent to 56-bit symmetric encryption).[91] In January 1999 the Electronic Frontier Foundation's "Deep Crack" computer won RSA Security's Challenge III by cracking

[88]Levin (1999).
[89]RSA Security Laboratory. See www.rsasecurity.com. RSA Security is a leading cryptography supplier.

[90]For a more detailed description of key recovery, see RSA Security's Web site (www.rsasecurity.com). For additional details see www.rsasecurity.com/rsalabs/faq/7-12.html.
[91]Asymmetric and symmetric encryption have different measurements. In general, asymmetric algorithms require longer keys to provide the same level of security as their symmetric key cousins.

a message encoded with 56-bit symmetric encryption in a record-breaking 22 hours and 15 minutes.

Experts now believe that hackers and technology specialists can break any code.[92] In 2000 RSA Security recommended 768-bit asymmetric encryption technology for personal use (80-bit symmetric encryption), 1024-bit asymmetric encryption for corporate use (128-bit symmetric encryption), and 2048-bit asymmetric encryption for highly sensitive information (256-bit symmetric encryption).[93]

## The Encryption Policy Issue

In the late 1990s the Clinton administration created an Interagency Group to work on data security issues, including encryption. The White House Office of Science and Technology Policy and the National Security Council chaired the group. The Interagency Group included representatives of the Office of Management and Budget, FBI, NSA, Department of Justice, Department of Commerce, State. The Administration argued that the proliferation of robust encryption products would make it easier for terrorists, spies, and criminals to conceal their activities and hence extremely difficult to gather intelligence, ensure national security, and enforce the law. The FBI and NSA cited the success of telephone wiretapping to support their argument. In addition to lawful wiretaps and searches, the government met its security objectives by clandestinely intercepting communications by criminals and terrorists. Each year wiretaps or electronic surveillance methods were responsible for the arrests of more than 2,000 people in the United States, of which approximately 20 percent resulted in conviction.[94]

The FBI and NSA generated concern in Congress and the Administration with accounts of terrorist attacks and global crime. These accounts were typically presented in closed briefings of congressional committees. In these closed briefings, technology companies and privacy advocates were prohibited from participating but could observe the proceedings. The observers were not allowed to provide any information on the content of the briefings to their organizations but were allowed to state whether anything discussed was important to their organizations. In support of continued export controls, the Interagency Group used a series of incidents to demonstrate their concern. The bombing of the World Trade Center by Ramzi Yousef was a case in point.[95] Yousef used over-the-counter encryption technology in his laptop computer, which took FBI experts more than a year to decipher. Once deciphered, the FBI discovered that among Yousef's terrorist projects was a plan to blow up 11 U.S. airliners in the Western Pacific in one day. A report by the National Strategy Information Center's Working Group on Organized Crime added to the Interagency Group's and the Administration's concerns. Two researchers estimated that in at least 500 cases worldwide criminals had used encryption. The study reported that the use of encryption by criminals was growing at a rate of 50 to 100 percent a year. Despite this growth the NSA told the House National Security committee in a classified briefing that a "good percentage" of the intelligence it received was still unencrypted, said Representative Patrick Kennedy (D-RI), a member of the committee.[96]

Technology companies, consumer privacy advocates, and some members of Congress, however, viewed the issue quite differently. U.S. companies contended that since strong encryption technology was already available around the world to legitimate users, terrorists, and criminals alike, the encryption export controls were doomed to failure. A study by the George Washington University School of Engineering and Applied Science found good encryption programs available outside the United States on more than 800 Web sites.[97]

Moreover, the companies argued that due to export policy, they and the United States were rapidly losing their leadership position in encryption technology. The technology sector was also losing potential sales and thus jobs, in addition to spending large sums to alter their operations to satisfy the export controls. For example, Sophis Networks had to offer its servers with three encryption systems—one for the open global market, one for the export-controlled segment of the global market, and one for the U.S. and Canadian markets. The

[92]RSA Security Laboratory. See www.rsasecurity.com.
[93]RSA Security Laboratory. See www.rsasecurity.com.
[94]Jim Puzzanghera, "Encryption Dealt a Blow," *San Jose Mercury News*, September 10, 1998, p. C1.

[95]Levin (1999).
[96]C4I News, "HNSC Revises Encryption Bill," September 11, 1997.
[97]"Enemies of the State," *News World Communications*, September 13, 1999.

companies also argued that the U.S. government was fighting a losing battle, since strong encryption was now being supplied by competitors in other countries. About 75 percent of the world's software was generated in the United States, but with the export controls on strong encryption products, U.S. companies had lost one-third of their market share in encryption software in 1998.[98]

Global customers preferred products and systems with strong encryption, but due to U.S. export restrictions, international customers were forced to purchase separate encryption devices and bolt them onto U.S. computer systems.[99] This was both expensive and clumsy and represented a competitive disadvantage for U.S. companies.[100] Brokat, a German company, provided strong encryption products for half the European Internet banking market and provided support for other forms of Internet commerce.[101] Analysts estimated that more than 500 non-U.S. encryption products were sold on the market by mid-1998, compared to only a handful in 1993.[102] "The U.S. really shot itself in the foot on this one," stated Stefan Roever, a managing partner at Brokat. Baltimore Technologies PLC, an Irish company selling encryption products, cited over 3,000 inquiries per day on its Web site. Siemens AG installed Baltimore's product at more than 500 corporate sites throughout Europe.[103] Microsoft claimed it had lost "hundreds of thousands" of potential users of its software. Consensus Development Corporation, which licensed encryption products to IBM, said it lost approximately 40 percent of new business leads because of U.S. encryption policy.[104]

U.S. software companies were also forced to alter their U.S. operations as a result of encryption export controls. For example, Netscape Communications continuously had to monitor its Internet site to prevent users from other countries from downloading the U.S. version of its browser, which featured 128-bit encryption.

Privacy advocates were also concerned about encryption policy. Information sent over the Internet passed through dozens of different computer systems on the way to its destination. A different system operator might manage each of these systems, and each system could be capable of capturing and storing the information. Furthermore, the online activities of Internet users could be monitored, both by their own service provider and by the system operator of any Web site they visited. Privacy advocates sought strong encryption products to protect the privacy of personal information and electronic transactions. They were particularly concerned that if communications and transactions over the Internet were subject to key recovery, the privacy of all Internet users would be jeopardized.

## Evolution of U.S. Encryption Policy

During the postwar period, the Central Intelligence Agency (CIA) and the FBI became increasingly concerned about the evolution of encryption technology. The NSA took the lead in the development and creation of encryption technology, employing a majority of the encryption experts.[105]

With the advent of the information economy, private companies began to develop encryption technologies outside the reach of the NSA. The U.S. government became increasingly concerned and tried to control the proliferation of encryption technology through export controls and escrowed encryption keys. The government classified all encryption technologies as "munitions" and subjected them to the Arms Export Control Act (AECA) and the International Traffic in Arms Regulations (ITAR), administered by the U.S. Department of State. Placing encryption products under the jurisdictions of the AECA and ITAR reflected the government's perception of the significant national security risk of exported encryption products.

## Export Controls

By the mid-1990s encryption policy had become more important to the Clinton administration and Congress. On November 15, 1996, the Administration removed encryption technology from the

---

98"Safe Encryption Bill Re-Introduced," *TechWeb News*, February 25, 1999.

99International customers also were confused by U.S. government policy and concerned that so-called "back doors" had been built into U.S. systems to allow U.S. law enforcement access to private information.

100As of 1996, there were more than 300 companies that developed and exported cryptographic products from within the United States and more than 355 outside the United States. *Source:* Computer Systems Policy Project, *op. cit.,* p. 10.

101President's Export Council Subcommittee on Encryption (PECSENC), September 18, 1998. See 209.122.145.150/presidentsexportcouncil/pecsenc/iwgfind.htm.

102Kimberley A. Strassel, "U.S. Rules Boost Europe's Encryption—European Competitors Cash in on U.S. Export Limits," *The Wall Street Journal*, July 7, 1998, p. B8.

103Ibid.

104Ibid.

---

105Levin (1999).

Munitions List and transferred jurisdiction from the Department of State to the Department of Commerce. Encryption was designated as a dual-use commodity subject to the Export Administration regulations, and specific encryption technology export controls were established. Within the United States any strength encryption technology could be used, but exports of encryption products were restricted. Fifty-six-bit symmetric encryption software could be exported freely once a one-time inspection showed that the technology incorporated key recovery. Foreign banks and foreign subsidiaries of U.S. companies were granted exceptions to the key recovery provision. The Administration's policy meant that the encryption exported was not really private, since a central administrator could turn keys over to law enforcement agencies when deemed necessary. Only "mass market software" with 40-bit or lower strength encryption could be freely exported after a 15-day review process.[106]

An export license for any encryption product or technology required a cumbersome and confusing application process. "What's written or published is only about 40 percent of what you need to know . . . from a regulatory standpoint, it's chaos," said Ken Bass, a partner at the Washington, D.C., law firm Venable, Baetjer, Howard & Civelletti. To receive export licenses for products incorporating strong encryption, multiple applications and extensive justifications were necessary. "You have to show a long-term relationship with the business partner and provide evidence, such as contracts."[107] Under the export rules, financial institutions received special permission to export strong 128-bit encryption technology but were restricted to encrypting only financial transactions and could not use the technology for general-purpose communication.

Technology companies and privacy advocates so strongly criticized this policy that the Administration established a task force to reshape the policy. On September 16, 1998, the Clinton administration announced a new encryption export policy containing four important changes:

1. Elimination of key recovery for "mass market" 56-bit encryption and permission to

export freely, except to the seven "terrorist" nations, after a one-time license exception.[108]

2. Expansion of the definition of "financial institution" to include worldwide subsidiaries of U.S. firms, insurance companies, health and medical organizations (not including biochemical/pharmaceutical manufacturers), and online merchants.

3. Continuation of the policy allowing key recovery products to be exported under a license exception.

4. Provision for other export requests to be approved on a case-by-case basis.

From the perspective of U.S. companies these changes were an improvement over earlier policies, but the new policy still did not allow the export of encryption stronger than 56-bit to individuals, companies, or government agencies in foreign countries, unless they were classified as a financial institution. Energy suppliers, telecommunications companies, the transportation industry, foreign governments, and human rights organizations were critical of the new policy.[109] Foreign governments were often the largest purchasers of strong encryption, but the U.S. government feared that some would use encryption technology to threaten U.S. national security.

As the complaints continued, members of Congress in 1997 introduced seven bills on encryption technology. No bill made it very far through the congressional process because the business, privacy, and national security concerns led to furious debates. One of these bills was SAFE.

## The Security and Freedom Through Encryption Act

SAFE was introduced by Representative Bob Goodlatte (R-VA) and subsequently gained and lost momentum a number of times. The original intent of the bill was the full relaxation of encryption export controls with no key escrow requirement or bit limit. The bill received strong support

[106] Levin (1999, pp. 530–532).
[107] Ellen Messmer, "Navigating the World of Government Encryption Export Rules," *Network World,* May 18, 1998, p. 8.

[108] The seven terrorist nations were Cuba, Iran, Iraq, Libya, Sudan, Syria, and North Korea.
[109] In a number of countries human rights organizations were the most common targets of government surveillance, since some governments viewed these organizations as security risks. Levin (1999, pp. 540–550).

from privacy advocates and technology companies alike. SAFE would

1. Permit the export of mass-market software and custom-designed software and hardware with encryption capabilities comparable to that already commercially available from foreign suppliers.

2. Impose stiff penalties for the use of encryption to commit or conceal a crime.

3. Allow U.S. companies to buy or sell any type of encryption within the United States and not require computer users to turn over copies of their keys to the U.S. government.

Because of its broad implications SAFE was referred to the House National Security (Armed Forces) Committee as well as to the International Relations, Intelligence, Judiciary, and Commerce committees. After the bill was reported, however, it stalled in the House Rules Committee as a result of opposition by the chair.

In 1999 SAFE was re-introduced by representatives Goodlatte and Zoe Lofgren (D-CA) with broader support and 258 co-sponsors. The bill was reported by the committees and given a rule by the House Rules Committee, preparing it for floor consideration. Even though the Senate had not yet considered the bill, President Clinton declared he would veto it.

### U.S. Encryption Policy in 1999: Continued Export Control

On September 16, 1999, the Clinton administration "announced a new approach to encryption."[110] The new strategy rested on three principles: "a one-time technical review of encryption products in advance of sale, a streamlined post-export reporting system, and a process that permits the government to review the exports of strong encryption to foreign government and military organizations and to nations of

concern . . . consistent with these principles, the government will significantly update and simplify export controls on encryption."[111] Under this new policy,

1. Any encryption commodity or software of any key length could be exported under license exception (i.e., without a license), after a technical review, to individuals, commercial firms, and other nongovernment end users in any country except for the seven state supporters of terrorism.

2. Any retail encryption commodities and software of any key length could be exported under license exception, after a technical review, to any end user in any country, except for the seven state supporters of terrorism.

3. Streamlined post-export reporting would provide government with an understanding of where strong encryption was being exported.

4. Sector definitions and country lists were eliminated.[112]

When privacy advocates, members of Congress, and technology companies read the details of Clinton's new approach to encryption, however, they were dismayed. For example, major customers of U.S. technology companies such as European telecommunications firms would be ineligible for unlicensed export sales because they were partly government-owned.[113] The new approach also continued to require an exporter to obtain permission to sell encryption products to foreign governments.

## Sophis Networks Company Background

Sophis Networks' Security Products Division, which included approximately 200 employees worldwide, developed security and encryption software for businesses, generating over $100 million in product revenue in 1999. The division provided end-to-end security solutions for organizations such as brokerage companies with Internet businesses, companies giving their employees access to privileged information, and ASPs (application service providers) that hosted services for customers. Sophis Networks' principal

---

[110]Statement released by the White House, "Administration Announces New Approach to Encryption," *U.S. Newswire*, September 16, 1999. In the same statement, Clinton transmitted to Congress the Cyberspace Electronic Security Act (CESA) to ensure that law enforcement agencies could access decrypted information, while protecting that information from inappropriate release. In addition, it authorized $80 million over 4 years for the FBI's technical support center, which would serve as a centralized technical resource for federal, state, and local law enforcement agencies for their use in responding to the increasing use of encryption by criminals.

[111]Ibid.
[112]Ibid.
[113]Bruce Seneier, "1999 Crypto: The Year in Review," *Cryptorhythms*, December 1999, p. 20.

activity was selling compatible and easily integrated security software technology to companies providing operating systems (e.g., Hewlett-Packard and Sun Microsystems). Its products helped companies authenticate users (similar to an ATM card with a PIN), authorize user access to certain information (according to a predetermined "profile" of the individual seeking access), provide services (supply information), and encrypt information as it was transmitted over public or private networks.

During the 1990s an increasingly important component of Sophis Networks' business had become the sale of enterprise servers, desktop systems, and network computing software. The company's customers and their customers needed to send secure information over a corporate network or through the Internet.[114] Sophis Networks recognized that intruders could potentially gain access to this information if strong encryption were not incorporated into their systems. Moreover, as the Internet continued to grow as a communication and commerce medium, the issue of data privacy was becoming a top priority for companies, individuals, and governments. In a not-so-bold forecast, Sophis Networks predicted that effective encryption security would not only be in great demand in all sectors of U.S. society, but also worldwide. The challenge for Joanne Mercer, other product managers, and the government affairs office at Sophis Networks was to sell Sophis Networks' servers and systems with strong integrated encryption software freely both in the United States and worldwide.

## Sophis Networks' Market Strategy

Because of the encryption export controls, companies such as Sophis Networks, Sun Microsystems, RSA Security, and Network Associates entered "into certain partnerships to build and foster [encryption] technologies and tried to anticipate the government regulations," according to Joanne Mercer. Network Associates acquired a Swiss computer company that developed a product at its

Dutch subsidiary that was "functionally equivalent" to its Pretty Good Privacy encryption software. Network Associates customers outside the U.S. could purchase the Dutch software and expect it to be fully compatible with Network Associates' U.S. version. Because Network Associates had provided no assistance in the development of the encryption product, export laws were not infringed, according to Kelly Blough, director of government relations at Network Associates. "There is no contact between our developers here with any developers in Europe," Blough said. "We are confident that [the Department of Commerce] will uncover nothing that is not in compliance with U.S. law."[115]

Sun Microsystems developed a product through a Russian subsidiary in which it had a 10 percent stake. Sun's Network Security Products Group Manager, Humphrey Polanen explained, "This is not being done to subvert export control laws but to deliver solutions to customers . . . We're doing this not to politicize encryption but to fulfill market demand."[116]

Sophis Networks formed similar partnerships with overseas companies. Joanne Mercer explained, ". . . we did not do this with an intent to circumvent the government rules or to defraud in any way, shape, or form. It was a way for us to develop technology outside the United States for the world to use."

Many of the technology companies affected by encryption export controls continued to develop their encryption technology capabilities in the United States, since companies could sell encryption products freely in the United States. Sophis Networks maintained its technology development budgets because it retained hope that the Administration would eventually relax the controls. The company built firewalls, encryption technologies, and authorization and authentication tools with the intention of exporting strong encryption products if the Administration were to relax its policies.

Joanne Mercer leaned back in her chair in frustration and wondered what else she and Sophis Networks could do to influence Administration policy on encryption exports controls. ∎

114"Network Associates," *Interactive Week*, February 7, 2000, p.35. Projections by International Data Corporation. The projections were (1) antivirus, $2.8 billion; (2) firewalls, $1.48 billion; and (3) encryption, $200 million.

115Matthew Nelson, "Network Associates Gets Around Export Laws," *Infoworld*, March 30, 1998, p.58.
116David Bank, "Sun Selling of Encryption to Skirt Policy," *The Wall Street Journal*, May 19, 1997, pp. A3–A4 and Michael Kanellos, "Sun Signs Deal with Russian Company," *Computer Reseller News*, June 9, 1997, p.68.

## PREPARATION QUESTIONS

1. Why has the U.S. government sought to restrict the export of strong encryption products? How serious are those concerns? What has been the nonmarket strategy of the FBI and NSA, and why has it been effective?
2. How serious are the controls for companies such as Sophis Networks?
3. Why have U.S. companies had only limited success in relaxing the controls? What should the companies have done differently?
4. If export controls were lifted, would U.S. companies likely be able to regain their former lead in encryption systems?
5. What should Sophis Networks do regarding President Clinton's threatened veto and the Administration's revised export control policy?

# Toys 'Я' Us and Globalization

Charles Lazarus began his career working in his father's used bicycle shop. He subsequently started selling children's furniture out of the shop, and when customers kept asking if he carried toys, he added some toys in addition to the children's furniture. He soon recognized, however, that he was not getting any repeat business. "Furniture lasts forever," Lazarus pointed out. "But toys," he continued with a laugh, "toys are great because they have built-in obsolescence. Kids break them."[1]

Lazarus was intrigued by the success of self-service supermarkets and conceived the idea of selling toys in a similar manner. He opened his first Toys 'Я' Us store in 1957 using shopping carts, a large selection, and low prices. Because toy sales were highly seasonal, he advertised to build a year-round demand. To raise funds for expansion, in 1966 he sold the company to Interstate Stores, a retailing conglomerate, for $7.5 million. Lazarus retained operating control, and when Interstate went bankrupt, the court made him president. After selling off the Interstate assets, in 1978 he renamed the company Toys 'Я' Us and launched a rapid expansion program. Toy industry analysts had estimated that over the next 10 years industry-wide sales of toys by specialty retailers would increase to $2.4 billion. Over that period, the sales of Toys 'Я' Us alone increased by over tenfold, reaching $4 billion in 1989, including clothing sales at Kids 'Я' Us stores. Profits were $268 million. Because of his vision and the company's tremendous success, Lazarus was widely viewed as a retailing genius.

The Toys 'Я' Us market strategy was built on three principles: price, selection, and stock. The original idea was to sell at discount prices in stores with supermarket-style service and limited sales staff. It soon became clear that consumers wanted one-stop shopping, leading to larger stores, more varieties of items, and a broad range of goods including items such as disposable diapers. Toys 'Я' Us then began to stock an average of 18,000 items in its stores. The key, of course, as Lazarus explained, was "to pick the right toy at the right time—the toys that sell. We're very much like the fashion industry. Customer tastes are very fickle, and you have to move quickly when they change. Otherwise, you'll be out of business. It's that simple."[2] The third principle was to have the goods on hand, so Toys 'Я' Us operated a sophisticated inventory tracking and supply system designed to avoid stock outs. The company used electronic point-of-purchase sales terminals in each store, which were linked to its central computers in its headquarters.

To supplement these principles, Toys 'Я' Us relied on advertising to get consumers to purchase toys year round, which both increased demand and reduced seasonality. It also provided a money-back guarantee policy under which a customer could return any item for any reason. In the United States, the location of stores was crucial. Toys 'Я' Us preferred locations with ample and adjacent parking so that customers could go out the door of the store and directly to their cars. Toys 'Я' Us also sought to keep its stores open 7 days a week, 365 days a year, where local ordinances permitted it. Toys 'Я' Us owned all its stores so as to maintain standardization and control.

## Globalization

By 1984 Toys 'Я' Us operated 169 stores in over 40 states and had revenue of $1.3 billion and profits of $92 million. Although it operated only within

[1] *Solutions*, March/April, 1988.

[2] *Solutions*, March/April, 1988.

the United States, it had developed a worldwide supply system, purchasing toys from around the world. East Asia represented the largest source of supply.

The company's initial international steps were cautious. It opened its first store outside the United States in Canada and then opened a store in England. Lazarus explained that "the Canadians seemed to be much like ourselves, and [our approach] seemed to work pretty well. And we went to England." Toys 'Я' Us continued to expand in Canada and the United Kingdom. Its other early international steps were serendipitous. Toys 'Я' Us had been approached by Jopie Ong, director of Singapore's Metro retail group, which wanted a franchise to open a store in Singapore. The Toys 'Я' Us policy was not to use franchisees, and hence it rejected the request. Ong persisted, however, and was eventually able to persuade the company to form a joint venture. Toys 'Я' Us–Metro opened its first Singapore store in 1984.

Its entry into Hong Kong was also serendipitous. Joseph Baczko, president of the Toys 'Я' Us international division, had met Victor Fung when they were both at Harvard. When Fung became chairman of Li & Fung Ltd., a Hong Kong trading company, the two companies were natural partners. The Toys 'Я' Us–Li & Fung joint venture was formed and opened a store in Hong Kong in 1985. The success of its stores in Singapore and Hong Kong led Toys 'Я' Us to develop a globalization strategy. Lazarus explained that the company was "interglobal." "Our registers in Hong Kong take eight currencies. . . . They just punch in what kind of currency you're giving them. It's a really international kind of thing. You have to see it to believe it." The company also preferred to hire locals as store and country managers.

Toys 'Я' Us viewed opportunity in a country as stemming from a large population and high income. Those factors "combined with the lack of any dominant toy retail competition in Europe and Asia, afford Toys 'Я' Us with an ideal climate for aggressive international expansion. . . ."[3] As Lazarus put it, "We can go anywhere there are supermarkets and kids because we are, after all, a supermarket for kids."[4]

---

[3]Toys 'Я' Us, Annual Report, 1991, p. 7.
[4]*Solutions,* March/April, 1988.

Each country posed different hurdles, however. Some were market based and others were nonmarket. Germany, Japan, and Sweden posed particular challenges.

## Germany[5]

With one of the highest standards of living in the world, Germany offered considerable potential. Although Germany had a relatively open economy, a number of rules, regulations, and traditional relationships presented difficulties for foreign entrants. Entry into retailing, in particular, was more difficult than might have been expected.

Toys 'Я' Us G.m.b.H. was formed in 1986, but as it attempted to enter the German market it encountered several hurdles. In contrast to the United States, a number of European countries had laws favoring employees over consumers. Germany protected employees in the retail trade by imposing strict rules on store-opening hours, except for gasoline stations and stores in railroad stations and airports. A federal law enacted in 1956 was intended to protect employees from having to work long hours, and it had continuing strong support from the 500,000-member union representing retail, banking, and insurance workers. Union members worked a 37.5-hour week. Many small retailers also supported the law, believing that extended hours would not increase sales enough to warrant the additional cost. Stores were required to close by 6:30 P.M. except on Thursday when they could remain open until 8:30 P.M. The 6:30 P.M. closing time gave employees little time to shop after work. Moreover, stores had to close by 2 P.M. on Saturday and were not allowed to open on Sunday.[6] In addition, in smaller towns many retailers closed at lunchtime.

Other federal laws also imposed hurdles. Not only were profits taxes the highest in Europe at 50 percent, but Germany also had regulations that were as strict as any in Europe, particularly in the retail sector. For example, German law prohibited discounts of more than 3 percent from previous prices except during certain restricted periods. German antitrust law also restricted the use of loss leader pricing, and the Cartel Office could order

---

[5]This section is based in part on an article in *The New York Times,* August 18, 1991, and on additional public sources.
[6]Stores could remain open until 4 P.M. on the first Saturday of every month and the four Saturdays before Christmas.

price increases. German law also prohibited lifetime guarantees.

German labor laws made it difficult to dismiss an employee and gave rights to employees on some policy issues. For example, employees had a say in any legislative effort to revise the store opening laws. In addition, the worker participation requirements in Germany were foreign to an American company and reduced a company's flexibility. Wages and benefits were very high—German workers typically had 6 weeks of vacation a year and received a thirteenth month of salary as a bonus. German employees were well educated and highly productive, however.

Most German toy retail stores were small, family-owned shops, and many were located in city centers. These retailers were often active members of local organizations. As managing director Arnt Klöser of Toys 'Я' Us G.m.b.H., who had been hired from a leading German department store chain, said, "When you ask a city for a construction permit, the first thing they do is ask the local chamber of commerce and retailers' association what they think of your idea. They always say the same thing: A toy store belongs in the city center, not the meadow on the edge of town."[7] To obtain store approval, Klöser's strategy was to try to convince the local toy retailers that the entry of Toys 'Я' Us would actually benefit them by expanding the market.

German toy manufacturers opposed the entry of Toys 'Я' Us because of concerns about the consequences for their current retail customers. To support local retailers, some manufacturers argued that a self-service retailer such as Toys 'Я' Us could place children in danger. They said that customers needed the assistance of a Fachmann to provide expert advice. The German Toy Manufacturers Association complained about the Toys 'Я' Us practice of selling such items as diapers, baby food, clothes, and sporting goods in addition to toys. Some manufacturers went further. The leading manufacturer of model trains, Gebruder Märklin, announced that it would not sell to Toys 'Я' Us because doing so would damage its image.

Toys 'Я' Us was willing to commit whatever resources were necessary to enter the German market, but it needed a strategy for dealing with the hurdles it faced.

---

7 *The New York Times*, August 18, 1991.

## Japan

By 1989 sales had reached $4 billion and net income was $238 million. The company operated nearly 500 Toys 'Я' Us and over 100 Kids 'Я' Us stores. Toys 'Я' Us operated over 70 stores in countries other than the United States. However, the company had not yet entered the Japanese market.

The opportunities in Japan were substantial. The Japanese toy market was over $5.5 billion, and personal income was growing rapidly. Less than 5 percent of the $5 billion toy market was accounted for by imported toys, however. Domestic toy manufacturers had a lock on the distribution system that supplied the thousands of small toy stores that accounted for virtually all the toy sales in the country.

One estimate was that over 50 percent of all retail sales in Japan was accounted for by shops with one or two employees. Many of these "mom and pop" shops were owned by retirees. The aging of shopowners and their children's reluctance to take over the businesses resulted in a decline of 9.3 percent in the number of shops from 1982 to 1985 and a 7 percent decline from 1985 to 1988. In spite of the decline, over 1.4 million small shops remained in Japan. These shops represented an important component of the clientistic and reciprocal exchange relationships with the Liberal Democratic Party (LDP) and the bureaucracy. Local merchants also often played an important role in the *koenkai* of many Diet members.

These small shops were an important part of the fabric of Japanese society, but they were also the cap of a very inefficient distribution system. Japan had several more layers to its distribution system than most other countries and two to three times the number of small shops per capita. This increased costs and prices. The high prices provided an important profit opportunity for an efficient, large-scale retailer such as Toys 'Я' Us.

Charles Lazarus saw a potential for 100 stores in Japan and hoped to open the first Toys 'Я' Us store in Niigata, 160 miles north of Tokyo. Toys 'Я' Us planned to supply the stores directly, bypassing the Japanese distribution system. Approximately 80 percent of the merchandise sold in its Japanese stores would be the same as that sold in the other Toys 'Я' Us stores.

Toys 'Я' Us' market opportunities were controlled by government regulations. As Vice President Michael Goldstein explained, "A lot will depend on whether the Japanese government will relax [its] rules. We think we're going to expand the market there for toys. It'll be good for us, good for our suppliers and will be good for Japan in that we're going to bring a diversity of consumer products for Japanese children."

Entry into the Japanese market was complicated by a variety of factors. The structure of Japanese retailing persisted in part because of the Large-Scale Retail Store Law (LSRSL), which made it difficult to open a large store. Notice had to be given to the Small and Medium-Size Enterprises Agency (SMEA) of MITI to open a store larger than 1,500 square meters.[8] SMEA typically recommended postponing the opening as it sought the advice of a local large-scale retail council. Notice of any store larger than 500 square meters also had to be given to the governor of the prefecture, which had authority similar to MITI's. Two laws enacted in 1977, the Coordinating Sphere of Activities Law and the Small and Medium-Size Business and Cooperative Law, strengthened the position of small enterprises by giving them a stronger voice in the local large-scale retail councils. Those councils sought the advice of the "commercial business arrangement committee," established by the local chamber of commerce. The committee's advice was often reflected in the decision of the governor or minister. Local councils played a role in setting not only store size but also store hours.[9] These laws and the local consultation process provided an opportunity for local merchants to oppose entry. As Tatsuki Kubo of McDonald's (Japan) explained, "It's a Japanese custom. If a big company wants to move into a local area, the people oppose it."[10]

These laws and the complex approval process did not preclude the opening of large stores, but they could result in long and often prohibitive delays. The laws placed no limit on the length of the consultation period, and there had been delays as long as 10 years. When faced with strong opposition some large-scale retailers had given up, whereas others had chosen to "negotiate" with the local store owners to overcome their opposition.

In spite of these restrictions, some supermarket and department store chains had expanded in Japan.

Isao Nakauchi founded the Daiei chain in 1957; by 1988 Daiei had 181 outlets that sold clothing and other merchandise as well as groceries. Nakauchi complained that opening a new store took from 5 to 7 years and that 73 applications had to be filed for 26 permits under 12 laws.

Because of the size of their outlets, companies such as McDonald's and 7-Eleven were often unaffected by the LSRSL.[11] Indeed, McDonald's, led by President Den Fujita, had expanded rapidly and by 1989 had 675 restaurants in Japan. McDonald's Japan was skilled at dealing with the relevant bureaucracy and the local government units whose approval was needed to open a restaurant. McDonald's (Japan) also employed *amakudari* bureaucrats for their relationships with and knowledge of the ministries from which they had descended.[12]

In recent years, the approval process had been somewhat streamlined, and in some cases the delays have been reduced to as little as 2 years. Restrictions on store hours and expansion had also been eased. Rumors of the possible entry of Toys 'Я' Us, however, stirred concern in the retail industry. A toy wholesaler in Niigata commented, "This is not just a local problem; Toys 'Я' Us will have a big impact on the entire toy industry. We are opposed to their plan."[13] He said he would be meeting with other members of the industry to formulate a strategy against Toys 'Я' Us. Masao Sakurai, a toy retailer with eight shops in Niigata, predicted, "If Toys 'Я' Us comes in, Japanese shops will be wiped out."[14]

In 1989 MITI issued a report, "Vision of the Japanese Distribution Industry in the 1990s," which criticized the inefficiency in the distribution system and explored possible improvements. One possibility would be to limit the ability of local governments to impose restrictions that favored local retailers. As was frequently the case in Japan, MITI could make some changes through "administrative guidance," although it would have to obtain the consent of the Ministry of Local Autonomy.

The Toys 'Я' Us market strategy was to attempt to bypass the Japanese distribution system by opening large stores and supplying them directly.

[8]Toys 'Я' Us stores were up to four times this size.

[9]Store hours and the number of employees permitted were regulated in the same manner.

[10]*The Wall Street Journal,* February 7, 1990.

[11]McDonald's Company (Japan) Ltd. was a 50–50 joint venture of the U.S. McDonald's Corporation and Fujita & Company. 7-Eleven stores were owned by Ito Yokuda, a supermarket and department store chain, which licensed the 7-Eleven name.

[12]*The Japan Economic Journal,* May 26, 1990.

[13]*The Wall Street Journal,* February 7, 1990.

[14]*The Wall Street Journal,* February 7, 1990.

To implement this strategy, the company faced not only the problem of the LSRSL but also a host of local regulations on retailing. One strategy Toys 'Я' Us could adopt was to attempt to place the issue of retailing restrictions on the agenda of the ongoing U.S.–Japan trade negotiations. U.S. Trade Representative Carla Hills was believed to be sympathetic to this issue and might make Toys 'Я' Us a cause célèbre. Toys 'Я' Us also faced the difficult problem of finding store locations because the price of land in Japan had reached astronomical levels.

## Sweden

Operating from its base in the United Kingdom, Toys 'Я' Us entered Sweden in September 1994, opening stores in Gothenberg, Malmo, and Skarholmen, a suburb of Stockholm.[15] In accord with its policies in other countries, the company required its 110 employees to sign the company handbook, which specified the work rules under which the company operated.

Unions were particularly strong in Sweden with over 90 percent of Swedish employees represented by a union. The Swedish model of labor relations had been an important factor in the country's long record of industrial peace. The Handelsanstallda Forbund, the Retail Workers Union, had signed up a number of workers in Toys 'Я' Us stores and demanded that the company sign the standard nationwide collective labor agreement. The objective of the collective agreement was to allow organized labor to bring broad pressure on employers as a means of balancing corporate power. "In all shops where we have members we want a collective agreement," said Mr. Bjorn Sjoblom of Handelsanstallda. 'This is quite normal in Sweden. We have not had any problems before with other companies.'[16]

Toys 'Я' Us refused to accept the collective agreement but remained willing to negotiate an agreement with the union. "Toys 'Я' Us does not have any difficulty in accepting an agreement with the union, but considers itself to have the right to participate in negotiations to formulate a firm-adapted agreement,' Sten Yetraeus, attorney with the business law firm Lagerlof & Leman, explained. '[Accepting the collective agreement] would mean

that we would be bound to a detailed book of regulations that is the product of many years of negotiations between the Retail Workers and the Retail Employers without us . . . ," "Yetraeus added.[17] Frank Heskjer, the company's head for Scandinavia, said, "We get by without such agreements in other countries and we'll do the same in Sweden." Retail Workers Union chairman Kenth Pettersson said, "We haven't had a conflict like this for years. Signing collective agreements is a virtual formality these days."[18] The Retail Workers Union and its chairman were at the more militant end of the labor spectrum in Sweden.

A government commission failed in its efforts to mediate a settlement, and the first strike by the union in 20 years began. Toys 'Я' Us stated, "[Unions] have forced our employees to strike solely because we will not unconditionally sign a collective agreement." David Rurka, managing director of the company for the United Kingdom and Scandinavia, said, "The problem is the culture here. Many of our people don't want to strike. But they say they have fathers or other family members in unions who say they must support the union. The union has motivated the staff with fear and fear alone."[19]

The union provided the strikers with 100 percent pay and took out national advertisements asking the public to support the strike and boycott Toys 'Я' Us stores. The union not only picketed each of the stores but attempted to blockade the stores from supplies. It enlisted the aid of the Transport Workers, and truckers refused to cross the picket lines. The Seamen's Union forced the Swedish flagged carrier Tor Lines to refuse to carry goods from the distribution facility in the United Kingdom to Sweden. The Seamen's Union also announced that it would take actions against Stena Line, Lion Ferry, and SweFerry AB. A Seamen's Union spokesperson said, "A struggle like this is well known within our own union." The expanded actions by the union were in part the result of shoppers who crossed the picket lines to buy low-priced diapers that the union learned were being imported from Denmark. Other unions also announced sympathy measures of support for the Retail Workers Union. For example, the financial sector union refused to handle the Toys 'Я' Us daily receipts.

[15]Toys 'Я' Us became one of the few foreign retail chains operating in Sweden.
[16]*Financial Times*, May 11, 1995.

[17]*Dagens Nyheter*, May 10, 1995.
[18]*The Reuter Business Report*, May 8, 1995.
[19]*Financial Times*, May 11, 1995.

Toys 'Я' Us paid a wage slightly higher than union members earned elsewhere and provided the same insurance. The principal concern, however, was job security. The employee handbook specified performance conditions that could lead to a firing, and one of the strikers explained, "You never felt really secure there, that you can stay." Therese Karlsson, who was let go by the company in Skarholmen during the provisional period, said, "Just prior to [being fired], management said that they were finished making cutbacks in personnel. Those of us who remained could feel secure, and a few were even promised permanent employment. Then they called me at home on a Saturday evening and told me 'you may leave.'"[20] Therese was one of the strikers on the picket line.

The conflict between Toys 'Я' Us and the union also involved other work rule issues. For example, the company handbook stated that employees were forbidden to "speak to or be interviewed by the mass media without special permission in advance from the managing director."[21] Gunnar Jonsson, manager of the Gothenberg store, explained, "Our rules about uniforms, searches at the end of the shift, about not talking to the media and so on do look hard on paper. But all stores demand a neat appearance from their staff, check purses and bags, and so on. Of course our employees may speak with the media — except when it has to do with the internal affairs of the company . . . ."[22] Fredrik Larsson, an employee since the store opened, commented, "In my personal opinion, the company's rules don't bother me. I don't see anything against a uniform, and the check that I have to undergo is not insulting, as I see it. After all, it's my own boss who does it. We know each other, and they do it mostly because they have to report to their manager that they have done it."[23]

In response to the strike Toys 'Я' Us halted its planned expansion in Sweden and speculated to the media that it might close its stores and leave the country. The company had planned 15 stores in Sweden employing 500 permanent and 1,000 seasonal workers.

As the strike continued, commentators viewed the conflict between Toys 'Я' Us and the union as a test for the Swedish model of collective bargaining in its new role as a member of the European Union. Peter Skogh, who managed the store in Malmo, said, "We are an international company coming into a new market. Of course we are trying to adapt to the conditions here. But Sweden, in order to survive, must also adapt to the European and international business climate."[24] "One self-employed mother who drove her four children past the pickets said, 'Swedish trade unions are inflexible and only interested in sticking to old principles. Sweden is sick to the back teeth of them.'"[25] Toys 'Я' Us began to receive expressions of support from other companies.

## PREPARATION QUESTIONS

1. What is the Toys 'Я' Us market strategy?
2. In what kinds of national markets are its opportunities the most attractive? Which companies are its natural competitors? Are any of them global?
3. What nonmarket forces potentially impede the success of its market strategy?
4. What overall market and nonmarket strategies should Toys 'Я' Us develop, and how should those components be integrated?
5. What specific strategy should it adopt to gain entry to the Japanese market?
6. What specific strategy should it adopt to enter the German market successfully?
7. What should it do about the situation in Sweden?

[20] *Dagens Nyheter*, May 24, 1995.
[21] *Dagens Industri*, May 10, 1995.
[22] *Dagens Nyheter*, May 10, 1995.
[23] *Dagens Nyheter*, May 10, 1995.
[24] *The Guardian*, May 13, 1995.
[25] *The Guardian*, May 13, 1995.

CHAPTER

# 18

# Corporate Social Responsibility

## Introduction

Through their market activities firms contribute to societal well-being by meeting consumer demand, providing jobs, developing new products, and paying taxes that fund public programs. Through their nonmarket activities firms shape their environment by, for example, supporting free trade and socially efficient approaches to environmental protection. Firms also give representation to stakeholders whose interests might not otherwise be represented in public processes. Although some market and nonmarket activities may at times raise concerns, business remains the principal engine for improving societal well-being.

Many firms go beyond what is required by their market and nonmarket environments and attempt to serve directly the needs of their stakeholders or, more broadly, of society. For these firms, successful performance not only requires compliance with laws and regulations but also requires fulfilling broader responsibilities. Firms make charitable contributions, provide pharmaceuticals to those in need, respect and support human rights, exercise self-regulation, and take measures beyond those required by law to protect the environment and the safety of employees and customers. Firms vary considerably in the extent of these activities, however. That extent depends on their conceptions of corporate social responsibility and the role of business in society.[1]

The previous chapters provide a basis for addressing issues in the market and nonmarket environments of business under the objective of maximizing shareholder value. The focus in those chapters was primarily on the nonmarket challenges that various interests directed at firms. Social responsibility focuses not on pressures from interests but on normative principles that identify duties based on conceptions of well-being, rights, and justice. These principles may require an objective broader than shareholder value maximization.

This part of the book thus adds a third consideration—moral concerns—to management in the environment of business. As illustrated in Figure 18-1, formulating integrated strategies requires consideration of the market and nonmarket environments

---

[1] Perspectives on the social responsibility issue are provided by, among others, Battacharya and Sen (2004), Carroll (1981), Engle (1979), Freeman (1984), Goodpaster (1983), Haas (1981), Jones (1980), Keim and Meiners (1978), Post (1978), Post, Preston, and Sachs (2002), Preston and Post (1975), Vogel (2005), and Wood (1991).

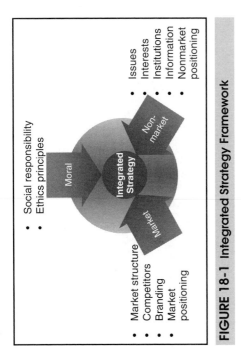

- Social responsibility
- Ethics principles

Moral

**Integrated Strategy**

Non-market

Market

- Market structure
- Competitors
- Branding
- Market positioning

- Issues
- Interests
- Institutions
- Information
- Nonmarket positioning

**FIGURE 18-1 Integrated Strategy Framework**

as well as attention to moral concerns and social responsibilities. This does not mean that the objective of shareholder value maximization is inappropriate; instead, it means that strategies and actions should be evaluated in terms of moral principles in addition to their effects on shareholder value.

This chapter examines the role of business in society and considers several conceptions of the objectives and responsibilities of business. The content of social responsibility is developed in the following chapters in terms of ethics systems and their application in management. Chapters 21 and 22 then address the implementation of ethics systems and concepts of corporate social responsibility.

Conceptions of corporate social responsibility vary considerably. For some firms it is a moral commitment to certain principles or to the altruistic redistribution of corporate wealth from shareholders to others. For other firms it is currently fashionable rhetoric for communicating with external stakeholders; for others it is a thin disguise for profit maximization or a strategy intended to avoid more stringent government regulations or standards of accountability.

There is no conclusive empirical evidence on the relation between actions taken in the name of corporate social responsibility (CSR) and corporate financial performance, as measured, for example, by competitiveness and profitability. Even if there were an empirical correlation, the direction of causality would have to be established. That is, do socially responsible actions lead to superior financial performance, or does superior financial performance allow a firm the luxury of taking socially responsible actions?

Advocates of CSR make three types of arguments. One is that normative or moral principles demand socially responsible actions by firms. This argument requires an identification of appropriate principles and an assessment of the duties imposed on a firm. A second argument is that if firms do not meet the expectations of society with regard to their social performance, they will face government action. A third argument made by some advocates is that firms that voluntarily take actions in the cause of CSR will be rewarded in the marketplace, for example, through increased demand for their products. As these arguments indicate, firms could adopt socially responsible policies for a variety of reasons. Some may do so because they believe it will increase profits. Others may do so for altruistic reasons. Others may do so defensively to avoid external pressure from interest groups and activists. One objective of this chapter is to examine motives arising from normative principles, self-interest, and threats.

This chapter also distinguishes between socially responsible policies and policies that simply represent sound business practice. Attention to consumer demand is a sound business practice and requires no justification other than the remuneration it provides. Similarly, creating a culture that builds mutual commitment between the firm and its employees requires no justification beyond the benefits it provides. In contrast, responding to a community need may go beyond the scope of sound business practice and requires justification.

The next section examines the responsibilities resulting from the law. The following section considers the role of business in society and identifies two conceptions of CSR. One is that of Milton Friedman, who argues that the social responsibility of business is to maximize profits, and the other argues that business is to be responsive to the needs of stakeholders. The strategic use of CSR is then considered along with a consideration of corporate social performance. A framework for reasoning about CSR is then presented, and a set of examples is provided to illustrate the use of the framework. The chapter concludes with a consideration of corporate governance and the market for the control of firms.

## Compliance with the Law

Any conception of the social responsibility of business must include compliance with just laws. Both civil and criminal law apply to firms and their managers. Criminal prosecution can occur under the antitrust laws, securities and exchange laws (as with insider trading), certain environmental laws, and many others. Individual managers and corporations are also subject to fines and can be liable for damages under both statutory and common law. These laws proscribe actions that legislatures and/or the courts have held to be socially unacceptable.

Compliance with the law is a fundamental component of responsible management, yet in recent years the number and size of corporate scandals and incidents of wrongdoing have been alarming. A partial list from the current decade includes Adelphia Communications, AIG, Arthur Andersen, Citigroup, Computer Associates, Crédit Lyonnais, Enron, Global Crossing, HealthSouth, ImClone, Marsh and McLennan, Merrill Lynch, Metallgesellschaft, The New York Stock Exchange, Parmalat, Qwest Communications, Rite Aid, Shell Oil, Sumitomo, Tyco, Vivendi, WorldCom, and Xerox. In addition, prominent executives including Jack Welch, former CEO of General Electric, were found to have received special treatment, and some such as Martha Stewart went to prison. The example on the next page provides an illustration.

Some individual companies have been involved in a series of wrongdoings. Citigroup agreed to the following recent settlements:

- 2002 paid $215 million to settle Federal Trade Commission charges on subprime lending
- 2003 paid $400 million on Securities and Exchange Commission (SEC) charges of biased research
- 2003 paid $145 million on SEC and New York State charges involving Enron
- 2003 paid $325 million to settle New York State charges of biased research
- 2004 paid $70 million on Federal Reserve charges on subprime lending
- 2004 paid $2.58 billion to settle a class action lawsuit on its involvement in the WorldCom scandal

In mid-2004 Citigroup increased its reserve for "Enron and pending litigation" to $6.7 billion. Chairman Sandy Weill received a $29 million cash bonus for 2003. In addition, as considered in Chapter 14, Japan ordered Citigroup's private banking group to close because of violations of banking rules, and shortly thereafter Citigroup fired three of its highest-ranking officers.

## Enron and Merrill Lynch: Go Directly to Jail

In December 1999 Enron was at risk of missing analysts' earnings projections. Missing the projections could cause a sharp drop in its high-flying share price. To increase reported earnings, Andrew Fastow, chief financial officer of Enron, and Merrill Lynch arranged a deal in which Merrill provided $7 million to an entity that acquired three electricity producing barges moored off the coast of Nigeria. Merrill agreed to participate in the deal because it wanted more of Enron's financing business. To ensure Merrill's participation Fastow made a secret oral pledge to buy the barges back from the entity at a prespecified price within 6 months, giving Merrill a 15 percent profit. In June 2000, as promised, the barges were acquird by LJM2, a special partnership investment fund used by Fastow to keep debt off Enron's books and manage its earnings.[1] The barge transaction was treated as a sale by Enron, allowing it to book a $12 million profit. Merrill, however, bore no risk in the deal, which meant that the deal was in effect a loan rather than a purchase. Since the barge deal had no risk, it had no eonomic substance, which meant that Enron could not treat it as a sale.

The Department of Justice filed criminal fraud charges against two Enron and four Merrill Lynch employees.[2] The jury convicted the Merrill employees and one of the Enron employees of conspiracy and wire fraud, and two of the defendants were also convicted of obstructing justice. An Enron accountant who had several times objected to the deal because she viewed it as without economic substance was acquitted. The four Merrill Lynch employees included the former heads of global investment banking and project and lease finance.

Federal sentencing guidelines specified prison sentences of 6 months for conspiracy and wire fraud, but the judge held a special postconviction hearing to determine if there were aggravating factors in the case that would warrant a longer sentence. If the jury concluded that the deal had caused substantial losses to Enron shareholders, the prison sentence could be increased by 4 years and possibly as much as 14 years.

[1]See the chapter case *The Collapse of Enron: Governance and Responsibility.*

[2]Neither Fastow nor Michael Kopper were among those charged, since they had previously pleaded guilty to criminal charges.

---

Whether there have been more such incidents recently than in the past is unclear, but what is clear is that a substantial number of major companies have violated the law or entered into settlements to end legal complaints. Responsible management requires compliance with laws, yet a company's policing of the actions of its managers cannot be perfect. Some managers violate the law because of greed, some because they think they "can get away with it," some because they believe others are doing the same thing without reprimands, and others because they are pushing into gray areas where there is ambiguity in the law. Regardless of the source of the problem, a foundation of responsible management is compliance with the law and caution in areas where the law is ambiguous. Moreover, violations of the law by business can lead to more stringent regulation, such as the Sarbanes-Oxley corporate governance requirements consider later in the chapter.

In addition to proscribing actions, the law assigns certain duties to firms and managers. For example, the Americans with Disabilities Act assigns an extensive set of duties to firms to provide for the disabled in the workplace. Duties assigned by law are not necessarily the limits of social responsibility, however. As considered later in this chapter and in subsequent chapters, duties also arise from moral considerations. The law thus is an essential guide for responsible management, but reliance solely on the law is rarely sufficient. The next section introduces the issue of whether responsible management requires more than compliance with the law and serving the interests of shareholders.

# The Role of Business in Society

This section presents and critiques perspectives on the role of business in society, and the following section presents two contrasting conceptions of corporate social responsibility.

## The Societal Efficiency Perspective

The classical view of the role of business in society is based on the rationale that the free enterprise system is the best means of achieving the efficient use of society's resources and maximizing human well-being. Particularly in a period of rapid technological progress, innovation, and the globalization of markets, efficiency and competitiveness are necessary for improvements in societal well-being. The best means of achieving economic efficiency is through the private enterprise system as implemented through the corporate form with incentives provided by the institutions of private property and markets as the institution for organizing economic activity. The failure of the economies of the former Soviet Union and Eastern Europe and the extensive privatization of government-owned corporations in both developed and developing countries reflect the conclusion that private enterprise and the reliance on markets are the keys to economic growth and social well-being.

Adam Smith (1776) wrote that the surest way to achieve well-being was to place resources in the hands of individuals and allow them to transact in markets. Not only are markets the best means of allocating scarce resources to society's needs, but they are also a source of protection for consumers who can turn to other suppliers if they become dissatisfied with a product or service. Markets also allow decentralized decision making and, coupled with the protection of private property, encourage innovation. Smith concluded that it was better to rely on the profit incentives that private ownership provides than to rely on goodwill:

It is not from the benevolence of the butcher, the brewer, or the baker, that we expect our dinner, but from their regard to their own self-interest. We address ourselves, not to their humanity but to their self-love, and never talk to them of their own necessities but of their advantages.

The corporate form is important to efficiency because share ownership and the limited liability of owners allow ownership and management to be separated. This allows a person working in one field to provide capital for enterprises in other fields with the capital markets coordinating the allocation of capital between investors and business opportunities. Managers of an enterprise are then the agents of the owners—the providers of capital—and serve their interests by maximizing the value of the capital they provide. When markets are competitive, value maximization by firms results in economic efficiency and maximizes aggregate societal well-being.

From this perspective, the role of business in society is to generate well-being through economic efficiency. Private property, the corporate form, and markets are the principal institutions for organizing economic activity. The maximization of shareholder value—or long-term profit maximization—is the objective that provides the strongest incentives, and competition directs those incentives toward efficiency.

## Concerns About the Efficiency Perspective

The efficiency perspective leaves unresolved a number of issues about the role of business in society. First, market imperfections as considered in Chapters 9, 10, and 11 can cause a divergence between private and social costs and can warrant a role for government regulation and antitrust. Some institutions, such as incentive-based regulation and the liability system, align private and social costs and direct economic activity toward efficiency even in the presence of market imperfections. Nevertheless, market imperfections remain.

Second, the reliance on private ownership and markets to generate well-being is justified by the moral philosophy of utilitarianism, considered in Chapter 19. Other conceptions of morality, such as those based on rights and justice considerations, however, are also important. They may call for limitations on private property, the restructuring of incentives, and government intervention for purposes other than the correction of market imperfections. For example, principles of distributive justice may warrant the redistribution of wealth and income to those who are less advantaged, and basic rights may require that the fair equality of opportunity be assured in society. Third, just as markets can be imperfect, so too can government. Because government may be ineffective in correcting market imperfections, providing social justice, and assuring rights, some critics of the societal efficiency perspective argue that business has an affirmative duty to address societal needs unfulfilled by government. A fourth concern results from agency problems considered next.

## Market Capitalism and Managerial Capitalism

The corporate form involves a separation of management from ownership. This separation is essential for the efficient allocation of capital, but it also gives managers a degree of discretion to pursue interests other than those of owners.[2] The separation of ownership from management and the resulting managerial discretion means that Adam Smith's market capitalism—the reliance on markets to direct the allocation of resources—coexists with managerial capitalism—the reliance on managers for the allocation of resources.[3]

The market for the control of firms, considered later in the chapter, provides one means of aligning the interests of managers with those of owners. Managers who do not serve the interests of shareholders can be replaced, either directly by the board of directors or through a takeover or proxy contest. The market for control, however, can be costly to exercise, so the alignment of the interests of managers with those of owners typically comes from managerial compensation systems such as performance bonuses and stock options. This alignment, however, is not perfect, giving managers a range of discretion in the objectives they pursue.

[2]Berle and Means (1932) first called attention to the issue of the separation of ownership and control and to its implication. Fama and Jensen (1983) provide a contractual perspective on the issue.
[3]See Chandler (1977) and Chandler and Tedlow (1985).

In principle, managerial capitalism could be more efficient than market capitalism. It allows the accumulation of resources through retained earnings and their allocation within the firm without having to incur the transactions costs of raising funds in the capital markets. It may also have advantages if management has information whose value would be dissipated if disclosed when raising capital. Managerial capitalism, however, can result in inefficiency when the incentives of management are not structured properly. For example, some firms cross-subsidize losses in one line of business with profits from another line of business. The more open are domestic and international markets, the stronger is competition; and the more active is the market for control, the greater are the pressures for efficiency and competitiveness, leaving less discretion to managers.

## The Social Responsibility Perspective

The social responsibility perspective focuses on roles for business identified by concerns that extend beyond economic efficiency. Those roles may stem from societal needs not otherwise adequately addressed, the consequences of market imperfections such as externalities, or distributive concerns such as the effect of international trade on workers in developing countries. They may also stem from concerns that government is either unable or unwilling to address. For example, companies have voluntarily instituted programs to reduce carbon dioxide emissions in response to global climate change. From this perspective social responsibilities arise from the needs and legitimate concerns of individuals and society, and business must assess those needs and concerns to determine the extent of its responsibilities.

Vogel (2005) defines corporate social responsibility as "policies and programs of private firms that go beyond legal requirements as a response to public pressures and societal expectations." His definition distinguishes CSR from compliance with laws and regulations and from "'normal' profit seeking activities." This definition focuses on the actions a firm takes independently of the motivation for the action, so it is a definition of corporate social performance, as considered in a later section. This definition includes both responses to pressures from the nonmarket environment and anticipation of societal expectations. The responsiveness issue is considered in the next section along with a more detailed conception of CSR.

Another perspective on CSR focuses more narrowly on the stakeholders in the firm's operations. From this perspective individuals such as employees have stakes that the firm is to take into account in its actions, and social responsibility requires balancing the legitimate interests of all stakeholders. The stakeholder perspective is examined in the next section, and a version of this perspective proposed by the Business Roundtable is presented in a following section.

## The Stakeholder Concept

A firm interacts with a number of constituencies, including employees, suppliers, customers, the communities in which it operates, and the public in general. To the extent that these constituents have an interest, or "stake," in their relationship with the firm, they are referred to as stakeholders.[4] Some stakes are protected by the law, as in the case of an employment contract or shareholder voting rights for approval of a merger. Most stakes, however, are protected by a relationship of mutual advantage. That is, a firm is attentive to the interests of stakeholders because it is advantageous to do so,

---

[4]See Freeman (1984) for an examination of stakeholder concepts and business strategy and Pfeffer and Salancik (1978) and Thompson (1967) for organizational perspectives.

and the stakeholders are attentive to the interests of the firm because they benefit from the relationship with it.

A stakeholder relationship centers on an exchange, as when an employee provides labor services to a firm in exchange for wages. Both parties presumably benefit from the continuation of the exchange relationship or else they would terminate it. Employees who have developed firm-specific human capital may earn a higher wage with their current employer than if they reentered the labor market.[5] Similarly, the firm may have a stake in the relationship with employees to the extent that wages are less than the value of employees' contributions plus the costs of finding and training replacements. Both the firm and the employees then have incentives to take into account the interests of the other party in the relationship. Their stakes are voluntarily maintained through mutual advantage.

Does a firm have a responsibility to stakeholders other than to maintain the relationship as long as it is advantageous to do so? Using the analogy to contract law (Chapter 12), an employee may have made reliance expenditures in the form of investing in firm-specific human capital that has little value to other prospective employers. Similarly, a supplier may change its workplace practices to satisfy the requirements of its customers. Responsibility in such cases is to create realistic expectations about the continuation of mutual advantage. It is those expectations that induce the firm-specific investments by stakeholders. Those expectations may incude how the firm will deal with the termination of the relationship. For example, the firm may compensate employees in the event of a plant closing and provide support to the community in which the plant was located. A firm thus has a responsibility to create and fulfill realistic expectations, and if it does not do so, it may have a further obligation to compensate stakeholders.[6]

Whether a firm has responsibility to stakeholders other than the creation of realistic expectations about the continuation of a relationship of mutual advantge is the subject of this part of the book. As argued in the following chapters, such a responsibility may arise from moral considerations that extend beyond mutual advantage.

## Corporate Social Responsibility or Responsiveness

In addition to creating realistic expectations regarding the continuation of a relationship of mutual advantage, firms may take into account the concerns of other groups. This may be in response to pressure that those groups exert on the firm. A firm may be targeted by an environmental group, confronted by a NIMBY movement, or face a threat of more stringent regulation. In such situations the firm may take actions that it would not otherwise take. In the Part I integrative case, *Anatomy of a Campaign: Rainforest Action Network and Citigroup,* Citigroup established environmental lending policies that went considerably beyond those in the Equator Principles (Chapter 11) for project finance in developing countries. Citigroup, arguably, was being responsive to the pressures it faced rather than voluntarily assuming an additional responsibility for the environmental consequences of its lending. Similarly, as discussed in Chapter 11, pressure from the local community led Shendahl Chemicals to reduce its toxic emissions below those allowed by environmental regulations. Similarly, the chemical industry established the Responsible Care initiative both to prevent another Bhopal tragedy and to avoid more stringent government regulation. The firms in these examples were being

[5]The magnitude of a stake is determined relative to the opportunities the stakeholder has through alternative relationships. For example, the stake of a supplier is the profits earned on the resources committed to the relationship relative to the opportunity cost of those resources.
[6]Post, Preston, and Sachs (2002) and Jensen (2001) provide opposing views of the stakeholder perspective.

responsive to the nonmarket pressures they faced. This responsiveness was likely good management given those pressures.

In contrast to this corporate social responsiveness, some companies take actions based on a sense of responsibility. BP stopped paying bribes in Russia, and Shell pulled out of the country because it believed participating in corruption is wrong. Similarly, BP dropped out of the lobby group working to open the Arctic National Wildlife Preserve for oil exploration. Levi Strauss & Company established workplace standards for its suppliers' factories before facing external pressures from activists and unions. As considered in Chapter 22 a group of Stanford University students established a company to supply LCD lights to people in developing countries. These companies assumed a responsibility or duty independently of the pressures they faced in their nonmarket environment.

Corporate social responsiveness differs from CSR in that the former is motivated by the potential harm that nonmarket pressure can cause and the latter is motivated by a conception of responsibility or duty that arises from moral principles or notions of good citizenship. The distinction is important for predicting how a firm will act in the future on issues with moral dimensions. Firms that are socially responsive would act only in response to, and to the extent of, the pressure they face, whereas firms that are socially responsible would also act in response to a moral concern or an unmet duty. The motivation in the former case comes from external pressure, whereas in the latter case it comes from internal considerations. Some firms may be motivated by both considerations, and others may act based on moral principles but still face external pressures. BP's actions have not relieved it from pressure by the opponents of oil exploration and production.

Understanding the motivation for an action is important to assessing whether a firm is socially responsive or socially responsible. Firms that are only responsive will act in proportion to the pressure they face, and firms that are responsible may act based on considerations beyond the pressure they face. Both may be proactive, but the former would do so to reduce the pressure it anticipates and the latter would do so to avoid moral infringements or breaches of duties.

Consistent with Vogel's definition many firms refer to actions taken in response to nonmarket pressure as CSR because they go beyond the dictates of government or the incentives provided by markets. Assessing the motivation for the actions, however, provides further depth to understanding, assessing, and predicting firm behavior. In some cases the motivation may have multiple sources. Procter & Gamble decided to market fair trade coffee under its Millstone brand coffee. P&G faced nonmarket pressure from Oxfam America and other NGOs, and it may also have recognized an opportunity to profit from consumers willing to pay more for fair trade coffee. It may also have believed that it was morally right to participate in a system that improved the situation of impoverished coffee producers in developing countries.

The example illustrates the difference between responsibility and responsiveness. Heinz's decision not to purchase tuna caught in purse seine nets was consistent with ethical consensus in the United States, but its decision was a response to the pressure it faced. Heinz's motive appears to have been to reduce the actual and potential damage from a boycott and the effect on its brand. Heinz was well aware of the fishing practices in the Eastern Pacific and the number of dolphins being killed. The company also understood the widespread concern about the issue once the videotape was broadcast in March 1988. That Heinz took 2 years to change its policy and not until it had become a boycott target suggests that its action was in response to the nonmarket pressure it faced.[7]

---

[7]In an interview in the film referenced in footnote 1 of the example, O'Reilly said, "I think it would be a poor chief executive officer that was not attentive to his customers . . . because of the affection children have for Flipper . . . there was a growing barrage of criticism, well-orchestrated, which I think served to convey a growing sentiment among schoolchildren that the previous fishing methods were no longer acceptable."

In contrast, Hobee's restaurants did not act in response to pressure. Its motive was to protect dolphins, even if doing so reduced its profits. Hobee's actions thus reflected its conception of its CSR.

## Tuna and Dolphins

Environmental and animal rights groups protested the use of purse seine nets to catch yellowfin tuna in the Eastern Pacific fishery. In the Eastern Pacific, tuna swim underneath dolphins, and fishing boats cast their nets around the dolphins knowing that the tuna will be caught. Environmental groups estimated that more than 100,000 dolphins a year were being caught in the nets and drowned. However, August Felando, president of the American Tuna Boat Association in San Diego, argued that the 30-vessel U.S. fleet accounted for the deaths of only 12,643 dolphins in 1989, compared with the U.S. limit of 20,500 established by the Marine Mammal Protection Act of 1972. He added that the number had been decreasing because U.S. fishermen had become skilled in freeing the dolphins from the nets. All U.S. tuna boats carried U.S. observers to monitor fishing practices. The United States also attempted to enforce its regulations on foreign tuna boats, with 30 percent of foreign tuna boats, mostly from Latin America, also carrying U.S. observers.

On April 12, 1990, H. J. Heinz President Arthur O'Reilly announced that its StarKist Seafood Company would purchase only "dolphin-safe" tuna and would no longer use tuna caught in purse seine nets.[1] StarKist planned to market its tuna under a "dolphin-safe" label. Heinz and other tuna companies had been under pressure for some time. The "save the dolphins" project had been working to convince tuna com-

panies to change their practices and had led a national boycott of yellowfin tuna products. The Humane Society, Greenpeace, the Earth Island Institute, and the Dolphin Coalition were also pressuring the tuna companies. The key event in the boycott campaign was a 1988 videotape taken by a biologist who had signed on as a crew member on a tuna boat. The videotape showed dolphins drowning in purse seine nets. The videotape was broadcast by the national television networks, and suddenly the public became involved. The Earth Island Institute, which had helped organize the boycott of StarKist, took out newspaper advertisements calling on Heinz to stop the "dolphin massacre." Some consumers responded, schoolchildren boycotted tuna, and the boycott even found its way into movies such as *Lethal Weapon 2*. Politicians also became interested in the issue, introducing legislation to require "dolphin-unsafe" labels on cans containing tuna caught with purse seine nets. O'Reilly said that his children had asked him to stop killing dolphins.

In 1988 Hobee's restaurants, a popular and growing chain, switched from yellowfin to Tongol tuna, which is not caught in a manner that contributes to dolphin deaths. In early 1990 the 10 Hobee's restaurants in the San Francisco Bay area began a boycott of all tuna products. Hobee's replaced many of its tuna items with chicken, placed pamphlets on each table explaining its policy, and provided training to its servers so that they could provide more information on the subject if asked. Hobee's also began a boycott of all Heinz products, substituting other brands for such staples as Heinz ketchup. The boycott sent a signal to Heinz.[2]

---

[1] O'Reilly's announcement was included in the film "Where Have All the Dolphins Gone?" produced by the Marine Mammal Fund and the American Society for the Prevention of Cruelty to Animals and narrated by George C. Scott and Charles Coburn. Shortly thereafter, Bumble Bee Seafoods and Van Camp Seafood Company, producer of Chicken of the Sea brand tuna, announced that they would do likewise. Bumble Bee was owned by Unicord of Thailand, and Van Camp was owned by the Mam Trust of Indonesia.

[2] Hobee's lifted its ban on other Heinz products after the April 12 announcement, but it continued its boycott of StarKist tuna, awaiting implementation of Heinz's program.

# Conceptions of the Social Responsibility of Business

To explore whether firms have responsibilities beyond those imposed by the law and the obligations from relationships of mutual advantage, the perspectives of Milton Friedman and the Business Roundtable are considered. Friedman may be thought of as an advocate of market capitalism, whereas the Business Roundtable adopts the perspective of managerial capitalism.

## Corporate Social Responsibility as Profit Maximization

Friedman (1970) argues that corporate responsibility is "to conduct the business in accordance with [owners'] desires, which generally will be to make as much money as possible while conforming to the basic rules of society, both those embodied in law and those embodied in ethical custom." The objective of a corporation thus is the maximization of its profits, or shareholder value, subject to the constraints imposed by the rules of society. Friedman concludes that those who argue that a "corporate executive has a 'social responsibility' . . . must mean that he is to act in some way that is not in the interest of his employers"; that is, the shareholders.

He argues further that corporate executives who serve some social purpose are acting as civil servants by imposing taxes on shareholders and making expenditures that shareholders would not approve. They act as if "political mechanisms, not market mechanisms, are the appropriate way to determine the allocation of scarce resources to alternative uses." According to Friedman, that amounts to socialism rather than capitalism. Furthermore, calls for a broader social responsibility may, in Friedman's view, actually promote that which corporations should seek to avoid. That is, by calling for the adoption of objectives other than profit maximization, managers are advocating the use of a political process to direct the allocation of corporate resources. Friedman believes that these calls for social responsibility will weaken the free enterprise system and the well-being that flows from it.

From Friedman's perspective, a corporation is a voluntary association of individuals who have joined together for a mutual purpose. That purpose may be the generation of profits in which they will share or the achievement of some social or nonprofit objective. In the case of a for-profit corporation, shareholders have a property right to its assets and hence to the return on those assets. As indicated in Figure 18-2, shareholders are

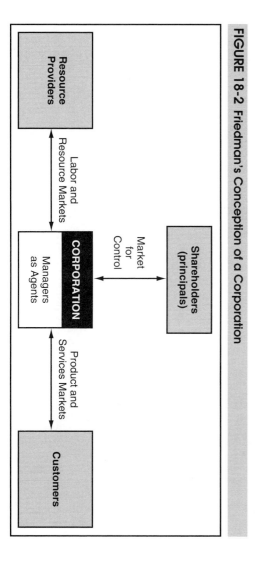

**FIGURE 18-2** Friedman's Conception of a Corporation

owners and hence principals and have the property rights to the profits earned by the corporation. The corporation is managed by agents—the managers—who are to operate it in the best interests of the principals. In an efficient capital market, shareholders will unanimously prefer that the firm be operated to maximize its market value. If one shareholder prefers to donate all his returns to charity and another prefers to spend all her returns on consumption, both will prefer that the firm be operated to make those returns as great as possible. If management does not maximize the value of the firm, the market for control will replace management through a takeover or proxy contest—if shareholders have not already done so.

From this perspective, the corporation engages in voluntary transactions with both resource providers and customers. As Figure 18-2 illustrates, labor and resource markets intermediate between resource providers and the corporation, and product and services markets intermediate between customers and the corporation. If markets are competitive, maximizing shareholder value is consistent with economic efficiency and yields the greatest aggregate well-being for society.

According to Friedman, then, the responsibility of managers, serving as agents of the owners of the firm, is to maximize profits (shareholder value) by engaging in free and open competition. In that competition, firms engage in voluntary exchanges with others, while abiding by the law and ethical custom.

## The Role of Government

It is impossible to have a conception of the responsibilities of business without also having a conception of the responsibilities of government. In Friedman's view, government is to impose taxes and determine expenditures, and the judiciary is to mediate disputes and interpret the law. Even when there are market imperfections and private costs diverge from social costs, the role of governments is to assign clear entitlements and protect them with a property or liability rule, as called for by the Coase theorem considered in Chapters 11 and 12. Individuals then will internalize the social costs of their actions and reach socially efficient decisions through private bargaining. When transactions costs are high, the government may equate private and social costs through market-like mechanisms such as tradable permits for pollution control, as considered in Chapter 11. These functions are reserved for government, with its coercive powers limited by a system of checks and balances, individual rights, and the popular election of representatives. According to Friedman, a call for corporate social responsibility "amounts to an assertion that those who favor the taxes and expenditures in question have failed to persuade a majority of their fellow citizens to be of like mind and that they are seeking to attain by undemocratic procedures what they cannot attain by democratic procedures."

Friedman does not indicate whether and to what extent firms should participate in political processes to influence government policies. The natural extension of his perspective, however, is that competition in political processes moves government toward social efficiency just as competition in markets drives firms toward social efficiency.[8]

## Philosophical Underpinnings

Friedman holds his view of a corporation as a voluntary association of individuals that maximizes the value of their property not only because of economic efficiency considerations but also because it is consistent with a philosophy of individual liberty and personal responsibility. From this perspective, society is a collection of individuals with

[8] See Becker (1983).

differing interests, who can be free only if they can own private property and act voluntarily in markets. The role of government then is to protect private property and other rights. Since individual liberty and voluntary actions take priority over government direction, resource allocation is to take place through markets rather than through a political process.[9] In this philosophy, competition not only promotes efficiency but also allows people to protect themselves by providing alternatives in the marketplace.

## The Social Responsibility Label

A firm operating in accord with Friedman's perspective may directly benefit others if doing so increases shareholder value. A value-maximizing firm may make philanthropic contributions because it strengthens the communities in which the firm operates, thereby helping it to attract and retain employees. A firm may institute worker-participation programs to improve productivity by enhancing worker satisfaction. A firm may design high-quality products and inform consumers of their safety and performance features because doing so reduces liability costs and increases profits. According to Friedman, when such actions increase shareholder value, they should not be given the label of social responsibility. Social responsibility must have a cost to the firm and its shareholders or else it is simply another component of a strategy of profit maximization.

From Friedman's perspective a conception of CSR that differs from shareholder value maximization can have only two interpretations—either a political process is to be used to make decisions or managers are to act as principals rather than as agents. Such political processes in the former case are to be reserved for government and not business. In the latter case, managers are determining who should bear the cost of that responsibility. When the markets in which the firm operates are competitive, the costs of social responsibility must ultimately be borne by shareholders. The firm then may become the target of a takeover attempt by investors who would operate it to maximize its value. In principle, unless restricted, the market for control should drive the firm toward value maximization.

## The Business Roundtable Statement on Social Responsibility

The Business Roundtable was founded in 1972 to "examine public issues that affect the economy and develop positions which seek to reflect sound economic and social principles."[10] The Roundtable is composed of the CEOs of 150 major corporations, with a combined employment of 10 million in the United States. In 1981 one of its task forces issued a "Statement on Corporate Responsibility." This statement reflects a constituency perspective and states that business is to "serve the public interest as well as private profit." The Roundtable stated that "some leading managers . . . believe that by giving enlightened consideration to balancing the legitimate claims of all its constituents, a corporation will best serve the interest of its shareholders."

9See Friedman (1962, Chapter 8). The moral underpinnings of Friedman's conception of corporate responsibility as profit maximization are a system of individual liberty and property rights similar to those of individualism. Lukes (1973) characterizes individualism as consisting of four elements: (1) accepting the intrinsic *moral worth* of individual human beings, (2) advocating the *autonomy* of individual thought and action, (3) acknowledging the existence and importance of individual *privacy*, and (4) expressing *self-development* or self-regulation as a desirable goal.
10See Business Roundtable (1981).

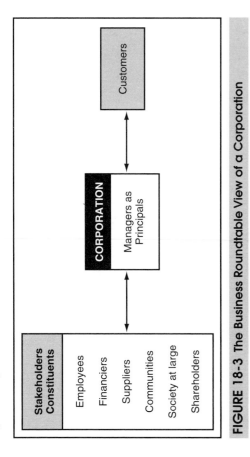

| Stakeholders Constituents |
| --- |
| Employees |
| Financiers |
| Suppliers |
| Communities |
| Society at large |
| Shareholders |

CORPORATION

Managers as Principals

Customers

**FIGURE 18-3 The Business Roundtable View of a Corporation**

The Roundtable's basic view of the firm is illustrated in Figure 18-3. The Roundtable identified seven constituencies: customers, employees, financiers, suppliers, communities, society at large, and shareholders. "Responsibility to all these constituencies in total constitutes responsibility to society, making the corporation both an economically and socially viable entity." The corporation thus is an entity whose existence depends on society's support. That is, a corporation is a legal entity granted certain privileges, including limited liability, indefinite life, and special tax treatment such as depreciation allowances. In exchange for these privileges, the corporation has a responsibility to the society that granted them.

According to the Roundtable, customers have "a primary claim for corporate attention," so in Figure 18-3 they are represented separately as the providers of revenue for the firm. Shareholders also "have a special relationship to the corporation" but are viewed as "providers of risk capital" rather than as principals, as Friedman views them. The Roundtable goes further and criticizes institutional investors because "a high proportion of [shareholders] is made up of institutionally grouped and often unidentified short-term buyers most interested in near term gain. This has affected their role among business constituencies." Ownership of the firm is never mentioned in the Roundtable statement, which suggests that the corporation exists as a legal entity, and shareholders are simply providers of risk capital. In contrast to Friedman's perspective, the principals in the Roundtable's view are managers.

The objective of a corporation is not as clearly identified in the Roundtable statement as it is in Friedman's theory. Instead, managerial decision making involves "weighing the impacts of decisions and balancing different constituent interests. . . ." The statement adds, "The shareholder must receive a good return but the legitimate concerns of other constituencies also must have the appropriate attention." Although the terms legitimate and good are not defined, this balancing is presumably different from shareholder value maximization. Management is to ensure that the corporation remains viable, but beyond a reasonable return on investment all constituents can have a claim to the resources and returns of the firm. The Roundtable statement intentionally provides little guidance about how a corporation makes trade-offs between the interests of various constituencies, since that is the responsibility of managers as principals.[11] As Vogel (1991, p. 114) noted, part of the "universal appeal of the concept

---

[11]The absence of specifics increased the support for the statement among members of the task force.

of corporate social responsibility rests on the concept's ambiguity," allowing management to formulate its own more specific objectives.

The Roundtable argues that the legitimate concerns of constituents are to be taken into account, but it does not want those constituents to participate in managerial decision making. Although "[i]t is important that all sides be heard . . . ," managers as principals are to give attention to constituents' interests and decide whether and how much to respond to those interests.

According to MacAvoy (1981), the Roundtable's concern for constituents "implies that the large corporation is a political entity subject to the votes of interest groups, rather than an economic organization subject to the market test for the efficient use of resources." He continued, "Political interests should not be served from corporate investment returns. If the stockholder wishes to support the local schools, or solutions to international problems, then he or she should do so with his or her own dividends." If managers operate their firms otherwise, they are acting as "politicians of the Roundtable," according to MacAvoy.

In a later statement "Corporate Governance and American Competitiveness," the Business Roundtable (1990, p. 5) stated, "It is important that all stakeholder interests be considered, but impossible to assure that all will be satisfied because competing claims may be mutually conflicting." In this statement, the Roundtable argued that corporate governance differs from political governance on several dimensions, including the speed and boldness with which businesses must act and the means through which shareholders can influence the course of management.

## Discussion

Business leaders advocate CSR for a variety of reasons. Some argue that there are societal objectives that can be achieved only through direct corporate action. Business, for example, may be more efficient than government or educational institutions at training workers for certain jobs. Other business leaders call for restraint on the pursuit of profits and for self-regulation in the hope that it will forestall additional government intervention and regulation. These calls are viewed by some as a necessary response to pressures arising in the nonmarket environment, which if ignored could lead to more serious threats to the free enterprise system. Some calls for CSR are directed to the public with the intent of increasing public support for business. Some who call for CSR believe that unless business uses the rhetoric of social responsibility, more onerous intervention by government will result. That intervention would not only harm business interests but would also impair efficiency, competitiveness, and the well-being of society.

Businesses thus advocate CSR for a variety of reasons, many of which are strategic. This has led skeptics to view as very limited what CSR can be expected to accomplish in meeting society's needs. Christian Aid, an agency of churches in the United Kingdom and Ireland, called "on the politicians to take responsibility for the ethical operation of companies rather than surrendering it to those from business peddling fine words and lofty sentiments."[12] In his comprehensive evaluation of CSR, Vogel also sees its impact as limited. He states that "while the CSR movement has measurably improved the performance of some firms in some areas, its overall impact has been and will remain more modest than many of its advocates claim, or hope—or some of their critics fear." If business is to do more, he concludes, government will have to prescribe conduct. At the

Many businesses support the notion of CSR as voluntary self-regulation. At the Earth Summit in Rio de Janeiro in 1992 this perspective was challenged by a United

---

[12]Christian Aid, Press release, January 21, 2004.

Nations recommendation for international regulation of corporate behavior. The World Council for Sustainable Development, a coalition of businesses, opposed the recommendation and succeeded in obtaining endorsement for a manifesto of voluntary self-regulation. Similarly, in its definition of CSR the European Commission stated that businesses are to take into account the social and environmental consequences of their operations on a voluntary basis.

The chapter cases, *Advanced Technology Laboratories, Inc.* and *Delta Instruments, Inc.*, and the Chapter 22 case, *University Games, Inc.*, concern the appropriate scope of social responsibility. The Chapter 19 cases, *Merck and Vioxx* and *Pfizer and Celebrex*, concern issues of responsibilities to patients.

## Strategic Corporate Social Responsibility

Some firms strategically use the rhetoric of CSR to maximize their profits. From a defensive perspective, some firms do so to reduce the likelihood that stakeholders will damage the firm through actions taken either in markets or in the nonmarket environment. Consumers may stop buying a product such as canned tuna; employees or communities may sue to block the closing of a plant; and consumer and environmental interest groups may intervene in regulatory proceedings. Conversely, if consumers will pay a premium for green products or for organic foods, a firm motivated by self-interest will supply those products regardless of its position on CSR. Similarly, if consumers prefer products produced from recycled materials or produced by a company with a reputation for environmentally friendly policies, a firm may find it profitable to develop such an environmental policy. If Internet users are hesitant to purchase online because of concerns about privacy, an ISP may invest in technology and practices to increase the security of information on its site, protect personal information, and prevent online profiling. These policies may have nothing to do with social responsibility and everything to do with profit maximization. Similarly, an ISP that adopts a strong privacy policy because of aggressive criticism by activists may be doing so defensively. Activists may be willing to praise a firm when it concedes to pressure, but if the motivation for the policy was to avoid the harm brought by activists, the firm may simply be maximizing profits.

Policies that respond to the interests of stakeholders or the concerns of advocacy groups can also build support in the market and the nonmarket environments. Firms may develop loyal customers, suppliers, and local communities whose support they can call on if they need to expand their facilities or influence government policy. For example, a firm may cooperate with stakeholder groups to attain greater efficiency through worker involvement programs or seek political support in the form of tax incentives or protection from imports. Furthermore, if the firm has invested in its relationships with stakeholders and understands the nature and extent of their interests, it may be able to bargain more effectively with them.

Policies such as allowing employees to volunteer in community organizations on company time can improve employee morale and may be rewarded through higher productivity and lower turnover. Similarly, charitable contributions to local organizations can strengthen a community and improve employee satisfaction and morale as well as attract better employees. Company policies that embrace principles of responsibility based on moral standards can reduce the likelihood that an employee will violate a law or a widely shared ethics principle.

Responsible policies may provide better access to government institutions and their officeholders. This may increase the effectiveness of lobbying and other political strategies, which can result in more favorable government policies or decisions.

Responsible policies may also result in activists having greater trust in a firm. This may provide an opportunity to communicate with them in the event of an emerging non-market issue. If the activists are willing to listen to the firm's position, the firm may be able to communicate its message in a less hostile setting.

The strategic use of CSR for the purpose of increasing shareholder value would be viewed by Friedman as just another strategy to maximize profits. If CSR actions reduced the value of the firm but increased the benefits to a stakeholder group, Friedman would view that as contrary to the role of business in society. The strategic response to the interests of stakeholders would be viewed as socially responsible by the Business Roundtable.

## Fulfilling Expectations

Consideration of stakeholder interests is at a minimum important because implicit relationships and understandings can in some cases be more efficient than explicit bargaining and contracting. This may involve the granting and honoring of trust and the creation of realistic expectations about how issues not covered by explicit agreements, such as labor contracts, will be addressed. To the extent that employees, customers, suppliers, and communities understand and can rely on the continuation of their relationships of mutual advantage, all parties can benefit.

Adopting socially responsible policies can carry risks. For policies to be sustainable the firm must meet the expectations it creates, and if those policies establish high standards, the firm can be held accountable for meeting them. Levi Strauss & Company had set high standards and successfully sustained those standards for decades. It also had continued to manufacture jeans in the United States, despite the high costs. In 1997 when it was forced by declining sales to lay off over 6,000 employees in the United States, the company was obliged by its reputation to provide generous severance packages for the employees who lost their jobs and for the communities in which plants were closed. The cost to Levi Strauss was over $200 million. In 2002 it closed another eight plants at a cost of $113 million, and in 2003 it was forced to close its last plants in Canada and the United States, eliminating 21 percent of its workforce. Again, the company provided a generous severance package for its former employees.

Reputations for socially responsible conduct can be dissipated. The Body Shop promoted its cosmetics business by emphasizing its policies of protecting the environment and purchasing natural ingredients from indigenous peoples. As discussed in Chapter 3 and considered further in Chapter 21, the Body Shop came under attack from critics who argued that it had failed to meet the expectations it had created.

# Corporate Social Performance

A number of researchers have investigated the relation between corporate social performance (CSP) and corporate financial performance (CFP).[13] Mahon and Griffin (1999), Roman, Hayibor, and Agle (1999), and Orlinsky, Schmidt, and Rynes (2003) examine and interpret many of these studies.[14] The authors conclude that although

---

[13]This section is based on Baron (2001a).
[14]See also Ullman (1985) for a different conclusion. Margolis and Walsh (2001) provide a summary of 75 studies of links between CSP and CFP. However, they do not attempt to assess the direction of causality. See Ilinitch, Soderstrom, and Thomas (1998) for a critique of the methods used in the literature.

there are considerable differences among the studies in terms of methods, measurement, and findings, the weight of evidence supports a positive correlation between CSP and CFP. McGuire, Sundgren, and Schneeweis (1988) review the research on the relationship between economic performance and CSR. In contrast, they conclude that the research is inconclusive.

In many of the studies CSP corresponds to taking into account the interests of stakeholders beyond that required by markets or the law. For example, a firm may reduce its toxic emissions below the allowable level. The measures used in these studies, however, leave open the issue of the motivation for the observed social performance. Maxwell, Lyon, and Hackett (2000) empirically studied firms' actions with regard to toxic emissions and concluded that the evidence is consistent with a theory that firms reduce their emissions below the levels allowed by environmental regulation so as to preempt more stringent regulation. They find that the reductions are more likely the greater the proportion of environmentalists in the state. The firms reduce their emissions because they hope to dampen the pressure from private and public politics; the firms are socially responsive.

Even if a positive correlation between CSR and CSP were documented, the direction of causation could run in either direction. Good CSR could cause good CSP, but good CSP could give a firm the slack to invest in CSR. McWilliams and Siegel (2001) present a conceptual model of a firm's investment in CSR and conclude that in equilibrium there should be a "neutral relationship" between CSR and CSP. Moreover, agency problems that allow managers to act as principals rather than as agents of shareholders can result in investment in CSR that is not rewarded in the marketplace. In contrast, a strategic CSR orientation could identify market niches that yield higher CSP. Whether either of the latter two effects would be sufficient to yield a statistically significant effect on CSP after controlling for other factors that affect financial performance is not clear.

Waddock and Graves (1997) evaluated the relationship between CSP and CFP and the direction of causation; that is, whether CSP causes better CFP or better CFP allows a firm to afford CSP. They measured CSP by an index of eight factors with weights determined by three members of the Social Issues in Management division of the Academy of Management.[15] Some of the factors, such as being a military contractor or participating in nuclear power, are curious inclusions apparently based on personal viewpoints, but lower weights were given to those factors than to factors such as employee relations and environmental performance. By regressing CSP on financial performance, controlling for several factors such as size and financial structure, they concluded that good financial performance leads to good CSP. They also regressed CFP on lagged CSP, but the coefficient on the return on equity was statistically insignificant.[16] Their study can be viewed as supporting the notion that good financial performance allows firms the luxury of socially responsible actions.

McGuire, Sundgren, and Schneeweis also suggest that "It may be more fruitful to consider financial performance as a variable causing social responsibility than the reverse." They and McGuire, Schneeweis, and Branch (1990) reach the same conclusion regarding causation as Waddock and Graves. In their assessment of 52 studies, Orlinsky, Schmidt, and Rynes conclude that causation runs in both directions: "financially successful companies spend more [on CSR] because they can afford it, but CSR also helps them become a bit more successful [in CFP]."

---

[15]The data were prepared by Kinder, Lydenberg, Domini & Co. of Cambridge, MA.
[16]They measure return on equity using accounting data rather than market value.

None of these studies distinguishes between corporate social responsibility and responsiveness, so little empirically is know about the motivation for CSP. CSP in these studies is measured in terms of actions taken and independently of motivation. Three firms that reduce their toxic emissions below the allowable level can receive the same CSP evaluation. Yet, one firm may do so because of moral principles, a second to pre-empt government regulation or because it faces an external threat by an activist group, and a third because doing so will increase the demand for its product. Researchers may evaluate all three firms as having good CSP, but assessing CSP through observed CSP should not be independent of motivation.

# A Framework for Assessing Corporate Social Responsibility

This section presents a framework for assessing CSR and distinguishing it from corporate social responsiveness and profit maximation. As with any subject in which the central concept is poorly defined and reasonable people have different conceptions of it, there are qualifications to the framework. Several of those qualifications are identified here.

One dimension of the framework is the motivation for the action. Why does motive matter in reasoning about CSR? If the objective is to assess CSP, then actions and not motives matter. It should not matter whether a firm takes an action to maximize profits, avoid a challenge from an activist group, or follow moral principles. If the objective is to predict the future behavior of firms, however, then motive matters. A firm that practices only strategic CSR will act only when there is an opportunity for profits. A firm that is only socially responsive will act when forced to by its nonmarket environment. A firm motivated by moral principles can act in the absence of a profit opportunity or of non-market pressure. From the perspective of predicting when a firm will act, it is important to understand motive as well as the market and nonmarket environments.

The second dimension of the framework is whether shareholder value is increased or decreased by the action. Shareholder value is important because Friedman argues that the extent of CSR is shareholder value maximization, and hence any action that decreases shareholder value is not responsible. Consequently, Friedman's perspective serves to anchor the framework. His perspective will be referred to as "shareholder responsibility."

In his conception of shareholder responsibility Friedman views firms and their managers as "smart" in the sense that they pursue every profit opportunity. Consequently, the reference point for the framework is the presumption that manage-ment is maximizing shareholder value. This means that the firm can identify and will pursue all opportunities for increasing shareholder value. If there is an opportunity to market green products profitably, the firm will recognize and pursue the opportunity independently of any influence from external parties. Similarly, a firm could use strate-gic CSR to increase shareholder value by lessening the risk from private or public politics, but Friedman would not refer to this as CSR. Conversely, if external pressure arises, the firm's response from Friedman's perspective must make the shareholder value higher than it would be if it did not respond. The resulting shareholder value, however, would be lower than if the pressure had not existed.

Friedman views managers as agents of shareholders and thus as exercising shareholder responsibility. If they were to act as principals and pursue objectives not preferred by shareholders, the capital markets would force their replacement either directly or through a control transaction. Friedman also requires that firms and their managers abide by the law and "ethical custom." Managers at Enron and Merrill Lynch thus would not have engaged in the barge deal. Ethical custom is neither defined nor illustrated by Friedman, and as indicated in Chapters 19 and 20, consensus on ethical custom is not assured. Ethics systems have different underlying principles and give attention to different considerations. Consequently, ethics and moral considerations will be treated as raising considerations and possibly imposing duties beyond the duty to maximize shareholder value.[17]

It is generally difficult to identify empirically both the motivation for an action and its effect on shareholders' value. Motivation is not observable, and mission statements and commitments to policies could be more rhetoric than substance. Motivation can best be assessed ex post by evaluating actions over time. Whether an action increases or decreases shareholders value is also difficult to assess empirically because many other factors also affect value. Moreover, corporate reports about the costs of their CSR programs are rare, and those presented typically fail to take into account opportunity costs.

The motivation for an action can be external or internal. External motivation can arise from either public or private politics. The threat that public politics could lead to more stringent regulation or new legislation that restricts the opportunities of a firm or industry could lead the firm to take action on an issue. Similarly, the threat or actuality of an activist campaign can lead a firm to act. Using the distinction developed above, this is corporate social responsiveness rather than responsibility.

Internal motivation could come in a variety of flavors. Friedman views managers as agents of shareholders, and given the discipline of the capital markets, those managers will serve their principals by exercising shareholder responsibility. The other form of internal motivation is moral. Morally motivated actions could increase shareholder value, but Friedman's managers would take those actions independently of moral considerations. Consequently, actions taken to maximize shareholder value are socially responsible when they are consistent with moral principles. Actions motivated by moral considerations could also reduce shareholder value. Friedman would view these as shareholder responsible if they were consistent with "ethical custom" but not otherwise. As developed in the following chapters, actions motivated by moral principles will be referred to as socially responsible.

Corporate social responsibility and responsiveness thus can be associated with situations in which shareholder value is lower. In the case of social responsiveness shareholder value is lower because of external pressure, whereas with social responsibility shareholder value is lower because of moral concerns. Citigroup's environmental principles were adopted under private politics pressure, and those principles in all likelihood reduced its shareholder value. Similarly, the chemical industry's Responsible Care initiative was motivated by the threat of public politics and may have reduced shareholder value but not as much as if the industry had done nothing. In contrast, BP's refusal to pay bribes in Russia was morally motivated and in all likelihood reduced shareholder value. That reduction was justified by avoiding a moral wrong.[18]

As with any framework several caveats and qualifications are relevant. One caveat is that a moral concern may be identified, but that does not necessarily imply that the duty to respond to it should be assigned to the firm. An approach to identifying where duties lie is developed in Chapters 19 and 20. A second caveat is that managers may not be as smart as assumed by Friedman and may not recognize or understand issues as well as do external parties. Those parties then can provide information and enlightenment by identifying issues and opportunities that require additional evaluation.

---

[17]The issue of when shareholder value maximization is morally justified is considered in Chapter 19.
[18]An analysis of bribery is presented in Chapter 22.

Another caveat comes from agency theory. If managers are protected from the discipline of the capital markets, they may view themselves as principals and serve their own interests or some other interests than shareholder value. Consequently, managers may not act in either a shareholder or socially responsible manner. A final caveat is that determining what is morally appropriate behavior can be difficult. What some people may view as appropriate behavior given one ethics system may be viewed by others as morally wrong from the perspective of a different system. For example, an action taken in accord with utilitarianism may violate what some people view as moral rights. This conflict is considered in Chapters 19 and 20.

## Examples of Corporate Social Responsibility?

This section presents and assesses three examples in the context of the framework.

### Unocal Corporation and the Dirty Car Bounty

Air quality in the Los Angeles basin was among the worst in the nation, and stringent measures were being prepared to address the problem. Proposals included restricting driving and shutting down factories when air quality reached potentially hazardous levels. Some firms began to take steps on their own to address the problem.

Unocal announced a novel program in which it offered to pay $700 cash for 7,000 pre-1971 automobiles, which would then be scrapped.[19] The scrap value of the cars was estimated to be $10 to $20, and their market value was believed to be considerably lower than $700.[20] In addition, Unocal offered to provide free tune-ups for pre-1975 cars. The cost of the program was estimated to be nearly $10 million. Unocal Chairman and CEO Richard J. Stegemeier explained, "Sixty percent of smog comes from mobile sources, cars and trucks. Thirty percent is coming from pre-1975 automobiles. If you want to make a big impact in a hurry, this is by far the quickest and most cost-effective way."[21] Although the impact on air quality depended on which modes of transportation replaced the old cars, Unocal estimated that emissions of pollutants would be reduced by 6 million pounds a year.[22] Within months, more than 10,000 car owners had applied to the program. Unocal also encouraged other companies to participate in the program. In July 1990 Ford announced that it would buy 1,000 old automobiles in the Los Angeles area and would offer the sellers an additional $700 rebate on the purchase of a new Ford.

The South Coast Air Resources Board, a state regulatory agency, subsequently adopted an old car scrap plan, which indicates that Unocal's innovation benefited society. The program has been adopted elsewhere by private parties and by governments and has become a serious instrument in pollution control programs. A study by Dixon and Garber (2001) concluded that continuing to scrap old cars and light trucks "would improve air quality in the greater Los Angeles area at a reasonable cost."[23]

Unocal also benefited from the program. Goodwill was generated, and it earned emissions credits for reducing pollutants.[24] The program may also have relieved pressure on environmental issues. Nevertheless, the Unocal old car program probably

[19]The 7,000 represented approximately 1.7 percent of the old cars in the Los Angeles area.
[20]Because of the attractiveness of the offer and its desire to focus on the Los Angeles basin, Unocal restricted the offer to autos registered in the area for at least the prior 6 months.
[21]*The New York Times*, April 27, 1990.
[22]Cars built before 1975, when catalytic converters were required on new automobiles, emit 50 grams of carbon monoxide per mile driven on average, whereas post-1975 models emit 20.7 grams per mile. Cars too old to have catalytic converters also emit many more hydrocarbons and nitrogen oxides than newer models.
[23]See, however, the Chapter 20 case *Environmental Justice and Pollution Credits Trading Systems.*
[24]Unocal sought to build goodwill by producing television commercials showing the crushing of old automobiles under its program.

made shareholders worse off, since it provided a public good with little likelihood of capturing benefits sufficient to cover its cost. That is, few consumers were likely to switch to Unocal gasoline because of the program. Unocal had identified an innovative alternative to more costly measures of reducing automobile emissions.

The motivation for Unocal's program is difficult to determine, but if the motivation was to mitigate a serious pollution problem, the program constituted social responsibility. If it was motivated by pressure from private or public politics, it represent social responsiveness. In either event it was beneficial social performance.

## Malden Mills Industries

In the 1980s employees at Malden Mills Industries discovered how to combine synthetic yarns to produce cloth with textured faces. The new synthetic fleece fabric, sold as Polartec, was featured in outerwear marketed by companies such as Patagonia, Lands' End, and L.L. Bean. The success of Polartec was interrupted in 1995 when a devastating fire destroyed the Polartec production facilities and a furniture upholstery unit at Malden's mill in Lawrence, Massachusetts. Aaron Feuerstein, owner of Malden Mills, pledged to get Polartec production restarted as soon as possible and quickly purchased new production equipment set up in a warehouse while the mill buildings were reconstructed. Feuerstein decided to rebuild in Lawrence rather than move production to a less expensive location with lower labor costs. He also rebuilt the mill's facilities in the original 19th-century style, including expensive details and finishings. The rebuilding cost $430 million, financed by $360 million in insurance payments and borrowing from GE Capital and other lenders. Feuerstein also pledged to reemploy the 2,700 mill workers and paid $25 million to 1,380 laid-off workers while the facilities were being rebuilt. Feuerstein explained, "I feel that I am a symbol of the movement against downsizing and layoffs that will ultimately produce an answer. People see me as a turning of the tide."[25] A company spokesperson stated, "We have to be profitable in the long run. But with Aaron we don't have to be two percentage points more profitable than the next guy. We are going to end up keeping more people than we would need if we were to run with flat-out efficiency."[26]

The upholstery unit lost several major customers, which forced Malden Mills to close the unit, leaving the company with 1,200 employees. Fleece imports and production by U.S. textile companies with lower costs began to eat away at Malden's sales, and the earnings problems worsened. In November 2001 the creditors forced Malden Mills to file for bankruptcy. The employees agreed to a wage freeze for 2 years and gave up their paid personal days. Mr. Feuerstein commented, "There are times in business when you don't think of the financial consequences but of the human consequences. There is no doubt that the company will survive."[27]

Malden Mills emerged from bankruptcy in 2003 under ownership by the former creditors led by GE Capital. A new CEO was hired and stated that jobs would likely be moved overseas. The company made an arrangement with a mill in China to produce fleece products. Mr. Feuerstein had been given an option to repurchase the company, and he obtained commitments for financing, but his offer was below the option price and was rejected. Malden Mills was on the verge of following the path of every other textile company in New England that left for the South and, more recently, Asia.

Malden Mills was privately owned by Mr. Feuerstein, and as the principal he could spend his funds as he pleased. He was morally motivated to transfer wealth to the

[25] *The New York Times*, July 4, 1996.
[26] *The New York Times*, July 4, 1996.
[27] *The New York Times*, November 28, 2001.

workers as part of his conception of individual responsibility. His actions, however, may have cost GE Capital and other creditors substantial amounts, and they finally took over the company by forcing bankruptcy when they lost confidence in Mr. Feuerstein's projections. Whether society as a whole was better off was not clear. Few shareholder-owned firms would not have done what he did.

### South Shore Bank and Community Development

In 1973 several corporations, foundations, and other organizations, including the Ford Foundation, Allstate Insurance, and the Episcopal Church, formed the ShoreBank Corporation to purchase the South Shore Bank in Chicago. The coalition's objective was for the bank to support community development by lending to small businesses and housing restoration groups. Over 90 percent of the residents in the local communities served were minority group members, and the housing stock was primarily apartment buildings.

Working with neighborhood groups, by 2001 South Shore Bank had been involved in the rehabilitation of over 1,000 multifamily buildings and had loaned over $600 million to 13,000 families and businesses. It also emphasized lending to small commercial establishments that might not qualify for regular bank loans. By 2003 its total community development investment was $275 million. The Bank also helped form affiliated banks and development corporations in Cleveland, Detroit, the Upper Peninsula of Michigan, Washington's Willapa Bay, and Portland, Oregon. ShoreBank maintained a strong balance sheet, but its profitability was low. In 2003 its profits were a record $7 million, compared to less than $2 million in 2000, and its shareholder equity was $91.5 million.

ShoreBank was the inspiration for the federal government's Community Development Financial Institution (CDFI) program to support financing for people without access to conventional financing. The program, administered by the Treasury Department, provided subsidized financing and grants to CDFIs that financed housing and businesses in poor areas. By 1998 approximately 350 CDFIs were in operation, and by 2001 the Treasury had provided grants of $534 million to support CDFIs.

The motivation for founding ShoreBank was primarily moral. In terms of performance the bank was not only successful in the communities in which it operated but it also was a model for other community development institutions. The initial funding of the bank was provided without expectation of a financial return, and all profits have been reinvested. The initial funders thus did not obtain a financial return, and their reward was a socially responsible investment that established a sustainable enterprise providing community development benefits.

# Corporate Governance

## Social Accountability

### Social Accountability

Accountability continues to be an issue for firms that adopt social responsibilities. Some firms experimented with independent "social audits" of their efforts, and some published those audits. The call for social audits faded in the 1980s as the impact of such reports was questioned, but in the mid-1990s they began to receive increased attention. As indicated in Chapter 3, the Body Shop decided to have an independent social audit as a means of quelling criticisms that its practices fell short of its pronouncements. This social audit is considered in Chapter 21.

Many firms now conduct their own assessments of social performance. Some of these assessments are comprehensive, and some focus on the environment or employee safety. BP provides an extensive and detailed report on its greenhouse gas emissions, including a report on an independent audit of its individual facilities. Dow Chemical provides a detailed report on its environment, health, and safety performance. In 1999 Ford began providing a report on its social performance and its commitments to future goals.

In 2004 the Gap, Inc., issued its first social responsibility report.[28] Along with reporting on the company's charitable and volunteer activity and its corporate governance policies, the report provided a detailed summary of the findings by its 90-person compliance team that conducted 8,500 inspections of over 3,000 garment factories that supplied the company. The inspections focused on compliance with the Gap's standards for suppliers. As a result of the compliance inspections, 136 suppliers were terminated. Many more suppliers were found to have deficiencies, and the Gap worked with them to correct the deficiencies. For example, between 10 and 25 percent of the factories in China, Saipan, and Taiwan were found to have used psychological coercion or verbal abuse. Half the factories in sub-Saharan Africa did not provide adequate safety equipment. The Gap also inspected 653 other garment factories that sought to supply the company and rejected 16 percent of them. The Reverend David Schilling of the Interfaith Center on Corporate Responsibility (ICCR) praised the report as a "major step forward."[29]

Social performance is not only self-assessed by firms but is also assessed through external monitoring and evaluation by activist and other groups. A number of "socially responsible" mutual funds have been established and refuse to hold shares in cigarette companies, weapons manufacturers, or firms that damage the environment. In 1994 Franklin Research & Development withdrew its highest rating for the Body Shop as a result of its evaluation of the company's social performance. Several independent organizations provide institutions, such as universities and pension funds, with evaluations of the social performance of firms. In preparing its social responsibility report, the Gap formed a public reporting working group with members from Domini Social Investments, the Calvert Group, the As You Sow Foundation, the Center for Reflection, Education and Action, and the ICCR. Organizations such as the ICCR provide evaluations of corporate policies on particular issues that are the subject of shareholder resolutions voted on at annual shareholder meetings.

Proponents of the stakeholder responsibility perspective, as, for example, articulated by the Business Roundtable, have argued for stakeholder representation on boards of directors to improve corporate social performance. Hillman, Keim, and Luce (2001) studied the relation between stakeholder directors and CSP.[30] Their statistical analysis revealed no aggregate relation between CSP and board representation, and when they disaggregated the components of CSP and types of board representatives, they also found little evidence of a relation. Even if an empirical relation had been found supporting a link between constituent representation and CSP, the direction of causality still would be unclear. As the authors noted, firms with poor CSP could be the ones that added constituent directors.

## The Duties of Boards of Directors

Corporations are "managed under the direction" of a board of directors, and board members have fiduciary responsibilities. The legal obligations of directors generally

[28]Gap Inc. Social Responsibility Report, 2004. www.gapinc.com.
[29]*The Wall Street Journal*, May 12, 2000.
[30]Performance was measured using the same data used by Waddock and Graves.

fall into categories referred to as the duty of loyalty and the duty of care. The duty of loyalty pertains to conflicts of interest and requires that directors serve the interests of the corporation and its shareholders. According to Clark (1985, p. 73), "Case law on manager's fiduciary duty of care can fairly be read to say that the manager has an affirmative, open-ended duty to maximize the beneficiaries' wealth.... " The duty of care requires directors to take care in their direction of the corporation under the "prudent person" standard and to make informed decisions. (Officers of the corporation have the same duty.) Directors are not expected to participate in the day-to-day management of the corporation.

The courts judge the discharge of the obligations of directors according to a common law standard referred to as the *business judgment rule*. Under this standard, actions taken by the board generally are not subject to judicial review if they are taken in accord with the duty of loyalty and the duty of care. The business judgment rule is based on the view that courts have no special expertise in second-guessing business decisions and that business decision making would be unduly hampered if it were subject to judicial review. Furthermore, the courts are likely to be less effective in monitoring managerial decisions than is the market for control.[31]

If directors do not exercise due care, they may be held liable.[32] In *Smith v. Van Gorkom* (1985), 488 A.2d 858 (Del.), the Delaware Supreme Court held that the directors of Trans Union Corporation were grossly negligent, and hence not protected by the business judgment rule, because they failed to independently value the firm in a leveraged buyout.[33] A subsequent case, *Hanson Trust PLC v. ML SCM Acquisition* (1986), 781 F.2d 264 (2nd Cir. 1986), established that being adequately informed is not sufficient to be protected by the business judgment rule. Directors must be well informed when they make decisions. Consequently, boards now seek the advice of independent experts in any valuation decision and in many other decisions as well. Reliance on experts is not sufficient, however, and directors are required to inquire into the content and quality of the reports given by management. The *Van Gorkom* and *Hanson* decisions caused the cost of directors and officers insurance to increase sharply. Most states responded by enacting statutes that allowed shareholders to limit the liability of directors and officers.

In addition to legal requirements, boards have a number of specific roles and functions. The Business Roundtable (1997, pp. 4–5) identified five principal functions of the board:

(i) Select, regularly evaluate and, if necessary, replace the chief executive officer, determine management compensation, and review succession planning.

(ii) Review and, where appropriate, approve the major strategies and financial and other objectives, and plans of the corporation.

(iii) Advise management on significant issues facing the corporation.

(iv) Oversee processes for evaluating the adequacy of internal controls, risk management, financial reporting and compliance, and satisfy itself as to the adequacy of such processes.

(v) Nominate directors and ensure that the structure and practices of the board provide for sound corporate governance.

---

[31] See Easterbrook and Fischel (1981).

[32] See Bagley (2002), Chapter 23.

[33] Corporations are incorporated under state law, and Delaware is the most popular state for incorporation.

The Roundtable also argued that board attention should focus on strategic decisions and the social impacts of corporate decisions, although it drew considerably narrower boundaries on social responsibility than did the task force statement on corporate social responsibility.

The Roundtable recommended a board composed of "a substantial majority of . . . outside (nonmanagement directors)" and recommended inclusion of more women and minorities on boards. The Roundtable also stated that "it is highly desirable for a board to have a central core of experienced business executives." Many corporations assign only nonmanagement directors to the audit, compensation, and nominating committees of their boards to ensure that the shareholders' interests are being served by management.

The IRRC (1993) surveyed institutional investors regarding their voting on corporate governance issues. A majority of the 85 institutional investors, which managed nearly half a trillion dollars of investments, responded that they routinely voted for shareholder proposals for a board with a majority of independent directors, a compensation committee composed entirely of outside directors, an independent nominating committee, and the annual election of directors.[34] By 1994 outside directors were a majority on the boards of 86 percent of U.S. corporations and 91 percent of financial institutions. A 1996 study by Korn/Ferry International reported that 36 percent of the largest industrial companies surveyed had a "lead director," 98 percent regularly evaluated the performance of a CEO, and 73 percent had outside directors meet without the CEO. Institutional investors clearly cast their votes for market capitalism. Dalton, Daily, Ellstrand, and Johnson (1998), however, surveyed 54 studies of the relation between corporate financial performance and board representation of independent and inside directors. They were unable to find any empirical relation between board composition and CFP.

The duty of loyalty supports both Friedman's position and the strategic use of CSR. The business judgment rule, however, means that management and the board have a substantial range of discretion in deciding the extent of that responsibility. Concerns about managerial capitalism and the objectives that management pursues have resulted in direct pressure from institutional investors for a more independent and vigilant board of directors. The nation's largest fund, the California Public Employees' Retirement System (CalPERS), for example, puts pressure on firms to have more independent boards and improve their financial performance. TIAA-CREF, a pension fund for teachers and professors, joined with CalPERS in seeking changes in boards of directors of companies such as Heinz, arguing that the board was not sufficiently independent. In 2004 CalPERS launched a campaign to withhold its vote for board members who were not sufficiently independent or who voted for auditors that also had consulting arrangements with the company. Commentators speculated that the campaign was intended to pressure the Securities and Exchange Commission to make it easier for shareholders to nominate directors.

## Sarbanes-Oxley

In the wake of the Enron and WorldCom bankruptcies Congress enacted the Public Company Accounting Reform and Investor Protection Act, known as Sarbanes-Oxley after its congressional sponsors. The law requires companies to identify an independent "financial expert" on its board audit committee and requires the CEO and CFO

---

[34]The other institutional investors generally vote on a case-by-case basis.

to certify the firm's financial statements. If those statements are found not to meet the standards in Sarbanes-Oxley, prison terms of up to 10 years and a fine of up to $1 million can be imposed. The law prohibits the audit firms from providing consulting services while conducting an audit. The law also established the independent Public Company Accounting Oversight Board as a watchdog over accounting firms. Penalties for destroying, falsifying, or altering records include prison terms of up to 20 years.[35] The National Association of Corporate Directors issued a report "Risk Oversight: Board Lessons for Turbulent Times" evaluating these board responsibilities.

Critics of Sarbanes-Oxley argued that it went too far. They worried that it would make it harder to recruit new board members, would spur a rash of lawsuits, impose heavy costs for meeting documentation requirements for financial controls, and make firms risk averse. Two years after enactment the first two concerns had not materialized. Firms, and particularly small firms, however, complained about the costs of documentation of their internal controls required by Section 404. Whether firms had become more risk averse was unclear, and the extent to which the law had discouraged fraud was difficult to assess.

## The Market for Control

The market for control disciplines management and directors to serve shareholder interests through mergers, acquisitions, hostile takeovers, proxy contests, and depressed market valuations.[36] However, many managers want to be insulated from the market for control, arguing that they are best able to chart the firm's course.[37] Investors often disagree and favor the discipline of the market to the discretion of management; that is, they prefer market capitalism to managerial capitalism. For example, through a series of acquisitions, United Airlines, which had renamed itself Allegis, had included in its system Hertz Rent-A-Car, Westin Hotels, and Hilton International. Pressure on the company for better financial performance caused its board of directors to replace the CEO. Under new management Allegis was broken up, with UAL, Inc., the surviving entity. In his letter to shareholders, the new chairman and CEO wrote, "My objective . . . has been . . . enhancing near-term stockholder values and the goal of permitting United Airlines to operate successfully and gain in value in the future in a very competitive environment. . . . We have determined to proceed immediately with the sale of all of our non-airline businesses—Hertz, Westin, and Hilton International—and to distribute the net proceeds from those sales to stockholders."[38]

Institutional investors are an increasingly important force in the market for control. During the 1970s and most of the 1980s, institutional investors were relatively passive and seldom attempted to influence the management of firms. Shareholder resolutions tended to focus on issues such as operating in South Africa, and institutional investors seldom initiated resolutions. Most institutions voted with management on proxy issues. With institutions now holding a majority of the shares of U.S. corporations, compared with slightly over 20 percent in 1970, institutional investors have been crucial in forcing management changes in companies such as General Motors and Eastman Kodak. Pension funds, such as CalPERS, have been concerned about the

[35]The law also separated stock analysis from deal-making of financial services firms. Sarbanes-Oxley increased the maximum prison sentence for mail and wire fraud from 5 to 10 years.
[36]See Weston, Chung, and Hoag (1990) for a comprehensive treatment of the market for control and Jensen (1988) for an analysis of the role of takeovers.
[37]See Coffee, Lowenstein, and Rose-Ackerman (1988).
[38]April 25, 1987, letter to Allegis Corporation stockholders from Frank A. Olson.

return on their investments and have increasingly opposed management on proxy challenges, anti-takeover charter amendments, and shareholder resolutions directed at forcing management to improve profitability. In addition, the Department of Labor has instructed pension fund managers to vote on proxy issues in the best interests of their beneficiaries.[39] In 1992 the Securities and Exchange Commission issued rules giving shareholders new powers, such as calling special meetings and maintaining confidentiality on proxy measures, that make it easier to take action against management. Although the market for control is active and limits the exercise of managerial capitalism, the imperfections in the market for control leave considerable room for management to guide a firm's decisions as it chooses.

Under pressure from corporations and organized labor, Pennsylvania enacted an anti-takeover law intended to protect its firms and the jobs they provided in the state. This action provided evidence on both the market for control and managerial responses to the protection of firms and their management. A unique feature of the law was that it gave corporations a window during which they could opt out of one or more of the law's protective provisions. The capital market reaction occurred soon after the bill was introduced in the state legislature. The price of a market basket of 60 companies incorporated in Pennsylvania fell over 5 percent relative to the Corporate Standard & Poor's 500 index. As the likelihood increased that the bill would pass, the gap increased — by January 1990, when the state senate passed the bill, the gap was 6.9 percent.[40] Since some firms were expected to opt out of the law, the decrease in market value for those firms that were expected to choose the protection of the law was considerably greater than the average. The capital markets penalized those companies that protected management from the market for control.

## Summary

The role of business in society and the extent of its social responsibilities remain subjects of disagreement. The duties of care and loyalty and the business judgment rule leave considerable discretion to directors and management, but management is not free to rely on its personal preferences for charting the paths of the firms they control. Management and directors face continuing pressure for improved financial performance, which limits management's discretion to pursue social objectives. The chapter case, *The Collapse of Enron: Governance and Responsibility*, addresses the responsibilities of directors when management pushes the envelope of acceptable practices.

In assessing what constitutes corporate social responsibility, it is important to consider the motive for an action, whether it was taken based on principles, in response to pressure, or to maximize profits. Corporate responsiveness is different from corporate responsibility, since the former means a firm acts when pressured whereas the latter means that a firm acts based on moral principles. Friedman would argue that strategic CSR is another form of profit maximization. Moreover, using the interests of constituents or moral arguments to justify actions taken independently of those considerations is not social responsibility. It is necessary to look behind the rhetoric of social responsibility to its content and motives.

The relation between social responsibility and financial performance remains unclear, but many companies argue that the two can, and do, go hand in hand. Even

[39]The Department of Labor has regulatory authority under the Employee Retirement Income Security Act of 1974.
[40]See Karpoff and Malatesta (1989).

Friedman's dictum to maximize profits is subject to the limits of the law and ethical custom, both of which leave a gray area between what is clearly responsible and what is clearly irresponsible. On such issues managers obtain guidance from two primary sources. The first is government, which proscribes as well as prescribes certain actions and provides incentives to adopt certain types of policies. The tax deductibility of philanthropic contributions and the tax advantages provided for hiring disadvantaged youths are examples of such incentives. The second source of guidance is ethics. Ethics provides a basis for reasoning about and evaluating actions and policies. The content of social responsibility ultimately is found in these principles and their moral foundations. Moral foundations, however, do not always provide unambiguous prescriptions nor are the prescriptions provided by different ethics frameworks necessarily the same. The following chapters develop these frameworks and consider applications within the scope of the corporate social responsibility debate.

# The Collapse of Enron: Governance and Responsibility

*In an interview with PBS in March 2001 when doubts were being raised about Enron, President and CEO Jeffrey Skilling said, "We are the good guys. We are on the side of the angels."*

*Addressing Jeffrey Skilling in a House hearing, Representative Edward J. Markey (D-MA), said, "You are employing the Sergeant Shultz defense of 'I see nothing. I hear nothing.'" (Sergeant Shultz was a character in the television series Hogan's Heroes.)*

*Representative James Greenwood (R-PA) referred to Enron CFO Andrew Fastow as the "Betty Crocker of cooked books."*

Enron was a great business success soaring to a market capitalization in excess of $60 billion and ranking seventh on the *Fortune* 500 list. It was frequently voted one of the most admired companies and one of the best companies to work for. Enron also had a cutthroat corporate culture in which pushing the envelope was routine and failure led to departure.

The company built its success on natural gas pipelines, energy production, and an innovative energy trading business. Some of its investments were failures, however. One was the Dabhol electric power generation plant that was subject to contentious contract disagreements with the government of India. Enron decided to walk away from the contract in 2000. Enron also acquired Portland General Electric and attempted to grow its Internet unit into a nation-wide fiber optics system. Enron acquired Wessex Water in the United Kingdom but failed in its attempt to develop it into a new line of business. Enron also invested in a broadband company that collapsed with the bursting of the telecom bubble.

Enron was creative in its financial arrangements, entering into numerous partnerships with a variety of entities. The purpose of some of the partnerships and their related-party transactions was to transfer certain assets, their associated borrowings, and their profits, or more often losses, to the partnership. This allowed Enron, with the approval of its auditor Arthur Andersen, to keep losses off its

income statement and debt off its balance sheet. Many of the partnerships were organized by Enron executives, some of whom invested in them with guaranteed returns. Negotiations with the partnerships were thus not at arms length, with Chief Financial Officer Andrew Fastow both representing Enron and participating through limited partnerships in deals with Enron. Fastow and several lower-level employees "were enriched, in the aggregate, by tens of millions of dollars they should never have received."[41] The participation of the employees other than Fastow had not been approved by the chairman and CEO.

The partnerships allowed Enron to keep substantial losses off its financial statements. From the third quarter of 2000 through the third quarter of 2001 Enron reported a before-tax profit of $1.5 billion, but if certain partnerships referred to as Raptors had been consolidated into its financial statement, its earnings would have been $429 million. Although Enron stated that the partnerships protected the company from risk, the risk was actually borne by Enron through guarantees to the Raptors. As Enron's share price declined in 2001 the Raptors' ability to protect Enron's earnings

---
[41]"The Report of Investigation by the Special Investigative Committee of the Board of Directors of Enron Corp., February 1, 2002 [Special Report], p. 3.

disappeared. CEO Jeffrey Skilling resigned abruptly in August 2001, while proclaiming that Enron was in good health.

Under increasing pressure from its own failed investments, facing difficulty in obtaining financing, and under scrutiny from Wall Street, on October 16 Enron reported a third-quarter pre-tax loss of $710 million and subtracted $1.2 billion from shareholders' equity. One billion dollars of the write-down was due to the correction of "accounting errors," and $200 million was due to the termination of the Raptors. In November Enron restated its earnings back through 1997. The restatements of earnings included the consolidation of a number of partnerships that had been used to keep debt and earnings fluctuations off Enron's financial statements. Fastow was asked to leave the company on October 23, and the Securities and Exchange Commission began an investigation. Revelation of the hidden losses destroyed any remaining confidence in the company, and its share price continued its decline from its peak of $81.39 on January 25, 2001, to less than a dollar in December 2001. Enron filed for Chapter 11 bankruptcy on December 2.[42] A flurry of class action and other lawsuits were filed against Enron and Andersen for securities fraud and other violations.

## History of the Company

After stints as a corporate economist, assistant professor, Federal Power Commission staff member, and undersecretary of the Department of Interior, Kenneth Lay became vice president of Florida Gas and then of the Continental Group. He then became president and CEO of Transco, a Houston-based gas company, and then of Houston Natural Gas. In 1985 he arranged the merger of Houston Natural Gas and Internorth, and the merged companies subsequently became Enron.[43] Enron operated fixed assets in power generation and natural gas transmission and organized an energy trading market in which it traded electricity and natural gas. Enron also had a large merchant investment business in structured transactions in fixed assets and trading. Enron was an aggressive advocate of deregulating energy markets.

In 2000 Enron had sales of $101 billion and assets of $47.3 billion. Enron operated 30,000 miles of pipelines and 15,000 miles of fiber optic cable and had 19,000 employees in 2002.

## Special Purpose Enterprises and Accounting Statements

A central component of Enron's strategy was to utilize subsidiaries and special purpose entities including partnerships for the funding and structuring of projects. Enron was estimated to have 3,000 partnerships and subsidiaries. It had over 140 subsidiaries in the Netherlands, where tax laws gave favorable treatment to holding companies with subsidiaries in other countries. The holding companies could loan funds to subsidiaries such as Enron Columbia Energy BV, and the interest on the loan was not taxable.

In partnerships named Marlin and Osprey, Enron formed an investment trust, lending its stock to the partnerships for use as collateral.[44] The partnership raised small amounts of outside equity and raised most of its funds by issuing debt with the Enron stock as collateral. The partnership then formed a joint venture with Enron in which Enron provided real assets to the joint venture in exchange for funds used to pay off debt on the assets. The debt in the joint venture did not appear on Enron's books, but if the joint venture were to fail or be unable to repay its debt obligations, Enron would have to provide shares to cover the debt payments. These partnerships were disclosed only in the fine print of Enron's annual report. In marketing such structured transactions Citigroup described one of the benefits as removing "certain items from 'plain view,'" thus enhancing the appearance of the balance sheet.[45]

Enron used a variety of other means to keep debt off its books, one of which was a prepaid swap. For example, in December 2000 Enron signed a contract to deliver natural gas to Mahonia Ltd. over a 5-year period and simultaneously signed a contract with Stonehill Aegean Ltd. to purchase the gas to be delivered to Mahonia. In the deals Mahonia prepaid the fair value of the contract, while Enron's payment to Stonehill was to be spread over 5 years. This in effect gave Enron a loan of $330 million at a 7 percent interest rate, but the loan did not appear on Enron's balance sheet. Mahonia and Stonehill

---

[42]Subsequent to filing for bankruptcy Enron agreed to a merger with Dynegy, but Dynegy backed out of the agreement shortly thereafter.

[43]*The New York Times*, February 3, 2002.

[44]*The New York Times*, February 14, 2002.

[45]*The New York Times*, February 14, 2002.

were affiliated companies linked to J P Morgan Chase, which structured the swap.[46] Citigroup reportedly loaned $2.4 billion to Enron through a series of prepaid swaps.[47]

Enron also established special purpose enterprises that participated in related-party transactions to keep certain assets and debt off its balance sheet and shield its earnings. Accounting for the enterprises was subject to generally accepted accounting principles. Enron could avoid having to consolidate these special purpose enterprises in its financial statements if they satisfied two conditions. One was that the enterprises were independently controlled, and the other was an SEC requirement that 3 percent of its assets be at risk; that is, outside equity of at least 3 percent was required.

## Chewco

In 1993 Enron established a partnership named JEDI (Joint Energy Development Investments) with the California Public Employees' Retirement System (CalPERS) as the limited partner. JEDI initially invested in natural gas pipelines and was not consolidated in Enron's financial statements because Enron and CalPERS exercised joint control.

In 1997 CalPERS wanted out of JEDI, and Fastow established Chewco Investments LP to buy CalPERS's interest for $383 million.[48] Accounting rules would have required disclosure of the partnership if an Enron senior executive, such as Fastow, were to manage Chewco, so Fastow assigned Michael J. Kopper, who reported to Fastow, to manage Chewco. Disclosure was not required because of Kopper's rank.

Chewco was financed by a $240 million loan from Barclays Bank PLC, guaranteed by Enron, and by an advance of $132 million from JEDI. To keep Chewco off Enron's books, a minimum 3 percent equity investment, or $11.5 million, had to be invested. To provide the outside equity, Fastow and Kopper established Big River Funding as Chewco's limited partner, and Little River Funding was established to own Big River Funding. Kopper invested $125,000 of his own funds in the two entities and arranged to borrow the remaining

$11.4 million "equity" from Barclays.[49] The credit document was written so that Barclays could treat it as a loan and Enron could treat it as equity for accounting purposes. For example, instead of referring to interest, the credit document referred to "yield." Barclays ultimately loaned only $6.8 million, so Chewco did not meet the SEC outside equity requirement.[50] Chewco thus was incorrectly kept off Enron's books with neither its debt nor its losses consolidated. Enron repurchased Chewco in March 2001, and Kopper and his partner Dodson received $10.5 million for their investment. In November 2001 Enron disclosed Chewco when it revised its financial statements.

Enron also engaged in a variety of questionable accounting practices regarding revenue and income from JEDI and Chewco. For example, Chewco held 12 million shares of Enron stock, which were carried at fair value. As its stock appreciated, Enron recorded a share of the appreciation as its own income, which is contrary to generally accepted accounting principles. Moreover, as its stock price began to fall, Enron's $90 million share of the loss on the shares held by Chewco was not recorded as a decrease in income. Arthur Andersen approved both the recognition of appreciation as income and not recognizing the decrease in value as a reduction in income.

## LJM Partnerships

In 1999 Fastow proposed establishing a partnership LJM Cayman LP (LJM1) for the ostensible purpose of hedging Enron's investment in Rhythms NetConnections by obtaining investments from outside investors.[51] Fastow would be the general partner, since, he explained, that would help attract outside investors. He said he would personally invest $1 million in LJM1. The proposal was approved by Lay, Skilling, and the Board, which determined that Fastow serving as managing partner of LJM1 would not "adversely affect the interests of Enron." Such a determination was required by Enron's code of conduct.

---

[49] Shortly thereafter Kopper transferred his financial interests to his domestic partner William Dodson.
[50] The remaining $6.6 million was funded from a distribution by JEDI from the sale of an energy company.
[51] Fastow named the LJM partnerships using the first letters of his wife's and children's names.

---

[46] *The New York Times*, February 19, 2002.
[47] *The New York Times*, February 17, 2002.
[48] Following a *Star Wars* theme, there were partnerships named JEDI, Obi 1, and Chewco after Chewbacca.

Enron also sought to take advantage of the "embedded" value resulting from a forward con-tract with an investment bank to purchase Enron shares at a fixed price. Enron restructured the contract, releasing 3.4 million shares of its stock to be used as collateral. To "hedge" Enron's invest-ment in Rhythms, LJM1 received these Enron shares in exchange for a note to pay $64 million to Enron. LJM1 then transferred the shares to a newly created limited partnership, Swap Sub, that gave Enron a put option on Enron's entire investment in Rhythms.[52] The put option entitled Enron to sell its Rhythms shares to Swap Sub at $54 per share in June 2004.[53] Enron had purchased its 5.4 million shares in Rhythms at $1.85 per share in March 1998, and when Rhythms went public in 1999 Enron's holding was valued at $300 million. This arrange-ment, however, did not provide a true hedge because if Enron's shares declined in value, Swap Sub would be unable to cover the put. In addition, Swap Sub did not have the required 3 percent equity investment. Arthur Andersen, which had not objected to the arrangement, concluded in October 2001 that it had made an error.

Enron began to unwind the hedging arrange-ment in the first quarter of 2000 in a series of complicated transactions. Five lower-level Enron employees plus Fastow formed a limited partner-ship, Southampton Place LP, to participate with LJM1 in the unwind. Within 2 months a $25,000 investment returned $4.5 million funneled into a "family foundation," whose limited partners were Fastow and the other five employees. Two of the five also invested $5,800 and received a return of $1 million in 2 months. These employees did not seek a determination from Lay and Skilling that their participation would not adversely affect the interests of Enron. The Report of the Special Committee established by the Board in the wake of the collapse stated, "Enron employees involved in the partnerships were enriched, in the aggregate, by tens of millions of dollars they should never have received—Fastow by at least $30 million, Kopper by at least $10 million, two others by $1 million each, . . ." The Special Committee report con-cluded, "We have not seen any evidence that any of

the employees, including Fastow, obtained approval from the chairman and CEO under the code of conduct to participate financially in the profits of an entity doing business with Enron. While every code violation is a matter to be taken seriously, these vio-lations are particularly troubling."

LJM1 was also used to take certain assets off Enron's balance sheet and increase its current income. Enron had a 65 percent interest in a Brazilian company building a power plant that was "experiencing significant construction problems." Enron sold a portion of its interest to LJM1, leaving it no longer technically in control of the company and allowing Enron to take its investment in the company off its balance sheet. This also allowed Enron to mark-to-market the value of a gas supply contract an Enron unit had with the Brazilian com-pany. This increased Enron's income for the second half of 1999 by $65 million.[54]

On Fastow's recommendation the Board approved the establishment of a second (LJM2) partnership with Fastow as the general partner.[55] LJM2 raised $394 million primarily from 50 limited partners, including Merrill Lynch, JP Morgan Chase, and Citigroup. In addition, Fastow and other Enron employees invested in LJM2 through two limited partnerships, one of which, Big Doe, was managed by Kopper, and the other by Fastow himself. The LJM partnerships were in a gray area of accounting standards and were not consolidated with Enron's financial statements.

## Raptors

Raptor was Enron's name for a partnership used to hedge its merchant investments portfolio in projects and companies. The Raptors were a result of the initial success of the Rhythms "hedge." Because its merchant investments were marked-to-market, changes in their value affected Enron's earnings on a quarterly basis. The first Raptor, named Talon, was established in April 2000. To pro-vide the 3 percent equity required to keep Talon off Enron's balance sheet, LJM2 provided $30 million. LJM2 was guaranteed a payment of $41 million before Talon could engage in hedging. For account-ing purposes the $41 million was treated as a return

---

[52]Enron could not sell its shares in Rhythms before the end of 1999.

[53]PricewaterhouseCoopers reviewed the transactions and concurred that the arrangement was fair to the parties.

---

[54]Special Report, pp. 136–137.

[55]The LJM partnerships participated in 20 transactions with Enron.

on LJM2's investment, leaving its $30 million to satisfy the 3 percent requirement. However, Enron, which contributed its shares to Talon, would keep 100 percent of its earnings. Talon's only assets were thus Enron's shares.

To pay LJM2 Enron signed a contract with Talon under which Enron paid $41 million in exchange for a put option, the right to sell Enron shares to Talon at a fixed price. Talon then paid the $41 million to LJM2, allowing Talon to begin operations. Enron and Talon then signed a contract under which Talon agreed to cover Enron's losses on certain investments in exchange for sharing in any appreciation of the investments. This protected Enron's income statement from losses on the merchant investments. The Raptor's ability to cover losses depended on the price of Enron shares, however. If Enron's share price were to decline to a $47 trigger, Talon would be unable to cover Enron's losses.

Four Raptors were used to keep $504 million of losses off Enron's books, but as its stock price fell, triggers were tripped that threatened their ability to protect Enron's reported earnings. Early in 2001 Enron restructured the Raptors to reestablish the façade that they were covering risks, but after the restructuring they were even more vulnerable. Within weeks of the restructuring Enron reported a profit of $425 million for the first quarter of 2001.

In referring to Talon the Board secretary wrote, "Does not transfer economic risk, but transfers P&L volatility."[56] The Board Special Committee stated, "Enron still bore virtually all of the economic risk. In effect, Enron was hedging risk with itself." The Special Committee concluded, "Especially after the restructuring, the Raptors were little more than a highly complex accounting construct that was destined to collapse."

As the Raptors were collapsing, Enron and Andersen accountants discovered that Enron's accounting for three of the Raptors was wrong. The shares Enron contributed to the Raptors had been treated as an increase in notes payable and a corresponding increase in shareholders' equity. This increased shareholders' equity by $1 billion during the first half of 2001. In October and November Enron restated its income and balance statements and consolidated the LJM partnerships.

In August Skilling abruptly resigned. After the resignation Sherron Watkins, an Enron vice president, wrote to CEO Kenneth Lay warning of the "inappropriateness" of some transactions. She wrote, "To the layman on the street it will look like we recognized funds flow of $800 million from merchant asset sales in 1999 by selling to a vehicle (Condor that we capitalized with a promise of Enron stock in later years."[57] She also wrote, "I am incredibly nervous that we will implode in a wave of accounting scandals."[58]

As a result of Watkins's letter Enron asked its outside law firm Vinson and Elkins to prepare a report on its transactions. The report presented on October 15 concluded that nothing wrong had been done, although it noted that both Enron and Andersen agreed that the accounting had been "creative and aggressive." Although the law firm found nothing wrong, the report stated, "Within Enron, there appeared to be an air of secrecy regarding the LJM partnerships and suspicion that those Enron employees acting for LJM were receiving special or additional compensation."

Not everyone was fooled by Enron. A few analysts issued warnings, but most analysts followed the herd. In a conference call with analysts, Enron released its first quarter 2001 earnings and proclaimed the quarter a great success. One skeptical analyst asked why the company was issuing an income statement without the accompanying balance sheet and cash flow statement. Skilling brushed aside the question, mocking the analyst.

Citigroup, a major lender to Enron, decided to hedge some of its risk. Fifteen months before Enron's collapse and again in May 2001 Citigroup sold 5-year notes to investors who were guaranteed a return plus their principal unless Enron went bankrupt or failed to repay a loan. In those events the investors would be paid in Enron debt. This was the largest hedge Citigroup had ever taken against a company.

## 401(k) Plans and Deferred Compensation

Enron employees participated in 401(k) retirement plans, and most of them held Enron shares. The

---

[56]The reference to "P&L volatility" meant that the profit and loss effects would not appear on Enron's books.

[57]Later in congressional testimony she referred to the culture at Enron as "arrogant."
[58]See Watkins (2003) for her analysis of moral responsibility in the Enron episode.

company matched employee contributions with equal contributions of Enron shares, and employees were prohibited from selling their shares until age 55.[59] Enron shares represented approximately 65 percent of the assets of the plans. During 2001 the company continued to tout its stock to employees as a good investment. Enron's collapse caused many employees to lose most of their retirement funds.

In addition to its 401(k) plans Enron had a deferred compensation plan under which managers could defer portions of their compensation. During 2001 before Enron filed for bankruptcy a number of executives withdrew funds from their deferred compensation plans, but others, including executives who had already retired, did not do so. As a result of the bankruptcy filing, those participating in the plan became unsecured creditors of the firm with their compensation to be determined by the bankruptcy court. Allegations were made that current executives were able to withdraw funds from their deferred compensation plans and were paid their bonuses in November prior to the bankruptcy filing, while others were not allowed to do so.

During Enron's slide in 2001 Kenneth Lay sold $100 million in Enron shares, including $70.1 million sold back to the company. Sales in public markets had to be disclosed in the month following the sale, whereas sales back to a company did not have to be disclosed until the following year.

Days before filing for bankruptcy, Enron paid $100 million in retention bonuses to 600 key employees deemed essential to the continued operation of the company. Enron also laid off 4,500 employees, giving them severance pay of $4,500.

## Political Contributions

Enron and its executives made substantial political contributions to members of Congress and state legislatures. Since 1989 it had given $5.7 million to members of Congress, with $2.0 million contributed in the 2000 election cycle. Approximately two-thirds went to Republicans. Approximately half the House and two-thirds of the Senate had received contributions from Enron executives. Enron also contributed substantially to state officeholders and parties. The company also lobbied intensely for the deregulation of energy markets and had participated in Vice President Richard Cheney's energy task force. Enron had also implemented a plan to cultivate a relationship with Vice President Al Gore during his presidential campaign.[60]

The contributions provided access in both Washington and state capitols for Enron's lobbying campaign. When it was collapsing, Enron executives sought relief from the Bush administration. Although he and President George W. Bush were well acquainted, Kenneth Lay went to the Secretaries of Commerce and Treasury, neither of whom contacted the President.[61] Secretary of Commerce Donald Evans rejected Lay's request for assistance. Evans commented on *Meet the Press*, "If I had stepped in, I think it would have been an egregious abuse of the office of Secretary of Commerce." Lay also called Secretary of Treasury Paul O'Neill and enlisted Robert Rubin, former Secretary of Treasury in the Clinton administration and currently a top executive at Citigroup, to call the Secretary urging assistance for Enron.[62] Secretary O'Neill rejected Enron's request.

Enron also attempted to lobby for deregulation with the Federal Energy Regulatory Commission headed by Pat Wood III, who had previously headed the Texas Public Utility Commission. Wood, however, was unresponsive to Enron and angered the company by imposing caps on wholesale prices of electricity in the West.

## The Board of Directors

The Board of Directors was responsible for the performance of the company and had a fiduciary duty to shareholders. As Enron increased its use of related-party transactions, the Board increased the control over those transactions and ordered annual reviews of all LJM transactions. The Special Committee (p. 12) concluded, however, "These controls as designed were not rigorous enough, and their implementation and oversight was inadequate at both the Management and Board levels." In addition, Enron's outside counsel "Vinson &

[59] Contributions in stock and restrictions on when the shares could be sold were common features of corporate retirement plans.

[60] *The New York Times*, February 18, 2002.
[61] Lay had been chair of then Governor Bush's business council.
[62] In 1999 Enron invited Rubin to join its board of directors, but he declined the offer.

Elkins should have brought a stronger, more objective and more critical voice to the disclosure process" (p. 26). Referring to Enron management and Arthur Andersen, outside director Robert K. Jaedicke, chairman of the Board Audit Committee, said in congressional testimony, "It now appears that none of them fulfilled their duty to [the Board]. We do not manage the company. We do not do the auditing. We are not detectives . . . I am not confident as I sit here today that we would have gotten to the truth with any amount of questioning and discussion."[63]

Throughout the rise and fall of Enron the Board apparently did not block the questionable transactions and financial arrangements that led to the collapse. The Board maintained that it was unaware of some of the deals and that data were withheld from it. For example, Chewco was approved by the Board during a telephone conference call without disclosure of the "equity" loan by Barclays to Chewco's limited partner. Kopper's management of Chewco was approved by Skilling, but Enron's code of conduct required it to be brought to the Board.

After the announcement of its third-quarter 2001 loss, Enron named William Powers, dean of the University of Texas School of Law, to its Board of Directors. The Board then appointed a Special Committee headed by Powers to produce a report on the collapse. The Special Committee concluded that the Board had failed in "its oversight duties."

The Special Committee assigned much of the responsibility to Kenneth Lay in his role as a Director. The report stated, "Lay approved the arrangements under which Enron permitted Fastow to engage in related-party transactions with Enron and authorized the Rhythms transaction and three of the Raptor vehicles. He bears significant responsibility for those flawed decisions, as well as for Enron's failure to implement sufficiently rigorous procedural controls to prevent the abuses that flowed from this inherent conflict of interest. In connection with the LJM transactions, the evidence we have examined suggests that Lay functioned almost entirely as a Director, and less as a member of Management. It appears that both he and Skilling agreed, and the Board understood, that Skilling was the senior member of Management responsible for

the LJM relationship." In the initial congressional hearings on the collapse, five Enron executives, Lay, Fastow, Kopper, chief accounting officer Richard Causey, and chief risk officer Richard Buy, exercised their constitutional right under the Fifth Amendment to protection against self-incrimination.[64] Jeffrey Skilling testified but had difficulty recalling what had happened.

## Arthur Andersen

Enron's auditor was Arthur Arthur Andersen, one of the big five accounting firms. Andersen also provided consulting services to the company. In 2000 Enron paid a total of $52 million to Andersen with approximately half for audit services. Enron paid $5.7 million to Andersen for nonaudit services provided to Chewco and the LJM partnerships.

Andersen issued no qualifications in its audit reports and apparently approved all transactions brought to it. Andersen claimed to be ignorant of most of the questionable partnership arrangements, however. Andersen indicated that it was not given access to data on Chewco, and if it had been it would have required a restatement of earnings.

Andersen CEO Joseph Berardino subsequently testified before Congress that it had questioned $51 million in earnings in 1997 and considered requiring adjustments in reported earnings. Andersen, however, decided that the adjustments were not "material" and did not require them. Berardino stated that the adjustments were "less than 8 percent" of normalized earnings. In November when Enron corrected its financial statements back to 1997, the $51 million adjustment was made. Berardino also stated that the Chewco/JEDI arrangements involved "possible illegal acts."

In October after the announcement of Enron's third-quarter loss and the write-down in its shareholders equity, Andersen's Houston office, which had the principal responsibility for the audits, began shredding documents associated with its audits.[65] The managing director said that he had consulted with a lawyer in Andersen's headquarters and had been advised to shred the documents.

---

[63]Six board members including Jaedicke resigned in March 2002.

[64]Causey and Buy were fired in February 2002.

[65]The managing director of the Houston office asked the staff to work overtime so that the shredding would not delay service to other clients.

After the telephone conversation the lawyer had sent an e-mail reminding the Houston office that Andersen policy required the retention of certain audit documents and allowed the shredding of other documents. The managing director was subsequently fired. ■

SOURCE: This case was prepared by Professor David P. Baron from public sources including the Report of Investigation by the Special Investigative Committee of the Board of Directors of Enron Corp., February 1, 2002 [Special Report], Copyright © 2002 by David P. Baron. All rights reserved. Reprinted with permission. This case was written in February 2002 when facts were still being revealed.

## PREPARATION QUESTIONS

1. What factors led to the collapse of Enron?
2. Should Enron have used partnerships in the manner it did? What, if anything, is wrong with using partnerships such as the Raptors, Chewco, and the LJMs?
3. What responsibilities does the board of directors have in such situations? What responsibilities did and should Enron and its directors have for its employees' 401(k) plans?
4. Why did Arthur Andersen and Vinson and Elkins not conclude that there were problems with Enron's structuring of transactions?
5. Is there an inherent conflict of interest for an outside auditor that also provides other services to its client?
6. What, if anything, was wrong with Enron's political contributions and lobbying? What assistance did the contributions buy Enron when it was collapsing?
7. How much of its financial arrangements should Enron have disclosed?
8. What responsibilities does an audit firm have?

# Advanced Technology Laboratories, Inc.

Advanced Technology Laboratories, Inc. (ATL), with worldwide headquarters in Bothell, Washington, and European headquarters in Munich, Germany, was a leader in digital diagnostic ultrasound technology and equipment. "Ultrasound is a noninvasive technology that uses high frequency sound waves to image the body's soft tissues, organs and fetal anatomy and to display blood flow in real time."66 ATL's ultrasound systems were used by cardiologists, radiologists, vascular surgeons, obstetricians, and gynecologists. Applications of ultrasound technology in gynecology included diagnosis of ovarian cysts, endometrial hyperplasia, endometrium, and ovarian flow.

ATL ultrasound systems were sold in 100 countries to village clinics and world-renowned medical research centers. The worldwide ultrasound market was estimated at $2.5 billion. In 1996 ATL earned $21.8 million on sales of $419 million. Its competitors included such companies as General Electric and Siemens.

ATL's principal subsidiaries were located in OECD countries as well as in Argentina and India.

66 ATL Web site: www.atl.com.

In other countries ATL sold its systems through agents. Demand in the United States was sluggish, and ATL's worldwide competitors had introduced new products during the past 2 years. ATL looked to developing countries for growth.

The most attractive growth opportunities were in large countries with high growth rates of spending for medical care and health services. India, with a population of 800 million and a forecasted growth rate of 15 to 20 percent a year for medical devices, represented a particularly attractive market. ATL India, a joint venture with an Indian company that made low-end ultrasound instruments, was responsible for sales in India and Nepal. China, with a population of 1.2 billion, also represented an attractive market, and the installed base of ultrasound equipment was lower in China than in India. In 1997 ATL formed ATL China, where it had sold ultrasound systems since 1978. ATL also had a technology transfer agreement with the Shantou Institute of Ultrasonic Instruments.

In 1997 ATL introduced its HDI 1000 system, which replaced 50 percent of the hardware components with multitasking software, making digital ultrasound technology available at a substantially lower cost. ATL's Handheld Systems Business Division had also developed its FirstSight high-resolution digital imaging technology that would bring "highly portable, handheld ultrasound devices . . . to the examining table, the bedside and the field." ATL Chairman and CEO Dennis C. Fill said, "We believe that in the next few years these handheld ultrasound devices could have the same impact on patient care as the stethoscope and have the potential to create entirely new markets across many medical disciplines."[67]

In certain cultures some parents valued sons more than daughters. In the 1990s ultrasound devices became an effective means of allowing parents to engage in sex selection. Ultrasound was capable of identifying the sex of a fetus as early as 16 weeks, and local ultrasound clinics began to spring up throughout a number of Asian countries. A study by the Indian government revealed that for every 1,000 baby boys born, only 929 baby girls were born. A study reported that of the 8,000 abortions performed at one Bombay hospital, all but one were female fetuses.

One explanation for the preference for boys was given in a *CNN World News* story. "Sons are favored in India because it is they who are expected to carry on the family name and take care of the parents in their old age. Daughters are seen as a liability, and an expensive one at that. Families pay small fortunes in dowries to get their daughters married. . . . For those Indians too poor to afford tests, there is a grimmer option. Skakuntala admits to killing her newborn daughter several years ago. She already had two girls and didn't want another. 'We were poor,' she says. 'I put my sari over her face and she stopped breathing. It was the only thing to do.'"[68] CNN also reported that 25 percent of the girls born in India did not reach the age of 25, and in some families boys are given disproportionate shares of food, medical care, and education.

In 1994 India responded to the practice of using ultrasound to identify the sex and abort female fetuses by enacting the Pre-Natal Diagnostic Techniques (Regulation and Prevention of Misuses) Act. The law limited the use of ultrasound to women who were at high risk due to age or other factors and banned abortions of female fetuses identified by either amniocentesis or ultrasound. However, the use of ultrasound combined with abortion for purposes of sex selection continued unabated. According to

*The New York Times,* "[f]or an investment amounting to a few thousand dollars, a mobile clinic operator can reap a small fortune from rural women, many of whom have never used a telephone or watched a television. Charges for the test can run as low as 150 rupees in poorer regions, about $5 . . . ."[69] The same report noted that the law did not require registration of ultrasound machines, so it was virtually impossible to control their use in mobile clinics.

Gender selection was also practiced in several other Asian countries, including China. The natural ratio of boys to girls at birth worldwide was 105 to 100, but in China it was 114 to 100 and was considerably higher in some rural districts.[70] Chinese law prohibited gender selection through abortion, infanticide, and child abandonment.

Sex selection was widely criticized. The United Nations International Conference on Population and Development opposed sex selection. In the United States the President's Commission for the Study of Ethical Problems in Medicine and Biomedical and Behavioral Research strongly opposed the practice, as did the American College of Obstetricians and Gynecologists' Committee on Ethics. The Ethics Committee of the American Society for Reproductive Medicine argued that doctors should use "moral suasion" to convince couples to avoid sex selection.

In 1995 the Canadian minister of health ordered Canadian doctors to cease providing sex selection services for nonmedical purposes, and the British Columbia College of Physicians and Surgeons issued guidelines urging doctors and sonographers not to reveal the sex of fetuses. Vancouver, which had a substantial population of Asian-Canadians, was concerned about people going to the United States for fetal sex identification and returning to Canada for an abortion paid for by the government. Dr. Dalip Sandhu said, "I tell them it's a sin. But they're not here to ask for my opinion. They want the information. They don't get it from me. It doesn't mean it stops them."[71] Shashi Assanand, director of the Lower Mainland Multicultural Family Support Services Centre in Vancouver, blamed the dowry system. "Besides paying for a lavish wedding, the bride's family is expected to buy her a complete

[67] ATL web site: www.atl.com.
[68] *CNN World News,* September 17, 1995.
[69] John F. Burns, *The New York Times,* August 27, 1994, section 1, p. 5.
[70] The ratio in South Korea was 114 to 100 and in Taiwan was 110 to 100.
[71] *Chicago Tribune,* August 3, 1997.

wardrobe and jewelry, as well as clothes and jewelry for the new son-in-law's family, with whom their daughter will be living. 'That's the minimum,' says Assanand. Those who can afford more are expected to give their new in-laws 'cash, furniture, appliances, a car and even property.'"[72]

Another group concerned with sex selection and women's issues was the Women's Environment and Development Organization (WEDO). WEDO and other women's groups were concerned about what was becoming known as the "missing women" of Asia.[73]

SOURCE: This case was written by Professors David P. Baron and Timothy J. Feddersen. Copyright © 1998 by the Board of Trustees of the Leland Stanford Junior University. All rights reserved. Reprinted with permission.

## PREPARATION QUESTIONS

1. Identify the moral concerns in using ultrasound for sex selection.
2. What possible reactions might ATL encounter on this issue?
3. Does ATL have any responsibility regarding the use of its products in sex selection?
4. Should ATL introduce its FirstSight handheld product in India?
5. Develop a strategy for ATL with respect to the issues discussed in the case. Be sure to include specific steps you would take to implement your strategy.

# Delta Instruments, Inc.

Delta Instruments, Inc., was founded in 1973 to produce a unique, patented mechanical pressure gauge for industrial and military use. The gauge design provided an accurate, long-life instrument that was extremely rugged and could be used in high vibration, pulsation, or corrosive service. Industrial applications were typically in the process industries, including power plants, refineries, and chemical plants. Military applications were quite broad, with the U.S. Navy the largest user (e.g., on aircraft-servicing nitrogen carts, diving chambers, and magazine sprinkler systems). Delta made no other products in significant volume.

Delta's total annual revenues were approximately $4.5 million. The firm employed 65 people in a single office-factory in Southern California. Approximately 45 employees worked in the factory. Delta had a three-person quality control department and a two-person engineering department. Delta was wholly owned by Jack Armstrong, who was actively involved in Delta's day-to-day operations.

Since its inception, Delta had supplied the government both directly and through prime contractors. Currently, Delta sold about $250,000 per year of military-specified gauges to various government prime contractors and about $200,000 per year directly to 10 to 15 government agencies or facilities. The Defense General Supply Center (DGSC) was the largest customer. Government sales, both direct and subcontract, were approximately 10 percent of Delta's total revenues. The direct contracts with the government were each usually small (under $50,000) and were often for standard Delta products.

Late in 1989 the DGSC awarded 19 contracts to Delta, worth $876,142, for the production of pressure gauges built to unique and rigorous specifications. Both Armstrong and the director of engineering concurred that although the gauge specifications were among the most difficult Delta had ever encountered, the specifications could be met. As was typical, each contract required that prototype gauges be tested to ensure compliance with required specifications and that the results of these preliminary tests be reported to the DGSC in the form of a First Article Test Report (FATR). Approximately 90 percent of the testing was to be conducted by independent testing laboratories with the remaining 10 percent being done by Delta. According to normal procedure, the testing labora-

[72]*Chicago Tribune*, August 3, 1997.

[73]See also *The Endangered Sex: Neglect of Female Children in Rural North India*, by Barbara Miller, 1981. Ithaca, NY: Cornell University Press.

tories were to submit their findings to Delta, which would add its findings to complete the FATRs and then submit them to the DGSC.

By July 1990 Delta had purchased the materials needed for production and had begun the first article testing on prototype gauges for 6 of the 19 contracts. After five of the six FATRs had been submitted to DGSC, Delta's pre-submission review of the sixth FATR revealed several anomalous data points. (For instance, an entry that should have read 90 was reported as 9). Further inspection by the junior engineer and the quality control director revealed that the original reports furnished by an outside laboratory differed from the copied reports included in the FATR submitted by Delta. When confronted with this inconsistency, the director of engineering, who was responsible for compiling the FATRs, admitted that he had altered the outside laboratory data included in the sixth FATR by using liquid paper whitener, changing the data, and then reproducing the page to mask the change. The effect of these alterations suggested that the prototype gauge produced under the sixth contract had passed the testing when, in fact, it had failed.

Following this discovery, Delta began an internal investigation of the five previously submitted FATRs. It found that three of the five reports also contained alterations of the data and the test results of outside testing laboratories. In general, these alterations overstated the performance of the tested gauges and claimed compliance with contract specifications even though no such compliance had actually been found. In a subsequent interview with Armstrong, the director of engineering stated that he had altered FATR data on "one or more reports," had acted alone, had not been asked to falsify data by anyone, and that these were the only test data he had ever altered at Delta. Both the quality control director and the junior engineer claimed no knowledge of this or any other incident of data falsification having previously occurred at Delta. No gauges had yet been produced or delivered to the DGSC. Delta had received no payments, nor had any been requested. Moreover, the problems found in the prototype gauges were correctable and compliance with the original contract specifications achievable.

Indeed, there appeared to be some method behind the director of engineering's madness. The data alterations reflected the anticipated performance of the gauges. The opinions of Armstrong, the quality control manager, and other engineers at Delta confirmed that the performance anticipated by the director of engineering would indeed be met when the problems in the prototypes were addressed.

Armstrong was shocked and embarrassed by this incident. Delta had an immaculate reputation based chiefly on the quality of its products and the integrity of its organization. Over nearly two decades, no other incident had the potential of impugning Delta's reputation. Furthermore, there had never been any contract disputes with the U.S. government. There also had been no contracts terminated for default. Moreover, the corporate culture at Delta embodied many of Armstrong's most deeply held values, including openness, honesty, and professionalism.

Armstrong was proud of his company's record and its culture and was anxious to preserve Delta's reputation. But how? Should he forget about the already submitted FATRs and strive to bring the gauges into compliance with the reported data? Should he simply withdraw the submitted FATRs, citing "technical difficulties" or "administrative errors," and resubmit the FATRs when the gauges performed as required? (An attorney claimed that both of these options were arguably within Armstrong's legal rights.) Or should he inform the DGSC of the inaccuracies in the FATRs, as well as the source of these errors?

Armstrong also felt a strong obligation to fairness in the treatment of the director of engineering. This obligation was enhanced by the fact that the director was a long-time friend, who often had accompanied Armstrong on skiing and fishing vacations. Moreover, he had recently developed a heart condition that required extensive, and sometimes expensive, medical treatments. Termination would deprive him of his medical insurance coverage and benefits. The director of engineering was an affable man, highly regarded and well liked by other Delta employees. ■

---

## PREPARATION QUESTION

**1.** Armstrong wanted to do the responsible thing, but what was responsible in this situation?

# CHAPTER 19

# Ethics Systems: Utilitarianism

## Introduction

Ethics is the study of moral judgments about the rightness of actions and rules of behavior. At the societal level, ethics is intended to contribute to mutually beneficial modes of conduct as an alternative to government regulation and enforcement. At the organizational level, ethics is a guide to managerial decision making and policy formulation. At the individual level, ethics provides a basis for justifying one's actions, evaluating the actions of others, and reasoning about moral issues.

This and the following chapter address the role of ethics in management and provide an overview of three principal ethics systems. The objective is to increase moral sensitivity and provide frameworks for reasoning about issues based on ethics principles and moral standards. No single ethics framework encompasses all the moral intuitions of people, so it is important to consider issues from the perspectives of several systems. The ethics systems considered are utilitarianism, rights, and justice. These systems correspond to basic ethical intuitions about the good and the right and are important guides to firms and managers in the evaluation of alternative courses of action.

Ethics and its application in management constitute a broad and deep subject. The approach taken here is to address the subject in a series of steps. This and the following chapter introduce the three ethics systems and evaluate nonmarket issues based on those systems. Chapters 21 and 22 focus on the implementation of these systems in domestic and international contexts, respectively. The chapter cases provide opportunities to reason from the perspectives of ethics systems and apply ethics principles and methods to managerial problems.

This chapter focuses on the nature of ethics in managerial contexts and on utilitarianism, an ethics system that evaluates actions in terms of the well-being they yield. The next two sections consider the role of ethics in management and the distinction between ethics and other forms of managerial decision making. The following sections address the relationship between ethics and self-interest, politics, and casuistry. The methodology of ethics and the relationship between ethics and moral and political philosophy are then considered. Utilitarianism, the principal consequentialist ethics system, is then introduced, and its application in the form of cost–benefit analysis is considered. The distinction between act and rule utilitarianism is identified, and a framework for applying utilitarianism in competitive situations is presented. The application of utilitarianism in managerial settings, and the difficulties in its application, are then considered. Examples

**693**

are presented of utilitarian reasoning, and those examples are then reconsidered in Chapter 20 from the perspectives of rights and justice.

## The Managerial Role of Ethics

Ethics has several managerial roles. Managers must address a variety of complex issues, and ethics provides guidance about how to take into account the interests, rights, and liberties of those affected by business decisions. As a normative approach, ethics provides principles for evaluating alternatives and formulating policies. In the context of the framework for nonmarket analysis presented in Chapter 2 and Figure 2-5, ethics in its normative role is used in both the choice and the screening stages. In the choice stage, ethics provides a basis for evaluating whether claims have moral standing and thus whether they are to be respected in the firm's actions. In the screening stage, ethics provides the underpinnings for policies that guide managers in determining which alternatives should be screened out and which should be considered further. Ethics also provides a basis both for assessing whether moral consensus is present and for justifying a firm's actions to stakeholders, government, and the public.

Ethics is also an important component of the positive analysis of nonmarket issues. Individuals, activists, interest groups, and government officeholders can be motivated by moral concerns about a firm's actions. In the analysis stage of the framework in Figure 2-5, ethics contributes to the prediction of morally motivated nonmarket action. Managers must be sensitive to how the moral determinants of nonmarket action can affect the firm and shape its nonmarket environment. Because individuals have a range of ethical intuitions, it is important to view issues from the perspectives of several ethics systems. In its normative and positive roles, ethics thus provides a basis for analysis, decision making, and the formulation of strategies to address nonmarket issues and the nonmarket actions associated with them.

## What Ethics Is and Is Not

Ethics is a systematic approach to moral judgments based on reason, analysis, synthesis, and reflection. Ethics addresses matters of importance to human well-being, autonomy, and liberty. Ethics is based on moral standards that are independent of the declarations of governments or other authoritative bodies. Moral standards are impartial, take precedence over self-interest, and are to apply to everyone; that is, they are to be universal.[1] Ethics thus is the discipline concerned with judgments based on moral standards and the reasoning therefrom.

Moral philosophers search for ethics systems that can withstand both philosophical scrutiny and the test of practical application. The result has been an array of ethics systems rather than consensus on a single system. On some issues, a decision alternative may be consistent with one ethics system and inconsistent with others. Random drug testing of employees may reduce social costs, and hence satisfy a utilitarian standard, yet it may violate an individual's right to privacy. Similarly, an absolute right to privacy could be unjust if it prevented drug testing of employees whose responsibilities affected public safety.

The issues considered in this and subsequent chapters involve significant moral concerns not easily resolved through approaches that are independent of moral standards. The focus thus is not on simple temptation. There are many managerial situations in which an action is contrary to the law, a well-established company policy, or widely shared ethics principles, yet managers may be tempted to take the action because they, or

---

[1]Moral claims are distinguished from prudential claims, which are based on considerations of self-interest.

the firm, may benefit from it. Since what is good or right is evident in these situations, they have only limited interest from the perspective of ethics. Addressing the issue of temptation remains important, however. One responsibility of management is to develop procedures to reduce the temptation that often arises, for example, from how performance is compensated. Approaches to reducing temptation and guiding managers through situations in which temptation may arise are considered in Chapters 21 and 22. The chapter case, *Enron Power Marketing and the California Market*, considers a company that succumbs to the temptation to manipulate a market for electricity.

Ethics is not the simple reliance on values or the search for value consensus. Values are expressions of desired outcomes or behavior. As a shortcut to ethical reasoning, individuals often rely on their values to guide their personal behavior. Values, however, differ among individuals, whereas ethics principles are to be universal. Moreover, there is little justification for concluding that because a majority has value X and a minority has value Y, value X should prevail. For a firm, policies must be both general and consistent and cannot be dictated by the personal values of whoever happens to occupy a particular managerial position at a particular point in time. Although statements of values by a firm, as considered in Chapter 21, are a useful guide for managers in the screening stage of the framework in Figure 2-5, managers must be able to reason from principles and assess whether current policies continue to be appropriate. Thus values are not a sufficient basis for ethical reasoning by management.

The focus of ethics also is not on issues involving direct mutual advantage. Such issues generally do not require ethics analysis. Every sale a firm makes benefits the firm and its customer. In the absence of external consequences, the transaction is generally free from moral objection. Mutual advantage may also control temptation. A consulting or investment banking firm often has an opportunity to serve its own rather than its clients' interests. To attract future clients, however, the firm has an incentive to establish a reputation for effectively serving client interests. Honoring expectations in such cases can be explained by self-interest independently of moral standards. Serving client interests, however, is not sufficient. Firms must assess whether client interests are consistent with ethics principles and the law, as illustrated by the Enron and Merrill Lynch example in Chapter 18.

# Business Ethics

Business ethics is the application of ethics principles to issues that arise in business. There is no separate discipline of business ethics. As opposed to personal ethics, where an individual is the principal in the sense of Chapter 18, business ethics pertains to situations in which individuals are in an organizational position and act as agents of the company and its owners.

Business ethics also differs from personal ethics because a manager has accepted the responsibilities associated with the position occupied. The set of issues faced thus differs from those one encounters in one's personal life. In an organizational setting an individual may have duties, such as preventing sexual harassment by others or meeting fiduciary responsibilities, that may not be encountered in one's personal life. Moreover, in one's personal life an individual may focus on the virtuous life in an Aristotelian sense or a life of propriety in a Confucian sense. In an organization role, however, a manager must reason about situations in which virtue is not always present, conceptions of what is good or right differ among individuals, and interests are in conflict. Consequently, the focus here is on ethics systems and their application to moral issues that arise in business.

The approach taken does not promote a particular moral vision nor use ethics to mold consensus on a particular set of standards. In the case of "hard" issues such as drug testing of employees, reasonable people of goodwill may disagree on the appropriate policy. The objective is thus to present ethics systems and methods of reasoning that deepen one's understanding of a situation, identify relevant moral concerns, and provide a means of evaluating alternative actions and policies. Even though many managerial actions are based on ethical intuitions rather than on explicit reasoning from ethics principles, that intuition often can be sharpened by ethics analysis, and consistency can be improved.

One reason for considering several ethics systems is that doing so helps sensitize managers to the variety of moral concerns that people may have about an issue. Considering several systems also aids managers in reasoning more broadly about the concerns raised. In particular, in addressing nonmarket issues it is important to understand and evaluate moral concerns from the perspectives of these in the nonmarket environment. To illustrate the moral concerns involved in nonmarket issues, consider the issue of integrity tests.

## Issue: Integrity Tests

In 1988 a federal law took effect prohibiting the use of pre-hiring polygraph tests, which had been given to approximately 2 million current and prospective employees annually.[2] The law also placed certain restrictions on the use of polygraph tests for employees suspected of violating laws or company policies. In response to the ban on pre-hiring polygraph tests, employers began to use more extensive background checks and written "integrity tests."

Integrity tests are paper-and-pencil tests intended to identify individuals with desirable or undesirable traits.[3] Examples of questions on the tests include, "Do you think a person should be fired by a company if it is found that he helped the employees cheat the company out of overtime once in a while?" and "If you found $100 that was lost by a bank truck on the street yesterday, would you turn the money over to the bank, even though you knew for sure that there was no reward?"[4] Firms use these tests, along with information about an applicant's ability, education, and experience, to screen for integrity and potential loyalty to the firm. Some firms have found the tests to be useful in identifying individuals who may be a problem on the job.

From the perspective of costs and benefits, integrity tests can produce benefits to the extent that they help better match potential employees to the jobs in which they will be most productive. The tests may yield substantial benefits for some jobs and few benefits for others. Firms thus must decide for which positions the tests provide net benefits that outweigh possible moral concerns.

Integrity tests raise concerns about rights. Integrity tests may invade privacy if the questions are personal. The tests also raise concerns about arbitrary treatment to the extent to which the tests are imperfect measures and hence may misclassify individuals. Employers, however, have a right to hire whomever they prefer as long as they do not engage in illegal discrimination, and they may use relevant means in making hiring decisions. The tests also raise justice considerations because they may deny opportunity to those who, for whatever reason, do not perform well on such tests. Justice considerations may also be involved if the tests put at a disadvantage individuals with past experiences that cause them to perform poorly on the tests.

---

[2]Exemptions from the law were provided for security guards and jobs that involved health and safety. Pharmaceutical companies were also exempt, as was government.
[3]See Sackett and Harris (1984).
[4]The questions are from the Integrity Attitude Scale published by Reid Psychological Systems. (*The New York Times*, November 28, 1997.)

The remainder of this chapter addresses the methodology of ethics and presents utilitarianism, which provides a basis for the evaluation of issues such as the use of integrity tests. The issue of integrity tests is also addressed in the next chapter from the perspective of moral rights and justice. The Chapter 20 case, *Genetic Testing in the Workplace*, raises related issues.

## Ethics and Private Interests

Ethical behavior enables society to realize the benefits from social interactions and individuals to rely on the word and conduct of others. Ethical behavior does not always make an individual or a firm better off, however. A policy of refusing to pay bribes to government officials can result in costly delays or the loss of sales in some countries. Furthermore, ethical behavior may not be self-evident to others and, even if it is, it may not be rewarded. Ethical behavior thus can conflict with profit objectives or with an individual's self-interest. That is, ethics principles prescribe behavior based on considerations that take precedence over self-interest. This is perhaps clearest in a utilitarian framework in which a person's own interests are given no greater consideration than the interests of any other person. Good ethics is thus not always beneficial to an individual or profitable for a firm; however, good ethics is good for society and is a requirement of good management.

Although good ethics may not always be profitable, unethical behavior can result in substantial losses, as evidenced by the series of business scandals and violations of the law considered in Chapter 18. Unethical actions by a firm can worsen the environment for all firms by causing the public to become suspicious of business and its motives. In the long run, harmony between business and society requires conduct consistent with the principles embodied in the social contract under which business operates. Business and its management thus are evaluated not only in terms of financial performance but also in terms of moral standards. The chapter cases, *Merck and Vioxx* and *Pfizer and Celebrex*, raise these issues.

## Ethics, Politics, and Change

Ethics involves an inquiry into whether a proposition has moral status. Propositions may be classified as claimed or granted. A granted proposition is one that has been established either by ethical consensus or by an authoritative body such as government. Claims often are made that a proposition has moral status. Frequently, these claims are intended to increase the likelihood that the proposition will be granted by government. For example, in some areas delivery services are plagued by robberies and threats to the safety of delivery personnel. As a result of reports from drivers concerned about their safety, a Federal Express district manager suspended after-dark pickups in Gary, Indiana. Similarly, a Domino's Pizza franchisee refused to deliver in certain high-risk areas in Miami. Consider the proposition that delivery services may not refuse to serve parts of their normal service area, even if the motive is to avoid possible harm to delivery personnel. One use of ethics is to determine whether such a proposition results in an injustice or a violation of rights. The use of ethics to establish the moral status of a proposition is illustrated by the horizontal arrows in Figure 19-1, which classifies propositions as claimed and granted and according to their moral status.[5]

---

[5]This figure was prepared by Keith Krehbiel.

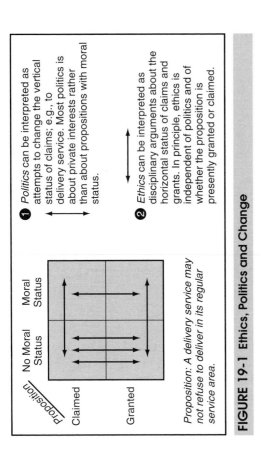

① *Politics* can be interpreted as attempts to change the vertical status of claims; e.g., to delivery service. Most politics focuses on propositions with moral status.

② *Ethics* can be interpreted as disciplinary arguments about the horizontal status of claims and grants. In principle, ethics is independent of politics and of whether the proposition is presently granted or claimed.

*Proposition: A delivery service may not refuse to deliver in its regular service area.*

**FIGURE 19-1 Ethics, Politics and Change**

Politics pertains to the vertical status of propositions in Figure 19-1. Most politics centers on private interests and is advanced in the absence of arguments about moral status, as illustrated by the three arrows in the left column of the figure. Some politics focuses on propositions with established moral status, as indicated by the arrow in the right column. The policies restricting deliveries were prohibited by the mayor of Gary and under court order by a U.S. district court judge in Miami. San Francisco passed an ordinance making it illegal to refuse to deliver in parts of the regular service area of a restaurant.

Change can come from both ethics and politics. The Chapter 20 case, *Environmental Justice and Pollution Credits Trading Systems*, focuses on the ethics and politics of the proposition that less-advantaged persons, including minorities and women, are adversely affected by certain environmental protection policies.

## Casuistry

Ethics is principled reasoning and is distinguished from casuistry, which is an approach to moral practice that seeks to balance competing considerations by making exceptions to principles in particular cases. Casuistry is an ancient approach that reemerged during the Reformation in the 16th century as the argument that different principles were applicable to different situations and in different roles. For example, a ruler might violate principles in an attempt to benefit his subjects. Casuistry was attacked by Pascal, who argued that although they may have been well intentioned, casuist methods were flawed and the results therefore questionable. Casuistry has been characterized as a false art of making exceptions in particular situations, resulting in the violation of underlying principles.[6] This approach is contrary to the ethics systems considered here, which are intended to apply universally. Thus, the familiar saying that "a diplomat is a person who lies abroad for the benefit of his country" may characterize politics but not ethics.

The following example illustrates casuist reasoning.

---

[6]See Jonsen and Toulmin (1988) for a history of casuistry and for its defense as a practical ethics.

## Saving the Division

Leyden Corporation was a small manufacturer of household appliances, including blenders, food processors, mixers, and coffee makers. Competition had intensified in all its lines of business, particularly as companies in the newly industrialized countries of Asia entered its markets. In 1997 Leyden incurred a loss of $1.2 million, and the first half of 1998 was worse. Leyden saw little opportunity to turn the situation around.

The most serious problem was with its line of blenders, which because of low-priced imports had experienced decreasing sales and was losing nearly $2 million a year. The blender division had done all it could to reduce costs, including freezing wage rates for the past year. If the profitability of the division could not be improved, Leyden's only alternative would be to close its plant. The general manager of the blender division formulated a plan that he believed would save the plant for a few years to buy time in the hope that something favorable, such as a change in exchange rates, might occur.

The general manager's plan involved cutting the quality of the blenders but marketing them like the previous models. The plan was to use a lower-quality motor and cheaper internal materials, which together would reduce costs by nearly 14 percent. This would enable the plant to remain open, as long as volume could be maintained. Although the blenders would not be as durable, a consumer would have no way of knowing that at the time of purchase. To conceal the lower quality, the general manager proposed keeping the same model numbers, charging the same price, advertising and marketing the blenders as before, and making certain that the new blenders had the same external appearance as the current ones. The general manager was confident that neither retailers nor customers would soon detect the changes.

The general manager reasoned that the plan would benefit employees and shareholders, and Leyden could be said to have a social responsibility to both groups of stakeholders. Consumers would be worse off compared to their expectations, but employees were a more immediate constituency, and consumers would still be getting a serviceable blender. From the point of view of responsibility to stakeholders, the general manager decided to implement the plan.

The general manager's reasoning is an example of casuistry. That is, the reasoning proceeds from a concept of responsibility to the particulars of a case without reliance on principles. From a utilitarianism perspective, selling a lower-quality product as if it were a higher-quality product reduces aggregate well-being because some consumers would be better off buying other blenders if they knew of the change. The plan also involves deception, which is difficult to support in any ethics system. Furthermore, it treats consumers as a means of saving the division. From a justice perspective, the company is unjustly taking advantage of them.

The casuist approach is dangerous precisely because it shortcuts the application of principles in favor of conceptions of responsibility that may be inconsistent with moral standards. Furthermore, those conceptions can be a disguise for the self-interest of the decision maker. Several factors indicate when casuistry is being practiced. It is often present in situations in which the action the manager wants to take is identified by self-interest, the firm's interest, or constituents' interests. Casuistry may be present when managers find themselves searching for a justification for the actions they wish to take based on self-interest. Casuistry may be present when a manager tries to rationalize around principles with the justification that constituents benefit. The chapter case, *Merck and Vioxx*, and the Chapter 18 case, *Delta Instruments, Inc*, raise such issues.

# The Methodology of Ethics

The methodology of ethics is illustrated in the left panel of Figure 19-2. It involves the identification of decision alternatives, evaluation of those alternatives in terms of ethics principles and moral standards, and choice based on those evaluations. Ethics analysis is to be applied early rather than late in the process. As illustrated in the right panel of Figure 19-2, ethics that serves only to explain decisions made on other bases is inappropriate. It encourages managers to choose actions that serve their and their firms' interests and then to search among the various ethics systems to find one that comes closest to justifying the already-chosen action. This does not mean that when correctly applied, ethics cannot be used to justify the action taken. That justification, however, should be consistent with the basis for the decision.

Figure 19-3 provides more detail on the methodology of ethics. The methodology begins with the identification of the facts about the issue, since if the facts are incorrectly understood, even a correct analysis can result in an inappropriate decision. Along with the facts, the moral concerns associated with the issue must be identified. They may involve concerns about well-being, rights and liberties, and fairness for those involved. Management also must identify alternatives for addressing the issue, and creativity should be used in generating alternatives.

Once the facts have been discerned, moral concerns identified, and alternatives generated, ethics principles and moral standards are used to analyze the alternatives. Analysis involves reasoning that is logical, systematic, consistent, and reflective. The results of the analysis are judgments about whether the alternatives are consistent with ethics principles and moral standards. When ethics is directed at decision making, the final stage involves choice and implementation. When ethics is used for positive purposes, the final stage involves predicting whether objections to a decision are likely

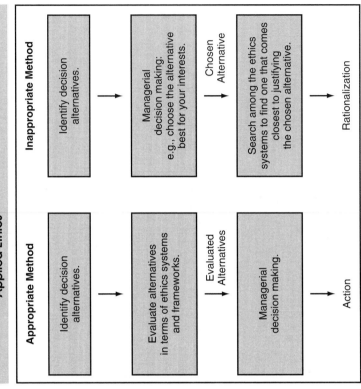

**FIGURE 19-2 Appropriate and Inappropriate Methods of Applied Ethics**

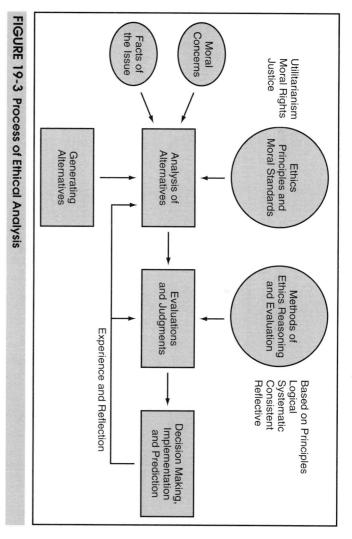

**FIGURE 19-3 Process of Ethical Analysis**

# The Relationships Among Moral Philosophy, Ethics, and Political Philosophy

Figure 19-4 illustrates the relationship between moral philosophy and ethics. Moral philosophy is concerned with deducing moral principles and standards from axioms or self-evident principles. The self-evident principle that what matters is human well-being is the basis for utilitarianism. From that principle, the standard of maximizing aggregate well-being is deduced. The action that maximizes aggregate well-being then has moral standing because it yields the greatest good in terms of well-being. As considered in Chapter 20, Kant's categorical imperative provides a basis for deducing maxims to guide behavior, which in turn provide a basis for identifying individual rights. Choosing a social contract from an impartial position provides the basis for principles of justice considered in Chapter 20.

As indicated in Figure 19-4, ethics is concerned with analysis and reasoning based on principles and standards. That reasoning may be directed at the design of society's institutions, such as the public education and justice systems, the identification of specific rights, and the identification of appropriate conduct. Analysis and reasoning may also be directed at determining which actions provide the greatest aggregate well-being or whether a right, such as a right to privacy, takes precedence over other considerations.

Political philosophy is related to ethics and moral philosophy but focuses on institutions to govern the interactions among individuals. Political philosophy naturally focuses on conceptions of the state, how the state should grant and limit liberties and ensure justice, and the extent to which markets or other institutions are used to organize economic activity.

and whether nonmarket action can be expected. Finally, experience and reflection provide lessons for refining the methods of analysis and evaluation.

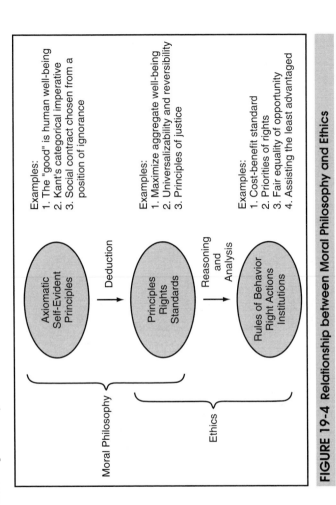

Examples:
1. The "good" is human well-being
2. Kant's categorical imperative
3. Social contract chosen from a position of ignorance

Examples:
1. Maximize aggregate well-being
2. Universalizability and reversibility
3. Principles of justice

Examples:
1. Cost-benefit standard
2. Priorities of rights
3. Fair equality of opportunity
4. Assisting the least advantaged

**FIGURE 19-4 Relationship between Moral Philosophy and Ethics**

Moral and political philosophy come together when they provide principles to govern the interactions among individuals. Utilitarianism provides a basis for a political philosophy in which the choice between private institutions, such as markets, and public institutions, such as government regulation, is made according to which maximizes aggregate well-being.

## Utilitarianism: A Consequentialist System

Utilitarianism has a rich history with its origins in the work of Jeremy Bentham (1789), who argued for a calculus of pain and pleasure, and then of John Stuart Mill (1861). The moral standing of utilitarianism, however, is better understood in more recent expressions to which the criticisms applied to hedonism are less applicable. Utilitarianism is better understood as a particular form of a consequentialist moral philosophy.

In a consequentialist system, an alternative is moral if it produces better consequences than any other alternative. Utilitarianism is a consequentialist system with two particular features. First, consequences are to be evaluated in terms of the preferences of individuals, and second, those preferences are to be aggregated. Aggregation is required because an action may make some individuals better off and others worse off. The standard of human well-being and the need to consider the consequences for all persons correspond to fundamental ethical intuitions.

As an example, because of the oil crisis of 1973 the United States adopted a national speed limit of 55 miles per hour. As oil prices dropped and Americans increased their driving, the pressure for higher speed limits mounted. In 1995 Congress abolished the federal speed limit, and by 1998 all but one state had increased their speed limits. Many increased their speed limit to 70 or 75 on rural stretches of interstate highways. Data subsequently indicated that the higher speed limits increased fatalities and injuries. The higher speed limits also saved motorists and their passengers many hours of travel time. The overwhelming revealed preference among the states for

higher speed limits suggests that the benefits from the time saved outweighed the safety costs. As one motorist said referring to the greater risks, "I'll take that trade-off."

Utilitarianism does not focus on the numbers of people who are better or worse off because of an action, nor is it equivalent to a vote among alternatives. If an action makes 100 people worse off by one unit each and makes one person better off by 101 units, the action should be taken. Utilitarianism also is not "the greatest good for the greatest number." That statement is ambiguous because, as the example indicates, one alternative could produce the greatest good yet another alternative could produce benefits for the greatest number. Utilitarianism chooses the action that yields the greatest good.

Table 19-1 illustrates the basic utilitarian approach. A decision maker is to choose between two alternatives, A and B. The well-being for each of the four members of society, measured in terms of their preferences or utilities for the consequences, is presented in the body of the table. The aggregate well-being is the sum of those utilities; that is, utilitarianism aggregates the utilities of the individuals. Alternative A yields an aggregate utility of 11, whereas action B yields a greater aggregate utility of 14. Utilitarianism identifies action B as the moral action, since it yields the greater good.

If one firm signs a supply contract with another firm to provide a product, both firms presumably are better off as a result of the transaction. From a utilitarian perspective the transaction is morally good provided there are no associated externalities. Moreover, as long as both parties agree to the contract, the price at which the product is exchanged is irrelevant. That is, if the value of the product to the buyer is 20 and the cost to the supplier is 15, the transaction results in a net benefit of 5 regardless of whether the price is 19 or 16. The price paid is a pure transfer between the buyer and the seller, and the transfer nets to zero in the utilitarian calculus.

## Utilitarianism and Self-Interest

Utilitarianism is nearly the antithesis of self-interest because one's own interests are to be given no more consideration than those of any other person. That is, decisions are to be impartial. The interests considered thus are not just those of the decision maker but those of everyone affected by the action. In the Leyden Corporation example marketing the blenders as proposed would likely make customers worse off by more than the company and employees would gain. In Table 19-1 individual 3 is worse off with action B than with A, but as a utilitarian decision maker, 3 has a moral duty to choose B over A. Note also that as utilitarians each of the four individuals will choose alternative B. That is, with utilitarianism there is unanimity about the moral action. Utilitarianism is also universalizable in the sense that each person would be willing to have everyone act in accord with its principle of maximizing aggregate well-being.

In the chapter case, *Merck and Vioxx*, Merck could not rule out the possibility that Vioxx might increase the risk of cardiovascular events such as heart attacks. Recognizing

**TABLE 19-1** Utilitarianism Example

| Individual | Utility from Alternative | |
|---|---|---|
| | A | B |
| 1 | 3 | 3 |
| 2 | 3 | 5 |
| 3 (the decision maker) | 3 | 2 |
| 4 | 2 | 4 |
| aggregate utility | 11 | 14 |

this, the company had the choice between marketing Vioxx only for patients at risk of stomach bleeding from over-the-counter pain relievers or marketing Vioxx broadly. The latter would yield billions of dollars more in profits while the company conducted clinical tests on a possible link between Vioxx and cardiovascular problems. Merck chose to market Vioxx broadly with heavy direct-to-consumer advertising. The case focuses on the initial marketing decision and subsequent decisions as new evidence on the possibility of coronary risk arrived.

## Aligning Self-Interest with Societal Well-Being

Utilitarianism coincides with self-interest only when societal consequences are aligned with private consequences. One role of government is to establish institutions that provide this alignment. When alignment has been achieved, individuals can evaluate actions in terms of the consequences for themselves rather than having to take into account the consequences for all others affected by an action.

Many of society's institutions are based on aligning the interests of firms and individuals with the aggregate interests of society. The institutions of private property and markets provide one means of alignment, since a voluntary transaction, such as the supply contract between the two firms, makes both the buyer and seller better off. A transaction that constitutes a Pareto improvement—making at least one person better off and no one worse off—thus is morally good from a utilitarian perspective. In the case of environmental protection, pollution credits trading systems as considered in Chapter 11 align the interests of polluters and society. The law of torts considered in Chapter 12 is an institution that assigns the social costs of accidents to individuals and firms, providing incentives to minimize the social costs of accidents. The Living Benefits example presented later in the chapter considers a market that arose in response to a demand for flexibility in the use of life insurance benefits.

When institutions that align self-interest with societal well-being are in place and markets are competitive, the maximization of profit by a firm results in the greatest aggregate societal well-being; that is, the greatest difference between societal benefits and societal costs. This alignment of private interests and societal interests forms one basis for Milton Friedman's view that the social responsibility of business is to maximize profits, as considered in Chapter 18.

## Utilitarianism, Distribution, and Altruism

Utilitarianism aggregates individuals' well-being as evaluated in terms of their preferences, and hence every person's utility is given equal weight. In the example in Table 19-1 the distribution of utility is more equal with alternative A than with alternative B, but since utilitarianism is concerned with aggregate well-being, it does not matter how that utility is distributed across individuals. Alternative B yields the greater aggregate utility and hence is the moral choice.

Although utilitarianism gives equal weight to the utilities of all persons, this does not mean that redistribution is irrelevant. The transfer of a dollar from a rich person to a poor person can increase aggregate well-being if the poor person is made better off by more than the rich person loses, that is, if the gain in the utility of the poor person is greater than the loss in the utility of the rich person. Utilitarianism thus evaluates redistribution as it does any other alternative—in terms of the aggregate utility of all persons. In the example of one firm supplying a product to another firm, the "marginal utilities" of the two firms are the same, so the price paid for the product does not affect the utilitarian conclusion that the transaction increases aggregate well-being.

Utilitarianism also takes into account altruistic preferences. If some individuals have altruistic preferences for the well-being of others, the well-being of those others receives greater consideration. For example, if a rich person has altruistic preferences for the well-being of the poor, the rich person has greater utility for alternatives that benefit the poor than for alternatives that do not, other things equal. The rich person's preferences for the well-being of the poor cannot be hypothetical, however. Instead, the rich person must be willing to act on those preferences by redistributing some of her wealth or contributing time to improving the well-being of the poor.

In evaluating two alternative government programs designed to benefit the poor, the preferences on which the rich person is willing to act are what is counted. Thus, a person concerned for the well-being of the poor is not able to assign a hypothetical or an arbitrary weight to their well-being. That rich person, however, may attempt to persuade others also to be altruistic or may engage in nonmarket action to have the government establish programs to provide benefits to the poor. If the resulting taxes reduce economic efficiency, the cost of that inefficiency must be taken into account in evaluating the programs to benefit the poor. Cost-benefit analysis incorporates these considerations.

Moreover, utilitarianism is the antithesis of self-interest, and the two are equivalent only if private and societal well-being are aligned.

## Summary of the Components of Utilitarianism

Utilitarianism is a moral philosophy that holds that

- moral good is judged in terms of consequences;
- consequences are evaluated in terms of human well-being;
- human well-being is evaluated in terms of individual preferences;
- the rightness of an action is judged by the aggregate well-being, or good, it yields; and
- the morally justified action maximizes aggregate well-being.

## Utilitarian Duty and the Calabresi and Melamed Principles

One of the most difficult aspects of applying utilitarianism, or any other ethics system, is determining who has the duty to take a moral action. For example, if aggregate utility would be increased by transferring a dollar to a poor person, from whom should that dollar come? The answer is that it should come from the person or persons with the smallest decrease in utility from giving up the dollar. If there are many people who could contribute, each could give up some portion of the dollar if that would result in a smaller decrease in their aggregate utility.

The Calabresi and Melamed principles introduced in Chapter 12 provide a framework for reasoning about the assignment of duty. The principles are intended to identify which party is in the best position to determine whether the benefits of an action outweigh its costs, which party is in the best position to induce others to take actions that yield benefits that exceed the costs, and which party is in the best position to induce others to act to correct a misassignment of entitlements. The party identified by those principles then has the duty to act.

For example, the appropriate level of safety to incorporate into a product depends on the safety features the manufacturer could incorporate and on the care the user of the product could take. To determine if the manufacturer or the user has the duty to add safety features or take care, respectively, the Calabresi and Melamed principles provide the following tests:

1. Assign the duty to the party—the manufacturer or the user—that can best achieve improvements in the difference between aggregate benefits and costs.

2. If it is not clear which party that is, the duty should be assigned to the party that is in the best position to assess the aggregate benefits and costs.

3. If that is unclear (and hence a mistake in the assignment of duty could be made), assign the duty to the party that can at the lowest cost induce the other party to take actions to improve the difference between aggregate benefits and aggregate costs.

In the case of product safety the duty is usually assigned to the manufacturer who is in the better position to assess aggregate costs and benefits and to reduce accidents through the incorporation of safety features. Moreover, the manufacturer is usually well positioned to induce the consumer through instructions and warnings to take care when the cost of that care is lower than the cost of adding additional safety features. Furthermore, a manufacturer may have a duty to anticipate carelessness and, in some situations, misuse of a product by a consumer. This assignment of duty is warranted when the manufacturer is better positioned to avoid the harm from carelessness and misuse through product design, the addition of safety features, and warnings.

In identifying the locus of duty in situations not involving government institutions, the Calabresi and Melamed principles can be simplified to answer the question, "Which party is best positioned to act or to induce others to act to yield benefits that exceed the costs?" For example, in the Chapter 21 case, *Citigroup and Subprime Lending,* Citigroup acquired The Associates, a large subprime lender that had been accused of predatory lending. Citigroup could continue to market subprime loans aggressively and rely on customers to determine whether they wanted to borrow or it could attempt to restrict its lending to customers who would actually benefit from the loans. The Calabresi and Melamed principles ask whether Citigroup or a borrower is better positioned to determine whether the loans were beneficial or predatory. In the Chapter 2 case, *Exclusive Resorts: Entrepreneurial Positioning and Nonmarket Defense,* customers were wealthy and in all likelihood had personal lawyers, tax advisors, and financial planners, so there was no need for the company to assess whether they would benefit. In the Citigroup case, however, many of the borrowers were poor or elderly and could easily succumb to aggressive marketing, which in many cases would leave them worse off with a loan. The Calabresi and Melamed principles suggest that Citigroup is better positioned than are some borrowers to assess whether a subprime loan would be beneficial. Hence, the duty is on Citigroup to ensure that its lending makes borrowers better off.

## Act and Rule Utilitarianism

Utilitarianism may be applied in two forms, *act utilitarianism* and *rule utilitarianism.* The classical distinction between these two forms is considered in this section, and the following section considers an alternative form applicable to settings in which consequences are jointly determined by more than one party.[7]

Act utilitarianism focuses on the consequences of a particular action in a particular situation and prescribes the action that yields the greatest aggregate well-being for everyone affected by that action. Rule utilitarianism focuses on a general rule of behavior to be followed by all individuals in all similar situations. A moral rule is then the one that

---

[7]See Brandt (1959, 1979) for the classical distinction.

does best in terms of its consequences for everyone affected in those similar situations. An action is then moral if it is consistent with the moral rule appropriate for that type of situation. As an example, in the Part V integrative case, *GlaxoSmithKline and AIDS Drug Policy*, a candidate for a rule could be:

*In the event of a public health emergency, a developing country may violate a patent and produce a life-preserving pharmaceutical under a compulsory license.*

The evaluation of this rule requires the specific information in the case and only a brief analysis is presented here. The benefits flowing from the rule are measured in terms of lives preserved. The costs are the production costs and the loss in well-being from the diminished incentives for pharmaceutical companies to conduct research and development when patents are not respected. In addition to aggregating the consequences, the rule must be compared to alternative rules such as having the pharmaceutical company provide the drug at preferential prices or developed countries purchase the drug and give it to the developing country. Further analysis is reserved for the case.

Rule utilitarianism is viewed by its advocates as providing a set of rules for guiding the behavior of all individuals in society in a mutually advantageous manner. Act utilitarianism focuses on individual actions and does not explain what the overall consequences would be for society if everyone were to act in that manner.

To illustrate the substantive and methodological distinctions between act and rule utilitarianism, suppose that in a particular situation deceiving rather than dealing with a person honestly would yield benefits that exceed the costs. Under act utilitarianism, deception is a morally justified action in this situation. If a general rule of behavior, however, were, "People may deceive others when it is beneficial to do so," relying on the word of others would be problematic. Aggregate well-being then would be lower because people would not be able to trust others. Thus, mutually advantageous reliance on the word of others would require costly enforcement mechanisms, such as explicit contracts. A rule such as "Always deal with people in an honest and forthright manner" would yield greater aggregate well-being if everyone followed the rule. This rule thus would have moral standing under rule utilitarianism.

Act utilitarianism also risks slipping into self-interest. Since act utilitarianism focuses on an individual's action in a specific situation rather than on general rules of behavior, individuals may be tempted to follow their self-interest. That is, the focus of act utilitarianism on the evaluation of specific actions can place the decision maker on the slippery slope leading to evaluating actions based on self-interest rather than the consequences for all affected.

The weakness of rule utilitarianism, however, is precisely the strength of act utilitarianism. If deception in a particular situation X yields benefits that exceed the costs, the following modification of the rule would yield greater aggregate well-being: "Always deal with people in an honest and forthright manner except in situation X in which deception is permitted." Amending the rule to allow an exception in situation X improves the utilitarian calculus and hence yields a morally superior rule. Then, any exception that yields benefits in excess of its costs would also yield a morally superior rule. Rule utilitarianism then degenerates into act utilitarianism.[8]

One response of a rule utilitarian is that utilitarian methods are necessarily applied in an imperfect world in which some facts are missing, information is incomplete, and not all consequences can be foreseen, let alone evaluated. In such a world, it is better to evaluate general rules of behavior to guide individuals than to apply utilitarian methods

_____
[8]See Lyons (1965).

separately to each action in each situation.[9] Rule utilitarianism encourages individuals to think about whether they would want everyone to follow the same rule of behavior in all similar situations. That is, rule utilitarianism encourages universalism. Rule utilitarianism thus is the preferred form of utilitarianism.

As an example, in the late 1980s American Airlines and United Airlines became concerned about the changes in medical standards adopted by the new federal air surgeon, an officer of the Federal Aviation Administration (FAA). The federal air surgeon has responsibility for granting medical waivers, referred to as "special issuances," that allowed reinstatement of pilots who had had their certification suspended. Under the new standards one pilot who had blacked out in the cockpit had been granted a special issuance, as had a pilot who had had bypass surgery. An airline was not required to put a pilot with a special issuance back in the cockpit, and American and United had kept their pilots grounded until receiving clearance from their own chief medical officers. The moral question was whether the airlines should take any action with regard to the new standards being followed by the federal air surgeon. Since the airlines could ground any of their pilots with special issuances that were questioned by their own medical officers, the airlines were not concerned about their own pilots. The broader concern was with general aviation pilots and other airlines that might not be aware of the changes made by the federal air surgeon. American and United extrapolated from their own situations to the broader population of pilots and airlines; that is, they considered a general rule. They concluded based on reasoning analogous to the Calabresi and Melamed principles that they had a duty to make their concerns public. The airlines went to the FAA and to the congressional committee with oversight responsibility for the FAA, which held hearings leading to a review of the medical standards.

## Jointly Determined Consequences

When consequences are jointly determined, a second form of act and rule utilitarianism is applicable.[10] As an example of such a situation, consider a firm seeking to sell telecommunication equipment to a government agency in a country in which corruption is known to be widespread. Suppose the firm believes that a competitor with inferior equipment is likely to be offering a bribe to the head of the agency. How should the firm reason about whether it should offer a matching bribe?

In act utilitarianism an individual chooses the action that maximizes aggregate well-being, taking the behavior of others as given. A matching bribe in this situation would increase aggregate well-being because the firm has superior equipment. In rule utilitarianism an individual chooses not only a rule for one's own action but also simultaneously for the actions of all individuals. In so doing the individual is choosing a rule of behavior to be followed by everyone, so the rule is universal. In addition, as utilitarians all persons would choose the same rule, since each person maximizes aggregate well-being. Each individual thus is choosing not only in an impartial manner but also chooses the same rule, so there is unanimity.[11] Since bribery and the resulting corruption reduce aggregate well-being, the moral rule is that neither firm offers a bribe. Bribery is considered in more detail in Chapter 22.

As a quantitative example, consider two individuals who each must decide whether to act honestly or dishonestly. Table 19-2 presents their utilities as a function

---

[9] See Hardin (1988).

[10] See Harsanyi (1982, p.57) for this characterization and also Harsanyi (1977).

[11] As developed further in the next chapter, such a rule meets the two higher order moral standards—universalizability and unanimous impartial choice—that give it moral standing.

of the actions each takes, where the first entry in each cell is the utility of person 1 and the second is the utility of person 2. Acting honestly is better for individual 1 if and only if individual 2 acts honestly, but acting dishonestly is better for 2 regardless of whether 1 acts honestly or dishonestly. With rule utilitarianism consider two alternative rules: (A) All act honestly and (B) All act dishonestly.[12] Rule A yields aggregate utility of 17, whereas rule B yields aggregate utility of 11. As rule utilitarians both individuals would choose rule A, so they are unanimous in their choice.

Act utilitarianism takes the other individual's action as given, so it is necessary to form a judgment about which action the other individual will take. In the example in Table 19-2 if 2 were to act dishonestly, as an act utilitarian individual 1 would act dishonestly, since that yields aggregate utility of 11 instead of 10. If 2 were to act honestly, 1 would act honestly. Individual 2 would reason in an identical manner, acting honestly if 1 were to act honestly, and acting dishonestly if 1 were to act dishonestly. Which actions would be taken thus depends on what the other individual can be expected to do. Suppose that 1 suspects that individual 2 might not be a utilitarian but instead might be motivated by self-interest. If 1 harbors such suspicions, the better action would be to act dishonestly. That is, if 2 were indeed motivated by self-interest, 2 would act dishonestly, since that is a dominant strategy; that is, acting dishonestly is better for 2 regardless of how 1 acts. If instead 2 were an act utilitarian but believed that 1 was suspicious and might believe that 2 was self-interested and act dishonestly, then 2 would act dishonestly. In this case incomplete information about what the other individual will do could easily cause act utilitarianism to degenerate into both being dishonest.[13]

## Decision Making in the Face of a Moral Transgression

Next consider the case in which individual 1 is a rule utilitarian and 2 is known to be self-interested and hence will act dishonestly. Is 1 morally justified in acting dishonestly? The answer at one level is no because the moral rule is for both to act honestly. It is 2 who is acting immorally. Under act utilitarianism 1 is morally right to act dishonestly, however, since doing so is justified by avoiding an even worse outcome. Rule utilitarianism, however, correctly indicates that the moral rule is for both to act honestly, so it is right for 1 to be honest. The moral obligation in such a case is to convince individual 2 to act honestly or more generally to initiate collective action to achieve a binding agreement for all to act honestly. In the case of bribery, the duty is on the firm, and all firms, to eliminate bribery and to reject extortion by government officials. This approach is considered in more detail in Chapter 22 in the case of bribery in international business where the collective action occurred through the OECD. Chapter 22 also considers a unilateral policy of the Cummins Engine Company to address such situations.

**TABLE 19-2 Rule Utilitarianism and Joint Determination**

|  |  | Individual 2 | |
|---|---|:---:|:---:|
|  |  | honest | dishonest |
| *Individual 1* | honest | 10,7 | 2,8 |
|  | dishonest | 7,2 | 4,7 |

---

12Note that there are other possible rules, such as, "Individual 1 is to act honestly and individual 2 dishonestly." The two rules A and B are considered because they are symmetric.

13Note that the situation in Table 19-2 is not a prisoners' dilemma.

## Utilitarianism and Rights

Rights may be classified as intrinsic or instrumental. Intrinsic rights are to be respected because they have moral standing independently of the consequences they yield. Instrumental rights are to be respected because they lead to desirable consequences. Instrumental rights are justified in a consequentialist system, such as utilitarianism, when in a wide variety of settings such rights improve well-being. Property rights are an example of instrumental rights in utilitarianism, since they facilitate beneficial economic transactions. Utilitarianism provides a means of evaluating instrumental rights but does not provide a basis for evaluating intrinsic rights, which must be justified by other considerations as identified in Chapter 20. The Chapter 20 case, *Genetic Testing in the Workplace*, includes issues of well-being and rights.

## Criticisms of Utilitarianism

### Philosophical Criticisms

One criticism of consequentialist systems is that they do not give adequate attention to intrinsic rights and liberties, which are said to be fundamentally important. A related criticism is that consequentialist systems treat all things alike in their calculus. Thus, aspirations, wants, needs, liberties, and opportunities are relevant only with regard to their effect on consequences. As Sen (1987, pp. 74–76) argues, however, consequences must remain an essential focus even of an ethics system that considers intrinsically important concepts.

Another concern with utilitarianism pertains to how duty is assigned when consequences are jointly-determined or transgressions are possible. If there is only one person who can take the moral action, the assignment of duty is clear. In some cases, however, there may be several parties who could take the action. One resolution is that the duty should be assigned to everyone who could take the action, but that leaves a collective choice problem that could be difficult to resolve. If there are costs associated with taking the action, the utilitarian resolution of the collective choice problem is that the person with the lowest cost of acting should be assigned the duty, as indicated previously. More generally, the assignment of duty can be based on the Calabresi and Melamed principles. In some cases the assignment may be either to a firm or to the government. For example, in the case of permanent layoffs, the duty to retrain laid-off employees could rest with the employer, the government, or the employees. The duty to retrain workers has been assigned primarily to government and the individuals themselves, whereas many companies have assumed the responsibility for upgrading the education and skills of their current employees.

The assignment of duty is more difficult when consequences are determined jointly through the actions of several, or many, persons, as in the discussion of the example in Table 19-2.[14] The link between actions and consequences also can involve more complicated strategic interactions, as in the case of a prisoners' dilemma or a free-rider problem. Identifying the moral rule may be straightforward, but assigning specific duties in strategic situations can be a complicated task.

Assigning duty is also difficult when circumstances change. Most employers provide health, life, and disability insurance for their employees, but if an employee becomes permanently disabled and unable to work, which party has the responsibility for the worker? An increasing number of employers fire permanently disabled workers, frequently after a specified time period such as 6 months. A Mercer Human Resource

---

[14]See Hardin (1988).

Consulting study found that 51 percent of the companies surveyed fired employees on long-term disability.[15] Disability insurance payments continue after firing, but health care and life insurance benefits are no longer provided, imposing a financial burden on the former employees. The employers argued that the fired workers were no longer employees, since they could not work. Moreover, the purpose of the disability insurance was to provide for the employee in the event of a disability. Who has the duty in such cases—the employer, the employee, or government?

Utilitarianism is also criticized for its focus solely on human well-being. Some critics claim that it should be expanded to include the well-being of other living creatures such as animals and trees and inanimate objects such as rocks and soil. This claim is the subject of much disagreement, but if the claim were accepted, the approach to taking these broader considerations into effect would be similar to how altruism is taken into account. Since the good is to be measured in terms of the preferences of individuals, the preferences of those individuals concerned with animate and inanimate objects would be taken into account, but only to the extent that they would act on those preferences on their own. Some go farther and argue that in the realms of conservation and the protection of nature what matters is not the pleasure that individuals obtain from an undisturbed mountain lake. Instead, the claim is that the well-being of the lake itself is to be taken into account.

## Interpersonal Comparisons of Utility

A fundamental problem with utilitarianism is the difficulty, if not the impossibility, of making interpersonal comparisons of preferences. The preferences considered in the discipline of economics are ordinal in the sense that they indicate only how an individual orders one consequence relative to another. Those preferences do not reflect intensity. The Pareto criterion avoids interpersonal comparisons, since it requires only that an action not make anyone worse off and make at least one person better off. A rule that produces a Pareto improvement thus has a strong claim to moral standing in a consequentialist ethics system. When actions make some individuals better off and others worse off, however, interpersonal comparisons are necessary to apply utilitarianism. Interpersonal comparisons are, however, problematic unless some common measure of preference intensity can be devised.[16]

In spite of the difficulties in making interpersonal comparisons of preferences, utilitarianism is regularly used to evaluate public policies by measuring benefits and costs in monetary units. Measurement may involve a direct estimate of how much individuals are willing to pay, or accept, for one consequence rather than another. Indirect estimates—using wage premiums to evaluate the cost of job hazards or housing price differentials as a function of the distance from an airport to estimate the cost of noise pollution—are also possible. Because of the difficulties in making interpersonal comparisons, cost-benefit calculations are often only one of several considerations used in public policy analysis. These issues are also present in business decisions as in the chapter case *Pricing the Norplant System*.

## Identifying Costs and Benefits

A difficulty in the application of a utilitarian system centers on whether well-being can be identified from observed actions; that is, from revealed preferences. If people choose to smoke or hang glide, actions that can reduce their life expectancy, is that

---

15 *The Wall Street Journal*, July 14, 2003.
16 Harsanyi (1982) argues that the problem of interpersonal comparisons of preferences can be overcome by applying a similarity postulate that holds that after allowing for differences in tastes, individuals can be viewed as reacting similarly when choosing among alternatives.

a benefit or a cost? If preferences are revealed by actions, these choices presumably have benefits that outweigh the costs of the reduced life expectancy. In a government cost-benefit analysis, however, the reduced life expectancy counts as a social cost, and the benefits generally are not counted. In the case of smoking, addiction can mean that actions are not voluntary and hence do not reveal preferences.

Since utilitarianism considers the consequences for everyone, certain consequences net to zero. Hence, in Chapter 12, the focus of the analysis of the liability system was on efficiency—that is, which party could reduce accidents at lowest cost—rather than on the distributive consequences. Similarly, in the tradable permits system for controlling sulfur dioxide emissions from power plants considered in Chapter 11, it did not matter from a utilitarian perspective whether the allowances were given free to power plants or were auctioned. Similarly, in the case of the supply contract, the price does not affect the aggregate benefits. It does matter, however, whether the FCC auctions licenses to use the radio spectrum rather than awarding them based on noneconomic criteria. An auction allocates the licenses to their highest valued use, which is consistent with utilitarianism. Auctioning also redistributes wealth from broadcast companies to the government and hence to the public, but that redistribution may net to zero in the utilitarian calculus.

## The Measurement Problem

Most applications of utilitarian analysis involve difficult measurement and estimation problems. Social costs and benefits typically are measured in monetary units based on the amount a person would accept in exchange for a beneficial consequence or would forgo to avoid a harmful consequence. Consequences are thus measured in terms of their monetary equivalents. The methods of measuring monetary equivalents in cost-benefit analysis in the public sector serve as guides for utilitarian analysis. These methods are presented in Boardman et al. (2001) and Gramlich (1998). Moore and Magat (1996, 1997) present cost-benefit analyses of product safety standards.

Economists look at what individuals reveal through their actions rather than what they say. That is, rather than asking people how costly is noise pollution, economists estimate the price differentials of homes on airline flight paths.[17] Wage differentials are used to measure certain social costs. Are the wage premiums paid for dangerous construction work an appropriate measure of the social costs of the accidents and deaths associated with that work? One answer is that workers have chosen those jobs in exchange for higher wages, and those choices reveal their trade-off of wages for risk.

The Food and Drug Administration routinely uses an age-adjusted value of a life saved because the elderly have a shorter remaining life expectancy than do younger persons. When the Environmental Protection Agency (EPA) conducted a secondary analysis in which it reduced the estimated health benefits for a person over 70 by 37 percent, activists labeled it "the senior citizen death discount." Private politics pressure led the EPA to stop using the measure.[18]

After an airline crash in 1989 safety activists led a movement to require the use of infant safety seats in aircraft. Children under the age of 2 years had been permitted to travel on airlines without tickets if they were held by a parent. Safety activists argued that parents should be required to purchase a ticket for the child and use an infant safety seat. The FAA conducted a cost-benefit analysis of the safety seat issue and concluded that requiring the use of safety seats would actually increase injuries and fatalities. The FAA estimated that the seats would save one infant's life over a decade. Requiring infant

---

[17]This approach takes into account the location decisions of people who have various tolerances for noise.
[18]The EPA uses a value of $6 million for prolonging a life.

safety seats, however, would increase the cost of air travel for families, which would cause some families to drive rather than fly. Since driving is considerably more dangerous than flying, deaths and injuries would increase. The FAA's estimate was nine additional highway fatalities, 52 serious injuries, and 2,300 minor injuries. The methods and conclusions of the FAA study were criticized on several dimensions including the estimated cost increase for air travel for families. Others attacked the conclusion itself. Representative Jim Lightfoot (R-IA) stated, "What's your child worth? Is it worth the price of an airline ticket?"[19] The FAA began a rule-making procedure in 1998, but refused to require safety seats despite pressure from the National Transportation Safety Board.

An alternative to a cost-benefit analysis in cases involving hazards is a cost-risk analysis or comparative risk analysis. Cost-risk analysis focuses on the costs required to reduce risks (e.g., to avoid the loss of a life) and compares the alternative in question with other alternatives. In evaluating the use of infant safety seats, the FAA estimated the lives that would be saved by the seats and the lives that would be lost because more families would drive rather than fly. The decision was then clear without even attempting to value a child's life. In the chapter case, *Pricing the Norplant System*, instead of attempting to measure social benefits, Wyeth-Ayerst Laboratories examined the relative effectiveness of its product compared with others on the market. The Chapter 20 case, *Genetic Testing in the Workplace*, provides an opportunity to use cost-risk analysis.

## The Information Problem

A serious problem in the managerial application of utilitarianism is obtaining the information required to evaluate the consequences for all those affected, either directly or indirectly. In the case of an action that affects only the firm and its immediate stakeholders, the required information may be available. If the action affects others or if the effects are indirect, as when intermediated by markets or other institutions, or when consequences depend also on the actions of other parties, the information problem can be more serious. The information problem also is more serious in the application of rule utilitarianism because the rule is intended to be applicable to many decision makers and many similar situations. Obtaining information about those other situations can be difficult and require assumptions.

One response to this information problem is extrapolation. If other firms are facing the same issue and if a firm is reasonably representative of the others, a firm may extrapolate to the broader set of firms based on its own information. If the issue is the potential radiation hazards to employees who use video display tubes or a chronic health problem, such as carpal tunnel syndrome resulting from repetitive tasks, the experiences of most firms and their employees may be similar. On such issues, extrapolation may be straightforward. The example of American Airlines and United Airlines and the special issuances is one example.

## Utilitarianism in Application

### Categories of Situations

In applying utilitarianism it is useful to distinguish between two categories of situations. The first includes those in which institutions are in place to align the interests of the decision maker with aggregate societal well-being. The second includes those in which institutions are either not in place or only imperfectly align private and social interests.

[19]*The Washington Post*, July 13, 1990.

In the first category, the interests of the firm and society are aligned, so the firm can act based on its own interests. If a firm makes a product that is hazardous when misused, and if misuse can be anticipated, the firm's decisions about safety features under a utilitarian standard can be made as considered in Chapter 12. The firm can maximize its profits and choose safety features based on their cost and the anticipated reductions in liability awards and legal costs. Even though these costs are not perfect measures of social costs, they represent the guidance of an institution, the law of torts, that has evolved over time in response to societal costs. The law of torts is an institution consistent with utilitarianism.

Similarly, if markets are competitive, a decision regarding closing a plant can be made on the basis of profitability. If the plant's costs are too high for it to be competitive, economic theory recommends that the resources used in that plant be reallocated to higher-valued uses. Furthermore, the government has established a set of institutions, such as unemployment insurance and job training programs, to deal with unemployment and reemployment. Decisions based on profitability then serve society's long-term interest in the efficient use of resources—although in some cases they do so only imperfectly. This does not mean, however, that the firm should not take measures to ease the transition for its former employees if it can do so at lower cost than can the employees. It also does not mean that other ethics considerations such as rights and justice are not relevant.

The second category of situations includes those in which institutions are not in place to align the interests of the firm and society. In these situations, utilitarian analysis must be applied directly, as considered in the following section. Government agencies use cost-benefit analysis to provide information to policymakers. Firms may also conduct a cost-benefit analysis, as the chapter case, *Pricing the Norplant System*, indicates. These analyses may not be without controversy, however.[20]

# Methodology

The framework for the application of utilitarianism is illustrated in Figure 19-3. It begins with the identification of the facts of the situation and the moral concerns. As applied in the form of cost-benefit analysis, the analysis then involves the following steps:

1. Identify the alternatives—rules of behavior and actions.
2. For each alternative, identify the set of consequences for all persons affected.
3. Determine which of the consequences are social costs and which are social benefits.
4. Evaluate and estimate the social costs and social benefits.
5. Choose the action or rule that yields the greatest difference between social benefits and social costs.

The objective of a complete utilitarian analysis is to arrive at the optimal decision in step 5. A more modest objective is to encourage managers to think broadly, rather than narrowly, about the consequences of actions. Even if a complete analysis cannot be conducted because, for example, of measurement and information problems, completing the first three steps can deepen the understanding of an issue and provide a sounder foundation for the application of ethical intuition and judgment. In particular, those steps encourage managers to consider the consequences of alternatives for all those affected.

To illustrate the analysis at this level, several examples are presented. These examples will also be considered again in Chapter 20 from rights and justice perspectives.

---

[20]See also the Chapter 4 case, *Shell, Greenpeace, and Brent Spar*, in which Shell conducted a consequentialist analysis of alternatives for the disposal of an oil platform.

## Living Benefits[1]

Herman H. Silverman, a high school English teacher, started a part-time business called Beat the Grim Reaper International, Inc. Silverman's company—and rival upstarts—bought the beneficiary rights to the life insurance policies of the terminally ill, principally people with acquired immune deficiency syndrome (AIDS), but some cancer patients as well.[2] Silverman was sanguine about his new enterprise: "I don't think there's anything as guaranteed as this is in terms of getting a return."

The following examples clarify the contractual arrangements surrounding what have come to be known generically as living benefits or viatical settlements. One of Silverman's new competitors, Living Benefits, Inc., purchased a $100,000 insurance policy for $53,000 from a 34-year-old Boston real estate salesman with AIDS. For 65 cents on the dollar, the company also purchased a $250,000 policy from a 59-year-old San Diego man with cancer. As the new legal beneficiary, Living Benefits paid the premiums on the policies and would receive all the proceeds upon their deaths. In the meantime, the former policyholders received $53,000 and $162,500, respectively, for use in their final years.

The benefits provided by these entrepreneurial enterprises did not go unnoticed by major public insurance companies. Robert Waldron, spokesman for the American Council of Life Insurance, said, "We recognize there's a desperate need. The high cost of dying just goes up every year." Indeed, the cost of prolonged illness frequently caused terminally ill individuals to stop their insurance premium payments before their deaths, causing their policies to lapse.[3] "As long as they're going soon anyway," added Silverman, "there's a service that I can

provide for people who want to have their money right now." Living Benefits customers were favorably disposed toward the provision of these services. "I think it's a great idea," said the salesman from Boston. "It benefits the person who is suffering." Likewise, the San Diego man dying of cancer was spending some of the proceeds to build a new house for his wife. "It's like having your cake and eating it too," he said. "As far as I'm concerned, I'm going to keep living."

The process of contracting for living benefits was somewhat more complicated than these examples might suggest. Applicants for living benefits from Beat the Grim Reaper typically endured an 8-week information-gathering process that began with a four-page questionnaire. Next, the applicant's medical and insurance records were transmitted to Grim Reaper. Grim Reaper employed a staff of consulting physicians who met with the applicant's attending physicians to determine the applicant's life expectancy. Grim Reaper then offered the applicant a price for the policy. The price was based on the applicant's life expectancy, the face value of the policy, the premiums required to maintain an active policy, and interest rates. Upon receipt of a waiver signed by the beneficiary, the policy and the proceeds of the sale were placed in escrow. Shortly thereafter, funds were transferred to the applicant. Grim Reaper had a policy of offering its services only to those with a "pronounced financial need."

A range of objections—emotional and moral—were raised about the provision of living benefits. Some observers claimed that this growing industry was exploiting the impaired judgment of the terminally ill and, in the process, trampling on the rights of the would-be beneficiaries. The president of Living Benefits, Rob T. Worley, conceded that some public reactions were negative: "We've had a few people that say this is ghoulish." Mr. Waldron of the American Council

---

[1] This example was written by Thomas Gilligan. Copyright © 1992 by Thomas Gilligan. All rights reserved. Reprinted with permission.

[2] AIDS advocacy groups had a well-developed national information network that informed members of the existence of such firms. Silverman also advertised the services of his company.

[3] A living-benefits spokesperson claimed that over 50 percent of those who died as a result of AIDS had let their life insurance policies lapse prior to death.

*(Continued)*

of Life Insurance took the argument a step farther: "This gives a third party who's not family an economic interest in a policyholder's death. As a concept, that is dangerous." Nevertheless, living benefits arrangements were increasingly common, and major insurance companies began offering living benefits to their policyholders.

## Analysis

Consider the following rule:

### *Life insurance policies of the terminally ill can be bought and sold.*

The sale of a life insurance policy by a terminally-ill policyholder is a voluntary decision, and the policyholder will sell the policy only if it makes him better off. Similarly, a company such as Living Benefits will purchase a policy only if doing so makes it better off. Consequently, a sale

is a Pareto improvement—both parties are better off, so from the perspective of utilitarianism the rule is moral. Another way to look at the issue is that a market for such life insurance policies increases economic efficiency by giving parties an opportunity to trade.

The principal caveat to this analysis is that a company might exploit the terminally ill person. That person, however, would be protected by friends and by the beneficiaries, who would reject the offer in that case. Exploiting a terminally ill person by inducing him to sell his life insurance policy against his will would be immoral. A second caveat is that the beneficiaries could block a sale to preserve the amount they would otherwise be paid in the event of the policyholder's death. The beneficiaries would in this case be acting immorally. Utilitarianism requires the company to take steps to avoid both of these cases.

---

## Integrity Tests

From the perspective of rule utilitarianism, the use of integrity tests is warranted if it better matches prospective employees to jobs. Integrity can be particularly important for jobs that involve security, as in defense industries; jobs that involve access to confidential information, such as that pertaining to clients; or jobs in which an employee is entrusted with resources, as with accountants, couriers, and bank tellers. Integrity tests may also be beneficial if they enable employers to select employees who are more likely to fit with the firm's culture. For these purposes, an integrity test may be one of several sources of information used in hiring decisions, alongside personal interviews and reference checks. Such tests can also be advantageous competitively. W. Thomas Van

Etten, senior vice president of Sun Bank in Miami, commented on his bank's use of an integrity test, a background check, and urinalysis for prospective employees, "People with a substance-abuse or integrity problem are more likely to look for work with our competitors who don't take as close a look as we do."[1]

If integrity tests are used for these purposes and if they are shown to be reasonably reliable, they pass the cost-benefit test and are morally good from the perspective of utilitarianism. In Chapter 20, integrity tests are reconsidered from rights and justice perspectives.

---

[1] *The New York Times*, October 1, 1989.

# Life Insurance Screening for Preexisting Conditions

To determine eligibility for individual life insurance policies, the insurance industry uses medical examinations to screen for such preexisting health problems as a heart condition or a stroke.[1] Once people have a life-threatening condition, they have an incentive to purchase life insurance to provide for dependents and others. Screening is intended to prevent someone from purchasing a large policy once his or her health is impaired. This provides incentives for people to purchase insurance ex ante, that is, before they have a life-threatening condition, rather than ex post, after they have such a condition.

The ethics issue is whether people with preexisting conditions should be able to purchase insurance in a pool with those with no preexisting conditions. The rule to be evaluated is

*Screening is permitted for preexisting conditions as a requirement for eligibility to purchase an individual life insurance policy.*

If this rule were not followed, insurance companies would have to increase the price of

insurance to cover the higher expected payments to the beneficiaries of those with preexisting conditions. The higher price would cause some individuals without preexisting conditions not to purchase insurance. This is an instance of adverse selection in which those with higher risks choose to buy life insurance, which increases the price of insurance and causes others who would have purchased insurance at the lower price not to do so.[2] If enough people with preexisting conditions were to buy life insurance, the price could ratchet up to the point at which those without preexisting conditions would drop out of the market. Those with preexisting conditions would then be alone in the pool, and the price would reflect solely the risks of their conditions. At that price, purchasing insurance likely would not be attractive to anyone.

Not screening for preexisting conditions thus would result in lower aggregate well-being because insurance would not be available to those who otherwise would be willing to pay for it. Utilitarian analysis thus supports a rule permitting screening for preexisting conditions. This analysis may be questioned from the perspective of ethics systems that take into account other considerations. Those considerations are addressed in Chapter 20.

[1] Group life insurance plans, such as those provided by an employer, typically do not require screening for preexisting conditions, but group policies are experience-related and premiums are adjusted annually. The cost of coverage for individuals with preexisting conditions is thus borne by the group members. In contrast, premiums for an individual life insurance policy are fixed at the time of purchase.

[2] Adverse selection is considered in Chapter 10.

# Redlining

An action that may be moral from the perspective of one ethics system may not be moral from the perspective of another ethics system. A significant problem in the insurance and banking industries arises from imperfect information about risks. The costs of investigating and assessing risks are often high, and risk assessment is

itself imperfect. The collateral for a mortgage on a home or a commercial establishment serves as a means of reducing the risk to the lender, and the value of the collateral depends on property values in the area in which the property is located.

Insurance companies have similar difficulties assessing property and casualty risks on

*(Continued)*

*(Continued)*

homes or automobiles when the risks depend on location as well as on the precautions taken by owners. Even if an applicant takes every measure of care, the likelihood that an automobile will be stolen or vandalized is higher in some neighborhoods than in others. When prices are required to be uniform over broad geographic areas, policies written on high-risk areas can result in losses for insurance companies.

To deal with the costs of risk assessment and evaluation, some financial institutions and insurance companies identified high-risk regions of cities and refused to lend or write policies in those regions. This practice, referred to as redlining, might have been efficient, and hence ethical from a utilitarianism perspective, if the costs of risk and credit evaluation were high and the likelihood was high that a loan or policy application would be rejected because of the risks. That is, if the average cost of credit evaluation were high and demographic data indicated that most residents in an area would not purchase insurance or qualify for a mortgage, it could be efficient for

the insurance company or financial institution not to consider applications from the area.[1]

Although redlining could be ethical from the perspective of costs and benefits, it is unethical from other perspectives. Redlining is said to violate a fundamental right, since it denies opportunity to those who would qualify for loans or insurance but who do not have the opportunity to do so because they happen to reside in a redlined area. Redlining is also said to result in unjust de facto discrimination against minorities and the poor to the extent that they are overrepresented in high-risk areas. Rights and justice frameworks thus bring important considerations to bear on issues such as redlining and have resulted in laws prohibiting the practice. The redlining issue illustrates that a practice could be acceptable from the perspective of one ethics system but unacceptable from the perspective of another.

---

[1]Similar practices exist in a number of other industries, as indicated by the previous discussion of delivery services.

## Summary

Ethics is intended to provide mutually beneficial rules of behavior without requiring government regulation and enforcement. Some of those rules are incorporated into constitutions and statutes, but ethics extends beyond the law to provide guidance to people in their behavior and to firms in their formulation of policies.

Ethics standards are impartial and are to be applied universally, in contrast to casuistry, which holds that leaders may violate ethics standards to fulfill responsibilities to constituents. Ethics generally differs from self-interest, and utilitarianism holds that every individual's well-being is given equal weight.

Utilitarianism is a consequentialist system of ethics that defines the good in terms of human well-being and evaluates that well-being in terms of individuals' preferences. Utilitarianism then aggregates those preferences to obtain a measure of societal well-being. The right action is the one that yields the greatest well-being. Utilitarianism's practical usefulness is in providing a system for evaluating actions that make some individuals better off and others worse off.

The two forms of utilitarianism are act and rule utilitarianism. Act utilitarianism focuses on an individual action taking the actions of others as given. Rule utilitarianism focuses on rules that all individuals are to follow in similar situations. Act utilitarianism is criticized for allowing exceptions to general rules of behavior, which can then degenerate into self-interest. Rule utilitarianism seeks rules of behavior that apply universally to all individuals. When consequences are a function of the actions of more than one individual, rule utilitarianism considers the actions of all individuals simultaneously. The moral rule is the one that yields the greatest aggregate well-being when everyone follows that rule.

An applied form of utilitarianism is cost-benefit analysis that evaluates actions and rules in terms of the costs and benefits they generate. The application of utilitarianism, however, involves three basic problems: (1) determining what counts as a benefit or a cost, (2) making interpersonal comparisons, and (3) conducting analysis with imperfect information about consequences and preferences. Utilitarian principles are applied in the form of cost-benefit analysis, but often, critics say, that approach fails to account for other important considerations. For example, utilitarianism considers rights only in their instrumental role of producing well-being.

# Pricing the Norplant System

Toward the end of the summer of 1993, Wyeth-Ayerst Laboratories, a unit of the American Home Products Corporation, was enjoying the continuing success of its contraceptive, the Norplant System. Introduced in 1991 in the United States, 1992 revenues from the Norplant System were $105 million, which exceeded initial projections by nearly 100 percent. Executives at Wyeth-Ayerst expected annual sales of the Norplant System to stabilize just below $165 million for the near term. Given the current hostile political and regulatory environment faced by the pharmaceutical industry, this success was indeed welcomed.

The Norplant System is a progestin (levonorgestrel) encased in six permeable polymer capsules (Silastic). The capsules, which are inserted in a woman's upper arm, continuously release the progestin into the bloodstream for 5 years. The progestin alters the chemical balance of a woman's own progesterone levels. This alteration prevents ovulation, decreases circulating sperm concentrations, and creates within the uterus an environment hostile for pregnancy.

The popularity of the Norplant System was not surprising. It exhibited several advantages over alternative forms of contraception. Clinical studies indicated that the Norplant System was a highly effective contraceptive method.[21] The average pregnancy rate for women using the system over the entire 5-year period was less than 1 percent, and the first-year pregnancy rate was less than 0.2 percent. In contrast, the first-year pregnancy rate was 3 percent for oral contraceptives and intrauterine devices (IUDs), 18 percent for diaphragms, and 0.4 percent for tubal ligation. The Norplant System also required no effort to use and was easily reversible. The Norplant System did, however, require surgical implantation and removal and provided no protec-

tion from sexually transmitted diseases. Clinical tests of the Norplant System were conducted on over 55,000 women in 46 countries prior to introduction in the United States.[22] The Norplant System had a strong record of safe use, having been used by 500,000 women worldwide for the past 20 years.

## Pricing the Norplant System

The Norplant System was developed jointly by Wyeth-Ayerst and the Population Council, a non-profit organization. In the development of the Norplant System, the Population Council received $10 million in grants from the federal government and private philanthropic organizations. The system used Wyeth-Ayerst's hormone levonorgestrel, which was licensed by Wyeth-Ayerst from its developer. Wyeth-Ayerst held the exclusive right to produce and distribute the Norplant System and could set its price. It paid the Population Council a royalty of no more than 5 percent of the sales price.

In its process of establishing a price for the Norplant System, Wyeth-Ayerst first conducted a study of the relative costs and benefits of alternative contraceptive methods. The direct costs to consumers included the financial costs of the contraceptive (i.e., average retail price), any additional costs related to the use of the contraceptive (i.e., fitting a diaphragm and spermicidal cream; inserting an IUD, insertion and removal of the Norplant System), additional physician follow-up visits (i.e., checkup and monitoring, recuperation, or development of side effects and complications), and the convenience and ease of use (i.e., the need to take oral contraceptives daily). The indirect costs included the need for medical treatment of the side effects resulting from contraceptive use (i.e., medical treatment of hypertension caused

[21]Population Council. *Norplant: A Summary of Scientific Data.* New York, January 1989.

[22]J. Sivin, "International Experience with Norplant® and Norplant®-2 Contraceptives." *Studies in Family Planning,* 1988: pp. 1981–1994.

by oral contraceptives), the possibility of hospitalization due to side effects (i.e., cost of hospitalization for treatment of pelvic inflammatory disease), supplies used to treat side effects (i.e., the costs of the prescription and nonprescription drugs and supplies needed post vasectomy), the loss of productivity due to side effects (i.e., absenteeism during recuperation), and the costs of contraceptive failure (i.e., the medical costs of abortion or delivery). Certain indirect benefits (i.e., the fact that oral contraceptives reduced the risk of ovarian and endometrial cancers) were also considered. Based on these studies and using the actual average retail price of other contraceptive methods, Wyeth-Ayerst concluded that even at an initial price of $600, the annual expected costs of the Norplant System would be 5 percent less than the IUD, 31 percent less than oral contraceptives, and 50 percent less than diaphragms. The annual expected costs of the Norplant System at an initial price of $600 were, however, 8 percent higher than tubal ligation and 375 percent higher than vasectomy.

Apart from scientific studies on the relative benefits of the Norplant System, Wyeth-Ayerst also had to consider the market for contraceptive devices in the United States. Marketing studies indicated that women perceived a benefit from the Norplant System that justified high initial retail prices in the $400 to $600 range. The scientific and practical advantages of the Norplant System were evident to potential consumers.

Two important features of the market complicated Wyeth-Ayerst's pricing decision, however. First, a significant percentage of all contraceptives were distributed through not-for-profit family planning clinics. These clinics financed their purchases of contraceptives and compensated their health professionals through grants from governments and philanthropic organizations. These clinics, which were usually strapped for funds, often enjoyed discounts from pharmaceutical manufacturers. For instance, Wyeth-Ayerst deeply discounted the price it charged these clinics for oral contraceptives. Such clinics would expect similar discounts on the Norplant System. Second, most contraceptives distributed in the United States were financed by third-party payers such as insurance companies, state, county, and city governments, and health maintenance organizations. In a world of rapidly escalating health care costs, these third-party payers were not simply price takers but, instead, engaged in tough negotiations with pharmaceutical companies to obtain as low as possible price on drugs. The discounted prices that some pharmaceutical companies offered family planning clinics were often used as targets in negotiations by third-party payers. Any discounts to family planning clinics would almost certainly be sought by medical insurers and government agencies.

The other consideration in the pricing of the Norplant System was cost. The actual costs of producing the Norplant System were quite small, less than $50 per unit including the insertion kit. An additional cost was the training of doctors and other health professionals in the insertion and use of the Norplant System. Wyeth-Ayerst estimated that these costs would be approximately $15 million annually. The other relevant cost was that of liability, since lawsuits followed from the use of virtually all contraceptive systems.

Under these circumstances, Wyeth-Ayerst adopted a uniform price of $350 for the introduction of Norplant. This price included the six progestin capsules and the disposable kit required for insertion. The patient also had to pay a doctor for the insertion and removal of Norplant. No discounts were given to family planning clinics or third-party payers. Wyeth-Ayerst, however, helped establish and fund the Norplant Foundation to distribute the Norplant System free of charge to indigent patients.

## Public Reaction to the Pricing of the Norplant System

Although commercial success of the Norplant System heartened Wyeth-Ayerst executives, public reaction to its pricing decision was not positive. Health professionals in family planning establishments criticized the pricing of the Norplant System on several grounds. Critics pointed to the $23 price per unit in bulk shipments of the Norplant System to developing countries (without the insertion kit) to highlight the glaring difference between the costs of production and average retail price of the Norplant System in the United States.[23] Critics charged that Wyeth-Ayerst was price-gouging American consumers. Whereas executives said that it was priced

[23] Wyeth-Amherst pointed out that these units were produced by a Danish manufacturer that held the exclusive right to distribute the Norplant System in certain African countries.

fairly, critics countered that the pricing reflected the monopoly Wyeth-Ayerst enjoyed on the supply of the Norplant System.[24] This monopoly position was particularly troublesome for critics, who charged that the bulk of the development cost of the Norplant System had been provided by public funds through the activities of the Population Council.

Critics also charged Wyeth-Ayerst with betrayal and creating a "financial nightmare" for family planning clinics. Many family planning officials believed that they were instrumental in gaining approval for the Norplant System in the United States. However, as a result of Wyeth-Ayerst's pricing decision, they claimed, their budgets had been ruptured. For example, the director of a family planning unit in a major hospital said that shortly after the introduction of the Norplant System, 500 women applied for it. The costs of supplying the system to all these women would have been $175,000, but the clinic's yearly budget for all contraceptives was $20,000. "All of the income for Norplant goes right to the drug company," said Mr. Salo of Planned Parenthood in San Diego. "We don't charge a margin on it. We lose money on each patient that we serve because Medicaid doesn't reimburse the full cost. Staff members have had to forgo raises, and plans for outreach have been shelved as a result."

Critics were also concerned about the implications of Wyeth-Ayerst's pricing of the Norplant System for the pricing of other advances in women's health care products scheduled for introduction in the coming years. For example, Upjohn introduced a new contraceptive, Depo-Provera, which was priced much higher in the United States than it was overseas; and some were concerned about the pricing of RU-486, the so-called abortion pill, scheduled to begin clinical tests in the United States the following year. "Are we going to see RU-486 come into this country at a price that makes it no cheaper than getting a first trimester abortion?" asked Mr. Kring, vice chairman and treasurer of the Norplant Foundation.

"It's a trend that scares me to death—that people are making huge profits in women's health care."

The pricing of the Norplant System also attracted the attention of lawmakers. Representative Ron Wyden (D-OR), a senior member of the Subcommittee on Health and the Environment of the House Energy and Commerce Committee, vowed to hold hearings on Wyeth-Ayerst's pricing decision. "You have a situation where clearly Americans are being charged more," said Representative Wyden. "We have a chance to expose these kinds of pricing practices and create a more competitive price."

## The Assignment

The Executive Committee on Pricing for Wyeth-Ayerst hastily gathered for a meeting. The members were concerned with the public criticisms directed at the pricing of the Norplant System and about the unfolding nonmarket threats. The committee, composed of the top executives of Wyeth-Ayerst, knew that a good deal of their time over the coming months would be spent on this issue.

They were also concerned with a more general issue that had become increasingly important as the health industry came under closer public scrutiny. The issue revolved around the pricing of proprietary medicines. What factors or principles should guide the Pricing Committee's decisions? Up to this point, the Pricing Committee's primary consideration was the relative quality and costs of available substitutes. In the view of the committee, if Wyeth-Ayerst could provide a better product at or below the costs of existing medicines, everyone would be better off. This focus had led to the comparison of the Norplant System with oral contraceptives in determining the $350 price. But were other factors important as well? For instance, would the pricing of the Norplant System continue to be a nonmarket issue, or would the issue dissipate with time? Did Wyeth-Ayerst's responsibilities extend beyond providing a more effective contraceptive at a price below those of available substitutes? Should the fact that contraceptives were primarily a women's health care product have a bearing on the price it charged?

Should the fact that family planning clinics play an important role in the distribution of contraceptives to poor women be a factor? Should the fact that the Norplant System was deeply discounted in developing countries play a role in determining the prices charged in the United States? Should the fact that Wyeth-Ayerst discounts oral contraceptives to

---

[24]Pharmaceutical prices generally involved a large markup above costs, since the prices of successful pharmaceuticals had to cover the research and development costs of both successful and unsuccessful attempts to discover new drugs. This also explained in part why prices of pharmaceuticals were higher in the United States and in other countries that have a pharmaceutical industry engaged in research and development than prices in countries that had no research-and-development-intensive pharmaceutical industry.

family planning clinics impact the decision of whether to discount the Norplant System to the poor? What should Wyeth-Ayerst do with respect to the family planning clinics?

The Pricing Committee has asked you to provide specific criteria for pricing proprietary medicines and to apply them to the pricing of the Norplant System. That is, you are to come up with a number that you would have adopted for the price of the Norplant System if it had been your decision to make. The Pricing Committee has asked you for an oral and written presentation of clarity sufficient to implement your proposed criteria. To help your analysis, the committee has set the following set of parameters:

1. The variable costs of the Norplant System (including insertion kit) was $50 per unit. This figure included all production and delivery costs as well as the expected costs of products liability claims. This cost also included the royalties Wyeth-Ayerst paid the developer of levonorgestrel and the Population Council.
2. Wyeth-Ayerst employed 2,700 staff, executives, health care professionals, and salespeople, who educated health professionals on the insertion and use of the Norplant System. To this point, Wyeth-Ayerst had trained over 28,000 doctors on the use of the Norplant System. With benefits, the average annual cost per employee was roughly $65,000. The Norplant System was expected to generate nearly 6 percent of Wyeth-Ayerst's total revenues of $2.8 billion. If the total labor costs were amortized to each of Wyeth-Ayerst's products based on their contribution to revenues, nearly $11 million in annual labor costs would be assigned to the sale of the Norplant System.
3. Wyeth-Ayerst allocated approximately $5 million annually for the advertising and promotion of the Norplant System. ■

SOURCE: This case was prepared by Thomas Gilligan from materials and information contained in *The Wall Street Journal*, August 30, 1993; the article "Contraceptive Pharmaco-Economics: A Cost Effectiveness Analysis of the Norplant System (levonorgestrel implants)," *Medical Interface*, a publication of the Medicom International, pp. 4–8; and other public sources. Copyright © 1994 by Thomas Gilligan. All rights reserved. Reprinted with permission.

# Enron Power Marketing, Inc., and the California Market

Using names such as Death Star, Get Shorty, Fat Boy, and Ricochet, Enron Power Marketing (EPM) deployed an array of electricity trading strategies to take advantage of imperfections in the design of the market for power in California. In a December 2000 memorandum an outside lawyer and an EPM lawyer reminded the company that the California market rules prohibited "gaming" the trading system and warned that penalties could include "fines and suspension" and actions by "the appropriate regulatory or antitrust enforcement agency."[25] In late April 2002 that memorandum and a later memorandum by lawyers engaged by Enron were discovered.[26] The Enron board of directors waived attorney-client privileges and confidentiality rights and turned the memos over to the Federal Energy Regulatory Commission (FERC).[27] An Enron attorney said that

[25] Memorandum from Christian Yoder of EPM and Stephen Hall, Stoel Rivers LLP, December 8, 2000.

[26] Memorandum from Gary Fergus (Brobeck, Phleger & Harrison, LLP) and Jean Frizzell (Gibbs & Bruns LLP), no date. The two memoranda were available at www.ferc.gov. The lawyers engaged by Enron reviewed the December memorandum and met with traders to discuss the strategies described. They concluded that some of the information in the December memorandum was incorrect. Both memoranda stated that other traders used some of the same strategies.

[27] In 2002 EPM and its trading technology were sold to UBS Warburg, a unit of UBS AG of Switzerland. Six hundred thirty-five employees moved from Enron to UBS.

it was "the responsible and honest thing" to do. FERC chairman Patrick Wood decided to make the memoranda public, stating, "We have to try to get to the bottom of this and tell the truth. If the capital markets perceive that regulators and customers and elected officials and everybody else are getting comfortable with understanding what went on in California, then you can restore confidence."[28]

Deregulation in the electricity market required establishing a market in which buyers and sellers could trade electricity on a continuous basis.[29] Markets for a nonstorable good such as electricity must be designed and regularized to allow supply and demand to be equilibrated almost minute by minute. One of the largest markets was established in California, where large customers were allowed to purchase electricity from any supplier. The efficiency of such markets can be improved by traders who act as middlemen between electricity producers and customers. EPM, Dynergy, El Paso, Reliant Resources, Duke Power, American Electric Power, Williams, and a number of other companies traded power. In 2000 EPM had an estimated 13.0 percent of the U.S. wholesale electricity market, and the next largest share was 8.9 percent.[30] Enron was believed to have had a significantly larger share of the California market.

No new electricity generation capacity had been built in California during the 1990s, and strong economic growth caused the state to import electricity from other states and Canada, particularly during peak periods. With reserve capacity in California below the minimum needed to ensure that demand could be met, the system was at risk. When a drought in the northwest reduced the power generated by hydroelectric facilities, the California market faced shortages and much higher wholesale prices. Despite the increases in wholesale power prices, the regulated retail prices remained fixed.[31]

The state's energy system and the market for electricity were coordinated by the Independent Service Organization (ISO), which operated the state's power grid. The power grid had a limited

capacity, since no new transmission capacity had been built in many years. Moreover, the system had bottlenecks that limited the amount of power that could be moved between the north and south of the state.

The ISO was responsible for ensuring that California's power needs would be met. The ISO attempted to forecast demand and supply and balance the system both in real time and in advance. A trader that contracted to supply large retail customers such as manufacturing plants submitted a daily "schedule" of deliveries for the day-ahead market, and the ISO checked whether there was both a buyer and a seller for each megawatt before scheduling its transmission across the state's power lines.

EPM's "inc-ing" strategy involved overscheduling power deliveries to Enron Energy Services, Enron's retail unit, which contracted with large retail customers. The overscheduling led the ISO to anticipate higher demand and to plan to buy power the next day. Often those purchases were from Enron at high prices. An EPM trader referred to this as the "oldest trick in the books." Enron was in effect speculating based on its forecasts of demand, scheduled power generation, and the ISO's predicted behavior, which was influenced by EPM's scheduling. According to the second memorandum, this strategy offset the practice of independently owned utilities that regularly underestimated their load (demand for their power). In addition to trading on its own account, EPM served as "scheduling coordinator" for other companies. Two power suppliers allegedly involved in the generation side of this practice were Puget Sound Electric and Powerex, a unit of BC Hydro of Canada. Both companies denied having violated either ISO or FERC rules. EPM's strategy was believed to be legal and, according to an ISO official, consistent with the ISO rules at the time. California politicians charged that the companies using this strategy reaped billions of dollars of profits from the California market.

The Get Shorty strategy took advantage of the ISO's policy of maintaining reserve capacity to handle unexpected surges in demand. The ISO referred to this reserve generating capacity as "ancillary services," and power generators were paid to maintain idle capacity that could be switched on at short notice. EPM used a strategy of shorting the ancillary services and then covering them the next morning at a lower price. This speculation was not always successful, since on at least one occasion the ISO asked EPM to deliver ancillary services it had shorted but

[28]*The New York Times,* May 12, 2002.

[29]The development of the wholesale electricity market was spurred by the Energy Policy Act of 1992.

[30]"Report on EnronOnline," FERC, May 16, 2002.

[31]Pacific Gas & Electric (PG&E) went bankrupt by buying power at wholesale prices with its customers paying at the fixed retail rate. When it filed for bankruptcy, PG&E was estimated to owe Enron $500 million.

failed to cover. The December memorandum stated, "This strategy might be characterized as 'paper trading' because the seller does not actually have the services to sell. . . . As a consequence, in order to short the ancillary services, it is necessary to submit false information that purports to identify the source of the ancillary services."

In the Death Star strategy EPM profited by relieving congestion in the power grid for deliveries between the north and south of the state. The ISO relieved congestion by paying power suppliers to reduce their deliveries on the congested part of the grid and sell their power elsewhere. EPM would overschedule power to be delivered, knowing that the ISO would not be able to determine whether there were actual users for the power. Since the power grid appeared to be overloaded, the ISO would pay power suppliers, including EPM, to relieve congestion by selling their power elsewhere, such as out of the state.

In its "load shift" strategy EPM overscheduled supply into a congested area and underscheduled power into a uncongested area. EPM then would "reduce" deliveries into the congested area, receiving congestion relief payments, and "increase" deliveries in the uncongested area. In this practice EPM did not have to actually contract for the power, and even if it had contracted for the power, it could sell the power at a loss and still profit. The December memorandum stated, "Because the congestion [relief] charges have been as high as $750 per megawatt-hour, it can often be profitable to sell power at a loss simply to be able to collect the congestion payment."

EPM also took advantage of a price cap imposed by California regulators to prevent price spikes due to shortages. The normal price for electricity was $30 to $40 a megawatt-hour, but price spikes of as high a $1,200 occurred in 2000 and in the spring of 2001 as the ISO desperately sought to obtain power. The price cap of $250, however, covered only California. During a price spike EPM could buy power at $250 in California, export it from the state, and sell it at a higher price. EPM referred to this as arbitrage. The December memorandum stated that this "appears not to present any problems, other than a public relations risk arising from the fact that such exports may have contributed to California's declaration of a Stage 2 Emergency yesterday."

Ricochet trades, or "megawatt laundering," involved completing the arbitrage opportunity by reselling the exported electricity back to the ISO, which was unconstrained in the price it could pay for imported power. In a Ricochet trade EPM would buy power at the $250 price cap during a price spike and sell the power to a party outside the state. That party would charge a small fee, and resell the power to EPM. EPM then would sell the power to the ISO at prices as high as $1,200. Ricochet trading involved other parties often without their knowledge of the nature of the trade. The ISO participated in a trade in which EPM sold power to a third party, which sold it to PGE, which then sold it to EPM. In June 2001 FERC imposed a price cap of $250 throughout the Western states, ending this arbitrage opportunity.

The December memorandum indicated that some of EPM's trading practices were "potentially criminal," and EPM reportedly halted the practices in December 2000. During the first several months of 2001 electricity prices in California continued to increase and shortages resulted in rolling blackouts and wholesale price spikes. To alleviate the energy crisis, or because he panicked as his critics contended, Governor Gray Davis committed $43 billion of state funds to buy power under long-term contracts at prices substantially above normal market prices. The energy crisis in California abated during the summer 2001 due to below normal temperatures, lower natural gas prices, and new generating capacity coming on line. The governor subsequently sought to renegotiate the contracts and obtain refunds from energy traders.

After the revelation of the two memoranda Senator Diane Feinstein (D-CA) wrote to U.S. Attorney General John Ashcroft asking for a criminal investigation of Enron's trading practices. She wrote that the memos from the Enron lawyers "indicate that Enron was not only manipulating prices in the West, but also engaged in a number of calculated strategies . . . to either receive payment for energy not delivered or increase price. In my book, this is outright fraud."[32]

R. Martin Chavez, CEO of Kiodex, an energy risk management company, said, "Energy trading is a football game; it ain't bridge. If you want a nice game because electricity is an important public good, then set up a nice game."[33] Recalling his days as head of

---

32 *The Wall Street Journal*, May 8, 2002.
33 *The New York Times*, May 12, 2002.

energy risk management at Goldman Sachs, he said, "The whole reason for the existence of traders is to make as much money as possible, consistent with what's legal. I lived through this: if you didn't manipulate the market and manipulation was accessible to you, that's when you were yelled at."[34] ■

[34]*The New York Times*, May 8, 2002.

## PREPARATION QUESTIONS

1. Was EPM doing anything wrong in its trading strategies? Was this not just taking advantage of opportunities available in the market?
2. What were the flaws in the California market design?
3. Were EPM's strategies different from the types of strategies used on Wall Street?
4. How should Enron have conducted its trading business?

# Merck and Vioxx

On September 30, 2004, Merck voluntarily withdrew its $2.5 billion blockbuster drug Vioxx (rofecoxib) because new clinical research showed a significantly higher probability of cardiovascular events, such as heart attacks, for patients who took the drug for over 18 months. Merck's market capitalization fell by 27 percent on the day of the announcement and subsequently fell another 13 percent. The withdrawal met with instant praise for the quick decision, but soon the praise turned to questions as information became available raising the issue of whether the company should have recalled the drug years earlier.

Merck defended itself in a series of full-page advertisements in major newspapers. In three full-page ads on November 21, 2004, Merck defended its actions, restated its commitments to patients, and attempted to assure investors about its financial strength and its future. The first ad stated:

**We extensively studied VIOXX** before seeking regulatory approval to market it.
**We promptly disclosed** the clinical data about VIOXX.

When questions arose, **we took additional steps, including conducting further prospective, controlled studies** to gain more clinical information about the medicine.

When information from these additional prospective, controlled trials became available, **we acted promptly** and made the decision to voluntarily withdraw VIOXX.

Vioxx, along with Pfizer's Celebrex and Bextra, were Cox-2 inhibitors used to treat patients with chronic pain. Traditional painkillers, such as aspirin and ibuprofen, blocked Cox-1 and Cox-2 enzymes that cause pain. Blocking Cox-1 enzymes had the benefit of reducing cardiovascular risks, such as blood clots and heart attacks, but it could contribute to intestinal and stomach problems including stomach bleeding and ulcers. Cox-2 inhibitors did not block Cox-1 enzymes, so relative to traditional painkillers they provide benefits to patients at risk from intestinal and stomach bleeding. Vioxx had sales of $2.5 billion in 2003, Celebrex had sales of $1.9 billion, and Bextra, a newer version of Celebrex, had sales of $687 million.

## The Initial Marketing Decision for Vioxx

Early Merck memoranda suggested that the company recognized that sales would be limited if Vioxx were restricted to patients with stomach or intestinal bleeding. If the drug were marketed as a general purpose painkiller for arthritis and other persistent ailments, sales would be much higher. If Merck were to market Vioxx as a general purpose painkiller, it would use heavy direct-to-consumer (DTC) advertising.

In designing clinical trials for Vioxx in the mid–1990s Merck recognized that to show its effectiveness trial subjects could not take aspirin. Consequently, the trials could show increased blood clots and cardiovascular events. A Merck scientist proposed that patients with a high risk of cardiovascular problems be kept out of the clinical trials. Information on the final design of the clinical trials was not available.[35]

The Food and Drug Administration (FDA) approved Vioxx for sale in 1999. The Phase III clinical trials required by the FDA for approval found "there was not an increased risk of cardiovascular events with VIOXX compared with placebo or VIOXX compared with other non-naproxen non-steroidal anti-inflammatory drugs (NSAIDS)."[36]

### PREPARATION QUESTIONS

1. Should Merck seek to market Vioxx as a general purpose painkiller with heavy DTC advertising or limit its marketing to those patients with gastrointestinal problems?

2. Should Merck conduct additional clinical trials to evaluate the risks of blood clots and cardiovascular events?

## The Success of Vioxx

Merck aggressively promoted Vioxx as a general purpose pain reliever for arthritis and other conditions. In 2000 it spent $161 million on DTC advertising for Vioxx. Continued heavy advertising and traditional marketing to doctors resulted in 2003 sales of $2.5 billion worldwide.

## The VIGOR Clinical Trials

In early 1999 Merck began a clinical study called VIGOR to demonstrate the effectiveness of Vioxx for patients with gastrointestinal problems. The control was naproxen, and participants were prohibited from taking aspirin. Patients with heart problems were not included in the trials. The results were released in March 2000 and showed that patients receiving Vioxx had fewer gastrointestinal problems than those receiving naproxen.[37] The results also showed that of the 4,047 people taking Vioxx, 101 had cardiovascular adverse events, such as blood clotting, whereas 46 of the 4,029 taking naproxen had such events. Because earlier studies had shown no greater cardiovascular problems with Vioxx than with a placebo, Merck suspected that the difference in cardiovascular adverse events was due to the beneficial effects of naproxen rather than to problems with Vioxx.[38] Merck and the FDA began discussions about what information from the VIGOR trial would be included in the new label for Vioxx.

### PREPARATION QUESTIONS

1. In light of the results of the VIGOR trials, should Merck issue a warning to doctors and patients?
2. Should Merck reduce its DTC advertising of Vioxx?
3. Should Merck conduct new clinical trials designed to identify any cardiovascular adverse effects of Vioxx?
4. What information should Merck support for inclusion on the new Vioxx label?

## The APPROVe Study

In August 2001 researchers at the Cleveland Clinic published an article in the *Journal of the American Medical Association* raising concerns about Vioxx's cardiovascular risks. In 2002 a researcher at the Catalan Institute of Pharmacology in Barcelona criticized Merck's handling of Vioxx. The same

[35]*The Wall Street Journal,* November 1, 2004.

[36]Merck, "Merck Announces Voluntary Worldwide Withdrawal of VIOXX®," www.vioxx.com/rofecoxib/vioxx/consumer/index.jsp. Naproxen is marketed over-the-counter as Aleve.
[37]The results of the study were published in the *New England Journal of Medicine* in November 2000.
[38]Ted Mayer, an attorney representing Merck, later explained, "The known antiplatelet properties of naproxen strongly suggested that a properly of naproxen was responsible for the differential rates in the Vigor trial." *The Wall Street Journal,* November 1, 2004.

criticism had been published in the British medical journal *The Lancet*.

The FDA was also concerned about the results of the VIGOR trial and particularly a Merck press release entitled "Merck Confirms Favorable Cardiovascular Safety Profile for Vioxx." In a September 17, 2001, letter to Merck the FDA called the press release "simply incomprehensible" and said that Merck had engaged "in a promotional campaign for Vioxx that minimizes the potentially serious cardiovascular findings that were observed . . ." The letter also stated, that "patients on Vioxx were observed to have a four-to five-fold increase" in heart attacks.[39] The new label for Vioxx mentioned both the gastrointestinal and cardiovascular results of the VIGOR trial.

As a result of the VIGOR trial, Merck researchers began discussing the possible risks associated with Vioxx and the other Cox-2 inhibitors. In May 2000 Merck considered conducting a cardiovascular study on Vioxx but decided not to do so. Earlier in 2000 Merck had begun enrolling patients for a 156-week study named APPROVe to demonstrate the effect of Vioxx on "the recurrence of neoplastic polyps of the large bowel" in patients with colorectal adenoma. In the study Merck used a placebo as the control and decided to monitor patients carefully for cardiovascular events. Merck established an external safety review board for the study. The board reviewed the interim results periodically and noted the cardiac risks. In May 2003 the panel noted a 20 percent higher risk of heart attack and stroke and by February 2004 the risk was 80 percent higher. Two of the five board members had consulting arrangements with Merck.[40]

An article published in *Circulation* in May 2004 found that Vioxx was "associated with an elevated relative risk" compared to Celebrex and to no pain reliever. Vioxx was also criticized at a medical conference in August by an FDA researcher.

In September 2004 the cardiovascular results in the APPROVe study showed 15 heart attack or strokes per 1000 patients with Vioxx compared to 7.5 with the placebo. Merck decided to withdraw Vioxx from the market. Merck reported, "In this study, there was an increased relative risk for confirmed cardiovascular (CV) events, such as heart attack and stroke, beginning after 18 months of treatment in the patients taking VIOXX compared to those taking placebo. The results for the first 18 months of the APPROVe study did not show any increased risk of confirmed CV events on VIOXX, and in this respect are similar to the results of two placebo-controlled studies described in the current US labeling for VIOXX."[41]

## PREPARATION QUESTIONS

1. In light of the criticism of Vioxx and the letter from the FDA, should Merck have withdrawn Vioxx or issued warnings to doctors and patients prior to learning the results of the APPROVe study?

2. Should Merck have conducted a specific cardiovascular study?

## The Lancet Article

In November 2004 researchers published a "meta-analysis" that combined the data from all the published studies on Vioxx.[42] Combining the data resulted in a larger sample size and narrower confidence intervals, which enabled the authors to conclude that the cardiovascular risk was higher with Vioxx. Merck criticized the statistical approach because the studies combined were not comparable, since some studies compared Vioxx with a placebo and non-naproxen NSAIDs, the VIGOR study used naproxen as the control, and the APPROVe study used a placebo. Merck stated that the meta-analysis showed nothing that had not already been published by Merck and that the increased cardiovascular risks were only due to the VIGOR study comparing Vioxx with naproxen. In its response to the article in *The Lancet*, Merck stated that "it was vigilant in monitoring and disclosing the cardiovascular safety of VIOXX and that the company absolutely disagrees with any implication to the contrary." Merck provided a detailed response to the article.

[39]*The Wall Street Journal*, October 5, 2004.
[40]*The Wall Street Journal*, February 7, 2005.
[41]Merck, "Merck Announces Voluntary Worldwide Withdrawal of VIOXX," September 30, 2004.
[42]Juni, et.al. *The Lancet*, November 5, 2004.

cardiac death was three times higher in patients that took high doses of Vioxx. He estimated that Vioxx was responsible for an additional 27,785 deaths from 1999 through 2003. His analysis was posted on the FDA Web site.

Another FDA official, Dr. Sandra Kweder, head of the Office of New Drugs, disagreed with Graham. Dr. Steven Galson, the FDA's director of drug evaluation and research, later said that Graham's numbers "constitute junk science" and were "irresponsible."[43] ∎

SOURCE: This case was prepared from public sources by David P. Baron. Copyright © 2004 by David P. Baron. All rights reserved. Reprinted with permission.

## Congressional Hearings

The Senate Finance Committee held hearings in November on whether the FDA was doing enough to assure post-approval safety of drugs. The FDA's Dr. David Graham stated, "I would argue that the FDA as currently configured is incapable of protecting America against another Vioxx." He testified that five drugs, Accutane, Meridia, Crestor, Bextra, and Serevent, should be reexamined to determine if they should be withdrawn. Earlier in the year Graham had examined the health records of 1.4 million Kaiser Permanente patients, including 40,405 who took Celebrex and 26,748 who took Vioxx. He found that the risk of heart attacks and sudden

### PREPARATION QUESTION

1. Should Merck provide testimony on the adequacy of the FDA's post-approval safety monitoring? How should it respond to Dr. Graham's study?

# Pfizer and Celebrex

On September 30, 2004, Merck withdrew from the market its Cox-2 inhibitor Vioxx because a clinic trial had found an increased risk of cardiac events such as strokes and heart attacks among patients taking the drug for over 18 months.[44] Commentators speculated that there could be problems with the entire class of Cox-2 inhibitors. Pfizer's Celebrex had become the best selling Cox-2 inhibitor with 21 million prescriptions written in 2003 and 2004 sales expected to reach $3.3 billion. The chemical formula for Celebrex was different from that of Vioxx, and none of the many studies of Celebrex had shown evidence of increased risk of cardiac events. Pfizer began a brief advertising campaign telling the public and doctors that Celebrex was safe and was not associated with an

increased risk of cardiac events. Pfizer considered beginning a clinical study to demonstrate that Celebrex did not cause adverse heart conditions and might even have beneficial effects.

Celebrex was discovered by Monsanto's Searle division, which was subsequently acquired by Pharmacia. In 2003 Pfizer acquired Pharmacia for $60 billion, in part because of Celebrex. Pfizer became the world's largest and most profitable pharmaceutical company. Celebrex's primary indication was for treating pain in patients subject to stomach bleeding, who could not take over-the-counter pain relievers such as aspirin and ibuprofen. Celebrex, however, had been marketed with heavy direct-to-consumer advertising as a more general pain reliever

### PREPARATION QUESTION

1. What more, if anything, should Merck do in response to the article in *The Lancer*?

[44] See the chapter case, *Merck and Vioxx*, for information on Cox-2 inhibitors and the withdrawal.

with an emphasis on arthritis pain. Pfizer spent $71 million on Clebrex ads during the first 9 months of 2004. Ads featuring figure skating champion Dorothy Hamill and other middle-aged people were common on television. The purpose of the ads was to have patients ask their doctors for the drug by brand name, and the results confirmed the strategy.

Approximately 40 studies sponsored by the National Institutes of Health (NIH) were underway, exploring other applications for Celebrex. For example, a 5-year study on 2,000 patients was being conducted by the National Cancer Institute (NCI)

to determine if high doses of Celebrex could prevent colon polyps and colorectal cancer. Three groups of clinical trial patients were given a placebo, 400 milligrams, and 800 milligrams of Celebrex. An earlier Pfizer study of patients taking 400 milligrams had shown no increase in cardiac events. The European Union had approved Pfizer's Cox-2 inhibitor Onsenal for treating intestinal polyps, and Pfizer planned to begin marketing the drug early in 2005. Onsenal used the same active ingredient celecoxib as Celebrex but was more potent.

## PREPARATION QUESTIONS

1. Should Pfizer review the clinical studies in progress to determine if there is any new evidence on cardiac events?
2. Should Pfizer stop its direct-to-consumer advertising of Celebrex?

## The National Cancer Institute Study

As a result of the Vioxx withdrawal the researchers conducting the cancer study for the NCI began a review of the patient trials in October. After 6 weeks of investigation the researchers had identified six patients with cardiac events in the placebo group, 15 in the 400 milligram group, and 20 in the 800 milligram group. The researchers presented their findings to a safety review panel of cardiologists on December 10. After reviewing the data, the panel was concerned. The NCI then informed the Food and Drug Administration (FDA), NIH, and Pfizer.[45] Pfizer learned of the results on Thursday, December 16, in a call from the NCI, and Pfizer CEO Henry McKinnell was called at his home at 7:00 P.M. that evening. McKinnell immediately

arranged a conference call with Pfizer's regulatory team for 8:00 P.M.[46] After the Vioxx withdrawal Pfizer had continued to market Celebrex to consumers and doctors. McKinnell had to decide what to do with Celebrex and how to present its decision to the FDA and the public. McKinnell and Pfizer had some experience with such issues. Shortly after it was marketed, patients taking both Viagra and angina medications reported cardiac events, including heart attacks.

Trial lawyers had scheduled a meeting for March 17 and 18, 2005, to plan their strategy for Vioxx, and Celebrex would certainly be added to their agenda. ∎

SOURCE: This case was prepared from public sources by professor David P. Baron. Copyright © 2004 by David P. Baron. All rights reserved. Reproduced by permission.

3. Should Pfizer withdraw Celebrex from the market as a precautionary measure?

## PREPARATION QUESTIONS

1. Should Pfizer stop its direct-to-consumer advertising of Celebrex?
2. Should Pfizer stop its marketing of Celebrex to doctors?
3. Should Pfizer withdraw Celebrex from the market?

4. What should Pfizer be prepared to do when it informs the FDA of its decision?
5. How should Pfizer present its decision to patients, doctors, and the public?

---

[45]The NIH notified the researchers conducting the other studies. The panel recommended that the NCI study be halted, and researchers did so.

[46]*The Wall Street Journal*, December 20, 2004.

# Ethics Systems: Rights and Justice

## Introduction

Consequentialist ethics systems such as utilitarianism focus on the good and evaluate the good in terms of individuals' preferences for consequences. Rights established under a consequentialist system are instrumental, since their justification is in terms of the consequences they yield. Some moral philosophies hold instead that there are certain rights and liberties justified by considerations independent of their consequences. Basic liberties such as freedom of speech and rights such as equal opportunity are fundamental concepts that express considerations of freedom, autonomy, and basic equality. Other moral philosophies emphasize comparisons of the situations of individuals. For example, in the redlining example in Chapter 19, concerns were raised about the violation of a right to opportunity and an injustice to individuals who happened to live in a redlined area. This chapter considers ethics systems that emphasize considerations of rights and justice.

This following two sections consider classes of ethics systems and rights. The following section introduces and critiques Kant's system of moral rules, which establishes intrinsic rights. An approach to rights analysis and to resolving conflicts among claimed rights is then presented. An alternative—neoclassical liberalism—to Kant's system is considered and critiqued. Categories of justice theories are then introduced with a focus on compensatory and distributive justice. Rawls's system of justice as fairness is presented, and his principles of justice are evaluated. The role of incentives in his system is identified and contrasted with utilitarianism and egalitarianism. The assignment of duty and the application of the justice principles are then considered. The chapter concludes with higher order principles used to evaluate ethics systems.

## Classification of Ethics Systems

Ethics systems are classified as teleological or deontological. Teleological, or consequentialist, systems define the rightness of an action in terms of the good its consequences yield. Deontological ethics systems hold that moral right takes precedence over the good and can be evaluated by considerations independent of, or in

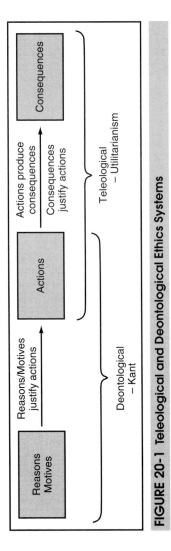

**FIGURE 20-1   Teleological and Deontological Ethics Systems**

addition to, consequences.[1] From a deontological perspective, the objective is to deduce from fundamental axioms a set of principles that have moral standing and then to identify rights and rules of behavior that correspond to those principles. Those rights and rules of behavior are intrinsic; that is, they are important in and of themselves. The principal deontological system considered here is Kant's theory of moral rules. Rawls's theory of justice brings together elements of deontological and consequentialist theories and prioritizes them.

As illustrated in Figure 20-1, both teleological and deontological systems are ultimately concerned with the evaluation of actions. Teleological systems approach this task by examining the relationship between actions and consequences. Deontological systems approach this task by examining the relationship between actions and the reasons or motives for taking those actions. In a teleological system, consequences are evaluated in terms of a value theory that is a part of the particular system. Utilitarianism, for example, uses a value theory based on individual preferences and their aggregation.

In deontological systems, the motive or reason for taking an action, or abiding by a principle, is required to have moral standing. A principle, for example, could be "respect each person's liberty by treating each person as he or she has freely consented to be treated." The reason to abide by the principle then is that individuals are willing to have everyone abide by it and are willing to have the principle applied to themselves.

Teleological and deontological systems are sufficiently different in their nature and structure that they do not necessarily yield the same evaluations of actions. Because no ethics system is immune to criticism, the objective here is not to decide which system is the most appropriate but instead to understand the guidance that each provides.

## Classes of Rights

Rights may be derived from moral principles or may be established through political choice. Rights established by political choice often reflect moral principles. The U.S. Constitution identifies individual liberties, such as the freedom of speech, and rights to political participation. Rights are also established through legislation, such as the Civil Rights Act of 1964, which prohibits discrimination on the basis of race, color, religion, sex, or national origin. Legislation has also established entitlements, such as the right of the poor to receive medical care under Medicaid. Rights are also established by private agreements, such as contracts, that specify mutual obligations and expectations that are enforceable by the courts. Rights may also be established by implicit contracts such as those associated with the employment policies of a firm.

---

[1]The root of deontology is *deon*, which means obligatory, to bind.

Rights are often categorized as negative or positive. Reflecting the intellectual tradition at the time it was written, the U.S. Constitution primarily establishes negative rights that impose duties on people and the state not to interfere with the actions of a person. Freedom of speech and assembly are negative rights because they prohibit others from interfering with those activities. A property right is a negative right because others are prohibited from compelling the holder to take an action with respect to that property. In contrast, positive rights impose affirmative duties on others to take particular actions. For example, a person has a positive right to some level of public education, and that right imposes duties on others to pay the corresponding taxes. Some individuals argue that people should have positive "economic rights" to food, housing, and medical care. Others believe that positive rights such as economic rights have lower standing than negative rights because positive rights impose duties that necessarily limit the liberty and autonomy of others.

An important difference between rights established by the state and those based on moral principles is that the former can be publicly enforced, whereas for moral rights there is no enforcement mechanism other than individual sanction. Rights granted by the state or by private agreements are generally specific; if ambiguity exists, an authoritative body such as a court clarifies the right. As considered in Chapter 12, for example, the common law has established precedents for determining remedies for the breach of contracts.

Rights and entitlements evolve over time as a consequence of demographic change, changes in preferences, and technological developments. Rights may also evolve because of changing perceptions about the appropriate extent of liberties, the dimensions of justice, or the relative importance of various rights. Rights also evolve as a consequence of interest group pressures acting through the institutions of government and public sentiment.

The evolution of the rights of university students provides an example. In the 1960s many universities followed the principle of in loco parentis, under which the distribution of rights between the university and the student was analogous to that between a parent and a child. The distribution of rights has evolved to the point at which enrollment now carries with it a well-defined set of rights and access to quasi-judicial mechanisms intended to ensure fair treatment.

Rent control is an example of a right resulting from the collective action of interest groups. Rent control, such as on apartments, is a means of redistributing wealth from landlords to renters. If apartment renters have sufficient political power, they may be able to institute rent control as a means of benefiting themselves at the expense of landlords. Rent control on apartments also affects those people who will be unable to find rental housing in the future, since rent control decreases the incentives to build apartments and spurs the conversion of apartments to condominiums.

## Kantian Maxims or Moral Rules

For Kant (1785, 1797) the foundations of a theory of morality are freedom and rationality. The expression of freedom is found in the concept of individual autonomy, and the requirement of rationality is found in the relationship between free will and maxims that govern actions. These maxims, or rules, are derived independently of their consequences by reasoning about the implications of freedom of the will. That is, maxims are evaluated based on the reasons or motives for them. The resulting maxims are thus impartial and universal—the person is to will universal rules, and the actions of others, from maxims is to allow individuals to judge their actions, and the actions of others, from the point of view of those maxims. As indicated in Figure 20-1, Kant's system is based on the motive, or mental disposition, and the reason for the action. Kant thus emphasizes the "right" over the "good."

Kant argued that because individuals are rational and each deduces maxims from a conception of freedom and autonomy that resides in everyone, all individuals will deduce the same maxims; that is, there will be unanimity. Reasoning in Kant's system is to be based on a fundamental axiom known as the categorical imperative.[2] The categorical imperative serves two basic functions. First, it provides a basis for determining moral rules. Second, it prescribes that individuals are to act in accord with those rules. Kant provides several formulations of the categorical imperative, but they basically hold that individuals are to be treated as autonomous beings, as ends rather than solely as means, and are to act based on a reason that each would will to be universal. Kant's basic formulation of the categorical imperative is:[3]

*Act according to the maxim that you would will to be a universal rule.*

According to Kant (1785, p. 39), "All rational beings stand under the law that each of them should treat himself and all others never merely as means but always at the same time as an end in himself." Morality for Kant then is the condition in which each individual can be an end, and ethics "is conceived as the law of one's own will, . . ." (1797, p. 47). This yields a second formulation of the categorical imperative:

*Treat individuals always as autonomous ends, and so never solely as means.*

This does not mean that a person cannot be treated as a means, for example, a means of production. An employee can thus be required to meet the standards for a particular job but has the right to quit or attempt to qualify for a better job.

The strength of Kant's conception of morality is that it focuses on motives or reasons for acting that are universal—apply to everyone—and thus are reversible—apply to oneself. The categorical imperative thus embodies two standards for the evaluation of maxims—universalizability and reversibility. Universalizability may be thought of as "Would I want everyone to behave according to that rule?" Reversibility may be thought of as "Would I want that rule applied to me?"[4] For example, if the rule under evaluation is "discrimination based on height is not allowed," reversibility requires that I do not discriminate based on height. Universalizability requires that I would will a society in which no one discriminated on the basis of height. The third standard for evaluating a candidate for status as a maxim or moral rule is, "Does it treat people always as ends and never solely as means, respecting their autonomy to choose?"

---

[2]The term *categorical* means that the imperative is not conditioned on any purpose other than the imperative itself. Kant (1785, p.26) wrote, "It is not concerned with the matter of the action and its intended result, but rather with the form of the action and the principle from which it follows: what is essentially good in the action consists in the mental disposition, let the consequences be what they may."

[3]This formulation applies to a broad class of maxims including some that could be contemplated but never acted on, so the categorical imperative is sharpened to pertain to rules that could be acted on. That is, the maxims must have meaning.

[4]Reversibility is implied by universalizability, but it is useful to state it separately as a reminder.

**EXAMPLE**

## Living Benefits

The Chapter 19 example Living Benefits focuses on the issue of whether it is right for companies to make viatical settlements; that is, to buy the life insurance policies of terminally ill individuals at a substantial discount from the face value of the policy. The magnitude of the discount depends on the estimated life expectancy of the individual, the risk the company bears in holding the policy, the premiums it must pay to keep the policy in force, and the competitiveness of the market for such policies. To assess whether such a practice is moral from a rights perspective, consider the maxim, "People may make viatical settlements." The categorical imperative asks whether this maxim treats people as autonomous ends and never solely as means. The policyholders are treated as a means to a profit for the companies

that buy the policies, but the policyholders also act autonomously in the sense that they can choose whether to sell their policies. That they have a free choice between holding and selling their policies means that they are treated as autonomous ends. As long as their capacity to choose is not impaired, living benefits satisfy this formulation of the categorical imperative. The other formulation of the categorical imperative is whether one would will the maxim to be a universal rule. Since all individuals reason rationally from the same conception of freedom and autonomy, Kant would conclude that they would will it to be universal. Whether in fact all individuals would reason in the same manner is difficult to assess, as considered in the later section on criticisms of moral rights.

## The Relationship between Maxims and Rights

Kant's system is expressed in terms of maxims, which individuals have a moral duty to respect. That duty establishes moral rights. Those moral rights are intrinsic, since they are derived from the categorical imperative and not from other considerations such as consequences. To illustrate the relationship between maxims, rights, and duties, consider the maxim, "A firm must sell its product to anyone who wants it, regardless of the price they are willing to pay."[5] This maxim violates the categorical imperative of treating individuals as autonomous ends, since the owners of the firm would be treated as means when forced to sell the product regardless of whether they wanted to do so.

Consider next the maxim, "A firm must sell its product to anyone who is willing to pay the price set by the firm." This maxim satisfies the categorical imperative of treating everyone as autonomous and as ends. Hence, it is a moral rule. This rule then has implications for rights and duties. First, it establishes property rights as moral rights. Second, it establishes the right of the firm to set the price for its product. Third, it does not allow the firm to distinguish, or discriminate, among buyers based on any considerations other than their willingness to pay the price set by the firm. This establishes a right not to be discriminated against and a corresponding duty not to discriminate on irrelevant considerations in making sales.

Consider another maxim, "A firm must sell its product to anyone who is willing to pay the cost of producing it." This rule violates the categorical imperative by not treating the owners of the firm as autonomous ends, since they are compelled to sell at a particular price. The regulation of a natural monopoly by setting price equal to cost thus would not be permitted in a Kantian system unless the owners of the firm were compensated sufficiently so that they would freely choose to set that price.

---

[5]This example was suggested by Daniel Diermeier.

Rights consistent with Kant's system include the freedoms of speech and conscience, since otherwise a person would not be autonomous. Rights also include political equality and the right to vote. Kantian rights require the opportunity to exercise individual autonomy, which includes the right not to be discriminated against on dimensions irrelevant to those opportunities. The categorical imperative draws a line between a right to opportunity without discrimination and the claim that individuals should be provided with the means to pursue opportunity and hence that others have a duty to provide those means. That claim may treat the recipients as ends and respect their autonomy and freedom, but it does not so treat those who have the duty since it uses them solely as means for serving others. Consequently, economic rights, such as rights to food or housing, are not consistent with Kant's ethics system. From this perspective, claims about economic rights are statements about political goals rather than moral rights.

There are thus few rather than many rights that follow from Kant's system. For example, Kant's system allows the voluntary provision of economic goods to individuals but does not compel anyone to provide those goods. In contrast, Rawls's system of justice, as considered later in the chapter, requires the fair equality of opportunity, and fairness requires that individuals have the means to realize opportunities.

As an example of Kant's framework, consider the nature of the relationship between an employer and an employee. In the 19th century, the employment relationship was governed by the "at-will" legal doctrine derived from the theory of free contract under which either party was free to terminate the relationship whenever it chose. The Kantian right to be treated as an end rather than solely as a means suggests that even though both human beings and machines are factors of production, human beings differ from machines in that they are also to be treated as ends. The employer's right to free contract and to dismiss an employee at will thus may be limited by an employee's right to be discharged only for cause. The maxim thus is, "An employer may dismiss an employee based only on considerations relevant to his or her performance on the job." A corresponding duty is associated with any right, and in this case the duty is assigned to the employer. An employer thus cannot dismiss an employee for her political views but can dismiss a disabled employee who can no longer work.[6] What constitutes "relevant to his or her performance," however, remains a matter of disagreement, particularly as it pertains to issues such as the testing of employees, as in the chapter case *Genetic Testing in the Workplace.*[7]

## Intrinsic and Instrumental Rights

Rights can be instrumental or intrinsic. Instrumental rights are to be respected because they contribute to achieving better consequences, by, for example, enabling individuals to pursue their interests. The right of free contract, that is, to enter into contracts, is intrinsic, but specific contract provisions are instrumental because they exist to facilitate mutually beneficial economic transactions by ensuring payment and the delivery of goods and services. Claims that individuals have economic rights to housing or food are claims about instrumental rights intended to improve their well-being.

Intrinsic rights are to be respected in and of themselves and do not require any justification in terms of consequences or other considerations. Intrinsic rights are derived from fundamental moral concepts such as autonomy and liberty, as in Kant's system. Examples of intrinsic rights are freedom of speech, equal protection including

[6]See the discussion in Chapter 19.
[7]Kupfer (1993) provides an ethics analysis of genetic testing.

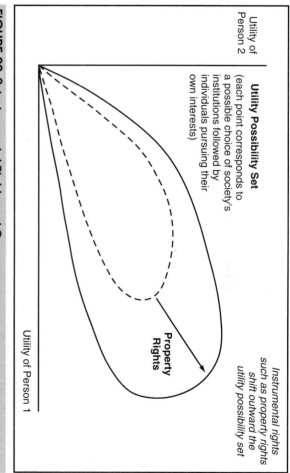

Utility of
Person 2

**Utility Possibility Set**
(each point corresponds to
a possible choice of society's
institutions followed by
individuals pursuing their
own interests)

Property
Rights

Instrumental rights
such as property rights
shift outward the
utility possibility set

Utility of Person 1

**FIGURE 20-2 Instrumental Rights and Consequences**

equal opportunity, and certain aspects of privacy. Some rights, such as property rights, are intrinsic when viewed from the perspective of autonomy and liberty and instrumental when viewed in terms of the consequences they yield. These rights may be stated in constitutions and laws, but intrinsic rights are to be respected independently of formal institutions. Intrinsic rights are frequently negative rights in the sense that respecting autonomy precludes others from infringing that autonomy. Many claims are made about the extent and scope of intrinsic rights, and formal institutions are often relied on to resolve conflicting claims. The extent of a right to privacy in the employment relationship, for example, remains a subject of competing claims as indicated in the example on privacy.

To illustrate the distinction between instrumental and intrinsic rights, consider a consequentialist example presented in Figures 20-2 and 20-3. These figures depict the possible combinations of utility, or well-being, for two individuals, 1 and 2, as a function of the activities in which they may engage, given society's institutions. That is, each point in the oblong shapes—the utility possibility sets—corresponds to the utilities the two individuals could attain if they acted to pursue their own interests, given the opportunities and incentives provided by a particular configuration of institutions. The institutions might correspond to various assignments of rights, the tax and transfer payment systems, the laws of torts and contracts, and public education. A point in the figure reflects the incentives provided by those particular institutions, so if the tax system dampens incentives for capital formation, aggregate output and the utility of both individuals could be lower than if stronger incentives were provided.

Instrumental rights affect the shape and size of the utility possibility set. For example, the dotted line might correspond to the set of institutions in communist countries such as the former Soviet Union and the nations of Eastern Europe under its control. The economies of those countries failed because the institutions of centralized state planning resulted in both insufficient capital formation and weak incentives for effort. As an instrumental right, a property right in which individuals keep the fruits of their

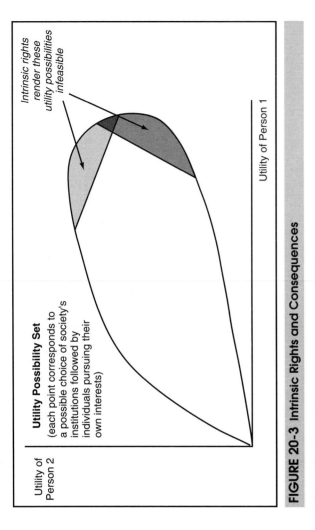

Utility of
Person 2

**Utility Possibility Set**
(each point corresponds to
a possible choice of society's
institutions followed by
individuals pursuing their
own interests)

*Intrinsic rights
render these
utility possibilities
infeasible*

Utility of Person 1

**FIGURE 20-3 Intrinsic Rights and Consequences**

labor provides stronger incentives for effort and capital formation and expands the utility possibility set, as illustrated in Figure 20-2. The privatization of companies in the former communist nations and in many other countries is one manifestation of this conclusion.

Intrinsic rights impose duties on individuals to respect those rights. Viewed from a Kantian perspective, property rights allow individuals to act as autonomous ends, and hence they have moral standing as intrinsic rights. In the context of Figure 20-2, the duty to respect those rights prevents others from moving from the larger to the smaller utility possibility set. Similarly, an intrinsic right to equal opportunity can expand the utility possibility set. An intrinsic right to equal opportunity, however, is not established in the Kantian system with reference to its effect on consequences but instead is established from the categorical imperative.

Other intrinsic rights may restrict the utility possibility set as illustrated in Figure 20-3. The claimed intrinsic right to privacy may limit the possible levels of utility attainable in a society. That is, intrinsic rights can constrain the set of available alternatives, and from a consequentialist perspective this can make at least some, and perhaps all, individuals worse off in terms of consequences. A right to privacy, for example, could be argued to prohibit genetic testing in the workplace, making it more difficult to move genetically susceptible individuals away from possible exposure to harmful chemicals.

The set of intrinsic rights established by Kant's ethics system is small and generally corresponds to negative rights that allow individuals to act as autonomous ends. The set of instrumental rights that enable people to pursue their interests is larger and may treat people solely as means. The right to some basic level of public education is one such right, and taxpayers are treated as a means. The set of rights established through political processes is larger still. That set includes measures such as rent control and the right to file an antidumping petition against imported goods. A right to file an international trade complaint is instrumental and is established by political authority.

## Privacy

Privacy is clearly important, but it remains controversial. In the employment relationship, for example, privacy pertains to issues such as whether employers can inspect the contents of an employee's locker, whether workplace surveillance of employees is permitted, whether supervisors can listen in on telephone order calls, and whether employees can be tested for substance abuse.

A right to privacy is said to arise both from moral standards and from legal guarantees. In the Kantian framework an intrinsic right to privacy can be viewed as arising from the notion of autonomy. Freedom of conscience is restricted when privacy is violated. In this sense people are said to have a sphere in which their thoughts can remain private. The question is the extent to which this personal sphere extends beyond thoughts to behavior.

The notion of autonomy pertains to the size of the sphere, since a person can choose to allow others access to information about himself or herself. For example, in an employment relationship management generally has the right to supervise and monitor an employee's performance. This right can extend beyond actual performance to factors that could affect that performance. For example, many employers require drug tests of their employees, even though such tests primarily provide information about or conduct outside the employment relationship. By accepting a job for which drug testing is required, individuals voluntarily sacrifice some of their personal sphere. Individuals thus can contract away some of their personal sphere. In that sense a right to privacy cannot be as important as inalienable rights such as speech and assembly. The intrinsic right in this example is a right not to be forced to accept or work in a job against one's will.

With regard to legal rights to privacy the U.S. Constitution does not mention privacy. The Fourth Amendment establishes a right "to be secure in their persons, houses, papers, and effects, against searches and seizures . . ." but that right is generally held to apply to searches and seizures by government. Thus, in the private sector there is no Constitutional prohibition against drug testing, but in the public sector in which government is an employer, employees have a right not to submit to drug tests unless they are in sensitive positions or are involved with public safety. The Supreme Court has concluded that other rights explicitly established by the Constitution imply that there is a right of privacy in a personal sphere.[1]

The extent of a right to privacy, or the size of the personal sphere, is difficult to identify. One has a right to the privacy of one's body and mind, but as the cases of drug tests and integrity tests indicate, that right is limited in an employment relationship. One has a right to the privacy of certain behavior, but surveillance is not generally prohibited. One also has privacy rights with respect to information about one's self, but many parties, such as doctors, employers, governments, and others, have records of that personal information. As mentioned in Chapter 13 over 40 percent of the Internet users surveyed said they would exchange their personal data, such as name, address, and contact information, for a $100 gift certificate. The Chapter 13 cases, *DoubleClick and Internet Privacy* and *Google and G-Mail*, and the Chapter 15 case, *The European Union Data Privacy Directive*, deal with the issue of data generated through Internet transactions and browsing. The chapter case, *RFID Tags*, concerns another privacy issue.

[1]See *Griswold v. Connecticut*, 381 U.S. 479 (1965).

## Criticisms of Kantian Rights

The criticisms of Kant's ethics system include both those that pertain to deontological systems in general and those specific to his system. The fundamental criticism of deontological systems is that they fail to explain why a principle or right should be respected. When one attempts to do so, one is often led to justifying it in terms of the extent to which it protects or promotes human interests. For example, why is treating individuals as ends important if it is not to give them the opportunity to pursue their interests? Thus, critics contend that consequences rather than motives actually underlie the moral standing of these principles.

More specific criticisms of rights-based ethics systems are that they may not (1) identify sufficiently precisely where the corresponding duty lies, (2) indicate the priority when one right conflicts with another, and (3) indicate when—if ever—it would be acceptable to violate a right. With respect to the first criticism, every right is accompanied by an associated duty, but who is to bear the burden of that duty is not always clear. Some negative rights, such as the right of free speech, impose a duty on everyone not to interfere with that speech. In the case of a claimed positive right, such as a right to medical care, however, the duty may fall on the individual, family, employer, or government. In such situations, legislation is often required to clarify where the duty lies. Legislation, however, reflects interests, and hence preferences and consequences.

A second criticism is that Kant's system does not clearly indicate whether or when one right has priority over another. The categorical imperative requires that individuals be treated as autonomous and so always as an end and never solely as a means. Kant's view was that there would be no conflict among the rights consistent with the categorical imperative. When a person, however, attempts to articulate the set of intrinsic rights, conflicts frequently appear. In such a case, Kant would argue that the person should examine those rights from the perspective of the categorical imperative, eliminating those inconsistent with it. In practice, this is difficult, and an approach to prioritizing rights, as presented in the section "Conflicts Among Rights," is needed.

A third criticism centers on whether there are any circumstances in which it would be acceptable to violate a maxim or right. For example, if rights are in conflict, it may be necessary to violate one to respect another. A violation of a right for whatever reason is a moral wrong, but the seriousness of the violation must be considered. In the language of justice theory, the issue is when it is acceptable to violate one right to avoid a violation of a more important right. Similarly, paternalism is a wrong, but there may be circumstances, as considered in Chapter 21, in which it may be acceptable to take an action to benefit a person even though that action violates the person's autonomy.

In spite of these criticisms, individual rights are a fundamental component of our ethical intuition. Rights are embedded in constitutions, statutes, and moral understandings. The duties corresponding to legal and moral rights provide fundamental constraints on the actions of managers and on the policies of firms.

The practical difficulties with the application of rights-based ethics systems pertain to the evaluation of claims about rights, the priority of various rights, and the relationship between rights and other concerns such as well-being and justice. The next section addresses these issues in the context of applied rights analysis.

## Applied Rights Analysis

In managerial decision making, rights have two effects. First, as illustrated in Figure 20-3, they rule out certain alternatives, such as those that would violate moral principles or constitutionally protected rights. Second, a right may impose an affirmative duty that requires a firm to take particular actions. The equal employment opportunity laws prohibit discrimination, whereas affirmative action regulations impose affirmative duties on employers to address the effects of past discrimination. The second effect is addressed later in the chapter in the context of equal employment opportunity, affirmative action, and the Americans with Disabilities Act. The focus here is on rights that rule out alternatives.

## Claimed and Granted Rights

A granted right is established by moral consensus or by government and is accompanied by a clear assignment of the corresponding duty. If the duty has not been clearly assigned, moral consensus is absent, or government has not spoken, the right in question is said to be claimed. Individuals claim rights and make demands on others by asserting moral justifications, but others may view those claims as morally unjustified.

To illustrate the distinction between claims and grants and their moral standing, consider the issue of foods containing genetically modified organism (GMO). A claim that a person has a right to ban imports of GMO foods neither has moral status nor is granted by government. A claim that a person has a right to have GMO food labeled as such may have moral standing because it enables persons to exercise their autonomy in their choice of foods. This right is not granted in the United States, but is in the European Union. Even if there were moral consensus that GMO foods should be labeled, government need not play a role. Some grocers could implement policies of selling GMO-free foods, and some food manufacturers could supply such products. A person then exercises autonomy by choosing where to shop.

Although it has no moral standing, people have a granted right through government to ban imports of GMO foods and to bear the sanctions authorized by the World Trade Organization (WTO), as in the case of the European Union and hormone-treated beef. People have a granted right (in the United States a Constitutional right to petition government) to lobby government to change WTO rules to require labeling or even the separation of GMO foods. The right to petition has moral standing as a form of free speech and representation by people acting as autonomous ends.

Private and public policy regarding GMO foods involves both ethics and politics, as illustrated in Figure 20-4. Ethics pertains to the moral standing of claims. Politics involves efforts to turn claimed rights into granted rights.

To address nonmarket issues where rights are claimed, managers must evaluate contesting arguments. To illustrate the evaluation of a claimed right, consider the claim that the poor have, or should have, entitlements different from those of other people. In *Kadrmas v. Dickinson Public Schools*, 487 U.S. 450 (1988), the Supreme Court affirmed its 1973 ruling that the equal protection clause of the Constitution does not give special protection due to income. Plaintiff Kadrmas challenged a North Dakota law that allowed school districts to charge a fee for school bus service. The Dickinson School provided bus service for rural students, picking them up at their doors, but charged them $97 per year for the service. The Kadrmas's income was close to the "officially defined poverty level," and Kadrmas refused to pay the fee. The school bus then no longer stopped for Sarita Kadrmas. Since the Kadrmases lived 16 miles from the school, they had to incur an additional expense for Sarita's transportation. They sued, and the case reached the Supreme Court. For the majority in a 5-to-4 decision, Justice Sandra Day O'Connor wrote,

The Constitution does not require that such [school bus] service be provided at all, and it is difficult to imagine why choosing to offer the service should entail a constitutional obligation to offer it for free. . . . We have previously rejected

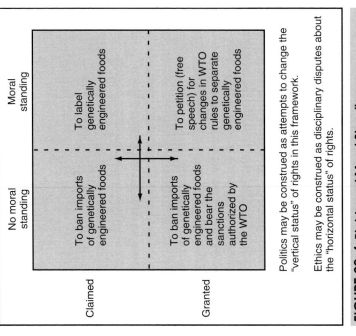

|  | No moral<br>standing | Moral<br>standing |
|---|---|---|
| Claimed | To ban imports<br>of genetically<br>engineered foods | To label<br>genetically<br>engineered foods |
| Granted | To ban imports<br>of genetically<br>engineered foods<br>and bear the<br>sanctions<br>authorized by<br>the WTO | To petition (free<br>speech) for<br>changes in WTO<br>rules to separate<br>genetically<br>engineered foods |

Politics may be construed as attempts to change the
"vertical status" of rights in this framework.

Ethics may be construed as disciplinary disputes about
the "horizontal status" of rights.

**FIGURE 20-4 Rights and Moral Standing**

the suggestion that statutes having different effects on the wealthy and the poor should on that account alone be subjected to strict equal protection. . . . Nor have we accepted the proposition that education is a "fundamental right," like equality of the franchise, which should trigger strict government scrutiny when government interferes with an individual's access to it.[8]

The majority's opinion thus distinguishes the constitutional grant of equal protection under the law from the claim that because of income individuals should be relieved of certain economic burdens. Equal protection is a right consistent with the Kantian system, whereas education and the economic right to free bus service are not. Managers must make similar judgments about claimed rights, and a method for the analysis of claims about rights is presented next.

## A Methodology for Rights Analysis

Rights analysis has two principal components. The first is determining whether a claimed right has moral standing. The second is determining how conflicts among rights are to be resolved. The methodology of rights analysis is as follows:

**1.** Identify the rights claimed and their claimed moral bases.
**2.** Determine which claimed rights satisfy moral standards; for example, Kantian standards or a utilitarian standard that establishes instrumental rights.
**3.** If a claim is not morally justified, check whether it is established by government. If it is, it is granted and is to be respected. If not, the claim need not be respected.[9]

[8]United States Law Week, (56), 6-21-88, 4777-4783, p. 4780.
[9]Claims should not be ignored, since they may motivate nonmarket action.

4. Identify the actions consistent with the protection or promotion of any morally justified rights.
5. Identify conflicts among rights. If there are none, those claimed rights with moral standing are to be respected.
6. If there are conflicts among rights with moral standing, investigate the importance of the interests those rights are intended to protect or promote.
7. Prioritize the rights based on the importance of those interests and determine the extent to which each is constrained by the others.
8. Choose the action that does best in terms of the priorities established.

The following example introduced in Chapter 19 illustrates the first four steps in the methodology; then conflicts among rights and prioritization are addressed.

## Life Insurance Screening for Preexisting Conditions

The reasoning in the *Kadrmas* decision suggests that individuals have no granted right to life insurance nor to purchase insurance at a particular price. Insurance companies thus need not provide insurance to everyone or anyone. When life insurance is offered, however, screening for preexisting conditions is claimed to be discriminatory and an invasion of privacy. In most jurisdictions, an insurance company has a granted right to screen for preexisting conditions and to deny or at least limit coverage.[1] That right can be withdrawn or limited through politics and government action, but in the absence of restrictions most insurance companies screen for preexisting conditions based on utilitarian considerations as considered in Chapter 19. Claims about privacy and discrimination, however, warrant examination because if they have moral standing in this situation, legal and moral rights would be in conflict.

_____
[1]The grant may extend considerably beyond screening. In 1990 a federal district court judge dismissed a lawsuit filed by an employee with AIDS who had charged that it was illegal for a firm that self-insured to limit medical coverage for AIDS. The judge held that the firm had complied with the requirements of the Employee Retirement Income Security Act (ERISA) by notifying employees that its medical plan could be revised on an annual basis. The Court of Appeals rejected the plaintiff's appeal, and in 1992 the Supreme Court let that decision stand.

## Conflicts Among Rights

### Rights and Interests

In the case of moral rights, or rights more generally, one approach to reasoning about, if not resolving, conflicts is to inquire into the importance of the rights by considering the interests they are intended to promote or protect. Rights established by deontological reasoning, conflicts is to inquire into the importance of the rights by considering the interests they are intended to promote or protect. Rights established by deontological approach addresses conflicts by examining the interests the rights are intended to protect or promote and by prioritizing those rights based on the importance of those interests. This approach thus adds considerations of consequences to the evaluation of rights.

Kant argued that the intrinsic rights established in accord with the categorical imperative do not conflict. When the set of rights is expanded to include instrumental rights and granted rights established by government through politics, however, rights can be in conflict. Those conflicts may mean that there is no action that respects all the rights. This section presents an approach to steps 5, 6, and 7 in the applied rights methodology. The approach addresses conflicts by examining the interests the rights are intended to protect or promote and by prioritizing those rights based on the importance of those interests. This approach thus adds considerations of consequences to the evaluation of rights.

systems are intrinsic, however, and are justified independently of the interests to which they contribute. They thus have high standing. Nevertheless, the approach of inquiring into interests is a practical method for addressing conflicts in managerial applications and is consistent with ethical intuition.

To illustrate the inquiry into the interests a claimed right is intended to promote, in his dissent in *Kadrmas* Justice Thurgood Marshall stated his view of the constitutional basis for a right:

The statute at issue here burdens a poor person's interest in an education. The extraordinary nature of this interest cannot be denied. By denying equal opportunity to exactly those who need it most, the law not only militates against the ability of each poor child to advance herself, but also increases the likelihood of the creation of a discrete and permanent underclass. Such a statute is difficult to reconcile with the framework of equality embodied in the Equal Protection Clause.

As I have stated on prior occasions, proper analysis of equal protection claims depends . . . upon identifying and carefully analyzing the real interests at stake.[10]

Justice Marshall thus turned to the interests of the individual in attempting to determine the priority of the claimed right to free school bus service. Justice O'Connor, in contrast, focused on whether a right has been granted by the Constitution rather than on the interests affected.

## Prioritization

The framework for analyzing conflicts among rights, as summarized in Figure 20-5 for the integrity tests example, begins with an identification of a right, an assessment of whether it is claimed or granted, and its bases. The possible bases for a right are moral and legal, where the latter includes the Constitution, statutes, and contracts. A granted

**FIGURE 20-5  Applied Rights Analysis: Integrity Tests**

| Right | Claimed/ Granted | Bases* | Addressing Conflicts | | |
|---|---|---|---|---|---|
| | | | Interests the Right Protects | Priority | Actions Consistent with the Right |
| Privacy | Claimed | Moral | Liberty Human dignity | 2†, 3‡ | Limited use of tests |
| Free from arbitrary treatment | Claimed | Moral | Opportunity to quality for jobs | 1 | Test verified; professional interpretation of results |
| To use test in hiring; (firm) | Granted | Moral/ Legal | Autonomy of employer Economic efficiency | 3†, 2‡ | Test where honesty is important to job performance |

*moral, legal (constitutional, statutory, common law)
†for jobs where the efficiency interest is not compelling
‡for jobs where the efficiency interest is compelling

---

[10]*California Reporter*, 829 (1987), p. 4782.

right is established by the state, by another individual or entity, or by moral consensus and has a clearly assigned duty. A claimed right either does not have a clearly assigned corresponding duty or has been established by neither a grant nor moral consensus.

The first four steps in the methodology presented earlier in the chapter identify rights and their status. Because moral and granted rights can be in conflict in managerial settings, they must be prioritized. Priorities are established by the institutions of society and by moral principles. The Constitution establishes certain priorities. For example, one has a right in one's home to prohibit others from trespassing for commercial purposes. However, one does not have the same right when its exercise denies others the opportunity to exercise their rights of free speech or religion. Consequently, home owners do not have the right to call on the state to prevent people from knocking on their doors to distribute religious materials. Constitutional rights also take precedence over legislatively granted rights, particularly because many constitutional rights also have a moral justification. Rights that are granted and have a moral basis have priority over moral claims that have a disputed moral basis. Intrinsic rights have priority over instrumental rights. More difficult are cases in which a granted right is in conflict with a claimed right.

To assess priorities in such a case, the interests those rights protect and promote are examined. Those interests may range from the opportunity to pursue one's own well-being to personal privacy, which has a moral basis in the right of conscience in a Kantian framework. The interests identified are intended to be fundamental, as in Justice Marshall's statement about the importance of education to opportunity. Once the interests have been identified, the rights that further those interests are to be assigned priority. At this point individuals may have differing assessments of priorities, but the assignment of priorities is intended to be impartial and based on the importance of the interest and not on the personal preferences of the person conducting the analysis. The final column in Figure 20-5 identifies actions that are consistent with a right.

The result of the analysis may be that there is no action that does not violate some right with legal or moral standing. Prioritization is then based on the seriousness of a violation. Given the assessment of priorities, the managerial task is to determine the extent to which a right should be limited to protect other rights and then to identify the actions that come the closest to meeting the priorities. The chapter case, *Genetic Testing in the Workplace*, and the Chapter 21 case, *Reporting of Clinical Trial Results*, involve the prioritization of rights.

## Integrity Tests

Integrity tests are currently legal under federal law and under the laws of at least 49 states, so the focus is on moral claims. The rights claimed are the prospective employees' right to privacy, their right not to be subject to arbitrary treatment as a consequence of an inaccurate test, and the employer's right to choose standards for hiring, as long as those standards do not discriminate on an illegal basis. Since these rights are in conflict, it is necessary to evaluate and prioritize them.

The right to privacy is granted by statute as it pertains to certain types of tests, such as polygraphs, but it is claimed as it pertains to integrity tests. Congress might in the future extend the right of privacy to integrity tests, but it has not yet done so. The right to be free from arbitrary treatment is based on the claim that the tests may misclassify individuals because of inherent inaccuracies. The firm's right to use the tests to select among prospective employees, as long as it

*(Continued)*

*(Continued)*

does not illegally discriminate, is granted and has both a moral and a legal basis. The moral basis derives from the autonomy of the employer (and employee) and the liberty to enter into contracts. The legal basis follows from property rights. The bases for the rights are indicated in Figure 20-5.

To investigate priorities, the interests the rights are intended to promote or protect must be identified. The claimed right to privacy is intended to promote liberty and protect human dignity. The claimed right to be free from arbitrary treatment protects the opportunity to qualify for positions. The employer's right to choose standards for hiring is, as an instrumental right, intended to promote economic efficiency by allowing employers to match prospective employees to jobs.

In addressing the conflicts among these rights, intrinsic rights have priority, because in a deontological system the right takes precedence over the good. The right not to be subjected to arbitrary treatment seems important in this case. In the last column in Figure 20-5, the actions consistent with this right center on ensuring accuracy in testing. In 1991 the American Psychological Association issued a report concluding that "the preponderance of the evidence" indicates that integrity tests can be useful, but it expressed concerns about some of the tests, the claims made for them, and their use in the absence of supervision by a qualified psychologist. Given these concerns, the tests should be carefully evaluated and supervised by trained personnel. Furthermore, because of possible inaccuracies, passing an integrity test should not be a necessary condition for employment but could be one of several factors considered.

With respect to privacy, the fundamental issue is whether it is morally acceptable to base employment and job assignments on psychological considerations. Integrity and other forms of psychological tests are said to invade privacy by asking questions that are too personal and not closely linked to job requirements. Such questions might pertain to lifestyle and off-the-job activities. Privacy can be limited, however, when there is a compelling reason, and individuals can choose whether to accept a position in which a degree of privacy is sacrificed. Consequently, the claimed right to privacy can be limited when the employer has an important interest served by the integrity test.

The employer's right to use tests to select employees on nondiscriminatory grounds is intended to respect autonomy and enhance the good of economic efficiency. In a deontological framework, the former right may be limited if otherwise the liberties or rights of individuals would be restricted. The good of economic efficiency is clearly important, but the right that promotes it is instrumental. Furthermore, deontological systems can require restrictions on that right to avoid infringing intrinsic rights, as illustrated in Figure 20-3. The actions consistent with this right to test thus might be to use the test depending on how important integrity and loyalty are for a particular position. A position such as security guard, bank teller, or purchasing agent might warrant an integrity test, whereas a custodial position might not.

Although there is ambiguity in the application of rights-based analysis in this case, the freedom from arbitrary treatment seems to have priority. The liberty and human dignity protected by a claimed right to privacy can be protected by not applying for a position for which an integrity test is required. This, however, would mean that opportunities are restricted by the tests. The interest that justifies the employer's use of an integrity test thus must be important to justify compromising the claimed right to privacy. For jobs in which integrity and loyalty are important to job performance, the employer's right to use the tests should have priority. For jobs in which integrity and loyalty are not important to job performance, the claimed right to privacy should have priority. Consequently, necessary conditions for the use of the tests is that they be reasonably accurate and administered by qualified individuals, that they be limited to jobs for which the tested traits are important to the interests of the firm, and that they be only one of several factors considered in employment decisions.[1] The chapter case, *Genetic Testing in the Workplace*, raises similar considerations about rights and their priorities.

---

[1] Dalton and Metzger (1993) reach a different conclusion based on concerns about the accuracy of the tests.

# Equal Employment Opportunity

Equal employment opportunity is a principle supported by virtually all ethics systems. Its importance is supported by legal grants that provide for its public enforcement. Its legal manifestation is Title VII of the Civil Rights Act of 1964, which prohibits discrimination on the basis of "race, color, sex, religion, or national origin." Most states have similar laws applicable to businesses operating within their state.

Concerns about illegal discrimination in the employment relationship now focus less on intentional discrimination and more on employment practices and policies that, while appearing neutral with respect to an identifiable group, have a disparate impact on the members of that group. An employment policy that is neutral with respect to race, for example, has a disparate impact if a lower proportion of minorities than whites are hired. Employers then must establish that the policy is required by business necessity—a bona fide occupational qualification (BFOQ). The concept of a disparate impact is broad and applies to hiring, promotion, and compensation. More subtly, it may also apply to grooming rules, physical requirements, language requirements, and information about an individual's past, such as an illness, criminal conviction, or a past substance abuse problem. Other laws have applied the same principles to other attributes, including age, disability, and pregnancy.

Title VII is administered by the Equal Employment Opportunity Commission (EEOC), an independent administrative commission with five members appointed by the president. The EEOC can act on its own or in response to a complaint filed by an individual. In addition, the EEOC has rule-making authority over compliance with Title VII and may file suit in federal court if conciliation fails. An individual may also file suit in federal court once the EEOC has attempted to resolve the issue. Because most states have laws similar to Title VII, the EEOC allows state agencies to handle many of the cases.

The remedies available to the EEOC or a court under Title VII include injunctions and mandated changes in practices. The complainant may be awarded reinstatement, promotion, payment of back wages, attorney fees, or other awards. As an example, in 1996 Texaco settled a racial discrimination lawsuit for $176.1 million and agreed to establish an "equality and tolerance task force." Texaco also settled a complaint by the EEOC, allowing it to scrutinize Texaco's hiring and promotion policies for 5 years.

The EEOC has been concerned with discrimination on Wall Street. In 2001 it filed a sex-discrimination lawsuit against Morgan Stanley Dean Witter. Private lawsuits can also be filed. A group of women employees had filed a class action sex-discrimination lawsuit against Merrill Lynch, and a settlement was reached in 1998 in which the company agreed to change its practices and compensate some 900 employees. A small group of women were dissatisfied with the changes and with the pace at which individual settlements were being made. The women decided to take their complaints to the sky. They arranged to have aircraft tow banners reading, "Merrill Lynch Discriminates Against Women" at events sponsored by Merrill, including golf tournaments, auto races, and vintage car shows.[11]

In 1993 Shoney's, Inc., agreed to a $105 million settlement in a case alleging discrimination against African Americans. Shoney's also agreed to institute an aggressive affirmative action program with a 10-year goal of 20 to 23 percent African American managers and assistant managers in its 754 company-owned restaurants. The Chapter 21 case, *Denny's and Customer Service,* addresses a discrimination case outside the employment relationship.

An employer has several defenses in a Title VII case. One is that of "business necessity," such as testing individuals for job-relevant skills. A second defense against a disparate impact charge is that of a BFOQ, but the EEOC and courts have interpreted this quite narrowly. A BFOQ defense pertains only to discrimination based on sex, religion, and national origin under Title VII and age under the Age Discrimination in Employment Act of 1967. Racial discrimination is never justified by a BFOQ. Third, seniority systems are not covered by Title VII, so a plaintiff must show intent of discrimination rather than a disparate impact. Seniority systems have been held to be protected against complaints under Title VII that they perpetuate the effects of discrimination.[12]

In addition to Title VII, the Civil Rights Act of 1866, codified as Section 1981 of Title 42 of the United States Code, provides protection against discrimination based on race. Section 1981 states that "all persons . . . have the same right to make and enforce contracts . . . as enjoyed by white persons." Since employment is viewed as a contract, Section 1981 covers the employment relationship. Protection from discrimination applies not only to minorities but to majorities as well. In *McDonald v. Santa Fe Trail Transportation Co,* 427 U.S. 274 (1976), the Supreme Court held that Section 1981 protects whites from discrimination.

In 1968 the Supreme Court held that Congress enacted the Civil Rights Act of 1866 pursuant to the 13th Amendment, which abolished slavery, rather than pursuant to the equal protection clause of the 14th Amendment. This meant that the act applies not only to government actions but also to private actions.[13] This considerably expanded the scope of application of Section 1981 and had a number of significant implications beyond those of Title VII. First, unlike Title VII, the act has no statute of limitations. Second, the act imposes no limit on the awards the courts may make, allowing both compensatory and punitive damages. Third, the act applies more broadly than Title VII, since it covers all employers whereas Title VII covers only those with at least 15 employees. Fourth, an individual can file a lawsuit directly without having to first go to the EEOC.

Title VII bars discrimination in employment but is silent about how a finding of discrimination is to be made. In *Griggs v. Duke Power,* 401 U.S. 424 (1971), the Supreme Court held that an employment policy that is "fair in form, but discriminatory in operation" is in violation of Title VII. Duke Power had required a high school diploma for employment, but its policy had a disparate impact on African Americans, who were less likely than white applicants to have graduated from high school. Griggs also established that the burden of proof rests on the employee or the EEOC to show that the policy in question has a disparate impact on a protected class.[14]

The Bush administration and Congress negotiated a compromise resulting in the Civil Rights Act of 1991, which amended several civil rights laws and overturned several Supreme Court decisions. It reversed one Supreme Court decision by placing the burden on the employer to show that a practice was a business necessity. The act also allowed punitive damages for intentional discrimination on the basis of sex, religion, national origin, or disability.[15] The act also overturned a 1989 Supreme Court decision that had restricted Section 1981 to hiring decisions. Section 1981 as amended now covers hiring, working conditions, promotion, and termination.

---

[12] See *International Brotherhood of Teamsters v. United States,* 431 U.S. 324 (1977); *American Tobacco Company v. Patterson,* 452 U.S. 937 (1982); and *Firefighters Local Union No. 1784 and Memphis Fire Department v. Carl W. Stotts et al.,* 467 U.S. 561 (1984).
[13] See Howell, Allison, and Henley (1987, p. 538).
[14] See also *McDonnell Douglas Corp. v. Green,* 411 U.S. 792 (1973) and *Texas Department of Community Affairs v. Burdine,* 447 U.S. 920 (1981).
[15] The Civil Rights Act of 1866 allowed punitive damages only for racial discrimination.

# Disabilities and Rights

The Americans with Disabilities Act (ADA) of 1990 bans discrimination on the basis of disability in virtually all aspects of the employment relationship for employers with 15 or more employees. The ADA also requires that businesses, including retail stores and restaurants, provide "reasonable accommodations" for the disabled. Disability is broadly defined to include "a physical or mental impairment that substantially limits one or more of that person's major life activities." Substance abuse is not considered a disability, but a person who no longer abuses substances and has completed a rehabilitation program could be considered disabled.

In the case of an employee fired for illegal drug use, the Supreme Court in 2003 upheld a Raytheon policy of refusing to rehire a person fired for misconduct. AIDS is considered by the courts as a handicap under the 1973 Vocational Rehabilitation Act and hence represents a disability, but HIV may not be a disability if it does not limit a major life activity. Employers are required to provide reasonable accommodation for an employee's disability.

The ADA is enforced by the EEOC and by private litigants. In an unusual settlement Wal-Mart agreed to pay $427,500 to a disabilities advocacy organization and to broadcast two television commercials in which two deaf individuals, who had filed a lawsuit under the ADA, described their difficulties in obtaining employment and reasonable accommodation from Wal-Mart. Courts can award compensatory but not punitive damages.

The coverage of the ADA is still being determined and has been the subject of numerous lawsuits. One issue is what limiting "major life activities" means. Another is what constitutes a "reasonable accommodation." A number of cases have been appealed to the Supreme Court, which has substantially limited the ADA's coverage. The court ruled that an impairment that limited a person's ability to do a particular job was not a disability under the ADA, which applies only when the impairment affects "the variety of tasks central to most people's daily lives."[16] The court also held that a company did not have to hire a person with liver disease for a job in an oil refinery where the person would be exposed to chemicals that could worsen his condition.[17] The court also held that a company was not required to violate a seniority system.[18] Although the courts have clarified the coverage of the ADA, considerable ambiguity remains.

# Neoclassical Liberalism

Liberalism emphasizes the liberty of individuals and is concerned with the relationships between liberty and morality and between that liberty and the state.[19] The former pertains to which rules or rights have moral standing, whereas the latter pertains to how individual liberty should be limited by the liberty of others and by the institutions individuals establish to govern their interactions. Liberal theory has a rich intellectual tradition including Hobbes (1651) and Locke (1690), but only a relatively recent version of that theory, that of Nozick (1974), is considered here. Nozick's theory is considered because it stakes out a position for a minimal state and because it provides a conception of rights and justice that is quite different from that of Kant and Rawls.

---

[16]*Toyota Motor Manufacturing, Kentucky Inc. V Williams*, 534 U.S. 184, 122 S.Ct. 681 (2002).

[17]*Chevron U.S.A. v. Echazabal*, 536 U.S. 73, 122 S.Ct. 2045.

[18]*US Airways v. Barnett*, 535 U.S. 391, 122 S. Ct. 1516.

[19]The term *liberal* is generally used in the United States to refer to positions that are to the left on a ideological dimension in which individual responsibilities and limited government are on the right and collectivist responsibilities and larger government are on the left. In many countries, liberalism refers to positions on the right of this dimension, and that is its use here.

As with Kant, Nozick attempts to deduce principles that define the scope of autonomy and liberty and then from those principles to derive a concept of justice. His starting point is the self-evident principle of requiring individuals' free consent to any restrictions that might be imposed on their personal liberty. Nozick derives his system based on the side constraint that "no moral balancing act can take place among us; there is no moral outweighing of one of our lives by others so as to lead to greater overall social good. There is no justified sacrifice of some of us for others" (p. 33). In Nozick's view, this side constraint ensures that individuals will be treated as ends—as the categorical imperative requires—and not as means. This is a stronger version of the categorical imperative than Kant employs, because Kant argues that individuals may be treated as means as long as they are also treated as ends.

Nozick recognizes that in the exercise of their own rights individuals could coerce or infringe the liberty of others. Individuals thus will form voluntary associations to protect their liberties. Such an association is one to which individuals freely consent, and it is the only entity allowed to use force to prevent violations of rights and liberties. That association may be viewed as a state, and the activities it is empowered to undertake have moral standing because it is the result of individuals exercising their autonomy. It thus satisfies the categorical imperative. Nozick concludes that the state would have minimal powers, limited to "protecting its citizens against violence, theft, and fraud, and to the enforcement of contracts . . ." (p. 26). Individuals thus have the negative right not to be coerced by others, and the state has the duty to enforce that right.

In Nozick's system the purpose of justice is to protect liberties. The fundamental principle of free consent provides his conception of distributive justice, which pertains to an individual's entitlements to goods and to the corresponding duties of others to satisfy those entitlements. Because any concept of distributive justice must be based on free consent, Nozick's conclusion is that what is just is whatever is the result of the voluntary actions of individuals. His maxim (p. 160) is expressed as, "From each as they choose, to each as they are chosen."

Nozick's theory has been criticized for its sole reliance on free consent. One line of criticism is based on the utilitarian perspective that actions should be evaluated in terms of their consequences. Another line of criticism is that his theory ignores the situation of those who are poorly off because of their initial endowments of abilities and resources. More importantly for applied purposes, Nozick's conception of a minimal state seems far removed from modern society. It does, however, provide a basis for the justification and extension of liberties.

# Categories of Justice Theories

Theories of justice add a comparative dimension to moral standards. Justice theories are concerned with how different individuals stand relative to each other on dimensions including, but not limited to, rights, liberties, and consequences. Rawls's theory of justice as fairness, for example, concludes that equality of moral and political rights is required but that economic rewards and burdens can be distributed unequally.

The three principal categories of justice theories are (1) distributive, (2) compensatory, and (3) retributive. Distributive justice is concerned with providing incentives to contribute to the well-being of society and with providing a fair and just distribution of the rewards of those contributions. Compensatory justice is concerned with determining how individuals should be compensated for the harm done by others. Retributive justice is concerned with punishment for actions that are contrary to a moral rule or societal well-being. Retributive justice may be used to justify deterring harmful actions. Only distributive and compensatory justice are considered here.

# Distributive Justice

Distributive justice is concerned with the distribution of the rewards and burdens of social interaction. A distributive standard is necessarily comparative, since it identifies how those rewards and burdens are assigned to individuals with particular attributes or in particular situations. Tax policy, for example, assigns the tax burden based on income, asset holdings, and consumption. Distributive justice is concerned with the question of which attributes are relevant for particular matters. Just as rights can rule out certain decision alternatives, as illustrated in Figure 20-3, justice principles can also rule out alternatives. Those principles can also impose duties to ensure that the distribution of rewards and burdens is just.

The basic comparative principle of distributive justice is that "Equals should be treated equally and unequals, unequally." Velasquez (1998, p. 105) elaborates by stating the principle,

> Individuals who are similar in all respects relevant to the kind of treatment in question should be given similar benefits and burdens, even if they are dissimilar in other irrelevant respects; and individuals who are dissimilar in a relevant respect ought to be treated dissimilarly, in proportion to their dissimilarity.

This principle implies that individuals should receive different pay if their productivity is different and should receive the same pay if their productivity is the same even though they differ in terms of irrelevant factors such as race or gender.

Distributive justice has a variety of conceptions. Egalitarianism requires the equal distribution of the rewards and burdens of society. This concept is typically rejected because an equal distribution of rewards would distort the incentives to produce those rewards. That is, at some point the more equally a society attempts to divide its pie the smaller the pie will be. Rawls's theory of justice concerns distributing the rewards and burdens of society in a manner that is fair yet gives attention to incentives to increase the size of the pie.

To illustrate the differences, consider the example in Table 20-1 of a three-person society in which individual 1 is more productive than individual 2 who is more productive than individual 3. The society has three possible systems of organizing the interactions of its members. A utilitarian system has the strongest incentives for individuals to use their abilities to pursue their interests, resulting in greater aggregate utility than the other systems. The distribution across individuals, however, is unequal due to the differences in productivity as indicated in the utilitarianism column of the table. Compared with the utilitarian system, an egalitarian system redistributes aggregate utility equally among the three individuals. To accomplish this, incentives have to be distorted by, for example, taxing the more productive individuals and redistributing the proceeds to the less productive individuals. In the example this reduces aggregate utility from 18 to 9. In contrast, Rawls's theory of justice considered below requires making the least advantaged individual, who in this society is individual 3, as well off as

**TABLE 20-1** Utilitarianism, Egalitarianism, and Rawlsian Justice

| Individual | Utilitarianism | Egalitarianism | Rawlsian Justice |
|---|---|---|---|
| 1 | 10 | 3 | 6 |
| 2 | 6 | 3 | 5 |
| 3 | 2 | 3 | 4 |
| *Aggregate utility* | 18 | 9 | 15 |

possible. In doing so Rawls seeks also to preserve incentives to the extent possible so that individuals can use their abilities to pursue their interests. This can also benefit the least advantaged individual through, for example, increased economic output. Aggregate utility is lower than that under utilitarianism, since incentives are distorted and there is redistribution in favor of individual 3. Aggregate utility is greater than under egalitarianism, however, since individuals have stronger incentives to pursue their interests and utilize their abilities.

## Compensatory Justice

Compensatory justice is concerned with whether and how a person should be compensated for an injustice. Compensatory justice has fairness and restitution as its goals. If a person is injured, the institutions of society may be designed to compensate the person. The principal institutions through which compensation for accidents is provided are the liability, workers' compensation, and insurance systems. Compensation serves two objectives. First, it provides restitution for the injury. Second, it provides incentives to reduce injuries and their social costs by imposing the burden on the parties responsible for the accident. If the institution of compensation is not well designed, however, it can result in a moral hazard problem that generates social costs by distorting the incentives for care. In such a case, the benefits of compensation must be weighed against the distortions of economic incentives the compensation causes. For example, the provision of government-backed flood insurance results in more home building in flood-prone areas than would be warranted by economic efficiency considerations.

Because of past injustices from discrimination in hiring and promotion practices, the courts ruled that compensation was owed to minority group members as a class, rather than solely to the identifiable victims of discrimination. Rawls's principle of fair equality of opportunity provides a different justification for this ruling by focusing not on the nature of past injustices but on ensuring that all individuals have fair equality of opportunity. This requires not only the absence of discrimination, but also the fair opportunity for all to qualify for positions and pursue their interests. From this perspective, measures to ensure opportunities are warranted even if they extend beyond the set of actual victims of past discrimination.

## Injustice

A general principle advanced in conceptions of justice is that an injustice is morally tolerated only if it is necessary to avoid a greater injustice. Such a principle requires an ordering of injustices. Gert (1988, pp. 110–111) offers a standard for when a violation of a moral rule is justified:

> A violation can be justified by providing reasons which would result in either some impartial rational persons advocating that that kind of violation be publicly allowed or less frequently, all impartial rational persons advocating that such a violation be publicly allowed.

Gert thus requires that the violator have reasons for the violation and that an impartial observer understand those reasons and be willing to have that form of violation publicly allowed.

An applied version of Gert's principle is the public disclosure test: "If I disclosed publicly that I had taken an action that violated a moral standard and explained my reasons for doing so, would the public understand and approve of my action?" One such explanation would be that a greater injustice was avoided. Since the public disclosure test is intended to be a hypothetical and reflective test for the person contemplating the action, it is important that the test not turn into a rationalization of a violation of a moral standard in the absence of a greater injustice. For this reason the public disclosure feature of the test is crucial. That is, others must agree that the injustice was warranted.

This principle is applied in Chapter 22 to the issue of whether avoiding a greater injustice justifies paying a bribe demanded as a condition for a sale. In the chapter case, *Genetic Testing in the Workplace*, a central issue is whether the injustice of the invasion of privacy through genetic testing is warranted to avoid the greater injustice of a person incurring serious physical harm from exposure to chemicals in the workplace. The Chapter 18 case, *Delta Instruments, Inc.*, raises justice issues in the wake of a moral wrong.

# Rawls's Theory of Justice

## The Framework for Justice as Fairness

Rawls (1971) provides a theory of distributive justice set in the tradition of the social contract theory of Locke (1690), Rousseau (1762), and Kant. Rawls argues for the priority of the right over the good, but he is less concerned with developing maxims for judging the reasons or motives that individuals have for their actions than with developing principles to guide the design of society's institutions. According to Rawls (1971, p. 7), "the primary subject of justice is . . . the way in which the major social institutions distribute fundamental rights and duties and determine the division of advantages from social cooperation . . . the legal protection of freedom of thought and liberty of conscience, competitive markets, private property in the means of production, and the monogamous family are examples of major social institutions."

Because any contemporaneous choice of principles by individuals would be based at least in part on who those individuals are and what roles they have in society, Rawls concludes that just principles are those that would be "chosen behind a veil of ignorance" from an "original position" in which one does not know one's personal characteristics and the place one will subsequently have in society. In this original position each individual is equal to every other individual, so the principles chosen will have moral standing, it is argued, because they will be deduced impartially where no one has an advantage.[20]

Rawls's contractarian method is illustrated in Figure 20-6. In the original position, individuals do not know which abilities they will have, which positions in society they will occupy, or what their tastes will be. What they do know is that there is a set of possible abilities, tastes, and positions they might be fortunate or unfortunate enough to have once the veil of ignorance has been lifted. They also know the laws of the natural sciences and the understandings gained from the social sciences, so they can predict the behavior that will result once society's institutions are in place and the veil has been lifted. Since in the original position all individuals are equal and the principles they choose will apply to everyone and so to themselves, the original position satisfies the Kantian standards of universalizability and unanimity. From the original position, individuals will also treat people always as ends and never solely as means. Since Kant's categorical imperative is satisfied, the principles chosen in the original position will have moral standing, according to Rawls.[21] Those principles constitute the social contract.

---

[20]One concern with deducing maxims in Kant's framework is that individuals, knowing their present positions in society, might not reason in an impartial manner. Kant argues that the sense of freedom and autonomy in everyone leads everyone to reason impartially and to will the same maxims, resulting in unanimity. Rawls seeks to ensure impartiality and unanimity through the device of the original position.
[21]See Rawls (1980) for a further analysis of the Kantian construction.

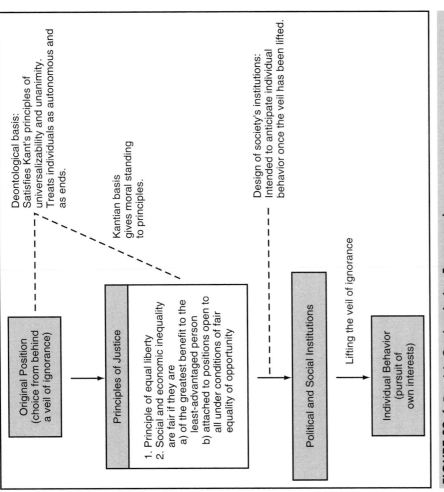

Original Position
(choice from behind
a veil of ignorance)

Deontological basis:
Satisfies Kant's principles of
universalizability and unanimity.
Treats individuals as autonomous and
as ends.

Kantian basis
gives moral standing
to principles.

Principles of Justice

1. Principle of equal liberty
2. Social and economic inequality
   are fair if they are
   a) of the greatest benefit to the
      least-advantaged person
   b) attached to positions open to
      all under conditions of fair
      equality of opportunity

Design of society's institutions:
Intended to anticipate individual
behavior once the veil has been lifted.

Political and Social Institutions

Lifting the veil of ignorance

Individual Behavior
(pursuit of
own interests)

**FIGURE 20-6 Rawls's Contractarian Framework**

Once the principles have been chosen, society's political and social institutions are to be designed based on those principles. Once those institutions are in place, the veil of ignorance is to be lifted, and individuals learn their abilities and tastes and may pursue whatever interests they have. An important feature of Rawls's theory is that it does not suppose that once the veil has been lifted people will necessarily behave according to a set of rules that take precedence over self-interest. Understanding that individuals may pursue their own interests, Rawls focuses on the role of institutions in guiding the pursuit of those interests in a mutually advantageous manner. The central task of Rawls's method then is to determine which principles and which institutions would be chosen in the original position.

The relevance of Rawls's system for management is found both in the principles of justice he identifies and in the concept of the design of institutions consistent with those principles. The principles provide a basis for reasoning about issues with moral dimensions. The choice of Rawls's institutions corresponds to the formulation of policies to guide managers in dealing with nonmarket issues with moral dimensions. These policies are used in the screening stage of the framework for nonmarket analysis and strategy formulation introduced in Chapter 2 and summarized in Figure 2-5. In the case of integrity tests, for example, the principles provide a basis for reasoning about whether such tests involve an unjustified intrusion on the liberties of prospective employees, whether they distort opportunities, and whether they have desirable distributive consequences.

## The Principles of Justice

Rawls argues that individuals would adopt two principles as a basis for justice as fairness:

First: each person is to have an equal right to the most extensive basic liberty compatible with similar liberty for others.

Second: social and economic inequalities are to be arranged so that they are both (a) to the greatest benefit of the least advantaged and (b) attached to positions and offices open to all under conditions of fair equality of opportunity.[22]

The first principle is referred to as the equal liberty principle, part (a) of the second is the difference principle, and part (b) is the fair equality of opportunity principle. Rawls's principles may be thought of as incorporating both deontological considerations (in the form of liberty and opportunity) and considerations of well-being (in terms of the benefit to the least advantaged).

Rawls argues that the principle of equal liberty has precedence over the fair equality of opportunity, which has precedence over the difference principle. By the first precedence, Rawls means "that liberty can be restricted only for the sake of liberty itself." The second precedence means that the difference principle is to be applied only after conditions ensuring the fair equality of opportunity are in place. In Rawls's system, no trade-off is permitted between basic liberties and social and economic benefits. Rawls thus concludes that society's institutions should be characterized by political equality but that social and economic inequalities can be tolerated as long as they are arranged in accord with the fair equality of opportunity and difference principles.

The equal liberty principle pertains to liberties such as the freedom of conscience and speech, the right to vote, the right to be eligible for office, freedom of assembly, freedom from arbitrary arrest, and the right to hold property. Such liberties can be limited only as necessary to maintain conditions of reasoned discourse and public order. For example, rules of recognition and procedure may be instituted to allow everyone to speak in a manner that allows that speech to be heard. With respect to political liberties, Rawls argues that there must be limits on "the scope of majority rule," such as limits like those in the Constitution and in the Bill of Rights.

Fair equality of opportunity is necessary to allow individuals to realize the worth of their liberty, and it requires that positions in society be open to all and that all individuals have a fair opportunity to qualify for those positions. When fair equality of opportunity has been assured, the difference principle requires that the least advantaged individuals be able to realize the worth of their liberty through the pursuit of their interests. The second principle thus is comparative and may require, for example, provisions for the disabled that provide them access to public facilities and to the same employment opportunities open to others. Rawls further argues that policies that improve the well-being of the least-advantaged individual would also improve the well-being of most, if not all, of the disadvantaged because their positions are "closely knit." Thus, a policy that benefits the least advantaged person also benefits other less advantaged persons.

To apply the difference principle, Rawls faces the task of determining who are the least-advantaged persons. This involves making comparisons among individuals, but as indicated in the discussion of utilitarianism in Chapter 19, such interpersonal

---

[22]Rawls (1971, pp. 60, 83). He gives a more extensive statement of the principles on pages 302–303.

comparisons are problematic. Rawls attempts to avoid this problem by identifying a set of "primary goods" that all individuals require to be able to pursue their interests, whatever those interests might be. The primary goods are divided into broad categories—rights and liberties, opportunities and powers, and income and wealth. Rawls argues that an index of these primary goods be used to assess the well-being of individuals. This allows for interpersonal comparisons. The difference principle thus takes well-being into account.

## The Role of Incentives

From Rawls's perspective, the institutions of society allow one individual to be better off than another if that is necessary to make the least-advantaged person better off. This is illustrated in Table 20-1 where the Rawlsian choice results in lower aggregate utility than utilitarianism, but makes the least-advantaged person better off than under the other two systems. The Rawlsian choice also allows more-advantaged persons to pursue their interests resulting in greater aggregate well-being than with egalitarianism. Rawls, however, is concerned with the well-being of the least advantaged rather than aggregate well-being.

The role of incentives and the comparison between the utilitarian, egalitarian, and Rawlsian systems are illustrated in Figure 20-7, where the utility possibility set corresponds to societal institutions that satisfy the equal liberty and fair equality of opportunity principles. In Figure 20-7, individual 1 is more advantaged than individual 2, since more of the alternatives result in a higher utility for 1 than for 2. Egalitarianism requires that the institutions be chosen to attain point A, which yields the greatest utility for each individual subject to the restriction that both are equally well-off. The difference principle states that it is just to move from A to B, even though individual 1 does relatively better than 2. It is just because the less advantaged person 2 is as well-off as possible at B. Rawls thus would choose institutions that provide incentives for economic efficiency to allow society to achieve B rather than A. Institutions that would allow C to be attained, however, would be unjust, since moving from B to C reduces the

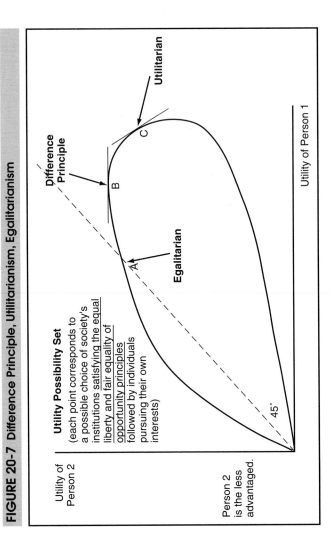

**FIGURE 20-7  Difference Principle, Utilitarianism, Egalitarianism**

well-being of the less-advantaged person even though the well-being of 1 increases by more than the well-being of 2 decreases. A utilitarian system that weights the well-being of each individual equally would choose institutions that result in point C.[23]

Rawls thus supports economic efficiency and the role of incentives and markets in attaining that efficiency. But his system of justice supports incentives and markets in a market system only in so far as they benefit the least advantaged. Economic efficiency and aggregate well-being thus can be sacrificed if doing so improves the situation of the least advantaged. The example evaluates living benefits from the perspective of Rawls principles.

---

### Living Benefits

Is the purchase of life insurance policies from the terminally ill, as considered in the Living Benefits example, consistent with Rawls's theory of justice? With respect to the principle of equal liberty, no liberties are infringed by the purchases, since a policyholder can freely choose to sell a policy or retain it.[1] Indeed, purchasing policies better enables the terminally ill to realize the worth of their liberty by providing funds for their use. Similarly, the purchases do not infringe the fair equality of opportunity, and if anything they expand the opportunities available to the terminally ill. The terminally ill can be regarded as the least advantaged, and allowing purchases of life insurance policies can make them better off. From a deontological perspective, the purchases allow the terminally ill to better realize the worth of their liberty, and from a consequentialist perspective the terminally ill can attain better consequences. The difference principle is thus satisfied. Under Rawls's theory the purchase of life insurance policies by the terminally ill is just and would be allowed in a choice in the original position from behind a veil of ignorance.

[1] As in the analysis of living benefits from the perspective of Kantian rights, the person must be competent to make a free choice.

---

## Duty in Rawls's Theory

The assignment of duty in Rawls's theory of justice is part of the choice of political and social institutions based on the principles of justice. Duty may be assigned to government, individuals, firms, or other organizations. All have a duty to respect and promote the basic liberties identified by the principle of equal liberty. The duty to ensure fair equality of opportunity is generally assigned to government and employers. Offices and positions are to be open to all, and employers may be assigned the duty to ensure that their employment practices provide all individuals with the opportunity to qualify for positions. The duty can extend further by requiring employers to take positive measures to ensure that employees have the means to qualify for better positions.

The duty to attend to the interests of the least advantaged under the difference principle should be assigned so that incentives are not distorted to the point that they jeopardize capital formation, investment, and the creation of jobs. That is, in the terminology of economics, incentives should be preserved so that society remains on the

---

[23] Rawls's difference principle requires that the choice of institutions be Pareto optimal. That is, any choice of institutions that yields a point in the interior of the utility possibility set in Figure 20-7 can be improved to make both persons better off.

frontier of the utility possibility set in Figure 20-7. Thus, the party that is best positioned to attend to the interests of the least advantaged, and to do so efficiently, should be assigned the duty. That duty is often assigned to government when the means is a transfer of income to the least advantaged. Assigning the duty directly to individuals would violate the equal liberty principle, but individuals may through their voluntary choice contribute time and money to charitable and related activities. Firms as the property of owners may also contribute to such activities on the same grounds. Some duties to attend to the interests of the least advantaged are assigned to firms. For example, injured workers are compensated through the workers' compensation system funded by taxes on employers. The duty to respond to the interests of the least advantaged rests on government and the free consent of individuals. The example on clinical trials provides another case.

On some matters, such as opportunity in employment, the duty naturally falls to the employer. Similarly, the duty to assure fair equality of opportunity and nondiscrim-

---

**EXAMPLE**

## Clinical Trial Obligations

CV Therapeutics, a small biotechnology company, developed a new drug, ranolazine, for treating angina.[1] Because it has become increasingly difficult to recruit participants for clinical trials in the United States, pharmaceutical companies began conducting trials in Eastern Europe and Russia where people were eager for Western medicines. CV Technologies was completing its successful clinic trials in Russia, and CEO Dr. Louis G. Lange was concerned about whether the company had a continuing duty to those participants in the trials who had benefited from its drug. In the United States companies typically continued to provide a drug for clinical trial participants until it was approved by the FDA for marketing. Also, many pharmaceutical companies had compassionate-use programs that made life-prolonging drugs available in poor countries. Ranolazine did not prolong life but improved the quality of life. Making it available for sale in Russia did not make economic sense, since few patients could afford it and obtaining approval and setting up a sales force would be prohibitively expensive for a company that did not yet have a product on the market. Providing the drug

for free in a compassionate-use program would also be very expensive. CV Therapeutics would have to train doctors in the use of the drug, set up a distribution system, and monitor use for any adverse side effects.

From the perspective of Kantian rights and Nozick's system CV Therapeutics seems to have no duty to the clinical trial participants as long as they were not promised that the drug would be provided after the trial was completed. The participants voluntarily entered into the trials and thus had acted as ends and exercised their autonomy. Given the infrastructure cost, providing the drug would likely not be required based on utilitarianism. From the perspective of Rawls's system basic liberties and the fair equality of opportunity principles seem not to be violated by not providing the drug, so is there a duty to provide it stemming from the difference principle? The Russian participants suffering from angina are certainly less advantaged, but providing the drug could result in an outcome in the interior of the utility possibility set in Figure 20-7. The cost of conducting clinical trials would be increased substantially, thus reducing the incentives for pharmaceutical R&D, particularly for start-ups and small companies. In that case any duty to provide the drug seems to rest with the U.S. or Russian governments or with private aid organizations.

[1]This example is based on an article in *The New York Times*, March 5, 2004.

ination in housing rests with landlords. But the duty to provide Rawls's primary goods, such as a minimum standard of living, so that individuals have a fair opportunity to realize the worth of their liberty, is a collective responsibility. As such, the assignment rests primarily with government.

## Criticisms of Rawls's Theory

One form of criticism centers on whether all individuals in the original position would choose the same principles and, if so, whether they would choose Rawls's principles rather than some other principles.[24] For example, if the first principle is to take precedence over the second, then the "most extensive basic liberty compatible with similar liberty for others" could be viewed as implying the neoclassical liberalism principle of a minimal role for government. Rawls, however, concludes that the role of government is extensive.

Another criticism centers on Rawls's conclusion that in the original position, once liberties and equal opportunity have been assured, society would choose institutions that provide the maximum benefit to the least advantaged. Some critics have argued that this principle would not be chosen because the chance of any one person being the least disadvantaged is minuscule. Harsanyi (1982) argues that in the original position people would choose a principle corresponding to average rule utilitarianism, since that maximizes the expected well-being of each person when in the original position. Rawls's use of primary goods as a means of assessing the advantages of individuals is also subject to the same criticisms as are interpersonal comparisons of utility.

As with utilitarianism and rights theories, a conceptual and applied difficulty in justice theories pertains to how duty is to be assigned. The issues pertaining to basic liberties are similar to those previously addressed. The assignment of the burden of assuring fair equality of opportunity and improving the position of the least advantaged is similar to the assignment of duty considered in Chapter 19 in the context of utilitarianism. Affirmative action is an institution that addresses these principles.

Nozick argues that any response to the least advantaged rests with the free choice of individuals who may, if they so choose, contribute to the well-being of others. Private charity is one reflection of this principle.

Nozick (1974) observes that Rawls's theory pertains to a "time slice" in which the allocation of rewards and burdens of society must necessarily be judged by "end results" and independently of history. That is, to apply the difference principle, the positions of people must be evaluated at a point in time, and Rawls does not inquire into how people came to be in those positions. Nozick argues that how individuals arrived at their current positions is important from a moral perspective. For example, if an injustice were done to a person in the past, it would be necessary to examine the subsequent chain of events to determine what compensation, if any, was warranted. If people had made voluntary choices that worked to their disadvantage, however, is there any duty to compensate them?

Nozick also argues that Rawls's system of justice is necessarily patterned according to characteristics of individuals or their situations, as required in the application of the difference principle. Whatever form of patterning is used, Nozick argues, must interfere with basic liberties.[25] This, he argues, means that no action can satisfy both Rawls's equal liberty principle and the difference principle.

Although Rawls's theory has been criticized on a variety of dimensions, it remains an important philosophical work and provides a useful framework for reasoning about

---

[24]The same criticisms may be made about Kant's system. Brandt (1979) argues that individuals could choose a variety of different principles. Gauthier (1986) provides a moral theory that addresses the issue of compliance with the initial choice. Binmore (1994) provides a strategic theory with a framework similar to Rawls's.
[25]See Nozick, (1974, pp. 160–164).

managerial problems. His theory brings together several considerations, including liberties, opportunities, and well-being, that ethical intuition recognizes as important. It also provides a degree of prioritization that can be used in resolving conflicts. The chapter case, *Environmental Justice and Pollution Credits Trading Systems*, provides an opportunity to reason from Rawls's perspective about both managerial policies and one of society's institutions.

## Affirmative Action

Affirmative action is a conscious attempt to realize equal opportunity. It includes steps to remedy the effects of past discrimination and may involve preferential treatment for individuals in protected classes. The EEOC oversees affirmative action plans and issues guidelines for their design. Affirmative action requires that employers adopt recruiting policies that ensure that minorities and women are included in the pool of candidates and that all those who meet the qualifications, or are qualifiable, are given fair consideration. Over 10,000 firms, as well as universities and nonprofit organizations, are required to have quantitative affirmative action goals. Compliance may require changes in recruitment, hiring, or promotion policies, additional training programs, and the establishment of explicit goals. Affirmative action plans have been adopted more broadly than required by law and have become part of the social fabric of many companies.

Compensatory justice and fair equality of opportunity provide foundations for affirmative action. Compensatory justice is intended to compensate individuals for injustices and, in the context of affirmative action, applies to both individuals and protected classes. From this perspective, compensation for the actual victims of illegal discrimination is justified. Compensation may also be justified for classes, even though the individuals receiving the compensation have not themselves been the subjects of discrimination. The rationale for compensation for a class is that its members' "starting positions" have been adversely affected by past discrimination.[1] This is consistent with the principle of fair equality of opportunity, which holds that individuals are to have a fair chance to qualify for positions. If individuals are at a disadvantage because of their education, training, or other conditions important for qualification, justice considerations may call for providing them additional education or other means to pursue opportunities.

Affirmative action is not immune to criticism on ethics grounds. Criticism centers on who is to bear the burden of the compensation and how the opportunities of others are to be altered to provide opportunity to those who have been disadvantaged. One means of compensation that generates little opposition is providing additional education and training. Other means have resulted in reverse discrimination resulting from the preferential treatment given to others.[2] Section 703(j) of Title VII of the Civil Rights Act of 1964 states: "Nothing contained in this title shall be interpreted to require any employer . . . to grant preferential treatment to any individual or to any group because of race, color, religion, sex, or national origin . . ."

An important attribute of many of the affirmative action programs that have withstood court scrutiny is that they are voluntarily agreed to. The court, however, may block a program that constitutes a permanent obstacle or barrier to those bearing the burden of an affirmative action program. In *Regents of University of California v. Bakke*, 438 U.S. 265, the Supreme Court struck down a voluntary policy that established a quota for minority admissions to a medical school because it precluded the admission of a qualified white male. In contrast, in *United Steelworkers*

---

[1]Groarke (1990) offers a moral justification for compensation and restitution.

[2]See Newton (1990) and Wasserstrom (1978) for perspectives on this issue.

*(Continued)*

*(Continued)*

of *America v. Weber*, 443 U.S. 193 (1979), the court upheld a voluntary agreement between an employer and a union that established numerical goals for minority inclusion in a company training program. The court ruled that the agreement did not constitute discrimination against a white male with more seniority who was denied inclusion, since the goals were temporary and did not constitute an absolute barrier to his future inclusion in the program or to promotion.

In contrast to the language of Title VII, the federal government has had a variety of programs that explicitly took race or sex into account. These include minority preference programs for broadcasting licenses, small business loans, college scholarships, and highway construction and defense contracts.[3] For example, federal law specified that 10 percent of the contract dollars on federally aided road projects be set aside for minorities. In 1988 Congress included women under the same program. On federal highway contracts a company qualified as "disadvantaged" was given up to a 10 percent price advantage over other firms.[4] When Adarand Construction lost a contract to a minority-owned firm even though it had the lowest bid, it sued the federal government, arguing that its right to equal protection under the Fifth Amendment had been violated. In 1995 the Supreme Court, in *Adarand Constructors v. Peña*. 515 U.S. 200 (1995), held in favor of Adarand, thereby forcing changes in federal set-aside programs.[5]

The courts had upheld minority preference programs when they served a compelling interest. As an example of a compelling interest, the Supreme Court in *Metro Broadcasting v. F.C.C.*, 110 SCt 2997 (1990), upheld an FCC policy that gave preference to minorities seeking to acquire a broadcasting license. The Court held that the FCC policy was important to the interest of providing a diversity of viewpoints and programming on the airways.[6] In 1998, however, a federal appeals court held that the *Adarand* decision implied a higher standard of scrutiny and concluded that the FCC policy was important but not compelling. Although the FCC policy was invalidated, many broadcasters vowed to continue following the FCC guidelines.[7]

Colleges and universities have affirmative action programs for student admissions, and in two 2003 decisions involving the University of Michigan, the Supreme Court clarified the legality of those programs. Relying on the *Bakke* decision, the court upheld a program of the Michigan Law School that considered minority applicants on an "individualized" basis.[8] The court, however, declared unconstitutional the university's affirmative action program for undergraduate admissions. That program automatically awarded 20 points on a 150-point admissions scale to African-American, Hispanic, and Native American applicants. In a 6-to-3 decision the court held that the program was quota-like.[9]

Although court scrutiny of government affirmative action and preference programs continues, the affirmative action programs of most companies are likely to remain intact since they are by now a part of the fabric of those companies. The objectives of many of those programs are as yet unrealized, however.

In addition to issues pertaining to employees, affirmative action may be extended to other constituencies. Many firms have a considerable underrepresentation of minorities and women among their distributors, franchisees, and agents, and civil rights advocates have worked to extend affirmative action goals to these positions.

---

[3]See Lodge (1990, pp. 409–421) for a description of a minority procurement program.
[4]That is, if a non-disadvantaged firm bids $100 on a contract and a disadvantaged firm bids $109, the contract is awarded to the disadvantaged firm at the bid of $109.
[5]In 2003 the Supreme Court refused to hear an appeal of lower court decision upholding a Denver city ordinance requiring a prime contractor to explain why a minority subcontractor was not selected when it had made the lowest bid.

[6]See Spitzer (1991) for an analysis of the justifications for minority preference in broadcasting. In 1992 the U.S. Court of Appeals ruled that the FCC policy giving preference to women constituted illegal discrimination against men.
[7]In 1995 Congress repealed a law that gave preference to broadcasters that sold a station to a minority-owned firm.
[8]*Gruter v. Bollinger*, 539 U.S. 982, 124 S.Ct. 35.
[9]*Gratz v. Bollinger*, 539 U.S. 244, 123 S.Ct. 2411.

## Applying the Principles of Justice

Although Rawls's system of justice is as much a political as a moral philosophy and is thus directed at the design of institutions more than at the evaluation of actions, it provides a set of considerations helpful to managers who must establish policies. Company policies are the managerial analogues of Rawls's institutions.

Because of its close relationship to Kantian rights, the application of Rawls's principle of equal liberty involves the same considerations found in rights analysis. This section thus focuses on fair equality of opportunity and the difference principle.

The principle of fair equality of opportunity is most directly applicable to policies associated with the employment relationship. As considered earlier in the chapter, Title VII of the Civil Rights Act of 1964 provides for equal opportunity by prohibiting discrimination in employment. Rawls's principle, however, goes beyond the prohibition of discrimination and requires the "fair equality" of opportunity. Fair equality requires not only that positions be open to all, but that individuals have the means to attempt to qualify for them. Justice Marshall's arguments in the *Kadrmas* case are consistent with this principle. Affirmative action programs may be viewed as one application of this principle.

The difference principle is applicable once liberties and fair equality of opportunity have been assured. That principle calls for affirmative consideration of those who are the least advantaged or who would be put in such a position by policies or actions. As Rawls argues, the position of the least-advantaged person is closely linked to the positions of other less-advantaged persons. Consequently, responding to the situation of the least-advantaged person affects many less-advantaged persons. The difference principle provides a justification, for example, for special programs that make facilities accessible to the disabled and provide opportunities for disadvantaged youths. It also provides a justification for policies that respond to the needs of laid-off employees and the communities in which they live.

The methodology for applying Rawls's framework involves the elimination of policy alternatives by using first the equal liberty principle and then the fair equality of opportunity principle. The remaining alternatives are then evaluated for fairness, and the choice among those remaining alternatives is based on the difference principle. The methodology may be summarized as follows:

1. Identify the liberties and rights involved.
2. The principle of equal liberty: Evaluate alternative policies in terms of how extensive are the corresponding liberties and rights of individuals consistent with equal liberties and rights for all. Prioritize rights and liberties when conflicts arise. Eliminate alternatives that limit liberties for reasons other than assuring other liberties and rights.
3. The principle of fair equality of opportunity: Identify the opportunities associated with each remaining alternative, and evaluate those alternatives in terms of how extensive are the corresponding opportunities. Eliminate alternatives that unnecessarily limit opportunities.
4. For the remaining alternatives, evaluate their fairness implications for the pursuit of opportunities by those affected.
5. Choose among the remaining policies based on the difference principle by favoring policies that benefit the least advantaged even if those policies reduce aggregate well-being.
6. Identify which parties have which duties.

In this methodology a departure from equal liberty cannot be justified by greater advantage in social or economic matters for any individual. The two examples illustrate the analysis.

## Integrity Tests

Much of the rights analysis of integrity tests presented earlier in the chapter is relevant from the perspective of justice as well, so the focus here is on the difference principle and fair equality of opportunity. One concern with an integrity test is whether it puts those who are already disadvantaged at a further disadvantage. If they are already disadvantaged for a reason that would be revealed by the integrity test and would result in a "failure" on the test, an objection on justice grounds could be raised if the reason were not relevant to the job. Similarly, if the test systematically affects the opportunities of individuals with particular attributes that are irrelevant to job performance, the test would be unjust. Such concerns are reflected in laws in a number of states that prohibit employers from inquiring about criminal records of job applicants or about their lifestyles.

The more compelling are the firm's interests and the more important are the tested traits for a particular position, however, the more likely the tests are justified. Justice principles require that the tests not adversely affect individuals on irrelevant grounds, but otherwise the tests may be used if they enable the firm to improve its performance; that is, to stay on the frontier in Figure 20-7.

## Life Insurance Screening for Preexisting Conditions

If screening for preexisting conditions for life insurance purposes is not a violation of the principle of equal liberty or the principle of fair equality of opportunity, it may conflict with the difference principle. Treatment of diseases such as AIDS can be very expensive, and to the extent that the cost is borne by the victim and the victim's family it can represent a heavy and in many cases insurmountable burden. To the extent that the cost of treatment substantially disadvantages some persons, the difference principle requires that institutions be designed to relieve at least some of that burden. Rawls then asks to which institution the duty should be assigned. The institution of life insurance seems less appropriate than the use of public funds, since adverse selection by those with preexisting conditions could substantially reduce the efficiency of the life insurance system. Screening for preexisting conditions thus seems consistent with Rawls's system.

# Higher Order Standards for Evaluating Ethics Systems

The ethics systems based on utilitarian, rights, and justice considerations use two general standards for determining which principles or rules have moral standing. The first is universalizability (which implies reversibility). A principle or rule has moral standing if one would be willing to have everyone, including oneself, behave in accord with it. This standard, however, does not necessarily imply that everyone would choose the same set of principles or rules. The second standard is unanimous impartial choice as in Rawls's original position. The notion of reasoning about principles from the original position is important because ethics principles are to be impartial and not based on the actual position a person occupies in society.

Rule utilitarianism and the rules derived from it have moral standing because each individual chooses a rule to be followed by everyone and, since each individual is maximizing aggregate well-being, everyone would choose the same rule. That is, the principle of maximizing aggregate well-being is universalizable, since one would will that everyone abide by it. The principle also would be chosen unanimously from the original position, since everyone would choose the rule that yields the greatest well-being.

Rawls's principles of equal liberty and fair equality of opportunity meet both the standards of universalizability and unanimous choice from the original position. Rawls's difference principle might meet the first standard, since some individuals could be willing to have everyone abide by it. It is not at all clear, however, that from the original position, everyone would choose the difference principle and not some other principle such as the utilitarian principle of maximizing aggregate well-being.

Kantian maxims meet both standards. The categorical imperative implies that maxims will be universal. The view that every individual is rational and deduces maxims from a conception of freedom and autonomy that resides in everyone means that each will choose the same rule, so unanimity results. Kant's view of rationality and a common conception of freedom and autonomy serve as the original position, so reasoning and choice are impartial.

In business applications these two higher order standards provide a basis for evaluating alternative policies and provide guidelines for managers to follow in nonmarket analysis and strategy formulation. These standards are used in Chapter 21 to evaluate the principles developed by Levi Strauss & Co. and Cummins Engine to guide their managers.

## Summary

Rights and justice are important concepts and correspond to fundamental ethical intuitions. Rights may be classified as intrinsic or instrumental. Intrinsic rights are justified independently of consequences by their consistency with conceptions of liberty and autonomy. Instrumental rights have moral standing because they lead to higher levels of well-being. Instrumental rights are an important component of teleological systems, which judge the good in terms of consequences. Intrinsic rights are a central component of deontological systems, which are based on considerations other than, or in addition to, consequences.

Kant's theory of moral rules is based on the categorical imperative, which holds that individuals are to be treated always as autonomous ends and never solely as means, and that rules of behavior are to be universal. Moral rules identify intrinsic rights of individuals and the corresponding duty to respect those rights. Intrinsic rights take precedence over considerations of well-being, but the ethical intuition that well-being is important remains strong.

Justice theories add an explicit comparative dimension to deontological systems. The three principal categories of justice theories are distributive, compensatory, and retributive. Distributive theories focus on the distribution of the rewards and burdens of social interactions. Compensatory theories are concerned with compensating for injustice. Retributive theories focus on punishment for moral wrongs. An injustice is a moral violation and is to be tolerated only if it is necessary to avoid a greater injustice.

Rawls provides a theory of justice as fairness that incorporates the Kantian framework and focuses on liberties, rights, and the comparative treatment of individuals. Rawls's theory prescribes that individuals are to be treated equally with respect to basic liberties but that individuals may be treated unequally in terms of rewards and burdens as long as the inequality satisfies conditions of fairness as embodied in the difference principle and in the principle of fair equality of opportunity. Rawls argues that liberties have first priority, and when they are assured, the provision of fair equality of opportunity is required. The difference principle, which requires that institutions and policies be designed to benefit the least-advantaged person, is then applied.

Higher order standards are used to evaluate ethics systems and principles. One such standard is universalizability, which requires that an individual would will that everyone follow the rule or abide by the principle. The second standard is unanimity, which requires that everyone would impartially choose the same rule or principle. Reasoning about which rules and principles would be unanimously supported is intended to be based on Kant's conceptions of autonomy, freedom, and rationality and is to take place impartially as if from the original position.

Managers must make decisions in situations in which there are competing moral claims that require judgments about the effects of decisions on individuals, their rights, and their well-being. An understanding of ethics systems and a sensitivity to the moral dimensions of issues are important for managers for several reasons. First, sensitivity to the ethics dimensions of issues and the use of ethics frameworks can help managers avoid wrongs that may otherwise result from a narrow focus on the firm's interests. Second, sensitivity to the moral concerns that others may have about the policies and practices of the firm can help management anticipate nonmarket actions and pressures. Third, managers will be more likely to make decisions that serve the long-run interests of society and ultimately of business itself. Fourth, the content of corporate social responsibility is found in ethics principles, as considered in the next chapter.

# Genetic Testing in the Workplace

Companies and their employees have an important interest in reducing health risks in the workplace. One approach to doing so is to alter production processes and the workplace to reduce hazards. For some companies, this is quite expensive, and in some work situations it is impossible to eliminate all health risks. Another approach is to choose the workforce to minimize the risk. This may be done through evaluating workers' qualifications and experience and through subsequent training. It may also be done by determining workers' susceptibility to certain diseases that could result from exposure in the workplace. Genetic testing is one means of determining susceptibility to certain hazards and can be done from a sample of blood or other bodily fluid. Such tests are generally accurate. Although they can be expensive, they offer a basis on which to select and assign workers to minimize the risks from exposure to certain health hazards and the possible tragedy of chronic or terminal diseases.

One genetic test is for G-6-PD (glucose-6-phosphate dehydrogenase) deficiency. G-6-PD is an enzyme required for the stability of red blood cells. "Those with the deficiency are highly susceptible to having their red-blood-cell membranes destroyed by certain drugs or other oxidizing agents. It is especially a problem for blacks and some Mediterranean people."[26] The G-6-PD deficiency is carried by a sex-linked recessive gene, and approximately 100 million males worldwide are estimated to have the deficiency.

Another genetic test is for alpha-1-antitrypsin (AAT) deficiency, which results in susceptibility to respiratory irritants such as those found in many workplaces. Treatment of the deficiency involves intravenous injections of AAT on a frequent basis.

Genetic testing can be used for either screening or monitoring purposes. In screening, genetic testing is used to select among job applicants for positions that may involve a potential health hazard. Screening can also be used in assigning current employees to jobs so as to minimize risks. Genetic testing can also be used to identify susceptible individuals who can take precautions to protect themselves or be moved to other jobs with less exposure to possible irritants such as oxidizing agents.

Genetic testing can also be used to monitor groups of employees over time to determine if they experience chromosome damage due to exposure in the workplace. This could be important for employees who work with lead, beryllium, and other potentially toxic metals and chemicals. In addition to providing information that could be used to reduce risks, some companies believe that genetic testing could give them a degree of protection from liability if a worker chose to stay in a job after being notified that he or she was genetically susceptible to a disease that could be triggered by exposure in the workplace.

With the advances in genetic mapping achieved by the Human Genome Project the possibilities for more accurate and extensive genetic testing in the workplace were seemingly unlimited. ■

SOURCE: Copyright © 1998 by the Board of Trustees of the Leland Stanford Junior University. All rights reserved. Reprinted with permission.

---

[26]*The Wall Street Journal*, February 24, 1986.

## PREPARATION QUESTIONS

1. Is genetic testing in the workplace warranted from a utilitarian perspective; that is, by the potential benefits it can yield? What ethics concerns does it involve?

2. Consider the use of genetic testing for screening job applicants, for assigning current employees to jobs, and for monitoring employees for genetic damage from exposure in the workplace. Which rights might be said to be violated by either the use or the prohibition of the use of genetic testing for these purposes? How would you prioritize those rights?

3. Is there a risk that an individual found to have a genetic deficiency might be subject to unfair discrimination? Who should be informed of the results of a genetic test? Is the use of genetic testing for monitoring more or less appropriate than its use for screening purposes?

4. Prepare a rights table as in Figure 20-5.

5. Organized labor and some activists oppose genetic testing on the grounds that the employer should ensure a safe workplace. Does an employer have a moral duty to reduce risks in the workplace to the point at which any qualified person regardless of his or her susceptibility can safely occupy the position?

6. If an employee with full understanding of his or her genetic susceptibility chooses (because, for example, of higher pay) to work in an area in which exposure is possible, should the employer assign the employee to that job?

7. Should there be a rule prohibiting the use of genetic information in determining eligibility for insurance or for setting premiums? Does basing insurance decisions on genetic characteristics differ from basing insurance decisions on preexisting health conditions?

8. Consider the case of a company with a production process that requires the processing of a metal, such as beryllium, that can be toxic to workers with a particular genetic deficiency. The company has installed dust collection and ventilation equipment, and the workplace meets all government safety requirements by a substantial margin. Nevertheless, an individual with a particular genetic deficiency can develop chronic and serious long-term illnesses from exposure to the metal. At an annualized cost of $1 million the company could install additional equipment that would reduce by half the risk to an employee with the genetic deficiency, but illness could still occur. For jobs in the metals processing unit, the company could also screen job applicants for the genetic deficiency and not hire those who have the deficiency. The cost of the screening would be approximately 10 percent of the cost of the additional equipment and would reduce the risk of disease by 90 percent. The company also has the alternative of replacing 80 percent of the workers in the metals processing unit with sophisticated and expensive robotic equipment at a net annualized cost of $3 million (net of the savings in labor costs). This would result in the layoff of 48 employees. What should the company do?

# Environmental Justice and Pollution Credits Trading Systems

As executive vice president for West Coast operations of Westco Oil Company, Jeremy Bentley was proud of the environmental accomplishments of his company in California. Emissions at the company's Long Beach refinery had been reduced, and oil spills at its marine terminal in El Segundo had been reduced dramatically.

Jeremy was aware of the Environmental Protection Agency's environmental justice campaign and supported its concern about the siting of facilities, such as hazardous waste disposal sites, in areas in which minorities and the poor were overrepresented. He was shocked, however, when Westco was confronted by the environmental justice movement. Not only were the arguments made by the activists novel, but they struck at the heart of the evolving system of air pollution control being implemented in the Los Angeles area and elsewhere in the United States. That system emphasized attaining environmental goals using the least costly means of abatement. Attaining the goals at least cost to society required greater reductions in emissions at facilities with low costs of abatement and smaller reductions at facilities with high costs of abatement.

To implement this system the South Coast Air Quality Management District (AQMD) had established a pollution credits trading program that allowed abaters to earn credits for emissions reductions and sell those credits to emitters of pollution that had high costs of abatement. The trading of credits reduced the aggregate costs of attaining environmental goals, and the AQMD had supported the development of markets in credits. Under one program approved by the AQMD, automobile scrap yards bought old, high-pollution automobiles for $600 to $700 and received a credit that they could sell either to the AQMD, a company such as Westco, or an environmental group. If a company purchased a credit, it would not have to reduce its emissions by as much as it would otherwise have to reduce them. Under Jeremy's leadership Westco had participated in the AQMD program and purchased credits that it used at its marine terminal. Jeremy had also purchased credits through other programs and used those credits at its Long Beach refinery.

Environmental justice and pollution credits trading systems collided in July 1997 in Southern California as environmental groups and advocates for low-income groups, led by the interest group Communities for a Better Environment, filed lawsuits seeking to force the EPA to rescind the authority granted to the AQMD and the California Air Resources Board to operate a pollution credits trading system. One focus of the lawsuits was the pollution credits trading system and the purchase and scrapping of old, high-pollution automobiles. One lawsuit filed by Communities for a Better Environment against five oil companies including Westco alleged that residents in San Pedro and El Segundo had been exposed to harmful hydrocarbon emissions because the companies violated the federal Clean Air Act by failing to reduce emissions at their marine terminals. Instead, the companies had earned pollution credits by purchasing and scrapping 7,400 old cars as allowed under the AQMD program. Westco had been one of the leading purchasers of the credits.

Unocal, which had initiated the program to purchase and scrap high-pollution cars, operated a subsidiary, Eco-Scrap, that purchased old cars for companies that wanted to earn pollution credits.

Spokesman Barry Lane said, "We still believe that the emission control program is of great value, it makes good sense."[27]

In another lawsuit, the Center on Race, Poverty and the Environment and the National Association for the Advancement of Colored People joined Communities for a Better Environment in alleging that the pollution credits trading system violated the civil rights of minorities by subjecting communities in which they were disproportionately represented to high levels of health-threatening pollutants. The lawsuit cited Title VI of the Civil Rights Act of 1964, which prohibits discrimination, such as against minorities and women, in programs and activities receiving federal funds.

In conjunction with the filing of the lawsuits, the activist and advocacy groups held a press conference at which local residents told of the harmful effects of the pollutants. Fifth-grader Laurie Johnson, who was on medical leave from Wilmington Park Elementary School, reported that she and other children at the school had health problems attributable to the emissions. She said, "It's time for our corporate neighbors to be responsible and give us a hand."[28] Sixty-nine year-old Lily Camarillo, who lived near a Texaco refinery, said, "I've raised several kids there, lost three others and you wouldn't believe the problems we've had. Headaches, sick stomachs; my daughter has leukemia."[29]

Richard Drury, attorney for Communities for a Better Environment, turned the pollution credits trading system principle on its head by arguing that it exposed residents to the equivalent of "thousands of cars idling at each marine terminal." He also said, "It's a good thing to get old cars off the road; they cause a lot of pollution. But you don't trade the health of workers and the residents who live near those facilities in exchange for that."[30] Later on CNN he said, "If you have enough money, you can buy enough pollution credits and pump out as much pollution as you want to. That's going to create toxic hot spots."[31]

AQMD spokesman Tom Eichorn stated, "These people think they're being affected by air pollution problems . . . our job is to respond to their

[27] *Los Angeles Times,* July 23, 1997.
[28] Copley News Service, July 23, 1997.
[29] Copley News Service, July 23, 1997.
[30] *All Things Considered,* National Public Radio, July 24, 1997.
[31] *CNN Today,* August 1, 1997.

32 Copley News Service, July 23, 1997.
33 CNN Today, August 1, 1997.
34 Los Angeles Times, July 23, 1997.

complaints." But he added that the agency did not believe that emissions were higher than before the pollution credits trading system was instituted.32 Barry Wallerstein of the AQMD said, "The preliminary analysis by our legal department indicates that we're in full compliance with federal law."33 "James Lents, the AQMD's outgoing executive officer, said he believes that the agency is not violating civil rights because toxic hot spots around industries are reduced under a separate rule, which prohibits fumes that pose a risk exceeding 100 cases of cancer among every million people exposed. However, that standard is less stringent than environmentalists and some health officials have wanted. AQMD board members, skeptical of the cancer danger posed by the [hydrocarbon] fumes, set the scaled-back standard in 1994."34

## Environmental Justice

The environmental justice movement began with concerns raised by activists that the poor and minorities were disproportionately affected by pollution. Since housing prices were naturally lower near industrial areas, low-income individuals tended to disproportionately locate in those areas. Concern for their well-being centered not only on issues of poverty and opportunity but also on the effects of pollution on their health. In 1992 the EPA issued a report raising the environmental justice issue. When President Clinton appointed Carol Browner, an environmentalist who had worked for Vice President Al Gore, she initiated an environmental justice program. In 1994 President Clinton issued an executive order directing federal agencies to ensure that public health and environmental programs were nondis-

Faced with moral accusations, lawsuits, and community pressure, Jeremy had to decide what to do. First he wanted to evaluate the moral claims being made by the activists and residents. Then, he would have to assess whether their claims, if morally supported, warranted a change in Westco's environmental protection programs. Jeremy also wondered whether he should meet with the residents or the activists to see if there was common ground from which they could work to resolve the issues.

criminatory and provided environmental justice. The president referred to Title VI of the Civil Rights Act in his order.

Many environmental interest groups and activists opposed the use of pollution credits trading systems. Some were suspicious of using incentive systems to control a social bad such as pollution. Some preferred uniform command-and-control regulations that forced a direct abatement requirement on all pollution sources and hence would result in a similar reduction in pollution in every locale rather than different levels of abatement across locales, depending on where the pollution credits were used. More fundamentally, however, most of the activists preferred lower emissions than allowed by legislation and EPA regulations.

As some commentators observed, with the mainstream environmental groups "under the thumb of Vice President Al Gore, their political patron," the cause of environmental justice has been led by some of the smaller and newer environmental interest groups.35 In the 1990s those groups emphasized the twin themes of health, particularly for those at risk, and of environmental justice. These groups argued that pollution control policies should take into account the special interests of low-income people who disproportionately live and work in areas of high pollution. President Clinton and Vice President Gore embraced both the concept of environmental justice and the use of pollution credits trading systems.

In 1997 the U.S. Court of Appeals gave individuals the right to challenge state environmental permits on the grounds of a disparate effect on low-income and minority groups. The Supreme Court, however, chose to review the decision.

As the EPA began its implementation planning, the environmental justice movement met with increasing opposition as business groups and members of Congress became concerned about the objectives of the movement and the consequences of such a policy. The U.S. Chamber of Commerce and the National Black Chamber of Commerce led a campaign to revoke the EPA's environmental justice program.36 "We fully support the U.S. Chamber's efforts to repeal the EPA's misguided policy," Black

35 *In These Times*, July 28, 1997.
36 The National Black Chamber of Commerce had 180 chapters representing 62,000 black-owned businesses.

Chamber President Harry Alford said. "This represents the beginning of a close working relationship between the U.S. Chamber and our organization to support black businesses around the country."[37] "It's an economics problem; it isn't race," Alford said. "If you're going to dump trash, you're going to dump it on land that's cheap. We feel the EPA is exploiting the Civil Rights Act and exploiting the black communities in an attempt to gather a vocal constituency in its ever-growing fight against big business."[38]

Alford was particularly concerned that the policy would drive jobs away from the areas in which minorities live. He pointed to the case of a permit sought by Shintech, a Japanese-owned company, to build a $700 million polyvinyl chloride plant in Louisiana's St. James Parish. Local activists had protested the plant, even though it would bring badly needed jobs to the parish.

Alford and others also argued that the EPA's environmental justice program would hinder attempts by cities to attract businesses to so-called "brownfields," some half million abandoned industrial sites, most of which were located in inner city areas. The U.S. Conference of Mayors spoke out against the EPA's environmental justice program, urging the EPA to develop a new policy that would encourage rather than hinder brownfield developments.

Congress also took an interest in the EPA program. The House Appropriations Committee inserted language in the EPA's fiscal 1999 appropriation barring it from taking any new civil rights actions under the program. The House Commerce Committee launched an investigation of the EPA's environmental justice program.

In a challenge to President Clinton, Carlos Porras, director of Communities for a Better Environment for Southern California, said. "[Environmental justice] is a defining issue for the president's administration. This has national significance and we're very interested to see where the Clinton administration draws the line."[39]

## Pollution Credits Trading Systems

For decades economists and business leaders had advocated the use of pollution credits trading systems to achieve environmental objectives at the least cost to society. Pollution credits trading systems had been implemented in the Midwest and Northeast for sulfur dioxide and nitrogen oxides, and several systems were in place in Southern California to control a number of pollutants. Many other states were considering using similar systems, and with the recent promulgation of costly new federal regulations regarding microscopic airborne particulates, additional states and regions were expected to consider these systems.

To illustrate the difference between pollution credits trading systems and the traditional command-and-control approach, consider an environmental objective of reducing emissions of hydrocarbons by 50 percent in the oil industry in the Los Angeles basin. Under a command-and-control system all pollution sources would be required to reduce their emissions by 50 percent. In a pollution credits trading system the 50 percent reduction would be achieved by requiring a source to hold a permit for each pound of hydrocarbons emitted. Permits would be issued equal to 50 percent of the pre-reduction emissions. For example, one permit could be issued for each pound of hydrocarbon emissions allowed with the permits allocated among the emitters according to some baseline such as their pre-reduction emissions. Then, an emitter with low costs of abatement that reduced its emissions below the number of permits it was allocated could sell its excess permits, or credits, to an emitter with high costs of abatement, which would reduce its emissions by less than 50 percent. Thus, low-cost abaters would reduce their emissions by more than high-cost abaters, allowing the environmental objective to be achieved at the lowest total cost. In characterizing pollution credits trading systems, David Roe, a senior attorney for Environmental Defense, said, "What this allows for the first time is that companies that have the technical ability to go beyond the law in reducing their emissions have a reason to do it."[40]

As an example, consider a region with three pollution sources $a$, $b$, and $c$ in locations $A$, $B$, and $C$, respectively. Suppose the sources each have been emitting 200 pounds of hydrocarbons and that the new environmental objective is to cut emissions by 50 percent to 300 pounds in total. Also assume that each source is allocated 100 permits. Suppose that

[37] *Washington Times*, July 20, 1998.
[38] *The National Journal*, July 11, 1998.
[39] *Los Angeles Times*, July 23, 1997.
[40] *The Wall Street Journal*, July 24, 1997.

**TABLE 20-2**

| Pounds Abated | Costs of Abatement by Source ($) | | |
|---|---|---|---|
| | *a* | *b* | *c* |
| 100 | 10 | 15 | 20 |
| 200 | 20 | 30 | 35 |

the costs of abatement for each source are as given in Table 20-2.

For example, if source *a* were to abate 100 pounds, its cost would be $10, and if it were to abate 200 pounds, the cost would be $20. The corresponding costs for source *c* are $20 and $35, respectively. If under a command-and-control system each source were to reduce its emissions by 100 pounds, the total cost of the 300 pounds of abatement would be $10 + 15 + 20 = $45.

The environmental objective of a 300-pound reduction can, however, be attained for $35 if *a* reduced its emissions by 200 pounds (at a cost of $20) and *b* reduced its emissions by 100 pounds (at a cost of $15). Source *a* would then have zero emissions, *b* would have emissions of 100, and *c* would have emissions of 200.

For this outcome to be realized, source *c* must purchase 100 credits. By purchasing the 100 credits, *c* would avoid the abatement cost of $20 that it would incur if it were to abate 100 pounds. By reducing its emissions by 200 rather than 100 pounds, *a* incurs a cost of only $10. Since *c* is willing

to pay up to $20 for 100 credits and *a* requires only $10 of compensation to reduce its emissions from 100 to 0 pounds, the two sources can reach an agreement. Thus, source *a* reduces its emissions by 200 pounds, source *b* reduces its emissions by 100 pounds, and source *c* purchases 100 credits from *a* rather than reducing its emissions. The equilibrium price for a credit is $15, since if *a* were to attempt to sell credits for more than $15, *b* would offer to sell credits for slightly less. Then, the competition between *a* and *b* would drive the price down to $15. Similarly, if the price were less than $15, *b* would offer to buy credits from *a*. Then *b* and *c* would compete for the credits, driving the price up to $15. The distribution of the cost of achieving the environmental objective with a price of $15 is then $5, $15, and $15, respectively, for sources *a*, *b*, and *c*.

In designing a pollution credits trading system, an important factor is the geographic region the system covers. The basic principle is that the region include those affected by the emissions, as in the Los Angeles basin. Then, the focus is on the aggregate reduction in emissions in that region rather than in specific locations. In the example, a reduction of 200 pounds was achieved by source *a* and 100 pounds at *b*. This result can also be stated in terms of the remaining emissions, which are 0, 100, and 200 pounds in locations A, B, and C, respectively. ∎

SOURCE: This case was written by Professor David P. Baron. Copyright © 1998 by the Board of Trustees of the Leland Stanford Junior University. All rights reserved. Reprinted with permission.

## PREPARATION QUESTIONS

1. Evaluate a pollution credits trading system from the perspective of utilitarianism.
2. Are the claims of the neighbors and activist groups actually claims about a Kantian right to have one's health protected from pollution?
3. Compare command-and-control and pollution credits trading approaches in terms of Nozick's imperative of free consent.
4. Evaluate the claims of the activist and advocacy groups based on Rawls's principles of justice. Is the AQMD's "separate rule" for hot

spots an appropriate response to justice concerns?
5. Do oil companies have a duty to reduce their emissions at their marine terminals and refineries rather than purchasing credits, even though doing so would reduce the efficiency of the pollution credits trading system?
6. What should Jeremy Bentley do and why? Should he voluntarily stop purchasing credits? Should he meet with the residents and activists?

# RFID Tags

Radio frequency identification (RFID) technology had been around for a long time, but recent advances in manufacturing reduced the unit cost by nearly 10 times and made it feasible to tag individual items. RFID tags could be used to track pallets, products, animals, and nearly anything imaginable. In a contract for up to 500 million RFID tags, Gillette was believed to have paid less than 10 cents a tag, although costs typically were 20 to 50 cents. The technology involved combining a small antenna with a computer chip with a unique ID number. When the item to which the tag was attached passed within 10 to 30 feet, the electromagnetic waves from a radio-frequency reader generated an electrical current that powered the transmitter and energized the tag. The tag then broadcasted information, such as item number, product description, and distribution history, to the reader, which transmitted it to a computer system. The tags could receive data, allowing the information to be updated. Because radio technology was used, no line of sight was required, and compared to barcodes, no human intervention was required to obtain the information.

RFID technology had been used for high-value activities such as inventory tracking, and Texas Instruments estimated that 40 to 50 million animals had been implanted with RFID tags. The tags were put in the shoes of marathon runners to time when they crossed the finish line, and the U.S. Navy incorporated them into the wristbands used on injured soldiers and sailors in the Iraq war to identify them and their conditions. ExxonMobil used the tags in its SpeedPass wireless payment system. Highway systems used RFID technology in fast lanes to determine billing when participants passed through a toll booth. The State of Virginia's Smart Tag system had the name, address, credit card number, driver's license number, and vehicle license number of every participant and recorded the day, time, and location of use of the tag. Applied Digital Solutions received Food and Drug Administration approval for ID chips that could be implanted under a person's skin and could be read with a handheld device. The implants could be used to identify an accident victim and retrieve his medical records.

Miniaturization and breakthroughs in production methods resulted in RFID tags smaller than a grain of rice, and some commentators predicted that the tags could be produced for 5 cents or less. Wal-Mart required its 100 largest suppliers to begin using RFID tags by January 2005 and not to pass on any costs. The European Monetary System was considering putting RFID tags in currency to reduce counterfeiting.

The cost reductions and innovations in applying the technology allowed manufacturers and retailers to improve the tracking of goods at the retail level. Researchers at the AutoID Center affiliated with the Massachusetts Institute of Technology developed "smart shelves" that could provide information to a retailer or manufacturer about how many items were on the shelf. The shelves could also provide site-of-purchase information and advertisements to shoppers. The Center was developing an electronic product code network (EPC™ Network) to provide open-source technology to developers and users. The ultimate objective of the Center was to develop an "Internet of Things."

The principal applications of the technology were expected to be in replacing barcodes and security devices on products and reducing theft and counterfeiting. The tags could be put on high-value items that were openly displayed without fear of theft. The primary markets for retail applications for RFID tags were expected to be in the European Union and the United States. The German retailer Metro had opened a demonstration store of the future that relied on RFID technology.

In one application Gillette planned to use the tags on products to deter shoplifting. If a customer picked up more than three packs of razor blades, a camera would take his picture. Another application was to use the tags to provide data on a consumer's habits and behavior by, for example, placing readers in store doors. The AutoID Center provided an Internet video displaying this application.

The AutoID Center illustrated another application for the tags. On a page titled "Managing Returns," an illustration stated, "Employees can scan an item to see if a returned item came from their store, when it was sold, what it sold for at the time or if it was stolen. No receipt is necessary."[41] The tags could also be used in product recalls by allowing manufacturers to identify the exact items in the lot of concern.

Benetton placed an order for 15 million RFID tags and planned to put RFID tags in the labels of sweaters. The tags could be used not only for check out but also to determine when a person wearing a Benetton garment entered the store. The store then could give special attention to repeat customers. In principle, shopping centers could place RFID readers in doorways and record the shopping patterns of people who purchased a tagged product. This could provide valuable information for store placement, promotions, and service configurations. The tags could also be used for post-sales support and other follow-up activity. Grover Ferguson of Accenture, Ltd., said, "When applied to business, they let us see the product at all times, from manufacturing through logistics to post-sales support."[42]

In an article on RFID tags *Forbes* began, "Stores have eyes. Now they're getting ears and brains. Soon tiny wireless chips stuck on shampoo bottles and jeans will track all that you wear and buy."[43] When RFID tags appeared at the retail level, privacy activists reacted. Katherine Albrecht of Caspian (Consumers Against Supermarket Privacy Invasion and Numbering) criticized the applications and said Benetton was creating "spy clothes." Caspian used the Internet to encourage a boycott of Benetton. Wayne Madsen of the Electronic Privacy Information Center (EPIC) warned of privacy invasion, and said, "There really needs to be legislation if companies are doing this. They say it's for internal

use. But what would prevent them from sharing it with third parties, with the government or criminal investigators?"[44] Benetton quickly rescinded its plan to put RFID tags in clothing but planned to use the tags in inventory tracking.

The State of Virginia provided its Smart Tag information to law enforcement officials and in response to court orders. The state had received requests to use the information from direct marketers, credit-collection companies, and estranged spouses.

Joe Tobolski of Accenture's silent commerce research center said, "Somebody with a decoder could sidle up and tell everybody where you buy your clothes." "Even worse, he says, rival retailers or crooks might stand outside with a reader and scan purchases as shoppers leave stores. The rival could use those data as market research, and the crook might be looking to swipe a high-end product."[45] In response to such complaints, Phillips, the supplier of Benetton, announced plans to put a kill feature in its tags.

Bobo Ischebeck of the Secure Mobile Solutions business group said, "Privacy is already challenged everywhere—with video surveillance cameras, mobile phones, GPS and credit cards. This [RFID issue] will go away very quickly." He warned, however, "Just because an engineer said he has just deactivated your RFID tag, would you believe him? I wouldn't trust an engineer, because there is no way to prove it. Trust no one."[46] Paula Rosenblum, an analyst with AMR, said, "The privacy issues loom large, but RFID will take a lot of cost and time out of the supply chain."[47] ∎

## PREPARATION QUESTIONS

1. Are the privacy claims about instrumental or intrinsic rights?
2. How serious are the privacy concerns associated with RFID tags? Are the objections raised mainly by people imagining the worst?
3. From a utilitarian perspective do the benefits of smart tags outweigh the privacy concerns?
4. What should the manufacturers and users of the tags do about the privacy concerns?
5. Should Benetton have rescinded its plans to put RFID tags in its clothing?

[41]The Auto-ID Center, "The ETC™ Network in the Retail Store."
[42]*Investor's Business Daily*, March 13, 2003.
[43]*Forbes*, March 18, 2002.

[44]Associated Press Worldstream, March 11, 2003.
[45]*Investor's Business Daily*, March 13, 2003.
[46]*Electronic Engineering Times*, April 28, 2003.
[47]*Investor's Business Daily*, March 13, 2003.

# CHAPTER 21

# Implementing Ethics Systems

## Introduction

Corporate statements of social responsibility and codes of ethics have become commonplace. In addition, many companies have established the position of ethics officer, and membership in the Ethics Officer Association increased from 12 in 1992 to 1,000 in 2004, including more than half of the *Fortune* 100 companies. Surveys by the Conference Board found that in 1987 only 21 percent of the members of boards of directors participated in creating codes of ethics; by 1998 the number had increased to 78 percent. Some codes and statements of responsibility are little more than public relations, whereas others reflect a strong corporate commitment to specific standards of conduct. That commitment increasingly involves not just policies but measurement and accountability. This chapter is concerned with the transformation of ethics principles into management practice.

The normative application of ethics includes the formulation of policies to be used in the screening stage of the framework for nonmarket analysis summarized in Figure 2-5 of Chapter 2. That is, policies based on ethics principles screen out alternatives that are unacceptable on moral grounds just as laws screen out alternatives. In the choice stage, ethics provides the basis for evaluating moral claims and for guiding choice among policy alternatives. Because all employees are expected to abide by a firm's policies, those policies must be implemented in a manner that ensures that real people in real situations will be able to act in accord with them. In the wake of a series of scandals, Chuck Prince, CEO of Citigroup, said, "I never thought that you had to say to people, 'We want to grow aggressively—and don't forget not to break the law.'"[1] In addition to the use of ethics in the screening and choice stages of the framework, in the analysis stage ethics provides a basis for anticipating nonmarket action motivated by moral concerns. For example, in the chapter case, *Citigroup and Subprime Lending*, Citigroup failed to anticipate the morally motivated nonmarket action directed against its subprime lending business.

Implementation requires measures ranging from developing and supporting personal integrity to providing guidance for the types of situations likely to be encountered by employees. For example, Boeing uses a training program entitled "Questions

---
[1]*Fortune*, November 29, 2004.

of Integrity: The Boeing Ethics Challenge."[2] The program includes 54 situations that provide a basis for discussion among employees. All Boeing employees are required to have at least 1 hour of ethics training every year, and management receives at least 5 hours of training.

Implementation requires a clear statement of the firm's policies so that employees can follow the rules and reason based on principles when they encounter new situations. Implementation may also involve compliance and audit programs capable of detecting violations and ensuring that standards are met. Compliance may involve institutional features such as an audit committee, an ombudsman, or a corporate ethics officer or department. Because structural approaches can be bureaucratic, less formal approaches emphasizing personal commitment and integrity are commonly used.

This chapter focuses on the managerial implementation of ethics principles and conceptions of corporate social responsibility. The Levi Strauss & Company example illustrates the basic approach to implementing the framework presented in Figure 2-5. The chapter considers the positive application of ethics in assessing the moral determinants of nonmarket action. Tensions in the application of ethics principles, including paternalism and the extent to which self-restraint should be exercised in corporate political activity, are then considered. The corporate social responsibility issue is reexamined, and examples of company programs are presented. A number of issues pertaining to implementing ethics principles and social responsibilities are examined, including compliance and accountability. The chapter concludes with a consideration of sources of unethical behavior.

---

[2] Boeing's "Ethics Challenge" can be found at http://active.boeing.com/companyoffices/ethicschallenge/cfm/intial/cfm.

---

## Levi Strauss & Company and Global Sourcing

Levi Strauss & Company is a privately owned firm that has integrated core values into its internal policies and earned a reputation for adherence to ethics principles and concern for the interests of its stakeholders.[1] In the 1980s the company made two important market decisions: to broaden its product lines, particularly into casual wear, and to expand internationally in both the markets in which it sells and in its sourcing of products.[2] The expansion of its markets and product lines, sales growth in the United States, and pressure for low-cost sources of supply resulted in a rapid expansion in the number of its suppliers. Levi Strauss soon found that a high percentage of its garments was no longer being produced in its own facilities but instead was being produced by over 700 foreign suppliers.

The company became concerned about whether its suppliers met the safety and other standards it maintained in its own production facilities. In addition, it was concerned about possible damage to its brand name resulting from conditions in its suppliers' facilities. The company had concerns pertaining to child labor, prison labor, plant safety, and environmental protection. The company also had concerns about the human rights conditions in several countries in which its suppliers were located. Its market strategy of expanding its markets and sourcing globally had generated a set of complex issues. Its problem was how to bring its supplier relationships into congruence with its ethics principles and core values.

---

[1] The company had backed its principles with action. It was a leader in integrating its factories in the South in the 1950s, and during the depression it kept employees on its payroll rather than laying them off. See Schoenberger (2000).

[2] This example is based on Baron (1995b).

*(Continued)*

(Continued)

Levi Strauss formed a task force to develop two policies to guide its managers: Terms of Engagement for suppliers and Guidelines for Country Selection for determining in which countries it would do business. The former focused on working conditions in suppliers' factories and covered dimensions such as safety, working hours, discrimination, child labor, dormitories for workers, and environmental protection. The latter focused on human rights concerns, political stability, the safety of company employees, and legal protection for trademarks and commercial interests.

These policies affected its market strategy in several ways. First, the company terminated its arrangements with suppliers in Burma because of widespread human rights violations in the country. Also due to human rights concerns, it decided to withdraw from China over several years. Not only did the China decision eliminate a low-cost, high-quality source of supply, it also precluded Levi Strauss from investing in its own facilities in China.[3] Second, the Terms of Engagement policy was implemented by audit teams that regularly visited each supplier and provided a detailed assessment of the conditions at the supplier's facilities.

The process used by Levi Strauss to develop the guidelines can be interpreted through the framework of Figure 2-5. The top panel of Figure 21-1 represents the development of

[3] Levi Strauss returned to China in 1998.

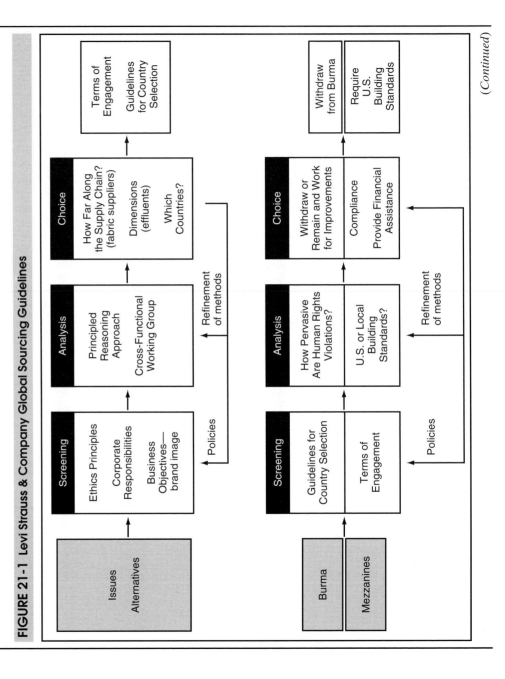

**FIGURE 21-1   Levi Strauss & Company Global Sourcing Guidelines**

(Continued)

*(Continued)*

policies to guide its managers, and the bottom panel represents the application to two issues: (1) whether to source in Burma and (2) how to address a safety issue in suppliers' factories. Referring to the top panel, Levi Strauss developed policies pertaining to suppliers and countries and considered alternatives ranging from complete withdrawal from countries to requiring suppliers to meet U.S. building codes. Screening involved the application of fundamental ethics principles in addition to its business objectives. Analysis involved the application of its "principled reasoning approach," in which stakeholder interests were explicitly taken into account.

The third stage involved developing recommendations and choosing among them. Choice included decisions about how broad the policies should be—should they cover effluents from washing operations—and how far down the supply chain they should go. Should the policies extend only to cutting and sewing operations or also to fabric producers? The results of this process were the Country Selection and Terms of Engagement policies to guide managers in their decision making about contractor practices and involvement in countries.

The bottom panel illustrates the application of the process to specific decisions about doing business in Burma and safety concerns about the construction of interior mezzanines in suppliers' factories in the Caribbean. The screening stage involved the application of the two policies, and analysis centered on the impact of alternatives on stakeholders as well as on specific concerns, such as how pervasive the human rights violations in Burma were and whether U.S. safety standards should be applied in the case of the mezzanines. Choices then were made between withdrawal and constructive engagement in the case of Burma and about who should pay for the safety improvements in the case of the mezzanines.

## Moral Determinants of Nonmarket Action

Although nonmarket action is often motivated by self-interest, on many issues it is motivated by moral concerns.[3] A broad set of activists, advocacy groups, public interest centers, religious groups, civil rights organizations, community groups, and politicians use the language of morality to advance their causes, mobilize those sympathetic to their causes, and set social and political agendas. Managers must understand the source and strength of the moral determinants of nonmarket behavior and must be able to assess the implications for the progress of issues in their life cycle.

The methodology for predicting nonmarket behavior based on moral concerns is less well developed than that for behavior based on self-interest. Furthermore, as indicated in the previous two chapters, unanimity about moral principles cannot be assumed. The task thus is to anticipate the types of issues for which morally based action is likely.

The first step involves assessing the range of moral concerns individuals may have about an issue. Since moral concerns are not the same as self-interest, individuals who are not directly affected by an issue may become aware of the issue through media coverage, as considered in Chapter 3. The activist and advocacy groups and the networks of NGOs and community groups considered in Chapter 4 are also an important source of information to the public and the media, and they often attempt to frame issues in moral terms.

The next step is to determine how members of the public are likely to evaluate an issue or company practice. Managers thus should assume the perspective of those in

---

3See Chapter 6.

the firm's environment and evaluate the issue as they might. Since individuals use a variety of moral standards, managers should examine the issue from utilitarian, rights, and justice perspectives. The objective of this step is to identify the range of moral concerns that may be raised about an issue or practice.

The link between moral concerns and nonmarket action is mediated by the cost of taking individual and collective action. These costs are difficult to assess, but it is clear that there are some individuals who have a high degree of commitment and low costs of acting based on moral concerns. The likelihood of collective action thus is governed by the same factors considered in Chapter 6. The costs of nonmarket and collective action are lower when people with similar moral perspectives are already organized, as in the case of an advocacy group or a union as in the Chapter 4 case *Nike in Southeast Asia.* The impact increases with the number of concerned individuals; their resources in terms of dollars, time, and energy; and the effectiveness of the strategies they employ.

An important factor in collective action is the extent to which the initial actions of those motivated by moral concerns spark a responsive chord with the public or attract the attention of politicians. In assessing this, it is useful to consider the claims and arguments made in attempting to attract broader support. Even when motivation is based on self-interest, moral claims may be used to advance a cause, and the media is often responsive to its perception of the societal significance of such claims.

The final step is to predict the likely individual and collective action. This involves an assessment of how many people may act and how their moral concerns might affect the behavior of institutional officeholders. Little systematic evidence is available on how many individuals participate in nonmarket activity as a function of moral concerns, so experience is important in assessing morally motivated behavior. The example illustrates the impact of morally motivated action. The chapter case, *Citigroup and Subprime Lending,* provides another opportunity to consider the moral determinants of nonmarket action.

## Circle K's Health Care Policy

The Circle K Corporation operated gasoline service stations and convenience marts in the Midwest, South, and West. Circle K had high turnover in its predominantly low-skilled positions, and its health care costs had doubled over the past 2 years and were twice that of some of its competitors. The company self-insured, so it directly bore the costs of employee health care. To control its costs, the company decided to limit health care coverage for certain conditions. In a letter to employees the CEO explained,

The company is concerned about certain personal lifestyle decisions regarding the use of alcohol, drugs, self-inflicted wounds, and sickness due to acquired immune deficiency syndrome. We believe that these personal lifestyle decisions could seriously impact

other participants' health care costs. Employees who are proven to suffer illness and accidents that result from the use of alcohol, drugs, self-inflicted wounds and AIDS, proven not to be contracted from blood transfusion, will not be eligible to receive company health care coverage in those circumstances. . . .

Circle K had thoroughly researched the issue and was confident that its new policy was in accord with the relevant law.

The reaction to Circle K's policy was swift. Moral objections included whether Circle K was making judgments about the morality of its employees, whether the policy was discriminatory, and whether it was unjust to deny coverage to those who were most in need of it. The particular lightning rod was coverage for AIDS.

*(Continued)*

*(Continued)*

AIDS activists and advocates were well organized and politically effective and were concerned that other companies might make similar changes in their health care policies. The activists brought the change to the attention of the public and the news media. AIDS had high societal significance and audience interest, so the news media provided extensive coverage. Circle K's CEO and its chairman were forced to defend the policy on national television. On the *Today* show

Bryant Gumbel asked the chairman, "What is it you're trying to police here—is it health or morality?"[1] The company soon withdrew its new policy. The failure to assess how others might evaluate the policy and whether morally motivated nonmarket action might arise resulted in a debacle that tarnished the company.

[1]*The Wall Street Journal*, August 18, 1988.

# The Challenge of Corporate Social Responsibility

The spread of codes of ethics and statements of social responsibility is due to three factors. The first is a belief by some firms that they should be accountable for conduct beyond profit maximization. The second is a defensive motivation intended to avoid private politics led by activists and other interest groups. The third is also defensive and is intended to pre-empt public politics and government regulation. Regardless of the motivation, these codes and statements commit firms to particular standards of conduct. The focus in this section is on the first motivation and how the resulting standards are implemented.

The social responsibilities of business are identified by ethics principles and reasoning based on those principles. The reliance on principles not only encourages managers to reflect on company policies and their own actions but also reduces the likelihood of reasoning in a casuist manner.

The reliance on principles, however, may not be sufficient to identify unambiguously the appropriate concept of corporate responsibility. Principles are stated generally, and translating them into rules of behavior and goals is challenging. Ethics systems are not sufficiently precise, for example, to determine how much corporations should contribute to charity. A system of justice might imply that some portion of profits be used for charitable purposes, whereas a rights-based system that emphasizes maximal liberty holds that the firm's owners as principals should choose whether and how much to contribute from their dividends or share price appreciation. On some issues the actions consistent with a utilitarian standard may differ from the actions consistent with rights or justice standards. From the perspective of utilitarianism, an integrity test is appropriate for a job if the benefits it yields are greater than its costs. An ethics system that holds that individuals have rights to privacy and freedom from arbitrary treatment, however, indicates that the use of the tests should be limited. The challenge for management is to formulate policies that respect these important considerations and resolve conflicts among them.

One frequently used approach to implementing corporate social responsibility is the "triple bottom line."[4] The triple bottom line is intended to measure corporate environmental, social, and financial performance. More importantly, it serves as a reminder to management and other employees that profits are not the only relevant measures of

[4]See Elkington (1997).

corporate performance. It also commits the firm to report on all three dimensions of performance. Much of this reporting could be done independently of the triple bottom line perspective, so the value of the triple bottom line may primarily be in terms of motivation and commitment.[5]

An important concern about the triple bottom line perspective is whether the capital markets will reward environmental and social performance. And, if it is rewarded, is it because it helps reduce the threat of private and public politics or because investors in the stock market reward socially responsible behavior? As indicated in Chapter 18, the empirical literature is inconclusive on this question. Even if it is not rewarded, ethical conduct is still right from a moral perspective.

One approach to measuring corporate social performance is the balanced scorecard.[6] The balanced scorecard was proposed as a system for evaluating overall performance by assessing financial performance, customer relationships, internal company processes, and learning and growth. Some companies have extended it to include ethics and social performance. The balanced scorecard has been used to assess corporate performance, business unit performance, and the performance of individual managers. Compensation can then be based on the resulting scores.

As an example, in the late 1990s Citibank introduced a balanced scorecard that broadened performance evaluation to include five components: financial performance, customer/franchise performance, strategic cost management, risk management, and people management. Its incentive compensation system, including bonuses and stock options, was also broadened to include performance along these five dimensions. One objective was to build teamwork with a focus on the overall performance of the corporation and its businesses. Each of its five businesses—consumer banking, credit cards, private banking, corporate banking, and emerging markets—were also evaluated in terms of these five measures. For the chairman and several other top executives, 100 percent of their variable compensation (bonus) was based on corporate scorecard performance. For the next group of 30 executives, 50 percent of their bonus was based on the corporate scorecard performance and 50 percent on individual scorecard performance. The balanced scorecard did not explicitly include corporate social responsibility, but compliance with the company's code of conduct was implicit in the evaluations.

In a potentially important case affecting corporate communication and the reporting of social performance, Nike was the subject of a lawsuit alleging that in defending its practices pertaining to its overseas suppliers' factories it had provided false and misleading information about its corporate social responsibility (see the Chapter 4 case *Nike in Southeast Asia*). Nike argued that its statements were speech protected by the First Amendment, but the California Supreme Court ruled that the case could go to trial under state consumer fraud laws pertaining to commercial speech, which receives less protection than individual and political speech. The U.S. Supreme Court refused to hear Nike's appeal on technical rather than substantive grounds. Although Nike's position was backed by businesses and a group of 32 publishing and broadcast companies that filed a supporting brief, the company was between a rock and a hard place. The only way it could get a Supreme Court ruling supporting corporate speech was to lose the case on trial, but it expected to win. Consequently, Nike decided to settle the case.[7] The California Supreme Court decision that such cases could be tried then remained in place.

---

[5] Norman and MacDonald (2003) provide a scathing criticism of the triple bottom line concept.
[6] See Kaplan and Norton (1992).
[7] Nike agreed to contribute $1.5 million to the Fair Labor Association (see Chapter 22) and continue its after-work educational programs in overseas suppliers' factories.

Nike said that "the case had a chilling effect on Nike's ability to speak out on issues of public importance." In response to the settlement Nike announced that it would no longer issue its corporate social responsibility report and it would limit its "participation in public events and media engagement in California."[8] In 2005 Nike resumed issuing its a corporate social responsibility report.

The implementation of social responsibility program can also be thwarted by private politics. Under Warren Buffett's leadership Berkshire Hathaway allowed shareholders to designate $18 a share of dividends to three charities of their choice. A woman who became an independent sales agent for Pampered Chef, a Berkshire company, in part because the company's mission statement encouraged its employees to "develop their God-given talents," learned that some of the profits she would generate would be donated to Planned Parenthood and other pro-choice groups. She launched a private politics campaign over the Internet. Customers complained, some sales agents resigned, and Pampered Chef was pressured to the point that Berkshire ended the dividend contributions program. The company, which had frequently been targeted by pro-life groups, said it ended the program because it was hurting Pampered Chef and its employees.

## Corporate Social Responsibility and Ethics in Practice

This section presents three examples of companies addressing challenges pertaining to stakeholders and social responsibility and then considers practices intended to improve the ethical conduct of business. In the three examples, BP was proactive in addressing nonmarket challenges; Wal-Mart acted soon after the nonmarket challenges began to spread; and Citigroup acted after a series of scandals had damaged its reputation.

### BP and Social Responsibility

In the early 1990s BP developed an oil field in Columbia in an area in which Marxist guerillas were active. Some oil companies in the area made direct payments to the guerillas, but BP decided to back the government. In 1997 the chairman of Exxon expressed the view that costly actions should not be taken until the scientific evidence was more conclusive. BP reviewed the scientific evidence on global warming and the policy alternatives for addressing it. The company, led by CEO Lord Browne of Madingley, decided that action was called for. Breaking ranks with the oil industry in 1997, Lord Browne (1997) stated in an address at Stanford University,

The time to consider the policy dimensions of climate change is not when the link between greenhouse gasses and climate change is conclusively proven—but when the possibility cannot be discounted and is taken seriously by the society of which we are part. We in BP have reached that point. It is an

produced to support the assignment of government troops to protect the oil field. It also made other payments to support the Columbian government. BP was widely criticized for its involvement and was accused of paying a war tax. The UK media provided extensive coverage of the situation, including a stinging television documentary, and while BP defended its action, it was clearly stung by the criticism.

At that time many businesses, and particularly those in the energy industries, had opposed taking strong measures to address global warming because of the costs that would be born by industry and the public. In 1997 the chairman of Exxon expressed the view that costly actions should not be taken until the scientific evidence was more conclusive. BP reviewed the scientific evidence on global warming and the policy alternatives for addressing it. The company, led by CEO Lord Browne of Madingley, decided that action was called for. Breaking ranks with the oil industry in 1997, Lord Browne (1997) stated in an address at Stanford University,

[8]Nike press release, "Kasky v. Nike," September 12, 2003. Nike also declined to release an undated version of the Chapter 4 case *Nike in Southeast Asia*.

important moment for us. We must now focus on what can and what should be done not because we can be certain climate change is happening but because the possibility cannot be ignored.[9]

BP participated in the World Business Council on Sustainable Development, and Lord Browne and other business leaders met with President Clinton to discuss measures to deal with global climate change. BP joined with Environmental Defense and other companies to develop an emissions trading system for greenhouse gasses, as discussed in Chapter 11. BP joined with the Nature Conservancy, American Electric Power, the U.S. and Bolivian governments, and a local conservation group to conserve a tropical forest in Bolivia. Flaring, the burning of natural gas released in conjunction with crude oil production, was a major source of carbon dioxide emissions, and BP, which had dramatically reduced flaring in its Norwegian operations, pledged to eliminate all flaring. BP already produced solar panels in Australia, Spain, and Saudi Arabia, and extended its commitment to solar power with a dozen plants in construction, including one in California. BP also served as the chair of the International Climate Change Partnership.

BP also decided to stop all nonmarket activity pertaining to opening the Arctic National Wildlife Refuge to oil exploration, although it did not pledge not to drill if the Refuge were opened.[10] BP stopped all corporate political contributions in the United States and elsewhere and, as considered in Chapter 22, refused to pay bribes in Russia.[11]

BP's concept of corporate social responsibility did not go far enough for some activist groups. Greenpeace sought the end to oil exploration and launched protests against BP. Matthew Spencer of Greenpeace said that BP has "made a valiant attempt to put a green sheen on [its] organization. Inevitably, if you scratch the surface, you find an aggressive company looking for new oil reserves."[12]

BP subsequently decided to reposition, or in its own terminology, rebrand the company. It changed its name from British Petroleum to BP, adopted the slogan "Beyond Petroleum," and replaced its corporate symbol with a sunburst. It also launched a major public relations campaign promoting its new image at a cost estimated at $200 million. BP hoped that its rebranding and its substantive actions would be rewarded in the marketplace, but many observers remained skeptical.

BP's slogan Beyond Petroleum led some people to believe that the company was committed to switching from oil and gas to alternative sources of energy. Lord Browne then had to clarify that BP's principal goal was "to create long-term—and I do stress long-term—shareholder value.[13] He also explained, "My view is that hydrocarbons will be the bulk of the energy supply for the next 30 to 50 years."[14] Skeptics wondered if BP's commitment to the environment would be sustained when Lord Browne stepped down from leadership of the company.

BP's commitment to corporate social responsibility included five components: ethical conduct; employees; relationships (customers and suppliers); health, safety, and environmental performance; and control and finance. To implement its policies and fulfill its commitments, it created a new staff function with seven regional directors

[9]Browne, John, "Speech at Stanford University, 19 May, 1997." *Review: The BP Quarterly Technology Magazine,* July/August, pp. 11–13.
[10]BP was the largest producer on the north slope of Alaska.
[11]BP halted corporate soft money contribution in the United States, as had a number of major U.S. corporations, although its U.S. employees continued their contributions to a corporate PAC.
[12]*The Wall Street Journal,* August 12, 1998.
[13]*The Wall Street Journal,* November 25, 2004.
[14]*Fortune,* December 8, 2002.

to encourage commitments. BP also reformulated its management performance contracts to include social and environmental performance including ethical conduct.[15]

## Wal-Mart: Reputation and Stakeholder Management

As indicated in Chapter 1, Wal-Mart was criticized by activists, unions, and politicians for allegedly depressing wages, providing inadequate health insurance for its 1.2 million associates, opposing unions, driving small merchants out of business, and adversely affecting the sense of community in small towns. Wal-Mart had become part of America's culture and as such received increasing attention. Wal-Mart had regularly been in television's *King of the Hill* as Megalo-Mart, and began to appear elsewhere on television. "Every Mart" was the setting for a *Without a Trace* episode, *South Park* had an episode on a "Wall-Mart" store coming to town, and the company was the butt of jokes on *The Daily Show*. Both CNBC and PBS's *Frontline* ran documentaries on the company.

Wal-Mart also experienced a host of labor incidents that generated criticism. In late 2003 Immigration and Customs agents raided several Wal-Mart stores, taking into custody 200 undocumented workers employed by custodial service companies that cleaned the stores. Some Wal-Mart employees were revealed to have been forced to punch out and continue working, and some minors had worked too many hours. The media reported that in high-crime areas Wal-Mart had a policy of locking night shift employees in the building to prevent "shrinkage" from theft. In many cases there was no one with a key to unlock the doors in the case of an emergency, and employees had to call a store manager to have the doors unlocked.[16] Wal-Mart was also criticized for refusing to sell some magazines and CDs and concealing parts of the covers of some magazines. Wal-Mart was also named in the largest-ever class-action lawsuit on behalf of 1.6 million women alleging job discrimination in promotions.[17]

Wal-Mart's strategy of entering urban markets and opening superstores that sold groceries directly threatened the Union of Food and Commercial Workers (UFCW). Because of growing competition from Wal-Mart, supermarket chains in Southern California demanded that their union employees pay a share of their health care costs. The UFCW struck, and after a lengthy strike an agreement was reached with the union members agreeing to share in the costs. The union then adopted a strategy of opposing the opening of Wal-Mart stores in urban areas. Backed by the California Labor Federation the California legislature passed a bill requiring an "economic impact" report for any new "superstore". Only Wal-Mart superstores would be affected. The governor vetoed the bill. In a public referendum, voters in Ingelwood, California, rejected a proposed change in a zoning requirement to allow Wal-Mart to build a superstore. The nonmarket pressure not only damaged the company's reputation but also threatened its expansion strategy, as considered in the Chapter 7 case, *Wal-Mart and Its Urban Expansion Strategy.*

Wal-Mart belatedly recognized that it had focused on only one primary stakeholder—its customers. Wal-Mart CEO H. Lee Scott, Jr., observed, "What we have found is that there is a different group of stakeholders today that are important, and that is a person who's not familiar with Wal-Mart stores, they're not familiar with what we stand for. So their view of Wal-Mart stores is what they read in the newspaper and what they see on TV. We have decided it is important for us to reach out to that

---

[15]See the case *British Petroleum (C): Social Responsibility* in Baron (2003c).
[16]Emergency exits were not locked, but employees were told to use them only in a true emergency.
[17]The Court of Appeals agreed to review the case to determine if it was eligible for class action status.

group."[18] Pointing to a change in direction, a spokesperson commented, "For too long, we thought that if we just focused on our customers then everything else would follow. We probably did not realize soon enough how important it was to work with the media. It is an acknowledgment that the media and others offer important venues for telling our story, and we need to continue to do a better job at that."[19] Wal-Mart had also ignored government and had not had a presence in Washington. Scott noted that Sam Walton "did not get involved in the political process; he prided himself on that."[20]

A spokeswoman for Wal-Mart explained, "The challenge to Wal-Mart is to change the way we do some things without changing who we are."[21] In 2004 Wal-Mart broadened its stakeholder focus and began to repair its tarnished reputation. It began a television and print advertising campaign featuring employees telling how happy they were working for Wal-Mart and how the company had provided opportunities for advancement. It sponsored PBS and NPR programs and began a $500,000 fellowship program for minority journalism students at nine universities. In California it took out full-page newspaper advertisements stating the facts with the introduction, "While we are always willing to consider constructive criticism, much of what has been said publicly about Wal-Mart in California is simply not true." Nationally, Wal-Mart took out full-page advertisements announcing its Teacher of the Year Program awards and stating that it would contribute $40 million to education in 2004. It also opened a Washington office to develop better relationships with the federal government. Wal-Mart also acted to deal with some of the community effects of its stores. Wal-Mart had closed hundreds of stores in the United States, with over 150 vacant. The company worked with local communities to find new businesses that could occupy the stores.

These steps were only the beginning.

# Citigroup: Responsibility Under Fire

Citigroup was one of the most profitable companies in the world with 2003 net earnings of $18 billion, compared to $21.5 billion for ExxonMobil and $15 billion for General Electric. Earnings were up again in 2004. Yet Citigroup's involvement in a series of scandals had continued unabated, and some commentators argued its seeming inability to stop the scandals had depressed its stock price. In addition to the regulatory judgments, settlements of lawsuits, and remaining lawsuits discussed in Chapter 18, which could ultimately cost Citigroup $10 billion, new scandals arose. In London Citigroup traders had dumped $13.3 billion of European government bonds on the market and then repurchased the bonds at depressed prices. The whipsawing of the bond market violated unwritten financial services industry standards and led to an investigation by British and German regulators. In Japan irregularities in Citigroup's private banking operations were identified in 2001 by Japanese regulators, but by 2003 the private banking group had returned to the same practices. The Japanese government ordered Citigroup's private bank to close, and Citigroup did so and also voluntarily closed its trust bank in Japan. Several Citigroup bankers in Japan were fired, and CEO Chuck Prince publicly apologized in Japan.

Some commentators argued that the source of Citigroup's problems was a culture emphasizing strong earnings growth and aggressive internal competition for performance. Citigroup had a very decentralized organizational structure with a matrix

[18] *The New York Times,* September 9, 2004.
[19] *The New York Times,* September 9, 2004.
[20] *The New York Times,* September 9, 2004.
[21] *The New York Times,* September 9, 2004.

overlay.[22] Bonuses were tied to balanced scorecard grades, but financial and earnings performance dominated. High-powered incentives were used in trading, as was standard practice in the industry.

As the scandals began to unfold Citigroup hired a new chief financial officer from outside the company, and Prince instituted tighter financial controls. He transferred responsibility for compliance with Citigroup's code of conduct from the legal department to the bank's senior risk manager. Citigroup established a new Policy Compliance Assessment Group, and multiple compliance reports to the board of directors were required. Prince subsequently fired three of the most senior Citigroup executives, all of whom had had some oversight responsibility for private banking in Japan. In a message to employees, Prince said, "We have to have the moral compass to deliver those profits and growth responsibly and honestly. Citigroup's culture must be synonymous with integrity."[23] Prince attempted to embed the message in Citigroup's culture by requiring ethics training of all employees and promoting an internal "ethics hotline." All finance, accounting, treasury, tax, and investor relations professionals worldwide were required to sign Citigroup's code of ethics. Prince also planned to include additional qualitative questions in its balanced scorecard evaluation system.

Prince, however, commented, "We want to maintain that aggressive nature. We're not going to turn ourselves into a charity, we're not going to become, you know, a big, bureaucratic government institution."[24] One observer commented, "The constraint on Citi's growth is not its market size, nor its capital. It may well be that Citi can't achieve its growth ambitions because it cannot safeguard itself properly from regulatory and reputation risk."[25] The challenge for Citigroup was whether it could conduct its business with integrity and avoid nonmarket limits to its growth. With 300,000 employees operating in over 100 countries, the challenge was substantial.

## Statements of Commitment and Expectations

Many companies specifically identify the set of responsibilities they assume and state those responsibilities in mission statements as both a form of commitment and an agenda for managerial action. One of the oldest of these statements is Johnson & Johnson's *Our Credo*, first issued in 1948, which identifies a set of responsibilities and forms the basis for the expectations of its constituents. Johnson & Johnson credits *Our Credo* for having guided its quick and successful actions in 1982 and 1986, when someone put cyanide in Tylenol capsules.

In accord with *Our Credo*, Johnson & Johnson implemented a program to reduce its workplace injuries and accidents with the goal of an injury-free work environment. As a result of both capital expenditures and safety programs, the company reduced its lost workday incidence rate from 1.81 in 1981 to 0.14 by 1989.

The safety program established goals in the following areas: injury prevention and loss control, environmental surveillance and control, medical surveillance and examination, work-related injury and illness management, and disease intervention and associated employee assistance programs. In addition to complying with regulations, operating units were to "establish health and safety guidelines where Credo commitments, scientific principles or regulatory inadequacies dictate." The operating companies of Johnson & Johnson then evaluated and reported their safety records.

[22]See Baron and Besanko (2001) for an analysis of Citigroup's organization of its global corporate banking business.
[23]*Business Week,* October 4, 2004.
[24]*The New York Times,* November 7, 2004.
[25]*Business Week,* October 4, 2004.

The safety program included a requirement that the head of the unit in which a serious, lost workday accident occurred file a report on the accident within 24 hours. The unit head then had to go to company headquarters to report in person to the operating board on the steps being taken to prevent similar accidents in the future. The purpose of the report was informational and was directed at measures that could be taken to reduce future accidents.

**EXAMPLE**

## Johnson & Johnson's Our Credo

We believe our first responsibility is to the doctors, nurses and patients, to mothers and fathers and all others who use our products and services. In meeting their needs everything we do must be of high quality. We must constantly strive to reduce our costs in order to maintain reasonable prices. Customers' orders must be serviced promptly and accurately. Our suppliers and distributors must have an opportunity to make a fair profit.

We are responsible to our employees, the men and women who work with us throughout the world. Everyone must be considered as an individual. We must respect their dignity and recognize their merit. They must have a sense of security in their jobs. Compensation must be fair and adequate, and working conditions clean, orderly and safe. We must be mindful of ways to help our employees fulfill their family responsibilities. Employees must feel free to make suggestions and complaints. There must be equal opportunity for employment, development and

advancement for those qualified. We must provide competent management, and their actions must be just and ethical.

We are responsible to the communities in which we live and work and to the world community as well. We must be good citizens—support good works and charities and bear our fair share of taxes. We must encourage civic improvements and better health and education. We must maintain in good order the property we are privileged to use, protecting the environment and natural resources.

Our final responsibility is to our stockholders. Business must make a sound profit. We must experiment with new ideas. Research must be carried on, innovative programs developed and mistakes paid for. New equipment must be purchased, new facilities provided and new products launched. Reserves must be created to provide for adverse times. When we operate according to these principles, the stockholders should realize a fair return.

## Core Principles and Their Evolution

Johnson & Johnson's *Our Credo* identifies commitments to a set of constituents and can be revised as the set of relevant issues evolves. Revisions of guiding principles such as *Our Credo* are based on a set of core principles that provides consistency over time. The relationship between core principles and current policies and practices can be illustrated using Figure 21-2. The relationship is based on three components: organizational values, corporate objectives, and strategies and practices. Organizational values serve as the core principles that guide the strategies and practices of the company as it strives to achieve its objectives.[26] Core principles can be viewed as unchanging. Organizational objectives are revised when necessary but only infrequently. Strategies and practices are revised frequently as a function of the salient issues in the market and nonmarket environments.

---

[26]This figure is due to Kirk Hanson.

Statements such as *Our Credo* serve as commitments to stakeholders and other constituents. They also communicate to employees a set of principles and values that they can follow in their jobs. The chapter case, *Denny's and Customer Service*, considers a company with serious allegations about racial discrimination that faces the challenge of developing a program for eliminating any discrimination and changing its culture. Seven years later Advantica Restaurant Group, Inc., the company formed to operate Denny's, Coco's, and Carrows restaurants, was ranked first in *Fortune* magazine's "America's 50 Best Companies for Minorities."

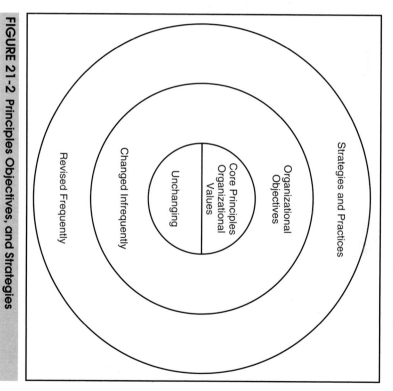

**FIGURE 21-2 Principles Objectives, and Strategies**

## The Body Shop and the Social Audit

By 1998 the Body Shop International PLC had grown from a single shop in Brighton, England, to over 1,500 stores in 47 countries. Founder Anita Roddick had propelled the growth of the Body Shop by positioning the company as an ethical and socially responsible merchandiser of cosmetics with environmentally friendly products and practices. The Body Shop developed a widely publicized Trade Not Aid program in which it sourced raw materials from indigenous peoples, purchasing, for example, blue corn from the Santa Ana Pueblo tribe in New Mexico and nuts from the Kayapo Indians in Brazil. In its promotional and public relations activities, the company highlighted these programs, along with other policies such as not testing its cosmetics on animals and pledging to "use our purchasing power to stop suppliers' animal testing." Anita Roddick appeared in an American Express advertisement touting its program of buying ingredients from developing countries. These programs brought the Body Shop rapid growth, as consumers responded to its image and cachet. The economic and social success of the company made an international celebrity of Anita Roddick, who used her podium to campaign for a variety of causes. To protest Shell Oil Company's failure to halt human rights abuses by the Nigerian government, she erected a large electronic sign reading STEER CLEAR OF SHELL—BOYCOTT NOW across from a Shell service station. The Body Shop also carried its campaigns into its stores.

In 1994 the Body Shop was criticized by a journalist in the magazine *Business Ethics*.[27] The criticism centered not on whether the Body Shop's record was better than that of other companies but instead on whether the company was living up to its lofty pronouncements. A company that had used its ethical and environmental policies to promote its business was held to meet a higher standard than other companies. The Body Shop and Anita Roddick aggressively attacked their critics, but when the concerns did not subside, the company commissioned a social audit of its policies and accomplishments. The report concluded that "The Body Shop has been an important and powerful example to many other businesses and to consumers that it is possible to serve both social as well as economic goals. It has also pioneered many social innovations that have stimulated others to try similar efforts. The company's impact as an exemplary business, however, has at times been weakened by some of the behaviors noted in this report."[28]

The audit evaluated the Body Shop's social performance on the following dimensions: company values and mission; relations with shareholders, customers, employees, franchisees, suppliers, community, and the trading with communities in need; concern for the environment; and contributions to social change. The audit gave high marks to the company's values, mission, and contributions to social change and the lowest mark to its reactions to criticisms. The audit also indicated several areas in which the company had not lived up to its proclamations. The company purchased only £2.25 million of supplies from communities in need, and the audit pointed to conflicts with its trading partners, including the Kayapo Indians. The report stated, "In this area more than any other, the company's performance lags behind what has been implied by its past promotions."

The Body Shop's financial performance began to slip as the cachet of retailing with a conscience faded and competition developed from other retailers using natural ingredients. In 1998 Anita Roddick was replaced as CEO by the board of directors, although she and her husband remained on the board of directors.

## Codes of Conduct

Ethics principles and corporate social responsibility commitments are implemented by individuals who may differ in their values, their ability to reason from ethics principles, and their moral fortitude. Firms therefore must provide guidance to their employees in the conduct of their duties. This guidance often is codified in a detailed set of procedures to which employees can refer when confronted with particular issues.[29] These codes include the requirements established by laws, prescriptions of behavior that go beyond the law, tests to determine whether an action should be taken, and, in some cases, principles from which the employee is to reason about a situation.

The Business Roundtable (1988, pp. 5–6) identified the topics covered by company codes of ethics and standards of conduct.

- Fundamental Honesty and Adherence to the Law
- Product Safety and Quality

[27]See Chapter 3.
[28]Kirk O. Hanson, "Social Evaluation: The Body Shop International 1995," The Body Shop International PLC, Watersmead, England, 1996.
[29]See Brooks (1989), Falsey (1989), Gorlin (1990), and Matthews (1987) for data on company codes. Williams (2000) addresses international codes of conduct.

- Health and Safety in the Workplace
- Conflicts of Interest
- Employment Practices
- Fairness in Selling/Marketing Practices
- Financial Reporting
- Supplier Relationships
- Pricing, Billing, and Contracting
- Trading in Securities/Using Inside Information
- Payments to Obtain Business/Foreign Corrupt Practices Act
- Acquiring and Using Information about Others
- Security
- Political Activities
- Protection of the Environment
- Intellectual Property/Proprietary Information

## Competitive and Proprietary Information

Practices specified in a code of conduct are often directed at situations particular to the industries in which the firm operates. In industries characterized by a high level of research and development, rapid technological progress, and intense competition, market and competitor intelligence activities can be important. Procter & Gamble decided to expand in the hair care market by purchasing Clairol and introducing a new brand, Physique. A major competitor was Unilever PLC; its brands included Sauve, Finesse, and Salon Selectives. P&G managers hired agents to obtain competitive intelligence on Unilever. The agents searched the trash of a Unilever office, obtaining 80 pages of confidential plans that they then gave to P&G. Searching the trash was not illegal, but it was prohibited by P&G's code of ethics. When top management of P&G learned about the espionage, P&G fired three of its managers and blew the whistle on itself. P&G notified Unilever that it had received the plans, and the two companies began negotiating a resolution of the issue. P&G agreed to pay $10 million to Unilever and submit to third-party audits to ensure that the confidential plans were not used.

In high-technology industries intellectual property is a crucial factor in competitive advantage. A temptation in such industries is to obtain information that may have intellectual property protection. Hewlett-Packard's policy on this issue was as follows:

HP must be well informed of competitive developments and is entitled to review all pertinent public information concerning competitive products (e.g., published specifications and prices and trade journal articles). However, HP may not attempt through improper means to acquire a competitor's trade secrets or other proprietary or confidential information, including information as to facilities, manufacturing capacity, technical developments or customers. Improper means include industrial espionage, inducing a competitor's present or former personnel to disclose confidential information, and any other means that are not open and aboveboard. HP must not use consultants to acquire information by improper methods.[30]

Competitive situations may also involve the temptation to obtain business by demeaning competitors rather than by promoting the virtues of a firm's own products.

[30]Hewlett-Packard Corporation, "Standards of Business Conduct," Palo Alto, CA, 1989.

Hewlett-Packard stated, "It is HP's policy to emphasize the quality of its products and to abstain from making disparaging comments or casting doubt on competitors or their products. If statements (oral or written) are made concerning a competitor or its products, they must be fair, factual and complete."

## Principles and Reasoning

The content of company codes depends on the set of issues employees are likely to encounter and the approach the individual company takes. The Cummins Engine Company has long had a reputation for its corporate social responsibility, based on ethics constructs that provide both consistency and a basis from which employees can reason.

Cummins's basic principle is a version of the Golden Rule:

For Cummins, ethics rests on a fundamental belief in people's dignity and decency. Our most basic ethical standard is to show respect for those whose lives we affect and to treat them as we would expect them to treat us if our positions were reversed. This kind of respect implies that we must:

1. Obey the law.
2. Be honest—present the facts fairly and accurately.
3. Be fair—give everyone appropriate consideration.
4. Be concerned—care about how Cummins's actions affect others and try to make those effects as beneficial as possible.
5. Be courageous—treat others with respect even when it means losing business. It seldom does. Over the long haul, people trust and respect this kind of behavior and wish more of our institutions embodied it.

An application of Cummins's fundamental principle is presented in Chapter 22 in the context of questionable foreign payments. That application is important because it provides a basis from which employees can reason about a situation based on moral principles.

The implementation of Cummins's principles is to be guided by the following standards:

1. Cummins Engine Company, Inc., competes on a straight commercial basis; if something more is required, the Company is not interested.
2. Cummins employees do nothing in search of business that they should not reveal willingly and publicly to any other member of the Cummins family or to any government official in any land.
3. Cummins neither practices nor condones any activity that will not stand the most rigorous public ethical examination.
4. If an employee has any doubt about the appropriateness or morality of any act, it should not be done. If an employee believes that there is a conflict between what his or her supervisors expect and what corporate ethical standards require, the employee should raise the issue with the Corporate Responsibility Department. The Company is prepared to help any employee resolve a moral dilemma and to ensure that no employee is put at a career disadvantage because of his or her willingness to raise a question about a corporate practice or unwillingness to pursue a course of action which seems inappropriate or morally dubious.[31]

[31]Cummins Practices, October 1, 1980.

The fourth point is particularly important because it identifies what the employee is to do in case of doubt. It also places the burden on the company to protect the employee in the fulfillment of his or her responsibility to raise concerns about its issues and practices.

The chapter case, *Reporting of Clinical Trial Results*, provides an opportunity to reason from principles.

## Ethics Programs

Upon revelation of illegal and unethical practices at General Dynamic's Electric Boat and Pomona divisions, Secretary of the Navy John Lehman ordered General Dynamics to institute a set of contract compliance measures and "to establish and enforce a rigorous code of ethics for all General Dynamics officers and employees with mandatory sanctions for violations." When asked which measure was the most important, Secretary Lehman answered, "Well, I think the code of ethics, because I think that the others are merely manifestations of an approach, an attitude, that has pervaded their doing business with the government. . . . It isn't the problem of one or two individuals doing the wrong things. It is a pervasive record of corporate policy that we want changed."[32]

In the wake of additional defense contracting scandals, the President's Blue Ribbon Commission on Defense Management recommended that defense contractors institute ethics programs. The commission concluded that self-regulation by defense contractors, rather than mandated requirements, was sufficient to achieve the objectives, and contractors were "asked" to develop codes of ethics. The defense contractors who agreed to the policies specified by the President's Blue Ribbon Commission (1986, p. 4) pledged to take the following measures to implement those policies:

- have and adhere to written codes of conduct;
- train their employees in such codes;
- encourage employees to report violations of such codes, without fear of retribution;
- monitor compliance with laws incident to defense procurement;
- adopt procedures for voluntary disclosure of violations and for necessary corrective action;
- share with other firms their methods for and experience in implementing such principles, through annual participation in an industry-wide "Best Practices Forum"; and
- have outside or nonemployee members of their boards of directors review compliance.

To implement the ethics codes, contractors developed companywide instructional and training programs to ensure that the policies were understood by all employees. All 103,000 General Dynamics employees participated in the training program.[33]

## Compliance

The Blue Ribbon Commission viewed a compliance system as an integral part of a corporate ethics program. Compliance with company practices begins with a commitment by management—particularly top management. Compliance also involves a structure,

32"The Ethics Program 1985/1986," General Dynamics Corporation, 1986.
33See Barker (1993) for an evaluation of the ethics program at General Dynamics.

including systems of internal auditing. Compliance may also involve a committee of the board of directors charged with oversight of the practices of the company. Such a committee often consists of independent directors. Personal commitment is often formalized by the requirement that managers annually sign a pledge of compliance with company policies. The final component of a compliance program is a disciplinary system to address violations. BP fires employees who violate its standards, and Citigroup fired both the employees directly responsible for the private banking scandal in Japan and the senior executives with responsibility for private banking and global banking.

Employees at General Dynamics were required to sign a card that read, "I have received and read the General Dynamics Standards of Business Ethics and Conduct. I understand that these Standards represent the policies of General Dynamics." General Dynamics identified the following set of disciplinary measures that could be taken in the case of violations of its code: "A warning; A reprimand (will be noted in individual's permanent personnel record); Probation; Demotion; Temporary suspension; Discharge; Required reimbursement of losses or damages; Referral for criminal prosecution or civil action."[34]

In 1991 the United States Sentencing Commission issued the Federal Sentencing Guidelines to govern fines for corporations that break laws. The Guidelines provided for varying levels of fines depending on whether the firm had instituted organizational procedures for prevention of crimes and compliance with laws and standards. Fines ranged from 5 percent of the damage to customers if a company had a complete compliance program to 400 percent if a company had no program and the crime involved top management.[35] Paine (1994, p. 109) summarized the components of a compliance program as identified in the sentencing guidelines:

Managers must establish compliance standards and procedures; designate high-level personnel to oversee compliance; avoid delegating discretionary authority to those likely to act unlawfully; effectively communicate the company's standards and procedures through training or publications; take reasonable steps to achieve compliance through audits, monitoring processes, and a system for employees to report criminal misconduct without fear of retribution; consistently enforce standards through appropriate disciplinary measures; respond appropriately when offenses are detected; and, finally, take reasonable steps to prevent the occurrence of similar offenses in the future.

The Sentencing Guidelines led many companies to institute compliance programs, and many established the position of ethics officer. In addition to the sentencing guidelines, the Chancery Court in Delaware, where many companies are incorporated, indicated that board directors could be liable if programs were not established to ensure compliance with the law.

Ethics is an integral part of any compliance program, but compliance with company codes can at times be in conflict with bottom-line pressures. Moreover, the law is not a sufficient guide for ethical practices. There is often a gray area between what is legal and what is ethical. Moreover, companies may assume duties and responsibilities that extend beyond the requirements of the law. Ethics principles as identified in Chapters 19 and 20 help guide actions in the gray areas and identify responsibilities.

---

[34]General Dynamics, "Standards of Business Ethics and Conduct," p. 19.
[35]See the example in Paine (1994).

# Tensions in the Implementation of Ethics Principles

## Paternalism

A basic issue for management is when, if ever, a firm is justified in acting paternalistically by taking an action intended to benefit another but in so doing violates a moral standard. For example, should firms institute substance abuse programs and drug testing for their employees or refuse to hire people who smoke?

Paternalism refers to actions taken to benefit a person without that person's consent. In any ethics system emphasizing individual autonomy and liberty, consent is essential for an action or a rule to have moral standing. Paternalism is thus a moral wrong. Paternalism is also objectionable from a consequentialist perspective because it denies individuals the opportunity to make choices that would further their interests. Gert (1988, pp. 286–287) provides a definition of paternalism.

One is acting paternalistically toward a person if and only if . . . :

**1.** one's action benefits that person,
**2.** one's action involves violating a moral rule with regard to that person,
**3.** one's action does not have that person's past, present, or immediately forthcoming consent, and
**4.** that person is competent to give consent (simple or valid) to the violation.

Actions taken on behalf of others are often justified by claims that if those others had the information that the action taker has, consent would have been granted. According to Gert's definition, an action taken to benefit a person who has incomplete information about a situation is not paternalistic if the person would grant consent once the action has been explained and the information presented.

In some cases, it is easy to know whether consent would be granted. Firms take a variety of actions to benefit their constituencies. A firm may bargain with HMOs over the price for health care services, and the firm's bargaining power can lower the cost to both employees and the firm. In such a case, it is in the interests of both employees and shareholders to have the firm represent them. Consent would surely be given.

In contrast, few companies endorse candidates for public office or try to influence how employees vote. Voting is an exercise of individual autonomy, and individuals have the fundamental right not to be coerced into associating with ideas, positions, or candidates with which they disagree. Consent by individuals to the endorsement of candidates by their employer likely would not be granted. Labor unions, however, regularly endorse candidates for office without the consent of their members. Labor unions differ from firms in an important dimension, however, since union members have the right to elect their leaders.

## Political Action and Restraint

In the United States, individuals, firms, interest groups, foreign governments, and others have broad granted rights to engage in political activity. Firms as well as other interests must decide whether and to what extent they should restrain themselves in the exercise of those rights.[36] On an issue such as the antitrust exemption sought by the soft drink industry, as discussed in Chapter 9, the right of bottlers to seek the exemption is clear, even if it would benefit the industry to the detriment of consumers and

---

[36] Reich (1998) offers a perspective on political restraint.

society. The issue then is when if ever a firm should restrain itself from pursuing its interests through political action.

In some cases, the political actions of business serve to uphold laws. The California constitution requires that a ballot proposition be limited to a single issue. When Proposition 105 was approved by the voters, the Chemical Specialties Manufacturers Association and the California Chamber of Commerce filed suit on the grounds that the proposition covered many different issues. The proposition pertained to the disclosure of toxic substances, apartheid, nursing home standards, the state election process, and protection for senior citizens against fraud. The court invalidated the proposition on the grounds that it was overly broad.

If a political alternative would result in a reduction in aggregate well-being, as is likely in the case of the antitrust exemption sought by the soft drink industry, a utilitarian standard calls for restraint. More generally, utilitarianism views political rights as instrumental and calls for their exercise only to maximize aggregate well-being. Even when the exercise of political rights is based on self-interest, the political competition among interests may work in the direction of maximizing aggregate well-being. The intense political competition over the ratification of NAFTA is one such example.

Pizza Hut's lobbying to retain the targeted-jobs tax credit for the employment of low-income youths was considered in Chapter 8. Subsequently, the inspector general of the Department of Labor (1993) released the results of a study of the program's impact indicating that instead of enhancing the employment prospects of those taking the subsidized jobs, the jobs "often appeared to be one more low-skilled, low-wage job in a succession of similar jobs in a worker's employment history." The recipients of the $2,400 tax credit were primarily large corporations in the fast-food and retail industries that had high turnover in low-wage jobs. Furthermore, the companies surveyed reported that they would have hired 95 percent of the people even without the tax credit. The program, estimated to cost $282 million in 1994, was described in the study as the "most wasteful of all programs, the kind where the federal government gets involved when people would have done something anyway."[37]

In light of this study, should Pizza Hut support this program? Certainly, a company has the right to accept tax credits offered by the government and has the political right to lobby the government in support of the tax credits with the objective of increasing its profits. The program was established without a test for whether those jobs would have been filled anyway and hence with the understanding that the tax credit would apply to such jobs. Pizza Hut was thus acting in accord with the law. Moreover, its support was consistent with the intent of the government, since the Clinton administration had proposed making the program permanent rather than requiring annual congressional authorizations.

Lobbying and other political activity by business and interest groups have become integral components of the democratic process in a pluralistic society. In participating in this process firms not only represent the interests of their owners but also can give voice to stakeholders and others who would not otherwise participate in the process because of the costs of individual and collective action. Support for the tax credits by Pizza Hut gave voice to low-income youths who otherwise might not be represented in the process. Participation by firms and other interest groups, however, must be guided by both the law and ethics principles.

Lobbying is the strategic advocacy of a position, and as in a court of law most lobbyists advocate their side of an issue and rely on the opposition to present the

---

[37]*The Wall Street Journal,* August 24, 1993.

other side. Lobbying and advocacy must be guided by principles, however, including avoiding false statements—for example, denying that tobacco can be addictive.[38] This may require acting against the firm's immediate interests when warranted by ethical consensus. For example, once the National Academy of Sciences issued its report concluding that CFCs damage the ozone layer, DuPont decided to stop CFC production earlier than called for by the government. British Petroleum viewed the growing scientific evidence on global climate change as sufficient to warrant actions to reduce its $CO_2$ emissions and promote sustainable energy sources such as solar power. Similarly, the coalition of Silicon Valley businesses that opposed Proposition 211, which would have made it easier for law firms to extract settlements from companies with volatile stock prices, acted in the interests of aggregate well-being by allowing more information to flow to the capital markets and by avoiding costly, frivolous lawsuits.[39]

Since political rights are granted, the issue of political restraint often focuses on actions that may be deceptive. As an illustration of the types of actions that raise concerns, firms and interest groups frequently support grassroots organizations that lobby, support candidates for office, and campaign on public referenda. On the issue of fuel economy standards, in 1990 General Motors sponsored an organization called Nevadans for Fair Fuel Economy Standards, which generated 10,000 letters to Senator Richard Bryan (D-NV) opposing his bill to raise CAFE standards. Senator Bryan accused the industry of conducting the letter-writing campaign "under false colors." GM spokesman William Noack defended the campaign as "a very straightforward, aboveboard educational program."[40] If Senator Bryan was correct in his assessment that the letter writers were uninformed and did not understand the issue, the campaign was unjustified, since it treated the letter writers as means and not also as ends. Moreover, such campaigns impose a negative externality in that they make it more difficult for informed letter writers to be heard.

## Sources of Unethical Behavior

Unethical behavior has a number of sources; some are idiosyncratic to the particular individuals involved and others are functions of the managerial setting or the policies of the firm itself. Codes of conduct provide useful guidance, but alone they may be insufficient to prevent unethical behavior and promote ethical behavior. If the culture in the organization encourages or condones questionable behavior or if incentive systems place self-interest before all else, ethical behavior will primarily rest on the personal integrity of employees. Personal integrity may be sufficient for most, but perhaps not all, employees, and for most, but perhaps not all, issues.[41]

Personal weakness and temptation can contribute to unethical behavior in business, as well as in other contexts. This includes situations in which an individual understands what is right but does not have the fortitude to take the right action, perhaps because it involves a degree of personal risk. In that case, the policies of the firm should be reexamined to lessen the personal risk associated with taking the right action. This may require revisions in incentive structures so that employees do not find themselves in positions in which their performance will be evaluated negatively as a result, for example, of a lost sale that could have been obtained only through an unethical act.

[38] See Hamilton and Hoch (1997) and Weber (1996).
[39] See the Chapter 8 case *Proposition 211: Securities Litigation Referendum (A)*.
[40] *The Wall Street Journal*, April 4, 1990.
[41] See Sonnenfeld and Lawrence (1978) for an analysis of the causes of price fixing in the folding-carton industry.

Cummins's fourth standard is one means of addressing this problem. The Sentencing Guidelines also recommend not delegating authority to individuals or positions when temptation may be strong or personal integrity weak.

The structure of both explicit and implicit incentives within a firm can be an important obstacle to ethical behavior. In 1990 Eastern Airlines and nine of its maintenance supervisors were indicted for failing to perform required maintenance and for falsifying maintenance records.[42] To improve its on-time performance, Eastern had instituted an incentive system for maintenance supervisors in which bonuses were paid for good on-time performance. Supervisors whose on-time and flight cancellation record was poor were transferred or in some cases fired. Not only did the supervisors face incentives and pressure from upper management, but the unions, which were incensed by layoffs and management's demands for wage reductions, often blocked supervisors' efforts to improve on-time performance. Under pressure from both sides, maintenance supervisors began to falsify records for maintenance that was not performed. The situation deteriorated to the point at which some pilots refused to fly aircraft that had accumulated maintenance problems. Believing that the complaints were part of the unions' struggle with management, Eastern executives reportedly continued to pressure the supervisors.

In 1992 charges were brought against Sears for allegedly recommending unneeded repairs, such as brake repairs and front-wheel alignments, in its auto centers. Service advisors reportedly recommended the repairs to earn higher commissions, and in settlements of charges in 41 states and 19 class action lawsuits, Sears agreed to eliminate commissions for its service advisors. After a corporate restructuring in 1993, the position of service advisor was eliminated and replaced by the position of service consultant, who was paid on a commission basis. The position of service consultant differed significantly from that of service advisor, however, because the consultants could not recommend repairs, whereas earlier the advisors had inspected cars and identified needed repairs. Repairs were recommended only by mechanics, who did not receive commissions. Because of its past problems, when its new system was announced, Sears received increased scrutiny by state attorneys general.

The problem of temptation can be exacerbated by several factors. First, if there is a belief that others are acting unethically or are succumbing to temptation, an individual may have more difficulty resisting. This is particularly true if employees find themselves in a prisoners' dilemma in which each has a dominant strategy of succumbing to temptation. For example, if a partnership will go to the associate with the highest billings, the competing associates may be induced to take unwarranted actions. What is required is a promotion system that considers factors in addition to billings. Second, succumbing to temptation is more likely if the prevailing attitude in the firm involves either short-cutting ethics analysis, using standards only to justify actions taken on other bases, or practicing casuistry. For example, the balancing of responsibilities can induce managers to underemphasize rights and principles of justice in favor of lessening constituent pressure. Third, temptation may be exacerbated by an aggressive culture of earnings growth, as in the case of Enron, or may have been in the case in the Citigroup example. Fourth, temptation combined with greed can lead to unethical conduct. The Chapter 19 case, *Enron Power Marketing and the California Market*, provides an example.

Unethical behavior can also result from too narrow a focus on the duties imposed by the law. The law identifies actions that an individual or firm must not take, but the

---

[42] The FAA had frequently cited Eastern for maintenance, safety, and record-keeping violations and fined it $12 million between 1987 and 1989.

# Summary

set of lawful actions can be considerably larger than the set of ethical actions. For example, Procter & Gamble's ethics standards prohibited espionage that was allowed by the law. The law provides minimum restraints on behavior. Another source of unethical behavior is reliance on an ethics framework that gives insufficient attention to important considerations. Relying only on utilitarianism and ignoring intrinsic rights can result in conduct that violates ethics standards that some individuals hold to be important. For this reason, each of the three ethics systems considered in the previous two chapters should be considered in managerial decision making.

A useful test in situations with moral dimensions is to assess whether an action can be explained both to others in the firm and to the public. This *public disclosure test* has two purposes. First, it forces the manager to articulate the reasons or basis for the action. This should involve an articulation of the reasoning used in arriving at the decision and should not be a search among ethics systems for arguments that come closest to justifying the action the manager prefers to take on other grounds. Second, it requires the manager to reflect on how others will evaluate the action. This does not mean that the action is subject to a vote among constituents. Instead, it focuses attention on the moral evaluations that others may have of the action.

Reliance on the personal integrity of employees is seldom sufficient to ensure ethical conduct, and employees should not be left to operate in an ethics vacuum. A commitment by top management is essential, and part of top management's responsibilities is to establish an environment in which ethical behavior is encouraged, supported, and rewarded. This requires formal and informal communication about exemplary conduct and leadership by deed as well as by word.

Statements of corporate responsibility, specific policies, and codes of conduct are useful guides for employees. These should identify principles, provide specific guidance for situations that are likely to be encountered, and indicate how to reason about situations and issues. A code should also indicate what an individual is to do when uncertain about whether an action is right. A compliance system is important in the implementation of ethics standards and should be designed to give top management confidence that unethical actions will be detected. A process that encourages and does not unduly punish self-disclosure can be an important component of a compliance system.

Temptation and pressure are principal causes of unethical behavior. Performance standards should be realistically attainable through means consistent with ethics principles. Incentive systems should be structured in a manner that encourages rather than hinders ethical conduct. In many firms, the selection, retention, and promotion of employees depend on the individual's integrity and record of conduct in addition to more traditional measures of performance.

# Denny's and Customer Service

Early on the morning of April 1, 1993, 21 members of the U.S. Secret Service arrived in Annapolis, Maryland, to prepare for President Bill Clinton's speech at the U.S. Naval Academy later that day. Before setting up security at the academy, the contingent, in full uniform, went to a local Denny's restaurant for breakfast. The group included six African American agents who sat at a table together, and an African American supervisor who, with the white agents, sat at other tables. After all the agents had ordered, the six black agents realized that the white agents and their supervisor had been served while they had not. Agent Robin Thompson went to ask the waitress about the order, and she said it was on its way. He then asked to talk with the manager and was told that the manager was on the phone. (White agents seated at other tables later reported that the waitress rolled her eyes after turning to leave the black agents' table.) After having waited an hour, the agents stood to leave, and only then, they said, were they offered a single tray of food. They refused the food because there was no time to eat. "We had to go to a Roy Rogers (a local fast-food restaurant) and eat in the van," said one of the African American agents.

Seven weeks after the incident, the six agents filed a lawsuit seeking unspecified monetary and punitive damages. The suit alleged that their civil rights had been violated because Denny's had denied them service because of their race. "It's a classic case of some kind of bias," Thompson said. The lawsuit immediately attracted nationwide media coverage. On the *CBS Evening News* Dan Rather summarized the incident by saying that the agents "put their lives on the line every day, but they can't get served at a Denny's."

Denny's, a unit of Flagstar, Inc., was a nationwide chain operating 1,487 restaurants throughout the United States. Flagstar was formed in 1989 when Coniston Partners headed a leveraged buyout of TW Services. In 1992 Kohlberg, Kravis, Roberts &

Company paid $300 million for a 47 percent interest in the highly leveraged Flagstar. Approximately 70 percent of the Denny's restaurants were owned by Flagstar and the rest were owned by franchisees. In contrast to fast-food chains such as McDonald's and Burger King, Denny's operated sit-down restaurants, so when a restaurant became crowded, customers did not wait in lines but instead waited to be seated, order, and be served.

In response to the agents' charges, Flagstar ordered an investigation of the incident. After questioning employees at the restaurant the day after the lawsuit was filed, the company fired the manager of the restaurant for failure to report the episode. Flagstar officials also defended their employees' actions. Steve McManus, a senior vice president who had questioned employees at the Annapolis restaurant, said the delay in the agents' service was caused by the size of their party and the complexity of their orders, which caused a backlog in the kitchen. The black agents were most affected by the delay because their table was the last to order. He said, "It's a service issue, not a discriminatory issue." In response, the agents said a group of white customers entered the restaurant after them, ordered, and was served while the agents waited. Flagstar CEO Jerome J. Richardson said, "We had one cook, and either two or three servers to serve the entire restaurant. If they say they were discriminated against, I apologize. But in my opinion, there was not an intent to not serve black people."[43]

The Annapolis incident was neither the beginning nor the end of Denny's troubles. "It's 1993 and certain things should not be happening. I just cannot imagine them not wanting to serve those children," said Randy Shepard, director of the all-black Martin Luther King All Children's Choir of Virginia. Shepard was referring to a June 1993 incident in

---

[43] *Newsweek*, July 19, 1993.

which 70 children and 54 adults were returning home by bus to Raleigh, North Carolina, after weekend performances in the Washington, D.C., area and were allegedly refused service at two Denny's restaurants. According to Shepard, the group first went to a Shoney's restaurant off Interstate 95 in Woodbridge, Virginia. "The manager there said he would be glad to accommodate us, but there was only 20 minutes before they closed, and service would take a long time," Shepard said. "He suggested we go to Denny's down the street." The three buses then stopped at a Denny's outside Dale City, Virginia, about 11:00 P.M. Shepard said he entered the restaurant and asked a manager if he could accommodate the group. "He said he couldn't accommodate us because he didn't have the staff and recommended a larger Denny's, the next exit down." At the second Denny's, Shepard said the manager met him in the parking lot and also told him he could not accommodate the group. "Some of the children had gone in to use the bathroom, so I went to get them," Shepard said. He added that the restaurant did not seem full, and "they seemed like they had ample enough staff around, and it appeared they had already started clearing tables to serve us." Prince William County Supervisor John Jenkins, whose district included one of the two Denny's restaurants, commented: "I feel like they ought to close that chain down. They have an interstate service route and ought to have enough help to serve those customers." Jenkins called for a county investigation of the incident.

Denny's officials and employees disputed many of Shepard's claims. "Our restaurant can't handle that kind of crowd—not with just two cooks and four servers. And I'm not prejudiced," said waitress Kimberly Marshall, who was white. However, her husband Dennis Marshall, an African American, said: "If you're open for business, you can't say you can't serve that many people. It doesn't make sense to me."[44] Denny's officials said that the first restaurant was full, the second was half full, and the bus driver had "indicated the group outside was in a hurry." Furthermore, a company spokesman stated that "in both Denny's restaurants, we offered to serve the large group and indicated there would be a lengthy wait," but the group left before the restaurant could serve them. Denny's officials stated that they were not equipped to serve 130 people with a staff appro-

priate for the off-peak time of 11:00 P.M. The officials acknowledged that the manager at the first Denny's suggested that the group try the other restaurant, but added that "he offered to phone the other restaurant to make the arrangements." Coleman Sullivan, vice president of communications of Flagstar, said, "It was 11:00 P.M. on a Sunday, and our manager told this bus group it would take a while to serve them. There was no discrimination."[45]

Eighteen months before the Annapolis incident, the Department of Justice (DOJ) had initiated an investigation of the Denny's chain in response to complaints from African American customers in California. After the investigation substantiated allegations of bias, Denny's and the DOJ entered into negotiations to settle the complaints. The complainants also took other action. Their lawyers had earlier established a toll-free number to encourage others to report racist episodes so they could qualify a class action suit.[46] On March 24, 1993, a group of 32 African American customers filed a class action civil suit in San Jose alleging several discriminatory practices, including the following:

- A group of 18 African American college students was forced to pay a cover charge of $2 each and pay for their meals in advance at a Denny's restaurant in San Jose, California, while six white students acquainted with one of the African American students were seated at a nearby table and were not required to pay the cover charge or pay in advance for their meals. According to the company, several Denny's restaurants had in the past implemented a "late night policy" requiring all groups of 10 or more to prepay for meals after 10 P.M. as a "security measure" to thwart the rising theft of meals, but the policy had "not been enforced in a discriminatory fashion."

- A racially mixed couple, Danny and Susan Thompson, took their three children to a Denny's restaurant in Vallejo, California, to celebrate their daughter Rachel's 13th birthday. According to the lawsuit, Denny's refused to serve Rachel their famous free birthday meal, despite the fact that she had both her baptismal certificate and school identification. "I felt violated, humiliated, and embarrassed,"

so we didn't eat there. I can't adequately describe the pain that you feel to see this happen to your child," Mrs. Thompson said.

- Denny's allegedly threatened or forcibly removed African American customers from several California restaurants.

- Denny's employed "a general policy of limiting black customers," using the term "blackout" to signal employees when too many blacks were in a restaurant. The suit also alleged that one district manager instructed store managers to "start cracking down and get rid of some of those blackouts." Some Denny's managers asked for prepayment of meals or told blacks that the restaurant would be closing soon.

- When an employee at a Denny's restaurant in San Jose, California, told a manager a customer's eggs needed to be recooked, he was told to "take it to the niggers, and if they have a complaint, tell them to come see me."

The class action lawsuit came only 5 months after a $105 million settlement of an employment discrimination suit against Shoney's, Inc., another leading national restaurant chain, which alleged that the company limited the number of African American employees at each location and restricted them to kitchen jobs by blackening the o in the word Shoney's on the job application to indicate an applicant was an African American. Lawyers for Saperstein, Mayeda, Larkin & Goldstein, the law firm that represented the plaintiffs in the Shoney's case and was currently negotiating for the plaintiffs in the Denny's suit, commented that the Denny's case may be more remarkable because it dealt with mistreatment of the most important element of any business, the customer. "These practices evoke the bald racism of the 1950s," the lawyers said in a statement. Former California Supreme Court Justice Cruz Reynoso, who had been recalled by California voters and was now a law professor at the University of California at Los Angeles, said he believed the Denny's case was the first "pattern and practice" racism case in the past 15 or 20 years involving a major public accommodation.

The service in a restaurant depended on a variety of factors, including Denny's policies, the practices of the restaurant managers, and the individual employees of the restaurant. The problem for Flagstar was twofold. First, although the company encouraged Denny's franchises to end practices that might be discriminatory, there was a limit to the control the company could exercise over the privately owned outlets. Second, the application of existing policies was problematic because policies intended to apply to all customers might instead be applied in a discriminatory fashion at individual locations by individual managers or employees.

While the negotiations with the DOJ were underway, Denny's addressed some of the issues by apologizing to customers, firing or transferring "bad-apple" employees, and creating a cultural diversity team. The "late night policy," which had been instituted to prevent diners from walking out without paying, was discontinued at all the chain's restaurants, both company owned and franchised. Mr. Richardson said, "The managers had problems with customers walking out on checks. Some required prepayment, which can be a problem when it's not applied to everyone."[47] In addition, Flagstar initiated meetings with civil rights groups.

Complicating the situation, Mr. Richardson, a former wide receiver for the Baltimore Colts who had started with a single hamburger restaurant in Spartansburg, South Carolina, had for 6 years been working to obtain one of the two National Football League franchises to be awarded in the fall of 1993. Denny's and Mr. Richardson had been criticized by the Reverend Jesse Jackson and his son, who headed the Rainbow Coalition. The younger Mr. Jackson had asked in a May 27 press release, "Are we seeing the beginning of a racist sports connection and pattern here?"[48] ∎

SOURCE: This case was prepared from public sources by Abraham Wu under the supervision of Professor David P. Baron. Copyright © 1994 by the Board of Trustees of the Leland Stanford Junior University. All rights reserved. Reprinted with permission.

[47]*Fortune*, July 12, 1993.
[48]*The Wall Street Journal*, July 1, 1993.

## PREPARATION QUESTIONS

1. What were the causes of the individual incidents at the Denny's restaurants? Were they more than incidents of bad service? What might they reflect? How serious are they?

2. What responsibilities does Flagstar have with regard to the incidents?

3. What roles have the media and plaintiffs' attorneys played in this issue?

4. What should Flagstar do about these incidents and allegations? What should Flagstar do about the lawsuits?

5. What policies should it adopt for its customer service and its employees, and how should those policies be implemented? How should it deal with independently owned Denny's restaurants?

# Citigroup and Subprime Lending

On September 6, 2000, Citigroup, Inc., announced an agreement to acquire Associates First Capital Corporation in an exchange of shares valued at $31.1 billion. The Associates was the largest publicly traded finance company with managed assets of $100 billion and shareholders equity of $10.4 billion. The Associates had 2,750 offices with approximately 1,000 in the United States and the rest in 13 other countries.[49] The Associates also did business through thousands of independent brokers. Citigroup had managed assets of $791 billion, and operations in 100 countries.

Citigroup chairman and CEO Sanford I. Weill said, "our consumer finance operations are very well regarded. We are excited about the prospects for the combined operations." Keith W. Hughes, chairman and CEO of the Associates, said, "We are excited to be joining forces in this effort, contributing the energy and drive that has led the Associates to twenty-five consecutive years of record earnings."[50] Citigroup planned to merge the U.S. operations of the Associates into its CitiFinancial unit, which also provided consumer finance. Hughes would be the head of CitiFinancial and join Citigroup's board of directors as vice chairman.

The acquisition of the Associates brought Sandy Weill back to his roots. In 1986 he became CEO of a Baltimore finance company, Commercial Credit Corporation, that lent to working class families. He built the company through internal growth

and acquisition and later merged The Travelers Group with Citicorp to form one of the largest financial institutions in the country. As a result of the merger Commercial Credit was succeeded by CitiFinancial, which in 2000 had $18.5 billion in loans and $390 million in profits. The Associates had profits of $409 million in the second quarter of 2000 and had 480,000 home equity loans outstanding. With the acquisition CitiFinancial would become the nation's largest finance company.

A major profit source for CitiFinancial and the Associates was subprime lending—lending to people who did not meet the customary credit requirements of banks. The growth of subprime lending during the 1990s had been spectacular, with lending increasing 13-fold between 1993 and 1999. Outstanding subprime loans were estimated at $150 billion in 1998. This lending had provided access to credit to many people who would not have qualified for prime loans because of their credit history. A study by Freddie Mac, however, estimated that perhaps one-third of subprime borrowers could have qualified for prime loans, and Freddie Mac chairman Franklin Raines believed that as many as half might be able to qualify. One study found that 35 percent of the subprime borrowers were over 55, and African Americans were twice as likely to borrow in the subprime market as in the prime market.

The growth in subprime lending was also driven by aggressive marketing by the subprime lenders. The lenders relied on both mass advertising and direct marketing. One form of subprime lending was home equity loans marketed to borrowers to consolidate their bills. *Business Week* commented on an example

---

[49] The Associates had been owned for a decade by the Ford Motor Company, which spun off the unit in 1998.
[50] Citigroup press release, September 6, 2000.

of such a loan on the CitiFinancial Web site: "I now can afford so much more than I thought possible," says Spencer L. of Worcester, Mass. A sample worksheet shows that Spencer can take out a $20,000 home-equity loan to consolidate his bills, pay off credit cards, and reap $310.57 in 'monthly savings.' The fine print notes that Spencer will pay that back in 120 months at a 13.49 percent interest rate. But nowhere on the Web site does it say that it would cost $36,500 to pay off starting debts of $17,000."[51]

Subprime lending had generated vocal complaints from consumer and activist groups, which referred to it as predatory lending. Many of the people who borrowed in the subprime market were lower income, minority, and elderly, and consumer advocates claimed that they often did not understand the loans and what was bundled with them. Some of these critics referred to the Associates as a "rogue company."

A second aspect of subprime lending was single-premium life insurance sold along with a loan to pay off the principal in the case of the death of the borrower. The insurance premiums for several years were typically charged up front and added to the loan principal. Moreover, the insurance often covered not only the loan principal but the insurance premiums and the interest on the loan. Frequently, the insurance did not cover the entire period of the loan. Because the premiums were packed into the loan principal, the insurance was financed at the high interest rates on the loans. The resulting cost of single-premium life insurance was considerably higher than the cost of term life insurance. This single-premium life insurance was criticized by community activists and government officials because many borrowers did not understand that it was included in the loan principal. The Consumer Federation of America called this "the worst insurance rip-off" in America.

As an example of a complaint involving insurance, Benny and Linda Mackey of Chocowinity, North Carolina, had fallen behind on their $519 monthly mortgage payments, and refinanced their $37,117.76 mortgage with the Associates. The Associates added a $4,231 "loan discount" to their principal and also added $4,910.08 in life insurance premiums to the loan. At a 14.99 percent interest rate the Mackey's monthly payment rose to $592. When they missed some payments, the Associates harassed them and threatened foreclosure, according to

the Mackeys. The Mackeys filed a complaint with State of North Carolina, and the Associates lowered their payments to $370 at a 9 percent interest rate. Alan Hirsch, a deputy attorney general of North Carolina, said that single-premium credit insurance was the most egregious practice, since "many borrowers don't understand it's been included in the loan." The attorney general of North Carolina had begun an investigation of the Associates in 1999 and subsequently filed a lawsuit against the company. The investigation focused on packing insurance premiums in the loan and financing it at high rates. North Carolina also enacted an antipredatory lending law.

Both the Associates and CitiFinancial sold single-premium life insurance. The Associates issued insurance through its subsidiary, Associates Corporation of North America, which over the past 5 years had collected $1.8 billion in insurance premiums and recorded earnings of $397.5 million.[52] Fannie Mae and Freddie Mac refused to buy first mortgages with single-premium credit insurance.

One of the principal critics of subprime lenders was ACORN (Association of Community Organizations for Reform Now). ACORN was an organization with 500 neighborhood chapters in 50 cities focusing on supporting low- and moderate-income families. It filed numerous lawsuits on behalf of people whom it viewed as victims. ACORN referred to subprime lending as "legalized robbery" and listed the following among the predatory lending tactics used by subprime lenders:[53]

- Charging excessive interest rates not justified by the risk involved.
- Charging and financing excessive points and fees.
- Packing loans with additional products like financial credit insurance or club memberships.
- Charging extended prepayment penalties that trap people in high-interest-rate loans.
- Financing single-premium credit insurance.
- Misrepresenting the terms and conditions of loans.
- Charging unfair and excessive late fees.
- Refinancings, and especially repeated refinancings, that result in no benefit to the borrower.
- Balloon payments and negative amortization schedules on high-cost loans.

[52]*The New York Times*, October 22, 2000.
[53]ACORN, "Predatory Lending: A Growing Problem," www.acorn.org.

- Targeting high-cost loans to vulnerable borrowers, including the elderly, low-income, and minority families.
- Using harassing and intimidating collection techniques.

In particular, ACORN had criticized Citi-Financial and the Associates for sales of single-premium life insurance, high up-front fees, and high prepayment fees. ACORN had asked the companies to stop these practices.[54]

AARP (American Association of Retired Persons) also was concerned about predatory mortgage lending because many people over 50 were using subprime borrowing. AARP was studying subprime lending and was considering a campaign against it. A campaign would involve both public education and support for stringent state legislation to curtail abuses.

Regulation of subprime lending was loose, and the relevant agencies were considering whether tighter supervision was warranted. The relevant regulators were the Comptroller of the Currency, the Federal Reserve Board, the Federal Deposit Insurance Corporation, and the Office of Thrift Supervision.

One lever of the community activists had been taken away in 1999 when Congress passed banking reform legislation. The legislation eliminated a requirement that in approving bank acquisitions the Federal Reserve Board had to solicit and consider consumer opinions on how well the banks met the requirements of the 1977 Community Reinvestment Act (CRA). That Act required banks to loan in the communities in which their offices were located. The legislation eliminated this requirement in the case of the acquisition of financial companies that did not take deposits. Since the Associates did not take deposits, Citigroup was only required to provide information to federal regulators about CRA performance. Groups such as ACORN had regularly used the CRA requirement to scrutinize the banks' lending data and extract lending pledges from the banks.

When the acquisition was announced, Representative Stephanie Tubbs Jones (D-OH) said, "Citigroup needs to know there are members of the House banking committee—particularly the Congressional Black Caucus members—who are concerned about the merger and they need to be concerned about our concerns." A North Carolina group had shown the Black Caucus a videotape of a man who had gone to an Associates office for a loan to buy groceries and over the next 10 years had been persuaded to refinance the loan 11 times, resulting in a $50,000 mortgage at an interest rate of 19 percent.[55]

The Associates had been named in approximately 700 lawsuits and had been fined $147,000 by the state of Georgia. The Department of Justice had filed a lawsuit against the Associates alleging that one of its credit card banks had violated fair lending laws in marketing credit cards to Hispanics.[56] The Federal Trade Commission (FTC) had initiated an investigation of the Associates in 1999 for allegations of deceptive marketing practices. Since 1998 the FTC had filed 14 lawsuits involving subprime lending, including complaints against the Associates.

Citigroup was surprised by the intensity of the criticisms of its acquisition of the Associates and more generally of subprime lending. The allegations of predatory lending and deception were serious, and they threatened a highly profitable business.

In response to the criticisms William Street, a Citigroup attorney, said, "Citigroup is committed to improving . . . the compliance systems and operation systems and anything else they determine needs improving to meet their standards."[57]

In a letter to the Comptroller of the Currency, the Superintendent of the New York State Banking Department, and the Chairman of the Federal Deposit Insurance Corporation, the regulators that had to approve the acquisition, Sandy Weill stated, "We prize our long-standing reputation for service to customers and communities and we recognize that CitiFinancial's position as the soon-to-be largest consumer finance company in the U.S. gives it the opportunity to play an even more important and valuable role in communities in which it does business."[58] The motto on Citigroup's 1999 annual report was "Leading by Example." ∎

SOURCE: Copyright © 2001 by David P. Baron. All rights reserved. Reprinted with permission.

---

[54] ACORN also launched a campaign against Household Finance for what it called abusive and predatory practices.

[55] *The Washington Post*, September 15, 2000.
[56] *The Washington Post*, September 15, 2000.
[57] *The Washington Post*, September 15, 2000.
[58] Citigroup, November 7, 2000.

**PREPARATION QUESTIONS**

1. Are there moral concerns associated with subprime lending? Are those moral concerns based on utilitarianism, rights, or justice considerations?

2. What are the moral determinants of nonmarket action in this case?

3. What should CitiFinancial do about single-premium life insurance?

4. What should CitiFinancial do about the other allegations of abuse?

5. Should Citigroup support the efforts of ACORN and AARP to weed out unscrupulous practices? Should it support tighter regulatory supervision of the subprime lending market?

6. What policies should Citigroup adopt for subprime lending?

# Reporting of Clinical Trial Results

Pharmaceutical companies conducted clinical trials in conjunction with the initial approval by the Food and Drug Administration (FDA) for marketing of a new drug. Approval was given for the specific indications (diseases, treatments, and patients; e.g., children) for which the trials had shown the drug to be safe and efficacious. Pharmaceutical companies also subsequently tested approved drugs for indications in addition to those for which approval had been given. For example, an antidepressant such as Prozac had been approved for use by adults and after additional clinical testing had been approved for treating children with depression.

Once a drug had been approved for one indication, doctors could prescribe it for any purpose. Although Prozac was the only antidepressant approved for children, doctors could prescribe other antidepressants for children. Pfizer's antidepressant Zoloft had been approved for treating obsessive-compulsive disorder in children, but doctors also prescribed it for depression. Estimates were that in 2002, 10.8 million prescriptions for antidepressants were written for patients under 18 years old, with 3 million of those for Zoloft.[59] Most of the antidepressants under testing for children were selective serotonin reuptake inhibitors (SSRIs), which had led to a revolution in the treatment of depression. Some doctors believed that the sharp decline in suicides among young people since 1994 was due to the use of antidepressants.[60]

Although the clinical trial data required by the FDA were proprietary, summaries and trial descrip-

tions, but not the underlying data, had to be made public. In the case of post-marketing clinical trials for approvals for new indications, pharmaceutical companies were required to report safety information to the FDA but were not required to disclose the data publicly. The data on efficacy did not have to be reported until an application for approval was submitted to the FDA. If no application were submitted, the efficacy data typically were not reported.

One incentive to conduct trials on children was a pediatrics-study law that provided a 6-month patent extension for a drug that was tested in two clinical studies on children. Pfizer, for example, had conducted two tests on Zoloft, neither of which found that Zoloft outperformed a placebo by a statistically significant level. Pfizer did not seek approval for treating depression in children but did receive a 6-month patent extension.[61] To obtain the patent extension, Pfizer filed the test results with the FDA, and a summary of the test results was made public.[62] The clinical trial data, however, remained proprietary, and by law the FDA was not permitted to make the data public without consent from the company.

GlaxoSmithKline (GSK) conducted five clinical studies of its antidepressant Paxil with mixed results. One study suggested that Paxil could be effective for children, and GSK publicized the results. A second study showed Paxil was no more effective than a placebo. Three clinical studies of Paxil on children showed evidence of possible suicide-related behavior

---

[59]Other antidepressants used for treating children were Wyeth's Effexor and GlaxoSmithKline's Paxil and Wellbutrin.
[60]*The Wall Street Journal*, August 5, 2004.

[61]*The Wall Street Journal*, August 6, 2004.
[62]The summaries were available at www.fda.gov/cder/pediatric. The FDA added to Zoloft's label that the drug had contributed to weight loss but that its effectiveness for depression "has not been established." (*The Wall Street Journal*, August 6, 2004.)

in patients.[63] One of the three studies was published, and based on that study the company wrote to doctors in the United Kingdom stating that Seroxat, the name of Paxil in the United Kingdom, "should not be prescribed as new therapy" for depression in children.[64] GSK did not write to doctors in the United States regarding Paxil.

Pressure mounted for pharmaceutical companies to make public all their data from clinical trials on children. Moreover, critics charged that the companies selectively released the results of clinical trials—making public the positive results for marketing purposes and not releasing the negative results.

Critics argued that all clinical trial data should be made public so that doctors and patients could be better informed about treatments. Antidepressant use for treating children was the flash point. Dr. Andrew Mosholder, an epidemiologist with the FDA's drug safety division, prepared a study of the risks of antidepressants for suicidal tendencies in children. The study was viewed as preliminary by the FDA and was not forwarded to the FDA advisory committee.[65] The FDA began an additional study on the issue, and as a precautionary measure required stronger warnings on labels. Senator Charles Grassley (R-IA) led a congressional investigation into whether the FDA had suppressed the study by Dr. Mosholder.

New York State Attorney General Eliot Spitzer filed a lawsuit against GSK alleging fraud because the company had concealed negative results on pediatric trials of Paxil. Spitzer said, "The point of the lawsuit is to ensure that there is complete information to doctors for making decisions in prescribing. The record with Paxil, we believe, is a powerful one that shows that GSK was making selective disclosures and was not giving doctors the entirety of the evidence."[66] The lawsuit disclosed an internal GSK memorandum that stated it would be necessary to "effectively manage the dissemination of these data in order to minimize any potential negative commercial impact."[67]

Data from Pfizer's two clinical trials were combined for an article published in the *Journal of the American Medical Association (JAMA)*. Because of

the larger sample size with the combined data, a statistically significant greater percent of the patients taking Zoloft had "responded" compared to the placebo.[68] The article did not report data on remission, a near absence of symptoms, among the study participants.[69] An article in the British journal *The Lancet* reviewed the unpublished data from the Pfizer studies along with data on other drugs, and stated that if remission data were available, "then they should publish it."[70]

Critics complained that positive test results were more commonly published in medical journals than were negative test results. Moreover, critics complained that companies selectively reported positive aspects of a test without reporting the full set of results. The *Washington Post* began an article on antidepressant trials as follows:

Makers of popular antidepressants such as Paxil, Zoloft, and Effexor have refused to disclose the details of most clinical trials involving depressed children, denying doctors and parents crucial evidence as they weigh fresh fears that such medicines may cause some children to become suicidal. The companies say the studies are trade secrets. . . . Although the drug-industry practice of suppressing data unfavorable to its products is legal, doctors and advocates say such secrecy distorts the scientific record. . . . "Conflicts of interest and the company control of the data have thrown out the scientific method," said Vera Hassner Sharav, a critic of the drugs and a patients' rights advocate. "If hundreds of trials don't work out, they don't publish them, they don't talk about them."[71]

In 2002 the 12 major medical journals whose editors belong to the Committee of Medical Journal Editors jointly published an editorial that stated, "The results of the unfinished trial may be buried rather than published if they are unfavorable to the sponsor's product. Such issues are not theoretical. There have been a number of recent public examples

63 *The Wall Street Journal*, June 3, 2004.
64 *The Washington Post*, January 29, 2004.
65 *The Wall Street Journal*, June 17, 2004.
66 *The New York Times*, June 3, 2004.
67 *The New York Times*, June 3, 2004.

68 The lead author on the *JAMA* article disclosed receiving financial support from the pharmaceutical industry for consulting and speaking services. (*The Wall Street Journal*, August 6, 2004.)
69 A subsequent review of the placebo on remission indicated that Zoloft did not outperform the placebo on remission.
70 *The Wall Street Journal*, August 6, 2004.
71 *The Washington Post*, January 29, 2004.

of such problems, and we suspect that many more go unreported."[72]

The *Canadian Medical Association Journal* (*CMAJ*) went further in a 2004 editorial:[73]

By concealing unfavorable evidence about efficacy and safety, pharmaceutical companies deceive physicians, their patients and, perhaps, shareholders. Worse, such concealment is a flagrant abuse of the trust freely offered to study investigators by research subjects. Nowhere is this more evident than in clinical trials of selective serotonin reuptake inhibitors (SSRIs) in children.

The *CMAJ* referred to the problem as the "file drawer" phenomenon. The *CMAJ* also disclosed that a researcher in a study of SSRIs in children had been required to sign a 10-year nondisclosure agreement in order to have access to company data. In the same issue of the *CMAJ* Merck announced, "Merck has adopted guidelines in which we commit to publish the results of hypothesis-testing clinical trials regardless of outcome."[74]

The Committee of Medical Journal Editors considered establishing a clinical trial registry as a prerequisite for the publication of test results in the journals. The Association of the British Pharmaceutical Industry had urged its members to voluntarily publish a registry of their trials but only 8 of the 80 members had done so.[75]

The American Medical Association approved a resolution asking the Department of Health and Human Services to begin a national clinical trials registry where pharmaceutical companies would be required to provide notice of any clinical trials to be conducted and report the results regardless of whether the results were positive or negative. Dr. Joseph M. Heyman stated, "We are concerned that this pattern of publication distorts the medical literature, affecting the validity and findings of systematic reviews, the decisions of funding agencies and, ultimately, the practice of medicine."[76] Merck quickly announced its support for the registry. The FDA said that it did not have the authority to establish a national registry and that congressional legislation would be required.

Dr. Mosholder's study reviewed data from 25 studies on nine antidepressant drugs, and evaluated the data using a number of levels of risk such as "suicide attempt," "preparatory actions towards imminent suicidal behavior," and "suicidal ideation."[77] The statistical significance of the results differed with the level of risk used and also varied between trials with the same drug. The overall pattern, however, suggested that suicidal tendencies might be somewhat higher with the antidepressants than with the placebo. The study had not yet been presented to the cognizant FDA advisory committee. ■

SOURCE: This case was prepared from public sources by Professor David P. Baron. Copyright © 2004 by David P. Baron. All rights reserved. Reprinted with permission.

## PREPARATION QUESTIONS

1. Do doctors and patients have a "right to know" about the results of all clinical trials? If so, is that right intrinsic or instrumental?

2. From the perspective of utilitarianism, should negative results be made public?

3. Identify the public and private politics pressures on pharmaceutical companies to disclose all clinical trial results.

4. As Pfizer or GlaxoSmithKline, should you make public negative or inconclusive clinical trial results?

5. Should you support a national registry of clinical trials and a requirement that trial results be made public?

[72] *The New York Times*, June 15, 2004.
[73] *Canadian Medical Association Journal*, February 17, 2004, p. 437.
[74] Laurence Hirsch, "Randomized clinical trials: What gets published and when?" *Canadian Medical Association Journal*, February 17, 2004, p. 481.
[75] *The New York Times*, June 15, 2004.
[76] *The New York Times*, June 16, 2004.
[77] *The Wall Street Journal*, August 5, 2004.

# Ethics Issues in International Business

## Introduction

Ethics issues abound within a country, but they take on added dimensions when a firm operates across national and cultural borders. Countries differ in the institutions that govern their political and economic activity as well as in their customs and culture. Countries also differ in their capacities to address issues of social and ethical concern. The capacities of many countries are limited by poverty, corruption, and political turmoil. Furthermore, their legal, health care, educational, and social services capabilities are often constrained by limited resources. World Bank (2004) data revealed that from 1980 to 2003 per capita real gross domestic product (GDP) in many countries in sub-Saharan Africa decreased substantially from an already impoverished level. In 2003, per capita income was 2 percent lower than in 1999 at only $490 compared to $37,610 in the United States, $39,980 in Switzerland, and $6,230 in Mexico. Life expectancy had fallen to 46 years in 2002 from 50 years in 1990. In contrast, the life expectancy in China in 2003 was 71 years and in Mexico was 74 years.

In contrast to the differences among countries, ethics principles are intended to be universal. Applying those principles in international settings with such major differences among countries, however, presents major challenges. Are the costs and benefits resulting from environmental protection in a low-income country the same as in a high-income country? Should a firm maintain the same safety and environmental standards in all countries? Do and should individuals in all countries have the same rights? Should practices that are morally unacceptable in one country be acceptable in other countries where they are legal? At a more general level, are the Western ethics systems considered in the previous chapters applicable in countries that do not have the Western intellectual and moral traditions?

Rather than attempt to address the broad range of ethics issues that arises in international business, emphasis here is on five specific issues—culture and moral standards, human rights, operating in developing countries, social entrepreneurship, and questionable foreign payments made to secure sales. The next section considers international law and institutions, and the following section addresses the perspective of cultural relativism and contrasts it with the universalism perspective. Issues associated with operating in developing countries are then considered, including social entrepreneurship and the development of private institutions to govern operating standards. The issues of corruption and questionable payments are then examined, and principles for reasoning about requests for payments are presented along with individual company and collective efforts to stop bribery and corruption.

# International Law and Institutions

Interactions between nations and foreign firms are governed by the laws of the host nation and by international law. International law consists of national laws that pertain to foreign persons, entities, and other nations; intergovernmental treaties and agreements; rulings by international courts; and actions of international bodies such as the United Nations and the Organization of American States.[1]

National laws include laws pertaining to international trade, official boycotts such as that against Cuba, the Foreign Corrupt Practices Act (FCPA), and required government approval for the acquisition by a foreign firm of a U.S. firm essential to national defense. Treaties and agreements include the North American Free Trade Agreement, the International Monetary Fund, the treaties of the European Union, the Geneva convention, the Kyoto Protocol on global climate change, reciprocal tax agreements, and accords on technical standards. International court rulings include those of the International Court of Justice, the World Court, the European Court of Justice, and the World Trade Organization's dispute resolution mechanism. Actions of international bodies include the United Nations' (UN) response to Iraq's invasion of Kuwait, the Law of the Sea, and the UN Convention on Contracts for the International Sale of Goods. Some international treaties are failures. The World Intellectual Property Organization treaty on intellectual property protection obtained fewer than 10 signatories, as developing countries refused to sign fearing that it would preclude them from having access to patented pharmaceuticals.

International agreements also provide frameworks within which continuing problems can be addressed. The 1985 Vienna Convention for the Protection of the Ozone Layer provided a framework for addressing ozone depletion and global warming.[2] The 1987 Montreal Protocol on Substances that Deplete the Ozone Layer resulted from this framework and committed the signatories to reduce CFCs to 50 percent of 1986 consumption. This reduction was judged insufficient, and the 1989 Helsinki Declaration committed the parties to eliminate all CFC production as soon as possible and no later than 2000.

The international law pertaining to global climate change began with UN action in 1988 and the 1989 Hague Declaration calling for the establishment of the UN Framework Convention on Climate Change. The convention covered greenhouse gasses not covered by the Montreal Protocol. The convention established a Conference of Nations as well as a secretariat and two advisory committees and committed the parties to concluding a more specific agreement by 1997. The result was the Kyoto Protocol on global climate change, which took effect in 2005.

International law differs from domestic law because sanctions may not be credible and enforcement is often left to individual nations. Some sanctions, such as the economic and military sanctions imposed on Iraq for the invasion of Kuwait and on the Taliban government of Afghanistan, have been shown to be credible. Many elements of international law, however, are respected not because of enforcement powers but because of mutual interests in preserving those laws. For example, the Dispute Settlement Body (DSB) of the World Trade Organization (WTO) rules on trade disputes, but it has no real

---

[1]See Shaw (2003) for a treatment of international law.
[2]See Shaw (1997, pp. 610–614).

enforcement powers. It can only authorize a country to impose duties on imports of another country that refuses to halt a trade violation. WTO members have generally accepted the DSB decisions.

In 1789 the first U.S. Congress passed the Alien Tort Claims Act (ATCA) to protect U.S. diplomats abroad from attacks and U.S. ships from pirates. In the 1990s activists sought to use the ATCA against U.S. corporations for alleged human rights violations abroad. In 1996, 12 refugees from Myanmar, formerly Burma, sued Unocal in the United States for alleged responsibility for murder, rape, forced labor, and torture. The actions were allegedly conducted by soldiers protecting the building of a natural gas pipeline by Unocal subsidiaries, the French oil company Total, and the government of Myanmar.

In 2004 the Supreme Court limited the grounds on which lawsuits could be filed under the ATCA, but allowed some cases involving serious human rights violations to go forward. A lawsuit against Unocal had been dismissed in federal court, but a California judge allowed the case to proceed. In another case a federal judge dismissed a lawsuit against 35 U.S. corporations alleging that their investments in South Africa had perpetuated crimes under apartheid. The application of the ATCA posed major uncertainties that would only be resolved by the Supreme Court.

Firms that operate internationally are subject to the laws of both their home country and their host countries, and at times those laws may be inconsistent. Moreover, practice and the law are often in conflict, as in the case of questionable foreign payments. The FCPA prohibits practices that are not uncommon in some countries. Because of the demands for payments, a number of companies adopted codes of conduct that go beyond the requirements of the law. Increasing and persistent corruption and pressure from the United States and other countries resulted in an international agreement to prohibit certain types of bribery.

Practices within a country pose both legal and ethical concerns. In some countries corruption is a fact (although not an inevitable fact) of life in many sectors of business activity.[3] In the mid-1980s Indonesia concluded that corruption and bribery in its ports were impeding economic growth by delaying imports and exports, at times for substantial periods. One report placed the amount of bribes at $200 million annually. To address the problem, the government ordered half the 13,000 employees in the Customs and Excise Service not to report to work. They continued to be paid their full wages, receive benefits, and even promotions, but they were not in a position to extract payments from importers and exporters.[4] A number of countries, including Indonesia, subsequently hired foreign firms to operate their customs services. The chapter case, *Complications in Marnera*, addresses management issues in a country with significant corruption.

## Cultural Relativism

In 1991 the Coalition for Justice in the Maquiladoras launched a campaign to improve conditions in the 2,000 U.S. plants (maquiladoras) located in the area near the U.S. border from Tijuana to Matamoros, Mexico. The coalition argued that although the firms met local standards in Mexico, they should meet the same health, safety, and environmental standards they met in the United States. "Moral behavior knows no borders. What would be wrong in the United States is wrong in Mexico," said Sister Susan Mika of the

---

[3]See Palmier (1989) for examples.
[4]*Far Eastern Economic Review,* June 6, 1990.

Interfaith Center on Corporate Responsibility (ICCR). Sister Mika expressed the view that moral standards are universal and that the standards in developed countries are the ones that should apply universally. The former is a rejection of cultural relativism, whereas the latter is a claim about particular standards.

Costs and benefits in the two countries differ, however, as is evident in the differences in per capita income. In 2001 the ICCR released a study of wages at maquiladoras. Reverend David Schilling said, "Our data show companies are nowhere paying a sustainable living wage."[5] Since wages and other costs differ, a utilitarianism or cost-benefit perspective could lead to different standards in Mexico and the United States. Differences also could be expected in terms of distributive justice as a result of the differences in standards of living between the countries.

Ethics, however, requires that firms, as well as individuals, not simply accept existing customs or prevailing practices in a country. Instead, firms and their managers are to evaluate issues of importance in terms of principles and standards that are universal.[6] Universal principles include respect for individual autonomy, improving aggregate well-being, and just actions regarding less-advantaged persons. Some cultural differences, such as in the institutions of political representation in democracies, are easily accepted. A democracy with a strong executive and a system of checks and balances, as in the United States, may be morally no better or worse than a parliamentary democracy. Some differences, such as the status of women in some fundamentalist Islamic societies, however, are not easily tolerated. Some differences, such as the suppression of political liberties and human rights in countries such as Myanmar and North Korea are not tolerated but are difficult to change.

In considering countries and cultures, Sen (1997) warned against generalizations that "hide more than they reveal." He advocated the simultaneous recognition of

- the significance of cultural variation
- the need to avoid cultural stereotypes and sweeping generalizations
- the importance of taking a dynamic rather than a static view of cultures
- the necessity of recognizing heterogeneity within given communities

In considering the relevance of differences in cultures and in the positions of peoples and nations in their development, it is useful to identify two extremes—cultural relativism and cultural imperialism—and to recognize that there is a considerable distance between the two. In its strongest version, cultural relativism holds that appropriate behavior in a country or culture is determined by its laws and customs.[7] That is, what is moral is defined by the customs within individual countries; when in Rome, do as the Romans do. If corruption is widespread in a country, then a firm should accept the functioning system and act as domestic firms do. At some level cultural differences and local practices surely are important, and it is clear that moral standards differ among cultures. Ethics principles, however, are to be universal rather than culturally determined.

Cultural imperialism in its strongest form means that in operating internationally a firm maintains the standards of its home country and judges others by those standards.[8]

---

[5]*The Wall Street Journal*, June 28, 2001. The study was titled, "Making the Invisible Visible: A Study of the Purchasing Power of Mexican Maquila Workers," ICCR, New York.
[6]See Donaldson (1989, Ch. 2) and Freeman and Gilbert (1988, Ch. 2) for analyses and rejections of cultural relativism. Brandt (1959) provides an extended evaluation of ethical relativism.
[7]See Bowie (1990).
[8]De George (1993) argues for an intermediate position in which the goal is not a set of ethics principles on which agreement is unlikely but rather is a set of international guidelines for business practice on which everyone can agree.

Cultural imperialism is surely not universally applicable, since the differences among cultures and countries are difficult to ignore. Donaldson (1996) cites the instance of a U.S. company that caught one of its employees in China stealing and turned the employee in to the authorities—who had the employee executed.

Donaldson identifies two fundamental conflicts between universal principles and local customs and practices. The first is a "conflict of relative development," which requires firms to recognize that countries and their peoples may differ in their capabilities due to their stages of economic development. He advocates that the following question be asked about local practices:

Would the practice be acceptable at home if my country were in a similar stage of economic development?

Levi Strauss & Company, for example, uses suppliers that pay the prevailing wage and employ children as young as 15, when that is consistent with host country laws. The answer to the question is that a firm is likely justified in paying the prevailing wage rate and legally hiring children. But, should it meet only local workplace safety standards? One answer is based on whether local safety standards are unreasonable to the point of jeopardizing a person's human dignity by failing to treat the person as an end as well as a means.

The second conflict is a "conflict of cultural tradition." In many cases, this conflict is more difficult to resolve. Donaldson (1996, p. 60) proposes,

Managers should deem a practice permissible only if they can answer no to both of the following questions: Is it possible to conduct business successfully in the host country without undertaking the practice? And is the practice a violation of a core human value?

For example, the arbitrary firing of employees is unlikely to be necessary to operate successfully and is a violation of basic principles. A company thus would not be justified in acting in such a manner. Bribery, however, is sufficiently pervasive in some countries that it might be required at times to operate successfully. If bribery is not a violation of a core human value, a company could be justified in providing "facilitating payments" in certain circumstances, as indicated later in the context of questionable foreign payments. In considering whether it should do business in a country where the answer is persistently no to the first question and yes to the second question, Levi Strauss refused to do business in Myanmar.

Donaldson (1996, pp. 61–62) argues that three general principles should guide companies in their global business activity:

1. Respect for core human values (human dignity, respect for basic rights, and good citizenship), which determine the absolute moral threshold for all business activities.
2. Respect for local traditions.
3. The belief that context matters when deciding what is right and wrong.

He also offers five guidelines for "ethical leadership": (1) Treat corporate values and formal standards of conduct as absolutes.[9] (2) Design and implement conditions of engagement for suppliers and customers. (3) Allow foreign business units to help formulate ethics standards and interpret ethics issues. (4) In host countries, support efforts to decrease institutional corruption. (5) Exercise moral imagination.

---

[9] For example, do not make exceptions to standards solely for the purpose of improving one's business prospects.

As an example of moral imagination, Levi Strauss faced a dilemma in Bangladesh. It learned that one of its suppliers was employing children younger than 14 years of age. The income earned by the children was important to their impoverished families, yet their working deprived them of the opportunity to attend school. Faced with this dilemma Levi Strauss convinced the supplier to pay the children their wages and benefits while they attended school and guarantee that they could return to their jobs once they completed their schooling.[10] Levi Strauss paid for their tuition, books, and school uniforms.

As indicated in Chapters 19 and 20, ethics frameworks can differ in terms of how the good and the right are conceived, as well as in their methods of analysis and their prescriptions. These differences, coupled with the differences among countries, suggest that at least some differences in practices and standards should be tolerated. Yet there are universal principles that are sufficiently important that firms should work toward their achievement. Donaldson (1989, pp. 81–86) proposes that respect for and promotion of rights should be universal and that all nations, firms, and individuals have a duty to respect a certain minimal set of rights. Those rights are the following:

1. Freedom of physical movement
2. Ownership of property
3. Freedom from torture
4. Fair trial
5. Nondiscriminatory treatment (freedom from discrimination on the basis of such characteristics as race and/or sex)
6. Physical security
7. Speech and association
8. Minimal education
9. Political participation
10. Subsistence

Using a distinction suggested by Shue (1980), Donaldson argues that firms have a duty not to deprive individuals of any of these rights and an affirmative duty to help protect individuals from being deprived of any of the last six. He also argues that the rights to nondiscriminatory treatment, political participation, and ownership of property are subject to cultural interpretation. One might disagree about which rights should be included in these sets, but the concept that respect for and promotion of certain rights constitutes minimal acceptable behavior is important. The next section considers two companies' attempts to address human rights issues.

# Human Rights and Justice

Some ethics issues arise not from the actions of individuals and firms, but instead from the policies of countries. Particularly in the case of countries that are not democracies, ethics concerns pertaining to human rights and justice can arise. In some countries, firms may be required to implement aspects of morally objectionable policies. For example, in China firms have responsibilities for enforcing aspects of the government's one-child-per-family law. Many people view this policy as violating basic human rights, such as those spelled out in the Universal Declaration of Human Rights proclaimed by the United Nations in 1948 and endorsed by many countries.

---

[10]See "Third-World Families at Work: Child Labor or Child Care?" *Harvard Business Review*, January–February, 1993.

Because of concerns about human rights in the countries in which their suppliers were located, several firms, including Levi Strauss and Reebok, formulated human rights statements pertaining to their business partners. Reebok's "Human Rights Production Standards," covered the following subjects: nondiscrimination, working hours/overtime, fair wages, child labor, freedom of association, and a safe and healthy work environment.

Reebok applied its standards at the level of its business partners, and Levi Strauss also developed guidelines for its business partners. In addition, the company applied its standards at the country level. It concluded that it should not do business with even an exemplary contractor if the policies of its home country resulted in pervasive violations of human rights.

To implement the guidelines, Levi Strauss established Country Assessment Guidelines and conducted an internal country review process that utilized information from a variety of public sources, such as the United Nations and the U.S. Department of State, as well as its own independent assessments. The review process led the company to withdraw immediately from Myanmar because of pervasive violations of human rights and to announce that it would withdraw over several years from China. The company also immediately canceled all contracts in China where prison labor was used, since the prisoners could have been convicted for political reasons. As the human rights conditions in China improved, the company reversed its decision in 1998.

## Slave Labor in Saipan?

Shortly after Levi Strauss adopted them, its guidelines underwent their first challenge. The issue involved a contractor based in the U.S. Territory of Saipan that worked for a number of apparel firms, including Levi Strauss, Liz Claiborne, and Eddie Bauer. Levi Strauss learned in late 1991 that the contractor was in legal trouble, and one of its vice presidents met with the contractor in San Francisco. He asked blunt questions about the contractor's legal problems, but the contractor assured him that there were only routine problems and that he need not be concerned.

A few months later the NBC television affiliate in Washington, D.C., broadcast a story about the Saipan contractor, alleging that he was using Chinese workers as "slave labor" and that the merchandise they produced was mislabeled as "Made in the U.S.A." In reality, products produced in Saipan are required to carry that label. The slave labor allegation, however, was more serious. It centered on the common practice in Saipan of bringing young women from China to work in the factories for a few years and then returning them to China. The young women were eager to come because the wages were high compared with wages in China. The story also reported that the contractor was about to plead no contest to a felony charge of denying workers compensation totaling several million dollars.

A day after the story made the national news, Levi Strauss executives met to begin their own investigation of the Saipan facilities. A group of senior executives visited the factory and found it to be an excellent facility—better than some in the United States. The dormitories where the workers were housed were substandard, but Levi Strauss concluded that the allegations of slave labor were unwarranted. What was clear, however, was that the contractor had consistently misled Levi Strauss. The recently approved Global Sourcing Guidelines called for business partners with standards consistent with the company's standards. Consequently, Levi Strauss canceled its contract with the Saipan contractor and paid several hundred thousand dollars in contract penalties to do so.

To Levi Strauss the Saipan incident indicated why guidelines were needed. They would protect the company's integrity and commercial success by preventing it from sourcing with contractors with questionable practices.

## Operating in Developing Countries

In developing countries, institutions are not always present to provide guidance to firms and their managers. Also, issues are more complex when people do not have the means to protect their rights and advance their interests. Poverty, lack of education, and inadequate health care create situations in which individuals cannot be expected to make the same decisions that would be made in a developed country. Furthermore, their governments may not have the means to provide the needed information, guidance, or regulation found in developed countries.

In developed countries, for example, the liability system assigns the social cost of injuries to producers and consumers, creating incentives for care and the reduction of hazards. In addition, regulation establishes safety standards and requires information and warnings about hazards. If institutions are not present or function imperfectly in a developing country, business is without a principal source of guidance. In such cases, the temptation may be to follow local practice. The consequences, however, may not be acceptable. Following local practice could lead to the exploitation of the ignorant and disadvantaged or the exposure of consumers or workers to serious hazards that they may not reasonably be able to avoid.

In such situations, ethics can provide guidance. To understand how a firm might reason in situations in which institutions are imperfect, consider the case of a safety decision about a product marketed in a developing country. Suppose that the product is safe under proper use but that misuse can result in injury. Also, suppose that many of the people who are likely to buy the product are impoverished and have a minimal formal education. There is no functioning liability system, and regulatory agencies are overburdened and cannot be expected to address the safety issue. The firm and its managers must provide their own guidance on appropriate action.

From the perspective of utilitarianism, the Calabresi and Melamed principles considered in Chapters 12 and 19 provide a basis for reasoning about the appropriate level of safety and how the product should be marketed. Those principles are intended to be applied in situations in which institutions are imperfect, entitlements and their protection are unclear, or transactions costs prohibit bargaining to resolve the issue. The principles first ask who is best placed to make a cost-benefit analysis of the product and its safety features. In a developed country, the answer is typically that the government is best placed to do so, as reflected in the institutions of liability and regulation. In the absence of those institutions, the responsibility falls on the firm and consumers. In a developing country, many consumers are poorly placed to evaluate hazards and exercise proper care. The firm thus has the moral responsibility to make the evaluation.

The Calabresi and Melamed principles also ask which party is best positioned to induce others to take actions that will improve the difference between social benefits and social costs. Consumers are certainly not in that position. The firm may be able to induce consumers to use the product properly and can take steps through product design to reduce the hazards from anticipated misuse. The former, for example, might require instructions presented in pictures as well as in words. In addition, marketing might focus on those market segments in which the product is most likely to be used properly. Similarly, distribution of the product might be restricted to outlets where instruction in proper use can be given. In a number of countries, however, such measures may not be sufficient.

The firm then is faced with the prospect of anticipatable misuse. Depending on the product in question, design and safety features can be effective means of reducing hazards from misuse, but the institutions of liability and regulation are not present to provide information on which safety features to incorporate.[11] The firm then is left with the issue of determining if the social costs of an injury in Bangladesh are the same as in Germany. Compensation for injuries is not the same even among developed countries, and the disparity between developed and developing countries can be considerable. The Calabresi and Melamed principles are incapable of resolving this issue. Utilitarianism evaluates alternatives using the preferences of those affected, which suggests using the trade-offs made in the developing country as the guide for deciding on the safety features to incorporate to reduce the hazards from anticipatable misuse. The chapter case, *University Games, Inc.*, addresses related issues facing a small business with limited resources.

Donaldson (1989, p. 116) addressed the issue of risks in developing countries and proposed a modification of Rawls's second principle to guide decisions about risks. He argued that the "difference principle would need to be adjusted to include freedom from risk as one of the primary goods normally covered by the principle." From this perspective a basic level of safety should be assured for all individuals, which could mean that higher standards than those practiced in developing countries should be used.

Firms are also guided by principles of rights and justice. When misuse can be anticipated, marketing a product to those who are likely to misuse it may constitute deception. This would violate moral rules focusing on treating individuals as ends whose ability to choose should be developed rather than their ignorance exploited. Advertising is frequently viewed as a culprit in such situations. Activists have campaigned for over 30 years against the practices used in marketing infant formula in developing countries. Similarly, critics argue that the promotion and advertising of cigarettes in developing countries not only causes health problems but also places an economic burden on the poor.

## AIDS and Developing Countries

Many developing countries lack the means to provide basic services for their people. Many of these same countries, particularly those in sub-Saharan Africa, have also been devastated by the AIDS pandemic. Some 20 million people worldwide have died from AIDS, and 40 million people are HIV positive, nearly three-quarters of whom are in sub-Saharan Africa. In some African countries the incidence is 30 to 40 percent.[12] AIDS has led to sharp declines in life expectancy and negative economic growth, since AIDS strikes the most productive age group. This has worsened impoverishment and countries' ability to address the pandemic.

The treatment of AIDS victims has been impeded by the high cost of AIDS drugs, all of which were under patent. Although there is no cure for AIDS, with a strict regimen of drugs AIDS had become a chronic treatable disease in developed countries. Those drugs, however, were priced high with many costing $10,000 or more a year. With the per capita income in sub-Saharan Africa averaging $1.50 a day, AIDS drugs were beyond the means of every country.

With many countries unable to provide care for AIDS victims, developed countries belatedly began to provide funds for treatment and prevention programs.[13] The United

[11]See the Chapter 12 case *California Space Heaters, Inc.*
[12]See the case "Note on AIDS and the Pharmaceutical Industry," P-41, Graduate School of Business, Stanford University, Stanford, CA.
[13]Private parties, and particularly the Gates Foundation, also funded care and prevention programs. Some, such as the AIDS Healthcare Foundation and Doctors without Borders, directly provided medical care. The Gates Foundation emphasized prevention programs and has spent over $1 billion in Africa.

Nations under the leadership of Secretary General Kofi Annan established the independent Global Fund to Fight AIDS, Tuberculosis and Malaria with $3 billion in funding financed by the developed countries. The United States pledged $3 billion a year for 5 years for AIDS treatment and prevention programs in developing countries, including a pledge to provide one-third of the Global Fund on a matching basis. The contributions from many countries lagged, however. Moreover, the Global Fund was unable to find enough well-organized recipient programs to spend the money it had.[14]

Some countries such as Brazil and Thailand used the "medical emergency" provisions of TRIPS to invoke compulsory licensing of AIDS drugs. In addition, India's pharmaceutical companies began to produce and export AIDS drugs under India's unique patent system.[15] The pharmaceutical companies argued vigorously that compulsory licensing weakened patent protection and diminished incentives to conduct research and development on AIDS drugs.[16]

Intense private and public politics were directed at pharmaceutical companies, and after many years they began to lower their prices under preferential pricing programs. Even at cost, however, the drugs were not affordable. The Part V integrative case, *GlaxoSmithKline and AIDS Drugs Policy*, addresses the challenges faced by the market leader in AIDS drugs in responding to the pandemic. The intensity of the private politics is illustrated in the following example.

[14]The Secretary General had said that $10 billion a year was needed to combat AIDS, but during the first 3 years the Global Fund allocated only $3 billion to 120 developing countries.
[15]See Chapter 12. India was forced by World Trade Organization rules to change its patent law.
[16]See Vachani and Smith (2004) for a perspective on AIDS drugs pricing.

---

**EXAMPLE**

## GlaxoSmithKline and Nonmarket Spillovers

For several years GlaxoSmithKline (GSK) had been under pressure from activists and the media for its pricing of AIDS drugs in the developing world, particularly in sub-Saharan Africa. Activists led by the AIDS Healthcare Foundation deployed a multipronged nonmarket strategy against GSK. One prong was to lobby investors to pressure GSK to lower its prices for AIDS drugs and make them more widely available. One of AHF's objectives was to enlist the aid of CalPERS, one of the largest funds in the United States, which held nearly $1 billion in GSK shares.

In 2003 an opportunity to pressure GSK was provided by a new United Kingdom (UK) law requiring a shareholder advisory vote on new compensation packages for executives of UK companies. The UK law reflected growing European opposition to American-style compensation systems. European opposition to lucrative compensation packages resulted in pressure against Germany's Mannesmann AG and France's Vivendi Universal SA. Percy Barnevik, former CEO and chairman of ABB Ltd., was forced to return $54.4 million of his pension package. Opposition also appeared in the United Kingdom to compensation plans at Vodafone PLC, Prudential PLC, and Marconi PLC.

GSK was a UK company, but CEO Jean-Pierre Garnier and GSK's top management team worked out of Philadelphia. Garnier and GSK argued that American-style compensation was necessary to compete for management talent in global competition. The component of the compensation package that served as a lightning rod was a "golden parachute" for Garnier estimated

*(Continued)*

*(Continued)*

to be worth $23.7 million. The compensation would be paid if Garnier lost his job due to an acquisition or resigned before 2007.

AIDS activists joined with British trade unions, including the union Amicus that represented GSK employees, to oppose the compensation package. AHF claimed that Garnier's golden parachute would buy AIDS treatment for 100,000 people. British mutual funds opposed the compensation package, and CalPERS joined in opposition. Sir Christopher Hogg, the non-executive chairman of GSK, wrote to shareholders telling them that

American-style compensation was required to compete with American pay scales and American companies.

At GSK's annual meeting the 2.8 billion votes were 50.72 percent to 49.28 percent against the compensation plan with CalPERS among those that voted against it. In addition, 17.69 percent of the shares were voted against election of Garnier to the board.

The vote was advisory, but management could not ignore it. Sir Christopher said, "The board takes this very seriously."

## Responsibility for Working Conditions in Suppliers' Factories

### Sweatshops

In the 1990s concern developed about "sweatshops" in Asia and Latin America that supplied U.S. footwear and apparel companies. The issue was propelled by poignant stories of poverty and abuse; nonmarket action by labor unions, human rights groups, and activists; and pressure from the U.S. Department of Labor. The media provided extensive coverage of the issue and advocated higher workplace standards. The pressure reached a crescendo when abuses at a Nike supplier in Vietnam were reported.[17] The president of Nike closed, many of the overseas factories were modern, as Levi Strauss had found in Saipan. The fear of many workers in the overseas factories was that higher standards would increase costs, causing purchasers to look elsewhere for lower cost suppliers. (See the Chapter 4 case *Nike in Southeast Asia*.) Yet in many of the countries in which the factories in question were located, few concerns over the working conditions were expressed. Moreover, since demand in those industries had grown rapidly as factories in the United States closed, many of the overseas factories were modern, as Levi Strauss had found in Saipan. The fear of many workers in the overseas factories was that higher standards would increase costs, causing purchasers to look elsewhere for lower cost suppliers.

To improve practices in suppliers' factories, President Clinton appointed an 18-member White House Apparel Industry Partnership, which included Nike, Reebok, L.L. Bean, Liz Claiborne, unions, human rights groups, and activist and advocacy representatives.[18] The task force was charged with producing a code and an enforcement mechanism to achieve standards including a 60-hour workweek, a minimum employment age of 14, and wage guidelines. The task force, however, became embroiled in strong disagreements about implementation details.

The Union of Needletrade, Industrial, and Textile Employees (UNITE) and activists sought a majority on the governing board of any organization the partnership created to audit compliance with the standards. The companies were worried that the groups that would conduct the audits of contractors' facilities would find that some met the standards and others did not, giving the former group a public relations advantage over the others. The companies were successful in having the board have an equal representation of companies and the other groups.

[17]One result was the 1997 enactment of the Sanders Amendment, which bans the import of foreign products produced with forced child labor.
[18]See Golodner (2000).

The other sources of disagreement proved to be more difficult, and the task force failed to reach an accord by the deadline. The two sides disagreed on the percent of supplier facilities to be inspected each year, and the labor and human rights groups pressed for "living wages," rather than the prevailing wages, for suppliers' employees. The labor and human rights groups also sought a provision directed at China requiring that workers have the right to form independent unions and engage in collective bargaining. Such a requirement could force companies not to source products in China, since China did not allow independent unions. Company representatives suggested that the motivation behind these labor provisions was protection of union jobs in the United States.

With the partnership deadlocked a group of committee members, including Liz Claiborne, Nike, Reebok, and a number of human rights groups, reached an agreement on standards and established a standing organization, the Fair Labor Association (FLA), to ensure compliance. The standards included a 60-hour workweek, a ban on employing children under the age of 15 unless the country explicitly allowed 14-year-olds to work, independent monitoring of suppliers' factories, and a requirement to pay the maximum of the official minimum wage and the prevailing market wage. The U.S. Secretary of Labor praised the agreement: "It is workable for business and creates a credible system that will let consumers know the garments they buy are not produced by exploited workers."[19]

Two members of the partnership, UNITE and an activist group, rejected the agreement. They joined with other activist groups, including the United Students Against Sweatshops, and other labor unions to form the Worker Rights Consortium (WRC) to work for more aggressive monitoring and higher standards including a living wage. Both the FLA and the WRC recruited affiliated members, primarily colleges and universities concerned about their licenses for sports apparel.

## Private Governance and Self-Regulation: The Fair Labor Association

The FLA was established in 1999 with many of the characteristics of a government institution. The FLA agreement specifies representation, decision rights, standards, monitoring, certification, public reporting, and amendment procedures. In 2004 the FLA included 12 companies with 31 labor and nongovernmental organizations (NGOs) on its advisory committee. The companies and the labor/NGOs each had six board seats, the 175 college and university affiliates held three board seats, and the chair had one seat. The FLA has a detailed code of workplace standards, as indicated in the previous section. The FLA code does not provide for a "living wage," as does the code for the WRC. A supermajority of two-thirds of the companies and two-thirds of the labor/NGOs is required to change the standards. This provides assurances to both sides that the standards will not be changed unless there is considerable consensus on both sides.

The FLA selected and certified a dozen independent third-party monitors to inspect a specified percent of the factories each year, and the companies chose from the set for the inspections. The FLA has also specified detailed procedures (Monitoring Guidance and Compliance Benchmarks) for the inspections. During the initial 2 to 3 years, independent monitoring of at least 30 percent of the participating companies' applicable facilities was required. Subsequently, 5 percent of a company's suppliers'

[19]*The New York Times*, November 5, 1998.

facilities were inspected annually. Inspections were unannounced, and the facilities inspected were chosen at random by the FDA staff and based on prior compliance reports. Any finding of noncompliance by an independent monitor was posted on the FLA Web site. The FLA also has a third-party complaint procedure that allows any person or organization to report "any situation of serious noncompliance" for any FLA member company. The FLA then reviews the complaint and investigates any verifiable violation of the code.

A number of industries have now established codes and certification processes for work practices, although they generally do not go as far as the FLA. The industries include coffee, diamonds, and chocolate. The number of organizations formed by industries to address working conditions and human rights will likely continue to increase to the extent that business is more responsive than governments to the underlying issues.

## Company Responses

Nike subsequently went beyond the FLA standards by pledging not to hire anyone under the age of 18 in its footwear plants and to meet U.S. air quality standards in the workplace. CEO Phil Knight stated, "The Nike product has become synonymous with slave wages, forced overtime and arbitrary abuse. I truly believe the American consumer doesn't want to buy products made under abusive conditions."[20] In 1999 Nike began a reporting system, "Transparency 101," under which it publicly released the external monitoring reports conducted by PricewaterhouseCoopers on 53 North American factories. It also posted information on the factories' efforts to implement the action plans developed as a result of the inspections. Nike also opened its contractors' facilities to student monitors and publicly released the reports on 32 contractors that produced college-licensed apparel. In 2005 in its corporate responsibility report Nike released the names of 700 of its suppliers and reviewed the problems remaining. In 2000 Phil Knight spoke at the United Nations about its participation in the UN-sponsored Global Alliance along with other companies and NGOs. The companies in the Global Alliance pledged to meet global labor and environmental standards.

Despite Nike's pledges and compliance efforts, Greenpeace refused to participate in the Global Alliance because companies such as Nike and Shell had been allowed to participate. Things were also contentious on a more personal level. Phil Knight had contributed $50 million to the University of Oregon, where he had been an undergraduate and had remained a "lifelong Duck." When the university joined the WRC, Knight, who had pledged an additional $30 million, withdrew his pledge and announced that "there will be no further donations of any kind to the University of Oregon." In 2001 Knight and the University reconciled their differences. The University of Oregon is no longer a member of the WRC.

The WRC claimed one success. After workers in a Mexican apparel maquiladora supplying Nike and Reebok boycotted the company cafeteria and staged a sit-in, the WRC sent a delegation to inspect the factory. It found violations of Mexican labor law and urged Nike and Reebok to ask the manufacturer to rehire all the workers that had been fired as a result of the sit-in. Nike, which had initiated its own inquiries when the strike began, independently called on the manufacturer to rehire the workers. Nike also called for independent monitoring of the factory. Media coverage resulted in worldwide attention to the situation and resulted in the rehiring of the employees and the ouster of the government-controlled union.

---

20 *The New York Times*, May 13, 1998.

## Social Entrepreneurship

The traditional business approach to addressing problems of poverty and illness involved voluntary donations to those in need. Merck developed a drug MECTIZAN for treating river blindness, which afflicts millions of people in developing countries. In 1987 Merck established a private-public partnership, the MECTIZAN Donation Program (MDP), to distribute the drug free to people in Africa where the disease was prevalent. The MDP now distributes the drug to 40 million people a year in 34 countries in Africa, Latin America, and Yemen. The MDP is complemented by a group of NGOs that support and provide treatment for river blindness. The NGOs obtain 50–50 matching grants from Merck to fund their treatment.

In contrast to the MDP, social entrepreneurship involves establishing commercially self-sustaining enterprises dedicated to improving the lives of people. The SouthShore Bank discussed in Chapter 18 was funded by donations of capital without the expectation of a financial return and has filled a market niche, lending to people who would not otherwise have been able to borrow from a bank. Requiring that the enterprise be commercially self-sustaining imposes the discipline of the market on the enterprise. Moreover, the lending supports small businesses and private housing rehabilitation projects that the borrowers have identified as commercially viable.

In 1974 Muhammad Yunus, an economics professor in Bangladesh, became concerned about the devastating poverty from which people were seemingly unable to escape. As he interviewed people he learned that many women made by hand small objects that they sold in local markets. Many borrowed in the morning from local lenders, purchased materials, made and sold the objects, and repaid the lender at the end of the day. The interest rates were usurious, leaving the women at best with a subsistence income and unable to improve their situation. He quickly identified 42 people in a similar situation and found that in total they needed only $27 a day in lending. Yunus began borrowing from a bank on his own account and lending to the people. The borrowers repaid the loans, and Yunus established the Grameen Bank to expand the number of people served. By 2004 Grameen Bank had loaned over $4 billion and had 3.5 million current borrowers, 95 percent of whom were women. Grameen loaned to groups of five women, who were responsible for allocating the borrowings among themselves and for ensuring that the borrowings were repaid. Grameen reported a 99 percent repayment rate. Grameen has enabled millions of people to rise out of abject poverty with many able to build their own homes and start businesses.[21] Microfinance was initiated in a number of other countries, and Nike initiated a microfinance program for workers in its suppliers' factories.[22]

Yunus also conceived an innovative approach to helping the poorest people— beggars. They could obtain a Grameen identity card that enabled them to borrow merchandise from stores and sell it door-to-door, with their borrowing financed by a loan from the bank. Yunus then turned to stationary beggars, many of whom were blind or missing a limb. Since they typically positioned themselves in strategic places, Grameen enabled them to sell drinks, food, and other objects from their places.

The fair trade movement was begun to improve the lives of poor farmers and workers trapped by market conditions. The fair trade movement can be understood as an approach to improving the well-being of poor farmers in developing countries by circumventing markets and coordinating market behavior. The fair trade system

---

[21]This account is based on a press release "Visionary Economist Mohammad Yunus Share Microfinance Success Stories," Graduate School of Business, Stanford University, May 2004.
[22]See Morduch (1999) for a survey of the literature on microfinance.

attempts to intervene directly on both the demand and the supply sides of the market by coordinating the flow of consumer revenue to participating producers. Coffee producers participating in the fair trade system are primarily organizations of small farmers that agree to meet certain production and environmental standards. Participating coffee brokers agree to pay a fixed, fair trade price, which exceeds the market price, so the income of coffee farmers is increased. The brokers charge a higher price for fair trade coffee, and retailers generally sell the coffee at a higher price.[23] Fair Trade certification allows consumers to participate, and the fair trade movement monitors the system to ensure that the higher prices actually benefit farmers. Fair Trade labels are now available for coffee, tea, rice, bananas, mangoes, cocoa, sugar, honey, fruit juices, and soccer balls.[24] The chapter case, *The Fair Trade Movement*, considers the origin of the movement, its organization, and its challenges.

The example describes a social entrepreneurship venture intended to bring light to people without electricity.

---

[23]See Argenti (2004) for a discussion of Starbucks and fair trade coffee.
[24]Fair Labeling Organizations International, www.fairtrade.net/sites/aboutflo/faq.html.

---

**EXAMPLE**

## Ignite Innovations

In 2003 four recent Stanford University graduates, two each from the Graduate School of Business and the School of Engineering, founded Ignite Innovations to produce and market a solar-charged LCD lamp for use by people without electricity in developing countries.[1] The idea for the lamp came from a Social Entrepreneurship Startup course taught by business school professor James Patell and engineering professors Bill Behrman and David Kelley. In conjunction with the Light Up the World Foundation students in the course took the challenge of developing a marketable product for the developing world. One-and-a-half billion people in the developing world had no electricity, and most used kerosene lamps for light. The lamps provided only minimal light and, worse, the fumes posed a health hazard. LCD lamps provided much more light and did so efficiently. With incandescent lamps 90 percent of the energy is converted into heat and 5 percent into light, but LCD lights reverse those numbers. Moreover, their batteries could be charged with a small solar panel.

One course objective was to develop a lamp that could be manufactured in quantity and sold at a price that would be economically attractive compared to using kerosene. A second objective was to research the potential markets to assess demand and determine how to get the product to those who needed it. The students decided that the venture should be subject not only to the discipline of the product market but also to the discipline of earning a profit. The enterprise thus had to be commercially self-sustaining, which meant that the price had to cover the cost of manufacturing, distribution, and marketing and provide a return to capital. The four graduates raised $280,000 from investors who expected the enterprise to earn a profit but not the usual market rate of return. Investors were morally committed to the venture.

The graduates decided to focus on India and conducted on-the-ground studies of the market. They also decided to have the lamps produced in India in conjunction with a local company.

[1]See "The Light Brigade," *Stanford Business*, September/October 2003, and "Coursework Brings Light to Poor in India," Graduate School of Business, Stanford University, June 2004.

*(Continued)*

*(Continued)*

The arrangement was similar to licensing and could be scaled to include producers in other countries. A major challenge was to produce the lamps at a low enough cost, and the venture made a major breakthrough when it found on the Internet a Chinese company that purchased old solar panels and cut them into smaller pieces and resold them. The venture planned to build 250 prototypes that would be used for field testing. Unfortunately, the founders had difficulty getting the prototypes produced in India, in part because of red tape associated with imports.

The founders of the venture were motivated by social objectives and were willing to work long hours for little compensation. The delays in producing the prototypes and the hardship of living in India were frustrating. Commercial self-sustainability was farther in the future that had been anticipated, and capital was limited. The future of Ignite hung in the balance.

# International Codes

As indicated in earlier sections, companies have developed their own codes of conduct for their global operations. In addition, industries such as the U.S. apparel and footwear industries and the worldwide chemical industry (Chapter 11) have developed codes. A number of broader attempts to establish global codes of conduct have also been undertaken to deal with human rights, labor conditions, the environment, and corruption.[25] The Global Reporting Initiative (GRI) goes further and has developed guidelines for sustainable reporting on the economic, environmental, and social performance of companies. Williams (2000) and the contributors to his volume review a variety of codes and include an appendix reproducing over 20 international codes. One of those codes is considered here.

In 1994 a group of business leaders and academics gathered to identify a set of transcultural values. The resulting Caux Round Table Principles for Business set forth both obligations and values derived from the western concept of human dignity and the Japanese concept of *kyosei*, or acting for the common good.[26] According to the Caux Round Table, "*kyosei* means living and working together for the common good—enabling cooperation and mutual prosperity to coexist with healthy and fair competition. 'Human dignity' refers to the sacredness or value of each person as an end, not simply as a means to the fulfillment of others' purposes or even majority prescription." The concept of *kyosei* can be understood in the traditional eastern focus on groups beginning with the family and extending outward to the work unit and universe. The concept of human dignity is based on Kant's categorical imperative.

The Caux Principles include a set of general principles and a set of stakeholder principles identifying responsibilities to customers, employees, owners/investors, suppliers, competitors, and communities.[27] These responsibilities are similar to those espoused by the advocates of corporate social responsibility. The general principles, presented in Figure 22-1, represent an attempt to identify a set of values that can be respected across western and eastern cultures, and they have a strong communitarian flavor.

---

[25]See Prakash and Hart (1999) for a broader focus on globalization and governance.
[26]See Skelly (1995) and Küng (1997, pp. 24–25).
[27]See Cavanagh (2000) and Goodpaster (2000) for background on and evaluation of the Caux principles.

1. *The Responsibilities of Business: Beyond Shareholders Toward Stakeholders . . .* Businesses have a role to play in improving the lives of all their customers, employees, and shareholders by sharing with them the wealth they have created. . . .

2. *The Economic and Social Impact of Business: Toward Innovation, Justice, and World Community . . .* Business also should contribute to human rights, education, welfare, and vitalization of the countries in which they operate. Business should contribute to economic and social development not only in the countries in which they operate, but also in the world community at large. . . .

3. *Business Behavior: Beyond the Letter of the Law Toward a Spirit of Trust . . .* businesses should recognize that sincerity, candor, truthfulness, the keeping of promises, and transparency contribute not only to their own credibility and stability, but also to the smoothness and efficiency of business transactions. . . .

4. *Respect for Rules . . .* business should respect international and domestic rules. In addition, they should recognize that some behavior, although legal, may still have adverse consequences.

5. *Support for Multilateral Trade . . .* businesses should cooperate in efforts to promote the progressive and judicious liberalization of trade and to relax those domestic measures that unreasonably hinder global commerce, while giving due respect to national policy objectives.

6. *Respect for the Environment* A business should protect and, where possible, improve the environment, promote sustainable development, and prevent the wasteful use of natural resources.

7. *Avoidance of Illicit Operations* A business should not participate in or condone bribery, money laundering, or other corrupt practices: indeed, it should seek cooperation with others to eliminate them. . . .

**FIGURE 22-1 Caux Principles of Business**

*Source:* Caux Round Table

# Questionable Foreign Payments and Corruption

Corruption is costly both tangibly and intangibly. Corruption distorts economic activity, resulting in a substantial cost to an economy. Corruption also undermines trust and confidence in government. As international trade and foreign direct investment expanded, the opportunities for corruption increased and more firms were exposed to demands for payments or temptations to offer payments when they believed competitors were likely to be offering payments. Both countries and companies wanted to reduce corruption, and in the 1990s international efforts began. One important development was the establishment of Transparency International, an NGO formed to combat corruption. Another development was the negotiation of an anti-bribery code under the auspices of the OECD. These developments are considered later in the chapter, after considering frameworks for evaluating the moral concerns about these questionable payments.

In a number of countries, the exchange of gifts and favors is customary, and in some cases favors may extend into the domain of unethical conduct. In a country in which small payments to low-level government employees are necessary to clear administrative hurdles, a firm may be justified in making the payments to avoid a greater injustice. When those payments are recurring and pervasive, however, the question is which is the greater injustice. A firm may decide to forgo sales if those sales necessitate a serious violation of ethics principles.

When corruption is pervasive, a company may go further and decide to withdraw from a country. A Unilever executive explained the company's decision to leave Bulgaria: "It was impossible for us to do business without getting involved in corruption. So we took the logical step and accepted the consequences. That meant packing our bags."[28]

## Questionable Payments and Ethics Principles

The disclosure in 1975 that the Lockheed Corporation had made payments of over $12 million to Japanese business executives and government officials to secure a sale of commercial aircraft led to revelations that over 450 U.S. companies had made similar payments totaling more than $300 million worldwide. The questionable foreign payments ranged from outright bribes to obtain sales to extortion payments made to customs officials to avoid delays in the clearance of imports. In response, Congress passed the Foreign Corrupt Practices Act (FCPA).

Some payments were made because firms, or their sales representatives, had reason to believe that competitors were offering payments to a customer. In an industry or a country in which such payments are customary, a firm may be unable unilaterally to change the practice, and the payments can be self-perpetuating.[29] This, however, does not provide a moral justification for the practice, and change can occur.[30] In Italy corruption and bribery were widespread and involved many of the country's prominent companies, business executives, and leaders of the major political parties. Revelations about the scope of the corruption resulted in widespread moral condemnation and led to prosecutions, a major restructuring of the electoral system, the formation of new political parties, and changes in government.

In a situation in which payments are either demanded or likely to be required to obtain a sale, firms and their managers have two sources of guidance—one is ethics and the other is the law. Ethics is considered first, and then the law is presented and interpreted. Corporate codes of conduct are then considered. The ethics analysis focuses on bribery and the question of when, if ever, a firm is morally justified in paying a bribe.

A bribe is a payment to an individual in an organization intended to influence that person's exercise of his or her responsibilities; that is, a bribe is intended to corrupt the behavior of the recipient. Bribery is ethically objectionable on a number of grounds. From a utilitarian perspective, bribery distorts markets and reduces economic efficiency. That is, when bribes replace value and merit as the basis for decisions, competition cannot be as efficient. From a rights perspective, bribery distorts the fair opportunity to compete in markets. Furthermore, bribes induce the recipients to violate a duty to the principals who employ them.

More fundamentally, the bases for Kant's moral rules are violated. First, a rule under which bribes are allowed is not universalizable because there is little reason to believe that individuals would will economic competition in bribes rather than competition without bribes. Second, bribery is not reversible. A firm would not want its own purchasing agents to make their decisions based on the bribes they received.

With respect to justice, bribes paid to government officials undermine the impartiality of government and hence the equality of political rights. A bribe also exploits the position a person occupies in the recipient organization and distorts the fair equality of opportunity to qualify for the position. Furthermore, the recipient may receive too much, having done nothing to deserve it. Bribes would also not be expected to benefit the least advantaged persons, even indirectly.

[28]*The Wall Street Journal*, February 16, 1999.
[29]See Carson (1987) and Philips (1984) for perspectives on bribery. Getz (2000) provides an overview and analysis of bribery and corruption.
[30]Klitgaard (1988) discusses the steps taken by the U.S. Army to overcome corruption in the construction and supply industries in Korea in the 1970s.

The remaining issue is whether bribes are justified if there is a greater injustice that can be avoided. This issue is considered next in the context of the Lockheed case.

## The Lockheed Case

The Lockheed case was described by Vice Chairman A. Carl Kotchian (1977), who authorized the payments in Japan. The $12 million payments in question represented less than 3 percent of the revenue on the L-1011 aircraft sold to All Nippon Airlines (ANA). The payments were made to the office of the prime minister, to seven other politicians and government officials, and to the president of ANA. The payments were not illegal under U.S. law at the time, and such payments were not unknown in the aircraft industry.[31] However, the payments were in violation of Japanese law. If Kotchian had been unsure of their legality in Japan, he could have contacted a Japanese lawyer or the commercial attaché at the U.S. embassy. Although it is customary in Japan to give gifts, an individual payment of $1.7 million cannot be viewed as a gift or as a routine political contribution.[32] Similarly, a payment of $50,000 per aircraft to the president of ANA could not be viewed as a part of the functioning system.

Mr. Kotchian offered several justifications for making the payments.[33] He argued that the payments were "worthwhile from Lockheed's standpoint" because "they would provide Lockheed workers with jobs, and thus redound to the benefit of their dependents, their communities, and stockholders of the corporation."[34] As considered in Chapter 19, this is casuist reasoning in that an unethical action is said to be justified by the benefits it provides to stakeholders. From a utilitarian perspective, the benefits to Lockheed's stakeholders are likely to be little different from the benefits to Boeing's or McDonnell Douglas's stakeholders if they were to obtain the sale. Furthermore, markets in which a competition in bribes takes place does not function as efficiently as when decisions are made on the basis of merit and value.

The ethics evaluation of this case depends on whether in the absence of payments ANA would have selected Lockheed aircraft. If ANA would have selected another aircraft supplier that did not offer a bribe, Lockheed's payments would be an explicit bribe, which cannot be ethically justified. To obtain the sale, Lockheed could have reduced the price of the aircraft, in which case the benefit would accrue to ANA and not to its officers and government officials.

A second possibility is that ANA would have purchased the L-1011 even if the payments were not made. The ethics issue then is whether Lockheed would be justified in making the payments, which, under this supposition, would be a response to extortion, as Kotchian claimed it was. He wrote: "From a purely ethical and moral standpoint I would have declined such a request [for payments]. However, in that case, I would most certainly have sacrificed commercial success."[35] Extortion involves the use of coercion to

---

[31] Lockheed's subsequent legal problems in the United States were due to a failure to disclose the payments as required by U.S. law. Lockheed later disclosed other payments made to secure sales, including a commission paid to Prince Bernard of the Netherlands. See Hay and Gray (1981) for a discussion of some of the Lockheed payments. In 1982, the Boeing Company pleaded guilty and paid a $400,000 fine for 40 counts of failure to disclose to the Export-Import Bank that it had paid "irregular commissions" to agents involved in foreign sales. (The Export-Import Bank required such disclosure on any sales it financed.) In 1981 the McDonnell Douglas Corporation pleaded guilty to fraud and making false statements and paid fines of over $1.2 million.

[32] It might also be argued that the payments were justified because they were a part of the functioning system in the aircraft industry. This, however, is not a moral justification, even if the competition often involves payments.

[33] See Drucker (1981) for another evaluation of this case.

[34] Kotchian (1977, p. 12).

[35] Kotchian (1977, p. 12).

extract a payment. Such a payment would be morally justified in the case of ransom paid in a kidnapping, for example. The difference between a ransom payment and the payments that Lockheed made, however, is that if after the fact Lockheed had publicly revealed the payments, the public would have reacted quite differently than it would in the case of a ransom payment. The Lockheed payments thus do not pass Gert's injustice test (Chapter 20) or the public disclosure test discussed in Chapter 21. Gert's test for when an injustice is warranted to avoid a greater injustice requires that a rational observer would understand the reason for the action. That test would surely not be met. As for the public disclosure test, Lockheed would never have been able to justify the payments to the Japanese or American publics.

A third possibility is that the payments were required to match payments offered by other aircraft manufacturers. This situation is considered next.

## A Utilitarian Analysis of Bribery

From a utilitarian perspective bribery is bad because it distorts economic activity away from producing the greatest well-being. To illustrate this, consider two companies, A and B, seeking a contract for a sale to country C. Suppose that Company A's product is likely better for C than is the product of company B and in the absence of bribes would likely be selected by C. If no bribes are offered, the expected utilities of A and B and country C are 4, 2, and 14, respectively, as presented in Table 22-1. For example, suppose that the profit on the sale would be $6 million, and in the absence of bribery the likelihood that A would be selected is two-thirds and the likelihood that B would be selected is one-third. The expected profits for A and B then are 4 and 2, respectively.

Consider next the possibility that the government officials responsible for selecting the contract winner can be bribed. If one company offers a bribe and the other does not, suppose its probability of winning the contract becomes one. Bribery involves transactions costs because both parties must conceal the payments and take measures to justify the selection. Suppose that the utilities if A does not bribe whereas B does bribe are 0, 5, and 9, respectively.[36] Suppose also the utilities if A bribes and B does not are 5, 0, and 11. If both companies pay bribes, the utilities are 2, 1, and 12.

Before considering the application of utilitarianism, suppose that the companies were self-interested. Inspection of Table 22-1 indicates that each company has a dominant strategy of paying a bribe. That is, if B were believed to be offering a bribe, then A is better off offering a bribe and obtaining a utility of 2 than not bribing and having a utility of 0. Similarly, if B were believed not to be offering a bribe, A is better off offering a bribe. Utilitarianism, however, requires that each company consider the aggregate utility of all three parties.

**TABLE 22-1 Utilities of A, B, and C**

|  |  | Company B | |
|---|---|---|---|
|  |  | *Not Bribe* | *Bribe* |
| *Company A* | *Not Bribe* | (4, 2, 14) | (0, 5, 9) |
|  | *Bribe* | (5, 0, 11) | (2, 1, 12) |

Under rule utilitarianism each of the three parties chooses actions for A and B simultaneously based on the greatest aggregate utility. The aggregate utilities are presented in Table 22-2. The moral rule thus is that neither A nor B bribes.

Suppose, however, that company B is not utilitarian but instead is purely self-interested. Since B has a dominant strategy, it will offer a bribe. Is a matching bribe ethically justified in this case? From the perspective of rule utilitarianism, the answer is no. As just demonstrated, everyone should choose the rule that no one is to offer or accept a bribe, and B is acting immorally. From an act utilitarianism perspective, however, is aggregate utility higher if A offers a matching bribe? From Table 22-2, if B is offering a bribe, A should offer a bribe because that results in an aggregate utility of 15 compared with 14 if it does not offer a bribe. Such reasoning can perpetuate bribery and is inappropriate.[37] This illustrates the weakness of act utilitarianism. Instead of offering the bribe, A could work for a collective agreement banning bribes.

Another test is whether a matching bribe is justified to avoid a greater injustice. The test provided in Chapter 20 is: "A violation of a moral rule [offering a bribe] can be justified by providing reasons which would result in either some impartial rational persons advocating that that kind of violation be publicly allowed, or less frequently, all impartial persons advocating that such a violation be publicly allowed." A more applied version of the test is: "If I disclosed publicly that I had taken the action, would the public understand and approve of my action?"

If a bribe were offered unilaterally, the public surely would not approve. If the payment represented extortion, the public might approve of it. The public, however, is more likely to demand that the extortion be stopped.

If the payment is to induce the recipient to take an action that the recipient has a duty to take and that action does not affect the outcome of a business transaction, the public may well approve of the payment. Such payments are allowed under the FCPA.

If one can show that the payment matches a payment that a competitor is offering, would the public approve? In some countries the answer might be yes. In the United States the FCPA requires the answer no. That is, pay no bribes but instead work to convince others not to offer or accept bribes. The OECD Anti-Bribery Convention reflects the success of such an approach.

A practical problem in applying the injustice standard is how to show that a competitor is offering a bribe. Both the offeror and the recipient have strong incentives to conceal it, which is one reason bribery is difficult to eradicate. More importantly, self-interest and the suspicion that a competitor may be offering a bribe may lead a company to offer a bribe. If both harbor such suspicions, the slippery slope can result in a competition in bribes.

**TABLE 22-2 Aggregate Utility**

|  | Company B | |
|---|---|---|
|  | Not Bribe | Bribe |
| **Company A** Not Bribe | 20 | 14 |
| Bribe | 16 | 15 |

---

[37]The same question can be posed regarding whether B should offer a bribe if A is offering a bribe. The answer is no, since the aggregate utility with only A bribing is 16, whereas if both offer bribes, it is 15.

Another reason not to pay bribes in situations in which there will be repeated encounters was given by an executive of a global company. He said, "If you pay once, you pay forever."

## The Foreign Corrupt Practices Act

In the Lockheed case the payments were made both through an official agent, the Marubeni Trading Company, and a confidential consultant. In conducting business in foreign countries, it is often advisable to retain the services of a national who is familiar with the system in the country and has contacts that will, at a minimum, save time in arranging appointments and may help speed permits and contracts through the host country's institutional structure. These agents are often compensated on a fee or commission basis, and the disposition of those monies may be known only to agents. If a portion of the commissions might be passed on to influence the actions of customers or government officials, the firm may be contributing to a corrupt act. Ethically, the firm has an obligation to instruct its agent about which practices are acceptable and which are unacceptable. Moreover, the firm has a duty to monitor the activities of its agents. The FCPA addresses these issues, among others.[38]

The FCPA makes bribery of foreign officials, political parties, candidates for office, and public international organizations a criminal offense. It provides for a fine of up to $1 million for the company and up to $10,000 and imprisonment for not more than 5 years for an individual making a payment or offer covered by the act. It assigns the burden of knowing whether illegal payments are being made to the company and imposes detailed record-keeping requirements. Under the FCPA, it is unlawful to make any "offer, payment, promise to pay, or authorization of the payment of any money, or offer, gift, promise to give, or authorization of anything . . ." to influence a decision, omit a required action, or give "any improper advantage" to the company. The term foreign official "does not include any employee of a foreign government or any department, agency, or instrumentality thereof whose duties are essentially ministerial or clerical." The FCPA thus allows small "facilitating payments" to low-level government employees such as customs inspectors, if the payments do not influence a decision.

The use of agents, intermediaries, or third parties is also covered, and they are subject to both criminal and civil penalties. In its original language, the act pertained to "any person, while knowing or having reason to know" about a payment for the purposes previously listed. This imposed a stringent duty on a company to know how fees paid to agents, intermediaries, and third parties were actually used. After the first few years of experience with the FCPA, a poll of 1,200 large businesses indicated that substantial sales had been lost in countries in which bribery was a common practice.[39] Although U.S. firms indicated that they supported the FCPA, 68 percent responded that the record-keeping burden should be reduced and that the law should be more specific about who in a foreign country can receive payments and for what purposes.

The Omnibus Trade and Competitiveness Act of 1988 amended the FCPA in several ways.[40] First, it altered the language about the use of third parties or intermediaries by eliminating the phrase "or having reason to know." Second, a payment to a foreign individual became illegal under the act if it was illegal in the foreign country. Third, if a

---

[38]See Pastin and Hooker (1988) and Alpern (1988) for ethics analyses of the FCPA.
[39]*Business Week*, September 19, 1983.
[40]The FCPA was also amended in the Anti-Bribery and Fair Competition Act of 1998 to bring it into accord with the OECD Convention considered later in the chapter. The preceding text includes these changes.

payment were legal in the foreign country, the defendant in an action brought under the act could use that legality as a defense. Fourth, the language of the act was clarified to indicate that payments that secured performance of routine government actions, such as signing customs documents and unloading or loading cargoes, were not illegal. Fifth, the amendments provided firms with a number of affirmative defenses, including consistency with host country laws and legitimate business expenses.

The FCPA does not prohibit payments to private businesses. The bribery of private businesses, or private-to-private bribery, is believed to be less common than the bribery of government officials. In 2001, however, the Department of Justice obtained guilty pleas from major international construction companies, including ABB and Phillipp Holtzman, for kickbacks and the payment of bribes on the U.S. Agency for International Development financing of water projects in Egypt. The companies met secretly to arrange for some of the companies to submit inflated bids or not to bid at all on certain contracts. In exchange the companies received monetary payments from the winning bidder or the remaining bidders.[41]

## Company Codes

Most firms have policies or codes to ensure compliance with the FCPA and international conventions and to clarify when foreign payments can be made and how they are to be accounted for. The three principal purposes of these codes are to provide guidance to employees, make it easier for them to say no to demands for payment, and ultimately discourage demands for payments.

The extent to which a firm encounters demands for payments depends on its lines of business, the countries in which it does business, and its organization. Some industries and some countries are characterized by a functioning system in which bribery and facilitating payments are not uncommon. A firm's lines of business and the countries in which it operates thus affect the scope of the problems it faces. That scope is also affected by the organizational structure of the firm. Firms can conduct their foreign business through a wholly owned subsidiary, a joint venture, a sales office that manages local dealers and distributors, or agents with whom the firm deals at arm's length. Controlling and monitoring payments generally become more difficult and making questionable payments becomes easier, the more independent is the firm's foreign unit.

Corruption in Russia is not uncommon, particularly in the oil industry. Demands for bribes were regularly made, and BP and Shell responded in quite different ways. Shell packed its bags and left the country. BP made a call to the chairman of Gazprom, the giant Russian natural gas producer, and complained about the demands for payments. Corruption in Russia is "organized," and the demands for payments stopped quickly. BP thanked the chairman and said to call if it could be any help. The son of the chairman now attends a university in the United Kingdom at no expense.

Company codes typically state the principal features of the FCPA; require that the representative of the firm know the local laws and the functioning system in the country; distinguish between gratuities, facilitating payments, and bribes; and specify record-keeping and reporting requirements. A code may also provide guidance for handling a request for a payment and indicate to whom an employee can turn if a payment's propriety is in question. Firms have also established audit procedures to detect illegal payments. In many firms, managers and sales representatives are required to pledge to abide by the FCPA and company guidelines.

---

[41]*The New York Times*, April 13, 2001.

Such policies not only provide guidance to managers and sales representatives, but they also establish a basis for a response when a government official or a customer demands a payment. A response that "company policy does not permit it" may, in some cases, lead to the demand being retracted. Furthermore, knowledge that the firm does not make such payments may eventually decrease the number of demands. For this to be effective, however, the firm must establish a reputation for not making payments.

BP has a policy of not paying bribes and also not making facilitating payments. CEO Lord Browne wrote to employees in 2002 stating, "We work within the law in every one of the 100 countries in which we operate and we work to our standards, which are often higher than the legal requirement. Those standards are universal in BP. We will not engage in bribery or corruption in any form including facilitating payments."[42]

As a result of the policy BP employees have been held "hostage" in Russia, but gradually the requests for facilitating payments decreased. The demands resurfaced from time to time, and BP has been forced to add an extensive audit and control staff in Russia to detect whether payments have been made. Some employees have been fired for making payments. Lord Browne explained that BP ran "a high cost operation in Russia."

BP also follows a policy of "publishing what you pay." That is, when contract payments are made to foreign governments, the amounts and the recipients are made public. With this information, citizens in the country can hold government officials accountable for the disposition of the funds.

## Cummins Practice

The Cummins Engine Company's policy on questionable foreign payments is striking in its articulation of a principle for reasoning about whether a payment should be made in a particular instance. Cummins states its "Primary Ethical Guide":

The key element which distinguishes ethically unacceptable payments is the corruption of [a] relationship of trust. When a company pays an agent of a buyer in order to influence that agent's purchasing decision, and when that payment is not known to the buyer, the company corrupts a relationship of trust between buyer and agent. The buyer's expectation that his agent will act with only the buyer's interest in mind is betrayed. Similarly, when a company pays a government agent in order to influence that agent's official decisions, the company corrupts a relationship of trust between the public and that official. The corruption of such a relationship of trust not only violates fundamental principles of fair dealing but also hampers efficient economic development and undermines social cohesion.[43]

Using the concept of higher order standards introduced in Chapter 20, Cummins's guide meets both the Kantian standard and the standard of rule utilitarianism. It treats the buyer as an autonomous end, and the rule of not corrupting a relationship of trust is one that people would will to be universal. From the perspective of rule utilitarianism the guide supports efficiency by requiring competition to be on a commercial basis rather than on bribes.

Figure 22-2 displays the framework of this principle. In contrast to Kotchian's analysis, which focuses on the consequences to the firm from making the payment,

[42]Lord Browne of Madingley, "to our employees," August, 2002. In 2003 BP fired 165 people for violating the company's ethics standards.

[43]Cummins Practices, October 1, 1980.

Cummins's principle focuses on the buyer and its agent. That agent is in a relationship of trust with its principal—shareholders in the case of private firms and citizens in the case of a government agency. In this relationship, the agent is to serve the interests of the principal; accepting a bribe sacrifices the interests of the principal for the interests of the agent. Cummins applies this reasoning in the tests that an employee is to use in determining if a payment is acceptable. "Does this payment undermine a relationship of trust? What expectations does the principal have of his agent in the particular transaction at issue? Is the payment known to the principal or is it not?"

Payments are allowable only if three conditions are met:

a. The payment is required to induce the official to perform a routine act which he is already under a duty to perform . . .
b. The payment is consistent with local practice. If the payment is consistent with local practice, it is reasonable to assume that it is consistent with public expectations of official behavior, and
c. There is no reasonable alternative available for obtaining the official act or service at issue.

Although the phrase "reasonable alternative" is not precise, condition c requires the company to consider such possibilities as reducing the price or expediting delivery to obtain the sale. Reducing the price to make the sale, rather than paying a bribe, causes the benefit to go to the principal rather than the agent, which is consistent with the relationship of trust. The relevant test is the requirement that the Cummins employee determine whether the principal knows of the payment, since then the principal can determine where the benefit should reside.

In cases in which the employee is uncertain whether a payment is allowed, Cummins states, "Where there is a question as to the propriety of a particular payment in view of the foregoing standards, the payment should not be made." To encourage compliance, Cummins also assures that "no employee is put at a career disadvantage because of his or her willingness to raise a question about a corporate practice or unwillingness to pursue a course of action which seems inappropriate or morally dubious." Cummins also provides its version of the public disclosure test: "Cummins employees do nothing in search of business that they should not reveal willingly and publicly to any other member of the Cummins family or to any government official in any land."

In addition to providing principles on which to reason and standards for assessing when a payment is allowable, Cummins's standards go beyond the FCPA by prohibiting corrupt payments to private, as well as to public, buyers. Recognizing that in some

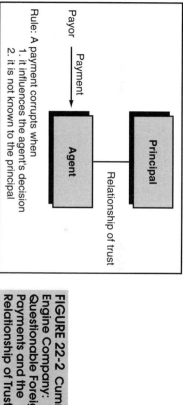

**FIGURE 22-2 Cummins Engine Company: Questionable Foreign Payments and the Relationship of Trust**

Payor → Payment

Principal

Agent

Relationship of trust

Rule: A payment corrupts when
1. it influences the agent's decision
2. it is not known to the principal

countries payments that do not satisfy its standards could be necessary to do business, Cummins states that it will "accept the loss of business." If the pattern of questionable payments continues, Cummins states that it will bring the matter to the attention of the host government to determine how the government wants the matter to be handled. If the demands for payments persist, Cummins is prepared to forgo the business. The chapter case, *Complications in Marnera*, raises similar issues.

## Transparency International

Concerned by what he had observed from his position in the World Bank, Peter Eiger founded Transparency International (TI) in Berlin in 1993 as an NGO to lead in the curtailment of corruption.[44] In his introduction to TI's "Global Corruption Report 2001" he wrote:

Corruption respects no national boundaries. It deepens poverty around the globe by distorting political, economic, and social life. Transparency International (TI) was born from the experience of people who witnessed first hand the real threat to human lives posed by corruption—and from its founders' frustration that nobody wanted to talk about it.

The instrument for TI's leadership in attacking corruption was the construction of a corruption index for countries as a way of calling attention to the issue and putting pressure on countries.

In conjunction with its Global Corruption Report TI publishes annually a Corruption Perception Index computed from existing surveys pertaining to corruption. The 2004 Index, for example, covered 146 countries using between 3 and 16 surveys for each country. The highest (least corrupt) on the Index was Finland followed by New Zealand, and the lowest were Bangladesh and Haiti preceded by Nigeria.[45] Nearly all of the highest ranked countries had small populations, and the highest ranked large country (over 30 million people) was the United Kingdom at 11. The United States was 17th.

The Corruption Perceptions Index pertains to the corruption in a country or the demand side of corruption. TI has also published a supply-side index. The Bribe Payers Index pertains to the countries whose companies pay bribes. TI hired Gallup International to conduct the survey on which the index is based. The survey asked private sector leaders in 15 emerging market countries about their perceptions of the extent to which the companies from 21 leading exporting countries pay bribes. Australia was ranked at the top (low bribery) and Russia at the bottom, with the United States tied with Japan for 13th.

The efforts of TI and other organizations as well as individual businesses contributed to an international effort to reduce corruption under the auspices of the OECD.

## The OECD Anti-Bribery Convention

For over two decades the FCPA stood alone among the developed countries with its imposition of both criminal penalties and stringent requirements for reporting and monitoring. The United States estimated that its companies lost billions of dollars a year in sales because of bribes paid by companies from other countries. In France,

---

[44]Transparency International now has chapters in 85 countries.
[45]According to its chairman, "Transparency International is not saying in this index that one country is more corrupt than another. We are reporting how business people, political analysts, and the general public around the globe perceive levels of corruption in different countries."

Germany, and many other European countries, bribes and other payments to foreign officials were tax deductible if required to secure a sale. With the growth in foreign direct investment in developing countries and increased trade, the scale of corruption expanded, and more countries became concerned about the effect of corruption not only on business activity but also on the countries where the payments were made. Pressure from the United States and European countries and from organizations such as Transparency International led to negotiations within the OECD. The result was the 1997 Anti-Bribery Convention (Convention on Combating Bribery of Foreign Public Officials in International Business Transactions), signed by the 30 OECD member countries plus Argentina, Bulgaria, Czech Republic, Poland, and Turkey.

The Convention requires signatories to make the act of bribery and the making of other forms of illicit payments to foreign public officials a criminal offense, whether paid directly or indirectly "in order to obtain or retain business or other improper advantage in the conduct of international business."[46] Small "facilitation" payments that are not made "to obtain or retain business" are not viewed as an offense. A foreign public official is defined to include not only those holding elective or appointive office, but also officials of public agencies and public enterprises at least 50 percent owned by the government. The Convention also imposes record-keeping obligations on businesses so that payments can be identified. The Convention does not pertain to private-to-private bribery, as in the case of the water projects in Egypt.

The bargaining on the Convention revealed the complexity of the issue. Since in many developing countries the government owns or controls many companies, the United States argued and eventually was successful in including government-controlled companies under the Convention. The United States also successfully obtained inclusion of elected members of parliament in the category of government officials, over the objections of several European countries that allowed payments to their members of parliament provided the payments were not to influence votes. The United States lost, however, in its attempt to include payments to political parties and party officials as an offense.

The European Union enacted a Criminal Law Convention on Corruption in 1999 that made criminal offenses of active bribery and passive bribery (extortion) that gives any "undue advantage" of domestic and foreign public officials and of private sector personnel. The United States signed the OECD Convention in 2000.

Countries differ considerably in terms of their history, culture, resources, and institutions, yet fundamental ethics principles are intended to be universal rather than country specific. Cultural relativism, in which one relies solely on host country laws and practices, is inappropriate, and universal relativism, in which one applies the same principles everywhere, ignores relevant differences among countries. The principles underpinning utilitarianism, rights theories, and theories of justice remain useful guides for operating across borders. The application of these principles, however, leaves unresolved issues about trade-offs between costs and benefits, how duties to ensure rights are assigned, and how justice considerations are to be taken into account.

---

[46]The Convention pertains to "active corruption" committed by the offerer of a bribe rather than to "passive corruption" committed by the recipient of the bribe. Like the FCPA the Convention pertains to the supply side of bribery.

Guidance for managers is provided by international, host country, and home country law and by ethics principles. International law is important, yet its enforcement is often irregular and its application to moral issues is often limited to general, rather than specific, matters. Host country law is an important guide, and when those laws are consistent with universal standards, they are to be respected. If they do not meet those standards, firms must develop policies guided by principles as well as law. Firms also must determine whether they will apply the same standards to their operations in all countries or adapt their policies and practices to the situation of each host country. This is a particular challenge in low-income countries that do not have the capacity to provide guidance through regulation or where people prefer economic growth over the safety and environmental standards of high-income countries.

The working conditions and human rights situation in the factories of overseas suppliers has raised moral concerns, and an innovative approach to addressing those concerns has been undertaken by the apparel and footwear industries. This approach has been institutionalized in the form of the Fair Labor Association, which provides for independent monitoring of factories.

Poverty can contribute to unethical behavior, and business is the principal engine for bringing people out of poverty. Social entrepreneurship seeks to better peoples' lives by responding to market failures through commercially self-supporting enterprises. Microfinance has improved the lives of millions by making credit available to people who cannot borrow from traditional sources. The fair trade movement has received support from both consumers and producers and has been extended to a variety of commodities. The challenge of social entrepreneurship is to create sustainable enterprises.

In some countries practices may violate fundamental principles, and those practices may be pervasive. Bribery and other forms of illicit payments are common in some countries. The FCPA and the OECD Convention provide guidance, assign duties, and impose penalties for violations. However, laws can leave a variety of issues, such as payments to private companies, unaddressed. In such cases, principles in addition to host country practices can provide guidance. Utilitarianism concludes that bribery is morally wrong. Some managers argue that bribes are required because of extortion by government officials or bribes offered by competitors. In such cases, the injustice standard is applicable and requires that the manager ask whether, if it were publicly disclosed, the publics in the host and home country would agree that the payment should be made.

The approach of Cummins Engine is useful for guiding managers in their reasoning about such issues, even if one does not reach the same conclusions the company reached. The approach involves a statement of principles, a method for reasoning from those principles to the specifics of a situation, standards that managers are to apply, and protection for individuals who raise corruption issues within the firm.

The range of ethics issues that arise in global operations is broader than those in a firm's home country, and in developing countries the institutions found in developed countries may be absent or may function imperfectly. Furthermore, the facts of the situations encountered internationally may be more difficult to uncover. These factors complicate the application of ethics principles and leave managers with the difficult task of formulating policies guided by a combination of law, ethics principles, and culture.

# Complications in Marnera

Pat Liu and her team of engineers from Bolton Engineering and Construction Company would be spending the next 6 months in Marnera while the government selected the contractor to develop a copper and gold mine in a remote part of the country. Development of the mine was likely to produce revenue of nearly $200 million over the next 7 years for Bolton. Bolton had just completed a successful mining project in a neighboring country, and Liu believed that the company was best qualified for the job because of that experience. The project in Marnera was particularly important because Bolton wanted to avoid laying off the engineers who had been working on the project in the neighboring country. Bolton had a modest local operation in Marnera, but Liu was the ranking Bolton official and would be in charge over the next 6 months. If Bolton were to win the contract, she would have responsibility for the mine project.

Upon arriving at the airport in Marnera, Liu and her team encountered an immediate problem. Each member of the team carried a top-of-the-line laptop computer, and in a traveling bag they had brought along three spares in case a computer were to develop problems due to the high humidity in Marnera. The customs official inspecting their bags expressed concern that Liu might try to sell the computers in Marnera. Selling the computers would violate import laws that required a license and customs duty for the sale of imported computers. Liu explained that the computers were for backup and would be used only by Bolton employees. The customs inspector remained concerned, however, and said that he would have to impound all their computers until either Bolton obtained a license and paid the customs duty or a hearing on the matter could be scheduled. The customs official said that he understood that they needed their computers and that the process of obtaining a license and paying the duty would take only a few weeks. A local Bolton employee who had met Liu and her party at the airport asked whether it would be possible for the customs inspector to take care of the matter if Bolton would entrust the customs

fee to him. The customs official nodded. Needing the computers Liu decided to give the fee to the customs official, who stamped their customs declarations allowing the team and their computers to enter the country.

Shortly thereafter Liu encountered the tax system in Marnera. The tax laws were clear, but their interpretation and enforcement were different matters. For corporations the typical approach was for the National Tax Service (NTS) to send a company a bill for its taxes. The tax bill was an estimate based on previous years or on projections of what the company might earn. The tax bill was understood by those familiar with the system as an invitation to negotiate with the NTS over the actual payment. Companies typically engaged the services of a licensed tax accountant or attorney to conduct the negotiations on their behalf. Bolton decided to seek the advice of a highly regarded and well-connected local attorney, who indicated that for a fee of 2 million richas he could take care of the matter and negotiate a quite reasonable tax bill. Liu expressed surprise at the size of the fee, and the attorney explained that much of the 2 million richas was for expenses that would be incurred during the negotiations with the NTS. The attorney said that this was the standard practice in Marnera and that the fee was tax deductible.

The attorney also explained to Liu that if she did not hire someone to handle the negotiations, Bolton would undoubtedly be assessed a final tax bill at least as high as the initial bill. He said that the NTS inspectors had a variety of means to increase tax bills, the easiest of which was to disqualify certain costs as nondeductible. Liu thanked the attorney for his advice and told him that she would get back to him within the week. Concerned about how the 2 million richas would be used, Liu decided to call the commercial attaché at the U.S. embassy whom she had met at a social event. The commercial attaché assured Liu that hiring an attorney to negotiate a company's tax bill was customary in Marnera. When Liu asked what the fee would be used for, the attaché avoided the question. Liu had to decide whether to hire the attorney or prepare Bolton's own tax statement.

In making final preparations for her presentation to the Ministry of Mining, Liu was surprised to learn from the managing director of Bolton's Marnera office that the bidding process had been changed. Instead of evaluating the bids directly, the Ministry would first select a preferred bidder based on its assessment of the technological capabilities of the bidders, costs, intangible factors, and their expressed willingness to utilize local suppliers. Then the Ministry would solicit final bids with the preferred bidder having the right to make the last bid—a right of first refusal. If the preferred bidder matched the highest bid of other contractors, it would be awarded the contract. If it did not match the highest bid, the selection process would be reopened.

One important factor was the level of safety to provide for workers. Bolton could maintain U.S. safety standards and procedures or it could use the prevailing practices in Marnera. With U.S. safety standards and procedures, the pace of work would be slower, adding 5 percent to the cost of the project. Much of the work involved in bringing in roads, power, and water to the mine site, as well as the work on the mine itself, was hazardous, and accidents could be expected. Following the prevailing practices would result in more accidents, and in Marnera there was neither a system of workers' compensation nor a functioning liability system that would allow injured workers to sue for damages. Instead, the local custom was that if an employee were injured on the job and unable to work, that employee's job would be given to another family member so that the family would be supported. Two questions entered Liu's mind. First, what was the right decision regarding safety? Second, if the right decision were to use U.S. standards, would Bolton be at a competitive disadvantage relative to its competitors?

Before leaving for Marnera Liu had been warned that one of Bolton's European competitors would undoubtedly offer payments directly to the top officials at the Ministry of Mining. Such payments were prohibited by U.S. law and by the recently negotiated OECD Anti-Bribery Convention, and countries were to bring their domestic laws into harmony with the Convention.[47] A number of countries, however, still had laws that allowed their companies to make such payments if necessary to obtain business, and the payments were tax deductible. Some countries were expected to move slowly in changing their laws. Then, the matter of enforcement remained.

As a precaution Liu wondered if she should engage the services of the local attorney to represent the company before the Ministry. She was particularly concerned about the effect that losing the bid would have on the employees of Bolton, many of whom would lose their jobs if she failed to get this contract. "It would be unfair if we lose this contract to one of our rivals because of questionable payments," she thought.

Thinking ahead to the possibility of Bolton being selected as the preferred bidder, Liu wondered how high competitors might bid. She mused that it would be nice if they confined their aggressiveness to the competition for selection as the preferred bidder.

In anticipation of the competition for the mining project, the managing director of Bolton's Marnera operations had been developing a relationship with the vice minister of Mining. He had recently attended a reception at the vice minister's home and had brought his wife and children expensive gifts. The vice minister had mentioned that he was hoping to send his eldest child to a university in England, but the cost seemed prohibitive. ∎

## PREPARATION QUESTIONS

1. How should Liu reason about these situations from the perspective of utilitarianism? What other considerations are relevant?
2. Should Liu have made the payment to the customs official?
3. Should Liu engage the services of the tax attorney to deal with the tax matter?
4. Should Liu use U.S. safety standards?
5. What, if anything, should Liu do given the likelihood that a competitor would offer a payment to officials at the Ministry of Mining? Consider the issue from the perspectives of act and rule utilitarianism.
6. Should Liu help the vice minister send his child to England?
7. What should Liu do if Bolton is selected as the preferred bidder?

[47]The OECD had no legislative or enforcement authority, which was the responsibility of the member countries.

# The Fair Trade Movement

Coffee production had been governed by the International Coffee Agreement (ICA), a cartel that attempted through export quotas for the producing countries to maintain prices within a range referred to as the corset. The quotas were waived in times of shortage when prices could rise substantially. Growing opposition to cartels led to criticism of the ICA, which collapsed in 1989 when the United States withdrew from the agreement. The ICA was succeeded by the International Coffee Organization (ICO), but it was unable to limit production. Prices began to fall, and with the exception of two periods of high prices due to frost in Brazil, prices remained below the corset levels. After a small price increase in 1999 coffee prices fell by 50 percent over the following three years.

The price drop was due to increased supply and slow growth in demand. In particular, Vietnam had provided incentives for farmers to grow coffee, and the country quickly became the second-largest exporter after Brazil. Brazil also had increased production as a result of increased mechanization and shifting away from frost-prone regions. Demand growth was slowed by increased competition from soft drinks and the movement to natural fruit drinks, particularly in the United States. From 1970 to 2000 coffee consumption per capita fell from 36 gallons to 17 gallons annually in the United States, while soft drink consumption increased from 23 to 53 gallons per capita.[48] Coffee retailers attempted to increase sales by introducing specialty and flavored coffees. The latter increased the demand for low-quality coffee.

OxfamAmerica reported that 70 percent of coffee production was accounted for by small farmers, who were devastated by the price drop. Oxfam reported that in 1980 a coffee grower could purchase a Swiss Army Knife with 4.171 kilograms of coffee, and in 2001, 10.464 kilograms were required. Oxfam estimated that 25 million coffee farmers were affected.

## The Fair Trade System

The fair trade movement began in the Netherlands in 1988 with the introduction of "Max Havelaar"

brand coffee, named after a 19th century Dutch novel depicting the exploitation of plantation workers in Dutch colonies. The objective of the movement was to protect small growers from fluctuating and falling prices. The movement grew in Europe and spread to the United States and other countries.

The fair trade coffee system paid farmers $1.26 a pound for their coffee or $1.41 for organic coffee. The market price for coffee in early 2004 was $0.65 a pound. To qualify for the fair trade system farmers had to form a producer organization such as a democratically operated cooperative or association.[49] The production practices of the producer organization were then monitored to ensure compliance with the fair trade standards.

The fair trade system had two wings. One focused on the certification of coffee producers, the monitoring of coffee brokers, and enforcement to ensure that funds reached the producers. The other focused on building a demand for fair trade products primarily in the consuming countries. The fair trade system was led by the Fairtrade Labeling Organizations (FLO), headquartered in Bonn, Germany. The FLO established FLO-Cert Ltd., which verified that the farmers benefited from the program.

The fair trade program in the United States was administered by TransFair USA, which tracked fair trade products from fair trade producers. TransFair was a member of the FLO. TransFair worked on the demand side of the market to increase the retail availability of fair trade coffee and other fair trade products. TransFair reported that 18.5 million pounds of fair trade coffee was sold in the United States in 2003 and projected 2004 sales at 29 million pounds. TransFair was financed by a 10 cents a pound fee paid by roasters for fair trade coffee as well as by grants from foundations.

[48]Oxfam International, "Mugged: Poverty in your coffee cup," 2002, p. 19.

[49]There are two sets of generic producer standards, one for small farmers and one for workers on plantations and in factories. The first set applies to smallholders organized in cooperatives or other organizations with a democratic, participative structure. The second set applies to organized workers, whose employers pay decent wages, guarantee the right to join trade unions and in factories, minimum health and safety as well as environmental standards must be complied with, and no child or forced labor may occur." Fair Labeling Organizations International, www.fairtrade.net/sites/aboutflo/faq.html.

In addition to TransFair and the FLO, NGOs worked to increase the availability of Fairtrade coffee. OxfamAmerica, Global Exchange, Co-Op America, and the Interfaith Fair Trade Initiative targeted coffee companies and retailers and sought to educate the public as well as coffee retailers. OxfamAmerica headed a private politics campaign to convince Procter & Gamble and Dunkin' Donuts to sell fair trade coffee. Adding to the direct pressure on the companies, the Center for Reflection, Education and Action (CREA) and Domini Social Investments registered for the P&G annual meeting the first-ever shareholder resolution on fair trade. The U.S. Senate and House approved resolutions calling for support of coffee farmers in developing countries.

Dunkin' Donuts agreed to sell fair trade expresso in the spring of 2003. After 2 years of efforts by the NGOs, in September 2003 Procter & Gamble agreed to sell Fair Trade Certified coffee through its Millstone specialty division and over the Internet. Sister Ruth Rosenbaum of CREA praised P&G: "P&G's action is an excellent example of what can be accomplished through collaboration of shareholder activists and nonprofit organizations. It's a win-win for the world's small-scale coffee farmers, for the environment, and for P&G itself."[50]

Oxfam established a rating systems for the four largest coffee companies, assessing for the past 12 months their actions to address the global coffee crisis. Procter & Gamble received a rating of 49 out of 100, Nestlé 43, Kraft 38, and Sara Lee 27. Phil Bloomer, the Make Trade Fair campaign director for Oxfam, said, "These companies continue to make massive profits while coffee farmers get poorer and poorer."[51]

## Challenges

One concern with the fair trade concept was whether retailers would charge such a large price premium that demand would be suppressed. "Supermarkets are taking advantage of the label to make more profit because they know that consumers are willing to pay a bit more because it is fair

trade," said Emily Daradaine, fruit-product manager" at the FLO.

At its 435 outlets Café Borders sold fair trade coffee for $16 a pound, whereas non-fair trade coffee was sold at $12 a pound. After an inquiry by a reporter for *The Wall Street Journal* Café Borders said it would lower the price for a bag of fair trade coffee by 20 percent. At the online site of the United Kingdom's largest supermarket chain Tesco PLC, fair trade coffee sold at 46 percent more than non-fair trade coffee. Luuk Laurens Zonneveld, managing director of the FLO, said he was concerned about high retail margins because they would reduce the market share for fair trade products. He said some of the FLO's affiliates might "approach" the companies about their practices.[52]

Whole Foods Markets had declined to participate in the fair trade program because it believed that the system was unfair to family farms that did not qualify as a producer's organization. Instead, Whole Foods started its own program, High Five for Farmers, under which it donated 5 percent of the price it paid for coffee to the farms that produced it.[53]

Royal Ahold NV of the Netherlands also set up an alternative certification program. "'If you are a large supermarket brand or a large roaster, to buy all your products under the fair-trade conditions is just not economically possible,' said David Rosenberg, director of Utz Kapeh," the foundation Royal Ahold helped establish to certify coffee.[54]

The fair trade movement claimed that fair trade coffee was higher quality. Tadesse Meskala, who managed a farmers' coffee cooperative in Ethiopia, commented, "Better payments leads us to make sure the coffee is a better quality." Farmers "care for the coffee because people care for us. They pay us a fair price."[55]

Ultimately, as the FTO stated, "The impact of Fair Trade in the end always depends on the goodwill and loyalty of the consumer."[56] Paul Rice, founder and chief executive of TransFair USA, said, "It is guilt-free coffee, but I would not call it

[50]OxfamAmerica, "Advocacy Groups and Shareholders Persuade Procter & Gamble to Offer Fair Trade Coffee," Press Release, September 15, 2003.
[51]OxfamAmerica, Press Release, December 9, 2003.

[52]*The Wall Street Journal*, June 8, 2004.
[53]*The Wall Street Journal*, June 8, 2004.
[54]*The Wall Street Journal*, June 8, 2004.
[55]*San Jose Mercury News*, April 28, 2004.
[56]www.fairtrade.net.

that. I would call it feel-good coffee."[57] Bill Conerly of the National Center for Policy Analysis commented, "It's a feel-good program. I don't

expect it to be a broad trend because people don't like to spend more money. I expect the impact to be trivial."[58] ∎

---

### PREPARATION QUESTIONS

1. Identify what fair trade accomplishes.
2. What are the important components of the fair trade system?
3. Will producers shirk on quality? Will the high price paid for fair trade coffee induce farmers

to clear forests to produce more coffee? Will retailers capture the surplus?
4. What are the opportunities for social innovation within the fair trade concept?

---

# University Games, Inc.

Bob Moog, president and founder of University Games, Inc., of Burlingame, California, returned from a 3-day trip to Chang Mai in Northern Thailand in January 1993. Bob received his MBA from the Graduate School of Business at Stanford in 1984 where he had been an informal student leader and creator of pranks, mischief, and camaraderie. After graduation he founded University Games to develop and market board games. By 1993 the company had U.S. sales of $8.5 million and worldwide sales of over $10 million. Not only was Bob the president of University Games, he was also the inventor of most of its proprietary board games. In addition to developing its own game themes, University Games licensed themes, such as Dick Tracy and Carmen Sandiego. University Games contracted out all the production of its games, and most of its sales were made through independent agents and representatives.

University Games had recently acquired exclusive U.S. distribution rights to a line of wooden puzzles under the Rain Tree label. The puzzles were produced in a factory in Chang Mai from a dark wood that gave them an attractive appearance. To obtain a higher margin, the puzzles were sold in specialty stores and not in discount stores. The puzzles were expected to produce revenue of nearly $700,000 in 1993. Moog planned to expand the line and had recently hired an outstanding new manager for the Rain Tree product line.

The factory in Chang Mai was owned by a Thai, who had received an engineering degree in the United States. After returning to Thailand he established a woodworking shop and began to create his own puzzles, which he sold locally. After struggling for many years, he began to achieve success when his puzzles were introduced in the United States. The factory's shipments increased rapidly from 500,000 baht in 1987 to 27 million baht in 1992 (25 baht to the dollar). He was particularly proud of being able to provide employment for over 300 people.

Moog's visit to the factory had two purposes. One was to discuss supply arrangements for the expansion of the product line and the production of other wooden game products that University Games was developing. The second purpose was to inspect the working conditions at the factory.

Although the working conditions were said to be good by the standards of northern Thailand, Moog described them as "pre–industrial revolution." The production process began with large pieces of wood being dried in kilns. Then, a group of men and boys sawed, drilled, and carved the dried wood in an open Quonset hut. The men were barefooted, and safety conditions were virtually nonexistent. For example, the men frequently used machetes to cut wood they held between their legs. Although the wood shop was cleaned and mopped every night, by 10:00 A.M. the men were covered with sawdust.

About half of them wore bandannas across their noses and mouths to avoid inhaling the dust.

Inside the main building of the factory, 50 to 60 young girls worked in the paint shop handpainting the wooden pieces. The girls sat in circles on the floor, talking and painting, and seemed to be having a good time. There were a few older women supervisors, but generally the employees seemed to work with little supervision. The factory owner was a tough employer who occasionally would fire employees who did not produce acceptable quality products, even though at times it may not have been the fault of employees, who sometimes did not know the standards they were expected to meet. He explained, "I don't give them a lot of chances."

The workers were thin but seemed to be in good health and quite happy. They worked 10 hours a day, 6 days a week, and had a 45-minute lunch break and three 20-minute breaks a day. They earned approximately $100 a month. In addition, many of the employees lived free of charge in a 3-year-old dormitory located on the factory premises. The factory owner believed that his was the only factory in Northern Thailand with a dormitory for its employees. The rooms in the dormitory were like those in a college dormitory and housed four to a room. The bathrooms in the dormitory were adequate, and the residents had access to a kitchen. The factory owner also provided food, which he sold to the employees at a fair price.

In addition to employing over 300 people, the factory owner contracted out some work to local villages. In effect, he staffed the factory for the base workload and subcontracted the extra work to the villages. In the villages people lived in houses built of wood or concrete block with thatched roofs. The houses had electricity and some had running water.

Work at the factory seemed inefficient. Sawdust covered much of the production floor and also covered the puzzle pieces waiting to be assembled. When workers cleaned the pieces to prepare them for painting, assembly, or shipping, some were damaged and had to be scrapped. In the paint shop, the girls wanted to sit in circles so they could talk as they worked. Rather than specializing, each girl performed each of the tasks. For example, instead of one girl painting only the yellow dots on each of the pieces, each painted a yellow dot, a red dot, a blue dot, and a green dot on each piece. One obstacle to improving productivity in the factory was the difficulty in getting the girls to work in a line or even to work at assembly and painting tables. Two years earlier the owner had put work tables in the paint shop, but as soon as he would leave the shop, the girls would either sit on the tables or push them aside and sit on the floor in circles to work. They preferred the social interaction to the higher wages that would accompany higher productivity.

Moog was concerned about the conditions at the factory and wondered what he could and should do about them. Although University Games was a small company, it was one of only two customers of the factory and accounted for 25 percent of its shipments. When Moog discussed the working conditions with the factory owner, it was clear that the owner was proud of what he had accomplished and did not want any meddling. When Moog asked about the conditions under which the wooden pieces were produced in the villages, the factory owner said, "I don't get involved in how the villages do the work for me, and you shouldn't get involved in how I do the work for you. All you should care about is do I get it done on time and do I get it done to the quality you want." Bob responded, "Look, if I were one of a hundred customers, I might agree with you. You are my only supplier for these puzzles, and I am one of only two customers you have and I represent 25 percent of your sales. We have to work together on this." Moog was also concerned about the impact of any higher costs on his company's profits, since his shareholders were pressing for higher profits. ∎

## PREPARATION QUESTIONS

**1.** How should Moog reason about his responsibility, if any, with respect to the factory in Thailand? Which practices should concern him?

**2.** What specifically should he do? Prepare a policy and plan of action.

**3.** How should he interact with the factory owner?

# GlaxoSmithKline and AIDS Drugs Policy

In Africa GlaxoSmithKline (GSK) confronted the reality of the AIDS pandemic every day, and its decisions impacted thousands. There were no ready answers to the crisis, but everyone—governments, nongovernmental organizations, the media, shareholders, and others—had an opinion. GSK had to determine how to address the crisis while maintaining business viability in developing countries in the midst of the pressures swirling around it.

Throughout the late 1990s, the CEO of GSK, Stanford Graduate School of Business alumnus Dr. Jean-Pierre Garnier, was at the forefront of the controversy over anti-retroviral drug pricing, patent protection, and drug access. Proactive in addressing critics, he was seen as the de facto spokesperson for the pharmaceutical industry in addressing these critical issues.

## AZT Discovery: The Source of Hope and the Root of Controversy

The controversy traced back to 1987 when the FDA approved Burroughs Wellcome's compound, Zidovudine, commonly known as AZT, as the first anti-retroviral (ARV) drug for the treatment of the HIV virus. Burroughs Wellcome, expecting a small market and short life cycle for the drug and hoping to recoup development and clinical trial costs, announced that a year of the treatment would cost patients $8,000 to $10,000. This resulted in an avalanche of criticism for excessive corporate profiteering and united a number of disparate parties against Burroughs Wellcome. Activist groups, the media, and government officials led the charge.

The controversy was further fueled by the assertion of critics that its development was funded by government grants and therefore AZT should enter generic production immediately. In 1991 Barr Laboratories filed for FDA approval to produce a generic version of AZT. Burroughs Wellcome spent 5 years in court fighting to protect its patent, and in the end prevailed. The eventual commercial success of AZT increased the public outcry. Despite Burroughs Wellcome's initial belief that the market for the drug was quite small and its life cycle short due to anticipated new drugs, by 1993 AZT, marketed under the brand name Retrovir, was Burroughs Wellcome's number two product with cumulative sales of over $1 billion.

## GlaxoSmithKline and AIDS Drugs

Because of the high costs and the risks of research and development, the pharmaceutical industry experienced a wave of mergers and acquisitions in the 1990s. In 1995 Glaxo acquired Burroughs Wellcome and AZT, making the company, now Glaxo Wellcome, the leader in AIDS therapy. Glaxo's own AIDS drug, Lamivudine (3TC) was expected to soon be approved by the FDA, and the company hoped to combine 3TC with AZT into a dual-drug combination. During the merger process management carefully evaluated its strategy for AIDS therapies and considered abandoning the market altogether. There were significant risks involved in pursuing new research in the controversial AIDS area, as indicated by Burroughs Wellcome's AZT experience. Some of the company's executives worried that the new company would expose itself to more public inquiry and scrutiny if it continued to pursue a leadership position in AIDS drugs.

The company's competitors were proceeding with their own efforts to develop AIDS therapies. Advanced trials were underway for a new class of protease inhibitors that showed promise when combined with the older AIDS drugs. Concerned about these new offerings and convinced that the market for AIDS therapies would remain sustainable, Glaxo Wellcome decided to continue its AIDS research. In 1995 and 1996 the FDA approved four new AIDS drugs from Roche, Merck, Abbott Laboratories, and Agouron. In 1999 Glaxo Wellcome added to its AIDS portfolio with Amprenavir.

In 2001 GlaxoSmithKline was formed by the merger of Glaxo Wellcome and SmithKline Beecham, becoming the world's second-largest pharmaceutical company. In 2002 GSK had net income of $6.941 billion on sales of $31.819 billion. Its return on equity was among the highest in the world. GSK was registered in the United Kingdom, but its top management was located in Philadelphia. GSK had been strategically pieced together through a number of mergers, combining the venerable pharmaceutical companies Glaxo, Wellcome, Burroughs, Beecham, and SmithKline & French and their drug portfolios, including some of the most successful AIDS therapies on the market.[1] In 2002 ARVs and AIDS drugs accounted for 7.9 percent of GSK's total revenues.

## Commitment to Developing Countries

After the merger, GSK reaffirmed its corporate commitment to developing countries. For the past 20 years GSK, as one of the leading worldwide producers of vaccines, had offered vaccines to developing markets at preferential prices. As an indication of its continuing pledge to remain in the sub-Saharan Africa market, GSK maintained more registered patents in the countries of that region than any other pharmaceutical company, even though 90 percent of its revenues came from the larger markets of the United States and Europe. It also maintained a presence in a majority of markets in Africa and continued to serve both the public sector and the small emerging private sector. However, despite lowering prices to offer access to a wider population, GSK found that the local sub-Saharan African governments were either uninterested in or financially unable to provide these drugs to their citizens. With each successive drug price decrease, the private market participants benefited, but few additional drugs reached the community at large.

As corporate policy GSK did not sell its drugs below production cost even in sub-Saharan Africa. In February 2002 Garnier announced that GSK would "not profit" from AIDS drugs sold in the

## The AIDS Drug Pricing Controversy

There was no known cure for AIDS. Nonetheless, the introduction of ARVs as part of HIV clinical care made AIDS a more manageable chronic illness by achieving dramatic reductions in viral load (the level of the HIV virus in the blood), thereby arresting immune system damage. Typically, ARV-based treatment consisted of a "cocktail" of at least three drugs from the various classes of ARV drugs. This three-drug cocktail was called "Highly Active Antiretroviral Therapy" (HAART). Each class of anti-HIV drugs in a cocktail attacked the virus at a different stage of its replication in the human host lymphocyte cell. GSK combined AZT and Epivir to form Combivir, which became the company's largest selling ARV. Combivir was typically used in a combination with a protease inhibitor. As of June 2000 there were 14 FDA-approved HIV/AIDS drugs. GSK held patents on four of them.

The introduction of ARVs widened the discrepancy in the quality of AIDS care between rich and poor countries. In the United States HAART therapy led to a 70 percent decline in deaths attributable to HIV/AIDS. However, most of the 36 million people in the developing world living with HIV/AIDS did not benefit from the therapy. The World Health Organization (WHO) conservatively estimated that in 2002, 6 million people in developing countries were in need of life-sustaining ARV therapy. Yet, fewer than 250,000 had access to these therapies, and half of those were in one country, Brazil.

## Pricing Pressure from Multiple Directions

As with other drugs the patents on the ARVs were owned by multinational pharmaceutical companies such as GSK, Bristol Myers Squibb, Pfizer, and Roche. Many observers argued that these patents resulted in high prices and kept needed drugs out of Africa and the rest of the developing world. Since most ARVs had been developed recently, the expiration of the patents would not occur soon. The

---

[1] Rick Mullin, "Pharma M & A declines, but financing picks up," *Chemical Week*, March 20, 2002.

[2] "AHF Reports GlaxoSmithKline Head Vows to Make 'No Profit' on AIDS Drugs in Poor Countries; Advocates Ask for Public Disclosure of Costs," *Business Wire*, February 27, 2002.

patent for AZT would expire in 2005, but the patents on many other ARVs extended until 2014. As a result few observers expected AIDS drugs to reach the developing world during the height of the AIDS pandemic.

The first negotiations over global access to AIDS drugs began in Geneva in 1991 when 18 drug companies met with WHO representatives for a series of talks. A key topic in these discussions was the cost of new AIDS drugs—estimated to be $10,000 or more a year. The talks ended in 1993 with no resolution.

The major producers of AIDS drugs steadfastly opposed the idea of lowering prices in poor countries such as in sub-Saharan Africa. The industry maintained that the real obstacles to AIDS treatment in Africa and other low-income regions were not inflated drug prices but social, managerial, and political barriers, such as the absence of roads, shortages of doctors and nurses, the limited use of contraceptive devices, and the lack of resources to provide even basic health care to many citizens. They asserted that treatment should be borne by governments and society and not the companies per se. Moreover, the companies argued that on a continent where nearly half the population lived on less than a dollar a day, there was no price at which AIDS drugs could be commercially distributed to victims. In addition, the companies worried that without the proper infrastructure and health monitoring, the widespread use of AIDS drugs would result in an even more virulent strain of HIV that would be drug-resistant.[3]

GSK and the other pharmaceutical companies believed their pricing policies were justified by the high costs of research and development. Patents were essential to pricing successful drugs, and without patent production, the economic model of the industry would fail, eliminating the incentive for future innovation in AIDS/HIV treatment. In the early 1990s the industry had lobbied the Clinton administration to extend domestic patent protection worldwide. These efforts were important in the creation of the Trade Related Aspects of Intellectual Property (TRIPS) agreement that was incorporated into the rules of the World Trade Organization

[3]The distribution of ARVs and supervision of their use was crucial, since if a person did not follow a strict regimen of taking them every day, drug resistant strains of HIV could develop. Moreover, if a patient stopped taking the ARVs for 2 weeks, resistance to the drug developed, and ARVs were then ineffective.

(WTO) when it was formed in 1995. GSK and other drug companies were also concerned that if they agreed to price concessions for developing countries, they would face increased price pressures in their core U.S. and European markets. Pressure could arise from the gray market importation of drugs from low-income countries or from activist campaigns that drew attention to the price differentials between developing countries and the U.S. and European markets.

The pressure on the industry continued for much of the 1990s, fueled by the unrelenting spread of HIV. Through agencies such as WHO and UNAIDS, the United Nations and its member countries exerted pressure on the pharmaceutical companies to reduce prices to improve access to drugs for HIV/AIDS victims. Activist groups like the AIDS Coalition to Unleash Power, or ACT UP! (which was formed in response to the initial launch price of AZT), Médicins sans Frontières, and the Consumer Project on Technology led protests and campaigns that charged the industry with profiteering from history's worst pandemic, using slogans like "Pfizer's Greed Kills," "Death Under Patent," and "GlaxoSmithKline! GlobalSerialKiller." These sentiments were exacerbated by the remarkable financial performance the drug industry experienced during this period. In 1999 the industry topped all three of *Fortune* magazine's measures of profitability and had one of the highest rates of return of any industry.

By the end of the decade public criticism had reached a crescendo. AIDS protestors badgered Vice President Gore's presidential campaign and chained themselves to desks in U.S. Trade Representative Charlene Barshefsky's office, demanding that the Clinton administration stop backing the industry against generic competitors. Activists became more aggressive and confrontational toward the drug companies, regularly taking actions such as storming into the offices of companies, including Pfizer and Bristol Myers, to disrupt their corporate events.

The media was also critical of drug companies and their handling of the AIDS drug pricing issue. Mainstream publications such as *The New York Times, Washington Post,* and *The Wall Street Journal* portrayed the pharmaceutical companies and their management as profit-centric and uncaring about the plight of poor countries. This public censure was echoed by journalists in both developed and developing countries and translated into antagonism against the drug companies and their pricing practices, domestically and internationally. The pharmaceutical industry had inadvertently become a primary recipient of the worldwide blame for the growing AIDS epidemic.

## Preferential Pricing Begins

In late 1999 the industry responded to the mounting criticisms. Prompted by the senior management of GSK and Bristol-Myers Squibb, the International Federation of Pharmaceutical Manufacturers Associations organized a meeting to explore solutions to the issue. Six of the major companies participated in a conference call in January 2000 at which executives at Glaxo and Bristol-Myers volunteered to draft a set of principles for an industry-led AIDS treatment initiative. After a series of talks and meetings, the companies agreed on a consensus draft to be presented to the United Nations agencies. By this time the original group of six companies had been reduced to five—Bristol-Myers Squibb, GlaxoSmithKline, Merck, Boehringer Ingelheim, and Roche. Pfizer had withdrawn, citing disagreement with the concept of preferential pricing.

Shortly after Pfizer's withdrawal, eight ACT UP! activists stormed the office of Pfizer CEO William Steere, Jr. They demanded that the company acquiesce to pressure from South African activists in the Treatment Action Campaign (TAC) and drop the price of fluconazole (diflucan) or issue a voluntary license for the importation of generic versions of the drug from a less expensive supplier. Fluconazole was effective in treating cryptococcal meningitis, the most common AIDS-related systemic fungal infection. Fluconazole was priced at $8.92 per pill in South Africa. In Thailand, where Pfizer did not have exclusive marketing rights, fluconazole cost only $0.29 per pill.[4] The average daily wage in South Africa in 1999 was about $7.00. The activists claimed that it was unacceptable for a corporation to maintain high prices while AIDS patients in poor countries were dying of treatable diseases. ACT UP! threatened to bring the issue to the attention of politicians and investors and claimed that Pfizer's actions were socially unconscionable. In April 2000 Pfizer announced that instead of lowering the price it would give away fluconazole to 3.6 million victims in South Africa.

Two months later Pfizer extended the offer to 50 other less-developed countries.

Pfizer's initiative was applauded by advocacy groups. It immediately shifted the onus to the remaining five companies to follow Pfizer's lead. In particular, TAC called on GSK to make AZT available to pregnant women to reduce the risk of mother-to-child transmission. The five remaining pharmaceutical companies lobbied the U.N. agencies—UNAIDS, WHO, UNICEF, U.N. Development Program—and the World Bank to consider their proposed preferential pricing policy. Finally on May 11, 2000, the five companies and the United Nations issued a joint Statement of Intent for an Accelerating Access initiative as a basis for preferential pricing for HIV/AIDS medicines in developing countries. The concessions were to be made on a country-by-country basis and involved significant restrictions on the resale and use of the drugs. The industry and the United Nations publicly hailed the initiative as a major step forward. Still, critics remained unhappy and charged the drug companies with continuing to maintain high prices by offering discounts selectively. The critics were angry that the language of the initiative was vague and that none of the drug companies, with the exception of GSK, had made firm commitments to exact price reductions.

In 2002 United Nations Secretary General Kofi Annan established the independent Global Fund to Fight AIDS, Tuberculosis and Malaria with $2.1 billion in funding to purchase AIDS drugs and conduct AIDS prevention programs in Africa. The funds came primarily from governments and the Gates Foundation. The Gates Foundation emphasized prevention programs over treatment of AIDS victims as the most cost effective means of addressing the AIDS pandemic.

## Compulsory Licensing

Another issue confronting GSK was the decision of countries such as Thailand and Brazil to invoke compulsory licensing under TRIPS and either allow local manufacturers to produce ARVs based on patented formulas or import generic substitutes for the patented drugs. Although not directly affected by the decisions in Thailand and Brazil, GSK watched with great interest the unfolding of negotiations in both countries. Together with other major drug producers, GSK was a strong proponent of intellectual property protection and for many years

[4]*ACT UP* Philadelphia/New York press release.

had lobbied the U.S. government to support patent rights and the TRIPS agreement. However, at the end of 1999 the U.S. government reversed its stance and announced that it would not object to compulsory licensing in situations where a medical emergency justified it.

This represented a potentially serious threat to GSK's ability to protect its patented products from generic competitors in overseas markets. Management feared that many countries might follow the examples of Thailand and Brazil and use the opportunity to import or make cheap imitation drugs at the expense of patent holders. The decision by the U.S. government meant that foreign governments would not face trade sanctions if they used compulsory licensing.

In 1997 the South African parliament granted its Ministry of Health the power to permit parallel importation of drugs produced under license in another country. In February 1998, 39 major drug companies (including GSK), represented by the Pharmaceutical Manufacturers Association of South Africa (PMA), filed a lawsuit against the Government of South Africa to strike down the law on the grounds that it breached international trade agreements such as TRIPS and was unconstitutional, since it gave the health minister arbitrary power to ignore patent rights. The lawsuit and subsequent trial drew strong criticism from the media and advocacy groups, and in April 2001 after the trial had been underway for 6 weeks, the PMA withdrew its lawsuit.

On February 7, 2001, Cipla, an Indian generic drug manufacturer, offered to supply a triple-combination therapy for HIV/AIDS at $350 per patient per year to Médicins sans Frontières, an independent medical and humanitarian aid agency working in Africa. Cipla was able to manufacture these drugs under Indian patent law and export them at a fraction of the price at which the drugs were available from their primary manufacturers. It also offered to sell the therapy for $600 per patient per year to the governments of poor countries on the condition that the recipient governments provide the drugs for free to those with HIV/AIDS. The comparative cost of this regimen in developed nations was $10,000 to $15,000 annually. Cipla's offer put pressure on other pharmaceutical companies to reduce their prices. Cipla also began to produce AZT and by the end of 2002 was producing 10 of the 14 most widely used AIDS drugs. In May Merck announced that it would sell its AIDS drug Crixivan for $600 per patient per year and Stocrin for $500 per patient per year in the developing world. According to the company, it made no profit at these prices. Shortly thereafter, Boehringer Ingelheim, Bristol-Myers Squibb, and Abbott Laboratories followed with similar discount offers.

Preferential pricing and compulsory licensing posed another challenge to the patent holders of AIDS drugs. Corrupt officials could intercept AIDS drugs and smuggle them into European countries and the United States, where they could be sold at market prices. GSK sought to avoid this by providing the preferentially priced drugs directly to health care providers. Nevertheless, corruption and re-exportation posed a problem for its markets in developed countries.

## Media Coverage

Extremely critical of the pharmaceutical industry on the drug pricing and access issue, the press had been relentless in its pressure on GSK. Beginning with Burroughs Wellcome's initial announcement of the price for AZT, the news media had successfully reframed HIV/AIDS drug pricing as a social justice and moral issue.

Even though GSK had lowered prices and negotiated with sub-Saharan African governments to provide the drugs to their citizens, the press reports continued to point to pricing as the primary barrier to drug access. In particular, the media in socially conscious Western countries faulted GSK and other pharmaceutical companies for not doing enough to ensure that those in sub-Saharan Africa had access to HIV/AIDS medicines. Initially, GSK was reactive in dealing with this pressure, often addressing questions and concerns with complex justifications about differential pricing and the specific positive steps that GSK had taken. Additionally, GSK was hesitant to fault publicly the governments that it had to work with on a regular basis.

## Activist Groups

The activist groups were concerned about a broad range of issues, from HIV/AIDS itself to social justice, consumer rights, and humanitarian relief. The challenge for GSK lay in how to address the concerns of these often hostile groups without impairing its business objectives. The power and influence of the advocacy organizations could not be ignored. They were well organized, had access to funds, and possessed considerable leverage in shaping public opinion. Their campaigns drew considerable attention from the media and politicians and were effective in galvanizing support from the public for their cause. GSK management recognized this and was responsive to the major activist groups. Those groups, however, were generally distrustful of major corporations and continued to publicly pressure the drug companies to change their policies.

The AIDS Healthcare Foundation (AHF), an NGO that was the world's largest specialized provider of HIV medical care, launched a multipronged campaign against GSK. First, AHF sought to convince CalPERS, the California state retirement system, which held $1 billion of GSK's shares, to pressure the company to lower ARV prices. Second, AHF filed a lawsuit challenging GSK's patent on AZT, arguing that the research had been financed by public funds. Third, AHF filed a complaint against GSK in South Africa, where AHF operated a clinic, challenging GSK's pricing and other policies in South Africa. Fourth, it filed a false advertising lawsuit in California against GSK. Fifth, it organized protests and demonstrations against GSK.

## GSK's Response

### Social Responsibility Committee

Despite the commitment made to the Accelerating Access initiative in 2000, GSK continued to receive negative press coverage of its response to the AIDS crisis. The company faced unrelenting pressure to cut further its prices and extend its discounts to a broader group of countries and organizations. The intense public scrutiny in turn triggered concern among the company's shareholders about the reputational risks involved in failing to address the issue of access to needed medicines. GSK spent considerable time in discussions with its key institutional shareholders to address these concerns.

In response to the pressure GSK established a corporate social responsibility committee, chaired by Sir Richard Sykes, GSK's new non-executive chairman, to review the company's policies on access. Specifically, the committee was charged with crafting a policy response for GSK not only to HIV/AIDS but to the broader issue of access to drugs in the developing world. The committee would also advise

the board of directors on issues of significance in the relationship between the company and society and would regularly review the company's policy on health care in the developing world.

On February 21, 2001, GSK announced that it would extend its preferential pricing offer for HIV/AIDS medicines beyond governments to include not-for-profit nongovernmental organizations (NGOs), such as international agencies, aid groups, and churches and charities that had facilities in place to appropriately monitor and treat patients. GSK also offered preferential prices on ARVs to employers in Africa that provided HIV/AIDS care and treatment directly to their employees through workplace clinics. Specifically, the price of Ziagen, which sold for $10.68 a day in the U.S. for the standard two-pill treatment, was reduced to $3.80 a day; Trizivir, a potent, triple-drug combination pill taken twice a day at a cost of $27.92 in the U.S. was priced at $6.60 in low-income countries; and Agenerase, a protease inhibitor that cost $18.50 a day for 16 pills in the U.S., was priced at $8.70 a day under the new preferential pricing plan. In addition to the AIDS drugs, GSK also reduced the price of its malarial pill Malarone from the U.S. list price of $52.71 for a full course of 12 tablets to $19.20 in the developing world.

Nonetheless, Garnier conceded that even with these steep discounts, the new prices would remain out of reach for most patients in the developing world. "We're not naive about the fact that compared to the means in these countries, everything is over-priced, even the generics," he said in an interview.

### Corporate Policy: "Facing the Challenge"

One unexpected result of the criticism of GSK's policies concerning access to ARVs in sub-Saharan Africa was the impact on the morale of employees, shareholders, and partners. In an effort to reassure its internal constituents, in June 2001 GSK published "Facing the Challenge," a report articulating the company's product, pricing, and partnership commitments to increased access to medicines for patients in need in developing countries. Reshaping the role of GSK as a partner in the global fight against AIDS, the report was a turning point for the company and its stakeholders. Garnier said of GSK's new partner role:

As a leading international research based pharmaceutical company, GlaxoSmithKline can make a real difference to health care in the developing

research and development costs? Should it make further reductions in its prices for its ARVs? How should GSK deal with the possibility of AIDS drugs supplied to Africa being diverted to Europe and the United States? Should GSK voluntarily license its ARVs to local drug producers in South Africa or other countries? Should it match Cipla's prices? How should it price its next AIDS drug currently in the pipeline? Should it continue to invest in research and development on drug therapies whose prices would likely be driven down by criticism from activists, governments, and the media or by patent infringements by companies in developing countries? GSK participated along with other pharmaceutical companies in TRIPS negotiations regarding compulsory licensing and parallel imports. What should GSK do to protect its intellectual property while providing access to drugs under patent for people and countries in need? More generally, what role should social concerns and societal pressure play in GSK's business strategy? And how could GSK better manage nonmarket considerations, both now and in the future? ∎

SOURCE: Deborah Liu (MBA 2002) and Soon Jin Lim (MBA 2002) prepared this case from public sources under the supervision of Professor David P Baron as the basis for class discussion rather than to illustrate either effective or ineffective handling of an administrative situation.

## GSK's Challenge Going Forward

GSK faced an enormous challenge at the beginning of 2003. How could it address the continuing concerns raised by activists, the media, and governments, while simultaneously serving the interests of GSK stakeholders? How should social responsibility be balanced against generating profits? Should it go further than its current commitment and begin to deliver health care in the poorest countries? What should be the cost basis on which it prices its ARVs—for example, the marginal cost of producing the drugs or the average cost, taking into account its

world. We believe this is both an ethical imperative and key to business success. "Facing the Challenge" is a signal of our intention and commitment to making access to medicines a continued priority of our company. We are extending our preferential pricing offers to more products, to more countries and to more customer groups, in an effort to secure greater access for patients to treatment that is both appropriate and sustainable. Our activities will be undertaken together with organizations that have relevant specialized knowledge, such as governments, international agencies, charities and academic institutions. The pharmaceutical industry can play an important role, but it does not have the mandate, expertise or resources to deliver health care unilaterally to developing countries.

---

## PREPARATION QUESTIONS

1. The European Union expressed concern about the availability of pharmaceuticals to poor countries. The Commission of the European Union held an annual meeting of its Health and TRIPS Issue Group on the subject of "Access to Essential Medicines." GSK was an active participant in the meetings; the next of which was scheduled for April 28, 2003. Garnier had agreed to attend the meeting and

understood that he would be questioned about GSK's AIDS drugs policy. In the role of CEO Garnier, would you announce any changes in the company's policy? What defense would you give in support of either the current policy or the new policy you plan to announce?

2. What position should Garnier take on TRIPS and compulsory licensing?

# References

Abegglen, James C., and George Stalk, Jr. (1985). *Kaisha, the Japanese Corporation.* New York: Basic Books.

Aggarwal, Vinod K. (Ed.) (2001). *Winning in Asia, European Style.* New York: Palgrave.

Akerlof, George A. (1970). "The Market for 'Lemons': Qualitative Uncertainty and the Market Mechanism." *Quarterly Journal of Economics,* 84, 488–500.

Alesina, Alberto, and Romain Wacziarg. (1999). "Is Europe Going Too Far?" Carnegie-Rochester Conference on Public Policy (*Journal of Monetary Economics*), 51, 1–42.

Alpern, Kenneth D. (1988). "Moral Dimensions of the Foreign Corrupt Practices Act: Comments on Pastin and Hooker." In Donaldson and Werhane (1988), 54–59.

Alt, James A., and Kenneth Shepsle (Eds.). (1990). *Perspectives on Positive Political Economy.* Cambridge, UK: Cambridge University Press.

Aoki, Masahiko (Ed.). (1984). *The Economic Analysis of the Japanese Firm.* Amsterdam, The Netherlands: North Holland.

American Society of Newspaper Editors. (1999). "Examining our Credibility: Examining Credibility, Explaining Ourselves." Reston, VA. www.asne.org.

Ansolabehere, Stephen, John de Figueiredo, and James M. Snyder. (2003). "Why Is There So Little Money in U.S. Politics?" Working paper, Massachusetts Institute of Technology, Cambridge, MA.

Areeda, Phillip, and Herbert Hovenkamp. 2002. *Fundamentals of Antitrust Law.* New York: Aspen Law & Business.

Areeda, Phillip, and Louis Kaplow. (1988). *Antitrust Analysis: Problems, Text, and Cases* (4th ed.). Boston: Little, Brown.

———. (1997) *Antitrust Analysis* (5th ed.). New York: Aspen Law and Business.

Areeda, Phillip, and Donald Turner. (1975, February). "Predatory Pricing and Related Practices under Section 2 of the Sherman Act." *Harvard Law Review,* 88, 697–733.

Argenti, Paul A. 2004. "Collaborating with Activists: How Starbucks Works with NGOs." *California Management Review.* 47: 91–116.

Arrow, Kenneth A. (1963). *Social Choice and Individual Values* (2d ed.). New York: Wiley.

Atsuyuki, Suzuta. (1978). "The Way of the Bureaucrat." *Japan Echo,* 5(3), 42–53. Reprinted in Okimoto and Rohlen (1988), 196–203.

Baerwald, Hans H. (1974). *Japan's Parliament: An Introduction.* London, UK: Cambridge University Press.

Bach, David. (2004). "The Double Punch of Law and Technology: Fighting Music Piracy or Remaking Copyright in a Digital Age?" *Business and Politics,* 6: Article 3.

Bagley, Constance E. (2002). *Managers and the Legal Environment: Strategies for the 21st Century* (4th ed.). St. Paul, MN: West Publishing Co.

Baker, Jonathan B. (1997). *Econometric Analysis in FTC v. Staples.* Washington, DC: Federal Trade Commission.

Bamberger, Gustavo E., and Dennis W. Carlton. (1999). "Antitrust and Higher Education: MIT Financial Aid (1993)." In John E. Kwoka, Jr. and Lawrence J. White, *The Antitrust Revolution: Economics, Competition, and Policy,* 264–285. New York: Oxford University Press.

Banner, Stuart. (1998). "The Origin of the New York Stock Exchange, 1791–1860." *Journal of Legal Studies,* 27, 113–140.

Barker, Richard A. (1993). "An Evaluation of the Ethics Program at General Dynamics." *Journal of Business Ethics,* 12, 165–177.

Baron, David P. (1983). *The Export-Import Bank: An Economic Analysis.* New York: Academic Press.

———. (1995a). "The Nonmarket Strategy System." *Sloan Management Review,* 37(Fall), 73–85.

———. (1995b). "Integrated Strategy: Market and Nonmarket Components." *California Management Review,* 37(Winter), 47–65.

———. (1996). *Business and Its Environment* (2d ed.). Upper Saddle River, NJ: Prentice Hall.

———. (1997a). "Integrated Strategy in International Trade Disputes: The Kodak-Fujifilm Case." *Journal of Economics and Management Strategy,* 6(Summer), 291–346.

———. (1997b). "Integrated Strategy, Trade Policy, and Global Competition." *California Management Review*, 39(Winter), 145–169.

———. (1999). "Integrated Market and Nonmarket Strategies in Client and Interest Group Politics." *Business and Politics*, 1(April), 7–34.

———. (2000). *Business and Its Environment* (3rd ed.). Upper Saddle River, NJ: Prentice Hall.

———. (2001). "Private Politics, Corporate Social Responsibility, and Integrated Strategy." *Journal of Economics & Management Strategy*, 10(Spring), 7–45.

———. (2003a). "Private Politics." *Journal of Economics & Management Strategy*, Vol. 12: 31–66.

———. (2003b). "Private Ordering on the Internet: The eBay Community of Traders." *Business and Politics*, 4: 245–274.

———. (2003c). *Business and Its Environment* (4th ed.). Upper Saddle River, NJ: Prentice Hall.

———. (2005a) "Competing for the Public Through the News Media," *Journal of Economics and Management Strategy*, (forthcoming).

———. (2005b) "Persistent Media Bias," *Journal of Public Economics*, (forthcoming).

Baron, David P. and David Besanko. (2001). "Strategy, Organization, and Incentives: Global Corporate Banking at Citibank." *Industrial and Corporate Change*, 10: 1–36.

Baron, David P. and John A. Ferejohn. (1989). "Bargaining in Legislatures." *American Political Science Review*, 83(December), 1181–1206.

Barone, Michael, and Richard E. Cohen. (2003). *The Almanac of American Politics 2004*, Washington, DC: National Journal.

Bartlett, Christopher A., and Sumantra Ghoshal. (1989). *Managing Across Borders: The Transnational Solution*. Boston, MA: Harvard Business School Press.

Battacharya, C. B., and Sankar Sen. (2004). "Doing Better by Doing Good: When, Why, and How Consumers Respond to Corporate Social Initiatives." *California Management Review*, 47:9–24.

Baysinger, Barry D., Gerald D. Keim, and Carl P. Zeithaml. (1985). "An Empirical Evaluation of the Potential for Including Shareholders in Corporate Constituency Programs." *Academy of Management Journal*, 28, 180–200.

Becker, Gary S. (1983). "A Theory of Competition and Pressure Groups for Political Influence." *Quarterly Journal of Economics*, 98, 371–400.

Bellis, Jean-Francois. (1989). "The EEC Antidumping System." In Jackson and Vermulst, *Antidumping Laws and Practice: A Comparative Study*, 41–97.

Bentham, Jeremy. (1789). *An Introduction to the Principles of Morals and Legislation*. Reprint Buffalo, NY: Prometheus Books (1988).

Berle, Adolph A., and Gardiner C. Means. (1932). "The Modern Corporation and Private Property." Reprint Buffalo, NY: W. S. Wein (1982).

Bernstein, Marver H. (1955). *Regulation by Independent Commission*. Princeton, NJ: Princeton University Press.

Besanko, David, David Dranove, Scott Schaefer, and Mark Shanley. (2004), *The Economics of Strategy* (3d ed.). New York: Wiley.

Binmore, Kenneth M. (1994). *Game Theory and the Social Contract*. Cambridge, MA: MIT Press.

Black, Henry C. (1983). *Black's Law Dictionary* (abridged 5th ed.). St. Paul: West Publishing Co.

Boardman, Anthony E., David H. Greenberg, Aidan R. Vining, and David L. Weimer. (2001). *Cost-Benefit Analysis: Concepts and Practice*. Upper Saddle River, NJ: Prentice Hall.

Bouchoux, Deborah E. (2001). *Protecting Your Company's Intellectual Property*. New York: AMACOM.

Bowie, Norman E. (1990). "Business Ethics and Cultural Relativism." In Peter Madsen and Jay M. Shafritz (Eds.), *Essentials of Business Ethics*, 366–382. New York: Penguin Books.

Brady, David, and Craig Volden. (1998). *Revolving Gridlock*. Boulder, CO: Westview Press.

Brandt, Richard B. (1959). *Ethical Theory*. Upper Saddle River, NJ: Prentice Hall.

———. (1979). *A Theory of the Good and the Right*. Oxford, UK: Clarendon Press.

Breyer, Stephen. (1982). *Regulation and Its Reform*. Cambridge, MA: Harvard University Press.

Brock, William A., and David S. Evans. (1986). *The Economics of Small Business*. New York: Holmes and Meyer.

Bronte, Stephen. (1982). *Japanese Finance: Markets and Institutions*. London, UK: Euromoney Publications.

Brooks, Leonard J. (1989). "Corporate Codes of Ethics." *Journal of Business Ethics*, 8, 117–129.

Browne, John. (1997). "Speech at Stanford University, 19 May, 1997." *Review: The BP quarterly technology magazine*, July/August, 11–13.

Budge, Ian, David Robertson, and Derek Hearl (Eds.). (1987). *Ideology, Strategy, and Party Change: Spatial Analyses of Post-War Election Programmes in Nineteen Democracies*. Cambridge, UK: Cambridge University Press.

Bulow, Jeremy, and Paul Klemperer. (1998). "The Tobacco Deal." *Brookings Papers on Economic Activity*. Washington DC: Brookings.

Business Roundtable. (1978). "The Role and Composition of the Board of Directors of the Large Publicly Owned Corporation." New York.

———. (1981, October). "Statement on Corporate Responsibility." New York.

——. (1988). "Corporate Ethics: A Prime Business Asset." New York.

——. (1990). "Corporate Governance and American Competitiveness." New York.

——. (1997, September). "Statement on Corporate Governance." New York.

Calabresi, Guido, and Douglas A. Melamed. (1972). "Property Rules, Liability Rules and Inalienability: One View of the Cathedral." *Harvard Law Review*, 85, 1089–1128.

Calingaert, Michael. (1993). "Government-Business Relations in the European Community." *California Management Review*, Winter, 118–133.

Campbell, Thomas J., Daniel P. Kessler, and George B. Shepherd. (1998). "The Link Between Liability Reforms and Productivity: Some Empirical Evidence." *Brookings Papers in Economic Activity: Microeconomics*. Washington, DC: Brookings.

Carp, Robert A., and Ronald Stidham. (2001). *The Federal Courts* (4th ed.). Washington, DC: CQ Press.

Carroll, Archie B. (1981). *Business & Society: Managing Corporate Social Performance*. Boston: Little, Brown.

Carson, Thomas L. (1987). "Bribery and Implicit Agreements: A Reply to Philips." *Journal of Business Ethics*, 6, 123–125. Reprinted in Newton and Ford (1990), 291–294.

Cater, Douglass. (1959). *The Fourth Branch of Government*. Boston: Houghton Mifflin.

Cavanagh, Gerald F. (2000). "Executives' Code of Business Conduct: Prospects for the Caux Principles," in Williams (2000), 169–182.

CBS News. (1980). *60 Minutes Verbatim*, 149–153. New York: Arno Press.

Cecchini, Paolo, with Michel Catinat and Alexis Jacquemin. (1988). *The European Challenge 1992: The Benefits of a Single Market*. Aldershot, UK: Wildwood.

Chandler, Alfred D. (1977). *The Visible Hand*. Cambridge, MA: Harvard University Press.

Chandler, Alfred D., and Richard S. Tedlow. (1985). *The Coming of Managerial Capitalism: A Casebook on the History of American Economic Institutions*. Homewood, IL: Richard D. Irwin.

Chang, Wejen. (1998). "Confucian Theory of Norms and Human Rights." In Wm. Theodore de Bary and Tu Weiming, *Confucianism and Human Rights*, 117–141, New York: Columbia University Press.

Cheng, Chung-ying. (1998). "Transforming Confucian Virtues into Human Rights: A Study of Human Agency and Potency in Confucian Ethics." In Wm. Theodore de Bary and Tu Weiming, *Confucianism and Human Rights*, 142–153, New York: Columbia University Press.

Christiansen, Flemming, and Shirin M. Rai. (1996). *Chinese Politics and Society: An Introduction*. Upper Saddle River, NJ: Prentice Hall.

Cini, Michelle, and Lee McGowan. (1998). *Competition Policy in the European Union*. London, UK: Macmillan.

Clark, Robert C. (1985). "Agency Costs versus Fiduciary Duties." In John W. Pratt and Richard J. Zeckhauser (Eds.), *Principals and Agents: The Structure of Business*, 55–79. Boston, MA: Harvard Business School.

Clarkson, Kenneth W., and Timothy J. Muris (Eds.). (1981). *The Federal Trade Commission Since 1970*. Cambridge, UK: Cambridge University Press.

Cline, Robert J., and Thomas S. Neubig. (1999). "Masters of Complexity and Bearers of Great Burden: The Sales Tax System and Compliance Costs for Multistate Retailers." Technical Report, Ernst and Young Economics Consulting and Quantitative Analysis.

Coase, Ronald H. (1960). "The Problem of Social Cost." *The Journal of Law and Economics*, 3(October), 1–44.

Coen, David. (1999). "The Impact of U.S. Lobbying Practice on the European Business-Government Relationship." *California Management Review*, 41, 27–44.

Coffee, John C., Jr., Louis Lowenstein, and Susan Rose-Ackerman. (1988). *Knights, Raiders & Targets: The Impact of the Hostile Takeover*. New York: Oxford University Press.

Cohen, Henry. (1990, November). "Products Liability: A Legal Overview." Washington, DC: Congressional Research Service, Library of Congress.

Committee for the Study of Economic and Monetary Union. (1989). *Report of Economic and Monetary Union in the European Community*. Brussels, Belgium.

Condorcet, Marquis de. (1785). *Essai sur l'Application de l'Analyse a la Probabilité des Decisions Rendues a la Pluralité des Voix*. Reprint New York: Chelsea, 1972.

Congressional Quarterly. (1994). *Federal Regulatory Directory* (7th ed.). Washington, DC: CQ Press.

——. (1997). *Politics in America: The 104th Congress*. Washington, DC: CQ Press.

Cook, Timothy E. (1989). *Making Laws & Making News: Media Strategies in the U.S. House of Representatives*. Washington, DC: Brookings.

Cooter, Robert, and Thomas Ulen. (1997). *Law and Economics* (2d ed.). Reading, MA: Addison-Wesley.

——. (2004). *Law and Economics* (4th ed.). Boston: Addison-Wesley.

Cramton, Peter. (1997). "The FCC Spectrum Auctions: An Early Assessment." *Journal of Economics & Management Strategy*, 6(Fall), 431–495.

Cummins Engine Company. (1980, October). Cummins Practice. Columbus, IN.

Curtis, Gerald L. (1975). "Big Business and Political Influence." In Ezra F. Vogel. *Modern Japanese Organization and Decision-Making*, 33–70. Berkeley: University of California Press.

———. (1999). *The Logic of Japanese Politics: Leaders, Institutions, and the Limits of Change.* New York: Columbia University Press.

Cusamano, Michael A., and David B. Yoffie. (1998). *Competing on Internet Time: Lessons from Netscape and Its Battle with Microsoft.* New York: The Free Press.

Dalkir, Serdar, and Frederick R. Warren-Boulton. (1999). "Prices, Market Definition, and the Effects of Merger: Staples-Office Depot (1997)." In Kwoka and White (1999), 143–164.

Dalton, D., C. Daily, A. Ellstrand, and J. Johnson. (1998). "Meta-analytic Reviews of Board Composition, Leadership Structure, and Financial Performance." *Strategic Management Review,* 19, 269–290.

Dalton, Dan R., and Michael B. Metzger. (1993). "Integrity Testing for Personnel Selection: An Unsparing Perspective." *Journal of Business Ethics,* 12, 147–156.

Davidson, Wallace N., Dan L. Worrell, and Abuzar El-Jelly. (1995). "Influencing Managers to Change Unpopular Corporate Behavior Through Boycotts and Divestitures." *Business & Society,* 34(August), 171–196.

De Bary, William T. (1991) *The Trouble with Confucianism.* Cambridge, MA: Harvard University Press.

DeGeorge, Richard T. (1993). "International Business Ethics." *Business Ethics Quarterly,* 4, 1–9.

Delmas, Magali. (2000). "Barriers and Incentives to the Adoption of ISO 14001 in the United States." *Duke Environmental Law and Policy Forum.* Fall: 1–38.

Delmas, Magali. (2001). "Stakeholders and Competitive Advantage: The Case of ISO 14001." *Production and Operation Management.* 10: 343–358.

Department of Labor, Office of Inspector General. (1993). "Targeted Jobs Tax Credit Program." State of Alabama, October 1, 1990–September 30, 1991.

Derthick, Martha, and Paul J. Quirk. (1985). *The Politics of Deregulation.* Washington, DC: Brookings.

———. (1997). *Renewing Fast-Track Legislation.* Washington, DC: Institute for International Economics.

Destler, I. M., and Peter J. Balint. (1999). *The New Politics of American Trade: Trade, Labor, and the Environment.* Washington, DC: Institute for International Economics.

Deyo, Frederic C. (Ed.) (1987). *The Political Economy of the New Asian Industrialism.* Ithaca, NY: Cornell University Press.

Diffie, Whitfield, and Susan Landau. (1998). *Privacy on the Line: The Politics of Wiretapping and Encryption.* Cambridge, MA: MIT Press.

Dixit, Avinash, and Susan Skeath. (2004). *Games of Strategy.* (2nd ed.). New York: Norton.

Dixon, Lloyd, and Steven Garber. (2001). *Fighting Air Pollution in Southern California by Scrapping Old Vehicles.* Santa Monica, CA: RAND.

Doi, Takeo. (1988). "Dependency in Human Relationships." In Okimoto and Thomas (1988), 20–25.

Dollinger, Marc J. (1988). "Confucian Ethics and Japanese Management Practices." *Journal of Business Ethics,* 7, 575–584.

Donaldson, Thomas. (1989). *The Ethics of International Business.* Oxford, UK: Oxford University Press.

———. (1996). "Values in Tension: Ethics Away from Home." *Harvard Business Review,* September–October, 48–49, 52–56, 58, 60, 62.

Donaldson, Thomas, and Patricia H. Werhane. (1988). *Ethical Issues in Business: A Philosophical Approach* (3d ed.). Upper Saddle River, NJ: Prentice Hall.

Dornbusch, Rudiger, and James M. Poterba (Eds.). (1991). *Global Warming: Economic Policy Responses.* Cambridge, MA: MIT Press.

Drucker, Peter B. (1981). "What Is 'Business Ethics'?" *The Public Interest,* 63(Spring), 18–36.

Durlabhji, Subhash. (1990). "The Influence of Confucianism and Zen on the Japanese Organization." *Akron Business and Economic Review,* 21(2), 31–45.

Duverger, Maurice. (1954). *Political Parties: Their Organization and Activity in the Modern State.* (Trans. Barbara and Robert North). New York: Wiley.

Easterbrook, Frank H., and Daniel R. Fischel. (1981). "The Proper Role of a Target's Management in Responding to a Tender Offer." *Harvard Law Review,* April, 1161–1204.

Edley, Christopher F., Jr. (1990). *Administrative Law.* New Haven, CT: Yale University Press.

Ellerman, A. Denny, Paul L. Joskow, and David Harrison, Jr. (2003). "Emissions Trading in the U.S.: Experience, Lessons, and Considerations for Greenhouse Gases." Pew Center for Global Climate Change.

Elkington, John. (1997). *Cannibals With Forks: The Triple Bottom Line of 21st Century Business.* Stony Creek, CT: New Society Publishers.

Elzinga, Kenneth G., and William Briet. (1976). *The Antitrust Penalties: A Study in Law and Economics.* New Haven, CT: Yale University Press.

Ellickson, Robert C. (1991). *Order Without Law.* Cambridge, MA: Harvard University Press.

Emerson, Michael, Michael Aujean, Michael Catinat, Phillippe Goybet, and Alexis Jacquemin. (1988). *The Economics of 1992.* Oxford, UK: Oxford University Press.

Engle, David L. (1979). "An Approach to Corporate Social Responsibility." *Stanford Law Review,* 32(November), 1–98.

Epstein, David, and Sharyn O'Halloran. (1999). *Delegating Powers.* Cambridge, UK: Cambridge University Press.

Epstein, Edward Jay. (1973). *News from Nowhere.* New York: Random House.

―――. (1981). "The Selection of Reality." In Elie Abel (Ed.), *What's News*, 119–132. San Francisco: Institute for Contemporary Studies.

Epstein, Marc J., and Karen E. Schnietz. 2002. "Measuring the Cost of Environmental and Labor Protests to Globalization: An Event Study of the Failed 1999 Seattle WTO Talks." *The International Trade Journal*, XVI: 129–160.

Epstein, Richard A. (1980). *A Theory of Strict Liability.* San Francisco: Cato Institute.

Esty, Daniel C. (1994). *Greening the GATT: Trade, Environment, and the Future.* Washington, DC: Institute for International Economics.

―――. (2001). "Bridging the Trade-Environment Divide." *Journal of Economic Perspectives*, 15, 113–130.

European Commission. (1988). "Social Dimensions of the Internal Market." Commission Working Paper, SEC (88) 1148, Brussels, Belgium.

Evans, Fred J. (1987). *Managing the Media.* New York: Quorum Books.

Fairbank, John K. (1992). *China: A New History.* Cambridge, MA: Harvard University Press.

Falsey, Thomas A. (1989). *Corporate Philosophies and Mission Statements.* New York: Quorum Books.

Fama, Eugene F., and Michael C. Jensen. (1983). "Separation of Ownership and Control." *Journal of Law & Economics*, 26(June), 301–325.

Federal Trade Commission. (1990). "The Hart-Scott-Rodino Antitrust Improvements Act of 1976." Washington, DC.

Feinstein, Alvan R. (1988). "Scientific Standards in Epidemiologic Studies of the Menace of Daily Life." *Science*, 242(December), 1257–1263.

Feldstein, Martin. (1997). "The Political Economy of the European Economic and Monetary Union: Political Sources of an Economic Liability." *Journal of Economic Perspectives*, 11(Fall), 23–42.

Fiorina, Morris P. (1989). *Congress: Keystone of the Washington Establishment* (2d ed.). New Haven, CT: Yale University Press.

Fisher, Franklin M., John J. McGowan, and Joen E. Greenwood. (1983). *Folded, Spindled, and Mutilated: Economic Analysis of U.S. v. IBM.* Cambridge, MA: MIT Press.

Fishwick, Frank. (1993). *Making Sense of Competition Policy.* London, UK: Kogan Page.

Fowler, Linda L., and Ronald G. Shaiko. (1987). "The Grass Roots Connection: Environmental Activists and Senate Roll Calls." *American Journal of Political Science*, 31(August), 484–510.

Fox, J. Ronald. (1982). *Managing Business-Government Relations: Cases and Notes on Business-Government Problems.* Homewood, IL: Richard D. Irwin.

Francis, John. (1993). *The Politics of Regulation: A Comparative Perspective.* Oxford, UK: Blackwell.

Frank, Reuven. (1991). *Out of Thin Air: The Brief Wonderful Life of Network News.* New York: Simon & Schuster.

Franklin, Marc A., and Robert L. Rabin. (1987). *Cases and Materials on Tort Law and Alternatives* (4th ed.). Mineola, NY: Foundation Press.

Freeman, R. Edward. (1984). *Strategic Management: A Stakeholder Approach.* Boston: Pitman.

Freeman, R. Edward, and Daniel R. Gilbert, Jr. (1988). *Corporate Strategy and the Search for Ethics.* Upper Saddle River, NJ: Prentice Hall.

Friedman, Milton. (1962). *Capitalism and Freedom.* Chicago: University of Chicago Press.

―――. (1970, September 13). "The Social Responsibility of Business Is to Increase Its Profits." *New York Times Magazine*, 32–33, 122, 126.

Friedman, Monroe. (1985). "Consumer Boycotts in the United States, 1970–1980: Contemporary Events in Historical Perspective." *Journal of Consumer Affairs*, 19(Summer), 96–117.

―――. (1999). *Consumer Boycotts.* New York: Routledge.

Fukui, Haruhiro. (1970). *Party in Power.* Berkeley: University of California Press.

Gale, Jeffrey, and Rogene A. Buchholz. (1987). "The Political Pursuit of Competitive Advantage: What Business Can Gain from Government." In Marcus, Kaufman, and Beam (1987), 31–42.

Galvin, Robert W. (1992, October). *International Business and the Changing Nature of Global Competition.* Oxford, OH: Miami University.

Graber, Doris A. (Ed.) 2000. *Media Power in Politics.* Washington, DC: CQ Press.

Gauthier, David. (1986). *Morals by Agreement.* Oxford, UK: Clarendon Press.

Gavil, Andrew I., William E. Kovacic, and Jonathan B. Baker. 2002. *Antitrust Law in Perspective: Cases, Concepts and Problems in Competition Policy.* St. Paul, MN: Thomson/West.

Gavil, Andrew I., William E. Kovacic, and Jonathan B. Baker. 2004. *Teacher's Update: Summer 2004, to Antitrust Law in Perspective.* St. Paul, MN: Thomson/West.

General Dynamics Corporation. "General Dynamics Standards of Business Ethics and Conduct." St. Louis, MO.

―――. "The Ethics Program 1985/1986." St. Louis, MO.

Gerlach, Michael L. (1992). *Alliance Capitalism: The Social Organization of Japanese Business.* Berkeley: University of California Press.

Gert, Bernard. (1988). *Morality: A New Justification of the Moral Rules.* New York: Oxford University Press.

Getz, Kathleen A. (2000). "International Instruments on Bribery and Corruption." In Williams (2000), 141–166.

Gibney, Frank (Ed.) (1998). *Unlocking the Bureaucrat's Kingdom: Deregulation and the Japanese Economy.* Washington, DC: Brookings.

Gilligan, Thomas W., and Keith Krehbiel. (1987). "Collective Decision-Making and Standing Committees: An Informational Rationale for Restrictive Amendment Procedures." *Journal of Law, Economics, and Organization*, 3(Fall), 287–335.

Gold, T. B. (1996). "Civil Society in Taiwan." In W. M. Tu, ed., *Confucian Traditions in East Asian Modernity.* Cambridge, MA: Harvard University Press.

Goldner, Linda F. (2000). "The Apparel Industry Code of Conduct: A Consumer Perspective on Social Responsibility." In Williams (2000), 241–252.

Goodman, John B. (1992). *Monetary Sovereignty: The Politics of Central Banking in Western Europe.* Ithaca, NY: Cornell University Press.

Goodpaster, Kenneth E. (1983). "The Concept of Corporate Responsibility." *Journal of Business Ethics*, 2, 1–22.

———. (2000). "The Caux Round Table Principles: Corporate Moral Reflection in a Global Business Environment." In Williams (2000), 183–208.

Goolsbee, Austan. (2000). "In a World Without Borders: The Impact of Taxes on Internet Commerce." *Quarterly Journal of Economics*, 115(2):561–76.

Gorlin, Rena A. (1990). *Codes of Professional Responsibility* (2d ed.). Washington, DC: Bureau of National Affairs.

Gramlich, Edward M. (1998). *A Guide to Benefit-Cost Analysis* (2d ed.). Prospect Heights, IL: Waveland Press.

Green, Edward, and Robert Porter. (1984). "Noncooperative Collusion under Imperfect Price Information." *Econometrica*, 52, 87–100.

Greve, Michael S., and Fred L. Smith, Jr. (1992). *Environmental Politics: Public Costs, Private Politics.* New York: Praeger.

Grieco, Joseph. (1990). *Cooperation Among Nations.* Ithaca, NY: Cornell University Press.

Griffin, Kelley. (1987). *Ralph Nader Presents More Action for a Change.* New York: Dembner Books.

Groarke, Leo. (1990). "Affirmative Action as a Form of Restitution." *Journal of Business Ethics*, 9, 207–213.

Groseclose, Timothy. (1996). "An Examination of the Market for Favors and Votes in Congress." *Economic Inquiry*, 34(April), 1–21.

Groseclose, Tim, and Jeff Milyo. (2004). "A Measure of Media Bias." Working Paper, UCLA, September.

Groseclose, Timothy, and James M. Snyder, Jr. (1996). "Buying Supermajorities." *American Political Science Review*, 90(June), 303–315.

Groves, Theodore, Yongmiao Hong, John McMillan, and Barry Naughton. (1994). "Autonomy and Incentives in Chinese State Enterprises." *Quarterly Journal of Economics*, 109 (February), 183–209.

———. (1995). "China's Evolving Managerial Labor Market." *Journal of Political Economy*, 103(August), 873–892.

Grub, Phillip D., and Jian Hai Lin. (1991). *Foreign Direct Investment in China.* New York: Quorum Books.

Haas, Walter A., Jr. (1981). "Corporate Social Responsibility: A New Term for an Old Concept with New Significance." In Bradshaw and Vogel (1981).

Haggard, Stephen. (1990). *Pathways from the Periphery: The Politics of Growth in the Newly Industrializing Countries.* Ithaca, NY: Cornell University Press.

Hall, Richard L., and Frank W. Wayman. (1990). "Buying Time: Moneyed Interests and the Mobilization of Bias in Congressional Committees." *American Political Science Review*, 84, 707–820.

Hamilton, Gary G. (1996). "Overseas Chinese Capitalism." In W. M. Tu (Ed.), *Confucian Traditions in East Asian Modernity.* Cambridge, MA: Harvard University Press.

Hamilton, J. Brooke, III, and David Hoch. (1997). "Ethical Standards for Business Lobbying: Some Practical Suggestions." *Business Ethics Quarterly*, 7, 117–129.

Hamilton, James T. (1993). "Politics and Social Costs: Estimating the Impact of Collective Action on Hazardous Waste Facilities." *RAND Journal of Economics*, 24(Spring), 101–125.

———. (1995). "Pollution as News: Media and Stock Market Reactions to the Toxics Release Inventory Data." *Journal of Environmental Economics & Management*, 28, 187–206.

———. (1997). "Taxes, Torts, and the Toxics Release Inventory: Congressional Voting on Instruments to Control Pollution." *Economic Inquiry*, 35(October), 745–762.

———. (1998). *Channeling Violence: The Economic Market for Violent Television Programming.* Princeton, NJ: Princeton University Press.

Hamilton, V. Lee, and Joseph Sanders. (1992). *Everyday Justice: Responsibility and the Individual in Japan and the United States.* New Haven, CT: Yale University Press.

Handler, Edward, and John R. Mulkern. (1982). *Business and Politics.* Lexington, MA: Lexington Books.

Hardin, Russell. (1982). *Collective Action.* Resources for the Future. Baltimore, MD: Johns Hopkins University Press.

Harding, Harry. (1987). *China's Second Revolution: Reform After Mao.* Washington, DC: Brookings.

Harris, Richard A., and Sidney M. Milkis. (1989). *The Politics of Regulatory Change: A Tale of Two Agencies.* Oxford, UK: Oxford University Press.

Harris, Robert G. (1989). "Telecommunications Policy in Japan: Lessons for the U.S." *California Management Review*, 31, 113–131.

**854** *References*

Harris, Robert G., and C. Jeffrey Kraft. (1997). "Meddling Through: Regulating Local Telephone Competition in the United States." *Journal of Economic Perspectives*, 11(Summer), 93–112.

Harsanyi, John C. (1982). "Morality and the Theory of Rational Behavior." In Sen and Williams (1982), 39–62.

———. (1977). "Rule Utilitarianism and Decision Theory." *Erkenntnis*, 11, 25–53.

Hawk, Barry E. (1988). "The American Antitrust Revolution: Lessons for the EEC?" *European Competition Law Review*, 9, 53–87.

Hay, Robert D., and Edmund R. Gray. (1981). *Business & Society: Cases and Text*. Cincinnati, OH: South-Western Publishing Co.

Heckathorn, Douglas D. and Steven M. Maser. (1990). "The Contractual Architecture of Public Policy: A Critical Reconstruction of Lowi's Typology." *Journal of Politics*. 52: 1101–1123.

Hewlett-Packard Company. (1984). "How to Deal with the Press." Palo Alto, CA.

———. (1989). "Standards of Business Conduct." Palo Alto, CA.

Hillman, Amy J. Gerald D. Keim, and Rebecca A. Luce. (2001). "Board Composition and Stakeholder Performance: Do Stakeholder Directors Make a Difference." *Business & Society*, 40, 295–314.

Hirschman, Albert O. (1970). *Exit, Voice, and Loyalty*. Cambridge, MA: Harvard University Press.

Hobbes, Thomas. (1651). *Leviathan*. Edited by C. B. Macpherson. Reprint London, UK: Pelican Books. 1968.

Holt, Charles A., and David T. Scheffman. (1989). "Strategic Business Behavior and Antitrust." In Larner and Meehan (1989), 39–82.

Hoscheit, J. M., and W. Wessels (Eds.). (1988). *The European Council 1974–1986: Evaluation and Prospects*. European Institute of Public Administration.

Howell, Rate A., John R. Allison, and N. T. Henley. (1987). *The Legal Environment of Business*. Chicago: Dryden Press.

Huber, Peter, and Robert E. Litan (Eds.). (1991). *The Liability Maze: The Impact of Liability Law on Safety and Innovation*. Washington, DC: Brookings.

Hufbauer, Gary C., Diane T. Berliner, and Kimberly Ann Elliot. (1986). *Trade Protection in the United States: 31 Case Studies*. Washington, DC: Institute for International Economics.

Hufbauer, Gary C., and Kimberly A. Elliott. (1994). *Measuring the Costs of Protection in the United States*. Washington, DC: Institute for International Economics.

Hufbauer, Gary C., Daniel C. Esty, Diana Orejas, Luis Rubio, and Jeffrey J. Schott. (2000). *NAFTA and the Environment: Seven Years Later*. Washington, DC: Institute for International Economics.

Huddleston, Jackson N. (1990). *Gaijan Kaisha: Running a Foreign Business in Japan*. Armonk, NY: M.E. Sharpe.

Ilinitch, Anne Y., Naomi S. Soderstrom, and Tom E. Thomas. (1998). "Measuring Corporate Environmental Performance." *Journal of Accounting and Public Policy*, 17, 383–408.

Inoguchi, Takashi, and Daniel I. Okimoto (Eds.). (1988). *The Political Economy of Japan: Volume 2, The Changing International Context*. Stanford, CA: Stanford University Press.

Investor Responsibility Research Center. (1993). "Voting by Institutional Investors on Corporate Governance Issues." Washington, DC.

Ito, Takatoshi. (1992). *The Japanese Economy*. Cambridge, MA: MIT Press.

Ivanhoe, Philip J. (1993). *Confucian Moral Self Cultivation*. New York: Peter Lang.

Iyengar, Shanto, and Donald R. Kinder. (1987). *News That Matters*. Chicago: University of Chicago Press.

Iyori, Hiroshi, and Akinori Uesuji. (1983). *The Antimonopoly Law in Japan*. New York: Federal Legal Publications.

Jackson, John H., and Edwin A. Vermulst. (1989). *Antidumping Laws and Practice*. Ann Arbor: University of Michigan Press.

Jensen, Michael J. (1988). "Takeovers: Their Causes and Consequences." *Journal of Economic Perspectives*. 2: 21–44.

———. (2001). "Value Maximization, Stakeholder Theory, and the Corporate Objective Function." *Journal of Applied Corporate Finance*. 14: 8–21.

Johnson, Chalmers. (1989). "MITI, MPT, and the Telecom Wars: How Japan Makes Policy for High Technology." In Johnson, Tyson, and Zysman (1989), 177–240.

Johnson, Chalmers, Laura D'Andrea Tyson, and John Zysman. (1989). *Politics and Productivity: The Real Story of Why Japan Works*. Cambridge, MA: Ballinger.

Jones, Thomas M. (1980). "Corporate Social Responsibility Revisited, Redefined." *California Management Review*, 22(Spring), 59–67.

Jonsen, Albert R., and Stephen Toulmin. (1988). *The Abuse of Casuistry*. Berkeley: University of California Press.

Joskow, Paul L., and Richard Schmalensee. (1983). *Markets for Power: An Analysis of Electric Utility Deregulation*. Cambridge, MA: MIT Press.

———. (1998). "The Political Economy of Market-Based Environmental Policy: The U.S. Acid Rain Program." *Journal of Law and Economics*, 41(April), 37–84.

Joskow, Paul L., Richard Schmalensee, and Elizabeth M. Bailey. (1998). "The Market for Sulfur Dioxide Emissions." *American Economic Review*, 88(September), 669–685.

Jury Verdict Research. (2001). *Personal Injury Valuation Handbook: Current Award Trends in Personal Injury, 2001 Edition*. LRP Publications.

Kahn, David. (1967). *The Codebreakers*. New York: Macmillan.

Kalt, Joseph P (1981). *The Economics and Politics of Oil Price Regulation*. Cambridge, MA: MIT Press.

Kaplan, Robert, and David Norton. 1992. "The Balanced Scorecard—Measures that Drive Performance." *Harvard Business Review*.

Kant, Immanuel. (1785). *Ethical Philosophy,* (a) *Grounding for the Metaphysics of Morals*; (1785) (b) *The Metaphysical Principles of Virtue* (1797). Translation by James W. Ellington, introduction by Warner A. Wick. Indianapolis, IN: Hackett. 1983.

Karpoff, Jonathan M., and Paul H. Malatesta. (1989). "The Wealth Effects of Second-Generation State Take-Over Legislation." *Journal of Financial Economics,* 25, 291–322.

Keim, Gerald D. (1985) "Corporate Grassroots Programs in the 1980s." *California Management Review,* 28(Fall), 110–123.

Keim, Gerald D. and Roger E. Meiners. (1978). "Corporate Social Responsibility: Private Means for Public Wants?" *Policy Review,* 5(Summer), 79–95.

Kelman, Steven. (1981). *What Price Incentives? Economics and the Environment.* Boston: Auburn House.

Kerwin, Cornelius M. (1994). *Rulemaking: How Government Agencies Write Law and Make Policy.* Washington, DC: CQ Press.

——. (1999) *Rulemaking: How Government Agencies Write Law and Make Policy* (2d ed.). Washington, DC: CQ Press.

King, Andrew A., and Michael J Lenox. (2000). "Industry Self-Regulation without Sanctions: The Chemical Industry's Responsible Care Program." *Academy of Management Journal.* 43: 698–716.

——. (2002). "Exploring the Locus of Profitable Pollution Reduction." *Management Science.* 48: 289–299.

Klitgaard, Robert. (1988). *Controlling Corruption.* Berkeley: University of California Press.

Kohler-Koch, Beate. (1998). *The Evolution and Transformation of European Governance.* Vienna: Institute for Advanced Studies.

Kneese, Alvin V., and Charles L. Schultze. (1975). *Pollution, Prices, and Public Policy.* Washington, DC: Brookings.

Koku, Paul Sergius, Aigbe Akhigbe, and Thomas M. Springer. (1997). "The Financial Impact of Boycotts and Threats of Boycotts." *Journal of Business Research,* 40, 15–20.

Konar, Shameek, and Mark A. Cohen. (1997). "Information as Regulation: The Effect of Community Right to Know Laws on Toxic Emissions." *Journal of Environmental Economics & Management,* 32, 109–124.

Kotchian, A. Carl. (1977, July 9). "The Payoff: Lockheed's 70-Day Mission to Tokyo." *Saturday Review,* 5–12.

Krehbiel, Keith. (1991) *Information and Legislative Organization.* Ann Arbor: University of Michigan Press.

——. (1996). "Institutional and Partisan Sources of Gridlock: A Theory of Divided and Unified Government." *Journal of Theoretical Politics,* 8, 7–40.

——. (1998) *Pivotal Politics: A Theory of U.S. Lawmaking.* Chicago, IL: University of Chicago Press.

——. (1999). "Pivotal Politics: A Refinement of Nonmarket Analysis for Voting Institutions." *Business and Politics,* 1 (April).

Kreps, David M. (1990). "Corporate Culture and Economic Theory." In Alt and Shepsle (1990), 90–143.

Kreps, David M., and Robert Wilson. (1982). "Reputation and Imperfect Information." *Journal of Economic Theory,* 27, 253–279.

Kridel, Donald J, David E. M. Sappington, and Dennis L. Weisman. (1996). "The Effects of Incentive Regulation in the Telecommunications Industry: A Survey." *Journal of Regulatory Economics,* 9, 269–306.

Kroszner, Randall S., and Thomas Stratmann. (1998). "Interest Group Competition and the Organization of Congress: Theory and Evidence from Financial Services Political Action Committees." *American Economic Review,* 88(December), 1163–1187.

Krugman, Paul (Ed.) (1986). *Strategic Trade Policy and the New International Economics.* Cambridge, MA: MIT Press.

Krugman, Paul R. (1990). *Rethinking International Trade.* Cambridge, MA: MIT Press.

Küng, Hans. (1997). "A Global Ethic in an Age of Globalization." *Business Ethics Quarterly,* 7, 17–32.

Küng-Shankleman, Lucy. (2000). *Inside the BBC and CNN: Managing News Organizations.* London: Routledge.

Kupfer, Joseph. (1993). "The Ethics of Genetic Screening in the Workplace." *Business Ethics Quarterly,* 3, 17–25.

Kwoka, John E., Jr., and Lawrence J White (Eds.). (1999), *The Antitrust Revolution: Economics, Competition, and Policy.* Oxford, UK: Oxford University Press.

Lake, Charles D. II (1998). "Liberalizing Japan's Insurance Market." In Gibney (1998), 116–141.

Lande, Stephen L., and Craig Vangrasstek. (1986). *The Trade and Tariff Act of 1984: Trade Policy in the Reagan Administration.* Lexington, MA: Lexington Books.

Lardy, Nicholas R. 1998. *China's Unfinished Economic Revolution.* Washington, DC: Brookings.

Levin, Staci. (1999). "Who Are We Protecting? A Critical Evaluation of United States Encryption Technology Export Controls." *Law and Policy in International Business,* Spring, 529–552.

Levine, S. I. (1997). "The United States and China: Managing a Stormy Relationship." In W. A. Joseph (Ed.), *China Briefing 1995–1996.* Armonk, NY: M. E. Sharpe.

Li, Shaomin. (2004). "Why Is Property Right Protection Lacking in China?" *California Management Review.* 46: 99–115.

Lieberthal, Kenneth. (1995). *Governing China.* New York: Norton.

Littlejohn, Stephen E. (1986). "Competition and Cooperation: New Trends in Corporate Public Issue Identification and Resolution." *California Management Review,* 29(Fall), 109–123.

Locke, John. (1690). *The Works of John Locke.* Reprint Westport, CT: Greenwood, 1989.

Lodge, George Cabot. (1990). *Comparative Business-Government Relations.* Upper Saddle River, NJ: Prentice Hall.

Lord, Michael D. (2000). "Constituency-based Lobbying as Corporate Political Strategy: Testing an Agency Theory Perspective." *Business and Politics,* 2, 289–308.

Lowi, Theodore J. (1964). "American Business, Public Policy, Case-Studies, and Political Theory." *World Politics,* 16(July), 677–693.

Lukes, Steven. (1973). *Individualism.* Oxford, UK: Basil Blackwell.

Lynn, Leonard H., and Timothy J. McKeown. (1988). *Organizing Business: Trade Associations in America and Japan.* Washington, DC: American Enterprise Institute.

Lyons, David. (1965). *The Forms and Limits of Utilitarianism.* Oxford, UK: Oxford University Press.

MacAvoy, Paul W. (1981, December 20). "The Business Lobby's Wrong Business." *The New York Times.*

Magat, Wesley A., Alan J. Krupnick, and Winston Harrington. (1986). *Rules in the Making: A Statistical Analysis of Regulatory Agency Behavior.* Washington, DC: Resources for the Future.

Magee, Stephen P., William A. Brock, and Leslie Young. (1989). *Black Hole Tariffs and Endogenous Policy Theory: Political Economy in General Equilibrium.* Cambridge, UK: Cambridge University Press.

Mahon, John F., and Jennifer J. Griffin. (1999). "Painting a Portrait: A Reply." *Business & Society,* 38(March), 126–133.

Mahoney, Richard J., and Stephen E. Littlejohn. (1989). "Innovation on Trial: Punitive Damages Versus New Products." *Science,* 15(December), 1398.

Manheim, Jarol B. (2001). *The Death of a Thousand Cuts.* Mahwah, NJ: Lawrence Erlbaum.

Marcus, Alfred A. (1980). *Promise and Performance: Choosing and Implementing Environmental Policy.* Westport, CT: Greenwood Press.

Marcus, Alfred A., Allen M. Kaufman, and David R. Beam (Eds.). *Business Strategy and Public Policy.* New York: Quorum Books.

Margolis, Joshua D., and James P. Walsh. (2001). *People or Profits? The Search for a Link Between a Company's*

*Social and Financial Performance.* Mahwah, NJ: Lawrence Erlbaum.

Mashaw, Jerry L., and Richard A. Merrill. (1985). *Administrative Law: The American Public Law System: Cases and Materials* (2d ed.). St. Paul, MN: West Publishing Co.

Mason, Mark. (1992). *Access Denied?: American Multinationals and Japan, 1899–1980.* Cambridge, MA: Harvard University Press.

Matthews, Marilyn C. (1987). "Codes of Ethics: Organizational Behaviour and Misbehaviour." In *Research in Corporate Social Performance* (vol. 9), 107–130. Greenwich, CT: JAI Press.

Maxwell, John W., Thomas P. Lyon, and Steven C. Hackett. (2000). "Self-Regulation and Social Welfare: The Political Economy of Corporate Environmentalism." *Journal of Law & Economics,* 43(October), 583–617.

Mayhew, David. (1974). *Congress: The Electoral Connection.* New Haven, CT: Yale University Press.

McCraw, Thomas K. (Ed.). (1981). *Regulation in Perspective: Historical Essays.* Boston: Harvard Business School.

McCubbins, Mathew, Roger Noll, and Barry Weingast. (1987). "Administrative Procedures as Instruments of Political Control." *Journal of Law, Economics and Organizations,* 3, 243–277.

McDonald's Corporation – Environmental Defense Fund, Waste Reduction Task Force. (1991). "Final Report," April.

McGuire, J. B., T. Schneeweis, and B. Branch. (1990). "Perceptions of Firm Quality: A Cause or Result of Firm Performance." *Journal of Management,* 16, 167–180.

McGuire, Jean B., Alison Sundgren, and Thomas Schneeweis. (1988). "Corporate Social Responsibility and Firm Financial Performance." *Academy of Management Journal,* 31, 854–872.

McMillan, John. (1991). "DANGO: Japan's Price-Fixing Conspiracies." *Economics and Politics,* 3(November), 201–218.

McWilliams, Abagail, and Donald Siegel. (2001). "Corporate Social Responsibility: A Theory of the Firm Perspective." *Academy of Management Review.* 26: 117–127.

Milgrom, Paul, and John D. Roberts. (1982). "Limit Pricing and Entry Under Incomplete Information." *Econometrica,* 50, 443–459.

Mill, John Stuart. (1859). *On Liberty.* Edited by David Spitz. New York: Norton. 1975.

—————. (1861). "Utilitarianism." In Alan Ryan (Ed.), *Utilitarianism and Other Essays: J. S. Mill and Jeremy Bentham.* New York: Penguin Books. 1987.

Milyo, Jeffrey, David Primo, and Timothy Groseclose. (2000). "Corporate PAC Campaigns Contributions in Perspective." *Business and Politics,* 2, 75–88.

Mitnick, Barry M. (1980). *The Political Economy of Regulation*. New York: Columbia University Press.

Moe, Terry M. (1980). *The Organization of Interests*. Chicago: University of Chicago Press.

——. (1985). "Congressional Control of the Bureaucracy: An Assessment of the Positive Theory of 'Congressional Dominance.'" Paper presented at the American Political Science Association annual meeting.

Moore, Barrington. (1966). *Social Origins of Dictatorship and Democracy*. Boston: Beacon Press.

Moore, Michael J., and Wesley A. Magat. (1996). "Labeling and Performance Standards for Product Safety: The Case of CPSC's Lawn Mower Standards." *Managerial and Decision Economics*, 17, 509–516.

——. (1997). "The Injury Risk Consequences of the All-Terrain Vehicles Consent Decree." *International Review of Law and Economics*, 17, 379–393.

Morduch, Jonathan. (1999). "The Microfinance Promise." *Journal of Economic Literature*. 37:1569–1614.

Morishima, Michio. (1988). "Confucianism as a Basis for Capitalism." In Okimoto and Rohlen (1988), 36–38.

Mroczkowski, Thomas, and Masao Hanaoka. (1989). "Continuity and Change in Japanese Management." *California Management Review*, 31, 39–53.

Mundo, Philip A. (1992). *Interest Groups: Cases and Characteristics*. Chicago: Nelson-Hall Publishers.

Muramatsu, Michio, and Ellis S. Krauss. (1987). "The Conservative Policy Line and the Development of Patterned Pluralism." In Kozo Yamamura and Yasukichi Yasuba, (Eds.), *The Political Economy of Japan: Volume 1. The Domestic Transformation*. Stanford, CA: Stanford University Press.

Natural Resources Defense Council. (1989, February 27). "Intolerable Risk: Pesticides in Our Children's Food." Washington, DC.

Newman, Edwin. (1984). "A Journalist's Responsibility." In Schumhl (1984) 19–38.

Newton, Lisa H., and Maureen M. Ford (Eds.). (1990). *Taking Sides: Clashing Views on Controversial Issues in Business Ethics and Society*. Guilford, CT: Dushkin.

Nivison, David S. (1996). *The Ways of Confucianism*. Chicago: Open Court.

Noll, Roger G. and Bruce M. Owen. (1983). *The Political Economy of Deregulation: Interest Groups in the Regulatory Process*. Washington, DC: American Enterprise Institute.

Norman, Wayne, and Chris MacDonald. (2003). "Getting to the Bottom of 'Triple Bottom Line.'" *Business Ethics Quarterly*.

Nozick, Robert. (1974). *Anarchy, State, and Utopia*. New York: Basic Books.

Nugent, Neill. (2003). *The Government and Politics of the European Union* (5th ed.). Durham, NC: Duke University Press.

O'Halloran, Sharyn. (1994). *Politics, Process, and American Foreign Policy*. Ann Arbor: University of Michigan Press.

Okimoto, Daniel I. (1989). *Between MITI and the Market: Japanese Industrial Policy for High Technology*. Stanford, CA: Stanford University Press.

Okimoto, Daniel I., and Thomas P. Rohlen (Eds.). (1988). *Inside the Japanese System: Readings on Contemporary Society and Political Economy*. Stanford, CA: Stanford University Press.

Oleszek, Walter J. (2004). *Congressional Procedures and the Policy Process* (6th ed.). Washington, DC: CQ Press.

Olson, Mancur J. (1965). *The Logic of Collective Action*. Cambridge, MA: Harvard University Press.

Ordover, Janusz A., and Robert D. Willig. (1983). "The 1982 Department of Justice Merger Guidelines: An Economic Assessment." *California Law Review*, 71, 535–574.

Orlitsky, Marc, Frank L. Schmidt, and Sara L. Rynes. (2003). "Corporate Social and Financial Performance: A Meta-analysis." *Organizational Studies*, 24: 403–411.

Ornstein, Norman J., Thomas E. Mann, and Michael J. Malbin. (1998). *Vital Statistics on Congress*. Washington, DC: American Enterprise Institute.

Oster, Sharon M. (1999). *Modern Competitive Analysis* (3rd ed.). Oxford, UK: Oxford University Press.

Overturf, Stephen F. (1986). *The Economic Principles of European Integration*. New York: Praeger.

Owen, Bruce M. and Ronald Braeutigam. (1978). *The Regulation Game: Strategic Use of the Administrative Process*. Cambridge, MA: Balinger.

Paine, Lynn Sharp. (1994). "Managing for Organizational Integrity." *Harvard Business Review*, March–April, 106–117.

Palmier, Leslie. (1989). "Corruption in the West Pacific." *The Pacific Review*, 2(1), 23.

Pastin, Mark, and Michael Hooker. (1988). "Ethics and the Foreign Corrupt Practices Act." In Donaldson and Werhane (1988), 48–53.

Pearson, Margaret M. (1991) *Joint Ventures in the Peoples Republic of China*. Princeton, NJ: Princeton University Press.

Pei, M. (1997). "Racing Against Time: Institutional Decay and Renewal in China." In William A. Joseph (Ed.) *China Briefing 1995–1996*, Armonk. NY: M. E. Sharpe.

Peltzman, Sam. (1975). "The Effects of Automobile Safety Regulation." *Journal of Political Economy*, 83(August), 677–725.

——. (1976). "Toward a More General Theory of Regulation." *Journal of Law and Economics*, 19, 211–240.

Peterson, Steven P., and George E. Hoffer. (1994). "The Impact of Airbag Adoption on Relative Personal

Injury and Absolute Collision Insurance Claims." *Journal of Consumer Research*, 20(March), 657–662.

Pfeffer, Jeffrey, and Gerald Salancik. (1978). *The External Control of Organizations*. New York: Harper and Row.

Philips, Michael. (1984). "Bribery." *Ethics*, 94(July). Reprinted in Newton and Ford (1990), 280–290.

Pierson, Paul. (1999). "Social Policy and European Integration." In Andrew Moravcsik (Ed.), *Centralization or Fragmentation: Europe Facing the Challenges of Deepening, Diversity, and Democracy*. New York: Council on Foreign Relations.

Polinsky, A. Mitchell. (2003). *An Introduction to Law and Economics* (3rd ed.). New York: Aspen Publications.

Popoff, Frank P. (1992). "Going Beyond Pollution Prevention." In *Business: Championing the Global Environment*, Report Number 995, The Conference Board, New York.

Porter, Michael E. (1980). *Competitive Strategy: Techniques for Analyzing Industries and Competitions*. New York: Free Press.

———. (1985). *Competitive Advantage*. New York: Free Press.

Porter, Michael E., and C. van der Linde. (1995). "Toward a New Conception of the Environment-Competitiveness Relationship." *Journal of Economic Perspectives*. 9: 97–118.

Posner, Richard A. (1974). "Theories of Economic Regulation." *Bell Journal of Economics*, 5(Autumn), 335–358.

———. (1976). *Antitrust Law: An Economic Perspective*. Chicago: University of Chicago Press.

———. (1981). *The Economics of Justice*. Cambridge, MA: Harvard University Press.

Post, James E. (1978). *Corporate Behavior and Social Change*. Reston, VA: Reston Publishing.

Post, James E., Lee F. Preston, and Sybille Sachs. (2002). "Managing the Extended Enterprise: The New Stakeholder View." *California Management Review*. 45: 6–28.

Poterba, James M. (1991). "Tax Policy to Combat Global Warming: On Designing a Carbon Tax." In Dornbusch and Poterba (1991), 71–98.

Potoski, Matthew, and Aseem Prakash. (2005). "Green Clubs and Voluntary Governance: ISO 14001 and Firms' Regulatory Compliance." *American Journal of Political Science*. (Forthcoming.)

Povich, Elaine S. (1996). *Partners and Adversaries*. Arlington, Va.: The Freedom Forum.

Prahalad, C. K., and Gary Hamel. (1990). "The Core Competencies of the Corporation." *Harvard Business Review*, May–June, 79–91.

Prakash, Aseem. (2001). "Beyond Seattle: Globalization, the Nonmarket Environment, and

Corporate Strategy." *Review of International Political Economy*, 8.

Prakash, Aseem, and Jeffrey A. Hart. (Eds.). (1999). *Globalization and Governance*. London, UK: Routledge.

President's Blue Ribbon Commission on Defense Management. (1986). "A Formula for Action." Washington, DC.

Preston, Lee E., and James E. Post. (1975). *Private Management and Public Policy*. Upper Saddle River, NJ: Prentice Hall.

Priest, George L. (1977). "The Common Law Process and the Selection of Efficient Rules." *Journal of Legal Studies*, 6(January), 65–82.

Pruitt, S. W., and Monroe Friedman. (1986). "Determining the Effectiveness of Consumer Boycotts: A Stock Price Analysis of Their Impact on Corporate Targets." *Journal of Consumer Policy*, 9, 375–387.

Pruitt, S. W., K. C. John Wei, and Richard E. White. (1988). "The Impact of Union-Sponsored Boycotts on the Stock Prices of Target Firms." *Journal of Labor Research*, 9, 285–289.

Putnam, Todd. (1993). "Boycotts Are Busting Out All Over." *Business and Society Review*, 47–51.

Pye, Lucian W. (1978). *China: An Introduction*. Boston: Little, Brown.

———. (1985). *Asian Power and Politics: The Cultural Dimensions of Authority*. Boston: Little, Brown.

———. (1988). *The Mandarin and the Cadre: China's Political Cultures*. Ann Arbor: University of Michigan Press.

Quirk, Paul J. (1981). *Industry Influence in Federal Regulatory Agencies*. Princeton, NJ: Princeton University Press.

Rawls, John. (1971). *A Theory of Justice*. Cambridge, MA: Belknap Press.

———. (1980). "Kantian Constructivism in Moral Theory." *The Journal of Philosophy*, 9(September), 515–572.

———. (1993). *Political Liberalism*. New York: Columbia University Press.

Redding, S. Gordon. (1996). "Societal Transformation and the Contribution of Authority Relations and Cooperative Norms in Overseas Chinese Business." In Wei-ming Tu (Ed.), *Confucian Traditions in East Asian Modernity*. Cambridge, MA: Harvard University Press.

Reed, Steven R. (1986). *Japanese Prefectures and Policymaking*. Pittsburgh, PA: University of Pittsburgh Press.

Reich, Robert B. (1998). "The New Meaning of Corporate Social Responsibility." *California Management Review*, 40(Winter), 8–17.

Reischauer, Edwin O. (1988). *The Japanese Today: Change and Continuity*. Cambridge, MA: Belknap Press.

Richards, Jonathon D. (1993). "Japan Fair Trade Commission Guidelines Concerning Distribution System and Business Practices: An Illustration of Why Antitrust Law Is a Weak Solution to U.S. Trade Problems with Japan." *Wisconsin Law Review*, 921–960.

Roman, Ronald M., Sefa Hayibor, and Bradley R. Agle. (1999). "The Relationship Between Social and Financial Performance: Repainting a Portrait." *Business & Society*, 38(March): 109–125.

Rose, Nancy L. (1985). "The Incidence of Regulatory Rents in the Motor Carrier Industry." *RAND Journal of Economics*, 16(Autumn), 299–318.

——— (1987). "Labor Rent Sharing and Regulation: Evidence from the Trucking Industry." *Journal of Political Economy*, 95, 1146–1178.

Rosenbaum, Walter A. (1995). *Environmental Politics and Policy* (3d ed.). Washington, DC: Congressional Quarterly.

Rosenthal, Douglas E. (1990). "Competition Policy." In Gary C. Hufbauer, *Europe 1992: An American Perspective*, 292–343. Washington, DC: Brookings.

Rousseau, Jean Jacques. (1762). *Of the Social Contract.* Reprint New York: Harper and Row. 1984.

Rubin, Paul H. (1983). *Business Firms and the Common Law: The Evolution of Efficient Rules.* New York: Praeger.

Rugman, Alan, John Kirton, and Julie Soloway. (1999). *Environmental Regulations and Corporate Strategy: A NAFTA Perspective.* Oxford, UK: Oxford University Press.

Sabato, Larry J. (1984). *PAC Power: Inside the World of Political Action Committees.* New York: Norton.

Sackett, P. R., and M. M. Harris. (1984). "Honesty Testing for Personnel Selection: A Review and Critique." *Personnel Psychology*, 37, 221–245.

Salisbury, Robert H. (1992). *Interests and Institutions.* Pittsburgh: University of Pittsburgh Press.

Saloner, Garth, Andrea Shepard, and Joel M. Podolny. (2001). *Strategic Management.* New York: Wiley.

Saloner, Garth, and A. Michael Spence. (2002). *Creating and Capturing Value: Perspectives and Cases on Electronic Commerce.* New York: Wiley.

Salop, Steven C., and Lawrence J. White. (1988). "Private Antitrust Litigation: An Introduction and Framework." In White (1988).

Schaede, Ultike. (1998). "Bureaucrats in Business." In Gibney (1998), 160–170.

Schmalensee, Richard, Paul L. Joskow, A. Denny Ellerman, Juan Pablo Montero, and Elizabeth M. Bailey. (1998). "An Interim Evaluation of Sulfur Dioxide Emissions Trading." *Journal of Economic Perspectives*, 12(Summer), 53–68.

Schmidt, Benno C., Jr. (1981). "The First Amendment and the Press." In Elie Abel (Ed.), *What's News,* 57–80. San Francisco: Institute for Contemporary Studies.

Schoenberger, Karl. (2000). *Levi's Children: Coming to Terms with Human Rights in the Global Marketplace.* New York: Grove Press.

Schuknecht, Ludger. (1992). *Trade Protection in the European Community.* Chur, Switzerland: Harwood Academic.

Schwartz, Benjamin I. (1985). *The World of Thought in Ancient China.* Cambridge, MA: Harvard University Press.

Sen, Amartya. (1987). *On Ethics & Economics.* Oxford, UK: Basil Blackwell.

——— (1997). "Economics, Business Principles and Moral Sentiments." *Business Ethics Quarterly*, 7, 5–15.

Sen, Amartya, and Bernard Williams (Eds.). (1982). *Utilitarianism and Beyond.* Cambridge, UK: Cambridge University Press.

Shaffer, Brian, and Daniel T. Ostas. (2001). "Exploring the Political Economy of Consumer Legislation: The Development of Automobile Lemon Laws." *Business and Politics*, 3, 65–76.

Shapiro, Carl, and Hal R. Varian. (1999). *Information Rules: A Strategic Guide to the Network Economy.* Boston: Harvard University Press.

Shaw, Malcolm W. (1997). *International Law* (4th ed.). Cambridge, UK: Cambridge University Press.

——— (2003). *International Law* (5th ed.). Cambridge, UK: Cambridge University Press.

Shepsle, Kenneth A., and Mark S. Bonchek. (1997). *Analyzing Politics: Rationality, Behavior, and Institutions.* New York: Norton.

Shils, Edward. (1996). "Reflections on Civil Society and Civility in the Chinese Intellectual Tradition." In Wei-ming Tu (Ed.), *Confucian Traditions in East Asian Modernity.* Cambridge, MA: Harvard University Press.

Shipper, Frank, and Marianne M. Jennings. (1984). *Business Strategy for the Political Arena.* Westport, CT: Quorum Books.

Shirk, Susan L. (1993). *The Political Logic of Economic Reform in China.* Berkeley: University of California Press.

Shue, Henry. (1980). *Basic Rights: Subsistence, Affluence, and U.S. Foreign Power.* Princeton, NJ: Princeton University Press.

Shue, Vivienne. (1988). *The Reach of the State.* Stanford, CA: Stanford University Press.

Shugart, William F. II. (1990). *Antitrust Policy and Interest-Group Politics.* New York: Quorum Books.

Sieg, Albert. (1994). *The Tokyo Chronicles.* Essex Junction, VT: Oliver Wright Publications.

Sigman, Betsy Ann, and Susan-Kathryn McDonald. (1987). "The Issues Manager as Public Opinion and Policy Analyst." In Marcus, Kaufman, and Beam (1987), 164–194.

Skelly, Joe. (1995). "The Rise of International Ethics: The Caux Round Table Principles for Business." *Business Ethics*, March–April Supplement, 2–5.

Smith, Adam. (1776). *An Inquiry into the Nature and Causes of the Wealth of Nations.* Edited by R. H. Campbell and A. S. Skinner. Oxford, UK: Clarendon Press. 1995.

———. (1991). "On Buying Legislatures." *Economics and Politics*, 3(July), 93–109.

Sonnenfeld, Jeffrey, and Paul R. Lawrence. (1978). "Why Do Companies Succumb to Price Fixing?" *Harvard Business Review*, 56(July–August), 145–157.

Spar, Deborah L., and Lane T. La Mure. (2003). "The Power of Activism: Assessing the Impact of NGOs on Global Business." *California Management Review*, 45: 78–101.

Sparrow, Batholomew H. (1999). *Uncertain Guardians: The News Media as a Political Institution.* Baltimore: Johns Hopkins University Press.

Spence, A. Michael. (1973). "Job Market Signaling." *Quarterly Journal of Economics*, 87: 355–374.

Spitzer, Matthew L. (1991). "Justifying Minority Preferences in Broadcasting." *Southern California Law Review*, 293, 334–336.

Spulber, Daniel F. (1989). *Regulation and Markets.* Cambridge, MA: MIT Press.

Stavins, Robert N. (1998). "What Can We Learn from the Grand Policy Experiment? Lessons from $SO_2$ Allowance Trading." *Economic Perspectives*, 12(Summer), 69–88.

Stender, Terrence. (1998). "Too Many Secrets: Challenges to the Control of Strong Crypto and the National Security Perspective." *Case Western Reserve Journal of International Law*, Winter, 287–337.

Stewart, Richard B. (1988). "Controlling Environmental Risks through Economic Incentives." *Columbia Journal of Environmental Law*, 13, 153–169.

Stigler, George. (1971). "The Theory of Economic Regulation." *Bell Journal of Regulation*, 2(Spring), 3–21.

Streeck, Wolfgang. (1984). *Industrial Relations in West Germany.* New York: St. Martin's Press.

Swire, Peter P., and Robert E. Litan. (1998). *None of Your Business.* Washington, DC: Brookings.

Tachibanaki, Toshiaki. (1984). "Labor Mobility and Job Tenure." In Aoki (1984), 77–102.

Taka, Iwao. (1994). "Business Ethics: A Japanese View." *Business Ethics Quarterly*, 4, 53–78.

Teece, David J. (2000). *Managing Intellectual Capital.* Oxford, UK: Oxford University Press.

Temin, Peter, with Louis Galambos. (1987). *The Fall of the Bell System.* Cambridge, UK: Cambridge University Press.

Teoh, Slew Hong, Ivo Welch, and C. Paul Wazzan. (1999). "The Effect of Socially Activist Investment Policies on the Financial Markets: Evidence from the South African Boycott." *Journal of Business*, 72, 35–89.

Thompson, James. (1967). *Organizations in Action.* New York: McGraw-Hill.

Tomlinson, R. (1997). "A Chinese Giant Forges a Capitalist Soul." *Fortune* (September 29): 184–192.

Trebilcock, Michael I., and Robert C. York. (1990). *Fair Exchange: Reforming Trade Remedy Laws.* Toronto, Canada: C. D. Howe Institute.

Tu, Wei-ming. (1979). *Humanity and Self-Cultivation.* Berkeley: University of California Press.

Ulmann, A. (1985). "Data in Search of a Theory: A Critical Examination of the Relationship Among Social Performance, Social Disclosure, and Economic Performance." *Academy of Management Review*, 10, 540–577.

Upham, Frank K. (1987). *Law and Social Change in Postwar Japan.* Cambridge, MA: Harvard University Press.

Urata, Shujiro. (2001). "Europe's Trade and Foreign Direct Investment in Asia." In Aggarwal (2001), 31–58.

Vachani, Sushil and N. Craig Smith. (2004). "Socially Responsible Pricing: Lessons from the Pricing of AIDS Drugs in Developing Countries." *California Management Review*. 47: 117–144.

Van Schendelen, M. P. C. M. (1993). "The Netherlands: Lobby It Yourself." In M. P. C. M. Van Schendelen (Ed.), *National Public and Private EC Lobbying.* Hants, UK: Aldershot.

Van Wolferen, Karel. (1989). *The Enigma of Japanese Power.* New York: Alfred A. Knopf.

Velasquez, Manuel G. (1998). *Business Ethics: Concepts and Cases* (4th ed.). Upper Saddle River, NJ: Prentice Hall.

———. Viscusi, W. Kip. (1991). *Reforming Products Liability.* Cambridge, MA: Harvard University Press.

Viscusi, W. Kip, and Michael J. Moore. (1993). "Product Liability, Research and Development, and Innovation." *Journal of Political Economy*, 101, 161–184.

Viscusi, W. Kip, John M. Vernon, and Joseph E. Harrington, Jr. (2000). *Economics of Regulation and Antitrust* (2d ed.). Cambridge, MA: MIT Press.

Vogel, David. (1978). *Lobbying the Corporation: Citizen Challenges to Business Authority.* New York: Basic Books.

———. (1986). *National Styles of Regulation: Environmental Policy in Great Britain and the United States.* Ithaca, NY: Cornell University Press.

———. (1991). "Business Ethics: New Perspectives on Old Problems." *California Business Review*, 33(Summer), 101–117.

Vogel, David. (2005). *Can Corporations Be Made Responsible? The Potential and Limits of Corporate Social Responsibility.* Washington, DC: Brookings.

Waddock, Sandra A., and Samuel B. Graves. (1997). "The Corporate Social Performance-Financial Performance Link." *Strategic Management Journal*, 18, 303–319.

Wang, L., and Joseph Fewsmith. (1995). "Bulwark of the Planned Economy: The Structure and Role of the State Planning Commission." In Carol L. Hamrin and Suisheng Zhao (Eds.), *Decision-Making in Deng's China*. Armonk, NY: M. E. Sharpe.

Wartick, Steven L., and Robert E. Rude. (1986). "Issues Management: Corporate Fad or Corporate Function?" *California Management Review*, 29(Fall), 124–140.

Wasserstrom, Richard (1978). "A Defense of Programs of Preferential Treatment." *National Forum: The Phi Kappa Phi Journal*, 58(Winter), 15–18.

Watkins, Sherron S. (2003). "Ethical Conflicts at Enron: Moral Responsibility in Corporate Capitalism." *California Management Review*. 45: 6–19.

Weaver, Suzanne. (1977) *Decision to Prosecute: Organization and Public Policy in the Antitrust Division*. Cambridge, MA: MIT Press.

Weber, Leonard J (1996). "Citizenship and Democracy: The Ethics of Corporate Lobbying." *Business Ethics Quarterly*, 6 (April), 253–259.

Weidenbaum, Murray L. (2004). *Business and Government in the Global Marketplace*, (7th ed.). Upper Saddle River, NJ: Pearson Prentice Hall.

Weingast, Barry M., and Mark Moran. (1983). "Bureaucratic Discretion or Congressional Control? Regulatory Policymaking by the Federal Trade Commission." *Journal of Political Economy*, 91(October), 765–800.

Weston. J. Fred, Kwand S. Chung, and Susan E. Hoag. (1990). *Mergers, Restructuring, and Corporate Control*. Upper Saddle River, NJ: Prentice Hall.

White, Lawrence J. (Ed.) (1988). *Private Antitrust Litigation: New Evidence, New Learning*. Cambridge, MA: MIT Press.

White, Michelle J. (2004). "Asbestos and the Future of Mass Torts." Working Paper 10308, National Bureau of Economic Research, Cambridge, MA.

White, Matthew W. (1997). "Power Struggles: Explaining Deregulatory Reforms in Electricity Markets." *Brookings Papers on Economic Activity: Microeconomics*, 201–250.

Williams, Oliver F. (Ed.). (2000). *Global Codes of Conduct: An Idea Whose Time Has Come*. Notre Dame, IN: Notre Dame University Press.

Williamson, Oliver E. (1975). *Markets and Hierarchies: Analysis and Antitrust Implications*. New York: Free Press.

Wilson, James Q. (1980). *The Politics of Regulation*. New York: Basic Books.

——. (1989). *Bureaucracy: What Government Agencies Do and Why They Do It*. New York: Basic Books.

Wilson, Robert. (2001). "Architecture of Power Markets." Working paper, Stanford University, Stanford, CA.

Wise, Mark, and Richard Gibb. (1993). *Single Market to Social Europe*. Essex, UK: Longman Scientific & Technical.

Wiseman, Alan E., and Jerry Ellig. (2004). "Market and Nonmarket Barriers to Internet Wine Sales: The Case of Virginia." *Business and Politics*. 6: Article 4.

Wolf, Charles, Jr. (1979). "A Theory of Nonmarket Failure." *Journal of Law and Economics*, 22(April), 107–139.

——. (1988) *Markets or Governments*. Cambridge, MA: MIT Press.

Wood, Donna J. (1991). "Corporate Social Performance Revisited." *Academy of Management Review*, 18, 691–718.

World Bank. (2004). *World Development Indicators*. Washington, DC.

Wu, Abraham H. (1994). "Contributions, Lobbying, and Participation." Working paper, Stanford University, Stanford, CA.

Yang, C. K. (1959). *Chinese Communist Society: The Family and the Village*. Cambridge, MA: MIT Press.

Yang, M. M. (1994). *Gifts, Favors, and Banquets*. Ithaca, NY: Cornell University Press.

Yayama, Taro. (1998). "Who Has Obstructed Reform?" In Gibney (1998), 91–115.

Yoffie, David B. (1987). "Corporate Strategies for Political Action: A Rational Model." In Marcus, Kaufman, and Beam (1987).

——. (1988a). "How an Industry Builds Political Advantage." *Harvard Business Review*, May-June, 82–89.

——. (1988b). Motorola and Japan and Motorola and Japan: Supplements I, II, III, 0-388-057, 0-388-058, 9-388-059. Boston, MA: Harvard Business School.

Young, Louis H. (1978, September 21). "Business and the Media: The Failure to Understand How the Other Operates." Speech delivered at the ITT Key Issues Lecture Series, Columbia, Missouri.

# Index

## A

Abbott Laboratories, 842, 845
ABC
  Disney, 352, 360
  *Home Show*, 68
  News, 92
  ownership, 74, 358
  *Primetime Live*, 78, 595
  Washington Post poll, 276
Absolute liability, 423
ACE Group of Companies (case),
  224–226
Acid rain, 194, 371–373
ACORN, 104, 802–803
Act utilitarianism, 706–709
Activist groups, 8
  boycotts by, 98–101
  environmental, 1
  generic strategy of, 106
  INFACT, 98
  interacting with, 109
  market environment and, 4
  negotiating with (example), 112
  Neighbor to Neighbor (example), 84
  Starbucks and, 45
  strategies, 103, 107, 125
  strength of, 97
  tuna and dolphins (example), 662
  *See also* Interest groups
Act utilitarianism, 706–708
Ad hoc coalitions, 247, 249, 255
Administrative Procedure Act (APA), 148, 327
Advanced Technology Laboratories, Inc. (case), 689–691
Adverse selection, 336, 763
Advocacy
  groups, 8, 16, 96, 431
  lobbying and, 794
  public, 252
  science, 104–105, 380
Affirmative action (example), 760–761
Age Discrimination in Employment Act of 1967, 748
Agendas
  Arrow's impossibility theorem and, 144–145
  Boeing's nonmarket, 185
  nonmarket issue, 5
  voting, 145

Agenda setting
  authority, 145
  majority building and, 215
  role of news media, 69
Agriculture, international trade and, 607–608
AIDS drugs policy (case), 841–847
Airbus, 182, 185, 218, 610
Air France, 531
Alar, 87
  activist groups and, 81
  case, 89–90
  media coverage, 77
  NRDC campaign on, 67–68
Aldeasa, EU duty free abolition and (case), 557–563
Allegis, 679
Alliance of Automobile Manufacturers (AAM), 6, 11, 271
All Nippon Airlines (ANA), 825
Altruism, utilitarianism, and distribution, 704–705
Amazon.com, 40, 269, 437, 458
American Association of Advertising Agencies, 194
American Association of Retired Persons (AARP),
  13, 141, 262, 803
American Chamber of Commerce (ACC),
  245, 511, 520, 543
American Express, 288, 542, 606, 787
American Federation of State, County, and Municipal
  Employees, 186
American Feed Industry Association (AF1A), 87
American Medical Association (AMA), 19
Americans with Disabilities Act (ADA), 27, 657
American Tort Reform Association, 432
Amnesty International, 110
Andean Community, 613
Antidumping
  Cemex and (case), 623–629
  international trade and, 608–609
Antimonopoly law, in Japan, 501–502
Antitrust law
  compliance with, 304
  enforcement of
    government enforcement, 286–288
    per se violations, 289–290
    private enforcement, 289
  exemptions, 284–285
  government enforcement of, 286–288
  monopoly (example), 285
  private enforcement of, 289